America
PAST AND PRESENT

ROBERT A. DIVINE
University of Texas

T. H. BREEN
Northwestern University

GEORGE M. FREDRICKSON
Stanford University

R. HAL WILLIAMS
Southern Methodist University

and

RANDY ROBERTS
Purdue University

BRIEF THIRD EDITION

HarperCollins*College*Publishers

Acquisitions Editor: Bruce Borland
Developmental Editor: Betty Slack
Project Coordination, Text and Cover Design: Proof
    Positive/Farrowlyne Associates, Inc.
Cover Illustration/Photo: "Johnson Hall," by E. L.
    Henry, Collection of Albany Institute of History and
    Art, gift of Laura Munsell Tremanine
Photo Researcher: Leslie Coopersmith
Manager: Willie Lane
Compositor: GTS Graphics
Printer and Binder: R. R. Donnelley & Sons Company
Cover Printer: The Lehigh Press, Inc.

America: Past and Present, Brief Third Edition

Library of Congress Cataloging-in-Publication Data
America, past and present / Robert A. Divine . . . [et. al.].—Brief
    3rd ed.
        p. cm.
    Includes bibliographical references and index.
    ISBN 0-673-46758-9
    1. United States—History. I. Divine, Robert A.
E178.1.A4894 1994   93-25161
973—dc20   CIP

    95 96 9 8 7 6 5 4

Contents in Brief

CONTENTS

MAPS

CHARTS, TABLES, AND GRAPHS

PREFACE TO BRIEF
THIRD EDITION

This Brief Third Edition of *America: Past and Present*, prepared by Professor Randy Roberts with the collaboration of the four authors of the full-length survey text, is intended to serve the needs of instructors in one-semester courses and those who supplement the main assigned text with a wide variety of other readings. Enriched by the use of primary sources, monographs, scholarly articles, and fiction, a foundation text helps the student grasp the sweep and complexity of the American past.

The full-length edition won acclaim for its skillful integration of political, diplomatic, economic, social, and cultural history; its clarity of organization; and its stylistic grace. The goal of this abridgment is to produce a condensation true to the original in all its dimensions—a miniaturized replica or *bonsai*, as it were—retaining the style and tone, and the interpretations, with their nuances and subtleties intact. To achieve that goal, factual coverage and thematic advancement have been closely monitored; we have gone over the text line by line, and the intent of every paragraph has been retained. This version contains about two thirds of the narrative of the full-length book, more than one half of the highly praised maps, charts, and graphs, and a commensurate proportion of the outstanding illustration program.

The Brief Third Edition of *America: Past and Present* reflects the major changes that were made in the third edition of the full-length text. Chapter 1 now includes discussion of preconquest Native American culture and African culture and society before American settlement. In Chapters 8–20 more material has been added on intellectual and cultural developments of the early and mid-nineteenth century. Chapters 22 and 23 on the Progressive Era have been reorganized for better integration and continuity. The chapters that cover the post–World War II and Cold War era have also been reorganized. Chapter 28 covers the Cold War under Truman; Chapter 29 focuses on domestic policy and developments during the Eisenhower, Kennedy, and Johnson administrations; and Chapter 30 deals with foreign policy, including the Vietnam War, during the 1950s and 1960s. The revised final chapter (33) covers political developments from Reagan through the election of 1992 and also includes new sections on social issues and problems of the 1980s. Also added to the Brief Third Edition are a number of new thematic, military, and current international maps and figures and several new summary tables, which summarize factual information related to social and economic change in a format designed to permit quick and easy review for students.

R.R.

PREFACE TO FULL-LENGTH THIRD EDITION

The third edition of *America: Past and Present* is a major revision that strives to achieve the shared goal of the previous editions—to present a clear, relevant, and balanced history of the United States as an unfolding story of national development, from the days of the earliest inhabitants to the present. We emphasize the *story* because we strongly believe in the value of historical narrative in providing a vivid sense of the past. In each chapter, we sought to blend the excitement and drama of the American experience with insights about the social, economic, and cultural forces that underlie it.

In this edition we have gone over each chapter carefully to sharpen the analysis and the prose and to offer new perspectives. Many suggestions proposed by those who used the previous editions in their classrooms have been adopted.

Among the revisions that take account of a growing body of excellent scholarly work are these:

• The opening chapter has been rewritten to provide an extensive discussion of preconquest Native American culture and a section on African culture and society before American settlement. Students are presented with the necessary information about pre-Columbian, European, and African societies to help them better understand the conjunction of these three cultures in the New World.

• Throughout this revised edition, the roles that Native Americans, as well as African Americans and women, played in the development of American society is emphasized. They continue to appear throughout the text, not as witnesses to the historical narrative, but as principals in its development.

• Chapters 5–7 discusss the Constitution and constitutional issues in greater depth than previous editions. The same chapters also present a fuller explication of republicanism in theory and in practice.

• Chapters 8–20 provide expanded coverage of intellectual and cultural developments of the early and mid-nineteenth century, including illuminating anecdotal material, and a revised section on the Texas Revolution that takes account of Mexican and Mexican-American perspectives of the conflict.

• The chapter on American overseas expansion in the late nineteenth and early twentieth centuries (Chapter 21) includes more material on anti-imperialist thinking; the two chapters on the Progressive Era (Chapters 22 and 23) have had a substantial overhaul; a great deal of new material drawn from the most recent studies has been added and the chapters have been reorganized to achieve greater concept integration and continuity. Chapter 22 now examines the economic and social conditions and the intellectual and cultural currents that gave rise to the Progessive movement; Chapter 23 explores progressivism in terms of political action on all govermental levels.

• The chapters that discuss the post-World War II period and the Cold War have been extensively revised and reordered. Chapter 28 now focuses on the Truman presidency and McCarthyism in the context of the early Cold War; a revised Chapter 29 deals with the domestic develpments—mainly civil rights and liberal reform measures—of the Eisenhower, Kennedy, and early Johnson years at the height of the Cold War. Chapter 30 is now devoted exclusively to exploring foreign policy of the 1950s and 1960s with special emphasis on the developing and intensifying Vietnam War. It enables students to see how the Vietnam conflict grew out of the containment policy of the 1950s.

Chapter 32 has updated demographics and new material on long-term social trends.
• A greatly expanded and revised final chapter covers the major political developments under Presidents Reagan and Bush, and analyzes the impact of these policies on both the American economy and the world. New sections on major social problems of the decade of the 1980s include discussions of the AIDS epidemic and the "war on drugs." The section concludes with a discussion of the momentous political changes in Europe that may very well mark the end of the Cold War.

APPROACH AND THEMES

As the title suggests, our book is a blend of the traditional and the new. The strong narrative emphasis and chronological organization are traditional; the incorporation of the many fresh insights that historians have gained from the social sciences in the past quarter-century is new. We have used significant incidents and episodes to reflect the dilemmas, the choices, and the decisions made by the people as well as by their leaders. After discussion of the colonial period, most of the chapters examine shorter time periods, usually about a decade, permitting us to view these major political and public events as points of reference and orientation around which social themes are integrated. This approach gives unity and direction to the text.

In recounting the story of the American past, we see a nation in flux. The early Africans and Europeans developed complex agrarian folkways that blended Old World customs and New World experiences; as new cultural identities evolved, the idea of political independence became more acceptable. People who had been subjects of the British Crown created a system of government that challenged later Americans to work out the full implications of theories of social and economic equality.

The growing sectional rift between the North and South, revolving around divergent models of economic growth and conflicting social values, culminated in civil war. In the post-Civil War period, the development of a more industrialized economy severely tested the values of an agrarian society, engendering a Populist reform movement. In the early twentieth century, Progressive reformers sought to infuse the industrial order with social justice. World War I demonstrated the extent of American power in the world. The resiliency of the maturing American nation was tested by the Great Depression and World War II. The Cold War ushered in an era of crises, foreign and domestic, that revealed both the strengths and the weaknesses of modern America.

The impact of change on human lives adds a vital dimension to our understanding of history. We need to comprehend the way the Revolution affected the lives of ordinary citizens; what it was like for both blacks and whites to live in a plantation society; how men and women fared in the shift from an agrarian to an industrial economy; and what impact technology, in the form of the automobile and the computer, has had on patterns of life in the twentieth century.

Our commitment is not to any particular ideology or point of view; rather, we hope to challenge our readers to rediscover the fascination of the American past and reach their own conclusions about its significance in their lives. At the same time, we have not avoided controversial issues; instead, we have tried to offer reasoned judgments on such morally charged subjects as the nature of slavery and the advent of nuclear weapons. We believe that while history rarely repeats itself, the story of the American past is relevant to the problems and dilemmas facing the nation today, and we have therefore sought to stress themes and ideas that continue to shape our national culture.

STRUCTURE AND FEATURES

The structure and features of the book are intended to stimulate student interest and to reinforce learning. Chapters begin with **vignettes** or incidents, many of them new, that establish direction for chapter themes stated in the introductory sections (which also serve as overviews to the topics covered) and with **expanded summaries.** Each chapter has a **chronology, recommended readings, bibliography** (redone for this edition), and a **two-page special feature essay** on a topic that combines high interest and instructional value. Nine of the special features are on new topics—some explore the Constitution and landmark cases, immigration, and the culture of the workplace; others relate to historiographical, environmental, and technological issues.

The extensive **full-color map program** has been enhanced to provide a greater global perspective and more integration of information and action. **New charts, graphs, and tables**—many with a capsulized format for convenient review of factual information—relate to social and economic change. The rich **full-color illustration program** bearing directly on the narrative advances and expands the themes, provides elaboration and contrast, tells more of the story, and generally adds another dimension of learning. The illustrations also present a mini-survey of American painting styles. **Five picture essays** explore diverse facets of American life and a **revised and expanded "Growth of America" series** at the front of the book with maps and accompanying narrative includes a **time line of parallel events.** The augmented **Appendix,** with updated presidential, electoral, cabinet, and Supreme Court charts and a statehood admission chart, also features a new chart of U.S. population by state and region with projections to the end of the century.

Although this book is a joint effort, each author took primary responsibility for writing one section. T. H. Breen contributed the first eight chapters from the earliest Native American period to the second decade of the nineteenth century; George M. Fredrickson wrote Chapters 9 through 16, carrying the narrative through the Reconstruction Era. R. Hal Williams is responsible for Chapters 17 through 24, focusing on the industrial transformation and urbanization, and the events culminating in World War I; and Robert A. Divine wrote Chapters 25 through 33, bringing the story through the Depression, World War II, and the Cold War to the present. Each contributor reviewed and revised the work of his colleagues and helped shape the material into its final form.

The Authors

ACKNOWLEDGMENTS

We are most grateful to our reviewers and consultants whose thoughtful and constructive work contributed greatly to the third edition of *America: Past and Present.*

James Axtell
College of William and Mary

David Bernstein
California State University, Long Beach

James Border
Berkshire Community College

Mary C. Brennan
Ohio State University

Daniel Patrick Brown
Moorpark College

Raphael Cassimere, Jr.
University of New Orleans

Charles L. Cohen
University of Wisconsin

Jerald Combs
San Francisco State University

Virginia Crane
University of Wisconsin, Oshkosh

James C. Curtis
University of Delaware

Charles Douglass
Florida Community College at Jacksonville

Thomas Dublin
SUNY-Binghamton

John P. Farr
Chattanooga State Technical Community College

William W. Freehling
Johns Hopkins University

Fred E. Freidel
Bellevue Community College

Richard Frey
Southern Oregon State College

Gary W. Gallagher
Pennsylvania State University

Sara E. Gallaway
Oxnard College

Louis S. Gomolak
Southwest Texas State University

Lewis L. Gould
University of Texas

Richard C. Haney
University of Wisconsin, Whitewater

Edward F. Hass
Wright State University

James A. Hurst
Northwest Missouri State University

Robert M. Ireland
University of Kentucky

Carol E. Jenson
University of Wisconsin, La Crosse

Robert R. Jones
University of Southwestern Louisiana

Stephen Lawson
University of South Florida

Henry Louis
Kansas City Kansas Community College

Karen Marcotte
Palo Alto College

Herbert Margulies
University of Hawaii at Manoa

James H. Merrell
Vassar College

Joseph C. Miller
University of Virginia

Harmon Mothershead
Northwest Missouri State University

John K. Nelson
University of North Carolina

Roger L. Nichols
University of Arizona

Michael Perman
University of Illinois, Chicago

Marlette Rebhorn
Austin Community College

Andrew W. Robertson
Louisiana State University

David Sandoval
University of Southern Colorado

Howard Schonberger
University of Maine

Ingrid Winther Scobie
Texas Women's University

Kathryn Kish Sklar
SUNY-Binghamton

Paul R. Taylor
Augusta College

Michael E. Thompson
South Seattle Community College

Nancy Unger
San Francisco State University

Donna L. Van Raaphorst
Cuyahoga Community College

Russell Veeder
Dickinson State University

Forrest A. Walker
Eastern New Mexico State University

James P. Walsh
Central Connecticut State University

Rosemarie Zagarri
Catholic University

Many thanks also to the following reviewers who gave generously of their time and knowledge to read the manuscript for the brief third edition of *America: Past and Present* and whose thoughtful evaluations and suggestions for revisions have proved extremely valuable in preparing the final product.

James Barringer
Hillsborough Community College

Sandra McGee Deutsch
University of Texas, El Paso

Gregory L. Goodwin
Bakersfield College

Robert C. Hilderbrand
University of South Dakota

James E. McMillan
New Mexico State University

Marguerite Renner
Glendale Community College

Megan Seaholm
University of Texas

William P. Short, Jr.
Cecil Community College

Grant W. Smart
Salt Lake Community College

Kay C. Starnes
University of North Carolina, Charlotte

Dean Wolfe
Kingwood College

A large number of instructors, too many to name individually, who used the previous editions were most helpful in reporting on the success of the text in the classroom. We heartily thank them all.

Finally, each author received aid and encouragement from many colleagues, friends, and family members. Randy Roberts wishes to acknowledge in particular his wife Suzy, Jason Tetzloff, Purdue University, and Terry Bilhartz, Sam Houston State University.

SUPPLEMENTS

FOR INSTRUCTORS

INSTRUCTOR'S RESOURCE MANUAL

This important resource manual by James P. Walsh of Central Connecticut State College begins with the essay "A Guide to Teaching History Through Films," by Randy Roberts of Purdue University. Each chapter contains interpretative essays, anecdotes, and references to biographical or primary sources, and a comprehensive summary of the text.

AMERICA THROUGH THE EYES OF ITS PEOPLE: A COLLECTION OF PRIMARY SOURCES

Prepared by Carol Brown of Houston Community College, this one-volume collection of primary documents portraying the rich and varied tapestry of American life contains documents of women, Native Americans, African Americans, Hispanics, and others who helped to shape the course of U.S. history. Designed to be duplicated by instructors for student use, the documents also have accompanying student exercises.

"THIS IS AMERICA" IMMIGRATION VIDEO

Produced by the American Museum of Immigration, these two 20-minute videos tell the story of American immigrants, relating their personal stories and accomplishments. By showing how the richness of our culture is due to the contributions of millions of immigrant Americans, the videos make the point that America's strength lies in the ethnically and culturally diverse backgrounds of its citizens.

DISCOVERING AMERICAN HISTORY THROUGH MAPS AND VIEWS

Created by Gerald Danzer, University of Illinois at Chicago, the recipient of the AHA's 1990 James Harvey Robinson Prize for his work in the development of map transparencies, this set of 140 four-color acetates is a unique instructional tool. It contains an introduction on teaching history through maps and a detailed commentary on each transparency. The collection includes cartographic and pictorial maps, views and photos, urban plans, building diagrams, and works of art.

AMERICAN HISTORY VIDEO LASER DISC

This is an all new HarperCollins video laser disc featuring photos, film clips, animated map segments, and videos of major events in American history.

VIDEO LECTURE LAUNCHERS

Prepared by Mark Newman, University of Illinois at Chicago, these video lecture launchers (each 2 to 5 minutes in duration) cover key issues in American history from 1877 to the present. The launchers are accompanied by an Instructor's Manual.

VISUAL ARCHIVES OF AMERICAN HISTORY

This video laser disc provides over 500 photos, and 29 minutes of film clips of major events in American history. Each photo or film clip may be instantly accessed, making this collection ideal for classroom use.

TEST BANK

Prepared by Carol Brown and Michael McCormick, Houston Community College, and James S. Olson, Sam Houston State University, this test bank contains over 1200 multiple-choice, true/false, matching, and completion questions.

TESTMASTER COMPUTERIZED TESTING SYSTEM

This flexible, easy-to-master computer test bank includes all the test items in the printed test bank. The TestMaster software allows you to edit existing questions and add your own items. Tests can be printed in several different formats and can include figures such as graphs and tables. Available for IBM and Macintosh computers.

QuizMaster

The new program enables you to design TestMaster generated tests that your students can take on a computer rather than in printed form. QuizMaster is available separate from TestMaster and can be obtained free through your sales representative.

Grades

A grade-keeping and classroom management software program that maintains data for up to 200 students.

For Students

Learning to Think Critically: Films and Myths about American History

Randy Roberts and Robert May of Purdue University use well-known films such as *Gone with the Wind* and *Casablanca* to explore some common myths about America and its past. Many widely held assumptions about our country's past come from or are perpetuated by popular films. Which are true? Which are patently not true? And how does a student of history approach documents, sources, and textbooks with a critical and discerning eye? This short handbook subjects some popular beliefs to historical scrutiny to help students develop a method of inquiry for approaching the subject of history in general.

Study Guide and Practice Tests

This two-volume study guide was created by Donald L. Smith, Houston Community College; Richard Bailey, San Jacinto College; Charles M. Cook and Jon V. Garrett, Houston

Community College; and Randy Roberts, Purdue University. Each volume begins with an introductory essay, "Skills for Studying and Learning History." Each chapter contains a summary, learning objectives, identification list, map exercises, glossary, and multiple-choice, completion, and essay questions.

SuperShell II Computerized Tutorial

Prepared by Ken L. Weatherbie, Del Mar College, this interactive program for IBM computers helps students learn the major facts and concepts through drill and practice exercises and diagnostic feedback. SuperShell II, which provides immediate correct answers and the text page number on which the material is discussed, maintains a running score of the student's performance on the screen throughout the session. This free student supplement is available to instructors through their sales representatives.

Mapping American History: Student Activities

Written by Gerald Danzer of the University of Illinois, Chicago, this free map workbook for students features exercises designed to teach students to interpret and analyze cartographic materials as historical documents. The instructor is entitled to a free copy of the workbook for each copy of the text that is purchased from HarperCollins.

TimeLink Computer Atlas of American History

This atlas, compiled by William Hamblin of Brigham Young University, is an introductory software tutorial and textbook companion. This Macintosh program presents the historical geography of the continental United States from colonial times to the settling of the West and the admission of the last continental state in 1912. The program covers territories in different time periods, provides quizzes, and includes a special Civil War module.

About the Authors

ROBERT A. DIVINE

Robert A. Divine, George W. Littlefield Professor in American History at the University of Texas at Austin, received his Ph.D. degree from Yale University in 1954. A specialist in American diplomatic history, he has taught at the University of Texas since 1954, where he has been honored by the Student Association for teaching excellence. His extensive published work includes *The Illusion of Neutrality* (1962), *Second Chance: The Triumphs of Internationalism in America During World War II* (1967), and *Blowing on the Wind* (1978). He is also the author of *Eisenhower and the Cold War* (1981), and editor of *Exploring the Johnson Years* (1981) and *The Johnson Years*, Vol. II (1987). He has been a fellow at the Center for Advanced Study in the Behavioral Sciences and has given the Albert Shaw Lectures in Diplomatic History at Johns Hopkins University.

T. H. BREEN

T. H. Breen, William Smith Mason Professor of American History at Northwestern University, received his Ph.D. from Yale University in 1968. He has taught at Northwestern since 1970. Breen's major books include *The Character of the Good Rule: A Study of Puritan Political Ideas in New England* (1974), *Puritans and Adventurers: Change and Persistence in Early America* (1980), *Tobacco Culture: The Mentality of the Great Tidewater Planters on the Eve of Revolution* (1985), and with S. Innes of the University of Virginia, *"Myne Owne Ground": Race and Freedom on Virginia's Eastern Shore* (1980). His *Imagining the Past* won the 1990 Historic Preservation Book Award. In addition to receiving an award for outstanding teaching at Northwestern, Breen has been the recipient of research grants from the American Council of Learned Societies, the Guggenheim Foundation, the Institute for Advanced Study (Princeton), and the National Humanities Center. He has served as the Fowler Hamilton Fellow at Christ Church, Oxford University (1987–1988) and the Pitt Professor of American History and Institutions, Cambridge University (1990–1991).

GEORGE M. FREDRICKSON

George M. Fredrickson is Edgar E. Robinson Professor of United States History at Stanford University. He is the author or editor of several books, including the *Inner Civil War* (1965), *The Black Image in the White Mind* (1971), and *White Supremacy: A Comparative Study in American and South African History* (1981), which won both the Ralph Waldo Emerson Award from Phi Beta Kappa and the Merle Curti Award from the Organization of American Historians. His most recent work is *The Arrogance of Race: Historical Perspectives on Slavery, Racism, and Social Inequality* (1988). He received both the A.B. and Ph.D. degrees from Harvard and has been the recipient of a Guggenheim Fellowship, two National Endowment for the Humanities Senior Fellowships, and a Fellowship from the Center for Advanced Studies in the Behavioral Sciences. Before coming to Stanford in 1984, he taught at Northwestern. He has also served as Fulbright lecturer in American History at Moscow University and as Harmsworth Professor of American History at Oxford.

late-nineteenth-century Speaker of the House, secretary of state, and Republican presidential candidate.

R. HAL
WILLIAMS

R. Hal Williams is Professor of History at Southern Methodist University. He received his A.B. degree from Princeton University (1963) and his Ph.D. degree from Yale University (1968). His books include *The Democratic Party and California Politics, 1880–1896* (1973), *Years of Decision: American Politics in the 1890s* (1978), and *The Manhattan Project: A Documentary Introduction to the Atomic Age* (1990). A specialist in American political history, he taught at Yale University from 1968 to 1975 and came to SMU in 1975 as Chair of the Department of History. From 1980 to 1988, he served as Dean of Dedman College, the school of humanities and sciences, at SMU. In 1980, he was a Visiting Professor at University College, Oxford University. Williams has received grants from the American Philosophical Society and the National Endowment for the Humanities, and he has served on the Texas Committee for the Humanities. He is currently at work on a biography of James G. Blaine, the

RANDY
ROBERTS

Randy Roberts teaches history at Purdue University where in 1991 he won the Murphy Award as the Outstanding Undergraduate Teacher and in 1993 the Society for Professional Journalists' Teacher of the Year Award. He received his Ph.D. from Louisiana State University in 1978. A specialist in cultural history and the history of sport, he has published widely in those fields. His books include *Jack Dempsey: The Manassa Mauler* (1979), *Papa Jack: Jack Johnson and the Era of White Hopes* (1983), and *Winning Is the Only Thing: Sports in America Since 1945* (1989) as well as *Where the Domino Fell: America and Vietnam 1945–1990* (1991). He is on the editorial board of the *Journal of Sport History* and *Arete: The Journal of Sport Literature,* and he is co-editor of the Illinois University Press series Studies in Sports and Society. He has received several grants from the National Endowment for the Humanities. He is currently finishing books on John Wayne and the Mike Tyson trial.

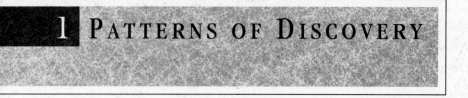

1 PATTERNS OF DISCOVERY

One day in 1908 while riding along a dry creek bed near Folsom, New Mexico, George McJunkin, a black cowboy, noticed some unusual bones protruding from the mud. Probing these remains with his knife, he uncovered several flint points as well that somewhat resembled Apache arrowheads. Archaeologists later concluded that McJunkin had stumbled across an ancient bison skeleton and the tips from the spears of the hunters who had killed the beast 10,000 years ago. This discovery of the "Folsom Man" demonstrated that Native American civilizations were far older than had been assumed. Later discoveries revealed that Stone Age hunters first migrated to North America from Siberia some 30,000 years ago.

Native Americans had inhabited the continent for millennia when European explorers crossed the Atlantic Ocean in the fifteenth century and proclaimed the discovery of a New World. But, as historian J. H. Parry observed, "Columbus did not discover a new world; he established contact between two worlds, both already old."

The dream of vast treasure first lured Europeans to the New World, but there was no typical pattern of settlement once they arrived. The experiences of the immigrants varied widely, as they attempted to transfer familiar institutions to America. They wanted to reproduce the particular societies that they had left behind.

Often the success of these ventures depended on factors over which the colonists had little control. The support of the mother countries and the availability of investment capital, for example, profoundly affected the character of colonial settlements. The land itself played an important role, for not all areas were equally fertile or rich in mineral deposits. Given the differences in game and timber alone, it is not surprising that English, French, and Spanish colonies developed in substantially different ways.

NATIVE AMERICAN CULTURES

When the peopling of America began some 30,000 years ago, the Earth's climate was considerably colder than it is today. Much of the world's moisture was transformed into ice. The oceans dropped several hundred feet below their current level, creating a land bridge between Asia and America. The first people to cross this land bridge were small bands of Siberian hunters in pursuit of giant mammals, woolly mammoths, and mastodons. The migration of these nomadic groups took place over thousands of years. By 8000 B.C. men and women had ventured to the tip of South America.

Survival in the harsh environment forced the separate groups to look inward. Native Americans did not think of themselves as representatives of a single people or race. Over the centuries relatively isolated tribal groups developed their own cultures, patterns of kinship, and spoken languages. By the time that Europeans first arrived, Native Americans who had settled north of Mexico had evolved between 300 and 350 separate languages. The concept of homogeneous Native American culture was invented in a much later period by persons largely ignorant of the complexity of the history of these early people.

The introduction of agriculture revolutionized the life of Native Americans. As early as 2000 B.C. some groups in the Southwest began farming, and over the centuries their knowledge spread north and east. The impact of agri-

Division of labor between the sexes is depicted in this sixteenth-century engraving by Jacques Le Moyne of Native Americans sowing beans and maize. The men prepare the ground with hoes; one woman digs holes with a dowel while the other two drop in the seeds. Le Moyne visited Florida between 1564 and 1565.

culture upon Native American societies was immense. Freed from the insecurity of an existence based solely upon hunting and gathering, Native Americans settled in permanent villages. An increased food supply led to a population boom, freeing some people for artistic endeavors. The Agricultural Revolution further divided North American tribes; groups in Mexico and the Southwest relied heavily on domesticated plants while those living in the Northeast, who had no agriculture or who acquired it late, continued to depend mainly on hunting and gathering.

DIVERSITY AND ACHIEVEMENT

The most advanced Native American cultures appeared in Mexico and Central America. The Maya and Toltec peoples built vast cities, organized sophisticated government bureaucracies, and developed an accurate calendar and a complex form of writing. When the Spanish conquerors first saw the impressive cities of the New World, they compared them to Venice, one of Italy's most stunning artistic and engineering achievements. One explorer even proclaimed one Mexican city "the most beautiful . . . in the world."

Over the centuries, Native American civilizations rose and fell. By the time Columbus set sail in 1492, the Aztec, an aggressive, militant people, dominated the Valley of Mexico. They ruled by the sword and carried out human sacrifice on a scale previously unknown in Mexico.

The people who inhabited the present-day territories of the United States and Canada were less technologically advanced than their Mexican neighbors. Although tribes in the Southwest and the Mississippi Valley practiced intensive agriculture, eastern tribes mixed farming with hunting and gathering. Small bands among the Algonquin tribes on the Atlantic coast, for example, formed villages and cultivated corn in the warm summer months. But with the hardships of winter, the bands dispersed, and each family lived off the land as

best it could. The dangers were great; survival could never be taken for granted.

Despite common linguistic roots, the members of the different Algonquin groups, such as the Narraganset and the Powhatan, communicated only with greatest difficulty. The distinct dialects that developed in the isolated environments were as different from one another as modern Romanian is from Portuguese.

Though the Indians of eastern North America may have found communication between tribes difficult, they shared many cultural values and assumptions. Most Native Americans, for example, defined their place in society within complex kinship systems. These personal bonds determined the character of economic and political relations. As James Axtell explains, "The basic unit of social membership in all the tribes was the exogamous clan, a lineal descent group determined through one parent." The farming tribes that lived in those areas eventually claimed by England were often matrilineal, for in these bands the women performed the agricultural labor, owned the planting fields, and maintained tribal customs. Descent took a patrilineal form among the tribes of the northern Great Lakes and Canada, which depended more heavily upon hunting. In these groups the men owned the hunting grounds that the family needed to survive.

PATTERNS OF CONTACT

The arrival of Europeans on this continent radically altered the lives of the native inhabitants. Whether English or Spanish, the colonizers regarded their own cultures as superior to those of the Native Americans, and they quickly tried to introduce their concept of civilization to those they considered savages. The attempt was a universal failure.

Some Native Americans—or Indians, as they came to be called by the Europeans—paid lip service to Christianity, but neither Catholic nor Protestant dogma deeply affected their inner convictions. Indian concepts of sin and the afterlife differed markedly from Christian theology. The white settlers' educational sys-

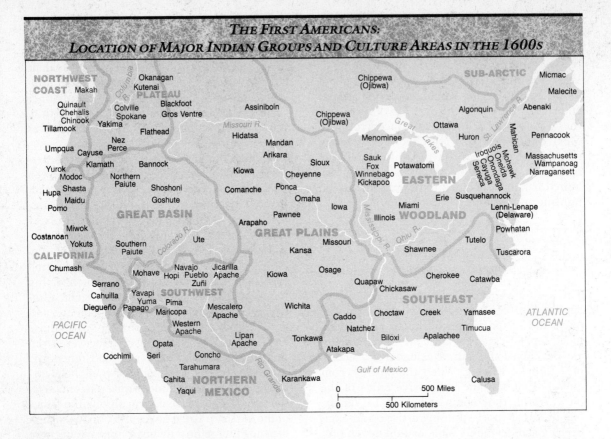

THE FIRST AMERICANS:
LOCATION OF MAJOR INDIAN GROUPS AND CULTURE AREAS IN THE 1600s

NORTHWEST COAST Makah
Okanagan
Kutenai
PLATEAU
Quinault
Chehalis
Chinook
Tillamook
Colville
Spokane
Yakima
Blackfoot
Gros Ventre
Flathead
Nez Perce
Cayuse
Umpqua
Yurok
Klamath
Modoc
Northern Paiute
Shasta
Hupa
Maidu
Pomo
Bannock
Shoshoni
Goshute
GREAT BASIN
Miwok
Costanoan
Yokuts
Southern Paiute
CALIFORNIA
Chumash
Serrano
Cahuilla
Diegueño
Yavapi
Yuma
Papago
Pima
Maricopa
SOUTHWEST
Mohave
Hopi
Navajo
Pueblo
Zuñi
Jicarilla Apache
Mescalero Apache
Western Apache
Opata
Cochimi
Seri
Concho
Tarahumara
Cahita
Yaqui
NORTHERN MEXICO

Assiniboin
Missouri R.
Hidatsa
Mandan
Arikara
Kiowa
Cheyenne
Comanche
Ponca
Arapaho
Omaha
Pawnee
Iowa
GREAT PLAINS
Ute
Missouri
Kansa
Kiowa
Osage
Wichita
Lipan Apache
Tonkawa
Caddo
Natchez
Atakapa
Karankawa
Colorado R.
Sioux
Rio Grande

Chippewa (Ojibwa)
Chippewa (Ojibwa)
SUB-ARCTIC
Micmac
Malecite
Algonquin
Abenaki
Ottawa
Huron
Menominee
Sauk
Fox
Winnebago
Kickapoo
Potawatomi
EASTERN WOODLAND
Iroquois
Mohawk
Oneida
Onondaga
Cayuga
Seneca
Mahican
Pennacook
Massachusetts
Wampanoag
Narragansett
Miami
Illinois
Erie
Susquehannock
Lenni-Lenape (Delaware)
Powhatan
Tutelo
Tuscarora
Shawnee
Cherokee
Catawba
Quapaw
Chickasaw
SOUTHEAST
Choctaw
Creek
Yamasee
Timucua
Biloxi
Apalachee
Calusa
Great Lakes
St. Lawrence R.
Mississippi R.
Ohio R.
Gulf of Mexico

PACIFIC OCEAN

ATLANTIC OCEAN

0   500 Miles
0   500 Kilometers

---

tem proved no more successful in winning converts to European culture. Stuffy classrooms held little attraction for young Indian scholars. And, as Benjamin Franklin was told by tribal leaders in 1753, college education did not teach Indian students "the true methods of killing deer, catching Beaver or surprising an enemy."

The Native Americans clung tightly to their own ways, showing little enthusiasm for European clothes, diet, or houses. And when an Indian married a white—unions that the English found less desirable than did the French or Spanish—the European partner usually elected to live among the Indians. Even slavery failed to achieve cultural conversion. Enslaved Indians either ran away or died; they did not become Europeans.

Indians did, however, covet the products of European technology. Arrows tipped with metal rather than flint were obviously superior. Hunting became more efficient, and with the introduction of firearms, Indian warfare became more deadly. The tribes located closest to the white settlements obtained firearms more quickly than those that lived farther west. This put the interior tribes at a great disadvantage, and it is not surprising that the tribes trading directly with the whites dominated other Native Americans armed only with bows and arrows.

At the same time, however, Indians who traded with the Europeans soon became dependent on the new commerce. To pay for the European goods, Indians hunted more aggressively, which reduced the population of fur-bearing animals at a time when European settlement was already having an impact on deer and other animals.

EFFECTS OF DISEASE

Disease ultimately destroyed the cultural integrity of many North American tribes. European explorers exposed North Americans to germs against which they possessed no natural immunities—smallpox, measles, and typhus. Settlers who possessed no knowledge of germ theory speculated that God had providentially cleared the wilderness of heathens.

Modern historians believe that some tribes suffered a 90 to 95 percent population loss within the first century of European contact. The death of so many Indians deprived the conquerors, especially the Spanish, of indigenous workers needed to operate new mines and plantations. This loss may have caused colonists throughout the New World to seek a substitute labor force in Africa.

The Indian survivors of the terrible epidemics often suffered profound psychological consequences.

Some tribes, the Iroquois, for example, withstood the threat of disease better than did others. On the whole this disaster reinforced racial stereotypes in the minds of Europeans already predisposed to view Indians as inferior and uncivilized. European colonists may have described Native Americans in derogatory terms because they were seeing sick and dispirited men and women whose lives had been shattered.

AFRICAN PEOPLE AND HISTORY

During the era of the European slave trade, a number of myths about sub-saharan Africa were propagated. Europeans maintained that the sub-Saharan Africans lived simple, isolated lives. Indeed, some scholars still depict this vast region stretching from the Senegal River south to modern Angola as a single cultural unit, as if at one time, all the men and women living there had shared a common set of political, religious, and social values.

Such was not the case. Sub-Saharan West Africa was rich in political, religious, and cultural diversity. Centuries earlier, the Muslim religion had slowly spread into black Africa, and although many West Africans resisted the Islamic faith, it was widely accepted in the Senegal Valley. The Muslim traders from North Africa and the Middle East who introduced their religion to West Africans also established sophisticated trade networks that linked the villagers of Senegambia with the urban centers of northwest Africa, Morocco, Tunisia, and Cyre-

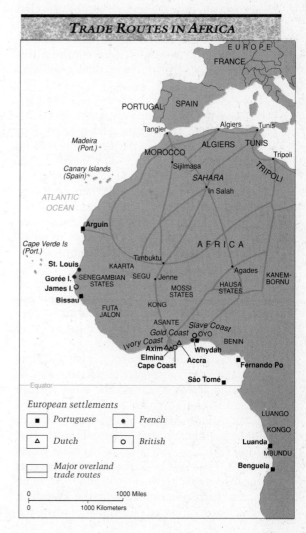

TRADE ROUTES IN AFRICA

European settlements
- ■ Portuguese
- ● French
- △ Dutch
- ○ British
- ▭ Major overland trade routes

0   1000 Miles
0   1000 Kilometers

naica. Great camel caravans regularly crossed the Sahara Desert carrying trade goods, which were exchanged for gold and slaves.

West Africans spoke many different languages and organized themselves into diverse political systems. As in Europe, kingdoms rose and fell, and when the first European traders arrived, Mali, Benin, and Kongo were among the major states. Other Africans lived in stateless societies organized along lineage structures. But whatever the form of government, men and women found their primary social identity within well-defined lineage groups, which consisted of persons claiming descent from a common ancestor. In these lineage groups, the clan elders made the important economic and social decisions—from who should receive land to who might take a wife. These communities were normally self-sufficient, producing both food and trade goods.

The first Europeans to reach the West African coast by sail were the Portuguese. In the fifteenth century, they journeyed to Africa in search of gold and slaves. Africans were willing partners in the commerce, but insisted that Europeans respect their trade regulations. They required the Europeans respect their trade regulations. They required the Europeans to pay tolls and other fees and restricted the foreign traders to conducting their business in small forts or castles located at the mouths of the major rivers. Local merchants acquired slaves and gold in the interior and transported them to the coast, where they were exchanged for European goods. Strong African armies and deadly diseases prevented Europeans from moving into the interior regions of Africa.

Even before Europeans colonized the New World, the Portuguese were purchasing almost a thousand slaves a year on the West African coast and sending them to Portuguese and Spanish Atlantic island plantations. Current estimates indicate that approximately 10.7 million Africans were taken to the New World as slaves. The slave trade was so extensive that during every year between 1650 and 1831, more Africans than Europeans came to the Americas. As one historian noted, "In terms of immigra-tion alone . . . America was an extension of Africa rather than Europe until late in the nineteenth century."

BACKGROUND OF EUROPEAN CONQUEST

In ancient times the West possessed a mythical appeal to people living along the shores of the Mediterranean Sea. Classical writers speculated about the fate of the legendary Atlantis, a great civilization that had mysteriously sunk beneath the ocean waves. In the fifth century A.D. an intrepid Irish monk, Saint Brendan, reporting finding enchanted islands far out in the Atlantic where he also met a talking whale. Such stories aroused curiosity but proved difficult to verify.

About 1000 A.D., Scandinavian seafarers known as Norsemen or Vikings actually established settlements in the New World. In the year 984 a band of Vikings led by Eric the Red sailed west from Iceland to a large island in the North Atlantic, which Eric inappropriately named Greenland in an effort to attract colonists to this icebound region. A few years later Eric's son, Leif, pushed even farther west to northern Newfoundland. Poor communications, hostile Indians, and political upheavals at home, however, made maintenance of these distant outposts impossible. The Viking adventurers were not widely known; when Columbus set out on his great voyage in 1492, he seemed to have been unaware of these earlier exploits.

RISE OF NATION-STATES

The Viking achievement went unnoticed partly because other Europeans were not prepared to sponsor trans-Atlantic exploration and settlement. Medieval kingdoms were loosely organized, and for several centuries fierce provincial loyalties, widespread ignorance of classical learning, and dreadful plagues such as the Black Death discouraged people from thinking about the world beyond their villages.

In the fifteenth century these conditions began to change. The expansion of commerce, a more imaginative outlook fostered by the Renaissance, and a general population growth after 1450 contributed to the exploration impulse. Land became more expensive, and landowners prospered. Demands from wealthy landlords for such luxury goods as spices and jewels, obtainable only in distant ports, introduced powerful new incentives for exploration and trade.

This period also witnessed the victory of the "new monarchs" over feudal nobles; political authority was centralized. The changes came slowly, and in many areas violently, but wherever they occurred, the results altered traditional political relationships between the nobility and the crown, between the citizen and the state. The new rulers recruited national armies and paid for them with national taxes. These rulers could be despotic, but they usually restored a measure of peace to communities tired of chronic feudal war.

The story was the same throughout most of western Europe. Henry VII in England, Louis XI in France, and Ferdinand of Aragon and Isabella of Castile in Spain forged strong nations from weak kingdoms. If these political changes had not occurred, the major European countries could not possibly have generated the financial and military resources necessary for worldwide exploration. Indeed, the formation of aggressive nation-states prepared the way for the later wars of empire.

TECHNOLOGY AND KNOWLEDGE

During this period naval innovators revolutionized ship design and technology. Before the fifteenth century the ships that plied the Mediterranean were clumsy and slow. But by the time Columbus sailed from Spain, they were faster, more maneuverable, and less expensive to operate. Most important of all was a new type of rigging developed by the Arabs, the lateen sail, which allowed large ships to sail into the wind, permitting trans-Atlantic travel and difficult maneuvers along the rocky, uncharted coasts of North America. By the end of the fifteenth century, seafarers set sail with a new sense of confidence.

The final prerequisite to exploration was knowledge. The rediscovery of classical texts and maps in the humanistic renaissance of the fifteenth century helped stimulate fresh investigation of the globe. And, because of the invention of the printing press in the 1430s, this new knowledge could spread across Europe. The printing press opened the European mind to exciting possibilities that had only been dimly perceived when the Vikings sailed the North Atlantic.

SPAIN AND THE NEW WORLD

In the early fifteenth century, Spain was politically divided, its people were poor, and its harbors were second-rate. There was little to indicate that this land would take the lead in conquering the New World. But in the early sixteenth century Spain came alive. The union of Ferdinand and Isabella sparked a drive for political consolidation which, because of the monarchs' militant Catholicism, took on the characteristics of a religious crusade. The new monarchs waged a victorious war against the Moslem states in southern Spain, which ended in 1492 when Granada, the last Moslem stronghold, fell. Out of this volatile political and social environment came the *conquistadores*, men eager for personal glory and material gain, uncompromising in matters of religion, and unswerving in their loyalty to the Crown. These were the men who first carried European culture to the New World.

ADMIRAL OF THE OCEAN

If it had not been for Christopher Columbus (Cristoforo Colombo), Spain might never had gained an American empire. Born in Genoa, Italy, in 1451 of humble parentage, Columbus devoured classical learning and became ob-

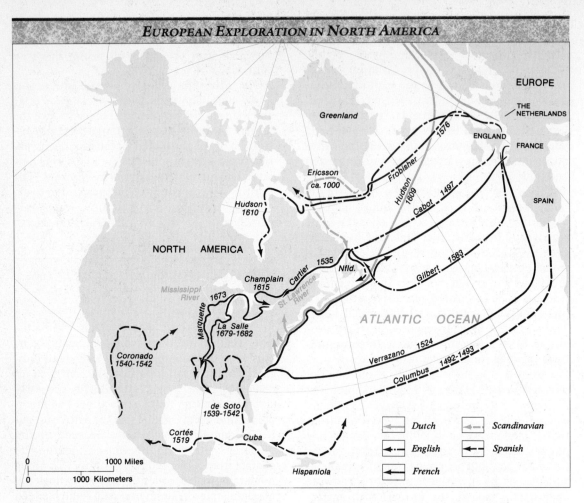

sessed with the idea of sailing west across the Atlantic Ocean to reach Cathay, as China was then known. In 1484 he presented his plan to the king of Portugal, who was also interested in a route to Cathay. But the Portuguese were more interested in the route that went around the tip of Africa. After a polite audience, Columbus was refused support.

Undaunted by rejection, Columbus petitioned Isabella and Ferdinand for financial backing. They were initially no more interested in his grand design than the Portuguese had been. But fear of Portugal's growing power as well as Columbus' confident talk of wealth and empire led the new monarchs to reassess his scheme. Finally the two sovereigns pro-

vided the supremely self-assured navigator with three ships, the *Niña, Pinta,* and *Santa Maria.* The indomitable admiral set sail for Cathay in August 1492, the year of Spain's unification.

Educated Europeans in the fifteenth century knew without question that the world was round. The question was size, not shape. Columbus estimated the distance to the mainland of Asia to be about 3000 nautical miles, a voyage that his small ships would have had no difficulty in completing. The actual distance is 10,600 nautical miles, however, and had the New World not been in his way, his crew would have run out of food and water long before they reached China.

After stopping in the Canary Islands for ship repairs and supplies, Columbus crossed the Atlantic in thirty-three days, landing on an island in the Bahamas. He searched for the fabled cities of Asia, never considering that he had stumbled upon a large land mass completely unknown in Europe. Since his mathematical calculations had been correct, he assumed he would soon encounter the Chinese. Instead he met friendly, though startled, Native Americans, whom he called Indians.

Three more times Columbus returned to the New World—in searched of fabled Asian riches. He died in 1506, a frustrated, impoverished dreamer, unaware that he had reached a previously unknown continent. The final blow came in December 1500 when an ambitious falsifier, Amerigo Vespucci, published a sensational travel account that convinced German mapmakers that he had beaten Columbus to the New World. Before the deception was discovered, *America* gained general acceptance throughout Europe as the name for the newly discovered continent.

The Rise of the Conquistadores

By the Treaty of Tordesillas (1494) Spain and Portugal divided the New World. Portugal gained Brazil, and Spain laid claim to all the remaining territories. Spain's good fortune unleashed a horde of conquistadores on the Caribbean. They came not as colonists but as fortune hunters seeking instant wealth, preferably gold, and they were not squeamish about the means they used to obtain it. The primary casualties of their greed were the Native Americans. In less than two decades the tribes that had inhabited the Caribbean islands had been exterminated, victims of exploitation and disease.

After a quarter century the rumors of fabulous wealth in Mexico lured the conquistadores from the islands Columbus had found to the mainland. On November 18, 1518, Hernán Cortés, a minor government functionary in Cuba, and a small army set sail for Mexico.

There Cortés soon demonstrated that he was a leader of extraordinary ability, a person of intellect and vision who managed to rise above the goals of his avaricious followers.

His adversary was the legendary Aztec emperor Montezuma. It was a duel of powerful

At first contact with Cortés's army, the Aztecs, led by Montezuma, thought the Spaniards were demigods. The psychological advantage of their perceived omnipotence helped Cortés to score a decisive victory in Mexico.

personalities. After burning his ships to cut off his army from a possible retreat, Cortés led his band of 600 followers across difficult mountain trails toward the Valley of Mexico. The sound of gunfire and the sight of armor-clad horses, both unknown to Native Americans, frightened the Indians. Added to these technological advantages was an important psychological factor. At first Montezuma thought that the Spaniards were gods, representatives of the fearful plumed serpent, Quetzalcoatl. By the time the Aztec ruler realized his error, it was too late to save his empire.

MANAGING AN EMPIRE

Cortés' victory in Mexico, coupled with other Spanish conquests, notably in Peru, transformed the mother country into the wealthiest nation in Europe. But the Spanish crown soon faced new difficulties. The conquistadores had to be brought under royal authority. Adventurers like Cortés were stubbornly independent, quick to take offense, and thousands of miles away from the seat of government. One solution was the *encomienda* system. Conquistadores were rewarded with Indian villages and control over native labor. They also had the responsibility of protecting the Indians, who suffered terribly under this cruelly exploitative system of labor tribute. The system did make the colonizers very dependent upon the king, however, for it was he who legitimized their title. As one historian has noted, the system transformed "a frontier of plunder into a frontier of settlement."

Bureaucrats dispatched directly from Spain soon replaced the aging conquistadores. Unlike the governing system that later existed in England's mainland American colonies, Spain's rulers maintained tight control over their American possessions through their government officials. After 1535 a viceroy, a nobleman appointed to oversee the king's colonial interests, ruled the people of New Spain. Working independently of the viceroy, an *audiencia*, the supreme judicial body, brought a measure of justice to the Indians and Spaniards and

The wife and daughter of an Algonquian chief, drawn by John White. The child is holding an English doll.

made certain that the viceroys did not slight their responsibilities to the king. Finally, the Council of the Indies in Spain handled colonial business. Although cumbersome and slow, somehow this rigidly controlled system worked.

The Spanish also brought Catholicism to the New World. The Dominicans and Franciscans, the two largest religious orders, established Indian missions throughout New Spain, and some barefoot friars protected the Native Americans from the worst forms of exploitation. One courageous Dominican, Fra Bartolomé de Las Casas, even published an eloquent defense of Indian rights, *Historia de las Indias*, that among other things questioned the European conquest of the New World. The book led to reforms designed to bring greater "love and moderation" to Spanish-Indian relations.

About 750,000 people migrated to the New World from Spain. Most of the colonists were impoverished, single males in their late twenties in search of economic opportunities. They generally came from the poorest agricultural regions of southern Spain. Since few Spanish women migrated, especially in the sixteenth century, the men often married Indians and, later, blacks, unions which produced "mestizos" and "mulattoes." The frequency of interracial marriage created a society of more fluid racial categories than there were in the English colonies, where the sex ratio of the settlers was more balanced and the racially mixed population comparatively small.

SETTLING THE BORDERLANDS

The lure of gold drew Spanish conquistadores to the unexplored lands to the north of Mexico. Between 1539 and 1541, Hernando de Soto trekked across the Southeast from Florida to the Mississippi River looking for gold and glory, and at about the same time, Francisco Vásquez de Coronado set out from New Spain in search of the fabled "Seven Cities of Cibola." Neither conquistador found what he was searching for. In the seventeenth century when Juan de Oñate established outposts in the Southwest, the Spanish came in open conflict with Native Americans in that region. In 1680 the Indians drove the whites completely out of the territory. Thereafter the decision was made to maintain only a token presence in present-day Texas and New Mexico in order to discourage French encroachment upon Spanish lands. For the same reason, the Spanish colony of St. Augustine was established in Florida in 1565. Little interest was shown by Spanish authorities in California, a land of poor Indians and even poorer natural resources. Had it not been for the work of a handful of priests, Spain would have had little claim to California.

Even so, Spain claimed far more of the New World than it could possibly manage. After the era of the conquistadores, Spain's rulers regarded the American colonies primarily as a source of precious metal, and between 1500 and 1650 an estimated 200 tons of gold and 16,000 tons of silver were shipped back to the Spanish treasury in Madrid. The resulting inflation hurt the common people in Spain and prevented the growth of Spanish industry. Unimaginative leadership and debilitating wars hastened the Spanish decline. As one insightful observer declared in 1603, "the New World conquered by you has conquered you in its turn." Nonetheless, Spain's great cultural contribution to the American people is still very much alive today.

FRENCH EXPLORATION AND SETTLEMENT

French interest in the New World developed more slowly. In 1534 Jacques Cartier first sailed to the New World in search of a northwest passage to China. At first he was depressed by the rocky, barren coast of Newfoundland. He grumbled, "I am rather inclined to believe that this is the land God gave to Cain." But the discovery of a large, promising waterway raised Cartier's spirits. He reconnoitered the Gulf of St. Lawrence, traveling up the river as far as Montreal, but he did not discover a northwest passage, gold, or other precious metals. After several voyages to Canada, Cartier became discouraged by the harsh winters and meager findings; he returned home for good in 1542. Not until seventy-five years later did the brilliant navigator Samuel de Champlain rediscover this region for France. He founded Quebec in 1608.

In Canada the French developed an economy based primarily on the fur trade, a commerce that required close cooperation with the Native Americans. They also explored the heart of the continent. In 1673 Père Jacques Marquette journeyed down the Mississippi River, and nine

In the dead of winter the streams of New France were frozen solid. French voyageurs built sledges, placed their canoes and their supplies on them, and proceeded down the frozen course into the heart of the continent.

years later Sieur de La Salle traveled all the way to the Gulf of Mexico. In the early eighteenth century, the French established small settlements in Louisiana, the most important being New Orleans.

Although the French controlled the region along the Mississippi and its tributaries, their dream of a vast American empire suffered from several serious flaws. From the first, the king remained largely indifferent to colonial affairs. An even greater problem was the nature of the land and climate. Few rural peasants or urban artisans wished to venture to the inhospitable northern country, and throughout the colonial period, New France was underpopulated. By the first quarter of the eighteenth century, the English settlements had outstripped their French neighbors in population as well as in volume of trade.

✦ BACKGROUND OF ENGLISH EXPLORATION

The first English visit to North America remains something of a mystery. Fishermen working out of the western English ports may have landed in Nova Scotia and Newfoundland as early as the 1480s. John Cabot (Giovanni Caboto), a Venetian sea captain, completed the first recorded trans-Atlantic voyage by an English vessel in 1497. Henry VII had rejected Columbus' enterprise for the Indies, but the first

Tudor monarch apparently experienced a change of heart after hearing of Spain's success.

Like other explorers of that time, Cabot believed that he could find a northwest passage to Asia. He doggedly searched the northern water for a likely opening, but a direct route to Cathay eluded him. Cabot died during a second attempt in 1498. Although Sebastian Cabot continued his father's explorations in the Hudson Bay region in 1508–1509, English interest in the New World waned. For the next three quarters of a century, the English people were preoccupied with more pressing domestic and religious concerns. The Cabot voyages did, however, establish an English claim to American territory.

THE REFORMATION IN EUROPE AND ENGLAND

The reign of Henry VII was plagued by domestic troubles. England possessed no standing army, a small, weak navy, and many strong and independent local magnates. During the sixteenth century, however, the next Tudor king, Henry VIII, and his daughter Elizabeth I developed a strong central government and transformed England into a Protestant nation. These changes propelled England into a central role in European affairs and were crucial to the creation of England's North American empire.

The Protestantism that eventually stimulated colonization was definitely not of English origin. In 1517 a relatively obscure German monk, Martin Luther, publicly challenged certain tenets and practices of Roman Catholicism, and within a few years the religious unity of Europe was forever shattered. Luther's message was straightforward. God spoke through the Bible, Luther maintained, not through the pope or priests. Pilgrimages, fasts, alms, indulgences, none of these traditional acts could assure salvation. Luther's radical ideas spread rapidly across northern Germany and Scandinavia.

Other Protestant reformers soon spoke out against Catholicism. The most important of these was John Calvin, a lawyer turned theologian, who lived in the Swiss city of Geneva.

Calvin stressed God's omnipotence over human affairs. The Lord, he maintained, chose some persons for "election," the gift of salvation, while condemning others to eternal damnation. Human beings were powerless to alter this decision by their individual actions.

Common sense suggests that such a bleak doctrine might lead to fatalism or hedonism. After all, why not enjoy worldly pleasures if they have no effect on God's judgment? But common sense would be wrong. Indeed, Calvinists were constantly busy searching for signs that they had received God's gift of grace. The uncertainty of their eternal state proved a powerful psychological spur, for as long as people did not know whether they were scheduled for heaven or hell, they worked diligently to demonstrate that they possessed at least the seeds of grace. This doctrine of "predestination" became the distinguishing mark of Calvin's followers throughout northern Europe. In the seventeenth century, they were known in France as Huguenots, and in England and America as Puritans.

Popular anticlericalism was the basis for the Reformation in England. The English people had long resented paying monies to a distant pope. Early in the sixteenth century, opposition

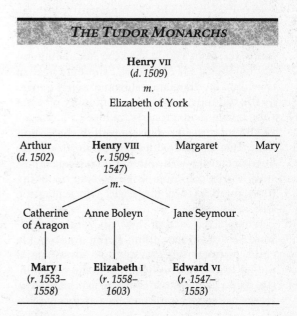

THE TUDOR MONARCHS

Henry VII
(*d. 1509*)
m.
Elizabeth of York

Arthur	**Henry VIII**	Margaret	Mary
(*d. 1502*)	(*r. 1509–1547*)		

m.

Catherine of Aragon	Anne Boleyn	Jane Seymour

Mary I	**Elizabeth I**	**Edward VI**
(*r. 1553–1558*)	(*r. 1558–1603*)	(*r. 1547–1553*)

to the clergy grew increasingly vocal. Cardinal Thomas Wolsey, the most powerful prelate in England, flaunted his immense wealth and became a symbol of spiritual corruption. Parish priests were ridiculed for their ignorance and greed. Anticlericalism did not run as deep in England as in Germany, but by the late 1520s the Roman Catholic clergy had strained the allegiance of the great mass of the population. Ordinary men and women throughout the kingdom were ready to leave the institutional church.

The catalyst for Reformation in England was Henry VIII's desire to end his marriage to Catherine of Aragon, daughter of the king of Spain. Their union in 1509 had produced a daughter, Mary, but no son. The need for a male heir obsessed Henry. He and his counselors assumed that a female ruler could not maintain domestic peace and that England would fall once again into civil war. Henry petitioned Pope Clement VII for a divorce. Unwilling to tolerate the public humiliation of Catherine, Spain forced the pope to procrastinate. In 1527 time ran out. Henry fell in love with Anne Boleyn, who later bore him a daughter, Elizabeth. The king divorced Catherine without papal consent.

The final break with Rome came swiftly. Between 1529 and 1536, the king, acting through Parliament, severed all ties with the pope, seized church lands, and dissolved many of the monasteries. In March 1534 the Act of Supremacy boldly named Henry VIII "supreme head of the Church of England." Land formerly owned by the Catholic church passed quickly into private hands, and property holders acquired a vested interest in Protestantism. In 1539 William Tyndale and Miles Coverdale issued an English edition of the Bible, which made it possible for the common people to read the Scriptures in their own language. The separation was complete.

When Henry died in 1547, his young son Edward VI came to the throne. But he was a sickly child. Militant Protestants took advantage of the political uncertainty to introduce Calvinism into England. In breaking with the papacy, Henry had shown little enthusiasm for theolog-

ical change; most Catholic ceremonies remained. But opponents now insisted that the Church of England remove every trace of its Catholic origins. Edward died in 1553, and these ambitious efforts came to a sudden halt. Henry's eldest daughter, Mary I, next ascended the throne. Fiercely loyal to the Catholic faith, she vowed to return England to the pope. Hundreds of Protestants were executed, others scurried off to Geneva and Frankfurt where they absorbed radical Calvinist doctrines. When Mary died in 1558 and was succeeded by Elizabeth I, these "Marian exiles" returned, more eager than ever to purify the Tudor church of Catholicism. Mary had inadvertently advanced the cause of Calvinism by creating so many Protestant martyrs. The Marian exiles controlled the Elizabethan church, which remained fundamentally Calvinist until the end of the sixteenth century.

THE PROTESTANT QUEEN

Elizabeth I was a woman of extraordinary talent. She governed England from 1558 to 1603, an intellectually exciting period during which some of her subjects took the first halting steps toward colonizing the New World.

Elizabeth's most urgent duty was to end the religious turmoil that had divided the country for a generation. She had no desire to restore Catholicism. After all, the pope openly referred to her as a woman of illegitimate birth. Nor did she want to re-create the church exactly as it had been in the final years of her father's reign. Rather, Elizabeth established a unique church, near-Catholic in ceremony, but Protestant in doctrine. The examples of Edward and Mary had demonstrated that neither radical change nor widespread persecution gained a monarch lasting popularity.

Elizabeth still faced serious religious challenges. Catholicism and Protestantism were warring faiths; each was an ideology, a body of deeply held beliefs that influenced the way that average men and women across the continent interpreted the experiences of everyday life. The confrontation between Protestantism and Catholicism affected Elizabeth's entire reign.

Militant Calvinists urged her to drop all Catholic rituals, and fervent Catholics wanted her to return to the Roman church. Pope Pius excommunicated her in 1570. Spain, the most intensely Catholic state in Europe, vowed to restore England to the "true" faith, and the Catholic terrorists constantly plotted to overthrow the Tudor monarchy.

RELIGION, WAR, AND NATIONALISM

English Protestantism and English nationalism slowly merged. A loyal English subject in the late sixteenth century loved the monarch, supported the Church of England, and hated Catholics, especially those who happened to live in Spain. Elizabeth's subjects adored their Virgin Queen, and they applauded when her famed "Sea Dogs"—dashing figures such as Sir Francis Drake and Sir John Hawkins—seized Spanish treasure ships in American waters. The English sailors' raids were little more than piracy, but they passed for grand victories. With each engagement, each threat, each plot, English nationalism took deeper root. By the 1570s, the English people were driven by powerful ideological forces similar to those that had moved the subjects of Isabella and Ferdinand almost a century earlier.

In the mid-1580s, Philip II of Spain constructed a mighty fleet carrying thousands of Spain's finest infantry. This Armada was built to cross the English Channel and destroy the Protestant queen. When one of Philip's lieutenants viewed the Armada at Lisbon in May 1588, he described it as "La felicissima armada," the invincible fleet. The king believed that with the support of England's oppressed Catholics, Spanish troops would sweep Elizabeth from power.

It was a grand scheme; it was an even grander failure. In 1588 a smaller, more maneuverable English navy dispersed the Armada and revealed Spain's vulnerability. Philip's hopes for a Catholic England lay wrecked along the rocky coasts of Scotland and Ireland. Elizabeth's subjects remained loyal throughout the crisis. In-spired by success in the Channel, bolder personalities dreamed of acquiring riches and planting colonies across the North Atlantic. Spain's American monopoly had been broken.

IRISH REHEARSAL FOR AMERICAN COLONIZATION

England's first colony was Ireland. On that island enterprising Englishmen first learned to subdue a foreign population and seize its lands. Ireland's one million inhabitants were scattered mainly along the coast, and there were few villages. To the English, the Irish seemed wild and barbaric. They were also fiercely independent. The English dominated a small region around Dublin, but much of Ireland remained in the hands of Gaelic-speaking Catholics who presumably lived beyond the reach of civilization.

During the 1560s and 1570s the English decided that money could be made in Ireland, despite the hostility of the Irish. English colonists moved in and forced the Irish either into tenancy or off the land altogether. Semi-military colonies were planted in Ulster and Munster.

Colonization produced severe cultural strains. The English settlers, however humble their own origins, felt superior to the Irish. After all, the English had championed the Protestant religion, constructed a complex market economy, and created a powerful nation-state. To the English, the Irish appeared lazy, lawless, superstitious, and ofttimes stupid. Even educated representatives of the two cultures found communication almost impossible. English colonists, for example, criticized Ireland's pastoral farming methods. It seemed perversely wasteful for the Irish to be forever moving about because this practice retarded the development of towns. Sir John Davies, a leading English colonist, declared that if the Irish were left to themselves, they would "never . . . build houses, make townships or villages or manure or improve the land *as it ought to be*." Such wastefulness became the standard English justification for seizing more land. No matter what the Irish did, they could never be sufficiently English to please their new masters.

English ethnocentrism was relatively benign so long as the Irish accepted subservient roles. But they rebelled frequently, and English condescension turned quickly to violence. Resistance smacked of disrespect, and for the good of the Irish and the safety of the English, it had to be crushed. Sir Humphrey Gilbert was especially brutal. A talented man who wrote treatises on geography, Gilbert explored the coast of North America and entertained Queen Elizabeth with witty conversation. But as military governor in Ireland, he tolerated no opposition.

In 1569, when the Irish rose up in Munster, he executed everyone he could catch, "mane, woman and childe." He cut off the heads of many enemy soldiers killed in battle, and in the words of one contemporary, Gilbert laid his macabre trophies "on the ground by each side of the way leading into his tent, so that none should come into his tent for any cause but commonly he must pass through a lane of heads." Instead of brining peace and security, such behavior generated a hatred so deep that Ireland remains divided to this day.

The Irish experiments served as models for later English colonies in the New World, shaping the English view of America and its people. English adventurers in the New World compared Native Americans to the "wild" Irish. This ethnocentrism was a central element in the transfer of English culture to America. The English, like the Spanish and the French, did not perceive America in objective terms. They had already constructed an image of America, and the people and objects that greeted them on the other side of the Atlantic were forced into Old World categories, some of them Irish.

❧ ENGLAND TURNS TO AMERICA

By the 1570s, England was ready to challenge Spain and reap the profits of Asia and America. Only dimly aware of Cabot's voyages and with very limited colonization experience in Ireland, the English adventurers made almost every mistake that one could possibly imagine between 1575 and 1600. They did, however, acquire valuable information about winds and currents, supplies and finance, which laid the foundation for later, more successful ventures.

GILBERT'S ADVENTURE AND THE ROANOKE TRAGEDY

The pioneer of English colonization in the New World was the same Sir Humphrey Gilbert who had experimented in colonization with Ireland. Gilbert originally set out to discover the northwest passage to Cathay. He published an entire book on the subject, showing exactly where the passages might be found. He tantalized readers and potential investors with stories of the fabulous riches awaiting those who first seized control of the short route to Asia. Gilbert also envisioned vast New World estates, much like those he had created in Ireland.

Gilbert's enterprise got off to a bizarre start. In 1576, he sent Martin Frobisher, a courageous sea captain, to find the passage. Frobisher missed it, but he returned with tons of "gold" from desolate Hall's Island. The sparkling dirt turned out upon closer analysis to be worthless chunks of iron pyrite (fool's gold).

In 1578 Gilbert tried a different approach. He persuaded Elizabeth to grant him a charter for "remote heathen and barbarous landes." After one abortive attempt and against the advice of the queen, Gilbert sailed to Newfoundland in 1583 and claimed the territory as his very own.

On the return voyage his ship was lost without a trace. The tough old adventurer was last sighted sitting on the open deck during a storm reading from the works of Sir Thomas More.

Sir Walter Raleigh shared Gilbert's dreams. The men was half brothers, and after Gilbert's death, Raleigh announced his own intention of establishing a colony in America. In 1585 the optimistic Raleigh dispatched two captains to the coast of the present-day North Carolina to claim land granted to him by Elizabeth. The men returned with glowing reports about the fertility of the soil. Diplomatically, Raleigh renamed this marvelous region Virginia, in honor of his patron, the Virgin Queen.

Raleigh's enterprise seemed ill-fated from the start. Though encouraged by Elizabeth, he received no financial backing from the crown, and despite careful planning, everything went wrong. In 1585 Sir Richard Grenville transported a group of men to Roanoke Island, but the colonists did not arrive in Virginia until nearly autumn. The settlement was also poorly located, and even experienced navigators found it dangerous to reach. Finally, Grenville alienated the local Indians when he senselessly destroyed an entire Indian village in retaliation for the theft of a silver cup.

Grenville hurried back to England in the autumn of 1585, leaving the colonists to fend for themselves. They performed quite well. But when an expected shipment of supplies failed to arrive on time, the colonists grew discontented. In the spring of 1586 Sir Francis Drake unexpectedly landed at Roanoke, and the colonists impulsively decided to return home with him.

In 1587 Raleigh launched a second colony. The new settlement was more representative, containing men, women, and even children. The settlers feasted upon Roanoke's fish and game and bountiful harvests of corn and pumpkin. Yet within weeks after arriving, the leader

CHRONOLOGY

30,000–25,000 B.C.	Indians cross the Bering Strait into North America
2000–1500 B.C.	Agricultural revolution transforms Native American life
1001 A.D.	Norsemen establish a small settlement in Vinland (Newfoundland)
1438	(Ca.) Invention of printing method using movable type

1469	Marriage of Isabella and Ferdinand leads to the unification of Spain
1492	Columbus lands at San Salvador
1497	Cabot leads first English exploration of North America
1502	Montezuma becomes emperor of the Aztecs
1506	Columbus dies in Spain after four voyages to America
1517	Martin Luther's protests set off Reformation in Germany
1521	Cortés achieves victory over the Aztecs at Tenochtitlán
1529–1536	Henry VIII provokes English Reformation
1534	Cartier claims Canada for France
1536	Calvin's *Institutes* published
1540	Coronado explores the Southwest for Spain
1558	Elizabeth becomes queen of England
1583	Sir Humphrey Gilbert dies
1585	First Roanoke settlement established on coast of North Carolina
1588	Spanish Armada defeated by the English
1603	Elizabeth I dies
1608	Champlain founds Quebec
1682	La Salle travels the length of the Mississippi River

of the settlement, John White, returned to England at the colonists' urging to obtain additional food and clothing and to recruit new immigrants.

Once again, Raleigh's luck turned sour. War with Spain pressed every available ship into military service. When rescuers eventually reached the island in 1590, they found the village deserted. The fate of the "lost" colonists remains a mystery. The best guess is that they paid for Grenville's attack upon the Indians with their lives.

The Roanoke debacle discouraged others from emulating Raleigh. He had squandered a fortune and had nothing to show for it. During the 1590s smart investors put their money into privateering or other less exhausting ventures. Had it not been for Richard Hakluyt, who publicized the explorers' accounts of the New World, the dream of American colonization by the English might have ended.

MIXING PEOPLES ON A NEW CONTINENT

Hakluyt, a supremely industrious man, never saw America. Nevertheless, his vision of the New World powerfully shaped public opinion. He interviewed captains and sailors and carefully collected their travel stories in a massive book entitled *The Principall Navigations, Voyages, and Discoveries of the English Nation* (1589). Although each tale appeared to be a straightforward narrative, Hakluyt edited each piece to drive home the book's central point: England needed American colonies. English settlers, he argued, would provide the mother country with critical natural resources, and in the process they would grow rich themselves.

As a salesman for the New World, Hakluyt was as misleading as he was successful. He failed to mention the rich cultural diversity of the Native Americans and the varied backgrounds of the Europeans. Nor did he say a word about the sufferings of Africans in America. Instead he led many ordinary men and women who traveled to America to expect nothing less than a paradise on earth. As the history of Jamestown was soon to demonstrate,

the harsh realities of America bore little relation to those golden dreams.

☙ RECOMMENDED READING

The events surrounding the exploration of the New World have been the subject of a rich historical literature. A particularly well-written account of the background of European expansion is J. H. Parry, *The Age of Reconnaissance* (1963). A book of narrower focus is Samuel E. Morison, *The European Discovery of America: The Southern Voyages, 1492–1616* (1971). The transformation of early modern Europe, especially economic shifts, is discussed in Ralph Davis' brilliant synthesis, *The Rise of Atlantic Economies* (1973). Alfred Crosby provides insights into the unintended results of exploration in *Columbian Exchange: Biological and Cultural Consequences of 1492* (1972). Spain's rise to a world power can be traced in J. H. Elliott, *Imperial Spain, 1469–1716* (1963), and J. H. Parry, *The Spanish Seaborne Empire* (1966). Charles Gibson provides an excellent introduction to the history of New Spain in *Spain in America* (1966). Two books by W. J. Eccles, *Canada Under Louis XIV, 1663–1701* (1964) and *The Canadian Frontier, 1534–1760* (1969), provide considerable insight into the development of New France.

There are many fine studies of sixteenth-century England, beginning with G. R. Elton, *England Under the Tudors* (1974), and J. E. Neale, *Queen Elizabeth I* (1934). A. G. Dickens examines England's religious transformation in *The English Reformation* (1964). One should also look at Patrick Collinson, *The Religion of Protestants: The Church in English Society, 1559–1625* (1982). The two best studies of Ireland in this period are Nicholas P. Canny, *The Elizabethan Conquest of Ireland* (1976), and David B. Quinn, *The Elizabethans and the Irish* (1966).

Two sensitive books on Native American cultures are Bruce Trigger, *The Children of Aataentsic: A History of the Huron People to 1660* (1976), and Cornelius Jaenen, *Friend and Foe: Aspects of French-Amerindian Cultural Contact in the Sixteenth and Seventeenth Centuries* (1976). Sherburne F. Cook and Woodrow Borah provide a comprehensive analysis of the demographic crisis in *The Aboriginal Population of Central Mexico on the Eve of the Spanish Conquest* (1963). See Calvin Martin, *Keepers of the Game: Indian-Animal Relationships and the Fur Trade* (1978) on the Indians' responses to white culture. Also of interest are Shepard Krech, ed., *Indians, Animals, and the Fur Trade: A Critique of Keepers of the Game* (1981), and James Axtell, *The Invasion Within: The Conquest of Culture in Colonial North America* (1985).

2 THE SPECTRUM OF SETTLEMENT

In the spring of 1644, John Winthrop, governor of Massachusetts Bay, learned that Indians had overrun the scattered tobacco plantations of Virginia, killing as many as 500 colonists. Winthrop never thought much of the Chesapeake settlements. He regarded the people who had migrated to that part of America as grossly materialistic, and because Virginia had recently expelled several Puritan ministers, Winthrop decided that the Indian hostilities were God's way of punishing the planters for their worldliness. He gave the Virginians neither help nor sympathy.

In 1675 Indian forces declared all-out war against the New Englanders, and reports of the destruction of Puritan communities were soon circulating in Virginia. Sir William Berkeley, Virginia's royal governor, was not displeased by the news of New England's adversity. He and his friends held the Puritans in contempt. Indeed, the New Englanders reminded them of the religious fanatics who had provoked civil war in the mother country and who, in 1649, had executed Charles I. In reasoning that echoed Winthrop's, Berkeley concluded that the Indian attacks were God's revenge on the Puritans. He, in turn, declined to send the New Englanders the necessary supplies or sympathy.

Unity and nationalism were not part of Winthrop's and Berkeley's America. English colonization in the seventeenth century did not spring from a desire to build a centralized empire in the New World similar to those in Spain or France. Instead, the English Crown awarded colonial charters to a wide variety of people including merchants, religious idealists, and aristocratic adventurers, all of whom established separate and profoundly different colonies.

LEAVING HOME

Changes in the mother country occurring throughout the period of settlement help explain the diversity of English colonization. Far-reaching economic, political, and religious transformation affected seventeenth-century England. Many people left the villages where they were born in search of fresh opportunities. Thousands traveled to London, by 1600 a city of several hundred thousand inhabitants. Others set out for more exotic destinations. A large number of English settlers migrated to Ireland; lucrative employment and religious freedom attracted others to Holland. The most adventurous individuals, however, went to the New World—to Caribbean islands such as Barbados or to the mainland colonies.

Various reasons drew the colonists across the Atlantic. The quest for a purer form of worship motivated many, while the dream of owning land attracted others. And a few came to escape

bad marriages, jail terms, and poverty. But whatever their reasons for crossing the ocean, English men and women who emigrated to America in the seventeenth century left a mother country wracked by recurrent, often violent, political and religious controversies. During the 1620s the Stuart monarchs—James I (1603–1625) and his son Charles I (1625–1649)—fought constantly with the elected members of Parliament. In 1640 the conflict escalated into a bloody civil war between the king and supporters of Parliament. Finally, in 1649 the victorious parliamentarians beheaded Charles, and for almost a decade Oliver Cromwell, a brilliant general and religious reformer, governed England.

The unrest did not end with the death of Charles I. After Cromwell's death the Stuarts were restored to the throne (1660). But through the reigns of Charles II (1660–1685) and James II (1685–1688) the political turmoil continued. When the authoritarian James openly favored his fellow Catholics, the nation rose up in the "Glorious Revolution" (1688), sent him into permanent exile, and placed his staunchly Protestant daughter and son-in-law (William and Mary) upon the throne.

Political turmoil, religious persecution, and economic insecurity determined the flow of emigration. Men and women thought more seriously about living in the New World at such times. Ever-changing conditions in England help to explain the diversity of American settlement.

Regardless of when they came, the colonists carried with them a bundle of ideas, beliefs, and assumptions that shaped the way they viewed their new environment. The New World tested and sometimes transformed their values, but never destroyed them. The different subcultures that emerged in America were determined largely by the interaction between these values and such physical elements as climate, crops, and soil. The Chesapeake, the New England Colonies, the Middle Colonies, and the Carolinas formed distinct regional identities that persisted long after the first settlers had passed from the scene.

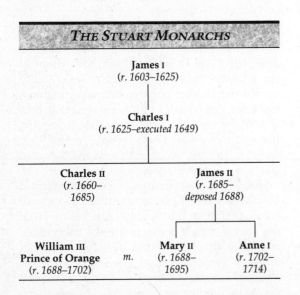

THE STUART MONARCHS

James I
(r. 1603–1625)

Charles I
(r. 1625–executed 1649)

Charles II
(r. 1660–1685)

James II
(r. 1685–deposed 1688)

William III
Prince of Orange
(r. 1688–1702)

m.

Mary II
(r. 1688–1695)

Anne I
(r. 1702–1714)

The Chesapeake: Dreams of Glory

The Roanoke debacle (see Chapter 1) raised questions about America's promise, but with the aid of visionaries like Richard Hakluyt the dream persisted. Writers insisted that there were profits to be made in the New World. In addition, goods from America would supply England with items that it would otherwise be forced to purchase from European rivals—Holland, France, and Spain. The three motives of making money, helping England, and annoying Catholic Spain constituted a powerful incentive. Shortly after James I ascended to the throne, the settlers were given an opportunity to test their theories in the Chesapeake colonies of Virginia and Maryland.

MISADVENTURE AT JAMESTOWN

Money had been an early obstacle to colonization. The "joint-stock company" removed the barrier. A business organization in which

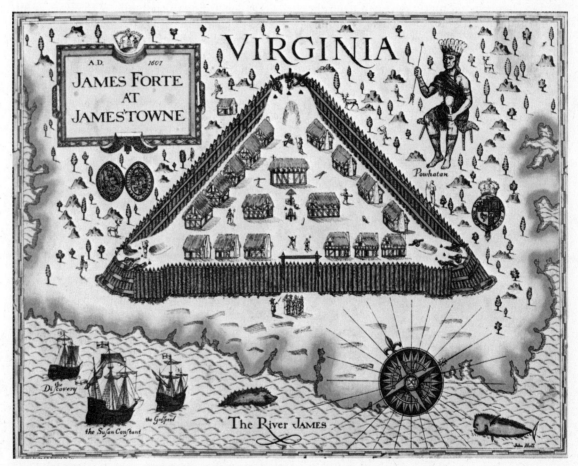

Surrounded by water on three sides, the marshy peninsula on the James River seemed an easy-to-defend location for the Jamestown fort.

scores of people could invest without fear of bankruptcy, it proved very successful. A person could purchase a share of stock at a stated price, and at the end of several years, could anticipate recovering the initial investment plus a portion of whatever profits the company had made. Within a very short time, some of these enterprises were able to amass large amounts of capital, enough certainly to finance a new colony. Virginia was the first such venture.

On April 10, 1606, James I issued a charter authorizing the London Company under the dynamic leadership of Sir Thomas Smith (no relation to Captain John Smith) to establish plantations in Virginia. Although the boundaries mentioned in the charter were vague, the London Company promptly renamed itself the Virginia Company and set out to find the treasure that Hakluyt had promised. In December 1606, the *Susan Constant*, the *Godspeed*, and the *Discovery*, with 104 men and boys aboard,

Pocahontas took the name Rebecka when she converted to Christianity. This portrait was painted during a visit to London in 1616.

sailed for America. The land the voyagers found was lush and well-watered with "faire meadowes and goodly tall trees."

They soon found something else—death and dissension. The low-lying ground on which they set up their base was thirty miles up the James River on a marshy peninsula they named Jamestown. It proved to be a disease-ridden death trap; even the drinking water was contaminated with salt. However, a peninsula was easier to defend and they feared a surprise attack more than sickness.

Almost instantly, the colonists began quarreling. Tales of beaches strewn with rubies and diamonds had lured them to Virginia. Once there, instead of cooperating for the common good—guarding the palisade or farming—each individual pursued personal interests. Meanwhile, disease, hostile Indians, and then starvation ravaged the hapless settlers.

Had it not been for Captain John Smith, Virginia might have gone the way of Roanoke. Smith told tales of fighting the Turks and being saved from certain death by various beautiful women, claims that modern historians have largely verified. In Virginia, Smith brought order out of anarchy. He traded with the Indians for food, mapped the Chesapeake Bay, and was even rescued from execution by a precocious Indian princess, Pocahontas. After seizing control of the ruling council in 1608, he instituted a tough military discipline, forcing the lazy to work and breathing life back into the dying colony.

Leaders of the Virginia Company in London soon recognized the need to reform the entire enterprise. A new charter in 1609 granted the company the right to make all commercial and political decisions affecting the colonists. Moreover, in an effort to obtain scarce capital, the original partners opened the "joint stock" to the general public. The company sponsored a spirited publicity campaign; pamphlets and sermons extolled the colony's potential and exhorted patriotic English citizens to invest in the enterprise.

This burst of energy came to nothing. Bad luck and poor planning plagued the Virginia

Company. A ship carrying settlers and supplies went aground in the Caribbean; the governor, Lord De La Warr, postponed his departure for America; and Captain Smith suffered a debilitating accident and had to return to England. As a result, between 1609 and 1611 the remaining settlers lacked capable leadership. Food supplies grew short. The terrible winter of 1609–1610—termed the "starving time"— drove a few desperate colonists to cannibalism. Smith reported that one crazed settler killed, salted, and ate parts of his wife before the murder was discovered. Many people lost their will to live.

Governor De La Warr finally arrived in June 1610. He and the deputy governors who succeeded him ruled by martial law. Men and women marched to work by the beat of the drum. These extreme measures saved the colony but Virginia did not flourish. In 1616, the year profits were to be distributed to shareholders, the company hovered near bankruptcy, with only a vast expanse of unsurveyed land 3000 miles from London to show for all its efforts.

A "Stinking Weed" Saves the Colony

The solution to Virginia's problems grew in the vacant lots of Jamestown. Only Indians cultivated tobacco—for religious purposes—until John Rolfe realized that this local weed might be a valuable export crop. Rolfe, who married Pocahontas, developed a milder tobacco leaf that greatly appealed to European smokers.

Virginians suddenly possessed a means to make money. Tobacco was easy to grow, and settlers who had avoided work now threw themselves into its production with single-minded diligence. James I initially considered smoking immoral and unhealthy; he changed his mind as the duties he collected on tobacco imports mounted.

The Virginia Company in 1618 launched one last effort to transform Virginia into a profitable enterprise, promising a series of reforms— relaxation of martial law and establishment of

The praises sung of tobacco and Virginia on this British tobacco label express the change in King James's attitude toward the "stinking weed" once he recognized the profit to be gained from it.

a representative assembly were among these. Sir Edwin Sandys (pronounced Sands), a gifted entrepreneur, led the faction of stockholders who pumped life into the faltering organization, encouraging private investors to develop their own estates in Virginia. Sandys even introduced a new method for distributing land. Colonists who paid their own way to Virginia were guaranteed a "headright," a fifty-acre lot for which they paid only a small annual rent. Additional headrights were granted to the adventurers for each servant that they brought to the colony. This procedure enabled planters to build up huge estates with dependent labor, a land system that persisted long after the company's collapse.

Sandys had only just begun. He also urged the settlers to diversify their economy. He envisioned colonists busily producing iron and tar, silk and glass, sugar and cotton, as well as tobacco. To finance such a huge project, Sandys relied upon a lottery. The final element in the grand scheme was people. Sandys sent thousands of hopeful settlers to Virginia, newcomers swept up by the same hopes as the original colonists of 1607.

Mortality in Virginia

Between 1619 and 1622 colonists arrived in Virginia in record numbers. Most of the 3570 individuals who emigrated to the colony during those years were single males in their teens or early twenties. Most of them came as indentured servants. In exchange for transportation across the Atlantic, they agreed to serve a master for a stated number of years. The younger the servant, the longer he or she was expected to serve. In return, the master promised to give the laborers proper care and, at the conclusion of their contracts, to provide them with tools and clothes according to "the custom of the country."

Since the Virginia masters needed strong servants able to do heavy field work, young males were preferred. Thus the sex ratio in Virginia was dramatically skewed. In the early decades, men outnumbered women by as much as six to one. Even if a man lived to the end of his indenture, he could not realistically expect to start a family of his own. Moreover, servants were often treated harshly. They were sold, traded, even gambled away in a hand of cards. It does not require much imagination to see that a society that tolerated such an exploitative labor system might later embrace slavery.

Most Virginians did not live long enough to worry about marrying and starting a family. Between 1618 and 1622 perhaps three out of every four persons in Virginia died. Contagious diseases killed the most. Salt poisoning also took a toll. And on Good Friday, March 22, 1622, the local Indians slew 347 settlers in a well-coordinated surprise attack. Those who survived must have lived with a sense of impermanence and a desire to escape Virginia with a little money before they too met an early death.

On both sides of the Atlantic people wondered who should be blamed for the debacle. The burden of responsibility lay with the Virginia Company. Neither food nor shelter awaited the settlers when they arrived in Virginia. Weakened by the long sea voyage, the malnourished colonists quickly succumbed to contagious diseases.

Officials in Virginia also shared the guilt. Their greed caused them to overlook both the common good and the public defenses. Jamestown took on the characteristics of a "boom town." Unrestrained self-advancement was the dominant feature of this highly individualistic, competitive society.

In 1624 the king took charge, dissolving the bankrupt enterprise and finally transforming Virginia into a royal colony. The Crown appointed a governor and a council, but made no provision for the continuation of Virginia's representative assembly. Even without the king's authorization, however, the House of Burgesses gathered annually, and in 1639 Charles belatedly recognized its existence.

He had no choice. The colonists who served on the council or in the assembly were strong-willed ambitious men. Having survived privation, disease, and Indian attacks, they were singlemindedly out to get rich and had no intention of surrendering their control over local affairs. Governors who opposed the council did so at considerable personal risk. Nor was Charles, encountering his own problems at home, much disposed to intervene. In 1634 the assembly divided the colony into eight counties, each of which was governed by a justice of the peace. The "county court"—as these officers were called—remained the center of Virginia's social, political, and commercial life long after the American Revolution.

The changes in government had little impact upon the character of daily life in Virginia. The isolated tobacco plantations that dotted Virginia's many navigable rivers were the focus of the settlers' lives. This dispersed pattern of settlement retarded the development of institutions such as schools and churches. And for more than a century Jamestown was the only place that could reasonably be called a town.

Maryland: A Troubled Sanctuary

Maryland's roots lay not in a wild scramble for wealth, but in a nobleman's desire to create a sanctuary for England's persecuted Catholics.

The driving force behind the settlement of Maryland was Sir George Calvert, later Lord Baltimore. Well-educated, charming, ambitious, and from an excellent family, he became a favorite of James I. Although he kept his religious beliefs private, he showed great interest in the progress of Virginia and New England. By the late 1620s it was clear that he longed to establish a colony of his own.

On June 30, 1632, Charles I granted George Calvert's son, Cecilius, a charter for a colony to be located on the Chesapeake Bay north of Virginia. George died while the negotiations were in progress, but his vision shaped the character of the new settlement, named "Mariland, in honor of the Queene." For his part, Charles wanted to halt the southward spread of Dutch influence from New Netherland and regarded Baltimore's project as a cheap and convenient way to do so.

The charter itself is an odd document, part medieval and part modern. Lord Baltimore held absolute authority over the colonists. He was as powerful in his colony as a lord on a feudal estate. As proprietor, Baltimore owned the land outright, but he subdivided it into manors where landed aristocrats could establish their own courts of law. The more land a person owned, the more privileges that person enjoyed in the government.

Embedded in this feudal scheme was a concept that broke boldly with the past. Unlike the European leaders of his day, Baltimore championed religious freedom for all people who accepted the divinity of Christ. Even though Maryland's early settlers—Catholics as well as Protestants—occasionally persecuted each other, Baltimore's commitment to toleration never flagged.

In 1634 the first of Maryland's immigrants landed at St. Mary's, near the mouth of the Potomac River. Maryland attracted both Catholics and Protestants, and for a brief period, the two groups seemed capable of living in peace. Unlike the Virginia settlers, these early colonists were not threatened by starvation, and they maintained friendly relations with the local Indians.

Lord Baltimore's feudal system never took root in Chesapeake soil. People simply refused to play the social roles that he had assigned. Most importantly, the elected assembly, which first met in 1635, insisted upon exercising traditional parliamentary privileges that eventually undermined Baltimore's authority. With each passing year, the proprietor's absolute control over the men and women of Maryland progressively weakened.

Despite Lord Baltimore's efforts to establish liberty of conscience, Maryland's gravest problems grew out of the colonists' religious intolerance. Aggressive Jesuits frightened Protestants, who in turn tried to unseat the proprietor on the grounds that he and his chief advisors were Catholic. In fact, Baltimore's experiment led to chronic instability during the first thirty years after settlement. Violence, not toleration, resulted from his efforts to put freedom of conscience into practice.

In this troubled sanctuary, planters cultivated tobacco on dispersed riverfront plantations. No towns developed. The tobacco culture permeated every aspect of society. A steady stream of indentured servants supplied the plantations with dependent laborers, until they were replaced at the end of the seventeenth century by slaves. Both Maryland and Virginia were peopled by settlers principally concerned with their individual concerns.

EUROPEAN SETTLEMENT OF NEW ENGLAND

Legend surrounds the Pilgrims. These brave refugees crossed the cold Atlantic in search of religious liberty, signed a democratic compact aboard the *Mayflower*, landed at Plymouth Rock, and gave us our Thanksgiving Day. As with most mythic accounts, this one contains only a core of truth.

The Pilgrims were not crusaders who set out to change the world. They were humble English farmers from Scrooby Manor. They believed that the Church of England retained too many traces of its Catholic origin, that its very rituals compromised God's true believers. And so, in the early years of the reign of James I, the Scrooby congregation formally left the state church. Like others who followed this logic, they were called "Separatists." Since English statute required citizens to attend established Church of England service, the Scrooby Separatists moved to Holland in 1608–1609 rather than compromise their souls.

The Netherlands provided the Separatists with a good home—too good. They feared that their distinct identity was threatened, that their children were becoming Dutch. By 1617 a portion of the Scrooby congregation vowed to sail to America. A group of English investors who were only marginally interested in Separatism underwrote their trip. In 1620 they sailed for Virginia aboard the *Mayflower*.

Hardship soon shattered the voyagers' optimism. Because of an error in navigation, the Pilgrims landed not in Virginia, but in New England, where their land patent from the Virginia Company had no validity. Without a patent, the colonists possessed no authorization to form a civil government, a serious matter since some sailors who were not Pilgrims threatened mutiny. To preserve the struggling community from anarchy, forty-one men agreed on November 11 to "covenant and combine our selves together into a civill body politick."

Unfortunately, the Mayflower Compact, as this voluntary agreement was called, could not ward off disease and hunger. During the first months at Plymouth, death claimed approximately half of the 102 people who had initially set out from England. Moreover, debts contracted in the mother country severely burdened the new colony. Through strength of will and self-sacrifice, their elected leader, William Bradford, persuaded frightened men and women that they could survive in America.

The Pilgrims never became very prosperous. But they did build a humble farm community and practice their Separatist beliefs. Although they experimented with commercial fishing and the fur trade, most families relied upon mixed husbandry, grain, and livestock. Not a populous colony, in 1691 Plymouth was ab-

sorbed into its thriving, larger neighbor, Massachusetts Bay.

PURITAN COMMONWEALTH

During the seventeenth century Puritan zeal transformed the face of England and America. The popular image of a Puritan—a carping critic who condemned liquor and sex, who dressed in drab clothes, and minded the neighbors' business—is based on a fundamental misunderstanding of the actual nature of Puritanism. Puritans were radical reformers committed to far-reaching institutional change, not Victorian prudes. Not only did they found several American colonies, but they sparked the English civil war and the bold new thinking about popular representation that accompanied it.

The Puritan movement came out of the Protestant Reformation. It accepted the notion that an omnipotent God predestined some people to salvation and damned others throughout eternity (see Chapter 1). Puritans constantly monitored themselves for signs of grace, hints that God had in fact placed them among his "elect." And their attempt to live as if they *were* saved—that is, according to the Scriptures— became the driving engine for reform on this earth.

They saw their duty clearly: to eradicate unscriptural elements and practices from the Church of England; to campaign vigorously against the sins of sexual license and drunkenness; and to inveigh against alliances with Papist (Catholic) states. Puritans were more combative than the Pilgrims had been. They wanted to purify the English Church from within, and before the 1630s at least, Separatism held little appeal for them.

From the Puritan perspective, the early Stuarts, James I and Charles I, seemed unconcerned about the spiritual state of the nation. The monarchs, Puritans believed, courted Catholic alliances and showed no interest in purifying the Church of England. As long as Parliament met, Puritan voters in the various boroughs and counties throughout the nation elected men sympathetic to their point of view. These outspoken representatives criticized royal policies. And because of their defiance, Charles decided in 1629 to rule England without Parliament. Four years later he named as Archbishop of Canterbury the Puritans' most conspicuous clerical opponent, William Laud. The last doors of reform slammed shut; the corruption remained.

John Winthrop, the future governor of Massachusetts Bay, was caught up in these events. A man of modest wealth and education, he believed God would punish England, although he was confident that the Lord would provide shelter somewhere for his Puritan flock. Other Puritans, some of them wealthier and better connected than Winthrop, reached similar conclusions about England's future. They turned their attention to the possibility of establishing a colony in America. On March 4, 1629, their Massachusetts Bay Company obtained a charter directly from the king.

The king may have believed that Massachusetts Bay would be simply another commercial venture, but Winthrop and his associates knew better. In the Cambridge Agreement (August 1629) they pledged to emigrate, knowing that their charter allowed the company to hold meetings wherever the stockholders desired, *even in America.* And if they were in America, the king could not easily interfere in their affairs.

"A City on a Hill"

The Winthrop fleet departed England in March 1630. By the end of the year, almost 2000 people had arrived in Massachusetts Bay, and before the "Great Migration" concluded in the early 1640s, almost 16,000 men and women would arrive in the new Puritan colony.

Unlike the early immigrants to Virginia and Maryland, they moved to Massachusetts Bay as nuclear families: fathers, mothers, and their dependent children. This guaranteed a more balanced sex ratio than in the Chesapeake colonies. Finally, and perhaps more significantly, these colonists survived. Indeed, their life ex-

pectancy compares favorably to that of modern Americans. This remarkable phenomenon alleviated the emotional shock of long-distance migration.

Their common sense of purpose provided another source of strength and stability. God, they insisted, had formed a special covenant with them. On his part, the Lord expected them to live according to scripture, to reform the church, in other words, to create a "city on a hill" that would stand as a beacon of righteousness for the rest of the Christian world. If everyone kept the covenant, the colonists could expect peace and prosperity. They fully expected to transform a religious vision into a social reality.

They arrived in Massachusetts Bay without a precise plan for their church, other than that they refused to separate formally from the Church of England. Reform, not separation, was their mission. Gradually, they came to accept a form of church government known as Congregationalism. Under this system, each congregation was independent of outside interference. The people (the "saints") *were* the church. They pledged as a body to uphold God's law. In Congregational churches, full members—men and women who testified that they were among the Lord's "elect"—selected a minister, punished errant members, and determined matters of theology. This loose structure held together for more than a century.

In creating a civil government, the Bay Colony faced a particularly difficult challenge. Their charter allowed the investors in a joint-stock company to set up a business organization. When the settlers arrived in America, however, company leaders—men like Winthrop—moved quickly to transform the commercial structure into a colonial government. In 1631 they expanded the franchise to include all adult males who had become members of a Congregational church. During the 1630s, at least 40 percent of the adult male population could vote in elections—a percentage far above the standards in England. These "freemen" elected their own governor, magistrates, local representatives, and even military officers.

Two popular misconceptions about the government should be dispelled. It was neither a democracy nor a theocracy. Magistrates ruled in the name of the electorate but believed their responsibilities as rulers were to God. And second, the Congregational ministers possessed no formal political authority. They could not even hold civil office.

Unlike in Virginia, the town, rather than the county, became the center of public life in the Bay colony. Groups of men and women voluntarily covenanted together to live by certain rules. They constructed their communities around a meetinghouse where church services and town meetings were held. Each townsman received land sufficient to build a house and to support a family. The house lots were clustered around the meetinghouse; the fields were located on the village perimeter. Land was free, but villagers were obliged to contribute to the minister's salary, to pay local and colony taxes, and to serve in the town militia.

DEALING WITH DISSENT

The settlers of Massachusetts Bay managed to live in peace. When differences arose, as they often did, the courts settled matters. People believed in a rule of law, as was illustrated in 1648 when the colonial legislature drew up the *Laws and Liberties*, the first alphabetized code of law printed in English. This code clearly stated the colonists' rights and responsibilities as citizens of the commonwealth. It engendered public trust in government and discouraged magistrates from the arbitrary exercise of authority.

The most serious challenges to Puritan orthodoxy in Massachusetts Bay came from two remarkable individuals. The first, Roger Williams, arrived in 1631. He was well liked and immediately attracted a body of loyal followers. But he preached extreme separatism. Moreover, he questioned the validity of the colony's charter since the king had not first purchased the land from the Indians. Williams also insisted that the civil rulers of Massachusetts had no business punishing settlers for their religious beliefs. The magistrates believed that Williams threatened the social and religious

foundation of the colony, and in 1636 they banished him. Williams then bought a tract of land from the Narraganset Indians and founded the Providence settlement in Rhode Island.

The magistrates of the Bay Colony believed that Anne Hutchinson posed an even greater threat to the peace of the commonwealth. Intelligent and outspoken, she questioned the authority and theology of some of the most respected ministers of the colony. As justification for her own views, known as Antinomianism, she cited divine inspiration, rather than the Bible or the clergy. In other words, Hutchinson's teachings could not be tested by Scripture, a position that Puritan leaders regarded as dangerously subjective. Without clear, external standards, one person's truth was as valid as that of anyone else's, and from Winthrop's perspective, Hutchinson's teachings invited civil and religious anarchy.

When she described some of the leading ministers as unconverted men, the General Court intervened. Hutchinson was cross-examined for two days in 1637, but she knew Scripture too well to be easily tripped up. Then she made a slip that led to her undoing. She stated that what she knew of God came "by an immediate revelation." She had heard a voice. This "heretical" declaration challenged the authority of the Bay rulers and they were relieved to exile Hutchinson and her followers to Rhode Island.

BREAKING AWAY

Massachusetts Bay spawned four new colonies, three of which survived to the American Revolution. New Hampshire became a separate colony in 1677, although its population grew slowly, and for much of the colonial period it remained economically dependent upon Massachusetts.

Far more people were drawn to the fertile lands of the Connecticut River valley. Populated by settlers from the Bay Colony under the ministry of Thomas Hooker, the valley took on the religious and cultural characteristics of Massachusetts. In 1639 representatives from the Connecticut towns drafted the Fundamental Orders, a blueprint for civil government;

and in 1662 Charles II awarded the colony a charter of its own. That same year Connecticut absorbed the New Haven colony, a struggling Puritan settlement on Long Island Sound.

Rhode Island experienced a wholly different history. From the beginning, it was populated by exiles and "troublemakers." One Dutch visitor uncharitably characterized it as "the receptacle of all sorts of riff-raff people." However, the colony's broad toleration attracted many men and women who held unorthodox religious beliefs.

Toleration, however, did not mean cooperation. Villagers fought over land and schemed with outside speculators to divide the tiny colony into even smaller pieces. Even a royal charter obtained in 1663 did not calm the political turmoil. For most of the seventeenth century, colonywide government existed in name only. But despite all the bickering, Rhode Island's population grew, and the colony's commerce flourished.

DIVERSITY IN THE MIDDLE COLONIES

New York, New Jersey, Pennsylvania, and Delaware were founded for quite different reasons. William Penn, for example, envisioned a Quaker sanctuary; the Duke of York worried chiefly about his own income. Despite the founders' intentions, however, some common characteristics emerged. Each colony developed a strikingly heterogeneous population, men and women of different ethnic and religious backgrounds. This cultural diversity became a major influence upon the economic, political, and ecclesiastical institutions of the Middle Colonies, and foreshadowed later American society.

ANGLO-DUTCH RIVALRY ON THE HUDSON

By the early decades of the seventeenth century, the Dutch had established themselves as

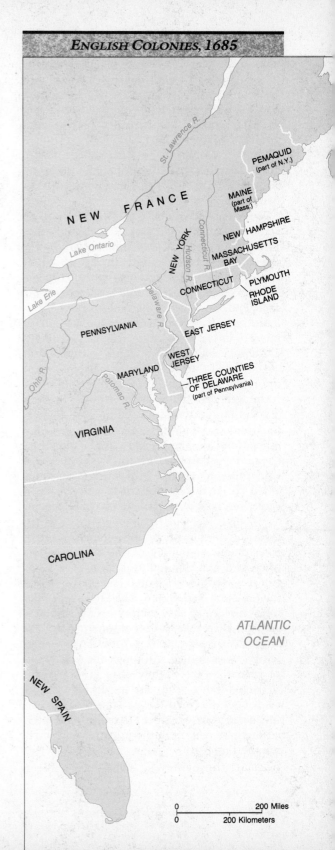

ENGLISH COLONIES, 1685

Europe's most aggressive traders. Holland's merchant fleet was second to none, trading in Asia, Africa, and America. While searching for the elusive Northwest Passage in 1609, Henry Hudson, an English explorer employed by a Dutch company, sailed up the river that bears his name and claimed the area for Holland. Hudson's sponsors, the Dutch West Indies Company, established two permanent settlements, Fort Orange (Albany) and New Amsterdam (New York City) in the colony of New Netherland.

The first Dutch settlers in New Netherland were not actually colonists. Rather they were salaried employees of the Company, who were expected to spend most of their time gathering animal fur pelts. They received no land for their efforts. Needless to say, this arrangement attracted relatively few Dutch immigrants.

Although the colony's population was small, only 270 in 1628, it contained an extraordinary ethnic mix. By the 1640s Finns, Germans, and Swedes lived there, along with a sizable community of free blacks. Another contribution to the hodgepodge of languages was added by New England Puritans who moved to New Netherland to stake out farms on Long Island.

The Company sent a succession of directors-general to oversee and govern. Without exception, these men were temperamentally unsuited to govern an American colony. They were autocratic, corrupt, and above all, inept. The Long Island Puritans complained bitterly about the absence of any sort of representative government, and none of the colonists felt much loyalty to the trading company.

In August 1664 the Dutch lost their tenuous hold on New Netherland. The English Crown, eager to score an easy victory over a commercial rival, dispatched a fleet of warships to New Amsterdam (renamed New York City). No real fighting was needed. Although the last director-general, Peter Stuyvesant (1647–1664), urged resistance, the settlers decided otherwise. They accepted the Articles of Capitulation, a generous agreement that allowed Dutch nationals to remain in the province and to retain their property.

Charles II had already granted his brother, James, the Duke of York, a charter for the newly captured territory and much else besides. He became absolute proprietor of Maine, Nantucket, Martha's Vineyard, and land extending from the Connecticut River to Delaware Bay. The duke was no more receptive to the idea of a representative government than the Dutch trading company had been; but to appease the complaining colonists, the governor, Colonel Richard Nicolls, drew up a legal code known as the Duke's Laws. It guaranteed religious toleration and created local governments.

There was no provision, however, for an elected assembly. Nor was there much harmony in the colony. The Dutch, for example, continued to speak their own language, worship in their own churches (Dutch Reformed Calvinists), and eye their English neighbors with suspicion. In fact, the colony seemed little different from what it had been under the Dutch West India Company, a loose collection of independent communities ruled by an ineffectual central government.

DIVISIONS IN NEW JERSEY

Only three months after receiving a charter for New York, the duke made a terrible blunder—something this stubborn, humorless man was quite prone to do. He awarded the land lying between the Hudson and Delaware rivers to two courtiers, John, Lord Berkeley, and Sir George Carteret. This colony was named New Jersey in honor of Carteret's birthplace, the Isle of Jersey in the English Channel.

The duke's impulsive act bred confusion. Before learning of James' decision, the governor of New York allowed migrants from New England to take up farms west of the Hudson River, promising them an opportunity to establish an elected assembly and liberty of conscience in exchange for the payment of a small annual quitrent to the duke. Berkeley and Carteret recruited colonists on similar terms. The new proprietors assumed, of course, that they would receive the rent money.

The result was chaos. Legally, only James could set up a colonial government or authorize an assembly. But knowledge of the law failed to quiet the controversy, and through it all, the duke showed not the slightest interest in the peace and welfare of the people of New Jersey.

Matters were further complicated in 1674 when Berkeley tired of the venture and sold his proprietary rights to a group of surprisingly quarrelsome Quakers. The colony was legally divided into East and West Jersey, but neither half prospered. When the West Jersey proprietors went bankrupt in 1702, the Crown mercifully reunited the two Jerseys into a single royal colony.

In 1700 the population of New Jersey stood at approximately 14,000. Its residents lived on scattered, often isolated farms; villages of more than a few hundred people were rare. And, as in New York, the ethnic and religious diversity of the settlers was striking. Yet the colonists of New Jersey somehow managed to live together peaceably.

QUAKERS IN AMERICA

Quakers founded Pennsylvania. This radical religious group gained its name from the derogatory term that English civil authorities used to describe those who "tremble at the word of the Lord." George Fox (1624–1691) was the tireless spokesman of the Society of Friends, as Quakers were formally known. He preached that every man and woman possessed a powerful, consoling "inner light." This was a wonderfully liberating message, especially for persons of lower class origin. Gone was the stigma of original sin; discarded was the notion of eternal predestination. Everyone could be saved.

Quakers practiced humility. They wore simple clothes and employed old-fashioned terms

One of the liberating aspects of the Quaker religion was the idea that the "Inner Light" of Christ was present in everyone. By implication, all men and women were equal before the Lord and required no intermediaries. This belief was reflected in the Quaker meeting, in which individuals rose to speak as the spirit moved them, without the formal guidance of a minister conducting a service.

of address that set them apart from their neighbors. They were also pacifists. According to Fox, all persons were equal in the sight of the Lord, a belief that annoyed people of rank and achievement. Moreover, they refused to keep their thoughts to themselves, spreading the light throughout England, Ireland, and America. Harassment, imprisonment, and even execution failed to curtail their activities. In fact, such measures proved counterproductive, for persecution only inspired the Quakers to redouble their efforts.

William Penn lived according to the Inner Light, a commitment that led eventually to the founding of Pennsylvania. He was a complex man: an athletic person interested in intellectual pursuits; a visionary capable of making pragmatic decisions; and an aristocrat whose religious beliefs involved him with the lower classes. Penn's religious commitment irritated his father, who hoped William would become a favorite at the Stuart court. Instead Penn was expelled from Oxford University for holding unorthodox religious views, moved to the forefront of the Quaker movement, and even spent two years in an English jail for his beliefs.

Precisely when Penn's thoughts turned to America is not known. In any case, Penn negotiated in 1681 one of the more impressive land deals in the history of American real estate. Charles II awarded Penn a charter making him the sole proprietor of a vast area called Pennsylvania (literally, Penn's woods), a name that embarrassed the modest Quaker. The next year, Penn purchased from the Duke of York the so-called Three Lower Counties that eventually became Delaware. This astute move guaranteed that Pennsylvania would have open access to the Atlantic and determined even before Philadelphia had been established that it would become a great commercial center.

Penn lost no time in launching his "Holy Experiment." His plan blended traditional notions about the privileges of a landed aristocracy with quite daring concepts of personal liberty. Penn guaranteed that the settlers would enjoy among other things liberty of conscience, freedom from persecution, no taxation without representation, and due process of law. He believed that both the rich and poor had to have a voice in political affairs; neither should be able to overrule the legitimate interests of the other class. In his Frame of Government (1682), he envisioned a governor appointed by the proprietor, a provisional council responsible for initiating legislation, and an assembly that could accept or reject the bills presented to it. Penn apparently thought that the council would be filled by the colony's richest landholders and that the assembly would be peopled by the smaller landowners. It was a fanciful, clumsy structure, and in America the entire edifice crumbled under its own weight.

Penn promoted his colony aggressively throughout England, Ireland, and Germany. The response was overwhelming. People poured into Philadelphia and the surrounding area. Most of the early settlers were Irish, Welsh, and English Quakers. But men and women from other lands soon joined the Quaker surge toward Penn's woods. One newcomer called the vessel that brought him to Philadelphia a "Noah's Ark" of nationalities and religions.

Penn himself emigrated to America in 1682. His stay, however, was unexpectedly short and unhappy. The council and assembly fought over the right to initiate legislation. Wealthy Quaker merchants dominated the council, and rural settlers unconcerned about the "Holy Experiment" controlled the assembly. Many colonists refused to pay quitrents, and the Baltimore family claimed that much of Pennsylvania actually lay in Maryland. In 1684, to defend his charter against Baltimore's attack, Penn returned to London.

Penn did not see his colony again until 1699. By that time, the settlement had changed considerably. Although it had prospered, a contentious quality pervaded its politics. Even the Quakers split into hostile factions. As the seventeenth century closed, few colonists still shared the founder's desire to create a godly, paternalistic society.

In 1701 legal challenges in England again forced Penn to depart for the mother country. Just before he sailed, Penn signed the Charter of Liberties, a new framework of government that established a unicameral or one-house legislature (the only one in colonial America) and gave the representatives the right to initiate legislation. The charter also provided for the political separation of the Three Lower Counties (Delaware) from Pennsylvania, something people living in this area had demanded for years. This hastily drafted document served as Pennsylvania's constitution until the American Revolution.

His experience in America must have depressed Penn, now both old and sick. In England Penn was imprisoned for debts incurred by dishonest colonial agents, and in 1718 Pennsylvania's founder died a broken man.

PLANTING THE CAROLINAS

In some ways Carolina society looked very much like the one that had developed in Virginia and Maryland. In both areas white planters forced unfree laborers to produce staple crops for a world market. But such superficial similarities masked substantial regional differences. In fact, "The South"—certainly the fabled solid South of the early nineteenth century—did not exist during the colonial period. The Carolinas, joined at a much later date by Georgia, stood apart from their Chesapeake neighbors.

Carolina owed its establishment to the restoration of the Stuarts to the English throne. Court favorites who had followed the Stuarts into exile during the civil war demanded tangible rewards for their loyalty. New York and New Jersey were obvious plums. So too was Carolina. On March 24, 1663, the king granted Sir John Colleton and seven other courtiers a charter to the vast territory between Virginia and Florida and running west as far as the "South Seas."

Unlike so many Englishmen before them, the eight proprietors did not think of America in terms of instant wealth. Their plan involved luring settlers from established American colonies by means of an attractive land policy and such other incentives as a representative assembly, liberty of conscience, and a liberal headright system. In exchange for their privileges, they demanded only a small annual quitrent.

After dividing their grant into three distinct jurisdictions, Albermarle, Cape Fear, and Port Royal, the proprietors waited for the money to roll in; to their dismay, no one seemed particularly interested in moving to the Carolina frontier. Plans for the settlement of Cape Fear and Port Royal fell through, and the majority of the surviving proprietors gave up on Carolina.

Anthony Ashley Cooper, later earl of Shaftesbury, was an exception. In 1669 he persuaded the remaining proprietors to invest their own capital in the colony. He then dispatched over 300 English colonists to Carolina. After a rough voyage that saw one ship destroyed by Atlantic gales, the settlers arrived at the Ashley River. Later the colony's administrative center, Charles Town (it did not become Charleston until 1783), was established at the junction of the Ashley and Cooper rivers.

Ashley also wanted to bring order to the new society. With assistance from John Locke, the famous English philosopher (1632–1704), Ashley devised the Fundamental Constitutions of Carolina. His goal was to create a landed aristocracy that governed the colony through the Council of Nobles, a body designed to administer justice, oversee civil affairs, and initiate legislation. A parliament in which smaller landowners had a voice could accept or reject bills drafted by the Council. The very poor were excluded from political activity altogether. Ashley's plans for a "balance of government" between aristocracy and democracy, however, never conformed to the realities of Carolina society, and his Council of Nobles remained a paper dream.

Before 1680 almost half the men and women who settled in the Port Royal area came from Barbados. This small Caribbean island, which produced an annual fortune in sugar, depended upon slave labor. By the third quarter of the seventeenth century, Barbados had become overpopulated, and Barbadians looked to Carolina for relief. These migrants, many of whom were quite rich, traveled to Carolina both as individuals and family groups. Some brought

Name	Original Purpose	Date of Founding	Principal Founder	Major Export	Estimated Population c. 1700
Virginia	Commercial venture	1607	Captain John Smith	Tobacco	64,560
New York (New Amsterdam)	Commercial venture	1613 (Made English colony, 1664)	Peter Stuyvesant, Duke of York	Furs, grain	19,107
Plymouth	Refuge for English Separatists	1620 (Absorbed by Massachusetts 1691)	William Bradford	Grain	Included with Massachusetts
New Hampshire	Commercial venture	1623	John Mason	Wood, naval stores	4958
Massachusetts	Refuge for English Puritans	1628	John Winthrop	Grain, wood	55,941
Maryland	Refuge for English Catholics	1634	Lord Baltimore (George Calvert)	Tobacco	34,100
Connecticut	Expansion of Massachusetts	1635	Thomas Hooker	Grain	25,970
Rhode Island	Refuge for dissenters from Massachusetts	1636	Roger Williams	Grain	5894

slave gangs with them. The Barbadians carved out plantations on the tributaries of the Cooper River and established themselves immediately as the colony's most powerful political faction. The society they created was closer to the slave-based plantation society they left than to any of the other English colonies.

Much of the planters' time was taken up with the search for a profitable crop. They experimented with a number of plants—tobacco, cotton, silk, and grapes. The most successful items in the early years turned out to be beef, cattle, furs, and naval stores (especially tar, used to maintain ocean vessels). It was not until the 1690s that the planters came to appreciate fully the value of rice, but once they had done so, it quickly became the colony's main staple.

Proprietary Carolina was in a constant political uproar. Barbadian settlers resisted the proprietors' policies, and the proprietors appointed a series of utterly incompetent governors. By the end of the century, the lower houses of assembly had assumed the right to initiate legislation. In 1719 the colonists overthrew the last proprietary government, and in 1729 the king created separate royal governments in North and South Carolina.

Name	Original Purpose	Date of Founding	Principal Founder	Major Export	Estimated Population c. 1700
Delaware (New Sweden)	Commercial venture	1638 (Included in Penn grant, 1681; given separate assembly, 1703)	Peter Minuit William Penn	Grain	2470
North Carolina	Commercial venture	1663	Anthony Ashley Cooper	Wood, naval stores, tobacco	10,720
South Carolina	Commercial venture	1663	Anthony Ashley Cooper	Naval stores, rice	5720
New Jersey	Consolidation of new English territory, Quaker settlement	1664	Sir George Cartaret	Grain	14,010
Pennsylvania	Refuge for English Quakers	1681	William Penn	Grain	18,950
Georgia	Discourage Spanish expansion; charity	1733	James Oglethorp	Silk, rice, wood, naval stores	5200 (in 1750)

Sources: U.S. Bureau of Census, Historical Statistics of the United States: Colonial Times to 1970, *Washington, D.C., 1975; John J. McCusker and Russell R. Menard*, The Economy of British America, 1607–1789, *Chapel Hill, 1985.*

FOUNDING OF GEORGIA

The early history of Georgia was strikingly different from that of Britain's other mainland colonies. Its settlement was really an act of aggression against Spain, a country that had as good a claim to this area as the English did. During the eighteenth century, the two nations were often at war (see Chapter 4), and South Carolinians worried that the Spaniards moving up from bases in Florida would occupy the disputed territory between Florida and the Carolina grant.

The colony owed its existence primarily to James Oglethorpe, a British general and member of Parliament who believed that he could thwart Spanish designs on the area south of Charleston while providing a fresh start for London's debtors. Although Oglethorpe envisioned Georgia as an asylum as well as a garrison, the military aspects of his proposal were especially appealing to the leaders of the British government. In 1732 the king granted Oglethorpe and a board of trustees a charter for a new colony. The trustees living in the mother country were given complete control over Georgia politics, a condition the settlers soon found intolerable.

CHRONOLOGY

1607	First English settlers arrive at Jamestown
1608–1609	Scrooby Congregation (Pilgrims) leaves England for Holland
1609–1611	"Starving time" in Virginia threatens survival of the colonists
1619	Virginia assembly, called House of Burgesses, meets for the first time First slaves sold at Jamestown
1620	Pilgrims sign the Mayflower Compact
1622	Surprise attack by local Indians devastates Virginia
1624	Dutch investors create permanent settlements along Hudson River James I, king of England, dissolves Virginia Company
1625	Charles I ascends English throne
1630	John Winthrop transfers Massachusetts Bay charter to New England
1634	Colony of Maryland is founded
1638	Anne Hutchinson exiled to Rhode Island
1639	Connecticut towns accept Fundamental Orders
1649	Charles I executed during English civil war

1660	Stuarts are restored to the English throne
1663	Rhode Island obtains royal charter Proprietors receive charter for Carolina
1664	English soldiers conquer New Netherland
1677	New Hampshire becomes a royal colony
1681	William Penn granted patent for his "Holy Experiment"

At first the colony did not fare very well. Few English debtors showed any desire to move there, and the trustees provided little incentive for emigration. No settler could amass more than 500 acres of land. Moreover, land could be passed only to an eldest son, and if a planter died without a son, the holding reverted to Oglethorpe and the trustees. Slavery and rum were prohibited.

The settlers wanted more—slaves, a voice in local government, unrestricted land ownership. Oglethorpe met their demands with angry rebuffs. Eventually, however, Oglethorpe lost interest in his colonial experiment, and the trustees were then forced to compromise their principles. In 1738 they eliminated all restrictions on the amount of land a person could own; they allowed women to inherit land. Slaves came next, then rum. In 1751 the trustees gave up on what had become a hard-drinking, slave-holding plantation society and returned Georgia to the king. That same year, the king authorized an assembly. But even with these social and political changes, Georgia attracted very few new settlers.

SEVENTEENTH-CENTURY LEGACY

The seventeenth-century English colonies had little in common beyond their allegiance to the king. A contemporary visitor could find along the Atlantic coast a spectrum of settlements, one that ranged from the almost feudal hierarchy of Carolina to the visionary paternalism of Pennsylvania to the Puritan commonwealth of Massachusetts Bay. The diversity of English colonization needs to be emphasized precisely because it is so easy to overlook. Even though the colonists eventually banded together and fought for independence and established a federal government, persistent differences separated New Englanders from Virginians, Pennsylvanians from Carolinians.

RECOMMENDED READING

The most detailed investigation of the founding of the early American colonies remains Charles M. Andrews, *The Colonial Period of American History*, 4 vols. (1934–1938). A full discussion of the historiography of colonial America is Jack P. Greene and J. R. Pole, eds., *Colonial British America* (1984), and D. W. Meinig, *The Shaping of America: A Geographical Perspective* (1986).

To understand the English background of colonization, see Carl Bridenbaugh, *Vexed and Troubled Englishmen, 1590–1642* (1968). T. H. Breen, *Puritans and Adventurers: Change and Persistence in Early America* (1980), explores the problem of cultural transfer. Also helpful is David Grayson Allen, *In English Ways: The Movement of Societies and the Transferal of English Local Law and Custom* (1981), and David Cressy, *Coming Over: Migration and Communication Between England and New England in the Seventeenth Century* (1987).

The best analysis of the early settlement of Virginia is Edmund S. Morgan, *American Slavery, American Freedom* (1975). An exciting account of the founding of Jamestown is *Captain John Smith: A Select Edition*, ed. Karen O. Kupperman (1988). On Roanoke, see D. B. Quinn, ed., *The Roanoke Voyages, 1584–1590* (1967). For a masterful analysis of current research see Thad W. Tate and David L. Ammerman, eds., *The Chesapeake in the Seventeenth Century* (1979). New insights are offered in Allan Kulikoff, *Tobacco and Slaves: The Development of Southern Cultures in the Chesapeake, 1680–1800* (1986).

Studies of early New England are Kenneth A. Lockridge, *A New England Town: The First Hundred Years* (1970), and E. S. Morgan, *Puritan Dilemma: The Story of John Winthrop* (1958). On Puritan ideas, see Perry Miller, *New England Mind: From Colony to Province* (1953), and Charles E. Hambrick-Stowe, *The Practice of Piety* (1982).

A good account of New York and the transition from Dutch to English rule is Michael Kammen, *Colonial New York* (1975). The best single book on the political history of early Pennsylvania is Gary B. Nash, *Quakers and Politics: Pennsylvania, 1681–1726* (1968). To understand the Quaker movement, read Frederick B. Tolles, *Quakers and the Atlantic Culture* (1960). William Penn's life and political thought are the subject of Mary M. Dunn, *William Penn, Politics and Conscience* (1967). A comprehensive general description of the early Carolina settlements can be found in Wesley F. Craven, *The Southern Colonies in the Seventeenth Century, 1607–1689* (1949).

3 PUTTING DOWN ROOTS: COLONISTS IN AN EMPIRE

TRADITIONAL SOCIETIES: THE NEW ENGLAND COLONIES
IN THE SEVENTEENTH CENTURY

THE PLANTERS' WORLD

THE AFRICAN-AMERICAN EXPERIENCE

BLUEPRINT FOR EMPIRE

POLITICAL UNREST, 1676–1691: COLONIAL GENTRY IN REVOLT

COMMON EXPERIENCES, SEPARATE CULTURES

The Witherspoon family moved from Great Britain to the South Carolina backcountry early in the eighteenth century. Their son, Robert, who was only a small child when his family moved to America, later produced an exceptional and candid account of their pioneer life. On arrival in South Carolina, the Witherspoons experienced a wave of despondency. Where they expected to find a fine-timbered house and the comforts of England, they discovered acres of wilderness and "a very mean dirt house." For many years, the Witherspoons feared that they would be killed by Indians, become lost in the woods, or be bitten by snakes.

The Witherspoons managed to survive these early difficult years on the Black River. Although the Carolina backcountry did not look very much like the world they had left behind,

Robert's father remained optimistic about the future. He assured his family that soon the trees would be cut down and the land would be populated by neighbors.

Robert Witherspoon's story serves as a reminder that early American history was in fact created by families. Neither the peopling of the Atlantic frontier, the cutting down of the forests, nor the creation of communities was part of what would be considered state policy today. Families determined much of the character of the American colonies. It was within this primary social unit that most colonists earned their livelihoods, educated their children, defined gender, sustained religious traditions, and nursed each other in sickness.

Early colonial families did not exist in isolation but were part of larger societies. The characteristics of the first English settlements in the New World varied substantially (see Chapter 2), and these initial differences grew stronger during the seventeenth century as each region acquired its own history and developed its own traditions. The characteristics of the local societies reflected their supply of labor, abundance of land, and commercial ties with European markets.

By 1660, these regional differences had nearly undermined any possibility of a unified English empire in America. During the reign of Charles II, however, a trend toward cultural convergence began. Such unifying forces as a common language and a common religion began to overcome the economic and cultural differences and pull the English colonists together. Parliament took advantage of this trend and began to establish a uniform set of rules for the expanding American empire. The process was slow and uneven, often sparking violent colonial resistance, but by the end of the seventeenth century, England had made significant progress toward its goal.

TRADITIONAL SOCIETIES: THE NEW ENGLAND COLONIES IN THE SEVENTEENTH CENTURY

The family was central to the development of social stability in early New England. This observation may seem commonplace, but the modern reader must remember that in the seventeenth century many activities now performed by the state were the responsibility of the family. It was within the family unit that men and women earned a livelihood, educated their children, maintained religious traditions, and nursed each other in sickness. New Englanders expected social institutions—church and state, in particular—to complement and support rather than to take over family functions. Any understanding of patterns of stabil-

ity in colonial New England, therefore, must begin with the character of the family.

IMMIGRANT FAMILIES AND NEW SOCIAL ORDER

Early New Englanders believed that God ordained the family for human benefit. It was essential to the maintenance of social order, since outside the family, men and women succumbed to carnal temptation. Such people had no one to sustain them, no one to remind them of Scripture. And just as Scripture taught obedience to the Lord, the godly seventeenth-century family was patriarchal in structure.

This familial experience exercised a powerful influence upon early New England life. Mature adults who migrated to America within nuclear families preserved local English customs more fully than did the youths who traveled to other parts of the continent as single men and women. Not only did traveling with one's family help to reduce the shock of migration, it ensured that the ratio between men and women would be fairly well balanced. In addition, persons who had not already married in England could expect to form nuclear families of their own.

The great migration of the 1630s and 1640s brought approximately 20,000 persons to New England. The English Civil War reduced this flood to a trickle, but by the end of the century, the population of New England had reached almost 120,000, an amazing increase considering the small number of original immigrants. Historians have long searched for the reason. Men and women in New England married no earlier than they did in England; for a first marriage men's average age was in the mid-twenties; women, the early twenties. Nor, for that matter, were Puritan families unusually large by the standards of the period.

The reason turned out to be longevity. Put simply, people who, under normal conditions, would have died in contemporary Europe survived in New England. Indeed, the life expectancy of seventeenth-century settlers was not very different from our own. Males who sur-

This painting depicts Anne Pollard at age 100. Her life span exemplifies the striking longevity of New England settlers.

The life cycle of the family in New England began with marriage. Young men and women generally selected their own partners, usually a neighbor. Prospective brides were expected to possess a dowry worth approximately one half what the bridegroom brought to the union. The overwhelming majority of the region's population married, for in New England, the single life was not only physically difficult, but also morally suspect.

The household was primarily a place of work—very demanding work. It has been estimated that a family of five needed seventy-five acres of cleared land just to feed itself. But a family also needed a surplus crop to pay for items that could not be manufactured at home—metal tools, for example. The belief that early American farmers were self-sufficient is a popular misconception.

During the seventeenth century, men and women generally lived in the communities of their parents and grandparents. Towns, in fact, were collections of families, not individuals. Over time, these families intermarried, so that the community became an elaborate kinship network. In many towns the original founders dominated local politics and economic affairs for several generations. Not surprisingly, newcomers who were not absorbed into the family system tended to move away from the village with greater frequency than did the sons and daughters of the established lineage groups.

Congregational churches were also built upon a family foundation. During the earliest years of settlement, the churches accepted persons who could demonstrate that they were among God's "elect." But when the sons and daughters of the "elect" failed to experience saving grace, a synod in 1662 adopted the so-called Half-Way Covenant. The compromise allowed the grandchildren of persons in full communion to be baptized even though *their* parents could not demonstrate conversion. Obsession with family meant that by the end of the century, Congregational churches often failed to meet the religious needs of New Englanders who were not members of the select families.

vived infancy could expect to see their seventieth birthday. The figures for women were only slightly lower. No one is sure why they lived longer, but pure drinking water, a cool climate that retarded the spread of fatal contagious disease, and a dispersed population promoted general good health.

Longer life altered family relations. New England may have been one of the first societies in recorded history in which a person could reasonably anticipate knowing his or her grandchildren. The traditions of particular families and communities, therefore, remained alive, literally, in the memories of the colony's oldest citizens.

Colonists regarded education as primarily a family responsibility. The ability to read was considered essential for learning the principles of Christianity. For this reason, the Massachusetts legislature ordered towns containing at least fifty families to open elementary schools supported by local taxes. Larger towns supported more advanced grammar schools, which taught a basic Latin curriculum. After 1638, young men could attend Harvard College, the first institution of higher learning founded in England's mainland colonies.

This family-based education system worked. A majority of the region's adult males could read and write, an accomplishment not achieved in the Chesapeake colonies for another century. The literacy rate for women was somewhat lower, but by the standards of the period, it was still impressive.

WOMEN IN PURITAN NEW ENGLAND

The status of women in colonial New England was complex. Although subordinate to men by law and custom, their productive labor was essential to the survival of most households. They cooked, washed, made clothes, milked cows, gardened, and raised poultry. Sometimes, by selling surplus food, wives achieved some economic independence. Women also joined churches in greater numbers than did men, and it is possible that their involvement in these institutions encouraged them to express their ideas.

In political and legal matters, society sharply curtailed the rights of colonial women. According to common law practice, a wife exercised no control over property. And since a divorce was extremely difficult to obtain, a woman married to a cruel or irresponsible spouse had little recourse but to run away or accept the unhappy situation.

Yet most women were neither prosperous entrepreneurs nor abject slaves. Like men, they generally accepted the roles that they thought God had ordained. Although Puritan couples worried that the affection they felt for a husband or a wife might turn their thoughts away from God's perfect love, this was a danger they were willing to risk.

RANK AND STATUS IN NEW ENGLAND SOCIETY

During the seventeenth century the New England colonies attracted neither noblemen nor paupers, an incomplete social structure by contemporary European standards. The lack of very rich, titled persons was particularly troublesome. According to the prevailing hierarchical view of the structure of society, well-placed individuals were *natural rulers*, people intended by God to exercise political authority over the rank and file. Migration forced the colonists, however, to choose their rulers from men of more modest status, ignoring the 'ordinariness of their persons."

The colonists gradually sorted themselves out into distinct social groupings. To become part of the ruling elite it helped to possess at least moderate wealth and education; it was also expected that leaders would belong to a Congregational church and defend religious orthodoxy. The Winthrops, Dudleys, and Pynchons fulfilled these expectations, and in public affairs they assumed dominant roles. They took their responsibility quite seriously and certainly did not look kindly upon anyone who spoke of their "ordinariness."

The problem was that while most New Englanders accepted a hierarchical view of society, they disagreed over their assigned places. Both Massachusetts Bay and Connecticut passed sumptuary laws—statutes that limited the wearing of fine apparel to the wealthy and prominent—designed to curb the pretensions of lower status individuals. By the end of the century, the character of the ruling class in New England had changed, and personal piety figured less importantly in social ranking than did family background and large estate.

Most northern colonists were yeomen (independent farmers), few of whom became rich and even fewer of whom fell hopelessly into debt. Possession of land gave agrarian families a sense of independence from external authority, but during the seventeenth century, this independence was balanced by an equally strong feeling of local identity. Not until the late eighteenth century, when a large number of New Englanders left their familial villages in search of new land, did many northern yeomen place personal material ambition above traditional community bonds.

It was not unusual for northern colonists to work as servants among their neighbors at some point in their lives. New Englanders recruited few servants from the Old World. Their forms of agriculture, which mixed cereal with dairy farming, made employment of large gangs of dependent workers uneconomical. New England servants more resembled apprentices than anything else, and servitude was more a vocational training program than an exploitive system. This was vastly different from the institutions that developed in the southern colonies.

❧ THE PLANTERS' WORLD

An entirely different regional society developed in England's Chesapeake colonies. Although the two areas were founded at roughly the same time by Protestant Englishmen, the two regions were worlds apart in terms of environmental conditions, labor systems, and agrarian economies. The most important reason for the distinctiveness of these early southern plantation societies, however, turned out to be the Chesapeake's death rate, a frighteningly high mortality that tore at the very fabric of family life.

FAMILY LIFE IN A PERILOUS ENVIRONMENT

Unlike New England settlers, the men and women who migrated to the Chesapeake region did not move in family units. Nor were most entirely free when they arrived. Between 70 and 85 percent of the white colonists who went to Virginia and Maryland during the seventeenth century owed four or five years' labor in exchange for the cost of passage to America. Most of these indentured servants were men, and although more women made the voyage after 1640, the sexual ratio in the Chesapeake was never as balanced as it had been in early Massachusetts.

Most immigrants to the Chesapeake region died soon after arriving. Malaria and other diseases took a frightful toll, and drinking water contaminated with salt killed many colonists living in low-lying areas. Life expectancy for Chesapeake males was about forty-three, some ten to twenty years less than for men born in New England! For women, life expectancy was even shorter. A full 25 percent of all children died in infancy. Another 25 percent did not see their twentieth birthday. The survivors were often weak or ill, unable to perform hard physical labor.

These demographic conditions retarded normal population increase. Young women who might have become wives and mothers could not do so until they had completed their terms of servitude. They thus lost several reproductive years, and in a society in which so many children died in infancy, late marriages greatly restricted family size. Moreover, the unbalanced sex ratio meant that many men could not find wives. Without a constant flow of immigrants, the population of Virginia and Maryland would have actually declined.

High mortality compressed the family cycle into a few short years. Marriages were extremely fragile, and one partner usually died within seven years. Not only did children not meet grandparents, they often did not even know their own parents. Widows and widowers quickly remarried, and children frequently grew up with persons to whom they had no blood relation. People had to adjust to the impermanence of family life and to cope with a high degree of personal insecurity.

The unbalanced sex ration in the Chesapeake may have provided women with the means to improve their social status. Because of the uneven sex ratio, women could be confident of finding husbands, regardless of their abilities, attractiveness, or moral character. Despite liberation from some traditional restraints, however, women as servants were still vulnerable to sexual exploitation by their masters. Moreover, childbearing was extremely dangerous; women in the Chesapeake usually died twenty years earlier than their New England counterparts.

RANK AND STATUS IN PLANTATION SOCIETY

Tobacco cultivation formed the basis of the Chesapeake economy. Although anyone with a few acres of cleared land could grow leaves for export, cultivation of the Chesapeake staple did not produce a society of individuals roughly similar in wealth and status. To the contrary, it generated inequality. The amassing of a large fortune involved the control of a large labor force. More workers in the fields meant larger harvests, and, of course, larger profits. Since free persons showed no interest in toiling away in another man's fields of tobacco, not even for wages, wealthy planters relied upon laborers who were not free as well as on slaves. The social structure that developed in the seventeenth-century Chesapeake reflected a wild, often unscrupulous scramble to bring men and women of three races—black, white, and Indian—into various degrees of independence.

Great planters dominated Chesapeake society. The group was small, and during the early decades of the seventeenth century, constantly changing. Not until the 1650s did the family names of those who would become famous eighteenth-century gentry appear on the records. These ambitious men arrived in America with capital. They invested immediately in laborers, and one way or another, they obtained huge tracts of the best tobacco-growing land. Although not aristocrats, but rather the younger sons of English merchants and artisans, they soon acquired political and social power. Over time, these gentry families—such as the Burwells, Byrds, Carters, and Masons—intermarried so frequently that they created a vast network of cousins. During the eighteenth century it was not uncommon to find a half dozen men with the same surname sitting simultaneously in the Virginia House of Burgesses.

Freemen formed the largest class in this society. Most came as indentured servants, unlike New England's yeomen farmers, and by sheer good fortune, managed to stay alive to the end of their contracts. When their period of indenture was over, many freemen lived on the edge of poverty. After 1660, opportunities for upward mobility decreased dramatically.

Below the freemen came indentured servants. Membership in this group was not demeaning; after all, servitude was a temporary status. But servitude in the Chesapeake colonies was not the benign institution it was in New England. Great planters purchased servants to grow tobacco, and they were not overly concerned with the well-being of these laborers. The unhappy servants regarded their servitude as a form of "slavery," while the planters worried that discontented servants and impoverished freemen would rebel at the slightest provocation. Later events would justify these fears.

The character of social mobility changed during the seventeenth century. Before the 1680s, movement into the planter elite by newcomers who possessed capital was relatively easy. After the 1680s, however, life expectancy rates improved in the Chesapeake colonies and the sons of great planters replaced their fathers in powerful government positions. The key to success was possession of slaves. Those planters who owned more blacks could grow more tobacco and thus purchase additional laborers. Over time, the rich not only became richer, they also formed a distinct ruling elite that newcomers found increasingly difficult to enter.

Opportunities for advancement also decreased for the region's freemen. As the gentry consolidated its hold on political and economic institutions, ordinary people discovered that it was much harder to rise in Chesapeake society. Men and women with more ambitious dreams headed for Pennsylvania, North Carolina, and western Virginia.

Social institutions that figured importantly in the New Englanders' daily lives were either weak or nonexistent in the Chesapeake, partly due to the high infant mortality rates. There was little incentive to build elementary schools, for example, since only half the children would reach adulthood. The development of higher education languished, too, and the great planters sent their sons to English or Scottish schools through much of the colonial period.

Tobacco also inhibited the growth of towns in this region. Owners of isolated plantations along the river banks traded directly with English merchants and had little need for local markets. People met sporadically at scattered churches, courthouses, and taverns. Seventeenth-century Virginia could not boast of even one printing press.

THE AFRICAN-AMERICAN EXPERIENCE

Many people who landed in the colonies had no desire to come to the New World; they were brought from Africa as slaves to cultivate rice, sugar, and tobacco. As the Native Americans were exterminated and the supply of white indentured servants dried up, white planters demanded ever more African laborers.

ROOTS OF SLAVERY

Between the sixteenth and nineteenth centuries, slave traders carried almost 11 million blacks from Africa to the New World, mainly to Brazil and the Caribbean. Only a small part

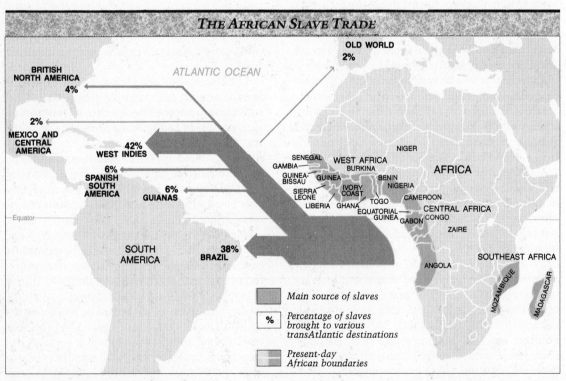

THE AFRICAN SLAVE TRADE

ATLANTIC OCEAN

OLD WORLD 2%

BRITISH NORTH AMERICA 4%

2% MEXICO AND CENTRAL AMERICA

42% WEST INDIES

6% SPANISH SOUTH AMERICA

6% GUIANAS

SOUTH AMERICA

38% BRAZIL

Equator

AFRICA

WEST AFRICA
SENEGAL
GAMBIA
GUINEA-BISSAU
GUINEA
SIERRA LEONE
LIBERIA
GHANA
IVORY COAST
TOGO
BURKINA
NIGER
BENIN
NIGERIA
CAMEROON
EQUATORIAL GUINEA
GABON
CONGO
CENTRAL AFRICA
ZAIRE
ANGOLA
SOUTHEAST AFRICA
MOZAMBIQUE
MADAGASCAR

Main source of slaves

% Percentage of slaves brought to various transAtlantic destinations

Present-day African boundaries

From Philip Curtin's The Atlantic Slave Trade

of this commerce involved British North America. Young black males predominated in the human cargo; the planters preferred this group for the hard physical labor of the plantations. In many early slave communities, black men outnumbered women by a ratio of two to one.

English colonists did not hesitate to enslave black people; the decision to import African slaves to the British colonies was based primarily upon economic considerations. But English masters never justified the practice purely in terms of planter profits. They associated blacks in Africa with heathen religion, barbarous behavior, sexual promiscuity, in fact, with evil itself. From such a perspective, the enslavement of African men and women seemed unobjectionable. Planters avowed that loss of freedom was a small price for the civilizing benefits of conversion to Christianity.

Africans first landed in Virginia in 1619. For the next fifty years, their status remained unclear. English settlers classified some black laborers as slaves for life, others as indentured servants. A few blacks purchased their freedom. Several seventeenth-century Africans even became successful Virginia planters.

One reason that Virginia lawmakers tolerated such confusion was that the black population remained very small. Planters wanted more African slaves, but during this period, slave traders sold their cargoes on Barbados or the other sugar islands of the West Indies, where they fetched a higher price than Virginians could afford. In fact, before 1680 most blacks who reached England's colonies on the North American mainland came from Barbados or through New Netherland rather than directly from Africa.

By the end of the seventeenth century, the status of Virginia's black people was no longer in doubt. They were slaves for life, as were their children after them. Slavery was unequivocally based on skin color alone. This transformation reflected an increase in the supply of Africans to British North America. After 1672 the Royal African Company undertook to meet the colonial planters' rising demands for black laborers, and during the eighteenth century many American merchants entered the lucrative trade.

The expanding black population apparently frightened white colonists, and lawmakers drew up ever stricter slave codes. The white planter could deal with his black property as he alone saw fit, and one extraordinary Virginia statute excused a master who killed a slave on the grounds that no rational person would purposely "destroy his own estate." Furthermore, children born to a slave woman became slaves regardless of the father's race. Nor did conversion to Christianity free blacks from bondage. Unlike the Spanish colonies where persons of lighter color enjoyed greater privileges in society, in the English colonies racial mixing was not tolerated, and mulattoes received the same treatment as did pure Africans.

AFRICAN-AMERICAN CULTURES IN ENGLISH AMERICA

The slave experience varied substantially from colony to colony. The size and density of the slave population determined in large measure how successfully blacks could maintain a separate cultural identity. On isolated rice plantations in South Carolina, where during the eighteenth century 60 percent of the population was black, African-Americans developed creole languages that blended English with words from African tongues. Slaves on these large plantations were also able to establish elaborate and enduring kinship networks that may have helped reduce the more dehumanizing aspects of bondage.

Blacks made up a smaller percentage of the population in New England and the Middle Colonies (less than 10 percent) and even in Virginia (40 percent). Most slaves in the northern colonies worked as domestics and lived in their masters' homes. Close contact with whites made it more difficult to preserve and reaffirm an African heritage and identity.

In eighteenth-century Virginia, native-born blacks had learned to cope with whites on a daily basis. They looked with disdain upon slaves who had just arrived from Africa. Blacks as well as whites pressed these "outlandish" newcomers to accept elements of English culture, especially to speak the English language.

Despite their wrenching experiences, black slaves did establish cultural traditions that involved an imaginative reshaping of African and European customs into something that was neither African nor European; it was African-American. For example, slaves embraced Christianity, but transformed it into an expression of religious feeling in which an African element remained vibrant.

During the early decades of the eighteenth century, blacks living in England's mainland colonies began to reproduce themselves suc-

cessfully; that is, live births exceeded deaths. This demographic shift did not take place in the Caribbean or South American colonies until a much later date. Historians believe that North American blacks enjoyed a healthier climate and better diet than did other New World slaves.

But longer lives did not make them any less slaves. Nor did it prevent slave protests, including organized revolt. The most serious slave rebellion of the colonial period was the Stono Uprising, which took place in September 1739. One hundred and fifty South Carolina blacks rose up and murdered several whites. They marched toward Florida and the promise of freedom, but the local militia overtook and

Old Plantation, watercolor by an unknown artist (about 1800), shows that some African identity and customs survived plantation life. The man and woman in the center dance (possibly to celebrate a wedding) to the music of drums and banjo. Instruments, turbans, and scarves have African elements.

crushed the rebellious slaves. Such rebellions were rare; in fact, the level of interracial violence in colonial North America was quite low. But the fear of slave rebellions was pervasive, prompting whites to take drastic defensive measures.

BLUEPRINT FOR EMPIRE

Just as the status of slaves changed during the seventeenth century, so did the status of white colonists. Until the middle of the seventeenth century, English political leaders largely ignored the American colonists. After the restoration of Charles II to the throne in 1660, however, intervention replaced indifference. The Crown, Parliament, and the mercantile interests decided that the colonies should be brought more tightly under the control of the mother country. Regulatory policies that evolved during this period formed a framework for empire that survived with only minor adjustments until 1765.

A NEW COMMERCIAL SYSTEM

The famous eighteenth-century Scottish economist Adam Smith coined the term *mercantilism* to describe the system on which England based its commercial regulations. As administered by the policymakers of the late seventeenth century, however, the system was not nearly as well thought out or organized as Smith suggested. Rather, it represented a series of individual responses to the needs of several powerful interest groups.

Each group looked to colonial commerce to solve a different problem. Charles wanted money to pay his enormous debts. English merchants were eager to exclude Dutch rivals from lucrative American markets, but without government assistance they could not compete successfully with the Dutch Merchant Marine. Parliament wanted to strengthen England's navy, and the expansion of the domestic shipbuilding industry was a fine starting place. And

almost everyone agreed with the mercantilistic view that the mother country should establish a more favorable balance of trade, that is, increase exports, decrease imports, and grow richer at the expense of other European states. Together, these ideas provided a blueprint for England's first empire, a complex set of regulations that shaped the character of Anglo-American cultural and economic relations until the American Revolution.

NAVIGATIONAL ACTS TRANSFORM COLONIAL SOCIETY

In 1660 parliament passed a Navigation Act, the most important piece of imperial legislation drafted before the American Revolution. Colonists from Maine to Georgia paid close attention to the act, which stated (1) that no ship could trade in the colonies unless it had been constructed in either England or America and carried a crew that was at least 75 percent English, and (2) that certain enumerated goods of great value that were not produced in England—tobacco, sugar, cotton, indigo, dye, wool, ginger—could be transported from the colonies *only* to an English or another colonial port. Early in the next century, Parliament added rice, molasses, wood resins, tars, and turpentines to the enumerated list.

The Act of 1660 was masterfully conceived. It encouraged the development of domestic shipbuilding, prohibited European rivals from obtaining enumerated goods anywhere except in England, and provided the Crown with added revenue. Parliament supplemented this act in 1663 with a second Navigation Act, known as the Staple Act, that closed off nearly all direct trade between European nations and the American colonies. With a few noted exceptions, nothing could be imported into America unless it had first been transshipped through the mother country, a process that greatly added to the price paid by colonial consumers.

During the 1660s Virginians showed little enthusiasm for the new imperial system. Not only did the collection of customs on tobacco greatly reduce profits, but with the exclusion of the Dutch as the middlemen in American commerce, tobacco planters had to sell their crops to English merchants at artificially low prices. Virginia's loss (£100,000 in import duties collected for the Crown by 1670) was Charles II's gain. At first, New England merchants ignored or cleverly circumvented the commercial restrictions. These crafty traders picked up cargoes of enumerated goods such as sugar or tobacco, sailed to another colonial port (thereby technically fulfilling the letter of the law), and then made directly for Holland or France. Along the way they paid no customs.

To plug this loophole, Parliament passed another Navigation Act in 1673. This statute established a plantation duty to be collected at the various colonial ports. New Englanders could no longer escape paying customs. And in 1675, as part of this new imperial firmness, the Privy Council formed a powerful subcommittee, the Lords of Trade, whose members monitored colonial affairs.

Despite these legal reforms, serious obstacles impeded the execution of imperial policy. The customs service did not have enough effective agents in American ports to enforce the Navigation Acts fully, and imperial officials of various independent agencies often worked at cross-purposes.

Parliament passed the last major piece of imperial legislation in 1696. Among other things, the statute tightened enforcement procedures, putting pressure specifically upon the colonial governors to keep England's competitors out of American ports. The Act of 1696 also expanded the American customs service and for the first time set up vice-admiralty courts in the colonies. This decision particularly rankled the colonists. Established to settle disputes that occurred at sea, vice-admiralty courts required neither juries nor oral cross-examination, both traditional elements of common law. On the eve of the American Revolution, a sudden expansion of the admiralty system raised a storm of protest.

The year 1696 witnessed one other significant change in the imperial system. William III replaced the ineffective Lords of Trade with a body of policy advisers that came to be known as the Board of Trade. This group was expected to monitor colonial affairs closely; and for several decades at least, it energetically carried out its responsibilities.

The members of Parliament believed that these reforms would belatedly compel the colonists to accept the Navigation Acts, and in large measure they were correct. By 1700 American goods transshipped through the mother country accounted for a quarter of *all* English exports, an indication that the colonists found it profitable to obey the commercial regulations. In fact, during the eighteenth century, smuggling from Europe to America dried up almost completely.

The Navigation Acts of the seventeenth century also shaped the colonists' material culture. Over time, Americans grew increasingly accustomed to purchasing English goods; they established close ties with specific merchant houses in London, Bristol, or Glasgow. It is not surprising, therefore, that by mid-eighteenth century the colonists preferred the manufactures of the mother country over those of England's commercial rivals. In other words, the Navigation Acts affected the development of consumer habits throughout the empire, and it is not an exaggeration to suggest that this regulatory system was in large part responsible for the anglicanization of eighteenth-century American culture (see Chapter 4).

POLITICAL UNREST, 1676–1691: COLONIAL GENTRY IN REVOLT

The Navigation Acts created an illusion of unity; these imperial statutes superimposed a system of commercial regulations on all the colonies. But within each society men and women struggled to bring order out of disorder, to establish stable ruling elites, to defuse ethnic and racial tensions, and to cope with population pressures that imperial planners only dimly understood. During the final decades of the seventeenth century, these efforts sometimes sparked revolt between factions of the local gentry, usually the "outs" versus the "ins," for political power.

CIVIL WAR IN VIRGINIA: BACON'S REBELLION

Virginia was the first colony to experience this political unrest. After 1660, the Virginia economy steadily declined. Returns from tobacco had not been good for some time, and the Navigation Acts reduced profits even further. Into this unhappy environment came thousands of ambitious indentured servants.

The reality bore little relation to their dreams. A hurricane destroyed one entire tobacco crop, and in 1667 Dutch warships captured the tobacco fleet just as it was about to sail for England. Indentured servants complained about lack of food and clothing. No wonder that Virginia's governor, Sir William Berkeley, despaired of ever ruling "a People where six parts of seven at least are Poor, Endebted, Discontented and Armed." In 1670 he and the House of Burgesses disenfranchised all landless freemen, persons they regarded as troublemakers, but the threat of social violence remained.

Enter Nathaniel Bacon. This ambitious young man arrived in Virginia in 1674. He came from a respectable English family and set himself immediately as a substantial planter. But he wanted more. Bacon envied the government patronage monopolized by Berkeley's cronies, a group known locally as the "Green Spring" faction. When Bacon attempted to obtain a license to engage in the fur trade, he was rebuffed. This lucrative commerce was reserved for the governor's friends. If Bacon had been willing to wait, he would probably have been accepted into the ruling clique, but as subsequent events would demonstrate, Bacon was not a man of patience.

In 1675, Indian attacks on outlying plantations thrust Bacon suddenly into the center of Virginia politics. Virginians expected the governor to send an army to retaliate. Instead, Berkeley called for the construction of a line of defensive forts. Settlers suspected that the governor was simply trying to protect his own fur interests and was rewarding his friends with contracts to build useless forts.

In response, Bacon boldly offered to lead a volunteer army against the Indians at no cost to the hard-pressed Virginia taxpayers. All he demanded was an official commission from Berkeley giving him military command. The governor steadfastly refused.

What followed would have been comic had not so many people died. Bacon thundered against the governor's treachery; Berkeley labeled Bacon a traitor. Bacon led several campaigns against the Indians, failing to kill any enemies, but managing to massacre some friendly Indians. Bacon also burned Jamestown to the ground, forcing Berkeley to flee to the colony's eastern shore. Charles II sent troops to aid the governor, but by the time they arrived, Berkeley had gained full control of the colony's government. In October 1676, Bacon died after a brief illness, and his band of rebels dispersed within a few months.

Order was soon restored, and in 1677 the Crown recalled the embittered Berkeley. The governors who followed were unusually greedy, and the local gentry formed a united front against them.

THE GLORIOUS REVOLUTION IN THE BAY COLONY

During John Winthrop's lifetime, the settlers of Massachusetts developed an inflated sense of their independence from the mother country. After the Restoration in 1660, however, the Crown put an end to that illusion. Royal officials demanded full compliance with the Navigation Acts, which were constant reminders of New England's colonial status. The growth of commerce attracted new merchants who were there to make money and were restive under

Metacomet, called King Philip by the whites, waged a war against the Massachusetts colonists that left at least a thousand New Englanders dead.

gional economy. "In proportion to population, King Philip's War inflicted greater casualties upon the people than any other war in our history," writes historian Douglas Leach.

Another shock followed. In 1684, the Court of Chancery, sitting in London and acting under a petition from King James II, annulled the charter of the Massachusetts Bay Company. The decision forced the most stubborn Puritans to recognize that they were part of an empire run by people who did not share their particular religious vision.

In the place of representative governments, James II created the Dominion of New England. In various stages from 1686 to 1689, it incorporated Massachusetts, Connecticut, Rhode Island, Plymouth, New York, New Jersey, and New Hampshire under a single appointed royal governor. For this demanding position, James selected Sir Edmund Andros (pronounced Andrews), a military veteran of tyrannical temperament. He quickly abolished elective assemblies and town meetings, and enforced the Navigation Acts so rigorously that he brought about a commercial depression. His high-handed methods alienated almost all the colonists.

Early in 1689 the news of the Glorious Revolution reached Boston. The English people had deposed James II, an absolutist monarch who openly espoused Catholicism. His daughter Mary and her husband William of Orange ascended the throne as joint monarchs in James' place. William and Mary had accepted a Bill of Rights that stipulated the constitutional rights of the English subject. Almost immediately the Bay colonists overthrew the hated Andros regime and jailed the governor. No one came to Andros' defense.

However united they were, the Bay colonists could not take the newly crowned monarchs' support for granted. But thanks largely to the tireless efforts of Increase Mather, a Congregational minister and father of Cotton Mather, who pleaded the colonists' case in London, King William abandoned the Dominion of New England and in 1691 conferred a new royal charter upon Massachusetts. This document

the Puritan strictures. These developments divided Bay leaders. A few Puritan ministers and magistrates regarded compromise with England as treason, a breaking of the Lord's covenant. Other spokesmen recognized the changing political realities within the empire and urged a more moderate course.

In 1675, the Indians dealt the New Englanders a terrible setback. Metacomet, a Wampanoag chief whom the whites called King Philip, declared war against the colonists; he was joined by the powerful Narragansets. In little more than a year of fighting, the Indians destroyed scores of frontier villages, killed hundreds of colonists, and disrupted the entire re-provided for a Crown-appointed governor and a franchise based on property ownership rather than church membership. On the local level, town government remained much as it had been in Winthrop's time.

CONTAGION OF WITCHCRAFT

During these politically troubled times, hysterical men and women living in Salem Village, a small, struggling farming community, created panic in Massachusetts Bay. In late 1691, during a very cold winter, several adolescent girls began to behave in strange ways. They cried for no apparent reason; they twitched on the ground. The girls attributed their suffering to the work of witches. The arrest of several alleged witches did not relieve the girls' "fits," and other arrests followed. At least one person confessed, providing a frightening description of the devil as "a thing all over hairy, all the face hairy, and a long nose." By the end of the summer, a specially convened court had hanged nineteen people; another was pressed to death. Many more suspects awaited trial.

Then suddenly, the storm was over. Led by Increase Mather, a group of prominent Congregational ministers urged leniency and restraint. Especially troubling to the clergymen was the court's decision to accept "spectral evidence," that is, reports of dreams and visions in which the accused appeared as the devil's agent. The colonial government accepted the minister's advice and convened a new court, which promptly acquitted, pardoned, or released the remaining suspects.

No one knows exactly what sparked the terror in Salem Village. The community had a history of discord, and during the 1680s the people split into angry factions over the choice of a minister. Jealousy and bitterness apparently festered to the point that adolescent girls who normally would have been disciplined were allowed to incite judicial murder. As often happens in incidents like this one, the accusers later came to their senses and apologized for the cruel suffering that they had inflicted.

THE GLORIOUS REVOLUTION IN NEW YORK AND MARYLAND

When news of the Glorious Revolution reached New York City in May 1689, Jacob Leisler, a German immigrant with mercantile ties to the older Dutch elite, raised a group of militiamen and seized a local fort in the name of William and Mary. For a short time he controlled the city. But English newcomers and powerful Anglo-Dutch families who had recently risen to prominence opposed the older Dutch group to which he was allied, and Leisler never was able to construct a secure political base.

In 1691 a new royal governor, Henry Sloughter, reached New York and ordered Leisler to surrender his authority. Leisler hesitated; he may have feared the vengeance of rival factions. The pause cost Leisler his life. He was declared a rebel, promptly tried, and executed in grisly fashion. Four years later, Parliament officially pardoned him, but the decision came a bit late. The bitter political factionalism that engendered this unfortunate episode plagued New York throughout the next century.

Tensions in Maryland between Protestants and Catholics ran high during the last third of the seventeenth century. When news of James' overthrow reached Maryland early in 1689, pent-up anti-proprietary and anti-Catholic sentiment exploded. John Coode, a member of the Assembly and an outspoken Protestant, formed a group called the Protestant Association, which forced the governor appointed by Lord Baltimore to resign.

The Protestant Association petitioned the newly crowned Protestant monarchs to transform Maryland into a royal colony, alleging many wrongs suffered at the hands of the Catholic-dominated upper house. William complied, sending a royal governor in 1691. The new Assembly then proclaimed the Church of England as the established religion and excluded Catholics from public office. Baltimore lost control of the colony's government. In 1715, however, the fourth Lord Baltimore, who had been raised a member of the Church of En-

CHRONOLOGY

1619	First blacks arrive in Virginia
1638	Harvard College established
1660	Charles II is restored to the English throne
	First Navigation Act passed by Parliament
1663	Second Navigation (Staple) Act passed
1673	Plantation duty imposed to close loopholes in commercial regulations
1675	King Philip's (Metacomet's) War devastates New England
1676	Bacon's Rebellion threatens Governor Berkeley's government in Virginia
1681	William Penn receives charter for Pennsylvania
1684	Charter of Massachusetts Bay Company revoked
1685	Duke of York becomes James II
1686	Dominion of New England established
1688	James II driven into exile during Glorious Revolution
1689	Rebellions break out in Massachusetts, New York, and Maryland
1691	Jacob Leisler executed
1692	Salem Village wracked by witch trials

gland, regained full proprietorship from the Crown. Maryland remained in the hands of the Calvert family until 1776.

COMMON EXPERIENCES, SEPARATE CULTURES

In the years since Winthrop had sailed to the New World, colonial Americans had become more, not less, English. They had been drawn into an imperial system—Carolinians, Virginians, New Englanders, all regulated now by the same commercial statutes. They had not, however, developed a sense of unity as Americans. Profound sectional differences remained, indeed had grown stronger, so that during the eighteenth century, the colonists felt increasingly torn between the culture of the mother country and the culture of their own region.

RECOMMENDED READING

The best account of seventeenth-century New Englanders' views on the family remains Edmund S. Morgan, *The Puritan Family* (1966). Morgan has also produced a masterful analysis of a southern colony; his *American Slavery, American Freedom: The Ordeal of Colonial Virginia* (1975) examines the impact of an extraordinarily high death rate upon an evolving triracial plantation society. Anyone interested in the history of slavery should start with David B. Davis, *The Problem of Slavery in Western Culture* (1966), and Winthrop D. Jordan, *White over Black: American Attitudes Toward the Negro, 1550–1812* (1968). A complete discussion of the drafting of the Navigation Acts and England's efforts to enforce them can be found in C. M. Andrews, *The Colonial Period of American History*, vol. 4 (1938). David S.

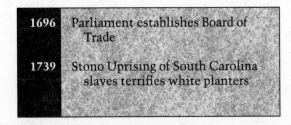

1696	Parliament establishes Board of Trade
1739	Stono Uprising of South Carolina slaves terrifies white planters

Lovejoy provides a comprehensive survey of the various late seventeenth-century rebellions in *The Glorious Revolution in America* (1972).

Stephen Foster, *Their Solitary Way* (1971), is a highly readable analysis of the ways in which Puritans perceived their society. Two books that examine the relationship between the life cycle and social structure are John Demos, *A Little Commonwealth* (1970), and Philip J. Greven, *Four Generations* (1969). The role of women in this society is the subject of Laurel T. Ulrich, *Good Wives: Image and Reality in the Lives of Women in Northern New England, 1650–1750* (1982).

The development of colonial society in the South is explored in T. W. Tate and D. L. Ammerman, eds., *The Chesapeake in the Seventeenth Century* (1979). Roger A. Ekirch, *Bound for America* (1987) discusses indentured servitude, but see also David W. Galenson, *White Servitude in Colonial America: An Economic Analysis* (1981). T. H. Breen speculates on the cultural values of early Virginians in *Puritans and Adventurers* (1980).

The black experience in colonial America has been the topic of several recent interdisciplinary studies: Philip D. Curtin, *The Atlantic Slave Trade: A Census* (1969); Peter Wood, *Black Majority* (1974); G. W. Mullin, *Flight and Rebellion* (1972); and T. H. Breen and Stephen Innes, *"Myne Owne Ground," Race and Freedom on Virginia's Eastern Shore* (1980).

The best study of King Philip's War is by Douglas Leach, *Flintlock and Tomahawk* (1958). One can better understand the Indians' perspective by reading William Cronon, *Changes in the Land: Indians, Colonists, and the Ecology of New England* (1983), and Neil Salisbury, *Manitou and Providence* (1982). Of the many studies of Salem Village witchcraft, the most imaginative are Paul Boyer and Stephen Nisenbaum, *Salem Possessed* (1974), and John Demos, *Entertaining Satan: Witchcraft and the Culture of Early New England* (1982).

4 EXPANDING HORIZONS: EIGHTEENTH-CENTURY AMERICA

PEOPLE AND TRADE IN AN EXPANDING EMPIRE

RELIGIOUS REVIVAL IN AN AGE OF REASON

POLITICS: BRITISH THEORY AND AMERICAN PRACTICE

CENTURY OF IMPERIAL WAR

FORGING A CULTURAL IDENTITY

Sometime early in December 1705, Isaac Pummatick and his friend Peter ran away. Isaac, an Indian, had deserted the royal army, and Peter, who was black, had fled the bonds of slavery. Starting in Maine, they journeyed south to the busy Massachusetts port of Newbury. There they boarded a ship bound for South Carolina, where they hoped to establish new identities.

They could leave Maine, but they could not escape the technology of their day. Peter's master placed an advertisement in the *Boston New-Letter*, the first weekly journal published in England's mainland colonies. He described Peter and offered a reward for the return of his slave. In the same issue of the weekly, an officer in His Majesty's Service announced the desertion of Isaac. The *Boston New-Letter* arrived in South Carolina about the same time as did Peter and Isaac. The two men were soon spotted, captured, and returned to Maine. The event marked a milestone in the history of colonial communications.

Although Peter and Isaac had no desire to be part of such a historical achievement, their fate was determined by the rapidly changing character of eighteenth-century colonial society. Americans were no longer as isolated as they had been during most of the seventeenth century. After 1690, men and women were gradually drawn into the larger Anglo-American world. Colonists whose parents or grandparents had tamed a "howling wilderness" relied increasingly upon imported goods, read London journals, traveled to the mother country, fought Britain's enemies, and sought favors from royal officials. Colonial women modeled themselves on the ideal of the English "genteel lady." A love–hate relationship with England began.

Tensions arose and there were many contradictions. It was not unusual for colonists who adopted the latest London fashions to condemn the corrupting influence of British life. Colonists eagerly read sophisticated English journals, yet extolled the virtues of simplicity and provincial society. Benjamin Franklin, one of the most cosmopolitan colonial figures of the age, championed American liberties. And William Byrd, a Virginia planter who spent most of his adult life in Great Britain chasing celebrities, insisted that America had purer air than England. Trapped between two cultures, the colonists were neither Englishmen nor Americans. In time, however, they would have to choose between the two worlds.

❧ PEOPLE AND TRADE IN AN EXPANDING EMPIRE

During the eighteenth century, the American population doubled approximately every twenty-five years. Not only was the total population increasing at a very rapid rate, it was also becoming more dispersed and heterogeneous. Each year witnessed the arrival of thousands of non-English Europeans, most of whom were soon scattered along the colonial frontier.

POPULATION EXPLOSION

The estimated white population of Britian's mainland colonies rose from about 250,000 in 1700 to 2,150,000 in 1770, an annual growth rate of 3 percent. Few societies in recorded history have expanded so rapidly. Natural reproduction was responsible for most of the growth. The population of the late colonial period was strikingly young; approximately one half of the population at any given time was under the age of sixteen.

Immigration further swelled the colonial population. The largest group of newcomers

consisted of Scotch-Irish. During the seventeenth century, English rulers sent thousands of Scottish Presbyterians as colonists to Catholic Ireland in an attempt to pacify that war-torn country. The plan failed, and after a short time, many of the Scotch-Irish elected to immigrate to America, where they hoped to find the freedom and prosperity that they had been denied in Ireland. By the time of the American Revolution, perhaps 250,000 Scotch-Irish had migrated to America.

Most Scotch-Irish immigrants landed initially in Philadelphia, but they soon headed for the fertile land on Pennsylvania's western frontier. They were welcomed, for the colony's proprietors believed that the Scotch-Irish would serve as a buffer between the Indians and the older, coastal communities. The Penn family soon had second thoughts, however. The Scotch-Irish settled wherever they found unoccupied land, regardless of who owned it, and challenged established authority.

ESTIMATED POPULATION, 1720–1760

		New England Colonies	Middle Colonies	Southern Colonies
1720	White	166,937	92,259	138,110
	Black	3,956	10,825	54,098
1730	White	211,233	135,298	191,893
	Black	6,118	11,683	73,220
1740	White	281,163	204,093	270,283
	Black	8,541	16,452	125,031
1750	White	349,029	275,723	309,588
	Black	10,982	20,736	204,702
1760	White	436,917	398,855	432,047
	Black	12,717	29,049	284,040

New England Colonies New Hampshire, Massachusetts, Rhode Island, and Connecticut
Middle Colonies New York, New Jersey, Pennsylvania, and Delaware
Southern Colonies Maryland, Virginia, North Carolina, South Carolina, and (after 1740) Georgia

Source: Adapted from R.C. Simmons, The American Colonies: From Settlement to Independence. © 1976 by R.C. Simmons. Reprinted by permission of the Harold Matson Company, Inc.

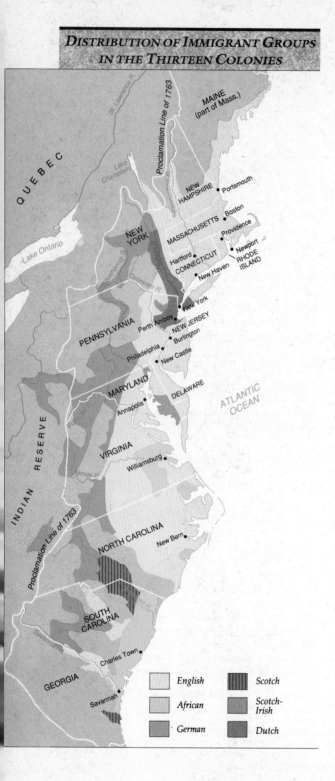

DISTRIBUTION OF IMMIGRANT GROUPS IN THE THIRTEEN COLONIES

QUEBEC

St. Lawrence R.

Lake Champlain

Proclamation Line of 1763

MAINE
(part of Mass.)

Lake Ontario

NEW
HAMPSHIRE
• Portsmouth

NEW
YORK

MASSACHUSETTS
• Boston

Connecticut R.

Susquehanna R.

Hudson R.

Hartford
CONNECTICUT
• New Haven

Providence
• Newport
RHODE
ISLAND

Delaware R.

PENNSYLVANIA

• New York

Perth Amboy
NEW JERSEY
• Burlington

Philadelphia •
• New Castle

MARYLAND

DELAWARE

Annapolis •

Potomac R.

ATLANTIC
OCEAN

INDIAN RESERVE

VIRGINIA

Williamsburg •

James R.

Proclamation Line of 1763

NORTH CAROLINA

New Bern •

SOUTH
CAROLINA

Savannah R.

GEORGIA

Charles Town •

Savannah •

	English		Scotch
	African		Scotch-Irish
	German		Dutch

A second large body of non-English settlers, more than 100,000 people, came from the Upper Rhine Valley, in the German Palatinate. Some of these people belonged to small pietist Protestant sects, and they came to America in search of religious toleration. Most Germans, however, sought the peace and good land of the colonies. By 1776 persons of German stock—mistakenly called Dutch—accounted for more than one third of Pennsylvania's total population. Even their detractors admitted that the Germans were the best farmers in the colony.

Ethnic differences in Pennsylvania bred disputes. The Scotch-Irish and the Germans preferred to live with people of their own background, and they sometimes fought to keep members of the other nationalities out of their neighborhood. Further complicating the problem, the English were suspicious of both groups. Indeed, many Pennsylvanians shared Benjamin Franklin's opinion that the Germans posed a threat to the primacy of the English language and government in that colony.

Prejudice and hostility may have persuaded the Germans and the Scotch-Irish to head for western Pennsylvania, the Shenandoah Valley of Virginia, and the backcountry of the Carolinas. The Germans usually remained wherever they found unclaimed fertile land. The Scotch-Irish tended to move two or three times and acquired a reputation as a rootless people.

Another large group of Europeans arriving in America during the eighteenth century came without any burning desire to do so. They were convicted felons, transported to America as punishment for their crimes. Between 1718 and 1775, judges in England, Ireland, and Scotland shipped approximately 50,000 convicts to the New World. Most were young males who had committed only minor crimes against property, and few prospered in the colonies. After the American Revolution the British redirected this flow of convicts to Australia.

CULTURE OF THE CITIES

Considering the rate of population growth, few eighteenth-century Americans lived in cities.

Boston, Newport, Philadelphia, New York, and Charleston—the five largest cities—contained only about 5 percent of the colonial population. In 1775 none had more than 40,000 persons. The explanation for the dearth of city dwellers can be found in the highly specialized nature of colonial commerce. Port towns served as intermediary trade and shipping centers where bulk cargoes were broken up for inland distribution; they did not support large-scale manufacturing. Also, men who worked for wages usually became farmers, rather than urban laborers.

Yet American cities profoundly affected colonial culture, for it was in the cities that the English influence was most· pronounced. Wealthy merchants and lawyers tried to emulate the culture of the mother country. They went to the theater, listened to concerts, and dressed in the high fashion of London society. The architectural splendor was especially noticeable. Homes of enduring beauty, modeled on English country houses, were constructed during the reign of Britain's early Hanoverian kings. Since all these kings were named George, the term *Georgian* was applied to this style of architecture.

Their owners filled these houses with fine furniture. Each city patronized certain skilled craftsmen, but the artisans of Philadelphia were known for producing magnificent copies of the works of Thomas Chippendale, Great Britain's most famous furniture designer. These developments gave American cities an elegance that they had not possessed in the previous century.

For some American artists colonial society did not fulfill their needs. They could not find the training they required, and America seemed devoid of the kind of subject matter that inspired the great European masters. John Singleton Copley, perhaps colonial America's finest and most highly regarded painter, always wondered whether the English would respect his work. Sir Joshua Reynolds, the preeminent English painter of the age, admired Copley's *Boy with the Squirrel* and urged the artist to pursue his career in England. In 1774 Copley moved to London.

John Singleton Copley's portraits convey a powerful sense of the subject's physical presence—a person, as he or she really is—as in Boy with the Squirrel.

ECONOMIC EXPANSION

The colonial economy kept pace with the stunning growth in population. Per capita income never fell behind the population explosion. An abundance of land and the extensive growth of agriculture accounted for this economic success. Each year more Americans produced more tobacco, wheat, and rice—just to cite the major export crops—and by this means, they maintained a high level of individual prosperity without developing an industrial base.

One half of American goods produced for export went to Great Britain. The Navigation Acts (see Chapter 3) were still in effect and "enumerated" items such as tobacco and furs had to be landed first at a British port. Over the

Estimated Population of Colonial Cities, 1720–1770
Showing Decennial Percentage Increases

	Boston	%	Newport	%	New York	%	Philadelphia	%	Charleston	%
1720	12,000	—	3,800	—	7,000	—	10,000	—	3,500	—
1730	13,000	8	4,640	22	8,622	23	11,500	15	4,500	29
1740	15,601	20	5,840	26	10,451	21	12,654	10	6,269	39
1750	—	—	6,670	14	14,225	36	18,202	44	7,134	14
1760	15,631	—	7,500	12	18,000	27	23,750	30	8,000	12
1770	15,877	2	9,833	31	22,667	26	34,583	46	10,667	33

Source: R.C. Simmons, The American Colonies: From Settlement to Independence. © 1976 by R.C. Simmons. Reprinted by permission of the Harold Matson Company, Inc.

years, specific legislation brought white pine trees, molasses, hats, and iron under imperial control as England regulated colonial trade to her advantage.

The statutes might have created tensions between the colonists and the mother country had they been rigorously enforced. Crown officials, however, generally ignored the new laws. But even without the Navigation Acts, a majority of colonial exports would have been sold on the English markets. The emerging consumer society in Great Britain was beginning to create a generation that possessed enough income to purchase American goods, especially sugar and tobacco. This rising demand was the major market force shaping the colonial economy.

Roughly one fourth of all American exports went to the West Indies. Colonial ships carrying food sailed for the Caribbean and returned *immediately* to the Middle Colonies or New England with cargoes of molasses, sugar, and rum. "Triangular trade" including the west coast of Africa was insignificant. In addition, the West Indies played a vital role in preserving American credit. Without this source of income, colonists would not have been able to pay for the manufactured items that they purchased in the mother country. The cost of goods imported from Great Britain normally exceeded the revenues collected on American exports to the mother country. To cover this small but recurrent deficit, colonial merchants relied upon profits made in the West Indies.

After mid-century, however, the balance of trade turned dramatically against the colonists. Americans began buying more English goods than their parents and grandparents had done. Between 1740 and 1770 English exports to the American colonies increased by an astounding 360 percent.

In part, this shift reflected the increased production of British industries. Because of technological advances in manufacturing, Great Britain was able to produce certain goods more efficiently and more cheaply than the colonists could. Americans started to buy as never before; Staffordshire china and imported cloth replaced crude earthenware and rough homespun. In this manner, British industrialization undercut American handicraft and folk art.

To help Americans purchase manufactured goods, British merchants offered generous credit. For many people, the temptation to acquire English finery blinded them to hard economic realities. Colonists deferred settlement by agreeing to pay interest on their debts, and by 1760 total indebtedness had reached £2 million. Colonial governments could delay the balance-of-payment crisis for a time by issuing paper money, but the problem was not resolved.

The eighteenth century brought a substantial increase in intercoastal trade. Southern planters sent tobacco and rice to New England and the Middle Colonies, where these staples were exchanged for meat and wheat as well as for goods imported from Great Britain. By 1760 approximately 30 percent of the colonists' total tonnage capacity was involved in this extensive "coast-wise" commerce. In addition, American colonists carried on a substantial amount of commerce over the rough, back-country highway known as the "Great Wagon Road," which stretched 735 miles along the Blue Ridge Mountains from Pennsylvania to South Carolina. The long, gracefully designed Conestoga wagon was vital to this overland trade.

These shifting patterns of trade had an immense effect on the development of an American culture. First, the flood of British imports eroded local and regional identities. Deep sectional differences remained, of course, but Americans from New Hampshire to Georgia were increasingly drawn into a sophisticated economic network centered in London.

Second, the expanding coastwise and overland trade brought colonists of different backgrounds into more frequent contact, exchanging ideas and experience as well as tobacco and wheat. New journals and newspapers appeared. Americans were kept abreast of the latest news in the colonies as well as in London. Americans were expanding their horizons, and slowly, sometimes painfully, a distinct culture was emerging.

RELIGIOUS REVIVAL IN AN AGE OF REASON

Two great forces—one intellectual, the other religious—transformed the character of eighteenth-century American life. Although both movements originated in Europe, they were redefined in a New World context and soon reflected the peculiarities of the colonial experience. The *Enlightenment* changed the way that educated urbane colonists looked at their world; the *Great Awakening* brought a rebirth to thousands of men and women scattered along the Atlantic coast. Both movements made Americans aware of other persons, often complete strangers, who shared their beliefs. These voluntary networks undercut traditional community ties and helped the colonists forge new culture identities.

AMERICAN ENLIGHTENMENT

European historians often refer to the eighteenth century as an Age of Reason. During this period a body of new ideas, called the Enlightenment, altered the way that educated Europeans thought about God, nature, and society. Enlightenment philosophers replaced the concept of original sin with a much more optimistic view of human nature. A benevolent God, they argued, having set the universe in motion, gave human beings the power of reason to enable them to comprehend the orderly workings of His creation. Everything, even human society, operated according to these mechanical laws. It was the duty of men and women, therefore, to make certain that insti-

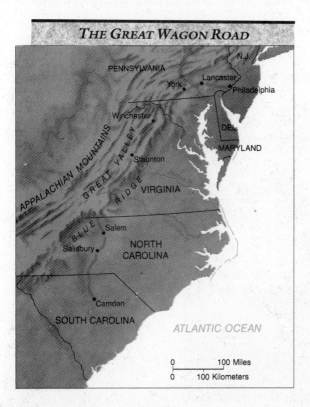

THE GREAT WAGON ROAD

PENNSYLVANIA
N.J.
York
Lancaster
Philadelphia
Winchester
DEL.
MARYLAND
APPALACHIAN MOUNTAINS
GREAT VALLEY
Staunton
BLUE RIDGE
VIRGINIA
Salem
Salisbury
NORTH CAROLINA
Camden
SOUTH CAROLINA
ATLANTIC OCEAN

0   100 Miles
0   100 Kilometers

tutions such as church and state conformed to self-evident natural laws. Through the use of reason, they asserted, human suffering could be eliminated and perfection could be achieved.

The American Enlightenment was a rather tame affair compared to its European counterpart. Colonists welcomed the advent of experimental science but stoutly defended the tenets of traditional Christianity. Americans emphasized the search for useful knowledge, ideas, and inventions. What mattered was practical experimentation, and the Enlightenment spawned scores of earnest scientific tinkerers, people who dutifully recorded changes in temperature, the appearance of strange plants or animals, and the particulars of astronomic phenomena.

The greatest of all these American experimenters was Benjamin Franklin (1706–1790). As a young man working in his brother's Boston printshop, he discovered a copy of a new British journal, the *Spectator*. It was like a breath of fresh air to a boy growing up in Puritan New England. In August 1721 he and his brother founded the *New-England Courant*, a weekly newspaper that satirized Boston's political and religious leaders in the manner of the contemporary British press. Proper Bostonians were not prepared for such a critical journal, and in 1723 Franklin left Massachusetts in search of a less antagonistic intellectual environment.

He settled in Philadelphia. There he devoted himself to the pursuit of useful knowledge. Franklin never denied the existence of God. Rather, he pushed the Lord aside, making room for the free exercise of reason. A naturally curious man, he was constantly experimenting and broadening his understanding of science, always with some practical end in mind. The lightning rod and a marvelously efficient stove are only two of Franklin's important contributions to material progress through human ingenuity.

Franklin energetically promoted the spread of Enlightenment ideas. In Philadelphia he formed "a club for mutual Improvement, which we call'd the Junto" and a library asso-

Experiments with electricity by Benjamin Franklin became world famous and motivated others to study this strange force. The people are rubbing rods together to produce static electricity.

ciation to discuss literature, philosophy, and science. The members of these groups communicated with Americans living in other colonies, providing them not only with the latest information from Europe, but also with models for their own clubs and associations. Such efforts broadened the intellectual horizons of many colonists, especially city dwellers.

GREAT AWAKENING

The Great Awakening had a far greater impact on the lives of the common people than did the Enlightenment. This unprecedented evangelical outpouring caused men and women to rethink basic assumptions about society, church, and state. In our own time we have witnessed the forces of religious revival in different regions throughout the world. It is no exaggeration to claim that a similar revolution took place in mid-eighteenth century America.

Only with hindsight does the Great Awakening seem a unified religious movement. Revivals occurred in different places at different times. The first signs of a spiritual awakening appeared in New England during the late 1730s. The intensity of the event varied from region to region. Revivals were most important in Massachusetts, Connecticut, Rhode Island, Pennsylvania, New Jersey, and in the 1750s and 1760s in Virginia. No single religious denomination or sect monopolized the Awakening; mainly Congregationalist churches were affected in New England, but elsewhere revivals involved Presbyterians, Methodists, and Baptists.

The evangelism of the Great Awakening infused a new sense of vitality into religions that had lost their fervor. People in New England complained that Congregational ministers seemed obsessed with dull, scholastic matters; their sermons no longer touched the heart. And in the southern colonies, there were simply not enough ordained ministers to tend to the religious needs of the population.

The Great Awakening began unexpectedly in Northampton, a small farm community in western Massachusetts, sparked by the preaching of Jonathan Edwards, the local Congrega-

tionalist minister. With fervent zeal, Edwards reminded his flock that their fate had been determined for all eternity by an omnipotent God. He thought his fellow ministers had grown soft and were preaching easy salvation. Edwards disabused his congregation of that false comfort. With calm self-assurance he described in vivid detail the torments of the damned, those whom God had not elected to receive divine grace.

Why this uncompromising Calvinist message set off religious revivals during the late 1730s is not known. Whatever the explanation for the sudden popular response to Edwards's preaching, young people began flocking to church. They experienced a searing conversion, a sense of "new birth" and utter dependence upon God. The excitement spread, and evangelical ministers concluded that God must be preparing Americans, His chosen people, for the millennium.

The best-known figure of the Great Awakening was George Whitefield, a young, inspiring preacher from England who toured the colonies from Georgia to New Hampshire. He was an extraordinary public speaker who cast a spell over the throngs who came to see and hear him.

Whitefield's audience came from all groups of American society, rich and poor, young and old, rural and urban. While Whitefield described himself as a Calvinist, he welcomed all Protestants, and he spoke from any pulpit that was available. "Don't tell me you are a Baptist, an Independent, a Presbyterian, a dissenter," he thundered, "tell me you are a Christian, that is all I want."

Other, American-born, itinerant preachers followed Whitefield's example. The most famous was Gilbert Tennent, a Presbyterian of Scotch-Irish background who had been educated in the Middle Colonies. He, and other revivalists of like mind, traveled from town to town, colony to colony challenging local clergymen who seemed hostile to evangelical religion. Many ministers remained suspicious of the itinerants and their methods. Some complaints may have amounted to little more than jealousy. Others raised serious questions: How could the revivalists be certain that God had

The fervor of the Great Awakening was intensified by the eloquence of touring preachers such as George Whitefield, who enthralled his audiences.

sparked the Great Awakening? And how could the revivalists be certain that the "dangers of enthusiasm" would not lead them astray? During the 1740s and 1750s, many congregations split between defenders of the new emotional preaching, the "New Lights," and those who regarded the entire movement as dangerous nonsense, the "Old Lights."

While Tennent did not condone the excesses of the Great Awakening, his attacks on formal learning invited the crude anti-intellectualism of such deranged revivalists as James Davenport. Davenport preached under the light of smoky torches; he danced and stripped, shrieked and laughed. He also urged people to burn books written by those who had not experienced the "new light."

To concentrate upon occasional anti-intellectual outbursts is to obscure the positive ways in which this vast revival changed American society. First, the New Lights founded several important centers of higher education. They wanted to train young men who would carry on the good works of Edwards, Whitefield, and Tennent. Princeton (1747), Dartmouth (1769), Brown (1764), and Rutgers (1766) were all colleges founded by revivalist leaders.

Second, the Great Awakening encouraged men and women who had been taught to remain silent before traditional figures of authority to take an active role in their own salvation. They could no longer rely upon ministers or institutions. The individual alone stood before God. This emphasis upon personal religious choices shattered the old harmony that existed among Protestant sects and in its place introduced a boisterous, often bitterly fought competition.

With religious contention, however, came an awareness of a larger community, a union of fellow believers that extended beyond the boundaries of town and colony. In fact, evangelical religion was one of several forces at work during the mid-eighteenth century that brought scattered colonists into contact with one another for the first time. In this sense, the Great Awakening was a "national" event long before a nation actually existed.

People who had been touched by the Great Awakening saw America as "an instrument of Providence." With God's help, social and political progress was achievable, and from this perspective, of course, the New Lights did not sound much different than the mildly rationalist American spokesmen of the Enlightenment. Both groups prepared the way for the development of a revolutionary mentality in colonial America.

POLITICS: BRITISH THEORY AND AMERICAN PRACTICE

The balanced constitution of Great Britain was an object of nearly universal admiration during the eighteenth century. According to its defenders, it protected life, liberty, and property better than did any other contemporary government. The constitution incorporated three distinct parts: the monarch, the House of Lords, and the House of Commons. Thus, in theory the government represented the socioeconomic interests of the king, nobility, and common people. Acting alone, each body would run to excess, even tyranny, but operating within a mixed system, they automatically checked each other's ambitions for the common good.

THE REALITY OF BRITISH POLITICS

The reality of daily political life, however, bore little relation to theory. The three elements of the constitution did not, in fact, represent distinct socioeconomic groups. Men elected to the House of Commons often came from the same social background as did those who served in the House of Lords. All represented the interests of Britain's landed elite. Moreover, there was no attempt to maintain strict constitutional separation. The king exerted considerable influence, for example, in the House of Commons.

The claim that the members of the House of Commons represented all the people of England also seemed farfetched. In 1715 only about 20 percent of British adult males had the right to vote, and there was no standard size for electorate districts. Some representatives to Parliament were chosen by several thousand voters; some, by only one handful of electors.

Before 1760 few people in England spoke out against these constitutional abuses. The main exception was a group of radical publicists whom historians have labeled the "Commonwealthmen." These writers decried the corruption of political life, warning that the nation that compromised its civic virtue deserved to lose its liberty and property. The most famous Commonwealthmen were John Trenchard and Thomas Gordon, who penned a series of essays entitled *Cato's Letters* between 1720 and 1723. They warned the nation to be vigilant against tyranny by England's rulers.

But however shrilly these writers protested, however any newspaper articles they published, the Commonwealthmen won little support for their potential reforms. Englishmen were not willing to tamper with a system of government that had so recently survived a civil war and a Glorious Revolution. Americans, however, took Trenchard and Gordon to heart.

AMERICAN POLITICAL CULTURE IN THE MID-EIGHTEENTH CENTURY

The colonists assumed—perhaps naively—that their governments were modeled upon the balanced constitution of Great Britain. They argued that within their political systems, the governor corresponded to the king, the governor's council to the House of Lords, and the colonial assemblies to the House of Commons. As the colonists discovered, however, English theories about the mixed constitution were no more relevant in America than they were in the mother country.

By mid-century royal governors appointed by the Crown ruled a majority of the mainland colonies. Many of the appointees were career army officers who through luck, charm, or family connection had gained the ear of someone close to the king. These patronage posts did not generate income sufficient to interest the most powerful or talented personalities of the period, but they did draw middle-level bureaucrats who were ambitious, desperate, or both.

Before departing for the New World, royal governors received an elaborate set of instructions drafted by the Board of Trade. The document dealt with almost every aspect of colonial life, political, economic, and religious, and no one knew for certain that these orders even possessed the force of law.

About the governors' powers, however, there was no doubt; they were enormous. In fact, royal governors could do certain things in America that a king could not do in eighteenth-century Britain. Among these were the right to veto legislation and dismiss judges. The governors also served as commanders in chief in each province.

Royal governors were advised by a council, usually a body of about twelve wealthy colonists selected by the Board of Trade in London upon the recommendation of the governor. By the eighteenth century, however, the council had lost most of its power. This body was certainly no House of Lords.

Nor were the colonial assemblies much like the House of Commons. A far greater proportion of men could vote in America than in Great Britain. In most colonies adult white males who owned a small amount of land could vote in county-wide elections. Although participation in government was not high, and most colonists were content to let gentry represent them in the assemblies, the potential for throwing the rascals out was always present.

THE COLONIAL ASSEMBLIES

Members of the assemblies were convinced that they had a special obligation to preserve colonial liberties. Any attack upon the legislature was perceived as an assault upon the rights of Americans. So aggressive were these bodies in seizing privileges, determining procedures, and controlling money bills that some historians have described the political development of eighteenth-century America as "the rise of the assemblies."

This political system seemed designed to generate hostility. There was simply no reason for the colonial legislature to cooperate with appointed royal governors. A few governors managed briefly to create in America a political culture of patronage akin to what they knew in England. But usually such efforts clashed with the colonists' perceptions of politics. They *really* believed in the purity of the balanced constitution, and attempts to revert to a patronage system were met by their loud protests in language that seemed to be directly lifted from the pages of *Cato's Letters*.

The major source of shared political information was the weekly journal, a new and vigorous institution in American life. In New York and Massachusetts especially, weekly newspapers urged readers to preserve civic virtue, and to exercise extreme vigilance against the spread of privileged power. Through such journals, a pattern of political rhetoric that in Britain had gained only marginal respectability became after 1765 America's normal form of political discourse.

The rise of the assemblies shaped American culture in other, subtler ways. Over the course of the century, the language of the law became increasingly anglicized. Varying local legal practices that had been widespread during the seventeenth century became standardized. Indeed, by 1750 there was little difference between the colonial legal system and that of the mother country. Not surprisingly, many men who served in colonial assemblies were either lawyers or persons who had received legal training. When Americans from different regions met they discovered that they shared a commitment to the preservation of the English common law.

But if eighteenth-century political developments drew the colonists closer to the mother country, they also brought Americans a greater awareness of each other. As their horizons widened, they learned that they operated within the same general imperial system and that they shared similar problems. Like the revivalists and merchants—people who crossed old boundaries—colonial legislators laid the foundation for a broader cultural identity.

CENTURY OF IMPERIAL WAR

The scope and character of warfare in the colonies changed radically during the eighteenth century. Local conflicts with the Indians, such as King Philip's War (1675–1676) in New England, gave way to hostilities that originated on the other side of the Atlantic, in rivalries between Great Britain and France over geopolitical considerations and commercial ambitions. The external threat to security forced people in different colonies to devise unprecedented measures of military and political cooperation.

By 1750 the French had established a chain of settlements southward through the heart of the continent from Quebec to New Orleans. But

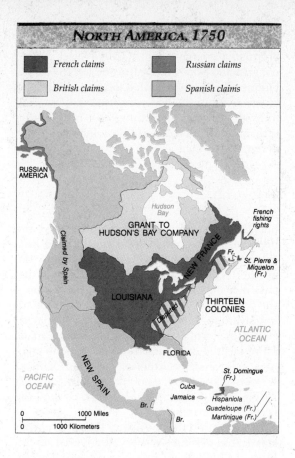

NORTH AMERICA, 1750

French claims
British claims
Russian claims
Spanish claims

RUSSIAN AMERICA

Claimed by Spain

Hudson Bay

GRANT TO HUDSON'S BAY COMPANY

NEW FRANCE

French fishing rights

Fr.

St. Pierre & Miquelon (Fr.)

LOUISIANA

Desired

THIRTEEN COLONIES

ATLANTIC OCEAN

NEW SPAIN

FLORIDA

PACIFIC OCEAN

St. Domingue (Fr.)

Cuba
Jamaica

Hispaniola
Guadeloupe (Fr.)
Martinique (Fr.)

Br.

Br.

0   1000 Miles

0   1000 Kilometers

sies with considerable skill. Moreover, the small population of New France was concentrated along the St. Lawrence, and it could easily mass the forces needed to defend Montreal and Quebec.

KING WILLIAM'S AND QUEEN ANNE'S WARS

Colonial involvement in imperial war began in 1689, when England's new king, William III, declared war on France's Louis XIV. Europeans called this struggle the War of the League of Augsburg, but to the Americans, it was simply King William's War. Canadians raided the northern frontiers of New York and New England, and although they made no territorial gains, they caused considerable suffering among the civilian population of Massachusetts and New York.

The war ended with the Treaty of Ryswick (1697), but the colonists were drawn almost immediately into a new conflict, Queen Anne's War, a dynastic conflict known in Europe as the War of the Spanish Succession (1702–1713). Colonists in South Carolina as well as New England battled against the French and Indians. The bloody combat along the American frontier was formally terminated in 1713 when Great Britain and France signed the Treaty of Utrecht. European concerns were paramount in the peace negotiations. Although two decades of fighting had taken a fearful toll in North America, neither France nor the English colonists had much to show for their sacrifice.

When George I, the first Hanoverian king of Great Britain, replaced Queen Anne in 1714, parliamentary leaders determined to preserve peace. But on the American frontier hostilities continued. At stake was the entire West, including the Mississippi Valley. English colonists believed that the French planned to "encircle" them, to confine them to a narrow strip of land along the Atlantic coast. As evidence they pointed to the French forts that had been constructed through the heart of America. On their part, the French suspected that their rivals intended to seize all of North America.

few French troops were stationed in the New World. The Crown left the defense of Canada and the Mississippi Valley to the companies engaged in the fur trade. This seemed an impossible task for the French outposts strung along the St. Lawrence River, the Great Lakes, and the Mississippi banks.

On paper, at least, the British settlements enjoyed military superiority. Nonetheless, for most of the first half of the eighteenth century, their advantage proved more apparent than real. While the British settlements possessed a larger and more prosperous population than the French—1,200,000 to 75,000—they were divided into separate governments that sometimes seemed more suspicious of each other than of the French. When war came, French officers and Indian allies exploited these jealou-

They noted that land speculators and Indian traders were pushing aggressively into territory claimed by France. And so the two sides lined up their Indian allies and made ready for war.

KING GEORGE'S WAR AND ITS AFTERMATH

In 1743 the Americans were dragged once again into the imperial conflict. During King George's War (1743–1748), known in Europe as the War of the Austrian Succession, the colonists scored a magnificent victory over the French. In June 1745, an army of New England troops under the command of William Pepperrell captured Louisbourg, a gigantic fortress on Cape Breton Island guarding the approaches to the Gulf of St. Lawrence and Quebec. The Americans, however, were in for a shock. When the war ended with the signing of the Treaty of Aix-la-Chapelle in 1748, the British government handed Louisbourg back to the French in exchange for concessions elsewhere! New Englanders saw this as an insult, one they did not soon forget.

By the conclusion of King George's War, the goals of the conflict had clearly changed. Americans no longer aimed simply at protecting their territory from attack. They now wanted to gain complete control over the West, a region obviously rich in economic opportunity. Vast tracts of land and lucrative trade with the Indians awaited ambitious colonists.

The French were not prepared to surrender an inch. But time was running against them. Not only were the English colonies growing more populous, they also possessed a seemingly inexhaustible supply of manufactured goods to trade with the Indians. The French decided in the early 1750s, therefore, to seize the Ohio Valley before their rivals could do so. They established forts throughout the region, the most formidable being Fort Duquesne, located at the strategic fork in the Ohio River near the modern city of Pittsburgh.

Although France and England had not officially declared war, British officials advised the governor of Virginia to "repel force by force." The Virginians, who had their eyes on the Ohio

Valley, needed no encouragement. In 1754 several militia companies under the command of a promising young officer, George Washington, constructed Fort Necessity not far from Fort Duquesne. The plan failed. French and Indian troops overran the badly exposed outpost (July 3, 1754). Among other things, this humiliating setback revealed that a single colony could not defeat the French.

ALBANY CONGRESS AND BRADDOCK'S DEFEAT

Benjamin Franklin, for one, understood the need for intercolonial cooperation. When British officials invited representatives from the northern colonies to Albany (June 1754) to discuss relations with the Iroquois, Franklin used the occasion to present a bold blueprint for colonial union. His so-called Albany Plan envisioned the formation of a Grand Council, made up of elected delegates from the various colonies, to oversee matters of common defense, western expansion, and Indian affairs. Most daring of all, he wanted to give the council the power of taxation.

First reaction to the Albany Plan was enthusiastic, but neither the separate colonial assemblies nor Parliament finally approved the plan.

The first political cartoon to appear in an American newspaper. Drawn by Benjamin Franklin in 1754, it portrays his belief in colonial union.

The assemblies were jealous of their fiscal authority, and the English thought the scheme undermined the Crown's power in the colony.

Even though there was still no formal declaration of war, the British resolved to destroy Fort Duquesne, and to that end, in 1755 they dispatched units of the regular army to the Ohio Valley under the command of Major General Edward Braddock. A poor leader who inspired no respect, on July 9 Braddock led his force of redcoats and colonists into one of the worst defeats in British military history. The French and Indians opened fire as Braddock's army was wading across the Monongahela River, about eight miles from Fort Duquesne. Enraged, Braddock ordered a senseless counterattack. In the end, nearly 70 percent of Braddock's troops were either killed or wounded, and Braddock himself was dead. The French remained in firm control of the Ohio Valley.

SEVEN YEARS' WAR

Britain's imperial war effort had hit rock bottom. No one in England or America seemed to possess the leadership necessary to drive the French from the Mississippi Valley. Still, on May 18, 1756, Great Britain declared war on France, a conflict called the French and Indian War in America and the Seven Years' War in Europe.

William Pitt, the most powerful minister in the cabinet of George II, finally provided Great Britain with what it needed most, a forceful leader. Arrogant and conceited, Pitt nevertheless offered a bold, new imperial policy. Rather than fight great battles in Europe, where France had the advantage, Pitt decided that the critical theater of the war would be in North America, where Britain and France were struggling for control of colonial markets and raw materials. His goal was clear; he was determined to expel the French from the continent, however great the cost.

To effect this ambitious scheme, Pitt took personal command of the army and navy. He mapped strategy; he promoted young promising officers over the heads of their superiors. He convinced Parliament to pour millions of

CHRONOLOGY

1689	William and Mary accede to the English throne
1702	Anne becomes queen of England
1706	Birth of Benjamin Franklin
1714	George I of Hanover becomes monarch of Great Britain
1727	George II accedes to the British throne
1732	Colony of Georgia is established Birth of George Washington
1734–1736	First expression of the Great Awakening at Northampton, Massachusetts
1740	George Whitefield electrifies his listeners at Boston
1745	Colonial troops capture Louisbourg
1754	Albany Congress meets
1755	Braddock is defeated by the French and Indians in western Pennsylvania
1756	French and Indian War (Seven Years' War) is formally declared
1759	British are victorious at Quebec Wolfe and Montcalm are killed in battle
1760	George III becomes king of Great Britain
1763	Peace of Paris ending French and Indian War is signed

Dates	European Name	American Name	Major Allies	Issues
1689–1697	War of the League of Augsburg	King William's War	Britain, Holland, Spain, their colonies, and Native American allies against France, its colonies, and Native American allies	Opposition to French bid for control of Europe
1702–1713	War of the Spanish Succession	Queen Anne's War	Britain, Holland, their colonies, and Native American allies against France, Spain, their colonies, and Native American allies	Austria and France hold rival claims to Spanish throne
1739–1748	War of the Austrian Succession (War of Jenkins's Ear)	King George's War	Britain, its colonies, Native American allies, and Austria against France, Spain, their Native American allies, and Prussia	Struggle among Britain, Spain, and France for control of New World territory; among France, Prussia, and Austria for control of central Europe
1756–1763	Seven Years' War	French and Indian War	Britain, its colonies, and Native American allies against France, its colonies, and Native American allies	Struggle among Britain, Spain, and France for worldwide control of colonial markets and raw materials

pounds into his imperial efforts, thus creating an enormous national debt that would soon haunt both Britain and its colonies.

To direct the grand campaign, Pitt selected two relatively obscure colonels, Jeffrey Amherst and James Wolfe. It was a masterful choice, one that soon proved sound. Forces under their direction captured Louisbourg on July 26, 1758, a victory that cut the Canadians' main supply line with France. Time was now on the side of the British. Two poor harvests, in 1756 and 1757, and a population too small to meet the military demands of the accelerated conflict, led to a desperate situation for the French empire in North America. Frontier forts began to fall; Fort Duquesne was abandoned in 1758. French and Indian troops retreated to Quebec and Montreal, surrendering key outposts at Ticonderoga, Crown Point, and Niagara as they withdrew.

The climax to a century of war came dramatically in September 1759. Wolfe, now a major general, assaulted Quebec, held by the brilliant French commander, the Marquis de Montcalm. It was a remarkable campaign, which saw Wolfe's men scale a cliff under the cover of darkness and launch a successful surprise attack at dawn on September 13, 1759. Both Wolfe and Montcalm were mortally wounded. When an aide informed Wolfe that the French had been routed, he signed, "Now, God be praised, I will die in peace." One year later, Amherst accepted the final surrender of the French army at Montreal.

The Peace of Paris signed on February 10, 1763, almost fulfilled Pitt's grandiose dreams. Great Britain took possession of an empire that stretched around the globe. After a century-long struggle, the French had been driven from the mainland of North America, retaining only

Major American Battle	Treaty
New England troops assault Quebec under Sir William Phips (1690)	Treaty of Ryswick (1697)
Deerfield Massacre (1704)	Treaty of Utrecht (1713)
New England forces capture Louisbourg under William Pepperrell (1745)	Treaty of Aix-la-Chapelle (1748)
British and Continental forces capture Quebec under Major General James Wolfe (1759)	Peace of Paris (1763)

their sugar islands in the Caribbean. The treaty gave Britain title to Canada, Florida, and all the land east of the Mississippi River. The colonists were overjoyed. It was a time of good feelings and imperial pride.

The Seven Years' War made a deep impression upon American society. The military struggle had forced the colonists to cooperate on an unprecedented scale. It also drew them into closer contact with the mother country. They became aware of being part of a great empire, but in the very process of waging war, they acquired a more intimate sense of an America that lay beyond the plantation and the village. Moreover, the war trained a corps of American officers, people like George Washington, who learned from firsthand experience that the British were not invincible.

British officials later accused the Americans of ingratitude. The English charged that they had sent troops and provided funds to liberate the colonists from the threat of French attack, but the Americans had refused to shoulder their fair share of the costs. The British used this argument to justify parliamentary taxation

The British soundly defeated the French at Quebec in 1759 with superior strategy and force of arms in a battle that proved to be the climax of the French and Indian War. However, it cost the British the life of their brilliant commander, General James Wolfe.

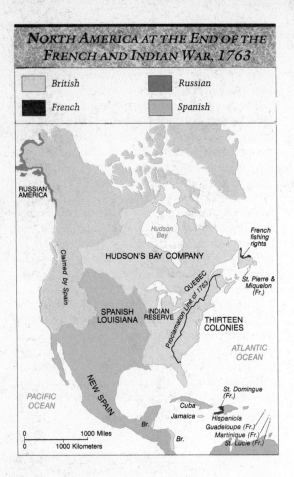

NORTH AMERICA AT THE END OF THE FRENCH AND INDIAN WAR, 1763

British
Russian
French
Spanish

RUSSIAN AMERICA

Claimed by Spain

Hudson Bay

French fishing rights

HUDSON'S BAY COMPANY

QUEBEC

St. Pierre & Miquelon (Fr.)

SPANISH LOUISIANA

INDIAN RESERVE

Proclamation Line of 1763

THIRTEEN COLONIES

ATLANTIC OCEAN

PACIFIC OCEAN

NEW SPAIN

St. Domingue (Fr.)

Cuba
Jamaica
Br.

Hispaniola
Guadeloupe (Fr.)
Martinique (Fr.)
St. Lucie (Fr.)
Br.

0   1000 Miles
0   1000 Kilometers

in America. In fact, the Americans had been slow in providing men and materials needed to fight the French. But in the end, they did contribute to the defense of the empire. The colonies supplied almost 20,000 soldiers and spent well over £2 million. Americans believed they had played a vital role.

FORGING A CULTURAL IDENTITY

In 1754 John Dickinson, a young American, visited Great Britain on the eve of a parliamentary election. He look forward to seeing and hearing the great English political leaders. What he saw, however, was the most corrupt sort of political activity. Vice had become virtuous in the sordid world of English society and politics. He left England disillusioned, but prouder than ever to be an American.

Dickinson's intellectual odyssey was not unusual. After 1760, other provincials, persons who had been attracted to Great Britain by the chance to advance their careers, denounced the luxury and corruption that seemed to have swept the mother country. Perhaps they resented being treated as cultural inferiors; perhaps they reflected the spirit of the Great Awakening. Whatever their personal motives, many colonial leaders had become convinced that Britain's rulers threatened what one Marylander called "the reign of American freedom."

RECOMMENDED READING

A well-written introduction to the topic of Anglo-American relations in the late colonial period is Richard Hofstadter, *America at 1750: A Social Portrait* (1971). For the wars of empire, see Howard H. Peckman, *The Colonial Wars, 1689–1762* (1964). The state of eighteenth-century religion is examined in Sydney E. Ahlstrom's encyclopedic *Religious History of the American People* (1972). A useful discussion of the revivals can be found in Patricia U. Bonomi, *Under the Cape of Heaven* (1986). Anyone curious about intellectual history should read Henry F. May, *The Enlightenment in America* (1976). The most imaginative analysis of eighteenth-century colonial politics is Edmund S. Morgan, *Inventing the People* (1988).

The growth of the American population in this period is traced in Carl Bridenbaugh, *Myths and Realities, Societies in the Colonial South* (1952); James T. Lemon, *The Best Poor Man's Country* (1972); and Gary B. Nash, *The Urban Crucible* (1979). The economic development of colonial America and England is discussed in John McCusker and Russell Menard, *The Economy of British America* (1985).

The most engaging account of the imperial wars is Francis Parkman's nineteenth-century work, *France and England in North America*. More recent studies include Fred Andersen, *A People's Army* (1984).

Esmond Wright, *Franklin of Philadelphia* (1986), is a good biography of the scientist/statesman. Several excellent editions of his *Autobiography* are also available.

Eighteenth-century English politics and society is the subject of J. H. Plumb, *Growth of Political Stability in England* (1987); Roy Porter, *English Society in the Eighteenth Century* (1982); and J. C. D. Clark, *English Society, 1688–1832* (1985). In addition, see Jack P. Greene, *Pursuits of Happiness: The Social Development of Early Modern British Colonies* (1989).

5 THE AMERICAN REVOLUTION: FROM GENTRY PROTEST TO POPULAR REVOLT, 1763–1783

AN EXPECTANT SOCIETY

ERODING THE BONDS OF EMPIRE: CHALLENGE AND RESISTANCE

DECISION FOR INDEPENDENCE

WAR FOR INDEPENDENCE

WINNING THE PEACE

REPUBLICAN CHALLENGE

During the Revolutionary War, a captured British officer spent some time at the plantation of Colonel Thomas Mann Randolph, a leader of Virginia's gentry. The Englishman described with a note of disgust the arrival of three farmers who were members of the local militia—the way the militiamen drew chairs up to the fire, pulled off their muddy boots, and began spitting. Randolph explained that such behavior demonstrated "the spirit of independency" in America. Indeed, every American who "bore arms" during the Revolution considered himself as good as his neighbors.

This chance encounter illuminates the character of the American Revolution. The initial stimulus for rebellion came from the gentry—from the rich and wellborn. They voiced their unhappiness in public statements and in speeches before elected assemblies. However, soon they lost control as the revolutionary movement generated a momentum of its own. As relations with the mother country deteriorated, the traditional leaders of colonial society were forced to invite the common folk to join the protest—as rioters, as petitioners, and finally as soldiers. What had begun as a squabble among the gentry had been transformed into a mass movement, and as Randolph learned, once the common people had become involved in shaping the nation's destiny, they could never again be excluded.

The incident at Randolph's plantation reveals a second, often overlooked, aspect of the American Revolution. It involved a massive military commitment. If mud-covered Virginia militiamen had not been willing to stand up to seasoned British troops, to face the terror of the bayonet charge, independence would have remained a dream of intellectuals. Proportionate to the population, a greater percentage of Americans died in military service during the Revolution than in any war in American history, with the exception of the Civil War. Liberty to them was more than an abstraction studied by political theorists, like Thomas Jefferson and John Adams, and those Americans who risked death and survived the ordeal saw new meaning in the concept of equality as well.

AN EXPECTANT SOCIETY

Only with hindsight can one see the coming of the American Revolution. The lives of most free colonists were filled with economic and political expectations. It was a period of optimism. The population continued to grow, and the standard of living continued to improve. To be sure, wealth was not evenly distributed. The southern colonies were richer than the northern colonies. But even the poorest colonists benefited from the rising standard of living. Economic and political discontent was out of step with the tempo of the age.

No one consciously set out in 1763 to achieve independence. The bonds of loyalty that had cemented the British empire dissolved slowly. At several points British rulers and American colonists could have compromised. Their failure to do so was the result of thousands of separate decisions, errors, and misunderstandings. The Revolution was, in fact, a complex series of events, full of unexpected turns, extraordinary creativity, and great personal sacrifice.

ROOTS OF IMPERIAL CRISIS

Ultimate responsibility for preserving the empire fell to George III, whose reign began in 1760. He was only twenty-two years old; had led a sheltered, loveless life; and was poorly educated. He displayed little understanding of the larger implications of government policy, and many people who knew him considered him dull-witted. Unfortunately, the king could not be ignored, and during a difficult period that demanded imagination, generosity, and wisdom, George muddled along as best he could.

Unlike the preceding Georges, George III decided to play an aggressive role in government. He selected as his chief minister the Earl of Bute, a Scot whose only qualification for office appeared to be his friendship with the young king and the young king's mother. The Whigs, a political faction that dominated Parliament, believed that George was attempting to turn back the clock, to reestablish a monarchy free from traditional constitutional restraints.

Despite his insecurity over an inadequate education, George III was determined to take over an active role in reigning over Parliament and the colonies.

George did not, in fact, harbor such arbitrary ambitions, but his actions threw customary political practices into doubt.

In 1763 Bute left office. What followed was a seven-year period of confusion, during which ministers came and went, often for no other reason than George's personal distaste. Because of this chronic instability, subministers, the minor bureaucrats who directed routine colonial affairs, did not know what was expected of them. In the absence of a long-range policy, the ministers showed more concern for their own future than for coping with the problems of empire building.

The king does not bear the sole blame for England's loss of empire in the American colonies. The members of Parliament, the men who actually drafted the statutes that drove a wedge between the colonists and the mother country, failed to respond creatively to the challenge of events. They clung doggedly to the principle of parliamentary sovereignty, and when Americans questioned whether that legislative body in London should govern colonial affairs, parliamentary spokesmen provided no constructive basis for compromise. They refused to see a middle ground between the preeminent authority of Parliament and complete American independence.

Parliament's attitude was in part a product of ignorance. Few men active in English government had visited America. For those who attempted to follow colonial affairs, accurate information proved extremely difficult to obtain. One could not expect to receive an answer from America to a specific question in less than three months. As a result of the lag in communication between England and America, rumors sometimes passed for true accounts, and misunderstanding influenced the formulation of colonial policy.

THE AMERICAN PERSPECTIVE

At the conclusion of the French and Indian War, it seemed inconceivable that the colonists would challenge the supremacy of Parliament. But the crisis in imperial relations that soon developed impelled the Americans first to define and then to defend principles that were rooted deeply in the colonial political culture.

For more than a century, the colonists' ideas about their role within the British empire had remained a vague, untested bundle of assumptions about personal liberties, property rights, and representative institutions. But by 1763 certain fundamental American beliefs had become clear. They accepted the authority of representative local assemblies to tax their constituents. But to declare that the House of Commons in London enjoyed the same right made no sense to them. Moreover, the colonists rejected the distinction that British officials sometimes made between taxes imposed directly on a person's estate and taxes on trade that could be passed on to consumers. Americans firmly believed that a tax was a tax by whatever name and that Parliament had no right to collect taxes on the American side of the Atlantic, especially since no Americans sat in Parliament.

Political thought in the colonies contained a strong moral component, one that British rulers and American Loyalists (people who sided with the king during the Revolution) never fully understood. The origins of this perspective on civil government are difficult to pinpoint but, certainly, the moral fervor of the Great Awakening and the reformist writings of the Commonwealthmen played a part (see Chapter 4). Whatever the intellectual sources may have been, colonists viewed *power* as extremely dangerous, unless it was countered by *virtue*.

Insistence upon civic virtue—sacrifice of self-interest to the public good—became the dominant theme of revolutionary political writing. American pamphleteers shared the outlook of those who regarded bad government not as human error, but as sin. They saw a host of external threats and plots—arbitrary taxation, standing armies, bishops sent over by the Church of England—all designed to crush American liberty. Popular writers seldom took a dispassionate, legalistic approach in their analysis of Anglo-American relations. They described events in conspiratorial terms, using language charged with emotion.

Colonial newspapers spread these ideas through a large, dispersed population. A majority of adult white males—a great majority in the northern colonies—were literate, and the number of journals in the country increased dramatically during the revolutionary period. The newspaper united the colonies, informing each colony about the political activities in the others, and provided the rhetoric that successfully roused ordinary folk to take up arms against Britain.

ERODING THE BONDS OF EMPIRE: CHALLENGE AND RESISTANCE

Following the Seven Years' War, more than 7000 British troops, members of the regular army, remained in North America. Their alleged purpose was to provide a buffer between Indians and frontiersmen and to preserve order in the newly conquered territories of Florida and Quebec. But not one person in the British government actually made the decision to keep an army in the colonies. The army was not recalled simply because of bureaucratic confusion and inertia.

The war had saddled Britain with a national debt so huge that over one half of the annual budget went to interest payments. A peacetime army, so far from the mother country, fueled the budgetary crisis. The growing financial burden weighed heavily on restive English taxpayers and sent government leaders scurrying in search of new sources of revenue.

For their part, colonists doubted the value of this very expensive army. First, British troops did not maintain peace effectively. This was demonstrated in 1763 when Ottawa Chief Pontiac, who had been allied with the French and hated the British, organized a general uprising along the western frontier. His warriors easily slipped by the redcoats and slew several thousand settlers. Second, the colonists resented the Proclamation of 1763 which attempted unsuccessfully to restrain Americans from moving into Indian lands west of the Appalachian Mountains, and they identified the hated policy with the British troops who guarded the frontier.

The task of reducing England's debt fell to George Grenville, the somewhat unimaginative chancellor of the exchequer who replaced Bute in 1763 as the king's first minister. He decided that the colonists would have to contribute to the maintenance of the army. The first bill he steered through Parliament was the Revenue Act of 1764, known as the Sugar Act.

This legislation represented a major break with the Navigation Acts that had governed the flow of colonial commerce for almost a century (see Chapter 3). The earlier acts were designed to force Americans to trade with the mother country; their primary purpose was not to raise money. The Sugar Act, on the other hand, was specifically designed to generate revenue. It imposed new import duties on sugar, coffee, wines, and other imports, instituted tougher customs collection methods, and expanded the jurisdiction of the vice-admiralty courts. The act also included provisions aimed at curbing colonial smuggling of molasses and bribery of customs officials.

American reaction came swiftly. James Otis, a fiery orator from Massachusetts, exclaimed that the legislation deprived Americans of "the rights of assessing their own taxes." Petitions of protest involved no violence, but to Grenville and persons of his temperament, even petitions smacked of ingratitude. After all, they reasoned, had not the mother country saved the Americans from the French? But Grenville's perspective overlooked the contribution of colonial staples such as rice and tobacco to the prosperity of the mother country. Moreover, American markets helped sustain British industry (see Chapter 4). The colonists saw no justification for Grenville's aggressive new policy now that the military emergency had passed.

THE STAMP ACT: A POLITICAL CRISIS

Even before the Sugar Act had gone into effect, Grenville put the final touches on a second revenue measure, the Stamp Act. Although a few members of Parliament warned that the Americans would bitterly resent the act, the majority of the House of Commons supported the legislation. Specifically, the Stamp Act required printed documents — such as legal contracts, newspapers, and marriage licenses — to bear revenue stamps purchased from royal stamp distributors. The act was to go into effect November 1, 1765.

Word of the Stamp Act reached America by May, and the colonial reaction against it was swift. In Virginia's House of Burgesses, eloquent young Patrick Henry introduced five resolutions protesting the act. He timed his move carefully. It was late in the session; many of the more conservative burgesses had already departed for their plantations. Even then, Henry's resolves declaring that Virginians had the right to tax themselves as they alone saw fit passed by narrow margins.

The Virginia Resolves might have remained a local matter had it not been for the colonial press. Newspapers throughout America printed Henry's resolutions. The newspaper accounts, however, were not always accurate. Some accounts said that all five of Henry's resolutions had passed, when, in fact, the fifth resolution, which announced that Britain's actions were "illegal, unconstitutional, and unjust," had been stricken from the legislative records. Several newspapers even printed two resolutions that Henry had not dared to introduce. The result of this misunderstanding, of course, was that the Virginians appeared to have taken an extremely radical position on the issue of the supremacy of Parliament, one that other Americans now trumpeted before their own assemblies.

Not to be outdone by Virginia, the Massachusetts assembly in June proposed a general meeting to protest Grenville's policy. Nine colonies sent representatives to the Stamp Act Congress that convened in New York City in October 1765. The delegates drafted petitions to the king and Parliament which restated the colonists' belief "that no taxes should be imposed on them, but with their own consent, given personally, or by their representatives." There

was no mention of independence or disloyalty to the Crown.

Resistance to the Stamp Act soon moved from assembly petitions to mass protests in the streets. In Boston, the Sons of Liberty burned the local stamp distributor in effigy. The violent outbursts of these mobs frightened colonial leaders; yet the evidence suggests that they encouraged the lower classes to intimidate royal officials. After 1765, it was impossible for either royal governors or patriot leaders to take the common folk for granted.

By November 1, 1765, stamp distributors in almost every American port had publicly resigned, and without distributors, the hated revenue stamps could not be sold. The Sons of Liberty convinced colonial merchants to boycott British goods. What most Americans did not yet know — communication with the mother country took months — was that in July Grenville had fallen from power. His replacement as first lord of the treasury, Lord Rockingham, envisioned a prosperous empire founded upon an expanding commerce, with local government under the gentle guidance of Parliament. Grenville, now simply a member of Parliament, urged a tough policy toward America, but important men, such as William Pitt, defended the colonists' position. Finally, Rockingham called for the repeal of the Stamp Act. On February 22, 1766, the House of Commons complied.

Repeal failed to restore imperial harmony. Lest its retreat on the Stamp Act be interpreted as weakness, the House of Commons passed the Declaratory Act (March 1766), a shrill defense of parliamentary supremacy over the Americans "in all cases whatsoever." The colonists' insistence upon no taxation without representation failed to impress British rulers. Clearly, if America thought it won the Stamp Act battle, Parliament was announcing that it fully expected to win the war.

In America, too, attitudes hardened. Respect for imperial officeholders as well as Parliament had diminished. Suddenly, royal governors, customs collectors, and military personnel appeared alien, as if their interests were not those of the people over whom they exercised authority. Indeed, it is testimony to the Americans' lingering loyalty to the British Crown and constitution that rebellion did not occur in 1765.

TOWNSHEND'S BOAST: TEA AND SOVEREIGNTY

Rockingham's ministry soon gave way to a government headed once again by William Pitt, now the Earl of Chatham. The aging Pitt suffered horribly from gout, and during his long absences from London, Charles Townshend, his chancellor of the exchequer, made important political decisions. Townshend's mouth often outran his mind, and in January 1767 he pleased the House of Commons by announcing that he knew a way to obtain revenue from the Americans.

His plan turned out to be a grab bag of duties on American imports of paper, glass, paint, and tea, collectively known as the Townshend Revenue Acts (June 1767). To collect these duties he created an American Board of Customs Commissioners, a body based in Boston and supported by reorganized vice-admiralty courts in port cities.

Americans were no more willing to pay Townshend's duties than they had been to buy Grenville's stamps. In major ports, the Sons of Liberty organized boycotts of British goods. Imported finery came to symbolize England's political corruption. Americans prided themselves on wearing homespun clothes, a badge of simplicity and virtue. Women were ardent supporters of the boycott, holding public spinning bees to produce more homespun.

On February 11, 1768, the Massachusetts House of Representatives drafted a circular letter, which it then sent to other colonial assemblies. The letter requested suggestions on how best to thwart the Townshend Acts. Although the letter was mild, Lord Hillsborough, England's secretary for American Affairs, took offense. He called the letter a "seditious paper" and ordered the Massachusetts representatives to rescind it; the legislators refused.

Suddenly, the circular letter became a *cause célèbre*. When the royal governor of Massachusetts dissolved the House of Representatives,

the other colonies demonstrated their support of the Bay Colony by taking up the circular letter in their assemblies. Hillsborough promptly dissolved more colonial legislatures. Parliament's challenge had brought about the very results it most wanted to avoid: a basis for intercolonial communication and a growing sense among the colonists of the righteousness of their position.

THE BOSTON MASSACRE HEIGHTENS TENSIONS

In October 1768 British rulers made another critical mistake. The issue was the army. In part to intimidate colonial troublemakers, the ministry stationed 4000 regular troops around Boston. The armed strangers camped on Boston Commons, sometimes shouting obscenities at citizens passing the site. To make relations

Outrage over the Boston Massacre was fanned by propaganda such as this etching by Paul Revere, which showed British redcoats firing on unarmed civilians. Blood spurting from dying patriots became more conspicuous in subsequent printings.

worse, the redcoats—soldiers who were ill-treated and underpaid—competed in their spare time for jobs with local dockworkers and artisans.

When citizens questioned why the army had been sent to a peaceful city, pamphleteers claimed that the soldiers in Boston were simply another phase of a conspiracy originally conceived by the Earl of Bute to oppress Americans, to take away their liberties, and to collect illegal revenues. Grenville, Hillsborough, Townshend were all, supposedly, part of the plot. To Americans raised on the political theories of the Commonwealthmen, the pattern of tyranny seemed obvious.

Colonists had no difficulty interpreting the violence that erupted in Boston on March 5, 1770. In the gathering dusk of that afternoon, young boys and street toughs used rocks and snowballs to bombard a small isolated patrol outside the offices of the hated customs commissioners in King Street. The details of this incident are obscure, but it appears that as the mob grew and became more threatening, the troops panicked and fired, leaving five Americans dead.

Pamphleteers promptly labeled the incident a "massacre." The victims were seen as martyrs. To the propagandists, what actually happened mattered little. Their job was to inflame emotions; they performed their work well. Confronted with such an intense reaction and with the possibility of massive armed resistance, Crown officials wisely moved the army to an island in Boston Harbor.

At this critical moment, the king's new first minister restored a measure of tranquility. Lord North, congenial, well-meaning, but not very talented, became the first minister in 1770, and for the next twelve years—indeed, throughout most of the American crisis—he managed to retain his office. His secret formula seems to have been an ability to get along with George III and to build an effective majority in Parliament.

One of North's first recommendations to Parliament was the repeal of the ill-conceived Townshend duties. Not only had the duties enraged Americans, they hurt British manufacturers by encouraging Americans to develop their own industries. Parliament responded by dropping all the duties with the notable exception of tea. But Parliament still maintained that it held total supremacy over the colonies. For a time, Americans drew back from the precipice of confrontation, frightened by the events of the past two years.

AN INTERLUDE OF ORDER, 1770–1773

For a brief moment, American colonists and British officials put aside their recent animosities. Merchants returned to familiar patterns of trade, and American indebtedness grew. Even in Massachusetts, the people decided that they could accept their new royal governor, an American, Thomas Hutchinson.

But appearances were deceiving. The bonds of imperial loyalty remained fragile, and even as Lord North attempted to win the colonists' trust, Crown officials in America created new strains. Customs commissioners abused their powers of search and seizure and in the process lined their own pockets. Any failure to abide by the Navigation Acts, no matter how minor, could bring confiscation of ship and cargo.

The commissioners were not only corrupt, they were also foolish. They harassed the wealthy and powerful as well as the common folk. The commissioners' actions drove members of the colonial ruling class, men like John Hancock of Boston, into opposition to the king's government. Eventually, the commissioners' greed brought the colonists closer together.

Samuel Adams (1722–1803) refused to accept the notion that the repeal of the Townshend duties had secured American liberty. During the early 1770s, while colonial leaders turned to other matters, Adams kept the cause alive with a drumfire of publicity. He never allowed the people of Boston to forget the many real and alleged wrongs perpetrated by the Crown. Adams was a genuine revolutionary, seemingly obsessed with the need to preserve civic virtue and moral values in the conduct of public affairs. With each new attempt by Parliament to assert its supremacy over the colonists, more and more Bostonians listened to what Adams had to say. By 1772 Adams had broad support for the formation of a committee of correspondence to communicate grievances to villagers throughout Massachusetts. People in other colonies soon copied his idea and established intercolonial committees as well. It was a brilliant stroke; Adams developed a structure of political cooperation completely independent of royal government.

THE FINAL PROVOCATION: THE BOSTON TEA PARTY

In May 1773 Parliament resumed its old tricks. It passed the Tea Act, a strange piece of legislation that Parliament thought the colonists would welcome. The statute was designed to save the floundering East India Company, not to raise revenue. It allowed the company to ship tea directly to America, thereby eliminating the colonial middlemen and permitting Americans to purchase tea at bargain rates. The plan, however, was flawed. First, since the Townshend duty on tea remained in effect, this new arrangement seemed like a devious way to win popular support for Parliament's right to tax the colonists without representation. Second, the act threatened to undercut tea smugglers and the powerful mercantile groups operating in Boston.

Americans soon registered their protest. Boston took the most dramatic stand. Although colonists in Philadelphia and New York City turned back tea ships before they could unload, in Boston Governor Hutchinson would not permit the vessels to return to England. Local patriots would not let them unload. So the ships sat in Boston Harbor crammed with tea until the night of December 16, 1773. That night a group of men in Indian dress boarded the ships and pitched 340 chests of tea worth £10,000 into the water.

When news of the Tea Party reached London in January 1774, the North ministry was stunned. The people of Boston had treated parliamentary supremacy with utter contempt, and British rulers saw no humor whatsoever in the destruction of private property by subjects of the Crown dressed in costume. To quell such rebelliousness, Parliament passed a series of laws called the Coercive Acts. (In America they were referred to as the Intolerable Acts.) This legislation (1) closed the port of Boston until the city fully compensated the East India Company for the lost tea; (2) restructured the Massachusetts government by transforming the upper house from an elective to an appointed body and restricting the number of legal town meetings to one a year; (3) allowed the royal governor to transfer British officials arrested for offenses committed in the line of duty to England or Canada, where there was little likelihood they would be convicted; and (4) authorized the army to quarter troops wherever they were needed, even if this required the compulsory requisition of uninhabited private buildings. George III enthusiastically supported this tough policy; he appointed General Thomas Gage to serve as the colony's new royal governor.

This sweeping series of laws confirmed the colonists' worst fears. The vindictiveness of the acts strengthened the influence of men like Samuel Adams and undermined the influence of colonial moderates. In Parliament, a saddened Edmund Burke, one of America's few remaining friends, warned his countrymen that the acts could lead to war.

In the midst of this constitutional crisis, Parliament announced plans to establish a new civil government for the Canadian province of Quebec (Quebec Act, June 22, 1774), which extended the province's boundaries all the way south to the Ohio River and west to the Mississippi. The act made no provision for an elective assembly, but it granted French-speaking Roman Catholics religious and political rights and a large voice in local affairs. These measures were seen by Americans as a denial of *their* rights to settle and trade in this fast-developing region.

Americans everywhere rallied to Massachusetts' defense. Few persons advocated independence, but they could not remain passive while Boston was destroyed. They sent food and money and, during the autumn of 1774, reflected more deeply than ever on what it meant to be a colonist in the British Empire. And the more they reflected, the more they objected to the idea of the sovereignty of Parliament.

CHRONICLE OF COLONIAL-BRITISH TENSION

Legislation	Date	Provisions	Colonial Reaction
Sugar Act	April 5, 1764	Revised duties on sugar, coffee, tea, wine, other imports; expanded jurisdiction of vice-admiralty courts	Several assemblies protest taxation for revenue
Stamp Act	March 22, 1765; repealed March 18, 1766	Printed documents (deeds, newspapers, marriage licenses, etc.) issued only on special stamped paper purchased from stamp distributors	Riots in cities; collectors forced to resign; Stamp Act Congress (October 1765)
Quartering Act	May 1765	Colonists must supply British troops with housing and other items (candles, salt, rum, etc.)	Protest in assemblies; New York Assembly punished for failure to comply (1767)
Declaratory Act	March 18, 1766	Parliament declares its sovereignty over the colonies "in all cases whatsoever"	Ignored in celebration over repeal of the Stamp Act
Townshend Revenue Acts	June 26, 29, July 2, 1767; all repealed except duty on tea, March 1770	New duties on glass, lead, paper, paints, tea; customs collections tightened in America	Nonimportation of British goods; assemblies protest; newspapers attack British policy
Tea Act	May 10, 1773	Parliament gives East India Company right to sell tea directly to Americans; some duties on tea reduced	Protests against favoritism shown to monopolistic company; tea destroyed in Boston (December 16, 1773)
Coercive Acts (Intolerable Acts)	March–June 1774	Closes port of Boston; restructures Massachusetts government; restricts town meetings; troops quartered in Boston; British officials accused of crimes sent to England or Canada for trial	Boycott of British goods; First Continental Congress convenes (September 1774)
Prohibitory Act	December 22, 1775	Declares British intention to coerce Americans into submission; embargo on American goods; American ships seized	Drives Continental Congress closer to decision for independence

DECISION FOR INDEPENDENCE

Samuel Adams had prepared Americans for this moment. Something had to be done. But what? The committees of correspondence endorsed a call for a continental congress, a gathering of fifty-five elected delegates from twelve colonies (Georgia sent none but agreed to support the action taken). This momentous gathering convened in Philadelphia on September 5, 1774, and included such respected leaders as John and Samuel Adams, Patrick Henry, Richard Henry Lee, and George Washington.

But the delegates were strangers to one another. They knew little about the customs and values, the geography and economy of Britain's other provinces. Differences of opinion soon surfaced. Delegates from the Middle Colonies wanted to proceed with caution, but before they knew what had happened, Samuel Adams maneuvered these moderates into a position far more radical than they found comfortable. Boston's master politician engineered congressional commendation of the Suffolk Resolves, a bold statement drawn up in Suffolk County, Massachusetts, that encouraged Americans to resist the Coercive Acts forcibly.

The tone of the meeting was set. The more radical delegates carried the day. They agreed to form an "Association" to halt all commerce with the mother country until Parliament repealed the Intolerable Acts. They also agreed to meet in the coming year. Meanwhile, in London, George III told his confidants, "blows must decide whether (New England governments) are to be subject to this country or independent."

"SHOTS HEARD AROUND THE WORLD"

Before Congress reconvened, "blows" fell at Lexington and Concord, two small farm villages in eastern Massachusetts. On the evening of April 18, 1775, General Gage dispatched troops from Boston to seize rebel supplies. Paul Revere, a renowned silversmith and active patriot, warned the colonists that the redcoats were coming. The militia of Lexington, a collection of ill-trained farmers, decided to stand on the village green the following morning, April 19, as the British soldiers passed on the road to Concord. No one planned to fight, but in a moment of confusion someone (probably a colonist) fired; the redcoats discharged a volley, and eight Americans lay dead.

Word of the incident spread rapidly. "Minutemen," special companies of Massachusetts militia prepared to respond instantly to military emergencies, went into action. The redcoats found nothing of significance in Concord, and turned back to Boston. The long march back became a rout; the minutemen swarmed all over the redcoats. On June 17 colonial militiamen again held their own against seasoned troops at the Battle of Bunker Hill (actually Breed's Hill). The British finally captured the hill, but after this costly "victory" in which he lost 40 percent of his troops, Gage took the American militiamen more seriously.

THE SECOND CONTINENTAL CONGRESS DIRECTS THE WAR EFFORT

Members of the Second Continental Congress gathered in Philadelphia in May 1775. They faced an awesome responsibility. British government in the mainland colonies had almost ceased to function; Americans were fighting redcoats; and the country desperately needed strong central leadership. Congress provided that leadership. The delegates formed a Continental army, appointed George Washington its commander, purchased military supplies, and, to pay for them, issued paper money. But they refused to take the final step—independence.

Indecision drove John Adams nearly mad with frustration. He and other like-minded delegates ranted against their timid colleagues. Haste, however, would have been a terrible mistake, for many Americans were not convinced that independence was either necessary or desirable. If Congress had moved too quickly, it might have faced charges of extremism and thereby lost mass support for its cause.

The British government appeared intent upon transforming colonial moderates into angry rebels. In December 1775 Parliament passed the Prohibitory Act, declaring war on American commerce. The British navy blockaded colonial ports and seized American ships on the high seas. Lord North also hired German mercenaries to put down the rebellion. And in America, royal governors like Lord Dunmore further undermined the possibility of reconciliation by urging Virginia's slaves to take up arms against their masters.

Thomas Paine (1737–1809) pushed the colonists even closer to independence. In January 1776, Paine, a recent arrival from England, published a pamphlet entitled *Common Sense*. In this powerful democratic manifesto, Paine urged the colonists to resist "tyranny and false systems of government." The essay became an instant best-seller. More than 120,000 copies were sold in the first three months after publication. *Common Sense* systematically stripped kingship of historical and theological justification. Contrary to traditional English belief, Paine said, monarchs could and did commit many wrongs. George III was simply a "royal brute," who by his arbitrary behavior had surrendered his claim to the colonists' obedience.

Paine's greatest contribution to the revolutionary cause was persuading common folk to sever their ties with Great Britain. "Europe, and not England," he exclaimed, "is the parent country of America. This new world hath been the asylum for the persecuted lovers of civil and religious liberty from *every part* of Europe." The time had come for the colonists to

This 1775 engraving by Amos Doolittle, an eyewitness, shows the attack on the British regulars as they marched from Concord back to Boston. The minutemen fired from cover. It is not certain who fired the first shot at Lexington.

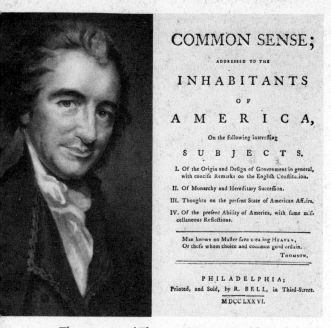

COMMON SENSE;

ADDRESSED TO THE

INHABITANTS

OF

AMERICA,

On the following interesting

SUBJECTS.

I. Of the Origin and Design of Government in general,
with concise Remarks on the English Constitution.

II. Of Monarchy and Hereditary Succession.

III. Thoughts on the present State of American Affairs.

IV. Of the present Ability of America, with some miscellaneous Reflections.

Man knows no Master save creating HEAVEN,
Or those whom choice and common good ordain.

THOMSON.

PHILADELPHIA;

Printed, and Sold, by R. BELL, in Third-Street.

MDCCLXXVI.

*The message of Thomas Paine's pamphlet,
Common Sense (title page shown), was easy to
follow. His stark phrases calling for "The Free and
Independent States of America" reverberated in
people's hearts and minds.*

form an independent republic. "We have it in our power," Paine wrote in one of his most moving statements, "to begin the world over again . . . the birthday of a new world is at hand."

On July 2, 1776, after a long and tedious debate, Congress finally voted for independence. The motion passed; twelve states *for*, none *against*. Thomas Jefferson, a young Virginia lawyer and planter who enjoyed a reputation as a graceful writer, drafted a formal declaration that was accepted two days later with only minor alterations. Much of the Declaration of Independence consisted of a list of specific grievances against George III and his government. But the document's enduring fame rests upon statements of principle that are tested anew in each generation of Americans; that "all men are created equal," that they are endowed with certain rights, among which are "life, liberty, and the pursuit of happiness," and that governments are formed to protect these rights.

WAR FOR INDEPENDENCE

Only fools and visionaries were optimistic about America's prospects of winning independence in 1776. The Americans had taken on a formidable military power whose population was perhaps four times greater than their own. Britain also possessed a strong industrial base, a well-trained regular army supplemented by thousands of hired German troops (Hessians), and a navy that dominated the world's oceans. Many British officers had battlefield experience. They already knew what the Americans would slowly learn, that waging war requires great discipline, money, and sacrifice.

The British government entered the conflict fully confident that it could beat the Americans. Lord North and his colleagues regarded the war as a police action. They anticipated that a mere show of armed force would intimidate the upstart colonists. Humble the rebels in Boston, they reasoned, and Americans will abandon independence like rats fleeing a burning ship.

As later events demonstrated, of course, Britain had become involved in an impossible military situation, somewhat analogous to that in which the United States found itself in Vietnam. Three separate elements neutralized advantages held by the larger power over its adversary. First, the British had to transport men and supplies across the Atlantic, a logistic challenge of unprecedented complexity. Second, America was too vast to be conquered by conventional military methods. Redcoats might gain control over the major port cities, but as long as the Continental army remained intact, the rebellion continued. And third, British strategies never appreciated the depth of the Americans' commitment to a political ideology. European troops before the French Revolution served because they were paid or because they were professional soldiers, but not because they hoped to advance a set of constitutional principles. Americans were different. Although some joined the army for the bounty money or to escape unhappy families or because they were drafted, a remarkable number of American troops were committed to republican ideals.

During the earliest months of rebellion, American soldiers—especially those of New England—suffered no lack of confidence. Indeed, they interpreted their engagements at Concord and Bunker Hill as evidence that brave, yeoman farmers could lick British regulars on any battlefield. George Washington spent the first years of the war disabusing the colonists of this foolishness. As he had learned during the French and Indian War, military success depended upon careful planning, endless drill, and tough discipline.

Washington insisted upon organizing a regular, well-trained field army. He rejected the idea of waging a guerilla war. He recognized that the Continental army served not only as a fighting force but also as a symbol of the republican cause. Its very existence would sustain American hopes, and so long as the army survived, American agents could plausibly solicit foreign aid. This thinking shaped Washington's cautious wartime strategy; he studiously avoided any "general actions" in which the Continental army might be destroyed.

If the commander in chief was correct about the army, however, he failed to comprehend the importance of local militia. These scattered, almost amateur, military units seldom altered the outcome of a battle, but they did maintain control over large areas of the country not directly affected by the British army. Throughout the war, they compelled men and women who would rather have remained neutral to support actively the American effort. Without their local political coercion, Washington's task would have been considerably more difficult.

EARLY DISASTERS: "TIMES THAT TRY MEN'S SOULS"

After the embarrassing losses in Massachusetts, the king appointed General Sir William Howe to replace the ill-fated Gage. British rulers now understood that a simple police action would not be sufficient to crush the American rebellion. Howe promptly evacuated Boston—

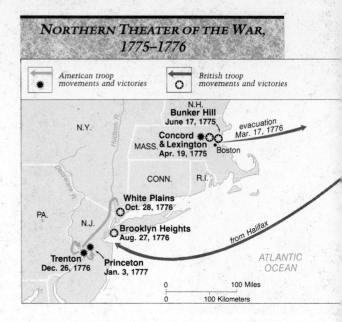

NORTHERN THEATER OF THE WAR, 1775–1776

American troop movements and victories

British troop movements and victories

N.Y.
N.H.
Bunker Hill June 17, 1775
evacuation Mar. 17, 1776
Concord & Lexington Apr. 19, 1775
MASS.
Boston
CONN.
R.I.
White Plains Oct. 28, 1776
PA.
N.J.
Brooklyn Heights Aug. 27, 1776
from Halifax
ATLANTIC OCEAN
Trenton Dec. 26, 1776
Princeton Jan. 3, 1777

0   100 Miles
0   100 Kilometers

an untenable strategic position—and on July 3, 1776, his forces stormed Staten Island in New York harbor. From this central position, he hoped to cut off New Englanders from the rest of America.

When Washington learned that the British were digging in at New York, he transferred many of his inexperienced soldiers to Long Island where they suffered a serious defeat (August 26, 1776). Howe drove the Continental army across the Hudson River into New Jersey, but he failed to annihilate Washington's entire army. Nevertheless, the Americans were on the run, and in the fall of 1776, contemporaries predicted that the rebels would soon capitulate.

His swift victories in New York and New Jersey persuaded General Howe that few Americans enthusiastically supported independence. He issued a general pardon, therefore, to anyone who would swear allegiance to George III. More than 3000 Americans responded to Howe's peaceful overtures. However, the pardon plan eventually failed partly because Howe's soldiers and officers regarded loyal Americans as inferior provincials, an attitude that did little to promote good relations, and partly because the rebel militia often retaliated against Americans who had deserted the patriots' cause.

In December 1776, Washington's bedraggled army retreated across the Delaware River into Pennsylvania. American prospects appeared bleaker than at any other time during the war. "These are the times that try men's souls," Tom Paine wrote in a pamphlet entitled *American Crisis*. "The summer soldier and the sunshine patriot will, in this crisis, shrink from the service of their country, but he that stands it *now* deserves . . . love and thanks of man and woman." Before winter, Washington determined to attempt one last desperate stroke.

Howe played into Washington's hands. The British army was strung out across New Jersey. On the night of December 25, Continental soldiers slipped over the ice-filled Delaware River and at Trenton took 900 sleeping Hessian mercenaries by complete surprise. Cheered by success, Washington returned a second time to Trenton, but on this occasion a large British force under Lord Cornwallis trapped the Americans. Washington secretly, by night, marched his little army around Cornwallis' left flank. On January 3, 1777, the Americans surprised a British garrison at Princeton. Having regained their confidence, Washington's forces then went into winter quarters. The British, fearful of losing any more outposts, consolidated their troops, thus leaving much of the state in the hands of the patriot militia.

VICTORY IN A YEAR OF DEFEAT

In 1777 England's chief military strategist, Lord George Germain, still perceived the war in conventional European terms. He believed that England could achieve a complete victory by crushing Washington's army in a major battle. Unfortunately, the Continental forces proved extremely elusive, and while one British army vainly tried to corner Washington in Pennsylvania, another was forced to surrender in the forests of upstate New York.

In the summer of 1777 General John Burgoyne marched south from Canada determined to clear the Hudson Valley of rebel resistance.

He intended to join Howe's army, which was to come up to Albany, thereby cutting New England off from the other states. Burgoyne moved slowly, weighed down by a German band, thirty carts filled with the general's liquor and belongings, and 2000 dependents and camp followers. The campaign was a disaster. American military units cut the enemy force apart in the deep woods north of Albany, and overwhelmed Burgoyne's German mercenaries at Bennington. After it became clear that Howe could provide no relief, the haughty Burgoyne was forced to surrender 5800 men to the American General Horatio Gates at Saratoga (October 17).

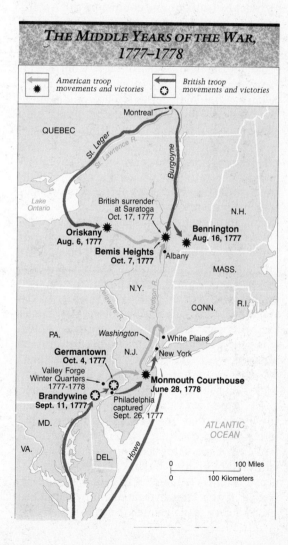

THE MIDDLE YEARS OF THE WAR, 1777–1778

American troop movements and victories

British troop movements and victories

QUEBEC

Montreal

St. Leger

St. Lawrence R.

Burgoyne

Lake Ontario

British surrender at Saratoga Oct. 17, 1777

N.H.

Oriskany Aug. 6, 1777

Bennington Aug. 16, 1777

Bemis Heights Oct. 7, 1777

Albany

MASS.

N.Y.

CONN.

R.I.

PA.

Washington

White Plains

Germantown Oct. 4, 1777

N.J.

New York

Valley Forge Winter Quarters 1777-1778

Monmouth Courthouse June 28, 1778

Brandywine Sept. 11, 1777

Philadelphia captured Sept. 26, 1777

MD.

ATLANTIC OCEAN

VA.

DEL.

Howe

0   100 Miles
0   100 Kilometers

General Howe could provide no support to Burgoyne because about the time Burgoyne left Canada, Howe quite unexpectedly decided to move this main army from New York City to Philadelphia, trying to devise a way to destroy Washington's forces. The British troops sailed to the head of the Chesapeake Bay and then marched north to Philadelphia. Washington's troops obstructed the enemy's progress, but they could not stop the British from entering the city on September 26, 1777.

Lest these defeats discourage Congress and the American people, Washington attempted one last battle before the onset of winter. In a curious engagement at Germantown (October 4), beset by bad luck and confusion, the Americans launched a major counterattack on a fog-covered battlefield, but just at the moment when success seemed assured, the Americans broke off the fight. A discouraged Continental army dug in for the winter at Valley Forge, twenty miles outside of Philadelphia, where camp diseases took 2500 American lives.

THE FRENCH ALLIANCE

Even before the Americans declared their independence, agents of the government of Louis XVI began to explore ways to aid the colonists, not so much because the French monarchy favored the republican cause, but because it hoped to avenge its defeat in the Seven Years' War and lessen the power of Britain. During the early months of the Revolution the French covertly sent tons of essential military supplies to the Americans, but refused to recognize American independence or sign an outright military alliance with the rebels. The international stakes were too great for the king to openly back a cause that had little chance of success.

The American victory at Saratoga convinced the French that the rebels had formidable forces and were serious in their resolve. Meanwhile, in Paris, American representative Benjamin Franklin hinted that Congress might accept a recently tendered British peace overture. Hence, if the French wanted the war to continue, if they really wanted to strike at their old rival, then they had to formally recognize the independence of the United States.

The stratagem paid off handsomely. On February 6, 1778, the French presented American representatives with two separate treaties. The first, called the Treaty of Amity and Commerce, established commercial relations between France and the United States. It tacitly accepted the existence of a new, independent republic. The Treaty of Alliance was even more generous. In the event that France and England went to war (they did so on June 14), the French agreed to reject any peace initiative until Britain recognized American independence. The Americans pledged that they would not sign a separate peace with Britain without first informing their new ally. Amazingly, France made no claim to Canada or any territory east of the Mississippi River.

French intervention instantly transformed British military strategy. What had been a colonial rebellion suddenly became a world conflict, a continuation of the great wars for empire of the late seventeenth century (see Chapter 4). Scarce military resources, especially newer fighting ships, had to be diverted from the American theater to guard the English Channel. England realized that the French navy posed a serious challenge to the overextended British fleet.

THE FINAL CAMPAIGN

British General Henry Clinton replaced Howe, who resigned after the battle of Saratoga. As a subordinate officer, Clinton was imaginative, but as commander of British forces in America, his resolute self-confidence suddenly dissolved. Perhaps he feared failure. Whatever the explanation for his vacillation, Clinton's record in America was little better than Howe's or Gage's.

Military strategists calculated that Britain's last chance of winning the war lay in the southern colonies, a region largely untouched in the early years of fighting. They believed that with proper support and encouragement the Loyalists in Georgia and South Carolina would take up arms for the Crown. The southern strategy devised by Germain and Clinton in 1779 turned the war into a bitter guerrilla conflict, and during the last months of battle, British officers worried that their search for an easy victory had inadvertently opened a Pandora's box of uncontrollable partisan furies.

The southern campaign opened in the spring of 1780. Savannah had already fallen, and Clinton reckoned that if the British could take Charleston, they would be able to control the entire South. Clinton and his second in command, General Cornwallis, gradually encircled the city, and on May 12, the 6000-man American army in Charleston surrendered.

The defeat took Congress by surprise, and without making proper preparations, it dispatched a second army to South Carolina under Horatio Gates, the hero of Saratoga. He, too, failed. At Camden, Cornwallis outmaneuvered the raw American recruits (August 16). Poor Gates galloped from the scene and did not stop until he reached Hillsboro, North Carolina, 200 miles away.

Even at this early stage of the southern campaign, the savagery of partisan warfare had become evident. Loyalist raiders plundered or occasionally killed neighbors against whom they harbored ancient grudges. Men who supported independence or who had merely fallen victim to the Loyalist guerrillas bided their time. On October 7 at King's Mountain, North Carolina, they struck back against a force of Loyalists and British regulars who had strayed too far from base. This was the most vicious fighting of the Revolution; the Americans gave no quarter.

Cornwallis, badly confused and poorly supported, proceeded to squander his strength senselessly chasing American forces across the Carolinas in the winter and early spring of 1781. When he did engage a freshly formed army under the command of Nathanael Greene, the most capable general on Washington's staff, Cornwallis was outmaneuvered and outfought at Cowpens and Guilford Courthouse. His army's strength sapped, Cornwallis pushed north into Virginia, planning apparently to establish a base of operations on the coast.

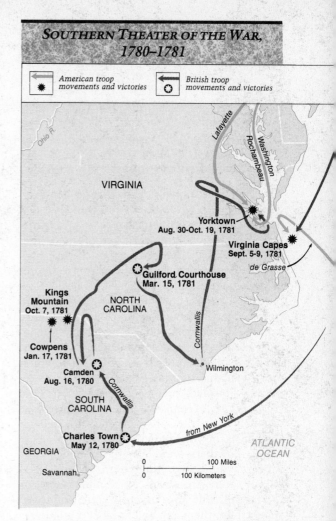

SOUTHERN THEATER OF THE WAR, 1780–1781

American troop movements and victories
British troop movements and victories

VIRGINIA

Ohio R.

Lafayette

Washington
Rochambeau

Yorktown
Aug. 30–Oct. 19, 1781

Virginia Capes
Sept. 5–9, 1781

de Grasse

Guilford Courthouse
Mar. 15, 1781

Kings Mountain
Oct. 7, 1781

NORTH CAROLINA

Cornwallis

Cowpens
Jan. 17, 1781

Camden
Aug. 16, 1780

Cornwallis

Wilmington

SOUTH CAROLINA

from New York

Charles Town
May 12, 1780

ATLANTIC OCEAN

GEORGIA

Savannah

0   100 Miles
0   100 Kilometers

He selected Yorktown, a sleepy tobacco market town located on a peninsula bounded by the York and James rivers. Washington watched these maneuvers closely. The canny Virginia planter knew this territory intimately, and he sensed that Cornwallis had made a serious blunder. When Washington learned that the French fleet could gain temporary dominance in the Chesapeake Bay, he rushed south from New Jersey. With him marched thousands of well-trained French troops commanded by the Comte de Rochambeau; they were joined along the way by a sizable contingent of forces led by the Marquis de Lafayette. All the pieces fell into place. The French admiral, Comte de

Grasse, cut Cornwallis off from the sea, while Washington and his lieutenants encircled the British on the land. On October 19, 1781, Cornwallis surrendered his entire army of 6000 men. The continental army had completed its mission; the task of securing independence now rested in the hands of American diplomats.

THE LOYALIST DILEMMA

The war lasted longer than anyone had predicted in 1776. While the nation won its independence, many Americans paid a terrible price. Indeed, a large number of men and women decided that however much they had loved colonial society, they could not accept the new government.

No one knows for certain how many Americans supported the Crown during the Revolution. But more than 100,000 men and women permanently left America. Although a number of these exiles had served as British office-holders, they came from all ranks and sections of society—farmers, merchants, tradesmen. The wealthier exiles went to London and begged for pensions from the king. Others relocated in Canada or the West Indies.

The Loyalists were caught in a difficult squeeze. The British did not trust them; after all, they were Americans. Nor could they trust the British, who after urgently soliciting their support, left them exposed to rebel retaliation. In England, the exiles found themselves treated as second-class citizens. Embittered and unwanted in America, they often found themselves just as embittered and unwanted in London.

Americans who actively supported independence saw these people as traitors. According to one patriot, "A Tory (Loyalist) is a thing whose head is in England, its body in America, and its neck ought to be stretched." In many states revolutionary governments confiscated Loyalist property. Some Loyalists were beaten, and a few were even executed. Long after the victorious Americans turned their attentions to the business of building a new republic, Loyalists remembered a comfortable, ordered

The fate of the Tories was an unhappy one. The patriots meted out harsh punishments to those who did not flee to England or Canada.

world that had been lost forever at Yorktown. Theirs was a sad, often lonely, fate.

WINNING THE PEACE

Congress appointed a splendid delegation to negotiate a peace treaty: Benjamin Franklin, John Adams, and John Jay. According to their official instructions, they were to insist only upon the recognition of the independence of the United States. On other issues, Congress ordered its delegates to defer to the counsel of the French government.

But in Paris there were grave problems. The French had formed a military alliance with Spain, and French officials announced that they could not consider the details of an American settlement until after the Spanish had recaptured Gibraltar from the British. The prospects for a Spanish victory were not good. More than anything the American representatives feared that some European intrigue might cost the United States its independence.

While the three American delegates publicly paid their respects to French officials, they secretly entered into negotiations with an English agent. These actions not only violated their instructions, they did not fool the French for a moment. French spies kept them informed of what occurred at these meetings, and while they could have protested the American breach of faith, they did not do so.

The negotiators drove a remarkable bargain. The preliminary agreement, signed on September 3, 1783, not only guaranteed the independence of the United States, it also transferred all the territory east of the Mississippi River— except Florida, which remained under Spanish

CHRONOLOGY

1763	Peace of Paris ends the Seven Years' War
1764	Parliament passes Sugar Act to collect American revenue
1765	Stamp Act receives support of House of Commons (March) Stamp Act Congress meets in New York City (October)
1766	Stamp Act repealed the same day that Declaratory Act becomes law (March 18)
1767	Townshend Revenue Acts stir American anger (June–July)
1768	Massachusetts assembly refuses to rescind circular letter (February)
1770	Parliament repeals all Townshend duties except one on tea (March) British troops "massacre" Boston civilians (March)
1772	Samuel Adams forms committee of correspondence
1773	Lord North's government passes Tea Act (May) Bostonians hold Tea Party (December)
1774	Parliament punishes Boston with Coercive Acts (March–June) First Continental Congress convenes (September)
1775	Patriots take stand at Lexington and Concord (April) Second Continental Congress gathers (May) Americans hold their own at Bunker Hill (June)
1776	Congress votes for independence; Declaration of Independence is signed British defeat Washington at Long Island (August) Americans score victory at Trenton (December)
1777	General Burgoyne surrenders at Saratoga (October)
1778	French treaties recognize independence of the United States (February)
1780	British take Charleston (May)
1781	Washington forces Cornwallis to surrender at Yorktown (October)
1783	Peace treaty signed (September) British evacuate New York City (November)

sovereignty—to the new Republic. The treaty established generous boundaries on the north and south and gave the Americans important fishing rights in the North Atlantic. In exchange, Congress promised to help British merchants collect debts contracted before the Revolution and to compensate Loyalists whose land had been confiscated by the various state governments. The preliminary treaty did not take effect until after the French reached their own agreement with Great Britain, thus formally honoring the Franco-American alliance. It is hard to imagine how Franklin, Adams, and Jay could have negotiated a more favorable conclusion to the war. In the fall of 1783, the last redcoats sailed from New York City, ending 176 years of colonial rule.

REPUBLICAN CHALLENGE

The American people had waged war against the most powerful nation in Europe and emerged victorious. The treaty marked the conclusion of a colonial rebellion, but it remained for the men and women who had resisted taxation without representation to work out the full implications of republicanism. What would be the scope of the new government? What powers would be delegated to the people, the states, the federal authorities? How far would the wealthy, wellborn leaders of the rebellion be willing to extend political, social, and economic rights? The war was over, but the drama of the American Revolution was still unfolding.

RECOMMENDED READING

The revolutionary era is one of the most heavily analyzed periods of American history. Two of the more readable syntheses of this vast literature are Merrill Jensen, *The Founding of a Nation: A History of the American Revolution, 1763–1789* (1968), and Robert Middlekauff, *The Glorious Cause: The American Revolution, 1763–1789* (1982). Edmund S. Morgan, *The Birth of the Republic, 1763–1789* (1956), is a short, provocative examination of the revolutionary era. The best introduction to military history remains Howard H. Peckham, *The War for Independence: A Military History* (1958).

The literature dealing with British politics on the eve of the American Revolution is particularly rich. One important study is John Brooke, *King George III* (1974). For information on the development of political associations, see John Brewer, *Party Ideology and Popular Politics at the Accession of George III* (1976). The American interpretation of changing British politics is imaginatively discussed in Bernard Bailyn, *The Ideological Origins of the American Revolution* (1967), and Pauline Maier, *From Resistance to Revolution: Colonial Radicals and the Development of American Opposition to Britain, 1765–1776* (1972).

The most perceptive work on the events leading to the Revolution is Edmund S. and Helen M. Morgan, *The Stamp Act Crisis* (1953), a book that provides an excellent account of American society in 1765. Other studies of these difficult years are John Shy, *Toward Lexington* (1965); Rhys Isaac, *The Transformation of Virginia, 1740–1790* (1982); T.H. Breen, *Tobacco Culture: The Mentality of the Great Tidewater Planters on the Eve of Revolution* (1986); and Benjamin W. Labaree, *The Boston Tea Party* (1964). Robert A. Gross, *The Minutemen and Their World* (1976), is a fine study of Concord. Edward Countryman explores the complex events in New York in *A People in Revolution: The American Revolution and Political Society in New York, 1760–1790* (1982). For information on Thomas Paine see Eric Foner, *Tom Paine and Revolutionary America* (1976).

The most detailed study of the war is Don Higginbotham, *The War of American Independence* (1971). The British side of the story is well told in Piers Mackesy, *The War for America, 1775–1783* (1964). The Loyalists are examined in Wallace Brown, *The King's Friends: The Composition and Motives of the American Loyalists Claimants* (1965), and William H. Nelson, *The American Tory* (1961). Richard B. Morris, *The Peacemakers: The Great Powers and American Independence* (1965), provides a comprehensive study of the peace negotiations.

6 THE REPUBLICAN EXPERIMENT

In 1785 the sons and daughters of some of Boston's wealthiest families announced the formation of a tea assembly or "Sans Souci Club." The members of this select group gathered once a week for the pleasure of good conversation, a game of cards, some dancing, and perhaps a glass of Madeira wine. These meetings outraged other Bostonians, many of them old patriots. For men like Samuel Adams, who dreamed of creating a "Christian Sparta," the club represented the worst excesses of British society. Thus the club's very existence threatened the *republican principles* for which Americans had so recently fought a revolution. Men who had lived through the tense years of the 1770s believed such "foolish gratifications" would erode public morality, substituting "luxury, prodigality, and profligacy" for "prudence, virtue, and economy."

However ridiculous it may now appear, this local tempest reflected deep tensions within postrevolutionary American society. Victory over the British forced people to translate abstract notions about republicanism into daily practice. The effort proved considerably more difficult than anyone had predicted in 1776. As students of classical history understood, republican government required public virtue, a commitment to self-sacrifice.

Yet during the 1780s, citizens of the new nation seemed caught up in a wild, destructive scramble for material wealth. Revolutionary leaders had boldly declared that all men were created equal, and yet African Americans languished in bondage. The patriots had condemned colonialism, and yet some Americans thought that people who settled west of the Appalachian Mountains should remain dependent upon the original thirteen states. Indeed, in 1785 it was not even clear whether the Americans would establish a strong central government or divide themselves into smaller, autonomous republics.

These challenges generated an outpouring of political genius. At other times in American history, persons of extraordinary talent have been drawn to theology, commerce, or science, but during the 1780s, the country's intellectual leaders—Thomas Jefferson, James Madison, Alexander Hamilton, and John Adams among them—focused their creative energies on the problem of how a free people ought to govern themselves.

REVOLUTIONARY SOCIETY

Revolution changed American society, often in ways that no one had planned. This phenomenon is not unusual. The great revolutions of modern times produced radical transformations in French, Russian, and Chinese society. By comparison, the immediate results of the American Revolution appear much tamer, less wrenching. Nevertheless, national independence compelled people to reevaluate social relations that they had taken for granted during the colonial period. However faltering their first steps, they raised fundamental questions about the meaning of equality in American society that still have not been answered to everyone's satisfaction.

SOCIAL AND POLITICAL REFORM

Following the war, Americans aggressively ferreted out and, with republican fervor, denounced any traces of aristocratic pretense. As colonists, they had long resented the claims that certain Englishmen made to special privilege simply because of noble birth. A society based on artificial status was contrary to republican principles.

The appearance of equality was as important as the actual achievement. In fact, the distribution of wealth in postwar America was more uneven than it had been in the mid-eighteenth century. Yet Americans attempted to root out the notion of a privileged class. States abolished laws of primogeniture and entail. In colonial times these laws allowed a landholder either to pass his entire estate to his eldest son or to declare that his property could never be divided, sold, or given away. Although America had never been affected greatly by such customs, their abolition was an important symbolic blow against the idea of a landed aristocracy.

Republican ferment also encouraged many states to lower property requirements for voting. After the revolutionary experience, such a step seemed logical. The concept of a representative government was well accepted in America. These reforms, however, did not significantly expand the American electorate. Long before the Revolution, an overwhelming percentage of free males had owned enough land to vote, and few leaders at that time were willing to entertain the idea of universal manhood suffrage.

The most important changes in voting patterns were the result of western migration. As Americans moved to the frontier, they received full political representation in their state legislatures, and because new districts tended to be poorer than established coastal settlements, their inhabitants selected representatives who seemed less cultured, less well trained than those sent by eastern voters. Moreover, western delegates resented traveling so far to attend legislative meetings, and they lobbied successfully to transfer state capitals to more convenient locations.

After independence, Americans also reexamined the relationship between church and state. Republican spokesmen such as Thomas Jefferson argued in favor of the disestablishment of state churches. They insisted that rulers had no right to interfere with the free expression of an individual's religious beliefs. Nor did they believe that churches should be supported with taxpayers' monies. Although Massachusetts and Connecticut did not disestablish their Congregational churches, most of the southern states did disestablish the Anglican church. Few Americans favored irreligion or secularism, though they championed religious toleration.

SLAVES AND WOMEN IN THE NEW REPUBLIC

Revolutionary fervor even forced Americans to confront the most appalling contradiction to the republican principles—slavery. Abolitionist sentiment ran high during the 1780s, especially among the Quakers of the middle states. In increasing numbers, other Americans agreed. They formed groups to end slavery from Massachusetts to Virginia that included such prominent figures as Alexander Hamilton, John Jay, and Benjamin Franklin.

The attack on slavery took a number of different forms. The Vermont constitution of 1777 specifically prohibited slavery. In 1780 the Pennsylvania legislature abolished the practice. Other states followed suit. By the decade after 1800 slavery was well on the road to extinction in the northern states.

Even in the South, where blacks made up a large percentage of the population, slavery embarrassed thoughtful republicans. Some planters followed James Madison's egalitarian example and simply freed their slaves. Despite these promising beginnings, however, the southern states did not abolish slavery. The economic incentives to maintain a servile labor force, especially after the invention of the cotton gin in 1793 and the opening up of the Alabama and Mississippi frontier, overwhelmed the abolitionist impulse. An opportunity to translate the rhetoric of the American Revolution into social practice had been lost, at least temporarily. Even Thomas Jefferson, the man who wrote the Declaration of Independence, could not bring himself to free his own slaves.

The currents of republicanism also raised the expectations of American women. For example, during this period women began to petition for divorce on new grounds. One case is particularly instructive concerning changing attitudes toward women and the family. In 1784, John Backus, an obscure Massachusetts silver-

In 1790, female property owners of New Jersey were granted suffrage. After only seventeen years, however, their right to vote was retracted by state lawmakers who viewed female suffrage as a threat to order. Though the Revolution had brought attention to the importance of equality, a broader definition of the term had yet to evolve.

smith, was hauled before a court and asked why he beat his wife. He responded that "it was Partly owing to his Education for his father treated his mother in the same manner." The difference was that Backus' wife refused to tolerate such abuse, and she sued successfully for divorce.

The war itself presented some women with fresh opportunities to employ their talents. In 1780 Esther DeBerdt Reed founded a large volunteer women's organization in Philadelphia— the first of its kind in the United States—that raised over $300,000 for Washington's army. Other women ran family farms and businesses while their husbands fought the British.

Despite these scattered gains, republican society still defined women's roles exclusively in terms of mother, wife, and homemaker. Other pursuits seemed unnatural, even threatening. It is perhaps not surprising that New Jersey, whose legislature in 1790 had voted to allow women who owned property to vote, in 1807 repealed female suffrage in the interests of "the safety, quiet, and good order and dignity of the state."

Although the Revolution did not bring about a massive restructuring of American society, it did raise issues of immense significance for the later history of the United States. Republican spokesmen insisted that equality, however narrowly defined, was an essential element of republican government. They failed to abolish slavery or institute universal manhood suffrage, true, but they vigorously articulated a set of assumptions about people's rights and liberties that challenged future generations of Americans to make good on the promise of the Revolution.

If the Revolution seems less radical than those of other nations, particularly that of France, it may be because eighteenth-century Americans had fewer entrenched barriers to overcome in the first place. Indeed, the Revolution confirmed many rights that colonial Americans had long enjoyed—broad suffrage, religious toleration, and freedom of movement. Nor was the traditional ruling class in America attacked, although new classes were soon challenging them for political and economic leadership. As one wealthy Bostonian complained in 1779, "Fellows who would have cleaned my shoes five years ago, have amassed fortunes and are riding chariots."

THE STATES: THE LESSONS OF REPUBLICANISM

In May 1776 the Second Continental Congress urged the states to adopt constitutions. Rhode Island and Connecticut already had republican governments by virtue of their unique charters, and the rest of the new states soon complied. Several constitutions were frankly experimental, and some states later rewrote documents that had been drafted in the first flush of independence. But if these early constitutions were provisional, they nevertheless provided the framers of the federal Constitution of 1787 with invaluable insights into the strengths and weaknesses of government based on the will of the people.

BLUEPRINTS FOR STATE GOVERNMENT

Despite disagreements over details, Americans who wrote the various state constitutions shared certain political assumptions. First, they insisted upon preparing *written* documents. As colonists, they had lived under royal charters, documents that described the workings of local government in detail, and they felt comfortable with the contractual language of legal documents.

However logical the decision to produce written documents may have seemed to the Americans, it represented a major break with English practice. Political philosophers in the mother country had long boasted of Britain's unwritten constitution, a collection of judicial reports and parliamentary statutes. Yet this highly vaunted system had not protected the colonists from oppression. It is understandable then why, after declaring independence, Americans demanded that their state constitutions explicitly define the rights of the people as well as the powers of their rulers. They desired more from public officials than simply assurances of good faith.

The authors of the state constitutions believed that men and women possessed certain natural rights over which government exercised no control whatsoever. So that future rulers—potential tyrants—would know the exact limits of their authority, these fundamental rights were carefully spelled out.

Eight state constitutions contained specific Declarations of Rights. In general, they affirmed three fundamental freedoms: religion, speech, and press. They protected citizens from unlawful searches and seizures; they upheld trial by jury. Ultimately, the best expression of this impulse is contained in the famed Bill of Rights of the federal Constitution.

In almost every state, delegates to constitutional conventions drastically reduced the power of the governor. He was allowed to make almost no political appointments, and while the state legislators closely monitored his activities, he possessed no veto over their decisions (Massachusetts being the lone exception). Most early constitutions lodged nearly all effective power in the legislature. In fact, the writers of the state constitutions were so fearful of the concentration of power in the hands of one person that they failed to realize that governors—like the representatives—were servants of a free people.

The legislature dominated early state government. Some states even questioned the need for a senate or upper house, and Pennsylvania and Georgia instituted a unicameral, or one-house, system. Many Americans believed that the lower house could handle all the state's problems. The two-house form survived the Revolution largely because it was familiar and because some persons had already begun to suspect that certain checks upon the popular will, however arbitrary they might appear, were necessary to preserve minority rights.

A SOVEREIGN PEOPLE

Perhaps the most significant state constitution was the one adopted by the people of Massachusetts because they hit upon a remarkable political innovation. Their state constitution was drafted by a specifically elected convention of delegates, not ordinary officeholders.

John Adams served as the chief architect of the governmental framework of the state. It included a house and senate, a popularly elected governor who—unlike the chief executives of the state—possessed a veto over legislative bills, and property qualifications for officeholders as well as voters. The most striking aspect of the 1780 constitution, however, was its opening sentence: "We . . . the people of Massachusetts . . . agree upon, ordain, and establish." This powerful vocabulary would be echoed in the federal Constitution.

The state constitutions ushered a different type of person into public office. When one Virginian surveyed the newly elected House of Burgesses in 1776, he discovered that it was "composed of men not quite so well dressed, not so politely educated, nor so highly born as some Assemblies I have formerly seen." They were indeed the people's people, representative republicans. Whether this new breed of representative would be virtuous enough to safe-

guard the fledgling republic remained a hotly debated question.

CREATING A NEW NATIONAL GOVERNMENT

When the Second Continental Congress convened in 1775, the delegates found themselves waging war in the name of a country that did not yet exist. As the military crisis deepened, Congress gradually—often reluctantly—assumed greater authority over national affairs, but everyone agreed that such narrowly conceived measures were a poor substitute for a legally constituted government. The separate states could not possibly deal with the range of issues that now confronted the American people. Indeed, if independence meant anything in a world of sovereign nations, it implied that creation of a central authority capable of conducting war, borrowing money, regulating trade, and negotiating treaties.

ARTICLES OF CONFEDERATION

The first attempt to produce a framework for national government failed miserably. Congress appointed a committee headed by John Dickinson, a lawyer who had written an important revolutionary pamphlet entitled *Letters from a Farmer in Pennsylvania*. Dickinson's plan for creating a strong central government shocked the delegates, who had assumed that the constitution would authorize a loose confederation of states.

Dickinson's plan called for equal state representation in Congress. This upset states such as Virginia and Massachusetts that were more populous than others and fueled tensions between large and small states. Also unsettling was Dickinson's recommendation that taxes be paid to Congress on the basis of a state's total population, black as well as white, a formula that angered Southerners.

Not unexpectedly, the draft that Congress finally approved in November 1777 bore little resemblance to Dickinson's original plan. The

Articles of Confederation jealously guarded the sovereignty of the states. The delegates who drafted this framework shared a general republican conviction that power—especially power so far removed from the people—was inherently dangerous and that the only way to preserve liberty was to place as many constraints as possible upon federal authority.

They succeeded marvelously; Congress created a government that many people regarded as powerless. The Articles provided for a single legislative body, consisting of representatives selected annually by the state legislatures. Each state possessed a single vote in Congress. There was no independent executive, and of course, no veto over legislative decisions. The Articles also denied Congress the power of taxation, a serious oversight in time of war. The national government could obtain funds only by asking the states for contributions, called requisitions. If a state failed to cooperate—and many did—Congress limped along without financial support. Amendments to this constitution required unanimous assent by all thirteen states. The authors of the new system apparently expected a powerless national government to handle foreign relations, military matters, Native American affairs, and interstate disputes. They most emphatically did not award Congress ownership of the lands west of the Appalachian Mountains.

MEETING A CRISIS

Once the new constitution had been sent to the states for ratification, the major bone of contention became the disposition of the vast, unsurveyed territory west of the Appalachians that everyone hoped the British would soon surrender. Some states, such as Virginia and Georgia, claimed land all the way from the Atlantic Ocean to the elusive "South Sea" by virtue of royal charters. People who lived in those states not blessed with vague or ambiguous royal charters seemed to be in danger of being permanently cut off from the anticipated bounty. In protest, these "landless" states stubbornly refused to ratify the Articles of Confederation. All states had sacrificed during the Revolution, they reasoned, and so all states

should profit from the fruits of victory, in this case, from the sale of western lands. Marylanders were particularly vociferous, fearing depopulation by settlers in search of cheap farmland.

The states resolved this bitter controversy in 1781 as much by accident as by design. Virginia, a "landed" state, realized that her position was not without its special problems. Republicans such as Thomas Jefferson worried about expanding their state beyond the mountains; with poor transportation links, it seemed impossible to govern such a large territory effectively from Richmond. The western settlers might even come to regard Virginia as a colonial power insensitive to their needs. Virginia, therefore, agreed to cede its western land claims to Congress, and the other landed states soon followed suit. These transfers established an important principle, for after 1781 there was no question that the West belonged not to the states but to the United States.

No one greeted ratification of the Articles with jubilation. Americans were still fully occupied with winning independence. In 1781 the new government began setting up a bureaucracy. It created the Departments of War, Foreign Affairs, and Finance. By far the most influential presence within the Confederation government was Robert Morris (1734–1806), a freewheeling Philadelphia merchant who was appointed the first superintendent of finance. His decisions provoked controversy. Contemporaries who feared the development of a strong national government identified Morris with efforts to undermine the authority of the states and to seize the power of taxation; at least one congressional critic labeled him a "pecuniary dictator."

THE CONFEDERATION'S MAJOR ACHIEVEMENT

Whatever Congress's weaknesses, it scored one impressive triumph. Congressional action brought order to western settlement, especially in the Northwest Territory, and incorporated frontier Americans into an expanded federal system.

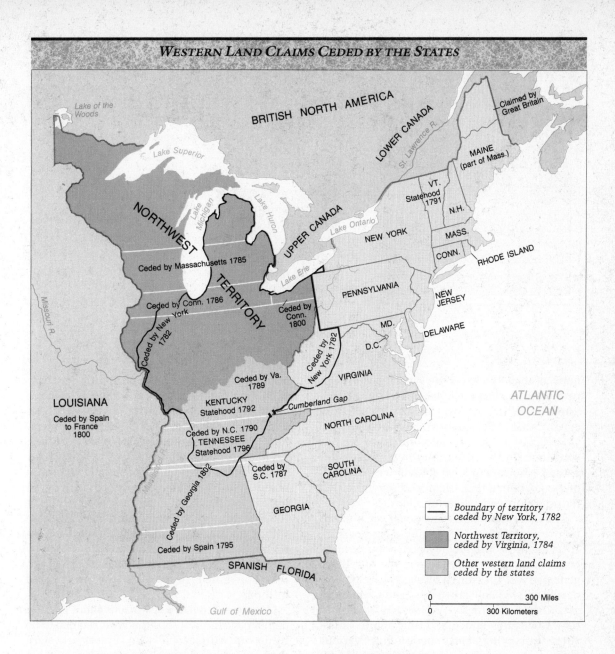

BRITISH NORTH AMERICA

Lake of the Woods

Lake Superior

LOWER CANADA

St. Lawrence R.

Claimed by Great Britain

MAINE (part of Mass.)

VT. Statehood 1791

N.H.

NORTHWEST

Lake Michigan

Lake Huron

UPPER CANADA

Lake Ontario

NEW YORK

MASS.

CONN.

RHODE ISLAND

Ceded by Massachusetts 1785

TERRITORY

Lake Erie

PENNSYLVANIA

NEW JERSEY

Ceded by Conn. 1786

Ceded by Conn. 1800

MD.

DELAWARE

Missouri R.

Ceded by New York 1782

D.C.

Ceded by New York 1782

VIRGINIA

ATLANTIC OCEAN

Ceded by Va. 1789

LOUISIANA

Ceded by Spain to France 1800

KENTUCKY Statehood 1792

Cumberland Gap

Ceded by N.C. 1790

TENNESSEE Statehood 1796

NORTH CAROLINA

Ceded by S.C. 1787

SOUTH CAROLINA

Ceded by Georgia 1802

GEORGIA

Ceded by Spain 1795

SPANISH FLORIDA

Gulf of Mexico

Boundary of territory ceded by New York, 1782

Northwest Territory, ceded by Virginia, 1784

Other western land claims ceded by the states

0   300 Miles

0   300 Kilometers

In 1781, however, the prospects for success did not seem promising. For years, colonial authorities had ignored people who migrated far inland, sending neither money nor soldiers to protect them from Indian attack. Tensions between the seaboard colonies and the frontier regions had occasionally flared into violence. With thousands of men and women, most of them squatters, pouring across the Appala-chian Mountains, Congress had to act quickly to avoid the past errors of royal and colonial authorities.

The initial attempt to deal with this explosive problem came in 1784. Jefferson, then serving as a member of Congress, drafted an ordinance that became a basis for later, more enduring legislation. He recommended carving ten new states out of the western lands located

Grid Pattern of a Township
36 sections of 640 acres (1 square mile each)

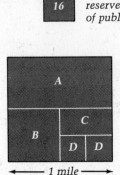

36	30	24	18	12	6
35	29	23	17	11	5
34	28	22	16	10	4
33	27	21	15	9	3
32	26	20	14	8	2
31	25	19	13	7	1

6 miles (vertical) — *6 miles* (horizontal)

16 Income of one section reserved for the support of public education

A Half-section   320 acres
B Quarter-section   160 acres
C Half-quarter section   80 acres
D Quarter-quarter sections   40 acres

← 1 mile →

north of the Ohio River. He specified that each new state establish a republican form of government. When the population of a territory equaled that of the smallest state already in the Confederation, the region could apply for full statehood. In the meantime, free adult males could participate in local government, a democratic guarantee that frightened several of Jefferson's more conservative colleagues.

The impoverished Congress was eager to sell off the western territory as quickly as possible. After all, the frontier represented a source of income that did not depend upon the unreliable generosity of the states. A second ordinance, passed in 1785 and called the Land Ordinance, established an orderly process for laying out new townships and marketing public lands. After surveying and subdividing various regions, the government planned to auction off its holdings in 640-acre sections (one square mile) at prices of not less than a dollar an acre, payable in coin only. Section 16 was set aside for the support of public education and four other sections were held for the government.

Public response disappointed Congress. Surveying the lands took far longer than anticipated, and few persons possessed enough hard currency to make even the minimum purchase of 640 acres. Finally a solution to the problem came from Manasseh Cutler, a land speculator and congressional lobbyist. He and his companions offered to purchase more than 6 million unsurveyed acres of land located in present-day southeastern Ohio by persuading Congress to accept at full face value government loan certificates that had been issued to soldiers during the Revolution. The speculators could pick up these certificates on the open market for as little as 10 percent of their face value. Like so many other get-rich-quick schemes, however, this one failed to produce the anticipated millions.

Congress also had reservations about frontier democracy. In the 1780s the West seemed to be filling up with people who, by eastern standards, were uncultured. The attitude was as old as the frontier itself. Indeed, seventeenth-century Englishmen had felt the same way about the earliest Virginians. The belief that the westerners were lawless, however, persisted, and even a sober observer like Washington insisted that the West crawled with "banditti." The Ordinance of 1784 placed the government of the territories in the hands of people about whom congressmen and speculators had second thoughts.

These various currents shaped the Ordinance of 1787, one of the final acts passed under the Confederation. This bill, also called the Northwest Ordinance, provided a new structure for government of the Northwest Territory. The plan authorized the creation of between three and five territories, each to be ruled by a governor, a secretary, and three judges appointed by Congress. When the population reached 5000, voters who owned property could elect an assembly, but the decisions were subject to the governor's absolute veto. Once 60,000 persons resided in a territory, they could write a constitution and petition for full statehood. While these procedures represented a retreat from Jefferson's original proposal, the Ordinance of 1787 contained several significant features. A bill of rights guaranteed the settlers trial by jury, freedom of religion, and due process of law. In addition, this act outlawed slavery, a prohibition that freed the future states of Ohio, Indiana, Illinois, Michigan, and Wisconsin from the curse of human bondage.

By contrast, the growing settlements south of the Ohio River seemed chaotic. Between 1775 and 1784, for example, the population of what was to become Kentucky jumped from approximately 100 to 30,000 persons. In this and other southwestern regions, land speculators were an ever-present problem. By 1796 the entire region south of the Ohio River had been transformed into a crazy quilt of claims and counterclaims that generated lawsuits for many years to come.

SEARCH FOR ORDER

Throughout the country, Americans became increasingly critical of the Articles of Confederation. Complaints varied from region to region, from person to person, but most disappointment reflected economic frustration. Americans had assumed that peace would restore prosperity. When such was not the case, they searched the political horizon for a reason.

THE NATIONALIST CRITIQUE

Renewed trade with Great Britain on a large scale undermined the stability of the American economy. Specie (coins) flowed eastward across the Atlantic, leaving the United States desperately short of hard currency, and when British merchants called in their debts, thriftless American buyers often fell into bankruptcy. Critics also pointed to the government's inability to regulate trade. Southerners in particular resisted any such attempts. They protested that any control on the export of tobacco, rice, and cotton smacked of the Navigation Acts.

To blame the Confederation alone for the economic depression would be unfair. Nevertheless, during the 1780s many people agreed that a stronger government could somehow have softened the blow. In their rush to acquire imported luxuries, Americans seemed to have deserted republican principles, and a weak Congress was helpless to restore national virtue.

The country's chronic fiscal instability increased public anxiety. During the war, Congress printed over $200 million in paper currency, but because of an extraordinarily high rate of inflation, the rate of exchange for Continental bills soon declined to a fraction of their face value. In 1781 Congress turned to the states for help, asking them to retire the worthless money. Instead, several states not only recirculated the Continental bills, they also issued worthless currency of their own.

A heavy burden of state and national debt compounded the general sense of economic crisis. Revolutionary soldiers had yet to be paid, and the government owed money to domestic and foreign creditors. The pressure to pay these debts grew, but Congress was unable to respond. Since Congress was prohibited from taxing the American people, it required little imagination to see that the Confederation would soon default on its legal obligations unless something was done quickly.

In response, an aggressive group of men announced that they knew how to save the Confederation. The "nationalists"—led by Alex-

"Not worth a Continental" became a common oath when inflation eroded the value of the Continental currency. Most currency issued by the states was equally valueless.

ander Hamilton, James Madison, and Robert Morris—called for major constitutional reforms, the chief of which was an amendment allowing Congress to collect a 5 percent tax on imported goods. Revenues generated by the proposed Impost of 1781 would be used by the Confederation to reduce the national debt. Twelve states accepted the impost, but Rhode Island resolutely refused to cooperate. One negative vote on this proposed constitutional change was enough to kill the taxing plan; amending the Articles required unanimous consent.

The nationalists sparked fierce opposition. Many Americans were apprehensive of their plans. The nationalists, for their part, regarded their opponents as economically naive and argued that a country with the potential of the United States required a complex, centralized fiscal system. But for all their pretensions to re-

alism, the nationalists of the early 1780s were politically inept. They underestimated the depth of republican fears, and in their rush to strengthen the Articles, they overplayed their hand.

A group of extreme nationalists even appealed to the army for support. To this day, no one knows the full story of the Newburgh Conspiracy of 1783. Officers of the Continental army stationed at Newburgh, New York, worried that Congress would disband them without funding their pensions and began to lobby intensively for relief. The officers' initial efforts were harmless enough, but frustrated nationalists such as Morris and Hamilton decided that if the army exerted sufficient pressure on the government, perhaps even threatened a military takeover, then stubborn Americans might be compelled to amend the Articles.

The conspirators failed to take George Washington's integrity into account. In a surprise visit, he confronted the officers directly at Newburgh. So great was his personal influence that a few words from him ended any chance of rebellion. Washington, indeed, deserves credit for preserving civilian rule in this country. He refused to consider any scheme that contemplated using the army as a political instrument.

In April 1783 Congress proposed a second impost, but it too failed to win unanimous ratification. Even a personal appeal by Washington could not save the amendment. With this defeat, nationalists gave up on the Confederation. Morris retired from government, and Madison returned to Virginia utterly depressed by what he had witnessed.

DIPLOMATIC HUMILIATION

In foreign affairs, Congress endured further embarrassment. American negotiators had promised Great Britain that its citizens could collect debts contracted before the Revolution. The states, however, dragged their heels, and several even passed laws obstructing the settlement of legitimate prewar claims. Congress was powerless to force compliance. The British responded to this apparent provocation by refusing to evacuate troops from posts located in the Northwest Territory. A strong central government would have driven the redcoats out, but without adequate funds, the weak Congress was powerless to act.

Congress' postrevolutionary dealings with Spain were equally humiliating. That nation refused to accept the southern boundary of the United States established by the Treaty of Paris. Spanish agents schemed with southern Indian tribes to resist American expansion, and on July 21, 1784, Spain added a further insult by closing the lower Mississippi River to citizens of the United States. This last event devastated western farmers who needed free use of the Mississippi to send their crops to the world's markets. Without the river, the economic development of the entire Ohio Valley was in jeopardy.

In 1785 a Spanish official, Don Diego de Gardoqui, opened talks with John Jay, a New Yorker appointed by Congress to obtain rights to navigation of the Mississippi. Jay soon discovered that Gardoqui would not compromise, but he pressed on, attempting to win concessions that would have commercially linked the United States to Spain and benefited northern traders while foregoing free navigation of the Mississippi for twenty-five years. When Congress learned of Jay's plans, it wisely terminated the negotiations with Spain.

By the mid-1780s, Congress had squandered whatever respect it may once have enjoyed. It met irregularly, and some states did not even bother to send delegates. The nation lacked a permanent capital, and Congress drifted from Philadelphia to Princeton to Annapolis to New York City, prompting one humorist to suggest that the government purchase an air balloon to allow members of Congress to "float along from one end of the continent to the other" and "suddenly pop down into any of the states they please."

RESTRUCTURING THE REPUBLIC

Thoughtful Americans, especially those who had provided leadership during the Revolution, agreed that something had to be done. By 1785 the country seemed to be drifting; the buoyant optimism that had sustained revolutionary patriots had dissolved into pessimism and doubt. By 1786 Washington was asking his countrymen exactly why they had fought the Revolution.

A CRISIS MENTALITY

The country's problems could be traced in part to the republicans' own ideology. More than anything else, they feared the concentration of power in the hands of unscrupulous rulers. They therefore created governments—national and state—with weak chief executives and strong assemblies. However, too many of the people who manned the state assemblies and Congress were not up to the task. The result was a government of excessive individualism where legitimate minority rights took a backseat to the desires of the majority.

Confronted with economic chaos, many states blithely churned out worthless currency, while others passed laws impeding the collection of debts. In Rhode Island the situation became absurd. State legislators made it illegal for merchants to reject Rhode Island money even though everyone knew it had no value. As Americans tried to interpret these experiences within a republican framework, they were checked by the most widely accepted political wisdom of the age. Baron de Montesquieu (1689–1755), a French political philosopher of immense international reputation, declared flatly that a republican government could not flourish in a large territory. For such a government to function properly, the people had to be able to keep a close eye on their representatives. Americans treated Montesquieu's theories as self-evident truths, and they were thus nervous about tampering with the sovereignty of the states.

James Madison rejected Montesquieu's argument, and in so doing, helped Americans to think of republican government in exciting new ways. This soft-spoken, rather unprepossessing Virginian was the most brilliant American political thinker of his generation. Based on his reading of the Scottish philosopher David Hume and others, Madison became convinced that Americans need not fear a greatly expanded republic. In fact, he believed that a republican form of government would work better in a large country than in a small one. In small states like Rhode Island, for example, legislative majorities tyrannized the propertied minority. In a large republic, these injustices could be avoided. With so many people scattered over a huge area, no one faction would be able to form an effective majority, and one powerful interest would be checked by some other equally powerful interest.

Madison did not, however, advocate a modern "interest-group" model of political behavior. Rather, he thought that the competing selfish factions would neutralize each other, leaving the business of governing the republic to the ablest, most virtuous persons that the nation could produce. In other words, the government Madison envisioned would be based on the will of the people and yet detached from their narrowly based demands. This thinking formed the foundation of Madison's most famous political essay, *The Federalist* No. 10.

A concerted movement to overhaul the Articles of Confederation began in the mid-1780s. The Massachusetts legislature asked Congress to call a convention for the purpose of revising the entire constitution. Nothing came of the suggestion until 1786 when Madison and his friends persuaded the Virginia assembly to recommend a convention to explore the creation of a unified system of "commercial regulation." Congress supported the idea. However, only five states sent delegates to the Annapolis convention. Rather than try to conduct any business, the Annapolis delegates advised Congress to hold a second meeting in Philadelphia to consider constitutional changes. Congress authorized a grand convention to gather in May 1787.

Events played into Madison's hands. Soon after the Annapolis meeting, an uprising known as Shays' Rebellion, involving several thousand impoverished farmers, shattered the peace of western Massachusetts. These farmers complained of high taxes, of high interest rates, and most of all, of a state government insensitive to their economic problems. In 1786 Dan-

Among the framers of the Constitution, James Madison, not yet forty, was the most effective advocate of a strong central government.

iel Shays, a veteran of the battle of Bunker Hill, and his armed neighbors closed a county courthouse where creditors were suing to foreclose farm mortgages. His band then marched to Springfield, site of a federal arsenal, but the state militia soon put down the rebellion.

Nationalists throughout the United States overreacted to news of Shays' Rebellion. From their perspective, the incident symbolized the breakdown of law and order that they had long predicted. And even more important, the event persuaded persons who might otherwise have ignored the Philadelphia meeting to participate in drafting a new constitution.

THE PHILADELPHIA CONVENTION

In the spring of 1787 fifty-five men representing twelve states traveled to Philadelphia. Only Rhode Island refused to take part in the proceedings. The delegates were practical men: lawyers, merchants, and planters, many of whom had fought in the Revolution and served in the Congress of the Confederation. The majority were in their thirties and forties. The gathering included George Washington, James Madison, George Mason, Robert Morris, John Dickinson, Benjamin Franklin, and Alexander Hamilton. Absent were John Adams and Jefferson, who were conducting diplomacy in Europe; Patrick Henry stayed home in Virginia because he "smelled a rat."

As soon as the convention opened on May 25, the delegates made several procedural decisions of utmost importance. First, they ruled that their discussions would be kept absolutely secret. This determination allowed delegates to speak their minds freely, without fear of criticism from people who had not actually witnessed the debates. The delegates also decided to vote by state, but to avoid the kinds of problems that had plagued the Confederation, they ruled that key proposals needed the support of only a majority instead of the nine states required in the Articles.

INVENTING A FEDERAL REPUBLIC

Madison understood that whoever sets the agenda, controls the meeting. Even before the delegates had arrived, he drew up a framework for a new federal system known as the "Virginia Plan." He wisely persuaded Edmund Randolph, Virginia's popular governor, to present this scheme to the convention on May 29. In his plan, Madison advocated a strong central government, one that could override the shortsighted local legislatures.

The Virginia Plan envisioned a national legislature consisting of two houses, one elected directly by the people, the other chosen by the first house from nominations made by the state assemblies. Representation in both houses was proportional to the state's population. The Virginia Plan provided for an executive elected by Congress. To the surprise of the states' rights supporters, the entire package carried easily, and the convention found itself discussing the details of "*a national* Government . . . consisting of a *supreme* Legislature, Executive, and Judiciary."

On June 15, William Paterson, a New Jersey lawyer, presented a counterproposal. The New Jersey Plan preserved the fundamental spirit of the Articles of Confederation, including the retention of a unicameral legislature. Paterson argued that his revisions, while more modest than Madison's plan, would have greater appeal for the American people. The delegates listened politely to his plan, which would have given Congress extensive new powers to tax and regulate trade, and then they soundly rejected it on June 19.

Rejection of the New Jersey Plan, however, did not clear the way for a final vote. Delegates from small states feared that Madison's plan would hurt their states. These men maintained that unless each state possessed an equal vote in Congress, the small states would find themselves at the mercy of their larger neighbors. Countering this claim, delegates from the large states argued that it was absurd to assert that Rhode Island with only 68,000 people should have the same voice in Congress as Virginia's 747,000 inhabitants.

COMPROMISE SAVES THE CONVENTION

The mood of the convention was tense. Hard work and frustration, coupled with Philadelphia's sweltering summer heat, frayed nerves. Although some members predicted that the meeting would accomplish nothing of significance, the gathering did not break up; the delegates desperately wanted to produce a constitution. On July 2, a "grand committee" of one person from each state was elected by the convention to resolve persistent differences between the large and small states.

And the grand committee did just that. It recommended that the states be equally represented in the upper house of Congress and proportionately by population in the lower house. Only the lower house could initiate money bills. The committee also decided that one member of the lower house should be selected for every 40,000 inhabitants of a state, and for this purpose, a slave was to be counted as three-fifths of a freeman. This compromise overcame the impasse between large and small states.

On July 26, the convention formed a Committee of Detail, a group that prepared a rough draft of the Constitution. When its work was done, the delegates debated each article. The task required the better part of a month.

During these sessions, the members of the convention concluded that the president, as they now called the executive, should be selected by an electoral college, a body of prominent men in each state chosen by local voters. The number of electoral votes held by each state equaled its number of representatives and senators. Whoever received the second largest number of votes in the electoral college automatically became vice-president. In the event that no person received a majority of the votes, the election would be decided by the lower house—the House of Representatives—with each state casting a single vote.

Delegates also armed the chief executive with a veto power over legislation as well as the right to nominate judges. Both privileges, of course, would have been unthinkable a decade earlier, but the state experiences revealed the importance of having an independent executive to maintain a balanced system of republican government. The Philadelphia convention thus telescoped into four months the process of constitutional education that had taken over four years to learn at the state level.

HINTS OF FUTURE CONTROVERSY

During the final days of August, two new issues suddenly disrupted the convention. One was a harbinger of the great sectional crisis of the nineteenth century. Many northern representatives detested the slave trade and wanted to end it immediately. In order to win southern support for the Constitution, however, the northern delegates promised that the legislature would not interfere with the slave trade until 1808 (see Chapter 8).

The second issue was the absence in the Constitution of a bill of rights. Such declarations had been included in most state constitutions. Virginians like George Mason insisted that the states and their citizens needed explicit protection from possible excesses by the federal government. While many delegates sympathized with Mason's appeal, they insisted that the proposed constitution provided sufficient security for individual rights. During the hard battle over ratification the delegates to the convention may have regretted passing over the issue so lightly.

The delegates adopted an ingenious procedure for ratification. Instead of submitting the Constitution to the various state legislatures, all of which had a vested interest in maintaining the status quo, they called for the election of thirteen state conventions especially chosen to review the new federal government. Moreover, the Constitution would take effect after the assent of only nine states. There was no danger, therefore, that the proposed system would fail simply because a single state like Rhode Island withheld approval.

On September 17, thirty-nine men signed the Constitution. A few members of the convention like Mason could not support the document. Others had already gone home. Out of the three months of heat and effort a new form of government had emerged.

WHOSE CONSTITUTION? THE STRUGGLE FOR RATIFICATION

Supporters of the Constitution recognized that ratification would not be easy. After all, the convention had been authorized only to revise the Articles. Instead, it produced a radical new plan that fundamentally altered relations between the states and the central government. The delegates dispatched a copy of the document to the Congress of Confederation which in turn referred it to the separate states. The fight for ratification had begun.

	Articles of Confederation	Constitution
Mode of ratification or amendment	Require confirmation by *every* state legislature	Requires confirmation by three fourths of state conventions or legislatures
Number of houses in legislature	One	Two
Mode of representation	One to seven delegates represent each state, each state holding only one vote in Congress	Two senators represent each state in upper house, each senator holds one vote; One representative to lower house represents every 30,000 people (in 1788) in a state, each representative holds one vote
Mode of election and term of office	Delegates appointed annually by state legislatures	Senators chosen by state legislatures for six-year term (direct election after 1913); representatives chosen by vote of citizens for two-year term
Executive	No separate executive: Delegates annually elect one of their number as president who possesses no veto, no power to appoint officers or to conduct policy. Administrative functions of government theoretically carried out by Committee of States; practically by various single-headed departments	Separate executive branch: President elected by electoral college to four-year term, granted veto, power to conduct policy, to appoint ambassadors, judges, and officers of executive departments established by legislation
Judiciary	Most adjudication left to state and local courts, Congress final court of appeal in disputes between states	Separate branch consisting of Supreme Court and inferior courts established by Congress to enforce federal law
Taxation	States alone can levy taxes, Congress funds the Common Treasury by making requisitions for state contributions	Federal government granted powers of taxation
Regulation of commerce	Congress regulates foreign commerce by treaty, but holds no check on conflicting state regulations	Congress regulates foreign commerce by treaty, all state regulations must obtain congressional consent

FEDERALISTS AND ANTI-FEDERALISTS

Proponents of the Constitution enjoyed great advantages over the unorganized opposition. In the contest for ratification, however, they took no chances. Their most astute move was the adoption of the label *Federalist*, a term that cleverly suggested that they stood for a confederation of states rather than for the creation of a supreme national authority. Critics of the Constitution—who tended to be somewhat poorer, less urban, and less well-educated than their opponents—cried foul, but there was little they could do. They were stuck with the name *Anti-Federalist*, an awkward term that made their cause seem far more obstructionist than it actually was.

The Federalists recruited the most prominent public figures of the day. In every state convention, speakers favoring the Constitution were more polished, better educated, more fully prepared than were their opponents. In New York the campaign to win ratification sparked publication of *The Federalist*, a remarkable series of essays written by Madison,

Hamilton, and Jay during the fall and winter of 1787 and 1788. The nation's newspapers threw themselves overwhelmingly behind the new government. In fact, few journals even bothered to carry Anti-Federalist writings. Nor were Federalists above using threats and even strong-arm tactics. They were determined to win. A nation was at stake.

With so many factors working against them, the Anti-Federalists still came very near victory. Voting was exceptionally close in three large states: Massachusetts, New York, and Virginia. Apparently those who resisted ratification were not so far removed from the political mainstream as has sometimes been suggested by scholars who dismiss the Anti-Federalists as "narrow-minded local politicians."

The Anti-Federalists spoke in the language of the Commonwealthmen (see Chapter 4). Like the extreme republicans who wrote the first state constitutions, the Anti-Federalists were deeply suspicious of political power. During the debates over ratification, they warned that public officials, however selected, would be constantly scheming to expand their authority. It seemed obvious to these critics of the Constitution that the larger the republic, the greater the opportunity for political corruption. Local

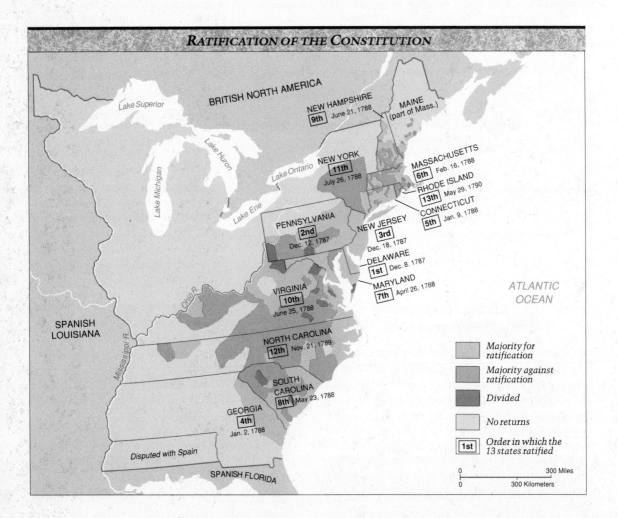

RATIFICATION OF THE CONSTITUTION

voters could not possibly know what their representatives in a distant capital were doing. Anti-Federalists possessed a narrow view of representation. They argued that elected officials should reflect the character of their constituents as closely as possible. They feared that in large congressional districts, representatives would lose touch with the people and the wealthy would win the elections. Older on the average than their opponents, they recalled how aristocrats in Britain had abused their power.

Federalist speakers mocked their opponents' limited perspective. The Constitution deserved general support precisely because it ensured that future Americans would be represented by "natural aristocrats," individuals possessing greater insights, skills, and training than did the average citizen. These talented leaders, Federalists insisted, could discern the interests of the entire population. They were not tied to the selfish needs of local communities. The first ten amendments to the Constitution are the major legacy of the Anti-Federalist argument. The absence of a bill of rights troubled many people. In almost every state convention, opponents of the Constitution pointed to the need for greater protection of individual liberties and rights that people presumably possessed naturally such as freedom of religion and the right to a jury trial. To counter this complaint, Federalists pledged to present a bill of rights to Congress as soon as the Constitution was ratified.

The Constitution drew support from many different types of people. In fact, historians have been unable to discover sharp correlations between wealth and occupation on the one hand and attitudes toward the proposed system of government on the other. In general, Federalists lived in more commercialized areas than did their opponents. Those men involved in commerce—artisans as well as merchants—tended to vote for ratification, while farmers only marginally involved in commercial agriculture frequently voted Anti-Federalist.

Despite passionate pleas from Patrick Henry and other Anti-Federalists, most state conventions quickly adopted the Constitution. Although the battle was close in several states, and although it took almost three years for Rhode Island to ratify, all the states eventually ratified the Constitution. And once the ratification process was over, Americans soon closed ranks behind the new government.

ADDING A BILL OF RIGHTS

After ratification Madison and other Federalists urged passage of a bill of rights to appease able men like Mason and Edmund Randolph, who might otherwise remain alienated from the new federal system. But they proceeded with caution. Madison certainly did not want Anti-Federalists to use the bill of rights as an excuse to revise the entire Constitution or to promote a second constitution.

Madison carefully reviewed the state recommendations as well as the various declarations of rights that had appeared in the early state constitutions, and on June 8, 1789, he placed before the House of Representatives a set of amendments designed to protect individual rights from government interference. Madison told the members of Congress that the greatest dangers to popular liberties came from "the majority [operating] against the minority." A committee compressed and revised his original ideas into twelve amendments, ten of which were ratified and became known collectively as the Bill of Rights.

The Bill of Rights protects the freedoms of assembly, speech, religion, and the press; guarantees speedy trial by an impartial jury; preserves the people's right to bear arms; and prohibits unreasonable searches. Other amendments deal with legal procedure. Only the Tenth Amendment addresses the states' relation to the federal system. This crucial article, designed to calm Anti-Federalists' fears, specifies that those "powers not delegated to the United States by the Constitution, nor prohibited by it to the States, are reserved to the States respectively, or to the people."

On September 25, 1789, the Bill of Rights passed both houses of Congress, and by December 15, 1791, these amendments had been ratified by three-fourths of the states. Madison was justly proud of his achievement. He had effectively secured individual rights without undermining the Constitution.

A NEW BEGINNING

By 1789 one phase of American political experimentation had come to an end. During these exciting years, the people gradually, often haltingly, learned that in a republican society they themselves were sovereign. They could no longer blame the failure of government on inept monarchs or greedy aristocrats. They bore a great responsibility. Americans had demanded a government of the people only to discover during the late 1780s that in some situations the people cannot be trusted with power, that majorities can tyrannize minorities, that the best government can abuse individual rights. They had the good sense, therefore, to establish a marvelous system of checks and balances that protected the people from themselves.

The country's prospects seemed brighter. Benjamin Franklin captured the national mood during the final moments of the constitutional convention. As the delegates came forward to

CHRONOLOGY

1776	Second Continental Congress authorizes colonies to create republican governments (May)
	Eight states draft new constitutions; two others already enjoy republican government by virtue of former colonial charters
1777	Congress accepts Articles of Confederation after long debate (November)
1780	Massachusetts finally ratifies state constitution
1781	States ratify Articles of Confederation following settlements of Virginia's western land claims
	British army surrenders at Yorktown (October)
1782	States fail to ratify proposed Impost tax
1783	Newburgh Conspiracy thwarted (March)
	Treaty of Peace signed with Great Britain (September)
1785	Land Ordinance for Northwest Territory passed by Congress
1786	Jay-Gardoqui negotiations over Mississippi navigation anger southern states
	Annapolis Convention suggests second meeting to revise the Articles of Confederation (September)
	Shays' Rebellion frightens American leaders

1787	Constitutional Convention convenes in Philadelphia (May)
	Northwest Ordinance passed by Congress; restructures territorial government
1787– 1788	The federal Constitution is ratified by all states except North Carolina and Rhode Island
1791	Bill of Rights (first ten amendments of the Constitution) ratified by states

sign the document, he observed that there was a sun carved on the back of Washington's chair. "I have . . . often in the course of the session . . . looked at the sun behind the President without being able to tell whether it was rising or setting: but now at length I have the happiness to know that it is a rising and not a setting sun."

RECOMMENDED READING

The best general accounts of this period have been written by Merrill Jensen and Jackson Turner Main. See especially Main's *The Sovereign States, 1775–1783* (1973), and *The Anti-Federalists, Critics of the Constitution, 1781–1788* (1961). Gordon S. Wood provides a penetrating analysis in *The Creation of the American Republic, 1776–1787* (1969). The failure of Congress during the 1780s is the subject of Jack N. Rakove's monograph, *The Beginnings of National Politics: An Interpretive History of the Continental Congress* (1979), and Peter S. Onuf, *The Origins of the Federal Republic* (1983).

The changing basis of political participation is discussed in Chilton Williamson, *American Suffrage from Poverty to Democracy, 1760–1860* (1960). On black Americans, see Winthrop Jordan, *White over Black: American Attitudes Toward the Negro, 1550–1812* (1968), and Benjamin Quarles, *The Negro in the American Revolution* (1961). On women, see Linda K. Kerber, *Women of the Republic: Intellect and Ideology in Revolutionary America* (1980), and Mary Beth Norton, *Liberty's Daughters: The Revolutionary Experience of American Women, 1750–1800* (1980).

The early state constitutions are discussed in Willi Paul Adams, *The First American Constitutions: Republican Ideology and the Making of the State Constitutions* (1980). The Newburgh Conspiracy is covered in Richard H. Kohn, *Eagle and Sword: The Federalists and the Creation of the Military Establishment in America, 1783–1802* (1975). On the financial problems that beset the Confederation, see E. J. Ferguson, *The Power of the Purse: A History of American Public Finance, 1776–1790* (1961). The day-to-day workings of Congress are examined in H. J. Henderson, *Party Politics in the Continental Congress* (1974). A good survey of western settlement is Peter S. Onuf, *Statehood and Union: A History of the Northwest Ordinance* (1987).

The best source on the Constitution is Max Farrand, ed., *Records of the Federal Convention of 1787*, 4 vols. (1911–1937). The intellectual background of the Founders is examined in Garry Wills, *Explaining America: The Federalist* (1981). To understand Madison's thinking about a large republic, see the essays in Douglass Adair, *Fame and the Founding Fathers*, edited by Trevor Colburn (1974). Also, Richard Beeman, et al., eds., *Beyond Confederation: Origins of the Constitution and American National Identity* (1987), and Leonard W. Levy, *Original Intent and the Framers' Constitution* (1988).

7 SETTING THE AGENDA: FEDERALISTS AND REPUBLICANS, 1788–1800

While presiding over the first meeting of the United States Senate in 1789, Vice-President John Adams raised a pressing procedural question: How should the senators address George Washington, the newly elected president? Adams insisted that Washington deserved an impressive title, a designation that would lend dignity and weight to his office. Adams recommended "His Highness, the President of the United States, and Protector of their Liberties," but some senators favored "His Elective Majesty" or "His Excellency."

Washington and many other people regarded the entire debate as ridiculous. Madison believed that such a discussion befit European aristocrats more than American republicans. When the senators learned that their efforts embarrassed Washington, they dropped the topic. The leader of the new Republic would be called President of the United States. One wag, however, dubbed the portly Adams, "His Rotundity."

The comic-opera quality of this debate should not obscure the participants' seriousness. During the 1790s, decisions about the use of power, about actual governmental policies and positions, had the potential to set a lasting precedent and thus to reinforce or imperil the Revolution itself. But the question of how best to put widely shared republican principles into practice divided Americans. Public figures increasingly gravitated to Alexander Hamilton or Thomas Jefferson, the two most powerful personalities of the decade, and before Washington retired from the presidency, these loose political affiliations had hardened into open party identification, either Federalist or Republican, a development that no one in 1787 had anticipated or desired.

The process was painful and the participants often became bitter. Contemporaries associated parties with faction, with conspiratorial efforts to undermine public virtue. The United States had not yet developed the concept of loyal party opposition. In the 1790s, therefore, sensible and honorable people sometimes mistook simple disagreement over policy for treason. Since Federalists and Republicans both claimed to speak for the common good, for a revolutionary heritage, people assumed that one group or the other had to be lying. Suspicion, verging on paranoia, permeated political discussion; before the end of this difficult decade, party spokesmen advocated blatantly partisan actions that could have involved the United States in international war, shattered the Union, and destroyed constitutional liberties. Few times in this country's history has politics so fully occupied the attention of the American people.

National leaders were surprised by the amount of public opinion that had been fostered by party politics. The people had been invited to participate in government, but it was generally assumed that the ordinary voters would defer to their social betters. Instead, the founders discovered that they presided over a rough-and-tumble political culture hungry for national discourse. The public followed the issues and debates in hundreds of highly partisan newspapers and magazines. Just as film, and later television, has done in our own century, print journalism brought politics to a larger audience than ever before.

ESTABLISHING GOVERNMENT

In 1788 George Washington enjoyed great popularity throughout the nation. In America's first presidential election, he received the unanimous support of the electoral college, an achievement that no subsequent president has duplicated. John Adams was selected vice-president.

The responsibility Washington bore was as great as his popularity. The political stability of the young Republic depended in large measure on how he handled himself in office. In the eyes of his compatriots, he had been transformed into a living symbol of the new government, and during his presidency (1789–1797), he carried himself with studied dignity and reserve—never ostentatious, the embodiment of classical republican virtues. A French diplomat who witnessed Washington's first inauguration reported in awe: "He has the soul, look and figure of a hero united in him." But the adulation of Washington—however well meant—seriously affected the conduct of public affairs, for criticism of his administration was regarded as an attack on the president, and by extension, on the Republic itself. During the early years of Washington's presidency, therefore, American public opinion discouraged partisan politics.

Washington created a strong, independent presidency. While he discussed pressing issues with the members of his cabinet, he left no doubt that he ultimately made policy. Moreover, the first president resisted congressional efforts to restrict executive authority, especially in foreign affairs.

The first Congress quickly established executive departments. Each department was headed by a secretary nominated by the president and serving at the president's pleasure. For the Departments of War, State, and the Treasury, Washington nominated Henry Knox, Thomas Jefferson, and Alexander Hamilton respectively. Edmund Randolph served as part-time attorney general, a position that ranked slightly lower in prestige than the head of a department. As head of the Treasury, which oversaw the collection of customs and other federal taxes, Hamilton could anticipate having several thousand political patronage jobs to dispense.

To modern Americans accustomed to a large federal bureaucracy, the size of Washington's government seems amazingly small. Jefferson, for example, ran the entire State Department with a staff of two chief clerks, two assistants, and a part-time translator. The situation in most other departments was similar. Overworked clerks scribbled madly just to keep up with the press of correspondence. Considering the workloads of men like Jefferson, Hamilton, and Adams, it is no wonder that the president had difficulty persuading able people to accept positions in the new government.

Congress also provided for a federal court system. The Judiciary Act of 1789 created a Supreme Court staffed by a chief justice and five associated justices. In addition, the statute set up thirteen district courts authorized to review the decisions of the state courts. John Jay, a leading figure in New York politics, agreed to serve as chief justice, but since federal judges in the 1790s were expected to travel hundreds of miles over terrible roads to attend sessions of the inferior courts, few persons of outstanding talent and training joined Jay on the federal bench.

Remembering the financial insecurity of the old Confederation government, the newly elected congressmen passed the tariff of 1789, a tax of approximately 5 percent on imports. The act generated considerable revenue, but it also sparked controversy. Southern planters, who relied heavily upon European imports, claimed the tariff discriminated against their interests in favor of those of northern merchants. These battle lines would re-form again and again in the years to come.

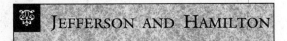

JEFFERSON AND HAMILTON

Washington's first cabinet included two extraordinary personalities, Alexander Hamilton and Thomas Jefferson. Both had served the country with distinction during the Revolution, were recognized by contemporaries as men of special genius as well as high ambition, and brought to public office a powerful vision of how the American people could achieve greatness. The story of their opposing views during the decade of the 1790s provides insight into the birth and development of political parties. It also reveals how a common political ideology, republicanism, could be interpreted in two vastly different ways, turning former friends into bitter adversaries. Indeed, the falling out of Hamilton and Jefferson reflected deep, potentially explosive, political divisions within American society.

Hamilton was a brilliant, dynamic young lawyer who had distinguished himself as Washington's aide-de-camp during the Revolution. Born in the West Indies, the child of an adulterous relationship, Hamilton employed charm, courage, and intellect to fulfill his inexhaustible ambition. He strove not for wealth but for reputation. Men and women who fell under his spell found him almost irresistible, but to enemies, Hamilton appeared a dark, calculating, even evil, genius. He advocated a strong central government and refused to be bound by the strict wording of the Constitution. He loved America, but he admired English culture, and during the 1790s he advocated closer commercial and diplomatic ties with Britain.

Jefferson possessed a profoundly different temperament. More reflective, he shone less brightly in society than did Hamilton. He thirsted not for power or wealth but for an opportunity to advance the democratic principles that he had stated so eloquently in the Declaration of Independence. He became secretary of state just after returning from Paris where he had witnessed the first exhilarating moments of the French Revolution. He believed that republicanism would everywhere replace absolute monarchy and aristocratic privilege. His European experiences biased Jefferson in favor of France over Great Britain when the two nations clashed.

Both Hamilton and Jefferson insisted that they were working for the creation of a strong, prosperous republic. Rather than seeing them as spokesmen for competing ideologies, one should view Hamilton and Jefferson as different kinds of republicans who during the 1790s attempted as best they could to cope with unprecedented political challenges.

The two men did seriously disagree on precisely how the United States should fulfill its

During the first years of Washington's administration, neither Hamilton (left) nor Jefferson recognized the full extent of their differences. But as events forced the federal government to make decisions on economic and foreign affairs, the two secretaries increasingly came into open conflict.

destiny. As head of the Treasury Department, Hamilton urged his fellow citizens to think in terms of bold commercial development, of farms and factories embedded within a complex financial network that would reduce the nations's reliance upon foreign trade. Because Great Britain had already established an elaborate system of banking and credit, the secretary looked to that country for economic models that might be reproduced on this side of the Atlantic.

Hamilton's pessimistic view of human nature caused him to fear total democracy. Anarchy, not monarchy, was his nightmare. The best hope for the survival of the Republic, Hamilton believed, lay with the country's monied classes. If the wealthiest people could be persuaded that their economic self-interest could be advanced by the central government, then they would strengthen it, and by so doing, bring a greater measure of prosperity to the common people. From Hamilton's perspective, there was no conflict between private greed and public good; one was the source of the other.

In almost every detail, Jefferson challenged Hamilton's analysis. The secretary of state assumed that the strength of the American economy lay not in its industrial potential, but in its agricultural productivity. He recognized the necessity of change, and while he thought that persons who worked the soil were more responsible citizens than those who labored in factories for wages, he encouraged the nation's farmers to participate in an expanding international market.

Unlike Hamilton, Jefferson expressed faith in the ability of the American people to shape policy. He had a boundless optimism in the judgment of the common folk. He instinctively trusted the people, feared that uncontrolled government power might destroy their liberties, and insisted that public officials follow the letter of the Constitution. The greatest threat to the young Republic, he argued, came from the corrupt activities of pseudo-aristocrats, persons who placed the protection of "property" and "civil order" above the preservation of "liberty." Under no circumstances did he want to mortgage the nation's future—through the creation of a large national debt—to the selfish interests of bankers, manufacturers, and financial speculators.

HAMILTON'S GRAND DESIGN

The unsettled state of the nation's finances presented a staggering challenge to the new government. Congress turned to Hamilton for a policy, and he eagerly accepted the assignment. He read deeply in abstruse economic literature, but the reports he wrote bore the unmistakable stamp of his own creative genius. The secretary synthesized a vast amount of information into an economic blueprint so complex, so innovative that even his allies were slightly baffled. Certainly, Washington never fully grasped the subtleties of Hamilton's plan.

The secretary presented his *Report on the Public Credit* to Congress on January 14, 1790. His research revealed that the nation's outstanding debt stood at approximately $54 million. This sum represented various foreign and domestic obligations that the United States government had incurred during the Revolutionary War. But that was not all. The states still owed creditors approximately $25 million. During the 1780s, Americans desperate for cash had been forced to sell government loan certificates to speculators at greatly discounted prices, and it was estimated that approximately $40 million of the nation's debt was owed to 20,000 people, only 20 percent of whom were the original creditors.

FUNDING AND ASSUMPTION

Hamilton's *Report on the Public Credit* contained two major recommendations covering the areas of funding and assumption. First, under his plan the United States promised to fund its foreign and domestic obligations at full face value. Current holders of loan certificates, whoever they were and no matter how they obtained them, could exchange the old certificates for new government bonds bearing a moderate rate of interest. Second, the secretary urged the federal government to assume responsibility for paying the remaining state debts.

Hamilton reasoned that his credit system would accomplish several desirable goals. It would significantly reduce the power of the individual states to shape national economic policy, something Hamilton regarded as essential in maintaining a strong federal government. Moreover, the creation of a fully funded national debt signaled to investors throughout the world that the United States was now solvent, that its bonds represented a good risk. Hamilton hoped that American investment capital would remain in America, providing a source of money for commercial and industrial growth, rather than flow to Europe. In short, Hamilton invited the country's wealthiest citizens to invest in the future of the United States.

To Hamilton's great surprise, his friend Madison attacked the funding scheme in the House of Representatives. He too wanted the United States to pay its debts, but he was more concerned with the original buyers of the certificates than with the speculators who had purchased them from the hard-pressed patriots. However, far too many records had been lost since the Revolution for the Treasury Department to be able to identify all the original holders. In the end, Congress sided with Hamilton's more practical position.

Assumption unleashed even greater criticism. Hamilton's program seemed designed to reward states that had not paid their debts. In addition, the secretary's opponents in Congress became suspicious that assumption was only a ploy to increase the power and wealth of Hamilton's immediate friends. On April 12, 1790, a rebellious House led by Madison defeated assumption.

The victory was short lived. Hamilton and congressional supporters resorted to legislative horse-trading to revive his foundering program. In exchange for locating the new federal capital on the Potomac River, a move that would stimulate the depressed economy of northern Virginia, several key congressmen who shared Madison's political philosophy changed their votes on assumption. In August Washington signed assumption and funding into law. The first element of Hamilton's design was now securely in place.

THE CONTROVERSIAL BANK OF THE UNITED STATES

The persistent Hamilton submitted his second report to Congress in January 1791. He proposed that the United States government charter a national bank, much like the Bank of England. This privately owned institution would be funded in part by the federal government. The bank not only would serve as the main depository of the United States government but also would issue currency acceptable in payment of federal taxes. Because of that guarantee, the money would maintain its value while in circulation.

Madison and others in Congress immediately raised a howl of protest. They feared that banks might "perpetuate a large monied interest" in America. And what about the Constitution? That document said nothing specifically about chartering financial corporations, and they warned that if Hamilton and his supporters were allowed to stretch fundamental law on this occasion, they could not be held back in the future. On this issue, Hamilton stubbornly refused to compromise.

This intense controversy involving his closest advisers worried the president. Even though the bank bill passed Congress (February 8), Washington seriously considered vetoing the legislation on constitutional grounds. Before doing so, however, he requested written opinions from the members of his cabinet. Jefferson's rambling attack on the bank was wholly predictable; Hamilton's defense was masterful.

He boldly articulated a doctrine of *implied powers*—that the "necessary and proper" clause of the Constitution (Article I, Section 8) gave Congress more power than it specified. Neither Madison nor Jefferson had anticipated this interpretation of the Constitution. Hamilton's so-called loose construction carried the day, and on February 25, 1791, Washington signed the bank act into law.

Hamilton triumphed in Congress, but the general public looked upon his actions with growing fear and hostility. Many persons associated huge national debts and privileged banks with the decay of public virtue. They believed that Hamilton was intent upon turning the future of America over to corrupt speculators. To back-country farmers, making money without actual engaging in physical labor appeared immoral, unrepublican, and certainly, un-American. When the greed of a former Treasury Department official led to several serious bankruptcies in 1792, people began to listen more closely to what Madison, Jefferson, and their associates were saying about growing corruption in high places.

SETBACK FOR HAMILTON

In his third major report, *Report on Manufactures*, submitted to Congress in December 1791, Hamilton revealed the final details of his grand design for the economic future of the United States. This lengthy document suggested ways by which the federal government might stimulate manufacturing and thus free itself from dependency upon European imports. What was needed was direct government intervention. Hamilton argued that protective tariffs and special industrial bounties would greatly accelerate the growth of a balanced economy, and with proper planning, the United States would soon hold its own with England and France.

In Congress the battle lines were clearly drawn. Hamilton's opponents ignored his economic arguments and instead engaged him on moral and political grounds. Madison took a states' rights position and railed against the dangers of "consolidation," a process that threatened to concentrate all power in the federal government, leaving the states defenseless. Jefferson argued that the development of manufacturing entailed urbanization and cities bred every sort of vice. Other southern congressmen saw tariffs and bounties as vehicles for enriching Hamilton's northern friends at the planters' expense. The recommendations in the *Report on Manufactures* were soundly defeated in the House of Representatives.

Washington detested political squabbling. In August 1792, he begged Hamilton and Jefferson to rise above their differences. The appeal came too late. Hamilton's reports eroded the goodwill of 1788, and by the conclusion of Washington's term, neither secretary trusted the other's judgment. Their sparring had produced congressional factions, but no actual parties had yet formed with permanent organizations that engaged in campaigning.

FOREIGN AFFAIRS: A CATALYST TO THE BIRTH OF POLITICAL PARTIES

During Washington's second term (1793–1797), war in Europe dramatically thrust foreign affairs into the forefront of American life. Officials who had disagreed over Hamilton's economic policies now were divided by the fighting between France and Britain. Bitter feelings, inflamed emotions, and accusations of treason were common. This poisonous atmosphere spawned the formation of formal political organizations—the Federalists and Republicans. The clash between these groups developed over how best to preserve the new Republic. The Republicans advocated states' rights, strict interpretation of the Constitution, friendship with France, and vigilance against "the avaricious, monopolizing Spirit of Commerce and Commercial Man." The Federalists urged a strong national government, central economic planning, closer ties with Great Britain, and maintenance of public order, even if that meant calling out federal troops.

THREATS TO UNITED STATES NEUTRALITY

Great Britain treated the United States with arrogance. Contrary to the instructions of the Treaty of 1783, British troops continued to occupy military posts in the Northwest Territory. Moreover, even though 75 percent of American imports came from Great Britain, that country refused to grant the United States full commercial reciprocity.

France presented a very different challenge. In the spring of 1789, the French Revolution began, and Louis XVI was dethroned. The men who seized power were militant republicans, ideologues eager to liberate all Europe from feudal institutions. Once the Revolution was set in motion, however, the leaders lost control of the movement. Constitutional reform turned into bloody purges, and one radical group, the Jacobins, guillotined thousands of people during the so-called Reign of Terror (October 1793–July 1794). These events left Americans confused. While those who shared Jefferson's views cheered the spread of republicanism, those who sided with Hamilton condemned French expansionism and political violence.

In the face of growing international tension, neutrality seemed the most prudent course for the United States. But the policy was easier for a weak country to proclaim than to defend. In February 1793 France declared war on Great Britain, and both countries immediately challenged the official American position on shipping: "free ships make free goods," meaning that belligerents should not interfere with the shipping of neutral carriers. To make matters worse, no one was certain whether the Franco-American Treaty of 1778 (see Chapter 5) legally bound the United States to support its old ally against Great Britain.

Both Hamilton and Jefferson wanted to avoid war. Jefferson believed that if Great Britain refused to honor America's neutrality and observe neutral shipping rights—in other words, if the Royal Navy seized American sailors—then the United States should award France special trade advantages. Hamilton thought Jefferson's scheme insane. He pointed out that

The execution of Louis XVI by French revolutionaries served to deepen the growing political division in America. Republicans, although they deplored the excesses of the Reign of Terror, continued to support the French people. Federalists feared that the violence and lawlessness would spread to the United States.

Britain possessed the largest navy in the world and was not likely to be coerced by American threats. The United States, he counseled, should appease the former mother country even if that meant swallowing national pride.

A newly appointed French minister to the United States, Edmond Genêt, precipitated the first major diplomatic crisis. This unstable young man arrived in Charleston, South Carolina, in April 1793. He found considerable popular enthusiasm for the French Revolution, and heartened by this reception, he authorized privately owned American vessels to seize British ships in the name of France. Such actions clearly violated United States neutrality and invited British retaliation. When government officials warned Genêt to desist, he threatened to take his appeal directly to the American peo-

ple, who presumably loved France more than the Washington administration did.

This confrontation particularly embarrassed Jefferson, the most outspoken pro-French member of the cabinet. He condemned Genêt's imprudent actions. Washington did not wait to determine if the treaties of 1778 were still in force. Even before he had formally received the French minister, the president issued a Proclamation of Neutrality (April 22).

JAY'S TREATY DIVIDES THE NATION

Great Britain failed to take advantage of Genêt's insolence. Instead, it pushed the United States to the brink of war. British forts on U.S. soil in the Northwest Territory remained a constant source of tension. In June 1793 a new element was added. The London government closed French ports to neutral shipping, and in November, its navy captured several hundred American vessels trading in the French West Indies. Outraged members of Congress, especially those who identified with Jefferson and Madison, demanded retaliation, an embargo, a stoppage of debt payment, even war.

Before this rhetoric produced violence, Washington made one final effort to preserve peace. In May 1794 he sent Chief Justice John Jay to London to negotiate a formidable list of grievances. Jay's major objectives were removal of the British forts, payment for ships taken in the West Indies, improved commercial relations, and acceptance of the American definition of neutral rights.

Jay's mission had little chance of success, partly because Hamilton had secretly informed British officials that the United States would compromise on most issues. Jay did persuade the British to abandon their frontier posts and to allow small American ships to trade in the British West Indies, but they rejected out of hand the United States position on neutral rights. The British would continue to search American vessels on the high seas for contraband and to seize sailors suspected of being British citizens. Moreover, there would be no compensation for the ships seized in 1793 until the Americans paid British merchants for debts contracted before the Revolution. And to the particular annoyance of Southerners, not a word was said about the slaves that the British army had carried off at the conclusion of the war. While Jay salvaged the peace, he appeared to have betrayed the national interest.

News of Jay's Treaty produced an angry outcry in the national capital. Even Washington was apprehensive. He submitted the document to the Senate without recommending ratification. After an extremely bitter debate, the upper house, controlled by Federalists, narrowly accepted a revised version of the treaty (June 1795).

The details of the Jay agreement soon leaked to the press. Throughout the country Jay was burned in effigy. Southerners announced they would not pay prerevoluntionary debts to British merchants. And when news of the treaty reached the House of Representatives, a storm of protest broke out. Followers of Jefferson— now called Republicans—in Congress thought they could stop Jay's Treaty by withholding funds for its implementation.

But the president still had a trump card to play. He raised the possibility that the House was really contemplating his impeachment. Such an action was, of course, unthinkable, and public support quickly swung toward Washington and the Federalists, as the followers of Hamilton were called. Jay's Treaty was saved, but the division between the two parties was beyond repair.

By the time that Jay's Treaty became law (June 14, 1795), the two giants of Washington's first cabinet had retired. Late in 1793 Jefferson returned to his Virginia plantation, Monticello, where despite his separation from day-to-day political affairs, he remained the chief spokesman for the Republican party. His rival, Hamilton, left the Treasury in January 1795 to return to private life in New York City. He maintained close ties with important Federalist officials, however, and even more than Jefferson, Hamilton concerned himself with the details of party organization.

DIPLOMACY IN THE WEST

Before Great Britain finally withdrew its troops from the western forts in 1796, its military officers encouraged local tribes to attack settlers and traders from the United States. The Indians won several impressive victories over federal troops in the area that would become western Ohio and Indiana. But the tribes were actually more vulnerable than they realized, for when confronted with a major United States army under the command of General Anthony Wayne, they received no support from their British allies. At the battle of Fallen Timbers (August 20, 1794), Wayne's forces crushed Indian resistance in the Northwest Territory, and the tribes were compelled to sign the Treaty of Greenville, formally ceding to the United States government the land that became Ohio.

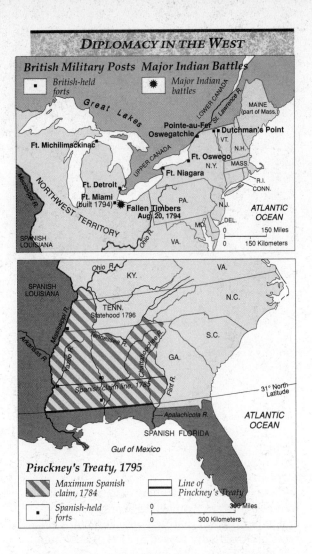

DIPLOMACY IN THE WEST

British Military Posts □ British-held forts

Major Indian Battles ✴ Major Indian battles

Great Lakes

LOWER CANADA

St. Lawrence R.

MAINE (part of Mass.)

Pointe-au-Fer
Oswegatchie
Dutchman's Point

VT.
N.H.

Ft. Michilimackinac

UPPER CANADA

Ft. Oswego

N.Y.
MASS.

Ft. Niagara

R.I.
CONN.

Ft. Detroit

Ft. Miami (built 1794)
Fallen Timbers
Aug. 20, 1794

PA.

N.J.

DEL.

MD.

Mississippi R.

NORTHWEST TERRITORY

Ohio R.

VA.

ATLANTIC OCEAN

SPANISH LOUISIANA

0 — 150 Miles
0 — 150 Kilometers

Ohio R.

KY.

VA.

SPANISH LOUISIANA

TENN.
Statehood 1796

N.C.

Mississippi R.

Yazoo R.

Tennessee R.

Chattahoochee R.

S.C.

Arkansas R.

GA.

Flint R.

Spanish claim line, 1785

31° North Latitude

Apalachicola R.

ATLANTIC OCEAN

SPANISH FLORIDA

Gulf of Mexico

Pinckney's Treaty, 1795

▨ Maximum Spanish claim, 1784

□ Spanish-held forts

— Line of Pinckney's Treaty

0 — 300 Miles
0 — 300 Kilometers

Shrewd negotiations mixed with pure luck helped secure the nation's southwestern frontier. For complex reasons having to do with the state of European diplomacy, Spanish officials in 1795 encouraged the United States representative in Madrid to discuss the navigation of the Mississippi River. Before this initiative, the Spanish government not only had closed the river to American commerce but also had incited the Indians of the region to harass United States settlers (see Chapter 6). Relations between the two countries would probably have deteriorated further had the United States not signed Jay's Treaty. The Spanish assumed—quite erroneously—that Great Britain and the United States had formed an alliance to strip Spain of its North American possessions.

To avoid this imagined disaster, officials in Madrid offered the American envoy, Thomas Pinckney, extraordinary concessions: the opening of the Mississippi, the right to deposit goods in New Orleans without paying duties, a secure southern boundary on the thirty-first parallel, and a promise to stay out of Indian affairs. An amazed Pinckney signed the Treaty of San Lorenzo (also called Pinckney's Treaty) on October 27, 1795, and in March the Senate ratified the document without a single dissenting vote.

POPULAR POLITICAL CULTURE

Ratification of Jay's Treaty generated intense political strife during Washington's administration. It divided Americans along party lines at a time when parties or factions were viewed as subversive. Party conflict also suggested that Americans had lost the sense of common purpose that had united them during the Revolution. Politicians agreed that opposition smacked of disloyalty and therefore should be eliminated by any means—fair or foul. But who should eliminate whom? That was the question that occupied both Federalists and Republicans.

More than any other single element, newspapers transformed the political culture of the United States. Americans were voracious readers and they were well supplied with newspapers. Most of these journals were fiercely partisan. Rumor and opinion were presented as fact, and public officials were regularly dragged through the rhetorical mud. Jefferson, for example, was accused of cowardice; Hamilton vilified as an adulterer.

Even poets and essayists were caught up in the political fray. The better writers often produced party propaganda. American writers sometimes complained that the culture of the young Republic was too materialistic, too un-

Tarring and feathering federal officials was one way in which western Pennsylvanians protested the tax on whiskey in 1794. Washington's call for troops to put down the insurrection drew more volunteers than he had been able to raise during most of the American Revolution.

appreciative of the subtler forms of art then popular in Europe. But it was clear that poets who ignored patriotism and politics simply did not sell well in the United States.

This decade also witnessed the birth of political clubs. Modeled on the political debating societies that sprang up in France during the early years of the French Revolution, the clubs emphasized political indoctrination. By 1794 at least twenty-four clubs were holding regular meetings. Along with newspapers, they provided the common people with highly partisan political information.

WHISKEY REBELLION LINKED TO REPUBLICAN INCENDIARIES

Political tensions became explosive in 1794. The Federalists convinced themselves that the Republicans were actually prepared to employ violence against the United States government.

Though the charge was without foundation, it took on plausibility in the context of growing party strife.

The crisis developed when a group of farmers living in western Pennsylvania protested a federal excise tax on distilled whiskey that Congress had originally passed in 1791. These men did not relish paying any taxes, but this tax struck them as particularly unfair. They made a good deal of money distilling their grain into whiskey, but the excise could seriously reduce the profits.

Largely because the Republican governor of Pennsylvania refused to suppress the angry farmers, Washington and other leading Federalists assumed that the insurrection represented a direct political challenge. The president called out 15,000 militiamen, and accompanied by Hamilton, he marched against the rebels. The expedition was an embarrassing fiasco. The distillers disappeared, and, predictably enough, no one living in the Pittsburgh region seemed to know where the troublemakers had gone. Two supposed rebels were convicted of high crimes against the United States, one reportedly a "simpleton" and the other insane. Washington eventually pardoned both men. As peace returned to the frontier, Republicans gained much electoral support from voters whom Federalists had alienated.

In the national political forum, however, the Whiskey Rebellion had just begun. Washington blamed the "Republican" clubs for promoting civil unrest. Jefferson labeled the entire episode a Hamiltonian device to create an army for the purpose of intimidating Republicans. How else could one explain the administration's gross overreaction to a few disgruntled farmers? The response of both parties reveals a pervasive fear of some secret, evil design to destroy the Republic. The clubs and newspapers fanned these anxieties, convincing many government officials that the First Amendment should not be interpreted as protecting political dissent.

WASHINGTON'S FAREWELL

In September 1796 Washington published his famed "Farewell Address," formally declaring his intention to retire from the presidency. Written largely by Hamilton, who drew upon a draft by Madison, it sought to advance the Federalist cause in the forthcoming election. By waiting until September to announce his retirement, Washington denied the Republicans valuable time to organize an effective campaign. There was an element of irony in this initiative. Washington had always maintained that he stood above party lines. While he may have done so in the early years of his presidency, events such as the signing of Jay's Treaty and the suppression of the Whiskey Rebellion transformed him in the eyes of many Americans into a spokesman solely for Hamilton's Federalist party.

In the address, Washington issued two warnings. First, he warned his country against all political factions. Second, he counseled the United States to avoid making any permanent alliances with distant nations that had no real interest in promoting American security. If few Americans paid attention to the first part of his message, the second part guided foreign relations for many years and became the credo of later American isolationists.

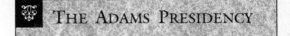

THE ADAMS PRESIDENCY

The election of 1796 took place in an atmosphere of mutual distrust. Jefferson, soon to be the vice-president, believed he was running against the American representatives of British aristocracy. On their part, the Federalists were convinced that their Republican opponents wanted to hand the government over to French radicals. By modern standards, the structures of both parties and the campaign methods employed were still primitive.

During the campaign the Federalists sowed the seeds of their eventual destruction. Party stalwarts agreed that John Adams should run against the Republican candidate, Thomas Jefferson. Hamilton, however, could not leave well enough alone. From his law office in New York City, he schemed to deprive Adams of the presidency. He apparently feared that an independent-minded Adams would be difficult to manipulate. He was correct.

Hamilton exploited an awkward feature of the electoral college. In accordance with the Constitution, each elector cast two ballots, and the person who gained the most votes became president. The runner-up, regardless of party affiliation, served as vice-president. Ordinarily the Federalist electors would have cast one vote for Adams and one for Thomas Pinckney, the party's choice for vice-president. Everyone hoped, of course, that there would be no tie. Hamilton secretly urged southern Federalists to support Pinckney with their first vote, which meant throwing away an elector's second vote. The strategy backfired when New Englanders loyal to Adams heard of Hamilton's maneuvering. They dropped Pinckney, and when the votes were counted, Adams had 71, Jefferson 68, and Pinckney 59. Hamilton's treachery not only angered the new president but also heightened tensions within the Federalist party.

Adams assumed the presidency under intolerable conditions. He found himself saddled with the members of Washington's old cabinet, who regularly consulted with Hamilton behind Adams' back. But to have dismissed them summarily would have called Washington's judgment into question, and Adams was not publicly prepared to take that risk. Adams also had to work with a Republican vice-president. Adams hoped that he and Jefferson could cooperate, but partisan pressures soon overwhelmed the president's good intentions. After a short time, Adams stopped consulting Jefferson.

THE XYZ AFFAIR AND DOMESTIC POLITICS

Foreign affairs immediately occupied Adams' full attention. The French government regarded Jay's Treaty as an affront. By allowing Great Britain to define the condition for neutrality, the United States had in effect sided with that nation against the interest of France.

Relations between the two countries steadily deteriorated. The French dismissed Charles Cotesworth Pinckney, the United States representative in Paris, and the French minister in Philadelphia openly supported Jefferson for president in 1796. In 1797 French privateers began seizing American ships. During this period, neither country bothered to declare war, and for that reason the hostilities came to be known as the Quasi-War.

Hamilton and his friends welcomed the popular outpouring of anti-French sentiment. They counseled the president to prepare for all-out war, hoping that war would purge the United States of French influence. Adams was not persuaded to escalate the conflict. Instead he sent a three-man commission—Charles Pinckney, John Marshall, and Elbridge Gerry—to Paris in a final attempt to remove the sources of antagonism. They were instructed to obtain compensation for the ships seized by French privateers as well as release from the treaties of 1778. In exchange, the commission offered France the same commercial privileges granted to Great Britain in Jay's Treaty.

The commission was shocked by the outrageous treatment it received in France. Instead of dealing directly with Talleyrand, the French minister of foreign relations, they met with obscure intermediaries who reported that Talleyrand would not open negotiations unless he was given $250,000. In addition, the French government expected a "loan" of millions of dollars. The Americans refused to play this insulting game.

The event set off a domestic political explosion. When Adams presented the commission's official correspondence before Congress —the names of Talleyrand's lackeys were labeled X, Y, and Z—the Federalists burst out with a war cry. At last, they would be able to even old scores with the Republicans. So tense was the atmosphere that old friendships between Federalists and Republicans were shattered. As Jefferson wrote to an old colleague: "Men who have been intimate all their lives, cross the streets to avoid meeting, and turn their heads another way, lest they should be obliged to touch their hats."

CRUSHING POLITICAL DISSENT

In the spring of 1798 the followers of Hamilton —called High Federalists—assumed that it was just a matter of time until Adams asked Congress for a formal declaration of war. In the meantime, they pushed for a general rearmament, new fighting ships, additional harbor fortifications, and most important, a greatly expanded United States army. About the need for land forces, Adams remained understandably skeptical. He saw no likelihood of a French invasion.

The president missed the political point. The army the Federalists wanted was intended not to thwart French aggression but to stifle internal opposition. Indeed, militant Federalists used the XYZ affair as the occasion to institute what Jefferson termed the "reign of witches." Jefferson was right; the threat to Republicans was real.

During the summer of 1798 a provisional army gradually came into existence. George

Washington agreed to lead the troops, but he would do so only on condition that Adams appoint Hamilton as second-in-command. Although Adams did not want to promote Hamilton to the command over others who outranked him and were more agreeable, he was not about to refuse Washington's request.

The chief of the High Federalists threw himself into the task of recruiting and supplying the troops. No detail escaped his attention. Only loyal Federalists received commission—even Adams' son-in-law was denied a post—as Hamilton put the finishing touches on his plan to restore domestic order. The mood of the nation grew tense, and many politicians predicted that a civil war would soon erupt.

Hamilton should not have treated Adams with such open contempt. After all, without presidential cooperation, Hamilton could not fulfill his grand military ambitions. Whenever pressing questions concerning the army arose, Adams was nowhere to be found. He delayed Hamilton at every step, making it quite clear that his first love was the navy. In May 1798,

the president even persuaded Congress to establish the Navy Department. Moreover, Adams steadfastly refused to ask Congress for a formal declaration of war. As the weeks passed, the American people increasingly looked upon the idle army as an expensive extravagance.

SILENCING POLITICAL OPPOSITION: THE ALIEN AND SEDITION ACTS

The Federalists did not rely solely upon the army to crush political dissent. During the summer of 1798, the party's majority in Congress passed a group of bills known collectively as the Alien and Sedition Acts. The legislation authorized the use of federal courts and the powers of the presidency to silence the Republicans. The acts were born of fear and vindictiveness, and in their efforts to punish the followers of Jefferson, the Federalists created the nation's first major crisis over civil liberties.

Congress drew up three separate Alien Acts. The first, the Alien Enemies Law, vested the

In the early years of the Republic, political dissent sometimes escalated to physical violence. This fistfight on the floor of Congress took place on February 15, 1798. The combatants are Republican Matthew Lyon and Federalist Roger Griswold.

president with extraordinary wartime powers. On his own authority he could detain or deport foreigners who behaved in a manner he thought suspicious. Since Adams refused to ask for a declaration of war, this legislation never went into effect. The second act, the Alien Law, empowered the president to expel any foreigner from the United States simply by executive decree. While Adams did not attempt to enforce the act, the mere threat of arrest caused some Frenchmen to flee the country. The third act, the Naturalization Law, was the most flagrantly political of the group. The act established a fourteen-year probationary period before foreigners could apply for full United States citizenship. This act was designed to limit the "hordes of wild Irishmen" and other immigrants who voted Republican.

The Sedition Law struck at the heart of free political exchange. It defined criticism of the United States government as criminal libel; citizens found guilty by a jury were subject to fines and imprisonment. Republicans were justly worried that the Sedition Law undermined rights guaranteed by the First Amendment. As far as the Federalists were concerned, if their opposition could be silenced, they were willing to restrict freedom of speech.

Americans living in widely scattered regions of the country soon witnessed political repression first hand. District courts staffed by Federalist appointees indicted seventeen people for criticizing the government. The most celebrated trial occurred in Vermont. A Republican congressman, Matthew Lyon, who was running for reelection, publicly accused the Adams administration of mishandling the Quasi-War. Lyon, an Irish immigrant, had earlier angered Federalists by spitting in the eye of a Federalist congressman during a heated exchange. Now a Federalist court was pleased to have the opportunity to convict him of libel. But Lyon enjoyed the last laugh. While he served his term in jail, his constituents reelected him to Congress.

As this and other cases demonstrated, the federal courts had become political tools. While the fumbling efforts at enforcement of the Sedition law did not silence opposition— indeed, they sparked even greater criticism and created martyrs—the actions of the administration persuaded Republicans that the survival of free government was at stake.

THE REPUBLICANS APPEAL TO THE STATES

By the fall of 1798 Jefferson and Madison were convinced that the Federalists envisioned the creation of a police state. Some extreme Republicans such as John Taylor of Virginia recommended secession from the Union; others advocated armed resistance. But Jefferson wisely counseled against such extreme strategies. Instead, he turned to the state legislatures for help.

As the crisis deepened, Jefferson and Madison drafted separate protests known as the Virginia and Kentucky Resolutions respectively. Both statements vigorously defended the right of individual state assemblies to interpret the constitutionality of federal law. Jefferson wrote the Kentucky Resolutions in November 1798, and in an outburst of partisan anger, he flirted with a doctrine as dangerous to the survival of the United States as anything advanced by Hamilton and his High Federalist friends.

In the Kentucky Resolutions, Jefferson described the federal union as a compact. The states transferred certain explicit powers to the national government, but in his opinion, they retained full authority over all matters not specifically mentioned in the Constitution. Jefferson rejected Hamilton's broad interpretation of the "general welfare" clause. He believed that individual states had the right to nullify any law that was not specifically within the charter of the Constitution. Carried to an extreme, Jefferson's logic could have led to the break-up of the federal government. Although Madison agreed that the Alien and Sedition Acts were unconstitutional, his Virginia Resolutions were more moderate than Jefferson's Kentucky Resolutions.

The Virginia and Kentucky Resolutions must be viewed in proper historical context. They were not intended as statements of abstract principles and most certainly not as a justification for southern secession. They were pure political party propaganda. Jefferson and Madison were simply reminding American voters during a period of severe domestic tension that the Republicans offered a clear alternative to Federalist rule.

ADAMS' FINEST HOUR

In February 1799 President Adams belatedly declared his independence from the Hamiltonian wing of the Federalist party. Throughout the confrontation with France, Adams had shown little enthusiasm for war, and after the XYZ affair, the French changed their tune. Talleyrand now sent word that he was ready to negotiate in good faith. The High Federalists ridiculed this report, but Adams decided to accept this peace initiative. In February he asked the Senate to confirm William Vans Murray as United States representative to France.

In November 1799, Murray and several other negotiators arrived in France. By then Napoleon Bonaparte had come to power, but he cooperated with the Americans. Together, they drew up an agreement known as the Convention of Mortefontaine. The French refused to compensate the Americans for vessels taken during the Quasi-War, but they did declare the treaties of 1778 null and void. Moreover, the convention removed annoying French restrictions on United States commerce. Not only had Adams avoided war, he had also created an atmosphere of mutual trust that paved the way for the purchase of the Louisiana Territory. The negotiations brought Adams personal satisfaction, but they cost him reelection.

THE PEACEFUL REVOLUTION: THE ELECTION OF 1800

On the eve of the election of 1800, the Federalists were fatally divided between the followers of both Adams and Hamilton. Once again the former secretary of the treasury attempted to rig the voting in the electoral college so that the party's vice-presidential candidate, Charles Cotesworth Pinckney, would receive more ballots than did Adams. Again the conspiracy backfired, and the Republicans carried the election.

But to everyone's surprise, the election was not resolved in the electoral college. When the ballots were counted, Jefferson and his running mate, Aaron Burr, had tied. This accident—a Republican elector should have thrown away his second vote—sent the selection of the next president to the House of Representatives, a body still controlled by members of the Federalist party.

As the House began its work on February 27, 1801, excitement ran high. Each state delegation cast a single vote, with nine votes needed to be elected. The drama dragged on for days. To add to the confusion, the ambitious Burr refused to withdraw. Finally, leading Federalists decided that Jefferson, whatever his faults, would make a more responsible president than would the shifty Burr. On the thirty-sixth ballot, Jefferson was elected. The Twelfth Amendment, ratified in 1804, saved the American people from repeating this potentially dangerous turn of events. Henceforth, the electoral college cast separate ballots for president and vice-president.

During the final days of his presidency, Adams appointed as many Federalists as possible to the federal bench. Jefferson protested the hasty manner in which these "midnight judges" were selected. One of them, John Marshall, became chief justice of the United States, a post he held with distinction for thirty-four years. But behind the last-minute flurry of activity lay bitterness and disappointment. On the morning of Jefferson's inauguration, Adams slipped away from the capital—now located in Washington—unnoticed and unappreciated.

In the address that Adams missed, Jefferson attempted to quiet partisan fears. "We are all Republicans; we are all Federalists," he declared. He did not mean that there were no longer any party differences, only that all politicians shared a deep commitment to a federal Union based upon republican ideals. Indeed, the president interpreted the election of 1800 as a fulfillment of the principles of 1776.

CHRONOLOGY

1787	Constitution of the United States signed (September)
1789	George Washington inaugurated (April) Louis XVI of France calls meeting of the Estates General (May)
1790	Congress approves Hamilton's plan for funding and assumption (July)
1791	Bank of the United States is chartered (February) Hamilton's *Report on Manufactures* rejected by Congress (December)
1793	France's revolutionary government announces a "war of all people against all kings" (February) Genêt affairs strains relations with France (April) Washington issues Proclamation of Neutrality (April) Spread of "Democratic" clubs alarms Federalists Jefferson resigns as secretary of state (December)
1794	Whiskey Rebellion put down by United States Army (July–November) General Anthony Wayne defeats Indians at Battle of Fallen Timbers (August)
1795	Hamilton resigns as secretary of the treasury (January) Jay's Treaty divides the nation (June) Pinckney's Treaty with Spain is a welcome surprise (October)
1796	Washington publishes "Farewell Address" (September) John Adams elected president (December)
1797	XYZ affair poisons United States relations with France (October)
1798–1800	Quasi-War with France
1798	Congress passes the Alien and Sedition Acts (June and July) Provisional army is formed Virginia and Kentucky Resolutions protest the Alien and Sedition Acts (November and December)
1799	George Washington dies (December)
1800	Convention of Mortefontaine is signed with France, ending Quasi-War (September)
1801	House of Representatives elects Thomas Jefferson president (February)

From a broader historical perspective, however, the election of 1800 seems noteworthy for what did not occur. There were no riots in the streets, no attempted coup by military officers, no secession from the Union, nothing except the peaceful transfer of government from the leaders of one party to those of the opposition. That in itself was a remarkable achievement.

RECOMMENDED READING

John C. Miller, *The Federalist Era, 1789–1801* (1960), provides a good political survey of this exciting period. Forrest McDonald has reinterpreted the politics of the 1790s in *The Presidency of George Washington* (1974) and *Alexander Hamilton* (1979).

See also Merrill D. Peterson, *Thomas Jefferson and the New Nation: A Biography* (1970), and Jacob Ernest Cooke, *Alexander Hamilton* (1982). Drew McCoy, *The Elusive Republic: Political Economy in Jeffersonian America* (1980), and Joyce Appleby, *Capitalism and a New Social Order: The Republican Version of the 1790s* (1984) provide important insights into the issues that divided Hamilton and Jefferson. Richard Hofstadter avoided taking sides in *The Idea of a Party System: The Rise of Legitimate Opposition in the United States, 1780–1840* (1969).

Political ideologies of this period are discussed in Lance Banning, *The Jeffersonian Persuasion: Evaluation of Party Ideology* (1978), and Richard Buel, Jr., *Securing the Revolution: Ideology in American Politics, 1789–1815* (1972). The problems associated with the developing political parties are examined in William N. Chambers, *Political Parties in a New Nation: The American Experience, 1776–1809* (1963).

Detailed treatments of the major negotiations and treaty fights are Alexander De Conde, *Entangling Alliance: Politics and Diplomacy Under George Washington* (1958); Jerald A. Combs, *The Jay Treaty: Political Battleground of the Founding Fathers* (1970); and William Stinchcombe, *The XYZ Affair* (1980). The new government's attempt to restrict civil rights is covered in James Morton Smith, *Freedom's Fetters: The Alien and Sedition Laws and American Civil Liberties* (1956).

8 REPUBLICANS IN POWER: THEORY AND PRACTICE

DEVELOPING REGIONAL IDENTITIES

REPUBLICAN ASCENDANCY

SOURCES OF POLITICAL DISSENSION

FAILURE OF FOREIGN POLICY

THE STRANGE WAR OF 1812

REPUBLICAN LEGACY

British visitors often disliked Jeffersonian society. Wherever they traveled in the young Republic, they met ill-mannered people inspired with a ruling passion for liberty and equality. Charles William Janson, an Englishman who lived in the United States for thirteen years, was particularly upset by the lack of deference in American society. He remembered one woman who worked for an acquaintance of his and who refused to acknowledge that any person was her master. She told Janson: "I'd have you know, *man*, that I am no *sarvant* [sic]; none but *negers* [sic] are *sarvants*."

This was the authentic voice of Jeffersonian republicanism—self-confident, assertive, blatantly racist, and having no intention of being relegated to low social status. The maid believed that she was her employer's equal. She may even have fostered dreams of having em-

ployees of her own some day. After all, for the men and women who believed in the vision that Jefferson and other Republicans offered, America was a land of boundless opportunity.

Yet the limits of the Jeffersonian vision were obvious even to contemporaries. The people who spoke most nobly about equality often owned slaves. It is not surprising that leaders of the Federalist party accused the Republicans, especially those who lived in the South, of hypocrisy. The race issue simply would not go away. Beneath the political maneuvering over the acquisition of the Louisiana Territory and of the War of 1812 lay fundamental disagreement about the spread of slavery to the western territories.

In other areas the Jeffersonians did not fulfill even their own high expectations. As members of the opposition party during the presidency of

John Adams, they insisted upon a strict interpretation of the Constitution, peaceful foreign relations, and a reduction of the role of the federal government in the lives of the average citizens. But following the election of 1800, Jefferson and his supporters discovered that unanticipated pressures, foreign and domestic, forced them to moderate these goals. Before he retired from public office, Jefferson interpreted the Constitution in a way that permitted the government to purchase the Louisiana Territory when the opportunity arose; he regulated the national economy with a rigor that would have made Alexander Hamilton blush, and he led the country to the brink of war. Some Americans praised the president's pragmatism; others felt betrayed.

DEVELOPING REGIONAL IDENTITIES

During the early decades of the nineteenth century, the population of the United States experienced substantial growth, more the result of natural reproduction than immigration. The 1810 census counted 7,240,000 Americans, a jump of almost 2 million in just ten years. Of this total, approximately 20 percent were blacks. It was a young population. The largest single group in this society was children, boys and girls who were born after Washington's administration and who came of age at a time when the nation's boundaries were rapidly expanding.

Even as Americans defended the rights of individual states, they were forming strong regional identifications. In commerce and politics they perceived themselves as representatives of distinct subcultures, namely, Southerners, New Englanders, or Westerners. Pride and defensiveness mingled together to produce sectional identities, which in time became stronger than even state loyalties.

This shifting focus of attention resulted not only from an awareness of shared economic interests but also from a sensitivity to outside attacks upon slavery. Long before Jefferson died

in 1826, Southerners raised the specter of secession and showed how fragile national unity was.

WESTERN CONQUEST

The most striking changes occurred in the West. Before the end of the American Revolution, only Indian traders and a few hardy settlers had ventured across the Appalachians. After 1790, however, a flood of people poured west to stake out farms on the rich soil. Pittsburgh and Cincinnati, both strategically located on the Ohio River, became important commercial ports. Congress rapidly formed new territories and admitted new states. Wherever they located, Westerners depended upon water transportation. Riverboats represented the cheapest and fastest way to get crops to market. The Mississippi River was the crucial commercial link for the entire region.

Families who moved west attempted to transplant familiar Eastern customs to the frontier. In some areas such as the Western Reserve, a narrow strip of land along Lake Erie in northern Ohio, the influence of New England remained strong. In general, however, a creative mixing of peoples of different backgrounds in a strange environment generated distinctive folkways. They developed their own heroic figures and prided themselves on their toughness, ambition, and self-confidence. Restless and excited by the challenges and opportunities of the frontier, these settlers thought little about packing up their belongings and moving further west.

Only one obstacle barred the way—Indians. Native Americans still lived in the region, and they insisted that they owned the land. The tragedy was that the Indians, many of them dependent on trade with whites and ravaged by disease and alcohol, lacked unity. Small groups allegedly representing the interests of an entire tribe sold off huge pieces of land, often for whiskey or trinkets.

These fraudulent transactions disgusted the brilliant Shawnee leaders, Tecumseh, and his brother, Tenskwatawa (known as the Prophet). These men desperately tried to revitalize tribal culture, encouraging Indians to avoid contact

The Prophet provided spiritual leadership for the union of Indian tribes he and his brother Tecumseh organized to resist white encroachment upon Indian lands.

with whites, to resist alcohol, and most important, to hold on to their land. Frontiersmen saw Tecumseh as a threat to progress, and during the War of 1812, they shattered the Indians' dream of cultural renaissance. North and south, American settlers pushing west swept away the Indian barrier.

Well-meaning Jeffersonians did not intend to exterminate the Indians. The president talked about creating a vast reservation beyond the Mississippi River. He planned to turn the Indians into yeoman farmers. But even the most enlightened thinkers of the day did not believe that the Indians possessed a culture worth preserving.

COMMERCIAL CAPITALISM

Before 1820 the prosperity of the United States depended primarily upon its agriculture and trade. Jeffersonian America was by no stretch of the imagination an industrial economy. Except for the cotton gin, important mechanical and chemical inventions did not appear in the fields for another generation. Southerners concentrated upon staple crops, tobacco, rice, and cotton. In the North people generally produced livestock and cereal crops. Regardless of location, however, the nation's farmers, who represented 84 percent of the population, followed a backbreaking work routine that did not differ substantially from that of their parents and grandparents. Probably the major innovation of this period was the agricultural fair, which was first introduced in hopes of improving animal breeding.

The merchant marine represented an equally important element in America's preindustrial economy. At the turn of the century ships flying the Stars and Stripes transported a large share of the world's trade. Merchants in Boston, New York, and Philadelphia received handsome profits from this commerce. Their ships provided essential links between European countries and their Caribbean colonies. This trade, along with the export of domestic staples, especially cotton, generated great fortunes. Unfortunately, the boom did not last. The success of the "carrying trade" depended in large measure upon friendly relations between the United States and the major European powers. When England and France began seizing American ships—as they both did after 1805—national prosperity suffered.

The cities of Jeffersonian America functioned chiefly as depots for international trade. Only about 7 percent of the nation's population lived in urban centers, and most of these people owed their livelihoods either directly or indirectly to the "carrying trade." Shipbuilders, stevedores, and artisans, as well as merchants, contributed to the shipping business. As the merchant families grew wealthy, their demand for luxury items drew a group of master craftsmen whose beautiful and intricate pieces—such as New England clocks—were perhaps the highest artistic achievement of the period.

American cities exercised only marginal economic influence upon the nation's vast hinterland. Because of the high cost of land transportation, urban merchants seldom purchased goods for export—flour and meat, for example—from a distance of more than 150 miles.

The separation between rural and urban Americans was far more pronounced during Jefferson's presidency than it was after the development of canals and railroads a few decades later.

The booming carrying trade may actually have retarded the industrialization of the United States. The lure of large profits drew investment capital—a scarce resource in a developing society—into commerce. By contrast, manufacturing seemed too risky.

Industry was not entirely forgotten, however. Samuel Slater, an English-born designer of textile machinery, did establish several cotton spinning mills in New England, but before the 1820s these plants employed only a small number of workers. Another farsighted inventor, Robert Fulton, sailed the first American steamship up the Hudson River in 1807. In time, this marvelous innovation opened new markets for domestic manufacturers, especially in the West.

REPUBLICAN ASCENDANCY

The District of Columbia seemed an appropriate capital for a Republican president. At the time of Jefferson's first inauguration, Washington was still an isolated rural village. Jefferson fit comfortably into Washington society. He despised formal ceremony and sometimes shocked foreign dignitaries by meeting them in his slippers or a threadbare jacket. Reading and reflection were his primary escapes from official duties.

The president was a poor public speaker. He wisely refused to deliver annual addresses before Congress. In personal conversation, however, Jefferson exuded considerable charm. His dinner parties were major social events, and in this forum, Jefferson regaled politicians with his knowledge of literature, philosophy, and science.

Notwithstanding his commitment to the life of the mind, Jefferson was a politician to the core. He ran for the presidency in order to achieve specific goals: the reduction of the size and cost of federal government, the repeal of the obnoxious Federalist legislation such as the Alien Acts, and the maintenance of international peace. Jefferson realized that he required the full cooperation of congressional Republicans, some of whom were fiercely independent men. To accomplish his program Jefferson developed friendships, wrote memoranda, and held intimate meetings with key Republicans. In two terms as president, Jefferson never had to veto a single act of Congress.

Although cotton was an important trade item in the early nineteenth century, technological advances in textile production were slow in taking hold. Some spinning mills such as the one pictured here were built in New England, but most cloth was still manufactured in home settings.

Jefferson carefully selected the members of his cabinet. During Washington's administration, he had witnessed—even provoked—severe infighting; as president, he nominated only those who enthusiastically supported his programs. James Madison became secretary of state, and Albert Gallatin, a Swiss-born financier who understood the complexities of the federal budget, accepted Jefferson's appointment as secretary of the treasury. Henry Dearborn, Levi Lincoln, and Robert Smith, all loyal to Jefferson, filled the other cabinet posts.

JEFFERSONIAN REFORMS

A top priority of the new government was cutting the national debt. Throughout American history, presidents have advocated such reductions, but in the twentieth century, few have achieved them. Jefferson succeeded. Both he and Gallatin associated debt with Alexander Hamilton's Federalist financial programs (see Chapter 7), measures they considered harmful to republicanism. Jefferson claimed that legislators elected by the current generation did not have the right to mortgage the future of unborn Americans.

Jefferson also wanted to diminish the activities of the federal government. He urged Congress to repeal all direct taxes. Gallatin linked federal income to the carrying trade. He calculated that the entire cost of national government could be borne by customs receipts. The only problem with Gallatin's plan was that it depended upon peaceful international relations, a factor that was not predictable.

To help pay the debt inherited from the Adams administration, Jefferson ordered substantial cuts in the national budget. He closed several embassies in Europe, slashed military spending, and during his first term, he reduced the size of the United States Army by 50 percent. In addition, he retired a majority of the navy's warships, a move he claimed promoted peace.

More than just budgetary considerations prompted Jefferson's military reductions. A product of the revolutionary experience, he was deeply suspicious of standing armies. In the event of foreign attack, he reasoned, the militia would rise in defense of the Republic. To ensure that the citizen soldiers would receive professional leadership in battle, Jefferson created the Army Corps of Engineers and the military academy at West Point in 1802.

Political patronage greatly annoyed the new president. Although he controlled several hundred jobs, he refused to dismiss all the Federalists. To transform federal hiring into an undisciplined spoils system, especially at the highest levels of the federal bureaucracy, seemed to Jefferson to be shortsighted. Moderate Federalists might be converted to the Republican party, and in any case, there was a good chance that they possessed the expertise needed to run the government.

Jefferson's political moderation helped hasten the demise of the Federalist party. But the Federalists also contributed to their own decline. The party's organization was loose, and Federalist leaders refused to adopt the popular forms of campaigning that the Republicans had developed so successfully during the late 1790s. The mere prospect of flattering the common people was odious enough to drive some Federalists into political retirement.

Many of them also sensed that national expansion worked against their interests. Western states inevitably seemed to send Republican representatives to Washington. By 1805 the Federalists retained only a few states in New England and Delaware.

Faced with the imminent death of their party, younger Federalists belatedly attempted to pump life into their organization. They experimented with popular election techniques, tightened party organization, held nominating conventions, and campaigned energetically for office. But the results of these activities were disappointing. Even the younger Federalists felt it was demeaning to appeal to voters.

LOUISIANA PURCHASE

When Jefferson first took office, he was confident that Louisiana as well as Florida would eventually become part of the United States. He hoped to persuade the notoriously weak

Spanish rulers to sell the territory, but failing in this, he was prepared to threaten forcible occupation.

In May 1801, however, prospects for the easy or inevitable acquisition of Louisiana suddenly darkened. Jefferson learned that Spain had secretly transferred title of the entire region to France. To make matters worse, the French ruler Napoleon Bonaparte seemed intent upon reestablishing an empire in North America. Napoleon dispatched a large army to put down a rebellion in France's sugar-rich Caribbean colony, Santo Domingo. From that island stronghold in the West Indies, French troops could seize New Orleans and close the Mississippi River to American trade.

A sense of crisis enveloped Washington. Tensions increased when the Spanish officials who still governed New Orleans announced the closing of that port to American commerce (October 1802). Jefferson and his advisers assumed that the Spanish had acted upon orders from France, but despite this serious provocation, the president preferred negotiations to war. In January 1803 he asked James Monroe, a loyal Republican from Virginia, to join the American Minister, Robert Livingston, in Paris. The president instructed the two men to explore the possibility of purchasing the city of New Orleans. If Livingston and Monroe failed, Jefferson realized that he would be forced to turn to Great Britain for military assistance.

By the time Monroe joined Livingston in France, Napoleon's army in Santo Domingo had succumbed to tropical disease, and he had lost interest in establishing an American empire. Knowing nothing of these developments, the American diplomats were taken by surprise

UNDER MY WINGS EVERY THING PROSPERS

President Jefferson recognized the strategic location of New Orleans and determined to buy it from France. By 1803, when this view was painted, New Orleans was already a thriving port and an important outlet for products from the growing frontier.

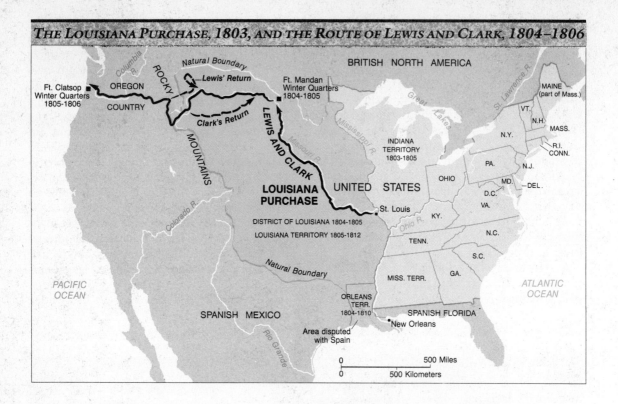

THE LOUISIANA PURCHASE, 1803, AND THE ROUTE OF LEWIS AND CLARK, 1804–1806

when they were offered the entire Louisiana Territory for only $15 million. At one stroke, the Americans doubled the size of the United States, although the boundaries were vague.

The American people responded enthusiastically to news of the treaty that formalized the Louisiana Purchase (May 1803). Jefferson, of course, was relieved that the nation had avoided war with France, but he worried that the treaty might be unconstitutional. The president pointed out that the Constitution did not specifically authorize the acquisition of vast new territories and the incorporation of thousands of foreign citizens. To escape this apparent legal dilemma, Jefferson proposed an amendment to the Constitution, but Napoleon's impatience for money convinced the president to forego the amendment and act quickly.

Jefferson's fears about the incorporation of this new territory were not unwarranted. The Spanish and French people who lived in the region were unfamiliar with America's customs, government, and laws. Jefferson frankly questioned whether these people would be loyal to the United States. He therefore recommended to Congress a transitional government consisting entirely of appointed officials. Some congressmen attacked this bill as anti-republican because it imposed taxes on the citizens of Louisiana without their consent. By a narrow margin the bill passed.

THE LEWIS AND CLARK EXPEDITION

In the midst of the Louisiana controversy, Jefferson dispatched a secret message to Congress requesting $2500 for the exploration of the Far West. How closely this decision was connected to the Paris negotiations is not clear. The president asked his talented private secretary, Meriwether Lewis, to discover whether the Missouri River offered a direct and practical "water communication across this continent for the purposes of commerce." Jefferson also regarded the expedition as a wonderful opportunity to collect precise data about flora and fauna. While preparing for this great adventure, Lewis' second in command, William Clark, assumed such a prominent role that the effort became known as the Lewis and Clark Expedition. Setting out from St. Louis in May 1804, the exploring party reached the Pacific Ocean in November 1805. The group returned safely the following September. The results of this expedition not only fulfilled Jefferson's scientific expectations, but also reaffirmed his faith in the future economic prosperity of the United States.

CONFLICT WITH THE BARBARY STATES

During this period, Jefferson dealt with another problem. For several decades, Morocco, Algiers, Tripoli, and Tunis—the Barbary states—had preyed on commercial shipping. Most European nations paid these pirates tribute, hoping thereby to protect merchants trading in the Mediterranean. In 1801, Jefferson responded to a demand for more tribute by dispatching a small fleet to the Barbary Coast to, as one commander commented, negotiate "through the mouth of a cannon." In the fighting that followed, Tripoli captured the United States frigate *Philadelphia* and Jefferson had to pay $60,000 for the safe return of the crew.

The war dragged on for four years. By 1805 the United States' vigorous naval blockade helped to end the Barbary War. One diplomat observed that the war demonstrated to Europe the proper way to negotiate with pirates.

Jefferson concluded his term on a wave of popularity. He had maintained the peace, reduced taxes, and expanded the boundaries of the United States. He overwhelmed Federalist Charles Cotesworth Pinckney in the election of 1804. So far, Jefferson's "revolution" had been successful.

SOURCES OF POLITICAL DISSENSION

At the moment of Jefferson's greatest electoral victory, a perceptive person might have seen signs of serious division within the Republican party and within the country. The president's heavy-handed attempts to reform the federal courts stirred deep animosities. Republicans had begun sniping at other Republicans, and one leading member of the party, Aaron Burr, became involved in a bizarre plot to separate the West from the rest of the nation. Congressional debates over the future of the slave trade revealed the existence of powerful sectional loyalties and profound disagreement on the issue.

ATTACK ON THE JUDGES

Jefferson's controversy with the federal bench commenced the moment he first became president. The Federalists, realizing that they would soon lose control over the executive branch, passed the Judiciary Act of 1801, which expanded the federal court system. Through his "midnight" appointments, Adams filled these posts with loyal Federalists. Jefferson opposed this attempt by Federalists to maintain their political control. Even more infuriating was Adams' appointment of John Marshall as the new chief justice. Marshall was one of the few men in the country who could hold his own against Jefferson.

In January 1802 Jefferson's congressional allies called for repeal of the Judiciary Act. Although they avoided the political issues, no one doubted that their attack was politically motivated. But the Constitution held that the judges could be removed only when they were found guilty of high crimes and misdemeanors. By repealing the Judiciary Act, Congress would in effect be dismissing judges without a trial, a clear violation of their constitutional rights. Unimpressed by this argument, in March Congress voted for repeal.

While Congress debated the Judiciary Act, another battle suddenly erupted. One of Adams' "midnight" appointees, William Marbury, complained that the new administration would not give him his commission for the office of justice of the peace for the District of Columbia. He sought redress before the Supreme Court, demanding that the federal justices compel James Madison, the secretary of state, to deliver the necessary papers. In his celebrated *Marbury* v. *Madison* decision (February 1803), Marshall berated the secretary of state for withholding Marbury's commission. Nevertheless, he concluded that the Supreme Court did not possess jurisdiction over such matters. Poor Marbury was out of luck. The Republicans proclaimed victory. However, they failed to examine the logic of Marshall's decision. He had ruled that part of the earlier judiciary act on which Marbury based his appeal, the one Congress passed in 1789, was unconstitutional. Thus *Marbury* v. *Madison* set an important precedent for judicial review of federal statutes.

Neither Marbury's defeat nor repeal of the Judiciary Act placated extreme Republicans. They insisted that federal judges should be made more responsible to the will of the people. One solution, short of electing federal judges, was impeachment. Early in 1803, John Pickering, an incompetent judge from New Hampshire, presented the Republicans with a curious test case. This Federalist appointee suffered from alcoholism as well as insanity. However, Pickering had not committed any high crimes against the United States government. Ignoring such legal niceties, Jefferson's allies in the Senate impeached Pickering (March 1804), and he was removed from the bench.

Jefferson had his sights set on bigger game even before Pickering's impeachment. In the spring of 1803, he accused Samuel Chase, a justice of the Supreme Court, of delivering a treasonous speech. Republican congressmen took the hint, agreeing that Chase, who had frequently attacked Republican policies, had committed an indictable offense.

At this stage, some members of Congress expressed uneasiness. The charges drawn up against the judge were purely political. Certainly Chase had been indiscreet, accusing Republicans of threatening "peace and order, freedom and property." But his attack on the Jefferson administration hardly seemed criminal. It was clear that if the Senate convicted Chase, every member of the Supreme Court, including Marshall, might also be dismissed.

Chase's impeachment trial before the United States Senate was one of the most dramatic events in American legal history. Aaron Burr, the vice-president, organized the proceeding, and he redecorated the Senate chamber for the event. In this luxurious setting, Chase and his lawyers conducted a masterful defense. By contrast, John Randolph, the congressman who served as chief prosecutor, behaved in an erratic manner, betraying repeatedly his ignorance of relevant points of law. On March 1, 1805, the Senate acquitted the justice of all charges. This trial, too, set a valuable precedent: While most Republican senators personally disliked the arrogant Chase, they refused to expand the constitutional definition of impeachable offenses.

POLITICS OF DESPERATION

The collapse of the Federalists on the national level encouraged dissension within the Republican party. Extremists in Congress insisted upon monopolizing the president's ear, and when he listened to political moderates, they rebelled. During Jefferson's second term, these critics—labeled "Tertium Quids"—argued that the president's policies, foreign and domestic, sacrificed virtue for pragmatism. Their chief spokesmen were two members from Virginia, John Randolph and John Taylor. They both despised commercial capitalism and urged Americans to return to a simple agrarian way of life.

The Yazoo controversy raised the Quids from political obscurity. This complex legal battle began in 1795 when a thoroughly corrupt Georgia assembly sold 35 million acres of western land, known as the Yazoo claims, to private companies at bargain prices. It soon became apparent that every member of the legislature had been bribed, and in 1796 state lawmakers rescinded the entire agreement. Unfortunately, some land had already changed hands. Jefferson inherited the entire mess when he became president. The special commission he appointed to look into the matter recommended that Congress set aside 5 million acres for buyers who had unwittingly purchased land from the discredited companies.

Randolph immediately cried foul. Such a compromise, however well-meaning, condoned fraud. Republican virtue hung in the balance. Finally, the Marshall Supreme Court ruled in *Fletcher* v. *Peck* (1810) that legislative fraud did not impair private contracts and that the Georgia assembly of 1796 did not have the authority to take away lands already sold to innocent buyers. This important case upheld the Supreme Court's authority to rule on the constitutionality of state laws.

THE BURR CONSPIRACY

Vice-President Aaron Burr created far more serious difficulties for the president. The two men had never been close, and Burr's refusal to bow out during the election of 1800 (see Chapter 7) further strained the relationship. During Jefferson's first term, the ambitious Burr played a distinctly minor role in shaping policy.

In the spring of 1804 Burr decided to run for the governorship of New York. Although he was a Republican, he curried the favor of High Federalists who were plotting the secession of New England and New York from the Union. Alexander Hamilton frustrated Burr's efforts, however, when he described the Republican as "a dangerous man . . . who ought not to be trusted with the reins of government." Burr blamed Hamilton for his subsequent defeat and challenged his tormentor to a duel. On July 11, 1804, at Weehawken, New Jersey, the vice-president shot and killed the former secretary of the treasury. Both New York and New Jersey indicted Burr for murder. His political career lay in shambles.

In his final weeks as vice-president, Burr hatched a scheme so audacious that the people with whom he dealt could not decide whether he was a genius or a madman. Although he told different stories to different men, he evidently planned a filibustering campaign against a Spanish colony, perhaps Mexico, and he envisioned separating the western states and territories from the Union. The persuasive Burr convinced a handful of politicians and adventurers to follow him. Even James Wilkinson, commander of the United States Army in the Mississippi Valley, joined Burr.

In the late summer of 1806 Burr put his ill-defined plan into action. It ended almost before it started. Wilkinson had a change of heart and denounced Burr to Jefferson. This started a general stampede, as conspirators rushed pell-mell to save their own skins. Federal authorities arrested Burr in February 1807 and took him to Richmond to stand trial for treason. Even before a jury had been called, Jefferson announced publicly that Burr's guilt was beyond question.

Jefferson spoke prematurely. The trial judge was John Marshall, who insisted upon a narrow constitutional definition of treason. He refused to hear testimony regarding Burr's supposed intentions and demanded two witnesses to each overt act of treason.

Burr, of course, had been too clever to leave this sort of evidence. While Jefferson complained bitterly about the miscarriage of justice, the jurors declared on September 1, 1807, that the defendant was "not proved guilty by any evidence submitted to us." Although Marshall had acted in an undeniably partisan manner, his actions inadvertently helped protect the civil rights of all Americans. If the chief justice had allowed circumstantial evidence into the Richmond courtroom, if he had listened to rumor and hearsay, he would have made it much easier for later presidents to use trumped-up conspiracy charges to silence legitimate political opposition.

THE SLAVE TRADE

Slavery sparked angry debate at the Constitutional Convention of 1787. If delegates from the northern states had refused to compromise on this issue, Southerners would not have supported the new government. At the convention, the South agreed that after 1808 Congress *might consider* banning the importation of slaves into the United States. In return, the North agreed to count a slave as three fifths of a free white male, which increased southern representatives in Congress and accounted for Jefferson's 1800 presidential victory.

In an annual message sent to Congress in December 1806, Jefferson urged the representatives to prepare legislation outlawing the slave trade. During the early months of 1807, congressmen debated various ways of ending this embarrassing commerce. Although northern representatives generally favored a strong bill, southern congressmen responded with threats and ridicule. They explained to their northern colleagues that no one in the South regarded slavery as evil. It appeared naive, therefore, to expect local planters to enforce a ban on the slave trade or to inform federal agents when they spotted a smuggler.

The bill that Jefferson finally signed in March 1807 probably pleased no one. The law prohibited the importation of slaves into the United States after the new year. Whenever customs officials captured a smuggler, the slaves were turned over to state authorities and disposed of according to local custom. Southerners did not cooperate, and for many years African slaves continued to pour into southern ports. Undoubtedly Great Britain, which outlawed the slave trade in 1807, was the greatest single force in limiting the number of African slaves shipped to the United States. Ships of the Royal Navy took British—and in this case, American—laws seriously.

FAILURE OF FOREIGN POLICY

During Jefferson's second term (1805–1809), the United States found itself in the midst of a world at war. A brief peace in Europe ended abruptly in 1803, and the two military giants of the age, France and Great Britain, fought for supremacy on land and sea. It was a total war, an ideological war, a type of war unknown in the eighteenth century. Britain was the master of the seas, but France held supremacy on land.

During the early stages of the war, the United States profited from European adversity. As "neutral carriers," American ships transported goods to any port in the world where they could find a buyer, and American merchants grew wealthy serving Britain and France.

Napoleon's successes on the battlefield, however, quickly strained Britain's economic resources. In response, Britain tightened its control over the seas. British warships seized American vessels engaged in trade beneficial to France, and British captains stepped up the impressment of sailors on ships flying the United States flag. Then in 1806, the British government issued a series of trade regulations known as "Orders in Council." These proclamations forbade neutral commerce with the Continent and threatened any ship that violated these orders with seizure. The declarations created what were in effect "paper blockades," for even the powerful British navy could not monitor the activities of every continental port.

Napoleon responded to Britain's commercial regulations with his own paper blockade, called the Continental System. In the Berlin Decree of November 1806 and the Milan Decree of December 1807, he announced the closing of all continental ports to British trade and decreed that neutral vessels carrying British goods were subject to seizure. Since French armies occupied most of the territory between Spain and Germany, the decrees obviously cut the British out of a large market. Americans were caught between two conflicting systems. To please one power was to displease the other.

This unhappy turn of international events baffled Jefferson. He had assumed that civilized countries would respect neutral rights; justice obliged them to do so. Appeals to reason, however, made little impression upon states at war. Jefferson tried to negotiate with Britain, but the agreement that resulted was unacceptable to the president.

The United States soon suffered an even greater humiliation. A ship of the Royal Navy, the *Leopard*, sailing off the coast of Virginia, commanded an American warship to submit to a search for deserters (June 21, 1807). When the captain of the *Chesapeake* refused to cooperate, the *Leopard* opened fire, killing three men and wounding eighteen. The attack clearly violated the sovereignty of the United States. The American people demanded revenge.

Despite the pressure of public opinion, Jefferson played for time. He recognized that the United States was unprepared for war against a powerful nation like Great Britain. The president worried that an expensive conflict with Great Britain would quickly undo the fiscal reforms of his first term. For Jefferson, war entailed deaths, debts, and taxes, none of which he particularly relished.

EMBARGO DIVIDES THE NATION

Jefferson found what he regarded as a satisfactory way to deal with European predators with a policy he called "peaceable coercion." If Britain and France refused to respect the rights of neutral carriers, then the United States would keep its ships at home. Not only would this action protect them from seizure, it would also deprive the European powers of much needed American goods, especially food. Jefferson predicted that a total embargo of American commerce would soon force Britain and France to negotiate with the United States in good faith. Congress passed the Embargo Act on December 22, 1807.

"Peaceable coercion" turned into a Jeffersonian nightmare. Americans objected strenuously to the legislation, and Jefferson had to push through a series of acts to force compliance. By the middle of 1808, Jefferson and Gallatin were involved in the regulation of the smallest details of American economic life. The federal government supervised the coastal trade and regulated the overland trade with Canada. When violations still occurred, Congress gave customs collectors the right to seize a vessel merely on suspicion of wrongdoing. Jefferson's eagerness to pursue a reasonable foreign policy blinded him to the fact that he and a Republican Congress would have to establish a police state to make it work.

Northerners hated the embargo and regularly engaged in smuggling. Persons living near Lake Champlain in upper New York State simply ignored the regulations, and they roughed up collectors who interfered with the Canadian trade. Jefferson was so determined to stop the illegal activity that he even urged the governor of New York to call out the militia. In a decision that George III might have applauded, Jefferson dispatched federal troops to overawe the citizens of New York.

New Englanders regarded the embargo as lunacy. Merchants preferred to take their chances on the high seas. Sailors and artisans were thrown out of work. The popular press maintained a constant howl of protest. One writer observed that embargo in reverse spelled "O grab me!" Opposition to the embargo caused a brief revival of the Federalist party in New England, and a few extremists suggested the possibility of state assemblies nullifying federal laws.

By 1809 the bankruptcy of Jefferson's foreign policy was obvious. The embargo never seriously damaged the British economy. Napoleon liked the embargo, since it seemed to harm Great Britain more than it did France. Finally, Republicans in Congress panicked and repealed the embargo a few days before James Madison's inauguration. Relations between the United States and the great European powers were much worse in 1809 than they had been in 1805.

A NEW ADMINISTRATION GOES TO WAR

James Madison followed his good friend Tom Jefferson into the White House. As president, Madison suffered from several personal and political handicaps. Although his intellectual abilities were great, he lacked the qualities necessary for effective leadership. His critics argued that his modest and unassuming manner indicated a weak, vacillating character.

Dolley Madison, a charming and vivacious woman, hosted popular informal entertainments at the White House and set the standard for future First Ladies.

During the election of 1808, Randolph and the Quids tried unsuccessfully to persuade James Monroe to challenge Madison's candidacy. Jefferson favored his old friend Madison. In the end, a caucus of Republican congressmen gave the official nod to Madison, the first time in American history that such a congressional group controlled a presidential nomination. Although Madison won the presidency, the Federalists made impressive gains in the House of Representatives. Madison compounded his difficulties by appointing cabinet members who actively opposed his policies.

The new president inherited Jefferson's foreign policy problems. Neither Britain nor France showed the slightest interest in respecting American neutral rights. Madison's solution was to implement a weak and clumsy Non-Intercourse Act (March 1, 1809) that Congress passed at the same time it repealed the embargo. The new bill authorized the resumption of trade between the United States and all nations of the world *except* Britain and France. Either of these countries could restore full commercial relations simply by promising to observe the rights of neutral carriers.

The British immediately took advantage of this offer. Their minister to the United States, David M. Erskine, informed Madison that the British government had modified its position on a number of sensitive commercial issues. Encouraged by these talks, Madison announced that trade with Great Britain could resume on June 10, 1809. Unfortunately, Erskine had not conferred with his superiors, who rejected the agreement out of hand. While an embarrassed Madison fumed in Washington, the Royal Navy seized the American ships that had already put to sea.

Britain's apparent betrayal led the artless Madison straight into a French trap. In May 1810 Congress passed Macon's Bill Number Two. In a complete reversal of strategy, this poorly drafted legislation reestablished trade with *both* England and France. It also contained a curious carrot-and-stick provision. As soon as either of these European states repealed restrictions upon neutral shipping, the United States government promised to halt all commerce with the other.

Napoleon spotted a rare opportunity. He announced that he would respect American neutral rights. Again, Madison acted impulsively, announcing that unless Britain repealed the Orders in Council by November, the United States would cut off all commercial relations. Only later did Madison learn that Napoleon had no intentions of living up to his side of the bargain. But humiliated by the Erskine experience, Madison decided to ignore French provocations and to pretend that the emperor was behaving in an honest manner.

Events unrelated to international commerce fueled anti-British sentiment in the newly settled parts of the United States. Westerners believed—incorrectly as it turned out—that British agents operating out of Canada had persuaded Tecumseh's warriors to resist the spread of American settlement. General William Henry Harrison, governor of the Indian Territory, marched an army to the edge of a large Shawnee village at the mouth of Tippecanoe Creek near the banks of the Wabash River. On the morning of November 7, 1811, the American troops bested the Indians at the battle of Tippecanoe. The incident forced Tecumseh to seek British military assistance, something he probably would not have done had Harrison left him alone.

FUMBLING TOWARD CONFLICT

In 1811 the anti-British mood of Congress intensified. A group of militant representatives, some of them elected to Congress for the first time in the election of 1810, announced that they would no longer tolerate national humiliation. These aggressive nationalists, many of them elected in the South and West, have sometimes been labeled the "War Hawks." Men like Henry Clay and John C. Calhoun spoke about honor and pride, as if foreign relations were some sort of duel between gentlemen. While the War Hawks were Republicans, they repudiated Jefferson's policy of peaceful coercion.

Madison surrendered to the War Hawks. On June 1, 1812, he sent Congress a message requesting a declaration of war against Great Britain. The timing of his action was peculiar. Over the preceding months, tensions between the two countries had relaxed, and the British government was suspending the Orders in Council.

However inadequately Madison communicated his goals, he was able to enforce a plan. His major aim was to force the British to respect American maritime rights, especially in Caribbean waters. The president's problem was to figure out how a small, militarily weak nation like the United States could bring effective pressure upon Great Britain. The answer, at least it was Madison's, seemed to be Canada. This colony supplied Britain's Caribbean possessions with much needed foodstuffs. The

president reasoned, therefore, that by threatening to seize Canada, the Americans might compel the British to make concessions on maritime issues. It was this logic that secretary of state James Monroe had in mind when he explained in June 1812 that "it might be necessary to invade Canada, not as an object of the war but as a means to bring it to a satisfactory conclusion."

Even contemporaries expressed confusion about the causes of the War of 1812. Madison's formal message to Congress listed Great Britain's violation of maritime rights, impressment of American seamen, and provocation of Indians. The War Hawks wanted war for other reasons. Some probably hoped to conquer Canada. For others the whole affair may have truly been a matter of national pride. Surprisingly, New Englanders, in whose commercial interests the war would supposedly be waged, ridiculed such chauvinism. Although Congress voted for war, the nation was clearly divided about the need to fight Britain. Madison's slim victory over De Witt Clinton, nominated by a faction of antiwar Republicans, in the election of 1812 indicated this split in America.

THE STRANGE WAR OF 1812

Optimism among the War Hawks ran high. However, they failed to appreciate how unprepared the country was for war, and they also refused to mobilize needed resources. The House rejected proposals for direct taxes and authorized naval appropriations only with the greatest reluctance. They did not seem to understand that a weak, highly decentralized government—the one that Jeffersonians championed—was incapable of waging an expensive war against the world's greatest sea power.

New Englanders refused to cooperate with the war effort. Throughout the war, they carried on a lucrative, though illegal, commerce with the enemy. The British government apparently believed that the New England states might negotiate a separate peace, and during the first year of the war, the Royal Navy did not bother to blockade the major northern ports.

American military operations focused initially upon the western forts, but the battles in this region demonstrated that the militia, no matter how enthusiastic, was no match for well-trained European veterans. American forces surrendered Detroit and Michilimackinac to the enemy, and poorly coordinated marches on Niagara and Montreal accomplished nothing. On the sea, the United States did much better. In August, Captain Isaac Hull's *Constitution* defeated the *H.M.S. Guerriere* in a fierce battle, and American privateers destroyed or captured a number of British merchantmen. These victories, however, indicate that Britain was more concerned with Napoleon than the United States. As soon as peace returned to Europe in the spring of 1814, Britain redeployed its fleet and easily blockaded the tiny United States Navy.

The campaigns of 1813 revealed that conquering Canada would be more difficult than the War Hawks ever imagined. Both sides in this war recognized that whoever controlled the Great Lakes controlled the West. On Lake Erie the Americans won the race for naval superiority. Oliver Hazard Perry won an important naval battle at Put-in-Bay, and General Harrison overran an army of British troops and Indian warriors at the battle of Thames River. During this engagement Tecumseh was killed. On the other fronts, however, the war went badly for the Americans.

In 1814 the British took the offensive. Following their victory over Napoleon, British strategists planned to increase pressure on three separate American fronts: the Canadian frontier, Chesapeake coastal settlements, and New Orleans. In the Canadian theater, the British suffered a setback. The American victory off Plattsburg on Lake Champlain accelerated peace negotiations, for after news of battle reached London, the British government concluded that major land operations along the Canadian border were futile.

Throughout the year, British warships harassed the Chesapeake coast. To their surprise, the British found the region almost totally un-

defended, and on August 24, 1814, a small force of British marines burned the nation's capital, a victory more symbolic than strategic. Encouraged by their easy success, the British launched a full-scale attack on Baltimore (September 14). To everyone's surprise, the fort guarding the harbor held out against a heavy bombardment, and the British gave up the operation. The survival of Fort McHenry inspired Francis Scott Key to write "The Star-Spangled Banner."

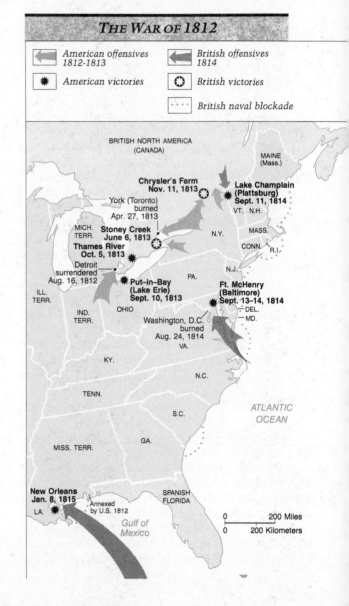

THE WAR OF 1812

American offensives 1812–1813

British offensives 1814

American victories

British victories

British naval blockade

BRITISH NORTH AMERICA (CANADA)

MAINE (Mass.)

Chrysler's Farm Nov. 11, 1813

Lake Champlain (Plattsburg) Sept. 11, 1814

York (Toronto) burned Apr. 27, 1813

VT. N.H.

MICH. TERR.

Stoney Creek June 6, 1813

N.Y.

MASS.

CONN. R.I.

Thames River Oct. 5, 1813

N.J.

Detroit surrendered Aug. 16, 1812

PA.

ILL. TERR.

Put-in-Bay (Lake Erie) Sept. 10, 1813

Ft. McHenry (Baltimore) Sept. 13–14, 1814

IND. TERR.

OHIO

DEL. MD.

Washington, D.C. burned Aug. 24, 1814

VA.

KY.

N.C.

TENN.

S.C.

ATLANTIC OCEAN

GA.

MISS. TERR.

New Orleans Jan. 8, 1815

LA.

Annexed by U.S. 1812

SPANISH FLORIDA

Gulf of Mexico

0   200 Miles

0   200 Kilometers

The battle of New Orleans should never have occurred. The battle took place after the diplomats in Europe had concluded their peace negotiations. General Edward Pakenham, the commander of the British forces, was not aware of these negotiations, however, and on January 8, 1815, he foolishly ordered a frontal attack against General Andrew Jackson's well-defended positions. In a matter of hours, the entire British force had been destroyed. The victory not only transformed Jackson into a national folk hero, it also provided the people of the United States with a much needed source of pride. Even in military terms, the battle was significant, for if the British had managed to occupy New Orleans, they would have been difficult to dislodge regardless of the specific provisions of the peace treaty.

HARTFORD CONVENTION: THE DEMISE OF THE FEDERALISTS

In the fall of 1814, a group of leading New England politicians, most of them moderate Federalists, gathered in Hartford to discuss relations between the people of their region and the federal government. The delegates were angered and hurt by the Madison administration's seeming insensitivity to the economic interests of the New England states.

The men who met at Hartford on December 15 did not advocate secession from the Union. Although people living in other sections of the country cried treason, the convention delegates only recommended changes in the Constitution. Frustrated by the three-fifths clause that gave southern slaveholders a disproportionately large voice in the House, the delegates proposed that congressional representation should be calculated on the basis of the number of white males living in a state. The convention also wanted to limit each president to a single term in office, a reform that New Englanders hoped might end Virginia's monopoly of the executive mansion. And finally, to protect their region from what they saw as the tyranny of southern Republicans, the delegates insisted that a two-thirds majority was necessary before Congress could declare war, pass commercial regulations, or admit new states to the Union.

The convention's recommendations arrived in Washington at the same time as the news of the Battle of New Orleans reached the capital. Republican leaders in Congress accused the hapless New Englanders of disloyalty, and people throughout the country were persuaded that a group of wild secessionists had attempted to destroy the Union. The Hartford Convention accelerated the final demise of the Federalist party.

TREATY OF GHENT ENDS THE WAR

On August 8, 1814, serious peace talks began in the Belgian city of Ghent. The United States sent a distinguished negotiating team: John Quincy Adams, Albert Gallatin, Henry Clay, James A. Bayard, and Jonathan Russell. The members of the British delegation were both more arrogant and more obscure. During the early weeks of negotiations, it seemed as if the American and English representatives were not speaking the same language, and they made little real progress.

Fatigue finally broke the diplomatic deadlock. The British government realized that no amount of military force could significantly alter the outcome of hostilities in the United States. Weary negotiators signed the Treaty of Ghent on Christmas Eve 1814. The document dealt with virtually none of the topics contained in Madison's original war message. Neither side surrendered territory; Great Britain refused even to discuss the topic of impressment. In fact, the treaty was simply an agreement to end fighting. The Senate apparently concluded that stalemate was preferable to continued conflict and ratified the treaty 35 to 0.

Most Americans thought the War of 1812 an important success. Even though the country's military accomplishments had been unimpressive, the people of the United States had been swept up in a contagion of nationalism. For many Americans, this "second war of independence" reaffirmed their faith in themselves and the revolutionary experience.

REPUBLICAN LEGACY

A remarkable coincidence occurred on July 4, 1826, the fiftieth anniversary of the Declaration of Independence. On that day, Thomas Jefferson died at Monticello. His last words were "Is it the Fourth?" On the same day several hundred miles to the north, John Adams also passed his last day on earth. His mind was on his old friend and sometime adversary, and during his final moments, Adams found comfort in the assurance that "Thomas Jefferson still survives."

CHRONOLOGY

1800	Thomas Jefferson elected president
1801	Adams makes "midnight" appointments of federal judges
1802	Judiciary Act is repealed (March)
1803	Chief Justice John Marshall rules on *Marbury* v. *Madison* (February); sets precedent for judicial review
	Louisiana Purchase concluded with France (May)
1804– 1806	Lewis and Clark explore the Northwest
1804	Aaron Burr kills Alexander Hamilton in a duel (July)
	Jefferson elected to second term
1805	Justice Samuel Chase acquitted by Senate (March)
1807	American warship *Chesapeake* fired upon by British *Leopard* (June)
	Burr is tried for conspiracy (August–September)
	Embargo Act passed (December)
1808	Slave trade is ended (January)
	Madison elected president
1809	Embargo is repealed; Non-Intercourse Act passed (March)
1810	Macon's Bill Number Two reestablishes trade with Britain and France (May)
1811	Harrison defeats Indians at Tippecanoe (November)

1812	Declaration of war against Great Britain (June)
	Madison elected to second term, defeating De Witt Clinton of New York
1813	Perry destroys British fleet at battle of Put-in-Bay (September)
	Harrison wins again at battle of Thames River (October)
1814	Jackson crushes Creek Indians at Horseshoe Bend (March)
	British marines burn Washington, D.C. (August)
	Americans turn back British at Plattsburg (September)
	Hartford Convention meets to recommend constitutional changes (December)
	Treaty of Ghent ends War of 1812 (December)
1815	Jackson routs British at battle of New Orleans (January)

Adams was correct. The political battles that occupied both men during their presidencies had already passed into history and were largely forgotten. But the spirit of the Declaration of Independence survived, and Jefferson's vision of a society in which "all men are created equal" challenged later Americans to make good on the promise of 1776.

❦ RECOMMENDED READING

The best-written and in many ways the fullest account of the first two decades of the nineteenth century remains Henry Adams' classic *History of the United States During the Administrations of Jefferson and Madison*, 9 vols. (1889–1891). A fine abridged edition has been prepared by Ernest Samuels (1967). A good general account of the period is Marshall Smelser, *The Democratic Republic, 1801–1815* (1968). Those interested in the problems that Jefferson faced as president should read Merrill D. Peterson, *Thomas Jefferson and the New Nation: A Biography* (1970), and Dumas Malone, *Jefferson and His Time*, vols. 4 and 5 (1970), (1974).

Several works focus more narrowly upon political problems: Noble E. Cunningham, Jr., *The Process of Government Under Jefferson* (1978); James Sterling Young, *The Washington Community, 1800–1828* (1966); and Robert M. Johnstone, Jr., *Jefferson and the Presidency: Leadership in the Young Republic* (1978). See also Richard E. Ellis's masterful *The Jeffersonian Crisis: Courts and Politics in the Young Republic* (1971). A good introduction to the political philosophy of the Jeffersonians is Daniel Boorstin, *The Lost World of Thomas Jefferson* (1948).

For Madison's life see Ralph Ketcham, *James Madison, A Biography* (1971). J.C. Stagg provides a full account of the War of 1812 in *Mr. Madison's War* (1983). Foreign policy problems are treated in Bradford Perkins, *Prologue to War, England and the United States, 1805–1812* (1961), and Burton Spivak, *Jefferson's English Crisis: Commerce, Embargo, and the Republican Revolution* (1979).

The economic developments of this period are the subject of several interesting studies. The most provocative is Thomas C. Cochran, *Frontiers of Change: Early Industrialization of America* (1981). Also see Stuart Bruchey, *The Roots of American Economic Growth, 1607–1861* (1965), and Robert H. Wiebe, *The Opening of American Society: From the Adoption of the Constitution to the Eve of Disunion* (1984). A good introduction to the history of the western settlements is Reginald Horsman, *The Frontier in the Formative Years, 1783–1815* (1970).

The Burr conspiracy is discussed in Milton Lomask's biography, *Aaron Burr* (1982). Problems facing the Federalist party are the subject of David Hackett Fisher, *The Revolution of American Conservatism* (1965), and Linda K. Kerber, *Federalists in Dissent: Imagery and Ideology in Jeffersonian America* (1970).

9 NATIONALISM AND NATION BUILDING

EXPANSION AND MIGRATION

TRANSPORTATION AND THE MARKET ECONOMY

THE POLITICS OF NATION BUILDING AFTER THE WAR OF 1812

When the Marquis of Lafayette revisited the United States in 1824, he marveled at how the country had changed in the more than forty years since he had served with George Washington. The country had grown remarkably, and steam-powered boats now united the various western outposts. Everywhere Lafayette was greeted with patriotic oratory celebrating the liberty, prosperity, and progress of the new nation. Always the diplomat, Lafayette told Americans what they wanted to hear. He hailed "the immense improvements" and "admirable communications" that he had witnessed and declared himself deeply moved by "all the grandeur and prosperity of these happy United States, which, at the same time they nobly seem the complete assertion of American independence, reflect on every part of the world the light of a far superior political civilization."

There were good reasons why Americans made Lafayette's return visit the occasion for patriotic celebration and reaffirmation. Free from foreign threats, America was growing rapidly in population, size, and wealth. Its republican form of government was apparently working well. In his first inaugural address, James Monroe had anticipated Lafayette's observations. It was a speech full of national self-satisfaction. "No country was ever happier with respect to its domain," Monroe said. As for the government itself, it was so near to perfection that "in respect to it we have no essential improvements to make."

Beneath the optimism and self-confidence, however, there were undercurrents of doubt and anxiety about the future. Almost all the Founders were dead. Could their example of republican virtue and self-sacrifice be maintained in an increasingly prosperous and materialistic society? Many Americans feared the answer. And what about the place of slavery in a "perfect" democratic republic? Lafayette himself wondered why the United States had not yet extended freedom and equality to the black slaves.

But the peace following the War of 1812 did open the way for a great surge of nation building. Transportation improvements created new markets, and advances in the processing of raw materials led to the first stirrings of industrialization. Political leadership provided little active direction for the process of growth and expansion, but an active judiciary took up part of the slack in a series of decisions that served to promote economic development and assert the priority of national over state and local interests. To guarantee the peace and security essential for internal progress, statesmen proclaimed a foreign policy designed to insulate America from external involvements. A new nation of great potential wealth and power was now emerging.

EXPANSION AND MIGRATION

The new peaceful relations with Great Britain in 1815 allowed the American people to shift their attention from Europe and the Atlantic to the vast lands of North America that lay before them. Although the British had withdrawn from the region north of the Ohio, they continued to lay claim to the Pacific Northwest. Spain still possessed Florida and much of the present-day American West. Between the Appalachians and the Mississippi and in the lower Mississippi Valley, settlement had already begun in earnest. Many parts of the region, however, were only sparsely settled by whites, and much good land remained in Indian hands. Diplomacy, military action (or at least the threat of it), and the western movement of vast

numbers of settlers were all needed before the continent would yield up its wealth.

EXTENDING THE BOUNDARIES

The first goal of postwar expansionists was to obtain Florida from Spain. In the eyes of the Spanish, their possession extended along the Gulf Coast to the Mississippi, but in 1812 the United States had annexed the area between the Mississippi and the Perdido rivers in what

NORTH AMERICA, 1819

United States

British possessions

Spanish possessions

Russian possessions

Mountain men and Indians met at an annual "rendezvous" to trade their furs to agents of the Rocky Mountain Fur Company for food, ammunition, and other goods. Feasting, drinking, gambling, and sharing exploits were also part of the event.

became Alabama. The remainder, known as East Florida, became the prime object of territorial ambition for President James Monroe and his energetic secretary of state, John Quincy Adams. Spanish claims west and east of the Mississippi blocked Adams' grand design for continental expansion.

General Andrew Jackson provided Adams with an opportunity to acquire the land. In 1816 United States troops touched off a conflict when they went into East Florida in pursuit of hostile Seminole Indians and the fugitive slaves that they were harboring. In April and May of 1818 Jackson exceeded his official orders and occupied East Florida. In addition, he court-martialed and executed two British subjects whom he accused of being enemy agents. Although his actions were widely criticized by government officials, no disciplinary action was taken.

Secretary Adams informed the Spanish government that the United States had acted in self-defense and that further conflict could be avoided only if East Florida was ceded to the United States. Weakened by Latin American revolutions and liberation movements, Spain was in no position to resist American bullying. Spanish minister Luis de Onís acceded. In addition to relinquishing Florida, de Onís agreed to a dividing line between Spanish and American territory that ran all the way to the Pacific, thus giving up Spain's claim to Pacific coastal areas north of California and opening a path for future American expansion. These understandings were formalized in the Adams-Onís Treaty (1819), which also became known as the Transcontinental Treaty. Great Britain and Russia still had competing claims to the Pacific Northwest, but the United States was now poised to acquire some frontage on a second ocean. Secretary Adams described the agreement on a definite boundary to the Pacific as "forming a great epoch in our history."

Interest in exploitation of the Far West continued to grow between 1810 and 1830. In 1811 a New York merchant, John Jacob Astor, founded the fur trading post of Astoria at the mouth of the Columbia River in the Oregon country. In the 1820s and 1830s fur traders operating out of St. Louis worked their way up the

Missouri to the northern Rockies and beyond. First they limited themselves to trading for furs with the Indians, but eventually these "mountain men" went after game on their own and sold the furs to agents of the Rocky Mountain Fur Company at an annual "rendezvous."

These colorful characters, who included such legendary figures as Jedediah Smith, Jim Bridger, Kit Carson, and Jim Beckwourth, accomplished prodigious feats of survival under harsh natural conditions. Although they actually depleted the animal resources on which the Indians depended, these mountain men projected an image of being part of their environment rather than destroyers of it. To later generations they typified a romantic ideal of lonely self-reliance in harmony with unspoiled nature.

The reports of military expeditions provided better information about the Far West than the tales of the mountain men, most of whom were illiterate. The most notable of the postwar expeditions was mounted by Major Stephen S. Long in 1819–1820. Long mapped some of the rivers of the Great Plains and endorsed the somewhat misleading view that the plains beyond the Missouri were a "great American desert" unfit for cultivation or settlement. The real focus of attention between 1815 and the 1840s, therefore, was the nearer West, the rich agriculture lands between the Appalachians and the Mississippi that were being opened up for settlement.

SETTLEMENT TO THE MISSISSIPPI

Complete occupation and exploitation of the trans-Appalachian interior required displacing the many Indian communities still inhabiting that region in 1815. In the Ohio Valley and the Northwest Territory, the Indians had already

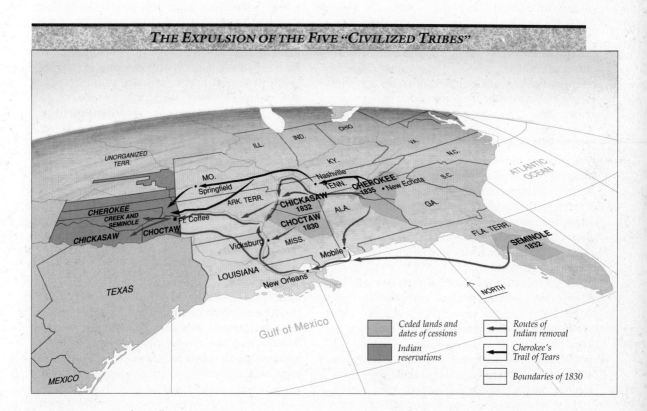

THE EXPULSION OF THE FIVE "CIVILIZED TRIBES"

been defeated. Consigned by treaty to reservations outside the main lines of white advance, most of the tribes were eventually forced west of the Mississippi. In 1831–1832 a faction of the confederated Sac and Fox Indians under Chief Black Hawk attempted to reoccupy lands east of the Mississippi previously ceded by another tribal faction. Federal troops and Illinois state militia routed the Indians. It was the last stand of the woodland Indians of the Midwest.

Uprooting the once populous Indian communities of the Old Northwest was part of a national program for removing Indians of the eastern part of the country to an area beyond the Mississippi. Whites believed that Indians impeded "progress." Furthermore, Indians held land communally and not in private parcels: white settlers regarded this practice as an insuperable obstacle to economic development. During the Monroe era it became clear that white settlers wanted the removal of all Indians. The issue was particularly pressing in the South, where greed combined with racism to doom the Indian tribes.

In the South, as in the Old Northwest, a series of treaties negotiated between 1815 and 1830 reduced tribal holdings and provided for the eventual removal of most Indians to the trans-Mississippi West. Not all tribes left quietly. The so-called five civilized tribes—the Cherokees, Creeks, Seminoles, Choctaws, and Chickasaws—had become settled agriculturalists, and they owned good land in the South. Pressure continued to mount. When deception, bribery, and threats by the federal government failed to induce land cessions, state governments took matters into their own hands. The stage was thus set for the forced removal of the five civilized tribes to Oklahoma during the 1830s. (See Chapter 10 for a more complete discussion.)

While Indians were being driven beyond the Mississippi, settlers poured into the agricultural heartland of the United States. This movement was the most dramatic and significant phase of the great westward expansion of population and settlement that began in the early colonial period and lasted until the 1880s.

In 1810 only about one seventh of the American population lived beyond the Appalachians; by 1840 more than a third did. Eight new states were added to the Union during this period. The government took care of Indian removal, but the settlers faced the difficult task of gaining a livelihood from the land.

Much of the vast acreage opened up by the western movement passed through the hands of land speculators before it reached those of the farmers and planters. After a financial panic in 1819 brought ruin to many who had purchased tracts on credit, the minimum price was lowered from $2.00 to $1.25 an acre, but full payment was required in cash. This change favored wealthy speculators who bought land at a massive rate.

Eventually most of the land did find its way into the hands of actual cultivators. In some areas squatters arrived before the official survey and formed claims associations that policed land auctions to prevent "outsiders" from bidding up the price and buying their farms out from under them. Squatters also insisted that they had the right to buy the land that they had already improved at the minimum price, a program called "preemption." In 1841 the right to farm on public lands with assurance of a *future* preemption right was formally acknowledged by Congress.

Settlers who arrived after speculators had secured title had to deal with land barons. Fortunately for the settlers, most speculators operated on credit and were forced to obtain a quick return on their investment. They did this by selling land at a profit to settlers who had some capital and by arranging finance plans for tenants who did not. Thus the family farm or owner-operated plantation was the typical unit of western agriculture.

Since debt was common in the West, most farmers found it necessary to do more than simply raise enough food to subsist; they had to produce something for market. Most of the earliest settlement was along rivers, which provided cheap transportation. But even in more remote areas, farmers managed to get their corn, wheat, cotton, or cured meat to market.

To meet the needs of farmers, local marketing centers quickly sprang up, usually at river junctions. Cities emerged seemingly overnight, and they in turn accelerated regional development.

THE PEOPLE AND CULTURE OF THE FRONTIER

Most of the hundreds of thousands of settlers who populated the West were farmers from the seaboard states. They migrated for all sorts of reasons, but prominent among them were overpopulation, rising land prices, and declining fertility of the soil in the older regions. Most moved as family units and tried to recreate their former way of life as soon as possible. Women were often reluctant to migrate in the first place, and when they arrived in new areas, they strove valiantly to recapture the comfort and stability that they had left behind.

New Englanders carried with them their churches, schools, notions of community uplift, and Puritan ideals of hard work and self-denial. Similarly, settlers from Virginia and the Carolinas retained their devotion to family honor, personal independence, and ideas of white supremacy. In the West, differences between the North and South soon emerged.

In general, the pioneers sought out the kind of terrain and soil with which they were already familiar. People from the eastern uplands favored the hill country of the West. Piedmont and tidewater farmers and planters usually made for the lower and flatter areas. Both groups avoided the fertile but unfamiliar prairies. Rather than being the bold and deliberate innovators of myth, the typical agricultural pioneers were deeply averse to changing their traditional habits.

Yet some adjustments were necessary simply to survive under frontier conditions. Initially, at least, a high degree of self-sufficiency was required on isolated homesteads. The settlers built their own homes and raised their own crops; they made their own clothes and manufactured their own household necessities, such as soap and candles.

But this picture of frontier self-reliance is not the whole story. Most settlers in fact found it extremely difficult to accomplish all the tasks using only family labor. A more common practice was the sharing of work by a number of pi-

The log cabin and split-rail fence of this typical frontier farmstead were cut from trees on the land. Other nearby trees have been burned to clear the land for farming.

oneer families. Assembling the neighbors to raise a house, harvest wheat, or sew quilts helped turn collective work into a rare festive occasion. The jug was passed, and various contests sped the work along. Sharing the work was a creative response to the shortage of labor that also provided a source for communal solidarity. These events probably tell us more about the "spirit of the frontier" than the conventional image of the pioneer as a lonely individualist.

Restlessness and geographic mobility also characterized many of these settlers. The wandering of young Abraham Lincoln's family from Kentucky to Indiana and finally to Illinois between 1816 and 1830 was fairly typical. Improved land could be sold at a profit and the proceeds used to buy new acreage beyond the horizon where the soil was reportedly richer. Hence few early-nineteenth-century American farmers developed the kind of attachment to the land that is often associated with rural populations in other parts of the world.

Transportation and the Market Economy

It took more than the spread of settlement to bring prosperity to new areas and ensure that they would identify with older regions or with the country as a whole. Along the eastern seaboard land transportation was so primitive that in 1813 it took seventy-five days for one wagon of goods drawn by four horses to make a trip of about a thousand miles, and traveling west over the mountains meant months on the trail.

After the War of 1812 political leaders realized that national security, economic progress, and political unity were all more or less dependent on binding the nation together through a greatly improved transportation network. Accordingly, President Monroe called for a federally supported program of "internal improvements" in 1815. In the ensuing decades, the nationalist's vision of a transportation revolution was realized to a considerable extent, although the direct role of the federal government turned out to be less important than anticipated.

A Revolution in Transportation: Roads and Steamboats

Americans who wished to get from place to place rapidly and cheaply needed new and improved roads. The first great federal transportation project was the building between 1811 and 1818 of the National Road between Cumberland, Maryland, on the Potomac, and Wheeling, Virginia, on the Ohio. This impressive, gravel-surfaced toll road was subsequently extended and reached Vandalia, Illinois, in 1838. Soon state governments promoted the building of other "turnpikes," as these privately owned toll roads chartered by the states were called. By about 1825 southern New England, upstate New York, much of Pennsylvania, and northern New Jersey were crisscrossed by thousands of miles of turnpikes.

But the toll roads benefited travelers more than they did transporters of bulky freight. The latter usually found that total expenses—toll plus the cost and maintenance of heavy wagons and great teams of horses—were too high to guarantee a satisfactory profit from haulage. Hence, traffic was less than anticipated, and investors were disappointed with returns. In the final analysis, turnpikes failed to link up the settled seaboard areas with the new West. What was desperately needed was a form of transportation that could inexpensively haul freight over long distance.

The fact that the United States had a great natural transportation system in its river network was one of the most significant reasons for the country's rapid economic development. The Ohio-Mississippi system in particular provided ready access to the rich agricultural areas of the interior and a natural outlet for their products. By 1815, flatboats loaded with wheat, flour, salt pork, and cotton were floating toward New Orleans. Even after the coming of the steamboat, flatboats continued to carry a major share of the downriver trade.

But the flatboat trade was necessarily a one-way traffic. A farmer from Ohio or Illinois, or someone hired to do the job, could float down to New Orleans easily enough, but there was generally no way to get back except by walking overland through rough country. Until the problem of upriver navigation was solved, the Ohio-Mississippi could not carry the manufactured goods that farmers desired in exchange for their crops.

Fortunately, a solution was readily at hand—the use of steam power for river transportation. Inventor Robert Fulton improved upon an idea that many men had toyed with for years. In 1807 he successfully propelled the *Clermont* 150 miles up the Hudson River. The first steamboat launched in the West was the *New Orleans*, which made the trip from Pittsburgh to New Orleans in 1811–1812. The steamboat revolutionized the commerce of the West. By 1820, sixty-nine steamboats with a total tonnage of 13,890 were plying western waters.

Steam transport was a great boon for farmers and merchants. It reduced costs, increased the speed of moving goods and people, and allowed a two-way commerce on the Mississippi and Ohio. Eastern manufacturers and merchants were now much more firmly linked to the interior markets.

The steamboat quickly captured the American imagination. The great paddle wheelers became luxurious floating hotels, the natural habitats of gamblers and confidence men. But the boats also had a lamentable safety record, frequently running aground, colliding, or blowing up. As a result of such accidents, the federal government began in 1838 to regulate steamboats and monitor their construction and operation. This legislation stands as the only instance in the pre-Civil War period of direct federal regulation of domestic transportation.

THE CANAL BOOM

A transportation system based solely on rivers and roads had one enormous gap—it did not provide an economical way to ship western

Man-made canals temporarily filled the gap in a developing transportation system of rivers and roads. This scene of the junction of the Erie and Northern canals (c. 1835) shows mules walking alongside the canal towing barges. The locks are seen in the background.

farm produce directly east to the growing urban market of the seaboard states. The solution offered by the politicians and merchants of the Middle Atlantic and Midwestern states was to build a system of canals to link seaboard cities directly to the Great Lakes, the Ohio, and ultimately the Mississippi.

The best natural location for a canal between a river flowing into the Atlantic and one of the Great Lakes was between Albany and Buffalo, a relatively flat stretch of 364 miles. When the New York legislature approved of the bold project in 1817, no more than about 100 miles of canal existed in the entire United States. Credit for the enterprise belongs to New York's governor, De Witt Clinton, who convinced the state legislature that the project could be successfully financed by issuing bonds. In 1825 the entire canal was opened with great public acclaim and celebration.

At 364 miles long, 40 feet wide, 4 feet deep, and containing 84 locks, the Erie Canal was the most spectacular engineering achievement of the young Republic. Furthermore, it was a great economic success. It reduced the cost of moving goods from Buffalo to Albany to one twelfth the previous rate. Easterners and Westerners could now buy each other's goods at a sharply reduced rate. The canal also helped to make New York City the unchallenged commercial capital of the nation.

The great success of the Erie Canal inspired other states to extend public credit for canal building. Between 1826 and 1834, Pennsylvania constructed an even longer and more elaborate canal, covering the 395 miles from Philadelphia to Pittsburgh. But the Pennsylvania Main Line Canal did not do as well as the Erie, partly because of the bottleneck that developed at the crest of the Alleghenies, where canal boats had to be hauled over a high ridge on an inclined-plane railroad. Other states followed suit, and the nation's rivers and lakes were linked by an elaborate canal network.

The canal boom ended when it became apparent in the 1830s and 1840s that most of these waterways were unprofitable. State credit had been overextended, and the panic and de-pression of the late 1830s and early 1840s forced retrenchment. Moreover, by this time railroads were beginning to compete successfully for the same traffic, and a new phase in the transportation revolution was beginning.

But canals should not be written off as economic failures that contributed little to the improvement of transportation. Some of them continued to be important arteries up to the time of the Civil War and well beyond. Furthermore, the failure of many of the canals was due solely to their inability to yield an adequate return on the money invested in them. This problem of financing tells us little or nothing about their public usefulness. Had the canals been thought of as providing a service rather than yielding a profit—in the manner, for example, of modern interstate highways—they might have maintained a high reputation for serving the economic interests of the nation. As it was, they contributed enormously to creating vital economic ties between the agricultural West and the industrializing Northeast.

EMERGENCE OF A MARKET ECONOMY

The desire to reduce the costs and increase the speed of shipping heavy freight over great distances laid the groundwork for a new economic system. With the advent of steamboats and canals, Western farmers could inexpensively ship their crops both to the Northeast and New Orleans. This improved transport led to an increase in farm income and provided a stimulus for commercial agriculture.

At the beginning of the nineteenth century, the typical farming household consumed most of what it produced and sold only a small surplus in nearby markets. Most manufactured articles were produced at home. Easier and cheaper access to distant markets caused a decisive change in this pattern. Between 1800 and 1840, agricultural output increased remarkably. The rise in productivity was partly due to technological advances. Iron or steel plows proved better than wooden ones, the grain cradle replaced the scythe, and better varieties of crops, grasses, and livestock were introduced. But the availability of good land and the revolution in marketing were the most important spurs to profitable commercial farming. Transportation facilities made distant markets available and plugged farmers into a commercial network that provided credit and relieved them of the need to do their own selling.

The emerging exchange network encouraged a movement away from diversified farming and toward regional concentration on staple crops. Wheat was the main cash crop in the North, and the center of its cultivation moved westward as soil depletion, pests, and plant disease lowered yields in older regions. On the rocky hillsides of New England, sheep raising was displacing the mixed farming of an earlier era. But the prime example of successful staple production in this era was the rise of the cotton kingdom in the South.

A number of factors made the South the world's greatest producer of cotton. First was the great demand generated by the rise of textile manufacturing in England and, to a lesser extent, in New England. Second was the effect of the cotton gin in processing. Invented by Eli Whitney in 1793, this simple device cut the labor costs involved in cleaning short-staple cotton. Third was the availability of good land in the Southeast. Similar to the movement of the center of wheat cultivation in the North, the center of cotton growing moved steadily west from mainly South Carolina and Georgia toward the fertile plantation areas of Alabama, Mississippi, and Louisiana.

A fourth factor—the existence of slavery, which provided a flexible system of forced labor—permitted operations on a scale impossible for the family labor system of the agricultural North. Finally, the cotton economy benefitted from the South's splendid natural transportation system, its great network of navigable rivers. The South had less need than other agricultural regions for artificial "internal improvements" such as canals and good roads. Planters could simply establish themselves on or near a river and ship their crops to market via natural waterways.

COMMERCE AND BANKING

As regions specialized in the growing of commercial crops, a new system of marketing emerged. During an early or pioneer stage in many areas, farmers did their marketing personally. With the growth of country towns, local merchants took over the crop near the source, bartering clothing and other manufactured goods for produce. These intermediaries shipped the farmers' crops to larger local markets such as Pittsburgh, Cincinnati, and St. Louis. Cotton growers in the South were more likely to deal directly with factors or agents in the port cities from which their crop was exported. But even in the South, intermediaries existed in such inland towns as Macon, Nashville, and Shreveport.

The extension of credit was a crucial element in the whole system. Farmers borrowed from local merchants, who received an advance of their own when they consigned the crop to a commission house or factor. The commission agents relied on credit from merchants or manufacturers at the ultimate destination, which might be Liverpool or New York City. The need for credit encouraged the growth of money and banking.

Before the revolutions in transportation and marketing, small-scale local economies could survive to a considerable extent on barter. But long-distance transactions involving credit and deferred payment required money and lots of it. Although the Constitution authorized only the federal government to issue money, in the early-to-mid-nineteenth century the government printed no paper money and produced gold and silver coins in such inappreciable quantities that it utterly failed to meet the expanding economy's requirement for a circulating currency.

Private or state banking institutions filled the void by issuing bank notes, promises to redeem their paper in *specie*—gold or silver—on the bearer's demand. The demand for money and credit during the economic boom after 1815 led to a vast increase in the number of state banks—from 88 to 208 in two years. The resulting flood of state bank notes caused this form of currency to depreciate well below its face value and threatened a runaway inflation. In an effort to stabilize the currency, Congress established a second Bank of the United States in 1816.

Whenever the national bank tried to enforce tight money policies by requiring that banks have adequate specie reserves to back their notes, state banks in the South and West—where national bank notes were scarce and the demand for credit was high—resisted vigorously. The result was a running battle between state and private banks and the national bank. The state banks were not as irresponsible or as out of tune with the real economic needs of their regions as they are often pictured as being. Their notes may have circulated at less than face value, but they nevertheless met a genuine need for currency and credit.

EARLY INDUSTRIALISM

The growth of a market economy also created new opportunities for industrialists. In 1815 most manufacturing in the United States was carried on in households, in the workshops of skilled artisans, or in small mills. The factory form of production, in which supervised workers tended or operated machines under one roof, was rare. Even in the American textile industry, most of the spinning of thread and weaving, cutting, and sewing of cloth was still done by women working at home.

Most of the clothing worn by Americans was made entirely in households by female family members. But a growing proportion was produced for market, rather than direct home consumption. Under the "putting-out system" of manufacturing, merchant capitalists provided raw material to people in their own homes, picked up the finished or semifinished products, paid the workers, and took charge of distribution. The putting-out system was centered in the Northeast, and besides textiles, such items as shoes and hats were made in this manner.

The making of articles that required greater skill was mostly carried on by artisans working in small shops in towns. But in the decades after 1815, the merchants who purchased from these workers gained greater control over production. Shops expanded in size, masters tended to become entrepreneurs rather than working artisans, and journeymen often became wage earners rather than aspiring masters. At the same time, the growing market for low-priced goods led to a stress on speed, quantity, and standardization of the methods of production.

A fully developed factory system emerged first in textile manufacturing. The establishment of the first cotton mills utilizing the power loom as well as spinning machinery—thus making it possible to turn fiber into cloth in a single factory—resulted from the efforts of a trio of Boston merchants, Francis Cabot Lowell, Nathan Appleton, and Patrick Tracy Jackson.

Under the name of the Boston Manufacturing Company, the associates began their Waltham operation in 1813. Their phenomenal success led to the erection of larger and even more profitable mills. The mill at Lowell became a great showplace for early American industrialization. Its large and seemingly contented work force of unmarried women residing in supervised dormitories, its unprecedented scale of operation, its successful mechanization of almost every stage of production— all captured the American middle-class imagination in the 1820s and 1830s. Other mills using similar methods sprang up throughout New England, and the region became the first important manufacturing area in the United States.

The shift away from the putting-out system to factory production changed the course of capitalistic activity in the region. Before the 1820s, New England merchants concentrated mainly on international trade. A major source of capital was the lucrative China trade carried on by fast, well-built New England vessels. When the success of Waltham and Lowell became clear, many merchants shifted their capital away from oceanic trade and into manufacturing. Politically, this change meant that representatives from New England no longer advocated a low tariff that favored exporters over importers. They now became leading proponents of a high duty rate designed to protect manufacturers from foreign competition.

The development of other "infant industries" of the postwar period was less dramatic and would not come to fruition until the 1840s and 1850s. But the first stirring of an iron industry and a small arms industry was felt during this period. And although most manufacturing was centered in the Northeast, the West also experienced modest industrial progress as the number and size of facilities such as grist mills, slaughterhouses, and tanneries increased. Distilleries in Kentucky and Ohio were particularly active.

One should not assume, however, that America had already experienced an industrial revolution by 1840. Most of the nation's labor force was still employed in agriculture; less than one out of every ten workers was directly involved in factory production. The revolution that did occur during these years was essentially one of distribution rather than production. The growth of a market economy of national scope was the principal economic development of this period. And it was one that had vast repercussions for all aspects of American life.

THE POLITICS OF NATION BUILDING AFTER THE WAR OF 1812

Geographic expansion, economic growth, and the changes in American life that accompanied them were bound in the long run to generate political controversy. Federal and state policies meant to encourage or control growth and expansion did not benefit farmers, merchants, manufacturers, and laborers equally. Conflicts inevitably arose. Northerners, Southerners, and Westerners were affected in different ways, too. But the temporary lack of a party system meant that politicians did not have to band together and offer the voters a choice of programs and ideologies. A myth of national harmony

prevailed, culminating in the "Era of Good Feelings" during James Monroe's two terms as president.

Behind the facade, individuals and groups fought for advantage, as always, but without the public accountability and need for broad popular approval that a party system would have required. As a result, popular interest in national politics fell to a low ebb.

The absence of party discipline and programs did not completely immobilize the federal government. The president took important initiatives in foreign policy; Congress legislated on matters of national concern; and the Supreme Court made far-reaching decisions. The common theme of the public policies that emerged between the War of 1812 and the Age of Jackson was an awakening nationalism—a sense of American pride and purpose that reflected the events of the period.

THE REPUBLICANS IN POWER

By the end of the War of 1812, the Federalist party was no longer a significant force in national politics, although the Republican party had adopted some of their rival's policies. Retreating from their original philosophy of states' rights and limited government, Republican party leaders now openly embraced a national bank, a protective tariff for industry, and a program of federally financed internal improvements.

In Congress, Henry Clay of Kentucky took the lead in advocating that the government take action to promote economic development. The keystone of what Clay called the "American system" was a high protective tariff to stimulate industrial growth and provide a "home market" for the farmers of the West, making the nation economically self-sufficient and free from a dangerous dependence on Europe.

In 1816 Congress took the first step toward Clay's goal by passing a tariff that raised import duties an average of 20 percent. The tariff was passed to protect American industry from British competition and received patriotic support in all sections of the country. Americans viewed the act as a move toward economic independence, a necessity to protect political independence.

Later the same year, Congress voted to establish the second Bank of the United States. Organized much like the first bank, it was a mixed public-private institution. The Bank served the government by providing a depository for its funds, an outlet for marketing its securities, and a source of redeemable bank notes that could be used for the payment of taxes or the purchase of public lands. The bank bill was opposed by state banking interests and strict constructionists, but the majority of Congress found it a necessary and proper means of promoting financial stability and meeting the constitutional responsibilities of federal government to raise money from taxation and loans.

Legislation dealing with internal improvements made less headway in Congress. Except for the National Road, the federal government undertook no major transportation projects during the Madison and Monroe administrations. Both presidents believed that internal improvements were desirable but that a constitutional amendment was required before federal monies could legally be used for the building of roads and canals within individual states. Both men vetoed internal improvement bills. Consequently, public aid for the building of roads and canals continued to come almost exclusively from state and local governments.

MONROE AS PRESIDENT

As had Jefferson before him, President Madison chose his own successor in 1816. James Monroe thus became the third successive Virginian to occupy the White House for a full two terms. Experienced, but stolid and unimaginative, he lacked the intellectual depth and agility of his predecessors, but he was reliable, dignified, and high-principled.

The keynote of Monroe's presidency was national harmony, which meant that he went out of his way to avoid controversy. Indeed, one newspaper writer announced that party strife was a thing of the past and that an "era of good feelings" had begun. The principal aim of Monroe's administrations was to see that these good feelings persisted. He wanted to end all sectional and economic differences and assert American power and influence on the world stage. His choice of a cabinet was well calculated to serve these purposes. His secretary of state, John Quincy Adams, was not only a diplomat of great experience and skill but also a New Englander. If recent precedent was to be followed, he would succeed Monroe as president and thus end the "Virginia dynasty." As secretary of war, Monroe chose John C. Calhoun, a leading Southerner who was at this time a fervent nationalist. To accommodate the old-line states' rights wing of the party, he appointed William C. Crawford of Georgia as secretary of the treasury.

The first challenge to Monroe's hopes for domestic peace and prosperity was the Panic of 1819, which ended the postwar boom. After a period of rampant inflation, easy credit, and massive land speculation, the Bank of the United States called in loans and demanded the immediate redemption in specie of the state bank notes in its possession. This retrenchment brought a drastic downturn in the economy, as prices fell sharply, businesses failed, and banks repossessed land bought on credit.

Congress responded slowly and weakly to the economic crisis. Monroe himself refused to exert strong leadership. He was able to remain above the battle and persuade the American public that he was in no way responsible for the state of the economy nor was he in a position to do anything about it. Unlike a modern president, Monroe could retain his full popularity during hard times.

Monroe prized national harmony even more than economic prosperity. But during his first administration a bitter controversy developed between the North and the South over the admission of Missouri to the Union. Once again Monroe remained above the battle and suffered little damage to his own prestige. It was left entirely to Congress to deal with the nation's most serious domestic political crisis between the War of 1812 and the late 1840s.

THE MISSOURI COMPROMISE

In 1817, the Missouri territorial assembly applied for statehood. It was clear that Missouri expected to be admitted into the Union as a slave state. Since Missouri was the first state, other than Louisiana, to be carved out of the Louisiana Purchase, the resolution of the status of slaves there would have implications for the rest of the trans-Mississippi West.

When the question came before Congress in early 1819, submerged sectional fears and anxieties came bubbling to the surface. Many Northerners resented southern control of the presidency and the three-fifths clause of the Constitution. Southerners feared for the future of what they regarded as a necessary balance of power between the sections. Up until 1819 a strict equality had been maintained by alternately admitting slave and free states. Because the North had a decisive majority in the House of Representatives, the South saw its equal vote in the Senate as essential for preservation of the balance.

In February 1819, Congressman James Tallmadge of New York introduced an amendment to the statehood bill banning further introduction of slaves into Missouri and providing for the gradual emancipation of those already there. The amendment was approved by the House but voted down by the Senate. The issue remained unresolved until a new Congress convened in December 1819. In the meantime, the measure elicited hot debate. Southern senators saw the Tallmadge amendment as an attack on the principle of equality between the states—a Northern ploy to upset the balance of power.

A separate statehood petition from the people of Maine suggested a way out of the impasse. In February 1820, the Senate voted to couple the admission of Missouri as a slave state with the admission of Maine as a free state. A further amendment was also passed

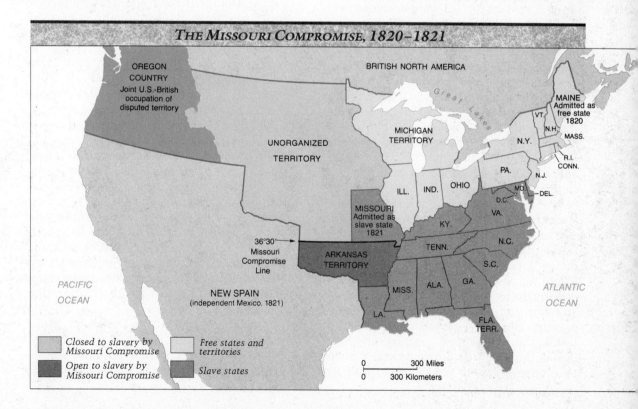

THE MISSOURI COMPROMISE, 1820–1821

OREGON COUNTRY
Joint U.S.-British occupation of disputed territory

BRITISH NORTH AMERICA

Great Lakes

MAINE
Admitted as free state 1820

UNORGANIZED TERRITORY

MICHIGAN TERRITORY

VT
N.H.
MASS.
N.Y.
R.I.
CONN.
PA.
N.J.

ILL. IND. OHIO

MD.
D.C.
DEL.

MISSOURI
Admitted as slave state 1821

VA.

KY.

36°30'
Missouri Compromise Line

ARKANSAS TERRITORY

TENN.

N.C.

S.C.

PACIFIC OCEAN

NEW SPAIN
(independent Mexico, 1821)

MISS. ALA. GA.

LA.

ATLANTIC OCEAN

FLA. TERR.

Closed to slavery by Missouri Compromise

Open to slavery by Missouri Compromise

Free states and territories

Slave states

0   300 Miles
0   300 Kilometers

prohibiting slavery in the rest of the Louisiana Purchase north of the southern border of Missouri, or above the latitude of 36° 30'. The Senate's compromise then went back to the House where Henry Clay—who broke the proposal into three separate bills—adroitly maneuvered it through to narrow victory.

A major sectional crisis had been resolved. But the Missouri affair had ominous overtones for the future of North–South relations. Thomas Jefferson described the controversy as "a fire bell in the night," threatening the peace of the Union. Clearly, the subject of slavery or its extension aroused deep sectional feeling. Emotional rhetoric about morality and fundamental rights issued from both sides. If the United States were to acquire any new territories in which the status of slavery had to be determined by Congress, renewed sectional strife would be inevitable.

POSTWAR NATIONALISM AND THE SUPREME COURT

While the Monroe administration was proclaiming national harmony and congressional leaders were struggling to reconcile sectional differences, the Supreme Court was making a more substantial and enduring contribution to the growth of nationalism and a strong federal government, thanks to Chief Justice John Marshall. A Virginian, a Federalist, and a devoted disciple of George Washington, Marshall served as chief justice from 1801 to 1835, and during that entire period he dominated the Court as no other chief justice has ever done.

As the author of most of the major opinions issued by the Supreme Court during its formative period, Marshall gave shape to the Constitution and clarified the crucial role of the Court in the American system of government. He placed the protection of individual liberty, especially the right to acquire property, above the attainment of political, social, and economic equality. Ultimately he was a nationalist, believing that the strength, security, and happiness of the American people depended mainly on economic growth and the creation of new wealth. As he saw it, the Constitution existed to provide the political ground rules for a society of industrious and productive individuals who could enrich themselves while adding to the strength of the nation as a whole.

The role of the Supreme Court, in Marshall's view, was to interpret and enforce these ground rules, especially against the efforts of state legislatures to interfere with the constitutionally protected rights of individuals or combinations of individuals to acquire property through productive activity. The Court also permitted the federal government to assume broad powers so that it could fulfill its constitutional responsibility to promote the general welfare by encouraging economic development and national prosperity.

In a series of major decisions between 1819 and 1824, the Marshall Court enhanced the power of the judicial branch and used the contract clause of the Constitution (which prohibited a state from passing a law "impairing the obligations of contracts") to limit the power of state legislatures. It also strengthened the federal government by sanctioning a broad or loose construction of its constitutional powers and by clearly affirming its supremacy over the states.

In *Dartmouth College* v. *Woodward* (1819) the Marshall Court made the far-reaching determination that any charter granted by a state to a private corporation was fully protected by the contract clause. In practical terms, the Court's ruling in the Dartmouth case meant that the kind of business enterprises then being incorporated by state governments—such as turnpike or canal companies and textile manufacturing firms—could hold on indefinitely to any privileges or favors that had been granted in their original charters. The decision therefore increased the power and independence of business corporations by weakening the ability of the states to regulate them or withdraw their privileges.

About a month after the Dartmouth ruling, in March 1819, the Marshall Court handed down its most important decision. In *McCulloch* v. *Maryland* the Court ruled that a

Maryland tax on the Bank of the United States was unconstitutional. The two main issues were whether Congress had the right to establish a national bank and whether a state had the power to tax or regulate an agency or institution created by Congress.

In response to the first question, Marshall set forth his doctrine of "implied powers," that the federal government could assume powers that helped it fulfill the "great object" for which it had been founded. Marshall thus struck a blow for "loose construction" of the Constitution. In answer to the second question, Marshall held that if a state had the power to tax a federal agency, it would also have the power to destroy it. Shot through the decision was the belief that the American people "did not design to make this government dependent on the states." In the continuing debate between states' righters and nationalists, the Marshall Court came down firmly on the side of the nationalists.

In *Gibbons* v. *Ogden* (1824) a steamboat monopoly granted by the state of New York was challenged by a competing ferry service. The Supreme Court declared the New York grant unconstitutional in a move that further broadened the power of the federal government at the expense of the states by bolstering the right of Congress to regulate interstate commerce. At the same time, the Court encouraged the growth of a national market economy. The actions of the Supreme Court provide the clearest and most consistent example of the main nationalistic trends of the postwar period—the acknowledgment of the federal government's major role in promoting the growth of a powerful and prosperous America and the rise of a nationwide capitalistic economy.

NATIONALISM IN FOREIGN POLICY: THE MONROE DOCTRINE

The new spirit of nationalism was also reflected in foreign affairs. The main diplomatic challenge facing Monroe after his reelection in 1820 was how to respond to the successful revolt of most of Spain's Latin American colonies after the Napoleonic wars. Henry Clay and many other Americans favored immediate recognition of the new republics, believing that their neighbors to the south were simply following the example of the United States in its own struggle for independence.

CHRONOLOGY

1813	Boston Manufacturing Company founds cotton mill at Waltham, Massachusetts
1815	War of 1812 ends
1816	James Monroe elected president
1819	Supreme Court hands down far-reaching decision in Dartmouth College case and in *McCulloch* v. *Maryland*
	Adams-Onís Treaty cedes Spanish territory to the United States
	Financial panic is followed by a depression lasting until 1823
1820	Missouri Compromise resolves nation's first sectional crisis
	Monroe reelected president unanimously
1823	Monroe Doctrine proclaimed
1824	Lafayette revisits the United States
	Supreme Court decides *Gibbons* v. *Ogden*
1825	Erie Canal completed; Canal Era begins

Before 1822, the administration struck a policy of neutrality. But Congress clamored for recognition. Starting in 1822 Monroe reversed his position, and during the next four years the United States officially recognized Mexico, Colombia, Chile, Argentina, Brazil, the Federation of Central American States, and Peru.

Recognizing the republics put the United States on a possible collision course with the major European powers. In 1822 Austria, Prussia, Russia, and France met in Verona and formed the "Grand Alliance," a reactionary union committed to rolling back the tides of liberalism, self-government, and national self-determination that had arisen during the French Revolution and its Napoleonic aftermath. Although the Grand Alliance did not undertake direct intervention in Latin America, it did give France the green light to invade Spain and, if so disposed, to reconquer the empire. Both Great Britain and the United States were alarmed by this prospect.

American policymakers were particularly troubled by Tsar Alexander I, who was attempting to extend Russian claims on the Pacific coast of North America south to the fifty-first parallel—into the Oregon country that the United States wanted for itself. The Russian threat weighed heavily on the mind of Secretary of State Adams as he formulated foreign policy during Monroe's second term.

The threat from the Grand Alliance forced America to move closer to Great Britain, which for trading reasons favored independent Latin American countries. In August 1823 the British foreign secretary George Canning broached the possibility of joint Anglo-American action against the designs of the Alliance to the U.S. minister to Great Britain. Monroe, as well as former presidents Jefferson and Madison, welcomed the suggestion and favored open cooperation with the British.

Secretary of State Adams, however, favored a different approach. He believed that the national interest would best be served by avoiding all entanglement in European politics while at the same time discouraging European intervention in the Americas. In addition, political ambition motivated Adams, and he did not want to be labeled pro-British. He therefore advocated unilateral action by the United States rather than some kind of joint declaration with the British.

In the end, Adams managed to swing Monroe around to his viewpoint. In his annual message to Congress on December 2, 1823, Monroe included a far-reaching statement on foreign policy that was actually written mainly by Adams. What came to be known as the Monroe Doctrine solemnly declared that the United States opposed any further colonization in the Americas or any effort by European nations to extend their political systems outside of their own hemisphere. In return, the United States pledged not to involve itself in the internal affairs of Europe or to take part in European wars.

Although the Monroe Doctrine made little impression on the great powers of Europe at the time it was proclaimed, it signified the rise of a new sense of independence and self-confidence in American attitudes toward the Old World. The Doctrine also reflected the inward-looking nationalism that had arisen after the War of 1812.

The Monroe Doctrine was the capstone of an era that celebrated American strength, prosperity, and independence. Self-satisfaction, geographic expansion, and genuine economic achievement were the keynotes of the age. The wider world was receding from view, but as Americans shifted their attention to internal matters the spirit of harmony and consensus that President Monroe had tried to call forth could not sustain itself. Ahead lay economic competition and political conflict. To a considerable extent these controversies involved the fruits of "progress"—the question of who would reap the benefits or pay the price—of a growing economy and a changing society.

The Era of Good Feelings turned out to be a passing phase and something of an illusion. The idea that an elite of nonpartisan statesmen could define common purposes and harmonize competing elements—the concept of leadership embodied in Monroe and Adams—would no longer be viable in the more contentious and democratic America of the Jacksonian era. Increasingly, the power of "the common man" and sectionalism would shape national debates and policy.

❧ RECOMMENDED READING

The standard surveys of the period between the War of 1812 and the Age of Jackson are two works by George Dangerfield—*The Era of Good Feelings* (1952) and *Awakening of American Nationalism, 1815–1828* (1965). For general accounts of the westward movement, see Ray A. Billington, *Westward Expansion* (1974), and Malcolm J. Rohrbough, *The Trans-Appalachian Frontier* (1978). On the removal of Native Americans, see Francis P. Prucha, *American Indian Policy in the Formative Years* (1962), and Dale Van Every, *Disinherited: The Lost Birthright of the American Indian* (1966). Insights into social, cultural, and economic life of settlers in the frontier areas can be derived from Frank Owsley, *Plain Folk of the Old South* (1948), and Allen G. Bogue, *From Prairie to Corn Belt* (1963). On the exploration of the trans-Mississippi West, see William H. Goetzmann, *Exploration and Empire* (1966). On popular and literary images of the West and the frontier, see Henry Nash Smith, *Virgin Land: The American West as Symbol and Myth* (1950), and Richard Slotkin, *The Fatal Environment: The Myth of the Frontier in the Age of Industrialization* (1985).

Outstanding studies of economic transformation are George R. Taylor, *The Transportation Revolution, 1815–1860* (1951), and Stuart Bruchey, *Growth of the American Economy* (1975). On the development of internal waterways, see Carter Goodrich, *Government Promotion of American Canals and Railroads* (1960), and Harry N. Scheiber, *Ohio Canal Era* (1969). Agricultural development is treated in Paul W. Gates, *The Farmer's Age: Agriculture, 1815–1860* (1960). On the early growth of manufacturing see Peter Termin, *Iron and Steel in Nineteenth-Century America* (1964); H. J. Habakkuk, *American and British Technology in the Nineteenth Century* (1962); and David J. Jeremy, *Transatlantic Industrial Revolution* (1981).

Insight into the politics of postwar nationalism can be derived from Shaw Livermore, Jr., *The Twilight of Federalism* (1962), and James S. Young, *The Washington Community, 1800–1828* (1966). The Marshall Court and legal-constitutional developments are covered in Robert K. Faulkner, *The Jurisprudence of John Marshall* (1968), and Morton J. Horwitz, *The Transformation of American Law, 1780–1860* (1977).

On diplomacy and the Monroe Doctrine, see Samuel F. Bemis, *John Quincy Adams and the Foundations of American Foreign Policy*, and Ernest May, *The Making of the Monroe Doctrine* (1976).

10 THE TRIUMPH OF WHITE MEN'S DEMOCRACY

DEMOCRACY IN THEORY AND PRACTICE

JACKSON AND THE POLITICS OF DEMOCRACY

THE BANK WAR AND THE SECOND PARTY SYSTEM

HEYDAY OF THE SECOND PARTY SYSTEM

As the number of travelers, transients, and other Americans on the move in this country increased during the 1820s and 1830s, enterprising businessmen began to erect a new type of hotel to provide lodging, food, and drink on a large scale in the center of many cities. A prototype of the new hotel was the Boston Exchange Hotel with its eight stories and three hundred rooms. The "first-class" hotel became a prominent feature of the American scene— soon every commercial center in the country had a grand hotel or two to brag about.

The "democratic" mingling of the social classes in these new hotels often caused foreigners to view them as "a true reflection of American society." Their very existence showed that people were on the move geographically and socially. Among their patrons were traveling salesmen, ambitious young men seeking to establish themselves in a new city, and restless pursuers of "the main chance" not yet ready to put down roots.

Hotel managers shocked European visitors by failing to enforce traditional social distinctions among their clientele. Under the "American Plan," guests were required to pay for their meals, and everyone, regardless of class, ate at a common table. With two crucial exceptions—unescorted women and people of color—almost anyone who could pay enjoyed the kind of personal service previously available only to a privileged class.

But the hotel culture also revealed some of the limitations of the new era of democratic ideals and aspirations. Blacks and women were excluded or discriminated against, just as they were denied the suffrage at a time when it was being extended to all white males. The genuinely poor simply could not afford to patronize the hotels and were consigned to squalid rooming houses. If the social equality *within* the hotel reflected a decline in traditional rigid class lines, the broad gulf between potential patrons and those who could not pay the rates signaled the growth of inequality based squarely on wealth rather than inherited status.

The hotel life also reflected the emergence of democratic politics. Professional politicians of a new breed, pursuing the votes of a mass electorate, spent much of their time in hotels as they traveled about. Those elected to Congress or a state legislature often lodged and conducted political transactions in hotels. In fact, when Andrew Jackson arrived in Washington to prepare for his administration in 1829, he took residence at the new National Hotel. The hotel was more than a public and "democratic" gathering place; it was also a haven where the rising men of politics and business could find rest and privacy. In its lobbies, salons, and private rooms the spirit of an age was expressing itself.

DEMOCRACY IN THEORY AND PRACTICE

Historians have often viewed Andrew Jackson's coming to power—his election in 1828 and the boisterous "people's" inauguration that followed—as the critical moment when a democratic spirit took possession of American culture and public life. But that oversimplifies a very complex movement. The rise of Jackson took place in an atmosphere of ferment and a changing climate of opinion that turned America in a more democratic direction.

During the 1820s and 1830s the term *democracy* first became generally accepted as a way of describing how American institutions were supposed to work. The Founders had defined democracy as direct rule by the masses of the people; most of them rejected that approach to government because it was at odds with their conception of a well-balanced republic led by a "natural aristocracy." For champions of popular government in the Jacksonian period, however, the people were truly sovereign and could do no wrong. "The voice of the people is the

voice of God" was their clearest expression of principle.

Besides evoking this heightened sense of "popular sovereignty," the democratic impulse seemed to stimulate a process of social leveling. Early Americans had usually assumed that the rich and wellborn should be treated with special respect and recognized as natural leaders of the community and guardians of its culture and values. By the 1830s the disappearance of inherited social ranks and clearly defined aristocracies or privilege groups struck European visitors as the most radical feature of democracy in America. The spirit of deference was dying in America.

"Self-made men" of lowly origins could now rise more readily to positions of power and influence. Exclusiveness and aristocratic pretension were now likely to provoke popular hostility or scorn. But economic equality, in the sense of an equitable sharing of wealth, was not part of the agenda of mainstream Jacksonianism. The watchword was equality of opportunity not equality of rewards.

THE DEMOCRATIC FERMENT

The supremacy of democracy was most obvious in the new politics of universal manhood suffrage and mass political parties. By the 1820s, most states had removed the last remaining barriers to political participation by all white males. This change was not as radical or controversial as it would be later in nineteenth-century Europe; ownership of land was so common in the United States that a general suffrage did not mean that men without property became a voting majority.

Accompanying this broadening of the electorate was a rise in the proportion of public officials who were elected rather than appointed. More and more judges, as well as legislative and executive officeholders, were chosen by the people. As a result, a new style of politicking developed, emphasizing dramatic speeches that played to the voters' fears and concerns.

Skillful and farsighted politicians—like Martin Van Buren in New York—began in the

1820s to build stable statewide political organizations out of what had been loosely organized factions of the Jeffersonian party. Earlier politicians had regarded parties as a threat to republican virtue and had embraced them only as a temporary expedient. But in Van Buren's opinion, regular parties were an effective check on the temptation to abuse power, a tendency deeply planted in the human heart. The major breakthrough in American political thought during the 1820s and 1830s was the idea of a "loyal opposition," ready to capitalize politically on the mistakes or excesses of the "ins," without denying their right to act in the same way when the "ins" became the "outs."

Changes in the method of nominating and electing a president fostered the growth of a two-party system on the national level. By 1828 presidential electors were chosen by popular vote rather than by state legislature in all but two of the twenty-four states. The need to mobilize grass-roots support behind particular candidates required some form of national organization. When national nominating conventions made their appearance in 1831, the choice of candidates became a matter for representative party assemblies rather than congressional caucuses or ad hoc political alliances. These democratic practices generated much more widespread interest in politics. Between 1824 and 1840 the percentage of eligible voters who cast their ballot in presidential elections tripled.

Economic questions dominated the political controversies of the 1820s and 1830s. The Panic of 1819 and the subsequent depression heightened popular interest in government economic policy. Americans advanced several solutions for keeping the economy healthy. Some, especially small farmers, favored a return to a simpler and more "honest" economy without banks, paper money, and the easy credit that encouraged speculation. Others, particularly emerging entrepreneurs, saw salvation in government aid and protection for venture capital. Politicians and eventually political parties responded to these conflicting views.

The party disputes that arose over corporations, traffics, banks, and internal improvements involved more than the direct economic concerns of particular interest groups. They were viewed in the context of republican fears of conspiracy against American liberty and equality. Charges of corruption and impending tyranny were common.

The notion that the American experiment was a fragile one, constantly threatened by power-hungry conspirators, eventually took two principal forms. For Jacksonians, it was "the money power" that endangered the survival of republicanism; for their opponents it was men like Jackson himself—alleged "rabble-rousers" who duped the electorate into ratifying high-handed and tyrannical action contrary to the true interests of the nation.

An object of increasing concern for both sides was the role of the federal government. National Republicans and later the Whigs believed the government should take active steps to foster economic growth; Jacksonians only wanted to eliminate "special privileges." How best to guarantee equality of opportunity—whether by active governmental promotion of commerce and industry or by strict laissez-faire policies—was a hotly debated issue of the period.

For one group of dissenters, democracy took on a more radical meaning. Leaders of the workingmen's parties and trade unions condemned the growing gap between the rich and the poor resulting from early industrialization and the growth of a market economy. Society, in their view, was divided between "producers"—laborers, artisans, farmers, and small business owners who ran their own enterprises—and nonproducing "parasites"—bankers, speculators, and merchant capitalists. Their aim was to give the producers greater control over the fruits of their labor. They advocated such things as abolition of inheritance and a redistribution of land, as well as educational reforms, a ten-hour day, abolition of imprisonment for debt, and a currency system based exclusively on hard money so that workers could no longer be paid in depreciated bank notes.

Northern abolitionists and early proponents of women's rights made another kind of effort to extend the meaning and scope of democracy.

Radical men and women advocated immediate emancipation for slaves and equal rights for blacks and women. But Jacksonian America was too permeated with racism and male chauvinism to listen to such reformers. In some ways, the civil and political status of both blacks and women deteriorated during "the age of the common *man.*" (See Chapter 11.)

DEMOCRACY AND SOCIETY

Although some inequalities persisted or even grew during the age of democracy, they did so in the face of a growing belief that equality was the governing principle of American society. What this meant in practice was that no one could expect special privileges because of family connections. The popular hero was "the self-made man" who had climbed the ladder of success through his own efforts without forgetting his origin.

Except for southern slaveholders, wealthy Americans could not depend on a distinctive social class for domestic service. Instead of keeping "servants," they hired "help"—household workers who sometimes insisted on sharing meals with their employers. No true American was willing to be considered a member of a servant class and those engaged in domestic work considered it a temporary stopgap. Except as a euphemistic substitute for the word *slave,* the term *servant* virtually disappeared from the American vocabulary.

Another sign of equality was the decline of distinctive modes of dress for upper and lower classes. The elaborate periwigs and knee breeches worn by eighteenth-century gentlemen gave way to short hair and pantaloons, a style that was adopted by men of all social classes. Those with a good eye for detail might detect subtle differences in taste or in the quality of materials, but the casual observer could easily conclude that all Americans belonged to a single social class.

Of course Americans were not all of one social class. In fact, inequality based on control of productive resources was increasing during the Jacksonian period. The rise of industrialization was creating a permanent class of landless, low-paid wage earners in America's cities. In the rural areas there was a significant division between successful commercial farmers or planters and those who subsisted on marginal land. Nevertheless, European observers commented upon the fact that all white males were equal before the law and at the polls.

Furthermore, traditional forms of privilege and elitism were indeed under strong attack, as evidenced by changes in the organization and status of the learned professions. State legislatures abolished the licensing requirements for physicians previously administered by local medical societies. As a result, practitioners of unorthodox modes of healing were permitted to compete freely with established medical doctors. The legal profession was similarly opened up to far more people. The result was not always beneficial.

For the clergy, "popular sovereignty" meant that they were increasingly under the thumb of the laity. Ministers had ceased to command respect merely because of their office, and to succeed in their calling, they were forced to develop a more popular and emotional style of preaching. Preachers, as much as politicians, prospered by pleasing the public.

Members of the upper class who could not adapt to the new politics and democratic rhetoric often found themselves stripped of the offices they had once held almost as a matter of right. Denied direct political power, they sought to exert influence through their control of philanthropic and charitable activities. But even in this area, local notables were challenged by national reform movements and philanthropic organizations that employed professional traveling agents and experimented with new forms of mass appeal.

DEMOCRATIC CULTURE

The democratic spirit also found expression in the rise of new forms of literature and art directed at a mass audience. The intonations of individual artists and writers varied considerably. But they all had one thing in common: They were aware that their audience was the broad citizenry of a democratic nation rather than a refined elite.

A mass market for popular literature was made possible by a rise in literacy and a revolution in the technology of printing. An increase in potential readers and a decrease in publishing costs led to a flood of lurid and sentimental novels, some of which became the first American best-sellers. Many of the new sentimental novels were written by and for women. Some female authors implicitly protested against their situation by portraying men in general as tyrannical, unreliable, or cruel and the women these men made miserable as resourceful individualists capable of making their own way. But the standard happy endings sustained the convention that a woman on her own is an unnatural thing, for a virtuous and protective man always turned up and saved the heroine from a truly independent life.

In the theater, melodrama became the dominant genre, involving the inevitable trio of beleaguered heroine, mustachioed villain, and a hero who arrives in the nick of time. Another favorite was the patriotic comedy in which the rustic Yankee foiled the foppish European aristocrat. Men and women of all classes went to the theater, and those in the cheap seats often openly voiced their displeasure with an actor or play.

The spirit of "popular sovereignty" expressed itself less dramatically in the visual arts, but its influence was nonetheless felt. Beginning in the 1830s, painters turned from portraying great events and famous people to the depiction of scenes from everyday life. Democratic genre painting captured the lives of plain folk with skill and understanding. Popular recreation and electioneering activity were common motifs.

Architecture and sculpture reflected the democratic spirit in another mode; they were viewed as civic art forms meant to extol the achievements of the Republic. In the 1820s and 1830s, the classical Greek style with its columned facades was favored for banks, hotels, and private dwellings as well as for public buildings. Similarly, sculpture was intended strictly for public admiration or inspiration, and its principal subjects were the heroes of the Republic.

Serious exponents of a higher culture and a more refined sensibility sought to reach the new public in the hope of elevating its taste or uplifting its morals. The "Brahmin poets" of New England—Henry Wadsworth Longfellow, James Russell Lowell, and Oliver Wendell Holmes—offered lofty sentiments to a receptive middle class; Ralph Waldo Emerson carried his philosophy of spiritual self-reliance to lyceums and lecture halls across the county; and great novelists like Nathaniel Hawthorne and Herman Melville experimented with the popular romantic genres. But the ironic and pessimistic view of life that permeated the fiction of these two authors clashed with the optimism of the age and their work failed to gain a large readership.

The ideal of art for art's sake was utterly alien to the instructional spirit of mid-nineteenth-century American culture. The responsibility of the artist in a democratic society, it was generally assumed, was to contribute to the gen-

With the Natty Bumppo series, James Fenimore Cooper became the first major American writer to use frontier settings and characters.

eral welfare by encouraging virtue and proper sentiments. Only Edgar Allan Poe seemed to fit the European image of romantic genius rebelling against middle-class pieties. The most original of the antebellum poets, Walt Whitman, sought to be a direct mouthpiece for the rising democratic spirit, but his abandonment of traditional verse forms and his freedom in dealing with the sexual side of human nature left him isolated and unappreciated during his most creative years.

JACKSON AND THE POLITICS OF DEMOCRACY

The public figure who came to symbolize the triumph of democracy was Andrew Jackson, although he came out a loser in the presidential election of 1824. His victory four years later, his actions as president, and the great political party that formed around him refashioned national politics in a more democratic mold. It may be an exaggeration to call the whole period from the 1820s to the 1840s "the age of Jackson," but Old Hickory occupied the center of the public stage during much of that turbulent and eventful era.

THE ELECTION OF 1824 AND J. Q. ADAMS' ADMINISTRATION

The election of 1824 was one of the most complicated and controversial in American history. As Monroe's second term ended, the ruling Republican party was in disarray and could not agree on who should succeed to the presidency. The party's congressional caucus chose William Crawford of Georgia, an old-line Jeffersonian. But a majority of congressmen showed their disapproval of this outmoded method of nominating candidates by refusing to attend the caucus. Soon John Quincy Adams, Henry Clay, John C. Calhoun, and Andrew Jackson had their hats in the ring.

Initially Jackson was not given much of a chance. He was a military hero, not a national politician, and few party leaders felt that wartime victories were enough to catapult him into the White House. But after testing the waters, Calhoun withdrew and chose instead to run for vice-president. Then Crawford suffered a debilitating stroke that weakened his chances. These events made Jackson the favorite in the South. He also found favor among those in the North and West who were disenchanted with the economic nationalism of Clay and Adams.

In the election Jackson won a plurality of the electoral votes. But since he lacked the necessary majority, the contest was thrown into the House of Representatives where the legislators were to choose from among the three top candidates. Here Adams emerged victorious over Jackson and Crawford. Clay, who had just missed making the final three, provided the winning margin by persuading his supporters to vote for Adams. When Adams proceeded to appoint Clay as his secretary of state, the Jacksonians charged that a "corrupt bargain" had deprived their favorite of the presidency. Even though the charges were unproven, Adams assumed office under a cloud of suspicion.

Although he was a man of integrity and vision, Adams was an inept politician. He refused to bow to the public antipathy toward nationalistic programs and called for an expansion of governmental activity. Congress, however, had no intention of following Adams' lead.

The new Congress that was elected in 1826 was clearly under the control of men hostile to the administration and favorable to the presidential aspirations of Andrew Jackson. The main business before Congress was the tariff issue. Pressure for greater protection came not only from manufacturers but also from many farmers. The cotton-growing South—the only section where tariffs of all kinds were unpopular—was already safely in the general's camp. In order to gain popularity in the other sections, Jackson tacitly lent his support to the tariff of 1828. This "tariff of abominations" was a congressional grab bag which contained substantial across-the-board increases in duties—gifts

A painting of Andrew Jackson in the heroic style by Thomas Sully. The painting shows the president as the common people saw him.

The most significant of these were Vice-President Calhoun, who now spoke for the militant states' rights sentiment of the South; Senator Martin Van Buren, who dominated New York politics through the political machine known as the Albany Regency; and two Kentucky editors, Francis P. Blair and Amous Kendall, who worked to mobilize opposition to Henry Clay and his "American system" in the West. These men and their followers laid the foundation for the first modern American political party—the Democrats. And from this time on, national parties existed primarily to engage in a contest for the presidency. Without this great prize, there would have been little incentive to create national organizations out of the parties and factions developing in the states.

The election of 1828 saw the birth of a new era of mass democracy. Jackson's supporters made widespread use of such electioneering techniques as huge public rallies, torchlight parades, and lavish barbecues or picnics paid for by the candidate's organization. Personalities and mudslinging dominated the campaign, which reached its low point when Adams' supporters accused Jackson's wife Rachel of bigamy and adultery and Jackson's associates charged that Adams' wife was born out of wedlock.

What gave Jacksonians the edge was their success in portraying their candidate as an authentic man of the people, despite his substantial fortune in land and slaves. They emphasized Jackson's backwoods upbringing, military record, and common sense unclouded by a fancy education. Adams, according to Democratic propagandists, was the exact opposite— an overeducated aristocrat, more at home in the salon and the study than among the plain people. Anti-intellectualism was a potent force, and Adams never really had a chance.

The result had the appearance of a landslide for Old Hickory. But the verdict of the people was not as decisive as the returns might suggest. Although Jackson had piled up massive majorities in some of the slave states, the voters elsewhere divided fairly evenly. Furthermore, it was not clear what kind of a mandate he had won. Most of the politicians in his camp

for all sections save the South. It was not, however, simply a ploy to get Jackson elected; it was in fact an early example of how special interest groups can achieve their goals in democratic politics through a process of legislative bargaining known as logrolling.

JACKSON COMES TO POWER

The campaign of 1828 actually began early in the Adams administration. Resurrecting the corrupt bargain charge, Jackson's supporters began to organize on the state and local level. So successful were their efforts that influential state and regional leaders who had supported other candidates in 1824 now rallied behind Jackson to create a formidable coalition.

favored states' rights and limited government as against the nationalism of Adams and Clay, but the general himself had never taken a clear public stand on such issues as banks, tariffs, and internal improvements. His victory was more a triumph of image and personality than the popular endorsement of a particular set of programs.

Jackson turned out to be one of the most forceful and domineering of American presidents. His most striking character traits were an indomitable will, an intolerance of opposition, and a prickly pride that would not permit him to forgive or forget an insult or supposed act of betrayal. His violent temper had led him to fight a number of duels, and as a soldier his critics claimed he was guilty of using excessive force. His frontier background and military experiences had made him tough and resourceful but had also deprived him of the flexibility normally associated with successful politicians. Yet he generally got what he wanted.

Jackson's presidency commenced with his open endorsement of rotation of officeholders or what his critics called "the spoils system." Although he did not actually depart radically from his predecessors in the degree to which he removed federal officeholders and replaced them with his supporters, he was the first president to defend this practice as a legitimate application of democratic doctrine. He contended that the duties of public officers were simple and that any man of intelligence could readily fill the positions.

Jackson also established a new kind of relationship with his cabinet. Cabinet members became less important than they had been in previous administrations. Old Hickory regarded himself as "the direct representative of the people" and his cabinet as an interchangeable set of administrators whose sole function was to carry out the will of the chief executive. He used his cabinet members more for consultation than for policymaking, and he diluted their influence even further by relying heavily on the advice of an unofficial and confidential set of advisors known as his Kitchen Cabinet.

Midway in his first administration Jackson completely reorganized his cabinet. The apparent cause of this upheaval was the Peggy Eaton affair. Peggy O'Neale Eaton, the daughter of a Washington tavern owner, married Secretary of War John Eaton in 1829. Because of gossip about her moral character, the wives of other cabinet members refused to receive her socially. Jackson became her champion. Eventually all but one of his cabinet members resigned over the incident, and Jackson formed a fresh cabinet. Perhaps the most important consequence of the affair was that Martin Van Buren, although he resigned with the rest, also supported Peggy Eaton, and therefore won Jackson's favor.

INDIAN REMOVAL

The first major policy question facing the Jackson administration concerned the fate of Native Americans. Jackson had long favored removing eastern Indians to lands beyond the Mississippi. His support of removal was no different from the policy of previous administrations. The only real issue was how rapidly and thoroughly the process should be carried out and by what means. At the time of Jackson's election, the states of Georgia, Alabama, and Mississippi were clamoring for quick action.

The greatest obstacle to voluntary relocation, however, was the Cherokee nation, which held land in Georgia, Alabama, North Carolina, and Tennessee. The Cherokees not only refused to move but also had instituted a republican form of government for themselves, achieved literacy in their own language, and made considerable progress toward adopting a settled agrarian way of life similar to that of southern whites. These were obviously not Indians in need of the "civilizing" benefits of the government's program, and missionaries and northeastern philanthropists argued that the Cherokee should be allowed to remain where they were.

The southern states disagreed. Georgia, Alabama, and Mississippi extended their state laws over the Cherokees, moves which defied provisions of the Constitution giving the federal government exclusive jurisdiction over Indian affairs and also violated specific treaties.

Jackson, however, endorsed the state actions. His own attitude was that Indians were children when they did the whites' bidding, and savage beasts when they resisted. In his December 1829 message to Congress he advocated a new and more coercive removal policy. He denied Cherokee autonomy, asserted the primacy of states' rights over Indian rights, and called for the speedy and thorough removal of all eastern Indians to designated areas beyond the Mississippi.

Early in 1830 the president's congressional supporters introduced a bill to implement this policy. The ensuing debate was vigorous and heated, but senators and House members from the South and western border states pushed through the bill. Jackson then moved quickly to conclude the necessary treaties, using the threat of unilateral state action to bludgeon the tribes into submission. In 1832 he condoned Georgia's defiance of a Supreme Court decision (*Worcester* v. *Georgia*) that denied the right of a state to extend its jurisdiction over tribal lands. The fate of the eastern Indians was sealed.

In 1838 a stubbornly resisting majority faction of the Cherokees were rounded up by federal troops and forcibly marched to Oklahoma. This trek—known as the "Trail of Tears"— was made under such harsh conditions that almost a quarter of the Indians died on the way. A ruthless land grab, the Cherokee removal exposed the prejudiced and greedy side of Jacksonian democracy.

THE NULLIFICATION CRISIS

During the 1820s Southerners became increasingly fearful of federal encroachment on the rights of the states. Behind this concern, in South Carolina at least, was a strengthened commitment to the preservation of slavery and a resulting anxiety about possible uses of federal power to strike at the "peculiar institution." Hoping to keep the explosive slavery issue out of the political limelight, South Carolinians seized on another genuine grievance— the protective tariff—as the issue on which to take their stand in favor of a state veto power over federal actions that they viewed as con-

Cherokee Indians, carrying their few possessions, are prodded along by U.S. soldiers on the "Trail of Tears." Several thousand Native Americans died on the ruthless, forced march from their homelands in the East to the newly established Indian Territory in Oklahoma.

trary to their interests. As a staple-producing and exporting region, the South was hurt by any tariff that increased the prices for manufactured goods and threatened to undermine foreign markets by inciting counter-protection.

Vice-President John C. Calhoun emerged as the leader of the states' rights insurgency in South Carolina. After the passage of the "tariff of abominations" in 1828, the state legislature declared the new duties unconstitutional and endorsed a lengthy disquisition—written anonymously by Calhoun—that affirmed the right of an individual state to nullify federal law. However, Calhoun and South Carolina hoped that Jackson would defend their position. In the president's position on Georgia's de facto nullification of federal treaties upholding Indian tribal rights and his veto of a major internal improvement bill (the Maysville Road in Kentucky) based upon a strict interpretation of the Constitution, South Carolinians saw room for hope.

In the meantime, a bitter personal feud developed between Jackson and Calhoun. As Calhoun lost favor with Jackson because of his position on the Eaton affair, it became clear that Van Buren would be Jackson's designated successor. The personal breach between Jackson and Calhoun colored and intensified their confrontation over nullification and the tariff.

But there were also differences of principle. Although generally a defender of states' rights and strict construction of the Constitution, Jackson opposed the theory of nullification as a threat to the survival of the Union. The differences between Jackson and Calhoun came into the open at the Jefferson Day Dinner in 1830, when Jackson offered the toast "Our Union: It must be preserved"; to which Calhoun responded: "The Union: next to Liberty most dear. May we always remember that it can only be preserved by distributing equally (its) benefits and the burdens . . . ."

In 1830 and 1831 the movement against the tariff gained strength in South Carolina. Calhoun resigned as vice-president and openly took the lead. In 1832 Congress passed a new tariff that lowered the rates slightly but retained the principle of protection. Supporters of nullification then succeeded in persuading the South Carolina state legislature to call a special convention. When the convention met in November 1832, the members voted overwhelmingly to nullify the tariffs of 1828 and 1832 and to forbid the collection of customs duties within the state.

Jackson reacted with characteristic decisiveness. He asked Congress to vote him the authority to use the army to enforce the tariff. At the same time, he sought to pacify the nullifiers somewhat by recommending a lower tariff. The Congress responded by enacting the Force Bill—which gave the president the military powers he sought—and the compromise tariff of 1833. Faced with this combination of force and compromise, South Carolina eventually rescinded the nullification ordinance. But to demonstrate that they had not conceded their constitutional position, the convention delegates concluded their deliberations by nullifying the Force Bill.

The nullification crisis revealed that South Carolinians would not tolerate any federal action that seemed contrary to their interests or raised doubts about the institution of slavery. The nullifiers' principle of state sovereignty implied the right of secession as well as the right to declare laws of Congress null and void. Although in many ways Jackson was a proslavery president, some farsighted southern loyalists were alarmed by the Unionist doctrines the president propounded in his proclamation against nullification. More strongly than any previous president, he had asserted that the federal government was supreme over the states and that the Union was indivisible. What was more, he had justified the use of force against states that denied federal authority.

THE BANK WAR AND THE SECOND PARTY SYSTEM

Jackson's most important and controversial use of executive power was his successful attack on the Bank of the United States. "The Bank War" revealed some of the deepest concerns of Jackson and his supporters and expressed their concept of democracy in a dramatic way. It also aroused intense opposition to the president and his policies, an opposition that crystallized in a new national party—the Whigs. The destruction of the Bank and the economic disruption that followed brought to the forefront the issue of the government's relationship to the nation's financial system. Differences on this question helped to sustain the new two-party system and provided the stuff of political controversy during the administration of Jackson's hand-picked successor—Martin Van Buren.

MR. BIDDLE'S BANK

The Bank of the United States had long been embroiled in public controversy. The South and West openly blamed it for the Panic of 1819 and the depression that followed. But after Nicholas Biddle took over the Bank's presidency in 1823, it regained public confidence. Cultured and able, Biddle probably understood the mysteries of banking and currency better than any other American of his generation. But he was arrogant and vain, as sure of his own judgment as Jackson himself.

Old-line Jeffersonians had always opposed the Bank on the grounds that its establishment was unconstitutional and it placed too much power in the hands of a small, privileged group. Its influence on the national economy was tremendous, and because of this, it was a convenient scapegoat for anything that went wrong with the economy. In an era of rising democracy, the most obvious and telling objection to the Bank was simply that it possessed great power and privilege without being under popular control.

THE BANK VETO AND THE ELECTION OF 1832

Jackson came into office with strong reservations about banking and paper money in general. He also harbored suspicions that branches of the Bank of the United States had illicitly used their influence on behalf of his opponent in the presidential election. In his annual messages in 1829 and 1830, he called on Congress to begin discussing ways of reducing the Bank's power.

Biddle began to worry about the fate of the Bank's charter when it came up for renewal in 1836. At the same time, Jackson's Kitchen Cabinet advised him that an attack on the Bank would provide a good party issue for the election of 1832. Biddle then made a fateful blunder. He determined to seek recharter by Congress in 1832, four years ahead of schedule. Senator Henry Clay, leader of the antiadministration forces on Capitol Hill, encouraged this move because he was convinced that Jackson had chosen the unpopular side of the issue. The bill to recharter, therefore, was introduced in the House and Senate in early 1832. It passed Congress with ease.

The next move was Jackson's, and he made the most of the opportunity. He vetoed the bill and defended his action with ringing statements of principle. The Bank was unconstitutional, he said, and even worse because it was a monopoly, it violated the fundamental rights of the people in a democratic society. Jackson believed that the government should guarantee equality of opportunity, not grant privileges that provided special interests with exclusive advantages.

Jackson thus called on the common people to join him fighting the "monster" corporation. His veto message was the first to go beyond strictly constitutional arguments to deal directly with social and economic issues. Congressional attempts to override the veto failed, and Jackson resolved to take the entire issue to the people in the upcoming presidential election, which he viewed as a referendum to decide whether he or the Bank would prevail.

The 1832 election pitted Jackson against Henry Clay, standard-bearer of the National Republicans. The Bank recharter was the major issue. In the end, Jackson won a great personal triumph, garnering 219 electoral votes to 49 for Clay. As far as Old Hickory was concerned, he had his mandate.

KILLING THE BANK

Not content with preventing the Bank from getting a new charter, the victorious Jackson now resolved to attack it directly by removing federal deposits from Biddle's vaults. Jackson told Van Buren, "The bank . . . is trying to kill me, but I will kill it." Old Hickory regarded Biddle's opposition during the presidential race as a personal attack, part of a devious plot to destroy the president's reputation and deny him the popular approval that he deserved. As always, Jackson believed his opponents were not merely wrong but evil besides and deserved to be destroyed. Furthermore, he viewed the election result as his popular mandate to go after the Bank.

In order to remove the deposits from the Bank, Jackson had to overcome strong resistance in his own cabinet. When one secretary of the treasury refused to support the policy, he was shifted to another cabinet post. When a second balked at carrying out removal, he was replaced by Roger B. Taney, a Jackson loyalist and dedicated opponent of the Bank. Beginning in late September 1833, Taney ceased depositing government money in the Bank and began to withdraw the funds already there. The funds were then ill-advisedly placed in selected state banks. Opponents charged that the banks had been chosen for political rather than fiscal reasons and dubbed them Jackson's "pet banks."

The Bank counterattacked by calling in outstanding loans and instituting a policy of credit contraction that helped bring on an economic recession. Biddle hoped to win support for recharter by demonstrating that weakening the Bank's position would be disastrous for the economy. But all he showed, at least to the president's supporters, was that they had been right all along about the Bank's excessive power. With some justice, they blamed the economic distress on Biddle, and the Bank never did regain its charter.

Even more serious than the conflict over the Bank was the strong opposition to Jackson's fiscal policies that developed in Congress. Led by Henry Clay, the Senate approved a motion of censure against Jackson, charging him with exceeding his constitutional authority in removing the deposits. Jacksonians in the House were able to block such action, but the president was further humiliated when the Senate refused to confirm Taney as secretary of the treasury. Anti-Jacksonians were gaining in strength.

EMERGENCE OF THE WHIGS

The coalition that passed the censure resolution in the Senate provided the nucleus for a new national party—the Whigs. The leadership of the new party and a majority of its support came from National Republicans and ex-Federalists. But the Whigs also picked up critical backing from southern proponents of states' rights who had been upset by Jackson's stand on nullification and now saw an unconstitutional abuse of power in his withdrawal of federal deposits from the Bank of the United States. The Whig label was chosen because of its associations with both English and American Revolutionary opposition to royal power and prerogatives; its rallying cry was "executive usurpation" by the tyrannical designs of "King Andrew."

The Whigs also gradually absorbed the Anti-Masonic party, a surprisingly strong northeastern political movement that exploited traditional American fears of secret societies and conspiracies. They also appealed successfully to the moral concerns of the northern middle class under the sway of an emerging evangelical Protestantism. Anti-Masons detested Jacksonianism mainly because it stood for a toleration of diverse life-styles. They believed that the government should restrict such "sinful" behavior as drinking, gambling, and breaking the Sabbath.

As the election of 1836 approached, the government's fiscal policies also provoked a localized rebellion among the urban, working-class elements of the Democratic coalition. This group favored a strict hard-money policy and condemned Jackson's transfer of federal deposits to the state banks as inflationary. Because they wanted working people to be paid in specie rather than inflated bank notes, the "Loco-Focos"—named for the matches they used for illumination when their opponents turned off the gaslights at a party meeting—went beyond opposition to the Bank of the United States and attacked state banks as well. Seeing no basis for cooperation with the Whigs, they established the independent Equal Rights Party and nominated a separate state ticket in 1836.

Jackson himself had hard-money sentiments and probably regarded the "pet banks" solution as a temporary expedient. Nonetheless, in early 1836 he surrendered to congressional pressure and signed legislation allocating surplus federal revenues to the deposit banks, increasing their numbers and weakening federal controls over them. The result was runaway inflation, wild land speculation, and irresponsible printing of paper money. Reacting somewhat belatedly to the speculative mania he had helped to create, Jackson pricked the bubble on July 11, 1836. He issued his "specie circular" requiring that after August 15 only gold and silver would be accepted in payment for public lands. This action served to curb inflation and land speculation but did so in such a sudden and drastic way that it helped precipitate the financial panic of 1837.

THE RISE AND FALL OF VAN BUREN

As his successor, Jackson chose Martin Van Buren, a master of practical politics. The Democratic National Convention of 1835 unanimously confirmed Jackson's choice. Van Buren promised to "tread generally in the footsteps of General Jackson."

The newly created Whig party, reflecting the diversity of its constituency, was unable to decide on a single standard-bearer and chose instead to run three regional candidates—Daniel Webster in the East, William Henry Harrison in the Old Northwest, and Hugh Lawson White in the South. The Whigs hoped to deprive Van Buren of enough electoral votes to throw the election into the House of Representatives where one of the Whigs might stand a chance.

This strategy proved unsuccessful. Van Buren won a clear victory. But the election foreshadowed future trouble for the Democrats, particularly in the South. There the Whigs ran virtually even. The emergence of a two-party-system in the previously solid South resulted from two factors—opposition to some of Jackson's policies and the image of Van Buren as an unreliable Yankee politician.

The main business of Van Buren's administration was to straighten out the financial disorder resulting from the destruction of the Bank of the United States and the issuing of Jackson's specie circular. As he took office Van Buren was immediately faced with a catastrophic depression. The Panic of 1837 was not exclusively, or even primarily, the result of government policies. It was in fact international in scope and reflected some complex changes in the world economy that were beyond the control of American policymakers.

But the Whigs were quick to blame the state of the economy on Jacksonian finance, and the administration had to make a politically effective response. Since Van Buren and his party were committed to a policy of laissez-faire on the federal level, there was little or nothing they could do to relieve economic distress through subsidies or relief measures. But the president could at least try to salvage the federal funds deposited in shaky state banks and devise a new system of public finance that would not contribute to future panics by fueling speculation and credit expansion.

Van Buren's solution was to establish a public depository for government funds with no connections whatsoever to commercial banking. His proposal for an "independent subtreasury" aroused intense opposition from the congressional Whigs, and it was not until 1840 that it was enacted into law. In the meantime the economy had temporarily revived in 1838 only to sink again into a deeper depression the following year.

Van Buren's chances for reelection in 1840 were undoubtedly hurt by the state of the economy. But the principal reason for his defeat was that he lacked the charisma of a Jackson and was thus unable to overcome the extremely ef-

A charismatic leader, a folksy man of the people—that was the image conveyed by the banners the Whig party created for the 1840 campaign of William Henry Harrison, the hero of Tippecanoe.

fective campaign mounted by the Whigs. The Whig party of 1840 was well-organized on a grass roots level, and they found their own Jackson in William Henry Harrison, a military hero of advanced age, who was associated in the public mind with the battle of Tippecanoe and the wining of the West.

Harrison's views on public issues were little known, and the Whigs ran him without a platform to avoid distracting the electorate from his personal qualities. They pretended that Harrison had been born in a log cabin—actually it was a pillared mansion—and that he preferred hard cider to more effete beverages. To balance the ticket and increase its appeal in the South they chose John Tyler of Virginia, a converted states' rights Democrat, to be Harrison's running mate.

Using the slogan, "Tippecanoe and Tyler, Too," the Whigs pulled out all stops in their bid for the White House. Imitating the Jacksonian propaganda against Adams in 1828, they portrayed Van Buren as a luxury-loving aristocrat and compared him with their own homespun candidate. The Democrats tried but were unable to project Van Buren as a man of the peo-

ple. Harrison won, and the Whigs gained control of both houses of Congress.

HEYDAY OF THE SECOND PARTY SYSTEM

America's "second party system" came of age in the election of 1840. The rivalry of Democrats and Whigs made the two-party pattern a permanent feature of the electoral politics in the United States. During the 1840s, the two national parties competed on fairly equal terms for the support of the electorate. Allegiance to one party or the other became an important source of personal identity for many Americans and increased their interest and participation in politics.

In addition to drama and entertainment, the parties offered the voters a real choice of programs and ideologies. Whigs stood for a "positive liberal state," in which the government had the right and duty to subsidize or protect enterprises that could contribute to general prosperity and economic growth. Democrats advocated a "negative liberal state," in which government keeps its hands off the economy.

Conflict over economic issues helped determine each party's base of support. In the Whig camp were most industrialists and merchants, plus a large proportion of those farmers and planters who had adapted successfully to a market economy. Democrats appealed mainly to small farmers, workers, declining gentry, and emerging entrepreneurs who were excluded from the established commercial groups that stood to benefit most from Whig programs. But issues like the tariff could further complicate this pattern; workers in protected industries often voted Whig, while importers normally voted for the Democrats and freer trade.

Economic interest was not the only factor behind the choice of parties. Life-styles and ethnic or religious identities strongly affected party loyalties during this period. In the northern states, one way to tell the typical Whig from the typical Democrat was to see what each did on Sunday. An evangelical Protestant

CHRONOLOGY

1824	House of Representatives elects John Quincy Adams president
1828	Congress passes "tariff of abominations" Jackson elected president over J.Q. Adams
1830	Jackson vetoes the Maysville Road bill Congress passes Indian Removal Act
1831	Jackson reorganizes his cabinet First national nominating conventions meet
1832	Jackson vetoes the bill rechartering the Bank of the United States Jackson re-elected defeating Henry Clay (National Republican candidate)
1832–1833	Crisis erupts over South Carolina's attempt to nullify the tariff of 1832
1833	Jackson removes federal deposits from the Bank of the United States
1834	Whig party comes into existence
1836	Jackson issues "specie circular" Martin Van Buren elected president
1837	Financial panic occurs, followed by depression lasting until 1843

was likely to be a Whig. A person who belonged to a ritualized church—Catholic, Lutheran, or Episcopalian—or did not go to church at all was probably a Democrat.

The Democrats were the favored party of immigrants, Catholics, free-thinkers, backwoods farmers, and those of all classes who enjoyed traditional amusements condemned by the new breed of moral reformers. One thing that all these groups had in common was a desire to be left alone, with freedom to think and behave as they liked. The Whigs welcomed a market economy but wished to restrain the individualism and disorder it created by enforcing cultural and moral values derived from the Puritan tradition. Most of those who sought to be "their brothers' keepers" were Whigs.

Nevertheless, party conflict in Congress continued to center on national economic policy. Whigs stood firm for a loose construction of the Constitution and positive federal guidance and support for business and economic development. The Democrats persisted in their defense of strict construction, states' rights, and laissez-faire. Debates over tariffs, banking, and internal improvements remained vital and vigorous during the 1840s.

True believers in both parties saw a deep ideological or moral meaning in the clash over economic or social issues. The Democrats were the party of individualism and personal liberty. The role of government was to remove obstacles to individual rights, which could mean the right to rise economically, the right to drink hard liquor, or the right to be unorthodox in religion. The Whigs, on the other hand, were the party of community. They believed that the propertied, the well-educated, and the pious were responsible for guiding the masses toward a common goal.

1840	Congress passes the Independent Sub-treasury Bill Harrison (Whig) defeats Van Buren (Democrat) for the presidency

Each, in a sense, reflected one side of a broader democratic impulse. This Jacksonian legacy was a stress on individual freedom and ethnic or cultural tolerance (except for blacks). The Whigs perceived that in a republic, strong government could serve the general interest and further the spirit of national unity.

TOCQUEVILLE'S WISDOM

The French traveler Alexis de Tocqueville, author of the most influential account ever written of the emergence of American democracy, visited the United States in 1831. He found much to praise in America, from the country's genius for local self-government to the participation of ordinary citizens in the affairs of their communities. But Tocqueville was also acutely aware of the limitations of American democracy and of the dangers facing the Republic. He believed that the nullification crisis foreshadowed the destruction of the Union and predicted that the problem of slavery would lead eventually to civil war and racial conflict. He also noted the power of white supremacy, providing an unforgettable first-hand description of the sufferings of an Indian community in the course of forced migration to the West as well as a graphic account of the way free blacks were segregated and driven from the polls in northern cities.

Tocqueville was equally aware that the kind of democracy white men were practicing in the Jacksonian era did not include women. The democratic ideal could not be so limited as to include only some of the people; its boundaries would soon begin to expand enough to exceed the restrictions of white male supremacy.

RECOMMENDED READING

The best general accounts of Jacksonian democracy are Arthur M. Schlesinger, Jr., *The Age of Jackson* (1945); Glyndon G. Van Deusen, *The Jacksonian Era, 1828–1848* (1959); and Edward Pessen, *Jacksonian America: Society, Personality, and Politics*, rev. ed. (1979). Alexis de Tocqueville's *Democracy in America* (2 vols., 1945) is the classic analysis of Jacksonian America by a perceptive foreign visitor.

The new political system is described in Richard P. McCormick, *The Second American Party System* (1966), and Richard Hofstadter, *The Idea of a Party System* (1970). On radical, working-class movements, see Edward Pessen, *Most Uncommon Jacksonians: The Radical Leaders of the Early Labor Movement* (1967), and Bruce M. Laurie, *Working People of Philadelphia, 1800–1850* (1980). Social manifestations of the democratic ethos are covered in Douglas T. Miller, *Jacksonian Autocracy: Class and Democracy in New York, 1830–1860,* and Joseph F. Kett, *The Formation of the American Medical Profession* (1968). On democratic culture, see David Grimstad, *Melodrama Unveiled: American Theater and Culture, 1800–1850* (1968); Neil Harris, *The Artist in American Society* (1966); and Russel B. Nye, *Society and Culture in America, 1830–1860* (1960).

The emergence of Andrew Jackson and the Democratic party is described in Samuel F. Bemis, *John Quincy Adams and the Union* (1956), and in books by Robert V. Remini: *Martin Van Buren and the Making of the Democratic Party* (1959) and *Andrew Jackson and the Course of American Empire, 1767–1821* (1977); *Andrew Jackson and the Course of American Freedom, 1822–1832* (1981); and *Andrew Jackson and the Course of American Democracy, 1833–1845* (1984). A good general account of Jackson's presidency is Richard B. Latner, *The Presidency of Andrew Jackson* (1979). On Jacksonian Indian Policy, see Bernard W. Sheehan, *The Seeds of Extinction: Jeffersonian Philanthropy and the American Indian,* and Michael Paul Rogin, *Fathers and Children: Andrew Jackson and the Subjugation of the American Indian* (1975). The standard works on the nullification crisis are William W. Freehling, *Prelude to Civil War* (1966), and Richard E. Ellis, *The Union at Risk: Jacksonian Democracy, States' Rights, and the Nullification Crisis* (1987).

The Bank War is discussed in Bray Hammond, *Banks and Politics in America from the Revolution to the Civil War* (1957), and Robert V. Remini, *Andrew Jackson and the Bank War* (1967). On Van Buren's administration see James C. Curtis, *The Fox at Bay: Martin Van Buren and the Presidency* (1970), and Donald B. Cole, *Martin Van Buren and the American Political System* (1984).

On the Whigs, see Clement Eaton, *Henry Clay and the Art of American Politics* (1957), and Daniel Walker Howe, *The Political Culture of the American Whigs* (1979). The growth of a two-party system in the South is described in William J. Cooper, Jr., *The South and the Politics of Slavery* (1978). On the cultural differences between Whigs and Democrats, see Ronald P. Formisano, *The Birth of Mass Political Parties: Michigan, 1827–1861* (1971).

11 THE PURSUIT OF PERFECTION

THE RISE OF EVANGELICALISM

DOMESTICITY AND CHANGES IN THE AMERICAN FAMILY

INSTITUTIONAL REFORM

REFORM TURNS RADICAL

In the winter of 1830–1831 a wave of religious revivals swept the northern states. For six months in Rochester, New York, evangelist Charles G. Finney preached almost daily, emphasizing that every man or woman had the power to choose Christ and a godly life. He converted hundreds, and he urged them in turn to convert relatives, neighbors, and employees. If enough people enlisted in the evangelical crusade, Finney proclaimed, the millennium would be achieved within months.

Finney's call for religious and moral renewal fell on fertile ground in Rochester. The leading families in this bustling boom town were divided into quarreling factions, and workingmen were breaking free from the control that their employers had previously exerted over their daily lives. More vigorous standards of proper behavior and religious conformity unified Rochester's elite and increased its ability to control the rest of the community. Evangelical Protestantism provided the middle class with a stronger sense of identity and purpose.

But the war on sin was not limited to such safe ground. Before long, religious and moral reformers took the logical step from individual to societal reformation. They demanded that all social and political institutions measure up to the standards of Christian perfection. They proceeded to attack such collective "sins" as the liquor traffic, war, slavery, and even government. Religiously inspired reformism cut two ways. On the one hand, it brought a measure of order and cultural unity to previously divided and troubled communities like Rochester. But it also inspired a variety of more radical movements or experiments that threatened to undermine established institutions and principles. One of these—abolitionism—would trigger political upheaval and help to bring on the Civil War.

Although both the evangelical reformers and the new democratic politicians sought popular favor and assumed that individuals were free agents capable of self-direction and self-improvement, the leaders differed in important respects. Jacksonians idealized common folk pretty much as they found them and saw no danger to the community if individuals pursued their worldly interests. Evangelical reformers, on the other hand, believed that the common people needed to be redeemed and uplifted. They did not trust a democracy of unbelievers and sinners. The Republic would be safe, they insisted, only if a right-minded minority preached, taught, and agitated until the mass of ordinary citizens was reborn into a higher life.

THE RISE OF EVANGELICALISM

American Protestantism was in a state of constant ferment during the early nineteenth century. The separation of church and state was now complete. Dissenting groups, like the Baptists and Methodists, welcomed full religious freedom because it offered a better chance to win new converts. But all pious Protestants were concerned about the spread of "infidelity"—their word for laxity in matters of faith and excessive worldliness.

Revivalism provided the best way to extend religious values and build up church membership. The Great Awakening of the mid-eighteenth century had shown the wonders that evangelists could accomplish, and the new revivalists repeated this success by increasing the proportion of the population that belonged to Protestant churches, forming voluntary organizations, and mobilizing the faithful into associations to spread the gospel and reform American morals.

THE SECOND GREAT AWAKENING: THE SOUTHERN FRONTIER PHASE

The Second Great Awakening began in earnest on the southern frontier around the turn of the century. Highly emotional camp meetings, organized usually by Methodists or Baptists, became a regular feature of religious life in the South and lower Midwest. On the frontier the camp meeting met social as well as religious needs. In the sparsely settled southern backcountry, for many people the only way to get baptized, married, or have a communal religious experience was to attend a camp meeting.

Rowdies and scoffers also attended. Mostly they drank whiskey, caroused, and fornicated on the fringes of the small city of tents and wagons. But sometimes they too fell into emotional fits and were converted. Evangelists loved to tell stories of such conversions or near conversions.

Camp meetings obviously provided an emotional outlet for rural people whose everyday lives were often lonely and tedious. But they could also promote a sense of community and social discipline. Conversion at a campaign meeting could be a rite of passage, signifying that a young man or woman had outgrown wild or antisocial behavior and was now ready to become a respectable member of the community. But for the most part frontier revivalism remained highly individualistic. It strengthened personal piety and morality but did not stimulate organized benevolence or social reform.

THE SECOND GREAT AWAKENING IN THE NORTH

Reformist tendencies were more evident in the distinctive kind of revivalism that originated in New England and western New York. The northern evangelists were mostly Congregationalists and Presbyterians, strongly influenced by the traditions of New England Puritanism. Their revivals, although somewhat less extravagant and emotional than those on

Frontier camp meetings in the early 1800s were attended by large crowds (sometimes thousands at a time) who sang, prayed, wept, and begged for divine mercy as the spirit moved them. The meetings served as an emotional outlet for rural people whose lives lacked color and human contact.

the frontier, found fertile soil in small-to-medium-sized towns and cities. The northern brand of evangelism resulted in the formation of societies devoted to the redemption of the human race in general and American society in particular.

The reform movement began in New England as an effort to defend Calvinism against the liberal views of religion fostered by the Enlightenment. The Reverend Timothy Dwight, who became president of Yale College in 1795, and other like minds were alarmed by the growing tendency to view the Deity as the benevolent master architect of a rational universe rather than as an all-powerful mysterious God. Some Congregationalist clergy reached the

point of denying the doctrine of the Trinity, proclaiming themselves "Unitarians." Horrified when the Unitarians won control of the Harvard Divinity School, Dwight battled this liberal tendency by reaffirming the old Calvinist belief that man was sinful and depraved. But the harshness and pessimism of orthodox Calvinist doctrine, with its stress on original sin and predestination, had limited appeal in a Republic committed to human freedom and progress.

Dwight himself made some concessions to the spirit of the age by agreeing that human beings had a limited control over their spiritual destiny. But a younger generation of Congregational ministers reshaped New England Puritanism to increase its appeal to people who shared the prevailing optimism about human capabilities.

The main theologian of early nineteenth-century neo-Calvinism was Nathaniel Taylor, a disciple of Dwight. Taylor softened the doctrine of predestination and contended that every individual was a "free agent" who had the ability to overcome a natural inclination to sin. This reconciliation of original sin with "free agency" enabled the neo-Calvinists to compete successfully with the revival denominations that preached that sinners had the ability to choose salvation.

The first great practitioner of the new evangelical Calvinism was Lyman Beecher, another of Dwight's pupils. In the period just before and after the War of 1812, Beecher helped to promote a series of revivals in the Congregational churches of New England. Using his own homespun version of free agency, he induced thousands of churchgoers to acknowledge their sinfulness and surrender to God.

During the late 1820s Beecher was forced to confront the new and more radical form of revivalism being practiced in western New York by Charles G. Finney. Upstate New York was a seedbed for religious enthusiasm. A majority of its population were transplanted New Englanders who had left behind their close-knit village communities and ancestral churches but not their Puritan consciences. Troubled by rapid economic changes and social dislocations, they were ripe for the assurances of a new faith and a sense of moral direction.

Although he worked within the Congregational and Presbyterian churches, Finney departed radically from traditional Calvinist doctrines. In his hands, the doctrine of free agency became unqualified free will. Indifferent to theological issues, Finney appealed strictly to emotion or to "the heart" rather than to doctrine or reason. He eventually adopted the extreme view that it was possible for redeemed Christians to be totally free of sin—to be perfect as their Father in Heaven is perfect.

Beginning in 1823, Finney conducted a series of highly successful revivals in the towns and cities of western New York. Even more contro-versial than his freewheeling approach to theology were the means he used to win converts. Finney sought instantaneous conversions through a variety of new methods including protracted meetings lasting all night or for several days in a row. He achieved dramatic results. Sometimes listeners fell to the floor in fits of excitement and immediately sought God's grace.

Beecher and the eastern evangelicals were disturbed by Finney's new methods and by the hysteria that they produced. They were also upset because he violated long-standing Christian tradition by allowing women to pray aloud in Church. But it soon became clear that Finney was not merely stirring people to temporary peaks of excitement, he was also leaving strong and active churches behind him, and eastern opposition gradually weakened.

FROM REVIVALISM TO REFORM

Northern revivalists inspired a great movement for social reform. Converts were organized into voluntary associations that sought to stamp out sin and social evil and win the world for Christ. Most of the converts of northern revivalism were middle-class citizens already active in the lives of their communities. They were seeking to adjust to the bustling world of the market revolution in ways that would not violate their traditional moral and social values. Given the generally optimistic and forward-looking attitudes of such Americans, it is understandable that a wave of conversions would lead to hopes for the salvation of the nation and the world.

In New England, Beecher and his evangelical associates were behind the establishment of a great network of missionary and benevolent societies. Foreign missionaries spread the gospel to remote parts of the world, and organizations such as the American Bible Society distributed Bibles in areas of the West where there was a scarcity of churches and clergymen. Missionaries even reached out to the many poor people in American cities.

Evangelicals formed moral reform societies as well as missions. Some of these aimed at curbing irreligious activity on the Sabbath; others sought to stamp out dueling, gambling, and prostitution. In the latter case, crusaders attempted to redeem the prostitutes as well as to curtail the activities of their patrons. Others felt that the cause of virtue would be better served by suppressing public discussion and investigation of sexual vices.

Beecher was especially influential in the temperance crusade, the most successful of the reform movements. The temperance movement was directed at a real social evil, more serious in many ways than the drug problem of today. Since the Revolution, whiskey had become the most popular American beverage. It was cheaper than milk or beer and safer than water (which was often contaminated). Per capita annual consumption of distilled beverages in the 1820s was almost triple what it is today, and alcoholism had reached epidemic proportions.

The temperance reformers viewed indulgence in alcohol as a threat to public morality. Drunkenness was seen as a loss of self-control and moral responsibility that spawned crime, vice, and disorder. Above all, it threatened the family. The main target of temperance propaganda was the husband and father who abused, neglected, or abandoned his wife and children because he was a slave to the bottle. The drinking habits of the poor and laboring classes also aroused great concern, for the "respectable" and propertied elements lived in fear that lower-class mobs, crazed with drink, would attack private property and destroy social order.

Many of the evangelical reformers regarded intemperance as the greatest single obstacle to the achievement of a Republic of God-fearing, self-disciplined citizens. In 1826 a group of clergymen organized the American Temperance Society to educate Americans about the evils of hard liquor. The society sent out lecturers, issued a flood of literature, and sponsored essay contests.

The campaign was enormously effective. Although it may be doubted whether large numbers of confirmed drunkards were actually cured, the movement did succeed in altering the drinking habits of middle-class Americans by making temperance a mark of respectability. Per capita consumption of hard liquor declined more than 50 percent during the 1830s.

Cooperating missionary and reform societies—collectively known as "the benevolent empire"—were a major force in American culture by the early 1830s. A new ethic of self-control and self-discipline was being instilled in the middle class that equipped individuals to confront a new world of economic growth and social mobility without losing their cultural and moral bearings.

By the 1830s the French traveler Alexis de Tocqueville could marvel at the power of Christian faith and morality in a land without an established church. It seemed to him that voluntaristic religions produced moral and law-abiding citizens without the need for governmental coercion. In religion and reform, and not in politics, many Americans saw the best and last hope for the Republic.

DOMESTICITY AND CHANGES IN THE AMERICAN FAMILY

The evangelical culture of the 1820s and 1830s influenced the family as an institution and inspired new conceptions of its role in American society. For many parents, child rearing was viewed as essential preparation for the self-disciplined Christian life. Women—regarded as particularly susceptible to religious and moral influences—were increasingly confined to the domestic circle, but assumed a greater importance within it.

MARRIAGE AND SEX ROLES

The American family underwent major changes in the decades between the revolution and the mid-nineteenth century. One was the triumph of marriage for love. Parents now exercised even less control over their children's selection of mates than they had in the colonial period. The prompting of the heart, so important to religious conversion, was now seen as the primary factor in choosing a mate. It seems likely, too, that relations between husbands and wives were becoming more affectionate. In the main, eighteenth-century correspondence between spouses had been formal and distant in tone. The husband, for example, rarely confessed that he missed his wife or craved her company. By the early nineteenth century first names, pet names, and terms of endearment like "honey" or "darling" were increasingly used by both sexes, and absent husbands frequently confessed that they felt lost without their mates. In return, wives assumed a more egalitarian tone and offered counsel on a wide range of subjects.

At its best, marriage had become more a matter of companionship and less an exertion of male dominance. But the change should not be exaggerated or romanticized. In law, and in cases of conflict between spouses, the husband remained the unchallenged head of the household. True independence or equality for women was impossible at a time when men held exclusive legal authority over a couple's property and children.

Such power as women exerted within the home came from their ability to affect the decisions of men who had learned to respect their moral qualities and good sense. The evangelical movement encouraged this quiet expression of feminine influence. Revivals not only gave women a role in converting men but made a feminized Christ the main object of worship. A nurturing, loving, merciful Savior, mediating between a stern father and his erring children, provided the model for woman's new role as spiritual head of the home. Membership in evangelical church-based associations inspired and prepared women for their new role as guardians of domestic culture and morality. Female reform societies taught them the strict ethical code they were to instill in other family members; organized mothers' groups gave instruction in how to build character and encourage piety in children.

Historians have described the new conception of woman's role as the "Cult of True Womanhood" or the "ideology of domesticity." In the view of most men, woman's place was in the home and on a pedestal. The ideal wife was a model of piety and virtue who exerted a wholesome moral and religious influence over members of the coarser sex.

The sociological reality behind the Cult of True Womanhood was an increasing division between the working lives of men and women. In the eighteenth century and earlier most economic activity had been centered in the home and nearby, and husbands and wives often worked together in a common enterprise. By early in the mid-nineteenth century this way of life was limited mainly to rural areas. In towns and cities, the rise of factories and counting-houses severed the home from the workplace. Men went forth every morning to their places of labor, leaving their wives at home to tend the house and the children. The cult of domesticity made a virtue of the fact that men were solely responsible for running the affairs of the world and building up the economy.

A new concept of sex roles justified and glorified this pattern. The "doctrine of two spheres"—set forth in novels, advice literature, and the new ladies' magazines—sentimentalized the woman who kept a spotless house, nurtured her children, and offered her husband a refuge from the heartless world of commerce and industry. From a modern point of view, it is easy to condemn the cult of domesticity as a rationalization for male dominance. But most women of the early to mid-nineteenth century probably did not feel oppressed or degraded by the new arrangement. Women had never enjoyed equality, and the new norm of confinement to the home did not necessarily imply that women were inferior. By the standards of evangelical culture, women in the domestic sphere could be viewed as superior to men since women were in a good position to cultivate the "feminine" virtues of love and self-sacrifice and thus act as official guardians of religious and moral values.

The domestic ideology had real meaning only for relatively affluent women. Working-class wives were not usually employed outside the home during this period, but they labored long and hard within the household, often taking in washing or piecework to supplement a meager family income. Their endless domestic drudgery made a sham of the notion that women had the time and energy for the "higher things in life."

For middle-class women whose husbands earned a good income, however, freedom from industrial or farm labor offered tangible benefits. They now had the leisure to read extensively in the new literature directed primarily at housewives, to participate in female-dominated charitable activities, and to cultivate deep and lasting friendships with other women. The result was a distinctively feminine subculture emphasizing "sisterhood" or "sorority." This growing sense of solidarity with other women often bridged economic and social gaps as demonstrated when upper- and middle-class women organized societies for the relief and rehabilitation of poor or "fallen women."

For some women, the domestic ideal even sanctioned ladylike efforts to extend their sphere until it conquered the masculine world outside the home. This domestic feminism was reflected in women's involvement in crusades to stamp out such masculine sins as intemperance, gambling, and sexual vice. It was also the motivating force behind the campaign to make schoolteaching a woman's occupation.

Women attempted to make the world a better place by properly rearing their children who were captive pupils for the mother's instructions. Since women were considered particularly well-qualified to transmit piety and morality to future citizens of the Republic, the cult of domesticity exalted motherhood and encouraged a new concern with childhood as the time of life when "character" was formed.

THE DISCOVERY OF CHILDHOOD

The nineteenth century has been called "the century of the child." More than before, childhood was seen as a distinct stage of life requiring the special and sustained attention of parents. The family now became "child-centered," which meant that the care, nurturing, and rearing of children was viewed as the family's prime function.

New customs and fashions heralded the "discovery" of childhood. Books aimed specifically at juveniles and others providing expert advice to parents on child rearing began to roll off the presses. The ideal family described in the advice manuals and sentimental literature was bound together by affection rather than authority. Firm discipline remained at the core of "family government," but there was a change in the preferred method of enforcing good behavior. Corporal punishment declined, partially displaced by shaming or withholding of affection. The intended result of punishment was often described as "self-government"; and to achieve it parents used guilt, rather than fear, as their main source of leverage.

Child-centered families also meant smaller families. If nineteenth-century families had remained as large as those of earlier times, it would have been impossible to lavish so much care and attention on individual offspring. Between 1800 and 1850 the average family size declined about 25 percent, beginning a long-range trend lasting to the present day.

The practice of various forms of birth control undoubtedly contributed to this demographic revolution. Ancestors of the modern condom and diaphragm were openly advertised and sold during the pre-Civil War period, but it is likely that most couples controlled family size by practicing the withdrawal method or limiting the frequency of intercourse. Abortion was also surprisingly common and was on the rise.

Parents seemed to understand that having fewer children meant that they could provide their offspring with a better start in life. Such attitudes were appropriate to a society that was beginning to shift from agriculture to commerce and industry.

INSTITUTIONAL REFORM

The family could not carry the whole burden of socializing and reforming individuals. Children needed schooling as well as parental nurture. Some adults, too, seemed to require special kinds of attention and treatment. Seeking to extend the advantages of "family government" beyond the domestic circle, reformers worked to establish or improve public institutions that were designed to shape individual character and instill a capacity for self-discipline.

THE EXTENSION OF EDUCATION

The period from 1820 to 1850 saw an enormous expansion of free public schools. The new resolve to put more children in school for longer periods reflected many of the same values that exalted the child-centered family. It was believed that formal training at a character-building institution would prepare children to make a living and bear the burdens of republican citizenship when they became adults. Purely intellectual training at school was regarded as less important than moral indoctrination.

Besides being an extension of the family, the school could also serve as a substitute for it. Educational reformers were alarmed at the masses of poor and immigrant children who allegedly lacked a proper home environment. The safety of the Republic depended on schools to make up for this disadvantage.

Before the 1820s, schooling in the United States was a haphazard affair. The wealthy sent their children to private schools, and some of the poor sent their children to charity or "pauper" schools that were usually financed in part by state or local government. Between the 1820s and the 1850s, the movement for publicly supported common schools made great headway in the North and had limited success in parts of the South. In theory, the common school was an egalitarian institution providing a free basic education for children of all backgrounds.

The agitation for expanded public education began in the 1820s and early 1830s as a central demand of the workingmen's movements in eastern cities. These artisans and tradespeople viewed free schools open to all as a way of countering the growing gap between rich and poor. Middle-class reformers soon seized the initiative, shaped educational reform toward the goal of social discipline, and provided the momentum needed for legislative success.

The most influential spokesman for the common school movement was Horace Mann of Massachusetts. As a lawyer and a member of the state legislature, Mann worked tirelessly for the establishment of a state board of education and adequate tax support for local schools. His philosophy of education was based on the premise that children were clay in the hands of teachers and school officials and could be molded to a state of perfection. Like the advocates of child rearing through moral influence rather than physical force, he discouraged corporal punishment except as a last resort.

LESSON XXI.

1. IN'DO-LENT; *adj.* lazy; idle.
2. COM-MER'CIAL; *adj.* trading.
3. COM'IC-AL; *adj.* amusing.
3. DRONE; *n.* an idler.
4. NAV'I-GA-BLE; *adj.* in which boats can sail.

THE IDLE SCHOOL-BOY.

PRONOUNCE correctly. Do not say *indorlunt* for in-do-lent; *creepin* for creep-ing; *sylubble* for syl-la-ble; *colud* for col-ored; *scarlit* for scar-let; *ignerunt* for ig-no-rant.

1. I WILL tell you about the ⁺laziest boy you ever heard of. He was indolent about every thing. When he played, the boys said he played as if the teacher told him to. When he went to school, he went creep-ing along like a snail. The boy had sense enough; but he was too lazy to learn any thing.

2. When he spelled a word, he ⁺drawled out one syllable after another, as if he were afraid the ⁺sylla-bles would quarrel, if he did not keep them a great way apart.

3. Once when he was ⁺reciting, the teacher asked him, "What is said of ⁺Hartford?" He answered, "Hartford is a ⁺flourishing *comical* town." He meant that it was a "flourishing *commercial* town;" but he was such a drone, that he never knew what he was about.

4. When asked how far the River ⁺Kennebec was navigable, he said, "it was navigable for *boots* as far as ⁺Waterville." The boys all laughed, and the teacher could not help laughing, too. The idle boy ⁺colored like scarlet.

The lessons and examples in McGuffy's Readers *upheld the basic virtues of thrift, honesty, and charity and taught that evil deeds never went unpunished.*

Against those who argued that school taxes violated the rights of property, Mann contended that private property was actually held in trust for the good of the community. Education, he stressed, saved children from drifting into lives of poverty and vice and prepared them to become good, law-abiding citizens. Mann's conception of public education as a means of social discipline converted the middle and upper classes to his cause.

In practice, the new or improved public schools often alienated working-class pupils and their families rather than reforming them. Compulsory attendance laws deprived poor families of needed wage earners without guaranteeing new occupational opportunities for those with an elementary education. Furthermore, Catholic immigrants complained quite correctly that Mann and his disciples were trying to impose a uniform Protestant culture on the pupils.

In addition to the "three Rs" of reading, writing, and arithmetic, the essence of what was being taught in the public schools of the mid-nineteenth century was the "Protestant ethic"—industry, punctuality, sobriety, and frugality. These were the virtues stressed in the famous McGuffey readers, which first appeared in 1836. Such moral indoctrination helped produce generations of Americans with personalities and beliefs adapted to the needs of an industrialized society. If the system did not encourage thinking for one's self, it did prepare people who could easily adjust to the regular routines of the factory or the office.

Fortunately, however, education was not limited to the schools nor devoted exclusively to dren. Every city and almost every town or village had a lyceum, debating society, or mechanic's institute where adults of all social classes could broaden their intellectual horizons. Young Abe Lincoln, for example, sharpened his intellect and honed his debating skills as a member of such an institute in New Salem, Illinois, in the early 1830s. Unlike the public schools, the lyceums and debating societies fostered independent thought and the spread of new ideas.

DISCOVERING THE ASYLUM

Some segments of the population were obviously beyond the reach of family government and character training provided in homes and schools. In the 1820s and 1830s, reformers became acutely aware of the dangers to society posed by an apparently increasing number of criminals, lunatics, and paupers. Their answer was to establish special institutions to provide a controlled environment in which the inmates could be reformed and rehabilitated.

In earlier times, the existence of paupers, law-breakers, and insane persons was viewed as the consequence of divine judgment or original sin. For the most part these people were dealt with in ways that did not isolate them from local communities. But dealing with deviants in a neighborly way broke down as economic development and urbanization made commu-

Inmates of asylums, prisons, and almshouses could have fared worse had it not been for the considerable efforts of Dorothea Dix to publicize inhumane conditions.

nities less cohesive. At the same time, reformers were concluding that all defects of mind and character were correctable—that the insane could be cured, criminals reformed, and paupers taught to pull themselves out of destitution. The result was the discovery of the asylum.

The 1820s and 1830s saw the emergence of state-supported prisons, insane asylums, and poorhouses. New York and Pennsylvania led the way in prison reform. In theory, prisons and asylums substituted for the family. The custodians were intended to act as parents by providing moral advice and training. In practice, these institutions were far different from the affectionate families idealized by the cult of domesticity. Their most prominent feature was the imposition of a rigid daily routine. The early superintendents and wardens believed that the enforcement of an inflexible and demanding set of rules and procedures would encourage self-discipline.

In retrospect, it is clear that the prisons, asylums, and poorhouses did not achieve the aims of their founders. A combination of naive theories and poor performance doomed these institutions to a custodial rather than a reformatory role. Public support was inadequate to meet the needs of the growing inmate population, and the personnel of these places of confinement lacked the training needed to help their charges. The result was overcrowding and the use of brutality to keep order.

But conditions would have been even worse without the efforts of a remarkable woman—Dorothea Dix—one of the most effective of all the pre-Civil War reformers. As a direct result of her skill in publicizing the inhumane treatment prevailing in prisons, almshouses, and insane asylums, fifteen states built new hospitals and improved supervision of penitentiaries and other institutional facilities.

REFORM TURNS RADICAL

During the 1830s, internal dissension split the great reform movement spawned by the Second Great Awakening. Efforts to promote evangelical piety, improve personal and public morality, and shape character through familial or institutional discipline continued and even flourished. But bolder spirits went beyond such goals and set their sights on the total liberation and perfection of the individual. Especially in New England and the upper North, a new breed of reformers, prophets, and utopians attacked established institutions and rejected all compromise with what they viewed as a corrupt society.

DIVISIONS IN THE BENEVOLENT EMPIRE

Early nineteenth-century reformers were generally committed to changing existing attitudes and practices gradually in ways that would not invite conflict or disrupt the fabric of society. But by the mid-1830s a new mood of impatience and perfectionism surfaced within the benevolent societies. The Temperance Society, for example, split between radicals who insisted on a total commitment to "cold water" and moderates who were willing to overlook moderate wine and beer drinking. The same sort of division arose in the American Peace Society between those insisting on absolute pacifism and those willing to sanction "defensive wars."

The new perfectionism realized its most dramatic and important success within the antislavery movement. Before the 1830s many of the people who expressed religious and moral concern over slavery were affiliated with the American Colonization Society, a benevolent organization founded in 1817. Most colonizationists admitted that slavery was an evil, but they felt it should be eliminated only gradually and with the cooperation of slaveholders. Reflecting the power of racial prejudice, they proposed to transport freed blacks to Africa as a way of relieving southern fears that a race war would erupt if slaves were simply released from bondage and allowed to remain in America. In 1821 the society established a colony in West Africa, named it Liberia, and settled several

Black leaders in the abolitionist movement included Frederick Douglass, who escaped from slavery himself and was one of the most effective voices in the antislavery campaign.

thousand American blacks there over the next decade.

Colonization proved to be grossly inadequate as a step toward the elimination of slavery. Slave-holders rarely cooperated with the movement, and free blacks rejected the whole process. Black opposition to colonization helped persuade William Lloyd Garrison and other white abolitionists to repudiate the Colonization Society and support immediate emancipation without emigration.

Garrison launched a new and more radical antislavery movement in 1831 when he began to publish a journal called the *Liberator* in Boston. Most of his early subscribers were free blacks, who were also a mainstay of support for the American Anti-Slavery Society he founded in 1833. Black orators, especially escaped slaves like Frederick Douglass, were featured at antislavery rallies. Garrison's rhetoric was as severe as his proposals were radical. As he wrote in the first issue of the *Liberator*, "I will be as harsh as the truth and as uncompromising as justice. . . . I will not retreat a single inch— AND I WILL BE HEARD."

THE ABOLITIONIST ENTERPRISE

The abolitionist movement, like the temperance crusade, was a direct outgrowth of the Second Great Awakening. Many leading abolitionists had undergone conversion experiences in the 1820s and were already committed to a life of Christian activism before they dedicated themselves to freeing the slaves. Several were ministers or divinity students seeking a mission in life that would fulfill their spiritual and professional ambitions.

The career of Theodore Dwight Weld exemplified the connection between revivalism and abolitionism. Influenced strongly by Charles G. Finney, Weld underwent a conversion experience in 1826. He then became an itinerant lecturer for various reform causes. By the early 1830s, his attention was focused on the moral issue raised by the institution of slavery. After a brief flirtation with the colonization movement, he became a convert to abolitionism. Traveling throughout Ohio, where he and his associates founded Oberlin College as a center for abolitionist activity, he used the tried and true methods of the revival—fervent preaching, protracted meetings, and the call for individuals to come forth and announce their redemption—in the cause of the antislavery movement. As a result of these efforts, northern Ohio and western New York became hotbeds of abolitionist sentiment.

Antislavery orators and organizers tended to have their greatest success in the smaller towns of the upper North. The typical convert came from an upwardly mobile family engaged in small business, the skilled trades, or market farming. In the cities, abolitionists were more likely to encounter fierce and effective opposition. Indeed, Garrison was once almost lynched in Boston.

Abolitionists who thought of taking their message to the fringes of the South had reason to pause, given the fate of the antislavery editor Elijah Lovejoy. In 1837 while attempting to defend himself and his printing press from a mob in Alton, Illinois, just across the Mississippi River from slaveholding Missouri, Lovejoy was shot and killed.

Racism was a major cause of antiabolitionist violence in the North. Rumors that abolitionists advocated or practiced interracial marriage could easily excite an urban crowd to destructive acts. Working-class whites tended to fear that economic and social competition with blacks would increase if abolitionists succeeded in freeing the slaves and making them citizens. But a striking feature of many of the mobs was that they were dominated by "gentlemen of property and standing." Upstanding citizens resorted to violence, it would appear, because abolitionism effectively threatened their conservative notions of social order and hierarchy.

By the end of the 1830s, the abolitionist movement was under great stress. Besides the burden of external repression, there was dissension within the movement. Becoming an abolitionist required an exacting conscience and unwillingness to compromise on matters of principle. These character traits also made it difficult for abolitionists to work together and maintain a united front against their opponents. Furthermore, relations between black and white abolitionists were tense. Whites tended to be condescending and paternalistic, unwilling to allow blacks to assume leadership positions or shape policy.

During the late 1830s, Garrison, the most visible spokesman for the cause, began to adopt positions that other abolitionists found extreme and divisive. He attacked government, clergy, and churches for refusing to take a strong antislavery stand, and he refused to work with any person or organization that did not fully support his crusade.

These positions alienated those members of the Anti-Slavery Society who continued to hope that organized religion and the existing political system could be influenced or even taken over by abolitionists. But it was Garrison's stand on women's rights that led to an open break at the national convention of 1840. Many of his followers separated from Garrison and his organization when the Boston editor engineered the election of a female abolitionist to the executive committee of the Anti-Slavery Society.

The schism weakened Garrison's influence within the movement. When he later repudiated the United States Constitution as a proslavery document and called for Northern secession from the Union, few antislavery people in the mid-Atlantic or midwestern states went along. Outside of New England, most abolitionists worked *within* churches and the political system. The Liberty party, organized in 1840, was their first attempt to enter the electoral arena under their own banner; it signaled a new effort to turn antislavery sentiment into political power.

Historians have debated the question of whether the abolitionist movement of the 1830s and early 1840s was a success or failure. It failed to convert a majority of Americans to its position on the evil of slavery. And in the South, it caused a strong counterreaction and helped inspire a more militant and uncompromising defense of slavery. The belief that peaceful agitation, or what abolitionists called "moral suasion," would convert slaveholders and their northern sympathizers to abolition was obviously unrealistic.

But in another sense the crusade was successful. It brought the slavery issue to the forefront of public consciousness and convinced a substantial and growing segment of the northern population that the South's peculiar institution was morally wrong and a potential danger to the American way of life. The politicians who later mobilized the North against the expansion of slavery into the territories drew their strength from the reservoir of antislavery attitudes and sentiment created by the abolitionists.

FROM ABOLITIONISM TO WOMEN'S RIGHTS

Abolitionism also served as a catalyst for the women's rights movement. From the beginning women were active participants in the abolitionist crusade. Some antislavery women defied conventional ideas of their proper sphere by becoming public speakers and demanding an equal role in the leadership of antislavery societies. The most famous of these were the Grimké sisters, Sarah and Angelina, who attracted enormous attention because they were the rebellious daughters of a South Carolina slaveholder.

The battle to participate equally in the antislavery crusade made a number of female abolitionists acutely aware of male dominance and oppression. For them, the same principles that justified the liberation of the slaves also applied to the emancipation of women from all restrictions on their rights as citizens. However, not all of the antislavery men agreed with the idea of equal rights for women.

Wounded by male reluctance to extend the cause of emancipation to include women, Lu-

Elizabeth Cady Stanton, a leader of the women's rights movement, is pictured here with one of her seven children. In addition to her pioneering work for women's rights, especially women's suffrage, she lectured on family life and child care.

cretia Mott and Elizabeth Cady Stanton organized a new and independent movement for women's rights. The high point of their campaign was the famous convention at Seneca Falls, New York, in 1848. In a "Declaration of Sentiments," the delegates condemned the treatment of women by men and demanded the right to vote and to control their own property, person, and children. Rejecting the cult of domesticity with its doctrine of separate spheres, these women and their male supporters launched the modern movement for sexual equality.

RADICAL IDEAS AND EXPERIMENTS

Hopes for individual or social perfection were not limited to reformers inspired by evangelicalism. Between the 1820s and 1850s, a great variety of schemes for human redemption came from those who had rejected orthodox Protestantism. Some were freethinkers carrying on the traditions of the Enlightenment, but most were seeking new paths to spiritual or religious fulfillment. These philosophical and religious radicals attacked established institutions, proscribed new modes of living, and founded utopian communities to put their ideas into practice.

A radical movement of foreign origin that gained a toehold in Jacksonian America was utopian socialism. In 1825–1826 the British manufacturer and reformer Robert Owen founded a community based on common and equal ownership of property at New Harmony, Indiana. About the same time Owen's associate, Frances Wright, gathered a group of slaves at Nashoba, Tennessee, and set them to work earning their freedom in an atmosphere of "rational cooperation." The rapid demise of both of these model communities suggests that utopian socialism did not easily take root in American soil.

The most successful and long-lived of the pre-Civil War utopias was established in 1848 at Oneida, New York, and was inspired by an unorthodox brand of Christian perfectionism.

Its founder, John Humphrey Noyes, believed that the Second Coming of Christ had already occurred; hence, human beings could be totally free from sin and were no longer obliged to follow the moral rules that their previously fallen state had required. At Oneida, traditional marriage was outlawed, and a carefully regulated form of "free love" prevailed.

It was a literary and philosophical movement known as transcendentalism that inspired the era's most memorable experiments in thinking and living on a higher plane. The main idea was that the individual could transcend material reality and ordinary understanding, attaining through a higher form of reason—or intuition—a oneness with the universe as a whole and with the spiritual forces that lay behind it. Transcendentalism was the major American version of the romantic and idealist thought that emerged in the early nineteenth century. Throughout the Western world, romanticism was challenging the rationalism and materialism of the Enlightenment in the name of exalted feeling and cosmic spirituality. Most American transcendentalists were dissatisfied with rationalistic religions but were unable to embrace evangelical Christianity because of intellectual resistance to its doctrines. Instead they sought inspiration from a philosophical and literary idealism of German origin. Their prophet was Ralph Waldo Emerson, a brilliant essayist and lecturer who preached that each individual could commune directly with a benign spiritual force that animated nature and the universe—he called it the "oversoul."

Emerson was an advocate of self-reliance and avoided all involvement in organized movements or associations. But in the vicinity of Emerson's home in Concord, Massachusetts, a group of like-minded seekers of truth and spiritual fulfillment gathered during the 1830s and 1840s. One group of transcendentalists, led by the Reverend George Ripley, rejected Emerson's radical individualism and founded a cooperative community at Brook Farm, near Roxbury, Massachusetts, in 1841. For the next four years they worked the land in common, conducted an excellent school on the principle that spontaneity rather than discipline was the key to education, and allowed ample time for conversation, meditation, communion with nature, and artistic activity of all kinds. The Brook Farm experiment ended in 1849.

Another experiment in transcendental living adhered more closely to the individualistic spirit of the movement. Between 1845 and 1847, Henry David Thoreau, a young disciple of Emerson, lived by himself in the woods along the shore of Walden Pond and carefully recorded his thoughts and impressions. In a sense, he pushed the ideal of "self-culture" to its logical outcome—a utopia of one. The result was *Walden* (published in 1854), one of the greatest achievements in American literature.

FADS AND FASHIONS

Not only venturesome intellectuals experimented with new beliefs and life-styles. Between the 1830s and 1850s, a number of fads, fashions, and medical cure-alls appeared on the scene, indicating that a large segment of the middle class was obsessed with the pursuit of personal health, happiness, and moral perfection. Dietary reformers like Sylvester Graham convinced many people to give up meat, coffee, tea, and pastries in favor of fruit, vegetables, and whole wheat bread. Amelia Bloomer advocated loose-fitting pantalettes as a healthful substitute for the elaborate structure of corsets, petticoats, and hooped skirts then in fashion. A concern with understanding and improving personal character and abilities was reflected in the craze for phrenology—a popular pseudoscience that involved studying the shape of the skull to determine natural aptitudes and inclinations.

In an age of perfectionism, even the dead could be enlisted on the side of universal reform. Seances were held in parlors all over the nation; spiritualists urged direct contact with the dead, who were viewed as having "passed on" to a purer state of being and a higher wisdom. Spiritual beliefs were a logical outgrowth of the perfectionist dream pursued so ardently by antebellum Americans.

COUNTERPOINT ON REFORM

One great American writer observed at close quarters the perfectionist ferment of the age but held himself aloof, suggesting in his novels and tales that pursuit of the ideal led to a distorted sense of human nature and possibilities. Nathaniel Hawthorne's sense of human frailty and sinfulness made him skeptical about the lofty claims of transcendentalism and utopianism. He satirized transcendentalism as unworldly and overoptimistic and lampooned life in such cooperative communities as Brook Farm. His greatest novels, *The Scarlet Letter* (1850) and *The House of Seven Gables* (1851), imaginatively probed people's futile efforts to escape sin and evil. The world was imperfect, he suggested, and one simply had to accept that reality.

To be sure, the dreams of perfectionist reformers promised more than they could possibly deliver. Revivals could not make all men like Christ; temperance could not solve all social problems; abolitionist agitation could not bring a peaceful end to slavery; and transcendentalism could not fully emancipate people from the limitations and frustrations of daily life. But the reformers could argue that Hawthorne's skepticism and fatalism was a prescription for doing nothing in the face of intolerable evils. If the reform impulse was long on inspirational rhetoric but somewhat short on durable, practical achievements, it did challenge Americans to improve their country.

❧ RECOMMENDED READING

Alice Felt Tyler, *Freedom's Ferment* (1944), gives a lively overview of the varieties of pre-Civil War reform activity. Ronald G. Walters, *American Reformers, 1815–1860* (1978), provides a modern interpretation of these movements. The best general work on revivalism is William G. McLoughlin, *Modern Revivalism* (1959). Paul E. Johnson, *A Shopkeeper's Millennium: Society and Revivals in Rochester, New York, 1815–1837* (1978), describes the impact of the revival on a single community.

Various dimensions of evangelical religion are covered in Donald G. Mathews, *Religion in the Old South* (1977); Whitney R. Cross, *The Burned-Over District* (1950); Perry Miller, *The Life of the Mind in America from the Revolution to the Civil War* (1965); and Timothy I. Smith, *Revivalism and Social Reform in Mid-Nineteenth-Century America* (1957). On the temperance movement, see Ian R. Tyrell, *Sobering Up: From Temperance to Prohibition in Antebellum America, 1800–1860* (1979).

A good introduction to the changing roles of women and the family in nineteenth-century America is Carl N. Degler, *At Odds: Women and the Family in America from the Revolution to the Present* (1980). The cult of domesticity is the subject of Barbara Welter, "The Cult of True Womanhood," *American Quarterly* 18 (1966): 217–40; Nancy F. Cott, *The Bonds of Womanhood: "Woman's Sphere" in New England, 1780–1835* (1977); Kathryn Kish Sklar, *Catherine Beecher: A Study in American Domesticity* (1973); and Mary Ryan, *The Cradle of the Middle Class: The Family in Oneida County New York, 1790–1865* (1981).

On educational reform, see Carl F. Kaestle, *Pillars of the Republic: Common Schooling and American Society, 1780–1860* (1983), Lawrence Cremin, *American Education: The National Experience, 1783–1876* (1980), and Michael B. Katz, *The Irony of Early School Reform: Educational Innovation in Mid-Nineteenth Century Massachusetts* (1968). David J. Rothman, *The Discovery of the Asylum: Social Order and Disorder in the New Republic* (1971), provides a penetrating analysis of the movement for institutional reform.

Among the most significant works on the abolitionist movement are John L. Thomas, *The Liberator: William Lloyd Garrison* (1963); Bertram Wyatt-Brown, *Lewis Tappan and the Evangelical War Against Slavery* (1969); Lewis Perry, *Radical Abolitionism: Anarchy and the Government of God in Antislavery Thought* (1973); Robert H. Abzug, *Passionate Liberator: Theodore Dwight Weld and the Dilemma of Reform* (1980); and Lawrence J. Friedman, *Gregarious Saints: Self and Community in American Abolitionism* (1982). Leonard L. Richards, *"Gentlemen of Property and Standing": Anti-Abolition Mobs in Jacksonian America* (1970), interprets violence against the abolitionists. On the connection between abolition and women's rights, see Gerda Lerner, *The Grimké Sisters from South Carolina: Rebels Against Slavery* (1967), and Blanche Glassman Hersh, *The Slavery of Sex: Feminist Abolitionists in America* (1978).

The utopian impulse is the subject of Arthur Bestor, *Backwoods Utopias* (1950), and Michael Fellman, *The Unbounded Frame: Freedom and Community in Nineteenth-Century Utopianism* (1973).

12 AN AGE OF EXPANSIONISM

MOVEMENT TO THE FAR WEST

MANIFEST DESTINY AND THE MEXICAN WAR

INTERNAL EXPANSIONISM

Orators and writers, responding to the surging nationalism of the 1840s, hailed the emergence of a mood or movement known as "Young America." The rhetoric of the Young Americans was as extravagant as their ambitions. They heralded a nation on the move— onward, upward, westward. Nothing, one writer noted, could "stop the advancement of this truly democratic and omnipotent spirit of the age." This identification of Young America with the extension of democracy reveals its roots in the Jacksonianism of the previous decade; the major voices for the expansionist spirit were young Democrats seeking a new way to recapture the political magic of Old Hickory. Their current hero was a "Young Hickory," who also came out of Tennessee to become a strong president—James K. Polk.

Those who identified with this image of an adolescent nation awakening to maturity favored an aggressive foreign policy, territorial acquisitions, and rapid economic growth. They called in turn for annexation of Texas, assertion of an American claim to all of Oregon, and the appropriation of vast new territories from Mexico. They also celebrated the technological advances that would knit this new empire together, especially the telegraph and the railroad.

Young America was an intellectual as well as a political movement. During the Polk administration, Young American writers and critics—mostly based in New York—called for a new and distinctive national literature, free of subservience to European themes or models and expressive of the democratic spirit. Their organ was the *Literary World,* founded in 1847, and its ideals influenced two of the greatest writers the nation has ever produced—Walt Whitman and Herman Melville.

Whitman captured much of the exuberance, optimism, and expansionism of Young America. He celebrated a nation whose limits were circumscribed only by the imagination. In *Moby Dick,* Herman Melville produced a novel sufficiently original in form and conception to more than fulfill the demand of Young Americans for "a New Literature to fit the New Man in the New Age." But he was too deep a thinker not to see the perils that underlay the soaring ambition and aggressiveness of the new age. In the character of Ahab, the whaling captain who brings destruction on himself and his ship by his relentless pursuit of the white whale, Melville symbolized—among other things—the dangers facing a nation that was overreaching itself by indulging its pride and exalted sense of destiny with too little concern for the moral and practical consequences.

MOVEMENT TO THE FAR WEST

In the 1830s and 1840s the westward movement of population left the valley of the Mississippi behind and penetrated the Far West all the way to the Pacific. Pioneers pursued fertile land and economic opportunities beyond the existing boundaries of the United States and thus helped set the stage for the annexations and international crises of the 1840s. Some went for material gain, others for adventure, and a significant minority sought freedom from religious persecution. They carried American attitudes and loyalties with them into regions that

TERRITORIAL EXPANSION BY THE MID-NINETEENTH CENTURY

Ceded by U.S. 1818
CANADA
WASH.
OREGON COUNTRY 1846
MONT.
Ceded by Great Britain 1818
N. DAK.
Ceded by Great Britain, 1842 (Webster–Ashburton Treaty)
MAINE
ORE.
IDAHO
MINN.
WIS.
MICH.
VT
N.H.
MASS.
R.I.
CONN.
WYO.
S. DAK.
N.Y.
PA.
N.J.
NEV.
UTAH
NEBR.
IOWA
IND.
OHIO
DEL.
MD.
MEXICAN CESSION 1848
COLO.
LOUISIANA PURCHASE 1803
ILL.
UNITED STATES 1783
W.VA.
D.C.
VA.
CALIF.
KANS.
MO.
KY.
N.C.
ARIZ.
N. MEX.
OKLA.
ARK.
TENN.
S.C.
ATLANTIC OCEAN
PACIFIC OCEAN
TEXAS ANNEXATION 1845
MISS.
ALA.
GA.
GADSDEN PURCHASE 1853
TEXAS
LA.
FLA.
1810 1812 Annexed by U.S.
Ceded by Spain, 1819 Ratified by U.S., 1821
Ceded by Spain 1819
Map shows present-day boundaries
MEXICO
0   300 Miles
0   300 Kilometers

were already occupied or at least claimed by Mexico or Great Britain. Whether they realized it or not, these pioneers were the vanguard of American expansionism.

BORDERLANDS OF THE 1830s

Territorial ambition lured Americans northward as well as westward, and for a time it seemed that Canada might be a few frontier for expansionism. Conflicts over the border between America and British North America led periodically to calls for diplomatic or military action to wrest the northern half of the continent from the English. During the 1830s tensions were particularly high as Americans and Canadians wrestled over the exact location of the border between Maine and New Brunswick. Finally in 1842, Secretary of State Daniel Webster concluded an agreement with the British government, represented by Lord Ashburton. The Webster-Ashburton Treaty gave over half of the disputed territory to the United States and established a definite northeastern boundary with Canada.

On the other side of the continent, the United States and Britain both laid claim to Oregon, a vast unsettled area that lay between the Rockies and the Pacific from the forty-second parallel (the northern boundary of California) to the latitude of 54°40' (the southern boundary of Alaska). Although in 1818 the two nations had agreed to joint occupation, the Americans had strengthened their claim by acquiring Spain's rights to the Pacific Northwest in the Adams-Onís Treaty (see Chapter 9), and the British had gained effective control of the northern portion of the Oregon country. Blocking an equitable division was the reluctance of both sides to surrender access to the Columbia River basin and the adjacent territory extending north to the forty-ninth parallel (which later became the northern border of the state of Washington).

The Oregon country was virtually unpopulated before 1840, but the same could not be said of the Mexican borderlands that lay directly west of Jacksonian America. By 1827 Mexican settlements in present-day New Mexico contained about 44,000 people. To save the province from economic stagnation, the Mexican authorities decided in 1822 to encourage trade between Santa Fe, the capital of New Mexico, and the United States. They succeeded in stimulating commercial prosperity, but they also whetted expansionist appetites on the Anglo side of the border.

California in the 1820s and 1830s was a more colorful, turbulent, and fragile northward expansion of Mexican civilization. Much less populous than New Mexico—there were only about 4000 Hispanic inhabitants in 1827—California was a land of huge estates and enormous herds of cattle. At the beginning of the 1830s most of the land and the wealth of the province was controlled by the chain of twenty-one mission stations of the Catholic Church that stretched from San Diego to San Francisco.

In 1833 the Mexican government confiscated the Church's lands and released the Indians from semislavery, but this in fact made their plight even worse. Rather than giving the land to the 30,000 Christian Indians in California, the government awarded immense tracts to Mexican citizens. During the fifteen years that they held sway, the *rancheros* (as the large landowners were called) captured the fancy and aroused the envy of Anglo traders and visitors to California through their flamboyant lifestyle, superb horsemanship, and taste for violent and dangerous sports.

The easterners who conveyed to the rest of the nation a romantic image of this sun-baked land of beautiful scenery and senoritas were mostly merchants and sailors involved in the oceanic trade between Boston and California ports. By the mid-1830s, several Yankee merchants had taken up permanent residence in towns like Monterey and San Diego in order to conduct the California end of the business. The reports that they sent back about the Golden West sparked great interest in eastern business circles.

THE TEXAS REVOLUTION

At the same time that some Americans were trading with California, others were taking possession of Texas. After Mexico became independent in 1821, it inherited Spain's claim to Texas, which the United States recognized. Both Adams and Jackson tried to buy Texas from Mexico, but their efforts were firmly rebuffed. Beginning in the early 1820s, however, American settlers began to move into Texas at the invitation of the Mexican government.

In 1823 Mexican officials agreed to the proposal of two Americans—Moses Austin and his son Stephen F. Austin—to populate Texas by granting huge tracts of land to a few individuals who would then act as colonizing agents. American immigrants were drawn by the offer of fertile and inexpensive land, and those from the southwestern states often brought slaves with them in the hope of extending the cotton kingdom.

Friction soon developed between the Mexican government and the American colonists over such issues as the status of slavery and the Catholic Church. In 1829 Mexico formally freed all slaves under its jurisdiction, but the Texans simply ignored the decree. Mexican law also required that immigrants accept the Catholic faith, but this regulation also became a dead letter. The abuses of Mexican law grew, along with the size of the American population in Texas, and in 1830 the Mexican Congress prohibited further American immigration and importation of slaves to Texas.

But enforcement of the new law was feeble, and the flow of settlers, slaves, and smuggled goods continued virtually unabated. A longstanding complaint of the Texans was the failure of the Mexican constitution to grant them local self-government. In 1832 Texans showed their displeasure with Mexican rule by rioting in protest against the arrest of several Americans by the commander of the Galveston garrison.

Stephen F. Austin went to Mexico City in 1833 to present the Texans' grievances and seek concessions from the central government. He succeeded in having the ban against American immigration lifted but failed to win agreement for self-government. Then, as he was about to return to Texas, Austin was arrested and imprisoned for more than a year for writing a letter recommending that Texans set up a state government without Mexico City's consent.

In 1835, some Texans revolted against Mexico. The insurrectionists claimed that they were fighting for freedom against a long experience of oppression. Actually, Mexican rule had not been harsh, although it was inefficient and ofttimes corrupt. Furthermore, the Texans' devotion to "liberty" did not prevent them from defending slavery against Mexico's attempt to abolish it. Texans had done pretty much what they pleased, despite laws to the contrary and angry rumblings from south of the Rio Grande.

A more plausible justification for revolution was the Texans' fear of the future under the latest regime to be established in Mexico City. In 1834 General Antonio López de Santa Anna made himself dictator of Mexico and abolished the federal system of government. When news of these developments reached Texas late in the year, they were accompanied by rumors of the impending disenfranchisement and even expulsion of American immigrants. Influenced by these rumors, the rebels tended to ascribe sinister motives to Santa Anna's new policy of enforcing tariff regulation by military force.

When he learned that the Texans were resisting customs collections, Santa Anna sent reinforcements. By October 1835 the two sides were engaged in a war. The first phase of the fighting ended when Stephen F. Austin laid siege to San Antonio with a force of 500 men and after six weeks forced its surrender, thereby capturing most of the Mexican troops then in Texas.

THE REPUBLIC OF TEXAS

While this early fighting was going on, delegates from the American communities met in convention and after some hesitation voted overwhelmingly to declare their independence on March 2, 1836. A constitution, based closely on that of the United States, was adopted for the new Republic of Texas, and a temporary government was installed to carry on the military struggle.

Although the ensuing conflict was largely one of Americans against Mexicans, some

After the battle of San Jacinto, its hero Sam Houston, lying wounded under a tree, accepts the surrender of General Santa Anna, at left in white breeches. The man cupping his ear at right is Erastus "Deaf" Smith, a famous scout and important man in Houston's army.

Texas-Mexicans or *Tejanos* joined the fray on the side of the Anglo rebels. They too wanted to be free from Santa Anna's heavy-handed rule, although after the rebellion many of them became victims of anti-Mexican prejudice.

Within days after Texas declared itself a republic, rebels and Mexican troops in San Antonio fought the famous battle of the Alamo. Myths about the battle have magnified the Anglo rebels' valor at the Mexicans' expense. True enough, 187 rebels fought off a far larger Mexican force, capitulating only after more than a week of battling. It is not true, however, that all of the rebels fought to the death—apparently eight men, including Davy Crockett, surrendered. Moreover, the rebels fought from inside a strong fortress with superior weapons

against march-weary Mexican conscripts. Nevertheless, their stand was brave, and their deaths gave the insurrection new inspiration.

A few days later another Texas detachment was surrounded and captured in an open plain near the San Antonio River and was marched to the town of Goliad where all 350 of its members were summarily executed. The "Goliad massacre" provoked the Texas rebels to even more desperate resistance.

The main Texas army, under General Sam Houston, moved quickly to avenge these early defeats. On April 21, 1836, Houston led his force of 700 men in a daring assault on Santa Anna's encampment near the San Jacinto River. Within fifteen minutes the battle was over, the Mexican force defeated, and Santa

Anna captured. The Mexican leader was marched to Velasco where he was forced to sign treaties recognizing the independence of Texas and its claim to territory all the way to the Rio Grande.

Sam Houston, the hero of San Jacinto, became the first president of the Texas republic. He sought annexation to the United States, but Andrew Jackson and others believed that domestic politics, the sectional issue of the expansion of slavery, and the possibility of a war with Mexico made such an action untenable. Congress and the Jackson administration, however, did formally recognize Texas sovereignty, and during the following decade of independence, the population of the "Lone Star Republic" soared from 30,000 to 142,000.

TRAILS OF TRADE AND SETTLEMENT

After New Mexico opened its trade to American merchants in 1822, a thriving commerce developed along the trail that ran from Independence, Missouri, to Santa Fe. To protect themselves from the hostile Indians whose territory they had to cross, the traders traveled in large caravans. The federal government assisted them by providing troops when necessary and by appropriating money to purchase rights of passage from various tribes. Even so, the trip across the Cimarron desert and the southern Rockies was often difficult and hazardous. But profits from the exchange of textiles and other manufactured goods for furs, mules, and precious metals were substantial enough to make the risk worth taking.

Relations between the United States and Mexico soured following the Texas revolution, and this had a devastating effect on the Santa Fe trade. Much of the ill feeling was caused by the Texans' blundering efforts to get a piece of the Santa Fe action. After several clashes with the Texans, the Mexican government in 1842 passed a new tariff banning the importation of many of the goods sold by American merchants and prohibiting the export of gold and silver.

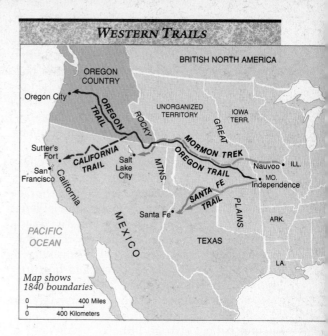

WESTERN TRAILS

Map shows 1840 boundaries

The famous Oregon Trail was the great overland route that brought the wagon trains of American migrants to the West Coast during the 1840s (see map). The journey took about six months; most parties departed in May, hoping to arrive in November before the great snows hit the last mountain barriers. After small groups had made their way to both Oregon and California in 1841 and 1842, a mass migration—mostly to Oregon—began in 1843. These migrants were quick to demand the extension of full American sovereignty over the Oregon country.

THE MORMON TREK

Among the settlers moving west were members, known as Mormons, of the most successful religious denomination founded exclusively on American soil—the Church of Jesus Christ of Latter Day Saints. The background of the Mormon trek was a history of persecution in the eastern states. Joseph Smith, founder of Mormonism, encountered strong opposition from the time he announced that he had received a new divine revelation, in Palmyra, New York, in 1820. This prophecy foretold the restoration of a purer Christianity that had once thrived on American soil. He and his followers were determined to establish a western Zion where they could practice their faith unmolested and carry out their special mission to convert the Native Americans.

In the 1830s the Mormons established communities in Ohio and Missouri, but the former went bankrupt in the Panic of 1837 and the latter was the target of angry mobs and vigilante violence. In 1839 the Mormons found a temporary haven at Nauvoo, Illinois. But Smith soon reported new revelations, which engendered dissension among his followers and hostility from neighboring "gentiles." Most controversial was his authorization of plural marriage. In 1844 Smith was killed by a mob while being held in jail in Carthage, Illinois.

The death of Smith confirmed the growing conviction of the Mormon leadership that they needed to move further west to establish their Zion in the wilderness. In late 1845, Smith's successor, Brigham Young, decided to send a party of 1500 men to assess the chances of maintaining a colony in the vicinity of the Great Salt Lake. In 1847 Young himself arrived in Utah and sent back word to the faithful that he had found the promised land.

The Mormon community that Young established in Utah is one of the great success stories of western settlement. In contrast to the extreme individualism and disorder that characterized the mining camps and other new communities, "the state of Deseret" (as Utah was originally called) was a model of discipline and cooperation. Because of its communitarian form of social organization, its centralized government, and the religious dedication of its inhabitants, this frontier society was able to expand settlement in a planned and efficient way and develop a system of irrigation that "made the desert bloom."

After Utah came under American sovereignty in 1848, the state of Deseret fought to maintain its autonomy and its custom of polygamy or "celestial marriage" against the efforts of the federal government to extend American law and set up the usual type of territorial administration. In 1857 the Mormons and the federal government almost came to blows, until President James Buchanan decided to use diplomacy rather than force.

MANIFEST DESTINY AND THE MEXICAN WAR

The rush of settlers beyond the nation's borders in the 1830s and 1840s inspired politicians and propagandists to call for annexation of those areas that the migrants were occupying. Some went further and proclaimed that it was the "manifest destiny" of the United States to expand until it had absorbed all of North America, including Canada and Mexico. Such ambitions—and the policies they inspired—led to a major diplomatic confrontation with Great Britain and a war with Mexico.

TYLER AND TEXAS

President John Tyler initiated the politics of Manifest Destiny. He was vice-president when William Henry Harrison died in office in 1841 after serving scarcely a month. Tyler was a states' rights, proslavery Virginian who had been picked as Harrison's running mate to broaden the appeal of the Whig ticket. Profoundly out of sympathy with the mainstream of his own party, he soon broke with the Whigs in Congress, who had united behind Henry Clay's nationalistic economic program. Despite the fact that he lacked a base in either of the major parties, Tyler hoped to be elected president in his own right in 1844. To accomplish this difficult feat, he needed a new issue around which he could build a following that would cut across established party lines.

In 1843 Tyler decided to put the full weight of his administration behind the annexation of Texas. He anticipated that this would be a popular move, especially in the slaveholding

South, and would give him a solid base of support for the 1844 election.

To achieve his objective, Tyler enlisted the support of John C. Calhoun, the leading political defender of slavery and southern rights. Success or failure in this effort would constitute a decisive test of whether the North was willing to give the southern states a fair share of national power and adequate assurances for the future of their way of life. If antislavery sentiment succeeded in blocking the acquisition of Texas, the Southerners would at least know where they stood and begin to "calculate the value of the union."

To prepare the public mind for annexation, the Tyler administration launched a propaganda campaign in the summer of 1843. Rumors were circulated that the British were preparing to guarantee Texas independence and make a loan to that financially troubled republic in return for the abolition of slavery. Although the reports were groundless, the stories were believed and used to give urgency to the annexation cause.

The strategy of linking annexation explicitly to the interests of the South and slavery backfired politically. Northern antislavery Whigs charged that the whole scheme was a proslavery plot meant to advance the interest of one section of the nation against the other—an allegation that has more substance than most historians have been willing to acknowledge. Consequently, the Senate rejected the treaty of annexation by a decisive vote in June 1844.

THE TRIUMPH OF POLK AND ANNEXATION

Tyler's initiative made the future of Texas the central issue in the 1844 campaign. But party lines held firm, and the president himself was unable to capitalize on it. Tyler tried to run as an independent, but his failure to gain significant support eventually forced him to withdraw from the race.

If the Democratic party convention had been held in 1843—as originally scheduled—ex-President Martin Van Buren would have won the nomination easily. But the convention was postponed until May 1844, and in the meantime the annexation question came to the fore. Van Buren persisted in the view he had held as president—that incorporation of Texas would arouse sectional strife and destroy the unity of the Democratic party. In an effort to keep the issue out of the campaign, Van Buren struck a gentleman's agreement with Henry Clay, the overwhelming favorite for the Whig nomination, that both of them would publicly oppose immediate annexation.

Van Buren's letter opposing annexation appeared before the Democratic convention and it cost him the nomination. Angry southern delegates invoked the rule requiring approval by a two-thirds vote. After several ballots a dark horse candidate—James K. Polk of Tennessee—emerged triumphant. Polk, a protege of Andrew Jackson, had been speaker of the House of Representatives and governor of Tennessee.

Polk was an avowed expansionist, and he ran on a platform calling for the simultaneous annexation of Texas and assertion of American claims to all of Oregon. He identified himself and his party with the popular cause of turning the United States into a continental nation, an aspiration that attracted support in the North as well as in the South. The Whig nominee, Henry Clay, was basically antiexpansionist, but his sense of the growing popularity of Texas annexation among southern Whigs caused him to waffle on the issue during the campaign. This in turn cost Clay the support of a small but crucial group of northern antislavery Whigs, who defected to the abolitionist Liberty party.

Polk won the fall election by a relatively narrow popular margin. His triumph in the electoral college was secured by victories in New York and Michigan, where the Liberty party candidate, James G. Birney, had taken away enough votes from Clay to affect the outcome. Although the election was hardly a clear mandate for expansionism, the Democrats claimed that the people were behind their aggressive campaign to extend the borders of the United States.

After the election, Congress reconvened to consider the annexation of Texas. The mood had changed as a result of Polk's victory, and leading Democratic senators were now willing to support Tyler's scheme for annexation by joint resolution of Congress. As a result, annexation was approved a few days before Polk took office.

THE DOCTRINE OF MANIFEST DESTINY

The expansionist mood that accompanied Polk's election and the annexation of Texas was given a name and a rationale in the summer of 1845. John L. O'Sullivan, a proponent of the Young America movement and influential editor, charged that foreign governments were conspiring to block the annexation of Texas in an effort to thwart "the fulfillment of our manifest destiny to overspread the continent allotted by providence for the free development of our yearly multiplying millions."

Besides coining the phrase *Manifest Destiny*, O'Sullivan pointed to the three main ideas that lay behind it. One was that God was on the side of American expansionism. A second idea, implied in the phrase *free development*, was that the spread of American rule meant the extension of democratic institutions. O'Sullivan's third premise was that population growth required the outlet that territorial acquisitions would provide. Behind this notion lurked the fear that growing numbers would lead to diminished opportunities and European-type socioeconomic class divisions if the restless and the ambitious were not given new lands to settle and exploit.

In its most extreme form, Manifest Destiny meant that the United States would someday occupy the entire North American continent; nothing less would appease its land-hungry population. The only question in the minds of fervent expansionists and Young Americans was whether the United States would acquire its vast new domain through a gradual, peaceful process of settler infiltration or through active diplomacy backed by force and the threat of war. The decision was up to President Polk.

POLK AND THE OREGON QUESTION

In 1845 and 1846 the United States came closer to armed conflict with Great Britain than at any time since the War of 1812. The willingness of some Americans to go to war over Oregon was expressed in the Democratic rallying cry "fifty-four forty or fight." Polk fed this expansionist fever by laying claim in his inaugural address to all of the Oregon country. Privately, however, he was willing to accept the forty-ninth parallel. What made the situation so tense was that Polk was dedicated to an aggressive diplomacy of bluff and bluster.

In July 1845 Polk authorized Secretary of State James Buchanan to reply to the latest British request for terms by offering a boundary along the forty-ninth parallel. Because this did not meet the British demand for all of Vancouver Island and free navigation of the Columbia River, the British ambassador rejected the pro-

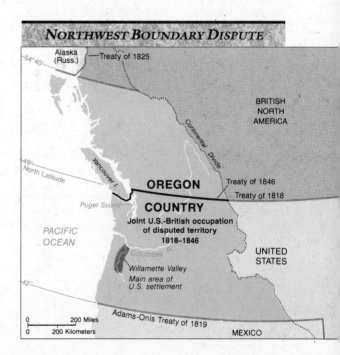

NORTHWEST BOUNDARY DISPUTE

posal out-of-hand. This rebuff infuriated Polk, who later called on Congress to terminate the agreement providing for joint occupation of the Pacific Northwest. Congress complied in April 1846.

Since abrogation of the joint agreement implied that the United States would attempt to extend its jurisdiction north to 54°40′, the British government decided to take the diplomatic initiative in an effort to avert war, while at the same time dispatching warships to the Western hemisphere in case conciliation failed. Their new proposal accepted the forty-ninth parallel as the border, gave Britain all of Vancouver Island, and provided for British navigation rights on the Columbia River. The Senate recommended that the treaty be accepted with the single change that British rights to navigate the Columbia be made temporary. It was ratified in that form on June 15.

Polk was prompted to settle the Oregon question because he now had a war with Mexico on his hands. His reckless diplomacy had brought the nation within an eyelash of being involved in two wars at the same time. American policymakers got what they wanted from the Oregon treaty, the splendid natural deep water harbor of Puget Sound. However, by agreeing to a compromise on Oregon, Polk alienated expansionist advocates in the Old Northwest who had supported his earlier call for "all of Oregon."

For many Northerners, the promise of new acquisitions of the Pacific Northwest was the only thing that made annexation of Texas palatable. They hoped that new free states could be created to counterbalance the admission of slaveholding Texas to the Union. As this prospect receded, the charge of antislavery defenders that Texas annexation was a southern plot drew more support; to Northerners Polk began to look more and more like a president concerned mainly with furthering the interests of his native region.

WAR WITH MEXICO

While the United States was avoiding a war with Great Britain, it was getting into one with Mexico. Although they had recognized Texas' independence in 1845, the Mexicans rejected the Lone Star Republic's unjustified claim to the unsettled territory between the Nueces River and the Rio Grande. When the United States annexed Texas and assumed its claim to the disputed area, Mexico broke off diplomatic relations and prepared for armed conflict.

Polk responded by placing troops in Louisiana on the alert and by dispatching emissary John Slidell to Mexico City. Polk hoped Slidell could resolve the boundary dispute and could persuade the Mexicans to sell New Mexico and California. Slidell's mission failed. In January 1846, Polk ordered General Zachary Taylor, commander of American forces in the Southwest, to advance well beyond the Nueces and proceed toward the Rio Grande, thus invading Mexican territory. By April, Taylor had taken up a position near Matamoras on the Rio Grande. On April 24, 1600 Mexican troops crossed the river from the south and the following day attacked a small American detachment. After learning of the incident, Taylor sent word to the president: "Hostilities may now be considered as commenced."

This news was neither unexpected nor unwelcome. Polk in fact was already preparing his war message to Congress when he learned of the fighting on the Rio Grande. A short and decisive war, he had concluded, would force the cession of California and New Mexico to the United States. Thus shortly after Congress declared war on May 13, American forces under Col. Stephen Kearny captured Santa Fe and took possession of New Mexico. Kearny's troops then set off for California where Anglo settlers and a so-called exploration expedition led by Capt. John C. Fremont, aided by U.S. naval vessels, had revolted against Mexican rule. With the help of Kearny's forces, the Americans wrested control of California from Mexico.

The war lasted much longer than expected because the Mexicans refused to make peace despite a succession of military defeats. In the first major campaign of the conflict, Taylor followed up his victory in two battles fought north of the Rio Grande by crossing the river,

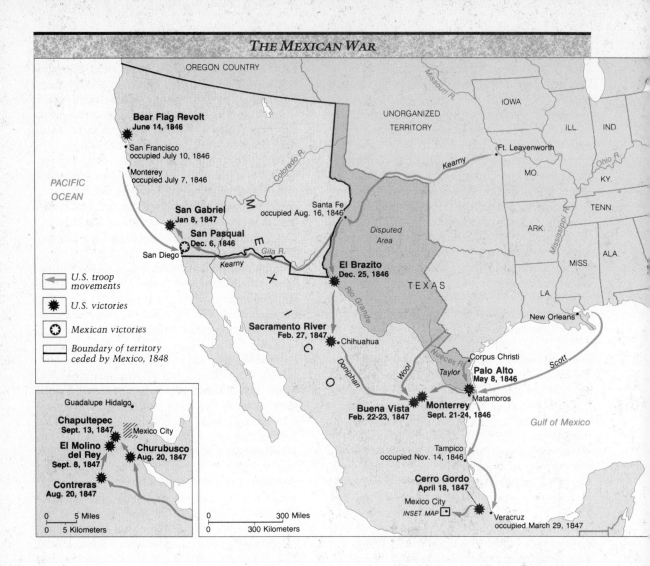

Map legend:
- → U.S. troop movements
- ✴ U.S. victories
- ◎ Mexican victories
- ▭ Boundary of territory ceded by Mexico, 1848

Map labels:

OREGON COUNTRY

Bear Flag Revolt
June 14, 1846

San Francisco
occupied July 10, 1846

Monterey
occupied July 7, 1846

PACIFIC OCEAN

San Gabriel
Jan 8, 1847

San Pasqual
Dec. 6, 1846

San Diego

Kearny

Gila R.

Santa Fe
occupied Aug. 16, 1846

Colorado R.

UNORGANIZED TERRITORY

IOWA

ILL.   IND

Ft. Leavenworth

Kearny

MO.   KY.

Missouri R.

Ohio R.

TENN.

ARK.

Disputed Area

El Brazito
Dec. 25, 1846

Rio Grande

TEXAS

MISS.   ALA.

LA.

New Orleans

Sacramento River
Feb. 27, 1847

Chihuahua

Doniphan

Wool

Taylor

Nueces R.

Corpus Christi

Palo Alto
May 8, 1846

Scott

Matamoros

Gulf of Mexico

Buena Vista
Feb. 22-23, 1847

Monterrey
Sept. 21-24, 1846

Tampico
occupied Nov. 14, 1846

Cerro Gordo
April 18, 1847

Mexico City
INSET MAP

Veracruz
occupied March 29, 1847

Inset map:

Guadalupe Hidalgo

Chapultepec
Sept. 13, 1847

Mexico City

El Molino
del Rey
Sept. 8, 1847

Churubusco
Aug. 20, 1847

Contreras
Aug. 20, 1847

0   5 Miles
0   5 Kilometers

0   300 Miles
0   300 Kilometers

---

taking Matamoras and marching on Monterrey. In September he captured this important northern city.

But Taylor's controversial decision to allow the Mexican garrison to go free and his unwillingness or inability to advance further into Mexico angered Polk and led him to adopt a new strategy for winning the war and a new commander to implement it. General Winfield Scott was ordered to prepare an amphibious attack on Vera Cruz with the aim of placing an American army within striking distance of Mexico City itself. Taylor was left to hold his

position in northern Mexico, where in February 1847 he defeated a sizable Mexican army at Buena Vista. Taylor was hailed afterwards as a national hero and conceivable presidential material.

The decisive Vera Cruz campaign was slow to develop because of the massive and careful preparations required. But in March 1847 the main American army, now under General Scott, finally landed near that crucial port city and laid siege to it. Vera Cruz fell after eighteen days, and then Scott began his advance on Mexico City. In the most important single battle of the war, Scott met forces under General Santa Anna at Cerro Gordo on April 17 and 18. In a well-commanded attack, Scott's forces defeated the Mexican army and opened the road to Mexico City. By August American troops were drawn up in front of the Mexican capital. After a temporary armistice, Scott ordered the massive assault that captured the city on September 14.

SETTLEMENT OF THE MEXICAN WAR

Accompanying Scott's army was a diplomat, Nicholas P. Trist, who was authorized to negotiate a peace treaty whenever the Mexicans decided they had had enough. Despite a sequence of American victories, however, no Mexican leader was willing to invite the wrath of an intensely proud and nationalistic citizenry by agreeing to the kind of terms Polk wanted to impose. By November, Polk was so irked by the delay that he ordered Trist to return to Washington.

Trist, to his credit, ignored Polk's instructions and continued to negotiate. On February 2, 1848, he signed a treaty that gained all the concessions he had been commissioned to obtain. The Treaty of Guadalupe Hidalgo ceded New Mexico and California to the United States for $15 million, established the Rio Grande as the border between Texas and Mexico, and promised that the United States government would assume the substantial claims of American citizens against Mexico. The Senate approved the treaty on March 10.

As a result of the Mexican War the United States gained half a million square miles of territory, including the present states of California, Utah, New Mexico, and Arizona, and parts of Colorado and Wyoming. In 1853, a dispute over the southern boundary of the cession was resolved by the Gadsden Purchase, through which the United States acquired the southernmost parts of present-day Arizona and New Mexico (see America at Mid-Century map on page 197). But one intriguing question remains. Why, given the expansionist spirit of the age,

didn't the United States take all of Mexico, as many Americans wished?

Racism and anticolonialism certainly help to account for the decision. It was one thing to acquire thinly populated areas that could be settled by Anglo-Saxon pioneers. It was something else again to incorporate a large population that was mainly of mixed Spanish and Indian origin. These "half-breeds," charged racist opponents of the "All Mexico" movement, could never be fit citizens of a self-governing republic. They would have to be ruled in the way that the British governed India, and the possession of colonial dependencies was contrary to American ideals and traditions.

Those actually making policy had more mundane and practical reasons for being satisfied with what was obtained at Guadalupe Hidalgo. What they had really wanted all along were the great California harbors of San Francisco and San Diego. From these ports Americans could trade directly with the Orient and dominate the commerce of the Pacific. Once acquisition of California had been assured, policymakers had little incentive to press for more Mexican territory.

The war with Mexico divided the American public and provoked political dissension. A majority of the Whig party opposed the war in principle, arguing (correctly) that the United States had no valid claims to the area south of the Nueces. Whig congressmen voted for military appropriations while the conflict was going on, but they constantly criticized the president for starting it. More ominous was the charge from antislavery Northerners of both parties that the real purpose of the war was to spread the institution of slavery and increase the political power of the southern states. While battles were being fought in Mexico, Congress was debating a proposal to prohibit slavery in any territories that might be acquired from Mexico. A bitter sectional quarrel over the status of slavery in new areas was a major legacy of the Mexican War.

The domestic controversies aroused by the war and the propaganda of Manifest Destiny revealed the limits of mid-nineteenth-century American expansionism and put a damper on additional efforts to extend the nation's boundaries. Concerns about slavery and race blocked further southern expansion, and the desire to remain at peace with Great Britain prevented northern expansion. After 1848, American growth usually took the form of populating and developing the vast territory already acquired.

INTERNAL EXPANSIONISM

The expansionists of the 1840s saw a clear link between acquisition of new territory and other forms of material growth and development. In 1844 Samuel F. B. Morse perfected and demonstrated his electric telegraph. Simultaneously, the railroad was becoming increasingly important as a means of moving people and goods over great distances. Improvements in manufacturing and agricultural methods led to an upsurge in the volume and range of internal trade, and the beginnings of mass immigration were providing human resources for the exploitation of brand new areas and economic opportunities.

The discovery of gold in California in 1848 encouraged thousands of emigrants to move to the West Coast. The gold they unearthed spurred the national economy, and the rapid growth of population centers on the Pacific Coast inspired projects for transcontinental telegraph lines and railroad tracks.

When the spirit of Manifest Destiny and the thirst for acquiring new territory waned after the Mexican War, the expansionist impulse turned inward. The technological advances and population increase of the 1840s continued during the 1850s. The result was an acceleration of economic growth, a substantial increase in industrialization and urbanization, and the emergence of a new American working class.

TRIUMPH OF THE RAILROAD

More than anything else, it was the rise of the railroad that transformed the American economy during the 1840s and 1850s. The technol-ogy for steam locomotives came from England, and in 1830 and 1831 two American railroads began commercial operation. Although these lines were practical and profitable, canals proved to be strong competitors, especially for the freight business. Passengers might prefer the speed of trains, but the lower unit cost of freight on the canal boats prevented most shippers from changing their habits. Furthermore, states like New York and Pennsylvania that had invested heavily in canals resisted chartering a competitive form of transportation.

During the 1840s rails extended beyond the northeastern and Middle Atlantic states, and mileage increased more than threefold, reaching a total of more than 9000 miles by 1850. Ex-

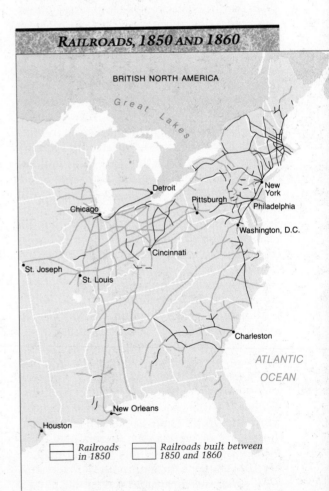

RAILROADS, 1850 AND 1860

BRITISH NORTH AMERICA

Great Lakes

Detroit
Chicago
Pittsburgh
New York
Philadelphia
Washington, D.C.
Cincinnati
St. Joseph
St. Louis

Charleston

ATLANTIC OCEAN

New Orleans
Houston

Railroads in 1850   Railroads built between 1850 and 1860

pansion was even greater in the following decade, and by 1860 all the states east of the Mississippi had rail service. In addition, throughout the 1840s and 1850s, railroads cut deeply into the freight business of the canals and succeeded in driving many of them out of business.

The development of railroads had an enormous effect on the economy as a whole. Although the burgeoning demand for iron rails was initially met mainly by importation from England, that demand eventually spurred development of the domestic iron industry. Since railroads required an enormous outlay of capital, their promoters pioneered new methods for financing business enterprise. Railroad companies sold stock to the general public and helped to set the pattern for the separation of ownership and control that characterizes the modern corporation.

But the gathering and control of private capital did not fully meet the needs of the early railroad barons. State and local governments, convinced that railroads were the key to their future prosperity, loaned the railroads money, bought their stock, and actively supported their development. Despite the dominant policy of laissez-faire, the federal government became involved by surveying the routes of projected lines and providing land grants. Thus a precedent was set for the massive land grants of the post-Civil War era.

THE INDUSTRIAL REVOLUTION TAKES OFF

While railroads were initiating a revolution in transportation, American industry was entering a new phase of rapid and sustained growth. The factory mode of production, which had originated before 1840 in the cotton mills of New England (see Chapter 9), was extended to a variety of other products. Between 1830 and 1860, wool and iron production moved toward the factory system, as did the shoemaking, firearms, clock, and sewing machine industries.

The essential features of this mode of production were the gathering of a supervised work force in a single place, the payment of cash wages to workers, the use of interchangeable parts, and manufacturing by "continuous process." Within a factory setting, standardized parts, manufactured separately and in bulk, could be efficiently and rapidly assembled into a final product by an ordered sequence of continuously repeated operations. Mass production, which involved the division of labor into a series of relatively simple and repetitive tasks, contrasted sharply with the traditional craft mode of production, in which a single worker produced the entire product out of raw materials.

New technology played an important role in the transition to mass production. Just as power looms and spinning machinery had made textile mills possible, the development of new and more reliable machines or industrial techniques revolutionized other industries. Elias Howe's invention of the sewing machine and Charles Goodyear's discovery of the process for the vulcanization of rubber opened the way for the mass production of a wide range of consumer items.

Perhaps the greatest triumph of American technology during the mid-nineteenth century was the development of the world's most sophisticated and reliable machine tools. Such advances as the invention of the extraordinarily accurate measuring device known as the vernier caliper in 1851 and the first production of turret lathes in 1854 were signs of a special American aptitude for the kind of precision toolmaking that was essential to efficient industrialization.

Progress in industrial technology and organization did not mean that the United States had become an industrial society by 1860. Agriculture retained first place both as a source of livelihood for individuals and as a contributor to the gross national product. But farming itself, at least in the North, was undergoing a technological revolution of its own. John Deere's steel plow enabled midwestern farmers to cultivate the tough prairie soils that had resisted cast iron implements, and Cyrus McCormick's mechanical reaper offered an enormous saving in the labor required for harvesting grain.

THE AGE OF PRACTICAL INVENTION, 1750–1860

(Dates refer to patent or first successful use)

Year	Inventor	Contribution	Importance/Description
1787	John Fitch	Steamboat	First successful American steamboat
1793	Eli Whitney	Cotton gin	Simplified process of separating fiber from seeds; helped make cotton a profitable staple of southern agriculture
1798	Eli Whitney	Jig for guiding tools	Facilitated manufacture of interchangeable parts
1802	Oliver Evans	Steam engine	First American steam engine; led to manufacture of high-pressure engines used throughout eastern United States
1813	Richard B. Chenaworth	Cast-iron plow	First iron plow to be made in three separate pieces, thus making possible replacement of parts
1830	Peter Cooper	Railroad locomotive	First steam locomotive built in America
1831	Cyrus McCormick	Reaper	Mechanized harvesting; early model could cut six acres of grain a day
1836	Samuel Colt	Revolver	First successful repeating pistol
1837	John Deere	Steel plow	Steel surface kept soil from sticking; farming thus made easier on rich prairies of Midwest
1839	Charles Goodyear	Vulcanization of rubber	Made rubber much more useful by preventing it from sticking and melting in hot weather
1842	Crawford W. Long	First administered ether in surgery	Reduced pain and risk of shock during operations
1844	Samuel F. B. Morse	Telegraph	Made long-distance communication almost instantaneous
1846	Elias Howe	Sewing machine	First practical machine for automatic sewing
1846	Norbert Rillieux	Vacuum evaporator	Improved method of removing water from sugarcane; revolutionized sugar industry and was later applied to many other products
1847	Richard M. Hoe	Rotary printing press	Printed an entire sheet in one motion, vastly speeded up printing process
1851	William Kelly	Air-boiling process	Improved method of converting iron into steel (usually known as Bessemer process because English inventor had more advantageous patent and financial arrangements)
1853	Elisha G. Otis	Passenger elevator	Improved movement in buildings; when later electrified, stimulated development of skyscrapers
1859	Edwin L. Drake	First American oil well	Initiated oil industry in the United States
1859	George M. Pullman	Pullman car	First sleeping car suitable for long-distance travel

Source: From Freedom and Crisis: An American History, Third Edition, *by Allen Weinstein and Frank Otto Gatell. Copyright © 1974, 1978, 1981 by Random House, Inc. Reprinted by permission of the publisher.*

RAILROAD MILEAGE, CA. 1860

Area	Miles
New England	3,660
Middle Atlantic	6,353
Old Northwest	9,592
Southeast	5,463
Southwest	4,072
Far West	1,495
Total	30,636

Source: Adapted from George R. Taylor and Irene D. Neu, The American Railroad Network, 1861 to 1890 (1956; reprint ed., Salem, N.H.: Arno, 1981).

A dynamic interaction between advances in transportation, industry, and agriculture gave great strength and resiliency to the economy of the northern states during the 1850s. Railroads offered western farmers better access to eastern markets. After Chicago and New York were linked by rail in 1853, the flow of most midwestern farm commodities shifted from the North-South direction based on riverborne traffic that had still predominated in the 1830s and 1840s to an East-West pattern.

The mechanization of agriculture did more than lead to more efficient and profitable commercial farming; it also provided an additional impetus to industrialization, and its labor-saving features released manpower for other economic activities. The growth of industry and the modernization of agriculture can thus be seen as mutually reinforcing aspects of a single process of economic growth.

MASS IMMIGRATION BEGINS

The original incentive to mechanize northern industry and agriculture came in part from a shortage of cheap labor. Compared with the industrializing nations of Europe, the United States of the early nineteenth century was a labor-scarce economy. Since it was difficult to attract able-bodied men to work for low wages in factories or on farms, women and children were used extensively in the early textile mills,

and commercial farmers had to rely heavily on the labor of their family members. Although labor-saving machinery helped ease the problem, by the 1840s and 1850s industrialization had reached a point where it needed far more unskilled workers. The growth of industrial-work opportunities helped attract a multitude of European immigrants between 1840 and 1860.

Between 1820 and 1840, an estimated 700,000 immigrants arrived in the United States. During the 1840s this substantial flow suddenly became a flood. No less than 4,200,000 crossed the Atlantic between 1840 and 1860. This was the greatest influx in proportion to total population—then about 20 million—that the nation has ever experienced.

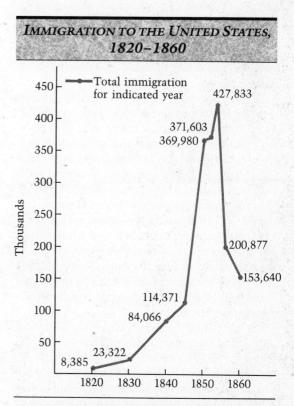

IMMIGRATION TO THE UNITED STATES, 1820–1860

Total immigration for indicated year

427,833
371,603
369,980
200,877
153,640
114,371
84,066
23,322
8,385

Source: U.S. Bureau of the Census, Historical Statistics of the United States, Colonial Times to 1970, Bicentennial Edition, Washington, D.C., 1975.

The largest single source of the new mass immigration was Ireland, but Germany was not far behind.

This massive transatlantic movement had many causes; some people were "pushed" out of their homes, while others were "pulled" toward America. The great potato famine in Ireland accounted for much of the emigration from that country. Escape to America was made possible by the low fares then prevailing on sailing ships bound from England to North America. Ships involved in the timber trade carried their bulky cargoes from Boston or Halifax to Liverpool. As an alternative to returning to America partly in ballast, they packed Irish immigrants into their holds.

Because of the ports involved in the lumber trade—Boston, Halifax, Saint John's, and Saint Andrews—the Irish usually arrived in Canada or the northeast states. Immobilized by poverty and a lack of skills required for pioneering in the West, most of them remained in the Northeast. Forced to subsist on low-paid menial labor and crowded into festering urban slums, they were looked down upon by most native-born Americans.

The million or so Germans who also came in the late 1840s and early 1850s were somewhat more fortunate. Most of them were also peasants, but they fled hard times rather than outright catastrophe. Unlike the Irish, they often escaped with a small amount of capital with which to make a fresh start in the New World. Many German immigrants were artisans and sought to ply their trades in cities like New York, St. Louis, Cincinnati, and Milwaukee. But a large portion of those with peasant backgrounds went back to the land. Many became successful midwestern farmers, and in general they encountered less prejudice and discrimination than the Irish.

What "pulled" most of the Irish, German, and other European immigrants to America was the promise of economic opportunity. Although a minority chose the United States because they admired its democratic political system, most immigrants were more interested in the chance to make a decent living than in voting or running for office. During times of prosperity and high demand for labor, America proved a powerful magnet to discontented Europeans.

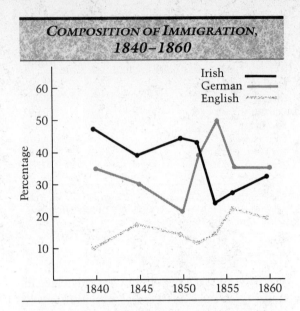

COMPOSITION OF IMMIGRATION, 1840–1860

Irish
German
English

Source: U.S. Bureau of the Census, Statistical Abstract of the United States: 1982–83 (103rd edition) Washington, D.C., 1982.

Yet the arrival of large numbers of immigrants worsened the already serious problems of America's rapidly growing cities. The old "walking city" in which rich and poor lived in close proximity near the center of town was changing to a more segregated environment. The advent of railroads and horse-drawn streetcars enabled the affluent to move to the first American suburbs, while areas nearer commercial and industrial centers became the congested settlements of newcomers from Europe. Emerging slums, such as the notorious "Five Points" district in New York City, were characterized by overcrowding, poverty, disease, and crime. Recognizing that these conditions created potential dangers for the entire urban population, middle-class reformers worked for the professionalization of police forces, introduction of sanitary water and sewage disposal systems, and the upgrading of housing standards. They made some progress in these endeavors in the period before the Civil War, but the lot of the urban poor, mainly immigrants, was not dramatically improved. For most of them urban life remained unsafe, unhealthy, and unpleasant.

THE NEW WORKING CLASS

A majority of the immigrants ended up as wage workers in factories, mines, and construction camps, or as casual day laborers doing the many unskilled tasks required by urban and commercial growth. By providing a vast pool of cheap labor, they fueled and accelerated the Industrial Revolution.

In the established industries and older mill towns of the Northeast, immigrants gradually

CHRONOLOGY

1822	Santa Fe opened to American traders
1823	Earliest American settlers arrive in Texas
1830	Mexico attempts to halt American migration to Texas
1831	American railroads begin commercial operation
1834	Cyrus McCormick patents mechanical reaper
1835	Revolution breaks out in Texas
1836	Texas becomes independent republic
1837	John Deere invents steel plow
1841	President John Tyler inaugurated
1842	Webster-Ashburton Treaty fixes border between Maine and New Brunswick
1843	Mass migration to Oregon begins Mexico closes Santa Fe trade to Americans
1844	Samuel F. B. Morse demonstrates electric telegraph James K. Polk elected president on platform of expansionism
1845	Mass immigration from Europe begins United States annexes Texas John L. O'Sullivan coins slogan *Manifest Destiny*
1846	War with Mexico breaks out United States and Great Britain resolve diplomatic crisis over Oregon
1847	American conquest of California completed Mormons settle Utah American forces under Zachary Taylor defeat Mexicans at Buena Vista Winfield Scott's army captures Vera Cruz and defeats Mexicans at Cerro Gordo Mexico City falls to American invaders
1848	Treaty of Guadalupe Hidalgo consigns California and New Mexico to United States Gold discovered in California
1849	"Forty-niners" rush to California to dig for gold
1858	War between Utah Mormons and United States forces averted

displaced the native-born workers who had predominated in the 1830s and 1840s. In the textile mills especially, native female labor was replaced by foreign male workers. Irish males, employers found, were willing to perform tasks that native-born men had generally regarded as women's work.

This trend reveals much about the changing character of the American working class. In the 1830s most male workers were artisans, while unskilled factory work was still largely the province of women and children. Both groups were predominantly of American stock. In the 1840s the proportion of men engaged in factory work increased, although the work force in the textile industry remained predominantly female. During that decade working conditions in many mills deteriorated. Relations between management and labor became increasingly impersonal, and workers were driven to increase their output. Workdays of twelve to fourteen hours were common.

The result was a new upsurge of labor militancy involving female as well as male factory workers. Workers' organizations petitioned state legislatures to pass laws limiting the workday to ten hours. Some such laws were actually passed, but they turned out to be ineffective because employers could still require a prospective worker to sign a special contract agreeing to longer hours as a condition of employment.

The employment of immigrants in increasing numbers between the mid-1840s and the late 1850s made it more difficult to organize industrial workers. Impoverished fugitives from the Irish potato famine tended to have lower economic expectations and little experience with labor organizations. Consequently the Irish immigrants were willing to work for less and were not so prone to protest bad working conditions or organize into unions.

But the new working class of former rural folk did not make the transition to industrial wage labor easily or without protesting in subtle and indirect ways. Tardiness, absenteeism, drunkenness, loafing on the job, and other forms of resistance to factory discipline reflected deep hostility to the unaccustomed and seemingly unnatural routines of "continuous process" production. The adjustment to new styles and rhythms of work was painful and took time.

By 1860 industrial expansion and immigration had created a working class of men and women who seemed destined for a life of low-paid wage labor. This reality stood in contrast to America's self-image as a land of opportunity and upward mobility. The ideal still had some validity in rapidly developing regions of the western states, but it was mostly myth when applied to the increasingly foreign-born industrial workers of the Northeast.

Both internal and external expansion had come at a heavy cost. Tensions associated with class and ethnic rivalries were only one part of the price of rapid economic development. The acquisition of new territories became politically divisive and would soon lead to a catastrophic sectional controversy. From the late 1840s to the Civil War, the United States was a divided society in more senses than one, and the need to control or resolve these conflicts presented politicians and statesmen with a monumental challenge.

RECOMMENDED READING

An overview of expansion to the Pacific is Ray A. Billington, *The Far Western Frontier, 1830–1860* (1956). On the impulse behind Manifest Destiny, see Frederick Merk, *Manifest Destiny and Mission in American History* (1963); Norman A. Graebner, *Empire on the Pacific: A Study in American Continental Expansionism* (1956); and Reginald Horsman, *Race and Manifest Destiny* (1981).

Other works on American penetration and settlement of the Far West include William H. Goetzmann, *Exploration and Empire: The Explorer and the Scientist in the Winning of the American West* (1966); John D. Unruh, Jr., *The Plains Across: The Overland Immigrants and the Trans-Mississippi West, 1840–1860* (1979); and Thomas O'Dea, *The Mormons* (1957). The politics and diplomacy of expansionism are treated in David M. Pletcher, *The Diplomacy of Annexation: Texas, Oregon, and the Mexican War* (1973), and Frederick Merk, *The Monroe Doctrine and American Expansion, 1843–1849* (1966). On the Mexican War, see Otis A. Singletary,

The Mexican War (1960), and John H. Schroeder, *Mr. Polk's War: American Opposition and Dissent* (1973).

Economic developments of the 1840s and 1850s are well covered in George R. Taylor, *The Transportation Revolution, 1815–1860* (1952); Albert Fishlow, *American Railroads and the Transformation of the Ante-Bellum Economy* (1965); Douglass C. North, *The Economic Growth of the United States, 1790–1860* (1961); and Merritt Roe Smith, *Harpers Ferry Armory and the New Technology* (1977).

For insight into immigrants, see Oscar Handlin, *Boston Immigrants: A Study in Acculturation*, rev. ed. (1959), and Marcus L. Hansen, *The Atlantic Migration, 1607–1860* (1976). Important recent works that deal with the working-class experience include Herbert G. Gutman, *Work, Culture, and Society in Industrializing America* (1976); Thomas Dublin, *Women at Work: The Transformation of Work and Community in Lowell, Massachusetts, 1826–1860* (1979); Sean Wilentz, *Chants Democratic: New York City and the Rise of the American Working Class, 1788–1850* (1984); Bruce Laurie, *Working People of Philadelphia, 1800–1850* (1980); and Steven J. Ross, *Workers on the Edge: Work, Leisure, and Politics in Industrializing Cincinnati, 1788–1890* (1985).

13 MASTERS AND SLAVES

SLAVERY AND THE SOUTHERN ECONOMY

THE SLAVEHOLDING SOCIETY

THE BLACK EXPERIENCE UNDER SLAVERY

On August 22, 1831, the worst nightmare of southern slaveholders became reality. A group of slaves in Southampton County, Virginia, rose in open and bloody rebellion. Their leader was Nat Turner, a preacher and prophet who believed that God had given him a sign that the time was ripe to strike for freedom. When white forces dispersed the rampaging slaves only forty-eight hours later, Turner's band had killed nearly sixty whites. The rebels were then rounded up and executed along with dozens of other slaves vaguely suspected of complicity. Nat Turner was the last to be captured, and he went to the gallows unrepentent, convinced that he had acted in accordance with God's will.

Southern whites were determined to prevent another such uprising. Their anxiety and determination were strengthened by the fact that 1831 also saw the emergence of a more militant northern abolitionism. Nat Turner and William Lloyd Garrison were viewed as two prongs of a revolutionary attack on the southern way of life. Afraid that abolitionist agitation might set about another revolt, southern whites launched a massive campaign to quarantine the slaves from possible exposure to antislavery ideas and attitudes.

A new series of laws severely restricted the rights of slaves to move about, assemble without white supervision, or learn to read and write. Other laws prevented white dissenters from publicly criticizing or even questioning the institution of slavery. The South rapidly became a closed society with a closed mind. Proslavery agitators sought to create a mood of crisis and danger requiring absolute unity and singlemindedness among the white population. This embattled attitude lay behind the growth of a more militant sectionalism and inspired threats to secede from the Union if security for slaveholding seemed to require it.

The campaign for repression apparently achieved its original aim. Nat Turner's revolt was the last mass slave uprising. Slave resistance, however, did not end; it simply took other and less dangerous forms. Slaves sought or perfected other methods of asserting their humanity and maintaining their self-esteem. This heroic effort to endure slavery without surrendering to it gave rise to an African-American culture of lasting value.

SLAVERY AND THE SOUTHERN ECONOMY

Slavery would not have lasted as long as it did—and Southerners would not have reacted so strongly to real or imagined threats to its survival—if an influential class of whites had not had a vital and growing economic interest in this form of human exploitation. Although forced labor had always been essential to the South's economy, between the 1790s and the Civil War, plantation agriculture expanded enormously and so did dependence on slave labor.

By the time of the Civil War, 90 percent of the South's 4 million slaves worked on plantations and farms. In the seven cotton-producing states of the lower South slaves constituted close to half of the total population and were responsible for producing 90 percent of the cotton and almost all of the rice and sugar. In the upper South whites outnumbered slaves by more than three to one and were less dependent on their labor. Thus even within the cotton kingdom there were important differences between the upper and lower South.

ECONOMIC ADJUSTMENT IN THE UPPER SOUTH

Tobacco, the plantation crop of the colonial period, continued to be the principal slave-cultivated commodity of the upper tier of southern states during the pre-Civil War era. But markets were often depressed, and profitable tobacco cultivation was hard to sustain for very long in one place because it rapidly depleted the soil. As a result, there were continual shifts in the areas of greatest production and much experimentation with new crops and methods of farming in the older regions. The heart of tobacco cultivation moved westward, so that by 1860 Kentucky had emerged as the major producer.

During the lengthy depression of the tobacco market that lasted from the 1820s to the 1850s, agricultural experimentation was widespread in Virginia and Maryland. Increased use of fertilizer, systematic rotation of tobacco with other crops, and the growth of diversified farming based on a mix of wheat, corn, and livestock contributed to a gradual revival of agricultural prosperity. Such changes increased the need for capital but reduced the demand for labor. Improvements were financed in part by selling surplus slaves in regions of the lower South where staple crop production was more profitable. The interstate slave trade was thus a godsend to the slaveholders of the upper South and a key to their survival and prosperity.

The fact that slave labor was declining in importance in the upper South meant that the peculiar institution had a weaker hold on public loyalty there than in the cotton states. Diversification of agriculture was accompanied by a more rapid rate of urban and industrial development than was occurring elsewhere in the South. As a result, Virginians, Marylanders, and Kentuckians were seriously divided on whether their ultimate future lay with the Deep South's plantation economy or with the industrializing, free labor system that was flourishing just north of their borders.

THE RISE OF THE COTTON KINGDOM

The warmer climate and good soils of the lower tier of southern states made it possible to raise crops more naturally suited than tobacco or cereals to the plantation form of agriculture and the heavy use of slave labor. Since the colonial

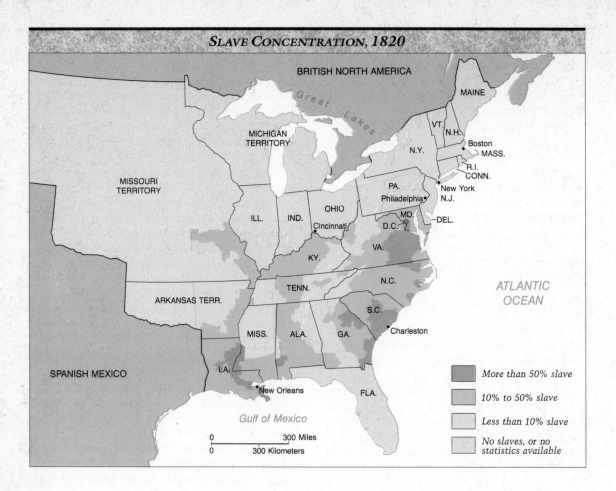

BRITISH NORTH AMERICA

Great Lakes

MAINE

MICHIGAN
TERRITORY

VT.
N.H.
N.Y.
Boston
MASS.
R.I.
CONN.

MISSOURI
TERRITORY

PA.
Philadelphia
New York
N.J.

ILL.   IND.   OHIO
Cincinnati
D.C.
MD.
DEL.

KY.
VA.

ARKANSAS TERR.
TENN.
N.C.

S.C.

MISS.   ALA.   GA.
Charleston

SPANISH MEXICO

LA.
New Orleans
FLA.

ATLANTIC
OCEAN

Gulf of Mexico

| 0 | | 300 Miles |
| 0 | | 300 Kilometers |

More than 50% slave

10% to 50% slave

Less than 10% slave

No slaves, or no
statistics available

period, rice and a special variety of fine cotton (known as "long-staple") had been grown profitably on the vast estates along the coast of South Carolina and Georgia. In lower Louisiana sugar was the cash crop, and it too required well-financed plantations and small armies of slave laborers. However, it was the rise of "short-staple" cotton as the South's major crop that strengthened the hold of slavery and the plantation on the southern economy.

Short-staple cotton differed from the long-staple variety in two important ways: its bolls contained seeds that were much more difficult to extract by hand, and it could be grown almost anywhere south of Virginia and Kentucky—the main requirement was a guarantee of 200 frost-free days. The invention of the cot-

ton gin in 1793 ended the seed extraction problem and made short-staple cotton the South's major crop. Unlike rice or sugar, cotton could be grown on small farms as well as on plantations. But large planters enjoyed certain advantages that made them the main producers. Only relatively large operators could afford their own gins or possessed the capital to acquire the fertile bottomlands that brought the highest yields. They also had lower transportation costs because they were able to monopolize the land along the rivers and streams that were the South's natural passageways of transportation.

Cotton was well suited to a plantation form of production. The required tasks were relatively simple and could be performed by supervised gangs of unfree workers. Furthermore, there was enough work to be done in all seasons to keep the force occupied throughout the year. Cotton requires constant weeding or "chopping" while growing and can be picked over an extended period. The relative absence of seasonal variations in work needs made the use of slave laborers advantageous.

The first major cotton-producing regions were inland areas of Georgia and South Carolina. The center of production shifted rapidly westward during the nineteenth century, first to Alabama and Mississippi and then to Arkansas, northwest Louisiana, and east Texas. The rise in total production that accompanied this geographical expansion was phenomenal. In 1792 the South's output of cotton was about 13,000 bales; in 1840 it was 1,350,000 bales; and in 1860 production peaked at the colossal figure of 4,800,000 bales. Most of this cotton went to supply the booming textile industry of Great Britain.

"Cotton is king!" proclaimed a southern orator in the 1850s, and he was right. By that time, three quarters of the world's supply of cotton came from the American South, and this single commodity accounted for over half of the total dollar value of American exports. Cotton growing and the network of commercial and industrial enterprises that marketed and processed this crop constituted the most important economic interest in the United

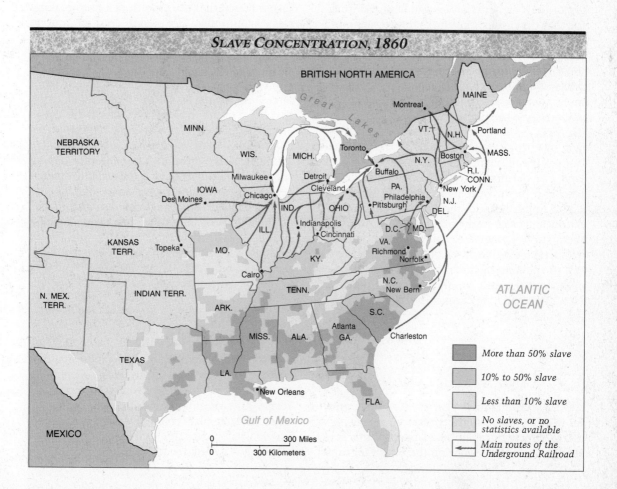

SLAVE CONCENTRATION, 1860

More than 50% slave

10% to 50% slave

Less than 10% slave

No slaves, or no statistics available

Main routes of the Underground Railroad

States on the eve of the Civil War. Since slavery and cotton seemed inextricably linked, it appeared self-evident to many Southerners that their peculiar institution was the keystone of national wealth and economic progress.

Despite its overall success, however, the rise of the cotton kingdom did not bring a uniform or steady prosperity to the lower South. Many planters worked the land until it was exhausted and then took their slaves westward to richer soils, leaving depressed and ravaged areas in their wake. In addition, planters were beset and sometimes ruined by fluctuations in markets and prices. The boom periods of 1815–1819 and 1832–1837 were each followed by a depression and a wave of bankruptcies. However, during the eleven years of rising output and high prices preceding the Civil War the planters gradually forgot their earlier troubles and began to imagine that they were immune to future economic disasters.

Despite the insecurities associated with cotton production, most of the time this crop represented the best chance for profitable investment that existed in the Old South. Prudent planters who had not borrowed too heavily during flush times could survive periods of depression by cutting costs and making their plantations self-sufficient. For those with worn-out land, two options existed: They could sell their land and move west or they could sell their slaves to raise capital for fertilization, crop rotation, and other improvements that could help them survive where they were. Hence planters had little incentive to seek alternatives to slavery, the plantation, and dependence on a single cash crop. From a purely economic point of view they had every reason to rally to the defense of slavery.

SLAVERY AND INDUSTRIALIZATION

As the sectional quarrel with the North grew more intense, Southerners became increasingly alarmed by their region's lack of economic self-sufficiency. Dependence on the North for capital, marketing facilities, and manufactured goods was seen as evidence of a dangerous subservience to "external" economic interests. Southern nationalists like J.D.B. DeBow, editor of the influential *DeBow's Review*, called during the 1850s for the South to develop its own industries, commerce, and shipping. But his call went unanswered. Men with capital were doing too well in plantation agriculture to risk much money in other ventures.

In the 1840s and 1850s, a debate raged among white capitalists over whether the South should use free whites or enslaved blacks as the basic labor force in the development of industry. Some leaders defended a white labor policy, arguing that factory work would provide new economic opportunities for a degraded class of poor whites. But other advocates of industrialization feared that the growth of a free working class would lead to social conflict among whites and preferred using slaves for all supervised manual labor. In practice, some factories employed slaves, others white workers, and a few even experimented with integrated work forces. As nearly as can be determined, mills that hired or purchased slave labor were just as profitable and efficient as those paying wages to whites.

It is clear, however, that the union of slavery and cotton that was central to the South's prosperity impeded industrialization and left the region dependent on a one-crop agriculture and on the North for capital and marketing. So long as plantations yielded substantial profits, there could be no major movement of slaves from agriculture to industry. If anything the trend was in the opposite direction.

THE "PROFITABILITY" ISSUE

Some Southerners were obviously making money, and a great deal of it, using slave labor to raise cotton. But did slavery yield a good return for the great majority of slaveholders who were not large planters? Did it provide the basis for general prosperity and a relatively high standard of living for the southern population in general, or at least for the two thirds of it who were white and free? In a word, was slavery profitable?

For many years historians believed that slave-based agriculture was, on the average, not very lucrative. Planters' account books seemed to show at best a modest return on investment. In the 1850s, the price of slaves rose at a faster rate than the price of cotton, allegedly squeezing many operators. Some historians even concluded that slavery was a dying institution by the time of the Civil War. Profitability, they argued, depended on access to new and fertile land suitable for plantation agriculture, and virtually all such land within the limits of the United States had already been taken up by 1860. Hence slavery had reached its natural limits of expansion and was on the verge of becoming so unprofitable that it would fall of its own weight in the near future.

A more recent interpretation holds that slavery was in fact still an economically sound institution in 1860 and showed no signs of imminent decline. During the 1850s planters could normally expect an annual return of 8 to 10 percent on capital invested. This yield was roughly equivalent to the best that could then be obtained from the most lucrative sectors of northern industry and commerce. Furthermore, it is no longer clear that plantation agriculture had reached its natural limits of expansion by 1860. Production in Texas had not yet peaked, and transportation improvements and flood control would certainly have opened up new areas for growing cotton. Those who now argue that slavery was profitable and had an expansive future have made a strong and convincing case.

But a larger question remains: What sort of economic development did a slave plantation system foster? What portion of the southern population benefited from the system? Did it promote efficiency and progressive change? Two recent economists, Robert Fogel and Stanley Engerman, have argued that slave plantation agriculture was much more efficient than northern family farming. However, critics of this thesis contend that Fogel and Engerman's sophisticated calculations are faulty and that there is no proof that the plantation was an internally efficient enterprise with good managers and industrious, well-motivated workers.

Other evidence suggests that only the large plantations were profitable. Because of various insecurities—lack of credit, high transportation costs, and a greater vulnerability to market fluctuations—smaller and nonslaveholding plantations had to devote a larger share of their acreage to subsistence crops. This kept their standard of living lower than that of most northern farmers. Slaves benefited from planter profits to the extent that they were better fed, housed, and clothed than they would have been had their owners been less prosperous. But to suggest that they were better off than northern wage laborers is proslavery propaganda rather than documented fact.

The South's economic development was skewed in favor of a single route to wealth, open only to the minority possessing both white skin and access to capital. The concentration of capital and business energies on cotton production foreclosed the kind of diversified industrial and commercial growth that would have provided wider opportunities. Thus, in comparison to the industrializing North, the South was an underdeveloped region in which neither slaves nor lower class whites had much incentive to work hard. A lack of public education for whites and the denial of even minimal literacy to slaves represented a critical failure to develop human resources. Good ground exists for concluding that the South's economy was condemned to backwardness so long as it was based on slavery.

THE SLAVEHOLDING SOCIETY

If the precise effect of slavery on the South's economic life remains debatable, there is less room for disagreement concerning its impact on social arrangements and attitudes. More than any other factor, the ownership of slaves determined gradations of social prestige and influence among whites. But the fact that all whites were free and that most blacks were slaves created a sharp cleavage between the races that could create the impression of a basic equality within "the master race." In the language of sociologists, inequality in the Old South was determined in two ways: by "class" and by "caste." An awareness of both systems of social ranking is necessary for an understanding of southern society.

THE PLANTERS' WORLD

Those who know the Old South only from modern novels, films, and television programs are likely to envision a land filled with majestic plantations, courtly gentlemen, elegant ladies, and faithful retainers. It is easy to conclude from such images that the typical white Southerner was an aristocrat who belonged to a family that owned large numbers of slaves. Certainly the great houses existed, some wealthy slaveholders did maintain an aristocratic lifestyle, and the great planters did set the tone and values for much of the society. But this was the world of only a small percentage of slaveowners and a minuscule portion of the total white population.

In 1860 only 25 percent of all white Southerners belonged to families owning slaves. Even in the cotton belt of the Deep South, slaveholders were a minority of whites on the eve of the Civil War. Planters, defined as agriculturalists owning twenty or more slaves, were the minority of a minority. In 1860 planters and their families constituted about 12 percent of all slaveholders and less than 4 percent of the total white population of the South. But even the master of twenty to fifty slaves could rarely live up to the popular image of aristocratic grandeur. To live this sort of life a planter had to own at least fifty slaves and preferably many more. In 1860 these substantial planters comprised less than 3 percent of all slaveholders and less than 1 percent of all whites.

Contrary to legend, most of the great planters of the pre-Civil War period were self-made rather than descendants of the old colonial gentry. For example, one Irish immigrant started out with a log cabin and a few acres in upland South Carolina around 1800. By the time of his death in 1854, he had built up an estate of 2000 acres, 114 slaves, and 4 cotton gins.

As the cotton kingdom spread westward from South Carolina and Georgia to Alabama, Mississippi, and Louisiana, the men who became the wealthiest planters were even less likely to have genteel backgrounds. A large proportion of them began as hard-driving businessmen who built up capital from commerce, land speculation, banking, and even slave trading. They then used their profits to buy plantations. The highly competitive, boom-or-bust economy of the Southwest put a greater premium on sharp dealing and business skills than on genealogy.

To be successful, a planter had to be a shrewd businessman who kept a careful eye on the market, the prices of slaves and land, and the extent of his indebtedness. Reliable "factors"—the agents who marketed the crop and provided advances against future sales—could assist him in making decisions, but a planter who failed to spend a good deal of time with his account books could end up in serious trouble. Managing the slaves and plantation production was also difficult and time consuming, even when overseers were available to supervise day-to-day activities. Hence few planters could be the men of leisure featured in the popular image of the Old South.

Some of the richest and most secure did aspire to live in the manner of a traditional landed aristocracy. Big houses, elegant carriages, fancy-dress balls, and excessive numbers of house servants all reflected aristocratic aspirations. Dueling, despite some efforts to repress it, remained the standard way to settle "affairs of honor" among gentlemen. Another sign of gentility was the tendency of planters' sons to avoid "trade" as a primary or secondary career in favor of law or the military. Planters' daughters were trained from girlhood to play the piano, speak French, dress in the latest fashions, and sparkle in the drawing room or on the dance floor. The aristocratic style originated among the older gentry of the seaboard slave states, but by the 1840s and 1850s it had spread southwest as a second generation of wealthy planters began to displace the rough-hewn pioneers of the cotton kingdom.

PLANTERS AND SLAVES

No assessment of the planters' outlook or "world view" can be made without considering their relations with their slaves. Planters owned more than half of all the slaves in the South and set the standards for treatment and management of them. Most of the planters liked to think of themselves as kindly and paternalistic. They tended to view slaves as per-petual children who were part of their extended patriarchal family. Paternalistic rhetoric increased greatly after abolitionists began to charge that most slaveholders were sadistic monsters. To some extent, the response was part of a defensive effort to redeem the South's reputation and self-respect.

There was, nevertheless, an element of truth in the planters' claim that their slaves were relatively well treated. Food, clothing, and shelter were normally sufficient to sustain life and labor at above a bare subsistence level; family life was encouraged and to some extent flourished; and average life expectancy, birth rate, and natural growth in population were only slightly below the average for southern whites. Certainly North American slaves of the pre-

Slave cabins, such as these on a prosperous plantation, were small and crude, but still were better than many that had only a doorway leading into a dirt-floored hovel.

Civil War period enjoyed a higher standard of living than those in other New World slave societies.

But relatively good physical conditions for slaves do not demonstrate that planters put ethical considerations ahead of self-interest. The ban on the transatlantic slave trade in 1808 was effective enough to make the domestic reproduction of the slave force an economic necessity if the system was to be perpetuated. Slaves were also valuable property and the main tools of production for a booming economy, and it was in the interest of masters to see that their property remained in good enough condition to work hard and bear large numbers of children.

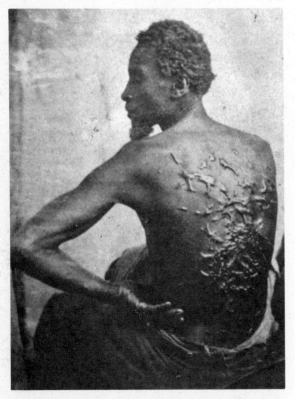

Not all slaves and masters had the benevolent relationship often cited in defense of slavery. Whippings that could produce scars like these were common on most plantations.

The testimony of slaves themselves and of some independent white observers suggests that masters of large plantations generally did not have close and intimate relations with the mass of field slaves. The kind of affection and concern associated with a father figure appears to have been limited mainly to relationships with a few favored house servants or other elite slaves. The field hands on large estates dealt mostly with overseers who were hired or fired on their ability to meet production quotas.

When they were being most realistic, planters conceded that the ultimate basis of their authority was force and intimidation, rather than the natural obedience due to a loving parent. Devices for inspiring fear included whipping—a common practice on most plantations—and the threat of sale away from family and friends. Planters and overseers maintained order and productivity by swift punishment for any infraction of the rules or even for a surly attitude.

Despite economic considerations, some masters inevitably yielded to the temptations of power or to their bad tempers and tortured or killed their slaves. Others raped slave women. Slaves had little legal protection against such abuse because slave testimony was not accepted in court. Human nature being what it is, such a situation was bound to result in atrocities. As Harriet Beecher Stowe, the author of *Uncle Tom's Cabin*, pointed out, there was something terribly wrong with any institution that gave one human being nearly absolute power over another.

THE WORLD OF THE COMMON WHITES

As we have seen, 88 percent of all slaveholders in 1860 owned fewer than twenty slaves and thus were not planters in the usual sense of the term. Of these, the great majority had fewer than ten. Many were simply farmers who used one or two slave families to ease the burden of their own labor. These slave owners lived spartan lives; their houses were simple and their lives were hard.

For better or worse, relations between owners and their slaves were more intimate than on larger estates. Unlike planters, these families often worked in the fields alongside their slaves and sometimes ate at the same table or slept under the same roof. But such closeness did not necessarily result in better treatment. Both the best and worst of slavery could be found on these farms, depending on the character and disposition of the master. Given a choice, most slaves preferred to live on plantations because they offered the sociability, culture, and kinship of the quarters, as well as better prospects for adequate food, clothing, and shelter.

Just below the small slaveholders on the social scale was a substantial class of yeoman farmers. Contrary to another myth about the Old South, most of these people did not fit the image of the degraded, shiftless, "poor white." The majority were proud, self-reliant farmers whose way of life did not differ markedly from that of family farmers in the Midwest during the early stages of settlement.

The yeomen were mostly concentrated in the backcountry where slaves and plantations were rarely seen. The foothills or interior valleys of the Appalachians and the Ozarks were unsuitable for plantation agriculture but offered reasonably good soil for mixed farming, and long stretches of "piney barrens," along the Gulf Coast were suitable for raising livestock. In such regions slaveless farmers concentrated, giving rise to the "white counties" that complicated southern politics.

The lack of transportation facilities, more than some failure of energy or character, limited the prosperity of the yeoman. A large part of their effort was devoted to growing subsistence crops, mainly corn. Their principal source of cash was livestock, especially hogs. But since the livestock was generally allowed to forage in the woods rather than being fattened on grain, it was of poor quality and did not bring high prices or big profits to raisers.

Although they did not benefit directly from the peculiar institution, most yeomen and other nonslaveholders tolerated slavery and were fiercely opposed to abolitionism in any form. Many abolitionists could not understand the reasons for their position, for undoubtedly yeomen were hurt economically by the existence of slavery and a planter class. In addition, most yeomen were staunch Jacksonians who resented aristocratic pretensions and feared concentrations of power and wealth in the hands of the few. On issues involving representation, banking, and internal improvements yeomen sometimes voted against the planters. Why, then, did they fail to respond to antislavery appeals that called for them to strike at the real source of planter power and privilege?

One reason was that some nonslaveholders hoped to get ahead in the world, and in the South this meant acquiring slaves of their own. Just enough of the more prosperous yeomen broke into the slaveholding classes to make the dream seem believable. Planters, anxious to ensure the loyalty of nonslaveholders, strenuously encouraged the notion that every white man was a potential master.

But the main reason why most nonslaveholders went along with the proslavery leadership was their intense fear and dislike of blacks. Although they had no natural love of planters and slavery, they believed that abolitionism would lead to disaster. In part their anxieties were economic; freed slaves would compete with them for land and jobs. But their racism went deeper than this. Emancipation was unthinkable because it would remove the pride and status that automatically went along with a white skin in this acutely race-conscious society. Slavery, despite its drawbacks, served to keep blacks "in their place" and to make all whites, however poor or underprivileged they might be, feel that they were superior to somebody.

A Closed Mind and a Closed Society

Despite the tacit assent of most nonslaveholders, the dominant class never lost its fear that lower class whites would turn against slavery. They felt threatened from two sides: from the slave quarters where a new Nat Turner might be gathering his forces and from the backcountry where yeomen and poor whites might heed the call of abolitionists to rise up against planter domination. Beginning in the 1830s, the ruling element tightened their grip on southern society and culture.

Before the 1830s, open discussion of the rights or wrongs of slavery had been possible in many parts of the South. Apologists commonly described the institution as "a necessary evil," and in the upper South there was support for colonization plans. By the end of 1832, however, all talk about emancipation had ended in the South. The argument that slavery was "a positive good"—rather than an evil slated for gradual elimination—won the day.

The "positive good" defense of slavery was an answer to the abolitionist charge that the institution was inherently sinful. The message was carried in a host of books, pamphlets, and newspaper editorials published between the 1830s and the Civil War. Who, historians have asked, was it meant to persuade? Partly, the argument was aimed at the North. But Southerners themselves were a prime target. In popularized forms, the message was used to arouse racial anxieties that tended to neutralize antislavery sentiment among the lower classes.

The proslavery argument was based on three main propositions. The first and foremost was that enslavement was the natural and proper status for people of African descent. Blacks, it was alleged, were innately inferior to whites and suited only for slavery. Biased scientific and historical evidence was presented to support this claim. Secondly, slavery was held to be sanctioned by the Bible and Christianity—a position made necessary by the abolitionist appeal to Christian ethics. Finally, efforts were made to show that slavery was consistent with the humanitarian spirit of the nineteenth century. The plantation was seen as a sort of asylum providing guidance and care for a race that could not rule itself.

By the 1850s, the proslavery argument had gone beyond mere apology for the South and its peculiar institution and featured an ingenious attack on the free labor system of the North. According to the Virginian George Fitzhugh, the master-slave relationship was more humane than the one prevailing between employers and wage laborers in the North. Slaves had security against unemployment and a guarantee of care in old age, while free workers might face destitution and even starvation at any time. Fitzhugh believed that on the whole slave societies were more orderly, just, and peaceful than free societies.

In addition to arguing against the abolitionists, proslavery Southerners attempted to seal off their region from antislavery ideas and influences. Whites who were bold enough to criticize slavery publicly were mobbed or persecuted. One of the bravest of the Southern abolitionists, Cassius Clay of Kentucky, armed himself with a brace of pistols when he gave speeches. Clergymen who questioned the morality of slavery were driven from their pulpits, and northern travelers suspected of being abolitionist agents were tarred and feathered. When abolitionists tried to send their literature through the mails during the 1830s, it was seized in southern post offices and publicly burned.

Such flagrant denials of free speech and civil liberties were inspired by fears that nonslaveholding whites and slaves would get the wrong ideas. Hinton R. Helper's book, *The Impending Crisis of the South*, an 1857 appeal to nonslaveholders to resist the planter regime, was suppressed with particular vigor. But the deepest fear was that slaves would hear the abolitionist talk or read antislavery literature and be inspired to rebel. Consequently, new laws were passed making it a crime to teach slaves to read and write. Free blacks, who were thought to be possible instigators of slave revolt, were denied basic civil liberties and were the object of growing surveillance and harassment.

All these efforts at thought control and internal security did not allay the fears of abolitionist subversion, lower class white dissent, and, above all, slave revolt. The persistent barrage of proslavery propaganda and the course of national events in the 1850s created a mood of panic and desperation. By this time an increasing number of Southerners had become convinced that safety from abolitionism and its associated terrors required a formal withdrawal from the Union—secession.

THE BLACK EXPERIENCE UNDER SLAVERY

Most blacks, if not most whites, experienced slavery on plantations; the majority of slaves lived on units owned by planters who had twenty or more slaves. The masters of these agrarian communities sought to ensure their personal safety and the profitability of their enterprises by using all the means—physical and psychological—at their command to make slaves docile and obedient. By word and deed, they tried to demonstrate their power, authority, and self-assumed superiority over their servants. As increasing numbers of slaves were converted to Christianity and attended white-supervised services, they were forced to hear, over and over again, that God had commanded slaves to obey their masters.

It is a great tribute to the resourcefulness and spirit of African Americans that most of them resisted these pressures and managed to retain an inner sense of their own worth and dignity. When conditions were right, they openly asserted their desire for freedom and equality and showed their disdain for white claims that slavery was "a positive good." But the struggle for freedom involved more than the confrontation of master and slave; free blacks, in both the North and the South, did what they could to speed the day when all African Americans would be free.

FORMS OF SLAVE RESISTANCE

Open rebellion, the bearing of arms against the white oppressors, was the most dramatic and clear-cut form of slave resistance. In the period between 1800 and 1831, a number of slaves participated in revolts that showed their willingness to risk their lives in a desperate bid for liberation. In 1800, for example, a Virginia slave named Gabriel Prosser mobilized a large band

of his followers to march on Richmond, but whites suppressed the uprising without any loss of white life. In 1811 another band of rebellious slaves was stopped as it moved toward New Orleans. In 1822 whites in Charleston, South Carolina, uncovered an extensive and well-planned conspiracy, organized by a free black man named Denmark Vesey, to arm the slave population and take possession of the city.

As we have already seen, the most bloody and terrifying of all slave revolts was the Nat Turner insurrection of 1831. Although it was the last slave rebellion of this kind during the pre-Civil War period, armed resistance had not ended. Hundreds of black fugitives fought in the Second Seminole War (1835–1842) alongside the Indians who had given them a haven. Many of the blacks eventually accompanied the Indian allies to the trans-Mississippi West.

Only a tiny fraction of all slaves ever took part in organized acts of violent resistance against white power. Most realized that the odds against a successful revolt were very high, and bitter experience had showed them that the usual outcome was death to the rebels. As a consequence, therefore, they characteristically devised safer or more ingenious ways to resist white dominance.

One way of protesting against slavery was to run away, and thousands of slaves showed their discontent and desire for freedom in this fashion. Although most fugitives never got beyond the neighborhood of the plantation, many escapees remained free for years by hiding in swamps or other remote areas, and a fraction made it to freedom in the North or Mexico.

For the majority of slaves, however, flight was not a real option. Either they lived too deep in the South to have any chance of reaching free soil, or they were reluctant to leave family and friends behind. The typical fugitive was a young, unmarried male from the upper South.

Slaves who did not revolt or run away often registered their opposition to their bondage in other ways. The normal way of expressing discontent was by engaging in a kind of indirect or passive resistance. Many slaves worked slowly and inefficiently, not because they were naturally lazy (as whites supposed), but as a gesture of protest or alienation. Others soundlessly voiced their protest by feigning illness or injury, stealing provisions, and committing such acts of sabotage as breaking tools, mistreating livestock, and setting barns on fire. The ultimate act of clandestine resistance was poisoning the master's food.

The basic attitude behind such actions was revealed in the folk tales that slaves passed down from generation to generation. The famous Bruh Rabbit stories showed how a small, apparently defenseless animal could overcome a bigger and stronger one through cunning and deceit. Such stories served as an allegory for the black view of the master-slave relationship. Other stories—which were not told in front of whites—openly portrayed the slave as a clever trickster outwitting the masters.

The Struggles of Free Blacks

In addition to the 4 million blacks in bondage, there were approximately 500,000 free African Americans in 1860, about half of them living in slave states. Whether they were in the North or the South, "free Negroes" were treated as social outcasts and denied legal and political equality with whites. Public facilities were strictly segregated, and after the 1830s blacks in the United States could vote only in four New England states. Nowhere but in Massachusetts could they testify in court cases involving whites.

Free blacks had difficulty finding decent jobs. Most states excluded blacks entirely from public school, and the federal government barred them from the militia, the postal service, and full access to public lands. Free blacks were even denied U.S. passports; in effect they were stateless persons even before the 1857 Supreme Court ruling that no Negro could claim American citizenship.

In the South, free blacks were subject to a set of direct controls that tended to make them semislaves. Invariably they were required to carry papers proving their free status and their movement was strictly limited. They were excluded from certain occupations, normally prohibited from holding meetings or forming organizations, and often forced into a state of

Harriet Tubman, on the extreme left, is shown here with some of the slaves she led to freedom on the underground railroad. Born a slave in Maryland, she escaped to Philadelphia in 1849. She is said to have helped as many as three hundred blacks to freedom. Many of them she took all the way to Canada, where they were beyond the reach of the Fugitive Slave Law.

economic dependency barely distinguishable from outright slavery.

Although beset by special problems of their own, most free blacks identified with the suffering of the slaves. Many of them had once been slaves themselves or were the children of slaves. Often they had close relatives who were still in bondage. Furthermore, they knew that as long as slavery existed, their own rights were likely to be denied and even their freedom was at risk. Kidnapping or fraudulent seizure by slave catchers was always a possibility.

Because of the elaborate system of control and surveillance, free blacks in the South were in a relatively weak position to work against slavery. The wave of repression that followed the Denmark Vesey episode revealed the dangers of revolutionary activity and the odds against success. Consequently, most free blacks found that survival depended on creating the impression of loyalty to the planter regime.

In the North, free blacks were in a better position to join the struggle for freedom. Despite all the prejudice and discrimination that they faced, they still enjoyed some basic civil liberties denied to southern blacks. They could protest publicly against slavery or white supremacy and could form associations for the advancement and liberation of African Americans. Beginning in 1830, northern African Americans regularly held conventions to protest the existence of human bondage.

Black newspapers, such as *Freedom's Journal*, first published in 1827, and *The North Star*, founded by Frederick Douglass in 1847, gave black writers a chance to preach their gospel of liberation to black readers. African-American authors also produced a stream of books and pamphlets attacking slavery, refuting racism, and advocating various forms of resistance. One of the most influential publications was David Walker's *Appeal . . . to the Colored Citizens of the World*, which appeared in 1829. Walker denounced slavery in the most vigorous language possible and called for a black revolt against white tyranny.

Free blacks in the North did more than make verbal protests against racial injustice. They were also the main conductors on the fabled "underground railroad" that opened a path for fugitives of slavery. Courageous ex-slaves such as Harriet Tubman and Josiah Henson made regular forays into the slave states to lead other blacks to freedom, and many of the "stations" along the way were manned by free Negroes. In northern towns and cities, free blacks organized "vigilance committees" to protect fugitives and thwart the slave catchers. Groups of blacks even used force to rescue recaptured fugitives from the authorities. In deeds as well as words, free blacks showed their unyielding hostility to slavery and racism.

AFRICAN-AMERICAN RELIGION

African Americans could not have resisted or even endured slavery if they had been utterly demoralized by its oppressiveness. What made the struggle for freedom possible were the inner resources and patterns of thought that gave dignity to their lives and hopes for a brighter future. From the realm of culture and fundamental beliefs blacks drew the strength to hold their heads high and look beyond their immediate condition.

Religion was the cornerstone of this emerging African-American culture, particularly among the slaves. Black Christianity was far from being a mere imitation of white religious form and beliefs. It was rather a distinctive variant of evangelical Protestantism that incorporated elements of African religion and stressed those portions of the Bible that spoke to the aspirations of an enslaved people thirsting for freedom.

Free blacks formed the first independent black churches by seceding from white congregations that discriminated against them in seating and church governance. Out of these secessions came a variety of autonomous Baptist groups and the highly successful African Methodist Episcopal (A.M.E.) Church organized under the leadership of Rev. Richard Allen of Philadelphia in 1816. But the mass of blacks did not have access to these independent churches.

Mostly they served only free blacks and urban slaves with indulgent masters.

Plantation slaves who were exposed to Christianity either attended neighboring white churches or worshipped at home. On large estates, masters or white missionaries often conducted regular Sunday services. But white-sanctioned religious activity was only a superficial part of the slaves' spiritual life. The true slave religion was practiced at night, often secretly, and was led by black preachers.

This covert slave religion was a highly emotional affair that featured singing, shouting, and dancing. In some ways the atmosphere resembled a backwoods revival meeting. But much of what went on was actually an adaption of African religious beliefs and customs. The chanting mode of preaching—with the congregation responding at regular intervals—and the expression of religious feelings through rhythmical movements, really a form of dance, were clearly African in origin. The emphasis on sinfulness and fear of damnation that were core themes of white evangelicalism played a lesser role among blacks. For them, religion was more an affirmation of the joy of life than a rejection of worldly pleasures and temptations.

Slave sermons and religious songs spoke directly to the plight of a people in bondage and implicitly asserted their right to be free. The most popular of all biblical subjects was the deliverance of the children of Israel from slavery in Egypt. Many sermons and songs referred to the crossing of Jordan and the arrival in the Promised Land. Other songs invoked the liberation theme in different ways. One recalled that Jesus had "set poor sinners free."

Most of the songs of freedom and deliverance can be interpreted as referring exclusively to religious salvation and the afterlife—and this was undoubtedly how slaves hoped their masters would understand them. But the slaves did not forget that God had once freed a people from slavery in this life and punished their masters. The Bible thus gave African Americans the hope that they, as a people, would repeat the experience of the Israelites and be delivered from bondage. During the Civil War, observers noted that freed slaves seemed to regard their emancipation as something that was preordained and were inclined to view Lincoln as the reincarnation of Moses.

Besides being the basis for a deep-rooted hope for eventual freedom, religion helped slaves endure bondage without losing their sense of inner worth. Religious slaves sometimes regarded themselves as superior to their owners and believed that all whites were damned because of their treatment of blacks.

More important, slave religion gave blacks a chance to create and control a world of their own. Preachers, elders, and other leaders of unofficial slave congregations could acquire a sense of status within their own community that had not been conferred by whites. Although religion did not inspire slaves to open rebellion (except in the case of Nat Turner), it must be regarded as a prime source of resistance to the dehumanizing effects of enslavement. It helped create a sense of community, solidarity, and self-esteem among slaves by giving them something of their own that they found infinitely precious.

THE SLAVE FAMILY

The black family was the other institution that prevented slavery from becoming unendurable and utterly demoralizing. Contrary to earlier beliefs, the majority of slaves lived in two-parent households. Although slave marriages were not legally binding, many masters encouraged stable unions, and the slaves themselves apparently preferred monogamy to more casual or promiscuous relationships. The black sexual ethic valued marital fidelity, an attitude strongly influenced by Christian teaching. But premarital sex was not regarded as a serious moral lapse, and it was common for a slave woman to bear one child out of wedlock before settling into a permanent union.

Relations between spouses and between parents and children were normally close and affectionate. Slave husbands and fathers did not, of course, have the same power and authority as free heads of families. But they did what they could, and this included supplementing the family diet by hunting, fishing, or pilfering plantation stores. Husbands and wives usually interacted on a basis of rough equality and did everything possible to relieve each other's burdens; together they taught their children how to survive slavery and plantation life.

The terrible anguish that usually accompanied the breakup of families through sale showed the depth of kinship feelings. After emancipation, thousands of freed slaves wandered about looking for spouses, children, or parents from whom they had been forcibly separated for years.

Feelings of kinship and mutual obligation extended beyond the nuclear family. Grandparents, uncles, aunts, and even cousins were known to slaves through direct contact or family lore. Nor were kinship ties limited to blood relations. When families were broken up by sale, individual members who found themselves on plantations far from home were likely to be "adopted" into new kinship networks.

What becomes apparent from studies of the slave family is that kinships provided a model for personal relationships and the basis for a sense of community. For some purposes, all the slaves on a plantation were in reality members of a single extended family. Slave culture was a family culture, and this was one of its greatest sources of strength and cohesion. Strong kinship ties, whether real or fictive, meant that slaves could depend on one another in times of trouble. The kinship network also provided a vehicle for the transmission of African-American folk traditions from one generation to the

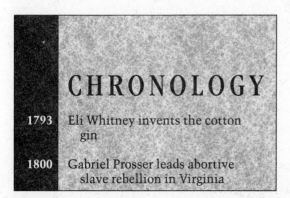

CHRONOLOGY

| 1793 | Eli Whitney invents the cotton gin |
| 1800 | Gabriel Prosser leads abortive slave rebellion in Virginia |

1811	Slaves revolt in Point Coupeé section of Louisiana
1822	Denmark Vesey conspiracy uncovered in Charleston, South Carolina
1829	David Walker publishes *Appeal . . . to the Colored Citizens of the World* calling for slave insurrection
1830	First National Negro Convention meets
1831	Slaves under Nat Turner rebel in Virginia, killing almost sixty whites
1832	Virginia legislature votes against gradual emancipation
1835–1842	Blacks fight alongside Indians in the Second Seminole War
1837	Panic of 1837 is followed by major depression of the cotton market
1847	Frederick Douglass publishes *The North Star*, a black antislavery newspaper
1849	Cotton prices rise, and a sustained boom commences
1852	Harriet Beecher Stowe's antislavery novel *Uncle Tom's Cabin* is published and becomes a best-seller
1857	Hinton R. Helper attacks slavery on economic grounds in *The Impending Crisis of the South*; the book is suppressed in the southern states
1860	Cotton prices and production reach all-time peak

next. Together with slave religion, kinship gave African Americans a feeling that they were members of a community, not just a collection of individuals victimized by oppression.

The sense of being part of a distinctive community was the key to black survival under slavery. Although slave culture did not normally provoke violent resistance to the slaveholder's regime, the inner world that the slaves made for themselves gave them the spiritual strength to thwart the masters' efforts to dominate their hearts and minds. After emancipation, this rich and resilient cultural heritage would combine with the tradition of open protest created by rebellious slaves and free black abolitionists to inspire and sustain new struggles for equality.

If slaves lived to some extent in a separate and distinctive world of their own, so did planters, less affluent whites, and even free blacks. The Old South was thus a deeply divided society. What held it together and provided some measure of unity was a booming plantation economy and a web of customary relationships and loyalties that could obscure the underlying cleavages and antagonisms. How fractured and fragile this society really was would become apparent after 1861 when it was subjected to the pressures of civil war.

✿ RECOMMENDED READING

Major works that take a broad view of slavery are Kenneth M. Stampp, *The Peculiar Institution: Slavery in the Ante-Bellum South* (1956), and Eugene D. Genovese, *Roll, Jordan, Roll: The World the Slaves Made* (1974).

Clement Eaton, *The Growth of Southern Civilization, 1790–1860* (1961), provides a good introduction to life in the Old South. Other general works on slavery and the Old South include Eugene D. Genovese, *The Political Economy of Slavery: Studies in the Economy and Society of the Slave South* (1965), and Leslie Howard Owens, *This Species of Property: Slave Life and Culture in the Old South* (1976). On the economics of slavery, see Gavin Wright, *The Political Economy of the Cotton South: Households, Markets, and Wealth in the Nineteenth Century* (1978); Robert William Fogel and Stanley L. Engerman, *Time on the Cross: The Economics of American Negro Slavery*, 2 vols. (1974); and Paul A. David et al., *Reckoning with Slavery: A Critical Study of the Quantitative History of American Negro Slavery* (1976). Nonagricultural slavery is examined in Robert S. Starobin, *Industrial Slavery in the Old South* (1970), and Richard C. Wade, *Slavery in the Cities* (1964).

On the society and culture of the southern white population, see W. J. Cash, *The Mind of the South* (1941); Frank L. Owsley, *Plain Folk of the Old South* (1949); Drew Gilpin Faust, *A Sacred Circle: The Dilemma of the Intellectual in the Old South, 1840–1860* (1977); Bertram Wyatt-Brown, *Southern Honor: Ethics and Behavior in the Old South* (1982); and James Oakes, *The Ruling Race: A History of American Slaveholders* (1982).

Proslavery consciousness is treated in William Summer Jenkins, *Pro-Slavery Thought in the Old South* (1935). Southern dissent and efforts to repress it are well covered in Carl N. Degler, *The Other South: Southern Dissenters in the Nineteenth Century* (1974).

On slave revolts, see Vincent Harding, *There Is a River: The Black Struggle for Freedom in America* (1981), and Herbert Aptheker, *American Negro Slave Revolts* (1943). The plight of Southern free blacks is covered in Ira Berlin, *Slaves Without Masters: The Free Negro in the Antebellum South* (1974). Slave culture and community are examined in Albert J. Raboteau, *Slave Religion* (1978); Herbert G. Gutman, *The Black Family in Slavery and Freedom, 1750–1925* (1976); and Lawrence W. Levine, *Black Culture and Consciousness: Afro-American Folk Thought from Slavery to Freedom* (1977).

14 THE SECTIONAL CRISIS

THE COMPROMISE OF 1850

POLITICAL UPHEAVAL, 1852–1856

THE HOUSE DIVIDED, 1857–1860

EXPLAINING THE CRISIS

On May 22, 1856, Representative Preston Brooks of South Carolina suddenly appeared on the floor of the Senate. He was looking for Charles Sumner, the antislavery senator from Massachusetts who had recently given a speech condemning the South for plotting to extend slavery to the Kansas Territory. When he found Sumner seated at his desk, Brooks proceeded to batter him over the head with a cane. Sumner made a desperate effort to rise, ripped his bolted desk from the floor, and then collapsed.

Sumner was so badly injured by the assault that he could not return to the Senate for three years. In parts of the North that were up in arms against the expansion of slavery, he was hailed as a martyr to the cause of "free soil." Brooks, denounced in the North as a bully, was lionized by his fellow Southerners and won re-election without opposition.

These contrasting reactions show how bitter sectional antagonism had become by 1856. Sumner spoke for the radical wing of the new Republican party, which was making a bid for national power by mobilizing the North against the alleged aggression of "the slave power." Southerners viewed the very existence of this party as an insult to their section of the country and a threat to its vital interests. Many Southerners believed that Sumner and his political friends were plotting against their way of life. By 1856, therefore, the sectional cleavage that would lead to the Civil War had already undermined the foundations of national unity.

The crisis of the mid-1850s came only a few years after the elaborate Compromise of 1850 had seemingly resolved the dispute over the future of slavery in the territories acquired as a result of the Mexican War. The renewed agitation over the extension of slavery was set in motion by the Kansas-Nebraska Act of 1854. This legislation revived the sectional conflict and led to the emergence of the Republican party. From that point on, a dramatic series of events heightened the mood of sectional confrontation and destroyed the prospects for a new compromise. The caning of Charles Sumner was one of these events, and violence on the Senate floor foreshadowed violence on the battlefield.

THE COMPROMISE OF 1850

During the late 1840s the leaders of the two major national parties, each with substantial followings in both the North and the South, had vested interest in resolving the sectional crisis. Furthermore, the less tangible features of sectionalism—emotion and ideology—were not yet as divisive as they would later become. Hence a fragile compromise was achieved through a kind of give-and-take that would not be possible after the emergence of strong sectional parties in the mid-1850s.

THE PROBLEM OF SLAVERY IN THE MEXICAN CESSION

The Founders, who were generally opposed to slavery, had attempted to exclude the slavery issue from national politics as the price of uniting states committed to slavery and those in the process of abolishing it. The Constitution gave the federal government no definite authority to regulate or destroy the institution where it existed under state law. Thus it was easy to condemn slavery in principle but very difficult to develop a practical program to eliminate it without defying the Constitution.

Radical abolitionists saw the problem clearly and resolved it by rejecting the law of the land in favor of a "higher law" prohibiting human bondage. But during the 1840s the majority of Northerners showed that while they disliked slavery, they also detested abolitionism. They were inclined to view slavery as a backward institution and slaveholders as power-hungry aristocrats. But they regarded the Constitution as a binding contract between slave and free states and were likely to be prejudiced against blacks and reluctant to accept large numbers of them as free citizens. Consequently, they saw no legal or desirable way to bring about emancipation within the southern states.

However, the Constitution had not predetermined the status of slavery in *future* states. Congress had the right to require the abolition of slavery as the price of admission into the Union. An effort to use this power had led to the Missouri crisis of 1819–1820 (see Chapter 9). The resulting Missouri Compromise line was designed to decide future cases and maintain a rough parity between slave and free states. Slavery was thus allowed to expand with the westward movement of the cotton kingdom but was discouraged or prohibited above the line of 36°30'.

This tradition of providing both the free North and the slave South with opportunities for expansion and the creation of new states broke down when new territories were wrested from Mexico in the 1840s. Many Northerners were unwilling to see California and New Mexico as well as Texas admitted into the Union as slave states. Since it was generally assumed in the North that Congress had the power to prohibit slavery in new territories, a movement developed in Congress to do just that.

THE WILMOT PROVISO LAUNCHES THE FREE-SOIL MOVEMENT

The "free soil" crusade began in August 1846, only three months after the start of the Mexican War, when Congressman David Wilmot, a Pennsylvania Democrat, proposed an amendment to the military appropriations bill that would ban slavery in any territory that might be acquired from Mexico.

Wilmot spoke for a large number of northern Democrats who felt neglected and betrayed by the policies of the Polk administration. Reductions in tariff duties and Polk's veto of an internal improvement bill upset many Democrats. Still others felt betrayed because Polk had gone back on his pledge to obtain "all of Oregon" up to 54°40' and then had proceeded to wage war to win all of Texas. This twist in the course of Manifest Destiny convinced northern expansionists that the South and its interests were dominating the party and the administration.

Nevertheless, these pioneer free-soilers had a genuine interest in the issue actually at hand— the question of who would control and settle the new territories. Combining an appeal to racial prejudice with opposition to slavery as an institution, Wilmot demanded that the new territories be opened only for white people. He wanted to give the common folk of the North a fair chance by excluding unfair competition with slavery and blacks from territory obtained in the Mexican cession.

Northern Whigs backed Wilmot's Proviso because they shared his concern about the outcome of an unregulated competition between slave and free labor in the territories. Many of the northern Whigs had opposed the annexation of Texas and the Mexican War. If expansion was inevitable, they were determined that it should not be used to increase the power of the slave states.

In the first House vote on the Wilmot Proviso, party lines crumbled and were replaced by a sharp sectional cleavage. After passing the House, the Proviso was blocked in the Senate by a combination of southern influence and Democratic loyalty to the administration. When the appropriation bill went back to the House without the Proviso, the administration's arm-twisting succeeded in changing enough northern Democratic votes to defeat the Proviso.

SQUATTER SOVEREIGNTY AND THE ELECTION OF 1848

After a futile attempt was made to extend the Missouri Compromise line to the Pacific—a proposal that was unacceptable to Northerners because most of the Mexican cession lay south of the line—a new approach was devised that appealed especially to Democrats. Its main proponent was Senator Lewis Cass of Michigan, an aspirant for the party's presidential nomination. He wanted to leave the determination of the status of slavery in a territory to the actual settlers. From the beginning this proposal contained an ambiguity that allowed it to be interpreted differently in the North and the South. For northern Democrats "squatter sovereignty"—or "popular sovereignty" as it was later called—meant that settlers could vote slavery up or down at the first meeting of a territorial legislature. For the southern wing of the party, it meant that a decision would only be made at the time a convention drew up a constitution and applied for statehood. It was in the interest of national Democratic leaders to leave this ambiguity unresolved for as long as possible.

Congress failed to resolve the future of slavery in the Mexican cession in time for the election of 1848. The Democrats nominated Cass on a platform of squatter sovereignty. The Whigs evaded the question by running war hero General Zachary Taylor without a platform. Northern Whigs favoring restrictions on the expansion of slavery took heart from the general's promise not to veto any territorial legislation passed by Congress. Southern Whigs supported Taylor because the general was a southern slaveholder.

Northerners who strongly supported the Wilmot Proviso were attracted by a third party movement. The Free-Soil party nominated former President Van Buren to carry their banner. Support for the Free-Soilers came mostly from Democrats and Whigs who opposed either the extension of slavery into the territories or the growing influence of the South in national policies. The founding of the Free-Soil party was the first significant effort to create a broadly based sectional party addressing itself to voters' concerns about the extension of slavery.

After a noisy and confusing campaign, Taylor came out on top, winning a majority of the electoral votes in both the North and the South. The Free-Soilers failed to carry a single state but were strong enough to run second behind Taylor in New York, Massachusetts, and Vermont.

TAYLOR TAKES CHARGE

Once in office, Taylor devised a bold plan to decide the fate of slavery in the Mexican cession. He tried to engineer the immediate admission of California and New Mexico to the Union as states, thus bypassing the territorial stage entirely and eliminating the whole question of the status of slavery in the federal domain. This proposal made practical sense in regard to California which was filling up rapidly with settlers drawn there by the lust for gold. Under the administration's urging, Californians convened a constitutional convention and applied for admission to the Union as a free state. In underpopulated New Mexico, it proved impossible to get a statehood movement off the ground.

Instead of resolving the crisis, President Taylor's initiative only worsened it. Fearing that New Mexico as well as California would choose to be a free state, Southerners of both parties accused the president of trying to impose the Wilmot Proviso in a new form. The prospect that only free states would emerge from the entire Mexican cession inspired serious talk of secession.

In Congress, Senator John C. Calhoun of South Carolina saw a chance to achieve his longstanding goal of creating a southern voting block that would cut across regular party lines. He warmly greeted each new sign of southern discontent and sectional unity. In the fall and winter of 1849–1850 several southern states agreed to participate in a convention to be held in Nashville in June, where grievances could be aired and demands made. For an increasing number of southern political leaders the survival of the Union would depend on the North's response to southern demands.

FORGING A COMPROMISE

When it became clear that the president would not abandon or modify his plan in order to appease the South, independent efforts began in Congress to arrange a compromise. Hoping once again to play the role of "great pacificator," Senator Henry Clay of Kentucky offered a series of resolutions meant to restore sectional harmony. On the critical territorial question, his solution was to admit California as a free state and organize the rest of the Mexican cession with no explicit prohibition of slavery. He also sought to resolve a major boundary dispute between New Mexico and Texas by granting the disputed region to New Mexico while compensating Texas through federal assumption of its state debt. As a concession to the North on another issue—the existence of slavery in the District of Columbia—he recommended prohibiting the buying and selling of slaves in the nation's capital. Finally, he called for more vigorous enforcement of the Fugitive Slave Law.

Clay proposed the plan in February 1850, but it received a mixed reception. One obstacle was President Taylor's firm resistance to the proposal; another was the difficulty of getting congressmen to vote for it in the form of a single package or "omnibus bill." The logjam was broken in July by two crucial developments. President Taylor died and was succeeded by Millard Fillmore, who favored the compromise; and a decision was made to abandon the omnibus strategy in favor of a series of measures that could be voted on separately. After the breakup of the omnibus bill, Democrats led by Senator Stephen A. Douglas replaced the original Whig sponsors as leaders of the compromise movement and maneuvered the separate provisions of the plan through Congress.

As finally approved, the Compromise of 1850 differed somewhat from Clay's original proposals. The popular sovereignty principle was included in the bills organizing New Mexico and Utah as the price of Democratic support. In addition, half of the compensation to Texas for giving up its claims to New Mexico was paid directly to holders of Texas bonds.

Abolition of the slave trade in the District of Columbia and a new fugitive slave law were also enacted. According to the provisions of the latter act, suspected fugitives were now denied a jury trail, the right to testify in their own behalf, and other minimal constitutional rights.

In the Senate chamber, its balconies overflowing with spectators, Henry Clay pleads for passage of the Compromise of 1850. John C. Calhoun (standing third from right) was by this time mortally ill; his speech denouncing the compromise was read by Senator James Mason of Virginia. Daniel Webster (seated at left with his head resting on his hand), himself ailing, argued in favor of the compromise plan.

As a result, there were no effective safeguards against false identification and the kidnapping of blacks who were legally free.

The compromise passed because its key measures were supported by both northern Democrats and southern Whigs. No single bill was backed by a majority of the congressmen from both sections and doubts persisted over the value or workability of a "compromise" that was really more like a cease-fire.

Yet the Compromise of 1850 did serve for a time as a basis for sectional peace. Southern moderates had carried the day, but southern nationalism was qualified at best. Southerners demanded strict northern adherence to the compromise, especially the Fugitive Slave Law, as a price for keeping threats of secession suppressed. In the North, the compromise received even greater support. The Fugitive Slave Law was unpopular in areas where abolitionism was particularly strong, and there were a few sensational rescues or attempted rescues of es-

caped slaves. But for the most part northern states adhered to the law during the early 1850s. By 1852, when the Democrats endorsed the compromise in their platform and the Whigs acceded to it in theirs, it appeared that sharp differences on the slavery issue had once again been banished from national politics.

POLITICAL UPHEAVAL, 1852–1856

The second party system—Democrats versus Whigs—survived the crisis over slavery in the Mexican cession, but in the long run the Compromise of 1850 may have weakened it. Although both national parties had been careful during the 1840s not to take stands on the slavery issue that would alienate their supporters in either section of the country, they had in fact offered voters alternative ways of dealing with the question. Democrats had endorsed head-long territorial expansion with the promise of a fair division of the spoils between slave and free states. Whigs had generally opposed annexation of acquisitions that were likely to bring the slavery question to the fore and threaten sectional harmony. Each strategy could be presented to southern voters as a good way to protect slavery and to Northerners as a good way to contain it.

The consensus of 1852 meant that the parties had to find other issues on which to base their distinctive appeals. Their failure to do so encouraged voter apathy and a disenchantment with the major parties. When the Democrats sought to revive the Manifest Destiny issue in 1854, they inadvertently reopened the explosive issue of slavery in the territories. By this time, the Whigs were too weak and divided to respond with a policy of their own, and a purely sectional free-soil party—the Republicans—gained prominence. The collapse of the second party system released sectional agitation from the earlier constraints imposed by the competition of strong national parties.

The Party System in Crisis

The presidential campaign of 1852 was singularly devoid of major issues. Both parties ignored the slavery question. Some Whigs tried to revive interest in nationalistic economic policies; but with business thriving under the Democratic program of laissez-faire, such proposals sounded empty and unnecessary.

Another tempting issue was immigration. Many Whigs were upset by the massive influx from Europe, partly because most of the new arrivals were Catholics, and the Whig following was largely evangelical Protestant. In addition, immigrants voted overwhelmingly Democratic. The Whig leadership was divided on whether to compete for the immigrant vote or to seek restrictions on immigrant voting rights.

The Whigs nominated General Winfield Scott of Mexican War fame who supported the faction that resisted nativism and sought to broaden the appeal of the party. However, Scott and his supporters were unable to break the Democratic grip on the immigrant vote, and some nativist Whigs apparently sat out the election to protest their party's disregard of their cultural prejudice.

But the main cause for Scott's crushing defeat was the support he lost in the South when he allied himself with the northern antislavery wing of the party, led by Senator William Seward of New York. The Democratic candidate, Franklin Pierce of New Hampshire, was a colorless nonentity compared to his rival, but he easily swept the Deep South and edged out Scott in most of the free states. The outcome revealed that the Whig party was in deep trouble because it lacked a program that would appeal to voters in both sections of the country.

Despite their overwhelming victory in 1852, the Democrats also had reasons for anxiety about the loyalty of their supporters. Voter apathy was strong, and Democratic leaders were placed in the uncomfortable position of having to appeal to both northern free-soilers and southern slaveholders.

The Kansas-Nebraska Act Raises a Storm

In January 1854, Senator Stephen A. Douglas proposed a bill to organize the territory west of Missouri and Iowa. Since this region fell within the area where slavery had been banned by the Missouri Compromise, Douglas hoped to head off southern opposition and keep the Democratic party united by disregarding the compromise line and setting up the territorial government in Kansas and Nebraska on the basis of popular sovereignty.

Douglas wanted to organize the area quickly because he was a strong supporter of the expansion of settlement and commerce. He hoped that a railroad would soon be built to the Pacific with Chicago (or another midwestern city) as its eastern terminus. A long controversy over the status of slavery in the Kansas-Nebraska area would delay the building of a railroad through the territory. Moreover, by trying to revive the spirit of Manifest Destiny, he hoped to strengthen the Democratic party and enhance his chances of becoming president.

The price of southern support, Douglas soon discovered, was the addition of an amendment explicitly repealing the Missouri Compromise. He reluctantly agreed. Although the bill then made its way through Congress, it split the Democratic party. A manifesto of "independent Democrats" denounced the bill as "a gross violation of a sacred pledge." For many Northerners, the Kansas-Nebraska Act was an abomination because it appeared to permit slavery in an area where it had previously been prohibited. More than ever, Northerners were receptive to the theme that there was a conspiracy to extend slavery.

Douglas' bill had a catastrophic effect on the prospects for sectional harmony. It repudiated a compromise that many in the North regarded as a binding sectional compact. In defiance of the whole compromise tradition, it made a concession to the South on the issue of slavery extension without providing an equivalent concession to the North. From now on, northern sectionalists would be fighting to regain what they had lost, while Southerners would be battling just as furiously to maintain rights already conceded.

The act also destroyed what was left of the second party system. The already weakened Whig party totally disintegrated when its congressional representation split cleanly along sectional lines on the Kansas-Nebraska issue. The Democratic party survived, but northern desertions and southern gains resulting from recruitment of proslavery Whigs destroyed its sectional balance and placed the party under firm southern control.

Finally, the furor over Kansas-Nebraska doomed the efforts of the Pierce administration to revive an expansionist foreign policy. Pierce

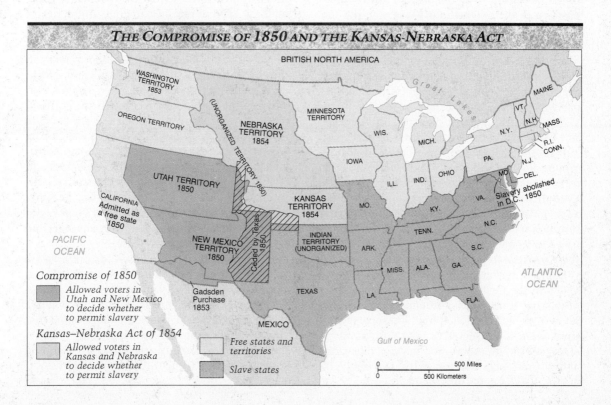

THE COMPROMISE OF 1850 AND THE KANSAS-NEBRASKA ACT

BRITISH NORTH AMERICA

WASHINGTON TERRITORY 1853

OREGON TERRITORY

(UNORGANIZED TERRITORY 1850)

NEBRASKA TERRITORY 1854

MINNESOTA TERRITORY

Great Lakes

MAINE

VT. N.H.

WIS. MICH. N.Y. MASS.

R.I. CONN.

IOWA PA. N.J.

UTAH TERRITORY 1850

ILL. IND. OHIO MO. DEL.

CALIFORNIA Admitted as a free state 1850

KANSAS TERRITORY 1854

MO. VA. Slavery abolished in D.C., 1850

KY.

PACIFIC OCEAN

NEW MEXICO TERRITORY 1850

Ceded by Texas 1850

INDIAN TERRITORY (UNORGANIZED)

ARK.

TENN. N.C.

S.C.

ATLANTIC OCEAN

Gadsden Purchase 1853

MISS. ALA. GA.

Compromise of 1850

Allowed voters in Utah and New Mexico to decide whether to permit slavery

TEXAS

LA. FLA.

MEXICO

Gulf of Mexico

Kansas–Nebraska Act of 1854

Allowed voters in Kansas and Nebraska to decide whether to permit slavery

Free states and territories

Slave states

0 500 Miles
0 500 Kilometers

and Secretary of State William Marcy were committed to acquiring Cuba from Spain. But Northerners interpreted the administration's plan, made public in a memorandum known as the "Ostend Manifesto," as an attempt to create a "Caribbean slave empire." The resulting storm of protest forced Pierce and his cohorts to abandon their scheme. The only tangible result of the southern expansionist dream of the 1850s was the purchase for $10 million of a 30,000 square-mile slice of Mexican territory south of the Gila River (the Gadsden Purchase, 1853). This acquisition rounded out the contiguous continental United States.

AN APPEAL TO NATIVISM: THE KNOW-NOTHING EPISODE

The collapse of the Whigs created the opening for a new political party. The anti-Nebraska sentiment of 1854 suggested that such a party might be organized on the basis of northern opposition to the extension of slavery to the territories. Before such a prospect could be realized, however, an alternative emerged in the form of a major political movement based on hostility to immigrants. For a time, it appeared that the Whigs would be replaced by a nativist party rather than an antislavery one.

Massive immigration of Irish and Germans (see Chapter 12), most of whom were Catholic, led to increasing tensions between ethnic groups during the 1840s and early 1850s. Protestants were suspicious and distrustful of the Catholics, whom they viewed as bearers of an alien culture. Nativist agitators charged that immigrants were agents of a foreign despotism, based in Rome, that was bent on overthrowing the American Republic.

Political nativism first emerged during the 1840s in the form of local "American" parties protesting immigrant influence in cities like New York and Philadelphia. These organizations were often secretive, and one group instructed its members to answer questions about their organization with the reply, "I know nothing." The political objective of the Know-Nothings was to extend the period of naturalization in order to undercut immigrant voting strength and to keep aliens in their place.

In 1854–1855 the movement surfaced as a major political force, calling itself the American party. Most of its backing came from Whigs looking for a new home, but it also attracted some ex-Democrats. Know-Nothingism also appealed to native-born workers fearful of competition from low-paid immigrants. Others supported the party simply as an alternative to the Democratic party.

The success of the new party was so dramatic that it was compared to a hurricane. In 1854 and 1855 Know-Nothings won control of a number of state governments, ranging from Massachusetts to Maryland to Texas. By late 1855 the Know-Nothings showed every sign of displacing the Whigs as the nation's second party.

Yet, almost as rapidly as it had arisen, the Know-Nothing movement collapsed. Its demise in 1856 is one of the great mysteries of American political history. Certainly as a national party it was unable to mend the deep sectional divisions over the question of slavery in the territories. Less clear is why Know-Nothings failed to become the major opposition party to the Democrats in the North. Political nativism may have contained the seeds of its own extinction. Know-Nothingism was in part a grass-roots protest against professional politicians. Most of the movement's spokesmen and elected officials were neither professional politicians nor established community leaders. Thus their very inexperience was a major source of their original attraction to voters and a factor in the movement's decline.

Furthermore, the Know-Nothings were never a real party. Because of the lack of organizational discipline and experienced leadership, the Know-Nothings were unable to make use of their power. Once voters discovered that the Know-Nothings also *did* nothing, they recovered from their antipolitical binge and looked for more competent leadership.

KANSAS AND THE RISE OF THE REPUBLICANS

The new Republican party was an outgrowth of the anti-Nebraska sentiment of 1854. The Republican name was first used in midwestern states to attract free-soil Democrats who refused to march under the Whig banner or even support any candidate for high office who called himself a Whig.

When the Know-Nothing party split over the Kansas-Nebraska issue in 1856, most of the northern nativists went over to the Republicans. Although Republicans were more concerned with "the slave power conspiracy" than any alleged "Popish plot," nativists did not have to abandon their religious prejudices; the party had the distinct flavor of evangelical Protestantism. On the local level Republicans sometimes supported causes that reflected an anti-immigrant or anti-Catholic bias—such as defense of Protestant Bible reading in schools and opposition to state aid for parochial education.

Unlike the Know-Nothings, the Republican party was led by seasoned professional politicians, men who had earlier been prominent Whigs or Democrats. Good organizers, they built up an effective party apparatus in an amazingly short time. By early 1856 the new party was well-established throughout the North and was preparing to make a serious bid for the presidency.

Underlying the rapid growth of the Republican party was the strong and growing appeal of its position on slavery in the territories. Republicans viewed the unsettled West as a land of opportunities, a place to which the ambitious and hard-working could migrate in the hope of improving their social and economic position. But if slavery were permitted to expand, the rights of "free labor" would be denied. Republicans emphasized that slave labor was unfair competition and retarded the commercial and industrial development of a region. They envisioned a West that was free and white.

Although passage of the Kansas-Nebraska Act raised the territorial issues and gave birth to the Republican party, it was the turmoil associated with attempts to implement popular sovereignty in Kansas that kept the issue alive and enabled the Republicans to increase their following throughout the North. In Kansas a bitter, violent contest was waged for control of the territorial government between transplanted New Englanders and Midwesterners who were militantly free-soil and slaveholding settlers from Missouri. Joining the slaveholders were proslavery residents of Missouri who crossed over the border to vote illegally in territorial elections. In the first territorial election, slavery was wholeheartedly endorsed.

Settlers favoring free soil were already a majority of the actual residents of the territory when the fraudulently elected legislature stripped them of their civil rights. To defend themselves and their convictions, they took up arms and established a rival territorial government under a constitution that outlawed slavery.

A small-scale civil war then broke out between the two regimes, culminating in May 1856 when proslavery adherents raided the free-state capital at Lawrence. Portrayed in Republican propaganda as "the sack of Lawrence," the incursion resulted in substantial property damage but no loss of life. In reprisal, antislavery zealot John Brown and several followers murdered five proslavery settlers in cold blood. During the next few months, a hit-and-run guerilla war raged between free-state and slave-state factions.

The national Republican press had a field day with the events in Kansas, exaggerating the extent of the violence but correctly pointing out that the Pierce administration was favoring rule by a proslavery minority over a free-soil majority. Since the "sack of Lawrence" occurred at about the same time that Charles Sumner was assaulted on the Senate floor, the Republicans launched their 1856 campaign under the twin slogans, "Bleeding Kansas and Bleeding Sumner." The image of an evil and aggressive "slave power" South proved a potent device for arousing northern sympathies and winning votes.

SECTIONAL DIVISION IN THE ELECTION OF 1856

The Republican nominating convention revealed the strictly sectional nature of the new party. With no delegates from the Deep South in attendance, the Republicans called for a congressional prohibition of slavery in all territories. The nominee was John C. Frémont, the western explorer who had helped in the conquest of California during the Mexican War.

The Democrats nominated James Buchanan of Pennsylvania, who had a long career in public service. Their platform endorsed popular sovereignty. The American party, a Know-Nothing remnant that survived mainly as the rallying point for anti-Democratic conservatives in the border states and parts of the South, chose ex-President Millard Fillmore as its standard-bearer and received the backing of those northern Whigs who hoped to revive the tradition of sectional compromise.

The election was really two separate races—one in the North between Frémont and Buchanan and the other in the South between Fillmore and Buchanan. With strong southern support and victories in four crucial northern states, Buchanan won. But the Republicans did remarkably well for a party that was scarcely more than a year old. Frémont swept the upper North with substantial majorities and won a larger proportion of the northern popular vote than either of his opponents. Since the free states had a substantial majority in the electoral college, a future Republican candidate could attain the presidency simply by overcoming a narrow Democratic margin in the lower North.

In the South the results of the election brought a momentary sense of relief tinged with deep anxiety about the future. For Southerners, the very existence of a sectional party committed to restricting the expansion of slavery constituted an insult to their way of life. They felt threatened. Only the continued success of a unified Democratic party under southern influence or control could maintain sectional balance and "southern rights."

THE HOUSE DIVIDED, 1857–1860

The sectional quarrel deepened and became virtually "irreconcilable" in the years between the elections of 1856 and 1860. A series of incidents provoked one side or the other, heightened the tension, and ultimately brought the crisis to a head. Behind the panicky reaction to public events lay a growing sense that the North and South were so different in culture and so opposed in basic interests that they could no longer coexist in the same nation.

CULTURAL SECTIONALISM

Signs of cultural and intellectual cleavage had appeared well before the triumph of sectional politics. As early as the mid-1840s, the slavery issue split the Baptist and Methodist churches into northern and southern wings. Instead of unifying Americans around a common Protestant faith, the churches became nurseries of sectional discord. Increasingly, northern preachers and congregations denounced slaveholding as a sin, while most southern church leaders rallied to a biblical defense of the peculiar institution and became influential apologists for the southern way of life. Both in the North and the South, ministers helped to turn political questions into moral issues and reduced the prospects for a compromise.

American literature also became sectionalized during the 1840s and 1850s. Southern men of letters such as William Gilmore Simms and Edgar Allen Poe wrote proslavery polemics, and lesser writers penned novels that seemed to glorify southern civilization at the expense of northern society. In the North, prominent men of letters—Emerson, Thoreau, and others—expressed strong antislavery sentiments in prose and poetry.

Literary abolitionism reached a climax in 1852 when Harriet Beecher Stowe published *Uncle Tom's Cabin*, a novel that sold more than 300,000 copies in a single year and fixed in the northern mind the image of the slaveholder as a brutal Simon Legree. Much of its emotional impact came from the book's portrayal of slavery as a threat to the family and the cult of domesticity. When the saintly Uncle Tom was sold away from his adoring wife and children, Northerners shuddered with horror and more than a few Southerners felt a painful twinge of conscience.

Southern defensiveness gradually hardened into cultural and economic nationalism. Southerners encouraged the use of proslavery textbooks, induced young men of the planter class to stay in the South for higher education, and sought to develop their own industry and commerce. Almost without exception, prominent southern educators and intellectuals of the late 1850s rallied behind the idea of a southern nation.

THE DRED SCOTT CASE

When James Buchanan was inaugurated on March 7, 1857, the dispute over the legal status of slavery in the territories was an open door through which sectional fears and hatreds could enter the political arena. Buchanan hoped to close that door by encouraging the Supreme Court to render a broad decision that would resolve the constitutional issue once and for all.

The Court was then about to render its decision in the case of *Dred Scott* v. *Sandford*. The case involved a Missouri slave whose owner had taken him to the Wisconsin Territory for a time during the 1830s. After his master's death, Dred Scott sued for his freedom on the grounds that he had lived for many years in an area where slavery had been outlawed by the Missouri Compromise. The Court, headed by Chief Justice Roger B. Taney, made several rulings in the case. First, it held that a slave was not a citizen and therefore had no right to sue in federal courts. Second, and more important for the general issue of slavery, the Court ruled that even if Scott had been a legitimate plaintiff, he would not have won his case. His residence in the Wisconsin Territory established no right to

freedom because Congress had no power to prohibit slavery there. The Missouri Compromise was thus declared unconstitutional and so, implicitly, was popular sovereignty—the main plank in the Republican platform.

In the North, and especially among Republicans, the Court's verdict was viewed as the latest diabolical act of the "slave power conspiracy." Five of the six justices who voted in the majority, Northerners argued, were proslavery Southerners. Furthermore, the fact that Bu-

The case of Dred and Harriet Scott resulted in a Supreme Court ruling that has been called the "most overturned decision in history."

chanan had played a role in the decision was widely known, and it was suspected that he had conspired with the justices in response to pressure from the prosouthern wing of the Democratic party.

Republicans denounced the decision as "a wicked and false judgment" and as "the greatest crime in the annals of the republic"; but they stopped short of openly defying the Court's authority. Instead, they argued on narrow technical grounds that the decision as written was not binding on Congress and that a ban on slavery in the territories could still be enacted. The decision actually helped the Republicans build support since it lent credence to their claim that an aggressive slave power was dominating all branches of the federal government and attempting to use the Constitution to achieve its own ends.

THE LECOMPTON CONTROVERSY

While the Dred Scott case was being decided, leaders of the proslavery faction in Kansas concluded that the time was ripe to draft a constitution and seek admission to the Union as a slave state. Since settlers with free-state views were now an overwhelming majority in the territory, the success of the plan required a rigged, gerrymandered election for convention delegates. When it became clear that the election was fixed, the free-staters boycotted it. The resulting constitution, drawn up at Lecompton, was certain to be rejected by Congress if a fairer election were not held.

To resolve the issue, supporters of the constitution decided to permit a vote on the slavery provision alone, giving the electorate the narrow choice of allowing or forbidding the future importation of slaves. Since there was no way to vote for total abolition, the free-state majority again resorted to boycott, thus allowing ratification of a constitution that protected existing slave property and placed no restriction on importations. In a second referendum, proposed by the free-staters and boycotted by the proslavery forces, the Lecompton constitution was overwhelmingly rejected.

The Lecompton constitution was such an obvious perversion of popular sovereignty that Stephen A. Douglas spoke out against it. But the Buchanan administration tried to push it through Congress in early 1858. The resulting debate was bitter and sometimes violent. The bill to admit Kansas into the Union as a slave state passed the Senate but was defeated in the House.

The Lecompton controversy seriously aggravated the sectional quarrel. The issue strengthened Republicans' belief that the Democratic party was dominated by Southerners, and at the same time it split the Democratic party between the followers of Douglas and the backers of Buchanan.

For Douglas the affair was a disaster; it destroyed his hopes of uniting the Democratic party and defusing the slavery issue through the application of popular sovereignty. In practice, popular sovereignty was an invitation to civil war. Furthermore, the Dred Scott decision protected Southerners' rights to own human property in federal territories. For his stand against Lecompton, Douglas was denounced as a traitor in the South, and his hopes of being elected president were greatly diminished.

DEBATING THE MORALITY OF SLAVERY

Douglas' more immediate problem was to win reelection to the Senate from Illinois in 1858. Here he faced surprisingly tough opposition from Republican candidate Abraham Lincoln, who set out to convince the voters that Douglas could not be relied upon to oppose consistently the extension of slavery.

In the famous speech that opened his campaign, Lincoln tried to distance himself from his opponent by taking a more radical position. He argued, " 'A house divided against itself cannot stand.' I believe this government cannot endure, permanently half *slave* and half *free*." He then described the chain of events between the Kansas-Nebraska Act and the Dred Scott decision as evidence of a plot to extend slavery, and he tried to link Douglas to that proslavery conspiracy by pointing to his rival's unwillingness to take a stand on the morality of slavery. Lincoln demanded that slavery be considered a moral, and not simply a political, issue.

In the subsequent series of debates that focused national attention on the Illinois senatorial contest, Lincoln hammered away at the theme that Douglas was a covert defender of slavery because he was not a principled opponent of it. Douglas responded by accusing Lincoln of endangering the Union by his talk of putting slavery on the path to extinction. Lincoln denied that he was an abolitionist but readily admitted that he, like the Founders, opposed any extension of slavery.

In the debate at Freeport, Illinois, Lincoln questioned Douglas on how he could reconcile popular sovereignty with the Dred Scott decision. Douglas responded that slavery could not exist without supportive legislation to sustain it and that territorial legislatures could simply refrain from passing a slave code if they wanted to keep it out. Coupled with his anti-Lecompton stand, Douglas' "Freeport Doctrine" hardened southern opposition to his presidential ambitions.

Douglas' most effective debating point was to charge that Lincoln's moral opposition to slavery implied a belief in racial equality. Lincoln, facing an intensely racist electorate, vigorously denied this charge and affirmed his commitment to white supremacy. He would grant blacks the right to the fruits of their own labor while denying them the "privileges" of citizenship. This was an inherently contradictory position, and Douglas made the most of it.

Although Republican candidates for the state legislature won a majority of the popular votes, the Democrats carried more counties and thus were able to send Douglas back to the Senate. Lincoln lost an office, but he won respect in Republican circles throughout the country. By stressing the moral dimension of the slavery question and undercutting any possibility of fusion between Republicans and Douglas Democrats, he had sharpened his party's ideological

Abraham Lincoln is shown here in his first full-length portrait. Although Lincoln lost the contest for the Senate seat in 1858, his participation in the Lincoln-Douglas debates established his reputation as a rising star of the Republican party.

focus and had stiffened its backbone against any temptation to compromise the free-soil position.

THE SOUTH'S CRISIS
OF FEAR

After Kansas became a free territory instead of a slave state in August 1858, slavery in the territories became a symbolic issue rather than a practical and substantive one. The remaining unorganized areas in the Rockies and northern Great Plains were unlikely to attract slaveholding settlers. Nevertheless, southerners continued to demand the "right" to take their slaves into territories, and Republicans persisted in denying it to them. Although they repeatedly promised not to interfere with slavery where it already existed, the Republicans did not gain the trust of the Southerners, who interpreted the Republicans' unyielding stand against the extension of slavery as a threat to southern rights and security.

A chain of events in late 1859 and early 1860 turned southern anxiety about northern attitudes and policies into a "crisis of fear." The first of these incidents was John Brown's raid on Harpers Ferry, Virginia, in October 1859. Brown was a fervent abolitionist with the appearance of an Old Testament prophet. He believed he was God's chosen instrument "to purge this land with blood" and eradicate the sin of slaveholding. On October 16, he led a small band of men across the Potomac River from his base in Maryland and seized the federal arsenal and armory in Harpers Ferry.

Brown's aim was to arm the local slave population and commence a guerilla war from havens in the Appalachians that would eventually extend to the planation regions of the lower South. But the neighboring slaves did not rise up to join him, and his plan failed. In the fight with U.S. marines that followed, ten of Brown's men were killed or mortally wounded, along with seven of the townspeople and soldiers who opposed them.

The wounded Brown and his remaining followers were put on trial for treason against the state of Virginia. The subsequent investigation produced evidence that several prominent northern abolitionists had approved of Brown's plan and had raised money for his preparations. This revelation seemed to confirm southern fears that abolitionists were actively engaged in fomenting slave insurrection. Southerners were further stunned by the outpouring of sympathy and admiration for Brown in the North. His actual execution on December 2 completed Brown's elevation to the status of a martyred saint of the antislavery cause.

Although Republican politicians were quick to denounce John Brown for his violent methods, Southerners interpreted the wave of northern sympathy as an expression of the majority opinion and the Republicans' "real" attitude. In the southern mind, abolitionists, Republicans, and Northerners were taking on one face. Within the South, the raid and its aftermath touched off a frenzy of fear. Southerners became increasingly vigilant for any sign of attack on their way of life, whether from without or from within.

Brown was scarcely in his grave when another set of events put southern nerves on edge. Next to abolitionist-abetted rebellions, the slaveholding South's greatest fear was that the nonslaveholding majority would turn against the master class and that the solidarity of southern whites would crumble. Hinton Rowan Helper's *The Impending Crisis of the South*, which called upon lower class whites to resist planter dominance and abolish slavery in their own interest, was regarded by slaveholders as even more seditious than *Uncle Tom's Cabin*. They feared the spread of "Helperism" among poor whites almost as much as the effect of "John Brownism" on the slaves.

The Republican candidate for Speaker of the U.S. House of Representatives, John Sherman of Ohio, had endorsed Helper's book as a campaign document. Southern congressmen threatened secession if Sherman was elected, and feelings became so heated that some House members began to carry weapons on the floor of the chamber. A more moderate Republican was elected, and the impasse over the speakership was resolved, but the contest helped persuade Southerners that the Republicans were committed to stirring up class conflict among southern whites. The identification of Republicans with Helper's ideas may have been decisive in convincing many conservative planters that a Republican president in 1860 would be intolerable.

THE ELECTION OF 1860

The Republicans, sniffing victory and generally unaware of the depth of southern feeling against them, met in Chicago on May 16 to nominate a presidential candidate. The initial front-runner, Senator William H. Seward of New York, proved unacceptable because of his reputation for radicalism and his long record of strong opposition to the nativist movement. What a majority of the delegates wanted was a less controversial nominee who could win two or three of the northern states that had been in the Democratic column in 1856. Abraham Lincoln met their specifications: He was considered more moderate than Seward and had kept his personal distaste for Know-Nothingism to himself. In addition, his rise to prominence from humble beginnings embodied the Republican ideal of equal opportunity for all.

The platform, like the nominee, was meant to broaden the party's appeal in the North. Although a commitment to halt the expansion of slavery remained, economic matters received more attention than they had in 1856. The platform called for a high protective tariff, free homesteads, and federal aid for internal improvements. The platform was cleverly designed to bring most ex-Whigs into the Republican camp while also accommodating enough renegade Democrats to give the party a solid majority in the northern states.

The Democrats failed to present a united front against this formidable challenge. When the party first met in the sweltering heat of Charleston in late April, Douglas was unable to win the nomination because of southern opposition. He did succeed in getting the convention to endorse popular sovereignty as its slavery platform, but the price was a walkout by southern delegates who favored a federal slave code for the territories.

Unable to agree on a nominee, the convention adjourned to reconvene in Baltimore in June. When the pro-Douglas force won most of the contested seats, another and more massive southern walkout took place. The result was a fracture of the Democratic party. The delegates who remained nominated Douglas, reaffirming their commitment to popular sovereignty; the southern bolters convened elsewhere to nominate John Breckinridge of Kentucky on a platform pledging federal protection of slavery in the territories.

By the time the campaign got underway, four parties were running presidential candidates. In addition to the Republicans, the Douglas Democrats, and the "Southern Rights" Democrats, a remnant of conservative Whigs and Know-Nothings nominated John Bell of Tennessee under the banner of the Constitutional Union party. Taking no explicit stand on slavery in the territories, Bell and his backers tried to represent the spirit of sectional compromise. In effect, the race became separate two-party contests in each section: In the North the real choice was between Lincoln and Douglas, and in the South the only candidates with a fighting chance were Breckinridge and Bell.

When the results came in, the Republicans had achieved a stunning victory. By gaining the electoral votes of all the free states except a fraction of New Jersey's, Lincoln won a decisive majority. The Republican strategy of seeking power by trying to win the majority section was brilliantly successful. Less than 40 percent of those who went to the polls throughout the nation actually voted for Lincoln, but his support in the North was so solid that he would have won in the electoral college even if his opponents had been unified behind a single candidate.

Most Southerners saw the results of the election as a catastrophe. A candidate and a party with no support in their own section had won the presidency on a platform viewed as insulting to southern honor and hostile to vital southern interests. For the first time in history, southern interests were in no way represented in the White House. Rather than accept permanent minority status in American politics and face the threat to black slavery and white "liberty" that was bound to follow, the political leaders of the lower South launched a movement for immediate secession from the Union.

❧ EXPLAINING THE CRISIS

Generations of historians have searched for the underlying causes of the crisis leading to the disruption of the Union but have failed to agree on an answer. Some have stressed the clash of economic interests between agrarian and industrializing nations. But this interpretation does not reflect the way people at the time expressed their concerns. The main issues in the sectional debates of the 1850s were whether slavery was right or wrong and whether it should be extended or contained. In the face of these issues, all economic considerations pale. Indeed, there was no necessity for producers of raw materials to go to war with those who marketed and processed them.

Another group of historians have blamed the crisis on "irresponsible" politicians and agitators on both sides of the Mason-Dixon line. Public opinion, they argue, was whipped into a frenzy over issues that competent statesmen could have resolved. But this viewpoint has been sharply criticized for failing to acknowledge the depths of feeling that could be aroused by the slavery question and for underestimating the obstacles to a peaceful solution.

The dominant modern view is that the crisis was rooted in profound ideological differences over the morality and utility of slavery as an institution. Most interpreters are now agreed that the conflict stemmed from the fact that the South was a slave society and was determined to stay that way, while the North was equally committed to a free labor system. It is hard to imagine that secessionism would have developed if the South had followed the North's example and abolished slavery in the postrevolutionary period.

Nevertheless, the existence or nonexistence of slavery will not explain why the crisis came when it did and in the way that it did. Why did the conflict become "irreconcilable" in the 1850s and not earlier or later? Why did it take the form of a political struggle over the future of slavery in the territories? Adequate answers to both questions require an understanding of political developments that were not directly caused by tensions over slavery.

By the 1850s, the established Whig and Democratic parties were in trouble because they no longer offered the voters clear-cut alternatives on the economic issues that had been the bread and butter of politics during the heyday of the second party system. This situation created an opening for new parties and issues. The Republicans used the issue of slavery in the territories to build the first successful sectional party in American history. They called for "free soil" rather than freedom for blacks because abolitionism conflicted with the northern majority's commitment to white supremacy and its respect for the original constitutional compromise that established a hands-off policy toward slavery in the southern states.

If politicians seeking new ways to mobilize an apathetic electorate are seen as the main instigators of sectional crisis, the reason why certain appeals were more effective than others must still be explained. Why did the slavery extension issue arouse such strong feelings in the two sections during the 1850s? After all, the same issues had arisen earlier and had proved adjustable.

Ultimately, therefore, the crisis of the 1850s must be understood as being deeply social and cultural as well as purely political. The North and South had diverged significantly in basic beliefs and values between the 1820s and the 1850s. In the free states, the rise of reform-minded evangelicalism had given a new sense of moral direction and purpose to a rising middle class adapting to the new market economy (see Chapter 11). In much of the South, the slave plantation system prospered, and the notion that white liberty and equality depended on having enslaved blacks to do menial labor became more deeply entrenched.

When politicians appealed to sectionalism during the 1850s, therefore, they could evoke conflicting views of what constituted a good society. The South—with its allegedly idle masters, degraded unfree workers, and shiftless poor whites—seemed to a majority of Northerners to be in flagrant violation of the Protestant work ethic and the ideal of open competition. From the dominant southern point of view, the North was a land of hypocritical money-grubbers who denied the obvious fact that the dependent laboring classes—especially racially inferior ones—had to be kept under the kind of rigid control that only slavery could provide. Once these contrary views of the world had become the main themes of political discourse, sectional compromise was no longer possible.

CHRONOLOGY

1846	David Wilmot introduces proviso banning slavery in the Mexican cession
1848	Free-Soil party is founded Zachary Taylor (Whig) elected president, defeating Lewis Cass (Democrat) and Martin Van Buren (Free-Soil)
1849	California seeks admission to the Union as a free state
1850	Congress debates sectional issues and enacts Compromise of 1850
1852	Harriet Beecher Stowe publishes *Uncle Tom's Cabin* Franklin Pierce (Democrat) elected president by a large majority over Winfield Scott (Whig)
1854	Congress passes Kansas-Nebraska Act, repealing Missouri Compromise Republican party founded in several northern states
	Anti-Nebraska coalitions score victories in congressional elections in the North
1854–1855	Know-Nothing party achieves stunning successes in state politics
1854–1856	Free-state and slave-state forces struggle for control of Kansas Territory
1856	Preston Brooks assaults Charles Sumner on Senate floor James Buchanan wins presidency despite strong challenge in the North from John C. Frémont
1857	Supreme Court decides Dred Scott case and legalizes slavery in all territories
1858	Congress refuses to admit Kansas to Union under the proslavery Lecompton constitution Lincoln and Douglas debate
1859	John Brown raids Harpers Ferry, is captured and executed
1859–1860	Fierce struggle takes place over election of a Republican as Speaker of the House (December–February)
1860	Republicans nominate Abraham Lincoln for presidency (May) Democratic party splits into northern and southern factions with separate candidates and platforms (June) Lincoln wins the presidency over Douglas (northern Democrat), Breckinridge (southern Democrat), and Bell (Constitutional Unionist)

❧ RECOMMENDED READING

The best general account of the politics of the sectional crisis is David M. Potter, *The Impending Crisis, 1848–1861* (1976). A provocative new analysis of the party system in crisis is Michael F. Holt, *The Political Crisis of the 1850s* (1978). The most thorough discussion of the events leading up to the Civil War is Allan Nevins, *The Ordeal of the Union*, vols. 1–4 (1947–1950). On southern responses to the events of the crisis period, see Avery Craven, *The Growth of Southern Nationalism 1848–1861* (1953), and William L. Barney, *The Road to Secession* (1972).

For the first phase of the sectional controversy, see Holman Hamilton, *Prologue to Conflict: The Crisis and Compromise of 1850* (1964). The rise of antislavery politics in the 1840s and 1850s is described in Richard Sewell, *Ballots for Freedom: Antislavery Politics in the United States, 1837–1860* (1976); Eric Foner, *Free Soil, Free Labor, Free Men: The Ideology of the Republican Party before the Civil War* (1970); and William E. Gienapp, *The Origins of the Republican Party, 1852–1856* (1987).

On nativism, see Ray Allen Billington, *The Protestant Crusade, 1800–1860* (1938) and Dale T. Knobel, *Paddy and the Republic* (1986). Major biographical studies of key participants in the crisis of the 1850s include Robert W. Johannsen, *Stephen A. Douglas* (1973); David Donald, *Charles Sumner and the Coming of the Civil War* (1960); and Don E. Fehrenbacher, *Prelude to Greatness: Lincoln in the 1850s* (1962). Another book by Don E. Fehrenbacher, *The Dred Scott Case: Its Significance in American Law and Politics* (1978), is the definitive work on the subject.

On the Lincoln-Douglas rivalry, see Harry V. Jaffa, *Crisis of the House Divided: An Interpretation of the Lincoln-Douglas Debates* (1959), and George B. Forgie, *Patricide in the House Divided: A Psychological Interpretation of Lincoln and His Age* (1979). On John Brown and his raid, see Stephen B. Oates, *To Purge This Land with Blood: A Biography of John Brown* (1970).

Perspectives on the intellectual and cultural aspects of the sectional conflict can be derived from William R. Taylor, *Cavalier and Yankee: The Old South and American National Character* (1961); John McCardell, *The Idea of a Southern Nation: Southern Nationalists and Southern Nationalism, 1830–1860* (1979); and Paul C. Nagel, *One Nation Indivisible: The Union in American Thought* (1964).

15 SECESSION AND THE CIVIL WAR

THE STORM GATHERS

ADJUSTING TO TOTAL WAR

FIGHT TO THE FINISH

President Abraham Lincoln was striking in appearance—at six feet four inches in height, he seemed even taller because of his disproportionately long legs and his habit of wearing a high silk "stovepipe" hat. His career prior to taking up residence in the White House in 1860 was less remarkable than his person, however. A look at his previous experience certainly provided no guarantee that he would one day tower over most of our other presidents in more than physical height.

Born to poor and illiterate parents on the Kentucky frontier in 1809, Lincoln received a few months of formal schooling in Indiana after the family moved there in 1816. But mostly he educated himself, reading and rereading a few treasured books by firelight. In 1831, when the family migrated to Illinois, he left home to make a living for himself. After failing as a merchant, he found a path to success in law and politics. Lincoln combined exceptional political and legal skills with a down-to-earth, humorous way of addressing jurors and voters. He became a leader of the Whig party in Illinois and one of the most sought after of the lawyers who rode the central Illinois judicial circuit.

The high point of his political career as a Whig was one term in Congress (1847–1849), but he alienated much of his constituency by opposing the Mexican War and wisely chose not to run for reelection. In 1848 he campaigned vigorously and effectively for Zachary Taylor, but the new president failed to appoint Lincoln to a patronage job he coveted. Disappointed by his political fortunes, Lincoln concentrated on building his law practice.

The Kansas-Nebraska Act of 1854, with its advocacy of popular sovereignty, provided Lincoln with an opportunity to reconcile his driving ambition for political success with his personal convictions. Lincoln had long believed that slavery was an unjust institution that should be tolerated only to the extent that the Constitution and the tradition of sectional compromise required. Attacking Douglas' plan on popular sovereignty, Lincoln threw in his lot with the Republicans and assumed leadership of the new party in Illinois. He attracted national attention in his bid for Douglas' Senate seat in 1858, and happened to have the right qualifications when the Republicans chose a presidential nominee in 1860.

After Lincoln's election provoked southern secession and plunged the nation into the greatest crisis in its history, there was understandable skepticism about his qualifications in many quarters. After all, the former rail-splitter from Illinois had never been a governor, senator, cabinet officer, or high-ranking military officer. But some of his training as a prairie politician would prove extremely useful in the years ahead.

Lincoln had shown himself adept at the art of party leadership, which meant being able to accommodate various factions and define party issues and principles in a way that would encourage unity and dedication to the cause. Holding the Republican party together by persuasion and patronage was essential to unifying the nation by force, and Lincoln succeeded in doing both.

Another reason for Lincoln's effectiveness as a war leader was that he identified wholeheartedly with the northern cause and could inspire others to make sacrifices for it. In his view, the issue in the conflict was nothing less than the survival of the kind of political system that gave men like himself a chance for high office. For Lincoln, a government had to be strong enough to maintain its own existence and guarantee equality of opportunity.

The Civil War tested America's ability to preserve its democratic form of government in the face of domestic foes. It put on trial the very principle of democracy at a time when most European nations had rejected political liberalism and accepted the view that popular government would inevitably collapse into anarchy. As Lincoln put it in the Gettysburg Address, the only cause great enough to justify the enormous sacrifice of life on the battlefields was the struggle to preserve the democratic ideal, or to ensure that "government of the people, by the people, and for the people, shall not perish from the earth."

THE STORM GATHERS

Lincoln's election provoked the secession of seven states of the Deep South but did not lead immediately to armed conflict. Before the sectional quarrel turned from a cold war into a hot one, two things had to happen. A final effort to defuse the conflict by compromise and conciliation had to fail, and the North needed to develop a firm resolve to maintain the Union by military action. Both of these developments may seem inevitable to us, but for most of those living at the time it was not clear until the guns blazed at Fort Sumter that the sectional crisis would have to be resolved on the battlefield.

THE DEEP SOUTH SECEDES

South Carolina, which had long been in the forefront of southern rights and proslavery agitation, was the first state to leave the Union (December 20, 1860). The constitutional theory behind secession was that the Union was a "compact" among sovereign states, each of which could withdraw from the Union by a vote of a convention similar to the one that had ratified the Constitution in the first place. The South Carolinians justified seceding at this time by charging that "a sectional party" had elected a president hostile to slavery.

In other states of the cotton kingdom there was similar outrage at Lincoln's election but less certainty about how to respond to it. Some Southerners, labeled "cooperationists," believed the South should respond as a unit, after holding a southern convention. South Carolina's unilateral action, however, set a precedent.

When conventions in six other states of the Deep South met during January 1861, delegates favoring immediate secession were everywhere in the majority. By February 1, seven states had removed themselves from the Union—South Carolina, Alabama, Mississippi, Florida, Georgia, Louisiana, and Texas. In the upper South, however, calls for immediate secession were unsuccessful; majority opinion in Virginia, North Carolina, Tennessee, and Arkansas did not subscribe to the view that Lincoln's election was a sufficient reason for breaking up the Union.

Delegates from the Deep South met in Montgomery, Alabama, on February 4 to establish the Confederate States of America. Relatively moderate leaders dominated the proceedings and defeated or modified some of the pet schemes of a radical faction composed of extreme southern nationalists. Voted down were proposals to reopen the Atlantic slave trade, to count *all* slaves in determining congressional representation, instead of three fifths, and to prohibit the admission of free states to the new Confederacy.

The resulting provisional constitution was surprisingly similar to that of the United States. Most of the differences merely spelled out traditional southern interpretations of the federal charter. The central government was denied the authority to impose protective tariffs, subsidize internal improvements, or interfere with slavery in the states, and was required to pass laws protecting slavery in the territories. As provisional president and vice-president, the convention chose Jefferson Davis of Mississippi and Alexander Stephens of Georgia, men who had previously resisted secessionist agitation.

The moderation shown in Montgomery resulted in part from a desire to win support for the cause of secessionism in the reluctant states of the upper South. But it also revealed that proslavery reactionaries had never succeeded in getting a majority behind them. Most Southerners were staunchly proslavery but had been opposed to dissolving the Union and repudiating their traditional patriotic loyalties so long as there had been good reasons to believe that slavery was protected from northern interference.

The panic following Lincoln's election destroyed that sense of security; but it was clear from the actions of the Montgomery convention that the goal of the new converts to secessionism was not to establish a slaveholders' reactionary utopia. They only wished to recreate the Union that existed before the rise of the Republican party, and they opted for secession only when it seemed clear that separation was the only way to achieve their aim. Some optimists even predicted that all of the North except New England would eventually join the Confederacy.

Secession and the formation of the Confederacy thus amounted to a very conservative and defensive kind of "revolution." The only justification for southern independence upon which a majority could agree was the need for greater security for slavery and the social relations that institution entailed.

THE FAILURE OF COMPROMISE

While the Deep South was opting for independence, moderates in the North and the border slave states were trying to devise a compromise that would stem the secessionist tide before it could engulf the entire South. In Congress, Senator John Crittenden of Kentucky presented a plan that served as the focus for discussion. Crittenden advocated extending the Missouri Compromise line to the Pacific to guarantee the protection of slavery in the southwestern territories. He also recommended a constitutional amendment that would forever prohibit the federal government from abolishing or regulating slavery in the states.

Initially, congressional Republicans showed some willingness to give ground and take these proposals seriously. However, Republican support quickly vanished when Lincoln sent word from Springfield that he was adamantly opposed to the extension of the compromise line. With Lincoln opposing the plan, Republicans voted against the compromise in committee. When the senators and congressmen of the seceding states also voted against the plan, it was doomed to defeat.

Some historians have blamed Lincoln and the Republicans for causing unnecessary war by rejecting a compromise that would have appeased southern pride without providing any practical opportunity for the expansion of slavery. But it is quite possible that the secessionists, who wanted slavery protected in *all* territories, would not have been satisfied even if the Republicans had approved the plan.

Furthermore, Lincoln and his followers had what they considered to be very good reasons for not making territorial concessions. They mistakenly believed that secessionism reflected a minority opinion in the South and that a strong stand would win the support of southern Unionists and moderates. In addition, Lincoln took his stand on free-soil seriously. He did not want to give slaveholders any chance to enlarge their domain.

Lincoln was also convinced that backing down in the face of secessionist threats would fatally undermine the democratic principle of majority rule. In his inaugural address of March 4, 1861, he recalled that during the winter many "patriotic men" had urged him to accept a compromise that would "shift the ground" on which he had been elected. But to do so would have signified that a victorious presidential candidate "cannot be inaugurated till he betrays those who elected him by breaking his pledges, and surrendering to those who tried and failed to defeat him at the polls." Making such a concession would mean that "this government and all popular government is already at an end."

AND THE WAR CAME

By the time of Lincoln's inauguration, seven states had seceded, formed an independent confederacy, and seized most federal forts and other installations in the Deep South without firing a shot. Lincoln's predecessor, James Buchanan, rejected the right of secession, but refused to use coercion to maintain federal authority. Many Northerners agreed with his stand.

The collapse of compromise efforts narrowed the choice to peaceful separation or war between the sections. By early March, the tide of public opinion was beginning to shift in favor of strong action to preserve the Union. Even in the business community sentiment mounted in favor of a coercive policy.

In his inaugural address, Lincoln called for a cautious and limited use of force. He would defend federal forts and installations not yet in Confederate hands but would not attempt to recapture the ones already taken. He thus tried to shift the burden for beginning hostilities to the Confederacy. As Lincoln spoke, only four military installations within the seceded states were still held by United States forces. The most important and vulnerable of these installations was Fort Sumter inside Charleston harbor. The Confederacy demanded the surrender of the garrison, and shortly after taking office, Lincoln was informed that Sumter could not hold out much longer without reinforcements and supplies.

After some initial indecision and opposition from his cabinet, Lincoln decided to reinforce the fort, and he so informed the governor of South Carolina on April 4. The Confederacy regarded the sending of provisions as a hostile act and began shelling the fort near dawn on April 12. After forty hours of bombardment, the commander of the Union forces surrendered, and the Confederate flag was raised over Fort Sumter. The South had won a victory but had also assumed responsibility for firing the first shot.

On April 15, Lincoln proclaimed that an insurrection existed in the Deep South and called upon the militia of the loyal states to provide 75,000 troops for short-term service to put it down. Two days later, a Virginia convention voted to join the Confederacy. Within the next five weeks, Arkansas, Tennessee, and North Carolina followed suit. Lincoln's policy of coercion forced them to choose sides, and they opted to join the other slave states in the Confederacy.

In the North, the firing on Sumter evoked strong feelings of patriotism and dedication to

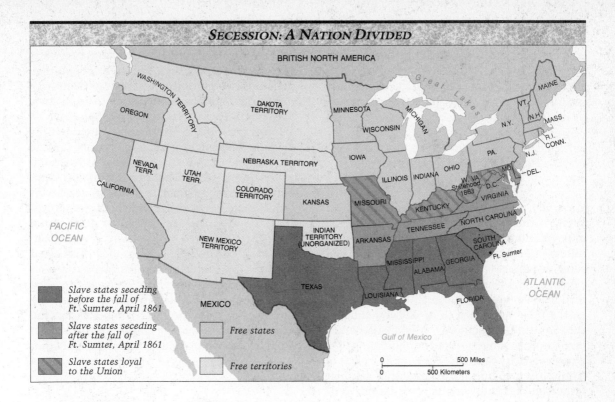

SECESSION: A NATION DIVIDED

BRITISH NORTH AMERICA

WASHINGTON TERRITORY

OREGON

DAKOTA TERRITORY

MINNESOTA

WISCONSIN

MICHIGAN

Great Lakes

MAINE

VT.

N.H.

N.Y.

MASS.

R.I.

CONN.

NEVADA TERR.

UTAH TERR.

NEBRASKA TERRITORY

IOWA

PA.

N.J.

CALIFORNIA

COLORADO TERRITORY

KANSAS

ILLINOIS

INDIANA

OHIO

W. VA. Statehood 1863

MD.

DEL.

D.C.

VIRGINIA

MISSOURI

KENTUCKY

PACIFIC OCEAN

NEW MEXICO TERRITORY

INDIAN TERRITORY (UNORGANIZED)

ARKANSAS

TENNESSEE

NORTH CAROLINA

SOUTH CAROLINA

Ft. Sumter

TEXAS

MISSISSIPPI

ALABAMA

GEORGIA

ATLANTIC OCEAN

MEXICO

LOUISIANA

FLORIDA

Gulf of Mexico

Slave states seceding before the fall of Ft. Sumter, April 1861

Slave states seceding after the fall of Ft. Sumter, April 1861

Slave states loyal to the Union

Free states

Free territories

0   500 Miles

0   500 Kilometers

the Union. Like many other Northerners, Stephen A. Douglas, Lincoln's former political rival, pledged his full support for the crusade against secession and literally worked himself to death rallying midwestern Democrats behind the government. Everyone assumed that the war would be short and not very bloody. It remained to be seen whether Unionist fervor could be sustained through a long and costly struggle.

The entire Confederacy comprised only eleven of the fifteen states in which slavery was lawful. In the border slave states of Maryland, Delaware, Kentucky, and Missouri, secession was thwarted by a combination of local Unionism and federal intervention. By taking care to respect Kentucky's neutrality, using martial law ruthlessly in Maryland, and stationing regular troops in Missouri, Lincoln kept these crucial border states in the Union.

Hence the Civil War was not, strictly speaking, a struggle between slave and free states.

More than anything else, conflicting views on the right of secession determined the ultimate division of states and the choices of individuals in areas where sentiment was divided. General Robert E. Lee, for example, was neither a defender of slavery nor a southern nationalist. But he followed Virginia out of the Union because he was the loyal son of a "sovereign state." Although concern about the future of slavery had driven the Deep South to secede in the first place, the war was seen less as a struggle over slavery than as a contest to determine whether the Union was indivisible.

ADJUSTING TO TOTAL WAR

The Civil War was a "total war" because the North could achieve its aim of restoring the Union only if the South was so thoroughly defeated that its separatist government was overthrown. It was a long war because the Confederacy put up "a hell of a fight" before it would agree to be put to death. A total war is a test of societies, economies, and political systems as well as a battle of wits between generals and military strategists.

PROSPECTS, PLANS, AND EXPECTATIONS

If the war was to be decided by sheer physical strength, then the North had an enormous edge in population, industrial capacity, and railroad mileage. Nevertheless, the South also had some advantages. To achieve its aim of independence, the Confederacy needed only to defend its own territory successfully. The North, on the other hand, had to invade and conquer the South. Consequently, the Confederacy faced a less serious supply problem, had a greater capacity to choose the time and place of combat, and could take advantage of familiar terrain and a friendly civilian population.

The nature of the war meant the southern leaders could define their cause as defense of their homeland against a Yankee invasion. It seemed doubtful in 1861 that Northerners would be willing to make an equal sacrifice for the relatively abstract principle that the Union was sacred and perpetual.

Confederate optimism on the eve of the war was also fed by other—and more dubious—calculations. It was widely assumed that Southerners who were accustomed to riding and shooting would make better soldiers than Yankees. When most of the large proportion of high-ranking officers in the U.S. Army who were of southern origin resigned to accept Confederate commands, Southerners confidently anticipated that their armies would be better led. Finally, Southerners assumed that if external help was needed, England and France would come to their aid, because those nations depended on southern cotton.

Both sides based their strategies on their advantages. The choice before President Davis, who assumed personal direction of the Confederate military effort, was whether to stay on the defensive or seek a sudden and dramatic victory by invading the North. He chose to wage an essentially defensive war in the hope that the North would soon tire of the blood and sacrifice and allow the Confederacy to go its own way.

Northern military planners had greater difficulty in working out a basic strategy, and it took a great deal of trial and error before there was a clear sense of what had to be done. Some optimists believed that the war could be won quickly and easily by sending an army to capture the Confederate capital of Richmond, scarcely a hundred miles from Washington. The early battles in Virginia ended this casual optimism. Other Northerners favored a plan called the "anaconda policy." Like a great boa constrictor, the North would squeeze the South into submission by blockading the southern coasts, seizing control of the Mississippi, and cutting off supplies of food and other

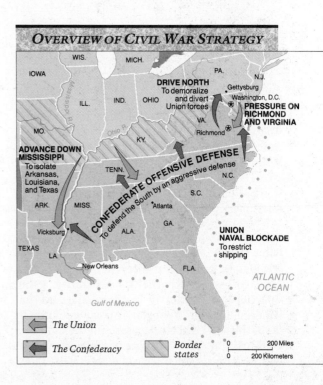

OVERVIEW OF CIVIL WAR STRATEGY

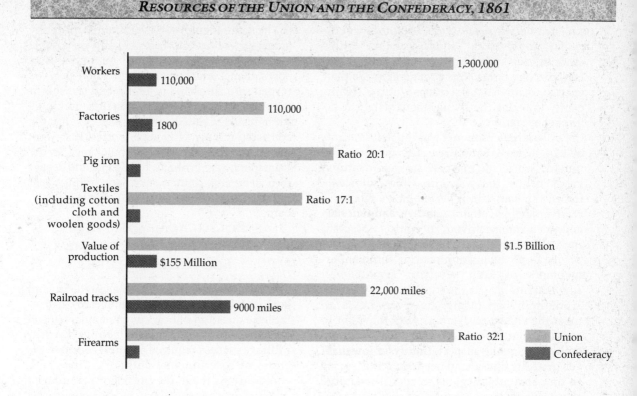

	Union	Confederacy
Workers	1,300,000	110,000
Factories	110,000	1800
Pig iron	Ratio 20:1	
Textiles (including cotton cloth and woolen goods)	Ratio 17:1	
Value of production	$1.5 Billion	$155 Million
Railroad tracks	22,000 miles	9000 miles
Firearms	Ratio 32:1	

essential commodities. This plan pointed to the West as the main focus of military operations.

Eventually Lincoln decided on a two-front war. He would keep the pressure on Virginia while at the same time authorizing an advance down the Mississippi Valley. He also attached great importance to the coastal blockade and expected naval operations to seize the ports through which goods entered and left the Confederacy. His basic plan of applying pressure and probing for weaknesses at several points simultaneously was a good one because it took maximum advantage of the northern superiority in manpower and material. But it required better military leadership than the North possessed at the beginning of the war and took a painfully long time to put into effect.

MOBILIZING THE HOME FRONT

The North and South faced very similar problems in trying to create the vast support systems needed by armies in the field. At the beginning of the conflict, both sides had more volunteers than could be armed and outfitted. But as it became clear that hopes for a short and easy war were false, the pool of volunteers began to dry up. To resolve this problem, the Confederacy passed a conscription law in April 1862, and the Union edged toward a draft in July when Congress gave Lincoln the power to assign manpower quotas to each state and resort to conscription if they were not met.

To produce the materials of war, both governments relied mainly on private industry. In the North, especially, the system of contracting with private firms and individuals to support the army often resulted in corruption, inefficiency, and "shoddy" goods. But the North's economy was strong at the core, and by 1863 its factories and farms were producing more than enough to provision the troops without significantly lowering the living standards of the civilian population.

The southern economy was much less adaptable to the needs of total war. Dependent on the outside world for most of its manufactured goods before the war, the Union blockade forced the southern government to sponsor a crash program to produce its own war materials and to encourage private enterprise. Astonishingly, the Confederate Ordnance Bureau succeeded in producing or procuring sufficient armaments to keep southern armies well supplied throughout the conflict.

Southern agriculture, however, failed to meet the challenge. Planters were reluctant to switch from cotton to foodstuffs, and the South's internal transportation system was inadequate. Its limited rail network was designed to link plantation regions to port cities rather than connect food-producing areas with centers of population. And when northern forces penetrated parts of the South, they created new gaps in the system. To supply the troops, the Confederate commissary resorted to impressment of agricultural produce, a policy so fiercely resisted by farmers and local politicians that it eventually had to be abandoned. By 1863 civilians in urban areas were rioting to protest food shortages.

Another challenge faced by both sides was how to finance an enormously costly struggle. Neither side was willing to resort to the heavy taxation that was needed to maintain fiscal integrity. Americans, it seems, were more willing to die for their government than to pay for it. Besides floating loans and selling bonds, both treasuries deliberately inflated the currency by printing large quantities of paper money that could not be redeemed in gold and silver. Runaway inflation was the inevitable result. But the problem was much less severe in the North, because of the overall strength of its economy and willingness of its citizens to buy bonds and pay taxes.

The Confederacy was hampered from the outset by a severe shortage of readily disposable wealth that could be tapped for public purposes. Land and cotton could not easily be turned into rifles and cannons, and the southern treasury had to accept payments "in kind." As a result, Confederate "assets" eventually consisted mainly of bales of cotton that were unexportable because of the blockade. As the Confederate government fell deeper and deeper into debt and printed more and more paper money, its rate of inflation soared out of sight.

POLITICAL LEADERSHIP: NORTHERN SUCCESS AND SOUTHERN FAILURE

Total war also forced political adjustment, and both the Union and the Confederacy had to face the question of how much democracy and individual freedom could be permitted when military success required an unprecedented exercise of governmental authority. Since both constitutions made the president commander in chief of the army and navy, Lincoln and Davis took actions that would have been regarded as arbitrary or even tyrannical in peacetime.

Lincoln was especially bold in assuming new executive powers. After the fighting started at Fort Sumter, he expanded the regular army and advanced public money to private individuals without authorization by Congress. On April 27, 1861, he declared martial law, which enabled the military to arrest and detain without trial civilians suspected of aiding the enemy, and suspended the writ of habeas corpus in the area between Philadelphia and Washington. This latter action was deemed necessary because of mob attacks on Union troops passing through Baltimore. In September 1862 Lincoln extended this authority to all parts of the United States where "disloyal" elements were active. He argued that preservation of the Union justified such actions.

For the most part, however, the Lincoln administration showed restraint and tolerated a broad spectrum of political dissent. "Politics as usual" persisted to a surprising degree. Antiadministration newspapers were allowed to criticize the president and his party almost at will, and opposition to Lincoln's programs was freely voiced in Congress.

Jefferson Davis proved to be a less effective war leader than Lincoln. He defined his powers as commander in chief narrowly and literally, which meant that he assumed personal direction of the armed forces but left policymaking for the mobilization and control of the civilian population primarily to the Confederate Congress. Unfortunately, Davis overestimated his capacities as a strategist and lacked the tact to handle field commanders who were as proud and testy as he was.

Davis' greatest failing, however, was his lack of initiative and leadership in dealing with the problems of the home front. He devoted little attention to a deteriorating economic situation that caused great hardship and sapped Confederate morale. In addition, although the South had a much more serious problem of internal division and disloyalty than the North, he chose to be extremely cautious in his use of martial law.

As the war dragged on, Davis' political and popular support eroded. He was opposed and obstructed by state governors who resisted conscription and other Confederate policies that violated the tradition of states' rights. The Confederate Congress and southern newspapers similarly criticized Davis' policies. His authority was further undermined because he did not even have an organized party behind him. As a result, it was difficult to mobilize the support required for hard decisions and controversial policies.

EARLY CAMPAIGNS AND BATTLES

The first campaign of the war was a minor triumph for the Union, as forces under General George McClellan succeeded in driving Confederate troops out of western Virginia during May and June 1861. McClellan's victory ensured that this region of predominantly Union-ist sentiment remained under northern control; out of it came the new "loyal" state of West Virginia, organized and admitted to the Union in 1863.

But the war's first major battle was a disaster for northern arms. Against his better judgment, General Winfield Scott responded to the "On to Richmond" clamor and ordered poorly trained Union troops under General Irvin McDowell to advance against the Confederate forces gathered at Manassas Junction, Virginia. They attacked the enemy position near Bull Run Creek on July 21. Confederate forces held the line against the northern assault until reinforcements arrived and then counterattacked. The routed northern forces quickly broke ranks and fled toward Washington and safety.

The humiliating defeat at Bull Run led to a shake-up of the northern high command. The man of the hour was George McClellan, who first replaced McDowell and then became general in chief when Scott was eased into retirement. A cautious disciplinarian, McClellan spent the fall and winter drilling his troops and whipping them into shape, much to the anxiety of a more and more impatient Lincoln.

Before McClellan moved, Union forces in the West won some important victories. In February 1862, a joint military-naval operation, commanded by General Ulysses S. Grant, captured Fort Henry on the Tennessee River and Fort Donelson on the Cumberland. The Confederate army was forced to withdraw from Kentucky and middle Tennessee, amassing its western forces at Corinth, Mississippi. The Union army slowly followed, but on April 6, the South launched a surprise attack. In the battle of Shiloh, one of the bloodiest of the war, only the timely arrival of reinforcements prevented the annihilation of Union troops backed up against the Tennessee River. After a second day of fierce fighting, the Confederates retreated to Corinth, leaving the enemy forces battered and exhausted.

Although the military effort to seize control of the Mississippi Valley was temporarily halted at Shiloh, the Union navy soon contributed dramatically to the pursuit of that objective. On April 26, a fleet coming up from the

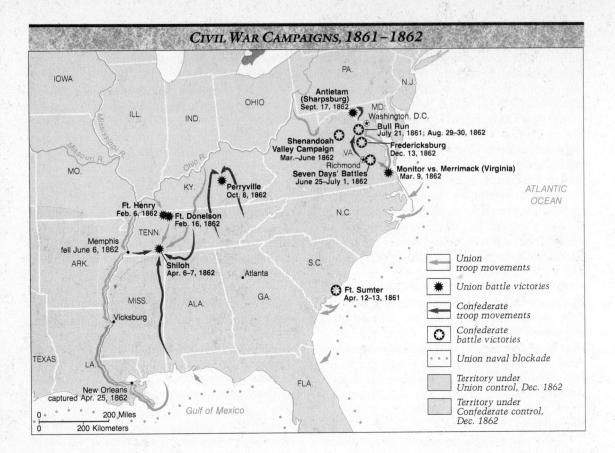

Gulf captured the port of New Orleans. The occupation of New Orleans, besides securing the mouth of the Mississippi, climaxed a series of naval and amphibious operations around the edges of the Confederacy that provided strategically located bases for the northern blockade. The last serious challenge to the North's naval supremacy ended on March 9, 1862, when the Confederate ironclad vessel *Virginia* (originally the U.S.S. *Merrimack*) was driven back by the *Monitor*, an armored and turreted Union gunship.

Successes around the edges of the Confederacy did not relieve northern frustration at the inactivity or failure of Union forces on the eastern front. Finally, at Lincoln's insistence, McClellan started toward Richmond. He moved his forces by water to the peninsula southeast

of the Confederate capital and began his march toward Richmond in early April 1862. By late May, his forces had pushed to within twenty miles of Richmond. There he stopped, awaiting the additional troops that he expected Lincoln to send.

These reinforcements were not forthcoming because the president felt that they were needed to defend Washington. While McClellan was inching his way up the peninsula, a relatively small southern force under General Thomas J. "Stonewall" Jackson was on the rampage in the Shenandoah Valley. When it appeared by late May that Jackson might be poised to march east and attack the Union capital, Lincoln decided to withhold troops from McClellan.

If McClellan had moved more boldly and decisively, he probably could have captured Richmond with the forces he had. But a combination of faulty intelligence reports and his own natural caution led him to falter in the face of what he wrongly believed to be superior numbers. At the end of May, the Confederates under Joseph E. Johnston took the offensive when they discovered that McClellan's army was divided on either side of the Chickahominy River. In the battle of Seven Pines, McClellan was barely able to withstand the assault. During the battle, General Johnston was severely wounded; succeeding him in command of the Confederate Army of Northern Virginia was native Virginian and West Point graduate Robert E. Lee.

Toward the end of June, Lee began an all-out effort to expel McClellan from the outskirts of Richmond. In a series of battles that lasted seven days, the two armies clawed at each other indecisively. Nevertheless, McClellan decided to retreat down the peninsula to a more secure base. This backward step convinced Lincoln that the peninsula campaign was an exercise in futility.

On July 11 Lincoln appointed General Henry W. Halleck to be the new general in chief and through Halleck ordered McClellan to withdraw his army from the peninsula to join a force under General John Pope that was preparing to move on Richmond by an overland route. Before the ever cautious McClellan could reach Pope, however, the Confederates attacked the overland army near Bull Run. In a battle superbly commanded by Lee, Pope was forced to retreat to Washington, where he was stripped of his command.

Lee proceeded to lead his exuberant troops on an invasion of Maryland, in the hope of isolating Washington from the rest of the North. McClellan caught up with him at Antietam, near Sharpsburg, and the bloodiest one-day battle of the war ensued. The result was a draw, but Lee was forced to fall back south of the Potomac. McClellan was slow in pursuit, and Lincoln blamed him for letting the enemy escape.

Convinced that McClellan was fatally infected with "the slows," Lincoln once again sought a more aggressive general and put Am-

brose E. Burnside in command of the Army of the Potomac. Aggressive but rather dense, Burnside's limitations were disastrously revealed at the battle of Fredericksburg, Virginia, on December 13, 1862, when he launched a deadly charge against a Confederate uphill position. The range and accuracy of small arms fire made such a charge utter folly. Thus ended a year of bitter failure for the North on the eastern front.

THE DIPLOMATIC STRUGGLE

The critical period of Civil War diplomacy was 1861–1862, when the South was making every effort to induce major foreign powers to recognize its independence and break the Union blockade. The hope that England and France could be persuaded to involve themselves in the war on the Confederate side stemmed from the fact that these nations depended on the South for three-quarters of their cotton supply.

The Confederate commissioners sent to England and France in May 1861 succeeded in gaining recognition of southern "belligerency," which meant that the new government could claim some of the international rights of a nation at war, such as purchasing and outfitting privateers in neutral ports. As a result, Confederate raiders, built and armed in British shipyards, devastated northern shipping to such an extent that insurance costs eventually forced most of the American merchant marine off the high seas for the duration of the war.

In the fall of 1861 the Confederate government dispatched James M. Mason and John Slidell to be its permanent envoys to England and France respectively and instructed them to push for full recognition of the Confederacy. They took passage on the British steamer *Trent*, which was stopped and boarded in international waters by a United States warship. Mason and Slidell were taken into custody by the Union captain, causing a diplomatic crisis that nearly led to war between England and the United States. After several weeks of international tension, Lincoln and Secretary of State

William H. Seward made the prudent decision to allow the Confederates to proceed to their destinations.

These envoys may as well have stayed at home; they failed in their mission to obtain full recognition of the Confederacy from either England or France. The anticipated cotton shortage was slow to develop, for the bumper crop of 1860 had created a large surplus in British and French warehouses. For a time in the fall of 1862, French ruler Napoleon III toyed with the idea of recognition, but he refused to act without British support. British leaders feared that recognition would lead to a war with the United States; the American minister to Great Britain, Charles Francis Adams, knew well how to play on those fears. Only if the South won decisively on the battlefield would Britain be willing to risk the dangers of recognition and intervention.

The cotton famine finally hit in late 1862, causing massive unemployment in the British textile industry. But, contrary to southern hopes, public opinion did not compel the government to abandon its neutrality and use force to break the Union blockade. Influential interest groups, which actually benefited from the famine, provided the crucial support for continuing a policy of nonintervention. Among these groups were owners of large cotton mills who had made bonanza profits on their existing stocks and were happy to see weaker competitors go under while they awaited new sources of supply. By early 1863 cotton from Egypt and India put the industry back on the track toward full production. Other obvious beneficiaries of nonintervention were manufacturers of wool and linen textiles, munition makers who supplied both sides, and shipping interests that profited from the decline of American competition on the world's sea lanes. Since the British economy as a whole gained more than it lost from neutrality, it is not surprising that there was little effective pressure for a change in policy.

By early 1863, when it was clear that "King Cotton Diplomacy" had failed, the Confederacy broke off formal relations with Great Britain. For the European powers, the advantages of getting involved in the conflict were not worth the risk of a war with the United States. Independence for the South would have to be won on the battlefield.

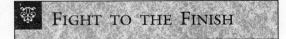

FIGHT TO THE FINISH

The last two and a half years of the struggle saw the implementation of more radical war measures. The most dramatic and important of these was the North's effort to follow through on Lincoln's decision to free the slaves and bring the black population into the war on the Union side. The tide of battle turned in the summer of 1863, but the South continued to resist valiantly for two more years, until finally overcome by the sheer weight of the North's advantages in manpower and resources.

THE COMING OF EMANCIPATION

At the beginning of the war, when the North still hoped for a quick and easy victory, only dedicated abolitionists favored turning the struggle for the Union into a crusade against slavery. But as it became clear how difficult it was going to be to suppress the "rebels," congressional and public sentiment developed for striking a fatal blow at the South's economic and social system by pressing for the freedom of its slaves.

Although Lincoln favored freedom for blacks as an ultimate goal, he was reluctant to commit his administration to a policy of immediate emancipation. In the fall of 1861 and again in the spring of 1862, he disallowed the orders of field commanders who sought to free slaves in areas occupied by their forces, thus angering the strongly antislavery Republicans known as "Radicals." Lincoln's caution stemmed from an effort to avoid alienating Unionist elements in the border slave states and from his own preference for a gradual, compensated form of emancipation.

Lincoln was also aware that one of the main obstacles to any program leading to emancipation was the strong racial prejudice of most whites in the North and South. Since he was pessimistic about the prospects of equality for blacks in the United States, Lincoln coupled his moderate proposals with a plea for government subsidies to support the voluntary "colonization" of free blacks outside the United States, and he actively sought places that would accept them.

But the slaveholding states that remained loyal to the Union refused to endorse Lincoln's gradual plan, and the failure of Union arms in the spring and summer of 1862 increased the public clamor for striking directly at the South's peculiar institution. Responding to political pressure, on September 22, 1862, Lincoln issued his preliminary Emancipation Proclamation. Had he failed to act, he would have split the Republican party, most of whose members favored emancipation. The proclamation gave the Confederate states one hundred days to give up the struggle without losing their slaves.

When there was no response from the South and no enthusiasm in Congress for Lincoln's gradual, compensated plan, the president on January 1, 1863, declared that all slaves in those areas under Confederate control "shall be . . . thenceforward, and forever free." He justified the final proclamation as an act of "military necessity" sanctioned by the war powers of the president and authorized the enlistment of freed slaves in the Union army. The language and tone of the document had "all the grandeur of a bill of lading," and made it clear that blacks were being freed for reasons of state and not out of humanitarian conviction.

Despite its uninspiring origin and limited application—it did not extend to loyal slave states or occupied areas—the proclamation did enunciate the abolition of slavery as a war aim. It also accelerated the breakdown of slavery as a labor system. As word spread among the slaves that emancipation was now official policy, larger numbers of them were inspired to run off and seek the protection of approaching northern armies. Approximately one quarter of the slave population gained freedom during the war under the terms of the Emancipation Proc-

lamation and thus deprived the South of an important part of its agricultural work force.

AFRICAN-AMERICAN ROLE IN THE WAR

Almost 200,000 African Americans, most of them newly freed slaves, eventually served in the Union armed forces and made a vital contribution to the North's victory. Although they were enrolled in segregated units under white officers, initially paid less than their white counterparts, and used disproportionately for garrison duty or heavy labor behind the lines, "blacks in blue" fought heroically in several major battles during the last two years of the war.

Those freed during the war who did not serve in the military were often conscripted to serve as contract wage laborers on cotton plantations owned or leased by "loyal" white planters within the occupied areas of the Deep South. Abolitionists protested that the coercion used by military authorities to get blacks back into the cotton fields amounted to slavery in a new form, but those in power argued that the necessities of war and the northern economy required such "temporary" arrangements. To some extent, regimentation of the freedmen within the South was a way of assuring racially prejudiced Northerners that emancipation would not result in an influx of black refugees to their region of the country.

The heroic performance of African-American troops and the easing of northern anxieties about massive black migration led to a deepening commitment to emancipation as a permanent and comprehensive policy. Realizing that his proclamation had a shaky constitutional foundation, Lincoln pressed for an amendment outlawing involuntary servitude. After supporting its inclusion as a central plank in the Republican platform of 1864, Lincoln used all his influence to win congressional approval for the new Thirteenth Amendment. The cause of freedom for blacks and the cause of the Union had at last become one and the same. Lincoln, despite his earlier hesitations and misgivings,

The 54th Massachusetts Colored Regiment charging Fort Wagner, South Carolina, July 1863. The 54th was the first black unit recruited during the war. Charles and Lewis Douglass, sons of abolitionist Frederick Douglass, both served with this regiment.

had earned the right to go down in history as "the great emancipator."

THE TIDE TURNS

By early 1863 the Confederate economy was in shambles, and its diplomacy had collapsed. The social order of the South was also showing signs of severe strain. Masters were losing control of their slaves, and nonslaveholding whites were becoming disillusioned with the hardships of a war that some of them described as a "rich man's war and a poor man's fight." Yet the North was slow to capitalize on the South's internal weaknesses; it had its own serious morale problems. The long series of defeats on the eastern front had engendered war weariness, and the new policies that "military necessity" forced the government to adopt encountered fierce opposition.

Although popular with Republicans, emancipation was viewed by most Democrats as a betrayal of northern war aims. Racism was a main ingredient in their opposition to freeing blacks. Especially in the Midwest, Democrats used the backlash against the proclamation to win political support. The Enrollment Act of March 1863, which provided for outright conscription, provoked a violent response from those unwilling to "fight for the niggers" and too poor to buy exemption from the draft. A series of antidraft riots culminated in the bloodiest domestic disorder in American history—the New York riot of July 1863. A New York mob, composed mainly of Irish-American laborers, burned the draft offices, the homes of leading Republicans, and an orphanage for black children. At least 120 people died before federal troops restored order.

To fight dissension and "disloyalty," the government used its martial law authority to arrest the alleged ringleaders. Patriotic private organizations also issued a barrage of propaganda aimed at what they believed was a vast secret conspiracy to undermine the northern war effort. Historians disagree about the real extent of covert and illegal antiwar activity, but militant advocates of "peace at any price"—popularly known as Copperheads—were certainly active in some areas, especially among the immigrant working classes of large cities and in southern Ohio, Indiana, and Illinois.

The only effective way to overcome the disillusionment that fed the peace movement was to start winning battles and thus convince the northern public that victory was assured. But before this could happen the North suffered one more humiliating defeat on the eastern front. In early May 1863, Union forces under General Joseph Hooker were routed at Chancellorsville, Virginia, by a much smaller Confederate army masterfully led by Robert E. Lee.

In the West, however, a major Union triumph was taking shape. For over a year, General Ulysses S. Grant had been trying to put his forces in position to capture Vicksburg, Mississippi, the almost inaccessible Confederate bastion that stood between the North and control of the Mississippi River. Finally, in late March 1863, he crossed the river north of the city and moved his forces to a point south of it, where he joined up with naval forces that had run the Confederate batteries mounted on Vicksburg's high bluffs. In one of the boldest campaigns of the war, Grant crossed the river, deliberately cutting himself off from his sources of supply, and marched into the interior of Mississippi. Living off the land and out of communication with an anxious and perplexed Lincoln, his troops won a series of victories and advanced on Vicksburg from the east. After unsuccessfully assaulting the city's defenses, Grant settled down for a siege on May 22.

In an effort to turn the tide of the war, President Davis approved Robert E. Lee's plan for an all-out invasion of the Northeast. Although this plan provided no hope for relieving Vicksburg, it might lead to a dramatic victory that would more than compensate for the probable loss of the Mississippi stronghold. Lee's army crossed the Potomac in June and kept going until it reached Gettysburg, Pennsylvania. There Lee confronted a Union army that had taken up strong defensive positions on Cemetery Ridge and Culp's Hill.

On July 2 a series of Confederate attacks failed to dislodge General George Meade's troops from the high ground they occupied. The following day Lee faced the choice of retreating to protect his lines of communication or launching a final, desperate assault. With more boldness than wisdom, he chose to make a direct attack on the strongest part of the Union line. The resulting charge on Cemetery Ridge was disastrous; advancing Confederate soldiers dropped like flies under the barrage of Union artillery and rifle fire.

Retreat was now inevitable, and Lee withdrew his battered troops to the Potomac, only to find that the river was at flood stage and could not be crossed for several days. For some reason, Meade failed to follow up his victory with a vigorous pursuit, and Lee was allowed to escape a trap that could have resulted in his annihilation. Vicksburg fell to Grant on July 4, the same day that Lee began his withdrawal, and Northerners rejoiced at the twin Independence Day victories. The Union had secured control of the Mississippi and had at last won a major battle in the East. But Lincoln's joy turned to frustration when he learned that his generals had missed the chance to capture Lee's army and bring a quick end to the war.

LAST STAGES OF THE CONFLICT

Later in 1863 the North finally gained control of the middle South, an area where indecisive fighting had been going on since the beginning of the conflict. The main Union target was Chattanooga, "the gateway to the Southeast."

In September Union forces maneuvered the Confederates out of the city but were in turn eventually surrounded and besieged there by southern forces. After Grant arrived from Vicksburg to take command, the encirclement was broken by daring assaults upon the Confederate positions on Lookout Mountain and Missionary Ridge. As a result of its success in the battle of Chattanooga, the North was poised for an invasion of Georgia.

Grant's victories in the West earned him promotion to general in chief of all the Union armies. After assuming that position in March 1864, he ordered a multipronged offensive to finish off the Confederacy. The main movements were a march on Richmond under his personal command and a thrust by the western armies, now led by General William T. Sherman, in the direction of Atlanta and the heart of Georgia.

In May and early June, Grant and Lee fought a series of bloody battles in northern Virginia that tended to follow a set pattern. Lee would take up an entrenched position in the path of the invading force, and Grant would attack it, sustaining heavy losses but also inflicting casualties that the shrinking Confederate army could ill afford. When his direct assault had failed, Grant would move to his left, hoping in vain to maneuver Lee into a less defensible position. After losing about 60,000 men, Grant decided to change his tactics and moved his army to the south of Richmond. There he drew up before Petersburg, a rail center that linked Richmond to the rest of the Confederacy; after failing to take it by assault, he settled down for a siege.

The siege of Petersburg was a long drawn-out affair, and the resulting stalemate in the East caused northern morale to plummet during the summer of 1864. Lincoln was facing reelection, and his failure to end the war dimmed his prospects. Although nominated with ease in June, Lincoln confronted growing opposition within his own party, especially from Radicals who disagreed with his apparently lenient approach to the future restoration of seceded states to the Union.

The Democrats seemed in a good position to capitalize on Republican divisions and make a strong bid for the White House. Their platform appealed to war weariness by calling for a cease-fire followed by negotiations to reestablish the Union. The party's nominee, General George McClellan, announced that he would not be bound by the peace plank and would pursue the war. But he promised to end the conflict soon because he would not insist on emancipation as a condition for reconstruction. By late summer Lincoln believed he would probably be defeated.

Northern military successes changed the political outlook. Sherman's invasion of Georgia went well. On September 2, Atlanta fell, and northern forces occupied the hub of the Deep South. The news unified the Republican party behind Lincoln. The election in November was almost an anticlimax; Lincoln won 212 of a possible 233 electoral votes and 55 percent of the popular vote. The Republican cause of "liberty and Union" was secure.

The concluding military operations revealed the futility of further southern resistance. Sherman marched almost unopposed through Georgia to the sea, destroying nearly everything of possible military or economic value in a corridor 300 miles long and 60 miles wide. The Confederate army that had opposed him at Atlanta moved northward into Tennessee, where it was defeated and almost destroyed by Union forces at Nashville in mid-December. Sherman captured Savannah on December 22. He then turned north and marched through the Carolinas, intending to join up with Grant at Petersburg.

While Sherman was tearing up the Carolinas, Grant finally ended the stalemate at Petersburg. When Lee's starving and exhausted army tried to break through the Union lines, Grant renewed his attack and forced the Confederates to abandon Petersburg and Richmond on April 2, 1865. A week later, Lee recognized that future fighting was pointless and surrendered his army at Appomattox Courthouse on April 9.

But the joy of the victorious North turned to sorrow and anger when actor John Wilkes

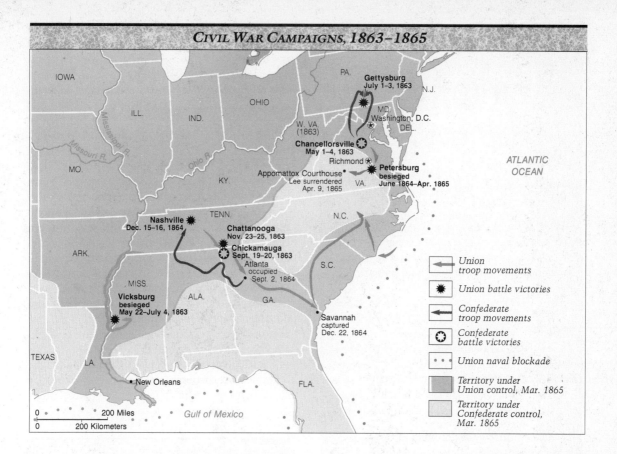

IOWA

ILL.

IND.

OHIO

PA.

Gettysburg
July 1–3, 1863

N.J.

MD.
Washington, D.C.

DEL.

W. VA.
(1863)

Chancellorsville
May 1–4, 1863

Richmond

Appomattox Courthouse
Lee surrendered
Apr. 9, 1865

VA.

Petersburg
besieged
June 1864–Apr. 1865

ATLANTIC
OCEAN

MO.

KY.

TENN.

N.C.

Nashville
Dec. 15–16, 1864

Chattanooga
Nov. 23–25, 1863

Chickamauga
Sept. 19–20, 1863

Atlanta
occupied
Sept. 2, 1864

S.C.

ARK.

MISS.

Vicksburg
besieged
May 22–July 4, 1863

ALA.

GA.

Savannah
captured
Dec. 22, 1864

TEXAS

LA.

New Orleans

FLA.

Gulf of Mexico

0 ——— 200 Miles
0 ——— 200 Kilometers

→ Union
troop movements

✳ Union battle victories

← Confederate
troop movements

✪ Confederate
battle victories

· · · Union naval blockade

Territory under
Union control, Mar. 1865

Territory under
Confederate control,
Mar. 1865

Booth assassinated Abraham Lincoln at Ford's Theater in Washington on April 14. Although Booth had a few accomplices, popular theories that the assassination was the result of a vast conspiracy involving Confederate leaders or (according to another version) Radical Republicans have never been substantiated and are extremely implausible. The man who had spoken at Gettysburg of the need to sacrifice for the Union cause had himself given "the last full measure of devotion." Four days after Lincoln's death the only remaining Confederate force of any significance, the troops under Joseph E. Johnston who had been opposing Sherman in North Carolina, laid down their arms. The Union was saved.

EFFECTS OF THE WAR

The nation that emerged from four years of total war was not the same America that had split apart in 1861. More than 618,000 young men were in their graves, and the widows and sweethearts they left behind temporarily increased the proportion of unmarried women in the population. Some members of this generation of involuntary "spinsters" sought new opportunities for making a living or serving the community that went beyond the purely domestic roles previously prescribed for women.

At enormous human and economic cost, the nation had emancipated 4 million African Americans from slavery, but it had not yet re-

CHRONOLOGY

1860	South Carolina secedes from the Union (December)
1861	Rest of Deep South secedes: Confederacy is founded (January–February)
	Fort Sumter is fired upon and surrenders to Confederate forces (April)
	Upper South secedes (April–May)
	South wins first battle of Bull Run (July)
1862	Grant captures Forts Henry and Donelson (February)
	Farragut captures New Orleans for the Union (April)
	McClellan leads unsuccessful campaign on the peninsula southeast of Richmond (March–July)
	South wins second battle of Bull Run (August)
	McClellan stops Lee at battle of Antietam (September)
	Lincoln issues preliminary Emancipation Proclamation (September)
	Lee defeats Union army at Fredericksburg (December)
1863	Lincoln issues final Emancipation Proclamation (January)
	Lee is victorious at Chancellorsville (May)
	North gains major victories at Gettysburg and Vicksburg (July)
	Grant defeats Confederate forces at Chattanooga (November)
1864	Grant and Lee battle in northern Virginia (May–June)

	Atlanta falls to Sherman (September)
	Lincoln is reelected president, defeating McClellan (November)
	Sherman marches through Georgia (November–December)
1865	Congress passes Thirteenth Amendment abolishing slavery (January)
	Grant captures Petersburg and Richmond
	Lee surrenders at Appomattox (April)
	Lincoln assassinated by John Wilkes Booth (April)
	Remaining Confederate forces surrender (April–May)

solved that they should be equal citizens. At the time of Lincoln's assassination, most northern states still denied blacks equality under the law and the right to vote. Whether the North would extend more rights to southern freedmen than it had granted to "free Negroes" was an open question.

The impact of the war on white working people was also unclear. Those in the industrializing parts of the North had suffered and lost ground economically because prices had risen much faster than wages during the conflict. But Republican rhetoric stressing "equal opportunity" and the "dignity of labor" raised hopes that the crusade against slavery could be broadened into a movement to improve the lot of working people in general. Foreign-born workers had additional reason to be optimistic; the fact that so many immigrants had fought and died for the Union cause had—for the moment—weakened nativist sentiment and encouraged ethnic tolerance.

What the war definitely decided was that the federal government was supreme over the states and had a broad grant of constitutional authority to act on matters affecting "the general welfare." The southern principle of state sovereignty and strict construction died at Appomattox, and the United States was on its way to becoming a true nation-state with an effective central government. Although the states retained many powers and the Constitution placed limits on what the national government could do, the war ended all questions about where ultimate authority rested.

A broadened definition of federal powers had its greatest impact in the realm of economic policy. During the war, Republican-dominated Congresses passed a rash of legislation designed to give encouragement and direction to the nation's economic development. Taking advantage of the absence of southern opposition, Republicans rejected the pre-Civil War tradition of laissez-faire and enacted a Whiggish program of active support for business and agriculture. In 1862 Congress passed a high protective tariff, approved a homestead act intended to encourage settlement of the West by providing free land to settlers, granted huge tracks of public land to railroad companies to support the building of a transcontinental railroad, and gave the states land for the establishment of agricultural colleges. The following year, Congress set up a national banking system. The notes that the national banks issued became the country's first standardized and reliable circulating currency.

These wartime achievements added up to a decisive shift in the relationship between the federal government and private enterprise. The Republicans took a limited government that did little more than seek to protect the marketplace from the threat of monopoly and changed it into an activist state that promoted and subsidized the efforts of the economically industrious and ambitious.

The most pervasive effect of the war on northern society was to encourage an "organizational revolution." Aided by government policies, venturesome businessmen took advantage of the new national market created by military procurement to build larger firms that could operate across state lines; some of the huge corporate enterprises of the postwar era began to take shape. Philanthropists also developed more effective national associations. Both the men who served in the army and those men and women who supported them on the home front became accustomed to working in large, bureaucratic organizations of a kind that had scarcely existed before the war.

Ralph Waldo Emerson, the era's most prominent man of letters, noted that the conflict encouraged a dramatic shift in American thought about the relationship between the individual and society. Before the war, Emerson championed the individual who stood apart from institutions and organizations and sought fulfillment in an inner world of imagination and cosmic intuition. During the conflict, he began to exalt the claims of organization, government, and "civilization" over the endeavors of "the private man." In purging his philosophy of extreme individualism and hailing the need to accept social discipline and participate in organized, cooperative activity, Emerson epitomized the way the war affected American thought and patterns of behavior.

The North won the war mainly because it had shown a greater capacity than the South to organize, innovate, and modernize. Its victory meant that the nation as a whole would now be ready to embrace the conception of progress that the North had affirmed in its war effort—not only advances in science and technology, but also bringing together and managing large numbers of men and women for economic and social goals. The Civil War was thus a catalyst for the great transformation of American society from an individualistic society of small producers into the more highly organized and incorporated America of the late nineteenth century.

🌿 RECOMMENDED READING

The best general survey of the Civil War era is James M. McPherson, *Battle Cry of Freedom: The Civil War Era* (1988). There are also two excellent textbooks on the period: J. G. Randall and David Donald, *The Civil War and Reconstruction*, 2nd ed. (1969), and James M. McPherson, *Ordeal by Fire: The Civil War and Reconstruction* (1981). An excellent shorter account is David Herbert Donald, *Liberty and Union* (1978). The best one-volume introduction to the military side of the conflict is Bruce Catton, *This Hallowed Ground* (1956). A brilliant study of the writings of those who experienced the war is Edmund Wilson, *Patriotic Gore: Studies in the Literature of the American Civil War* (1962).

For detailed accounts of the war, see Allan Nevins, *The War for the Union*, 4 vols. (1959–1971), and Bruce Catton, *Centennial History of the Civil War*, 3 vols. (1961–1965). The Confederate experience is well covered in Clement Eaton, *A History of the Southern Confederacy* (1954); Emory M. Thomas, *The Confederate Nation: 1861–1865* (1979); and Frank E. Vandiver, *Their Tattered Flags: The Epic of the Confederacy* (1970).

Lincoln's career and wartime leadership are treated in two excellent biographies: Benjamin P. Thomas, *Abraham Lincoln* (1954) and Stephen B. Oates, *With Malice Toward None: The Life of Abraham Lincoln* (1977). The most detailed works on Lincoln's stewardship of the Union cause are James G. Randall, *Lincoln the President*, 4 vols. (1945–1955, vol. 4 completed by Richard N. Current), and Carl Sandburg's less reliable *Abraham Lincoln: The War Years*, 4 vols. (1939).

Events leading up to the outbreak of hostilities are covered in Kenneth M. Stampp, *And the War Came: The North and the Sectional Crisis* (1950), and David M. Potter, *Lincoln and His Party in the Secession Crisis*, 2nd ed. (1962). The literature on military commanders, campaigns, and battles is enormous, but mention must be made of Douglas Southall Freeman's outstanding works on southern generalship: *R. E. Lee: A Biography*, 4 vols. (1934–1935), and *Lee Lieutenants*, 3 vols. (1942–1944). On the common soldier's experience of the war, see two books by Bell I. Wiley, *The Life of Johnny Reb* (1943) and *The Life of Billy Yank* (1952).

Major works on northern politics during the war include Hans Trefousse, *The Radical Republicans: Lincoln's Vanguard for Racial Justice* (1969); David Donald, *Charles Sumner and the Rights of Man* (1970); Joel Sibley, *A Respectable Minority: The Democratic Party in the Civil War Era* (1977); and Jean Baker, *Affairs of Party: The Political Culture of the Democratic Party in the Mid-Nineteenth Century* (1983). On legal and constitutional issues, see James G. Randall, *Constitutional Problems under Lincoln*, rev. ed. (1961), and Harold M. Hyman, *A More Perfect Union: The Impact of the Civil War and Reconstruction on the Constitution* (1973).

On the cultural impact of the war, see George M. Fredrickson, *The Inner Civil War: Northern Intellectuals and the Crisis of the Union* (1965); Daniel Aaron, *The Unwritten War: American Writers and the Civil War* (1973); and James H. Morehead, *American Apocalypse: Yankee Protestants and the Civil War* (1978).

For an understanding of the South's internal problems, see Frank Owsley, *States' Rights in the Confederacy* (1925); Curtis A. Amlund, *Federalism in the Southern Confederacy* (1966); and Bell I. Wiley, *The Plain People and the Confederacy* (1934).

Emancipation and the role of blacks in the war are the subject of a number of excellent studies, including Benjamin Quarles, *The Negro in the Civil War* (1953) and *Lincoln and the Negro* (1962); Bell I. Wiley, *Southern Negroes, 1861–1865* (1938); James M. McPherson, *The Struggle for Equality: Abolitionists and the Negro in the Civil War and Reconstruction* (1964); LaWanda Cox, *Lincoln and Black Freedom* (1981); Willie Lee Rose, *Rehearsal for Reconstruction: The Port Royal Experiment* (1964); and Herman Belz, *A New Birth of Freedom: The Republican Party and Freedmen's Rights, 1861–1866* (1976).

16 THE AGONY OF RECONSTRUCTION

THE PRESIDENT VERSUS CONGRESS

RECONSTRUCTION IN THE SOUTH

THE AGE OF GRANT

REUNION AND THE NEW SOUTH

The Yankees who went south immediately after the Civil War and became known as "carpetbaggers" have often been portrayed as vultures preying on the "prostrate South." Some were indeed rogues and swindlers, but a large number were ambitious men, no less honest than the average, who migrated south in search of a fair chance to better themselves, just as other people went west. Some tried growing cotton, failed, and returned to the North. But a minority of Northerners stayed on to pursue political careers during the period of Republican dominance that lasted from 1868 to the mid-1870s.

Some carpetbaggers were not simply seeking economic and political advantage for themselves but were also sincere champions of equality and opportunity for the newly freed slaves. One such was Albion W. Tourgée, an ex-Union officer from Ohio who settled in North Carolina in 1865. Tourgée advocated black suffrage, and as a superior court judge he acquired a reputation for honesty, fairness, and courage. He also risked his life to bring nightriding Klansmen to justice. But the white resistance to Reconstruction was eventually successful, and Tourgée and other Republicans were driven from office amid charges of corruption (which in his case at least were clearly trumped up).

In 1879, Tourgée returned to the North and wrote a best-selling novel about his southern experiences. Entitled *A Fool's Errand*, it details how the "wise men" in Washington blundered in their attempt to reconstruct the South. He described how the North had first offended the deep-seated racism of southern whites by declaring that blacks had "equality of political right." But northern policymakers had failed to establish an effective mechanism to enforce and protect black rights. Instead, they had readmitted the "rebellious states" to the Union and left the freedom to fight for equality "without the possibility of national interference." They told blacks to sink or swim—in the language of the time, to "root, hog, or die!"

As the novel makes clear through its vivid depiction of violence and intimidation against black voters, the freedmen were at a great disadvantage in this struggle; their poverty and illiteracy made them no match for the white supremacists who retained control of land and other sources of wealth and power. In Tourgée's view, "Radical Reconstruction" failed to achieve its goal of equality because it was not radical enough. Guaranteeing equality to the freed slaves required methods that were more thoroughgoing and revolutionary than those that Congress was prepared to accept and sustain.

THE PRESIDENT VERSUS CONGRESS

The problem of how to reconstruct the Union in the wake of the South's military defeat was one of the most difficult challenges ever faced by American policymakers. The Constitution provided no firm guidelines, and once emancipation became a northern war aim, the problem was compounded by a new issue: How far should the federal government go to secure freedom and civil rights for 4 million former slaves?

The debate that evolved led to a major political crisis. Advocates of a minimal Reconstruction policy favored quick restoration of the Union with no protection for the freed slaves beyond the prohibition of slavery. Proponents of a more radical policy wanted readmission of the southern states to be dependent on guarantees that "loyal" men would replace the Confederate elite and that blacks would acquire some of the basic rights of American citizenship. The White House favored the minimal approach, while Congress came to endorse the more radical policy. The resulting struggle between Congress and the chief executive was the most serious clash between two branches of government in the nation's history.

WARTIME RECONSTRUCTION

Tension between the president and Congress over how to reconstruct the Union began during the war. Although Lincoln did not set forth a final and comprehensive plan, he did indicate that he favored a lenient and conciliatory policy toward Southerners who would give up the struggle and repudiate slavery. In December 1863 he offered a full pardon to all Southerners (with the exception of certain classes of Confederate leaders) who would take an oath of allegiance to the Union and acknowledge the legality of emancipation. Once 10 percent or more of the voting population of any occupied state had taken the oath, they were authorized to set up a loyal government. By 1864 Louisiana and Arkansas had established fully functioning Unionist governments.

Lincoln's policy was meant to shorten the war by offering a moderate peace plan. It was also intended to further his emancipation policy by insisting that the new governments abolish slavery. When constitutional conventions operating under the 10 percent plan in Louisiana and Arkansas dutifully abolished slavery in 1864, emancipation came closer to being irreversible.

But Congress was unhappy with the president's reconstruction experiments and in 1864 refused to seat the Unionists elected to the House and Senate from Louisiana and Arkansas. A minority of congressional Republicans—the strongly antislavery Radicals—favored strong protection for black civil rights and provision for their enfranchisement as a precondition for the readmission of southern states. A larger group of moderates also opposed Lincoln's plan, but they did so primarily because they did not trust the repentant Confederates who would play a major role in the new governments.

Also disturbing Congress was a sense that the president was exceeding his authority by using executive powers to restore the Union. Lincoln operated on the theory that secession, being illegal, did not place the Confederate states outside the Union in a constitutional sense. Since individuals and not states had defied federal authority, the president could use his pardoning power to certify a loyal electorate, which could then function as the legitimate state government. The dominant view in Congress, however, was that the southern states had definitely forfeited their place in the Union and that it was up to Congress to decide when and how they would be readmitted.

After refusing to recognize Lincoln's 10 percent governments, Congress passed a Reconstruction bill of its own in July 1864. Known as the Wade-Davis Bill, this legislation required that 50 percent of the voters must take an oath of future loyalty before the restoration process could begin. Once this had occurred, those who could swear that they had never willingly supported the Confederacy could vote in an election for delegates to a constitutional convention. Lincoln exercised a pocket veto by refusing to sign the bill before Congress adjourned, angering many Congressmen.

Congress and the president remained stalemated on the Reconstruction issue for the rest of the war. During his last months in office, however, Lincoln showed a willingness to compromise. But he died without clarifying his intentions, leaving historians to speculate on whether his quarrel with Congress would have worsened or been resolved. Given Lincoln's past record of political flexibility, the best bet is that he would have come to terms with the majority of his party.

ANDREW JOHNSON AT THE HELM

Andrew Johnson, the man suddenly made president by an assassin's bullet, attempted to put the Union back together on his own authority in 1865. But his policies eventually put him at odds with Congress and the Republican party and provoked a serious crisis in the system of checks and balances among the branches of the federal government.

Johnson's approach to Reconstruction was shaped by his background. Born in dire poverty in North Carolina, he migrated as a young man to eastern Tennessee where he made his living as a tailor. Although poorly educated (he did not learn to write until adulthood), Johnson was an effective stump speaker who railed against the planter aristocracy. Entering politics as a Jacksonian Democrat, he became the political spokesman for Tennessee's nonslaveholding whites. He advanced from state legislator to congressman to governor and in 1857 was elected to the United States Senate.

When Tennessee seceded in 1861, Johnson was the only senator from a Confederate state who remained loyal to the Union and continued to serve in Washington. But his Unionism did not include antislavery sentiments or friendship for blacks. He wished that "every head of family in the United States had one slave to take the drudgery and menial service off his family."

During the war, while acting as military governor of Tennessee, Johnson implemented Lincoln's emancipation policy as a means of destroying the power of the hated planter class rather than as a recognition of black humanity. He was chosen as Lincoln's running mate in 1864 in order to strengthen the ticket. No one expected that this southern Democrat and fervent white supremacist would ever become president.

Some Radical Republicans initially welcomed Johnson's assent to the nation's highest office. Like the Radicals themselves, he was loyal to the Union and believed that ex-Confederates should be severely treated. He seemed more likely than Lincoln to punish southern "traitors" and prevent them from regaining political influence. Only gradually did Johnson and the Republican majority in Congress drift apart.

The Reconstruction policy that Johnson initiated on May 29, 1865, created some uneasi-

Nearly insurmountable problems with a Congress determined to enact its own Reconstruction policy plagued Andrew Johnson through his presidency. Impeached in 1868, he escaped conviction by a single vote.

ness among the Radicals, but most other Republicans were willing to give it a chance. Johnson placed North Carolina and eventually other states under appointed provisional governors mainly chosen from among prominent southern politicians who had opposed the secession movement and had rendered no conspicuous service to the confederacy. They were then responsible for calling constitutional conventions to elect "loyal" officeholders. Johnson's plan was especially designed to prevent his longtime adversaries—the planter class—from participating in the reconstruction of southern state governments.

Johnson urged the conventions to declare the ordinances of secession illegal, repudiate the Confederate debt, and ratify the Thirteenth Amendment abolishing slavery. After governments had been reestablished under constitutions meeting these conditions, the president assumed that the process of Reconstruction would be complete and that the ex-Confederate states would regain their full rights under the Constitution.

Many congressional Republicans were troubled by the work of the southern conventions, which balked at fully implementing Johnson's recommendations. Furthermore, in no state was even limited black suffrage approved. Johnson, however, seemed eager to give southern white majorities a free hand in determining the civil and political status of freed slaves.

Republican uneasiness turned to disillusionment and anger when the state legislatures elected under the new constitutions proceeded to pass "Black Codes" subjecting the former

slaves to a variety of special regulations and restrictions on their freedom. Especially troubling were vagrancy and apprenticeship laws that forced blacks to work and denied them a choice of employers. To Radicals, the Black Codes looked suspiciously like slavery under a new guise.

The growing rift between the president and Congress came into the open in December when the House and Senate refused to seat the recently elected southern delegation. Instead of endorsing Johnson's work and recognizing the state governments he had called into being, Congress established a joint committee, chaired by William Pitt Fessenden of Maine, to review Reconstruction policy and set further conditions for readmission of the seceded states.

CONGRESS TAKES THE INITIATIVE

The struggle over how to reconstruct the Union ended with Congress doing the job all over again. The clash between Johnson and Congress was a matter of principle and could not be reconciled. Johnson's stubborn and prideful nature did not help his political cause. But the root of the problem was that he disagreed with the majority of Congress on what Reconstruction was supposed to accomplish. An heir of the Democratic states' rights tradition, he wanted to restore the prewar federal system as quickly as possible, except for the prohibition on slavery and secession.

Most Republicans, however, believed that the North would be cheated of the full fruits of victory if the old southern ruling class were to regain regional power and national influence by devising new ways to subjugate blacks. (Since emancipation had nullified the three-fifths clause of the Constitution, all blacks were now to be counted in determining representation. Consequently, the Republicans worried about increased southern strength in Congress and the electoral college.) Congress thus sought a Reconstruction policy that would limit the political role of ex-Confederates and provide some protection for black citizenship.

Except for a few extreme Radicals, Republican leaders were not convinced that blacks were inherently equal to whites. They were convinced, however, that all citizens should have the same basic rights and opportunities. Principle coincided easily with political expediency; southern blacks were likely to be loyal to the Republican party that had emancipated them and thus increase that party's political power in the South.

The disagreement between the president and Congress became irreconcilable in early 1866 when Johnson vetoed two bills that had passed with overwhelming Republican support. One, the Freedmen's Bureau Bill, extended the life of the agency charged with providing former slaves with relief, legal help, and educational and employment assistance. The second, a civil rights bill, was intended to nullify the detested Black Codes and guarantee "equal benefit of all laws."

The vetoes shocked moderate Republicans who had expected Johnson to accept these relatively modest measures. Congress promptly passed the Civil Rights Act over Johnson's veto, signifying that the president was now hopelessly at odds with most of the congressmen from what was supposed to be his own party.

Johnson soon revealed that he intended to abandon the Republicans and place himself at the head of a new conservative party uniting the small minority of Republicans who supported him with a reviving Democratic party that was rallying behind his Reconstruction policy. As the elections of 1866 neared, Johnson stepped up his criticism of Congress.

Meanwhile, the Republican majority on Capitol Hill passed the Fourteenth Amendment. This, the most important of our constitutional amendments, gave the federal government responsibility for guaranteeing equal rights under the law to all Americans. The major section de-

RECONSTRUCTION AMENDMENTS, 1865–1870			
Amendment	Main Provisions	Congressional Passage (two-thirds majority in each house required)	Ratification Process (three fourths of all states including ex-Confederate states required)
13	Slavery prohibited in United States	January 1865	December 1865 (twenty-seven states, including eight southern states)
14	1. National citizenship extended; federal government given responsibility for guaranteeing equal rights	June 1866	Rejected by twelve southern and border states, February 1867
	2. State representation in Congress reduced proportionally to number of voters disenfranchised		Radicals make readmission of southern states hinge on ratification
	3. Former Confederates denied right to hold office		Ratified July 1868
15	Denial of franchise because of race, color, or past servitude expressly prohibited	February 1869	Ratification required for readmission of Virginia, Texas, Mississippi, Georgia
			Ratified March 1870

fined national citizenship for the first time as extending to "all persons born or naturalized in the United States." The states were prohibited from abridging the rights of American citizens and could not "deprive any person of life, liberty, or property, without due process of law; nor deny to any person . . . equal protection of the laws." The amendment was sent to the states with an implied understanding that Southerners would be readmitted to Congress only if their states ratified it.

The congressional elections of 1866 served as a referendum on the Fourteenth Amendment. With the support of Johnson, all the southern states except Tennessee rejected the amendment. But bloody race riots in Memphis and New Orleans and maltreatment of blacks throughout the South made it painfully clear that southern state governments were failing abysmally to protect the "life, liberty, or property" of the ex-slaves.

Johnson further weakened his cause by taking the stump on behalf of candidates who supported his policies. His undignified speeches and his inflexibility enraged northern voters. The Republican majority in Congress increased to a solid two thirds in both houses, and the radical wing of the party gained strength at the expense of moderates and conservatives.

CONGRESSIONAL RECONSTRUCTION PLAN ENACTED

Congress was now in a position to implement its own plan of Reconstruction. In 1867 it passed a series of acts that reorganized the South on a new basis. Generally referred to as "Radical Reconstruction," these measures actually represented a compromise between genuine Radicals and the more moderate elements within the party.

Consistent Radicals, such as Charles Sumner of Massachusetts and Thaddeus Stevens of Pennsylvania, wanted to reshape southern society before readmitting ex-Confederates to the Union. Their program required an extended period of military rule, confiscation and redistri-

bution of large landholdings among freedmen, and federal aid for schools that would educate blacks for citizenship. But the majority of Republican congressmen found such a program unacceptable because it broke with American traditions of federalism and regard for property rights.

The First Reconstruction Act, passed over Johnson's veto on March 2, 1867, did place the South under military rule—but only for a short period. The act opened the way for the readmission of any state that framed and ratified a new constitution providing for black suffrage. Since blacks (but not ex-Confederates) were allowed to participate in this process, Republicans thought they had found a way to ensure that "loyal men" would dominate the new governments.

"Radical Reconstruction" was based on the false assumption that once blacks had the vote, they would have the power to protect themselves against the efforts of white supremacists to deny them their rights. The Reconstruction Acts thus signaled a retreat from the true Radical position that a sustained use of federal authority was needed to complete the transition from slavery to freedom and prevent the resurgence of the South's old ruling class.

Even so, congressional Reconstruction did have a radical aspect. It strongly endorsed black suffrage. The principle that even the poorest and most underprivileged should have access to the ballot box was a noble and enlightened one. The problem was how to enforce it under conditions then existing in the postwar South.

THE IMPEACHMENT CRISIS

President Johnson was unalterably opposed to the congressional Reconstruction program, and he did everything within his power to prevent its full implementation. Congress responded by passing laws designed to limit presidential authority over Reconstruction matters. One of these measures was the Tenure of Office Act, requiring Senate approval for the removal of cabinet officers and other officials whose appointment had needed the consent of the Senate. Another measure sought to limit Johnson's authority to issue military orders.

Johnson objected vigorously to these restrictions on the grounds that they violated the constitutional doctrine of the separation of powers. Faced with Johnson's opposition, some congressmen began to call for his impeachment. When Johnson tried to discharge Secretary of War Edwin Stanton—the only Radical in his cabinet—the proimpeachment forces grew.

In January 1868 Johnson ordered General Grant to take over Stanton's job as head of the War Department. But Grant had his eye on the Republican presidential nomination and refused to defy Congress. Johnson then appointed General Lorenzo Thomas. Faced with this apparent violation of the Tenure of Office Act, the House of Representatives voted overwhelmingly to impeach the president, and he was placed on trial before the Senate.

Johnson narrowly avoided conviction and removal from office when the impeachment effort fell one vote short of the necessary two thirds. This outcome resulted in part from a skillful defense. Responding to the charge that Johnson had deliberately violated the Tenure of Office Act, the defense contended that the law did not apply to the removal of Stanton because he had been appointed by Lincoln.

The prosecution was more concerned that Johnson had abused the powers of his office in an effort to sabotage the congressional Reconstruction policy. Obstructing the will of the legislative branch, they claimed, was sufficient grounds for conviction. The Republicans who broke ranks to vote for acquittal feared that removal of a president for essentially political reasons would threaten the constitutional balance of powers and open the way to legislative supremacy over the executive.

The impeachment episode helped create an impression in the public mind that the Radicals were ready to turn the Constitution to their own use to gain their objectives. But the evidence of congressional ruthlessness and illegality is not as strong as most historians used to think. Modern legal scholars have found merit in the Radicals' claim that their actions did not violate the Constitution.

The failed conviction effort was an embarrassment to congressional Republicans, but the episode did ensure that Reconstruction in the South would proceed as the majority in Congress intended. During the trial Johnson helped influence the verdict by pledging to enforce the Reconstruction Acts, and he held to this promise during his remaining months in office.

RECONSTRUCTION IN THE SOUTH

The Civil War left the South devastated, demoralized, and destitute. Slavery was dead, but what this meant for future relationships between whites and blacks was still in doubt. Most whites were determined to restrict the freedmen's rights, and many blacks were just as set on achieving real independence. For blacks the acquisition of land, education, and the vote seemed the best means of achieving their goal. The thousands of Northerners who went south after the war for economic or humanitarian reasons hoped to extend Yankee "civilization" to what they viewed as a barbarous region. For most of them this reformation required the aid of the freedmen.

The struggle of these groups to achieve their conflicting goals bred chaos, violence, and instability. It was not the ideal setting for an experiment in interracial democracy. When the federal government's support of reform faltered, the forces of reaction and white supremacy were unleashed.

SOCIAL AND ECONOMIC ADJUSTMENTS

The Civil War scarred the southern landscape and wrecked its economy. Many plantations were ruined and several major cities—including Atlanta and Richmond—were gutted by fire. Most factories were dismantled or destroyed, and long stretches of railroad were torn up.

Nor was there adequate investment capital for rebuilding. The substantial wealth represented by Confederate currency and bonds had melted away, and emancipation of the slaves had divested the propertied classes of their most valuable and productive assets. According to some estimates, the South's per capita wealth in 1865 was only about half what it had been in 1860.

Recovery could not even begin until a new labor system replaced slavery. The lack of capital hindered the rebuilding of plantations, and most Americans assumed that Southern prosperity would depend on plantation-grown cotton. In addition, southern whites believed that blacks would work only under compulsion, and freedmen resisted labor conditions that recalled slavery.

Blacks strongly preferred to be small independent farmers rather than plantation laborers. For a time they had reason to hope that the federal government would support their ambitions. Some forty-acre land grants were given by federal authorities to freedmen. By July 1865, 40,000 black farmers were at work on 300,000 acres of what they thought would be their own land.

But the dream of "forty acres and a mule" was not to be realized. Neither President Johnson nor most Congressmen favored an effective program of land confiscation and redistribution. Consequently, the vast majority of blacks in physical possession of small farms failed to acquire title and were left with little or no prospect of becoming landowners.

Despite their poverty and landlessness, ex-slaves were reluctant to settle down and commit themselves to wage-labor for their former masters. Many took to the road, hoping to find something better. Some were still expecting grants of land, but others were simply trying to increase their bargaining power. As the end of 1865 approached, many freedmen had still not signed up for the coming season; anxious planters feared that they were plotting to seize the land by force. Within a few weeks, however, most of the holdouts signed for the best terms they could get. The most common form of agricultural employment in 1866 was a contract labor system. Under this system workers committed themselves for a year in return for fixed wages. Although blacks occasionally received help from the Freedmen's Bureau, more often than not they were worked hard and paid little, and the contracts normally protected the employers more than the employees.

Growing up alongside the contract system and eventually displacing it was the alternative capital-labor relationship of sharecropping— the right to work a small piece of land independently in return for a fixed share of the crop produced on it, usually one half. A shortage of labor gave the freedmen enough leverage to force this arrangement on those planters who were unwilling, but many landowners found it advantageous because it did not require much capital and forced the tenant to share the risks of crop failure or a fall in cotton prices.

Blacks initially viewed sharecropping as a step up from wage labor in the direction of landownership. But during the 1870s this form of tenancy evolved into a new kind of servitude. Croppers had to live on credit until their cotton was sold, and planters or merchants seized the chance to "provision" them at high prices and exorbitant rates of interest. Soon croppers discovered that debts multiplied faster than profits. Furthermore, various methods were eventually devised to bind indebted tenants to a single landlord for extended periods, although some economic historians argue that considerable movement was still possible.

Blacks in towns and cities found themselves living in an increasingly segregated society. Through legal and illegal methods, they were separated from whites in most public places and often forced to use separate facilities. Most hotels, restaurants, and other privately owned establishments catered only to whites. When black-supported Republican governments came to power in 1868, some of them passed civil rights acts requiring equal access to public facilities, but little effort was made to enforce the legislation. Some forms of racial separation were not openly discriminatory, and blacks accepted and even endorsed them. For the first time, blacks could organize all-black churches, an opportunity that had been denied to them during slavery. They tolerated segregated schools.

The upshot of all forms of racial separation was to create a divided society, one in which blacks and whites lived much of the time in separate worlds. But there were two exceptions to this pattern: One was at work, where blacks necessarily dealt with white employers; the other was in the political sphere, where blacks sought to exercise their democratic rights.

POLITICAL RECONSTRUCTION IN THE SOUTH

The state governments that emerged in 1865 had little or no regard for the rights of the freed slaves. Some of their codes made black unemployment a crime and limited the rights of blacks to own property or engage in occupations other than those of servant or laborer. Although federal authorities attacked these codes, private violence and discrimination against blacks continued on a massive scale. Hundreds, perhaps thousands, of blacks were murdered by organized terror groups as well as by acts of individual whites in 1865–1866, and few of the perpetrators were brought to justice.

The imposition of military rule in 1867 was designed in part to protect former slaves from violence and intimidation, but the task was beyond the capacity of the few thousand troops stationed in the South. When new constitutions were approved and states readmitted to the Union under the congressional plan in 1868, the problem became more severe. Armed white supremacists used systematic terrorism to discourage blacks from voting and to crush the new Republican regimes.

Hastily organized in 1867, the southern Republican party dominated the constitution making of 1868 and the regimes that came out of it. The party was an attempted coalition of three social groups: businessmen seeking aid for economic development, poor white farmers, and blacks. Although all three groups had different goals, their opposition to the old planter ruling class appeared to give them a solid basis for unity.

To be sure, the coalition faced difficulties even within their own ranks. Small farmers of the yeoman class had a bred-in-the-bone resistance to black equality. And conservative businessmen questioned costly measures for the elevation or relief of the lower classes of either race. In some states, astute Democratic politicians exploited these divisions by appealing to disaffected white Republicans.

But during the relatively brief period when they were in power in the South, the Republicans chalked up some notable achievements. They established (on paper at least) the South's first adequate system of public education, democratized state and local government, and appropriated funds for an enormous expansion of public services and welfare responsibilities.

Important though it was, social and political reform took second place to the major effort that Republicans made to foster economic development and restore southern prosperity by subsidizing the construction of railroads and other internal improvements. Although it addressed the region's real economic needs, and was initially very popular, the policy of aiding railroads turned out disastrously. Extravagance, corruption, and the determination of routes based on political rather than sound economic considerations meant an increasing burden of public debt and taxation; the policy did not produce the promised payoff of reliable, cheap transportation. Subsidized railroads frequently went bankrupt, leaving the taxpayers holding the bag. When the Panic of 1873 brought many southern state governments to the verge of bankruptcy and railroad building came to an end, it was clear that the Republicans' "gospel of prosperity" through state aid to private enterprise had failed miserably. Their political opponents, most of whom had originally favored these policies, now saw an opportunity to make gains by charging that Republicans had ruined the southern economy.

These activities were often accompanied by inefficiency, waste, and corruption. State debts and tax burdens rose enormously, mainly because governments had undertaken heavy new responsibilities, but partly as a result of waste and graft. In short, the Radical regimes brought needed reforms to the South, but they were not always model governments.

Southern corruption, however, was not exceptional, nor was it a special result of the extension of suffrage to uneducated blacks, as critics of Radical Reconstruction have claimed. It was part of a national pattern during an era when private interests considered buying government favors a part of the cost of doing business, and many politicians expected to profit by obliging them.

Blacks bore only a limited responsibility for the dishonesty of the Radical governments because they never controlled a state government and held few major offices. The biggest grafters were opportunistic whites—some of the most notorious were carpetbaggers but others were native Southerners. Some black legislators went with the tide and accepted "loans" from those railroad lobbyists who would pay most for their votes, but the same men could usually be depended on to vote the will of their constituents on civil rights or educational issues. Contrary to myth, the small number of blacks elected to state or national office during Reconstruction demonstrated on the average more integrity and competence than their white counterparts. Most were fairly well educated, having been free Negroes or unusually privileged slaves before the war. Many battled tirelessly to promote the interests of their race. It was unfortunate that Democratic critics of Radical Reconstruction were able to capitalize on racial prejudice and persuade many Americans that "good government" was synonymous with "white supremacy."

THE AGE OF GRANT

Ulysses S. Grant was the only president between Jackson and Wilson to serve two full and consecutive terms (1869–1877). But unlike other chief executives so favored by fortune and the electorate, Grant is commonly regarded as a failure. His administration was riddled with corruption, and his southern policy failed to achieve its goals. Faced with the demands of the presidency, Grant found that he had no strong principles to guide him except

loyalty to old friends and politicians. But the problems he faced seemed insoluble. A president with a clearer sense of duty and purpose might have done little better.

RISE OF THE MONEY QUESTION

In 1868 the question of how to manage the nation's currency and more specifically what to do about "greenbacks"—paper money issued during the war—competed with Reconstruction and spoilsmen issues for public attention. Defenders of "sound" money, mostly financial interests in the East, wanted the greenbacks withdrawn from circulation and Civil War debts redeemed in specie payments (silver and gold). Opponents of this hard-money policy and the resulting deflation of the currency were mainly credit-hungry Westerners and expansionist-minded manufacturers, who wanted to keep greenbacks in circulation. Both political parties had hard- and easy-money factions, preventing the money question from becoming a heated presidential election issue in 1868 and 1872.

But the Panic of 1873, which brought much of the economy to its knees, led to agitation to inflate the currency by issuing more paper money. Debt-ridden farmers, who would be the backbone of the greenback movement for years to come, now joined the easy-money clamor for the first time. Responding to the money and credit crunch, Congress moved in 1874 to authorize a modest issue of new greenbacks, but Grant vetoed the bill. In 1875, Congress enacted the Specie Resumption Act, which provided for a gradual reduction of greenbacks leading to full resumption of specie payment by 1879. The act was interpreted as deflationary, and farmers and workers, who were already suffering from deflation, reacted with dismay and anger.

The Democratic party could not capitalize adequately on these sentiments because of the influence of its own hard-money faction, and in 1876 an independent Greenback party entered the national political arena. Greenbackers kept the money issue alive through the next decade.

RETREAT FROM RECONSTRUCTION

The Republican effort to make equal rights for blacks the law of the land culminated in the Fifteenth Amendment, ratified in 1870, which prohibited any state from denying a citizen the right to vote because of race, color, or previous condition of servitude. Much to the displeasure of advocates of women's rights, however, the amendment made no provision for female suffrage. And states could still limit male suffrage by imposing literacy tests, property qualifications, or poll taxes allegedly applying to all racial groups; such devices would eventually be used to strip southern blacks of the right to vote. But the makers of the amendment did not foresee this result.

The Grant administration was charged with enforcing the amendment and protecting black voting rights in the reconstructed states. Since survival of the Republican regimes depended on black support, political partisanship dictated federal action, even though the North's emotional and ideological commitment to black citizenship was waning.

Between 1868 and 1872, the main threat to southern Republican regimes came from the Ku Klux Klan and other secret societies bent on restoring white supremacy by intimidating blacks who sought to exercise their political rights. A grass-roots vigilante movement, not a centralized conspiracy, the Klan thrived on local initiative and gained support from whites of all social classes. Its secrecy, decentralization, popular support, and utter ruthlessness made it very difficult to suppress. Blacks who voted ran the risk of being verbally intimidated, whipped, or even murdered.

These methods were first used effectively in the presidential election of 1868. Terrorism by white supremacists cost Grant the electoral votes of Louisiana and Georgia. In Louisiana political violence claimed hundreds of lives, and in Arkansas more than 200 Republicans were assassinated. Thereafter, Klan terrorism was directed mainly at Republican state governments. Virtual insurrections broke out in Arkansas, Tennessee, North Carolina, and parts of South Carolina. In Tennessee, North Carolina, and Georgia, Klan activities helped undermine Republican control, thus allowing the Democrats to come to power in all those states by 1870.

Faced with the violent overthrow of the southern Republican party, Congress and the Grant administration were forced to act. A series of laws passed in 1870–1871 sought to enforce the Fifteenth Amendment by providing federal protection for black suffrage and authorizing use of the army against the Klan. Although the Ku Klux Klan Acts or Force Acts did not totally destroy the Klan, the enforcement effort was vigorous enough to put a damper on hooded terrorism and ensure relatively fair and peaceful elections in 1872.

In these elections, a heavy black turnout enabled the Republicans to hold on to power in most states of the Deep South, despite efforts of the Democratic-Conservative opposition to woo Republicans by taking moderate positions on racial and economic issues. As a result of this setback, the Democratic-Conservatives

Susan B. Anthony (left) and Lucy Stone (right), feminist leaders whose adherents split over support for the Fifteenth Amendment. A militant wing of the women's rights movement led by Anthony was so angered that the 15th Amendment to the Constitution did not extend suffrage to women that they campaigned against its ratification. Stone led another group of feminists who supported the amendment on the grounds that this was the "Negro's hour" and that women could afford to wait. This disagreement divided the woman's suffrage movement for a generation to come.

made a significant change in their strategy and ideology. No longer did they try to take votes away from the Republicans by proclaiming their support of black suffrage and government aid to business. They began instead to appeal openly to white supremacy and to the traditional Democratic agrarian hostility to governmental promotion of economic development. Consequently, they were able to bring back to the polls a portion of the white electorate, mostly small farmers, who had not been turning out because they were alienated by the leadership's apparent concessions to Yankee ideas.

This new and more effective electoral strategy dovetailed with a resurgence of violence meant to reduce Republican, especially black Republican, voting. The new reign of terror differed from the previous Klan episode; its agents no longer wore masks but acted quite openly. They were effective because the northern public was increasingly disenchanted with federal intervention on behalf of what were widely viewed as corrupt and tottering Republican regimes. Grant used force in the South for the last time in 1874. When an unofficial militia—in Mississippi—instigated a series of bloody race riots prior to the state elections in 1875, Grant refused the governor's request for federal troops. As a result, intimidation kept black voters away from the polls.

By 1876 Republicans held on to only three southern states—South Carolina, Louisiana, and Florida. Partly because of Grant's hesitant and inconsistent use of presidential power but mainly because the northern electorate would no longer tolerate military action to sustain Republican governments and black voting rights, Radical Reconstruction was falling into total eclipse.

SPOILSMEN VERSUS REFORMERS

One reason Grant found it increasingly difficult to take strong action to protect southern Republicans was the charge by reformers that his administration was propping up bad governments in the South for personal and partisan advantage. And in some cases, the charges held a measure of truth.

The Republican party in the Grant era was rapidly losing the idealism and high purpose associated with the crusade against slavery. By the beginning of the 1870s, men who had been the conscience of the party had been replaced by a new breed of Republicans, such as Senator Roscoe Conkling of New York, whom historians have dubbed "spoilsmen" or "politicos." More often than not, Grant sided with the spoilsmen of his party.

During Grant's first administration, an aura of scandal surrounded the White House but did not directly implicate the president. In 1869 the financial buccaneer Jay Gould enlisted the aid of a brother-in-law of Grant to further his fantastic scheme to corner the gold market. Gould failed in the attempt, but he did manage to come away with a huge profit.

Grant's first-term vice-president, Schuyler Colfax of Indiana, was directly involved in the notorious Crédit Mobilier scandal. Crédit Mobilier was a construction company that actually served as a fraudulent device for siphoning off profits that should have gone to the stockholders of the Union Pacific Railroad, which was the beneficiary of massive federal land grants. In order to forestall government inquiry into this arrangement, Crédit Mobilier stock was distributed to influential congressmen. The whole business came to light just before the campaign of 1872.

Republicans who could not tolerate such corruption or had other grievances against the administration broke with Grant in 1872 and formed a third party committed to "honest government" and "reconciliation" between the North and the South. The "Liberal Republicans," led initially by such high-minded reformers as Senator Carl Schurz of Missouri, endorsed reform of the civil service to curb the corruption-breeding patronage system and advocated strict laissez faire economic policies—which meant low tariffs, an end to government subsidies for railroads, and hard money.

The Liberal Republicans' national convention nominated Horace Greeley, editor of the respected *New York Tribune*. This was a curious and divisive choice since Greeley was at odds with the founder of the movement on the tariff question and indifferent to civil service reform. The Democrats also endorsed Greeley, mainly because he vowed to end Radical Reconstruction. Greeley, however, did not attract support and was soundly defeated by Grant.

Grant's second administration bore out the reformers' worst suspicions about corruption in high places. In 1875 the public learned that federal revenue officials had conspired with distillers to defraud the government of millions of dollars in liquor taxes. Grant's private secretary, Orville E. Babcock, was indicted as a member of the "Whiskey Ring" and was saved from conviction only by the president's personal intercession. The next year, Grant's secretary of war William E. Belknap was impeached by the House after an investigation revealed that he had taken bribes for the sale of Indian trading posts. He avoided a Senate conviction by leaving office before the trial.

There is no evidence that Grant profited personally from any of the misdeeds of his subordinates. Yet he is not entirely without blame for the corruption of his administration. He failed to take action against the malefactors and even after the guilt had been clearly established tried to shield them from justice.

REUNION AND THE NEW SOUTH

The end of Radical Reconstruction in 1877 opened the way to a reconciliation of North and South. But the costs of reunion were high for less privileged groups in the South. The civil and political rights of blacks, left unprotected, were stripped away by white supremacist regimes. Lower class whites saw their interests sacrificed to those of capitalists and landlords. Despite the rhetoric hailing a prosperous "New South," the region remained poor and open to exploitation by northern business interests.

THE COMPROMISE OF 1877

The election of 1876 pitted Rutherford B. Hayes of Ohio, an honest Republican governor, against Governor Samuel J. Tilden of New York, a Democratic reformer. Honest government was apparently the electorate's highest priority. When the returns came in, Tilden had clearly won the popular vote and seemed likely to win a narrow victory in the electoral college. But the result was placed in doubt when the returns from the three southern states still controlled by the Republicans were contested. If Hayes were to be awarded these three states, plus one contested electoral vote in Oregon, Republican strategists realized, he would triumph in the electoral college by a single vote.

The outcome of the election remained undecided for months. To resolve the impasse, Congress appointed a special electoral commission of fifteen members to determine who would receive the votes of the disputed states. The commission split along party lines and voted 8 to 7 to award Hayes the disputed states. But this decision still had to be ratified, and in the House there was strong Democratic opposition.

To ensure Hayes' election, Republican leaders negotiated secretly with conservative southern Democrats, some of whom seemed willing to abandon their opposition if the last troops were withdrawn and "home rule" was restored to the South. Vague pledges of federal support for southern railroads and internal improvements were made, and Hayes assured southern negotiators that he had every intention of ending Reconstruction. Eventually an informal bargain, dubbed the "Compromise of 1877" was struck. What precisely was agreed to and by whom remains a matter of dispute; but one thing at least was understood by both sides—Hayes would be president and southern Republicans would be abandoned to their fate.

With southern Democratic acquiescence, the main opposition was overcome and Hayes took the oath of office. He immediately ordered the army not to resist a Democratic takeover in South Carolina and Louisiana. Thus fell the last of the Radical governments.

THE NEW SOUTH

The men who came to power after the ending of Radical Reconstruction in one southern

CHRONOLOGY

1863	Lincoln sets forth 10 percent Reconstruction plan
1864	Wade-Davis Bill passes Congress, is pocket-vetoed by Lincoln
1865	Johnson moves to reconstruct the South on his own initiative Congress refuses to seat representatives and senators elected from states reestablished under presidential plan (December)
1866	Congress passes Fourteenth Amendment (June) Republicans increase their congressional majority in the fall elections
1867	First Reconstruction Act is passed over Johnson's veto (March)
1868	Johnson is impeached; he avoids conviction by one vote (February–May) Grant wins presidential election, defeating Horatio Seymour
1869	Congress passes Fifteenth Amendment, granting blacks the right to vote
1870–1871	Congress passes Ku Klux Klan Acts to protect black voting rights in the South
1872	Grant reelected president, defeating Horace Greeley, candidate of Liberal Republicans and Democrats
1873	Financial panic plunges nation into depression

state after another are usually referred to as the "Redeemers." They had differing backgrounds and previous loyalties. Some were members of the Old South's ruling planter class who had warmly supported secession and now sought to reestablish the old order with as few changes as possible. Others, of middle-class origin or outlook, favored commercial and industrial interests over agrarian groups and called for a "New South," committed to diversified economic development. A third group were professional politicians bending with the prevailing winds.

Rather than supporters of any single ideology or program, these leaders can perhaps best be understood as power brokers mediating among the dominant interest groups of the South in ways that served their own political advantage. In many ways, the "rings" that they established on the state and county levels were analogous to the political machines developing at the same time in northern cities.

They did, however, agree on and endorse two basic principles: laissez-faire and white supremacy. Laissez-faire, the notion that government should be limited and neutral in its economic activities, could unite planters, frustrated at seeing direct state support going to businessmen, and capitalist promoters, who had come to realize that low taxes and freedom from government regulation were even more advantageous than state subsidies. It soon became clear that the Redeemers responded only to privileged and entrenched interest groups,

1875	Congress passes Specie Resumption Act "Whisky Ring" scandal exposed
1876–1877	Disputed presidential election resolved in favor of Republican Hayes over Democrat Tilden
1877	"Compromise of 1877" results in end to military intervention in the South and fall of the last Radical governments

SUPREME COURT DECISIONS AFFECTING BLACK CIVIL RIGHTS, 1875–1900

Hall v. *DeCuir* (1878)	Struck down Louisiana law prohibiting racial discrimination by "common carriers" (railroads, steamboats, buses). Court declared the law a "burden" on interstate commerce, over which states had no authority.
United States v. *Harris* (1882)	Declared federal laws to punish crimes such as murder and assault unconstitutional. Such crimes declared to be the sole concern of local government. Court ignored the frequent racial motivation behind such crimes in the South.
Civil Rights Cases (1883)	Struck down Civil Rights Act of 1875. Congress may not legislate on civil rights unless a *state* passes a discriminatory law. Court declared the Fourteenth Amendment silent on racial discrimination by private citizens.
Plessy v. *Ferguson* (1896)	Upheld Louisiana statute requiring "separate but equal" accommodations on railroads. Court declared that segregation is *not* necessarily discrimination.
Williams v. *Mississippi* (1898)	Upheld state law requiring a literacy test to qualify for voting. Court refused to find any implication of racial discrimination in the law. Using such laws, southern states rapidly disfranchised blacks.

especially landlords, merchants, and industrialists, and offered little or nothing to tenants, small farmers and working people. As industrialization began to gather steam in the 1880s, Democratic regimes became increasingly accommodating to manufacturing interests and hospitable to agents of northern capital who were gaining control of the South's transportation system and its extractive industries.

White supremacy was the principal rallying cry that brought the Redeemers to power in the first place. Once in office, they found that they could stay there by charging that opponents of ruling Democratic cliques were trying to divide "the white man's party" and open the way for a return to "black domination." Appeals to racism could also deflect attention away from the economic grievances of groups without political clout.

The new governments were more economical than those of Reconstruction, mainly because they cut back drastically on appropriations for schools and other needed public services. But they were scarcely more honest. Embezzlement of public funds and bribery of public officials continued at an alarming extent.

The Redeemer regimes of the late 1870s and 1880s badly neglected the interests of small white farmers. Whites, as well as blacks, were suffering from the notorious "crop lien" system, which gave local merchants who advanced credit at high rates of interest during the growing season the right to take possession of the harvested crop on terms that buried farmers deeper and deeper in debt. As a result, increasing numbers of whites lost title to their homesteads and were reduced to tenancy.

But the greatest hardships imposed by the new order were reserved for blacks. The Redeemers had pledged, as part of the Compromise of 1877, that they would respect the rights of blacks as set forth in the Fourteenth and Fifteenth Amendments. But when blacks tried to vote Republican in the "redeemed" states, they encountered renewed violence and intimidation. Moreover, white Democrats now controlled the election machinery. By the 1890s blacks were virtually disfranchised throughout the South.

The dark night of racism that fell on the South after Reconstruction seemed to unleash all the baser impulses of human nature. Between 1889 and 1899 an average of 187 blacks were lynched every year for alleged offenses against white supremacy. Those convicted of petty crimes against property were often little better off; many were condemned to be leased out to private contractors whose brutality rivaled that of the most sadistic slaveholders. Finally, the dignity of blacks was cruelly affronted by the wave of Jim Crow (strict segregation) laws passed in the 1890s.

The North and the federal government did little or nothing to stem the tide of racial oppression in the South. A series of Supreme Court decisions between 1878 and 1898 gutted the Reconstruction amendments and the legislation passed to enforce them, leaving blacks virtually defenseless against political and social discrimination.

At the same time, the wounds of the Civil War were healing for white Americans. "Reunion" became a cultural and political reality. But whites could come back together only because Northerners had tacitly agreed to give Southerners a free hand in their efforts to reduce blacks to a new form of servitude. It was the African Americans of the South who paid the heaviest price for sectional reunion and reconciliation.

❧ RECOMMENDED READING

One general survey of the Reconstruction era clearly stands out: Eric Foner, Reconstruction: America's Unfinished Revolution (1988). Two excellent short accounts of what happened during Reconstruction are Kenneth Stampp, The Era of Reconstruction, 1865–1877 (1965), and John Hope Franklin, Reconstruction: After the Civil War (1961). W. E. B. DuBois, Black Reconstruction in America, 1860–1880 (1935), a longer and more detailed study, remains brilliant and provocative. Recent reconsiderations of Reconstruction issues can be found in J. Morgan Kousser and James M. McPherson, eds., Region, Race and Reconstruction: Essays in Honor of C. Vann Woodward (1982), and Eric Foner, Nothing But Freedom: Emancipation and Its Legacy (1983). Morton Keller, Affairs of State: Public Life in Late Nineteenth Century America (1977), provides a splendid analysis of American government and politics during Reconstruction and afterward.

For an understanding of the conflict between the president and Congress, see Eric L. McKitrick, An-drew Johnson and Reconstruction, 1865–1867 (1960), and Michael Les Benedict, A Compromise of Principle: Congressional Republicans and Reconstruction (1974). On constitutional issues, Stanley I. Kutler, Judicial Power and Reconstruction Politics (1968), and Harold M. Hyman, A More Perfect Union: The Impact of the Civil War and Reconstruction on the Constitution (1973) are especially useful.

Dan T. Carter's When the War Was Over: Self-Reconstruction in the South (1985) and Michael Perman's two books, Reunion Without Compromise: The South and Reconstruction, 1865–1868 (1973) and The Road to Redemption: Southern Politics, 1869–1879 (1984), deal effectively with southern politics in the postwar years. A major aspect of politics during the Radical era is dealt with in Mark W. Summers, Railroads, Reconstruction, and the Gospel of Prosperity (1984). On the activities of the Freedmen's Bureau, see William McFeeley, Yankee Godfather: General O. O. Howard and the Freedmen (1968), and Donald G. Nieman, To Set the Law in Motion: The Freedmen's Bureau and Legal Rights for Blacks, 1865–1868 (1979).

The changing situation of blacks in the postwar South is treated in Leon Litwack, Been in the Storm So Long: The Aftermath of Slavery (1979); Harold O. Rabinowitz, Race Relations in the Urban South, 1865–1890 (1977); and C. Vann Woodward, The Strange Career of Jim Crow, 3rd rev. ed. (1974). Economic adjustments are analyzed in Lawrence N. Powell, New Masters: Northern Planters During the Civil War and Reconstruction (1980), and Roger L. Ransom and Richard Sutch, One Kind of Freedom: The Economic Consequences of Emancipation (1977).

A provocative study of American labor during the Reconstruction period is David Montgomery, Beyond Equality: Labor and the Radical Republicans, 1861–1872 (1967). The best introduction to the Grant era is William S. McFeeley, Grant: A Biography (1981).

Studies of the decline and fall of Reconstruction include C. Vann Woodward, Reunion and Reaction, rev. ed. (1956) and Keith I. Polakoff, The Politics of Inertia (1977). C. Vann Woodward, Origins of the New South, 1877–1913 (1951) remains the standard work on the post-Reconstruction South, but see also Paul M. Gaston, The New South Creed (1970); Jonathan M. Weiner, Social Origins of the New South: Alabama, 1860–1885 (1978); and J. Morgan Kousser, The Shaping of Southern Politics: Suffrage Restriction and the Establishment of the One-Party South (1974).

17 THE WEST: EXPLOITING AN EMPIRE

In the last three decades of the nineteenth century, a flood of settlers ventured into America's newest and last West. Prospectors poured into unsettled areas in search of "paydirt," railroads crisscrossed the continent, eastern and foreign capitalists invested in cattle and land bonanzas, and farmers took up the promise of free western lands. In the rhetoric of the day, the West was a land of hope and abundance.

With the end of the Civil War, white Americans again claimed a special destiny to expand across the continent. In the process they crushed the culture of the American Indians and ignored the special contributions of those of other nationalities, such as the Chinese miners and laborers and the Mexican herdsmen. As millions moved west, new states were carved out of the vast lands across the Mississippi. By 1900 only Arizona, New Mexico, and Oklahoma remained as territories.

The West became a great colonial empire, harnessed to eastern capital and tied increasingly to national and international markets. Western economies depended to an unusual degree on the federal government, which subsidized their railroads, distributed their land, and spent millions of dollars for the upkeep of soldiers and Indians. Although regional variations persisted, Westerners increasingly imitated the East's social, cultural, and political patterns.

By the 1890s the West of the buffalo and Indian was gone, replaced by cities, health resorts, Paris fashions, and the latest magazines. As Francis Parkman, a New Englander who had made the dangerous crossing to Oregon in

1846, reflected sadly in 1892: "The Wild West is tamed, and its savage charms have withered."

in enormous herds from Mexico to Canada. In 1865 perhaps 15 million buffalo lived on the Plains.

BEYOND THE FRONTIER

The frontier line had reached the edge of the timber country of Missouri by 1840. Beyond lay an enormous land of rolling prairies, parched deserts, and rugged, majestic mountains. Emerging from the timber country, travelers first encountered the Great Plains. The Prairie Plains, the eastern part of the region, enjoyed rich soil and good rainfall. To the west were the High Plains, rough, semiarid, rising gently to the foothills of the Rocky Mountains.

Running from Alaska to central New Mexico, the Rockies presented a formidable barrier. Although the passes were rich in beaver and gold, most travelers hurried through them, emerging in the desolate basin of present-day southern Idaho and Utah. Indians lived there, scrabbling out a bare subsistence by digging for roots, seeds, and berries. On the west, the lofty Coast ranges—the Cascades and Sierra Nevada—held back rainfall; beyond were the temperate lands of the Pacific Coast.

Early explorers and mapmakers thought the country beyond the Mississippi was uninhabitable. Between 1815 and 1860 American maps showed this land as "The Great American Desert." Settlement paused on the edge of the Plains, which daunted even those settlers hurrying across them for California and Oregon.

Few rivers cut through the Plains. Those that did flooded in spring and trickled in summer. The land lacked rainfall for crops, lumber for homes and fences, and the cast-iron plow and ax—the tools of eastern settlement—were virtually useless on the tough and treeless Plains soil.

Hot winds seared the Plains in summer, and northers, blizzards, and hailstorms froze them in winter. Despite these extremes, wildlife roamed in profusion—antelope, wolves, coyote, jackrabbits, and prairie dogs. The American bison, better known as the buffalo, grazed

CRUSHING THE INDIANS

In 1867 when Horace Greeley, editor of the *New York Tribune,* urged New York City's unemployed to head West, where "you will crowd nobody, starve nobody," he—like most of his countrymen—ignored the fact that large numbers of people already lived there. In 1865 nearly a quarter of a million Indians lived in the western half of the country. The Cherokee and other tribes were resettled there after being forced out of their eastern lands by advancing white settlement. Other tribes, such as the Hopi, Zuni, Navajo, Apache, Chinook, and Shasta, were native to the region. By the 1870s most of these tribes had been destroyed or beaten into submission. The powerful Ute, crushed in 1855, ceded most of their Utah lands to the United States and settled on a small reservation near Great Salt Lake. The Navajo and Apache fought back desperately, but between 1865 and 1873 they too were confined to reservations. California Indians succumbed to the contagious diseases carried by whites during the Gold Rush of 1849. By 1880 there were less than 20,000 Indians in all of California.

LIFE OF THE PLAINS
INDIANS

Nearly two thirds of the Indians west of the Mississippi lived on the Great Plains. The Plains tribes included the Sioux, Blackfoot, Cheyenne, Crow, Arapaho, Pawnee, Kiowa, Apache, and Comanche. Nomadic and warlike, the Plains Indians depended upon the buffalo, and later the horse as well, for their existence. A skilled horseman and warrior, the Plains Indian was the superior adversary in conflicts with white settlers and cavalry. Even the introduction of the new Colt six-shooters during the 1850s did not entirely offset the Indians' advantage.

Migratory in culture, the Plains Indians formed tribes of several thousand people but lived in smaller "bands" of 300 to 500. Each band was governed by a chief and a council, and each acted independently, which caused difficulties for the United States government. The bands followed and lived off the buffalo, using every part of the animal to provide food, clothing, shelter, and even fuel.

Warfare between tribes usually took the form of brief raids and skirmishes. Plains Indians fought few prolonged wars and rarely coveted territory. Most conflicts involved only a few warriors intent on stealing horses or "counting coups"—touching an enemy's body with the hand or a special stick. Tribes did develop, however, a fierce warrior class.

The Plains tribes divided labor by sex. Men hunted, traded, supervised ceremonial activities, and cleared ground for planting. Women were responsible for childrearing and artistic creativity. They also performed the camp work, grew vegetables, prepared buffalo meat and hides, and gathered roots and berries. Men were respected for their prowess in hunting and war, women for their skill with quill and paint.

"As Long as Waters Run"

Before the mid-nineteenth century Americans used the land west of the Mississippi as "one big reservation." The government named the area "Indian Country," moved eastern tribes there with firm treaty guarantees, and in 1834 passed the Indian Intercourse Act which prohibited any white person from entering Indian country without a license.

The situation changed in the 1850s. Americans pushed toward the gold fields and the rich farmland of the West Coast. To clear the way for settlement, the federal government in 1851 abandoned "One Big Reservation" in favor of a new policy of "concentration." For the first time it assigned definite boundaries to each tribe. The land was given to the tribes for "as long as waters run and the grass shall grow."

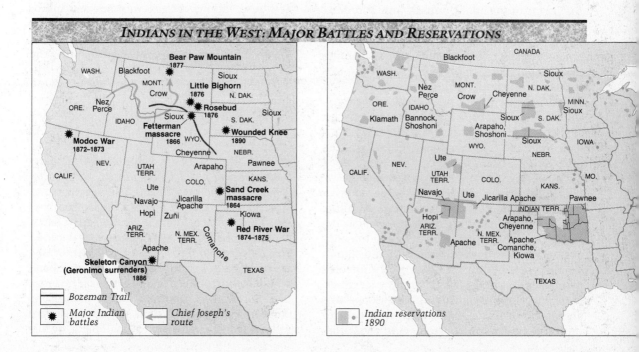

INDIANS IN THE WEST: MAJOR BATTLES AND RESERVATIONS

The "concentration" policy lasted only a few years. Accustomed to hunt widely for buffalo, many Indians refused to stay within their assigned areas. White settlers poured into Indian lands, then called on the government to protect them. In the 1850s Indians were pushed out of Kansas and Nebraska; in 1859 gold miners moved into the Pikes Peak country, touching off warfare with the Cheyenne and Arapaho.

Although the two tribes fought hard, they were no match for the federal government. In 1864 they asked for peace. Certain that the war was over, Chief Black Kettle led his 700 followers to camp on Sand Creek in southeastern Colorado. Early on the morning of November 29, 1864, a group of Colorado militia led by Colonel John M. Chivington attacked the sleeping Indians. The militiamen clubbed, stabbed, and scalped Indian men, women, and children.

The Chivington massacre set off angry protests in Colorado and the East. The government condemned "the gross and wanton outrages." Still, the two tribes were forced to surrender their Sand Creek reservation in exchange for lands elsewhere.

Before long the powerful Sioux were on the warpath in the great Sioux War of 1865–1867. An invasion of gold miners in Montana touched off the war, which flared even more intensely when the federal government announced plans to connect the various mining towns by building the Bozeman Trail through the heart of the Sioux hunting grounds. Red Cloud, the Sioux chief, was determined to stop the trail. In December 1866, pursued by an army column under Captain William J. Fetterman, he lured the incautious Fetterman deep into the wilderness, ambushed him, and wiped out all eighty-two soldiers in his command.

The Fetterman massacre, coming so soon after the Chivington massacre, sparked a public debate over the nation's Indian policy. The debate reflected differing white views of the Indians. In the East some humanitarian and church groups wanted a humane peace policy, directed toward educating and "civilizing" the tribes. Many people, East and West, questioned this approach, convinced that Indians were savages unfit for civilization. Westerners in general favored firm control over the Indians, including swift punishment of any who rebelled.

In 1867 the peace advocates won the debate. Halting construction on the Bozeman Trail, Congress created a Peace Commission to end the Sioux War. After studying the situation, the Peace Commission agreed that only one policy offered a permanent solution: a policy of "small reservations" to isolate the Indians on distant lands, teach them to farm, and gradually "civilize" them.

The commission chose two areas to hold all the Plains Indians. The 54,000 Indians on the northern Plains would be moved north of the Black Hills in Dakota Territory. On the southern Plains the 86,000 Indians would be moved into present-day Oklahoma. Both regions were considered unattractive to whites. In both areas tribes would be assigned specific reservations where government agents could supervise them.

FINAL BATTLES ON THE PLAINS

Few Indians settled peacefully into life on the new reservations. Young warriors and minor chiefs denounced the treaties and drifted back to the open countryside. In the Southwest the Kiowa and Comanche rampaged through the Texas Panhandle until the army crushed them into submission in the Red River War of 1874–1875.

On the northern Plains fighting resulted from the Black Hills Gold Rush of 1875. As prospectors tramped across Indian hunting grounds, the Sioux—led by Rain-in-the-Face, the great war chief Crazy Horse, and the famous medicine man Sitting Bull—gathered to stop them. One army column, under flamboyant Lieutenant Colonel George A. Custer, pushed recklessly ahead in pursuit of the Indians, eager to claim the victory. On the morning of June 25, 1876, thinking he had a small band of Indians surrounded on the banks of the Little Bighorn River in Montana, Custer divided his column and took 265 men toward the Indian village. Instead of fighting a small band, he dis-

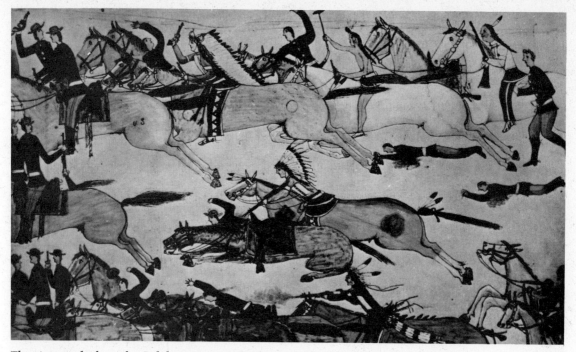

The pictograph above, by Oglala Sioux Amos Bad Heart Bull, is an Indian version of the battle between the Sioux, led by Sitting Bull, and the U.S. cavalry, led by Lt. Col. George A. Custer, at the Little Bighorn River in Montana in 1876.

covered that he had stumbled on the main Sioux camp of 2500 warriors. By mid-afternoon it was over: Custer and his men were dead. Custer was largely responsible for the loss, but "Custer's Last Stand," set in blazing headlines across the country, signaled a nationwide demand for revenge. Within a few months the Sioux were surrounded and beaten.

The Sioux War ended the major Indian warfare in the West, but occasional outbreaks occurred for several years thereafter. In 1877 the Nez Percé tribe of Oregon, a people who had warmly welcomed Lewis and Clark in 1805, rebelled under Chief Joseph but were defeated and sent to barren lands in the Indian Country of Oklahoma, where most of them died from disease. In 1890 the Teton Sioux of South Dakota, bitter and starving, became restless. Many of them turned to the "Ghost Dances," a set of dances and rites designed to bring back Indian lands and cause the whites to disappear.

The army intervened to stop the dancing, touching off violence that killed Sitting Bull and a number of other warriors. Frightened Indians fled southwest to join other Ghost Dancers under the aging chief Big Foot. Moving quickly, troops caught up with Big Foot's band, who agreed to come to the army camp on Wounded Knee Creek in South Dakota. An Indian, it is thought, fired the first shot, which was returned by the Army's new machine guns. Firing a shell a second, they shredded tepees and people. About 200 men, women, and children were massacred in the snow.

THE END OF TRIBAL LIFE

The final step in Indian policy came in the 1870s and 1880s. Some reformers had long argued against segregating the Indians on reservations, urging instead that the nation assimilate them individually into white culture.

These "assimilationists" wanted to use education, land policy, and federal law to eradicate tribal society.

Congress began to adopt the policy in 1871 when it ended the practice of treaty making with Indian tribes. Since tribes were no longer separate nations, they lost many of their political and judicial functions, and the power of the chiefs was weakened. Increasingly Indians became answerable in regular courts for certain crimes.

While Congress worked to break down the tribes, educators trained young Indians to adjust to white culture. Schools such as the Carlisle Indian School in Carlisle, Pennsylvania, taught students to fix machines and farm. They also forced them to trim their long hair, speak English, dress like "civilized" whites, and discontinue tribal ceremonies and dances. "Kill the Indian and save the man," said the founder of the Carlisle School.

Land ownership was the final and most important link in the new policy. Indians who owned land, it was thought, would become responsible, self-reliant citizens. Deciding to give each Indian a farm, Congress in 1887 passed the Dawes Severalty Act, the most important legal development in Indian-white relations in over three centuries.

Aiming to end tribal life, the Dawes Act divided tribal lands into small plots for distribution among members of the tribe. Each family head received 160 acres, single adults 80 acres, and children 40 acres. To keep the Indians' land from falling into the hands of speculators, the federal government held it in trust for twenty-five years. In addition, American citizenship was granted to Indians who accepted their land, lived apart from the tribe, and "adopted the habits of civilized life."

Through the Dawes Act, 47 million acres of land were distributed to Indians and their fam-

The Buffalo Hunt by *Charles M. Russell. At first the Plains Indian hunted the buffalo on foot; when the horse was introduced by Spanish explorers in the 1500s, the Indians adapted their hunting techniques to take advantage of its speed and agility. Unfortunately, by the time this painting was completed (1899), the way of life of the Plains Indian had vanished.*

ilies. There were another 90 million acres in the reservations, and these lands, often the most fertile, were sold to white settlers. To evade the twenty-five year rule, speculators leased rather than purchased the land from the Indians. Many Indians knew little about farming. Their tools were rudimentary, and in the culture of the Plains Indians, farming was women's work. In 1934 the government returned to the idea of tribal land ownership, but by then 138 million acres of Indian land had shrunk to 48 million acres, half of which was barren.

The final blow to tribal life came with the virtual extermination of the buffalo, the Plains Indians' chief resource and the basis for their unique way of life. The slaughter began in the 1860s as the transcontinental railroads pushed west and accelerated after 1871 when a Pennsylvania tannery discovered that buffalo hides made valuable leather. Professional hunters such as William F. "Buffalo Bill" Cody swarmed across the Plains, killing millions of the helpless beasts—3 million a year between 1872 and 1874. A good hunter killed a hundred buffalo a day; skinners took off the hides, removed the tongue, hump, and tallow, and left the rest. The waste was incredible, and by 1883 the buffalo were almost gone. When the government later set out to produce the famous "buffalo nickel," the designer had to go to the Bronx Zoo in New York City in order to find a living specimen.

By 1900 there were only 200,000 Indians in the country, most of them on reservations. Poverty, alcoholism, and unemployment were growing problems. Indians, no longer able to live off the buffalo, became wards of the state. Once possessors of the entire continent, they had been crowded into smaller and smaller areas, overwhelmed by the demand to become settled, literate, and English-speaking, like the white man.

Even as the Indians lost their identity, they entered the romantic folklore of the West. Dime novels told exciting tales of Indians fighting on the Plains. Buffalo Bill Cody turned it all into a profitable business. Beginning in 1883, Cody's Wild West Show ran for over three decades, playing to viewers in the United States and Europe. Perhaps the end of an era was most fittingly symbolized in 1885 when Sitting Bull himself, victor over Custer at the battle of Little Big Horn, performed in the show.

SETTLEMENT OF THE WEST

Between 1870 and 1900 white—and some black—Americans settled the enormous total of 430 million acres west of the Mississippi; they occupied more land than in all the years before 1870. People moved West for many reasons. Some sought adventure; others wanted to escape the drab routine of the factory or city life. Many moved to California for their health. The Mormons settled Utah to escape religious persecution.

Whatever the specific reason, most people moved West to better their lot. On the whole, their timing was good, for as the nation's population grew, so did demand for the livestock and the agricultural, mineral, and lumber products of the expanding West. Contrary to older historical views, the West did not act as a major "safety valve," an outlet for social and economic tensions. The poor and unemployed did not have the means to move there and establish farms; most people moved West in periods of expanding demand, when the prospects for making money from this new land looked brightest.

MEN AND WOMEN ON THE OVERLAND TRAIL

The first movement west aimed not for the nearby Plains but for California and Oregon. Between 1848 and 1878 perhaps as many as half a million individuals made the long journey. Some walked; others rode horses alone or in small groups. About half joined great caravans that inched across the 2000 miles between the Missouri River and the Pacific Coast.

More often than not, men made the decision to make the crossing; wives either went along or faced being left behind. Four out of five men on the overland trail had moved before. Most had little cash, but they needed only strong legs, a few staples, and a willingness to tighten the belt when game was scarce. The majority of people traveled in family groups, including in-laws, grandchildren, aunts, and uncles, meaning that their "quest for something new would take place in the context of the very familiar."

Individuals and wagon trains set out from various points along the Missouri River. Leaving in the spring and traveling through the summer, they hoped to reach their destination before the first snowfall. During April, travelers gradually assembled in spring camp. There they carefully packed their wagons, elected the train's leaders, and decided upon the rules that they would observe during their trip west.

Setting out in early May, travelers divided the enormous route into manageable portions. From a distance the white-topped wagons seemed driven by a common force, but in fact, internal discipline was a constant problem. Arguments erupted over the pace of the march, the choice of campsites, whether to rest or push on. Elected leaders quit; new ones were chosen.

Men, women, and children had different tasks on the trail. Men concerned themselves almost entirely with hunting, guard duty, and transportation. The women prepared the food, and the children kindled the fire, brought water to camp, and searched for wood and other fuel. Rising before the sun and walking fifteen miles a day, in searing heat and mountain cold, travelers were exhausted by late afternoon.

For women the trail was lonely, and they worked to exhaustion. Before long they adjusted their clothing to the harsh conditions, adopting the new bloomer pants or shortening their skirts. Like men, they carried firearms in case of Indian attacks. Most emigrants, however, saw few Indians en route.

The first stage of the journey was deceptively easy, and travelers usually reached Fort Kearney by late May. From there the trip became more demanding. Summer heat baked the route to Fort Laramie on the eastern edge of the Wyoming Territory. Anxious to beat the early snowfalls, travelers rested a day or two at the fort, then hurried on to South Pass, the best route through the forbidding Rockies. Although still summer, the mountain nights were so cold that ice formed at the top of the water buckets.

Beyond South Pass, emigrants went different directions; some headed south through Utah, some headed toward Fort Hall in Idaho and then on to California. Months of hard traveling were still in front of them. They had to cross deserts and the towering Sierra Nevada. Not until September or October would they reach the verdant Sacramento Valley.

Under the best of conditions the trip took almost six months, sixteen hours a day, dawn to dusk, of hard, grueling labor. Walking halfway across the continent was a never-to-be-forgotten experience for those who did it. The wagon trains, carrying the dreams of thousands of individuals, reproduced society in small focus: individualistic, hopeful, mobile, divided by age and sex roles, apprehensive, yet willing to strike out for the distant and new.

LAND FOR THE TAKING

As railroads pushed west in the 1870s and 1880s, locomotive trains replaced wagon trains, but the shift was gradual. Like many Americans, thousands of Europeans traveled by rail to designated outfitting places, and then continued their trek with wagons and oxen. Traffic flowed in both directions; eager settlers heading West passed defeated ones returning East.

Why did they come? In a word—land. Specifically, the land that the federal government promised to give to the head of each family who settled in the new territories. A popular camp song reflected this motive.

> Come along, come along—don't be alarmed.
> Uncle Sam is rich enough to give us all a farm.

Uncle Sam owned about 1 billion acres of land in the 1860s, much of it mountain and desert land unsuited for agriculture. By 1890 the government had distributed 48 million acres under the Homestead Act of 1862. But far more acres were sold—to private citizens, corporations, and to the states. Huge tracts were granted to railroad companies to tempt them to build across the unsettled West.

The Homestead Act of 1862, a law of great significance, gave 160 acres of land to anyone who would pay a $10 registration and pledge to live on it and cultivate it for five years. The offer set off a mass migration of land-hungry Europeans dazzled by a country that gave its land away. Americans also seized on the act's provisions, and between 1862 and 1900 nearly 600,000 families claimed free homesteads under it.

Yet the Homestead Act did not work as Congress had hoped. Tailored to the timber and water conditions of the East, the act was not suited to the semiarid West. Without irrigation, a 160-acre farm was simply not large enough to be self-supporting on the Great Plains.

The Timber Culture Act of 1873 attempted to adjust the Homestead Act to western conditions. It allowed homesteaders to claim an additional 160 acres if they planted trees on a quarter of it within four years. A successful act, it encouraged forestation and expanded farms to a workable size. On the other hand, the Desert Land Act of 1877, which allowed individuals to obtain 640 acres in the arid states for $1.25 an acre, provided they irrigated part of it within three years, invited wholesale fraud; irrigation was sometimes interpreted by ranchers as a bucket of water dumped on the ground.

The Timber and Stone Act of 1878 permitted anyone in California, Nevada, Oregon, and Washington to buy up to 160 acres of forestland, deemed "unfit for cultivation," for $2.50 an acre. As the ranchers had, timber companies used employees to file false claims and other fraudulent practices to acquire more land than the law allowed.

Speculators made ingenious use of the land laws. Sending agents in advance of settlement, they moved along choice river bottoms or irrigable areas, accumulating large holdings to be held for high prices. In the arid West, where control of water meant control of the surrounding land, shrewd ranchers plotted their holdings accordingly. In Colorado one cattleman, John F. Iliff, owned only 105 small parcels of land, but by placing them around the few waterholes, he effectively dominated an empire stretching over 6000 square miles.

Half a billion acres of western land were given or sold to speculators and corporations. At the same time only 600,000 homestead patents were issued, covering 80 million acres. Thus, only one acre in every nine initially went to individual pioneers, the intended beneficiaries of the nation's largesse.

As beneficiaries of the government's policy of land grants for railway construction, the railroad companies were the West's largest landowners. Eager to have immigrants settle on the land they owned, and eager to boost their freight and passenger business, the companies sent out attractive sales brochures to the East and Europe, touting life in the West. Union Pacific's advertisement described the rocky Platte Valley in Nebraska as "a flowery meadow clothed in nutritious grasses."

As new areas of the West opened, they were organized as territories under the control of Congress and the president. The president appointed the governor and judges in each territory; Congress detailed their duties, set their budgets, and oversaw their activities. Territorial officials had almost absolute power over the territories.

THE SPANISH-SPEAKING SOUTHWEST

In the nineteenth century almost all Spanish-speaking people in the United States lived in California, Arizona, New Mexico, Texas, and Colorado. Their numbers were small, but the influence of their culture and institutions was large. In some respects the Southwestern frontier was more Hispanic-American than Anglo-American.

Pushing northward from Mexico, the Spanish brought to the Southwest irrigation, stock raising, weaving, and mining. Both the Spanish and, later, the Mexicans created the legal framework for distributing land and water. They gave large grants of land to communities for grazing, to individuals as rewards for ser-

Charros at the Round-up by James Walker (1877). As Spaniards and Mexicans moved north, they brought with them ranching methods, irrigation, chaps, the burro, as well as the legal framework for distributing land and water in the arid Southwest. Evidence of this Spanish-Mexican heritage remains strong today.

vice, and to the various Indian pueblos (villages).

The Californios, descendants of the original colonizers of California, began to lose their once vast landholdings to drought and mortgages after the 1860s. Some turned to banditry, others lived in poverty and remembered better days. But as the Californios died out, Mexican-Americans continued the Spanish-Mexican influence. In 1880 one quarter of the residents of Los Angeles County were Spanish speaking.

In New Mexico Hispanic culture dominated the territory. The movement of Anglo ranchers onto contested Spanish land grants met with resistance by hooded nightriders in the 1880s. Spanish-speaking citizens remained the majority ethnic group in New Mexico until the 1940s.

Throughout the Southwest the Spanish-Mexican heritage gave a distinctive shape to so-ciety. Men headed the family and dominated economic life. Women had substantial economic rights (though few political ones), and they enjoyed a status their English-American counterparts did not have. Wives kept full control of property acquired before marriage; they also held half-title to all property in a marriage, which later caused many southwestern states to pass community property laws.

In addition, the Spanish-Mexican heritage fostered a modified economic caste system, a strong Roman Catholic influence, and the primary use of the Spanish language. Continuous immigration from Mexico kept language and cultural ties strong. Spanish names and customs spread, even among Anglos. Confronted by Sheriff Pat Garrett in a darkened room, New Mexico's famous outlaw, Billy the Kid, died saying *"Quien es? Quien es?"* ("Who is it? Who is it?")

Between 1850 and 1900 wave after wave of newcomers swept over the trans-Mississippi West. There were riches for the taking, hidden in goldwashed streams, spread lushly over grass-covered prairies, or available in the gullible minds of greedy newcomers. The nineteenth-century West took shape in the search for mining, cattle, and land bonanzas that drew eager settlers from the East and around the world.

As with all bonanzas, the consequences in the West were uneven growth, boom-and-bust economic cycles, and wasted resources. As a society it seemed constantly in the making. People moved here and there, following river bottoms, gold strikes, railroad tracks, and other opportunities. "Instant cities" such as San Francisco, Salt Lake City, and Denver arose, and cow towns and mining camps sprang up seemingly overnight. San Francisco grew to a third of a million people in a little more than two decades; Boston took more than two centuries to do the same.

The Mining Bonanza

Mining was the first important magnet to attract people to the West. Many came to "strike it rich" in gold and silver, but at least half the newcomers had no intention of working in the mines. Instead, they provided food, clothing, and services to the thousands of miners. For example, Leland Stanford and Collis P. Huntington, who later built the Central Pacific Railroad, set up a general store in Sacramento where they sold shovels and supplies.

The California Gold Rush of 1849 began the mining boom and set the pattern for subsequent experience. Individual prospectors made the first strikes, discovering pockets of gold along streams flowing westward from the Sierra Nevada. Practicing a simple process called placer mining, they needed only a shovel, a washing pan, and a good claim. As the placers gave out a great deal of gold remained, but it was locked in quartz or buried deep in the earth. Mining became an expensive business, far beyond the reach of the average miner.

Large corporations moved in to dig the deep shafts and finance costly equipment. Eastern and European financiers assumed control, labor became unionized, and mining towns took on some of the characteristics of the industrial city. Individual prospectors meanwhile dashed on to the next find. Unlike other frontiers, the mining frontier moved from west to east, as the original California miners hurried eastward in search of the big strike.

In 1859 fresh strikes were made near Pikes Peak in Colorado and in the Carson River valley of Nevada. News of both discoveries set off wild migrations, and the gold near Pikes Peak quickly played out. But the Nevada find uncovered a thick, bluish black ore that was almost pure silver and gold. A quick-witted drifter named Henry T. P. Comstock talked his way into partnership in the claim, and word of the Comstock Lode flashed over the mountains.

Thousands of miners climbed the Sierra Nevada that summer of 1859. But the biggest strike was yet to come. In 1873 John W. Mackay and three partners formed a company to dig deep into the mountain, and at 1167 feet they hit the Big Bonanza, a seam of gold and silver more than 54 feet wide. It was the richest discovery in the history of mining. Although most of the profits went to financiers and corporation, Mackay himself became the richest person in the world.

In the 1860s and 1870s important strikes were made in Washington, Idaho, Nevada, Colorado, Montana, Arizona, and the Dakota Territory. Miners flocked from strike to strike, and new camps and mining towns sprang up overnight. The miners were extremely mobile, usually moving on when the paydirt played out.

The final fling came in the Black Hills rush of 1874–1876. The army had tried to keep miners out of the area, the heart of the Sioux hunting grounds, and even sent a scientific party under Colonel George A. Custer to disprove the rumors of gold. Instead, Custer found gold all over the hills, and the rush was on. Miners, gamblers, desperadoes, and prostitutes flocked to Deadwood, the most lawless of all the mining camps.

Towns such as Deadwood, in the Dakota Territory; Virginia City, Nevada; Leadville, Colorado; and Tombstone, Arizona, began a new process in the frontier experience. Unlike the rural setting of the farming frontier, the mining camp became the germ of a city, and theaters, the latest fashions, schools, and lending libraries came quickly to them, providing civilized refinements not available on other frontiers. But urbanization also created the need for municipal government, sanitation, and law enforcement.

Mining camps were governed by a simple democracy. Soon after a strike, the miners in the area met to organize a mining "district" and adopted rules governing behavior in it. Rules regulated the size and boundaries of claims, established procedures for settling disputes, and set penalties for crimes. Petty criminals were banished from the district; serious offenders were hanged. Early visitors to the mining country were struck by the way miners, solitary and competitive, joined together, founded a camp, and created a society.

The camps were mostly male, made up of "men who can rough it" and a few women of "spirit and energy." Prostitutes followed the camps around the West, and "respectable" women were an object of curiosity. Some women worked claims, but more often they took jobs as cooks, housekeepers, and seamstresses—for wages considerably higher than in the East.

The lure of gold drew large numbers of Chinese, Chileans, Peruvians, Mexicans, French, Germans, and English to the mining camps. The Latin Americans brought valuable mining techniques, and the painstaking Chinese profitably worked claims others had abandoned. In the 1860s almost one third of the miners in the West were Chinese.

Hostility often surfaced against foreign miners, particularly the French, Latin Americans, and Chinese. In California, special taxes were levied to drive away foreign competition. Fi-

nally, after several riots and intense political pressure, Congress passed the Chinese Exclusion Act of 1882, which suspended immigration of Chinese laborers for ten years.

By the 1890s the early mining bonanza was over. All told, the western mines contributed billions of dollars to the economy. They helped finance the Civil War and provided needed capital for industrialization. The vast boost in the silver production from the Comstock Lode changed the relative value of gold and silver, the base of American currency. Bitter disputes over the currency affected politics and led to the famous "battle of the standards" during the presidential election of 1896 (see Chapter 20).

The mining frontier populated portions of the West and sped its political organization. Nevada, Idaho, and Montana were granted early statehood because of mining. Merchants, editors, lawyers, and ministers flocked to the frontier and established permanent settlements. But the industry also left behind painful scars in the form of ravaged Indian reservations, pitted hills, and lonely ghost towns.

GOLD FROM THE ROOTS UP

"There's gold from the grass roots down," said California Joe, a guide in the gold districts of the Dakota Territory in the 1870s, "but there's more gold from the grass roots up." Ranchers began to recognize the potential of the vast grasslands of the West. The Plains were covered with buffalo or grama grass, a wiry variety with short, hard stems. Cattle thrived on it.

For twenty years after 1865, cattle ranching dominated the "open range," a vast, fenceless area extending from the Texas Panhandle north into Canada. Such techniques of the business as branding, roundups, and roping came from Mexico. The cattle themselves, the famous Texas longhorns, also came from Mexico. Although their meat was coarse and stringy, they fed a nation hungry for beef at the end of the Civil War.

The problem was to get the beef to eastern markets, and Joseph G. McCoy, a livestock

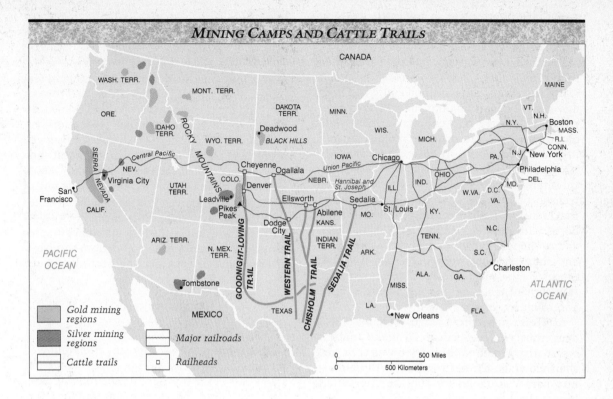

Gold mining regions

Silver mining regions

Cattle trails

Major railroads

Railheads

shipper from Illinois, solved it. Looking for a way to market Texas beef, McCoy conceived the idea of taking the cattle on "long drives" to railheads in Kansas. After several rebuffs, the persistent McCoy signed a contract in 1867 with the Hannibal and St. Joseph Railroad. Searching for an appropriate rail junction, he settled on the sleepy Kansas town of Abilene.

In September 1867, McCoy shipped the first train of twenty cars of longhorn cattle. By the end of the year a thousand carloads had followed, all headed for Chicago markets. In 1871 700,000 head of Texas cattle reached Abilene. The profits were enormous; drivers bought cheap Texas steers for $7 a head and sold them for $60 or $70 a head at a northern railhead.

Cowboys pushed steers northward on the Chisholm and other trails in herds of 2000 to 3000. Novels and films have portrayed these mounted herdsmen as white, but at least one

quarter of them were black and possibly another quarter were Mexicans. A typical crew on the trail north might have eight men, half of them black or Mexican. Most of the trail bosses were white; they earned about $125 a month.

Like miners, cattlemen lived beyond the formal reach of the law and so established their own. A cowboy who shot another was hanged on the spot. Ranchers adopted rules for cattle ownership, branding, roundups, and drives; and they formed associations to enforce them. The Wyoming Stock Growers' Association, the largest and most formidable, was often "the law" in Wyoming and extended its reach well into Colorado, Nebraska, Montana, and the Dakota Territory.

Hollywood to the contrary, there was little violence in the booming cow towns. Doc Holliday and William B. (Bat) Masterson never killed anyone, and the number of homicides in a year never topped five in any cattle town. In fact, famous western sheriffs like Wild Bill Hickok and Wyatt Earp repaired streets and sidewalks far more frequently than they used their guns.

By 1880 more than 6 million cattle had been driven to northern markets. But the era of the great cattle drive was ending. Farmers were planting wheat on the old buffalo ranges; barbed wire, a recent invention, cut across the trails and divided up the big ranches. Mechanical improvements in slaughtering, refrigerated transportation, and cold storage modernized the industry. Ranchers bred the Texas longhorns with heavier Hereford and Angus bulls, and as the new breeds proved profitable, more and more ranches opened on the northern ranges. By the mid-1880s large investments had transformed ranching into big business, often controlled by absentee owners.

By 1885 the northern ranges were becoming dangerously overcrowded. To make matters worse, the winter of 1885–1886 was cold, and the following summer was one of the hottest on record. Waterholes dried up; the grass turned brown. Beef prices fell. The winter of 1886–1887 was one of the worst in western history. Temperatures dropped to 45 degrees below zero, and cattle that once would have saved themselves by drifting ahead of the storms perished when they came up against the new barbed wire fences. When the snows thawed, ranchers found tens of thousands of carcasses stacked up against fences.

The cattle business recovered, but it took different directions. Outside capital, so plentiful in the boom years, dried up. Ranchers began fencing their lands, reducing the size of their herds, and growing hay for winter food. To the dismay of cowboys, mowing machines and hay rakes became as important as chuck wagons and branding irons. The last roundup on the northern ranges took place in 1905. Ranches grew smaller, and some ranchers switched to raising sheep. Homesteaders, armed with barbed wire and new strains of wheat, pushed onto the Plains, and the day of the open range was over.

FARMING ON THE FRONTIER

Like miners and cattlemen, millions of farmers moved West in the decades after 1870 to seek crop bonanzas and new ways of life. Some realized their dreams; many fought just to survive.

Between 1870 and 1900 farmers cultivated more land than ever before in American history. They peopled the Plains from the Dakota Territory to Texas, pushed the Indians out of their last sanctuary in Oklahoma, and poured into the basins and foothills of the Rockies. By 1900 the western half of the nation contained almost 30 percent of the population, compared to less than 1 percent just a half-century earlier.

SODBUSTERS ON THE PLAINS

Unlike mining, farm settlement often followed predictable patterns, taking population from states east of the frontier line and moving gradually westward. The movement slumped during the depression of the 1870s, but after several years of above-average rainfall on the Great Plains a new wave of optimism carried thousands more west. Between 1870 and 1900 the population on the Plains tripled. Farming there presented new problems. There was little surface water, and wells ranged between 50 and 500 feet deep. Lumber for homes and fences was also scarce. Water could be brought to the surface by windmills and lumber could be imported, but both solutions required more money than most farmers had.

Unable to afford wood, farmers often started out in dreary sod houses. Cut into three-foot sections, the thick prairie sod was laid like brick. Since glass was scarce, cloth hung over the windows; a blanket was hung from the ceiling to make two rooms. A sod house provided little light or air but cost only $2.78 to build.

Outside, the Plains environment sorely tested the men and women who moved there. Neighbors were distant; the land stretched on

Black homesteaders, photographed in front of their sod house in Custer County, Nebraska, about 1887. No doubt this family was drawn to the Plains, as were millions of other farmers in the last decades of the nineteenth century, by the promise of a new opportunity, only to find themselves struggling to survive the harsh conditions and loneliness of their new life.

as far as the eye could see. Always the wind blew. The sense of loneliness and desolation pervaded prairie life.

In the winters savage storms swept the open grasslands. Summertime temperatures stayed near 110 degrees for weeks at a time. Fearsome rainstorms, building in the summer's heat, beat down the young corn and wheat. The summers also brought grasshoppers, flying in swarms so huge they shut out the sun. The grasshoppers ate everything in sight: crops, clothing, mosquito netting, tree bark, even plow handles.

NEW FARMING METHODS

Farmers embraced new technology to meet these difficult conditions. Cheap and effective fencing material became available with the invention of barbed wire by an Illinois farmer, Joseph Glidden, in 1874. Other inventions, similarly designed to meet the new conditions, included James Oliver's patented chilled-iron plow with a smooth-surface mold board that did not clog in the thick prairie soils.

Farming techniques also adapted to the new environment. Dry farming helped compensate for the lack of rainfall. By plowing furrows twelve to fourteen inches deep, and creating a dust mulch to fill the furrow, farmers loosened the soil and slowed evaporation. New milling methods were developed in the 1870s to process the hard-kerneled imported varieties of wheat. Scientific agriculture advanced with new discoveries linking soil minerals and plant growth. The Hatch Act, passed in 1887, established a network of agricultural experiment stations that provided information about these new discoveries to farmers.

In the late 1870s huge bonanza farms arose, run by the new machinery and financed with outside capital. Oliver Dalrymple, the most famous of the bonanza farmers, hired armies of workers, bought machinery by the carload, and planted on a scale that dazzled the West. Using 200 pairs of harrows, 155 binders, and 16 threshers, Dalrymple produced 600,000 bushels of wheat in 1881. He and other bonanza managers profited from the economics of scale, buying materials at wholesale prices and receiving rebates from the railroads.

Then a period of drought began. Rainfall dropped between 1885 and 1890, and the large-scale growers found it hard to compete with smaller farmers who diversified their crops and cultivated more intensively. Many of the large bonanzas slowly disintegrated, and Dalrymple himself went bankrupt in 1896.

DISCONTENT ON THE FARM

Struck by the drabness of rural life, Oliver H. Kelley, a clerk in the Department of Agriculture, in 1867 founded the National Grange of the Patrons of Husbandry, known simply as the Grange. The Grange provided social, cultural, and educational activities for its members. Its constitution banned involvement in politics, but Grangers often ignored it and supported railroad regulation and other measures.

The Grange grew rapidly during the depression of the 1870s, and by 1875 it had over 800,000 members. Local Granges set up cooperative stores, grain elevators, warehouses, insurance companies, and farm machinery factories. Many failed, but in the meantime the organization made its mark. Discontent grew, spilling over into the turbulent Populist movement of the 1890s. (See Chapter 20 for a more detailed discussion.)

Like the cattle boom, the farming boom ended sharply after 1887. A severe drought that year cut harvests, and other droughts followed in 1889 and 1894. Thousands of new farmers were wiped out on the western Plains. Between 1888 and 1892 more than half the population of western Kansas left.

Farmers grew angry and restless. They complained about declining crop prices, rising railroad rates, and heavy mortgages. In the wheatgrowing Plains the economic problems were persistent. Returning home to Iowa in 1889, the author Hamlin Garland found his farming friends caught up "in a sullen rebellion against government and against God."

The peopling of the West transformed American agriculture. The states beyond the Mississippi became the garden land and bread basket of the nation. Soon the western states produced more than Americans could consume. By 1890 American farmers were exporting abundant amounts of wheat and other crops. As their operations became more commercialized and scientific, farmers were tied ever closer to the national future.

THE FINAL FLING

As the West filled in with people, pressure mounted on the federal government to open the last Indian territory, Oklahoma, to settlers. Congress and the president responded, forcing the Creeks and Seminoles to surrender their rights. President Benjamin Harrison announced the opening of the Oklahoma District as of noon, April 22, 1889.

Preparation was feverish all along the frontier. On the morning of April 22, nearly 100,000 people lined the Oklahoma borders. At noon the starting flag dropped, and horses and wagons loaded with people and hopes moved into the "last" territory. By sunset that day settlers claimed 12,000 homesteads, and the 1,920,000 acres of the Oklahoma District were officially settled. Reflecting the speed of western settlement, a character in Edna Ferber's novel *Cimarron* declared: "Creation! Hell! That took six days. This was done in one."

Between the Civil War and 1900 the West witnessed one of the greatest migrations in history. With the Indians driven into smaller and smaller areas, farms, ranches, mines, and cities rose up on the vast lands from the Mississippi to the Pacific. The 1890 census noted that for the first time in the country's history, "there can hardly be said to be a frontier line."

Picking up the theme, historian Frederick Jackson Turner, in an influential 1893 paper, claimed that the existence of the frontier and of free land explained American development. It shaped customs and character; gave rise to independence, self-confidence, and individualism; and fostered invention and adaptation. Historians have substantially modified Turner's thesis by pointing to frontier conservatism and imitativeness, the influence of varying racial groups, and the persistence of European ideas and institutions. Yet there can be no doubt that the West was the first American empire and that it had a profound impact on the American mind and imagination.

CHRONOLOGY

1849	Gold rush to California
1859	More gold discoveries, in Colorado and Nevada
1862	Congress passes Homestead Act, encouraging western settlement
1864	Nevada admitted to the Union Colonel John Chivington leads massacre of Indians at Sand Creek, Colorado
1865– 1867	Sioux fight against white miners and U.S. army in Great Sioux War
1866	"Long drive" of cattle touches off cattle bonanzas
1867	Horace Greeley urges Easterners to "Go West, young man" National Grange of the Patrons of Husbandry (the Grange) founded to enrich farmers' lives
1867– 1868	Policy of "small reservations" for Indians adopted
1873	Congress passes Timber Culture Act Big Bonanza discovered on the Comstock Lode in Nevada
1874	Joseph F. Glidden invents barbed wire Discovery of gold in Dakota Territory sets off Black Hills Gold Rush
1876	Colorado admitted to the Union Custer and his men defeated and killed by the Sioux at battle of Little Bighorn
1883	Museum expedition discovers fewer than 200 buffalo in the West Buffalo Bill Cody organizes and begins touring with his Wild West Show
1886– 1887	Severe drought and winter damage cattle and farming bonanzas
1887	Congress passes Dawes Severalty Act, making Indians individual landowners Hatch Act provides funds for establishment of agricultural experiment stations
1889	Washington, Montana, and the Dakotas admitted to the Union Oklahoma Territory opened to settlement
1890	Idaho and Wyoming admitted to Union Teton Sioux massacred at battle of Wounded Knee, South Dakota
1893	Young historian Frederick Jackson Turner analyzes closing of the frontier

✿ RECOMMENDED READING

The best general account of the movement west is Ray Allen Billington, *Westward Expansion* (1967). See also Frederick Merk, *History of the Westward Movement* (1978). Rodman W. Paul surveys the mining bonanza in *Mining Frontiers of the Far West* (1963); Fred A. Shannon provides similar coverage for agriculture in *The Farmer's Last Frontier* (1945). Lewis Atherton, *The Cattle Kings* (1961), and E. S. Osgood, *The Day of the Cattlemen* (1929), cover the cattle industry. Louis B. Wright, *Culture on the Moving Frontier* (1955), and Henry Nash Smith, *Virginia Land: The American West as Symbol and Myth* (1950), trace cultural and literary development.

Recent authors have taken fresh looks at older or ignored questions. Robert R. Dykstra, *The Cattle*

Towns (1968), examines five Kansas cattle towns, with interesting results. Gunther Barth, *Instant Cities* (1975), Earl Pomeroy, *The Pacific Slope* (1965), Kathleen Underwood, *Town Building on the Colorado Frontier* (1987), look at urban development in the Far West. Julie Roy Jeffrey, *Frontier Women: The Trans-Mississippi West* (1979), and Joanna L. Stratton, *Pioneer Women: Voices From the Kansas Frontier* (1981), are perceptive works, and John Mack Faragher, *Women and Men on the Overland Trail* (1979), examines social and other relationships on the trails west. Faragher's *Sugar Creek: Life on the Illinois Prairie* (1986), is an outstanding case study.

On the Indians, there are a number of valuable works, including William T. Hagan, *American Indians* (1961); Frederick E. Hoxie, *A Final Promise: The Campaign to Assimilate the Indians* (1984); Robert M. Utley, *The Last Days of the Sioux Nation* (1963); R. K. Andrist, *The Long Death* (1964); and Russell Thornton, *American Indian Holocaust and Survival: A Population History since 1492* (1987). Dwight W. Hoover, *The Red and the Black* (1976),

and Leonard Dinnerstein, Roger L. Nichols, and David M. Reimers, *Natives and Strangers* (1979), contrast Indian policy with the treatment of other minorities. Leonard Pitt looks at *The Decline of the Californios: A Social History of the Spanish-Speaking Californians* (1966), and Gunther Barth at the treatment of the Chinese in *Bitter Strength* 1964. Also see Arnoldo DeLeon, *The Tejano Community, 1836–1900* (1983), and *They Called Them Greasers: Anglo Attitudes Toward Mexicans in Texas* (1983).

Books on the mining bonanza include Rodman W. Paul, *California Gold* (1948); William T. Jackson, *Treasure Hill: Portrait of a Silver Mining Camp* (1963); Odie B. Faulk, *Tombstone: Myth and Reality* (1972). On the cowboy, see E.E. Dale, *Cow Country* (1942). Gene M. Gressley, *Bankers and Cattlemen* (1966), details outside investment in cattle. Roger D. McGrath, *Gunfighters, Highwaymen and Vigilantes: Violence on the Frontier* (1984) is a recent study. Valuable studies of farming include Allan G. Bogue, *From Prairie to Corn Belt* (1963), and H. M. Drache, *The Day of the Bonanza* (1964).

18 THE INDUSTRIAL SOCIETY

INDUSTRIAL DEVELOPMENT

AN EMPIRE ON RAILS

AN INDUSTRIAL EMPIRE

THE SELLERS

THE WAGE EARNERS

In 1876 Americans celebrated their first century of independence. Survivors of a recent civil war, they observed the centenary proudly and rather self-consciously in song, speech, and above all, in a grand Centennial Exposition, spread over thirteen acres, held in Philadelphia, Pennsylvania.

The exposition focused more on the present than the past, featuring machines, inventions, and new products. Fairgoers saw linoleum, a new, easy-to-clean floor covering. For the first time they tasted root beer and the rare banana, wrapped in foil and selling for a dime. They saw their first bicycle, an awkward high-wheeled contraption with solid tires.

In the entire exposition, machinery was the focus and Machinery Hall the most popular building. Here were the products of an ever-improving civilization. Long lines of the curious waited to see the telephone, Alexander Graham Bell's new device. Thomas A. Edison displayed several recent inventions. The typewriter, the elevator, and the Westinghouse railroad air brake similarly amazed the fairgoers.

But the exhibit drawing the largest crowds was the mighty Corliss engine, the focal point of the exposition. A giant steam engine, it dwarfed everything in Machinery Hall. Alone it supplied power for the 8000 other machines on the exposition grounds. The Corliss captured the nation's imagination, symbolizing America's swift movement toward an industrial and urban society.

At the start of the Civil War the United States lagged well behind industrializing nations such as Great Britain, France, and Germany. By 1900 it had vaulted far into the lead, with a manufacturing output that exceeded the *combined* output of its three European rivals. Over the same years cities grew, technology advanced, and farm production rose. Developments in manufacturing, mining, agriculture, transportation, and communication transformed society.

INDUSTRIAL DEVELOPMENT

American industry owed its remarkable growth to several considerations. It fed on an abundance of natural resources: coal, iron, timber, petroleum, waterpower. Labor was also abundant, drawn from American farm families and the hosts of European immigrants who flocked to America. Nearly 8 million immigrants arrived in the 1870s and 1880s; another 15 million came between 1890 and 1914.

The burgeoning population led to expanded markets, which new devices like the telegraph and telephone helped to exploit. The swiftly growing urban populations devoured goods, and the railroads linked the cities together and opened a natural market. Within its boundaries the United States had the largest free-trade market in the world, while tariff barriers partially protected its producers from outside competition.

Expansive market and labor conditions buoyed the confidence of European and American investors who provided large amounts of capital. Technological progress and invention increased productivity in many important industries and also helped foster a firm agricultural base, on which industrialization depends.

Eager to promote economic growth, government at all levels—federal, state, and local—gave manufacturers money, land, and other resources. Other boons to industry, too, flowed from the American system of government: stability, commitment to the concept of private property, and a reluctance to regulate industrial activity.

In this atmosphere entrepreneurs flourished. Taking steps crucial for industrialization, they organized, managed, and assumed the financial risks of the new enterprises. Admirers called them "captains of industry"; foes labeled them "robber barons." To some degree they were both—creative *and* acquisitive. If sometimes they seemed larger than life, it is because they dealt in concepts, distances, and quantities often unknown to earlier generations.

Industrial growth, it must be remembered, was neither a steady nor an inevitable process. Growth varied from industry to industry and from year to year. It was concentrated in the North and East. The more sparsely settled West provided raw materials, while the South had to rebuild after wartime devastation.

Still, industrial development proceeded at an extraordinary pace. Between 1865 and 1914 the real Gross National Product (GNP)—the total monetary value of all goods and services produced in a year, with prices held stable—grew at an average rate of more than 4 percent a year. As one economic historian noted: "Never before had such rapid growth continued for so long."

AN EMPIRE ON RAILS

Genuine revolutions happen rarely, but a major one occurred in the nineteenth century: a revolution in transportation and communication. The steamship sliced in half the time of the Atlantic crossing. The telegraph, flashing messages almost instantaneously along miles of wire, transformed communications, as did the telephone a little later. But the railroad worked the largest changes of all. Along with Bessemer steel, it was the most significant technical innovation of the century.

More than most innovations, the railroad dramatically affected economic and social life. It contributed advantages that canals and other inland waterways could not match. Those advantages included more direct routes, greater speed, greater safety and comfort than other modes of land travel, more dependable schedules, a larger volume of traffic, and year-round service. A day's land travel on stagecoach or horseback might cover fifty miles. The railroad covered fifty miles in little more than an hour. It went where canals and rivers did not go—directly to the loading platforms of great factories or across the arid West.

Linking widely separated cities and villages, the railroad ended the relative isolation and self-sufficiency of the country's "island communities." It tied people together, brought in outside products, fostered greater interdependence, and encouraged economic specialization. The railroad made possible a national market and in so doing pointed the way toward mass production and mass consumption, two of the hallmarks of twentieth-century society.

It also pointed the way toward a new kind of business development. Railroads were America's first big business, stretching over thousands of miles, employing thousands of people, dealing with countless consumers, and requiring a scale of organization and decision making unknown in earlier business. Year by year railroad companies consumed great quan-

tities of iron, steel, coal, lumber, and glass; such purchases stimulated growth and employment in numerous industries.

No wonder, then, that the railroad captured so completely the country's imagination. Walt Whitman, the poet, chanted the locomotive's praises:

> emblem of motion and power—pulse of the continent . . .
> Fierce-throated beauty!

For nearly a hundred years children gathered at depots, paused in the fields to wave as the fast express flashed by, listened at night to far-off whistles, and wondered what lay down the tracks. They lived in a world grown smaller.

BUILDING THE EMPIRE

When the Civil War ended, the country already had 35,000 miles of track, and much of the rail-

RAILROAD CONSTRUCTION, 1830–1920

Miles of Track	10,000	20,000	30,000	40,000	50,000	60,000	70,000
1830–1840							
1841–1850							
1851–1860							
1861–1870							
1871–1880							
1881–1890							
1891–1900							
1901–1910							
1911–1920							

Source: U.S. Bureau of the Census, Historical Statistics of the United States, Colonial Times to 1970, Bicentennial Edition, Washington, D.C., 1975.

road system east of the Mississippi River was in place (see Chapter 12). Farther west, the rail network stood poised on the edge of settlement. Although America already had nearly as much railroad track as the rest of the world, after 1865 rail construction increased spectacularly. Trackage peaked at 254,037 miles in 1916, just before the industry began its long decline into the mid-twentieth century.

To build such an empire took vast amounts of capital. American and European investors provided some of the money; government supplied the rest. Altogether local and state governments gave railroad companies about $525 million. In addition, the federal government donated millions of acres of public land to the railroad companies. Federal land grants helped build 18,738 miles of track, less than 8 percent of the rail system. The companies sometimes sold the land to raise cash but more often used it as security for bonds or loans.

Beyond doubt, the grants of cash and land promoted waste and corruption. The companies built fast and wastefully, eager to collect the subsidies that went with each mile of track. The corruption involved in the Crédit Mobilier is but one example of the excesses of the railroad companies (see Chapter 16).

Yet, on balance, the grants probably worked more benefits than evils. As Congress had hoped, the grants were the lure for railroad building across the rugged, unsettled West, where it would be years before the revenues would repay construction. The grants seemed necessary in a nation which, unlike Europe, expected private enterprise to build the railroads. In return for aid, Congress required the railroads to carry government freight, troops, and mail at substantially reduced rates.

LINKING THE NATION VIA TRUNK LINES

The early railroads may seem to have linked different regions, but in fact they did not. Built with little regard for through traffic, they were designed more to protect local interests than to tap outside markets. To avoid cooperating with other lines, they adopted conflicting schedules, built separate depots, and above all, used tracks of varying widths.

The Civil War showed the value of fast, long-distance transportation, and after 1865 railroad managers worked to provide it. In a burst of consolidation the large swallowed the small; integrated rail networks became a reality. Railroads also adopted standard schedules, signals, equipment, and finally in 1866, the standard track width (or gauge) of 4 feet 8½ inches.

In the Northeast four great trunk lines took shape, all intended to link eastern seaports with the rich traffic of the Great Lakes and western rivers. Like a massive river system, trunk lines drew traffic from dozens of tributaries (feeder lines) and carried it to major markets. The Baltimore and Ohio Railroad was one. The Erie Railroad, running from New York City to Chicago, ran parallel to the New York Central Railroad built by Cornelius Vanderbilt. The fourth line, the Pennsylvania Railroad, initially ran from Philadelphia to Pittsburgh, but it was expanded to unite Cincinnati, Indianapolis, Saint Louis, Chicago, New York City, Baltimore, and Washington. In the war-damaged South, consolidation took longer. But by 1900, just four decades after secession, the South had five major systems that tied into a national transportation network.

Over the rail system, passengers and freight moved in relative speed, comfort, and safety. Automatic couplers (1868), air brakes (1869), refrigerated cars (1867), dining cars, heated cars, Pullman sleeping cars, and stronger locomotives transformed railroad service. Passenger miles per year increased from 5 billion in 1870 to 16 billion in 1900. The railroads even changed time, establishing a standard system of four time zones for the country.

RAILS ACROSS THE CONTINENT

The dream of a transcontinental railroad stretched back many years but had always succumbed to sectional quarrels over the route. In 1862 and 1864, with the South out of the pic-

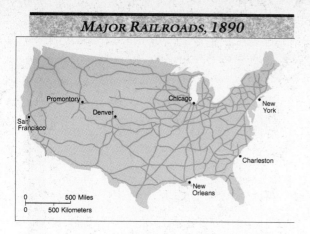

Promontory · Chicago · New York · San Francisco · Denver · Charleston · New Orleans

0   500 Miles
0   500 Kilometers

knit the world together. Bret Harte, the exuberant poet of the West, wrote of the coupling at Promontory:

> *What was it the Engines said,*
> *Pilots touching,—head to head*
> *Facing on the single track,*
> *Half a world behind each back?*

In the next twenty-five years, four more railroads reached the coast. By the 1890s business leaders talked comfortably of railroad systems stretching deep into South America and across the Bering Strait to Asia, Europe, and Africa. In an age of progress, anything seemed possible.

PROBLEMS OF GROWTH

Overbuilding during the 1870s and 1880s caused serious problems for the railroads. Lines paralleled each other, and where they did not, speculators like Jay Gould often laid one down to force a rival line to buy the new one out at inflated prices. Speculators like Gould bought and sold railroads like toys and watered their stock—distributed it in excess of the real value of the assets—in the process.

Competition was severe, and managers fought desperately for traffic. They offered special rates and favors: free passes for large shippers; low rates on bulk freight, carload lots, and long hauls; and above all, rebates—secret, privately negotiated reductions below published rates. Soon fierce rate wars convinced managers that ruthless competition helped no one.

At first, managers tried to control competition by sharing traffic, but intense competitive pressures killed every agreement. Customers grew adept at bargaining for rebates and other privileges, and railroads rarely felt able to refuse them.

Failing to cooperate, railroad owners next tried to consolidate. Through purchase, lease, and merger, they gobbled up competitors and built "self-sustaining systems" that dominated entire regions. But many of these systems, expensive and unwieldy, collapsed in the Panic of 1893.

ture, Congress passed legislation to build the first transcontinental. The act incorporated the Union Pacific Railroad Company to build westward from Nebraska to meet the Central Pacific Railroad Company, building eastward from the Pacific Coast. The federal government directly subsidized construction with grants of land and cash loans.

Construction began simultaneously at Omaha and Sacramento in 1863, lagged during the war, and moved vigorously ahead in 1865. It became a race, each company vying for land, loans, and potential markets. Along the way, construction crews for both companies confronted dangerous and difficult obstacles. Workers of the Union Pacific encountered frequent Indian attacks but had the advantage of building over flat prairie. Central Pacific crews faced more trying conditions in the high Sierra Nevada along California's eastern border. Under the most difficult conditions Central Pacific workers, most of whom were Chinese, dug, blasted, and pushed their way slowly east.

On May 10, 1869, the two lines met at Promontory, Utah, near the northern tip of the Great Salt Lake. The Union Pacific and Central Pacific presidents hammered in a golden spike (both missed it on the first try), and the dreamed-of connection was made.

The transcontinental railroad symbolized American unity and progress. Along with the Suez Canal, completed the same year, it helped

Needing money, railroads turned naturally to bankers, who finally imposed order on the industry. J. Pierpont Morgan, head of the New York investment house of J. P. Morgan and Company, took the lead. The most powerful figure in American finance, Morgan liked efficiency, combination, and order. He disliked "wasteful" competition. In 1885, during a bruising rate war between the New York Central and the Pennsylvania, Morgan invited the combatants to a conference aboard his palatial steam yacht. There he arranged a traffic-sharing agreement and collected a million-dollar fee. Bringing peace to an industry could be profitable. It also satisfied Morgan's passion for stability.

After 1893 Morgan and a few other bankers refinanced ailing railroads, and in the process they took control of the industry. Their methods were direct: Fixed costs and debt were ruthlessly cut; new stock was issued to provide capital; rates were stabilized; rebates and competition were eliminated; and control was vested in a "voting trust" of hand-picked trustees. By 1900 Morgan and his methods dominated American railroading.

As the new century began, the railroads had pioneered the pattern followed by most other industries. Seven giant systems controlled nearly two thirds of the mileage, and they in turn answered to a few investment banking firms like the house of Morgan. For good and ill, a national transportation network, centralized and relatively efficient, was now in place.

❧ AN INDUSTRIAL EMPIRE

Along with railroads, the new industrial empire was based on steel. Harder and more durable than other kinds of iron, steel wrought changes in manufacturing, agriculture, transportation, and architecture. It permitted longer bridges, taller buildings, stronger railroad track, better plows, heavier machinery, and faster ships. From the 1870s onward, steel output became the worldwide accepted measure of industrial progress.

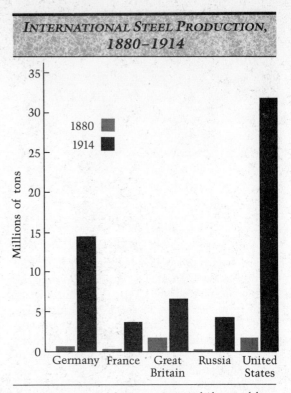

INTERNATIONAL STEEL PRODUCTION, 1880–1914

Source: U.S. Bureau of the Census, Statistical Abstract of the United States: 1982–83 (103rd edition) Washington, D.C., 1982.

The Bessemer process, developed in the late 1850s by Henry Bessemer in England and independently by William Kelly in the United States, made it possible. Both men discovered that a blast of air through molten iron burned off carbon and other impurities, resulting in steel of a more uniform and durable quality. The discovery transformed the industry. Earlier methods had produced amounts a person could lift; a Bessemer converter dealt with five tons of molten metal at a time. The mass production of steel was now possible.

CARNEGIE AND STEEL

Bessemer plants demanded extensive capital investment, abundant raw material, sophisticated production techniques, and modern research departments. Costly to build, they limited entry into the industry to the handful who could afford them.

Great steel districts arose in Ohio, Alabama, and Pennsylvania—especially near Pittsburgh, which became the center of the industry. Output shot up; by 1890 the United States took the world lead in production.

Iron ore abounded in the fabulous deposits near Lake Superior, the greatest deposits in the world. Through a series of intricate steps involving large and complex machines, such as giant steam shovels, the raw ore was transported to the steel mills.

Like the railroads, steel companies grew larger and larger. As operations expanded, managers needed greater skills. Product development, marketing, and consumer preferences became important. Competition was fierce, and steel companies, like the railroads, tried secret agreements, pools, and consolidation. During the 1880s and 1890s they moved toward *vertical integration*, a type of organization in which a single company owns and controls the entire process from unearthing of the raw materials to the manufacture and sale of the finished product.

Andrew Carnegie emerged as the undisputed master of the industry. Born in Scotland, he came to the United States in 1848 at the age of twelve. Settling near Pittsburgh, he went to work as a bobbin boy in a cotton mill, earning $1.20 a week. In 1852 his hard work and skill in a telegraph office caught the eye of Thomas A. Scott of the Pennsylvania Railroad. By 1859 Carnegie had become a divisional superintendent with the company. He was twenty-four.

Soon rich from shrewd investments, Carnegie plunged into the steel industry in 1872. On the Monongahela River south of Pittsburgh he built the giant J. Edgar Thomson Steel Works. With his warmth and salesmanship, he attracted able subordinates whom he drove hard and paid well. Carnegie kept the wages of the laborers in his mills low, disliked unions, and crushed a violent strike at his Homestead works in 1892 (see p. 319).

In 1878 Carnegie won the steel contract for the Brooklyn Bridge. As city building boomed during the 1880s, he converted the huge Homestead works near Pittsburgh to the manufacture of structural beams and angles, which went into the first skyscrapers. Carnegie profits mounted: from $2 million in 1888 to $40 million in 1900. Employing 20,000 people, it was the largest industrial company in the world.

In 1901 Carnegie sold it. Believing that wealth brought social obligations, he wanted to devote his full time to philanthropy. J. Pierpont Morgan, who in the late 1890s had put together several rival steel companies, paid Carnegie almost a half billion dollars for Carnegie Steel.

Drawing other companies into the combination, Morgan on March 3, 1901, announced the creation of the United States Steel Corporation. The first billion-dollar company, it employed 168,000 people, produced 9 million tons of iron and steel a year, and controlled three fifths of the country's steel business. Soon there were other giants, and as the nineteenth century ended, steel products—rare just thirty years before—had altered the landscape. Huge firms, investment bankers, and professional managers dominated the industry.

ROCKEFELLER AND OIL

Petroleum worked comparable changes in the economic and social landscape, although mostly after 1900. Distilled into oil, it lubricated the machinery of the industrial age. Kerosene, another major distillate of petroleum, brought inexpensive illumination into almost every home. Since tallow candles and whale oil were expensive to burn, many people went to bed at nightfall. Kerosene lamps opened the evenings to activity, which altered the patterns of life.

Like other changes in these years, the oil boom happened with surprising speed. In the mid-1850s petroleum was a bothersome, smelly fluid that occasionally rose to the surface of springs and streams. But in 1859 Edwin L. Drake drilled the first oil well near Titusville in northwest Pennsylvania, and the "black

John D. Rockefeller, satirized in a 1901 Punch *cartoon, is enthroned on oil, the base of his empire; his crown is girdled by other holdings. Rockefeller was not above using unsavory methods to discourage competitors.*

gold" fever struck. Chemists soon discovered ways to make lubricating oil, grease, paint, wax, varnish, naphtha, and paraffin. Within a few years there was a world market in oil.

At first, growth of the oil industry was chaotic. Early drillers and refiners produced for local markets, and since drilling wells and even erecting refineries cost little, competition flourished. Output fluctuated dramatically; prices rose and fell with devastating effect.

A young merchant from Cleveland named John D. Rockefeller imposed order on the industry. Beginning in 1863, at the age of twenty-four, he built a titan of corporate business, the Standard Oil Company. Like Morgan, Rockefeller considered competition wasteful, small scale enterprise inefficient, and consolidation the path of the future. Methodically, Rockefeller absorbed or destroyed competitors in Cleveland and elsewhere. As ruthless in his methods as Carnegie, he lacked the steel master's spontaneous charm. Like Carnegie, he demanded efficiency, relentless cost-cutting, and the latest technology. He was man of great vision, and he attracted exceptional lieutenants.

Paying careful attention to detail, Rockefeller realized that in large-scale production even small reductions meant huge savings. In one famous incident, he reduced the number of drops of solder on kerosene cans from forty to thirty-nine. In the end, Rockefeller triumphed over his competitors by marketing products of high quality at the lowest unit cost. But he employed other, less savory methods as well. He threatened rivals and bribed politicians, exploited railroad rebates, and employed spies to harass the customers of competing refiners. By 1879 he controlled 90 percent of the country's oil-refining capacity.

Vertically integrated, Standard Oil owned wells, timberlands, barrel and chemical plants, refineries, warehouses, pipelines, and fleets of tankers and oil cars. Its marketing organization served as a model for the industry, and it exported oil throughout the world.

To manage it all, the company developed a new plan of business organization, the trust, which had profound significance for American business. In 1882 Samuel T. C. Dodd, Standard's attorney, set up the Standard Oil Trust, with a board of nine trustees empowered "to hold, control, and manage" all Standard's properties. The first of the modern trusts was born. As Dodd intended, it immediately centralized control of Standard's far-flung empire.

Competition almost disappeared; profits soared. A trust movement swept the country, as industries with similar problems—whiskey, lead, and sugar, among others—followed Standard's example. The word *trust* became synonymous with monopoly, amid vehement public protests. Antitrust became a watchword for a generation of reformers from the 1880s through 1920. But Rockefeller's purpose had been *management* of a monopoly, not monopoly itself, which he had already achieved.

During the 1890s, Rockefeller helped pioneer another form of industrial consolidation, the holding company. Taking advantage of an 1889 New Jersey law that allowed companies to purchase other companies, he moved Standard Oil to New Jersey and bought up his own subsidiaries to form a holding company. The trust, he had learned, was cumbersome, and it was under attack in Congress and the courts. Holding companies offered the next step in industrial development. They were simply large scale mergers, in which a central corporate organization purchased the stock of the member companies and established direct, formal control. Soon other companies followed Rockefeller's example, and by 1900, 1 percent of the nation's companies controlled more than one third of its industrial production.

In 1897 Rockefeller retired with a fortune of nearly $900 million, but for Standard Oil and petroleum in general, the most expansive period was yet to come. The great oil pools of Texas and Oklahoma had not yet been discovered. There were only four usable automobiles in the country, and the day of the gasoline engine lay just ahead.

THE BUSINESS OF INVENTION

During the last third of the nineteenth century an extraordinary group of American inventors added to the world's knowledge. Some inventions gave rise to new industries; a few actually changed the quality of life. The number of patents issued to inventors reflected the trend. Between 1790 and 1860 the Patent Office issued just 36,000 patents; in the decade of the 1890s alone, it issued more than 200,000.

Some of the inventions transformed communications. In 1866 Cyrus W. Field improved the transatlantic cable linking the telegraph networks of Europe and the United States. By 1900 land and submarine cables reached around the world. Diplomats and business leaders could now "talk" to their counterparts in Berlin or Hong Kong. Even before the telephone, the cables quickened the pace of diplomacy, revolutionized journalism, and allowed businesses to expand and centralize.

The typewriter (1867), stock ticker (1867), cash register (1879), and adding machine (1888) helped business transactions. High-speed looms and sewing machines transformed the clothing industry, which for the first time in history turned out ready-made clothes for the masses.

Other innovations improved the diet. There were new processes for flour, canned meat, vegetables, condensed milk, and even beer. Refrigerated railroad cars, ice-cooled, brought fresh fruit from Florida and California to all parts of the country. In the 1870s Gustavus F. Swift, a Chicago meatpacker, hit on the idea of using the cars to distribute meat nationwide. Setting up "dissembly" factories to butcher meat (Henry Ford later copied them for his famous "assembly" lines), he started what a newspaper called an "era for cheap beef."

No innovation, however, rivaled in importance the telephone and the use of electricity for light and power. The telephone was the work of Alexander Graham Bell, a teacher of the deaf. Bell experimented with ways to transmit speech electrically, and after several years developed electrified metal disks that converted sound waves to electrical impulses and back again. On March 10, 1876, he transmitted the first sentence over a telephone: "Mr. Watson, come here; I want you." By 1905 there were 10 million telephones in the country— one for almost every ten people.

Thomas Alva Edison invented an array of processes and products of incalculable significance. Born in 1847, Edison had little formal education, although he was an avid reader. After earning a reputation for his work in telegraphy, Edison built and organized the first modern research laboratory at Menlo Park, New Jersey.

In 1877 Edison invented a "telephone repeater," which became the phonograph. Those unable to afford a phone, he thought, could record their voices for replay from a central telephone station. Using tin foil wrapped around a grooved, rotating cylinder, he shouted the verses of "Mary had a little lamb" and then listened in awe as the machine played them back. Within a generation Edison's invention had evolved into the phonograph record in its modern form. For the first time in history, people could listen again and again to a favorite piece of music. The phonograph made human experiences repeatable in a way never before possible.

In 1879 came an even larger triumph, the incandescent lamp. In tackling this idea, Edison set out to do nothing less than change light. A trial-and-error inventor, he tested 1600 materials before producing the carbon filament he wanted. With the financial backing of J. Pierpont Morgan, he organized the Edison Illuminating Company and built the Pearl Street power station in New York City. Power stations soon opened in Boston, Philadelphia, and Chicago. In a nation alive with light, the habits of centuries changed. A flick of the switch lit homes and factories at any hour of the day or night.

In a rare blunder, Edison based his system on low-voltage direct current, which could be transmitted only about two miles. George Westinghouse demonstrated the advantages of high-voltage alternating current, transmitted over great distances. With the inventor Nikola Tesla, Westinghouse developed an alternating-current motor that could convert electricity into mechanical power. Electricity could light a lamp or illuminate a skyscraper; pull a streetcar or drive an entire railroad; run a sewing machine or power a mammoth assembly line. Buried under pavement or strung from pole to pole, wires of every description—trolley, telephone, and power—soon distinguished the modern city. Electricity, in short, brought a revolution.

Alexander Graham Bell making the first telephone call between New York City and Chicago in 1892.

THE SELLERS

The increased output of the industrial age was one thing, but the products still had to be sold, and that gave rise to a new "science" of marketing. Some business leaders built extensive marketing organizations of their own. Others relied on retailers, merchandising techniques, and advertising, developing a host of methods to convince consumers to buy.

In 1867 businesses spent about $50 million on advertising; in 1900 they spent over $500 million, and the figure was increasing rapidly. The rotary press (1875) churned out newspapers and, with rotogravure illustrations, began a new era in newspaper advertising. Brand names became popular; already Kellogg was promising cornflake eaters "Genuine Joy, Genuine Appetite, Genuine Health and therefore Genuine Complexion."

Bringing producer and consumer together, nationwide advertising was the final link in the national market. Humorist Finley Peter

Dunne's Irish characters poked fun at the ads for breakfast cereals: "We all have our little tastes an' enthusyasms in th' matter iv breakfast foods, dependin' on what pa-a-pers we read an' what billboords we've seen iv late."

R. H. Macy in New York, John Wanamaker in Philadelphia, and Marshall Field in Chicago turned the department store into a national institution. There people could browse (a relatively new concept) and buy. Innovations in pricing, display, and advertising helped customers develop wants they did not know they had. In 1870 Wanamaker took out the first full-page newspaper ad.

The "chain store"—an American term—spread across the country. The A & P grocery stores began in 1859, and by 1915 there were a thousand of them. In 1880 F. W. Woolworth opened the first "Five and Ten Cent Store." He had fifty-nine stores in 1900. In similar fashion, Sears, Roebuck and Montgomery Ward sold to rural customers through mail-order catalogs—a means of selling that depended on effective transportation and a high level of customer literacy. By the early 1900s, Sears distributed 6 million catalogs annually.

Advertising, brand names, chain stores, and mail-order houses brought Americans of all varieties into a national market. Even as the country grew, a certain homogeneity of goods bound it together. There was a common language of consumption. The market, some contemporaries thought, bridged regional, class, and even ethnic differences.

The theory had limits; ethnic and racial differences remained deep in the society. But Americans *had* become a community of consumers, surrounded by goods unavailable just a few decades before, and able to purchase them. They had learned to make, want, and buy. As Arthur Miller, a twentieth-century playwright, said in *The Price*:

> Years ago a person, he was unhappy, didn't know what to do with himself—he'd go to church, start a revolution—something. Today you're unhappy? Can't figure it out? What is the salvation? Go shopping.

THE WAGE EARNERS

While entrepreneurs were important, it was the labor of millions of men and women that built the new industrial society. Their individual stories, nearly all unrecorded, reflected the achievement, drama, and pain of these years. In a number of respects, their lot improved during the last quarter of the nineteenth century. Real wages rose, working conditions got better, and the workers' influence in national affairs increased. Like others, workers also benefited from expanding health and educational services.

But life was not easy. Before 1900 most wage earners worked ten hours a day, six days a week. If skilled, they earned about twenty cents an hour; if unskilled, just about half that. On average they earned between $400 and $500 a year. It took about $600 to live decently. Construction workers, machinists, government employees, printers, clerical workers, and western miners made more than the average. Eastern coal miners, agricultural workers, garment workers, and unskilled factory hands made considerably less.

There were few holidays or vacations and little respite from the grueling routine. Work was not only grueling, it was often highly dangerous. Safety standards were low, and accidents were common. On the railroads, 1 in every 26 workers was injured, 1 in every 399 killed per year. Thousands suffered from chronic illness, unknowing victims of dust, chemicals, and other pollutants.

The breadwinner might be a woman or child; both worked in increasing numbers. Between 1870 and 1900 the number of working children rose nearly 130 percent; the percentage of working women rose from 15 to 20 percent. Most working women were young and single. Many began work at sixteen or seventeen, worked a half-dozen years or so, married, and quit. As clerical work expanded, women learned new skills like typing and stenography. Moving into formerly male occupations, they became secretaries, bookkeepers, typists, telephone operators, and clerks in the new department stores. The number of women gainfully employed rose from 2.6 million in 1880 to 4 million in 1890.

A few women—very few—became ministers, lawyers, and doctors. But change was slow, and in the 1880s some law schools were still refusing to admit women because they "had not the mentality to study law." Among women entering the profession, the overwhelming majority became nurses, schoolteachers, and librarians. In such professions a process of *feminization* occurred, in which women became a majority of the workers, a small number of men took the management roles, and most men left for other jobs, lowering the profession's status.

In most jobs, status and pay were divided unequally between men and women. Many of both sexes thought a woman's place was in the home. When employed in factories, women tended to occupy jobs that were viewed as natural extensions of household activity. They made clothes and textiles, processed food, and made cigars, tobacco, and shoes.

In general, adults earned more than children, the skilled more than the unskilled, native-born more than foreign-born, Protestants more than Catholics or Jews, and whites more than blacks or Asians. On average, women made a little more than half as much as men. These economic realities reflected bias against race, creed, or sex. In the industrial society white, native-born Protestants—the bulk of the population, though by 1900 no longer the bulk of the work force—reaped the greatest rewards.

Blacks labored on the fringes, usually in menial occupations. They earned less than other workers at almost every level of skill. On the

The typing pool of the audit division of the Metropolitan Life Insurance Co., New York, 1897. As clerical work expanded and more and more women learned new skills in order to move into this area of employment, men moved on to other jobs.

Pacific Coast, the Chinese—and later the Japanese—lived in enclaves and suffered periodic attacks of discrimination. At times immigration of both Chinese and Japanese was prohibited.

CULTURE OF WORK

Among almost all groups, industrialization shattered age-old patterns, including work habits and the culture of work. It made people adapt "older work routines to new necessities and strained those wedded to premodern patterns of labor." Men and women fresh from farms were not accustomed to the factory's disciplines. Now they worked indoors rather than out, paced themselves to the clock rather than the movements of the sun, and followed the needs of the market rather than the natural rhythms of the season. They had foremen and hierarchies and strict rules. Piece work determined wages, and always there was the relentless clock.

As industries grew larger, work became more impersonal. Machines displaced skilled artisans, and the unskilled tended them for employers they never saw. Workers picked up and left their jobs with startling frequency, and factories drew on a churning, highly mobile labor supply. Many workers were seemingly rootless, moving wherever new opportunity beckoned.

Substantial economic and social mobility accompanied the geographic mobility. The Horatio Alger stories, of course, had always said so, and careers like Andrew Carnegie's seemed to confirm it. The actual record was considerably more limited. Most business leaders in the period came from well-to-do or middle-class families of old American stock. Still, many workers made major progress during their lifetimes. Movement from the working class to the middle class was not an uncommon occurrence.

The chance for advancement played a vital role in American industrial development. It gave workers hope, wedded them to the system, and, at the same time, tempered their response to the appeal of labor unions and working-class agitation. Very few workers rose from rags to riches, but a great many rose to better jobs and higher status.

LABOR UNIONS

Weak throughout the nineteenth century, labor unions never included more than 2 percent of the total labor force nor more than 10 percent of industrial workers. To many workers, unions seemed "foreign," radical, and out of step with the American tradition of individual advancement. Craft, ethnic, and other differences fragmented the labor force, and its extraordinary mobility made organization difficult. Employers strongly opposed unions. Said one U.S. Steel executive, "If a worker sticks up his head, hit it." As the national economy emerged, however, national labor unions gradually took shape. The early unions often represented skilled workers in local areas, but in 1866 William H. Sylvis united several unions into a single national organization, the National Labor Union. Sylvis sought long-range humanitarian reforms rather than specific, bread-and-butter goals. A talented propagandist, he attracted many members, but he died in 1869, and the organization did not long survive him.

The year Sylvis died, Uriah S. Stephens and a group of Philadelphia garment workers formed a far more successful organization, the Noble and Holy Order of the Knights of Labor. A secret fraternal order, it grew slowly through the 1870s, until Terence V. Powderly ended the secrecy and embarked on an aggressive program. The Knights welcomed all laborers, regardless of skill, creed, sex, or color.

Harking back to the Jacksonians, the Knights set the "producers" against monopoly and special privilege. As members they excluded only "nonproducers"—bankers, lawyers, liquor dealers, and gamblers. Since employers were "producers," they could join; and since workers and employers had common interests, workers should not strike. The order's program included the eight-hour day and the abolition of child and prison labor, but more often it focused on uplifting, utopian reform, such as ending drunkenness and establishing worker-run factories, railroads, and mines.

Membership grew steadily—from 42,000 in 1882 to a peak of 725,000 in 1886. But neither Powderly nor the union's loose structure could handle the growth, and when Jay Gould crushed their strike on the Texas and Pacific Railroad, the Knights crumbled. In 1886 the Haymarket riot turned public sympathy against unions like the Knights. By 1890 the order had shrunk to 100,000 members. A few years later it was virtually defunct.

As the Knights waxed and waned, another organization emerged that was to endure. Founded in 1881, the American Federation of Labor (AFL) was a loose alliance of national craft unions. Unlike the Knights, it organized only skilled workers along craft lines, avoided politics, and worked for specific practical objectives. Samuel Gompers, the founder and long-time president, was determined to better the material lives of the workers. He accepted capitalism, and for labor he wanted simply a recognized place within the system and a greater share of the rewards.

Unlike Powderly, Gompers and the AFL assumed that most workers would remain workers throughout their lives. The task, then, lay in improving lives in "practical" ways: higher wages, shorter hours, and better working conditions. The AFL offered some attractive assurances to employers. As trade unionists, they would use the strike and boycott, but only to achieve limited gains, and if treated fairly, they would provide a stable labor force.

By the 1890s the AFL was the most important labor group in the country. By 1901 the organization had over a million members, or almost a third of the country's skilled workers, and by 1914 it had more than 2 million. The great majority of workers—skilled and unskilled—remained unorganized, but Gompers and the AFL had become a significant force in national life.

Although two of the AFL's national affiliates accepted women as members, others prohibited them outright, and Gompers himself often complained that women workers undercut the pay scales for men. Conditions improved after 1900, but even then unions were largely a man's world. The AFL did not expressly forbid black workers from joining, but member unions used high initiation fees, technical examinations, and other means to discourage black membership.

LABOR UNREST

Workers used various means to adjust to the factory age. To the dismay of managers and "efficiency" experts, they often dictated the pace and quality of their work, and they set the tone of the workplace. Newly arrived immigrants got jobs for friends and relatives, taught them how to deal with factory conditions, and humanized the workplace.

Many employers believed in an "iron law of wages" in which supply and demand, not the welfare of their workers, dictated wages. Wanting a docile labor force, employers fired workers who joined unions, hired scabs to replace strikers, and used a powerful new weapon, the court injunction, to quell strikes. The injunction, which forbade workers to interfere with their employers' business, was used to break the great Pullman strike of 1894 (see Chapter 20), and the Supreme Court upheld use of the injunction in *In re Debs* (1895).

As employers' attitudes hardened, strikes and violence broke out. Between 1880 and 1900 there were more than 23,000 strikes involving 6.6 million workers. The railroad strike of 1877 paralyzed railroads from West Virginia to California, resulting in the deaths of more than 100 workers, and required federal troops to suppress it. In another year, 1886, 610,000 workers were off the job because of strikes and lockouts.

The worst incident took place in Chicago. In early May 1886, police, intervening in a strike at the McCormick Harvester works, shot and killed two workers. The next evening, May 4, labor leaders called a protest meeting at Haymarket Square near downtown Chicago. The meeting was peaceful, but police ordered the crowd to disperse. Someone threw a dynamite bomb, instantly killing one policeman and fatally wounding six others. Police fired into the crowd, killing four.

No one ever discovered who threw the bomb, but many Americans demanded action against labor "radicalism." Cities strengthened their police forces and armories. Chicago police rounded up eight anarchists who were found guilty of murder on the basis of incendiary opinions. Although there was no evidence of

Anarchists called for a protest meeting and distributed these bilingual handbills (right) on the day of the Haymarket Square bombing in Chicago in 1886. This scene from Harper's Weekly *(left) was drawn from sketches and photographs made at the site moments after the bomb exploded.*

their complicity in the bomb-throwing incident, four were hanged, one committed suicide, and three were jailed.

Violence again broke out in the unsettled conditions of the 1890s. In 1892 Carnegie and Henry Clay Frick, his partner and manager, lowered wages nearly 20 percent at the Homestead steel plant. The Amalgamated Iron and Steel Workers, and AFL affiliate, struck, and Frick responded by locking the workers out of the plants. The workers surrounded it, and Frick, furious, hired a small private army of Pinkerton detectives to drive them off. Before the battle ended, the detectives were forced to surrender and thirteen people were killed.

A few days later the Pennsylvania governor ordered the state militia to impose peace at Homestead. On July 23 an anarchist named Alexander Berkman, who was not one of the strikers, walked into Frick's office and shot and stabbed him. Incredibly, Frick survived, watched the police take Berkman away, called in a doctor to bandage his wounds, and stayed in the office until closing time. In late July the Homestead works reopened under military guard, and in November the strikers gave up.

Events like those at Homestead troubled many Americans who wondered whether industrialization, for all its benefits, might carry a heavy price in social upheaval, class tensions, and even outright warfare. Most workers did not share in the immense profits of the industrial age, and as the nineteenth century came to a close, there were some who rebelled against the inequity.

In the half-century after the Civil War, the United States became the leading industrial nation in the world. On one hand, industrializa-

CHRONOLOGY

1859	First oil well drilled near Titusville, Pennsylvania
1866	William Sylvis establishes National Labor Union
1869	Transcontinental railroad completed at Promontory, Utah Knights of Labor organize
1876	Alexander Graham Bell invents the telephone Centennial Exposition held in Philadelphia
1877	Railroads cut workers' wages, leading to bloody and violent strike
1879	Thomas A. Edison invents the incandescent lamp
1881	Samuel Gompers founds American Federation of Labor (AFL)
1882	Rockefeller's Standard Oil Company becomes nation's first trust Edison opens first electric generating station in New York
1886	Labor protest erupts in violence in Haymarket Riot in Chicago Railroads adopt standard gauge
1892	Workers strike at Homestead steel plant in Pennsylvania
1901	J. P. Morgan announces formation of U.S. Steel Corporation, nation's first billion-dollar company

tion meant "progress," growth, world power, and in some sense, fulfillment of the American promise of abundance. For the bulk of the population, the standard of living—a particularly American concept—rose. But industrialization also meant rapid change, social instability, exploitation of labor, and growing disparity in income between rich and poor. Industry flourished, but control rested in fewer and fewer hands. Maturing quickly, the young system became a new corporate capitalism: giant businesses, interlocking in ownership, managed by a new professional class, and selling an expanding variety of goods in an increasingly controlled market. As goods spread through the society, so did a sharpened and aggressive materialism. Workers felt the strains of the shift to a new social order.

In 1902, a well-to-do New Yorker named Bessie Van Vorst decided to see what it was like to work for a living in a factory. Disguising herself in worn, inexpensive clothes, she went to Pittsburgh and got a job in a canning factory. She worked ten hours a day, six days a week, including four hours on Saturday afternoons when she and the other women, on hands and knees, scrubbed the tables, stands, and entire factory floor. She worked until her body ached and her hands blistered, until the noise of the machines and monotony of the labor made her dazed and weary. She earned $4.20 a week, $3 of which went for food alone. Van Vorst was lucky; she could return to her comfortable life in New York. The working men and women around her were not so fortunate. They stayed on the factory floor, and by the dint of their labor, created a new industrial society.

❧ RECOMMENDED READING

Samuel P. Hays, *The Response to Industrialism: 1885–1914* (1957) is an influential interpretation of the period. Other valuable overviews include Douglass C. North, *Growth and Welfare in the American Past: A New Economic History* (1966), and Stuart Bruchey, *Growth of the Modern Economy* (1975). Sean Dennis Cashman, *America in the Gilded Age* (1984), is a recent study.

The railroad empire is treated in G. R. Taylor and I. D. Neu, *The American Railroad Network, 1861–*

1890 (1956), and John R. Stilgoe, *Metropolitan Corridor: Railroads and the American Scene* (1983).

On the steel industry, see Peter Temin, *Iron and Steel in Nineteenth-Century America* (1964); Joseph F. Wall, *Andrew Carnegie* (1970); and John Ingham, *The Iron Barons: A Social Analysis of an American Urban Elite, 1874–1965* (1978). Edward N. Akin, *Flagler* (1968), traces the rise of Standard Oil.

For the techniques of selling see Daniel J. Boorstin, *The Americans: The Democratic Experience* (1973). Two superb books by Sam B. Warner, Jr., *Streetcar Suburbs: The Process of Growth in Boston, 1870–1900* (1962) and *The Urban Wilderness: A History of the American City* (1973), examine technology and city development. The wage earner is examined in Herbert G. Gutman, *Work, Culture, and Society in Industrializing America* (1976); Walter Licht, *Working for the Railroad: The Organization of Work in the Nineteenth Century* (1983); and Shelton Stromquist, *A Generation of Boomers: The Pattern of Railroad Labor Conflict in Nineteenth-Century America* (1987). Philip S. Foner, *Women and the American Labor Movement* 2 vols. (1979); Lois W. Banner, *Women in Modern America: A Brief History* (1974); and Milton Cantor and Bruce Laurie, eds., *Class, Sex, and the Woman Worker* (1977) are excellent.

On organized labor, see David Brody, *Steelworkers in America: The Nonunion Era* (1960); Gerald N. Grob, *Workers and Utopia: A Study of Ideological Conflict in the American Labor Movement, 1865–1900* (1961); S. B. Kaufman, *Samuel Gompers and the Origins of the American Federation of Labor* (1973); and Cindy Sondik Aron, *Ladies and Gentlemen of the Civil Service: Middle-Class Workers in Victorian America* (1987). John Laslett, *Labor and the Left: A Study of Socialist and Radical Influences in the American Labor Movement, 1881–1924* (1970) is illuminating. Paul Avrich, *The Haymarket Tragedy* (1984) is a detailed account of that event.

19 TOWARD AN URBAN SOCIETY, 1877–1890

THE LURE OF THE CITY

LIFE IN AMERICA, 1877

THE STIRRINGS OF REFORM

One day around 1900, Harriet Vittum, a settlement house worker in Chicago, went to the aid of a young Polish girl who lived in a nearby slum. The girl had discovered she was pregnant and had taken poison. When Vittum arrived at the girl's squalid three-room apartment, she found the rooms crammed with at least fourteen boarders and young children. Glancing out the window, Vittum saw the wall of another building so close she could reach out and touch it. She was struck by the girl's life in the crowded tenement, with its lack of light and air. Did she have the right, Vittum asked herself, to bring the girl back "to the misery and hopelessness of the life she was living in that awful place?"

The girl's life in the slum reflected the experience of millions of other people in the late nineteenth century. The glitter and excitement of the cities attracted people from rural America, Europe, South America, and Asia. Between 1860 and 1910 the number of people living in American cities increased sevenfold. They were lured by the prospects of greater economic opportunities, but their lives were often bleak and painful.

Two major forces reshaped American society between 1870 and 1920: *industrialization* and *urbanization*. By 1920, the city had become the center of American economic, social, and cultural life.

THE LURE OF THE CITY

Between 1870 and 1900 the city—like the factory—became a symbol of a new America. Drawn from farms, small towns, and foreign lands, newcomers swelled the population of older cities and created new ones almost overnight. At the beginning of the Civil War only one sixth of the American people lived in cities of 8000 people or more. By 1900, one third did; by 1920, one half did.

The movement to urban life brought explosive growth. Thousands of years of history had produced only a handful of cities with more than a half-million in population. In 1900 the United States had six such cities, including three—New York, Chicago, and Philadelphia—with a population over a million.

STRANGERS IN A NEW LAND

While some of the new city dwellers came from farms and small towns, many of them came from abroad. Most came from Europe, where unemployment, food shortages, and increasing threats of war sent millions fleeing across the Atlantic to make a fresh start in the United States. Italians first came in large numbers to escape an 1887 cholera epidemic in southern Italy; tens of thousands of Jews sought refuge from the pogroms (anti-Semitic massacres) that swept Russia and Poland after 1880. The immigration was so great that by 1890 about 15 percent of the population was foreign-born.

Most newcomers were job seekers. Nearly two thirds were males; most were between the ages of fifteen and forty and unskilled. They tended to crowd into northern seaboard cities, settling in areas where others of their nationality or region had settled.

They were often dazzled by what they saw. They stared at electric lights, indoor plumbing, streetcars, ice cream, lemons, and bananas. America's teeming markets, department stores, and Woolworth's new five-and-dime stores offered goods unknown in the homeland.

Cities had increasingly large foreign-born populations. In 1900 three fourths of Chicago's population was foreign-born or of foreign-born parentage, two thirds of Boston's, and one half of Philadelphia's. In New York City, where most immigrants arrived and many stayed, four out of five residents in 1890 were of foreign birth or foreign parentage.

Beginning in the 1880s, the sources of immigration shifted dramatically away from northern and western Europe, the chief source of immigration for over two centuries. More and more immigrants came from southern and eastern Europe: Italy, Greece, Austria-Hungary, Poland, and Russia. These "new" immigrants tended to be Catholic or Jews rather than Protestants, and they often spoke "strange" languages. Most were poor and uneducated; sticking together in communities, they clung to their native customs, languages, and religions.

More than any previous group, the so-called new immigrants troubled the mainstream society. Could they be assimilated? Did they share "American" values? Sneering epithets became part of the national vocabulary: "wop" and "dago" for Italians, "bohunk" for Bohemians, Hungarians, and other Slavs, "grease-ball" for Greeks, and "kike" for Jews. Anti-Catholicism and anti-Semitism led to shameful treatment of the immigrants. In 1889 the head of the Fresh Air Fund, a program that sent New York City children on vacations to the suburbs, noted that "no one asked for Italian children." By the end of the 1890s a number of organizations worked to restrict or end immigration.

IMMIGRANTS IN THE CITY

Industrial capitalism—the world of factories and machines—tested the immigrants and placed an enormous strain upon their families. Many immigrants came from peasant societies where life proceeded according to outdoor routine and age-old tradition. In their new city homes, they found both new freedoms and a novel set of customs and expectations. Historians have only recently begun to discover the remarkable ways in which they learned to adjust.

Like native-born families, most immigrant families were nuclear in structure—they consisted of two parents and their children. Generally, men were wage earners, women household managers and mothers. The father normally played a minor role in child-rearing or managing the family finances. "His to earn and hers to spend," was the standard of domestic virtue.

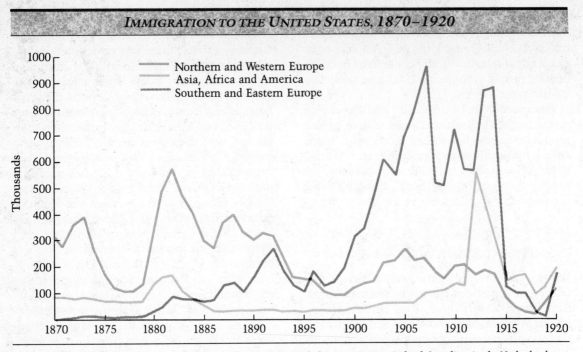

IMMIGRATION TO THE UNITED STATES, 1870–1920

Northern and Western Europe
Asia, Africa and America
Southern and Eastern Europe

Note: *For purposes of classification,* Northern and Western Europe *includes Great Britain, Ireland, Scandinavia, the Netherlands, Belgium, Luxembourg, Switzerland, France, and Germany.* Southern and Eastern Europe *includes Poland, Austria-Hungary, Russia and the Baltic States, Rumania, Bulgaria, European Turkey, Italy, Spain, Portugal, and Greece.* Asia, Africa, and America *includes Asian Turkey, China, Japan, India, Canada, the Caribbean, Latin America, and all of Africa.*

Source: U.S. Bureau of the Census, *Historical Statistics of the United States, Colonial Times to 1970,* Bicentennial Edition, Washington, D.C., 1975.

Although patterns varied between ethnic groups, and between economic classes within ethnic groups, immigrants tended to marry within the group more than did the native-born. Immigrants also tended to marry at a later age than natives, and they tended to have more children, a fact that worried nativists opposed to immigration.

Most immigrants tried to retain their traditional culture for themselves and their children while at the same time adapting to life in their new country. To do this, they spoke their native language, practiced their religious faith, read their own newspapers, established their own schools, and formed a myriad of social organizations to maintain ties between members of the group.

Immigrant associations offered fellowship in a strange land. They helped newcomers find jobs and homes; they provided important services such as unemployment and health insurance. Some groups were no larger than a neighborhood; others spread nationwide. Many women belonged to and participated in the work of the immigrant associations; in addition, there were groups exclusively for women. Such associations as the Polish National Alliance helped to keep alive Old World traditions while helping members become accustomed to American life.

Church, school, and fraternal societies shaped the way in which immigrants adjusted to life in America. East European Jews established synagogues and religious schools wherever they settled in order to preserve their ancient heritage. Among groups like the Irish and the Poles, the Roman Catholic Church provided spiritual and educational guidance. In the parish schools, Polish priests and nuns taught Polish-American children in the Polish language about Polish as well as American culture. By preserving language, religion, and heritage, they shaped the city—and the country itself—as much as it shaped them.

SKYSCRAPERS AND SUBURBS

Beginning in the 1800s a revolution in technology transformed American cities. The age of steel and glass produced the skyscraper; the streetcar produced the suburbs and new residential patterns.

On the eve of the change, American cities were a crowded jumble of small buildings. Buildings were usually made of masonry, and since the massive walls had to support their own weight, they could be no taller than a dozen or so stories. Steel frames and girders ended that limitation and allowed buildings to soar higher and higher. "Curtain walls," which concealed the steel framework, were no longer load-bearing; they were pierced by many windows that let in fresh air and light.

To a group of talented Chicago architects the new trends served as a springboard for innovative forms. The leader of the movement was Louis H. Sullivan, who had studied at M.I.T. and in Paris before settling in Chicago, attracted by the chance to rebuild the city after the great fire of 1871. In 1866, at the age of thirty, he began work on the Chicago Auditorium, one of the last great masonry buildings. Then, in a flash of imagination, he conceived the skyscraper. Sullivan's skyscrapers changed the urban skyline.

Architects must discard "books, rules, precedents," Sullivan announced; responding to the new, they should design for a building's function. "Form follows function," Sullivan believed, and he passed the idea on to a talented disciple, Frank Lloyd Wright. The modern city should stretch to the sky, "rising in sheer exaltation."

Electric elevators carried passengers upward in the new skyscrapers. During the same years streetcars carried them outward to expanded boundaries that transformed urban life. Cities were no longer largely "walking cities," confined to a radius of two or three miles, a distance an individual might walk. Streetcar systems extended the radius and changed the urban map. Cable lines, electric surface lines, and elevated rapid transit brought shoppers and workers into central business districts and sped them home again. Cheap to ride, these mass transit systems fostered commuting; widely separated business and residential districts sprang up. The middle class moved farther and farther out to the leafy greenness of the suburbs.

As the middle class moved out of the cities, the immigrants and working class poured in. They took over the older brownstones, row houses, and workers' cottages, turning them under the sheer weight of numbers into the slums of the central city. In the cities of the past classes and occupations had been thrown together. The streetcar city, sprawling and specialized, became a more fragmented and stratified society with middle-class residential rings surrounding a business and working-class core.

TENEMENTS AND PRIVIES

In the shadow of the skyscrapers grimy rows of tenements filled the central city. As Jacob Riis in *How the Other Half Lives* (1890) illustrated in words and pictures, it was a world of dark halls, poor ventilation, and squalid conditions.

Tenement houses on small city lots crowded people into cramped apartments. In 1890 nearly half the dwellings in New York City were tenements. That year more than 1.4 million people lived on Manhattan Island, one of whose wards had a population density of 334,000 people per square mile. Many people lived in alleys and basements so dark they could not be photographed until flashlight photography was invented in 1887.

Everywhere was the smell of poverty and neglect. In the 1870s and 1880s cities stank. One problem was horse manure, hundreds of tons of it a day in every city. Another was the privy, "a single one of which," said a leading authority on public health, "may render life in a whole neighborhood almost unendurable in the summer."

Cities dumped their wastes into the nearest body of water, then drew drinking water from the same site. Many built modern, purified waterworks but could not keep pace with spiraling growth. Factories, the pride of the era, polluted the urban air. At night Pittsburgh looked and sounded like "Hell with the lid off," according to contemporary observers. Smoke poured from hundreds of glass factories, iron and steel mills, and oil refineries.

Crime was another growing problem. The nation's homicide rate nearly tripled in the 1880s, much of the increase coming in the cities. Slum youths formed street gangs and committed crimes. In San Francisco the gangs gave rise to the new word "hoodlums," described by a disgusted English traveler as "young embryo criminals" who robbed and murdered at night.

After remaining constant for many decades, the suicide rate rose steadily between 1870 and 1900. Alcoholism was also on the rise, especially among men. A 1905 survey of Chicago counted as many drinking establishments as grocery stores, meat markets, and dry goods stores combined.

A view of Orchard Street, looking south from Hester Street on New York City's lower East Side in 1898. As millions emigrated to the United States during the last quarter of the nineteenth century, they crammed into already overpopulated ethnic neighborhoods, seeking others who spoke their language, practiced their religion, and followed their customs.

THE HOUSE THAT
TWEED BUILT

Closely connected with explosive urban growth was the emergence of the powerful city political machine. As cities grew, lines of responsibility in city governments became hopelessly confused, increasing the opportunity for corruption and greed. Burgeoning populations required streets, buildings, and public services; immigrants needed even more services. In this situation party machines played an important role.

The machines traded services for votes. Loosely knit, they were headed by a strong, influential leader—the "boss"—who tied together a network of ward and precinct captains, each of whom looked after his local constituents. During the second half of the nineteenth century such cities as New York City, Chicago, Philadelphia, and San Francisco developed powerful political machines.

William M. Tweed, head of the famed Tweed Ring in New York, provided the model for them all. Nearly six feet tall, weighing almost 300 pounds, Tweed rose through the ranks of the New York Democratic machine known as Tammany Hall. A man of culture and warmth, he moved easily between the rough back alleys of New York and the parlors and clubs of the city's elite. Behind the scenes he headed a ring that plundered New York for tens of millions of dollars.

The New York County Courthouse was his masterpiece. The three-story "House that Tweed Built" was designed to cost $250,000, but the bill ran a bit higher. Furniture, carpets, and window shades alone came to more than $5.5 million. In the end the building cost over $13 million—and in 1872, when Tweed fell, it was still not finished.

Some bosses were plainly corrupt; others believed in "honest graft," a term Tammany's George Washington Plunkitt coined to describe "legitimate" profits made from advance knowledge of city projects. Why did voters keep them in power? The answers are complex, but for the most part the bosses stayed in power because they paid attention to the needs of the least privileged city voters. They offered valued services in an era when neither government nor business lent a hand.

If an immigrant, tired and bewildered after the long crossing, came looking for a job, bosses like Tweed found him one in city offices or local business. If a family's breadwinner died or was injured, the bosses donated food and clothing and saw to it that the family made it through the crisis. They contributed to hospitals, orphanages, and dozens of worthy neighborhood causes.

Most bosses became wealthy; they looked after their own needs first. Reformers occasionally ousted them. But reformers rarely stayed in power long. Drawn mainly from the middle and upper classes, they had little understanding of the needs of the poor. Before long they returned to private concerns, and the bosses cheerily took power again.

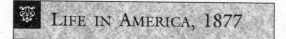

LIFE IN AMERICA, 1877

From 1877 to the 1890s the nation underwent sweeping changes that affected economic, political, and social life. Technology changed mores; bright lights and new careers drew young men and women to the cities; family ties loosened. Cities, suburbs, and factories took new forms. While many people worked harder and harder, others had increased leisure time. Thanks to advancing technology, news flashed quickly across the oceans, and for the first time in history people shook open their evening newspapers to read of that day's events in distant lands.

Old issues—those of racial, social and economic justice, and of federal-state relations— were not settled, but people wanted new directions. Political issues lost the sharp focus of the Civil War and Reconstruction. With the end of Reconstruction, concern over the Union and slavery faded into the past.

In 1877 the country had 47 million people. A little more than a decade later there were nearly 63 million. Nine tenths of the population was white; just under one tenth was black. The bulk of the white population, most of whom were Protestant, came from the so-called Anglo-Saxon countries of northern Europe. WASPS—White Anglo-Saxon Protestants—dominated American society.

Most people still lived on farms or in small towns. Their lives revolved around the farm, the church, and the general store. In 1880 nearly 75 percent of the population lived in communities of fewer than 2500 people. In 1900, in the midst of city growth, 60 percent still did. The average family in 1880 had three children, and life expectancy was about forty-three years. By 1900 it had risen to forty-seven years, the result of improved health care. For blacks and other minorities, often living in unsanitary rural areas, life expectancy was substantially lower: thirty-three years in 1900.

Toward the end of the century eating habits changed. New packaged breakfast cereals became popular, fresh fruit and vegetables came in on fast trains from Florida and California, and commercially canned food processing became safer and cheaper. The newfangled ice box, cooled by blocks of ice, kept food fresher.

Medical science was in the midst of a major revolution. Louis Pasteur's recent discovery that germs cause infection and disease created the new science of microbiology and led the way to the development of vaccines and other preventive measures. But tuberculosis, typhoid, diphtheria, and pneumonia—all now curable—were still the leading causes of death. Many families knew the wrenching pain of a child's death. Infant mortality declined between 1877 and 1900, but the great drop did not come until after 1920.

There were few hospitals and no hospital insurance. Most patients stayed at home, although medical practice expanded rapidly. In the field of surgery, anesthetics—ether and chloroform—eliminated pain, and antiseptic practices helped prevent postoperative infections. An earlier discovery—nitrous oxide, called laughing gas—eased the discomfort of dentistry. The new science of psychology began to explore the mind, hitherto uncharted. Wil-liam James, a leading American psychologist and philosopher, stressed the importance of the environment on human development.

MANNERS AND MORES

The code of Victorian morality set the tone for the era. The code prescribed stern standards of dress, manners, and sexual behavior. It was both obeyed and disobeyed, and it reflected the tensions of a generation that was undergoing a change in moral standards.

In 1877 children were to be seen and not heard. They spoke when spoken to, listened rather than chattered—or at least that was the ideal. Older boys and girls were often chaperoned, although they could always find moments alone. They played post office and spin the bottle; they puffed cigarettes behind the barn. Counterbalancing such youthful exuberance was strong pride in virtue and self-control. "Thank heaven I am absolutely pure," Theodore Roosevelt wrote in 1880 after proposing to Alice Lee. "I can tell Alice everything I have ever done."

Gentlemen of the middle class dressed in heavy black suits, derby hats, and white shirts with paper collars. Women wore tight corsets; long, dark dresses; and black shoes reaching well above the ankles. As with so many things, styles changed dramatically toward the end of the century, spurred in part by new sporting fads such as golf, tennis, and bicycling, which required looser clothing. Middle-class women adopted tailored suits and "shirtwaist" blouses modeled after men's shirts.

Religious and patriotic values were strong. One of the centers of community life, the church often set the tenor for family and social relationships. In the 1880s eight out of ten church members were Protestants; most of the rest were Roman Catholics. Evangelists like Dwight L. Moody conducted successful mass revival meetings across the country.

With slavery abolished, reformers turned their attention to new moral and political issues. One group, known as the Mugwumps, worked to end corruption in politics. Drawn mostly from the educated and upper class, they included important newspaper and magazine editors. Other zealous reformers campaigned for prohibition of the sale of intoxicating liquors, hoping to end the social evils that stemmed from drunkenness. In 1874 the Women's Christian Temperance Union was formed to combat the consumption of alcohol. By 1898 the WCTU had 10,000 branches and 500,000 members.

In New York City, Anthony Comstock formed the Society for the Suppression of Vice, which supervised public morality. At his behest Congress passed the Comstock Law (1873) prohibiting the mailing or transporting of "obscene, lewd or lascivious" articles. The law was not successful, and Comstock reported frequent violations of the act.

LEISURE AND ENTERTAINMENT

In the 1870s people tended to rise early. After dressing and eating, they went off to work and school; housewives marketed daily. In the evenings, families gathered in the "second parlor" or living room, where the children did their lessons, played games, sang around the piano, and listened to the day's verse from the Bible.

Indoor popular games included cards, dominoes, backgammon, chess, and checkers. Many of them were instructional as well as entertaining. The newest outdoor game was croquet, so popular that candles were mounted on the wickets to allow play at night. It was the first outdoor game designed for play by both sexes, and it frequently served as a setting for courtship.

New York's Broadway was the center of the theater, but road shows took popular plays to many cities and towns. American taste in the theater ran to intrigue, swordplay, melodrama, and grandiloquent language. Most plays were imported from Europe; the United States had few serious playwrights.

Sentimental ballads remained the most popular musical form, but the insistent syncopated rhythms of ragtime were being heard. By the time the strains of Scott Joplin's "Maple Leaf Rag" (1899) popularized ragtime, critics complained that "a wave of vulgar, filthy and suggestive music has inundated the land." Critics of ragtime took more comfort from the growth of classical music, which flourished during these years.

In the hamlets and small towns of America traveling circuses were enormously popular. The larger circuses, run by entrepreneurs like P. T. Barnum and James A. Bailey, played the cities, but every town attracted its own smaller versions. When the circus left town, Buffalo Bill's Wild West Show arrived, reenacting Indian field battles and displaying frontier marksmanship.

Football and baseball contests attracted avid fans. The years between 1870 and 1900 saw the rise of organized spectator sports, a trend reflecting the new uses of leisure. Baseball's first professional team, the Cincinnati Red Stockings, appeared in 1869, and baseball soon became the preeminent national sport. In 1869 Princeton and Rutgers played the first intercollegiate football game. Soon other schools picked up the sport, and by the early 1890s crowds of 50,000 or more attended the most popular contests. Boxing, although outlawed in most states, also gained a large following. John L. Sullivan, the era's most popular champion, won the last bare-knuckle heavyweight championship fight when he defeated Jake Kilrain in 1889 in a brutal seventy-five-round contest.

As gas and electric lights brightened the night, and streetcars crisscrossed city streets, leisure habits changed. With so many things to do, people stayed home less often. New York City's first electric sign appeared in 1881, and people filled the streets on their way to the theater, vaudeville shows, dance halls, or just out for an evening stroll.

FAMILY LIFE

Industrialization and urbanization changed family relationships. On the farm parents and children worked more or less together, and the family was a producing unit. In factories, family members rarely worked together. In working-class families, mothers, fathers, and children separated at dawn and returned, ready for sleep, at dark. Middle-class fathers began to move their families out of the city to the suburbs; they commuted to work on the new streetcars, leaving wives and children at home and school.

Increasingly, middle-class wives and children became isolated from the world of work. Unlike the rural or urban working-class—where mothers and children as well as fathers labored to support the family economy—middle-class families turned inward. Older children spent more time in adolescence, and periods of formal schooling were lengthier. Fewer wives participated directly in their husbands' work. As a result, they and their children occupied what contemporaries called a "separate sphere of domesticity," a place apart from the crass materialism of the outside world.

As the middle-class family's economic function declined, it took on increased emotional significance. "In the old days," said a woman in 1907, "a married woman was supposed to be a frump and a bore and a physical wreck. Now you are supposed to keep up intellectually, to look young and well and be fresh and bright and entertaining." Nonetheless, while society's leaders spoke fondly of the value of homemaking, the status of housewives declined under the factory system, which emphasized money rewards and devalued household labor.

Underlying all these changes was one of the modern world's most important trends, a major decline in fertility rates that lasted from 1800 to 1939. Though blacks, immigrants, and rural dwellers continued to have more children than white native city dwellers, the trend affected all races and classes. Late marriages partially accounted for the decline, but a more important factor was the conscious decision by women and men to postpone or limit families. In some cases, women decided to devote greater attention to a smaller number of children, in other cases to pursue their own careers. In large part, the decline in fertility stemmed from people's responses to the social and economic forces around them, the rise of cities and industry. As a result, they reshaped some of the fundamental attitudes and institutions of American society.

CHANGING VIEWS: A GROWING ASSERTIVENESS AMONG WOMEN

In and out of the family, there was a growing recognition of the self-sufficient working woman who was entering the work force in increasing numbers. Most were single and worked because of economic necessity. For many Americans, this "New Woman" was regarded as a threat, a corruption of the ideal woman of men's imaginations who was viewed as innocent, helpless, and good.

Views changed, albeit slowly. One important change occurred in the legal codes pertaining to women, particularly in the common law doctrine of *femme couverte*. Under that doctrine, wives were chattel of their husbands; they could not legally control their own earnings, property, or children unless they had drawn up a specific contract before marriage. By 1890 many states had substantially revised the doctrine to allow wives control of their own earnings and inherited property. In cases of divorce, which rose sharply in the last third of the century, the new laws also recognized women's rights to custody or joint custody of their children.

In the 1870s and 1880s a growing number of women were asserting their humanness and seeking self-fulfillment. Increasing interest in medical and psychological studies led women like Charlotte Perkins Gilman, author of *Women and Economics* (1898) to argue that what men called womanly "innocence" was really ignorance; they began approaching old taboos—menstruation, sexual intercourse, and childbirth—as natural functions and appropriate subjects of open inquiry.

More and more women were willing to voice their opinions about public policy, too, espousing causes with new fervor. They fought for the vote, lobbied for equal pay, and protested against price-gouging by merchants, sometimes taking to the streets in organized demonstrations. Susan B. Anthony, fined $100 (which she refused to pay) when she tried to vote in the presidential election of 1872, helped form the National American Woman Suffrage

Association in 1890 to work for female enfranchisement (see Chapter 22).

EDUCATING THE MASSES

Continuing a trend that stretched back a hundred years, childhood was becoming a distinct time of life. There was still only a vague concept of adolescence, but the role of children was changing. Children were perceived less as "little adults" valued for the additional financial gain they might bring into the family. Now children were to grow and learn and be nurtured rather than rushed into adulthood.

As a result, schooling became more important, and American educators came closer than ever before to universal education. More states and territories made school attendance compulsory, more public schools were constructed, and more money was spent on education. Between 1870 and 1900 illiteracy declined from 20 percent to just over 10 percent of the population. Still, even as late as 1900, the average adult had only five years of schooling.

Most schools stressed a highly structured curriculum, focused on discipline and routine in a rigid environment. School began early; boys attended all day, but girls often stayed home after lunch, since it was thought they needed less in the way of learning. On the teacher's command, students stood and recited from *Webster's Spellers* and *McGuffey's Readers*, the period's two most popular textbooks, which taught ethics, values, and religion as well as reading. In the *Readers* boys grew up to be heroes, girls to be mothers, and hard work always meant success.

The South lagged far behind in education. Family size was about twice as large as in the North, and a greater proportion of the population lived in isolated rural areas. Many southern states refused to adopt compulsory education laws. Most important, Southerners insisted on maintaining separate school systems to segregate the races. Supported by the 1896 United States Supreme Court decision in *Plessy* v. *Ferguson*, segregated schooling added a devastating financial burden to education in the South.

North Carolina and Alabama mandated segregated schools in 1876, South Carolina and Louisiana in 1877, Mississippi in 1878, and Virginia in 1882. The laws often implied that the schools would be "separate but equal," but they rarely were. In 1890 only 35 percent of black children attended school in the South; 55 percent of white children did. That year nearly two thirds of the country's black population was illiterate.

Educational techniques changed after the 1870s. Educators paid more attention to early elementary education. The kindergarten movement, started in St. Louis in 1873, spread across the country. In kindergartens, four- to six-year-olds learned by playing, not by rigid discipline. For older children, social reformers advocated "practical" courses in manual training and homemaking. For the first time education became a field of university study. Teacher training became increasingly professional. By 1900 there were 345 normal schools, or teacher-training institutions, throughout the United States.

HIGHER EDUCATION

Nearly 150 new colleges and universities opened in the twenty years between 1880 and 1900. The Morrill Land Grant Act of 1862 gave large grants of land to the states for the establishment of colleges to teach "agriculture and the mechanic arts." The act fostered sixty-nine "land-grant" institutions. Private philanthropy, born of the large fortunes of the industrial age, also spurred growth in higher education. Leland Stanford gave $24 million to endow Stanford University, and John D. Rockefeller gave $34 million to found the University of Chicago.

As universities increased, their function changed, and their curriculum broadened. No longer did they exist primarily to train young men for the ministry. They moved away from the classical curriculum of rhetoric, mathematics, Latin, and Greek toward "reality and practicality." The Massachusetts Institute of Technology (M.I.T.), founded in 1861, focused on science and engineering.

Influenced by the new German universities, which emphasized specialized research, Johns Hopkins University in Baltimore opened the nation's first separate graduate school in 1876. By 1900 more than 9000 Americans had studied in Germany, and some of them returned home to become presidents of institutions such as Harvard, Yale, Columbia, the University of Chicago, and Johns Hopkins.

One of them, Charles W. Eliot, who became president of Harvard in 1869 at the age of thirty-five, set up an elective system in which students chose their own courses rather than following a rigidly prescribed curriculum. Lectures and discussions replaced rote recitation, and courses in the natural and social sciences, fine arts, and modern languages multiplied.

Educational opportunities also increased for women. A number of women's colleges opened, including Vassar (1865), Wellesley (1875), Smith (1875), and Radcliffe (1893). The landgrant colleges of the Midwest, open to women from the outset, spurred a nationwide trend toward coeducation. By 1900 women made up about 40 percent of college students.

Fewer opportunities existed for blacks and other minorities. Most colleges did not accept minorities, and few applied. W.E.B. Du Bois, the brilliant black sociologist and civil rights leader, attended Harvard in the late 1880s but found the society of Harvard Yard closed against him. Black students turned to black colleges such as Hampton Normal and Industrial Institute in Virginia, which were often supported by whites who favored manual training for blacks. At the Tuskegee Institute in Alabama, which opened in 1881, Booker T. Washington, an ex-slave, put into practice his educational ideals. By 1900 Tuskegee was a model industrial and agricultural training school. It offered instruction in thirty trades to 1400 students.

Washington stressed patience, manual training, and hard work. Rather than fighting for equal rights, blacks should acquire property and show they were worthy of their rights. Outlined most forcefully in Washington's speech in Atlanta, the philosophy became known as the Atlanta Compromise; many whites and some blacks welcomed it. Acknowledging white domination, it called for slow progress through self-improvement, not through lawsuits or agitation. But Washington did believe in black equality. Often secretive in his methods, he

The printing shop at Booker T. Washington's Tuskegee Institute in Alabama. Although Washington emphasized the importance of vocational training, students at Tuskegee also received instruction in the liberal arts and sciences.

worked behind the scenes to organize black voters and lobby against harmful laws. In his own way, he bespoke a racial pride that contributed to the rise of black nationalism in the twentieth century.

Du Bois wanted a more aggressive strategy. Born in 1868, the son of poor parents, he studied at Fisk University in Tennessee and the University of Berlin before he went to Harvard. Unable to find a teaching job in a white college, he took a low-paying research position at the University of Pennsylvania. He had no office but did not need one. Du Bois used the new discipline of sociology, which emphasized factual observation in the field, to study the condition of blacks.

Notebook in hand, he set out to examine crime in Philadelphia's black Seventh Ward. He interviewed 5000 people, mapped and classified neighborhoods, and produced *The Philadelphia Negro* (1898), a book of nearly a thousand pages. The first study of the effect of urban life on blacks, it cited a wealth of statistics, all suggesting that crime in the ward stemmed not from inborn degeneracy but from the environment in which blacks lived. Change the environment, and people would change, too; education was a good way to go about it. Calling for integrated schools with equal opportunity for all, Du Bois also urged blacks to educate their "talented tenth," a highly trained intellectual elite, to lead them.

Throughout higher education there was increased emphasis on professional training, particularly in medicine, dentistry, and law. Enrollments swelled, even as standards of admissions tightened. Doctors, lawyers, and others became part of a growing middle class that shaped the concerns of the Progressive era (see Chapter 22).

Although fewer than 5 percent of the college-age population attended college between 1877 and 1890, the new trends had great impact. A generation of men and women encountered new ideas that changed their views of themselves and society. Many students emerged from American colleges with a heightened sense of the social problems facing the nation and the belief that they could help cure society's ills.

THE STIRRINGS OF REFORM

Intellectual beliefs of the period emphasized the slow process of evolution rather than radical reform. This stress on the slow pace of change reflected the doctrine of Social Darwinism, based on the evolutionary theories of Charles Darwin and the writings of English social philosopher Herbert Spencer. In several influential books Spencer applied Darwinian principles of natural selection to society, combining biology and sociology in a theory of "social selection" that explained human progress. Like animals, society evolved, slowly, by adapting to the environment. The "survival of the fittest"—a term Spencer, not Darwin, invented—preserved the strong and weeded out the weak.

Social Darwinism had a number of influential followers in the United States, including William Graham Sumner, a prominent professor at Yale University and forceful writer. He argued that government action on behalf of the poor or weak interfered with evolution and sapped the species. Reform tampered with the laws of nature and was ultimately harmful to society as a whole.

The influence of Social Darwinism on American thinking has been exaggerated, but in the powerful hands of Sumner and others it did influence some journalists, ministers, and policymakers. Between 1877 and the 1890s, however, it came under increasing attack. In fields such as religion, economics, politics, literature, and law, thoughtful people raised questions about established conditions and suggested the need for reform.

NEW CURRENTS IN SOCIAL THOUGHT

Henry George's nationwide best-seller *Progress and Poverty* (1879) led the way to a more critical appraisal of American society in the 1880s and beyond. The book jolted traditional thought by questioning the assumptions of Social Darwinism.

"The present century," he wrote, "has been marked by a prodigious increase in wealth-producing power. . . . It was natural to expect, and it was expected, that . . . real poverty [would become] a thing of the past." Such, however, was not the case. Instead, he argued, "the wealthy class is becoming more wealthy; but the poorer class is becoming more dependent."

George proposed a simple solution. Land formed the basis for wealth; a "single tax" on it, replacing all other taxes, would equalize wealth and raise revenue to help the poor. "Single-tax" clubs sprang up around the country, but George's solution, simplistic and unappealing, had much less impact than his analysis of the problem itself. He raised questions a generation of readers set out to answer.

George's emphasis on deprivation in the environment excited a young country lawyer in Ashtabula, Ohio, Clarence Darrow. Unlike the Social Darwinists, Darrow was sure that criminals were made and not born. They grew out of "the unjust condition of human life." In the mid-1880s he left for Chicago and a forty-year career working to convince people that poverty lay at the root of crime.

As Darrow rejected the implications of Social Darwinism, in similar fashion did Richard T. Ely and a group of young economists poke holes in traditional economic thought. Ely attacked classical economics for its dogmatism, simple faith in laissez-faire, and reliance on self-interest as a guide for human conduct. He refused to "acknowledge laissez-faire as an excuse for doing nothing while people starve."

In 1885 Ely led a small band of rebels in founding the American Economic Association, which linked economics to social problems and urged government intervention in economic affairs. Social critic Thorstein Veblen saw economic laws as a mask for human greed. In *The Theory of the Leisure Class* (1899), Veblen analyzed the "predatory wealth" and "conspicuous consumption" of the business class.

Lawyer Edward Bellamy dreamed of a cooperative society where poverty, greed, and crime no longer existed. Bellamy published *Looking Backward, 2000–1887* in 1887 and became a national reform figure virtually overnight. The novel's protagonist, Julian West, falls asleep in 1887 and awakes in the year 2000. He finds himself in a socialist utopia where cooperation, rather than competition, is the watchword. The vision captured the imagination of many Americans, who responded by calling for the nationalization of public utilities and a wider distribution of wealth.

Walter Rauschenbusch, a young Baptist minister, read widely from the writings of Bellamy, George, and other social reformers. When he took his first church post in Hell's Kitchen, a blighted area of New York City, he soon discovered the weight of the slum environment. In the 1890s Rauschenbusch became a professor at the Rochester Theological Seminary, and he began to expound on the responsibility of organized religion to advance social justice.

Some Protestant sects stressed individual salvation and a better life in the next world, not in this one. Poverty was evidence of sinfulness; the poor had only themselves to blame. Wealth and destitution, suburbs and slums—all formed part of God's plan.

Challenging those traditional doctrines, a number of churches in the 1880s began establishing missions in the city slums. Living among the poor and homeless, the urban missionaries grew impatient with religious doctrines that endorsed the status quo. Instead, many of them supported the emerging religious philosophy known as the "Social Gospel," which focused on improving living conditions as well as saving souls. Churches became centers for social uplift as well as religious activity.

The most active Social Gospel leader was Washington Gladden, a Congregational minister and prolific writer. Linking Christianity to the social and economic environment, Gladden spent a lifetime working for "social salvation." Emphasizing a fellowship of love, he denounced competition, urged an "industrial partnership" between employers and employees, and called for efforts to help the poor.

THE SETTLEMENT HOUSES

A growing number of social workers, living in the urban slums, shared Gladden's concern.

Jane Addams (right) founded Hull House in Chicago in 1889. The settlement house
provided recreational and day-care facilities, offered extension classes in academic,
vocational, and artistic subjects, and above all, sought to bring hope to poverty-stricken
slum dwellers. A member of Addams' staff (left) admires the work of a participant in a Hull
House painting class.

Like Tweed and Plunkitt, they appreciated the dependency of the poor; unlike them, they wanted to eradicate the conditions that underlay it.

Youthful, idealistic, and mostly middle-class, these social workers established settlement houses to help the poor. In 1886 the first such house was opened in New York City; by 1910 there were more than 400. Reformers such as Jane Addams, who established the famous Hull House in Chicago (1889), wanted to bridge the socioeconomic gap between rich and poor and to bring education, culture, and hope to the slums. They sought to create in the heart of the city the values and sense of community of small-town America.

Many of the settlement workers were women, some of them college graduates who found that society had little use for their tal-

ents and energy. When Jane Addams opened Hull House she was twenty-nine years old. Endowed with a forceful and winning personality, she intended "to share the lives of the poor" and humanize the industrial city. Her staff stressed education, offering classes in elementary English and Shakespeare, lectures on ethics and the history of art, and courses in cooking, sewing, and manual skills.

Like settlement workers in other cities, Addams and her colleagues studied the immigrants in nearby tenements. Finding people of eighteen different nationalities living within one square mile of Hull House, they taught them American history and the English language, yet also encouraged them—through folk festivals and arts—to preserve their heritage. Other settlement workers—among them Robert Woods in Boston and Lillian Wald in New

CHRONOLOGY

1862 Morrill Land Grant gives land to states for establishment of colleges

1869 Rutgers and Princeton play in nation's first intercollegiate football game
Cincinnati Red Stockings, baseball's first professional team, organized

1873 Comstock Law bans obscene articles from U.S. mail
Nation's first kindergarten opens in St. Louis, Missouri

1874 Women's Christian Temperance Union formed to crusade against evils of liquor

1876 Johns Hopkins University opens first separate graduate school

1879 Henry George analyzes problems of urbanizing America in *Progress and Poverty*
Salvation Army arrives in United States

1881 Booker T. Washington opens Tuskegee Institute in Alabama

1883 Metropolitan Opera opens in New York

1885 Home Insurance Building, country's first metal-frame structure, erected in Chicago

1887 Edward Bellamy promotes idea of socialist utopia in *Looking Backward, 2000–1887*

1889 Jane Addams opens Hull House in Chicago

1890 National American Woman Suffrage Association formed to work for women's right to vote

1894 Immigration Restriction League formed to limit immigration from southern and eastern Europe

1896 Supreme Court decision in *Plessy* v. *Ferguson* establishes constitutionality of "separate but equal" facilities
John Dewey's Laboratory School for testing and practice of new educational theory opens at University of Chicago

York City—concentrated on such social and human problems as hunger, school dropout, exploitive child labor, and the health care of the poor.

A CRISIS IN SOCIAL WELFARE

When the depression of 1893 struck (see Chapter 20), it jarred the young settlement workers, many of whom had just begun their work. In cities and towns across the country traditional methods of helping the needy foundered in the crisis. Gradually, a new class of professional social workers arose to fill the need. Unlike the church and charity volunteers, these social workers wanted not only to feed the poor but also to study their condition and alleviate it. Revealingly they called themselves "case workers" and daily collected data on the income, housing, jobs, health, and habits of the poor. Prowling tenement districts, they gathered information about the number of rooms, number of occupants, ventilation, and sanitation, putting together a fund of useful data.

Studies of the poor popped up everywhere. Walter Wyckoff embarked in 1891 on what he called "an experiment in reality." For eighteen months he worked as an unskilled laborer in jobs from Connecticut to California. Wyckoff summarized his findings in *The Workers* (1897), a book immediately hailed as a major contribution to sociology. Following Wyckoff's lead, other investigators examined the lives of domestic servants, miners, lumberjacks, and factory laborers. Calls for reform of urban life grew louder, spawning numerous task forces and civic organizations committed to that purpose.

"The United States was born in the country and moved to the city," historian Richard Hofstadter said. Much of that movement occurred during the nineteenth century when the United States was the most rapidly urbanizing nation in the Western world. American cities bustled with energy; they absorbed millions of migrants from Europe and other parts of the world. The migration, and the urban growth that accompanied it, reshaped American politics and culture.

By 1920 the census showed that, for the first time, most Americans lived in the cities. By then, too, almost half the population was descended from people who arrived after the American Revolution. As European, African, and Asian cultures met in the American city, a culturally pluralistic society emerged. Dozens of nationalities produced a culture whose members considered themselves Polish Americans, African Americans, and Irish Americans. Still, the metaphor of the melting pot clearly depicted a new national image. In the decades after the 1870s a jumble of ethnic and racial groups responded to the challenges of industrialization and urbanization.

❧ RECOMMENDED READING

On urban America, see Sam Bass Warner, Jr., *Streetcar Suburbs* (1962) and *The Urban Wilderness* (1972); Constance M. Green, *The Rise of Urban America* (1975); and Patricia Mooney Melvin, *The Organic City: Urban Definition & Community Organization, 1880–1920* (1987). Kenneth T. Jackson, *Crabgrass Frontier: The Suburbanization of the United States* (1985), is a recent treatment of the growth of suburbs. For youth, age, and family life see Carl N. Degler, *At Odds: Women and the Family in America From the Revolution to the Present* (1980); Joseph Kett, *Rites of Passage: Adolescence in America* (1977); and Carole Haber, *Beyond Sixty-Five: The Dilemma of Old Age in America's Past* (1983).

Robert V. Bruce, *The Launching of Modern American Science, 1846–1876* (1987); Wolfgang Schivelbusch, *Disenchanted Night: The Industrialization of Light in the Nineteenth Century* (1988); and Cecelia Tichi, *Shifting Gears: Technology, Literature, Culture in Modernist America* (1987), are helpful on science and technology.

For education see L. A. Cremin, *The Transformation of the School: Progressivism in American Education, 1876–1956* (1961); Lawrence Veysey, *The Emergence of the American University* (1965); Wayne E. Fuller, *The Old Country School* (1982); and David B. Tyack, *The One Best System: A History of American Urban Education* (1974). Donald Spivey, *Schooling for the New Slavery: Black Industrial Education, 1868–1915* (1978), Louis R. Harlan, *Booker T. Washington: The Making of a Black Leader, 1865–1901* (1973); Robert L. McCaul, *The Black Struggle For Public Schooling in Nineteenth-Century Illinois* (1987); James D. Anderson, *The Education of Blacks in the South, 1860–1935* (1988); and Gerald David Jaynes, *Branches Without Roots: Genesis of the Black Working Class in the American South, 1862–1882* (1986) are good.

Oscar Handlin, *The Uprooted* (1973), and John Higham, *Strangers in the Land: Patterns of American Nativism* (1955), are classic studies. Robert H. Bremner, *From the Depths: The Discovery of Poverty in the United States* (1956); Dorothy Rose Blumberg, *Florence Kelley: The Making of a Social Pioneer* (1971); Judith Ann Trolander, *Professionalism and Social Change: From the Settlement House Movement to Neighborhood Centers, 1886 to the Present* (1987); Allen F. Davis, *Spearheads for Reform: The Social Settlements and the Progressive Movement, 1890–1914* (1967); and *American Heroine: The Life and Legend of Jane Addams* (1973), also by Allen F. Davis, examine urban reform.

On leisure and entertainment, see Gunther Barth, *City People* (1980). David J. Pivar, *Purity Crusade: Sexual Morality and Social Control, 1868–1900* (1973); Susan Estabrook Kennedy, *If All We Did Was to Weep at Home: A History of White Working Class*

Women in America (1979); Alice Kessler-Harris, *Out to Work: A History of Wage-Earning Women in the United States* (1982); Faye E. Dudden, *Serving Women: Household Service in Nineteenth-Century America* (1983); Lois W. Banner, *American Beauty* (1983); Golora Moldow, *Women Doctors in Gilded-Age Washington: Race, Gender, and Professionalization* (1987); and Martha Banta, *Imaging American Women: Idea and Ideals in Cultural History* (1987), are helpful.

For immigration and urban growth, consult Barbara Solomon, *Ancestors and Immigrants* (1956); Josef J. Barton, *Peasants and Strangers: Italians, Rumanians, and Slovaks in an American City* (1975); and Moses Rischin, *The Promised City: New York's Jews* (1962). For one of the era's leading architects, see Robert Twombly, *Louis Sullivan: His Life and Work* (1986).

20 POLITICAL REALIGNMENTS IN THE 1890s

POLITICS OF STALEMATE

REPUBLICANS IN POWER: TARIFFS, TRUSTS, AND SILVER

THE RISE OF THE POPULIST MOVEMENT

THE CRISIS OF THE DEPRESSION

CHANGING ATTITUDES

THE PRESIDENTIAL ELECTION OF 1896

THE MCKINLEY ADMINISTRATION

In mid-February 1893, panic suddenly hit the New York stock market. In one day investors dumped a million shares of a leading company, the Philadelphia and Reading Railroad, and it went bankrupt. Business investment dropped sharply in the railroad and construction industries, touching off the worst economic turndown to that point in the country's history.

Frightened, people hurriedly sold stocks and other assets to buy gold, which depleted the gold reserve of the United States Treasury. On April 22, for the first time since the 1870s, the Treasury's reserve fell below $100 million.

The news shattered business confidence— the stock market broke. On May 3 railroad and industrial stocks plummeted, and the next day several major firms went bankrupt. On May 5

leading stocks plunged to record lows, and there was pandemonium on the floor and in the streets outside. It was a day of terrible strain.

Afterward, banks cut back on loans. Unable to get capital, businesses failed at an average rate of two dozen a day during the month of May. Banks closed their doors; people hoarded their money. On July 26 the Erie Railroad, one of the leading names in railroading history, failed.

August 1893 was the worst month. Across the country factories and mines shut down. In Orange, New Jersey, Thomas A. Edison, the symbol of the country's ingenuity, laid off 240 employees at the Edison Phonograph Works. On August 15 the Northern Pacific Railroad went bankrupt; the Union Pacific and the Santa Fe soon followed. Some economists estimated

A run on a New York bank during the panic of 1893. The stock market crashed on June 27, and by the end of the year, nearly 500 banks had closed.

unemployment at 2 million people or nearly 15 percent of the labor force.

Homeless and starving people crowded every city. Charity societies and churches tried to help, but they could not handle the huge numbers of needy in the cities, and they did not even reach the farms. One woman in Kansas wrote in June 1894: "I take my pen in hand to let you know we are starving."

Continuing through 1897, the depression was the decisive event of the decade. At its height, 3 million people were unemployed. The human costs were enormous, even among the well-to-do. Thanks to city lights and new entertainment, the decade became known as the Gay Nineties, but it was hardly that. When it was over, prosperity had returned, and the

United States had crushed Spain in a brief and popular war (see Chapter 21). Yet the depression had profound and lasting effects. Attitudes changed, above all in politics. A realignment of the American political system, which had been developing since the end in Reconstruction, finally reached its fruition in the 1890s, establishing new patterns that lasted well into the twentieth century.

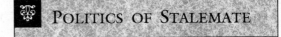

POLITICS OF STALEMATE

Electoral politics was a major fascination of the Gilded Age, its mass entertainment and favorite sport. Millions of Americans read party newspapers, listened to three-hour speeches by party leaders, and in elections turned out in enormous numbers to vote. In the six presidential elections between 1876 and 1896, an average of almost 80 percent of the electorate voted.

White males made up the bulk of the electorate; until after the turn of the century women could vote in national elections in only four western states. In 1875 the Supreme Court (*Minor* v. *Happersett*) upheld the power of the states to deny this right to women, while Congress continued to refuse to pass a constitutional amendment for women's suffrage. In addition, black men were increasingly kept from the polls by various methods. In 1877 Georgia adopted the poll tax, which forced voters to pay an annual tax for the right to vote. It was a tax few blacks could afford to pay. In 1898 Louisiana adopted the famous "grandfather clause," demanding a literacy test for all voters except the sons and grandsons of those who had voted in the state before 1867—a time, of course, when no blacks could vote. The number of registered black voters in Louisiana decreased from 130,334 in 1896 to 1342 in 1904.

THE PARTY DEADLOCK

The 1870s and 1880s were still dominated by the Civil War generation, the unusual group of people who rose to power in the turbulent 1850s. Five of the six presidents elected between 1865 and 1900 had served in the war, as had many civic, business, and religious leaders.

Party loyalties—rooted within Civil War traditions, ethnic and religious differences, and perhaps class distinctions—were remarkably strong. Although linked to the defeated Confederacy, the Democrats revived quickly after the war. In 1874 they gained control of the House of Representatives, which they maintained for all but four of the succeeding twenty years. While identification with civil rights and military rule cut Republican strength in the South, the Democratic party's principles of states' rights, decentralization, and limited government won supporters everywhere.

The Republicans pursued policies in which local interests merged into nationwide patterns, and government became an instrument to promote moral well-being and material wealth. The Republicans passed the Homestead Act (1862), granted subsidies to the transcontinental railroads, and pushed other measures to encourage economic growth. They also enacted legislation to protect civil rights and advocated a high protective tariff as a tool of economic policy.

In national elections, sixteen states, mostly in New England and the North, consistently voted Republican; fourteen states, mostly in the South, consistently voted Democratic. Elections, therefore, depended on a handful of "doubtful" states—New York, New Jersey, Connecticut, Ohio, Indiana, and Illinois—which received special attention at election time. Presidential candidates usually came from these states. From 1868 to 1912 eight of the nine Republican presidential candidates and six of the seven Democratic candidates came from the "doubtful" states, especially New York and Ohio.

The two parties were evenly matched, and elections were closely fought. In three of the five presidential elections between 1876 and 1892, the victor won by less than 1 percent of the vote; in 1876 and 1888 the losing candidates actually had more popular votes than the winners but lost in the electoral college. Knowing that small mistakes could lose elections,

politicians became extremely cautious. It was difficult to govern. Only twice during these years did one party control both the presidency and the two houses of Congress.

Historians once believed that politicians accomplished little between 1877 and 1900, but they were wrong. With the impeachment of Andrew Johnson, the authority of the presidency dwindled in relation to congressional strength. For the first time in many years power rested in Congress and, even more importantly, in state and local governments.

EXPERIMENTS
IN THE STATES

Across the country, state bureaus and commissions were established to regulate the new industrial society. Commodities shippers, especially farmers and merchants, in protest against the railroads' policies of rate discrimination and other corrupt practices, turned to the states for government action. By 1900 twenty-eight states had established commissions to oversee the railroads. Most of the early commissions, experimental in nature, served as models for later policy at the federal level.

Illinois had one of the most thoroughgoing provisions. Responding to local merchants who were upset with existing railroad rate policies, the Illinois state constitution of 1870 declared railroads to be public highways and authorized the state legislature to pass laws establishing maximum rates and preventing rate discrimination. In the important case of *Munn* v. *Illinois* (1877), the Supreme Court upheld the Illinois legislation.

But the Court soon weakened that judgment. In the *Wabash* case of 1886 (*Wabash, St. Louis & Pacific Railway Co.* v. *Illinois*) it narrowed the *Munn* rule and held that states could not regulate commerce extending beyond their borders. Only Congress could. The *Wabash* decision spurred Congress to pass the Interstate Commerce Act (1887), which created the Interstate Commerce Commission to investigate and oversee railroad activities. The act outlawed rebates and pooling agreements, the ICC became the prototype of the federal commissions that today regulate many parts of the economy.

REESTABLISHING PRESIDENTIAL POWER

Johnson's impeachment, the scandals of the Grant administrations, and the controversy surrounding the 1876 election (see Chapter 16) weakened the presidency. During the last two decades of the nineteenth century presidents fought to reassert their authority, and by 1900 they had largely succeeded. The late 1890s, in fact, mark the birth of the modern powerful presidency.

Rutherford B. Hayes entered the White House with his title clouded by the disputed election of 1876. Although opponents called him "His Fraudulency," he worked to reassert the authority of the presidency. Hayes worked for reform in the civil service, placed well-known reformers in high offices, and by ordering the last troops out of South Carolina and Louisiana, ended military Reconstruction. Committed to the gold standard, in 1878 he vetoed the Bland-Allison Silver Purchase Bill, which called for the partial coinage of silver, but Congress passed it over his veto.

James A. Garfield, a Union army hero and long-time member of Congress, succeeded Hayes. Ambitious and eloquent, Garfield planned to reunite the Republican party, lower the tariff to reduce surplus revenues, and assert American economic and strategic interests in Latin America. But he was soon besieged by office seekers. Each one wanted a government job, and each one thought nothing of cornering the president on every occasion. Then on July 2, 1881, Charles J. Guiteau, a deranged lawyer and disappointed office seeker, shot Garfield. Suffering through the summer, Garfield died on September 19, 1881, and Vice-President Chester A. Arthur became president.

Arthur was a better president than many had expected. He modernized the navy and worked to lower the tariff; in 1883, with his backing, Congress passed the Pendleton Act to reform the civil service. In part a reaction against Garfield's assassination, the act created a bipartisan Civil Service Commission to administer competitive examinations and appoint officeholders on the basis of merit.

In the election of 1884 Grover Cleveland, the Democratic governor of New York, narrowly defeated Republican nominee James G. Blaine. The first Democratic president since the outbreak of the Civil War, Cleveland was known for his honesty, stubbornness, and hard work. His first term in the White House (1885–1889) reflected the Democratic party's desire to curtail federal activities. Cleveland vetoed more bills than all his predecessors combined. Late in 1887 he committed himself and the Democratic party to lower the tariff. The Republicans accused him of undermining American industries, and in 1888 they nominated for the presidency Benjamin Harrison, a defender of the tariff. Although Cleveland garnered 90,000 more popular votes, Harrison won in the electoral college (see the "Choosing the President" chart in the Appendix).

REPUBLICANS IN POWER: TARIFFS, TRUSTS, AND SILVER

Despite Harrison's narrow margin, the election of 1888 was the most sweeping victory for either party in almost twenty years; it gave the Republicans the presidency and both houses of Congress. Eager to block Republican-sponsored laws, the Democrats in Congress used minority tactics, especially the "disappearing quorum" rule, which let members of the House of Representatives join in debate but then refuse to answer the roll call to determine if a quorum was present.

After two months of such tactics, the Republicans had had enough. On January 29, 1890, they fell two votes short of a quorum, and Speaker of the House Thomas B. Reed made congressional history. "The Chair," he said, "directs the Clerk to record the following names of members present and refusing to vote." Tumult continued for days, but in mid-

February 1890 the Republicans adopted the Reed rules and proceeded to enact the party's program.

As if a dam had burst, law after law poured out of the Republican Congress during 1890. The Republicans passed the McKinley Tariff Act, which raised tariff duties about 4 percent, higher than ever before. In addition, the act used duties to promote new industries.

The Republicans also passed the Sherman Antitrust Act, the first federal attempt to regulate big business. As the initial attempt to deal with the problem of trusts and industrial growth, the act shaped all later antitrust policy. It declared illegal "every contract, combination in the form of trust or otherwise, or conspiracy, in restraint of trade or commerce." Penalties for violation were stiff, including fines and imprisonment and the dissolution of guilty trusts."

One of the most important laws Congress has enacted, the Sherman Antitrust Act made the United States virtually the only industrial nation to regulate business combinations. It tried to restore competition in the marketplace to appease small businessmen. But the Supreme Court crippled the act in *U.S. v. E. C. Knight Co.* (1895) by ruling that it applied only to commerce and not to manufacturing. Not until after the turn of the century did it gain fresh power.

Another measure, the Sherman Silver Purchase Act, was intended to end the troublesome problem of silver as part of the nation's currency. Support for silver coinage was especially strong in the South and West, where people thought it might inflate the currency, raise wages and crop prices, and challenge the hated power of the gold-oriented Northeast. Eager to avert the free coinage of silver, which would require the coinage of all silver presented at the United States mints, President Harrison and other Republican leaders pressed for a compromise that took shape in the Sherman Silver Purchase Act of 1890.

The act directed the Treasury to purchase 4.5 million ounces of silver a month and to issue legal tender in the form of Treasury notes in payment for it. The act was a compromise; it satisfied both sides. Opponents of silver were pleased that it did not include free coinage. Silverites were delighted that the monthly purchases would buy up most of the country's silver production and move the country toward a bimetallic system based on silver and gold.

As a final measure, Republicans in the House passed a federal elections bill to protect the voting rights of blacks in the South. It set off a storm of denunciation among the Democrats, who called it a "force bill" that would station Army troops in the South. Defeated in the Senate, it was the last major effort until the 1950s to enforce the Fifteenth Amendment to the Constitution.

The 1890 elections crushed the Republicans, who lost seventy-eight seats in the House, an extraordinary loss. Political veterans went down to defeat, and new leaders vaulted into sudden prominence. In the Midwest state elections, as well as the national elections, Democrats made substantial gains.

The Rise of the Populist Movement

The elections of 1890 drew attention to a fast-growing movement among farmers that soon came to be known as Populism. The movement had begun rather quietly, and for a time it went almost unnoticed in the press. But during the summer of 1890 thousands of hardpressed farmers from the South and West made their problems known. At campgrounds they picnicked, talked, and listened to recruiters from an organization called the National Farmers' Alliance and Industrial Union, which promised unified action to solve agricultural problems.

The Farm Problem

Farm discontent was a worldwide phenomenon between 1870 and 1900. With the new means of transportation and communication, farmers everywhere were caught up in a complex international market they neither controlled nor entirely understood.

American farmers complained bitterly about declining prices for their products, rising railroad rates for shipping them, and burdensome mortgages. Some of the grievances were valid. Farm profits were certainly low, and the prices of farm commodities fell between 1865 and 1890. But they did not fall as low as did other commodity prices. Farmers received less for their crops, yet their purchasing power increased.

Neither was the farmers' second grievance—rising railroad rates—entirely justified. Railroad rates actually fell during these years, benefiting shippers of all products. Farm mortgages, while certainly burdensome, were common since many farmers mortgaged their property to expand their holdings or buy new farm machinery. Most mortgages were short, and the new machinery enabled farmers to triple their output and increase their income.

The actual situation varied from area to area and year to year. Still, many farmers were sure their condition had declined, and this perception sparked a growing anger. In an age excited about factories, farmers were seen as "hayseeds," a word that first appeared in 1889. A literature of rural disillusionment emerged, most notably Hamlin Garland's writings, which described the grimness of farm life.

THE FAST-GROWING FARMERS' ALLIANCE

By the end of the 1880s farmers had formed into two major organizations: the National Farmers' Alliance, located on the Plains west of the Mississippi and known as the Northwestern Alliance; and the Farmers' Alliance and Industrial Union, based in the South and known as the Southern Alliance.

The Southern Alliance began in Texas in 1875 but did not assume major proportions until Dr. Charles W. Macune took over the leadership in 1886. Its agents spread across the South where farmers were fed up with crop liens, depleted lands, and sharecropping. By 1890 the Southern Alliance claimed more than a million members. Like the Grange, the Alliance distributed educational materials, and it also established cooperative grain elevators, marketing associations, and retail stores.

Loosely affiliated with the Southern Alliance, a separate Colored Farmers' National Alliance and Cooperative Union enlisted black farmers in the South. Claiming over a million members, it probably had closer to 250,000. Blacks organized at considerable peril. In 1891 when black cotton pickers struck for higher wages near Memphis, the strike was violently put down; fifteen strikers were lynched. The abortive strike ended the Colored Farmers' Alliance.

On the Plains, the Northwestern Alliance, a smaller organization, was formed in 1880. But it lacked the centralized organization of the Southern Alliance. In 1889 the Southern Alliance changed its name to the National Farmers' Alliance and Industrial Union and persuaded the three strongest state alliances on the Plains to join. Thereafter, the new organization dominated the Alliance movement.

The Alliance turned early to politics. In the West its leaders rejected both the Republicans and Democrats and organized their own party. The Southern Alliance resisted the idea of a new party for fear it might divide the white vote, thus undercutting white supremacy. Instead, the Southerners wanted to capture control of the dominant Democratic party. But regardless of their political positions, such figures as Leonidas Polk, president of the National Farmers' Alliance; Jeremiah Simpson of Kansas; and Mary E. Lease provided the movement with forceful leadership.

Meeting in Ocala, Florida, in 1890, the Alliance adopted the Ocala Demands, the platform it pushed for as long as it existed. First and foremost, the demands called for the creation of a "sub-treasury system," which would allow farmers to store their crops in government warehouses. In return, they could claim Treasury notes for up to 80 percent of the local market value of the crop, a loan to be repaid when the crops were sold. Farmers could thus hold their crops for the best price. The Ocala Demands also urged the free coinage of silver, an end to protective tariffs and national banks, a federal income tax, the direct election of sena-

Populist Mary E. Lease advised farmers to "raise less corn and more hell." She also said ". . . if one man has not enough to eat three times a day and another man has $25 million, that last man has something that belongs to the first."

tors, and stricter regulation of the railroad companies.

The Alliance strategy worked well in the elections of 1890. Alliance leaders claimed thirty-eight Alliance supporters elected to Congress, with at least a dozen more pledged to Alliance principles.

THE PEOPLE'S PARTY

After the 1890 elections, Northern Alliance leaders urged the formation of a national third party to promote reform. In July 1892, a convention in Omaha, Nebraska, established the new People's party. Disillusioned with the response of the Democrats to agrarian difficulties, Southern Alliance leaders joined the new party. In the South the Populists worked with some success to unite black and white farmers under the same party banner.

The delegates at the Omaha convention nominated James B. Weaver of Iowa to run for president in 1892. As its platform, the People's party adopted many of the Ocala Demands. Weaver won 1,039,000 votes, the first third-party presidential candidate ever to attract more than a million votes, and he carried several western states for a total of twenty-two electoral votes. The Populists elected governors in Kansas and North Dakota, ten congressmen, five senators, and about 1500 members of state legislatures.

Despite the Populists' victories, the election brought disappointment. Using fraud and manipulation, Southern Democrats deflected the Populists' efforts; Weaver was held to less than a quarter of the vote in almost every Southern state. He lost heavily in most urban areas and failed to win over most farmers in the settled Midwest. In no midwestern state except Kansas and North Dakota did he win as much as 5 percent of the vote. Although the Populists did run candidates in the next three presidential elections, their heyday was over.

While it lived, the Populist party was one of the most powerful protest movements in American history. Catalyzing the feelings of hundreds of thousands of farmers, it attempted to solve specific economic problems, while at the same time advancing a larger vision of harmony and community, in which people who cared about each other were rewarded for what they produced.

THE CRISIS OF THE DEPRESSION

Building on the Democratic party's sweeping triumph in the midterm elections of 1890, Grover Cleveland decisively defeated incumbent President Benjamin Harrison in 1892. For the first time since the 1850s, the Democrats controlled the White House and both branches of Congress.

Unfortunately for Cleveland, the panic of 1893 struck almost as he took office. The economy had expanded too rapidly in the 1870s and

1880s. The mood changed early in 1893. Business confidence sagged, and investors became timid and uneasy. Panic hit the stock market. During 1893, 15,000 business firms and more than 600 banks closed.

The year 1894 was even worse. By midyear the number of unemployed stood at 3 million. One out of every five workers was unemployed, and unprecedented numbers of needy people taxed the ability of churches and charities to help. In the summer a heat wave and drought struck the farm belt west of the Mississippi River. Corn withered in the fields. In the South the price of cotton fell below five cents a pound, far under the break-even point.

People became restless and angry. There was even talk of revolution and bloodshed. "Everyone scolds," Henry Adams, the historian, wrote a British friend. "Everyone also knows what ought to be done. Everyone reviles everyone who does not agree with him, and everyone differs, or agrees only in contempt for everyone else. As far as I can see, everyone is right."

COXEY'S ARMY AND THE PULLMAN STRIKE

Some of the unemployed wandered across the country—singly, in small groups, and in small armies. During 1894 there were some 1400 strikes involving more than a half million workers. On Easter Sunday, 1894, an unusual "army" of perhaps 300 people left Massillon, Ohio. At its head rode "General" Jacob S. Coxey, a middle-aged businessman who wanted Congress to print $500 million to fi-

The great Pullman strike prevented needed supplies from reaching the nation's markets. Here the United States Cavalry escorts a meat train leaving the Chicago stockyards on July 10, 1894.

nance a massive road-building program that would put the nation's jobless to work.

Other armies sprang up around the country, and all headed for Washington armed with other demands and hopes. Coxey himself reached Washington on May 1, 1894, after a difficult, tiring march. Police were everywhere. Coxey made it to the foot of the Capitol steps, but before he could do anything, the police were on him. He was clubbed, arrested for trespassing, and sentenced to twenty days in jail.

The armies melted away, but discontent did not. The great Pullman strike—one of the largest strikes in the country's history—began just a few days after Coxey's arrest when the employees of the Pullman Palace Car Company struck to protest wage cuts, continuing high rents for company-owned housing, and layoffs. On July 26, 1894, the American Railway Union (ARU) under Eugene V. Debs joined the strike by refusing to handle trains that carried Pullman sleeping cars.

Within hours the strike paralyzed the western half of the nation. Grain and livestock could not reach markets. Factories shut down for lack of coal. The strike renewed talk of class welfare. In Washington, President Cleveland decided to break it because it obstructed delivery of the mail.

On July 2 he secured a court injunction against the ARU and ordered troops to Chicago. When they arrived on Independence Day, violence broke out, and mobs composed mostly of nonstrikers overturned freight cars, looted, and burned. Restoring order, the army occupied railroad yards in Illinois, California, and other points. By late July the strike was over; Debs was jailed for violating the injunction.

The Pullman strike had far-reaching consequences for the development of the labor movement. Upholding Debs' sentence in *In re Debs* (1895), the Supreme Court endorsed the use of the injunction in labor disputes, thus giving business and government an effective antilabor weapon that hindered union growth in the 1890s. The strike also catapulted Debs into prominence. Working people resented Cleveland's actions in the strike.

THE MINERS OF THE MIDWEST

The plight of miners in the Illinois, Indiana, and Ohio coalfields illustrated the personal and social impact of the depression. Even in the best of times, mining was a dirty and dangerous business. Mines often closed for as long as six months, and wages fell with the depression.

Mining was often a family occupation, passed down from father to son. It demanded delicate judgments about when to blast, where to follow a seam, and how to avoid rockfalls. Until 1890 English and Irish immigrants dominated the business, migrating from mine to mine. They were poorly paid and usually lived in flimsy shacks that were owned by the mining company. After 1890 immigrants from southern and eastern Europe came to the mines to find work.

As the depression deepened, tensions grew between miners and their employers and between "old" miners and the "new." The new miners, who usually spoke no English and lacked the skills handed down by the old miners, were often blamed for accidents, and they worked longer hours for less pay.

In April 1894 a wave of wage reductions sparked an explosion of labor unrest in the mines. The United Mine Workers, a struggling union formed just four years earlier, called for a strike of bituminous coal miners, and on April 21 virtually all midwestern and Pennsylvania miners quit working. The flow of coal slackened; cities faced blackouts; factories closed.

The violence that soon broke out followed a significant pattern. The new miners were much more prone than the old miners to violent action to win a strike. The depression hit them especially hard. In many areas, anger and frustration turned the 1894 strikes into outright war.

For nearly two weeks in June 1894 fighting rocked the coalfields. Mobs ignited mine shafts, dynamited coal trains, and defied the state militias. While miners of all backgrounds participated in the violence, the new miners led the most radical and violent assaults.

Shocked by the violence, public opinion shifted against the strikers. The strike ended in a matter of weeks, but its effects lingered. English and Irish miners moved out into other jobs or up into supervisory positions. Jokes and songs poked cruel fun at the new immigrants. The United Mine Workers, dominated by the older miners, began in 1896 to persuade Congress to stop the "demoralizing effects" of immigration.

The Pullman strike, which occurred at the same time, pulled attention away from the crisis in the coalfields, even though the miners' strike involved three times as many workers and provided a revealing glimpse of the tensions within American society. The miners of the Midwest were the first large group of skilled workers seriously affected by the flood of immigrants from southern and eastern Europe. Buffeted by depression, they reflected the social and economic discord that permeated every industry.

A BELEAGUERED PRESIDENT

President Cleveland was sure that he knew the cause of the depression. The Sherman Silver Purchase Act of 1890, he believed, had damaged business confidence, exhausted the Treasury's gold reserve, and caused the panic. The solution to the depression was equally simple: repeal the act.

In June 1893, Cleveland summoned Congress into special session. Rejecting the silverites' pleas for a compromise, Cleveland pushed the repeal bill through Congress, and on November 1, 1893, he signed it into law. Always sure of himself, he had staked everything on a single measure.

Repeal of the Sherman Silver Purchase Act was probably a necessary action. It responded to the realities of international finance, reduced the flight of gold out of the country, and over the long run boosted business confidence. Unfortunately, it contracted the currency at a time when inflation might have helped. It also did not bring economic revival. The stock mar-

ket remained listless, businesses continued to close, unemployment spread, and farm prices dropped.

The repeal battle of 1893 discredited the conservative Cleveland Democrats who had dominated the Democratic party since the 1860s. Reshaping the politics of the country, it confined the Democratic party largely to the South, helped the Republicans become the majority party in 1894, and strengthened the position of the silver Democrats in their bid for the presidency in 1896. By 1896 it appeared to most Americans that Cleveland's economic policies had not benefited the country.

DEPRESSION POLITICS

In 1894 Cleveland and the Democrats tried to fulfill their long-standing promise to reduce the tariff. The Wilson-Gorman Tariff Act, passed by Congress in 1894, contained only modest reductions in duties. It also imposed a small income tax, a provision the Supreme Court overturned in 1895. Discouraged, Cleveland let the bill become law without his signature.

The Democrats were buried in the elections of 1894, suffering the greatest defeat in congressional history. Wooing labor and the unemployed, the Populists made striking inroads in parts of the South and West, yet it was far from enough. Across the country the discontented tended to vote for the Republicans, not the Populists, a discouraging sign for the Populist party.

For millions of people, Grover Cleveland became a scapegoat for the country's economic ills. The Democratic party split, and southern and western Democrats deserted him in droves. At Democratic conventions Cleveland's name evoked jeers.

The elections of 1894 marked the end of the party deadlock that had existed since the 1870s. The Democrats lost, the Populists gained somewhat, and the Republicans became the majority party in the country. The Republican doctrines of activism and national authority, repudiated in the elections of 1890, became more attractive in the midst of depression.

CHANGING ATTITUDES

Across the country people were rethinking older ideas about government, the economy, and society. The depression, brutal and far-reaching, undermined traditional views. As men and women concluded that established ideas had failed to deal with the depression, they looked for new ones.

In prosperous times Americans had thought of unemployment as the result of personal failure, affecting primarily the lazy and immoral. Now, in the midst of depression, everyone knew people who were both worthy *and* unemployed. People began to debate issues they had long taken for granted. New discussion clubs, women's clubs, reform societies, university extension centers, church groups, farmer's societies—gave people a place to discuss alternatives to the existing order. Pressures for reform increased, and demand grew for government intervention to help the poor and unemployed.

EVERYBODY WORKS BUT FATHER

As husbands and fathers lost their jobs, more and more women and children went to work. Even as late as 1901, well after the depression had ended, a study of working-class families showed that more than half the principal breadwinners were out of work. So many women and children worked that in 1905 there was a popular song, "Everybody Works but Father."

During the 1890s the number of working women rose from 4 million to 5.3 million. Trying to make ends meet, they took in boarders and found jobs as laundresses, cleaners, or domestics. Where possible they worked in offices and factories. Far more black urban women than white worked to supplement their husbands' meager earnings. Women worked as telegraph and telephone operators, clerks in the new five-and-tens and department stores, as nurses, typists, and teachers.

The depression also caused an increasing number of children to work. During the 1890s boys and girls under sixteen years of age made up nearly a third of the labor force of the southern textile mills. In most cases children worked not in factories but in farming and city street trades like peddling and shoe shining. In 1900 the South had more than half the child laborers in the nation.

Concerned about child labor, middle-class women in 1896 formed the League for Protection of the Family, which called for compulsory education to get children out of factories and into classrooms. Soon other organizations were started to fight for reforms in the fields of child welfare, education, and sanitation.

CHANGING THEMES IN LITERATURE

The depression also gave impetus to a growing movement in literature toward realism and naturalism. In the years after the Civil War, literature often reflected the mood of romanticism—sentimental and unrealistic. But after the 1870s a number of talented authors rejected romanticism in favor of realism. Determined to portray life as it was, they studied local dialects, wrote regional stories, and emphasized the "true" relationships between people. In doing so, they reflected broader trends in the society: industrialism; evolutionary theory, which emphasized the effect of the environment on humans; and the new philosophy of pragmatism, which stressed the relativity of values. (See Chapter 22 for a more detailed discussion of pragmatism.)

A regionalist author who soon outgrew that genre, Mark Twain went on to become the country's most outstanding realist writer. Growing up along the Mississippi River in Hannibal County, Missouri, the young Samuel Langhorne Clemens observed life around him with a humorous and skeptical eye. Adopting a pen name from the river term *mark twain* (two fathoms), he drew on his own experiences. In such books as *The Adventures of Huckleberry Finn* (1884), Twain used dialect and common speech instead of literary language, touching off a major change in American prose style.

William Dean Howells came more slowly to the realistic approach. Writing initially about the happier side of life, he grew worried about the impact of industrialization. In his more powerful works he portrayed an urban society that produced great riches but only at a terrible price. In the poem "Society" (1895) he compared society to a splendid ball in which men and women danced on flowers covering the bodies of the poor.

Other writers became impatient even with realism. Pushing Darwinian theory to its limits, they wrote of a world in which a cruel and merciless environment determined human fate. Often focusing on economic hardship, naturalist writers scrutinized the poor, the lower classes, and the criminal mind; they brought to their writing the social worker's passion for direct and honest experience.

Stephen Crane spent a night in a seven-cent lodging house on the Bowery and in "An Experiment in Misery" captured the smells and sounds of the poor. Crane depicted the carnage of war in *The Red Badge of Courage* (1895). Frank Norris assailed the power of big business in two dramatic novels, *The Octopus* (1901) and *The Pit* (1903), both the story of individual futility in the face of the heartless corporations. Jack London traced the power of nature over civilized society in novels like *The Sea Wolf* (1904) and *The Call of the Wild* (1903).

Theodore Dreiser, the foremost naturalist writer, grimly portrayed a dark world in which human beings were tossed about by forces beyond their understanding or control. In his great novel, *Sister Carrie* (1901), he followed a young farm girl who took a job in a Chicago shoe factory. Like other naturalists, Dreiser focused on environment and character. He thought writers should tell the truth about human affairs, not fabricate romance.

Literary themes and illustrations of the day included "From the Depths," a powerful drawing from J. Ames Mitchell's The Silent War *(1906), which dealt with class struggle.*

THE PRESIDENTIAL ELECTION OF 1896

The election of 1896 was known as "the battle of the standards" because it involved the gold and silver standards of value in the monetary system of the nation. New voting patterns replaced old, the new majority party confirmed its control of the country, and national policy shifted to suit the new realities.

THE MYSTIQUE OF SILVER

People wanted quick solutions to the economic crisis. During 1896 unemployment shot up; farm income and prices fell to the lowest point in the decade. The silverites offered a solution, simple but compelling: the free and independent coinage of silver at the ratio of sixteen to one. Free coinage meant that the United States

Frank Baum's The Wonderful Wizard of Oz *(1900) was written as an allegory of the silver movement—from drought-stricken Kansas to a land of riches. In the original version of the story, Dorothy's magical slippers were silver rather than ruby.*

mints would coin all the silver offered to them. Independent coinage meant that the country would coin silver regardless of the policies of other nations, nearly all of which were on the gold standard.

Above all, the silverites believed in a quantity theory of money: The amount of money in circulation determined the level of activity in the economy. A shortage of money meant declining activity and depression. Silver meant more money and thus prosperity. Added to the currency, it would increase the money supply and stir new economic activity.

By 1896 silver was a symbol. It had moral and patriotic dimensions and stood for a wide range of popular grievances. For many, it reflected rural values rather than urban ones, suggested a shift of power away from the Northeast, and spoke for the downtrodden instead of the well-to-do.

Silver was a social movement, one of the largest in American history, but its life span turned out to be brief. As a mass phenomenon, it flourished between 1894 and 1896, then succumbed to electoral defeat, the return to prosperity, and the onset of fresh concerns. But in its time it bespoke a national mood and won millions of followers.

THE CAMPAIGN AND ELECTION

Scenting victory over the discredited Democrats, numerous Republicans fought for the party's presidential nomination. In the end, William McKinley, an able, calm Civil War veteran, won the nomination. As a congressman he had been the chief sponsor of the tariff act named for him. In the months before the 1896 national convention, Marcus A. Hanna, his campaign manager and trusted friend, raised $16 million, and built up a powerful national organization that proved successful. McKinley's platform favored the gold standard.

Despite President Cleveland's opposition, more than twenty Democratic states' platforms came out for free silver in 1894. Power in the party shifted to the South, where it remained for decades. The party's base narrowed; its outlook increasingly reflected southern views on silver, race, and other issues. In effect, the Democrats became a sectional—no longer a national—party.

The anti-Cleveland Democrats had their issue, but they lacked a leader. Out in Nebraska, William Jennings Bryan saw the opportunity. He was barely thirty-six years old and had relatively little political experience. But he had spent months wooing support, and he was a captivating public speaker.

From the outset of the 1896 Democratic convention, the silver Democrats were in charge, and they put together a platform that stunned the Cleveland wing of the party. It demanded the free coinage of silver, attacked Cleveland's actions in the Pullman strike, and censured his 1895 and 1896 gold bond sales. On July 9, as delegates debated the platform, Bryan's moment came. Striding to the stage, he stood for an instant, a hand raised for silence, waiting for the applause to die down.

He spoke with confidence, captivating the delegates. The country, he said, praised businessmen but forgot that laborers, miners, and farmers were businessmen, too. He defended silver, and in his famous closing said, "Having behind us the producing masses of this nation and the world . . . we will answer their demand for a gold standard by saying to them: 'You shall not press down upon the brow of labor this crown of thorns, you shall not crucify mankind upon a cross of gold.' " He ended with his arms outstretched as on a cross. Suddenly there was pandemonium. When the tumult subsided, the delegates adopted the anti-Cleveland platform, and the next day, Bryan won the presidential nomination.

The Democratic convention presented the Populists with a dilemma. The People's party had staked everything on the assumption that neither major party would endorse silver. Now it faced a painful choice: Nominate an independent ticket and risk splitting the silverite forces or nominate Bryan and give up its separate identity as a party.

The choice was unpleasant, and it shattered the People's party. Meeting late in July, the party's national convention nominated Bryan, but the Populists' endorsement probably hurt Bryan as much as it helped. It won him relatively few votes, since many Populists would have voted for him anyway. It identified him as a Populist, which he was not, and allowed the Republicans to accuse him of heading a ragtag army of malcontents.

In August 1896, Bryan set off on a campaign that became an American legend. Much of the conservative eastern press had deserted him, and he took his campaign directly to the voters, the first presidential candidate to do so in a systematic way. By his own count, Bryan traveled 18,009 miles, visited 27 states, and spoke 600 times to a total of some 3 million people. He built skillfully on a new "merchandising" style of campaign in which he worked to educate and persuade voters.

Bryan summoned voters to an older America: a land where farms were as important as factories, where the virtues of rural and religious life outweighed the doubtful lure of the city, where common people still ruled, and opportunity existed. He drew on the Jeffersonian tradition of rural virtue, distrust of central authority, and abiding faith in the powers of human reason.

McKinley let voters come to him. Railroads brought them by the thousands into his hometown of Canton, Ohio, and he spoke to them from his front porch. Never had a party spent so much money on a campaign. Through use of the press, he reached fully as many people as Bryan's more strenuous effort. Appealing to labor, immigrants, wealthy farmers, businessmen, and the middle class, McKinley defended economic nationalism and the advancing urban-industrial society.

On election day, voter turnout was extraordinarily high, a measure of the intense interest, but McKinley won a clear victory, capturing 50 percent of the vote to Bryan's 46 percent. The election struck down the Populists, whose totals sagged nearly everywhere. Although many Populist proposals were later adopted—the graduated income tax, crop loans to farmers, the secret ballot, for example—the party never again could win a majority of the voters. It vanished after 1896.

THE McKINLEY ADMINISTRATION

The election of 1896 cemented the voter realignment of 1894 and initiated a generation of Republican rule. For more than three decades after 1896, with only a brief Democratic resurgence under Woodrow Wilson, the Republicans remained the country's majority party.

McKinley took office in 1897 under favorable circumstances. To everyone's relief, the economy had begun to revive. The stock market rose, factories once again churned out goods, and farmers prospered. Discoveries of gold in Australia and Alaska and new extraction techniques enlarged the world's gold supply, decreased its price, and inflated the currency as the silverites had hoped.

McKinley and the Republicans basked in the glow. They became the party of progress and prosperity, an image that helped them win victories until the 1930s. McKinley's popularity soared. An activist president, he set the policies of the administration. He maintained close ties with Congress and worked hard to educate the public on national choices and priorities. McKinley struck new relations with the press and traveled far more than previous presidents. In some ways he began the modern presidency.

In July 1897, with his support, Congress passed the Dingley Tariff, which raised average tariff duties to a record level. As the final burst of nineteenth-century protectionism, it caused trouble for the Republican party. By the end of

CHRONOLOGY

1876	Mark Twain publishes *The Adventures of Tom Sawyer;* sets off major change in American literary style
1877	Disputed election of 1876 results in awarding of presidency to Republican Rutherford B. Hayes
1880	Republican James A. Garfield elected president
1881	Garfield assassinated; Vice-President Chester A. Arthur becomes president
1884	Democrat Grover Cleveland elected president, defeating Republican James G. Blaine
1887	Cleveland calls for lowering of tariff duties
1888	Republican Benjamin Harrison wins presidential election
1889	National Farmers' Alliance and Industrial Union formed to address problems of farmers
1890	Republican-dominated "Billion-Dollar" Congress enacts McKinley Tariff Act, Sherman Antitrust Act, and Sherman Silver Purchase Act Farmers' Alliance adopts the Ocala Demands
1892	Democrat Cleveland defeats Republican Harrison for presidency People's Party formed
1893	Financial panic touches off depression lasting until 1897 Sherman Silver Purchase Act repealed World Columbian Exposition opens in Chicago
1894	Coxey's army marches on Washington Employees of Pullman Palace Car Company strike
1896	Republican McKinley defeats William Jennings Bryan, Democratic and Populist candidate
1897	Gold discovered in Alaska Dingley Tariff Act raises tariff duties
1900	McKinley reelected, again defeating Bryan Gold Standard Act establishes gold as standard of currency
1901	McKinley assassinated; Vice-President Theodore Roosevelt assumes presidency Naturalist writer Theodore Dreiser publishes *Sister Carrie*

the 1890s, however, even some Republicans themselves had begun to conclude that the tariff had outlived its usefulness in the maturing American economy.

From the 1860s to the 1890s the Republicans had built their party on a pledge to *promote* economic growth through the use of state and national power. By 1900, with the industrial system firmly in place, the focus had shifted. The need to *regulate,* to control the effects of industrialism, became a central public concern of the new century.

McKinley prodded his party to move toward regulation, but he died before his plans matured. One problem was the government's need for revenue. Tariff duties were one of the few taxes the public would support. The Spanish-American War of 1898 (see Chapter 21) persuaded people to accept greater federal power and, with it, new forms of taxation. By the end of the nineteenth century, McKinley realized that economic nationalism, the creed on which he was raised, was a dying concept.

In 1898 and 1899, the McKinley administration focused on the war with Spain, the peace treaty that followed, and the dawning realization that the war had thrust the United States into a position of world power. In March 1900, Congress passed the Gold Standard Act, which declared gold the standard of currency and ended the silver controversy that had dominated the 1890s.

The presidential campaign of 1900 was a replay of the McKinley-Bryan fight of 1896. McKinley's running mate was Theodore Roosevelt, hero of the Spanish-American War (see Chapter 21), and former governor of New York, who was nominated for vice-president to capitalize on his popularity and, his enemies hoped, to sidetrack his political career into oblivion. McKinley won in a landslide. But on September 6, 1901, a few months after his second inauguration, McKinley was shot while standing in a receiving line at the Pan-American Exposition in Buffalo, New York. His assailant was Leon Czolgosz, a twenty-eight-year-old unemployed laborer and anarchist. On September 14, McKinley died, and Vice-President Theodore Roo-

sevelt became president. A new century had begun.

Reform movements begun in the 1890s flowered in the Progressive period after 1900. Political pattern shifted, the presidency acquired fresh power, and massive unrest prompted social change. The war with Spain brought worldwide responsibilities.

Technology continued to alter the way Americans lived. In 1896 Henry Ford produced a two-cylinder, four-horsepower car. At Kitty Hawk, North Carolina, Wilbur and Orville Wright, two bicycle manufacturers, neared the birth of powered flight. The pace of the world was quickening.

The realignments in the 1890s shaped nearly everything that came after them. In character and influence, the 1890s are as much a part of the twentieth century as they are of the nineteenth.

☙ RECOMMENDED READING

The most thorough account of the 1890s is in Harold U. Faulkner, *Politics, Reform and Expansion, 1890–1900* (1959), but see also Robert H. Wiebe, *The Search for Order, 1877–1920* (1967), and Samuel P. Hays, *The Response to Industrialism, 1855–1914* (1957). The best study of the 1890s depression is Charles Hoffman, *The Depression of the Nineties: An Economic History* (1970). On politics, see H. Wayne Morgan, *From Hayes to McKinley: National Party Politics, 1877–1896* (1969); Richard J. Jensen, *The Winning of the Midwest: Social and Political Conflict, 1888–1896* (1971); R. Hal Williams, *Years of Decision: American Politics in the 1890s* (1978); Paul Kleppner, *The Cross of Culture* (1970); Michael E. McGerr, *The Decline of Popular Politics: The American North, 1865–1928* (1986); and Richard L. McCormick, *The Party Period and Public Policy: American Politics From the Age of Jackson to the Progressive Era* (1986).

For the presidents and their policies, see Ari Hoogenboom, *The Presidency of Rutherford B. Hayes* (1988); Justus D. Doenecke, *The Presidencies of James A. Garfield and Chester A. Arthur* (1981); Richard E. Welch, *The Presidencies of Grover Cleveland* (1988); Homer E. Socolofsky and Allan B. Spetter, *The Presidency of Benjamin Harrison* (1987); and Lewis L. Gould, *The Presidency of William McKinley* (1981).

Larzer Ziff, *The American 1890s: Life and Times of a Lost Generation* (1966); Henry Steele Commager, *The American Mind* (1950); and Justin Kaplan, *Mr. Clemens and Mark Twain: A Biography* (1966), examine literary currents. On populism, see John D. Hicks, *The Populist Revolt: A History of the Farmers' Alliance and the People's Party* (1931), Lawrence Goodwyn, *Democratic Promise: The Populist Movement in America* (1976); Bruce Palmer, *"Man Over Money": The Southern Populist Critique of American Capitalism* (1980); and Norman Pollack, *The Just Polity: Populism, Law, and Human Welfare* (1987). C. Vann Woodward, *Tom Watson: Agrarian Rebel* (1938), is a superb biography.

Charles A. Lofgren, *The Plessy Case: A Legal-Historical Interpretation* (1987), and Bess Beatty, *A Revolution Gone Backward: The Black Response to National Politics, 1876–1896* (1987), are valuable. Social and labor unrest is covered in Stanley Buder, *Pullman: An Experiment in Industrial Order and Community Planning, 1880–1930* (1967); Dorothy Schweider, *Black Diamonds: Life and Work in Iowa's Coal Mining Communities, 1895–1925* (1983); and Carlos A. Schwantes, *Coxey's Army: An American Odyssey* (1985). Walter T. K. Nugent, *Money and American Society* (1968), and Allen Weinstein, *Prelude to Populism: Origins of the Silver Issue, 1867–1878* (1970), explain the silver-gold controversy.

21 TOWARD EMPIRE

AMERICA LOOKS OUTWARD

WAR WITH SPAIN

DEBATE OVER EMPIRE

When war with Spain began in April 1898, many Americans regretted it, while many others welcomed it. War was different then, shorter and more personal than the all-encompassing, lengthy, and mechanistic wars of the twentieth century. There were many people who thought that nations must fight every now and then to prove their power and test the national spirit.

Theodore Roosevelt, thirty-nine years old in 1898, was one of them. For months Roosevelt argued strenuously for war with Spain, first on grounds of freeing Cuba and expelling Spain from the hemisphere; second, to take Americans' minds from material gain; and third, because the army and navy needed the practice.

When the war broke out Roosevelt resigned his post as assistant secretary of the navy and joined the army. In 1898 officers supplied their own uniforms, and Roosevelt, the son of well-to-do parents, wanted his to be stylish. He ordered it from Brooks Brothers, the expensive New York clothier. He also chose to enlist his own regiment, and after a few telephone calls to friends and telegrams to several western governors asking for "good shots and good riders," he had more than enough men. The First United States Volunteer Cavalry, known as the Rough Riders, an intriguing mixture of Ivy League athletes and western frontiersmen, was born.

Eager for war, the men trained hard and played harder. Discipline was lax, and officers and enlisted men got along well together. Everyone howled with joy when orders came to join the invasion army for Cuba, and the Rough

Riders set sail on June 14, 1898. Lieutenant Colonel Roosevelt performed a war dance for the troops the night before.

America Looks Outward

The overseas expansion of the 1890s differed in several important respects from earlier expansionist moves of the United States. The American Republic had grown from its beginnings, but as settlers pushed westward, most of the lands they moved into were contiguous with existing territories of the United States and were intended for settlement.

The expansion of the 1890s involved the acquisition of island possessions, the bulk of them already thickly populated. The new territories were held less for settlement than as naval bases, trading outposts, or commercial centers on major trade routes. They were viewed primarily as colonies, not as states-in-the-making. Recent historians have tended to view this late-nineteenth-century expansion as the culmination of a half century of expansionist tendencies in thought and foreign policy, rather than a spur-of-the-moment expansionist path.

CATCHING THE SPIRIT OF EMPIRE

Most people in most times in history tend to look inward, and Americans in these years following the Civil War were no exception. They focused on Reconstruction, the movement westward, and the growing industrial system. Throughout the nineteenth century Americans enjoyed "free security" without fully appreciating it. Sheltered by two oceans, and the British navy, they could enunciate bold policies like the Monroe Doctrine while remaining virtually impregnable to foreign attack.

In those circumstances, some people urged the abolition of the foreign service, considering it an unnecessary expenditure, a dangerous profession that might lead to entanglement in the struggles of the world's great powers. But such voices lost much of their force by the 1870s and after when Americans took an increased interest in events abroad. There was a growing sense of internationalism, which stemmed in part from the telegraphs, telephones, and undersea cables that kept people better informed about political and economic developments in distant lands. And although there was little interest in American imperialism, most Americans continued to be interested in the expansion of the country's borders.

Several developments in these years combined to shift attention outward across the seas. The end of the frontier, announced officially in the census report of 1890, sparked fears about diminishing opportunities at home. Further growth, it seemed, must take place abroad.

Factories and farms multiplied, producing more goods than the domestic market could consume. Both farmers and industrialists looked for new overseas markets, and the growing volume of exports changed the nature of U.S. trade relations. American exports of merchandise amounted to $393 million in 1870, $858 million in 1890, and $1.4 billion in 1900.

Political leaders began to argue for the vital importance of foreign markets to continue economic growth. Some of them—James G. Blaine, secretary of state under Garfield and Harrison, for one—were caught up in the exhilaration of a worldwide scramble for empire. Like the European powers, they coveted the markets of Latin America, Asia, and Africa. The idea of imperialistic expansion was in the air, and great powers measured their greatness by the colonies they acquired. Inevitably, some Americans succumbed to the spirit and wanted to enter the international hunt for territory.

Intellectual currents that supported expansion drew on Charles Darwin's theories of evolution. Applied to human and social development, Darwin's biological concepts seemed to call for the triumph of the fit and the elimination of the unfit. Theodore Roosevelt, and many like-minded people, lauded virile and adventurous qualities and regarded them as a sign of America's greatness.

Entitled "The World Is My Market, My Customers Are All Mankind," this cartoon of the 1870s reflects America's growing interest in foreign markets.

Haeckel's Biogenetic Law, then a popular theory, suggested that the development of the individual repeated the development of the race. Primitive people thus were in the arrested stages of childhood or adolescence; they needed supervision and protective treatment. In a similar vein, John Fiske, a popular writer and lecturer, argued for Anglo-Saxon racial superiority, a result of the process of natural selection. The English and Americans, Fiske said, would occupy every land on the globe that was not already "civilized," bringing the advances of commerce and democratic institutions.

Such views were widespread among the lettered and unlettered alike. The career of Josiah Strong, a Congregational minister and fervent expansionist, suggested the strength of the developing ideas. A champion of overseas missionary work, in 1885 he published a book entitled *Our Country: Its Possible Future and Its Present Crisis.* An immediate best-seller, the book called upon foreign missions to civilize the world under the Anglo-Saxon races. Strong also believed that American commerce should follow the missionary. The result, he maintained, would be good for everyone involved.

Taken together, these developments in social, political, and economic thought prepared Americans for a larger role in the world. The change was gradual, and there was never a day when people awoke with a sudden realization of their interests overseas. But the change was there, and by the 1890s Americans were ready to reach out into the world in a more determined and deliberate fashion than ever before. For almost the first time, they felt the need for an outward direction in foreign policy.

FOREIGN POLICY APPROACHES, 1867–1900

Rarely consistent, American foreign policy in the last half of the nineteenth century took different approaches to different areas of the world. In relation to Europe, where the dominant world powers were, policymakers promoted trade and tried to avoid diplomatic entanglements. In North and South America, they based policy on the Monroe Doctrine, a recurrent dream of annexing Canada or Mexico, a hope for extensive trade, and Pan-American unity against the nations of the Old World. In the Pacific, they coveted Hawaii and other outposts on the sea lanes to China.

Secretary of State William Henry Seward, who served from 1861 to 1869, aggressively pushed an expansive foreign policy. He developed a vision of an American empire stretching south into Latin America and west to the shores of Asia. He wanted Canada and Mexico, islands in the Caribbean as strategic bases to protect a canal across the isthmus, and Hawaii and other islands as stepping-stones to Asia.

Seward tried unsuccessfully to negotiate a commercial treaty with Hawaii in 1867, the same year he annexed the Midway Islands. Also in 1867, he concluded a treaty with Russia for the purchase of Alaska (which was promptly labeled "Seward's Folly"), partly to sandwich western Canada between American territory and lead to its annexation. In all this, Seward's target remained the Asian market, which he and many others considered a virtually bottomless outlet for farm and manufactured goods. As the American empire spread, he thought, Mexico City would become its capital.

Hamilton Fish followed Seward as secretary of state, serving under President Ulysses S. Grant. An avid expansionist, Grant wanted to extend American influence in the Caribbean and Pacific, though Fish often restrained him. They moved first to repair relations with Great Britain, which had been strained during the Civil War. Negotiating patiently, Fish signed the Treaty of Washington in 1871, providing for arbitration of the *Alabama* claims issue—U.S. demands that Britain pay for damages caused by the Confederate vessel, *Alabama*, which had been built and outfitted in British shipyards—and other nettlesome controversies. The treaty, one of the landmarks in the peaceful settlement of international disputes, marked a significant step in cementing Anglo-American relations.

Grant and Fish looked most eagerly to Latin America. In 1870 Grant became the first president to proclaim the nontransfer principle— "hereafter no territory on this continent shall be regarded as subject to transfer to a European power." Fish also promoted the independence of Cuba, restive under Spanish rule.

James G. Blaine's first stint as secretary of state lasted only six months, until Garfield's assassination, but he laid extensive plans to establish closer commercial relations with Latin America. When he returned to the State Department in 1889 under President Benjamin Harrison, he moved to expand markets in Latin America. He envisaged a hemisphere system of peaceful intercourse, arbitration of disputes, and expanded trade. He also wanted to annex Hawaii.

In general Harrison and Blaine focused on Pan-Americanism and tariff reciprocity. Blaine presided over the first Inter-American Conference in Washington on October 2, 1889, which Blaine hoped would unite Latin America and the United States in a customs union and create a way to settle conflicts. Although the nineteen countries that were represented refused to accept Blaine's full program, the conference was a major step in hemisphere relations and led to later meetings promoting trade and other agreements. It created an international bureau that later became the Pan-American Union for the exchange of political, scientific, and cultural information.

Reciprocity, Harrison and Blaine hoped, would divert Latin American trade from Europe to the United States. Working hard to sell the idea in Congress, Blaine lobbied for a reciprocity provision in the McKinley Tariff Act of 1890 (see Chapter 20). Once that was enacted, he negotiated important reciprocity treaties with most Latin American nations, resulting in greater American exports of flour, grain, meat, iron, and machinery. But the Wilson-Gorman Tariff Act (1894) ended reciprocity.

Grover Cleveland, Harrison's successor, pursued an aggressive policy toward Latin America. In 1895 he brought the United States precariously close to war with Great Britain over a boundary dispute between Venezuela and British Guiana. Cleveland sympathized with Venezuela, and he and Secretary of State Richard Olney urged Britain to arbitrate the dispute. When Britain failed to act, Olney drafted a stiff diplomatic note affirming the Monroe Doctrine and denying European nations the right to meddle in Western Hemisphere affairs.

Lord Salisbury, the British foreign secretary, rejected Olney's arguments, whereupon, Cleveland asked Congress for authority to appoint a commission to decide the boundary and enforce its decision. This veiled threat of war coupled with British diplomatic problems in Africa and Europe forced Britain to change its position, and the dispute was peacefully arbitrated.

The Venezuelan incident demonstrated growing American power of persuasion in the Western Hemisphere. Cleveland and Olney had forced Great Britain to recognize United States dominance, and they had sharpened American influence in Latin America. The Monroe Doctrine assumed new importance.

The Lure of Hawaii and Samoa

The islands of Hawaii offered a tempting way station to Asian markets. In the early 1800s they were already called the "Crossroads of the Pacific," and trading ships of many nations stopped there. In 1820 the first American missionaries arrived to convert the islanders to Christianity. Like missionaries elsewhere, they advertised Hawaii's economic and other benefits and attracted new settlers, whose children later came to dominate Hawaiian political life and play an important role in annexation.

After the Civil War, the United States tightened its connections with the islands. The reciprocity treaty of 1875 allowed Hawaiian sugar to enter the United States free of duty and increased Hawaiian economic dependence on the United States. In addition, its political clauses effectively made Hawaii an American protectorate.

Following the 1875 treaty, white Hawaiians became more and more influential in the islands' political life. The McKinley Tariff Act of 1890 ended the special status given Hawaiian sugar, and in addition awarded American producers a bounty of two cents a pound. Hawaiian sugar production dropped dramatically, unemployment rose, and property values fell. Soon thereafter, Queen Liliuokalani, a strong-willed nationalist, retaliated by decreeing a new constitution that gave greater power to native Hawaiians.

Unhappy, the American residents revolted in early 1893 and called on the United States for help. John L. Stevens, the American minister in Honolulu, sent 150 marines ashore, and within three days the bloodless revolution was over. On February 14, 1893, Harrison's secretary of state John W. Foster and delegates of the new government signed a treaty annexing Hawaii to the United States. But only two weeks remained in Harrison's term, and the Senate refused to ratify the treaty. The new president, Cleveland, who disapproved of the American-instigated rebellion, withdrew the treaty and demanded that the queen be restored to her throne. However, the provisional government in Hawaii politely refused and instead established the Republic of Hawaii.

The debate over Hawaiian annexation continued through the 1890s. Those in favor of annexation pointed to Hawaii's strategic location, argued that Japan or other powers might seize the islands if the United States did not, and suggested that Americans had a responsibility to civilize and Christianize the native Hawaiians. Opponents warned that annexation might lead to a colonial army and colonial problems, the inclusion of a "mongrel" population in the United States, and rule over an area not destined for statehood.

Annexation came swiftly in July 1898 in the midst of excitement over victories in the Spanish-American War. Even before the war, President William McKinley had called for annexation, but opposition was still strong. The outbreak of war caused annexationists to redouble their efforts. McKinley and congressional leaders sought a joint resolution for annexation, which required only a majority of both houses. The annexation measure moved quickly through Congress, and McKinley signed it on July 7, 1898. His signature, giving the United States a naval and commercial base in the mid-Pacific, realized a goal of policymakers since the 1860s.

Hawaii represented a step toward China; the Samoan Islands, 3000 miles to the south, sat astride the sea lanes of the South Pacific. In 1878 the United States acquired the use of Pago Pago, a harbor on the island of Tutuila. Great Britain and Germany also secured treaty rights in Samoa, and thereafter the three nations jockeyed for position.

The situation grew tense in 1889 when warships from all three countries gathered in a Samoan harbor. But a sudden typhoon destroyed the fleets, and tensions eased. A month later delegates from the three countries met in Berlin to negotiate the problem. For a time the indigenous population was granted some degree of authority, but in 1899 the United States and Germany divided Samoa and compensated Britain with lands elsewhere in the Pacific.

THE NEW NAVY

Large navies were vital in the scramble for colonies, but in the 1870s the United States had almost no navy. One of the most powerful fleets in the world during the Civil War, the American navy had fallen into rapid decline. Ships rotted, and many officers left the service.

Conditions changed during the 1880s. A group of rising young officers, steeped in a new naval philosophy, argued for an expanded navy equipped with fast, aggressive ships capable of fighting battles across the seas. Big-navy proponents pointed to the growing navies of Great Britain, France, and Germany, arguing that the United States needed greater fleet strength to protect its interests in the Caribbean and Pacific.

In 1888 Congress authorized construction of four steel ships, marking the beginning of the new navy. The initial building program focused on lightly armored, fast cruisers for raiding enemy merchant ships and protecting American shores, but after 1890 the program shifted to the construction of a seagoing, offensive battleship navy capable of challenging the strongest fleets of Europe.

Alfred Thayer Mahan and Benjamin F. Tracy were major influences behind the new navy. Austere and scholarly, Mahan was the era's most influential naval strategist. He devoted a lifetime to studying the role of sea power in history, summarizing his beliefs in three major books: *The Influence of Sea Power Upon History, 1660–1783* (1890), *The Influence of Sea Power Upon the French Revolution and Empire, 1793–1812* (1892), and *The Interest of America in Sea Power* (1897).

Mahan's reasoning was simple and persuasive. Industrialism, he argued, produced vast surpluses of agricultural and manufactured goods, for which markets must be found. Markets involved distant ports; reaching them required a large merchant marine and a powerful navy to protect it. Navies, in turn, needed coaling stations and repair yards. Coaling stations meant colonies, and colonies became strategic bases, the foundation of a nation's wealth and power. The bases might serve as markets themselves, but they were more important as stepping-stones to other objectives, the markets of Latin America and Asia.

Mahan called attention to the worldwide race for power, a race, he warned, the United States could not afford to lose. To compete in the struggle, the United States needed strategic bases; a powerful, oceangoing navy; a canal across the isthmus connecting North and South America, to link the East Coast with the Pacific; and Hawaii as a way station on the route to Asia.

One of the many men Mahan impressed was Benjamin F. Tracy, who became Harrison's secretary of the navy in 1889. Tracy joined with big-navy advocates in Congress to push for a far-ranging battleship fleet that would be capable of attacking distant enemies. He actually wanted two fleets: eight battleships in the Pacific and twelve in the Atlantic. He got four first-class battleships.

In 1889, when Tracy entered office, the United States ranked twelfth among world navies; in 1893, when he left, it ranked seventh and was climbing rapidly. By the end of the decade the navy had seventeen steel battleships and six armored cruisers, and it ranked third in the world.

WAR WITH SPAIN

The war with Spain in 1898 built a mood of national confidence; altered older, more insular patterns of thought; and reshaped the way Americans saw themselves and the world. When the war ended, American possessions stretched into the Caribbean and deep into the Pacific.

The Spanish-American War established the United States as a world power for the twentieth century. It brought colonies and millions of colonial subjects, and confirmed the longstanding belief in the superiority of the New World over the Old. Americans felt sure they were touched with a special destiny.

A WAR FOR PRINCIPLE

By the 1890s Cuba and the nearby island of Puerto Rico comprised nearly all that remained of Spain's once vast empire in the New World. Several times Cuban insurgents had rebelled against Spanish rule, but they had failed to free their country. The depression of 1893 damaged the Cuban economy, and the Wilson-Gorman Tariff of 1894 prostrated it. Duties on sugar, Cuba's lifeblood, were raised 40 percent. With the island's sugar market in ruins, discontent with Spanish rule heightened, and in late February 1895 revolt again broke out.

Cuban insurgents established a junta in New York City to raise money, purchase weapons, and wage a propaganda war to sway American public opinion. Conditions in Cuba were grim. The insurgents engaged in a hit-and-run, scorched-earth policy to force the Spanish to leave while the Spanish commander tried to corner the rebels in the eastern end of the island and destroy them.

After initial failures, Spain in January 1896 sent General Valeriano Weyler y Nicolau to Cuba. Relentless and brutal, Weyler gave the rebels ten days to lay down their arms. He then put into effect a "reconcentration" policy designed to move the native population into camps and liquidate the rebels' popular base. Herded into fortified areas, Cubans died by the thousands—victims of unsanitary conditions, overcrowding, and disease.

There was a wave of compassion for the insurgents stimulated by the newspapers. The so-called yellow press, a group of circulation-hungry New York City newspapers led by Joseph Pulitzer's *New York World* and William Randolph Hearst's *New York Journal*, printed lurid stories of Spanish atrocities.

But yellow journalism did not cause the war. It stemmed from larger conflicts in policies and perceptions between Spain and the United States. Throughout his presidency, Grover Cleveland counseled neutrality, and initially President McKinley, who came into office in March 1897, did the same. But McKinley tilted more toward the insurgents. Before the end of 1897, the new president was criticizing Spain's "uncivilized and inhuman" conduct. The United States, he made clear, did not contest Spain's right to fight the rebellion but insisted it be done within humane limits.

Late in 1897 a change in government in Madrid brought a temporary lull in the crisis. The new government recalled Weyler and agreed to offer the Cubans some form of autonomy. The new initiatives pleased McKinley, though he again warned Spain that it must find a humane end to the rebellion. Then, in January 1898 Spanish army officers led riots in Havana against the new autonomy policy and shook the president's confidence in Madrid's control over conditions in Cuba.

McKinley ordered the battleship *Maine* to Havana to "show the flag" and to evacuate American citizens if necessary. On February 9, 1898, the *New York Journal* published a private letter stolen from Enrique Dupuy de Lôme, the Spanish ambassador in Washington. In the letter de Lôme called McKinley "weak" and "a would-be politician." Many Americans were angered by the insult; McKinley himself was more worried about other sections of the letter which revealed Spanish insincerity in the negotiations. De Lôme immediately resigned and went home, but the damage was done.

A few days later, on February 15, an explosion tore through the hull of the *Maine*, sinking the ship and killing 266 sailors. McKinley cautioned patience, but Americans cried "war!" Soon there was a new slogan, "Remember the *Maine* and to Hell with Spain!"

The most recent study of the *Maine* incident blames the sinking on an accidental internal explosion, but in 1898 Americans suspected Spain, especially after the report of an investigating board attributed the sinking to an external (and thus presumably Spanish) explosion.

In early March 1898, McKinley asked Congress for $50 million in emergency defense appropriations, a request Congress promptly approved. On March 27 McKinley cabled Spain his final terms. He asked Spain to declare an armistice, end the reconcentration policy, and—implicitly—move toward Cuban independence. The Spanish answer conceded some things, but not, in McKinley's judgment, the

Headlines like these in William Randolph Hearst's New York Journal *left little doubt among his readers that Spain had sunk the* Maine.

important ones. It made no mention of a true armistice, McKinley's offer to mediate, or Cuba's independence.

Reluctantly McKinley prepared his war message, which Congress heard on April 11, 1898. On April 19 Congress passed a joint resolution declaring Cuba independent and authorizing the president to use the army and navy to expel the Spanish from Cuba. An amendment by Colorado Senator Henry M. Teller pledged that the United States had no intention of annexing the island. On April 25 Congress passed a declaration of war, and late that afternoon McKinley signed it.

Some historians have suggested that McKinley was weak and indecisive in confronting the war hysteria in the country; others have called him a wily manipulator for war and imperial gains. In truth he was neither. Throughout the

Spanish crisis McKinley pursued a moderate middle course that sought to protect American interests, promote Cuba's independence, and allow Spain time to adjust to the loss of the remnant of empire. He also wanted peace, but in the end the conflicting national interests of the two countries brought them to war.

"A SPLENDID LITTLE WAR"

Ten weeks after the declaration of war, the fighting was over. For Americans they were ten glorious, dizzying weeks, with victories to fill every headline and slogans to suit every taste. Relatively few Americans died, and the quick victory seemed to verify burgeoning American power. John Hay, soon to be McKinley's secretary of state, called it "a splendid little war."

At the outset the United States was militarily unprepared. Like the navy, the army had shrunk drastically since the end of the Civil War. In 1898 the regular army consisted of only 28,000 officers and men, most of them more experienced in quelling Indian uprisings than fighting large-scale battles.

When McKinley called for 125,000 volunteers, as many as 1 million young Americans responded. Men clamored to join the newly formed National Guard units. The secretary of war feared "there is going to be more trouble to satisfy those who are not going than to find those who are willing to go."

Problems of equipment and supply quickly appeared. Some units went into battle carrying Civil War Springfield rifles whose cartridges gave off a puff of smoke when fired, neatly marking the troops' position. Food was also a problem, as was sickness. Tainted food and tropical diseases felled more American troops than enemy bullets.

Americans then believed that "a foreign war should be fought by the hometown military unit acting as an extension of their community." Soldiers identified with their hometowns and thought of themselves as members of a town unit in a national army. Not surprisingly, then, National Guard units mirrored the social patterns of their communities. Since everyone knew each other, there was an easy-going familiarity. Enlisted men resented officers who grabbed too much authority and expected officers and men to call each other by their first names.

Each community thought of the hometown unit as *its* unit, an extension of itself. In later wars the government censored news and dominated press relations; there was little censorship in the war with Spain, and the freshest news arrived in the latest letter home. Small-town newspapers printed news of the men, and towns sent food, clothing, and occasionally even local doctors to the front.

"SMOKED YANKEES"

When the invasion force sailed for Cuba, nearly one fourth of it was black. In 1898 the regular army included four regiments of black soldiers, the Twenty-fourth and Twenty-fifth Infantry and the Ninth and Tenth Cavalry. Black regiments had served with distinction in campaigns against the Indians in the West. Most black troops were posted in the West; no eastern community would accept them. When McKinley called for volunteers, more than 10,000 black troops volunteered for the National Guard.

Orders quickly went out to the four black regular-army regiments in the West to move to camps in the South to prepare for the invasion of Cuba. Crowds and cheers followed the troop trains across the Plains, but as they crossed into Kentucky and Tennessee, the cheering stopped. Station restaurants refused to serve the troops; all waiting rooms were segregated.

Many soldiers were not prepared to put up with the shameful treatment. Those stationed near Chickamauga Park, Tennessee, shot at some whites who insulted them and desegregated the railroad cars on the line in Chattanooga. Similar incidents broke out elsewhere in the South. Just before the army's departure for Cuba, the tensions in Tampa, Florida, erupted in a night of rioting during which three white and twenty-seven black soldiers were wounded. Such events demonstrated the irony of black American soldiers committed to fight for Cuban independence. As one black wondered, "Is America any better than Spain?"

Segregation continued on some of the troop ships. But the confusion of war often ended the problem, if only temporarily. Blacks took command as white officers died, and Spanish troops soon came to fear the "smoked Yankees," as they called them. Black soldiers played a major role in the Cuban campaign and probably staved off defeat for the Rough Riders at San Juan Hill. In Cuba they won twenty-six Certificates of Merit and five Congressional Medals of Honor.

THE COURSE OF THE WAR

Mahan's Naval War College had begun studying strategy for a war with Spain in 1895. By 1898 it had a detailed plan for operations in the Caribbean and Pacific. Naval strategy was simple: Destroy the Spanish fleet, damage Spain's merchant marine, and harry the colonies or the coast of Spain. The army's task was more difficult. It must defend the United States, invade Cuba and probably Puerto Rico, and undertake possible action in far-flung places like the Philippines or Spain.

At first McKinley moved cautiously. On the afternoon of April 20, 1898, he summoned the strategists to the White House, and to the dismay of those who wanted a more aggressive policy, decided on the limited strategy of blockading Cuba, sending arms to the insurgents, and annoying the Spanish with small thrusts by the army.

Victories soon changed the strategy. In the case of war, long-standing naval plans had called for a holding action against the Spanish base in the Philippines. On May 1, 1898, with the war barely a week old, Commodore George Dewey, commander of the Asiatic Squadron located at Hong Kong, crushed the Spanish fleet in Manila Bay. Suddenly, Manila and the Philippines lay within American grasp. Dewey had no troops to attack the Spanish army in Manila, but the War Department, stunned by the speed and size of the victory, quickly raised an expeditionary force. On August 13, 1898, the troops accepted the surrender of Manila, and with it, the Philippines.

McKinley and his aides were worried about Admiral Pascual Cervera's main Spanish fleet, thought to be headed across the Atlantic for an attack on Florida. In mid-May Cervera slipped secretly into the harbor of Santiago de Cuba, a city on the island's southern coast. But a spy in the Havana telegraph office alerted the Americans, and on May 28, a superior American force under Admiral William T. Sampson bottled Cervera up.

On June 14 an invasion force of about 17,000 men set sail from Tampa. Seven days later they landed at Daiquiri on Cuba's southeastern coast. All was confusion, but the Spanish offered no resistance. Immediately the Ameri-

cans pushed west toward Santiago, which they hoped to surround and capture. At first the advance was peaceful, through the lush tropical countryside.

The first battle broke out at Las Guasimas, a crossroads on the Santiago road. After a sharp fight, the Spanish fell back. On July 1 the Rough Riders, troops from the four black regiments, and the other regulars reached the strong fortifications at El Caney and San Juan Hill. Black soldiers of the Twenty-fifth Infantry charged the El Caney blockhouses. For the better part of a day the defenders fought stubbornly and held back the army's elite corps. In the confusion of battle, Roosevelt rallied an assortment of infantry and cavalry to take Kettle Hill, adjacent to San Juan Hill.

Chromolithograph depicting the charge of the 24th and 25th Colored Infantry Regiments and rescue of the Rough Riders at San Juan Hill on July 2, 1898.

They charged directly into the Spanish guns, Roosevelt at their head. Losses were heavy. Dense foliage concealed the enemy; smokeless powder gave no clue to their position. At nightfall the surviving Spanish defenders withdrew, and the Americans prepared for the counterattack. The worst, many soldiers feared, was yet to come.

American troops now occupied the ridges overlooking Santiago. They were weakened by sickness, a fact unknown to the Spanish, who decided the city was lost. The Spanish command in Havana ordered Cervera to run for the open sea, although he knew the attempt was hopeless. On the morning of July 3 his squadron steamed down the bay and out through the harbor's narrow channel, but the waiting American fleet closed in, and in a few hours every Spanish vessel was destroyed. Two weeks later Santiago surrendered.

Soon thereafter army troops, meeting little resistance, occupied Puerto Rico. Cervera had commanded Spain's only battle fleet, and when it sank, Spain was helpless against attacks on the colonies or even its own shores. The war was over. Lasting 113 days, it took relatively few lives, most of them the result of accident, yellow fever, malaria, and typhoid in Cuba. Of the 5500 Americans who died in the war, only 379 were killed in battle. The navy lost one man in the battle at Santiago Bay, and one sailor died of heat prostration in the stunning victory in Manila Bay.

❧ DEBATE OVER EMPIRE

The United States emerged from the war with an expansion of its territory and an even larger expansion of its responsibilities. According to the preliminary peace agreement, Spain granted independence to Cuba, ceded Puerto Rico and the Pacific island of Guam to the United States, and allowed Americans to occupy Manila until the two countries reached final agreement on the Philippines. To McKinley, the Philippines were the problem. Unlike

Puerto Rico, which was close to the U.S. mainland, and Guam, which was small and unknown, the Philippines were a large, sprawling archipelago thousands of miles from America.

McKinley weighed a number of alternatives for the Philippines, but he liked none of them. He did not want to give the islands back to Spain; public opinion would not allow it. Nor did he want to turn them over to another world power. Germany, Japan, Great Britain, and Russia had all expressed interest in them. He considered independence for the islands but was soon talked out of it. Nearly everyone who had been there believed the people were not ready for independence. Sifting the choices, McKinley decided there was only one practical policy: Annex the Philippines, with an eye to future independence after a period of tutelage.

At first hesitant, American opinion was swinging to the same conclusion. Religious and missionary organizations appealed to McKinley to hold on to the Philippines in order to "Christianize them." Some merchants and industrialists saw them as the key to the China market and the wealth of Asia. Many Americans simply regarded them as the legitimate fruits of war.

In October 1898, representatives of the United States and Spain met in Paris to discuss a peace treaty. Spain agreed to recognize Cuba's independence, assume the Cuban debt, and to cede Puerto Rico and Guam to the United States. Acting on instructions from McKinley, the American representatives demanded the cession of the Philippines. In return, the United States offered a payment of $20 million. Spain resisted but had little choice, and on December 10, 1898, the American and Spanish representatives signed the Treaty of Paris.

Submitted to the Senate for ratification, the treaty set off a storm of debate throughout the country. Such prominent Americans as Andrew Carnegie, Jane Addams, William Jennings Bryan, and Mark Twain argued forcefully against annexation of the Philippines. While some anti-imperialists feared the importation of cheap labor from new Pacific colonies and others argued against assimilation of different races, most anti-imperialists focused on a different argument: The exercise of tyranny abroad, they argued, would result in tyranny at home; the very principles of independence and self-determination on which the country was founded would be violated by annexation.

In November 1898, opponents of expansion formed the Anti-Imperialist League to fight against the peace treaty. Membership centered in New England; the cause was less popular in the West and South. It enlisted more Democrats than Republicans, though never a majority of either. The anti-imperialists lacked a coherent program. Most simply wished that Dewey had sailed away after beating the Spanish at Manila Bay.

The debate in the Senate lasted a month. McKinley pressed hard for ratification, and William Jennings Bryan, though opposed to annexation, supported ratification in order to end the war. Still, on the final weekend before the vote, the treaty was two votes short. That Saturday night, news reached Washington that fighting had broken out between American troops and Filipino insurgents who demanded immediate independence. The news increased pressure to ratify the treaty, which the Senate did on February 6, 1899. The United States had a colonial empire.

GUERRILLA WARFARE IN THE PHILIPPINES

Historians rarely write of the Philippine-American War, but it was an important event in American history. The war with Spain was over in a few months; war with the Filipinos lasted more than three years. For the first time Americans fought men of a different color in an Asian guerrilla war. The Philippine-American War of 1899–1902 took a heavy toll: 4300 Americans and perhaps as many as 57,000 Filipinos.

Emilio Aguinaldo, the Filipino leader, had welcomed the Spanish-American War. Certain that the United States would grant independence, he had worked for an American victory. On June 12, 1898, the insurgents proclaimed their independence from Spain. Then, cooperating with the Americans, they drove the Spanish out of many areas of the islands. In the liberated regions Aguinaldo established local governments. He waited impatiently for American recognition, but McKinley and others doubted the Filipinos were ready. Shortly thereafter, fighting broke out between the Filipinos and Americans.

Although by late 1899 the American army had defeated and dispersed the organized Filipino army, Aguinaldo and his followers continued to wage a guerrilla war. The Americans used Weyler-like tactics. After any attack on an American patrol, they burned all the houses in the nearest district. They established protected "zones" and herded Filipinos into them. Seizing or destroying all food outside the zones, they starved many guerrillas into submission.

Bryan tried to turn the election of 1900 into a debate over imperialism, but his attempt failed. For one thing, he himself refused to give up the silver issue, which cost him support among anti-imperialists in the Northeast, who were for gold. McKinley, moreover, was able to take advantage of the surging economy, and he could defend expansion as an accomplished fact. Riding a wave of patriotism and prosperity, McKinley won the election handily.

In 1900 McKinley sent a special Philippine Commission under William Howard Taft to establish a civil government. The following year Aguinaldo was captured. Back in Manila, he signed a proclamation urging his people to end the fighting. On July 4, 1901, authority was transferred from the army to Taft, who was named the civilian governor of the islands, and his civil commission.

Given broad powers the Taft Commission introduced many changes. The Americans built new schools, roads, and bridges. They reformed the judiciary, reconstructed the tax system, and introduced sanitation and vaccination programs. Taft also encouraged Filipino participation in government. Slowly the Filipinos moved toward independence, which came on July 4, 1946, nearly fifty years after Aguinaldo proclaimed it.

Governing the Empire

Ruling the colonies raised new and perplexing questions. How could—and how should—the distant dependencies be governed? Did their inhabitants have the rights of American citizens? Did "the Constitution follow the flag?"

In a series of cases between 1901 and 1904, the Supreme Court asserted the principle that the Constitution did not automatically and immediately apply to the people of an annexed territory and did not confer upon them all the privileges of United States citizenship. Instead, Congress could specifically extend such constitutional provisions as it saw fit.

Four dependencies—Hawaii, Alaska, Guam, and Puerto Rico—were organized quickly. In 1900 Congress granted territorial status to Hawaii and gave American citizenship to all citizens of the Hawaiian republic. A similar maneuver made Alaska a territory in 1912. Guam and the Samoan island of Tutuila were simply placed under the control of naval officers.

Puerto Ricans readily accepted the war's outcome, and in 1900 the Foraker Act established civil government in Puerto Rico. It organized the island as a territory. In 1917 United States citizenship was extended to the residents of the island.

Cuba proved a trickier matter. McKinley asserted the authority of the United States over conquered territory and promised to govern the island until the Cubans had established a firm and stable government of their own. To oversee this process, McKinley sent General Leonard Wood to Cuba. Wood moved quickly to bring order to the country. Early in 1900 he conducted municipal elections and arranged the election of delegates to a constitutional convention. The convention adopted a constitution modeled on the U.S. Constitution and, at Woods' prodding, included provisions for future relations with the United States. Known as the Platt Amendment, the provisions stipulated that Cuba should make no treaties that might impair its independence and acquire no debts it could not pay; most important, it empowered the United States to intervene in Cuba to maintain orderly government.

Between 1898 and 1902 the American military government worked hard for the economic and political revival of the island. It repaired the damage of the civil war, built roads and schools, and established order in rural areas. A public health campaign headed by Dr. Walter Reed, an army surgeon, wiped out yellow fever. When the last troops left in May 1902, the Cubans at last had their independence, although they were under the clear domination of their neighbor to the north.

The Open Door

Poised in the Philippines, the United States had become an Asian power on the doorsteps of China. Weakened by years of warfare, China in 1898 and 1899 was unable to resist foreign influence. Japan, England, France, Germany, and Russia eyed it covetously, dividing the country into "spheres of influence." They forced China to grant "concessions" that allowed them exclusive rights to develop particular areas and threatened American hopes for extensive trade with the country.

McKinley first outlined a new China policy in September 1898. He wanted Asian trade to be conducted on the basis of an "open door," where all countries would have an equal opportunity to compete for the Asian markets. In September 1899 Secretary of State John Hay addressed identical diplomatic notes to England, Germany, and Russia, and later to France, Japan, and Italy, asking them to join the United States in establishing the "Open Door." The policy urged three agreements: Nations possessing a sphere of influence would respect the rights and privileges of other nations in that sphere; the Chinese government would continue to collect tariff duties in all spheres; and nations would not discriminate against other nations in levying port dues and railroad rates within their respective spheres of influence.

Under the Open Door policy, the United States could retain many commercial advantages that were endangered by the partition of China into spheres of influence. McKinley and Hay also attempted to preserve for the Chinese some semblance of national authority. None of

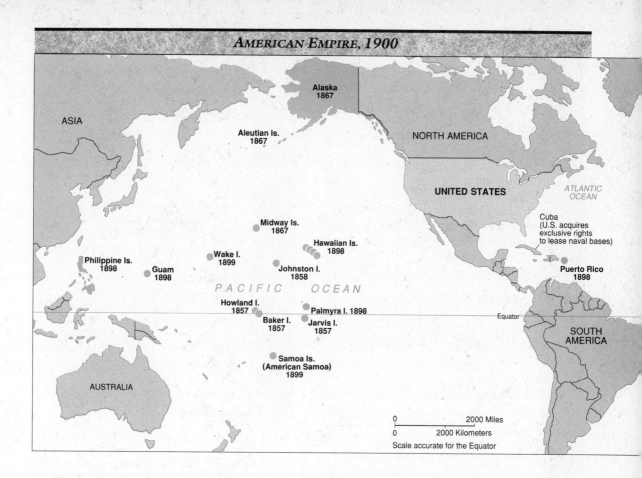

ASIA

Alaska
1867

Aleutian Is.
1867

NORTH AMERICA

UNITED STATES

ATLANTIC
OCEAN

Cuba
(U.S. acquires
exclusive rights
to lease naval bases)

Midway Is.
1867

Hawaiian Is.
1898

Wake I.
1899

Philippine Is.
1898

Guam
1898

Johnston I.
1858

Puerto Rico
1898

PACIFIC   OCEAN

Howland I.
1857

Palmyra I. 1898

Equator

Baker I.
1857

Jarvis I.
1857

SOUTH
AMERICA

Samoa Is.
(American Samoa)
1899

AUSTRALIA

0   2000 Miles
0   2000 Kilometers
Scale accurate for the Equator

the countries fully accepted the Open Door policy, but Hay turned the situation to American advantage by boldly announcing in March 1900 that all the powers had agreed to it.

The policy's first test came just three months later with the outbreak of the Boxer Rebellion in Peking (now Beijing). In June 1900 a secret, intensely nationalistic Chinese society called the Boxers tried to oust all foreigners from their country. Overrunning Peking, they drove foreigners into their legations and penned them up for nearly two months. In the end the United States joined Britain, Germany, and other powers in sending troops to lift the siege.

Fearing that the rebellion gave some nations, especially Germany and Russia, an excuse to expand their spheres of influence, Hay took quick action to emphasize American policy. In July he sent off another round of Open Door notes affirming U.S. commitment to equal commercial opportunity and respect for China's independence. While the first Open Door notes had implied recognition of China's continued independence, the second notes explicitly stated the need to preserve it. Together the two notes composed the Open Door policy, which became a central element in American policy in the Far East.

The war was over. Roosevelt, now famous, was elected governor of New York. He would soon become McKinley's vice-president and then president of the United States. For other Americans, heroism was not so profitable. Bravery in Cuba and the Philippines won some recognition for black soldiers, but the war itself set back the cause of civil rights. It spurred talk

CHRONOLOGY

1867	United States purchases Alaska from Russia Midway Islands are annexed
1871	Treaty of Washington between United States and Great Britain sets precedent for peaceful settlement of international disputes
1875	Reciprocity treaty with Hawaii binds Hawaii economically and politically to United States
1878	United States acquires naval base in Samoa
1883	Congress approves funds for construction of first modern steel ships; beginning of modern navy
1887	New treaty with Hawaii gives United States exclusive use of Pearl Harbor
1889	First Inter-American Conference meets in Washington, D.C.
1893	American settlers in Hawaii overthrow Queen Liluokalani; provisional government established
1895	Cuban insurgents rebel against Spanish rule
1898	Battleship *Maine* explodes in Havana harbor (February) Congress declares war against Spain (April) Commodore Dewey defeats Spanish fleet at Manila Bay (May)
	United States annexes Hawaii (July) Americans defeat Spanish at El Caney, San Juan Hill (actually Kettle Hill), and Santiago (July) Spain sues for peace (August) Treaty of Paris ends Spanish-American War (December)
1899	Congress ratifies Treaty of Paris United States sends "open-door" notes to Britain, Germany, France, Russia, Japan, and Italy Philippine-American War erupts
1900	Foraker Act establishes civil government in Puerto Rico Boxer Rebellion in China
1901	Platt Amendment authorizes American intervention in Cuba
1902	Philippine-American War ends with American victory

about "inferior" races, at home and abroad, and reunited whites in the North and South. A fresh outburst of segregation and lynching occurred during the decade after the war.

In a little more than a century, the United States had grown from thirteen states stretched along a thin strip of Atlantic coastline into a world power that reached from the Caribbean to the Pacific. As Seward and others had hoped, the nation now dominated its own hemisphere, dealt with European powers on equal terms, and exerted great influence in Asia.

✿ RECOMMENDED READING

The best general account of the development of American foreign policy in these years is Walter LaFeber, *The New Empire: An Interpretation of American Expansion, 1860–1898* (1963). Ernest R. May analyzes the causes of the Spanish-American War in *Imperial Democracy: The Emergence of*

America as a Great Power (1961); for a briefer treatment, see H. Wayne Morgan, *America's Road to Empire: The War with Spain and Overseas Expansion* (1965).

Graham A. Cosmas presents a detailed account of military organization and strategy in *An Army for Empire: The United States Army in the Spanish-American War* (1971), while Willard B. Gatewood, Jr., *"Smoked Yankees" and the Struggle for Empire: Letters from Negro Soldiers, 1898–1902* (1971), offers a fascinating glimpse of the thoughts of some black soldiers in the war. Gerald F. Linderman relates the war to the home front in *The Mirror of War: American Society and the Spanish-American War* (1974).

On American foreign policy, see David M. Pletcher, *The Awkward Years: American Foreign Relations Under Garfield and Arthur* (1962), and Milton Plesur, *America's Outward Thrust: Approaches to Foreign Affairs, 1865–1890* (1971).

For policies toward China see Thomas J. McCormick, *China Market: America's Quest for Informal Empire, 1893–1901* (1967); Marilyn B. Young, *Rhetoric of Empire: American China Policy, 1895–1901* (1968); and David L. Anderson, *Imperialism and Idealism: American Diplomats in China, 1861–1898* (1985).

Books on naval developments include William R. Braisted, *The United States Navy in the Pacific,* *1897–1909* (1958), and Benjamin J. Cooling, *Gray Steel and Blue Water Navy* (1979).

For the background of the war with Spain, see David F. Trask, *The War with Spain in 1898* (1981), and Philip S. Foner, *The Spanish-Cuban-American War and the Birth of American Imperialism, 1895–1902,* 2 vols. (1972). The course of the war itself can be followed in Frank Freidel, *The Splendid Little War* (1958); Charles H. Brown, *The Correspondents' War: Journalists in the Spanish-American War* (1967); and David A. Gerber, *Black Ohio and the Color Line, 1860–1915* (1976).

For the debate over expansion and the treaty with Spain, consult E. Berkley Tompkins, *Anti-Imperialism in the United States: The Great Debate, 1890–1920* (1970); Daniel B. Schirmer, *Republic or Empire: American Resistance to the Philippine War* (1972); Thomas J. Osborne, *"Empire Can Wait": American Opposition to Hawaiian Annexation, 1893–1898* (1981).

Policy toward Cuba and the Philippines is covered in Richard E. Welch, Jr., *Response to Imperialism: The United States and the Philippine-American War, 1899–1902* (1979); and Stuart Creighton Miller, *"Benevolent Assimilation": The American Conquest of the Philippines, 1899–1903* (1984). Willard B. Gatewood, Jr., *Black Americans and the White Man's Burden, 1898–1903* (1975) is a thought-provoking study.

22 THE PROGRESSIVE ERA

THE CHANGING FACE OF INDUSTRIALISM

SOCIETY'S MASSES

CONFLICT IN THE WORKPLACE

LIFE IN AMERICA, 1920

THE USES OF LEISURE

In 1902 Samuel S. McClure, the shrewd owner of *McClure's Magazine*, sensed something astir in the country that his reporters were not covering. Like *Life*, the *Ladies' Home Journal*, and *Cosmopolitan*, *McClure's* was reaching more and more people—more than a quarter of a million readers a month. Americans were snapping up the new popular magazines filled with eye-catching illustrations and up-to-date fiction.

McClure was always chasing new ideas and readers, and in 1902, certain that something was happening in the public mood, he told one of his staff editors, thirty-six-year-old Lincoln Steffens, "Get out of here, travel, go—somewhere. . . ."

Following McClure's suggestion, Steffens boarded a train and headed west, determined to understand the temper of the nation. In St. Louis he came across a young district attorney named Joseph W. Folk who had found a trail of corruption linking politics and some of the city's respected business leaders. "It is good business men," Folk stressed, "that are corrupting our bad politicians." Steffens' story, "Tweed Days in St. Louis," appeared in the October 1902 issue of *McClure's*.

The November *McClure's* carried the first installment of Ida Tarbell's scathing "History of the Standard Oil Company," and in January 1903 Steffens was back with "The Shame of Minneapolis," another tale of corrupt partnership between business and politics. McClure had what he wanted. In an editorial in the January issue he deplored the corruption in American life, "Capitalists, working men, politicians, citizens—all breaking the law, or letting it be broken."

Readers were enthralled, and articles and books by other muckrakers—Theodore Roosevelt coined the unflattering term in 1906 to describe the practice of exposing the corruption of public and prominent figures—spread swiftly. Muckraking flourished from 1903 to 1909, and while it did, good writers and bad investigated almost every corner of American life: government, labor unions, big business, Wall Street, health care, the food industry, child labor, women's rights, prostitution, ghetto living, and life insurance.

The muckrakers were a journalistic voice of a larger movement in American society. Called *progressivism*, it lasted from the mid-1890s through World War I. Like muckraking itself, it reflected concern with the state of society and a conviction that human compassion and scientific investigation could bring problems to light and solve them. Progressivism took on the character of Theodore Roosevelt and Woodrow Wilson, two important national spokesmen, but it affected large numbers of people and expressed at many levels the excitement of progress and change.

As McClure had hoped, Steffens *had* found something astir in the country, something so important and pervasive that it altered the course of American history. This chapter will examine in detail the economic, social, and intellectual conditions that gave rise to progressivism. Chapter 23 will examine progressivism itself, in the cities, states, and nation.

THE CHANGING FACE OF INDUSTRIALISM

Significant changes occurred in the industrial system during the years between the 1890s and World War I. The rapid growth of businesses gave rise to a widely-feared "trust" movement and the progressives' desire to regulate it. Importantly, both progressives and business leaders drew on similar visions of the country: complex, expansive, hopeful, managerially minded, and oriented toward results and efficiency. In working for reform, the progressives drew on the managerial methods of a business world they sought to regulate.

Businesses were large in the three decades after the Civil War, but in the years between 1895 and 1915 they became mammoth, employing thousands of workers and equipped with assembly lines to turn out huge numbers of the company's product. Inevitably, management attitudes changed, as did business organization and worker roles.

THE INNOVATIVE MODEL T

Mass production of automobiles began in the first years of the century. Using an assembly-line system that foreshadowed later techniques, Ransom E. Olds turned out 5000 Olds runabouts in 1904. More important, however, in 1903 Henry Ford and a small group of associates formed the Ford Motor Company, the firm that transformed the business.

Ford was forty years old. At first, like many others in the industry, he concentrated on luxury and racing cars. He even raced his own cars; in 1904 he set the world's land speed record—more than ninety miles per hour. However, his expensive cars found few buyers.

In 1907 he lowered the price, and sales picked up. Ford learned an important lesson of the modern economy: A smaller unit profit on a large number of sales meant enormous revenues. Early in 1908 he introduced the Model T, a four-cylinder, twenty-horsepower "Tin Lizzie," costing $850, and available only in black. Eleven thousand were sold the first year.

"I am going to democratize the automobile," Ford proclaimed. The key was mass production, and after many experiments, Ford copied the techniques of meat packers who moved animal carcasses along overhead trolleys from station to station. Adapting the process to automobile assembly, Ford in 1913 set up moving assembly lines in his plant in Highland Park, Michigan, that dramatically reduced the time and cost of producing cars. In 1914 he sold 248,000 Model T's. That year it took ninety-three minutes to assemble a car. By 1925 the

Changes in industry brought the start of mass production. Shown here is an early automobile assembly line at the Ford Motor Company's Michigan plant in 1913. Employees pushed the chassis from point to point by hand.

Ford plant turned out a new car every ten seconds of the working day.

While Ford was putting more and more cars on the road, the 1916 Federal Aid Roads Act set the framework for road building in the twentieth century. Removing control from county governments, it required every state desiring federal funds to establish a highway department to plan routes, oversee construction, and maintain roads. Providing for a planned highway system, the act produced a national network of two-lane, all-weather intercity roads.

THE BURGEONING TRUSTS

As businesses like Ford's grew, capital and organization became increasingly important, and the result was the formation of a growing number of trusts. Standard Oil started the trend in 1882 (see Chapter 18), but the greatest momentum came between 1898 and 1903. A series of mergers and consolidations swept the economy. Many smaller firms disappeared, swallowed up in giant corporations. By 1904 large-scale corporations of one form or another controlled nearly two fifths of the capital in manufacturing in the country.

The result was not monopoly, but *oligopoly*—control of a commodity or service by a small number of large, powerful companies. Six great financial groups dominated the railroad industry; a handful of holding companies controlled utilities and steel. Rockefeller's Standard Oil owned about 85 percent of the oil business. Copper, tobacco, rubber, and other products likewise were held by only a few producers.

By 1909 just 1 percent of the industrial firms were producing nearly half of the manufactured goods. Giant businesses reached abroad for raw materials and new markets. United Fruit, an empire of plantations and steamships in the Caribbean, exploited opportunities created by victory in the war with Spain. U.S. Steel worked with overseas companies to fix the price of steel rails, an unattainable dream just a few years before.

Though the trend has been overstated, finance capitalists like J. P. Morgan tended to replace the industrial capitalists of an earlier era. Able to finance the mergers and reorganizations, investment bankers played a greater and greater role in the economy. A multibillion-dollar financial house, J. P. Morgan and Company operated a network of control that ran from New York to every industrial and financial center in the nation. Like other investment firms, it held directorships in many corporations, creating "interlocking directorates" that allowed it to control many businesses.

Massive business growth set off a decade-long debate over what government should do about the trusts. Some critics wanted simply to break them up. Others argued that large-scale business was a mark of the times; it produced more goods and better lives. The debate over the trusts influenced politics throughout the Progressive Era.

MANAGING THE MACHINES

Mass production changed the direction of American industry. Size, system, organization, and marketing became increasingly important. Management focused on speed and product, not on workers. Assembly-line technology changed tasks and, to some extent, values. The goal was no longer to make a unique product that would be better than the one before. The goal now was to make each product come off the line exactly alike.

In a development that rivaled assembly lines in importance, businesses established industrial research laboratories where scientists and engineers developed new products. General Electric founded the first one in 1900 in a barn. It proved so successful that Du Pont, Eastman Kodak, and Standard Oil soon established research laboratories of their own. As the source of new ideas and technology, the labs altered life in the twentieth century.

Through all this, business became large-scale, mechanized, and managed. By 1920 close to one half of all industrial workers labored in factories employing more than 250 people. More than a third worked in factories that were part of multiplant companies.

Industries that processed materials—iron and steel, paper, cement, and chemicals—were increasingly continuous and automatic. In the glass industry, new machines ended the domination of highly skilled and well-paid craft workers. The machines turned out plate glass and ribbons of automobile window glass, and workers tending them could not fall behind. Foremen still managed the laborers on the factory floor, but more and more the rules came down from a central office where trained, professional managers supervised production flow. Workers lost control of the work pace. Employers successfully sped up the conveyor belt to heighten production. In the automobile industry, output per man-hour multiplied an extraordinary four times between 1909 and 1919.

Folkways of the work place—workers passing job-related knowledge to each other, setting their own pace, and in effect running the shop—gave way to "scientific" labor management. More than anyone else, Frederick Winslow Taylor, an inventive mechanical engineer, strove to extract maximum efficiency from each worker. Taylor proposed two major reforms. First, management must take responsibility for job-related knowledge and classify it into "rules, laws, and formulae." Second, management should control the work place "through *enforced* standardization of methods, *enforced* adoption of the best implements and working conditions, and *enforced* cooperation."

Taylor's methods included time-and-motion studies, training workers for particular tasks, and differential pay rates that rewarded those who worked fastest. Armed with stopwatches, his disciples reduced a factory's operations to the simplest tasks, then devised the most efficient way to perform them. The doctrine of scientific management spread throughout American industry.

Workers caught up in the changing industrial system experienced the benefits of efficiency and productivity; in some industries they earned more. But they suffered important losses as well. Performing repetitive tasks, they seemed part of the machinery, to whose pace and needs they moved. Bored, they might easily have lost pride of workmanship, though many workers, it is clear, did not. Jobs became not only monotonous but dangerous. Under pressure of speed, boredom or miscalculation could bring disaster. Meat cutters sliced fingers and

Fire nets were of no avail to the Triangle garment workers who jumped from the upper stories to escape the flames.

hands. Forty-six steel workers were killed on the job in just one mill in 1906. Injuries were part of many jobs.

In March 1911 a fire at the Triangle Shirtwaist Company in New York focused attention on unsafe working conditions. Seamstresses were trapped in the building because exit doors had been closed and locked by the company to prevent theft and to shut out union organizers. Many died in the stampede down the narrow stairways or the single fire escape. Others leaped from the building's top floors to escape the flames. One hundred and forty-six people died.

A few days later 80,000 people marched silently in the rain in a funeral procession up Fifth Avenue. The protests impelled New York's governor to appoint a State Factory Investigating Commission that recommended laws to shorten the workweek and improve safety conditions in factories and stores.

SOCIETY'S MASSES

National networks of products and consumers helped fuel the mass society which depended on an enormous increase in the labor force to work in the factories, mines, and forests. Immigration soared, and women, blacks, and Mexican Americans played larger roles.

WOMEN AT WORK

Women worked in larger and larger numbers. In 1900 more than 5 million worked. Of those employed, single women outnumbered married women by seven to one. Most women held service jobs. Only a small number held higher paying jobs as professionals or managers.

In the 1890s women made up over a quarter of medical school graduates. Adopting rigid standards, men gradually squeezed them out. Few women taught in colleges and universities, and those that did were expected to resign if they married. Men believed that once a woman became a "homemaker," she should have no other job.

More women than men graduated from high school, and with professions like medicine and science largely closed to them, they often turned to the new "business schools" that offered training in stenography, typing, and bookkeeping. In 1920 over a quarter of all employed women held clerical jobs. Many others taught school.

In 1907 and 1908 investigators studied 22,000 women workers in Pittsburgh; 60 percent of them earned less than $7 a week, a minimum for "decent living." Fewer than 1 percent held skilled jobs; most tended machines, wrapped and labeled, or did handwork that required no particular skill.

Critics charged that women's employment endangered the home, threatened reproductive functions, and even robbed them of their "special charm." Adding to the fears, the birth rate continued to drop between 1900 and 1920, and the divorce rate soared. By 1916 there was one divorce for every nine marriages as compared to one for twenty-one in 1880.

Many children worked. In 1900 about 3 million children—nearly 20 percent of those between the ages of five and fifteen—held full- or almost full-time jobs. Thousands of children worked in mines and southern cotton mills.

Gradually the use of child labor shrank when states passed compulsory education and minimum age laws. Families focused greater and greater attention on the children, and child-rearing became a central concern of family life.

As the middle-class family changed from an economic to an emotional unit, middle-class women claimed increasing pride in homemaking and motherhood. Mother's Day, as a national holiday, was formally established in 1913. With families preferring fewer children, birth control became a more acceptable practice. Margaret Sanger, a nurse and outspoken social reformer, led a campaign to give physicians broad discretion in prescribing contraceptives. Her efforts were resisted by the imposition of a ban on interstate transportation of contraceptive devices and information under the federal Comstock Law (see Chapter 19).

THE NIAGARA MOVEMENT AND THE NAACP

At the turn of the century eight of every ten blacks lived in rural areas, mainly in the South. Most were poor sharecroppers. "Jim Crow" laws segregated many schools, railroad cars, hotels, and hospitals. Poll taxes and other devices disfranchised blacks and many poor whites. Violence was common; between 1900 and 1914, white mobs murdered over a thousand black people, often mutilating them and burning them alive.

Many blacks labored in the cotton farms, railroad camps, sawmills, and mines of the South under conditions of peonage—trading their lives and labor for food and shelter. Often illiterate, they were forced to sign contracts which tied them to their jobs. Armed guards patrolled the camps and whipped those trying to escape. Few unions admitted blacks to their ranks, and almost always blacks earned less than whites in the same job. The illiteracy rate among blacks dropped from 45 percent in 1900 to 30 percent in 1910, but nowhere were they given equal school facilities, teachers' salaries, or educational materials.

In 1905 a group of black leaders met near Niagara Falls, New York, and pledged action on behalf of voting, equal access to economic opportunity, integration, and equality before the law. At their head was sociologist W.E.B. Du Bois, professor of history and economics at Atlanta University. Rejecting Booker T. Washington's gradualist approach, the Niagara movement claimed for blacks "every single right that belongs to a freeborn American, political, civil, and social; and until we get these rights we will never cease to protest." It kept alive a program of militant action focusing on equal rights and the education of black youth, and it spawned later civil rights movements. In *The Souls of Black Folk* (1903) and other works, Du Bois eloquently called for justice and equality.

Race riots broke out in Atlanta, Georgia, in 1906 and in Springfield, Illinois, in 1908. White mobs invaded black neighborhoods, burning, looting, and killing. William E. Walling, a wealthy southerner and settlement-house worker, Mary Ovington, a white anthropology student, and Oswald Garrison Villard, grandson of the famous abolitionist William Lloyd Garrison, were outraged. Along with other reformers, white and black, they issued a call for the conference that organized the National Association for the Advancement of Colored People, which swiftly became the most important civil rights organization in the country. Created in 1910, within four years the NAACP grew to over 6000 members. The eight top officers included one black—Director of Publicity and Research W.E.B. Du Bois.

Joined by the National Urban League, which was created in 1911, the NAACP pressured employers, labor unions, and the government on behalf of African Americans. It won some victories, but blacks continued to experience disfranchisement, poor job opportunities, and segregation. Little of progressivism's progress came their way.

IMMIGRANTS IN THE LABOR FORCE

Between 1901 and 1920 the extraordinarily high total of 14.5 million immigrants entered the country, more than in any previous twenty-year period. Continuing the recent trend (see

Chapter 19), many came from southern and eastern Europe. Still called the "new" immigrants, they met hostility from "older" immigrants of northern European stock who questioned their values and appearance.

Many of the immigrants came from Italy, Austria-Hungary, Poland, and Russia. Most were Catholic or Jewish in religion. More than a third were illiterate, and most, coming from peasant backgrounds, were unskilled. More than two thirds were males.

Labor agents—called *padroni* among the Italians, Greeks, and Syrians—recruited immigrant workers, found them jobs, and deducted a fee from their wages. Headquartered in Salt Lake City, Leonidas G. Skliris, the "Czar of the Greeks," provided workers for the Utah Copper Company and the Western Pacific Railroad. Agents similarly distributed immigrant workers to major eastern and midwestern cities.

Immigration moved both ways. Fifty percent or more of some groups returned "to the old country." Many Italian men virtually commuted, "birds of passage" who returned home every slack season. However, the outbreak of World War I interrupted this practice and trapped hundreds of thousands of Italians and others in the United States who had planned to return to Europe.

Older residents lumped the newcomers together, ignoring geographic, religious, and other differences. Preserving important regional distinctions, Italians tended to settle as Calabreses, Venetians, Abruzzis, and Sicilians. Native-born Americans viewed them all simply as Italians. Henry Ford and other employers tried to erase the difference through English classes and deliberate "Americanization" programs. In similar fashion, the International Harvester Corporation taught Polish laborers to speak English, but it had other lessons to impart as well. Factory Americanization programs were designed to produce good factory workers as well as good American citizens.

Nativist sentiment, which had accompanied earlier waves of immigration, intensified. Old-stock Americans sneered at the newcomers' dress and language. Racial theories emphasized

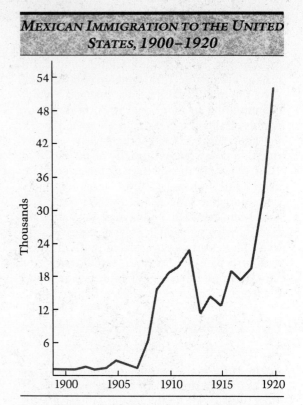

MEXICAN IMMIGRATION TO THE UNITED STATES, 1900–1920

Source: U.S. Bureau of the Census, Statistical Abstract of the United States: 1982–83 (103rd edition) Washington, D.C., 1982.

the superiority of northern Europeans, and the new "science" of eugenics suggested controls over the population growth of "inferior" peoples. Hostility against Catholics and Jews was common but touched other groups as well. In 1902 immigration from China—which had been suspended in 1882—was entirely prohibited.

Congress passed statutes requiring literacy tests designed to curtail immigration from southern and eastern Europe, but they were vetoed by Presidents Taft and Wilson. In 1917 Congress passed such a measure over Wilson's veto. Other measures tried to limit immigration from Mexico and Japan.

At the beginning of the twentieth century, Mexicans for the first time immigrated in large numbers, especially after a revolution in Mexico in 1910 forced many to flee across the northern border. (The exact number is unknown.) Almost all came from the Mexican lower class, eager to escape peonage and violence in their native land. Labor agents usually in the employ of large corporations or working for ranchers, recruited Mexican workers. After the turn of the century, almost 10 percent of the total population of Mexico moved to the American Southwest.

The Mexican immigrants helped to transform the Southwest. They built highways, dug irrigation ditches, laid railroad track, and picked cotton and vegetables. Yet American society imposed harsh rules on these people. Segregation laws and practices often kept them out of hotels and other public accommodations. Schools either barred them or, ironically, tried to anglicize them in segregated facilities. Yet again, Mexican Americans clung to their culture.

CONFLICT IN THE WORKPLACE

Assembly lines, speed-ups, long hours, and low wages produced a dramatic increase in American industrial output and profits after 1900; they also gave rise to numerous strikes and other kinds of labor unrest. Sometimes strikes took place through actions of unions; sometimes workers just decided that they had had enough and walked off the job. Whatever the cause, strikes were frequent.

Strikes and absenteeism increased after 1910; labor productivity dropped 10 percent between 1915 and 1918, the first such decline in memory. Workers changed jobs in droves. Union membership grew. In 1900 only about 1 million workers belonged to unions; by 1920, 5 million belonged, about 13 percent of the work force. But only 1.5 percent of female workers belonged to unions in 1910 due to sex discrimination.

Although it never had many members, the Women's Trade Union League, founded in 1903, led the effort to organize women into trade unions, lobby for legislation protecting female workers, and educate the public on the problems and needs of working women.

As tensions grew between capital and labor, some middle-class Americans became fearful that, unless something was done to improve the workers' situation, there might be violence or even revolution. This fear, along with some genuine desire to improve labor's lot, motivated some of the labor-oriented reforms of the Progressive Era.

Samuel Gompers' American Federation of Labor (AFL), by far the largest union organization, remained devoted to the interests of skilled craftsmen. While it aimed partly at better wages and working conditions, it also sought to limit entry into the craft and protect worker prerogatives. Within limits, the AFL found acceptance among giant business corporations eager for conservative policies and labor stability.

Unlike the AFL, the Industrial Workers of the World (IWW) tried to organize the unskilled and foreign-born laborers working in the mass-

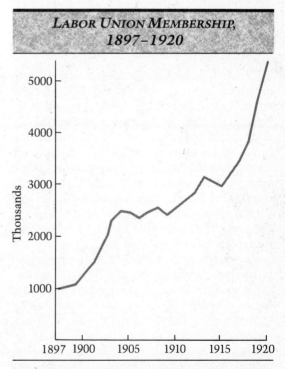

LABOR UNION MEMBERSHIP, 1897–1920

Source: U.S. Bureau of the Census, Statistical Abstract of the United States: 1982–83 (103rd edition) Washington, D.C., 1982.

production industries. Founded in Chicago in 1905, it aimed to unite the American working class into a mammoth union to promote labor's interests. The IWW, or Wobblies as they were known, urged social revolution to create a workers' world.

The IWW led a number of major strikes. The Lawrence, Massachusetts (1912), and Paterson, New Jersey (1912), strikes attracted national attention. Lawrence seized the limelight when the strikers sent off their ill-clad and hungry children out of the city to stay with sympathetic families; Paterson did so when they rented New York's Madison Square Garden for a massive labor pageant. They believed that a series of local strikes would intensify capitalists' repression, then bring about a general strike, and eventually usher in a workers' commonwealth.

The IWW fell short of these objectives, but during its lifetime—from 1905 to the mid-1920s—it made major gains among immigrant workers in the Northeast, migrant farm labor on the Plains, and loggers and miners in the South and Far West. In factories like Ford's, it recruited workers resentful of the speed-ups on the assembly lines.

Concerned about labor unrest, business leaders turned to the new fields of applied psychology and personnel management. A school of industrial psychology emerged. A few businesses established industrial-relations departments, hired public relations firms to improve their corporate image, and linked productivity to job safety and happiness. Ivy L. Lee, a pioneer in the field of corporate public relations, advised such corporate clients as Standard Oil and the Pennsylvania Railroad on how to improve relations with labor and the public.

On January 5, 1914, Ford took another significant step. He announced the Five-Dollar Day. With a single stroke, he doubled the wage rate for common labor, reduced the working day from nine hours to eight, and established a personnel department to place workers in appropriate jobs. As a result, Ford had the pick of the labor force. Turnover declined; absenteeism fell to 0.3 percent. Output increased; the IWW at Ford collapsed. At first scornful of the "uto-pian" plan, business leaders across the country soon copied it.

LIFE IN AMERICA, 1920

For many Americans, the quality of life improved significantly between 1900 and 1920. Jobs were relatively plentiful, and in a development of great importance, more and more people were entering the professions as doctors, lawyers, teachers, and engineers (see Chapter 23). With comfortable incomes, a growing middle class could take advantage of new lifestyles, inventions, and forms of entertainment. Mass consumption, promoted by a mushrooming advertising industry, fueled industry's mass production. Advertisers used sampling techniques, market testing, and research in their effort to sell products.

Mass production swept the clothing industry and dressed more Americans better than any people ever before. Manufacturers developed standard clothing and shoe sizes that fit most bodies. These "off-the-rack" items resulted in less expensive clothes and blurred the distinctions between rich and poor. By 1900, 90 percent of men and boys wore the new "ready-to-wear" clothes.

The income of people who worked in manufacturing rose from an average of $418 a year in 1900 to $1342 a year in 1920. While the middle class expanded, the rich also grew richer. By 1920, 5 percent of the population received almost one fourth of all income.

In 1920, the median age of the population was only twenty-five. (It is now nearly thirty-three.) Immigration accounted for part of the youthfulness, since most immigrants were young, and so did death rates. Thanks to medical advances and better living conditions, death rates dropped in the early years of the century; the average life span increased. Between 1900 and 1920 life expectancy rose dramatically: for white women, from forty-nine to fifty-six years; for white males, from forty-seven to fifty-four years; for blacks and other minorities, from thirty-three to forty-five years.

Infant mortality remained high. In comparison to today, fewer babies on average survived to adolescence, and fewer people survived beyond middle age. As a result, there were relatively fewer older people—in 1900 only 4 percent of the population was older than sixty-five compared to 13 percent today. Still, improvements in health care helped people live longer, and as a result, the incidence of cancer and heart disease increased.

In 1900 six of every ten Americans lived on farms or in towns of fewer than 2500 people. But the flight from the farms continued, and a decade later only five in ten still lived there. By 1920 fewer than a third of Americans lived on farms; fewer than half lived in rural areas.

Cities grew, and by any earlier standards, they grew on a colossal scale. Downtowns became a central hive of skyscrapers, department stores, warehouses, and hotels. Strips of factories radiated from the center. As street railways spread, cities took on a systematic pattern of socioeconomic segregation, usually in rings. Immigrants lived in the innermost ring, and wealthy suburbs occupied the outermost rings.

The giants were New York, Chicago, and Philadelphia—industrial cities that turned out every kind of product. Smaller cities like Rochester, New York, or Cleveland, Ohio, specialized in manufacturing a specific line of goods or processing regional products for the national market. Railroads instead of highways tied things together.

Step by step cities adopted their twentieth-century forms. Between 1909 and 1915 Los Angeles passed a series of ordinances that gave rise to modern urban zoning. For the first time the ordinances divided a city into three districts of specified use: a residential area, an industrial area, and an area open to residence and a limited list of industries. Other cities followed. The New York Zoning Law of 1916 became a model copied across the nation.

Zoning gave order to city development, keeping skyscrapers out of factory districts, factories out of the suburbs. It also had powerful social repercussions. In the South zoning became a tool to extend racial segregation; in northern cities it acted against ethnic minorities. Jews in

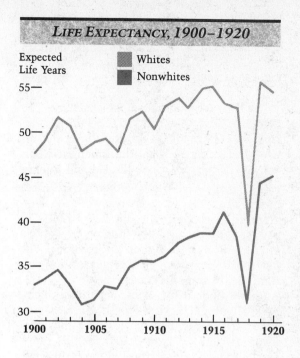

LIFE EXPECTANCY, 1900–1920

Expected Life Years

Whites
Nonwhites

New York, Italians in Boston, Poles in Detroit, blacks in Chicago—zoning laws held them all at arm's length.

While many people fled the farm, farmers themselves prospered, the beneficiaries of greater production and expanding urban markets. Rural Free Delivery (RFD), begun in 1893, helped diminish the farmers' sense of isolation. The delivery of mail to the farm door opened that door to a wider world; it exposed farmers to urban thinking, national advertising, and political events. In addition, parcel post (1913) permitted the sending of packages through the U.S. mail, while better roads, mail-order catalogs, and other innovations knit farmers into the larger society.

Land prices rose with crop prices, and farm tenancy increased, especially in the South. Many southern tenant farmers were black, and they suffered from farm-bred diseases. In 1909 the Rockefeller Sanitary Commission began a sanitation campaign that eventually wiped out hookworm, a farm-bred disease widespread among poor farmers in the South, and in 1912 the U.S. Public Health Service began work on rural malaria. Improvements in microscopes allowed scientists to concentrate on the cell; chromosome, gene, and hormone became household words.

THE USES OF LEISURE

Thanks to changing work rules and mechanization, many Americans benefited from more leisure time. The average work week for manufacturing laborers fell from sixty hours in 1890 to fifty-one in 1920. White-collar workers often spent even less time at the office. The new leisure time gave more people more opportunity for pleasurable diversions.

People flocked to places of entertainment. Baseball entrenched itself as the national pastime. Attendance at major-league games doubled between 1903 and 1910. Football also drew fans, although critics attacked the sport's violence and the use of "tramp athletes," nonstudents whom colleges paid to play. In 1905, the worst year, 18 players were killed and 150 seriously injured. Prodded by Theodore Roosevelt, representatives of the major colleges formed the Intercollegiate Athletic Association to clean up the sport; in 1910 that organization was renamed the National Collegiate Athletic Association.

Movie theatres opened everywhere. By 1910 there were 10,000 of them, drawing a weekly audience of 10 million people. Admission was usually five cents, and movies stressing laughter and pathos appealed to a mass market. In 1915 D. W. Griffith, a talented and creative director, produced the first movie spectacular, *The Birth of a Nation.*

Before 1910 band concerts were the country's most popular entertainment. As many as 20,000 amateur bands played in parks on summer Sunday afternoons. John Philip Sousa, the famous "March King," led a touring band that profited from the self-confident nationalism that followed the Spanish-American War. Robust, patriotic marches like "The Stars and Stripes Forever" (1896) earned him wealth and popularity.

Soon, automobiles and phonographs began to lure audiences away from the concerts. Early phonograph records were usually of vaudeville skits; orchestral recordings began in 1906. In 1919, 2.25 million phonographs were produced; two years later more than 100 million records were sold. People sang less and listened more.

The faster rhythms of syncopated ragtime became the rage, especially after 1911 when Irving Berlin, a Russian immigrant, wrote "Alexander's Ragtime Band." Ragtime set off a nationwide dance craze. Waltzes and polkas gave way to a host of new dances, many with animal names: the Fox Trot, Bunny Hop, Turkey Trot, Snake, and Kangaroo Dip. Partners were not allowed to dance too close; bouncers tapped them on the shoulder if they got closer than nine inches.

Vaudeville, increasingly popular after 1900, reached maturity around 1915. Drawing on the immigrant experience and the rich variety of city life, it included skits, songs, comics, acrobats, and magicians. Dances and jokes ex-

Although they were denounced as indecent and disgusting, the turkey trot and other "animal" dances were extremely popular. A young woman in New Jersey was jailed for fifty days for doing the turkey trot.

pressed an earthiness new to mass audiences. By 1914 stage runways extended into the crowd; female performers had bared their legs, and costumes revealed the midriff as well.

In songs like "St. Louis Blues" (1914), W. C. Handy took the black southern folk music of the blues to northern cities. Gertrude "Ma" Rainey sang in black vaudeville for nearly thirty-five years, and she discovered the twelve-year-old Bessie Smith, who became the "Empress of the Blues." Another musical innovation came from New Orleans. Charles (Buddy) Bolden, Ferdinand "Jelly Roll" Morton, and Louis Armstrong played an improvisational music that had no formal name. Reaching Chicago, it was finally named "jazz." Jazz jumped, and jazz musicians relied on feeling and mood.

Popular fiction reflected changing interests. Kate Douglas Wiggins' *Rebecca of Sunnybrook Farm* (1903) showed the continuing popularity of rural themes. Westerns also sold well, but readers turned more and more to detective thrillers with hard-bitten city detectives and science fiction tales featuring the latest dream in technology. The Tom Swift series, begun in 1910, looked ahead to spaceships, ray guns, and gravity nullifiers. Edward L. Stratemeyer, the mind behind Tom Swift, brought the techniques of mass production to book writing. He employed a stable of writers to turn out hundreds of Tom Swift, Rover Boys, and Bobbsey Twins stories for young readers.

EXPERIMENTATION IN THE ARTS

"There is a state of unrest all over the world in art as in all other things," the director of New York's Metropolitan Museum said in 1908. "It is the same in literature, as in music, in painting, and in sculpture." Isadora Duncan and Ruth St. Denis transformed the dance. Departing from traditional ballet steps, both women stressed improvisation, emotion, and the human form. Draped in flowing robes, Duncan told her students to "listen to the music with your soul. . . . Unless your dancing springs from an inner emotion and expresses an idea, it will be meaningless." After a triumphant performance with the New York Symphony in 1908, her ideas and techniques swept the country.

The lofts and apartments of New York's Greenwich Village attracted artists, writers, and poets interested in experimentation and change. To these artists, the city was the focus of national life and the sign of a new culture. Robert Henri and the realist painters—known to their critics as the Ashcan School—relished the city's excitement. They wanted "to paint truth and to paint it with strength and fearlessness and individuality." With the same feel for the environment that Brandeis and other reformers had shown, their paintings depicted street scenes, colorful crowds, and slum children swimming in the river.

In 1913 a show at the New York Armory presented 1600 modernist paintings, prints, and sculptures. The work of Picasso, Cézanne, Matisse, Brancusi, Van Gogh, and Gauguin dazed and dazzled American observers. Critics attacked the show as worthless and depraved, but it was a clear look at the future of art. The Post-Impressionists changed the direction of twentieth-century art and influenced adventuresome American painters. John Marin, Max Weber, Georgia O'Keeffe, Arthur Dove, and other modernists experimented in ways foreign to Henri's realists. Using bold colors and abstract patterns, they defied convention and worked to capture the energy of urban life.

There was an extraordinary outburst of poetry. In 1912 Harriet Monroe started the magazine *Poetry* in Chicago, the hotbed of the new poetry; Ezra Pound and Vachel Lindsay, both daring experimenters with ideas and verse, published in the first issue. T. S. Eliot published the classic "Love Song of J. Alfred Prufrock" in *Poetry* in 1915. Attacked bitterly by conservative critics, the poem established Eliot's leadership among a group of poets who rejected traditional meter and rhyme as artificial constraints. Eliot, Pound, and Amy Lowell, among others, believed that the poet's task was to capture fleeting images in verse. Others experimenting with new techniques in poetry included Robert Frost, Edgar Lee Masters, and Carl Sandburg. True to the increasingly urban

CHRONOLOGY

1898	Mergers and consolidations begin to sweep the business world, leading to fear of trusts
1900	General Electric founds the first industrial research laboratory
1903	Ford Motor Company formed W.E.B. DuBois calls for justice and equality for African Americans in *The Souls of Black Folk* Women's Trade Union League formed to organize women workers
1905	Industrial Workers of the World (IWW) established African-American leaders inaugurate Niagara movement, advocating integration and equal opportunity for African Americans
1909	Campaign by Rockefeller Sanitary Commission wipes out hookworm disease
1910	NAACP founded National Collegiate Athletic Association formed
1911	Frederick Winslow Taylor publishes *The Principles of Scientific Management* Fire at the Triangle Shirtwaist Company kills 146 people Irving Berlin popularizes rhythm of ragtime with "Alexander's Ragtime Band" National Urban League created
1912	IWW leads strikes in Massachusetts and New Jersey Harriet Monroe begins publishing magazine *Poetry*
1913	Ford introduces the moving assembly line in Highland Park, Michigan, plant Mother's Day becomes national holiday Show at New York Armory presents modernist paintings, prints, and sculptures
1915	D. W. Griffith produces the first movie spectacular, *The Birth of a Nation* T. S. Eliot publishes "The Love Song of J. Alfred Prufrock"
1916	Federal Aid Roads Act creates national road network Margaret Sanger forms New York Birth Control League
1917	Congress passes law requiring literacy test for all immigrants

vision of America, Sandburg's poem "Chicago" celebrated the vitality of the city.

Manners and morals change slowly, yet in the first two decades of this century sweeping change was underway; anyone who doubted it could visit a gallery, see a film, listen to music, or read one of the new literary magazines. Garrets and galleries were filled with a breathtaking sense of excitement about new forms of expression.

The ferment of progressivism in the city, state, and nation reshaped the country. In a burst of reform, people built playgrounds, restructured taxes, regulated business, won the vote for women, shortened working hours, altered political systems, opened kindergartens, and improved factory safety. They tried to fulfill the national promise of dignity and liberty.

Across America there was a mood of excitement, a feeling expressed in the best efforts of artists and politicians. Racism, repression, and labor conflict were present, but there was also talk of hope, progress, and change. In politics, science, journalism, education, and a host of other fields, people believed for a time that they could make a difference, and in trying to do so, they became part of the progressive generation.

RECOMMENDED READING

There are several important analyses of the Progressive Era, including Robert H. Wiebe, *The Search for Order, 1877–1920* (1967); Richard Hofstadter, *The Age of Reform* (1955); Samuel P. Hays, *The Response to Industrialism* (1957); Gabriel Kolko, *The Triumph of Conservatism* (1963); and James T. Kloppenberg, *Uncertain Victory: Social Democracy and Progressivism in European and American Thought, 1870–1920* (1986). C. Vann Woodward, *Origins of the New South, 1877–1913* (1951), is a superb account of developments in the South. Intellectual currents are traced in Charles Forcey, *The Crossroads of Liberalism* (1961); social justice reforms in Harold U. Faulkner, *The Quest for Social Justice, 1898–1914* (1931).

Work, workers, and the industrial society are treated in Herbert G. Gutman, *Work, Culture and Society in Industrializing America* (1977); David Montgomery, *Workers' Control in America: Studies in the History of Work, Technology, and Labor Struggles* (1979); and David Brody, *Workers in Industrial America: Essays on the Twentieth Century Struggle* (1980). Alfred D. Chandler, *Strategy and Structure: Chapters in the History of American Industrial Enterprise* (1962); Samuel Haber, *Efficiency and Uplift: Scientific Management in the Progressive Era* (1964); and Peter Conn, *The Divided Mind: Ideology and Imagination in America, 1898–1917* (1984) are useful overviews. Sam Bass Warner, Jr., *Streetcar Suburbs* (1962) and *The Urban Wilderness* (1972) are excellent on urban developments, including zoning and industrial growth.

On women's rights see Eleanor Flexner, *Century of Struggle: The Women's Rights Movement in the United States* (1959); William L. O'Neill, *Everyone Was Brave: The Rise and Fall of Feminism in America* (1969); Leslie Woodcock Tentler, *Wage-Earning Women: Industrial Work and Family Life in the United States, 1900–1930* (1979); Sheila M. Rothman, *Woman's Proper Place* (1978); Ellen Condliffe Lagemann, *A Generation of Women: Education in the Lives of the Progressive Reformers* (1979); and Theodora Penny Martin, *The Sound of Our Own Voices: Women's Study Clubs, 1860–1910* (1987).

On Du Bois, see Elliott M. Rudwick, *W.E.B. Du Bois* (1968). Other useful books include George M. Fredrickson, *The Black Image in the White Mind* (1971), and Charles F. Kellogg, *NAACP: A History of the National Association for the Advancement of Colored People, 1909–1920* (1967).

Donald B. Cole, *Immigrant City: Lawrence, Massachusetts, 1845–1921* (1963), and Thomas Kessner, *The Golden Door, Italian and Jewish Immigrant Mobility in New York City, 1880–1915* (1977), are helpful. Leonard Dinnerstein, Roger L. Nichols, and David M. Reimers, *Natives and Strangers: Ethnic Groups and the Building of America* (1979), offer a useful overview of Mexican American and the "new" immigrants.

The labor movement is covered in Harold Livesay, *Samuel Gompers and Organized Labor in America* (1978); Melvyn Dubofsky, *We Shall Be All: A History of the Industrial Workers of the World* (1969); Susan Estabrook Kennedy, *If All We Did Was to Weep at Home: A History of White Working Class Women in America* (1979); Barbara Mayer Wertheimer, *We Were There: The Story of Working Women in America* (1977); Patricia A. Cooper, *Once a Cigarmaker: Men, Women, and Work Culture in American Cigar Factories, 1900–1919* (1987); Martha Vicinus, *Independent Women: Work and Community For Single Women, 1850–1920* (1985); Joanne J. Meyerowitz, *Women Adrift: Independent Wage Earners in Chicago, 1880–1930* (1988); and Mary Drake McFeely, *Lady Inspectors: The Campaign for a Better Workplace, 1893–1921* (1988).

Studies of family life include W. Andrew Achenbaum, *Old Age in the New Land* (1978); William L. O'Neill, *Divorce in the Progressive Era* (1967); Tamara K. Hareven, ed., *Anonymous Americans* (1971) and *Transitions: The Family and Life Course in Historical Perspective* (1978). For birth control, see David M. Kennedy, *Birth Control in America: The Career of Margaret Sanger* (1970).

For the ways in which Americans entertained themselves, see Gunther Barth, *City People* (1980); Allison Danzig, *History of American Football* (1956), Russel B. Nye, *The Unembarrassed Muse: The Popular Arts in America* (1970); John E. DiMeglio, *Vaudeville U.S.A.* (1973); Ronald L. Davis, *A History of Music in American Life, Volume II: The Gilded Years, 1865–1920* (1980); and Robert Sklar, *Movie-Made America: A Social History of the American Movies* (1975).

23 FROM ROOSEVELT TO WILSON IN THE AGE OF PROGRESSIVISM

THE SPIRIT OF PROGRESSIVISM

REFORM IN THE CITIES AND STATES

THE REPUBLICAN ROOSEVELT

THE ORDEAL OF WILLIAM HOWARD TAFT

WOODROW WILSON'S NEW FREEDOM

On a sunny spring morning in 1909, Theodore Roosevelt left New York for an African safari. An ex-president at the age of fifty, he had turned over the White House to his chosen successor, William Howard Taft, and now he was off to hunt wild game. Some hoped he would not return. "I trust some lion will do its duty," Wall Street magnate J. P. Morgan said. Though he had built a reputation as an ardent conservationist, Roosevelt shot numerous lions, elephants, hippos, and rhinoceri, acquiring nearly 300 trophies in all.

It was good fun, and afterward Roosevelt set off on a tour of Europe. He argued with the pope, dined with the king and queen of Italy, and happily spent five hours reviewing troops of the German empire. Less happily, he followed events back home where, in the judgment of many friends, Taft was not working out as president.

Taft was puzzled by it all. Honest and warm-hearted, he had intended to continue Roosevelt's policies. But events turned out differently. The conservative and progressive wings of the Republican party split, and Taft often sided with the conservatives. Progressive Republicans urged Roosevelt to take control again of the party and the country.

Roosevelt came back to New York harbor on June 18, 1910, to the sound of naval guns and loud cheers. Greeting Gifford Pinchot, a close friend and one of Taft's leading opponents, with a hearty "Hello, Gifford," Roosevelt slipped away to his home in Oyster Bay, New York, where other friends awaited him.

Taft, who still viewed himself as a disciple of Roosevelt's, invited Teddy to spend a night or two at the White House, but the ex-president declined. Relations between the two friends cooled. "It is hard, very hard," Taft said in 1911, "to see a devoted friendship going to pieces like a rope of sand."

A year later there was no longer thought of friendship, only a desperate fight between Taft and Roosevelt for the Republican presidential nomination.

Taft won the nomination, but angry and ambitious, Roosevelt bolted and helped form a new party, the Progressive (or "Bull Moose") party, to unseat Taft and capture the White House. With Taft, Roosevelt, Woodrow Wilson (the Democratic party's candidate), and Socialist party candidate Eugene V. Debs all in the race, the election of 1912 became one of the most exciting in American history.

It was also one of the most important. The election of 1912 became a forum for Americans' concerns about the social and economic effects of urban-industrial growth. Each candidate offered a different vision for the future, and each expressed an aspect of progressive reform.

THE SPIRIT OF PROGRESSIVISM

For more than two decades progressivism dominated American life and in one way or another, it influenced almost everything that came after it. Politically, it fostered a reform movement that sought solutions for the problems of city, state, and nation. Intellectually, it drew on the expertise of the new social sciences and reflected a shift from older absolutes of class and religion to newer schools of thought that emphasized physiological explanations for behavior, the role of the environment in human development, and the relative nature of truth. Culturally, it inspired fresh modes of expression in dance, film, painting, literature, and architecture. Touching individuals in different ways, progressivism became a set of attitudes as well as a definable movement.

Unlike Populism, which grew mostly in the rural South and West, progressivism drew support across society. Progressivism appealed to the expanding middle class, prosperous farmers, and skilled laborers; it also attracted significant support in the business community.

Leadership came mainly from young, educated men and women. Many of them belonged to the professions—law, medicine, religion, business, teaching, and social work—and they thought they could use their expertise to improve society. They believed in progress and disliked waste. No single issue or concern united them all, but they shared a desire for change. Some wanted to purify municipal politics, others to clean up city streets, or to eradicate prostitution. They were Democrats, Republicans, Socialists and independents.

Progressives believed that if people knew the truth, they would act on it. Progress depended on knowledge. The progressives stressed individual morality and collective action, the scientific method, and the value of expert opinion. Like contemporary business leaders, they valued system, planning, management, and predictability. They wanted not only reform but efficiency.

Progressivism also fed on an organization impulse that encouraged people to join forces, share information, and solve problems. Between 1890 and 1920, a host of national societies and associations took shape—nearly 400 of them in just three decades. Some, such as the American Medical Association (1901), reflected the increasingly authoritative voice of the professions; others, such as the National Child Labor Committee, lobbied for legislation to regulate or reform specific issues.

Historians once viewed progressivism as the triumph of one group in society over another: urban reformers challenged city bosses; farmers took on powerful railroads. Now they stress the way progressivism brought people together rather than driving them apart. Disparate groups united in an effort to improve the well-being of many groups in society.

THE SOCIAL-JUSTICE MOVEMENT

Progressivism began in the cities during the 1890s. It first took hold among settlement workers and others interested in freeing individuals from the crushing impact of the slum and the factory. Ministers, intellectuals, social workers, and lawyers joined in a social-justice

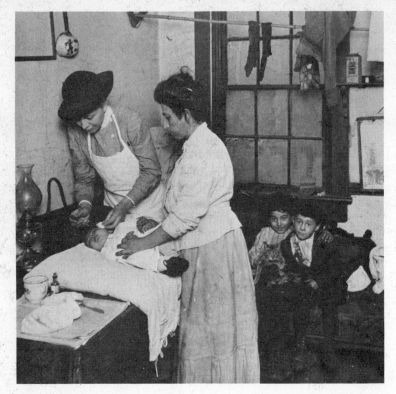

An Infant Welfare Society nurse treats the baby of an immigrant family in Chicago. A host of medical discoveries and improvement in the quality of medical education fostered an interest in public health work among social-justice reformers.

movement that focused national attention on the need for tenement house laws, more stringent child-labor legislation, and better working conditions for women. They brought pressure on municipal agencies for more and better parks, playgrounds, day nurseries, schools, and community services. Blending private and public action, settlement leaders turned increasingly to government aid.

Social-justice reformers were more interested in societal cures than individual charity. Unlike earlier reformers, they saw problems as endless and interrelated; individuals became part of a city's larger patterns. With that insight, social-service casework shifted from a focus on an individual's well-being to a scientific analysis of whole neighborhoods, occupations, and classes.

In 1900 Lawrence Veiller, a young social worker, put together a tenement-house exhibi-

tion that included over a thousand photographs, detailed maps of slum districts, statistical tables and charts, and graphic cardboard depictions of tenement blocks. Veiller correlated data on poverty and disease with housing conditions. Stirred by the public outcry, Governor Theodore Roosevelt appointed the New York State Tenement House Commission to do something about the problem.

With Veiller's success as a model, study after study analyzed the condition of the poor. Seeing their common problems, social-justice reformers formed the National Conference of Charities and Corrections, which in 1915 became the National Conference of Social Work. Through it, social workers discovered each other's efforts, shared methodology, and tried to establish themselves as a separate field within the social sciences. They formed professional schools at Harvard, the University of Chicago, and other major universities, and in 1909 they published their own magazine, the *Survey*. Instead of piecemeal reforms, they aimed at a comprehensive program of minimum wages, maximum hours, workers' compensation, and widows' pensions.

WOMAN SUFFRAGE, WOMAN'S RIGHTS

Women played a very large role in the social-justice movement. Feminists were particularly active, especially in the political sphere, between 1890 and 1914. Working-class as well as college-educated women pushed for reforms. From 1890 to 1910 the work of a number of national women's organizations, including the National Council of Mothers and the Women's Trade Union League, furthered the aims of the progressive movement. The National Association of Colored Women, the first black-sponsored social service agency in the nation, was founded in 1895.

Organizations such as the General Federation of Women's Clubs transformed literary meetings into social action gatherings. Drawing attention to women's concern for social reform, Mrs. Sarah P. Decker, who became president of the federation in 1904, told the members of her organization, "Dante is dead. . . . I think it is time that we dropped the study of his *Inferno* and turned our attention to our own."

Reluctant at first, the federation eventually lent support to woman suffrage, a cause that dated back to 1848. The suffrage movement suffered from disunity, male opposition, disagreement over whether to seek action at the state or national level, resistance from the Catholic Church, and opposition from liquor interests, who linked the cause to prohibition.

Women in the social-justice movement needed to influence elected officials—most of them men—whom women could not reach since they could not vote. Because politics was an avenue for reform, women activists became involved in the suffrage movement in growing numbers. After years of disagreement, the two major suffrage organizations, the National

Woman Suffrage Association and the American Woman Suffrage Association, merged in 1890 to form the National American Woman Suffrage Association. The merger opened a new phase of the suffrage movement, characterized by unity and a tightly controlled national organization.

In 1900 Carrie Chapman Catt became president of the National American Woman Suffrage Association, which by 1920 had nearly 2 million members. The association believed in peaceful lobbying to win the vote. Members of the Congressional Union, such as Alice Paul, were more militant. They interrupted public meetings, focused on Congress rather than the states, and in 1917 picketed the White House. The issue attracted many progressives who believed woman suffrage would purify politics. In 1918 the House passed a constitutional amendment stating simply that the right to vote shall not be denied "on account of sex." The Senate and enough states followed and, after three generations of suffragist efforts, the Nineteenth Amendment took effect in 1920.

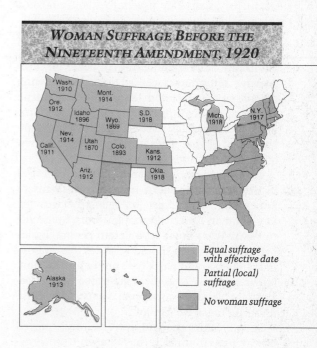

WOMAN SUFFRAGE BEFORE THE NINETEENTH AMENDMENT, 1920

Wash. 1910
Ore. 1912
Mont. 1914
Idaho 1896
Wyo. 1869
S.D. 1918
Mich. 1918
N.Y. 1917
Nev. 1914
Calif. 1911
Utah 1870
Colo. 1893
Kans. 1912
Ariz. 1912
Okla. 1918

Alaska 1913

- ■ Equal suffrage with effective date
- □ Partial (local) suffrage
- ▨ No woman suffrage

The social-justice movement had the most success in passing state laws limiting the working hours of women. By 1913 thirty-nine states set maximum working hours for women or banned the employment of women at night. As early as 1900 twenty-eight states had laws regulating child labor. But the courts often ruled against such laws, and families—needing extra income—sometimes ignored them.

In 1916 President Woodrow Wilson backed a law to limit child labor, the Keating-Owen Act, but in *Hammer* v. *Dagenhart* (1918) the Supreme Court overturned it as an improper regulation of local labor conditions. In 1919 Congress tried again in the Second Child Labor Act, also struck down by the Court in *Baily* v. *Drexel Furniture Company* (1922). Not until the 1930s did Congress succeed in passing a national child-labor law that the Supreme Court allowed to stand.

A FERMENT OF IDEAS

A dramatic shift in ideas became one of the most important forces behind progressive reform. Building on the developments of the 1890s (see Chapter 19), writers in law, economics, history, sociology, psychology, and a host of other fields advanced ideas that together challenged the status quo and called for change.

Most of the ideas focused on the role of the environment in shaping human behavior. Progressive reformers accepted society's growing complexity and called for a more scientific approach to social problems, allowed room for new theories, and above all rejected age-encrusted divine or natural "laws" in favor of ideas and actions that worked.

A new doctrine, called pragmatism, emerged in this ferment of ideas. It came from William James, the Harvard psychologist who was the key figure in American thought from the 1890s to World War I. A warm, tolerant person, James believed that truth should work for the individual, and it should work best not in abstraction, but in action. "True ideas are those we can assimilate, validate, corroborate, and verify. False ideas are those we cannot."

People, James thought, were not only shaped by their environment; they shaped it. In *Prag-* *matism* (1907), a book so popular it went through many editions, he praised "tough-minded" individuals who could live effectively in a world with no easy answers. The tough-minded accepted change; they knew how to pick manageable problems, gather facts, discard ideas that did not work, and act on those that did. Ideas that worked became truth. "What is the 'cash value' of a thought, idea or belief?" James asked. Does it work? Does it make a difference to the individual who experiences it? "The ultimate test for us of what a truth means," said James, "is the conduct it dictates."

The most influential educator of the Progressive Era, John Dewey, applied pragmatism to educational reform. He introduced an educational revolution, stressing children's needs and capabilities. Dewey argued that thought evolves in relation to the environment and that education is directly related to experience. New ideas in education, he said, are "as much a product of the changed social situation, and as much an effort to meet the needs of the society that is forming, as are changes in modes of industry and commerce." He opposed memorization and dogmatic, authoritarian teaching methods; he emphasized personal growth, free inquiry, creativity and cooperative learning. Providing an overarching framework within which others could fit, William James and Dewey had a great effect on other thinkers.

Rejecting the older view of the law as universal and unchanging, lawyers and legal theorists instead viewed it as a reflection of the environment—an instrument for social change. A movement grew among judges for "sociological jurisprudence" that related the law to social reform. Increasingly, judges and lawyers began to consider crime as much the result of problems in society as individual weakness.

Louis D. Brandeis' career illustrated the change. A rich corporate lawyer, he changed his mind about social issues during the depression of the 1890s, and as the "People's Attorney," he fought corporate abuses and political corruption. In 1908 he accepted an invitation from the National Consumers' League to defend an Oregon law limiting working hours for women to ten hours a day.

Brandeis decided on a new kind of argument. With the help of Lillian Wald (see Chapter 19), he compiled masses of medical and sociological data, and when he submitted to the Court a 104-page brief, only 2 pages examined traditional legal precedents. The balance included reports from factory inspectors, health and hygiene commissioners, and expert commissions—all showing that the ten-hour law was necessary to protect the health, safety, and morals of women in Oregon.

Agreeing, the Supreme Court in *Muller* v. *Oregon* (1908) upheld the Oregon statute, and the famous "Brandeis Brief," based on environmental data rather than legal precedent, influenced lawyers and courts across the country. Like so many other reform efforts during these years, it assumed that changes in the environment could improve the lives of people and produce a better society.

Socialism, a reformist political philosophy, grew dramatically before the First World War. Organized in 1901, the Socialist party of America doubled in membership between 1904 and 1908, then tripled in the four years after that. By 1911 there were socialist mayors in thirty-two cities. Although its doctrines were aimed at an urban proletariat, the Socialist party also drew support in parts of the rural South and West.

Eugene V. Debs, five times the party's presidential candidate, offset the popular image of the wild-eyed radical. A gentle and reflective man, Debs never developed a cohesive platform, but he was an eloquent, passionate, and visionary leader. He led the ARU into the Pullman strike. Running for president, he gained 100,000 votes in 1900; 400,000 in 1904; and 900,000 in 1912, the party's peak year.

REFORM IN THE CITIES AND STATES

Believing in government as an agent of change, the progressives wanted to curb the influence of "special interests" and make government follow the public will. Once this goal had been achieved, they welcomed government action at whatever level was appropriate. The use of federal power increased, along with the power and prestige of the presidency. Most important, the progressives believed in the ability of experts to solve problems. At every level, thousands of commissions and agencies took form. Staffed by trained experts, they oversaw a multitude of matters from railroad rates to public health.

REFORM IN THE CITIES

In the early years of the twentieth century, urban reform movements spread across the nation. In 1894 the National Municipal League was organized, and it became the forum for debate over civic reform, changes in the tax laws, and municipal ownership of public utilities. Within a few years nearly every city had a variety of clubs and organizations directed at improving the quality of city life.

In the 1880s reformers would call an evening conference, pass resolutions, and then go home; after 1900 they formed associations, adopted long-range policies, and hired employees to achieve them. In the mid-1890s only Chicago had an urban reform league with a full-time paid executive; within a decade there were such leagues in every major city.

In city after city, reformers reordered municipal government. They broadened the scope of utility regulation, restricted city franchises, updated tax assessments, and tried to clean up the electoral machinery. Committed to efficiency, and above all, results, they developed a trained civil service to oversee planning and day-to-day operations.

In constructing their model governments, urban reformers often turned to recent advances in business management and organization. They stressed continuity and expertise, a system in which professional experts staffed a government overseen by elective officials. They hired engineers to manage utility and water systems, physicians and nurses to improve public health, and city planners to supervise park and highway development. The growing number of experts and commissions widened the gap between voters and decision makers but dramatically improved the efficiency of government.

As cities exploded in size, they freed themselves from the tight controls of state legislatures and began to experiment with their governments. Struggling to recover from a devastating hurricane in 1900, Galveston, Texas, pioneered the commission form of government: a form of municipal government in which commissions of appointed experts, rather than elected officials, ran the city. Other cities simply hired a city manager.

In the race for reform, a number of city mayors won national reputations working to modernize taxes, clean up politics, lower utility rates, and control the awarding of valuable city franchises. In Toledo, Ohio, Mayor Samuel M. ("Golden Rule") Jones labored to improve the quality of life for the people in his city. In Cleveland, Ohio, Mayor Tom L. Johnson also fought to improve city life. He cut down on corruption, cut off special privilege, updated taxes, and gave Cleveland a reputation as the country's best-governed city.

Finding it difficult to regulate powerful city utilities and keep their costs down, Johnson and mayors in other cities turned more and more to public ownership of gas, electricity, water, and transportation. Called "gas and water socialism," the idea spread swiftly. In 1896 fewer than half of American cities owned their own waterworks; by 1915 almost two thirds did.

ACTION IN THE STATES

Reformers soon discovered, however, that many problems lay beyond a city's boundaries, and they turned for action to the state government. From the 1890s to 1920 they worked to stiffen state laws regulating the labor of women and children, create and strengthen commissions to regulate railroads and utilities, impose corporate and inheritance taxes, improve mental and penal institutions, and allocate more funds for state universities, the training ground for the experts and educated citizenry needed for the new society.

Maryland passed the first workers' compensation law in 1902; soon most industrial states had such legislation. Between 1900 and 1920, states also increasingly adopted factory inspection laws, mandated insurance for the victims of factory accidents, and enacted employers' liability laws.

New York was one of the states that led the way. Around 1905 a series of dramatic investigations revealed a systematic and corrupt alliance between politicians and business leaders in the gas, electricity, and insurance industries. An angry public responded immediately, supporting greater state regulation and management by independent expert commissions. In 1905 and 1906, the state established regulatory boards to oversee utilities and insurance; it also outlawed corporate contributions to political campaigns and restricted business lobbying in the state legislature.

To regulate business, virtually every state created regulatory commissions, empowered to examine corporate books and hold public hearings. Building on earlier experience, after 1900 they were given new power to initiate actions, rather than await complaints, and in some cases to set maximum prices and rates. State regulatory commissions pioneered methods later adopted in federal legislation of 1906 and 1910. Some business leaders supported the federal laws, preferring one regulatory agency to dozens of separate state commissions.

Historians have long praised the regulation movement, but the commissions did not always act wisely or even in the public interest. Elective commissions often produced commissioners who had little knowledge of corporate affairs. Appointive commissions sometimes fared better, but they too had to oversee extraordinarily complex businesses like the railroads, shaping everything from wages to train schedules.

Emphasizing people's involvement in politics, progressives, like the Populists, backed three measures to make officeholders responsive to popular will: the initiative, which allowed voters to propose new laws; the referendum, which allowed them to accept or reject a law at the ballot box; and the recall, which gave them a way to remove an elected official from office. They also backed the direct election of senators and direct primaries as instruments to expand the role of the electorate.

As attention shifted from the cities to the states, reform governors throughout the country won growing reputations. Robert M. La Follette of Wisconsin—talented, aggressive, and a superb stump speaker—became the most famous of a group that included Hiram Johnson in California, Charles Evans Hughes in New York, and Woodrow Wilson in New Jersey. In 1901 La Follette became governor of Wisconsin. In the following six years, he put together the "Wisconsin Idea," one of the most important reform programs in the history of state government. He established an industrial commission to regulate factory safety and sanitation; improved education, workers' compensation, public utility controls, and resource conservation; and lowered railroad rates. In addition, under La Follette, Wisconsin also became the first to adopt a state income tax.

Like other progressives, La Follette drew on expert advice and relied on academic figures like Richard Ely at the University of Wisconsin to provide facts and figures to support the measures he favored. Theodore Roosevelt called La Follette's Wisconsin "the laboratory of democracy" and the "Wisconsin Idea" soon spread to many other states.

After 1905, the progressives looked more and more to Washington. For one thing, Theodore Roosevelt was there. But progressives also had a growing sense that many concerns—corporations and conservation, factory safety, and child labor—crossed state lines. Federal action seemed desirable; specific reforms fit into a larger plan perhaps best seen from the nation's center. Within a few years, La Follette and Hiram Johnson became senators, and while reform went on back home, the focus of progressivism shifted to Washington.

THE REPUBLICAN ROOSEVELT

When President William McKinley died of gunshot wounds in September 1901 (see Chapter 20), Vice-President Theodore Roosevelt succeeded him in the White House. Roosevelt continued some of McKinley's policies, developed others of his own, and brought to them all the particular exuberance of his own personality.

Theodore Roosevelt is shown here addressing a group of African-American businessmen in 1910. Booker T. Washington is seated next to Roosevelt.

At age forty-two Roosevelt was then the youngest president in American history. Open, aggressive, and high-spirited, he worked long hours; a steady procession of politicians, labor leaders, industrialists, poets, artists, and writers paraded through the White House. Most of the people who met Roosevelt were captivated by his charming manner and impressed by the breadth of his knowledge.

If McKinley cut down on presidential isolation, Roosevelt virtually ended it. The presidency, he thought, was "the bully pulpit," a forum of ideas and leadership for the nation. The president was a "steward of the people." Self-confident, Roosevelt enlisted talented associates to help him lead the nation.

In 1901 Roosevelt invited Booker T. Washington, the prominent black educator, to lunch at the White House. Many Southerners protested, and they protested again when Roosevelt appointed several blacks to important federal offices in South Carolina and Mississippi. At first Roosevelt tried to build a biracial, "black-and-tan" southern Republican party. He also denounced lynching and ordered the Justice Department to act against peonage.

But Roosevelt soon retreated, a position consistent with his own belief in black inferiority. He joined others in blaming black soldiers stationed near Brownsville, Texas, after a night of violence there in August 1906. Acting quickly and on little evidence, he discharged "without honor" three companies of black troops. Six of the soldiers who were discharged held the Congressional Medal of Honor.

BUSTING THE TRUSTS

Like most people, Roosevelt wavered on the trusts. Large-scale production and industrial growth, he believed, were natural and beneficial; they needed only to be controlled. Still he distrusted the trusts' impact on local enterprise and individual opportunity. Distinguishing between "good" and "bad" trusts, he pledged to protect the former while controlling the latter.

At first Roosevelt hoped the glare of publicity would be enough to uncover and correct business evils, and in public he both praised and attacked the trusts. To aid him in this task, in 1903 he asked Congress to create a department of Commerce and Labor, with a Bureau of Corporations empowered to investigate corporations engaged in interstate commerce. When Congress hesitated, Roosevelt mustered public opinion behind the legislation, which then easily passed.

Roosevelt also undertook more direct legal action. On February 14, 1902, he instructed the Justice Department to bring suit against the Northern Securities Company for violation of the Sherman Antitrust Act. It was a shrewd move. A mammoth holding company, Northern Securities controlled the massive rail networks of the Northern Pacific, the Great Northern, and the Chicago, Burlington & Quincy railroads. Some of the most prominent names in business were behind the giant company, including J. P. Morgan and Company and the Rockefeller interests. Morgan was shocked; he complained that the president had not acted like a "gentleman."

In 1904 the Supreme Court, in a five to four decision, upheld the suit against Northern Securities and ordered the company dissolved. Roosevelt was jubilant, and he followed up the victory with several other antitrust suits. Between 1902 and 1907, he moved against the beef trust, the American Tobacco Company, the Du Pont Corporation, and Standard Oil.

But Roosevelt's policies were not always clear, nor his actions always consistent. He frequently took the advice of important business leaders, and he asked for (and received) business support in his bid for reelection in 1904 (including $150,000 from Morgan). In 1907 he even permitted Morgan's U.S. Steel to absorb the Tennessee Coal and Iron Company, an important competitor.

Roosevelt, in truth, was not a "trust buster," although he was frequently called that. William Howard Taft, his successor in the White House, initiated forty-three antitrust indictments in four years—nearly twice as many as the twenty-five Roosevelt initiated in the seven years of his presidency.

"SQUARE DEAL" IN THE COALFIELDS

A few months after announcing the Northern Securities suit, Roosevelt intervened in a major labor dispute involving the anthracite coal miners of northeastern Pennsylvania. Led by John Mitchell, a moderate labor leader, the United Mine Workers demanded wage increases, an eight-hour workday, and company recognition of the union. The coal companies refused, and in May 1902, 140,000 miners walked off the job. The mines closed.

As the months passed and the strike continued, coal prices rose. With winter coming on, schools, hospitals, and factories ran short of coal. Public opinion turned against the companies. Morgan and other industrial leaders privately urged them to settle, but George F. Baer, head of one of the largest companies, refused: "The rights and interests of the laboring man," Baer said, "will be protected and cared for—not by the labor agitators, but by the Christian men to whom God in his infinite wisdom has given the control of the property interests of this country."

Roosevelt was furious. Complaining of the companies' arrogance, he invited both sides in the dispute to an October 1902 conference at the White House. There, Mitchell took a moderate tone and offered to submit the issues to arbitration, but the companies refused to budge. Roosevelt ordered the army to prepare to seize the mines and then leaked word of his intent to Wall Street leaders.

Alarmed, Morgan and others again urged a settlement, and at last the companies agreed to accept the recommendations of an independent commission to be appointed by the president. In late October the strikers returned to work, and in March 1903 the commission awarded them a 10-percent wage increase and a cut in working hours. It recommended, however, against union recognition. The coal companies, in turn, were encouraged to raise prices to offset the wage increase.

More and more Roosevelt saw the federal government as an honest and impartial "broker" between powerful elements in society. Rather than leaning toward labor, he pursued a middle path to curb corporate or labor abuses, abolish privilege, and enlarge individual opportunity. Often he backed reforms in part to head off more radical measures.

During the 1904 campaign Roosevelt called his actions in the coal miners' strike a "square deal" for both labor and capital, a term that stuck to his administration. Roosevelt was not the first president to take a stand for labor, but he was the first to bring opposing sides in a labor dispute to the White House to settle it. He was the first to threaten to seize a major industry, and he was the first to appoint a commission whose decision both sides agreed to accept.

ANOTHER TERM

In the election of 1904, the popular Roosevelt soundly drubbed his Democratic opponent, Alton B. Parker of New York, and the Socialist party candidate, Eugene V. Debs of Indiana. In a landslide victory, he received 57 percent of the vote to Parker's 38 percent. Overjoyed, he pledged that "under no circumstances will I be a candidate for or accept another nomination," a statement he later regretted.

Following his election, Roosevelt laid out a reform program that included railroad regulation, employers' liability for federal employees, greater federal control over corporations, and laws regulating child labor, factory inspection, and slum clearance in the District of Columbia. He turned first to railroad regulation. In 1903 he had worked with Congress to pass the moderate Elkins Act to prohibit railroad rebates and increase the powers of the Interstate Commerce Commission (ICC). In 1904 and 1905 he wanted much more, and he urged Congress to empower the ICC to set reasonable and nondiscriminatory rates and prevent inequitable practices.

Widespread demand for railroad regulation strengthened Roosevelt's hand. He maneuvered cannily, skillfully trading congressional support for a strong railroad measure in return for his promise to postpone a reduction of the tariff. The result was the passage of the Hepburn Act of 1906, strengthening the ratemaking power of the ICC. It made ICC orders binding, pending any court appeals, thus placing the burden of proof upon the companies. Delighted, Roosevelt viewed the Hepburn Act as a major step in his plan for continuous, expert federal control over industry.

President Roosevelt signed two important laws to regulate the food and drug industries. Both laws reflected public outcry over adulterated and poisonous food and drugs. Muckraking articles had touched frequently on filthy conditions in meat-packing houses, and Upton Sinclair's *The Jungle* (1906) described them in terms graphic enough to send people reeling from the dinner table.

After reading *The Jungle*, Roosevelt ordered an investigation. The result, he said, was "hideous." Meat sales plummeted in the United States and Europe. Alarmed, the meat packers themselves supported a reform law. The Meat Inspection Act of 1906, stiffer than the packers had wanted, set rules for sanitary meat packing and government inspection of meat products.

A second measure, the Pure Food and Drug Act, passed more easily. Samuel Hopkins Adams, a reporter for *Collier's* who had once considered a medical career, exposed the dangers of patent medicines. He sent medicine samples to Dr. Harvey W. Wiley, the chief chemist in the Department of Agriculture, for analysis. Wiley and his "Poison Squad" had previously tested various food preservatives, determined to put an end to adulterated foods. The evidence in hand, Wiley pushed for regulation, Roosevelt joined the fight, and the act passed on June 30, 1906, helped along by the appearance in February of Sinclair's *The Jungle*. It represented a pioneering effort, through required labeling information, to ban the manufacture and sale of adulterated, misbranded, or unsanitary food or drugs.

An expert on birds, Roosevelt loved nature and the wilderness, and some of his most enduring accomplishments came in the field of conservation. Working closely with Gifford Pinchot, Chief of the Forest Service, he established the first comprehensive national conservation policy. He undertook a major reclamation program and strengthened the forest preserve program. Broadening the concept of conservation, he placed power sites, coal lands, and oil reserves as well as national forests in the public domain.

As 1908 approached, Roosevelt became increasingly strident in his demand for sweeping reforms. He attacked "malefactors of great wealth," urged greater federal regulatory powers, criticized the conservatism of the federal courts, and called for laws protecting factory workers. Many business leaders blamed him for a severe financial panic in the autumn of 1907, and conservatives in Congress stiffened

Early twentieth-century meat-processing scenes like this are idyllic compared to those described in Upton Sinclair's The Jungle, *which became the most successful of the muckraking books.*

their opposition. Divisions between Republican conservatives and progressives grew.

Immensely popular, Roosevelt prepared in 1908 to turn over the White House to William Howard Taft, his close friend and colleague. He assured Americans that Taft would carry on his policies. As expected, Taft soundly defeated the Democratic standard-bearer William Jennings Bryan. The Republicans retained control of Congress. Taft prepared to move into the White House, ready and willing to carry on the Roosevelt legacy.

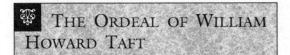

THE ORDEAL OF WILLIAM HOWARD TAFT

The Republican national convention that nominated Taft satisfied neither Roosevelt nor Taft. The conservative Republicans controlled the convention, and the platform reflected conservative views on labor, the courts, and other issues. La Follette and other progressive Republicans were openly disappointed.

Taking office in 1909, Taft felt "just a bit like a fish out of water." A graduate of Yale Law School and a distinguished judge, Taft's public service record was impressive. As the head of the Philippine Commission and later as the first governor general of the Philippines, he had shown a talent for organization. In 1904 Roosevelt appointed him secretary of war, a post that again highlighted Taft's administrative skill. A good-natured man, Taft preferred diplomacy to warfare, and he liked to work behind the scenes rather than in the spotlight.

Weighing close to 300 pounds, Taft enjoyed conversation, golf and bridge, good food, and plenty of rest. He was also honest, kindly, and amiable, and in his own way he knew how to get things done. Next to Roosevelt, however, he seemed lazy and spiritless.

Taft's years as president were not happy. He presided over a Republican party torn with tensions that Roosevelt had either brushed aside or concealed. The tariff, business regulation, and other issues split conservatives and progressives, and Taft often wavered or sided with the conservatives. He never had Roosevelt's faith in the ability of government to impose reform and alter individual behavior, and his ear was attuned more toward business than labor and the unions.

PARTY INSURGENCY

Taft started his term with an attempt to curb the powerful Republican Speaker of the House, crusty Joseph "Uncle Joe" Cannon of Illinois. Using the powers of his position, Cannon set House procedures, appointed committees, and virtually dictated legislation. He often opposed reform. In March 1909 thirty Republican congressmen joined Taft's efforts to curb Cannon's power, but Cannon retaliated and, threatening to block all tariff bills, forced a compromise. Taft stopped the anti-Cannon campaign for Cannon's pledge to help with tariff cuts.

The House quickly passed a bill providing for lower rates, but in the Senate, protectionists raised them. Senate leader Nelson A. Aldrich of Rhode Island introduced a revised bill that added over 800 amendments to the House rates. Angry, La Follette and other Republicans attacked the bill as the child of special interests and urged Taft to defeat the high-tariff proposal. Taft wavered but in the end backed Aldrich. The Payne-Aldrich Act, passed in November 1909, called for higher rates than the original House bill, though it lowered them from the Dingley Tariff of 1897 (see Chapter 20). An unpopular law, it helped discredit Taft and revealed the tensions in the Republican party.

Republican progressives and conservatives drifted apart. Taft tried to find middle ground but leaned more and more toward the conservatives. By 1910 progressive Republicans no longer looked to Taft for leadership. To the president's embarrassment, progressive congressmen were able, without presidential support, to curtail Speaker Cannon's authority to dictate committee assignments and schedule debates. In progressive circles there was growing talk of a Roosevelt return to the White House.

The Ballinger-Pinchot Affair

The conservation issue dealt another blow to the relations between Roosevelt and President Taft. In 1909 Richard A. Ballinger, Taft's secretary of the interior, offered for sale a million acres of public land that Pinchot, Taft's chief forester, had withdrawn from sale. Pinchot protested. After investigating, Taft supported Ballinger, although he asked Pinchot to remain in office.

Pinchot refused to drop the matter. He secretly provided material for two anti-Ballinger magazine articles, and he wrote a critical public letter that was read to the Senate by Senator Dolliver of Iowa. Taft fired the insubordinate Pinchot, an appropriate action, but again lost some standing in the process. Newspapers wrongly portrayed the president as an opponent of conservation.

The Ballinger-Pinchot controversy obscured Taft's important contributions to conservation. He won from Congress the power to remove lands from sale, and he used it to conserve more land than Roosevelt did. Still, the controversy tarred Taft; it also upset Roosevelt and widened the gulf between the two men.

Taft's Final Years

Interested in railroad regulation, Taft backed a bill in 1910 to empower the ICC to fix maximum railroad rates. Although it was hotly debated, the Mann-Elkins Act of 1910 gave something to everyone. It gave the ICC power to set rates, stiffened long- and short-haul regulations, and placed telephone and telegraph companies under ICC jurisdiction. These provisions delighted progressives. The act also created a Commerce Court to hear appeals from ICC decisions, an addition that pleased conservatives; progressive Republicans wanted to amend the bill to strengthen it, but Taft raised the issue of party loyalty and further alienated the progressives.

Withholding patronage, Taft attempted to defeat the progressive Republicans in the 1910 elections. He helped to establish antiprogressive organizations, and he opposed progressive Republican candidates for the Senate—Hiram Johnson, of California, for one. Progressive Republicans retaliated by organizing a nationwide network of anti-Taft Progressive Republican Clubs.

The 1910 election results were a major setback for Taft and the Republicans—both conservatives and progressives. In party primaries, progressive Republicans overwhelmed most Taft candidates, and in November, the Democrats beat virtually everyone. For the first time since 1894, Republicans lost control of both the House and the Senate.

Despite the defeat, Taft pushed through several important progressive measures before his term ended. With the help of the new Democratic House, he backed laws to regulate safety in mines and on railroads, create a Children's Bureau in the federal government, establish employers' liability for all work done on government contracts, and mandate an eight-hour workday for government workers.

In 1909 Congress initiated a constitutional amendment authorizing an income tax, perhaps the most significant legislative measure of the twentieth century. The Sixteenth Amendment took effect early in 1913. A few months later another important progressive goal was realized when the direct election of senators was ratified as the Seventeenth Amendment to the Constitution.

An ardent supporter of competition, Taft relentlessly pressed a campaign against trusts. In 1911 the Supreme Court in cases against Standard Oil and American Tobacco established the "rule of reason," which allowed the Court to determine whether a business was a "reasonable" restraint on trade. Taft thought the decisions gave the Court too much discretion, and he pushed ahead with the antitrust effort.

In October 1911, he sued U.S. Steel for its acquisition of the Tennessee Coal and Iron Company in 1907. Roosevelt had approved the acquisition, and the suit seemed designed to impugn his action. Furious, Roosevelt listened more and more to anti-Taft Republicans who urged him to run for president. In February 1912 he announced: "My hat is in the ring."

DIFFERING PHILOSOPHIES IN THE ELECTION OF 1912

Delighted Democrats looked on as Taft and Roosevelt fought for the Republican nomination. As the incumbent president, Taft controlled the party machinery, and when the Republican convention met in June 1912, he took the nomination. In early July the Democrats met in Baltimore, and after a forty-six ballot struggle, nominated Woodrow Wilson, the reform-minded governor of New Jersey.

A month later the anti-Taft and progressive Republicans—now calling themselves the Progressive party—whooped it up in Chicago. Naming Roosevelt for president, the Progressive—soon known as the "Bull Moose"—party convention set the stage for a lively three-cornered presidential contest.

Taft was out of the running before the campaign even began. He stayed at home and made no speeches before the election. Roosevelt campaigned strenuously for his Bull Moose platform, a program he called New Nationalism. It demanded a national approach to the country's affairs and a strong president to deal with them. The New Nationalism exalted the execution and the expert; urged social-justice reforms to protect workers, women, and children; and accepted "good" trusts. The New Nationalism encouraged large concentrations of labor and capital, serving the nation's interests under a forceful federal executive. Roosevelt's call for New Nationalism gained the support of many women. (For the first time in the history of a political party, the Progressive campaign enlisted women in its organization.) Some labor and business leaders, who saw relief from destructive competition and labor strife, supported the new party.

Wilson, in contrast, set forth a program called the New Freedom that emphasized business competition and small government. A states' rights Democrat, he wanted to rein in federal authority, using it only to sweep away special privilege, release individual energies, and restore competition. He echoed the Progressive party's social-justice objectives, while continuing to attack Roosevelt's planned state.

For Wilson, the vital issue was not a planned economy but a free one.

In the New Nationalism and New Freedom, the election of 1912 offered competing philosophies of government. Both Roosevelt and Wilson saw the central problem of the American nation as the effect of economic growth on individuals and society. Both focused on the government's relation to business; both believed in bureaucratic reform; and both wanted to use government to protect the ordinary citizen. But Roosevelt welcomed federal power, national planning, and business growth; Wilson distrusted them all.

On election day Wilson won 6.3 million votes to 4.1 million for Roosevelt, 3.5 million for Taft, and 900,000 for Eugene V. Debs, the Socialist party candidate. In one of the worst defeats ever suffered by an incumbent, Taft garnered only 8 electoral votes. The Democrats also won outright control of both houses.

WOODROW WILSON'S NEW FREEDOM

If under Roosevelt social reform took on the excitement of a circus, "under Wilson," one historian said, "it acquired the dedication of a sunrise service." Born in Virginia in 1856, the son of a Presbyterian minister, Wilson was a moralist; he reached judgments easily that, once reached, were rarely discarded.

After graduating from Princeton University and the University of Virginia Law School, Wilson found that practicing law bored him. Shifting to history and political science, from 1890 to 1902 he taught at Princeton. In 1902 he became president of the university. Eight years later he was governor of New Jersey, where he compiled a strong record as a reformer. Although Wilson's rise was rapid and he knew relatively little about national issues and personalities, he learned fast. In some ways the lack of experience served him well. He had few political debts to repay, and he brought fresh perspectives to older issues.

Wilson loved ideas but was sensitive to criticism and prone to self-righteousness. He often turned differences of opinion into bitter personal quarrels. Like Roosevelt, he believed in strong presidential leadership. He cooperated closely with Democrats in Congress, and his legislative record places him among the most effective presidents. Cold and aloof in individual conversation, Wilson could move crowds with graceful oratory. Unlike Taft, and even more than Roosevelt, he could inspire.

THE NEW FREEDOM IN ACTION

On the day of his inauguration, Wilson called Congress into special session to lower the tariff. When the session opened on April 8, 1913, Wilson himself was there, the first president since John Adams in 1801 to appear personally before Congress. In forceful language, he urged Congress to reduce tariff rates.

Wilson worked hard and skillfully to get the bill through Congress. The result was a triumph for Wilson and the Democratic party. The Underwood Tariff Act passed in 1913. The first tariff cut in nineteen years, it lowered rates about 15 percent and removed duties from sugar, wool, and several other consumer goods. To make up for lost revenue, the act also levied a modest, graduated income tax, authorized under the just-ratified Sixteenth Amendment. Marking a significant shift in the American tax structure, it imposed a 1 percent tax on individuals and corporations earning more than $4000 annually and an additional 1 percent tax on incomes over $20,000.

The act reflected the new unity of the Democratic party and the ability of Wilson as a leader. Encouraged by his success, Wilson decided to keep Congress in session through the hot Washington summer. Now he focused on banking reform, and the result in December 1913 was the Federal Reserve Act, the most important domestic law of his administration.

Meant to provide the United States with a sound yet flexible currency, the act established the country's first efficient banking system since Andrew Jackson killed the Second Bank of the United States in 1832 (see Chapter 10). It created twelve regional banks, each to serve a district. These banks answered to a Federal Reserve Board, appointed by the president, which governed the nationwide system.

A compromise law, the act blended public and private control of the banking system. Private bankers owned the federal reserve banks but answered to the presidentially appointed Federal Reserve Board. The reserve banks were authorized to issue currency and through the discount rate—the interest rate at which they loaned money to member banks—could raise or lower the amount of money in circulation. Monetary affairs no longer depended solely on the price of gold. Within a year nearly half the nation's banking resources were in the Federal Reserve System.

The Clayton Antitrust Act (1914) completed Wilson's initial legislative program. Partially motivated by the revelations of a congressional committee about the power of *interlocking directorates*—management (and control) of competing companies by executives from an interrelated business group—the Clayton Act outlawed such directorates and prohibited unfair trade practices. It forbade pricing policies that created monopoly, and it made corporate officers personally responsible for antitrust violations. Delighting Samuel Gompers and the labor movement, the act declared that unions were not conspiracies in restraint of trade, outlawed the use of injunctions in labor disputes unless necessary to protect property, and approved lawful strikes and picketing.

A related law established a powerful Federal Trade Commission to oversee business methods. The commission could demand special and annual reports, investigate complaints, and order corporate compliance, subject to court review. Although Wilson initially opposed the commission concept, he soon came to see it as the cornerstone of his antitrust plan. To reassure business leaders, he appointed a number of conservatives to the new commission and to the Federal Reserve Board.

In November 1914 Wilson proudly announced the completion of his New Freedom program. Tariff, banking, and antitrust laws promised a brighter future, he said. Many progressives, however, believed the process of reform had only begun.

RETREAT AND ADVANCE

Distracted by the start of war in Europe, Wilson gave less attention to domestic issues for more than a year. When he returned to concern with reform, he adopted more and more of Roosevelt's New Nationalism and blended it with the New Freedom in ways that set it off from his earlier policies.

One of Wilson's problems was the Congress. To his dismay the Republicans gained substantially in the 1914 elections. At the same time a recession struck the economy, which had been hurt by the outbreak of the European war in August 1914. Some business leaders blamed the tariff and other New Freedom enactments. On the defensive, Wilson began to cooperate more with bankers and industrialists. He refused to support a bill providing minimum wages for women workers, sidetracked a child-labor bill on the ground that it was unconstitutional, and opposed a bill to establish long-term credits for farmers. He also refused to endorse woman suffrage, arguing that it was a matter for the states to decide.

Wilson's record on race disappointed blacks and many progressives. He had appealed to black voters during the 1912 election, but did little to justify their support once in office. A Virginian himself, he appointed many Southerners to high office, and for the first time since the Civil War, southern segregationist views on race dominated the nation's capital.

As the year 1916 began, Wilson again pushed for reform, and the result—a virtual river of reform laws—began the second, national-minded phase of the New Freedom. In part Wilson was motivated by the approaching presidential election; he was, after all, a minority president. Moreover, many progressives were voicing disappointment with Wilson's limited reforms and his failure to support more advanced reform legislation such as farm credits, child labor, and woman suffrage.

Moving quickly to patch up the problem, Wilson named Louis D. Brandeis to the Supreme Court in January 1916. Popular among progressives, Brandeis was also the first person of Jewish faith to serve on the Court. In May Wilson reversed his stand on federally backed farm loans. The Federal Farm Loan Act of 1916 created a Federal Farm Loan Board to give farmers credit similar to the Federal Reserve's benefits for trade and industry.

Wilson was already popular within the labor movement. He had defended union recognition and collective bargaining. In 1913 he appointed William B. Wilson, a respected leader of the United Mine Workers, as the first head of the Labor Department. In 1914 in Ludlow, Colorado, state militia and mine guards fired machine guns into a tent colony of coal strikers, killing twenty-six men, women, and children. Outraged, Wilson stepped in and used federal troops to end the violence while negotiations to end the strike went on.

In August 1916 a threatened railroad strike again revealed Wilson's sympathies with labor. Like Roosevelt, he invited the two sides to the White House, where he urged the railroad companies to grant an eight-hour workday, while asking labor leaders to abandon the demand for overtime pay. Labor leaders accepted the proposal; railroad leaders did not. Soon Wilson signed the Adamson Act (1916) that imposed the eight-hour workday on interstate railways. The act ended the threat of a strike and expanded the federal government's authority to regulate industry.

With Wilson leading the way, the flow of reform legislation continued until the election. The Federal Workmen's Compensation Act established workers' compensation for government employees. The Keating-Owen Act, the first federal child-labor law, prohibited the shipment in interstate commerce of products manufactured by children under the age of fourteen. The Warehouse Act authorized licensed warehouses to issue negotiable receipts for farm products deposited with them. During the campaign Wilson endorsed the eight-hour workday for all the nation's workers and came out in support of woman suffrage.

The 1916 presidential election was close, but Wilson won it on the issues of peace and progressivism (see Chapter 24). By the end of 1916 he and the Democratic party had enacted most of the important parts of Roosevelt's Progressive party platform of 1912. To do it, Wilson abandoned portions of the New Freedom and

The strikers' tent colony at Ludlow, Colorado, after the militia and mine guards charged it on April 20, 1914.

accepted much of the New Nationalism, including greater federal power and commissions governing trade and tariffs. In mixing the two programs, he blended some of the competing doctrines of the progressive era, established the primacy of the federal government, and foreshadowed the pragmatic outlook of Franklin D. Roosevelt's New Deal.

The election of 1916 showed how deeply progressivism had reached into American society. Candidates were vying for the reform-minded vote, and the future seemed to belong to reform. In retrospect, however, 1916 marked the beginning of progressivism's sad decline into the 1920s. Many problems the progressives addressed, they did not solve; and some important ones, like race, they did not even tackle. Yet their regulatory commissions, direct primaries, city improvements, and child-labor laws marked an era of important and measured reform.

In 1909 Taft rode to his inauguration in a horse and carriage, in 1913 Wilson rode in an automobile, and change was evident throughout the country. The institution of the presidency expanded. Independent commissions, operating within flexible laws, supplemented executive authority.

These developments owed a great deal to both Roosevelt and Wilson. Wanting to manage a complex society, TR developed a simple formula: expert advice; growth-minded policies; a balancing of business, labor, and other interests; the use of publicity to gather support; and stern but often permissive oversight of the economy. TR strengthened the executive office, and he called upon the newer group of professional, educated, public-minded citizens to help him. "I believe in a strong executive," he said. "I believe in power."

At first Wilson had different ideas, wanting to dismantle much of Roosevelt's governing apparatus. But driven by outside forces and changes in his own thinking, Wilson soon moved in directions similar to those Roosevelt had championed. Starting out to disperse power, he consolidated it. Against his earlier policies, Wilson created a Federal Trade Commission to oversee business, a Tariff Commission to regulate overseas trade, and a powerful Federal Reserve Board to control money and banking.

Through such movements, government at all levels accepted responsibility for the welfare of

CHRONOLOGY

1894	National Municipal League formed to work for reform in cities
1900	Galveston, Texas, is first city to try commission form of government
1901	Theodore Roosevelt becomes president Robert M. La Follette elected reform governor of Wisconsin Doctors reorganize the American Medical Association Socialist party of America organized
1902	Roosevelt sues the Northern Securities Company for violation of the Sherman Antitrust Act Coal miners in northeastern Pennsylvania strike Maryland is first state to pass workers' compensation law
1903	Department of Commerce and Labor created
1904	Roosevelt elected to second term
1906	Hepburn Act strengthens ICC Upton Sinclair attacks meat-packing industry in *The Jungle* Congress passes Meat Inspection and Pure Food and Drug Acts
1908	Taft elected president Supreme Court upholds Oregon law limiting working hours for women in *Muller* v. *Oregon*
1909	Payne-Aldrich Tariff Act divides Republican party
1910	Mann-Elkins Act passes to regulate railroads Taft fires Gifford Pinchot, head of U.S. Forest Service Democrats sweep midterm elections
1912	Progressive party formed; nominates Roosevelt for president Woodrow Wilson elected president
1913	Underwood Tariff Act lowers rates Federal Reserve Act reforms U.S. banking system Sixteenth Amendment authorizes Congress to collect taxes on incomes
1914	Clayton Antitrust Act strengthens antitrust legislation
1916	Wilson wins reelection
1918	Supreme Court strikes down federal law limiting child labor in *Hammer* v. *Dagenhart*
1920	Nineteenth Amendment gives women the right to vote

various elements in the social order. A reform-minded and bureaucratic society took shape, in which men and women, labor and capital, political parties and social classes competed for shares in the expansive framework of twentieth-century life. But there were limits to reform. As both TR and Wilson found, the new government agencies, understaffed and underfinanced, depended in the end on the responsiveness of those they sought to regulate.

Soon there was a far darker cloud on the horizon. The spirit of progressivism rested upon a belief in human potential, peace, and progress. After Napoleon's defeat in 1815, a century of peace began in western Europe, and as the decades passed, war seemed a dying institution. It was not to be. In 1914 the most devastating of wars broke out in Europe, and in 1917 Americans were fighting on the battlefields of France.

℞ RECOMMENDED READING

George Mowry, *The Era of Theodore Roosevelt* (1958) and Arthur S. Link, *Woodrow Wilson and the Progressive Era* (1954), trace the social and economic conditions of the period. See also Henry F. Pringle's biography, *Theodore Roosevelt* (1931), John M. Blum's perceptive and brief *The Republican Roosevelt* (1954), and William H. Harbaugh's thoughtful *The Life and Times of Theodore Roosevelt*, rev. ed. (1975). Donald E. Anderson, *William Howard Taft* (1973) and Paolo E. Coletta, *The Presidency of William Howard Taft* (1973), study Taft. The definitive biography of Wilson is Arthur S. Link, *Wilson*, 5 vols. (1947–1965).

On specific issues, see O. E. Anderson, *The Health of a Nation: Harvey W. Wiley and the Fight for Pure Food* (1958); James G. Burrow, *Organized Medicine in the Progressive Era: The Move Toward Monopoly* (1977); Morris J. Vogel, *The Invention of the Modern Hospital: Boston, 1870–1930* (1980); Craig West, *Banking Reform and the Federal Reserve, 1863–1923* (1977); Eugene Nelson White, *The Regulation and Reform of the American Banking System, 1900–1929* (1983); Aileen Kraditor, *The Ideas of the Woman Suffrage Movement, 1890–1920* (1981); Christine A. Lunardini, *From Equal Suffrage to Equal Rights: Alice Paul and the National Woman's Party, 1910–1928* (1986); David W. Southern, *The Malignant Heritage: Yankee Progressives and the Negro Question, 1901–1914* (1968); James H. Timberlake, *Prohibition and the Progressive Crusade*

(1963); and Walter I. Trattner, *Crusade for the Children* (1970).

On urban reform, see John D. Buenker, *Urban Liberalism and Progressive Reform* (1973); Roy M. Lubove, *The Progressive and the Slums* (1962); and Martin J. Schiesl, *The Politics of Efficiency: Municipal Administration and Reform in America, 1880–1920* (1977). Also, Robert M. Crunden, *Ministers of Reform: The Progressives' Achievements in American Civilization, 1889–1920* (1982); James T. Patterson, *America's Struggle Against Poverty, 1900–1980* (1981); and Stephen Skowronek, *Building a New American State: The Expansion of National Administrative Capacities, 1877–1920* (1982). Bradley R. Rice, *Progressive Cities: The Commission Government Movement in America, 1901–1920* (1977) is helpful.

Books on specific cities include Melvin Holli, *Reform in Detroit: Hazen S. Pingree and Urban Politics* (1969); Carl V. Harris, *Political Power in Birmingham, 1871–1921* (1977); James B. Crooks, *Politics and Progress: The Rise of Urban Progressivism in Baltimore, 1895–1911* (1968); Zane L. Miller, *Boss Cox's Cincinnati* (1968); and Jack Tager, *The Intellectual as Urban Reformer: Brand Whitlock and the Progressive Movement* (1968).

Statewide movements are covered in George E. Mowry's influential study, *The California Progressives* (1951); Spencer C. Olin, Jr., *California's Prodigal Sons: Hiram Johnson and the Progressives, 1911–1917* (1968); David P. Thelen, *The New Citizenship: Origins of Progressivism in Wisconsin, 1885–1900* (1972); Herbert Margulies, *The Decline of the Progressive Movement in Wisconsin, 1890–1920* (1968); Ransom E. Noble, Jr., *New Jersey Progressivism Before Wilson* (1946); John F. Reynolds, *Testing Democracy: Electoral Behavior and Progressive Reform in New Jersey, 1880–1920* (1988); James Wright, *The Progressive Yankees: Republican Reformers in New Hampshire, 1906–1916* (1987); Robert F. Wesser, *Charles Evans Hughes: Politics and Reform in New York, 1905–1910* (1967); Richard L. McCormick, *From Realignment to Reform: Political Change in New York State, 1893–1910* (1981); Sheldon Hackney, *Populism to Progressivism in Alabama* (1969); Richard M. Abrams, *Conservatism in a Progressive Era: Massachusetts Politics, 1900–1912* (1964); and H. L. Warner, *Progressivism in Ohio, 1897–1917* (1964).

On politics, see George E. Mowry, *Theodore Roosevelt and the Progressive Movement* (1946); Richard L. McCormick, *The Party Period and Public Policy: American Politics from the Age of Jackson to the Progressive Era* (1986); Michael E. McGerr, *The Decline of Popular Politics: The American North, 1865–1928* (1986); Kenneth W. Hechler, *Insurgency:*

Personalities and Politics of the Taft Era (1940); David Sarasohn, *The Party of Reform: Democrats in the Progressive Era* (1989); Norman M. Wilensky, *Conservatives in the Progressive Era: The Taft Republicans of 1912* (1965); George Juergens, *News from the White House: The Presidential-Press Relationship in the Progressive Era* (1981); and L. J. Holt, *Congressional Insurgents and the Party System, 1909–1916* (1967).

Helpful biographies include Edmund Morris, *The Rise of Theodore Roosevelt* (1979); William Manners, *TR and Will* (1969); G. Wallace Chessman, *Theodore Roosevelt and the Politics of Power* (1969); John M. Blum, *Woodrow Wilson and the Politics of Morality* (1962), John M. Mulder, *Woodrow Wilson: The Years of Preparation* (1978); Kendrick A. Clements, *Woodrow Wilson* (1987); Henry F. Pringle, *Life and Times of William Howard Taft*, 2 vols. (1939); David P. Thelen, *Robert M. La Follette and the Insurgent Spirit* (1976); Fred Greenbaum, *Robert Marion La Follette* (1975); Philippa Strum, *Louis D. Brandeis* (1984); Alpheus Thomas Mason, *Brandeis: A Free Man's Life* (1946); and Harold W. Currie, *Eugene V. Debs* (1976).

24 THE NATION AT WAR

A NEW WORLD POWER

FOREIGN POLICY UNDER WILSON

TOWARD WAR

OVER THERE

OVER HERE

THE TREATY OF VERSAILLES

On the morning of May 1, 1915, the German government printed an important advertisement in the *New York World*. It warned American travelers that a state of war existed in Europe and that waters adjacent to Great Britain were part of the zone of war. It emphasized that "travellers sailing in the war zone on ships of Great Britain or her allies do so at their own risk." At 12:30 that afternoon, the British steamship *Lusitania* set sail from New York to Liverpool. The passenger list of 1257 was the largest since the outbreak of war in Europe. Alfred G. Vanderbilt, the millionaire sportsman, was aboard; so were several other famous Americans. While some passengers chose the *Lusitania* for speed, others liked the unmatched comfort of its modern staterooms.

Six days later, the *Lusitania* reached the coast of Ireland. German U-boats patrolled these dangerous waters. When the war began in 1914, Great Britain imposed a naval blockade of Germany. In return, Germany in February 1915 declared the area around the British Isles a war zone; all enemy vessels, armed or unarmed, were at risk. Germany had only a handful of U-boats, but submarine warfare was new and frightening. On behalf of the United States, President Woodrow Wilson protested the German action, and on February 10 he warned Germany of its "strict accountability" for any American losses resulting from U-boat attacks.

As in peacetime, the *Lusitania* sailed straight ahead, with no zigzag maneuvers to throw off pursuit. But the submarine U-20 was there, and the commander, seeing a large ship, fired a single torpedo. Seconds after it hit, a boiler exploded and blew a hole in the *Lusitania's* side. In eighteen minutes it sank. Nearly 1200 people died, including 128 Americans.

The sinking, the worst since the loss of the *Titanic*, horrified Americans. On the French front the Germans had just introduced poison gas, another alarming new weapon, and there were reports of German atrocities in Belgium. Still, most Americans wanted to stay out of war; like Wilson, they hoped negotiations could solve the problem.

In a series of diplomatic notes Wilson demanded a change in German policy. The first *Lusitania* note (May 13, 1915) called on Germany to abandon unrestricted submarine warfare, disavow the sinking, and compensate for lost American lives. Germany sent an evasive reply, and Wilson drafted a second *Lusitania* note (June 9) insisting on specific pledges. A third note (July 21)—almost an ultimatum— warned Germany that the United States would consider similar sinkings as "deliberately unfriendly."

Unbeknown to Wilson, Germany had already ordered U-boat commanders not to sink passenger liners without warning. In August 1915 a U-boat mistakenly torpedoed the British liner *Arabic*, killing two Americans. Wilson protested, and Germany, eager to keep the United States out of war, backed down. In the *Arabic* pledge (September 1) Germany promised to stop and warn liners, unless they tried to resist or escape.

Although Wilson's diplomacy had achieved his immediate goal, the *Lusitania* and *Arabic* crises contained the elements that led to war. Trade and travel tied the world together, and Americans no longer hid behind safe ocean barriers. New weapons, such as the submarine, strained old rules of international law. But while Americans sifted the conflicting claims of Great Britain and Germany, they hoped for peace. A generation of progressives, inspired with confidence in human progress, did not easily accept war.

Wilson also hated war, but he found himself caught up in a worldwide crisis that demanded the best in American will and diplomacy. In the end diplomacy failed, and in April 1917 the United States entered a war that changed the nation's history.

A NEW WORLD POWER

As they had in the late nineteenth century, Americans after 1900 paid little attention to

With the sinking of the Lusitania, *the American people learned first-hand of the horrors of total war. President Wilson's decision to protest the incident through diplomacy kept the United States out of war—temporarily.*

foreign affairs. People paid closer attention to what was going on at home. Foreign affairs, they reasoned, was the job of the president, an attitude that suited the interests of Roosevelt, Taft, and Wilson.

American foreign policy from 1901 to 1920 was aggressive and nationalistic. During these years the United States dominated the Caribbean and intervened in Europe, the Far East, and Latin America.

In 1898 the United States left the peace table possessing the Philippines, Puerto Rico, and Guam. Holding distant possessions required a colonial policy and a more outward approach in foreign policy. From the Caribbean to the Pacific, policymakers paid attention to issues and countries they had earlier ignored. Like other nations in these years, the United States built a large navy, protected its colonial empire, and became increasingly involved in international affairs.

The nation also became more and more involved in economic ventures abroad. Turning out goods from textiles to steel, mass-production industries sold products overseas, and financiers invested in Asia, Africa, Latin America, and Europe. While investments and trade never wholly dictated American foreign policy, they fostered greater involvement in foreign lands.

"I TOOK THE CANAL ZONE"

Convinced the United States should take a more active international role, Theodore Roosevelt spent his presidency preparing the nation for world power. Along with Secretary of War Elihu Root, he modernized the army, established the Army War College, imposed stiff tests for the promotion of officers, and created a general staff to oversee military planning and mobilization. Determined to end dependency on the British fleet, Roosevelt doubled the navy's strength during his term in office.

Stretching his authority to the limit, Roosevelt took steps to consolidate the country's new position in the Caribbean and Central America. European powers, which had long resisted American initiatives there, now accepted American supremacy. Preoccupied with problems elsewhere, Great Britain agreed to United States plans for an isthmian canal in Central America, withdrawing much of its military force from the area. Secretary of State John Hay negotiated with Britain the Hay-Pauncefote Treaty of 1901 that permitted the United States to construct and control an isthmian canal, providing it would be free and open to ships of all nations.

Delighted, Roosevelt began selecting the route. One route, fifty miles long, wandered through the rough, swampy terrain of the Panama region of Colombia. A French company had recently tried and failed to dig a canal there. Another possible route, through mountainous Nicaragua, was four times as long but followed natural waterways, which would make construction easier. An Isthmian Canal Commission decided in 1899 that the shorter route through Panama was preferable.

Roosevelt backed the idea, and he authorized Hay to negotiate an agreement with the Colombian chargé d'affaires, Thomas Herrán. The Hay-Herrán Convention (1903) gave the United States a ninety-nine-year lease, with option for renewal, on a canal zone six miles in width. In exchange, the United States agreed to pay Colombia a one-time fee of $10 million and an annual rental of $250,000.

To Roosevelt's dismay, the Colombian Senate rejected the treaty. Calling the Colombians "contemptible little creatures," Roosevelt considered seizing Panama, then hinted he would welcome a Panamanian revolt from Colombia. In November 1903 the Panamanians took the hint, and Roosevelt moved quickly to support them. Sending the cruiser *Nashville* to prevent Colombian troops from putting down the revolt, he promptly recognized the new Republic of Panama.

Two weeks later the Hay-Bunau-Varilla Treaty with Panama granted the United States control of the canal zone ten miles wide across the Isthmus of Panama. In return, the United States guaranteed the independence of Panama and agreed to pay the same fees offered Colom-

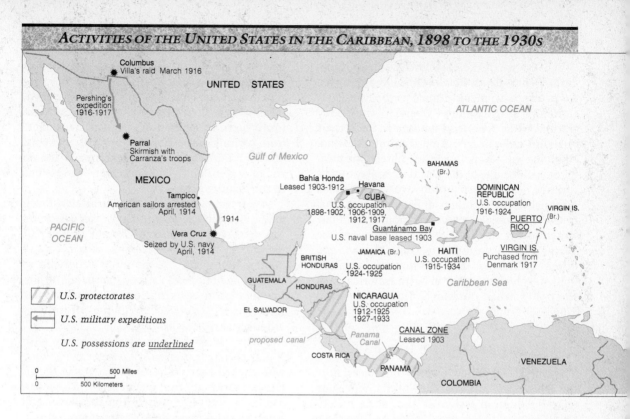

Columbus
Villa's raid March 1916

UNITED STATES

ATLANTIC OCEAN

Pershing's
expedition
1916-1917

Parral
Skirmish with
Carranza's troops

Gulf of Mexico

BAHAMAS
(Br.)

MEXICO

Tampico
American sailors arrested
April, 1914

Bahía Honda
Leased 1903-1912

Havana

DOMINICAN
REPUBLIC
U.S. occupation
1916-1924

VIRGIN IS.
(Br.)

CUBA
U.S. occupation
1898-1902, 1906-1909,
1912, 1917

PUERTO
RICO

PACIFIC
OCEAN

1914

Vera Cruz
Seized by U.S. navy
April, 1914

Guantánamo Bay
U.S. naval base leased 1903

JAMAICA (Br.)

HAITI
U.S. occupation
1915-1934

VIRGIN IS.
Purchased from
Denmark 1917

BRITISH
HONDURAS

U.S. occupation
1924-1925

Caribbean Sea

GUATEMALA

HONDURAS

U.S. protectorates

NICARAGUA
U.S. occupation
1912-1925
1927-1933

U.S. military expeditions

EL SALVADOR

U.S. possessions are underlined

proposed canal

Panama
Canal

CANAL ZONE
Leased 1903

0   500 Miles

COSTA RICA

VENEZUELA

0   500 Kilometers

PANAMA

COLOMBIA

The Roosevelt Corollary

bia. On August 15, 1914, the first ocean steamer sailed through the completed canal, which cost $375 million to build.

Roosevelt's actions angered many Latin Americans. Colombian-American relations remained strained until 1921, when the United States agreed to pay Colombia $25 million in cash and give it preferential treatment in using the canal. For his part, however, Roosevelt stoutly defended his actions. "I took the Canal Zone" he said, "and let Congress debate; and while the debate goes on, the Canal does also."

THE ROOSEVELT COROLLARY

With interests in Puerto Rico, Cuba, and the canal, the United States developed a Caribbean policy to ensure its dominance in the region. It established protectorates over some countries

and subsidized others to keep them dependent. When necessary, it even purchased islands to keep them out of the hands of other powers, as in the case of the Virgin Islands, bought from Denmark in 1917 to prevent Germany from acquiring them.

From 1903 to 1920 the United States intervened often in Latin America to protect the canal, promote regional stability, and exclude foreign influence. One problem worrisome to American policymakers was the scale of Latin American debts to European powers. Many countries in the Western Hemisphere owed money to European governments and banks, yet these same nations were poor, prone to revolution, and unable to pay. The situation invited European intervention. In 1902 Venezuela defaulted on debts; England, Germany, and Italy sent Venezuela an ultimatum and blockaded its ports. American pressure forced a settlement of the issue, but the general problem remained.

In 1904 when the Dominican Republic defaulted on its debts, Roosevelt was ready with a major announcement. Known as the Roosevelt Corollary of the Monroe Doctrine, the policy warned Latin American nations to keep their affairs in order or face American intervention. Applying the new policy immediately, the president took charge of the Dominican Republic's revenue system, and within two years he also established protectorates in Panama and Cuba. In Cuba, Roosevelt tied the action to the Platt Amendment to the Cuban constitution (see Chapter 21). Continued by Taft, Wilson, and other presidents, the Roosevelt Corollary guided American policy in Latin America until the 1930's, when Franklin D. Roosevelt's Good Neighbor Policy replaced it.

VENTURES IN THE FAR EAST

The Open Door policy toward China (see Chapter 21) and possession of the Philippine Islands shaped American actions in the Far East. Roosevelt wanted to balance Russian and Japanese power in the area, and he was not unhappy at first when war broke out between them in 1904. As Japan won victory after victory, however, Roosevelt became concerned. He accepted Japan's request to mediate the conflict, and in August 1905 convened a peace conference at Portsmouth, New Hampshire. The conference ended the war, but Japan emerged as the dominant force in the Far East. Adjusting policy, Roosevelt sent Secretary of War Taft to Tokyo to negotiate the Taft-Katsura Agreement (1905), which recognized Japan's dominance over Korea in return for its promise not to invade the Philippines. Giving Japan a free hand in Korea violated the Open Door policy, but Roosevelt argued that he had little choice.

In a show of strength, he sent the American fleet around the world, including a safe stop in Tokyo in October 1908. For the moment Japanese-American relations improved, despite Japan's resentment over the segregation of Asian children in San Francisco's public schools in 1906. In 1908 the two nations signed the comprehensive Root-Takahira Agreement in which they promised to maintain the status quo in the Pacific, uphold the Open Door, and support Chinese independence.

In later years tensions grew in the Far East. Japan's anger mounted in 1913 when the California legislature prohibited Japanese residents from owning property in the state. By the start of the First World War Japan longed for an Asian empire and eyed American possessions in the Pacific.

In foreign as well as domestic affairs, President Taft tried to continue Roosevelt's policies. For secretary of state he chose Philander C. Knox, and together they pursued a policy of "dollar diplomacy" to promote American financial and business interests abroad. The policy had profit-seeking motives, but it also aimed to substitute economic ties for military alliances and bring lasting peace.

In the Far East, Knox worked closely with Willard Straight, an agent of American bankers, who argued that dollar diplomacy was the financial arm of the Open Door. However, Knox's attempt to convince England, Japan, and Russia to join the United States in an international syndicate to loan China money to purchase the Manchurian railroads failed. The outcome was a blow to American policy and prestige in Asia. Instead of cultivating friendship, as Roosevelt had envisioned, Taft started an intense rivalry with Japan for commercial advantage in China.

FOREIGN POLICY UNDER WILSON

When he took office in 1913, Woodrow Wilson knew little about foreign policy. "It would be the irony of fate if my administration had to deal chiefly with foreign affairs," he told a friend. And so it was. During his two terms Wilson faced crisis after crisis in this area, including the outbreak of World War I.

A supremely self-confident man, Wilson conducted his own diplomacy. He had little respect for the party regulars who received diplomatic posts as patronage plums. He composed important diplomatic notes on his own typewriter, sent personal emissaries abroad, and carried on major negotiations without the knowledge of his secretary of state. The idealistic Wilson believed in a principled, ethical world in which militarism, colonialism, and war were brought under control. Rejecting the policy of dollar diplomacy, Wilson initially chose a course of moral diplomacy, designed to bring right to the world, preserve peace, and extend to other people the blessings of democracy.

CONDUCTING MORAL DIPLOMACY

William Jennings Bryan, whom Wilson appointed as secretary of state, was also an amateur in foreign relations. A populist who put his trust in the common people, he was skeptical of experts in the State Department. Bryan was a fervent pacifist, and like Wilson, he believed in the American duty to "help" less favored nations.

In 1913 and 1914 he embarked on an idealistic campaign to negotiate treaties of arbitration throughout the world. Known as "cooling-off" treaties, they provided for submitting all international disputes to permanent commissions of investigation. Neither party could declare war or increase armaments until the investigation ended. The idea drew on the popularity of commissions and a sense that reasonable people could settle disputes without resorting to war. Bryan negotiated cooling-off treaties with thirty nations, but none was ever used.

Wilson and Bryan promised a dramatic new approach in Latin America, concerned not with the "pursuit of material interest" but with "human rights" and "national integrity." Their promise, however, went unfulfilled, and in the end, they continued the Roosevelt-Taft policies. Wilson defended the Monroe Doctrine, gave unspoken support to the Roosevelt Corollary, and intervened in Latin America more than had either Roosevelt or Taft. By 1917 American troops "protected" Nicaragua, Haiti, the Dominican Republic, and Cuba.

TROUBLES ACROSS THE BORDER

Porfirio Diaz, president of Mexico for thirty-seven years, was overthrown in 1911. Diaz had encouraged foreign investments in Mexican mines, railroads, oil, and land; by 1913 Americans had invested over $1 billion. His overthrow led to a decade of violence that tested Wilson's policies and brought the United States close to war with Mexico.

A liberal reformer, Francisco I. Madero, followed Diaz as president. But Madero soon lost control of the troubled country. With support from wealthy landowners, the army, and the Catholic church, General Victoriano Huerta ousted Madero in 1913, threw him in jail, and arranged his murder. Most European nations immediately recognized Huerta, but Wilson refused to do so. Instead, he announced a new policy toward revolutionary regimes in Latin America. To win American recognition, they must not only exercise power, but reflect "a just government based upon law, not upon arbitrary or irregular force."

On that basis, Wilson withheld recognition from Huerta and maneuvered to oust him. Early in 1914 he stationed naval units off Mexico's ports to cut off arms shipments to the Huerta regime. On April 9, 1914, several American sailors, ashore in Tampico to purchase supplies, were arrested. They were promptly released, but the American admiral demanded an apology and a twenty-one-gun salute to the American flag. Huerta agreed—if the Americans also saluted the Mexican flag.

Shortly after Wilson asked Congress for authority to use military force if needed, he learned that a German ship was landing arms at Vera Cruz on Mexico's eastern coast. With Wilson's approval, American warships shelled the harbor, and marines took the city. Outraged, Mexicans of all factions denounced the invasion, and for a time the two countries hovered on the edge of war. Only a hasty diplomatic retreat by Wilson avoided more serious hostilities.

In July 1914, cut off from funds, Huerta resigned. Wilson recognized the new government, headed by Venustiano Carranza. Early in 1916, Francisco ("Pancho") Villa, one of Carranza's generals, revolted. Hoping to goad the United States into an action that would help him seize power, he raided border towns, injuring American civilians. Stepping up his assault, Villa murdered thirty-three Americans both in Mexico and the United States.

Stationing militia along the border, Wilson ordered General John J. Pershing on a punitive expedition to seize Villa in Mexico. Pershing led 6000 troops deep into Mexican territory. The expedition was a failure. Carranza protested, Villa eluded Pershing, and Wilson finally ordered his general home.

Wilson's policy had laudable goals; he wanted to help the Mexicans achieve political and agrarian reform, but his motives and methods were condescending. With little forethought, he interfered in the affairs of another country, and in doing so he revealed the themes—moralism, combined with pragmatic self-interest and a desire for peace—that also shaped his policies in Europe.

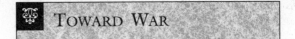

TOWARD WAR

By May 1914 the mood was tense in Europe. Large armies dominated the European continent. A web of alliances entangled nations, maximizing the risk that a local conflict could produce a wider war. Germany and its allies Austria-Hungary and Turkey dominated Central Europe. Linked in another alliance, England, France, and Russia agreed to aid each other in case of attack.

On June 28, 1914, a Balkan assassin in the service of Serbia murdered Archduke Franz Ferdinand, heir to the Austro-Hungarian throne. Within weeks Germany, Turkey, and Austria-

EUROPEAN ALLIANCES AND BATTLEFRONTS, 1914–1917

Allied Powers

Central Powers

Neutral nations

Hungary (the Central Powers) were at war with England, France, and Russia (the Allied Powers). Americans were shocked at the events. Wilson immediately proclaimed neutrality and asked Americans to remain "impartial in thought as well as in action." Privately, Wilson was stunned. A lifelong admirer of the British parliamentary system, he said "everything I love most in the world is at stake."

THE NEUTRALITY POLICY

In general Americans accepted neutrality. They saw no need to enter the conflict, especially after the Allies in September 1914 halted the first German drive toward Paris. Among progressives, there was added reason to resist. War violated the very spirit of progressive reform. Why demand safer factories and then kill men by the millions in war? Progressives and others tended to put the blame for war on the greed of "munition manufacturers, stockbrokers, and bond dealers" eager for wartime profits. Above all, progressives were sure that war would end reform. It consumed money and attention; it inflamed emotions. As a result, many progressives—such as Jane Addams, Frederick C. Howe, and Lillian Wald—fought to keep the United States out of war.

The war's outbreak also tugged at the emotions of millions of immigrant Americans. Those who came from the British Isles tended to support the Allies; those from Ireland tended to support Germany, hoping that Britain's wartime troubles might free their homeland from British domination. The large population of German-Americans often sympathized with the Central Powers.

At the deepest level, a majority in the country, bound by common language and institutions, sympathized with the Allies and blamed Germany for the war. When the war began, Germany invaded Belgium to strike at France and violated a treaty which the German chancellor called "just a scrap of paper." Many Americans resented the violation, and they liked it even less when German troops executed Belgian civilians who resisted. Both sides sought to sway American opinion, and fierce propaganda campaigns flourished. But in the end, the propaganda probably made little difference. Ties of heritage and the course of the war, not propaganda, decided the American position. At the outset, whichever side they cheered for, Americans of all persuasions preferred simply to remain at peace.

FREEDOM OF THE SEAS

The demands of trade tested American neutrality and confronted Wilson with difficult choices. Under international law, neutral countries were permitted to trade in nonmilitary goods with all belligerent countries. But Great Britain controlled the seas, and it intended to cut off shipments of war materials to the Central Powers.

As soon as war broke out, Britain blockaded German ports and limited the goods Americans could sell to Germany. As time passed, Britain stepped up the economic sanctions by forbidding the shipment to Germany of all foodstuffs and most raw materials. British ships often stopped U.S. ships and confiscated cargoes.

Again and again Wilson protested against such infringements of neutral rights. Sometimes Britain complied, sometimes not, and Wilson often grew angry. But needing American support and supplies, Britain pursued a careful strategy to disrupt German-American trade without disrupting Anglo-American relations. When necessary it paid (or promised to pay) American businesses for lost trade with Germany.

Other than the German U-boats, there were no constraints on trade with the Allies, and a flood of Allied war orders fueled the American economy. To finance the purchases, the Allies turned to American bankers for loans. By 1917 loans to Allied governments exceeded $2 billion, while loans to Germany came to only $27 million.

Loans and trade drew the United States ever closer to the Allied cause. And even though Wilson often protested English maritime policy, the protests involved American goods and money whereas Germany's submarine policy threatened American lives.

THE U-BOAT THREAT

A relatively new weapon, the submarine, strained the guidelines of international law. Traditional law required a submarine to surface, warn the target to stop, send a boarding party to check papers and cargo, then allow time for passengers and crew to board lifeboats before sinking the vessel. Flimsy and slow, submarines could ill-afford to surface while the prey radioed for help. If they did surface, they might be rammed or blown up by deck guns.

When Germany announced the submarine campaign in February 1915, Wilson protested sharply. The Germans promised not to sink American ships, and thereafter the issue became the right of Americans to sail on the ships of belligerent nations. Bryan urged Wilson to forbid Americans to travel in the war zones, but the president, determined to stand by the principles of international law, refused.

Wilson reacted more harshly in May and August of 1915 when U-boats sank the *Lusitania* and *Arabic*. He demanded that the Germans protect passenger vessels and pay for American losses. Fearing war, Bryan resigned as secretary of state and was replaced by Robert Lansing, a State Department counselor who favored the Allies. He urged strong stands against German violations of American neutrality.

In February 1916 Germany declared unrestricted submarine warfare against all *armed* ships. A month later, a U-boat torpedoed the unarmed French channel steamer, *Sussex*, without warning, injuring several Americans. Lansing urged Wilson to break relations with Germany. Wilson rejected the advice, but on April 18 sent an ultimatum to Germany that unless it immediately called off attacks on cargo and passenger ships, the United States would sever relations. Germany's Kaiser, convinced he did not yet have enough submarines to risk war, yielded. In the *Sussex* pledge of May 4, 1916, he agreed to Wilson's demands and promised to shoot on sight only ships of the enemy's navy. He tried to impose the condition that the United States compel the Allies to end their blockade.

The *Sussex* pledge marked the beginning of a short period of friendly relations between Germany and the United States. The agreement applied not only to passenger liners, but to *all* merchant ships, belligerent or not. There was one problem: Wilson had taken such a strong position that if Germany renewed submarine warfare on merchant shipping, war with the United States was likely. Nevertheless, most Americans viewed the agreement as a diplomatic stroke for peace by Wilson, and the issues of peace and preparedness dominated the presidential election of 1916.

"HE KEPT US OUT OF WAR"

The "preparedness" issue pitted antiwar groups against those who wanted to ready themselves for war. The American Rights Committee and other groups urged stepped-up military measures. In the summer of 1915 they persuaded the War Department to hold a training camp in Plattsburg, New York, in which regular army officers trained civilian volunteers in modern warfare.

Bellicose as always, Teddy Roosevelt led the preparedness campaign. He called Wilson "yellow" for not pressing Germany harder. Defending the military's state of readiness, Wilson refused to be stampeded just because "some amongst us are nervous and excited."

Wilson's position was attacked from both sides: Preparedness advocates charged cowardice, while pacifists denounced any attempt at military readiness. The difficulty of his position, plus the growing U-boat crisis, soon changed Wilson's mind. In mid-1915 he asked the War Department to increase military planning, and he quietly notified congressional leaders of a switch in policy. Later that year, Wilson approved large increases in expenditures for the army and navy, a move that upset many peace-minded progressives.

For their standard-bearer in the presidential election of 1916, the Republicans nominated Charles Evans Hughes, a moderate justice of the Supreme Court. Hughes, a dull campaigner, called for a tougher line against Germany. The Democrats nominated Wilson in a convention marked by spontaneous demonstrations for peace. Picking up the antiwar theme, perhaps with reservation, Wilson said in October: "I am not expecting this country to get into war." The campaign slogan, "He kept us out of war," was repeated again and again.

On election night, Hughes had swept most of the East, and Wilson retired at 10 P.M., thinking he had lost. During the night the results came in from California, New Mexico, and North Dakota; all supported Wilson. Holding the Democratic South, Wilson carried key states in the Midwest and West and won reelection. He took large portions of the labor and progressive vote, and women—who could vote in presidential elections in twelve states—voted heavily for him.

THE FINAL MONTHS OF PEACE

Just before election day Great Britain further limited neutral trade, and there were reports from Germany of a renewal of unrestricted submarine warfare. Fresh from his election victory, Wilson redoubled his efforts for peace.

In December 1916, he sent messages to both sides asking them to state their war aims. The Allies refused, although they promised privately to negotiate if the German terms were reasonable. The Germans replied evasively but in January 1917 revealed their real objectives. Close to forcing Russia out of the war, Germany sensed victory and craved territory—in eastern Europe, Africa, Belgium, and France.

On January 22, in an eloquent speech before the Senate, Wilson called for a "peace without victory." Outlining his own aims, he urged respect for all nations, freedom of the seas, arms limitations, and a league of nations to keep the peace. The speech made a great impression on many Europeans, but it was too late. The Germans had decided a few weeks before to unleash the submarines and gamble on a quick end to the war.

On January 31, the German ambassador in Washington informed Lansing that beginning February 1, U-boats would sink on sight all ships—passenger or merchant, neutral or belligerent, armed or unarmed—in the waters around England and France. German leaders estimated that if their submarine campaign were successful, they could win the war in six months. As he had pledged in 1916, Wilson broke off relations with Germany, although he still hoped for peace.

On February 25 the British government privately gave Wilson a telegram intercepted from Arthur Zimmermann, the German foreign minister, to the German ambassador in Mexico. A day later, Wilson asked Congress for authority to arm merchant ships to deter U-boats attacks. To prevent a filibuster, Wilson divulged the contents of the Zimmermann telegram. It proposed an alliance with Mexico in case of war with the United States, offering financial support and recovery of Mexico's "lost territory" in New Mexico, Texas, and Arizona.

Spurred by a wave of public indignation, the House passed Wilson's measure, but La Follette and others still blocked action in the Senate. On March 9, 1917, Wilson ordered merchant ships armed on his own authority. Between March 12 and March 21, U-boats sank five American ships, and Wilson decided to wait no longer. He called Congress into special session and at 8:30 in the evening on April 2, 1917, asked for a declaration of war. Americans, he said, "shall fight for the things which we have always carried nearest our hearts—for democracy. . . ."

OVER THERE

With a burst of patriotism, the United States entered a war its new allies were in danger of losing. That same month, the Germans sank 881,000 tons of Allied shipping, the highest amount of the war. There were mutinies in the French army; a costly British drive in Flanders stalled. In November the Bolsheviks seized power in Russia and soon signed a separate peace treaty with Germany (see the map on p. 412), freeing German troops to fight in the West. German and Austrian forces routed the Italian army on the southern flank, and the Allies braced for a spring 1918 offensive.

The United States was not prepared for war. Some Americans hoped the declaration of war itself might daunt the Germans; others hoped money and arms, not troops, would be sufficient to produce victory. Bypassing older generals, Wilson named "Black Jack" Pershing to head the American Expeditionary Force (AEF). Pershing inherited an army unready for war. It was small and poorly equipped. Its most recent battle experience had been chasing Pancho Villa unsuccessfully around northern Mexico. Nor did the armed forces have any war plans to fight Germany in Europe.

Although some in Congress preferred a voluntary army of the kind that had fought in the Spanish-American War, Wilson turned to conscription, which he felt was both efficient and democratic. In May 1917 Congress passed the Selective Service Act, providing for the registration of all men between the ages of twenty-one and thirty. The act eventually accounted for the induction of about 2.8 million men into the army.

The draft included black men as well as white and four African-American regiments were among the first sent into action. Despite their contributions, however, no black soldiers were allowed to march in the victory celebration that eventually took place in Paris.

WAR IN THE TRENCHES

World War I may have been the most terrible war of all time. After the early offensive, the European armies dug themselves into trenches, in places only hundreds of yards apart. Artillery, poison gas, hand grenades, and a new weapon—rapid-fire machine guns—kept them pinned down. Even in moments of respite, the mud, rats, cold, fear, and disease took a heavy toll. Deafening bombardments shook the earth, and there was a high incidence of shell shock. From time to time troops went "over the top" in an effort to break through, but the costs were enormous and the gains slight.

The first American soldiers reached France in June 1917. By the war's end, 2 million men had crossed the Atlantic. No troop ships were sunk, a credit to the British and American navies. After the summer of 1917 a convoy system developed by Admiral William S. Sims that

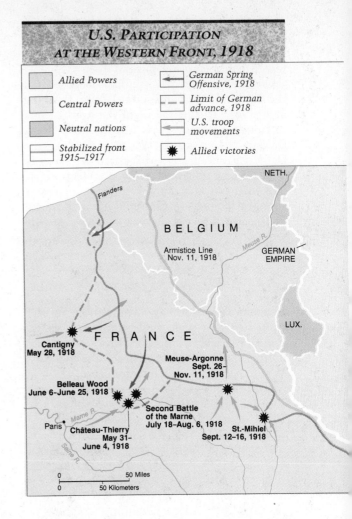

U.S. PARTICIPATION AT THE WESTERN FRONT, 1918

- Allied Powers
- Central Powers
- Neutral nations
- Stabilized front 1915–1917
- German Spring Offensive, 1918
- Limit of German advance, 1918
- U.S. troop movements
- Allied victories

NETH.

BELGIUM

Armistice Line Nov. 11, 1918

Meuse R.

GERMAN EMPIRE

LUX.

Flanders

FRANCE

Cantigny May 28, 1918

Meuse-Argonne Sept. 26– Nov. 11, 1918

Belleau Wood June 6-June 25, 1918

Second Battle of the Marne July 18–Aug. 6, 1918

St.-Mihiel Sept. 12–16, 1918

Paris

Marne R.

Château-Thierry May 31– June 4, 1918

Seine R.

0   50 Miles
0   50 Kilometers

used Allied destroyers to escort merchant vessels across the ocean cut shipping losses in half.

As expected, on March 21, 1918, the Germans launched a massive assault in western Europe. By May they had driven Allied forces back to the Marne River, just fifty miles from Paris. More than 27,000 Americans saw their first action. They blocked the Germans at the town of Château-Thierry, and four weeks later forced them out of Belleau Wood, a crucial strongpoint. On July 15 the Germans threw everything into a last drive for Paris, but in three days they were finished.

With the German drive stalled, the Allies counterattacked along the entire front. On September 12, 1918, half a million Americans and a smaller contingent of French drove the Germans from the St. Mihiel salient. Two weeks later, 896,000 Americans attacked between the Meuse River and the Argonne Forest. Focusing on the main railroad supply line for the German army in the West, they broke through in early November, cut the line, and drove the Germans back along the whole front.

The German high command knew that the war was lost. At 4 A.M. on November 11, Germany signed the armistice. The AEF lost 48,909 soldiers, and there were 230,000 wounded; losses to disease brought the total dead to over 112,000. The American contribution was vital, although small in comparison to the enormous costs to European nations, who lost more than 3 million soldiers. Fresh, enthusiastic American troops raised Allied morale; they helped turn the tide at a crucial point in the war. American soldiers, white and black, distinguished themselves during the last months of the terrible war.

OVER HERE

Victory at the front depended on economic and emotional mobilization at home. Consolidating federal authority, Wilson moved quickly in 1917 and 1918 to organize war production and distribution. An idealist who knew how to sway public opinion, he also recognized the need to enlist American emotions. To him, the war for people's minds, the "conquest of their convictions," was as vital as events on the battlefield.

THE CONQUEST OF CONVICTIONS

A week after war was declared, Wilson formed the Committee on Public Information (CPI) and asked George Creel, an outspoken progressive journalist, to head it. Creel recruited thousands of people in the arts, advertising, and film industries to publicize the war. He worked out a system of voluntary censorship with the press, plastered walls with colorful posters, and issued more than 75 million pamphlets.

Creel also enlisted 75,000 "four-minute men" to give quick speeches at public gatherings and places of entertainment on "Why We Are Fighting" and "The Meaning of America." By 1918 they were portraying the Germans as bloodthirsty Huns bent on world conquest. Exploiting a new medium, the CPI promoted films like *The Kaiser, the Beast of Berlin.* Creel secretly subsidized several prowar groups and formed the CPI's Division of Industrial Relations to rally labor to the war.

Helped along by the propaganda campaign, anti-German sentiment spread rapidly. Many schools stopped offering instruction in the German language, sauerkraut was renamed "liberty cabbage," and orchestral works by Bach, Beethoven, and Brahms vanished from some symphonic programs. German-Americans and antiwar figures were badgered, beaten, and in some cases killed.

Vigilantism, sparked often by superpatriotism of a ruthless sort, flourished. Frequently it focused on radical antiwar figures like Frank Little, an IWW official in Butte, Montana, who was taken from his boardinghouse in August 1917, tied to the rear of an automobile, and dragged through the street until his kneecaps were scraped off. He was then hanged.

Rather than curbing the repression, Wilson encouraged it. At his request, Congress passed the Espionage Act of 1917, which authorized sentences of up to twenty years in prison for persons found guilty of aiding the enemy, obstructing the recruitment of soldiers, or encouraging disloyalty. It allowed the postmaster general to remove from the mails materials that incited treason or insurrection.

In 1918 Congress passed the Sedition Act, imposing harsh penalties on anyone using "disloyal, profane, scurrilous, or abusive language" about the government, flag, or uniform. In all, more than 1500 persons were arrested under the new laws, some for such trivial offenses as laughing at rookies drilling at an army camp.

The sedition laws clearly went beyond any clear or present danger. There were German spies in the country, to be sure. The danger did not warrant a nationwide program of repression. Conservatives seized on the laws to stamp out socialists. In 1918 Eugene V. Debs, the Socialist party leader, delivered a speech denouncing capitalism and the war. He was convicted for violation of the Espionage Act and spent the war in a penitentiary in Atlanta. Nominated as the Socialist party candidate in the presidential election of 1920, Debs—then prisoner 9653—won nearly a million votes, but the Socialist movement never fully recovered from the repression of the war.

In fostering hostility toward anything that smacked of dissent, the war also gave rise to the great "Red Scare" that began in 1919 (see Chapter 25). Pleased at first with the Russian Revolution, Americans in general turned quickly against it, especially after Lenin and the Bolsheviks seized control late in 1917. The Americans feared Lenin's anticapitalist program, and they denounced his decision in early 1918 to make peace with Germany because it freed German troops to fight in France. In the summer of 1918, Wilson even cooperated with the Allied leaders and sent American troops into Russia in an attempt to bring down the fledgling Bolshevik government. Although the plan failed to achieve its goals, Wilson joined in an economic blockade of Russia, sent weapons to anti-Bolshevik insurgents, and refused to recognize Lenin's government. His actions soured Russian-American relations for decades to come.

A BUREAUCRATIC WAR

Quick, effective action was needed to win the war, and to meet the need, Wilson and Congress set up an array of new federal agencies, nearly 5000 in all. Staffed largely by businessmen, the agencies drew on funds and powers of a hitherto unknown scope.

The War Industries Board, one of the most powerful of the agencies, oversaw the production of all American factories. Headed by millionaire Bernard M. Baruch, it determined priorities, allocated raw materials, and fixed prices. It told manufacturers what they could and could not make. Working closely with

business, Baruch for a time acted as the dictator of the American economy.

Herbert Hoover, the hero of a campaign to feed starving Belgians, headed a new Food Administration, and he set out with customary energy to supply food to the armies overseas. Appealing to the "spirit of self-sacrifice," Hoover convinced people to save food by observing "meatless" and "wheatless" days. He fixed prices to boost production, bought and distributed wheat, and encouraged people to plant "victory gardens" at their homes, churches, and schools.

Other agencies rationed fuel and regulated railroads, shipping, and foreign trade. As never before, the government intervened in American life: When strikes threatened the telephone and telegraph companies, it simply seized and ran them. The partnership between government and business grew closer. As government expanded, business expanded as well, responding to wartime contracts. Industries like steel, aluminum, and cigarettes boomed in a war that displayed the triumph of large-scale industrial organization.

LABOR IN THE WAR

The war also brought organized labor into the partnership with government, although the results were more limited than in the business-government alliance. Samuel Gompers, president of the AFL, served on Wilson's Council of National Defense, an advisory group formed to unify business, labor, and government. Gompers hoped to trade labor peace for labor advances, and he formed a War Committee on Labor to enlist workers' support for the war. With the blessing of the Wilson administration, union membership grew rapidly during the war.

Hoping to encourage production and avoid strikes, Wilson adopted many of the objectives of the social-justice reformers. He supported an eight-hour workday in war-related industries and improved wages and working conditions. The War Labor Board, headed by Felix Frankfurter, standardized wages and hours, and at Wilson's direction, it protected the right of labor to organize and bargain collectively. Although it did not forbid strikes, it used various tactics to discourage them.

The WLB also ordered that women be paid equal wages for equal work in war industries. Women, blacks, and Mexican Americans filled the labor shortage caused by the draft and the end of large-scale European immigration to America. A million women worked in war industries. Although most held "women's jobs," there were some new opportunities and in some cases higher pay. There was also a new sense of confidence and increased expectations.

Looking for more people to fill wartime jobs, corporations found another major source among southern blacks. Beginning in 1916, northern labor agents traveled across the South, promising jobs, high wages, and free transportation. The movement northward became a flood. Between 1916 and 1918 over 450,000 blacks left the Old South for the booming industrial cities of St. Louis, Chicago, Detroit, and Cleveland.

Most of the newcomers were young, unmarried, and semiskilled. The men found jobs in factories, railroad yards, steel mills, packing houses, and coal mines; the women worked in textile factories, department stores, and restaurants. In their new homes, blacks found greater racial freedom but also different living conditions. Northern industrial society struck many blacks as impersonal and lonely, a society ruled by clocks and shop foremen.

Racial tensions increased, resulting in part from growing competition for housing and jobs. In mid-1917 a race war in East St. Louis, Illinois, killed nine whites and about forty blacks. In 1919 race riots occurred in Washington, D.C., Chicago, New York City, and Omaha. Lynch mobs killed forty-eight blacks in 1917, sixty-three in 1918, and seventy-eight in 1919. Ten of the victims in 1919 were war veterans, several still in uniform.

Blacks were more and more inclined to fight back. Two hundred thousand blacks had served in France—42,000 as combat troops. Returning home, they expected better treatment. W.E.B. Du Bois spoke of a "New Negro," proud and more militant: "We return. We return from fighting. We return fighting."

Eager for cheap labor, farmers and ranchers in the Southwest persuaded the federal government to relax immigration restrictions, and between 1917 and 1920 more than 100,000 Mexicans migrated into Texas, Arizona, New Mexico, and California. Tens of thousands of Mexican-Americans moved to Chicago, St. Louis, Omaha, and other northern cities to take wartime jobs. Often scorned and insecure, they created urban *barrios*, similar to the Chinatowns and Little Italys around them.

Like most wars, World War I affected patterns at home as much as abroad. Business profits grew, factories expanded, and industries turned out huge amounts of war goods. Government authority swelled, and people came to expect

War brought the mobilization of American factories. This woman worker in a defense plant welds with an acetylene torch.

different things of their government. Labor made some gains, as did women and blacks. Society assimilated some of the shifts, but social and economic tensions continued to grow, and when the war ended, they spilled over in the strikes and violence of the "Red Scare" of 1919 (see Chapter 25).

The United States emerged from the war the strongest economic power in the world. In 1914 it was a debtor nation; American citizens owed foreign investors about $3 billion. Five years later the United States had become a creditor nation. Foreign governments owed over $10 billion, and foreign citizens owed American investors nearly $3 billion. The war marked a drastic shift in economic power between Europe and America.

❧ THE TREATY OF VERSAILLES

Long before the fighting ended, Wilson began to formulate plans for the peace. On January 8, 1918, appearing before Congress to rebut Bolshevik arguments that the war was merely a struggle among imperialists, the president outlined terms for a far-reaching, nonpunitive settlement. Wilson's Fourteen Points were generous and farsighted, but they failed to satisfy wartime emotions.

England and France distrusted Wilsonian idealism as the basis for peace. They wanted Germany disarmed and crippled; they wanted its colonies; and they were skeptical of the principle of self-determination. As the end of the war neared, the Allies, who had made secret commitments with one another, balked at making the Fourteen Points the basis of peace. When Wilson threatened to negotiate a separate treaty with Germany, however, they accepted. Wilson had won an important victory, but difficulties lay ahead.

A PEACE AT PARIS

Just before the peace conference began, Wilson appealed to voters to elect a Democratic Con-

gress in the 1918 elections. The Democrats lost both the House and Senate, enabling Wilson's opponents to announce that voters had rejected his policies. In fact, the Democratic losses stemmed largely from domestic problems, but they hurt Wilson, who soon would be negotiating with European leaders buoyed by rousing victories at their own polls.

Two weeks after the election, Wilson announced that he would attend the peace conference. This was a dramatic break from tradition, and his personal involvement drew attacks from Republicans. They renewed the criticism when Wilson named no member of the Senate, and no prominent Republican, to the delegation to attend the conference. Wilson passed over Henry Cabot Lodge, the powerful Republican senator from Massachusetts who opposed the Fourteen Points and would soon head the Senate Foreign Relations Committee. Wilson wanted a delegation he could control—an advantage at the peace table but not in any battle over the treaty at home.

Upon his arrival in Europe, Wilson received a tumultuous welcome in England, France, and Italy. Overwhelmed, Wilson was sure that people shared his goals, but he was wrong: Like their leaders, they hated Germany and wanted victory unmistakably reflected in the peace plan.

Opening in January 1919, the Peace Conference at Paris continued until May. Although twenty-seven nations were represented, the "Big Four" dominated it: Wilson; Georges Clemenceau, the stubborn French premier who was determined to end the German threat forever; David Lloyd George, the crafty British prime minister who had pledged to squeeze Germany "until the pips squeak"; and the Italian prime minister, Vittorio Orlando. A clever negotiator, Wilson traded various "small" concessions for his major goals—national self-determination, a reduction in tensions, and a League of Nations to enforce the peace.

Wilson had to surrender some important principles. Instead of peace without victory, the treaty made Germany accept responsibility for the war and demanded enormous reparations. It made no mention of disarmament, free trade, or freedom of the seas, and it violated the goal of self-determination. Instead of an open covenant openly arrived at, the treaty was drafted behind closed doors.

But Wilson deflected some of the most extreme Allied demands, and he won his coveted Point 14, a League of Nations, designed "to achieve international peace and security." The League included a general assembly; a smaller council composed of the United States, Great Britain, France, Italy, Japan, and four nations to be elected by the assembly; and a court of international justice. League members pledged to submit to arbitration every dispute threatening peace and to enjoin military and economic sanctions against nations resorting to war. Article X, for Wilson the heart of the League, obligated members to protect each other's independence and territorial integrity.

The draft treaty in hand, Wilson returned home in February 1919 to discuss it with Congress and the people. Public opinion polls showed that most Americans favored the League, but there was strong congressional opposition to it. Thirty-seven senators, including Lodge, said they would not vote for the treaty without amendment. Should those numbers hold up, Lodge had enough votes to defeat it.

Returning to Paris, Wilson attacked his critics, while privately he worked for changes to improve the chances of Senate approval. The Allies won major concessions in return, but they amended the League draft treaty, agreeing that domestic affairs remained outside the League's jurisdiction, exempting the Monroe Doctrine, and allowing nations to withdraw after two years' notice. On June 28, 1919, they signed the treaty in the Hall of Mirrors at Versailles, and Wilson started home for his most difficult fight.

REJECTION IN THE SENATE

There were ninety-six senators in 1919, forty-nine of them Republicans. Fourteen Republicans, led by William E. Borah of Idaho, were the "irreconcilables" who opposed the League on any grounds. Frank B. Kellogg of Minnesota led a group of twelve "mild reservationists" who accepted the treaty but wanted to insert several reservations that would not greatly weaken it. Finally, there were the Lodge-led "strong reser-

---

WOODROW WILSON'S FOURTEEN POINTS, 1918: SUCCESS AND FAILURE IN IMPLEMENTATION

1. Open covenants of peace openly arrived at	Not fulfilled
2. Absolute freedom of navigation upon the seas in peace and war	Not fulfilled
3. Removal of all economic barriers to the equality of trade among nations	Not fulfilled
4. Reduction of armaments to the level needed only for domestic safety	Not fulfilled
5. Impartial adjustment of colonial claims	Not fulfilled
6. Evacuation of all Russian territory; Russia to be welcomed into the society of free nations	Not fulfilled
7. Evacuation and restoration of Belgium	**Fulfilled**
8. Evacuation and restoration of all French lands; return of Alsace-Lorraine to France	**Fulfilled**
9. Readjustment of Italy's frontiers along lines of Italian nationality	Compromised
10. Self-determination for the former subjects of the Austro-Hungarian Empire	Compromised
11. Evacuation of Rumania, Serbia, and Montenegro; free access to the sea for Serbia	Compromised
12. Self-determination for the former subjects of the Ottoman Empire; secure sovereignty for Turkish portion	Compromised
13. Establishment of an independent Poland, with free and secure access to the sea	**Fulfilled**
14. Establishment of a League of Nations affording mutual guarantees of independence and territorial integrity	Not fulfilled

Source: Data from G. M. Gathorne-Hardy, The Fourteen Points and the Treaty of Versailles (Oxford Pamphlets on World Affairs, no. 6, 1939), pp. 8–34; Thomas G. Paterson et al., American Foreign Policy, A History Since 1900, 2d ed., Vol. 2, pp. 282–93.

CHRONOLOGY

1901	Hay-Pauncefote Treaty empowers United States to build isthmian canal
1904	Theodore Roosevelt introduces corollary to Monroe Doctrine
1904–1905	Russo-Japanese War
1905	Taft-Katsura Agreement recognizes Japanese power in Korea
1908	Root-Takahira Agreement vows to maintain status quo in the Pacific Roosevelt sends the fleet around the world
1911	Revolution begins in Mexico
1913–1914	Bryan negotiates "cooling-off" treaties to end war
1914	World War I begins U.S. Marines take Vera Cruz Panama Canal completed
1915	Japan issues Twenty-One Demands to China (January) Germany declares waters around British Isles a war zone (February) *Lusitania* torpedoed (May) Bryan resigns; Robert Lansing becomes secretary of state (June) *Arabic* pledge restricts submarine warfare (September)
1916	Germany issues *Sussex* pledge (March)
	General John J. Pershing leads punitive expedition into Mexico to seize Pancho Villa (April) Wilson wins reelection
1917	Wilson calls for "peace without victory" (January) Germany resumes unrestricted U-boat warfare (February) United States enters World War I (April) Congress passes Selective Service Act (May) First American troops reach France (June) War Industries Board established (July)
1918	Wilson outlines Fourteen Points for peace (January) Germany asks for peace (October) Armistice ends the war (November)
1919	Peace negotiations begin in Paris (January) Treaty of Versailles defeated in Senate
1920	Warren G. Harding elected president

vationists," twenty-three of them in all, who wanted major changes that the Allies would have to approve.

With only four Democratic senators opposed to the treaty, the Democrats and compromise-minded Republicans had enough votes to ratify it, once a few reservations were inserted. Playing for time to allow public opposition to grow, Lodge scheduled lengthy hearings on the treaty. Democratic leaders urged Wilson to appeal to the Republican "mild reservationists," but he angrily refused.

Fed up with Lodge's tactics, Wilson set out in early September to take the case directly to the people. In Pueblo, Colorado, toward the end of his tour, he delivered one of the most eloquent speeches of his career. That night Wilson felt ill. He returned to Washington and on October 2, Mrs. Wilson found him lying unconscious on the floor of the White House, the victim of a stroke that paralyzed his left side.

After the stroke, Wilson could not work more than an hour or two at a time, and he saw very few people. For seven months he did not meet with the cabinet. Secretary of State Lansing convened the cabinet, but was ordered to stop and resign. Focusing his remaining energy on the fight over the treaty, Wilson lost touch with other issues, and critics charged that his wife, Edith Bolling Wilson, administered the government.

On November 6, 1919, Lodge finally reported the treaty out of committee, along with "Fourteen Reservations," one for each of Wilson's points. The most important reservation stipulated that implementation of Article X, Wilson's key article, required the action of Congress in each case.

Even though the Democrats could not pass the treaty without reservations, Wilson refused to compromise. When Mrs. Wilson urged her husband to accept the Lodge reservations, he said: "Better a thousand times to go down fighting than to dip your colors to dishonorable compromise."

On November 19, the treaty—with the Lodge reservations—failed, 39 to 55. Following Wilson's instructions, the Democrats voted against it. A motion to approve without the reservations lost 38 to 53, with only one Republican voting in favor. Neither Wilson nor Lodge would compromise. When the treaty with reservations again came up for vote on March 19, 1920, twenty-one Democrats defied Wilson and voted for it. But by a vote of 49 to 35, seven votes short of the necessary two-thirds majority, the treaty was defeated.

To Wilson one chance remained: the presidential election of 1920. The Democrats nominated Governor James M. Cox of Ohio. Wilson called for "a great and solemn referendum" on the treaty. The Democratic platform endorsed the treaty but agreed to accept reservations to clarify the American role in the League.

On the Republican side, Senator Warren G. Harding of Ohio won the presidential nomination. Harding waffled on the treaty, but it made little difference. Voters wanted a change. Harding won in a landslide. Without a peace treaty, the United States remained technically at war, and it was not until July 1921, almost three years after the last shot was fired, that Congress passed a joint resolution ending the war.

After 1919 there was disillusionment. World War I was feared before it started, popular while it lasted, and hated when it ended. To a whole generation that followed, it appeared futile, killing without a cause, sacrifice without benefit. Books, plays, and movies—Hemingway's *A Farewell to Arms*, John Dos Passos' *Three Soldiers*, Lawrence Stallings and Maxwell Anderson's *What Price Glory?*, among others—showed it as waste, horror, and death.

The war and its aftermath damaged the humanitarian, progressive spirit of the early years of the century. It killed "something precious and perhaps irretrievable in the hearts of thinking men and women." Progressivism survived well into the 1920s and the New Deal, but it no longer had the old conviction and broad popular support. Bruising fights over the war and the League drained most people's energy and enthusiasm.

Woodrow Wilson died in Washington in 1924, three years after Harding, the new president, promised "not heroics but healing; not nostrums but normalcy; not revolution but restoration." Nonetheless, the "war to end all wars," and the spirit of Woodrow Wilson left an indelible imprint on the country.

✿ RECOMMENDED READING

American foreign policy between 1901 and 1921 has been the subject of considerable study. Richard W. Leopold, *The Growth of American Foreign Policy* (1972), is balanced and informed. William Appleman Williams, *Roots of The Modern American Empire* (1969), explores the forces underlying American foreign policy. David H. Burton, *Theodore Roosevelt,*

Confident Imperialist (1968), and Frederick Marks III, *Velvet on Iron: The Diplomacy of Theodore Roosevelt* (1979), trace Roosevelt's policies. On Taft, see Ralph E. Minger, *William Howard Taft and United States Foreign Policy* (1975), and Walter V. Scholes and Marie V. Scholes, *The Foreign Policies of the Taft Administration* (1970). Arthur S. Link examines Wilson's foreign policy in *Woodrow Wilson: Revolution, War and Peace* (1979). N. Gordon Levin, Jr., *Woodrow Wilson and World Politics: America's Response to War and Revolution* (1968), places Wilson in the larger context of world events. Ernest R. May studies American policy before the war in *The World War and American Isolation, 1914–1917* (1959). Bradford Perkins, *The Great Rapprochement: England and the United States, 1895–1914* (1968), examines the growing friendship between the two countries.

Studies of events at home during the war include David M. Kennedy, *Over Here* (1980); Valerie Jean Conner, *The National War Labor Board: Stability, Social Justice and the Voluntary State in World War I* (1983); William Preston, Jr., *Aliens and Dissenters: Federal Suppression of Radicals, 1903–1933* (1963); Stephen Vaughn, *Holding Fast the Inner Lines: Democracy, Nationalism, and the Committee on Public Information* (1980); Maurine W. Greenwald, *Women, War, and Work* (1980); Neil A. Wynn, *From Progressivism to Prosperity: World War I and American Society* (1968); and John Whiteday Chambers II, *To Raise An Army: The Draft Comes to Modern America* (1967).

For relations with Latin America, see Dana G. Monro, *Intervention and Dollar Diplomacy in the Caribbean, 1900–1920* (1964); Richard L. Lael, *Arrogant Diplomacy: U.S. Policy toward Colombia, 1903–1922* (1987); and three books by Lester D. Langley: *Struggle for the American Mediterranean* (1975), *The United States and the Caribbean, 1900–1970* (1980), and *The Banana Wars: An Inner History of American Empire, 1900–1934* (1983).

On Mexico, see Peter Calvert, *The Mexican Revolution, 1910–1914* (1968), and Lloyd Gardner, *Wilson and Revolutions, 1913–1921* (1976). Several books deal with policies in the Far East, including Raymond A. Esthus, *Theodore Roosevelt and Japan* (1966), and Jerry Israel, *Progressivism and the Open Door: America and China, 1905–1921* (1971).

Historians have long debated the reasons for America's entry into the war; see, for example, Patrick Devlin, *Too Proud to Fight: Woodrow Wilson's Neutrality* (1974), and Ross Gregory, *The Origins of American Intervention in the First World War* (1971).

Arthur Walworth, *America's Moment, 1918: American Diplomacy at the End of World War I* (1977), examines Wilson's attempt to create a peaceful world order. The Treaty of Versailles and the struggle for ratification are covered in Arno J. Mayer, *Politics and Diplomacy of Peacemaking* (1967); Charles L. Mee, Jr., *The End of Order, Versailles, 1919* (1980); Warren F. Kuehl, *Seeking World Order* (1969); and Ralph A. Stone, *The Irreconcilables* (1970).

Wesley M. Bagby, *The Road to Normalcy* (1962), is an excellent study of domestic policies of the era.

25 Transition to Modern America

The moving assembly line that Henry Ford developed in 1913 (in Highland Park, Michigan) for manufacture of the Model T marked only the first step toward full mass production and the beginning of America's worldwide industrial supremacy. He already had a vision of a vast industrial tract where machines, moving through a sequence of carefully arranged manufacturing operations, would transform raw materials into finished cars, trucks, and tractors. By the mid-1920s at River Rouge, his plant southeast of Detroit, his vision had been realized.

Ford expanded his industrial dream in 1919 when he built a blast furnace and foundry to make engine blocks for both the Model T and his tractors. By 1924, more than 40,000 workers were turning out nearly all the metal parts used in making Ford vehicles.

Visitors from all over the world came to marvel at River Rouge. Some were disturbed by the jumble of machines and the apparent congestion on the plant floor, but industrial experts recognized that the arrangement led to incredible productivity because "the work moves and the men stand still." As a whole, the plant was "one huge, perfectly-timed, smoothly-operating industrial machine."

In 1927 Ford closed the assembly line at Highland Park. For the next six months, his engineers worked on designing a more compact and efficient assembly line at River Rouge for the Model A, which went into production in November. By then River Rouge had more than justified Ford's vision. For a generation of engineers, wrote historian Geoffrey Perrett, the River Rouge plant was "a monument."

Mass production, born in Highland Park in 1914 and perfected at River Rouge in the 1920s, became a hallmark of American industry. Soon Ford's emphasis on the flow of parts moving past stationary workers became the standard in nearly every American factory. The moving assembly line took away the last vestige of craftsmanship and turned workers into near robots. It also led to amazing efficiency that produced both high profits for manufacturers and low prices for buyers.

Most important, mass production founded a consumer-goods revolution. American factories turned out a flood of automobiles and electric appliances that made life easier and more pleasant for the vast majority of the American people. The result was the creation of a new America, one in which individualism was sacrificed to conformity as part of the price to be paid for a new era of abundance.

The twenties, often seen as a time of escape and frivolity before the onset of the Depression, actually marked a beginning, a time when the American people learned to adapt to life in the city, when they decided to center their existence upon the automobile, and when they rejected their rural past while still longing for the old values it had created. It is in the 1920s that we can find the roots of modern America.

THE SECOND INDUSTRIAL REVOLUTION

The first Industrial Revolution in the late nineteenth century had catapulted the United States into the forefront of the world's richest and most highly developed nations. With the advent of the new consumer-goods industries, the American people by the 1920s enjoyed the highest standard of living of any nation on earth. From 1922 to 1929 the economy boomed. The American industrial output nearly doubled, and the gross national product rose by 40 percent. Most of this explosive

growth took place in industries producing goods for consumers. Equally important, the national per-capita annual income increased by 30 percent to $681 in 1929. American workers became the highest paid in history and thus were able to buy the flood of new goods they were turning out on the assembly lines.

The key to the new affluence lay in technology. Electric motors replaced steam engines as the basic source of energy in factories, and efficiency experts helped to maximize labor's output. Production per man-hour increased an amazing 75 percent over the decade.

THE AUTOMOBILE INDUSTRY

The nature of the consumer-goods revolution can best be seen in the automobile industry, which became the nation's largest in the 1920s. Rapid growth was its distinguishing feature. In 1920, there were 10 million cars in the nation; by the end of the decade, 26 million autos were on the road.

Ford continued to lead the way, but General Motors and Chrysler Corporation offered stiff competition. Small manufacturers began to disappear, victims of the huge costs involved in mass production. *Oligopoly*, control of an industry by a few large companies, became the dominant pattern in all the consumer-goods industries.

The automobile boom depended on the apparently insatiable appetite of the American people for cars. But as the decade continued, the market became more saturated as more and more of those who could afford the novel luxury had become car owners. Marketing became as crucial as production. Automobile makers began to rely heavily on advertising and annual model changes, seeking to make customers dissatisfied with their old vehicles and eager to order new ones. And installment buying helped prolong the boom.

Despite these efforts, sales slumped in 1927 when Ford stopped making the Model T, picked up again the next year with the introduction of the Model A, but began to slide again in 1929. The automobile industry revealed a basic

Intensified manufacturing, promotional advertising, and installment buying made it possible for over 20 million Americans to own cars in the 1920s. Highway construction lagged behind auto sales.

weakness in the consumer-goods economy; once people bought an item with a long life, they were out of the market for a few years.

Few noticed the emerging economic instability during the affluent 1920s. Instead, contemporary observers focused on the great stimulus the automobile industry had on the steel, rubber, paint, glass, and road construction industries. Filling stations, tourist cabins (forerunners of the modern motel), and drive-ins of all kinds began to dot the landscape along the major and minor highways. The auto changed the whole pattern of city life, leading to a suburban explosion as real-estate developers could now build houses in ever wider concentric circles around the central cities.

PATTERNS OF ECONOMIC GROWTH

Automobiles were the most conspicuous of the consumer products that flourished in the 1920s

but certainly not the only ones. The electrical industry grew nearly as quickly. Two thirds of all American families enjoyed electricity by the end of the decade, and they spent vast sums on washing machines, vacuum cleaners, refrigerators, and ranges. The new appliances eased the burdens of the housewife and ushered in an age of leisure.

Radio broadcasting and motion-picture production also boomed in the 1920s. The early success of KDKA in Pittsburgh stimulated the growth of more than 800 independent radio stations, and by 1929 NBC had formed the first successful radio network. The film industry thrived in Hollywood, reaching its maturity in the mid-1920s. With the advent of the "talkies" in 1929, average weekly movie attendance climbed to nearly 100 million.

Other industries prospered as well. Production of light metals, chemicals, and synthetics grew into major businesses. Americans found a whole new spectrum of products to buy—cigarette lighters, wristwatches, heat-resistant glass cooking dishes, and rayon stockings to name just a few.

The corporation continued to be the dominant economic unit in the 1920s. Growing corporations now had hundreds of thousands of stockholders. The enormous profits generated by these corporations enabled their managers to finance growth and expansion internally, thereby freeing companies from their earlier dependence on investment bankers such as J. P. Morgan. Operating independently of outside restraint, the corporate managers were accountable only to other managers.

Another wave of mergers accompanied the growth of corporations during the 1920s. By the end of the decade, the 200 largest nonfinancial corporations owned almost half of the country's corporate wealth. The greatest abuses took place in public utilities where promoters like Samuel Insull built vast paper empires by gaining control of power companies and then draining them of their assets.

The most distinctive feature of the new consumer-oriented economy was the stress on advertising. Skillful practitioners like Edward Bernays and Bruce Barton sought to control public taste and consumer spending by identifying the good life with the possession of the latest product of American industry, whether a car, a refrigerator, or a cigarette.

Uniformity and standardization, the characteristics of mass production, now prevailed. Chain stores proliferated at the expense of "mom-and-pop" small retail establishments. Kansas farmers bought the same items as Pennsylvania factory workers. Sectional differences in dress, food, and furniture began to disappear. Radio and films even threatened regional accents by promoting a standard national dialect devoid of any local flavor.

ECONOMIC WEAKNESSES

The New Era, as businessmen labeled the decade, was not as prosperous as it first appeared. The revolution in consumer goods disguised the decline of many traditional industries in the 1920s. Railroads suffered from poor man-agement and from the competition of the growing trucking industry. Coal was being replaced by petroleum and natural gas. Cotton textiles declined with the development of rayon and other synthetic fibers.

Hardest hit of all was agriculture. American farmers had expanded production to meet the demands of World War I. After the war, farm prices and exports fell sharply. Throughout the 1920s, the farmers' share of the national income dropped until by 1929 the per-capita annual farm income was only $273, compared to the national average of $681.

Workers, although better off than farmers, did not share fully in the decade's affluence. The industrial labor force remained remarkably steady for a period of economic growth; the technical innovations meant that the same number of workers could produce far more than before. Most of the new jobs came in the lower-paying service industry. Although wages rose slowly, conditions of life for the worker did improve. Prices remained stable, so that workers enjoyed a gain in real wages.

Organized labor proved unable to advance the interests of workers in the 1920s. Many businessmen used the injunction and "yellow-dog" contracts, which forbade employees from joining unions, to establish open shops and deny workers the benefits of collective bargaining. Other employers wooed their workers away from unions using techniques of welfare capitalism, spending money to improve plant conditions and winning employee loyalty with pensions, paid vacations, and company cafeterias. The net result was a decline in union membership from a postwar high of 5 million to less than 3 million by 1929.

Black workers remained on the bottom, both economically and socially. Many of the blacks who migrated northward during World War I found jobs only in menial service areas, collecting garbage, washing dishes, and sweeping floors. Yet even these jobs offered them a better life than they found on the depressed southern farms, and so the migration continued. The black population in Chicago, New York, and other northern cities more than doubled in the decade of the 1920s.

Middle- and upper-class Americans were the groups who thrived in the 1920s. The rewards of a second Industrial Revolution went to the managers—the engineers, bankers, and executives who directed the new industrial economy. These were the people who bought the fine new homes in the suburbs and who could afford more than one car. Their conspicuous consumption helped fuel the prosperity of the 1920s, but their disposable income eventually became greater than their material wants. The result was speculation, as those with idle money began to invest heavily in the stock market to reap gains from the industrial growth.

The economic trends of the decade had both positive and negative implications for the future. On the one hand, there was the solid growth of new consumer-based industries. Automobiles and appliances were not passing fancies but part of the modern American way of life. The future pattern of American culture—cars and suburbs, shopping centers and skyscrapers—was determined by the end of the 1920s.

But at the same time there were ominous signs of danger. The unequal distribution of wealth, the saturation of the market for consumer goods, and the growing speculation all created economic instability. The boom of the twenties would end in a great crash; yet the achievements of the decade would survive even that dire experience.

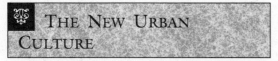

THE NEW URBAN CULTURE

The city replaced the countryside as the focal point of American life in the 1920s. The 1920 census revealed that for the first time slightly more than half the population lived in cities, defined broadly to include all places of more than 2500 people. Between 1920 and 1930 cities with populations of 250,000 or more had added some 8 million people to their ranks.

The skyscraper soon became the most visible feature of the city. Faced with inflated land prices, builders turned upward—developing a distinctively American architectural style in the process. By 1929, there were 377 buildings over 70 stories tall across the nation. Most significantly, the skyscraper came to symbolize the new mass culture.

In the metropolis, life was different. The old community ties of home, church, and school were loosening, but there were important gains—new ideas, new creativity, new perspectives. Some city dwellers became lost and lonely without the old institutions; others thrived in the urban environment.

WOMEN AND THE FAMILY

The urban culture of the 1920s witnessed important changes in the American family, which began to break down under the impact of economic and social change. A new freedom for women and children seemed to be emerging in its wake.

Women had already begun to leave the home in the early twentieth century as the second Industrial Revolution opened up new jobs for them. World War I speeded up the process, but in the 1920s there was no great permanent gain in the number of working women. Most women workers, however, had lower-paying jobs, ranging from stenographers and retail store clerks to maids. For the most part, the professions were reserved for men, with women relegated to such stereotypical fields as teaching and nursing.

To be sure, women had won the right to vote in 1920, but the Nineteenth Amendment proved to have less impact than its proponents had hoped. Once achieved, it robbed women of a unifying cause, and the suffrage itself did little to change the prevailing sex roles in society. Men remained the principal breadwinners in the family; women cooked, cleaned, and reared the children.

The feminist movement, however, still showed signs of vitality in the 1920s. In 1923 the National Woman's Party succeeded in having an Equal Rights Amendment introduced in Congress. Other women's organizations opposed the amendment on the ground that

September 11, 1920

Price—15 Cents
Subscription Price $7.00 a year

Leslie's

Illustrate *vaper*

VOTING
BOOTH NO 1

Women finally realized the hard-won right to vote. Leslie's Illustrated Newspaper cover of September 11, 1920, celebrates the fact.

women needed legal protection, especially laws guaranteeing them at least a minimum wage and limiting the maximum length of the workday. The drive for the ERA failed in the twenties, but social feminists were more successful in pushing for such humanitarian reforms as the Sheppard-Towner Act of 1921, which provided federal aid to establish state programs for maternal and infant health care.

A generational change had a profound impact on feminism in the 1920s. Instead of crusading for social progress, young women concentrated on individual self-expression by rebelling against Victorian restraints. In the cities, some quickly adopted what critic H. L. Mencken called the flapper image. Cutting their hair short, raising their skirts above the knee, and binding their breasts, "flappers" set out to compete on equal terms with men on the golf course and in the speakeasy. Shocking to their elders, the flappers assaulted the traditional

double standard in sex, demanding that equality with men should include sexual fulfillment before and during marriage. The new permissiveness led to a sharp rise in the divorce rate.

The sense of women's emancipation was heightened by a drop in the birthrate and the abundance of consumer goods. Yet appearances were deceptive. Many women could not enjoy the new labor-saving devices. The typical childless woman spent between forty-three and fifty hours a week on household duties; for mothers, the average work week was fifty-six hours, far longer than that of their husbands. And despite the talk of the "new woman," traditional sex roles remained unshaken. As one historian has concluded, "In the 1920s, as in the 1790s, marriage was the only approved state for women."

The family, however, did change. It became smaller as new techniques of birth control enabled couples to limit their offspring. More and more married women took jobs outside the home. Young people, who had once joined the labor force when they entered their teens, now discovered adolescence as a stage of life.

This prolonged adolescence led to new strains on the family in the form of youthful revolt. Freed of the traditional burden of earning a living at an early age, youth in the 1920s went on a great spree. Heavy drinking, casual sex encounters, and a constant search for excitement became the hallmarks of the upper-class youth immortalized by F. Scott Fitzgerald. The theme of rebellion against parental authority, which runs through all aspects of the 1920s, was at the heart of the youth movement.

THE ROARING TWENTIES

Frivolity and excitement ran high in the cities as crime waves and highly publicized sports events flourished. Prohibition ushered in such distinctive features of the decade as speakeasies, bootleggers, and bathtub gin. Crime rose sharply as middle- and upper-class Americans willingly broke the law to gain access to alcoholic beverages. City streets became the scene of violent shootouts between rival bootleggers, and underworld czars like Al Capone controlled illicit empires.

Sports became a national mania in the 1920s as people found more leisure time. Golf boomed, with some 2 million men and women playing the sport. Spectator sports attracted even more attention. Millions of Americans found drama in the exploits of Jack Dempsey, Red Grange, and Babe Ruth. New massive stadiums had to be built to satisfy the growing numbers of sports fans.

In what Frederick Lewis Allen called "the ballyhoo years," the popular yearning for excitement led people to seek various thrills in all kinds of ways—applauding Charles Lindbergh's solo flight across the Atlantic and flocking to such bizarre events as six-day bicycle races, dance marathons, and flagpole-sittings. Hero worship of sport and entertainment stars became an escape from the drabness of life on the assembly line.

Sex became another focal point in the 1920s as Victorian standards began to crumble. Sophisticated city dwellers seemed to be intent on exploring a new freedom in sexual expression. Plays and novels focused on adultery, and the new urban tabloids delighted in telling their readers about love nests and kept women. Hollywood exploited the obsession with sex by producing movies with such provocative titles as *A Shocking Night* and *Women and Lovers.* Young people embraced the new permissiveness joyfully, with the automobile providing couples an easy way to escape parental supervision.

There is considerable debate, however, over the extent of the sexual revolution in the 1920s. Actual changes in sexual behavior are beyond the historian's reach, hidden in the privacy of the bedroom, but the old Victorian prudery was a clear casualty of the 1920s. At least in urban areas, sex was no longer a taboo subject; men and women now could and did discuss it openly.

THE LITERARY FLOWERING

The greatest cultural advance of the 1920s was the outpouring of literature. The city gave rise to a new class of intellectuals—writers who commented on the new industrial society. Many were bewildered by the rapidly changing social patterns of the 1920s and appalled by the materialism of American culture. Some fled to Europe to live as expatriates. Others stayed at home, observing and condemning the excesses of a business civilization. All shared a sense of disillusionment and wrote pessimistically of the flawed promise of American life. Yet, ironically, their body of writing revealed a profound creativity that suggested that America was coming of age intellectually.

The exiles included the poet T. S. Eliot and the novelist Ernest Hemingway. In *The Waste Land,* which appeared in 1922, Eliot evoked images of fragmentation and sterility that had a powerful impact on the other disillusioned writers of the decade. He reached the depths of despair in *The Hollow Men* (1925), a biting description of the emptiness of modern man.

Ernest Hemingway sought redemption from the modern plight in the romantic individualism of his heroes. He wrote of men alienated from society who found a sense of identity in their own courage and quest for personal honor. His greatest impact on other writers came from his sparse, direct, and clean prose style.

Writers who stayed home were equally critical of contemporary American life. F. Scott Fitzgerald chronicled American high society in *The Great Gatsby* (1925), emphasizing the emptiness and lack of human concern. Sinclair Lewis became the most popular of the critical novelists. *Main Street* (1920) satirized the values of small-town America as dull, complacent, and narrow-minded, while *Babbitt* (1922) poked fun at the commercialism of the 1920s.

Most savage of all was H. L. Mencken, the Baltimore newspaperman and literary critic who founded the *American Mercury* in 1923. He mocked everything he found distasteful in America, from the Rotary Club to the Ku Klux Klan. A born cynic, he served as a zealous guardian of public integrity in an era of excessive boosterism.

The cultural explosion of the 1920s was surprisingly broad. It included novelists like Sherwood Anderson and John Dos Passos—who described the way the new machine age undermined such traditional American values as craftsmanship and a sense of community—and playwrights such as Eugene O'Neill and

Maxwell Anderson. Women writers were particularly effective in dealing with regional themes. Edith Wharton continued to write penetratingly about eastern aristocrats, while Willa Cather and Ellen Glasgow focused on the plight of women in the Midwest and the South, respectively. The greatest contribution to American music, imbuing it with a new vitality, came from the spread of jazz as blacks migrated northward. The form of jazz known as the blues became an authentic national folk music.

The cultural growth of the 1920s was the work of blacks as well as whites. W.E.B. Du Bois became the intellectual voice of the black community developing in New York City's Harlem. Along with James Weldon Johnson, a gifted black poet, Du Bois became the leader of the Harlem Renaissance. The NAACP moved its headquarters to Harlem, and in 1923 the Urban League began publishing *Opportunity*, a magazine devoted to scholarly studies of racial issues.

A black literary flowering quickly developed. In stark images, Claude McKay in *White Shadows* (1922) expressed both his resentment against racial injustice and his pride in blackness. Countee Cullen and Langston Hughes won critical acclaim for the beauty of their poems and the eloquence of their portrayal of the black tragedy.

During Harlem's golden age "almost everything seemed possible," wrote historian David Lewis. "You could be black and proud, politically assertive and economically independent, creative and disciplined—or so it seemed." Moreover, in a short time the mood of the Harlem Renaissance spread to black communities in other cities.

In retrospect, there is a striking paradox about the literary flowering of the twenties. Nearly all the writers, black as well as white, cried out against the conformity and materialism of the contemporary scene. Although highly critical, few took any interest in politics or in social reform. They retreated instead into individualism, seeking an escape from the prevailing business civilization in their art.

Whether they went abroad or stayed home, the writers of the 1920s turned inward to avoid being swept up in the consumer-goods revolution. Yet despite their withdrawal, and indeed perhaps because of it, they produced an astonishingly rich and varied body of work. American writing had a greater intensity and depth than in the past; American writers, for the first time, were taken seriously by Europeans.

THE RURAL COUNTERATTACK

Dominance by the urban centers led to a response that produced an ugly side of the twenties—a side where prejudice and bigotry, hate and intolerance flourished. For millions of Americans who lived in small towns and on farms, the city came to represent all that was evil in contemporary life. Largely Anglo-Saxon and steeped in traditional Protestantism, these rural folk condemned the urban-centered crime, radicalism, and modernism which they felt were threatening their own way of life. Saloons, whorehouses, little Italys and little Polands, Communist cells, free love, and atheism—all were identified with the city. As the urban areas grew in population and influence, the countryside struck back in a deliberate if doomed attempt to restore a lost purity to American life.

Other factors contributed to the intensity of rural counterattack. The war had unleashed a nationalistic spirit that craved unity and conformity. When the war was over, groups like the American Legion tried to root out "un-American" behavior and insisted on cultural as well as political conformity. And the prewar progressive reform spirit added to the social tension. Stripped of much of its former idealism, progressivism focused on social problems such as drinking and illiteracy to justify repressive measures like Prohibition and immigration restriction. The result was tragic, for often it pitted rural America against urban America in ugly conflicts.

The "Red Scare"

The first and most intense outbreak of national alarm came in 1919. The heightened nationalism of World War I found a new target in bolshevism. The Russian Revolution and the growth of communism in America frightened many Americans. Although the number of American Communists was never great, they were located in the cities, and their influence appeared to be magnified with the outbreak of widespread labor unrest.

A general strike in Seattle, a police strike in Boston, and a violent strike in the iron and steel industry thoroughly alarmed the American people in the spring and summer of 1919. A series of bombings and attempted bombings led to panic. On June 2, a bomb shattered the front of Attorney General A. Mitchell Palmer's home. Although the man who delivered it was blown to pieces, authorities quickly identified him as an Italian anarchist from Philadelphia.

Attorney General A. Mitchell Palmer ordered raids in 1919 on "dangerous aliens" and "foreign subversives," with flagrant disregard for due process of law and basic civil liberties.

In the public outcry that followed, Attorney General Palmer led the attack on the alien threat. In a series of raids that began on November 7, federal agents seized suspected anarchists and Communists and held them for deportation with no regard for due process of law. In December, 249 aliens were shipped to Russia. Nearly all were innocent of the charges against them. A month later, Palmer rounded up nearly 4000 suspected Communists in a single evening. Aliens rounded up were deported without hearings or trials.

For a time, it seemed that this Red Scare reflected the prevailing views of the American people. Instead of condemning their government's actions, citizens voiced their approval and even urged more drastic steps. In one particularly revolting episode, a group of war veterans in Centralia, Washington, dragged a radical from the town jail, castrated him, and hanged him from a railway bridge. The coroner's report stated that the victim "jumped off with a rope around his neck and then shot himself full of holes."

The very extremism of the Red Scare led to its rapid demise. Courageous government officials and prominent citizens spoke out against the government's violations of constitutional guarantees and the acts of terror. Finally, Palmer himself, with evident presidential ambition, went too far. In April 1920, he warned of a vast revolution to occur on May 1. When no bombings or violence took place on May Day, the public began to react against Palmer's hysteria, trying hard to forget their momentary loss of balance.

Yet the Red Scare exerted a continuing influence on American society in the 1920s. The foreign-born lived with the uneasy realization that they were viewed with hostility and suspicion. Two Italian aliens in Massachusetts, Nicola Sacco and Bartolomeo Vanzetti, were arrested in May 1920 for a payroll robbery and murder. They faced a prosecutor and jury who condemned them more for their ideas than for any evidence of criminal conduct and a judge who referred to them as "those anarchist bastards." Despite a worldwide effort that became the chief liberal cause of the 1920s, the two died in the electric chair on August 23, 1927. Their fate symbolized the bigotry and intolerance that lasted through the 1920s and made this decade one of the least attractive in American history.

PROHIBITION

In December 1917, Congress adopted the Eighteenth Amendment, prohibiting the manufacture and sale of alcoholic beverages. A little over a year later, Nebraska became the necessary thirty-sixth state to ratify, and Prohibition became the law of the land.

As implemented under the Volstead Act, beginning January 16, 1920, it was illegal for anyone to make, sell, or transport any drink that contained more than half of 1 percent alcohol by volume. Prohibition was the result of both a rural effort of the Anti-Saloon League and the urban progressive concern over the social disease of drunkenness. Although a number of states had already enacted Prohibition laws by 1920, the real tragedy resulted from the effort to extend this "noble experiment" to the growing cities, where it was deeply resented by many ethnic groups and nearly totally disregarded by the well-to-do and the sophisticated.

Prohibition did in fact lead to a decline in drinking. The consumption of alcohol dropped sharply in rural areas and among the lower classes, who could not afford the high prices of bootleg liquor. Among the middle class and the wealthy, however, drinking became fashionable. Bootleggers supplied whiskey, which quickly replaced lighter spirits like wine and beer. Despite the risk of illness or death from drinking the unregulated alcohol, Americans consumed some 150 million quarts of liquor a year in the twenties as bootleggers took in nearly $2 billion annually, about 2 percent of the gross national product.

Urban resistance to Prohibition finally led to its repeal in 1933. But in the intervening years, it damaged American society by breeding a profound disrespect for the law. In city after city, police openly tolerated the traffic in liquor, and judges and prosecutors agreed to let bootleggers pay merely token fines. The countryside felt vindicated, yet rural and urban America alike suffered from this overzealous attempt to legislate morals.

THE KU KLUX KLAN

The most ominous expression of rural protest against the city was the rebirth of the Ku Klux Klan. On Thanksgiving night in 1915, on Stone Mountain in Georgia, Colonel William J. Simmons and thirty-four followers founded the modern Klan. Only "native-born, white, gentile Americans" were permitted to join. Membership grew slowly during World War I, but after 1920 the Klan mushroomed. In villages, towns, and small cities across the South and West, the Klan attracted men seeking to relieve their anxiety over a changing society.

The Klan of the 1920s was not just antiblack; the tensions and conflicts in American society, as Klansmen perceived it, came from aliens—Italians and Russians, Jews and Catholics. The Klan punished blacks who did not know their place, women who practiced the new morality, and aliens who refused to conform. Beatings, floggings, burning with acid—even murder—were condoned. But they also tried more peaceful methods of coercion, formulating codes of behavior and seeking community-wide support. In addition, the Klan entered politics, showing remarkable strength in Texas, Oklahoma, Oregon, and Indiana.

Its appeal lay in the sanctuary it offered to insecure and anxious people. It gave its members reassurance and an exotic world of titles and practices. Members found a sense of identity in the group activities, whether they were peaceful picnics, ominous parades in white robes, or fiery crosses blazing in the night. By the mid-1920s, the Klan boasted a membership of nearly 5 million, and it had separate orders for women, boys, and girls.

The Klan fell even more quickly than it rose. Its more violent activities began to offend the nation's conscience. Misuse of funds and sexual scandals among Klan leaders, notably in Indiana, repelled many of the rank and file. Membership declined sharply after 1925; by the end of the decade, the Klan had virtually disappeared. But the spirit lived on, testimony to the recurring demons of nativism and racist hatred that have surfaced periodically throughout the American experience.

IMMIGRATION RESTRICTION

The nativism that permeated the Klan found its most successful outlet in the immigration legislation of the 1920s. The sharp increase in immigration in the late nineteenth century had led to a broad-based movement to restrict the flow of people from Europe. In 1917, over Wilson's veto, Congress enacted a literacy test that reduced the number of immigrants, and the war caused an even more drastic decline.

After armistice, however, rumors began to spread of an impending flood of people seeking to escape war-ravaged Europe. Worried congressmen spoke of a "barbarian horde" that would inundate the United States with "dangerous and deadly enemies of the country." Even though the actual number of immigrants fell below the prewar yearly average, Congress responded in 1921 by passing an emergency immigration act.

The 1921 act failed to satisfy the nativists. It still permitted more than 500,000 Europeans to come to the United States in 1923, nearly half of them from southern and eastern Europe. The declining percentage of Nordic immigrants alarmed writers like Madison Grant, who warned the American people that the Anglo-Saxon stock that had founded the nation was about to be overwhelmed by lesser breeds with inferior genes. Psychologists, relying on primitive IQ tests used by the army in World War I, confirmed this judgment.

Responding to such theories, in 1924 Congress adopted the National Origins Quota Act, which limited immigration from Europe to 150,000 a year; allocated most of the places to immigrants from Great Britain, Ireland, Germany, and Scandinavia; and banned all Asian

immigrants. The measure passed Congress with overwhelming rural support.

The new restrictive legislation marked the most enduring achievement of the rural counterattack. Unlike the Red Scare, Prohibition, and the Klan, the quota system would survive until the 1960s. Yet even here the rural victory was not complete. A growing tide of Mexican laborers, exempt from the quota act, flowed northward across the Rio Grande to fill the continuing need for unskilled workers on the farms and in the service trades. The Mexican immigration marked the strengthening of an element in our national ethnic mosaic that would grow in size and influence until it became a major force in modern American society.

THE FUNDAMENTALIST CONTROVERSY

The most famous of all the rural attacks on the new urban culture was the Scopes trial held in Dayton, Tennessee. There, in 1925, William Jennings Bryan engaged in a crusade against the theory of evolution, appearing as a chief witness against John Scopes, a high school biology teacher who had deliberately violated a new Tennessee law that forbade the teaching of Darwin's theory.

In the trial, Bryan testified under oath that he believed Jonah had been swallowed by a big fish and declared, "It is better to trust in the Rock of Ages than in the age of rocks." Chicago defense attorney Clarence Darrow succeeded in making Bryan look ridiculous. The court found Scopes guilty but let him off with a token fine; Bryan, exhausted by his efforts, died a few days later. H. L. Mencken, who covered the trial in person, rejoiced in the belief that fundamentalism was dead.

In reality, however, the traditional rural religious beliefs were stronger than ever. As middle- and upper-class Americans drifted into genteel Christianity that stressed good works and respectability, the fervid evangelical denominations continued to hold on to the old faith, and more aggressive fundamentalist

GATHERING DATA FOR THE TENNESSEE TRIAL

Religious fundamentalism, which enjoyed a resurgence after World War I, clashed with current scientific theory in the Scopes trial.

sects, such as the Jehovah's Witnesses, grew rapidly.

Many of those who came to the city in the twenties brought their religious beliefs with them and found new outlets for their traditional ideas. Thus evangelist Aimee Semple McPherson enjoyed amazing success in Los Angeles with her "Four-Square Gospel." Far from dying out, biblical fundamentalism remained remarkably strong in the cities as well as the country. The rural counterattack, while challenged by the city, did enable some older American values to survive in the midst of the new mass-production culture.

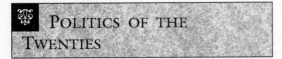

POLITICS OF THE TWENTIES

The tensions between the city and the countryside also shaped the course of politics in the 1920s. On the surface, it was a Republican de-

cade. The GOP controlled the White House from 1921 to 1933 and had majorities in both houses of Congress from 1918 to 1930. The Republicans halted further reform legislation and established a friendly relationship between government and business. Important shifts were taking place, however, in the American electorate. The Democrats, although divided into competing urban and rural wings, were laying the groundwork for the future by winning over millions of new voters, especially among the ethnic groups in the cities. The rising tide of urban voters indicated a fundamental shift away from the Republicans toward a new Democratic majority.

HARDING, COOLIDGE, AND HOOVER

The Republicans regained the White House in 1920 with the election of Warren G. Harding of Ohio. Handsome and dignified, Harding reflected both the virtues and blemishes of small-town America. Limited in outlook, Harding was a genial man who lacked the capacity to govern and who delegated power broadly as president.

He made some good cabinet choices, notably Charles Evans Hughes as secretary of state and Herbert C. Hoover as secretary of commerce, but two corrupt officials—Attorney General Harry Daugherty and Secretary of the Interior Albert Fall—sabotaged his administration. Daugherty became involved in a series of questionable deals that led ultimately to his forced resignation; Fall was the chief figure in the Teapot Dome scandal. Two oil promoters gave Fall nearly $400,000 in loans and bribes; in return, he helped them secure leases on naval oil reserves in Elk Hills, California, and Teapot Dome, Wyoming. The scandal came to light after Harding's death from a heart attack in 1923. Fall eventually served a year in jail, and the reputation of the Harding administration never recovered.

Vice-President Calvin Coolidge assumed the presidency upon Harding's death, and his honesty and integrity quickly reassured the nation. A reserved, reticent man of Yankee stock,

Coolidge became famous for his epigrams, which contemporaries mistook for wisdom. "The business of America is business," he proclaimed. Consistent with his philosophy, he believed his duty was simply to preside benignly, not govern the nation. Satisfied with the prosperity of the mid-twenties, the people responded favorably. Coolidge was elected to a full term by a wide margin in 1924.

When Coolidge announced in 1927 that he did not "choose to run" for reelection, Herbert Hoover became the Republican choice to succeed him. By far the ablest GOP leader of the decade, Hoover epitomized the American myth of the self-made man. Orphaned as a boy, he had worked his way through Stanford University and had gained both wealth and fame as a mining engineer. Sober, intelligent, and immensely hard-working, Hoover embodied the nation's faith in individualism and free enterprise.

He used his office to assist American manufacturers and exporters in expanding their overseas trade, and he strongly supported a trade association movement to encourage cooperation rather than cutthroat competition among smaller American companies. He saw business and government as partners, working together to achieve efficiency and affluence for all Americans.

REPUBLICAN POLICIES

During the 1920 campaign, Warren Harding had urged a return to "normalcy," a coined word that became the theme for the Republican administrations of the 1920s. Aware that the public was tired of zealous reform-minded presidents, Harding and his successors sought a return to traditional Republican policies. In some areas they were successful, but in others they were forced to adjust to the new realities of a mass-production society.

The most obvious attempt to go back to the Republicanism of William McKinley came in tariff and tax policy. Fearful of a flood of postwar European imports, Congress passed an emergency tariff act in 1921 and followed it a year later with the protectionist Fordney-McCumber Tariff Act.

Secretary of the Treasury Andrew Mellon, a wealthy Pittsburgh banker and industrialist, worked hard to achieve a similar return to "normalcy" in taxation. He pressed for repealing excess-profits tax on corporations and slashing personal rates on the very rich. He also reduced government spending from its World War I peak of $18 billion to just over $3 billion by 1925, thereby creating a slight surplus. Congress cooperated by cutting the highest income-tax bracket to a modest 20 percent.

The growing crisis in American farming during the decade forced the Republican administrations to seek new solutions. The end of the war led to a sharp decline in farm prices and a return to the problem of overproduction.

In this cartoon, Attorney General Daugherty struggles to keep the skeletons of corruption—the scandals of the Harding administration—hidden in the closet.

Southern and western lawmakers formed a farm bloc in Congress to press for special legislation for American agriculture. Although the farm bloc helped pass several laws, they failed to get at the root problem of overproduction. Farmers then supported more controversial measures designed to raise domestic crop prices by having the government sell the surplus overseas at low world prices. Coolidge vetoed the legislation on grounds that it involved unwarranted government interference in the economy.

Yet the government's role in the economy increased rather than lessened in the 1920s. Republicans widened the scope of federal activity and nearly doubled the ranks of government employees. Herbert Hoover led the way in the Commerce Department, establishing new bureaus to help make American industry more efficient in housing, transportation, and mining. Instead of going back to the laissez-faire tradition of the nineteenth century, the Republican administrations of the twenties were pioneering a close relationship between government and private business.

THE DIVIDED DEMOCRATS

While the Republicans ruled in the 1920s, the Democrats seemed bent on self-destruction. The pace of the second Industrial Revolution and the growing urbanization of the twenties split the party in two. One faction centered in the rural South and West. Traditional Democrats who had supported Wilson stood for Prohibition, fundamentalism, the Klan, and other facets of the rural counterattack against the city. In contrast, a new breed of Democrat was emerging in the metropolitan areas of the North and Midwest. Immigrants and their descendants began to participate actively in the Democratic party. Catholic and Jewish in religion and strongly opposed to Prohibition, they had little in common with their rural counterparts.

The split within the party surfaced dramatically at the national convention in New York in 1924. Held in Madison Square Garden, the convention soon degenerated into what one ob-

server described as a "snarling, cursing, tenuous, suicidal, homicidal roughhouse." Urban and rural factions of the party opposed each other at every turn. The delegates divided between Alfred E. Smith, the governor of New York, and William G. McAdoo of California, Wilson's secretary of the treasury. When it became clear that neither the city nor the rural candidate could win a majority, both men withdrew; on the 103rd ballot, the weary Democrats finally chose John W. Davis as their compromise nominee. Senator Bob La Follette of Wisconsin ran on an independent Progressive party ticket. His campaign was ineffective, as was Davis'. Both were easily defeated by Coolidge.

Yet the Democrats were in far better shape than this setback indicated. Beginning in 1922, the party had made heavy inroads into the GOP majority in Congress. Even in 1924, the Republican vote in the nation's largest cities declined. By 1926, the Democrats were within one vote of controlling the Senate and had picked up more seats in the House. The largest cities were swinging clearly into the Democratic column; all the party needed was a charismatic leader who could fuse the older rural elements with the new urban voters.

THE ELECTION OF 1928

The selection of Al Smith as the Democratic candidate in 1928 indicated the growing power of the city. Born on the lower east side of Manhattan of mixed Irish-German ancestry, Smith was the prototype of the urban Democrat. He was Catholic; he was associated with a big-city machine; he was a "wet" who wanted to end Prohibition. Rejected by rural Democrats in 1924, he still had to prove that he could unite the South and West behind his leadership. His lack of education, poor grammar, and distinctive New York accent hurt him, as did his eastern provincialism.

The choice facing the American voter in 1928 seemed unusually clear-cut. Herbert Hoover was a Protestant, a "dry," and an old-stock American who stood for efficiency and individualism. Just as Smith appealed to new voters in the cities, so Hoover won the support of many old-line Democrats who feared the city and the pope.

Yet beneath the surface, as historian Allan J. Lichtman points out, there were "striking similarities between Smith and Hoover." Both were self-made men who embodied the American belief in freedom of opportunity and upward mobility. Neither advocated any significant degree of economic change nor any redistribution of national wealth or power. Though Smith's religion hurt him the most, his failure to spotlight the growing cracks in prosperity and offer alternative economic policies ensured his defeat.

The 1928 election was a dubious victory for the Republicans. Hoover won easily, but Smith succeeded for the first time in winning a majority of votes for the Democrats in the nation's twelve largest cities. A new Democratic electorate was emerging, consisting of Catholics and Jews, Irish and Italians, Poles and Greeks. Now the task was to unite the traditional Democrats of the South and West with the urban, ethnic populations of the Northeast and Midwest.

The 1920s marked a major transition in American politics as well as in social and economic development. An old America founded on rural values had given way to a new urban society in which the production and use of consumer goods led to a very different way of life. Just as the nineteenth-century culture had revolved around the farm and the railroad, so the automobile and the city became the central features of modern America. Yet despite the very real economic progress achieved in the 1920s, the decade ended in a severe depression that lasted all through the 1930s. Only after World War II would the American people enjoy an abundance and prosperity rooted in the industrial transformation that began in the 1920s.

❧ RECOMMENDED READING

William Leuchtenberg provides the best overview of the 1920s in *The Perils of Prosperity, 1914–1932* (1958). The essays in John Braeman, Robert H. Bremner, and David Brody, eds., *Change and Continuity*

CHRONOLOGY

1919   U.S. agents arrest 1700 in Red Scare raids
Congress passes Volstead Act over Wilson's veto (October)

1920   Republican Warren G. Harding elected
Nineteenth Amendment passed, granting women the right to vote

1921   Congress enacts quotas for European immigrants

1923   Harding dies; Vice-President Calvin Coolidge assumes presidency
Newspapers expose KKK graft, torture, murder

1924   Coolidge elected to full term
Senate probes Teapot Dome scandal

1925   John Scopes convicted of teaching theory of evolution in violation of Tennessee law (July)

1927   Charles Lindberg completes first nonstop transatlantic flight from New York to Paris (May)
Coolidge vetoes farm price-control bill
Sacco and Vanzetti executed (August)
The movie *The Jazz Singer* features singing-talking soundtrack

1928   Republican Herbert Hoover defeats Democrat Al Smith for presidency

in *Twentieth Century America: The 1920s* (1968), illuminate important aspects of the period.

A fully detailed account of economic developments in the decade is George Soule, *Prosperity Decade* (1947). Other books on economic themes are John B. Rae, *The American Automobile* (1965); James J. Flink, *The Car Culture* (1975); James J. Flink, *The Automobile Age* [1988]; Roland Marchand, *Advertising the American Dream, 1920–1940* (1985); and James Prothro, *The Dollar Decade* (1954). The best book on labor is Irving Bernstein, *The Lean Years* (1960). James Shideler discusses the postwar agricultural depression in *Farm Crisis* (1957).

Social history is covered in Frederick Lewis Allen, *Only Yesterday* (1931); Helen Lynd and Robert Lynd, *Middletown* (1929); Paul Carter, *Another Part of the Twenties* (1976); and Paula S. Fass, *The Damned and the Beautiful* (1977).

The role of women in the 1920s is examined in William Chafe, *The American Woman* (1972); Susan D. Becker, *The Origins of the Equal Rights Amendment* (1981); Winifred D. Wandersee, *Women's Work and Family Values, 1920–1940* (1981); and Dorothy M. Brown, *Setting a Course: American Women in the 1920s* (1987). For blacks in the 1920s, see Nathan Huggins, *Harlem Renaissance* (1971); Gilbert Osofsky, *Harlem* (1966); and David Levering Lewis, *When Harlem Was in Vogue* (1981), a lively account of black culture.

Frederick Hoffman, *The Twenties* (1955), and Alfred Kazin, *On Native Ground* (1942), survey the literary trends during the decade. Other studies of this subject are Roderick Nash, *The Nervous Generation* (1969); Malcolm Cowley, *Exile's Return* (1934); and Edmund Wilson, *Shores of Light* (1952).

Studies of political fundamentalism include Robert K. Murray, *Red Scare* (1955); Andrew Sinclair, *Prohibition* (1962); David Chalmers, *Hooded Americans* (1965); and Lawrence Levine, *Defender of the Faith* (1965).

For political developments during the 1920s, see David Burner, *The Politics of Provincialism* (1968); Robert Murray, *The Harding Era* (1969); Burl Noggle, *Teapot Dome* (1962); and Joan H. Wilson, *Herbert Hoover* (1975).

26 FRANKLIN D. ROOSEVELT AND THE NEW DEAL

THE GREAT DEPRESSION

FIGHTING THE DEPRESSION

ROOSEVELT AND REFORM

IMPACT OF THE NEW DEAL

END OF THE NEW DEAL

The prosperity of the twenties came to an abrupt halt in October 1929. The stock market, which had boomed during the decade, suddenly faltered. Investors who had borrowed heavily to take part in the speculative mania that swept Wall Street suddenly were forced to sell their securities to cover their loans. The wave of selling triggered an avalanche. On October 24, later known as Black Thursday, nearly 13 million shares were traded. Bankers had only brief success in trying to stem the decline; panic overcame their feeble efforts on October 29, the worst day in stock-exchange history, when the industrial average fell by forty-three points. The panic ended in November, with stocks at 1927 levels. For the next four years, there was a steady drift downward, until by 1932 prices were 80 percent below their 1929 highs.

The Great Depression which followed the crash of 1929 was the most devastating economic blow that the nation ever suffered. It lasted for ten years, dominating every aspect of American life during the thirties. Unemployment rose to 12 million by 1932, and children grew up thinking that economic deprivation was the norm in America. Intractable and all-encompassing, the Depression loosened its grip on the nation only after the outbreak of World War II. And even then, it left enduring psychological scars on the millions of people who lived through it.

The Depression led to a profound shift in American political loyalties. The Republicans, dominant since the 1890s, gave way to a new Democratic majority. Millions of pre-World War I immigrants and their children became politically active. The result was the election of Franklin D. Roosevelt to the presidency and the development of the New Deal, a broad program of relief, recovery, and reform that increased the role of government in American life.

THE GREAT DEPRESSION

The economic collapse altered American attitudes. In the twenties, optimism had prevailed as people looked forward to an ever-increasing flow of consumer goods and a better way of life. But after 1929, bleak despair set in. Factories closed, machines fell silent, and millions upon millions of people walked the streets, looking for jobs that did not exist.

THE GREAT BULL MARKET

The consumer-goods revolution contained the seeds of its own collapse. The steady expansion of the automobile and appliance industries led gradually to a saturation of the market. At that point, production began to falter, and in 1927, the nation underwent a mild recession. The sale of durable goods declined, and construction of houses and buildings fell slightly. If corporate leaders had heeded these warning signs, they might have responded by raising wages or lowering prices, both effective ways to stimulate purchasing power and sustain the consumer-goods revolution. Or if government officials had recognized the danger signals and forced a halt in installment buying and slowed bank loans, the nation might have experienced a sharp but brief depression.

Neither government nor business leaders were so farsighted. The Federal Reserve Board lowered the discount rate, charging banks less for loans in an attempt to stimulate the economy. Much of this additional credit, however, went not into solid investment in factories and machinery but instead into the stock market, touching off a new wave of speculation that obscured the growing economic slow-down and ensured a far greater crash to come.

Individuals with excess cash began to invest heavily in the stock market, and the market moved upward. The strongest surge began in the spring of 1928, when investors ignored the declining production figures in the belief that they could make a living in the market. People took their savings and bet on speculative stocks. Corporations used their large cash reserves to supply money to brokers who in turn loaned it to investors on margin.

Investors could now play the market on credit, buying stock listed at $100 a share with $10 down and $90 on margin (the broker's loan for the balance). If the stock advanced to $150, the investor could sell and reap a gain of 500 percent on the $10 investment; in the bull (rising) market climate of the twenties, everyone was sure that the market would go up.

By 1929, it seemed that the whole nation was engaged in speculation. So great was the public's interest in the stock market that newspapers carried the stock averages on the front pages. Although more people were spectators than speculators, the bull market became a national obsession, assuring everyone that the economy was healthy and preventing any serious analysis of its underlying flaws.

The great crash in October 1929 put a sudden and tragic end to the speculative mania. The false confidence that had kept the economy from collapsing in 1927 evaporated overnight. Suddenly, corporations and financial institutions were no longer willing to provide capital for stock-market purchases. More important, investors and bankers cut off consumer credit as well, drying up buying power and leading to a sharp decline in the sales of consumer goods. Factories began to cut back production, laying off some workers and reducing hours for others. The layoffs and cutbacks lowered purchasing power even further, so fewer people bought cars and appliances. More factory layoffs resulted, and plants closed entirely, leading to even less money for the purchase of consumer goods.

This downward economic spiral continued for four years. By 1932, unemployment had swelled to 25 percent of the work force. Steel production was down to 12 percent of capacity, and the gross national product fell to 67 percent of the 1929 level. The bright promise of mass production had ended in a nightmare.

The basic explanation for the Great Depression lies in the fact that U.S. factories produced more goods than the American people could consume. There were other contributing causes—unstable economic conditions in Europe, the agricultural decline since 1919, corporate mismanagement, and excessive speculation—but at bottom people simply did not have enough money to buy the consumer products coming off the assembly lines.

The failure of the new economic system to distribute wealth more broadly was the chief difficulty. Too much money had gone into profits, dividends, and industrial expansion, and not enough into the hands of the workers, who were also consumers. Factory productivity had increased 43 percent during the decade, but the wages of industrial workers had gone up only 11 percent. If the billions that went into stock-market speculation had been used instead to increase wages—which would then have increased consumer purchasing power—production and consumption could have been brought into balance. Unfortunately for the prophets and pioneers of the New Era, it took the bitter experience of the Great Depression to give them an understanding of the full dynamics of the consumer-goods economy.

EFFECT OF THE DEPRESSION

It is difficult to measure the human cost of the Great Depression. The material hardships were bad enough. Families lived in lean-tos made of scrap wood and metal and went without meat and fresh vegetables for months, existing on a diet of soup and beans. The psychological burden was even greater: Americans suffered through years of grinding poverty with no letup in sight. The unemployed stood in line for hours waiting for a relief check; veterans sold apples or pencils on street corners, their manhood now in question. In the country, crops rotted in the fields because prices were too low to make harvesting worthwhile.

Few escaped the suffering. Blacks were often the first to lose their jobs. Mexican-Americans were deported in droves, now that citizens were willing to do stoop labor in the fields and

work as track layers on the railroads. The poor—black, brown, and white—survived because they knew better than most Americans how to exist in poverty. They stayed in bed in cold weather, both to keep warm and to avoid unnecessary burning up of calories. They patched their shoes with rubber from old tires, heated only their kitchens, and ate scraps of food others would reject.

The middle class, which had always lived with high expectations, was hit hard. Many professional and white-collar workers refused to ask for charity even while their families went without food. People who fell behind on their mortgage payments lost their homes, and health care declined as middle-class families stopped going regularly to doctors and dentists, unable to make the required cash payments in advance.

Even the well-to-do were affected, weighed down with guilt as they watched former friends and business associates join the ranks of the

Unemployment devastated thousands, some of whom walked the streets advertising their labor.

impoverished. "My father lost everything," became an all-too-familiar refrain among young people who dropped out of college.

Many Americans sought escape in movement. Men and boys, and some women, rode the rails in search of jobs, hopping freights to move south in the winter or west in the summer. Those who became tramps had to keep on the move to avoid arrest for vagrancy, but they did find a sense of community in the hobo jungles that sprang up along the major railroad routes. Here the homeless could find a place to eat and sleep and people with whom to share their misery.

FIGHTING THE DEPRESSION

The Great Depression presented an enormous challenge for American political leadership. The inability of the Republicans to overcome the economic catastrophe provided the Democrats with the chance to regain power. Although they failed to achieve full economic recovery before the outbreak of World War II, the Democrats did succeed in alleviating the suffering and establishing their political dominance.

HOOVER AND VOLUNTARISM

Herbert Hoover was the Depression's most prominent victim. Expressing complete faith in the American economic system, he relied primarily on voluntary cooperation with business to halt the slide. He called the leaders of industry to the White House and secured their agreement to maintain prices and wages at high levels. Yet within a few months, employers were reducing wages and cutting prices in a desperate effort to survive.

Hoover also believed in voluntary efforts to relieve the human suffering brought about by the Depression. He called on private charities and local governments to help feed and clothe those in need. But when these resources were exhausted, he rejected all requests for direct federal relief, asserting that such handouts would undermine the character of proud American citizens.

As the Depression deepened, Hoover reluctantly began to move beyond voluntarism to undertake more sweeping governmental measures. A new Federal Farm Board loaned money to aid cooperatives and bought up surplus crops in the open market in a vain effort to raise farm prices. At Hoover's request, Congress cut taxes and adopted a few federal public-works projects. To help imperiled banks and insurance companies, Hoover proposed and Congress established the Reconstruction Finance Corporation. The RFC loaned money to financial institutions to save them from bankruptcy. Hoover's critics, however, pointed out that while he favored aid to business, he still opposed measures such as direct relief and massive public works that would help the millions of unemployed.

By 1932, Hoover's efforts to overcome the Depression had clearly failed. His public image suffered its sharpest blow in the summer of 1932 when he ordered General Douglas MacArthur to clear out a group of ragged World War I veterans who had marched on Washington in a vain effort to get a bonus bill passed in Congress. Mounted troops drove the bonus marchers out of their shanties in Anacostia Flats along the Potomac, blinding the veterans with tear gas and burning their shacks.

Meanwhile, the nation's banking structure approached collapse. Bank customers responded to rumors of bankruptcy by rushing in to withdraw their deposits, thereby causing bank failures to rise steadily. Everywhere, Americans longed for a new president.

THE EMERGENCE OF ROOSEVELT

The man who stepped forward to meet this national need was Franklin D. Roosevelt, a distant cousin of the Republican Teddy. Born into a wealthy New York family, he enjoyed a privileged life of private tutors and trips to Europe. Well-educated and supremely secure, he had served in a number of elected and appointed offices. In 1921 he was crippled by polio. Refusing to give in, he fought back bravely, and though he never again walked unaided, he was elected governor of New York in 1928.

Roosevelt's dominant trait was his ability to persuade and convince other people. He possessed a marvelous voice, deep and rich, a winning smile, and a buoyant confidence that he could easily transmit to others. His bout with polio gave him both an understanding of human suffering and a broad political appeal as a man who had faced heavy odds and overcome them. A master politician with an agile mind, he had little patience with philosophical nuances. He dealt with the appearance of issues, not their deepest substance, and he displayed a flexibility toward political principles that often dismayed even his warmest admirers.

Roosevelt took advantage of the political opportunity offered by the Depression. With the Republicans discredited, he united the Democratic party. After winning the party's nomination in 1932, he broke with tradition by flying to Chicago and accepting in person, telling the cheering delegates, "I pledge myself to a new deal for the American people."

In the fall, he defeated Herbert Hoover in a near landslide for the Democrats. Roosevelt not only met the challenge of the Depression but also solidified the shift to the Democratic party that would dominate American politics for a half-century.

THE HUNDRED DAYS

When Franklin Roosevelt took the oath of office on March 4, 1933, the nation's economy was on the brink of collapse. Unemployment stood at nearly 13 million—one fourth the labor force—and banks were closed in thirty-eight states. Speaking from the steps of the capital, FDR declared boldly, "First of all, let me assert my firm belief that the only thing we have to fear is fear itself—nameless, unreasoning, unjustified terror." Then he announced that he would call Congress into special session and request "broad executive power to wage a war against the emergency, as great as

the power that would be given to me if we were in fact invaded by a foreign foe."

Within the next ten days, Roosevelt won his first great New Deal victory by saving the nation's banks. First he closed all the banks; then he presented new banking legislation to Congress, which it promptly passed. The measure provided for government supervision and aid to the banks. Strong ones would be reopened with federal support, weak ones closed, and those in difficulty bolstered by government loans.

On March 12, FDR addressed the nation by radio in the first of his fireside chats. In conversational tones, he told the public what he had done. He assured Americans that the government now stood behind the banks. The next day, March 13, the nation's largest and strongest banks opened their doors; at the end of the day, customers had deposited more cash than they withdrew. The banking crisis was over.

"Capitalism was saved in eight days," boasted one of Roosevelt's advisors. Most surprising was the conservative nature of FDR's action. Instead of nationalizing the banks, he had simply thrown the government's resources behind them and preserved private ownership. Though some other New Deal measures would be more radical, Roosevelt set the tone in the banking crisis. He was out to reform and restore the American economy system, not change it drastically.

For the next three months, Congress responded to a series of presidential initiatives. During the Hundred Days, Roosevelt sent fifteen major requests to Congress and received back fifteen pieces of legislation. One of these, the Tennessee Valley Authority (TVA), proved to be the most successful and enduring of all Roosevelt's New Deal measures. This innovative effort at regional planning resulted in the building of a series of dams in seven states along the Tennessee River to control floods, ease navigation, and produce electricity. This last feature created cheap and abundant power that helped transform the poverty-stricken upper South into a relatively prosperous industrial area.

Other New Deal agencies were temporary in nature, designed to meet the specific economic

Through his fireside chats, FDR became the first president to use radio broadcasts effectively to reach and reassure the American public.

problems of the Depression. None were completely successful; the Depression would continue for another six years. But psychologically the nation turned the corner in the spring of 1933. Under FDR, the government seemed to be responding to the economic crisis, enabling people for the first time since 1929 to look to the future with hope.

ROOSEVELT AND RECOVERY

Two major New Deal programs launched during the Hundred Days were aimed at industrial and agricultural recovery. The first was the National Recovery Administration (NRA), FDR's attempt to achieve economic advance through planning and cooperation between government, business, and labor. Businessmen were intent on stabilizing production and raising prices for their goods. Spokesmen for labor were equally determined to spread work through maximum hours and to put a floor under workers' income with minimum wages.

The NRA hoped to achieve both goals by permitting companies in each major industry to cooperate in writing codes of fair competition

that would set realistic limits on production, allocate percentages to individual producers, and set firm guidelines on prices. Section 7a of the enabling act mandated protection for labor in all the codes by establishing maximum hours, minimum wages, and the guarantee of collective bargaining by unions. No company could be compelled to join, but the New Deal sought complete participation by appealing to patriotism. Each firm that took part could display a blue eagle and stamp this symbol on its products. Led by Hugh Johnson, the NRA quickly enrolled the nation's leading companies and unions.

The NRA soon bogged down in a huge bureaucratic morass. The codes proved difficult to enforce and favored big business at the expense of smaller competitors. In addition, labor quickly became disenchanted with Section 7a. By 1934, more and more businessmen were complaining about the new agency. When the Supreme Court finally invalidated the NRA in 1935 on constitutional grounds, few mourned its demise. The idea of trying to overcome the Depression by relying on voluntary cooperation between competing businessmen and labor leaders had collapsed in the face of individual self-interest and greed.

The New Deal's attempt at farm recovery fared a little better. Henry A. Wallace, FDR's secretary of agriculture, came up with an answer to the farmer's old dilemma of overproduction. The government would act as a clearinghouse for producers of major crops, arranging for them to set production limits for wheat, cotton, corn, and other leading crops. Under the Agricultural Adjustment Administration (AAA), the government would allocate acreage among individual farmers, encouraging them to take land out of production by paying them subsidies.

After initial problems in 1933, the AAA program worked better in 1934 and 1935 as land removed from production led to smaller harvests and rising farm prices. Farm income rose for the first time since World War I. Most of the gain came from the subsidy payments themselves rather than from higher market prices.

On the whole, large farmers benefited most from the program. Possessing the capital to buy machinery and fertilizer, they were able to farm more efficiently than before on fewer acres of land. Small farmers, tenants, and sharecroppers did not fare as well, receiving very little of the government payments and often being driven off the land as owners took the acreage previously cultivated by tenants and sharecroppers out of production. In the long run, the New Deal reforms improved the efficiency of American agriculture, but at a real human cost.

The Supreme Court eventually found the AAA unconstitutional in 1936, but Congress reenacted it in modified form that year and again in 1938. The system of allotments became a standard feature of the farm economy. In another effort to assist the rural poor, the Farm Security Administration (FSA) loaned tenant farmers and sharecroppers money to buy their own land. But congressional appropriations were so modest that only about 2 percent got loans. The result of the New Deal for American farming was to hasten its transformation into a business in which only the efficient and well-capitalized would thrive.

The New Deal was far more successful in meeting the most immediate problem of the 1930s—relief for the millions of unemployed and destitute citizens. Roosevelt never shared Hoover's distaste for direct federal support; in May 1933, Congress authorized the Reconstruction Finance Corporation to distribute $500 million to the states to help individuals and families in need.

Roosevelt brought in former social worker Harry Hopkins to direct the relief program. By the end of 1933, Hopkins had cut through red tape to distribute money to nearly one sixth of the American people. The relief payments were modest in size, but they enabled millions to avoid starvation and stay out of humiliating breadlines.

Another, most imaginative, early effort was the Civilian Conservation Corps (CCC), which enrolled youth from city families on relief and sent them to parks and recreational areas to build trails and improve public facilities. The program contributed both to their families' incomes and to the nation's welfare.

Hopkins realized the need to do more than just keep people alive, and he soon became an advocate of work relief. Hopkins argued that the government should put the jobless to work, not just to encourage self-respect, but also to enable them to earn enough to purchase consumer goods and thus stimulate the entire economy. A Public Works Administration (PWA) headed by Secretary of the Interior Harold Ickes had been authorized in 1933, but Ickes failed to put many people to work.

The final commitment to the idea of work relief came in 1935 when Roosevelt established the Works Progress Administration (WPA) to spend nearly $5 billion authorized by Congress for emergency relief. The WPA put the unemployed on the federal payroll so that they could earn enough to meet their basic needs and help stimulate the stagnant economy. The WPA provided work for skilled and unskilled alike. It also tried to preserve the skills of American artists, actors, and writers by paying them to practice their craft.

The WPA, in addition to hiring workers for the usual construction and conservation projects, made use of the skills of artists, writers, and performers in the Federal Theatre Project.

The WPA helped ease the burden for the unemployed, but it failed to overcome the Depression. Rather than spending too much, as his critics charged, Roosevelt's greatest failure was not spending enough to prime the American economy by increasing consumer purchasing power. By responding to basic human needs, Roosevelt had made the Depression bearable but the New Deal's failure to go beyond relief to achieve prosperity led to a growing frustration and the appearance of more radical alternatives that challenged the conservative nature of the New Deal and forced FDR to shift to the left.

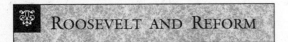

ROOSEVELT AND REFORM

In 1935 the focus of the New Deal shifted from relief and recovery to reform. During the first two years in office, FDR had concentrated on fighting the Depression by shoring up the sagging American economy. He was developing a "broker-state" concept of government, responding to pressures from organized elements such as corporations, labor unions, and farm groups while ignoring the needs and wants of the dispossessed who had no clear political voice.

The continuing depression and the high unemployment began to build pressures for more sweeping changes. Roosevelt faced the choice of either providing more radical programs—ones designed to end historical inequities in American life—or deferring to others who put forth solutions to the nation's ills. Bolstered by an impressive Democratic victory in the 1934 congressional elections, FDR responded by embracing a reform program that marked the climax of the New Deal.

ANGRY VOICES

The signs of discontent were visible everywhere by 1935. In the upper Midwest, progressives and agrarian radicals, led by Minnesota Governor Floyd Olsen, were demanding substantial changes to raise farmers', and workers', incomes. Textile plant strikes shut down mills in twenty states. The most serious challenge to Roosevelt's leadership, however, came from three demagogues who captured national attention in the midthirties.

The first was Father Charles Coughlin, a Roman Catholic priest from Detroit, who had originally supported FDR. Speaking to a rapt nationwide radio audience, Coughlin appealed to the discontented with a strange mixture of crank monetary schemes and anti-Semitism. He broke with the New Deal in late 1934, calling for monetary inflation and the nationalization of the banking system.

A more benign but equally threatening figure appeared in California. Dr. Francis Townsend, a sixty-seven-year-old physician, came forward in 1934 with a scheme to assist the elderly, who were suffering greatly during the Depression. The Townsend Plan proposed giving everyone over the age of sixty a monthly pension of $200 with the provision that it must be spent within thirty days. It would thus provide an old-age pension and stimulate the economy. Although impractical, more than 10 million people signed petitions endorsing the Townsend Plan.

A third new voice of protest was that of Huey Long, the flamboyant senator from Louisiana. An early New Deal supporter, Long turned against FDR and by 1935 had become a major political threat to the president. In 1934 he announced a nationwide "Share the Wealth" movement. He spoke grandly of taking from the rich to make "Every Man a King," guaranteeing each American a home worth $5000 and an annual income of $2500. To finance the plan, Long advocated seizing all fortunes of more than $5 million and levying a tax of 100 percent on income over $1 million. Millions of Americans responded favorably to Long's plan. Threatening to run as a third-party candidate in 1936, Long generated fear among Democratic leaders that he might attract 3 or 4 million votes, possibly enough to swing the election to the Republicans. Although he was assassinated in 1935, his popularity showed the need for the

New Deal to do more to help those still in distress.

SOCIAL SECURITY

When the new Congress met in January 1935, Roosevelt was ready to support a series of reform measures designed to take the edge off national dissent. Many of the Democrats in Congress were to the left of Roosevelt, favoring increased spending and more sweeping federal programs. Congress was prepared to enact virtually any proposal that Roosevelt offered.

The most significant reform enacted in 1935 was the Social Security Act. Unlike other modern industrial nations, the United States had never developed a welfare system to aid the aged, the disabled, and the unemployed. FDR's plan had three major parts. First, it provided for old-age pensions financed equally by a tax on employers and workers, with no government contributions. Second, it set up a system of unemployment compensation on a federal-state basis, with employers paying a payroll tax and with each state setting the benefit levels and administering the program locally. Finally, it provided for direct federal grants to the states, on a matching basis, for welfare payments to the blind, handicapped, needy elderly, and dependent children. Despite some criticism from the right and the left, Congress passed the Social Security Act by overwhelming margins.

Since its passage, critics have pointed out its shortcomings. The old-age pensions and handicapped and dependent children grants were paltry, and not everyone was covered. Those who most needed protection in their old age, such as farmers and domestic servants, were not included. The regressive feature of the act was even worse. All participants, regardless of income or economic status, paid in at the same rate, with no supplement from the general revenue. The trust fund also took out of circulation money that was desperately needed to stimulate the economy in the 1930s.

The conservative nature of the legislation reflected Roosevelt's own fiscal orthodoxy, but even more it was a product of his political realism. Despite the severity of the Depression, he realized that establishing a system of federal welfare went against deeply rooted American convictions. He insisted on a tax on participants to give those involved in the pension plan a vested interest in Social Security. He wanted them to feel that they had earned their pensions and that in the future no one would dare take them away. Above all, FDR had succeeded in establishing the principle of governmental responsibility for the aged, the handicapped, and the unemployed. Whatever the defects of the legislation, Social Security stood as a landmark of the New Deal, creating a system to provide for the welfare of individuals in a complex industrial society.

LABOR LEGISLATION

The other major reform achievement in 1935 was passage of the National Labor Relations Act. Senator Robert Wagner of New York introduced legislation in 1934 to outlaw company unions and other unfair labor practices in order to ensure collective bargaining for unions. Although initially opposed by Roosevelt, the bill gained support in Congress and was signed into law in July 1935.

The Wagner Act, as it became known, created a National Labor Relations Board to preside over labor-management relations and enable unions to engage in collective bargaining with federal support. The act outlawed a variety of union-busting tactics, and in its key provision decreed that whenever the majority of a company's workers voted for a union to represent them, management would be compelled to negotiate with the union on all matters of wages, hours, and working conditions. With this unprecedented government sanction, labor unions could now proceed to recruit the large number of unorganized workers throughout the country. The Wagner Act, the most far-reaching of all New Deal measures, led to the revitalization of the American labor movement and a permanent change in labor-management relations.

Three years later, Congress passed a second law that had a lasting impact on American workers—the Fair Labor Standards Act. A long-sought goal of the New Deal, this measure aimed to establish both minimum wages and maximum hours of work per week. The act was aimed at unorganized workers and met with only grudging support from unions. Southern conservatives opposed it strongly, both on ideological grounds and because it threatened the very low wages in the South that had attracted northern industry since Reconstruction.

Roosevelt finally succeeded in winning passage of the Fair Labor Standards Act in 1938, but only at the cost of exempting many key industries from its coverage. Despite its loopholes, the legislation did lead to pay raises for the 12 million workers earning less than the newly set minimum wage of forty cents an hour. More important, like Social Security it set up a system on which Congress could build in the future to reach more generous and humane levels.

All in all, Roosevelt's record in reform was similar to that in relief and recovery—modest success but no sweeping victory. A cautious and pragmatic leader, FDR moved far enough to the left to overcome the challenges of Coughlin, Townsend, and Long without venturing too far from the mainstream. His reforms improved the quality of life in America significantly, but he made no effort to correct all the nation's social and economic wrongs.

IMPACT OF THE NEW DEAL

The New Deal had a broad influence on the quality of life in the United States in the 1930s. Government programs reached into areas hitherto untouched. Many of them brought about long overdue improvements, but others failed to make any significant dent in historic inequities. The most important advances came with the dramatic growth of labor unions; conditions for working women and minorities showed no comparable advance.

RISE OF ORGANIZED LABOR

Trade unions were weak at the onset of the Depression, with a membership of fewer than 3

Union members in some companies resorted to sit-down strikes to achieve union recognition—as they did at General Motors in 1936.

million workers. Most were in the American Federation of Labor (AFL), composed of craft unions that served the needs of skilled workers. The nation's basic industries like steel and automobiles were unorganized; the great mass of unskilled workers thus fared poorly in terms of wages and working conditions.

John L. Lewis, head of the United Mine Workers, took the lead in organizing unskilled workers in mass-production industries by forming the Committee on Industrial Organization (CIO) in 1935. Dynamic and ruthless, Lewis first battled with the conservative leadership of the AFL, and then—after being expelled—he renamed his group the Congress of Industrial Organizations and announced in 1936 that he would use the Wagner Act to extend collective bargaining to the nation's auto and steel industries.

Within five years, Lewis had scored a remarkable series of victories. The big steel companies, led by U.S. Steel, surrendered without a fight in 1937, although the smaller firms en-

gaged in violent resistance, as did the automobile industry. When General Motors resisted, members of the newly created United Automobile Workers (UAW) simply sat down in the factory, refusing to leave until the company recognized their union and threatening to destroy the valuable tools and machines if they were removed forcibly. General Motors conceded defeat and signed a contract with the UAW. Chrysler quickly followed suit, and after a hard fight so too did Ford.

By the end of the 1930s, the CIO had some 5 million members, slightly more than the AFL. The successes were remarkable; organizers for the CIO and the AFL had been successful in auto-making, steel, textile, rubber, electrical, and metal industries. For the first time, unskilled as well as skilled were unionized. Because women and blacks made up a substantial proportion of the unskilled work force, they too benefited from the creation of the CIO.

Yet despite these impressive gains, only 28 percent of all Americans (excluding farm workers) belonged to unions in 1940. Employer resistance and traditional hostility to unions blocked further progress, as did the aloof attitude of President Roosevelt. The Wagner Act had helped open the way, but labor leaders deserved most of the credit for the gains that were achieved.

THE NEW DEAL RECORD ON HELP TO MINORITIES

The Roosevelt administration's attempts to aid the downtrodden were least effective with blacks and other racial minorities. The Depression had hit blacks with special force. The fall in the price of cotton had ruined many sharecroppers and tenant farmers, and by 1933, over 50 percent of urban blacks were unemployed. To make matters worse, hard times sharpened racial prejudice.

The New Deal helped blacks survive the Depression, but it never tried to confront squarely the racial injustice built into the federal relief programs. Although the programs served blacks as well as whites, in the South the weekly payments blacks received were much smaller. Neither the minimum wage nor Social Security covered those working as farmers or domestic servants, categories that comprised 65 percent of all black workers. In almost every agency, including the TVA, the interests of blacks counted little or not at all.

Despite this bleak record, blacks rallied behind Roosevelt's leadership, abandoning their historic ties to the Republican party. In part, this switch came in response to Roosevelt's appointment of a number of prominent blacks to high-ranking government positions. The president's wife, Eleanor Roosevelt, spoke out eloquently throughout the decade against racial discrimination. But perhaps the most influential factor in the blacks' political switch was the color-blind policy of Harry Hopkins. He had over 1 million blacks working for the WPA by 1939. Uneven as his record was, Roosevelt had still done more to aid this oppressed minority than any previous president since Lincoln.

The New Deal did far less for Mexican-Americans. Engaged primarily in agricultural labor, these people found their wages in California fields dropping steadily. The Roosevelt administration cut off any further influx from Mexico, and local authorities rounded up and shipped migrants back to Mexico to reduce the welfare rolls. Despite a few benefits from New Deal relief programs, the overall pattern was one of very great economic hardship and relatively little federal assistance for Mexican-Americans.

The American Indian, after decades of neglect, fared slightly better under the New Deal. Roosevelt appointed John Collier, a social worker who championed Indian rights, to serve as commissioner of Indian affairs. In 1934, Congress passed the Indian Reorganization Act, a reform measure designed to stress tribal unity and autonomy instead of attempting (as previous policy had done) to transform Indians into self-sufficient farmers by granting them small plots of land (see Chapter 17). Modest gains also occurred in education, but more than 300,000 Native Americans remained the nation's most impoverished citizens.

WOMEN AT WORK

The decade witnessed a continued decline in the status of American women. Since men were considered the major breadwinners, women were often the first fired. A Gallup poll revealed that 82 percent of the people disapproved of working wives, with 75 percent of the women polled agreeing.

Many of the working women in the 1930s were either single or the sole support of an entire family. Yet their wages remained lower than those for men, and their unemployment rate ran higher than 20 percent throughout the decade. The New Deal offered little encouragement. NRA codes sanctioned lower wages for women. The minimum wage did help those women employed in industry, but too many worked as maids and waitresses, jobs not covered by the law. The percentage of women in the work force was no higher in 1940 than it had been in 1910, and the sexist inequities in the marketplace were as great as ever.

The one area of advance in the 1930s came in government. Eleanor Roosevelt set an example that encouraged millions of American women.

Government employment was one of the few areas in which working women made advances in the 1930s. Secretary of Labor Frances Perkins, shown here inspecting the Golden Gate Bridge, was the first woman cabinet member, one of a number of women appointed by FDR to posts previously held only by men.

She traveled continually around the country, always eager to uncover wrongs and bring them to the president's attention. Frances Perkins, the secretary of labor, became the first woman cabinet member; FDR appointed women as ambassadors and federal judges for the first time; and women were elected to the Senate and the House of Representatives. In sum, a decade that was grim for most Americans was especially hard on American women.

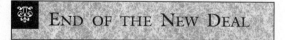

END OF THE NEW DEAL

The New Deal reached its high point in 1936, when Roosevelt was overwhelmingly reelected and the Democratic party strengthened its hold on Congress. But this political triumph was deceptive. In the next two years, Roosevelt met with a series of defeats in Congress. Yet despite these setbacks, he remained a popular political leader who had restored American self-confidence as he attempted to meet the challenges of the Depression.

THE ELECTION OF 1936

Franklin Roosevelt enjoyed his finest political hour in 1936. A man who loved the give-and-take of politics, FDR faced challenges from both the left and the right as he sought reelection. Father Coughlin and Gerald L. K. Smith organized a Union party, with North Dakota Progressive Congressman William Lemke heading the ticket. At the other extreme, a group of wealthy industrialists formed the Liberty League to fight what they saw as the New Deal's assault on property rights. In 1936 the Liberty League endorsed the Republican presidential candidate, Governor Alfred M. Landon of Kansas. A moderate, colorless figure, Landon disappointed his backers by refusing to campaign for repeal of the popular New Deal reforms.

Roosevelt ignored Lemke and the Union party, focusing attention instead on the assault from the right. Democratic spokesmen condemned the Liberty League as a "millionaire's union" and reminded the American people of how much Roosevelt had done for them in fighting unemployment and providing relief. In his speeches, FDR said he welcomed the hatred of the "economic royalists." This frank appeal to class sympathies proved enormously successful, and Roosevelt scored an easy victory at the polls.

Equally important, the election marked the stunning success of a new political coalition that would dominate American politics for the next three decades. FDR, building on the inroads into the Republican majority that Al Smith had begun in 1928, carried urban areas by impressive margins, held on to the traditional Democratic votes in the South and West, and added to them by appealing strongly to the diverse religious and ethnic groups in the northern cities. The strong support of labor and blacks indicated that the nation's new alignment followed economic as well as cultural lines. The poor and the oppressed became attached to the Democratic party, leaving the GOP in a minority position, limited to the well-to-do and to rural and small-town Americans of native stock.

THE SUPREME COURT FIGHT

FDR proved to be far more adept at winning electoral victories than in achieving his goals in Congress. In 1937, he attempted to use his recent success to overcome the one obstacle remaining in his path—the Supreme Court. During his first term, the Court had ruled several New Deal programs unconstitutional. The justices were elderly men who generally opposed New Deal measures; one Justice Van Devanter,

postponed retirement because of his strong opposition.

When Congress convened in 1937, the president offered a startling proposal to overcome the Court's threat to the New Deal. Declaring that the Court was falling behind schedule because of the age of its members, he asked Congress to appoint a new justice for each member of the Court over the age of seventy, up to a maximum of six.

Although this "court-packing" scheme, as critics quickly dubbed it, was perfectly legal, it outraged not only conservatives but liberals as well, who realized it could set a dangerous precedent for the future. Republicans wisely kept silent, letting prominent Democrats lead the fight against Roosevelt's plan. Despite all-out pressure from the White House, resistance in the Senate blocked early action on the proposal.

The Court defended itself well, pointing out that it was not behind schedule. The Court then surprised observers with a series of rulings approving such controversial New Deal measures as the Wagner Act and Social Security. In the midst of the struggle Justice Van Devanter resigned, enabling FDR to make his first appointment to the Court since taking office in 1933. Feeling that he had proved his point, FDR allowed his court-packing plan to die in the Senate.

Although Roosevelt made four more appointments during the next few years, the Court fight had badly weakened his relations with Congress, opening up deep rifts with members of his own party. Many senators and representatives, mostly Southerners, who had voted reluctantly for Roosevelt's measures during the depths of the Depression now felt free to oppose any further New Deal reforms.

THE NEW DEAL IN DECLINE

The legislative record during Roosevelt's second term was meager. Aside from the minimum wage and a maximum-hour law passed in 1938, Congress did not extend the New Deal into any new areas. Disturbed by growing congressional resistance, Roosevelt set out in the spring of 1938 to defeat a number of conservative Democratic congressmen and senators. His efforts were unsuccessful, however, and the failure of this attempted purge further underscored Roosevelt's strained relations with Congress.

The worst blow came in the economic sector. The slow but steady improvement in the economy suddenly gave way to a sharp recession in the late summer of 1937. In the next ten months, industrial production fell by one third, and nearly 4 million workers lost their jobs. Critics of the New Deal quickly labeled the downturn "the Roosevelt recession."

Actually, Roosevelt was at fault. In an effort to reduce expanding budget deficits, he had cut back sharply on WPA and other government programs after the election. This led to a reduction of consumer spending. Urged by economists, Roosevelt finally requested a $3.75 billion relief appropriation in April 1938, and the economy began to revive. But FDR's premature attempt to balance the budget meant two more years of hard times and marred his reputation as the energetic foe of the Depression.

The political result of the attempted purge and the recession was a strong Republican upsurge in the 1938 elections. In addition, after 1938, more and more often anti-New Deal Southerners voted with Republican conservatives to block social and economic reform measures. Thus not only was the New Deal over by the end of 1938, but a new bipartisan conservative coalition that would prevail for a quarter century had formed in Congress.

EVALUATION OF THE NEW DEAL

The New Deal lasted a brief five years, and most of its measures came in two legislative bursts in the spring of 1933 and the summer of 1935. Yet its impact on American life was enduring. Nearly every aspect of economic, social, and political development in the decades that followed bore the imprint of Roosevelt's leadership.

CHRONOLOGY

1932	Franklin D. Roosevelt elected president
1933	Emergency Banking Relief Act passed in one day (March) Twenty-first Amendment repeals Prohibition (December)
1934	Securities and Exchange Commission authorized (June)
1935	Works Progress Administration (WPA) hires unemployed (April) Wagner Act grants workers collective bargaining (July) Congress passes Social Security Act (August)
1936	FDR wins second term as president
1937	Auto Workers' sit-down strike forces General Motors contract (February) FDR loses Court-packing battle (July) Roosevelt recession begins (August)
1938	Congress sets minimum wage at forty cents an hour (June)

The least impressive achievement of the New Deal came in the economic realm. Whatever credit Roosevelt is given for relieving human suffering in the depths of the Depression must be balanced against his failure to achieve recovery in the 1930s. The moderate nature of his programs led to only slow and

Year Created	Act or Agency	Provisions
1933	Agricultural Adjustment Administration (AAA)	Attempted to regulate agricultural production through farm subsidies; reworked after the Supreme Court ruled its key regulatory provisions unconstitutional in 1936; coordinated agricultural production during World War II, after which it was disbanded.
	Banking Act of 1933 (Glass-Steagall Act)	Prohibited commercial banks from selling stock or financing corporations; created FDIC.
	Civilian Conservation Corps (CCC)	Young men between the ages of 18 and 25 volunteered to be placed in camps to work on regional environmental projects mainly west of the Mississippi; they received $30 a month, of which $25 was sent home; disbanded during World War II.
	Civil Works Administration (CWA)	Emergency work-relief program put over 4 million people to work during the extremely cold winter of 1933–34, after which it was disbanded.
	Federal Deposit Insurance Corporation (FDIC)	A federal guarantee of savings bank deposits initially of up to $2,500, raised to $5,000 in 1934, and frequently thereafter; continues today with a limit of $100,000.
	Federal Emergency Relief Administration (FERA)	Combined cash relief to needy families with work relief; superseded in early 1935 by the extensive work relief projects of the WPA and unemployment insurance established by Social Security.
	National Recovery Administration (NRA)	Attempted to combat the Depression through national economic planning by establishing and administering a system of industrial codes to control production, prices, labor relations, and trade practices among leading business interests; ruled unconstitutional by the Supreme Court in 1935.
	Public Works Administration (PWA)	Financed construction of over 34,000 federal and nonfederal construction projects at a cost of over $6 billion; initiated the first federal public housing program, made the federal government the nation's leading producer of power, and advanced conservation of the nation's natural resources; discontinued in 1939 due to its ineffectiveness at reducing unemployment and promoting private investment.
	Tennessee Valley Authority (TVA)	An attempt at regional planning, including provisions for environment and recreational design, architectural, educational, and health projects as well as its controversial public power projects; continues today to meet the Tennessee Valley's energy and flood control needs.
1934	Federal Communications Commission (FCC)	Regulatory agency with wide discretionary powers established to oversee wired and wireless communication; reflected growing importance of radio in everyday lives of Americans during the Depression; continues to regulate television as well as radio.
	Federal Housing Administration (FHA)	Expanded private home ownership among moderate income families through federal guarantees of private mortgages, the reduction of down payments from 30 to 10 percent, and the extension of repayment from 20 to 30 years; continues to function today.
	Securities and Exchange Commission (SEC)	Continues today to regulate trading practices in stocks and bonds according to federal laws.

Year Created	Act or Agency	Provisions
1935	National Labor Relations Board (NLRB); established by Wagner Act	Greatly enhanced power of American labor by instituting legal and procedural apparatus for overseeing collective bargaining; continues to arbitrate labor-management disputes today.
	National Youth Administration (NYA)	Established by the WPA to reduce competition for jobs by supporting education and training of youth; paid grants to over 2 million high school and college students in return for work performed in their schools; also trained another 2.6 million out-of-school youths at skilled labor to prepare them for later employment in the private sector; disbanded during World War II.
	Rural Electrification Administration (REA)	Transformed American rural life by making electricity available at low rates to American farm families in areas private power companies refused to service; closed cultural gap between rural and urban everyday life by making modern amenities, such as radio, available in rural areas.
	Social Security Act	Guaranteed retirement payments for enrolled workers beginning at age 65, set up federal-state system of unemployment insurance and care for dependent mothers and children, the handicapped, and public health; continues today.
	Works Progress Administration (WPA)	Massive work-relief program funded projects ranging from construction to acting; disbanded by FDR during World War II.
1937	Farm Security Administration (FSA)	Granted loans to small farmers and tenants for rehabilitation and purchase of small-sized farms; Congress slashed its appropriations during World War II when many poor farmers entered the armed forces or migrated to urban areas.
1938	Fair Labor Standards Act	Established a minimum wage of 40 cents an hour and a maximum work week of 40 hours for businesses engaged in interstate commerce.

halting industrial recovery. Although much of the advance came as a result of government spending, FDR never embraced the concept of planned deficits, striving instead for a balanced budget. As a result, the nation had barely reached the 1929 level of production a decade later, and there were still nearly 10 million men and women unemployed.

Equally important, Roosevelt refused to make any sweeping changes in the American economic system. Aside from the TVA program of dam construction and electrification, there were no broad experiments in regional planning and no attempt to alter free enterprise beyond imposing some limited forms of gov-

ernmental regulation. The New Deal did nothing to alter the basic distribution of wealth and power in the nation. The outcome was the preservation of the traditional capitalist system with a thin overlay of federal control.

More significant change occurred with the adoption of Social Security. The government acknowledged for the first time its responsibility to provide for the welfare of those unable to care for themselves in an industrial society. The Wagner Act helped stimulate the growth of labor unions to balance corporate power, and the minimum-wage law provided a much-needed floor for many workers. Yet the New Deal tended to help only the more vocal and organized groups, such as union members and commercial farmers. Those without effective voices or political clout received little help from the New Deal. Roosevelt did little more than Hoover in responding to the long-term needs of the dispossessed.

The most lasting impact of the Roosevelt leadership came in politics. FDR proved to be a genius at forging a new coalition. He united rural and urban Democrats and attracted new groups to the Democratic party, principally blacks and organized labor. His political success led to a major realignment that lasted long after he left the scene.

His political achievement also reveals the true nature of Roosevelt's success. He was a brilliant politician who recognized the essence of leadership in a democracy—appealing directly to the people and infusing them with a sense of purpose. Thus despite his limitations as a reformer, Roosevelt proved to be the man the American people needed in the 1930s—the leader who gave them the psychological lift that helped them endure and survive the Great Depression.

❧ RECOMMENDED READING

The best overall account of political developments in the 1930s is William Leuchtenburg, *Franklin D. Roosevelt and the New Deal* (1963). For a more critical view, see James MacGregor Burns, *Roosevelt: The Lion and the Fox* (1956), and Paul Conkin, *The New Deal* (1967). An exhaustive study of the New Deal through 1936 is Arthur M. Schlesinger, Jr., *The Age of Roosevelt*, 3 vols. (1957–1960), written from a sympathetic point of view.

General accounts of the 1930s include Broadus Mitchell, *Depression Decade* (1947), and John Braeman, Robert H. Bremner, and David Brody, eds., *The New Deal*, 2 vols. (1975). Books on the Great Depression include John Kenneth Galbraith, *The Great Crash* (1955); Robert Sobel, *The Great Bull Market* (1968); Studs Terkel, *Hard Times* (1970); and Robert S. McElvaine, *The Great Depression* (1984).

Frank Freidel, *Franklin D. Roosevelt*, 4 vols. (1952–1976) is the most comprehensive biography of FDR. The rich memoir literature for the New Deal includes Frances Perkins, *The Roosevelt I Knew* (1946); Raymond Moley, *The First New Deal* (1966); and Samuel I. Rosenman, *Working with Roosevelt* (1952).

The best of many books dealing with farm problems in the 1930s are Richard Kirkendall, *Social Scientists and Farm Politics in the Age of Roosevelt* (1966); Paul Conkin, *Tomorrow a New World* (1959); Van Perkins, *Crisis in Agriculture* (1969); and Donal Worster, *Dust Bowl* (1979). For labor developments, see Sidney Fine, *Sit Down: The General Motors Strike of 1936–37* (1969), and two books by Irving Bernstein, *The Turbulent Years* (1970) and *A Caring Society* (1985).

Studies of critics of the New Deal include George Wolfskill, *Revolt of the Conservatives* (1962); T. Harry Williams, *Huey Long* (1969); and Alan Brinkley, *Voices of Protest: Huey Long, Father Coughlin, and the Great Depression* (1982). For intellectual radicalism in the 1930s, see Daniel Aaron, *Writers on the Left* (1960), and Richard Pells, *Radical Visions and American Dreams* (1973).

Raymond Wolters offers a critical view of Roosevelt's policies toward African Americans in *Negroes and the Great Depression* (1970); Harvard Sitkoff is more positive in *A New Deal for Blacks* (1978). For the impact of the Depression on women, see Lois Sharf, *To Work and to Wed* (1980), and Susan Ware, *Holding Their Own: American Women in the 1930s* (1982).

27 AMERICA AND THE WORLD, 1921–1945

RETREAT, REVERSAL, AND RIVALRY

ISOLATIONISM

THE ROAD TO WAR

TURNING THE TIDE AGAINST THE AXIS

THE HOME FRONT

VICTORY

On August 27, 1928, U.S. Secretary of State Frank B. Kellogg, French Foreign Minister Aristide Briand, and representatives of twelve other nations met in Paris to sign a pact outlawing war. Spectators watched and photographers recorded the historic ceremony. In the United States, a senator called the Kellogg-Briand Pact "the most telling action ever taken in human history to abolish war."

In reality, the Pact of Paris was the result of a determined American effort to avoid involvement in the European alliance system. In June 1927, Briand had sent a message to the American people inviting the United States to join with France in signing a pact to outlaw war between the two nations. The invitation struck a sympathetic response, but the State Depart-

ment feared correctly that Briand's true intention was to establish a close tie between France and the United States. France believed that an antiwar pact with the United States would at least ensure American sympathy, if not involvement, in case of another European war. Kellogg outmaneuvered Briand by proposing that the pledge against war not be confined just to France and the United States, but instead be extended to all nations. An unhappy Briand had no choice but to agree, and so the diplomatic charade finally culminated in the elaborate signing ceremony in Paris.

Eventually the signers of the Kellogg-Briand Pact included nearly every nation in the world, but the effect was negligible. All promised to renounce war as an instrument of national policy, except in matters of self-defense. The pact relied solely on the moral force of world opinion.

Unfortunately, the pact was symbolic of American foreign policy in the years after World War I. Instead of asserting the role of leadership its resources and power commanded, the United States kept aloof from other nations. America went its own way, extending trade and economic dominance but refusing to take the lead in maintaining world order. This retreat from responsibility seemed unimportant in the 1920s when the very exhaustion from World War I ensured relative peace and tranquility. But in the 1930s, when threats to world order arose in Europe and Asia, the American people retreated even deeper, searching for an isolationist policy that would spare them the agony of another great war.

There was no place to hide in the modern world. The Nazi onslaught in Europe and the Japanese expansion in Asia finally led to American entry into World War II in late 1941, at a time when the chances for an Allied victory seemed most remote. With incredible swiftness, the nation mobilized its military and industrial strength. American armies were soon fighting on three continents, the U.S. Navy controlled the world's oceans, and the nation's factories were sending a vast stream of war supplies to more than twenty Allied countries.

When victory came in 1945, the United States was by far the most powerful nation in the world. But instead of the enduring peace that might have permitted a return to a less active foreign policy, the onset of the Cold War with the Soviet Union brought on a new era of tension and conflict. This time the United States could not retreat from responsibility. World War II was a coming of age for American foreign policy.

RETREAT, REVERSAL, AND RIVALRY

A bitter disillusionment ran through every aspect of American foreign policy in the 1920s. In contrast to Wilsonian idealism, American diplomats made loans, negotiated treaties and agreements, and pledged the nation's good faith, but they were careful not to make any binding commitments on behalf of world order. The result was neither isolation nor involvement but rather a cautious middle course that managed to alienate friends and encourage foes.

RETREAT IN EUROPE

The United States emerged from World War I as the richest nation on earth, displacing England from its prewar position of economic primacy. Each year of the 1920s saw the nation increase its economic lead as the balance of trade tipped heavily in America's favor. The war-ravaged countries of Europe borrowed enormous amounts from American bankers to rebuild their economies, and American exports and overseas investments far exceeded prewar levels.

The European nations could no longer compete on equal terms. The high American tariff, first imposed in 1922 and then raised again in 1930, frustrated attempts by England, France, and a defeated Germany to earn the dollars necessary to meet their American financial obligations. Although the Allied partners in World War I asked Washington to cancel the $10 billion in war debts, American leaders from Wilson to Hoover indignantly refused this request.

Only a continuing flow of private American capital to Germany allowed the payment of reparations to the Allies and the partial repayment of the war debts in the 1920s. The financial crash of 1929 halted the flow of American dollars across the Atlantic and led to subsequent default on the debt payments, with accompanying bitterness on both sides of the ocean.

Political relations fared little better. The United States never joined the League of Nations, nor did it take part in the attempts by England and France to negotiate European security treaties. The Republican administrations of the twenties refused to compromise American freedom of action by embracing collective security, the principle on which the

League was founded. And FDR made no effort to renew Wilson's futile quest. Remaining aloof from the European balance of power, the United States refused to stand behind the increasingly shaky Versailles settlement.

The United States ignored the Soviet Union throughout the 1920s. American businessmen, however, actively traded with Russia and pressed for diplomatic recognition of the Bolshevik regime. In 1933, Roosevelt finally signed an agreement opening up diplomatic relations between the two countries.

COOPERATION IN LATIN AMERICA

United States policy in the Western Hemisphere was both more active and more enlightened than in Europe. The State Department sought new ways in the 1920s to pursue traditional goals of political dominance and economic advantage in Latin America. Both Republican and Democratic administrations worked hard to limit American military involvement and to extend American trade and investment in the nations to the South. Under Harding, Coolidge, and Hoover, American marines were withdrawn from Haiti, the Dominican Republic, and Nicaragua. Renewed unrest in Nicaragua in 1925, however, led to a second intervention that lasted until the early 1930s.

Showing a new sensitivity, the State Department released the Clark Memorandum in 1930, a policy statement repudiating the controversial Roosevelt Corollary to the Monroe Doctrine. The United States had no right to intervene in neighboring states under the Monroe Doctrine, declared Undersecretary of State J. Reuben Clark, although he asserted a traditional claim to protect American lives and property under international law.

When FDR took office in 1933, relations with Latin America were far better than they had been under Wilson, but American trade in the hemisphere had fallen drastically as the Depression worsened. Roosevelt moved quickly to solidify the improved relations and gain economic benefits. He proclaimed a policy of the "good neighbor" and then proceeded to win good will by renouncing the imperialism of the past.

Starting in 1933, Roosevelt's secretary of state, Cordell Hull, moved toward a policy of nonintervention. A year later the United States loosened its grip on Cuba (renouncing the Platt Amendment) and Panama. By 1936, American troops were no longer occupying any Latin American nation. But the United States had not changed its basic goal of political and economic dominance in the hemisphere. Rather, the new policy of benevolence reflected Roosevelt's belief that cooperation and friendship were more effective tactics than threats and armed intervention.

The Good Neighbor Policy opened up new trade opportunities. American commerce with Latin America increased fourfold in the 1930s, and investment rose substantially from its Depression low. More important, FDR succeeded in forging a new policy of regional collective security between the nations of the Western Hemisphere and the United States.

RIVALRY IN ASIA

In the years following World War I, the United States and Japan were on a collision course in the Pacific. The Japanese, lacking the raw materials to sustain their developing industrial economy, were determined to expand onto the Asian mainland. They had taken Korea by 1905 and during World War I had extended their control over the mines, harbors, and railroads of Manchuria, the industrial region of northeast China. The American Open Door policy remained the primary obstacle to complete Japanese domination over China. The United States thus faced the clear-cut choice of either abandoning China or forcefully opposing Japan's expansion. American efforts to avoid making this painful decision postponed the eventual showdown but not the growing rivalry.

The first attempt at a solution came in 1921 when the United States convened the Washington Conference. The major objective was a political settlement of the tense Asian situation, but the most pressing issue was a dangerous naval race between Japan and the United States. Projected construction indicated that both countries would overtake the British navy by the end of the decade. Japan, spending nearly one third of its budget on naval construction, was eager for an agreement; in the United States, too, growing congressional concern over appropriations suggested the need for slowing the naval buildup.

Secretary of State Charles Evans Hughes outlined a specific plan for naval disarmament. After three months of discussion, the delegates signed a Five Power Treaty limiting capital ships (battleships and aircraft carriers) in a ratio of 5–5–3 for the United States, Britain, and Japan respectively and 1.67–1.67 for France and Italy. Japan agreed to the lower ratio only in return for an American pledge not to fortify Pacific bases such as the Philippines and Guam. The treaty cooled off the naval race even though it did not include cruisers, destroyers, or submarines.

The Washington Conference also produced a Nine Power Treaty that pledged the signators to uphold the Open Door policy and a Four Power Treaty that created a new Pacific security pact. Neither document contained any enforcement provision beyond a promise to consult in case of violation. In essence, the Washington treaties formed a parchment peace, a pious set of pledges that attempted to freeze the status quo in the Pacific.

This compromise lasted less than a decade. In September 1931, Japanese forces overran Manchuria in a brutal act of aggression. The United States, paralyzed by the Depression, responded feebly. In January 1932, Secretary of State Henry L. Stimson vowed that the United States would not recognize the legality of the Japanese seizure of Manchuria. Despite ultimate concurrence by the League of Nations on nonrecognition, the Japanese ignored the American moral sanction and incorporated the former Chinese province into their expanding empire.

Aside from the good-neighbor approach in the Western Hemisphere, American foreign policy faithfully reflected the prevailing disil-lusionment with world power that gripped the country after World War I. The United States avoided taking any constructive steps toward preserving world order, preferring instead the empty symbolism of the Washington treaties and the Kellogg-Briand Pact.

ISOLATIONISM

The retreat from an active world policy in the 1920s turned into a headlong flight back to isolationism in the 1930s. Two factors were responsible. First, the Depression made foreign policy seem remote and unimportant to most Americans. Second, the danger of war abroad, when it did finally penetrate the American consciousness, served only to strengthen the desire to escape involvement.

Three powerful and discontented nations were on the march in the 1930s—Germany, Italy, and Japan. In Germany, Adolf Hitler came to power in 1933 as the head of the National Socialist, or Nazi, movement. A shrewd and charismatic leader, Hitler capitalized on both domestic discontent and bitterness over World War I. Blaming the Jews and Communists for all of Germany's ills and asserting the supremacy of the "Aryan" race of blond, blue-eyed Germans, he quickly imposed a totalitarian dictatorship in which the Nazi party ruled and the führer was supreme. As he consolidated his power, his ultimate threat to world peace became clear. Hitler took Germany out of the League of Nations, reoccupied the Rhineland, and formally denounced the Treaty of Versailles.

In Italy, another dictator, Benito Mussolini, had come to power in 1922. Emboldened by Hitler's success, he embarked on an aggressive foreign policy in 1935. His invasion of Ethiopia led its emperor, Haile Selassie, to call upon the League of Nations for support. The League's halfway measures utterly failed to halt Mussolini's conquest. Collective security had failed its most important test.

Japan formed the third element in the threat to world peace. Militarists began to dominate

Millions of Germans idolized Adolf Hitler, portrayed in this German painting as a white knight. After the painting came into American hands, a GI slashed Hitler's face to indicate his displeasure with the mystique of the führer.

nations signed an anti-Comintern pact completing a Berlin-Rome-Tokyo axis. Their alliance ostensibly was aimed at the Soviet Union, but in fact it threatened the entire world. Only a determined American response could unite the other nations against this Axis threat. Unfortunately, the United States deliberately abstained from assuming this role of leadership until it was nearly too late.

THE LURE OF PACIFISM AND NEUTRALITY

The growing danger of war abroad led to a rising American desire for noninvolvement. Memories of the horrors of World War I contributed heavily. Historians began to treat the Great War as a mistake, criticizing Wilson for failing to preserve American neutrality and claiming that the clever British had duped the United States into entering the war.

American youth made clear their determination not to repeat the mistakes of their elders. Pacifism swept across college campuses. In April 1934, students and professors alike walked out of class to attend massive antiwar rallies, which became an annual rite of spring in the 1930s. Pacifist orators urged students to sign a pledge not to support their country "in any war it might conduct."

The pacifist movement found a scapegoat in the munitions industry. The publication of several books exposing the unsavory business tactics of the large arms dealers such as Krupps in Germany and Vickers in Britain led to the demand to curb these "merchants of death." Senator Gerald Nye of North Dakota headed a special Senate committee that spent two years investigating the dealings that brought enormous profits to munitions firms such as Du Pont. Nye went further, charging that bankers and munitions makers were responsible for American intervention in 1917. Although he offered no proof, the public—prepared to believe the worst of business during the Depression—accepted the merchants-of-death thesis.

The Nye Committee's revelations culminated in neutrality legislation aimed at avoiding involvement in European conflicts. In Au-

the government in Tokyo by the mid-1930s, using tactics of fear and even assassination against their liberal opponents. By 1936, Japan had left the League of Nations and had repudiated the Washington treaties. A year later, its armies began an invasion of China that signified the beginning of the Pacific phase of World War II.

The resurgence of militarism in Germany, Italy, and Japan undermined the Versailles settlement and threatened to destroy the existing balance of power. In 1937, the three totalitarian

gust 1935, Congress passed the first of three neutrality acts. The 1935 law banned the sale of arms to nations at war and warned American citizens not to sail on belligerent ships. In 1936, a second act added a ban on loans, and in 1937, a third neutrality act made these prohibitions permanent and required, on a two-year trial basis, that all trade other than munitions be conducted on a cash-and-carry basis.

President Roosevelt played a passive role in the adoption of the neutrality legislation. Privately, he expressed some reservations, but publicly he bowed to the prevailing isolationism. Yet FDR did take a few steps to try to limit the nation's retreat into isolationism. His failure to invoke the neutrality act after the Japanese invasion of China in 1937 enabled the hard-pressed Chinese to continue buying arms from the United States. In January 1938, he used his influence to block a proposal by Rep. Ludlow of Indiana to require a nationwide referendum before Congress could declare war. FDR's strongest public statement came earlier, in Chicago in October 1937; he denounced "the epidemic of world lawlessness" and called for an international effort to "quarantine" this disease.

WAR IN EUROPE

The neutrality legislation played directly into the hands of Adolf Hitler. Bent on the conquest of Europe, he could now proceed without worrying about American interference. In March 1938, he seized Austria in a bloodless coup. Six months later, he was demanding the Sudentenland, a province of Czechoslovakia with a large German population. When British and French leaders approved Hitler's move at the Munich conference, FDR gave his tacit consent.

Within one half year of the meeting at Munich, Hitler violated his promises by seizing nearly all of Czechoslovakia. In the United States, the State Department, with FDR's approval, pressed for neutrality revision, hoping to place *all* trade with belligerents, including munitions, on a cash-and-carry basis. The House, however, rejected the proposal aware that it would favor England and France, who controlled the sea.

In July 1939, Roosevelt finally abandoned his aloof position and held a meeting with Senate leaders to plead for reconsideration. Even with the threat of war in Europe, strong isolationist sentiment prevailed. Congressional leaders refused to alter the neutrality acts.

On September 1, 1939, Hitler began World War II by invading Poland. England and France responded two days later by declaring war. Russia had played a key role by signing a non-aggression treaty with Hitler in late August. The Nazi-Soviet pact enabled Germany to avoid a two-front war; the Russians were rewarded with a generous slice of eastern Poland.

President Roosevelt reacted to the outbreak of war by proclaiming American neutrality, but the successful aggression by Nazi Germany brought into question the isolationist assumption that American well-being did not depend upon the European balance of power. Strategic as well as ideological considerations began to undermine the earlier belief that the United States could safely pursue a policy of neutrality and noninvolvement. Americans came to realize that their own democracy and security were at stake in the European war.

THE ROAD TO WAR

For two years the United States tried to remain at peace while war raged in Europe and Asia. In contrast to Wilson's attempt to be impartial during most of World War I, however, the American people displayed an overwhelming sympathy for the Allies and total distaste for Germany and Japan. Roosevelt made no secret of his preference for an Allied victory, but a fear of isolationist criticism compelled him to move slowly, and often deviously, in adopting a policy of aid for England and France—short of actually entering the war.

FROM NEUTRALITY TO UNDECLARED WAR

Two weeks after the outbreak of war in Europe, Roosevelt called Congress into special session to revise the neutrality legislation. His aim was to repeal the arms embargo in order to supply weapons to England and France, but he refused to state this openly. Instead he asked Congress to replace the arms embargo with cash-and-carry regulations. Congress passed the revised neutrality policy by heavy margins in early November 1939.

A series of dramatic German victories had a profound impact on American opinion. In the spring of 1940, Germany seized Denmark and Norway and unleashed the *blitzkrieg* (lightning war) on the western front. Using tanks, armored columns, and dive bombers in close coordination, the German army drove the British off the continent in three weeks; three weeks later, France fell to Hitler's victorious armies.

Americans were stunned. Hitler had taken only six weeks to achieve what Germany had failed to do in four years of fighting in World War I. Suddenly they realized that they did have a stake in the outcome; if England fell, Hitler might well gain control of the British navy and the Atlantic, thus opening up the New World to German penetration.

Roosevelt responded by invoking a policy of all-out aid to the Allies short of war. Denouncing Germany and Italy as representing "the gods of force and hate," he pledged American support for England and its allies. In early September, FDR announced the transfer of fifty old destroyers to England in exchange for rights to build air and naval bases on eight British possessions in the Western Hemisphere. Giving warships to a belligerent nation was clearly a breach of neutrality, but Roosevelt stressed the importance of the United States guarding its Atlantic approaches.

Isolationists protested against this departure from neutrality. Roosevelt's opponents in the Midwest formed the America First Committee to oppose the drift toward war. Such diverse individuals as aviator-hero Charles Lindbergh, conservative Senator Robert A. Taft, and socialist leader Norman Thomas condemned FDR for involving the United States in a foreign conflict that they claimed in no way threatened America.

To support the administration's policies, moderate New Dealers, Eastern seaboard An-

glophiles, and liberal Republicans joined forces to organize the Committee to Defend America by Aiding the Allies. Kansas newspaper editor William Allen White served as chairman of this interventionist organization, which advocated unlimited assistance to England short of war. Above all, the interventionists challenged the isolationist premise that events in Europe did not affect American security. As White declared, "The future of western civilization is being decided upon the battlefield of Europe."

In the ensuing debate, the American people gradually came to agree with the interventionists. Frightened by the events in Europe, Congress approved large sums for preparedness, increasing the defense budget from $2 billion to $10 billion during 1940. Roosevelt courageously asked for a peacetime draft, the first in American history, to build up the army, and Congress consented.

The sense of crisis affected domestic politics. Roosevelt ran for an unprecedented third term in 1940 because of the war; the Republicans nominated Wendell Willkie, who shared FDR's commitment to aid for England. Roosevelt's decisive victory made it clear that the nation supported his departure from neutrality.

After the election, FDR took his boldest step. Responding to British Prime Minister Winston Churchill's warning that England was running out of money, the president asked Congress to approve a new program to lend and lease goods and weapons to countries fighting against aggressors. Roosevelt's call for America to become "the great arsenal of democracy" seemed straightforward enough, but he acted somewhat deviously by naming the program Lend-Lease and by comparing it to loaning a garden hose to put out a fire.

Isolationists angrily denounced Lend-Lease as both unnecessary and untruthful. In March 1941, however, Congress voted by substantial margins to authorize the president to "sell, transfer title to, exchange, lease, lend, or otherwise dispose of" war supplies to "any country the president deems vital to the defense of the United States." The accompanying $7 billion appropriation ended the "cash" part of cash-and-carry and ensured Britain full access to American war supplies.

The "carry" problem still remained. German submarines were sinking over 500,000 tons of shipping a month. England desperately needed the help of the American navy in escorting convoys across the U-boat-infested waters of the North Atlantic. Roosevelt responded with naval patrols as far east as Iceland. Hitler placed his submarine commanders under strict restraints to avoid drawing America into the European war. Nevertheless, incidents were bound to occur.

Undeclared naval war quickly followed. A German submarine damaged the U.S. destroyer *Kearney*, and another sank the *Reuben James*. FDR issued orders for the destroyers to shoot U-boats on sight. At Roosevelt's request, Congress repealed the "carry" section of the neutrality laws and permitted American ships to deliver supplies to England. Now American merchant ships as well as destroyers would become targets for German attacks. By December 1941, war with Germany seemed close.

In leading the nation to the brink of war in Europe, Roosevelt opened himself to criticism from both sides in the domestic debate. Interventionists felt he was too cautious; isolationists claimed that he had misled the American people by professing peace while plotting for war. Roosevelt was certainly less than candid, relying on executive discretion to engage in highly provocative acts in the North Atlantic. Although he clearly saw the threat Germany offered, he was also aware that most Americans wanted to stay out of World War II. Realizing that leading a divided nation into war would be disastrous, FDR played for time, inching the country toward war while waiting for the Axis nations to make the ultimate move. Japan finally obliged at Pearl Harbor.

SHOWDOWN IN THE PACIFIC

Japan had taken advantage of the war in Europe to expand further in Asia. The defeat of France and the Netherlands in 1940 left French and Dutch colonial possessions in the East Indies and Indochina vulnerable and defenseless. Japan now set out to incorporate these territories—rich in oil, tin, and rubber—into a Greater East Asia Co-Prosperity Sphere.

The Roosevelt administration countered with economic pressure. Japan was heavily dependent upon the United States for shipments of petroleum and scrap iron and steel. In July 1940, FDR signed an order setting up a licensing and quota system for the export of these crucial materials to Japan and banned the sale of aviation gasoline altogether. The United States was now employing economic sanctions to block Japanese expansion in Southeast Asia.

Tokyo appeared unimpressed. In early September 1940, Japanese troops occupied strategic bases in the northern part of French Indochina. Later in the month, Japan signed the Tripartite Pact with Germany and Italy, a defensive treaty that confronted the United States with a possible two-ocean war and a global totalitarian threat. Roosevelt and his advisors, however, saw Germany as the primary danger; thus they pursued a policy of all-out aid to England while hoping that economic measures alone would deter Japan.

The embargo on aviation gasoline, extended to include scrap iron and steel, was a burden Japan could bear, but a possible ban on all oil shipments was a different matter. Entirely dependent on oil imports from the United States and the Dutch East Indies, Japan tried to negotiate with the United States, but these talks broke down. Tokyo wanted nothing less than a free hand in China and an end to American sanctions, while the United States insisted on an eventual Japanese evacuation of all China.

In July 1941, Japan invaded southern Indochina, beginning the chain of events that led to war. Washington knew of this aggression before it occurred. Naval intelligence experts had broken the Japanese diplomatic code and were intercepting and reading all messages between Tokyo and the Japanese embassy in Washington. FDR responded on July 25, 1941, with an order freezing all Japanese assets in the United States. Trade with Japan, including the vital oil shipments, came to a complete halt. When the Dutch government-in-exile took similar actions, Japan faced a dilemma: In order to have oil shipments resumed, Tokyo would have to

War headline in extra editions on the morning of December 8 (above). FDR addressing Congress and the nation that afternoon (right). Congress immediately declared war on Japan.

end its aggression; the alternative would be to seize the needed petroleum supplies in the Dutch East Indies, an action that would mean war.

With General Hideki Tojo, an army militant, as the premier of Japan, the Tokyo government moved toward war. To mask its war preparations, Tokyo sent yet another envoy to Washington with new peace proposals, a mission both Japan and the United States knew was futile. Army and navy leaders urged FDR to seek a temporary settlement with Japan to give them time to prepare American defenses in the Pacific. Secretary of State Cordell Hull, however, refused to allow any concessions, sending a stiff ten-point reply to Tokyo that included a demand for Japanese withdrawal from China.

Two weeks later, on the evening of December 6, 1941, the first thirteen parts of the Japanese reply to Hull's note arrived in Washington. After reading the decoded text late that night, President Roosevelt said, "This means war."

The fourteenth part of Japan's reply arrived the next day, December 7, revealing Japan's complete rejection of the American position. Officials in Washington tried to warn American bases in the Pacific, but they were too late.

Just before 1 P.M. Washington time, squadrons of Japanese carrier-based planes caught the American fleet at Pearl Harbor totally by surprise. In a little more than an hour, the Japanese crippled the American Pacific fleet and destroyed their base at Pearl Harbor, sinking eight battleships and killing more than 2400 American sailors.

Speaking before Congress the next day, President Roosevelt termed December 7 "a date which will live in infamy" and asked for a declaration of war against Japan. With only one dissenting vote, both chambers did so. On December 11, Germany and Italy declared war against the United States; the nation was now fully involved in World War II.

The whole country united behind Roosevelt's leadership to seek revenge for Pearl Harbor and to defeat the Axis threat to American security. After the war, however, critics charged that FDR had entered the conflict by a back door, claiming that the president had deliberately exposed the Pacific fleet to attack. Subsequent investigations uncovered negligence in both Hawaii and Washington but no evidence to support the conspiracy charge. Both military experts and FDR had badly un-

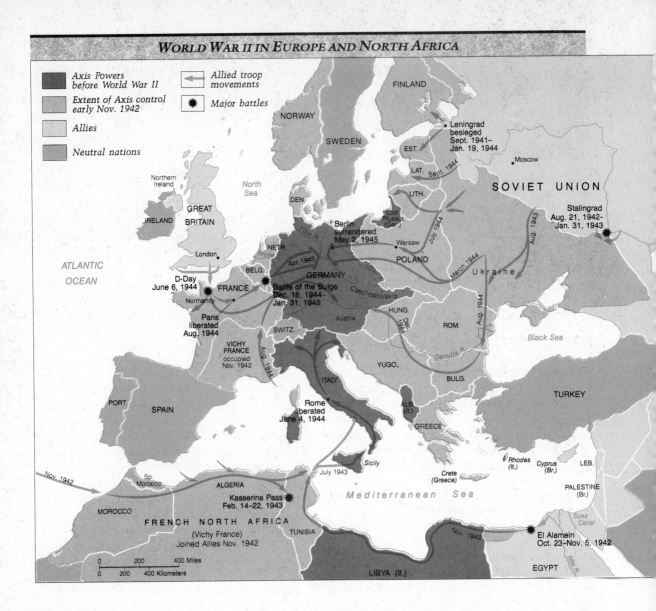

Axis Powers before World War II

Extent of Axis control early Nov. 1942

Allies

Neutral nations

Allied troop movements

Major battles

FINLAND

NORWAY

SWEDEN

EST.

LAT. Sept. 1944

LITH.

Moscow

SOVIET UNION

Leningrad besieged Sept. 1941– Jan. 19, 1944

Northern Ireland

North Sea

DEN.

East Prussia (Ger.)

Warsaw

July 1944

Aug. 1943

Stalingrad Aug. 21, 1942– Jan. 31, 1943

IRELAND

GREAT BRITAIN

London

NETH.

Elbe R.

Berlin surrendered May 2, 1945

POLAND

March 1944

Ukraine

BELG.

Rhine

Apr. 1945

GERMANY

Czechoslovakia

Aug. 1944

ATLANTIC OCEAN

D-Day June 6, 1944

FRANCE

Normandy

Battle of the Bulge Dec. 16, 1944– Jan. 31, 1945

HUNG.

Dec. 1944

ROM.

Black Sea

Austria

Danube R.

Paris liberated Aug. 1944

SWITZ.

Aug. 1944

VICHY FRANCE occupied Nov. 1942

YUGO.

BULG.

PORT.

SPAIN

ITALY

Rome liberated June 4, 1944

ALB. (It.)

GREECE

TURKEY

Rhodes (It.)

Cyprus (Br.)

LEB.

Sicily

July 1943

Crete (Greece)

PALESTINE (Br.)

Nov. 1942

Sp. Morocco

ALGERIA

Kasserine Pass Feb. 14–22, 1943

Mediterranean Sea

Suez Canal

MOROCCO

FRENCH NORTH AFRICA

(Vichy France) Joined Allies Nov. 1942

TUNISIA

Nov. 1942

El Alamein Oct. 23–Nov. 5, 1942

Nile R.

0   200   400 Miles
0   200   400 Kilometers

LIBYA (It.)

EGYPT

derestimated the daring and skill of the Japanese, but there was no plot. Perhaps the most frightening aspect of the whole episode is that it took the shock of the Japanese sneak attack to make the American people aware of the full extent of the Axis threat to their well-being and persuade them out of the long fruitless effort to stay out of the war.

TURNING THE TIDE AGAINST THE AXIS

In the first few months after the United States entered the war, the outlook for victory was bleak. In Europe, Hitler's armies controlled virtually the entire continent, from Norway in the north to Greece in the south. Despite the non-aggression pact, German armies had penetrated deep into Russia after an initial invasion in June 1941. In North Africa, General Erwin Rommel's Afrika Korps had pushed the British back into Egypt and threatened the Suez Canal (see map on p. 468).

The situation was no better in Asia. The Pearl Harbor attack had enabled the Japanese to move unopposed across Southeast Asia. Within three months they had conquered Malaya and the Dutch East Indies, with its valuable oil fields, and were pressing the British back both in Burma and New Guinea. American forces under General Douglas MacArthur had tried but failed to block the Japanese conquest of the Philippines. With the American navy still recovering from the devastation at Pearl Harbor, Japan controlled the western half of the Pacific (see map on p. 471).

Within the next two years, the United States and its allies finally halted the German and Japanese offensives in Europe and Asia. But then they faced the difficult process of driving back the enemy, freeing the vast conquered areas, and finally defeating the Axis powers on their home territory. It was a difficult and costly struggle requiring great sacrifice and heavy losses; World War II tested American will and resourcefulness to the hilt.

WARTIME PARTNERSHIPS

The greatest single advantage that the United States and its partners possessed was their willingness to form a genuine coalition to bring about the defeat of the Axis powers. In striking contrast was the behavior of Germany and Japan, each fighting a separate war without any attempt at cooperation.

The United States and Britain achieved a complete wartime partnership. Prewar military talks led to the formation of a Combined Chiefs of Staff, which directed Anglo-American military operations. The close cooperation between FDR and Prime Minister Churchill ensured a common strategy. The leaders decided at the outset that a German victory posed the greater danger and thus gave priority to the European theater in the conduct of the war.

Relations with the other members of the coalition in World War II were not quite so harmonious. The decision to defeat Germany first displeased the Chinese, who had been at war with Japan since 1937. Roosevelt tried to appease Chiang Kai-shek with a trickle of supplies. France posed a more delicate problem. FDR virtually ignored the Free French government in exile under General Charles de Gaulle. Roosevelt preferred to deal with the Vichy regime, despite its collaboration with Germany, because it still controlled the French fleet and retained France's overseas territories.

The greatest strain of all within the wartime coalition was with the Soviet Union. Although Roosevelt had ended the long period of nonrecognition in 1933, close ties had failed to develop. The great Russian purge trials and the temporary Nazi-Soviet alliance from 1939 to 1941, along with deep-seated cultural and ideological differences, made wartime cooperation difficult.

Ever the pragmatist, Roosevelt tried hard to break down the old hostility and establish a more cordial relationship with Russia during the war. He was quick to give Lend-Lease aid to Russia, and in May 1942, he promised a visiting Russian diplomat that the United States would create a second front in Europe by the end of that year, a pledge he could not fulfill. In January 1943, Roosevelt joined with Churchill at the Casablanca conference to declare a policy of unconditional surrender, vowing that the Western Allies would fight on until the Axis nations were completely defeated.

Despite these promises, the Soviet Union bore the brunt of the battle against Hitler in the early years of the war. The United States and England, grateful for the respite to build up their forces, could do little more than offer promises of future help and send Lend-Lease supplies. The result was a rift that never fully healed—one that did not prevent the defeat of Germany but did ensure future tensions and uncertainties between the Soviet Union and the Western nations.

HALTING THE GERMAN BLITZ

From the outset, the United States favored an invasion across the English Channel as the key to victory in Europe. Roosevelt and his leading military advisors were convinced that such a frontal assault would be the quickest way to win the war. Army Chief of Staff George C. Marshall placed his protégé, Dwight D. Eisenhower, in charge of drawing up and implementing the invasion.

But the British preferred a perimeter approach, with air and naval attacks around the edge of the continent, until Germany was properly softened up for the final invasion. Roosevelt temporarily consented to this plan, and in November 1942, American and British troops landed on the Atlantic and Mediterranean coasts of Morocco and Algeria.

The British launched an attack against Rommel at El Alamein in Egypt and soon forced the Afrika Korps to retreat across Libya to Tunisia. American forces then hit Rommel in Tunisia. After a humiliating defeat at the Kasserine Pass, General George Patton rallied the demoralized American soldiers, and by May 1943, Germany had been driven from Africa, leaving behind nearly 300,000 troops. During these same months, the Red Army broke the back of German military power after Hitler poured in division after division in what was ultimately a critical defeat at the battle of Stalingrad.

At Churchill's insistence, FDR agreed to follow up the North African victory with the invasion first of Sicily and then Italy in the summer of 1943. Italy dropped out of the war when Mussolini fled to Germany, but the Italian campaign proved to be a strategic dead end. Germany sent in enough divisions to establish a strong defensive line in the mountains south of Rome; American and British troops were forced to fight their way slowly up the peninsula, suffering heavy casualties.

More important, these Mediterranean operations delayed the second front, postponing it eventually to the spring of 1944. Meanwhile, the Soviets began to push the Germans out of Russia and looked forward to the liberation of Poland, Hungary, and Romania, where they could establish "friendly" Communist regimes. Having borne the brunt of the fighting against Nazi Germany, Stalin was ready to claim his reward—the postwar domination of Eastern Europe, a region which had been the historic pathway for Western invasion into Russia.

CHECKING JAPAN IN THE PACIFIC

The decision to defeat Germany first and the vast expanses of the Pacific dictated the nature of the war against Japan—amphibious, island-hopping campaigns rather than any attempt to reconquer the Dutch East Indies, Southeast Asia, and China. There would be two separate American operations. One, led by Douglas MacArthur based in Australia, would move from New Guinea back to the Philippines, while the other, commanded by Admiral Chester Nimitz from Hawaii, was directed at key Japanese islands in the Central Pacific. The original plan called for the two offensives to come together for the final invasion of the Japanese home islands.

Success in the Pacific depended above all else on control of the sea. In the battle of the Coral Sea in May 1942, American naval forces blocked a Japanese thrust to outflank Australia. The turning point came one month later at Midway. In this important battle, superior American air power enabled Nimitz's forces to engage the enemy at long range. The battle of Midway ended with the loss of four Japanese aircraft carriers compared to just one American. It was the first defeat the modern Japanese navy had ever suffered, and it left the United States in control of the Central Pacific.

Encouraged by this victory, American forces launched their first Pacific offensive in the Solomon Islands, east of New Guinea, in August 1942. Six months later the last Japanese were driven from the key island of Guadalcanal. At the same time, MacArthur began the long,

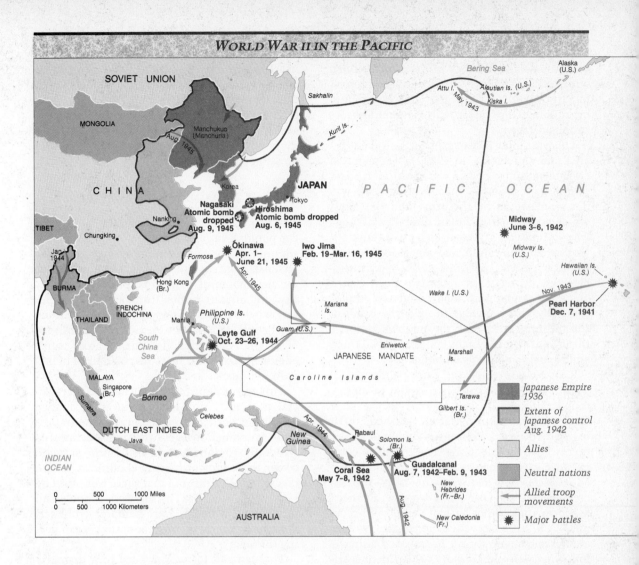

SOVIET UNION

MONGOLIA

Manchukuo
(Manchuria)

Aug. 1945

CHINA

TIBET

Chungking

BURMA

Jan.
1944

THAILAND

FRENCH
INDOCHINA

Nanking

Formosa

Hong Kong
(Br.)

Korea

JAPAN

Tokyo

Nagasaki
Atomic bomb
dropped
Aug. 9, 1945

Hiroshima
Atomic bomb dropped
Aug. 6, 1945

Okinawa
Apr. 1–
June 21, 1945

Iwo Jima
Feb. 19–Mar. 16, 1945

Apr. 1945

Manila

Philippine Is.
(U.S.)

Leyte Gulf
Oct. 23–26, 1944

South
China
Sea

MALAYA

Singapore
(Br.)

Borneo

Celebes

DUTCH EAST INDIES

Java

INDIAN
OCEAN

Sumatra

New
Guinea

Coral Sea
May 7–8, 1942

Rabaul

Solomon Is.
(Br.)

Guadalcanal
Aug. 7, 1942–Feb. 9, 1943

New
Hebrides
(Fr.–Br.)

New Caledonia
(Fr.)

AUSTRALIA

Apr. 1944

Aug. 1942

PACIFIC   OCEAN

Bering Sea

Alaska
(U.S.)

Sakhalin

Attu I.
May 1943

Aleutian Is. (U.S.)
Kiska I.

Kuril Is.

Midway
June 3–6, 1942

Midway Is.
(U.S.)

Hawaiian Is.
(U.S.)

Nov. 1943

Pearl Harbor
Dec. 7, 1941

Wake I. (U.S.)

Mariana
Is.

Guam (U.S.)

Eniwetok

JAPANESE MANDATE

Marshall
Is.

Caroline Islands

Tarawa

Gilbert Is.
(Br.)

Japanese Empire
1936

Extent of
Japanese control
Aug. 1942

Allies

Neutral nations

→ Allied troop
movements

✴ Major battles

0   500   1000 Miles
0   500   1000 Kilometers

---

bloody job of driving the Japanese back along the north coast of New Guinea.

By early 1943, the defensive phase of the war with Japan was over. The enemy surge had been halted in both the Central and the Southwest Pacific, and the United States was ready to move back toward the Philippines. Just as Russia had broken German power in Europe, the United States had halted the Japanese. And, like the Soviet plans for Eastern Europe, America expected to reap the rewards of victory by dominating the Pacific in the future.

✦ THE HOME FRONT

World War II had a greater impact than the Depression on the future of American life. While American soldiers and sailors fought abroad, the nation underwent sweeping social and economic changes at home.

American industry made the nation's single most important contribution to victory. The manufacturing plants that had run at half-capacity through the 1930s now hummed with activity. In Detroit, automobile assembly lines were converted to produce tanks and airplanes with the same efficiency as they once turned out cars. Shipmakers were just as productive. In part, America won the battle of the Atlantic by building ships faster than German U-boats could sink them.

This vast industrial expansion, however, created many problems. In 1942, FDR appointed Donald Nelson to head a War Production Board (WPB). An easy-going man, Nelson soon was out-maneuvered by the army and the navy, which preferred to negotiate directly with large corporations. Shortages of such critical materials as steel, aluminum, and copper led to an allocation system based on military priorities. However, through tax incentives for industrialists and rationing of import products, American industries were able to meet the needs of the military. All in all, the nation's factories turned out twice as many goods as did German and Japanese industry combined.

Roosevelt revealed the same tendency toward compromise in directing the economic mobilization as he had in shaping the New Deal. When administrators clashed, FDR worked toward a consensus and fair settlements. The president was also forced to compromise with Congress, which pared down the administration's requests for large tax increases. Half the cost of the war was financed by borrowing; the other half came from revenues. A $7 billion revenue increase in 1942 included so many first-time taxpayers that in the following year the Treasury Department instituted a new practice—withholding income taxes from workers' wages.

The result of this wartime economic explosion was a growing affluence. Despite the federal incentives to business, heavy excess-profit taxes and a 94-percent tax rate for the very rich kept the wealthy from benefiting unduly. The huge increase in federal spending, from $9 billion in 1940 to $98 billion in 1944, spread through American society. A government agreement with labor unions in 1943 held wage rates to a 15-percent increase, but the long hours of overtime doubled and sometimes tripled the weekly paychecks of factory workers.

Farmers shared in the new prosperity as their incomes quadrupled between 1940 and 1945. Most important, this rising income ensured postwar prosperity. Workers and farmers saved their money, channeling much of it into government war bonds, waiting for the day when they could buy the cars and home appliances they could not have during the long years of depression and war.

A NATION ON THE MOVE

The war led to a vast migration of the American population. Young men left their homes for training camps and then for service overseas. Defense workers and their families moved to the new booming shipyards, munitions factories, and aircraft plants. Rural areas lost population while coastal regions, especially along the Pacific and Gulf of Mexico, drew millions of people. California had the greatest gains, adding nearly 2 million to its population in less than five years.

This movement of people caused severe social problems. Housing was in short supply. Migrating workers crowded into house trailers and boardinghouses, bringing unexpected windfalls to landlords. Family life suffered under these crowded living conditions; an increase in the number of marriages was offset by a rising divorce rate. In addition, schools and other social agencies were hardpressed to service the remarkable baby boom that began during the war.

The demand for workers led to a dramatic rise in female employment. Women entered industries once viewed as exclusively male; by the end of the war, they worked alongside men tending blast furnaces in steel mills and welding hulls in shipyards. The wartime experience helped undermine the concept that woman's only proper place was in the home.

African Americans shared in the wartime migration, but their social and economic gains were limited by persistent racial prejudice. Nearly 1 million served in the armed forces, but few saw combat. The army placed blacks in segregated units and used them for service and construction tasks. The navy was even worse,

"Rosie the Riveter," a song extolling women workers, was very popular during the war. This photograph from Life *was taken by Margaret Bourke-White.*

relegating them to menial jobs until late in the war.

Black civilians fared a little better. In 1941, black labor leader A. Philip Randolph threatened a massive march on Washington to force Roosevelt to end racial discrimination in defense industries and government employment and to integrate the armed forces. FDR compromised, persuading Randolph to call off the march and drop his integration demand in return for an executive order creating a Fair Employment Practices Committee (FEPC) to ban racial discrimination in war industries. As a result, black employment by the federal government rose sharply; the FEPC proved less successful in the private sector. The nationwide shortage of labor was more influential than the FEPC in the rise in black employment during wartime. Blacks moved from the rural South to northern and western cities, finding occupa-

tions in the automobile, aircraft, and shipbuilding industries.

This movement of an estimated 700,000 people helped transform black/white relations from a regional issue into a national concern that could no longer be ignored. The limited housing and recreational facilities for both black and white war workers created tensions that led to urban race riots. The worst riot took place in Detroit in June 1943; twenty-three blacks and nine whites died in the fighting. These outbursts of racial violence fueled the resentments that would grow into the postwar civil rights movement. For most blacks, despite the economic gain, World War II was a reminder of the inequality of American life.

One-third of a million Mexican Americans served in the armed forces and shared some of the same experiences as blacks. At home, Spanish-speaking people left the rural areas of the Southwest for jobs in the cities. Despite low wages and union resistance, they managed to improve their economic position substantially. But they still faced discrimination based both on skin color and language, most notably in the Los Angeles "zoot suit" riots in 1943, when white servicemen attacked Mexican-American youths dressed in their distinctive long jackets and pegged trousers. The racial prejudice heightened feelings of ethnic identity and led

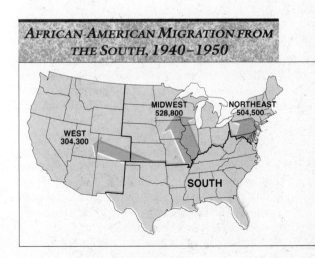

AFRICAN-AMERICAN MIGRATION FROM THE SOUTH, 1940–1950

MIDWEST 528,800

NORTHEAST 504,500

WEST 304,300

SOUTH

returning Mexican-American veterans to form organizations to press for equal rights in the future.

A tragic counterpoint to the voluntary movement of American workers in search of jobs was the forced relocation of 120,000 Japanese Americans from the West Coast. Responding to racial fears in California after Pearl Harbor, FDR approved an army order in February 1942 to move both the Issei (Japanese Americans who had emigrated from Japan) and the Nisei (people of Japanese ancestry born in the United States and therefore American citizens) to concentration-camp-like detention centers in the interior. Forced to dispose of their farms and businesses at distress prices, the Japanese Americans lost not only their liberty but also most of their worldly goods. Herded into detention centers, they lived as prisoners in tar-papered barracks behind barbed wire, guarded by armed troops.

Appeals to the Supreme Court proved fruitless; the justices upheld relocation on the grounds of national security in wartime. Beginning in 1943, individual Japanese Americans could win release by pledging their loyalty and finding a job away from the West Coast, but the camps were not closed down until March 1946. Although the Japanese Americans never experienced the torture and mass death of the German concentration camps, their treatment was a disgrace to a nation fighting for freedom and democracy.

WIN-THE-WAR POLITICS

Roosevelt used World War II to strengthen his leadership and maintain Democratic political dominance. As war brought about prosperity and removed the economic discontent that had sustained the New Deal, FDR announced that "Dr. New Deal" had given way to "Dr. Win-the-War." Congress, already controlled by a conservative coalition of southern Democrats and northern Republicans, had almost slipped into GOP hands in 1942. With very low voter turnout, the Republicans won 44 new seats in the House and 9 in the Senate.

In 1944, Roosevelt responded to the Democratic slippage by dropping Henry Wallace, his liberal vice-president, for Harry Truman, a moderate and down-to-earth Missouri senator who was acceptable to all factions of the Democratic party. Equally important, FDR received increased political support from organized labor.

The Republicans nominated Thomas E. Dewey, a moderate from New York who made Roosevelt's age and health the primary issues, along with the charge that the Democrats were soft on communism. His foreign policy statements were far more internationalist than previous Republican policy. Indeed, Dewey pioneered a bipartisan approach to foreign policy. He accepted wartime planning for the future United Nations and kept the issue of an international organization out of the campaign.

FDR's vitality impressed the voters, however, and in November 1944 he swept back into office for a fourth term. But the war years had taken their toll. The president, suffering from high blood pressure and congestive heart failure, had only a few months left to lead the nation.

VICTORY

World War II ended with surprising swiftness. Once the Axis tide had been turned by 1943 in Europe and Asia, it did not take long for Russia, the United States, and Britain to mount the offensives that drove Germany and Japan back across the vast areas they had conquered and set the stage for their final defeat.

The long-awaited second front finally came on June 6, 1944. For two years, the United States and England had concentrated on building up an invasion force of nearly 3 million troops and a vast armada of ships and landing craft to carry them across the English Channel. In hopes of catching Hitler by surprise, Eisenhower chose the Normandy peninsula, where the absence of good harbors had led to lighter German fortifications.

D-Day was originally set for June 5, but bad weather forced a delay. At dawn on June 6, the British and American troops fought their way ashore along a forty-mile stretch of beach, encountering stiff German resistance at several points. By the end of the day, however, Eisenhower had won his beachhead; a week later, more than 300,000 men were slowly pushing back the German forces through the hedgerows of Normandy. The breakthrough came on July 25 at Saint Lô, opening a gap for General George Patton's Third Army. Soon American forces liberated Paris and reached the Rhine River, but a shortage of supplies, especially gasoline, forced a three-month halt.

Hitler took advantage of this breathing spell to deliver a daring counterattack. In mid-December, the remaining German armored divisions burst through a weak point in the Allied lines in the Ardennes Forest, planning to cut off nearly one third of Eisenhower's forces. The gamble, however, failed. By committing nearly all his reserves to the Battle of the Bulge, Hitler had delayed Eisenhower's advance into Germany, but he had fatally weakened German resistance in the West.

The end came quickly. During the spring of 1945, both Russian and American troops moved toward Berlin. A massive Russian offensive began in mid-January and swept across the Oder River. General Bradley's troops crossed the Rhine, and allied forces captured the industrial Ruhr basin. In April the two armies met at the Elbe River. With the Red Army already in the suburbs of Berlin, Adolf Hitler committed suicide on April 30. A week later, on May 7, 1945, Eisenhower accepted the unconditional surrender of all German forces. Just eleven months and a day after the landing in Normandy, the Allied forces had brought the war in Europe to a successful end.

War Aims and Wartime Diplomacy

The American contribution to Hitler's defeat was relatively minor compared to the damage inflicted by the Soviet Union. As his armies overran Poland and the Balkan countries, Joseph Stalin was determined to retain control over this region, which had been the historic pathway for Western invasion into Russia. Delay in opening the second front and an innate distrust of the West convinced the Soviets that they should maximize their territorial gains by imposing Communist regimes on Eastern Europe.

American postwar goals were quite different. Now believing that the failure to join the League of Nations in 1919 had led to the coming of World War II, the American people and their leaders vowed to put their faith in a new attempt at collective security. At Moscow in 1943, Secretary of State Hull won Russian agreement to participate in a future world organization at the war's end. In the first wartime Big Three conference, held at Teheran, Iran, in late 1943, Stalin reaffirmed his commitment and also indicated to FDR that Russia would enter the war against Japan once Germany was defeated.

By the time the Big Three met again at Yalta, in February 1945, the military situation favored the Russians. Stalin drove a series of hard bargains. He refused to give up his plans for Communist domination of Poland and the Balkans, although he did agree to hold free elections in Eastern Europe. More important for the United States, Stalin promised to enter the Pacific war three months after Germany surrendered. In return, Roosevelt offered extensive concessions in Asia, including Russian control over Manchuria. While neither a sellout nor a betrayal, as some critics have charged, Yalta was a diplomatic victory for the Soviets—one that reflected Russia's major contribution to a victory in Europe.

For the President, the long journey to Yalta proved to be too much. In early April 1945, FDR left Washington for Warm Springs, Georgia, where he had always been able to relax. He was sitting for his portrait at midday on April 12, 1945, when he suddenly complained of a "terrific headache," then slumped forward and died. The nation mourned a man who had gallantly met the challenges of depression and global war but had not lived to see the final victory. Unfortunately, he had taken no steps to prepare his successor for the difficult problems that lay ahead.

The defeat of Nazi Germany dissolved the bond between the United States and the Soviet Union in World War II. With very different histories, cultures, and ideologies, the two nations had little in common beyond their enmity toward Hitler. It was now up to the inexperienced Harry Truman to deal with the growing rift that was destined to develop into the future Cold War.

TRIUMPH AND TRAGEDY IN THE PACIFIC

The total defeat of Germany in May 1945 turned all eyes toward Japan. The American forces were moving swiftly; by the end of 1944 they had secured bases for further advances and were building airfields for American B-29s to begin a deadly bombardment of the Japanese home islands. In addition, by the end of the year, General MacArthur had retaken the Philippines. The Japanese navy, in a Pacific version of the Battle of the Bulge, launched a daring three-pronged attack on the American invasion fleet in Leyte Gulf. The U.S. Navy rallied to blunt all three Japanese thrusts, sinking four carriers and ending any further Japanese naval threat.

The defeat of Japan was now only a matter of time. The United States had three possible ways to proceed. The military favored a full-scale invasion and estimated that they would

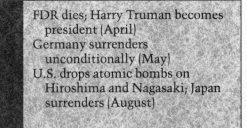

These traumatized victims of the first A-bomb blast, August 6, 1945, over Hiroshima seek first aid a few hours after the explosion.

suffer hundreds of thousands of casualties. Diplomats suggested a negotiated peace, urging that the United States modify the unconditional-surrender formula to permit Japan to retain the institution of the emperor.

The third possibility involved the highly secret Manhattan Project. Since 1939, the United States had spent $2 billion to develop an atomic bomb based on the fission of radioactive uranium and plutonium. Scientists, many of them refugees from Europe, worked at the University of Chicago, Oak Ridge, Tennessee, Hanford, Washington, and a remote laboratory in Los Alamos, New Mexico, to perfect this deadly new weapon. On July 16, 1945, they successfully tested the first atomic bomb in the New Mexico desert, creating a fireball brighter than several suns and a telltale mushroom cloud that rose some 40,000 feet above an enormous crater in the desert floor.

Informed of this achievement upon his arrival at Potsdam, President Truman authorized the army air force to use the atomic bomb against Japan. He followed the recommendation of a committee headed by Secretary of War Henry L. Stimson to drop the bomb on a Japanese city without any prior warning. Both Truman and Stimson viewed the decision as a legitimate wartime measure, one designed to save the hundreds of thousands of American and Japanese lives that would be lost in a full-scale invasion.

Weather conditions on the morning of August 6 dictated the choice of Hiroshima as the bomb's target. The explosion incinerated four square miles of the city and killed more than 60,000 people instantly. Two days later, Russia entered the war against Japan, and the next day, August 9, the United States dropped a second bomb on Nagasaki. There were no more atomic bombs available, but no more were needed. Japan surrendered unconditionally on August 14, 1945. Three weeks later, Japan signed a formal capitulation agreement on the decks of the battleship *Missouri* in Tokyo Bay to bring World War II to its official close.

For the first time, the nation's military potential had been reached; in 1945, it was unquestionably the strongest country on the earth. In the future, the United States would be involved in all parts of the world. And despite its enormous strength in 1945, the nation's new world role would encompass failure and frustration as well as power and dominion.

The legacy of war was equally strong at home. Four years of fighting brought about industrial recovery and unparalleled prosperity. The old pattern of unregulated free enterprise was as much a victim of the war as of the New Deal; big government and huge deficits had now become the norm as economic control passed from New York and Wall Street to Washington and Pennsylvania Avenue. The war led to far-reaching changes in American society that would only become apparent decades later. Such distinctive patterns of recent American life as the baby boom and the growth of the Sunbelt can be traced back to wartime origins. The war was a watershed in twentieth-century

America, ushering in a new age of global concerns and domestic upheaval.

☙ RECOMMENDED READING

The best general account of American attitudes toward the world in the 1920s can be found in Warren I. Cohen, *America Without Tears* (1987). On American foreign policy in the period between the wars, see Selig Adler, *The Uncertain Giant 1921–1941* (1965); Robert H. Ferrell, *Peace in Their Time* (1952); Michael J. Hogan, *Informal Entente* (1977); Melvin P. Leffler, *The Elusive Quest* (1978); and Roger Dingman, *Power in the Pacific* (1976).

Diplomatic developments in the 1930s are covered in Robert Dallek, *Franklin D. Roosevelt and American Foreign Policy, 1932–1945* (1979); Dorothy Borg, *The United States and the Far Eastern Crisis of 1933–1938* (1964); Irwin F. Gellman, *Good Neighbor Diplomacy* (1979); Manfred Jonas, *Isolationism in America, 1935–1941* (1966); and Robert A. Divine, *The Illusion of Neutrality* (1962).

Examinations of Roosevelt's policies during World War II include Robert Sherwood, *Roosevelt and Hopkins* (1948); James M. Burns, *Roosevelt: Soldier of Freedom* (1970); and Gaddis Smith, *American Diplomacy during the Second World War* (1964). For details of the American entry into the war, see William L. Langer and S. Everett Gleason, *The Challenge to Isolation* (1950) and *The Undeclared War* (1953); Robert A. Divine, *The Reluctant Belligerent*, 2 ed. (1979); Waldo Heinrichs, *Threshold of War* (1988); Roberta Wohlstetter, *Pearl Harbor: Warning and Decision* (1962); and Gordon W. Prange, *At Dawn We Slept* (1981).

Military and strategic aspects of World War II are covered in A. Russell Buchanan, *The United States and World War II*, 2 vols. (1964). For wartime diplomacy, see Herbert Feis, *Churchill, Roosevelt and Stalin* (1957); Michael Schaller, *The U.S. Crusade in China, 1936–1945* (1979); and Ralph B. Levering, *American Opinion and the Russian Alliance, 1939–1945* (1976). David Wyman assesses American responsibility for the Holocaust in *The Abandonment of the Jews* (1985).

On the atomic bomb, see Richard G. Hewlett and Oscar E. Anderson, *The New World, 1939–1946* (1962); Richard Rhodes, *The Making of the Atomic Bomb* (1987); and Martin Sherwin, *A World Destroyed* (1975). The two best accounts of the home front are Richard Polenberg, *War and Society* (1972), and John W. Blum, *V Was for Victory* (1976). Social developments during World War II are examined in Roger Daniels, *Concentration Camps USA* (1971); Karen Anderson, *Wartime Women* (1981); and Neil A. Wynn, *The Afro-Americans and the Second World War* (1976).

28 TRUMAN AND THE COLD WAR

THE COLD WAR BEGINS

CONTAINMENT

THE COLD WAR EXPANDS

THE COLD WAR AT HOME

"I am getting ready to go see Stalin and Churchill," President Truman wrote to his mother in July 1945, "and it is a chore." On board the cruiser *Augusta*, the new president continued to complain about the trip to Potsdam in his diary. Halfway around the world, Joseph Stalin left Moscow a day late because of a slight heart attack. Obsessed with security and hating to fly, he traveled to Potsdam, a suburb of Berlin, by rail. He was ready to claim the spoils of war.

The two men, one the veteran revolutionary who had been in power for two decades, the other an untested leader in office for barely three months, symbolized the enormous differences that now separated the wartime allies. Stalin was above all the realist. Brutal in securing total control at home, he was more flexible

in his foreign policy, bent on exploiting Russia's victory in World War II rather than aiming at world domination. Cunning and caution were the hallmarks of his diplomatic style. Truman, in contrast, personified traditional Wilsonian idealism. Lacking Roosevelt's guile, the new president placed his faith in international cooperation. Like many Americans, he believed implicitly in his country's innate goodness. Self-assured to the point of cockiness, he came to Potsdam clothed in the armor of self-righteousness.

Truman accepted Stalin at face value, believing he could deal with the Soviet leader. Together with Winston Churchill and his replacement, Clement Attlee, whose Labor party had just triumphed in British elections, Truman and Stalin clashed over such difficult issues as reparations, the Polish border, and the fate of eastern Europe. Truman tried to move the agenda along briskly, and he was upset by the constant delays. In an indirect, roundabout way, he informed Stalin of the existence of the atomic bomb. Truman offered no details, and the impassive Stalin asked for none, commenting only that he hoped the United States would make "good use of it against the Japanese."

Reparations proved to be the crucial issue at Potsdam. The Russians wanted to rebuild their war-ravaged economy with German industry; the United States feared it would be saddled with the entire cost of caring for the defeated Germans. A compromise was finally reached. Each side would take reparations primarily from its own occupation zone, a solution that foreshadowed the future division of Germany. "Because they could not agree on 'how to govern Europe'," wrote historian Daniel Yergin, Truman and Stalin "began to divide it."

The conference thus ended on an apparent note of harmony; beneath the surface, however, the bitter antagonism of the Cold War was festering. America and Russia, each distrustful of the other, were preparing for a long and bitter confrontation. A dozen years later, Truman reminisced to an old associate about Potsdam. He recalled his innocence and Stalin's duplicity. Then he added ruefully, "And I liked the little son of a bitch. . . ."

THE COLD WAR BEGINS

The conflict between the United States and the Soviet Union began gradually. For two years, the nations tried to adjust their differences, over the division of Europe, postwar economic aid, and the atomic bomb, through discussion and negotiation. The Council of Foreign Ministers provided the forum. Beginning in London during the fall of 1945, and meeting with their Russian counterparts in Paris, New York, and Moscow, American diplomats searched for a way to live in peace with a suspicious Soviet Union.

THE DIVISION OF EUROPE

The fundamental disagreement was over who would control postwar Europe. In the east, the Red Army had swept over Poland and the Balkans, laying the basis for Soviet domination there. American and British forces had liberated Western Europe, from Scandinavia to Italy. The Russians were intent on imposing Communist governments loyal to Moscow in the Soviet sphere. The United States, on the other hand, upheld the principle of national self-determination. The Soviets saw this demand for free elections as subversive. Suspecting American duplicity, Stalin brought down an "Iron Curtain" (Churchill's phrase) from the Baltic to the Adriatic as he created a series of satellite governments.

Germany was the key. The temporary zones of occupation gradually hardened into permanent lines of division. Ignoring the Potsdam Conference agreement that the country be treated as an economic unit, the United States and Great Britain by 1946 were refusing to permit the Russians to take reparations from the industrial Western zones. The United States and England merged their zones and championed the idea of the unification of all Germany. Russia, fearing a resurgence of German military power, responded by intensifying the communization of its zone, which included the jointly occupied city of Berlin. By 1947, England, France, and the United States were laying plans to transfer their authority to an independent West Germany.

The Soviet Union consolidated its grip on Eastern Europe in 1946 and 1947. One by one, Communist governments took power in Poland, Hungary, Rumania, and Bulgaria, each ultimately controlled by Stalin. The climax came in March 1948 when a coup in Czechoslovakia overthrew a democratic government and gave the Soviets a strategic foothold in Central Europe.

The division of Europe was an inevitable outgrowth of World War II. Both sides were intent on imposing their values—the Soviets stood in Eastern Europe, and the United States and Brit-

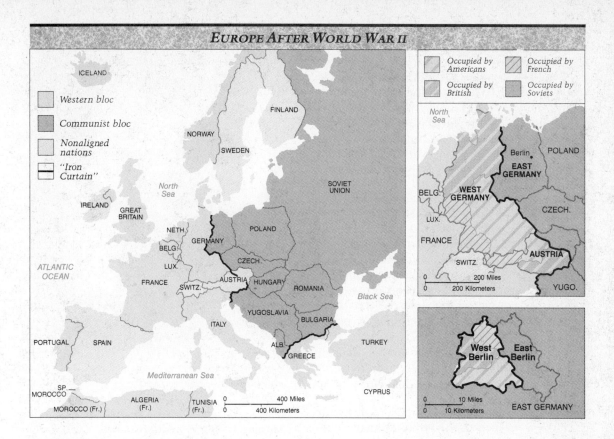

Western bloc

Communist bloc

Nonaligned nations

"Iron Curtain"

Occupied by Americans

Occupied by British

Occupied by French

Occupied by Soviets

ain were present in Germany, France, and Italy. A frank recognition of competing spheres of influence might have avoided further escalation of tension. But the Western nations, remembering Hitler's aggression in the 1930s, began to see Stalin as an equally dangerous threat to their well-being. Instead of accepting him as a cautious leader bent on protecting Russian security, they perceived him as an aggressive dictator leading a Communist drive for world domination.

WITHHOLDING ECONOMIC AID

The Second World War had inflicted enormous damage on Russia in terms of lost lives, de-

stroyed factories, and torn up railroad track. The industrialization that Stalin had achieved at such great sacrifice in the 1930s had been badly set back; even agricultural production had fallen by half during the war. Outside aid and assistance were vital for the reconstruction of the Soviet Union. American leaders knew of Russia's plight and hoped to use it to good advantage. Truman was convinced that economically "we held all the cards and the Russians had to come to us."

There were two possible forms of postwar assistance—loans and Lend-Lease. In January 1945, the Soviets requested a $6-million loan to finance postwar reconstruction. Despite initial American encouragement, FDR deferred action on this request; as relations with Russia cooled, the chances for action dimmed. By the war's end, the loan request, though never formally turned down, was dead.

Lend-Lease proved no more successful. On May 11, 1945, Truman terminated all Lend-Lease shipments to Russia, including those already at sea. The State Department saw the action as applying "leverage against the Soviet Union"; Stalin termed it "brutal." Heeding Russian protests, Truman resumed Lend-Lease shipments, but only until the war was over in August. After that, all Lend-Lease ended.

Deprived of American assistance, the Russians were forced to rebuild their economy through reparations, which they extracted from their zone of Germany, Eastern Europe, and Manchuria. Slowly the Russian economy recovered from the war, but the bitterness over the American refusal to extend aid convinced Stalin of Western hostility and thus deepened the growing antagonism.

The Atomic Dilemma

Overshadowing all else was the atomic bomb. The new weapon raised problems that would have been difficult for friendly nations to resolve. Given the uneasy state of Russian-American relations, the effect was disastrous.

The wartime policy followed by Roosevelt and Churchill insured a postwar nuclear arms race. Instead of informing their major ally of the developing atomic bomb, they kept it a closely guarded secret. Stalin learned of the Manhattan Project through espionage and responded by starting a Soviet atomic program in 1943. By the time Truman told Stalin of the weapon's existence at Potsdam, the Russians were well on the way to making their own bomb.

After the war, the United States developed a disarmament plan based on turning control of fissionable material, then the processing plants, and ultimately its stockpile of bombs over to an international agency. Later, Bernard Baruch, whom Truman chose to present the plan to the UN, added provisions aimed at imposing sanctions against violators and exempt-

"Don't mind me—just go right on talking."

Cartoonist Herblock warns of the worldwide menace of nuclear warfare. Mr. Bomb measures the earth for a coffin, negotiators and all.

ing the international agency from the UN veto. Ignoring scientists who pleaded for a more cooperative position, Baruch followed instead the advice of Army Chief of Staff Dwight D. Eisenhower, who cited the rapid demobilization of American armed forces to argue that "we cannot at this time limit our capability to produce or use this weapon." In effect, the Baruch Plan, with its multiple stages and emphasis on inspection, would preserve the American atomic monopoly for the indefinite future.

The Soviets responded predictably. They called for a total ban on the production and use of the new weapon as well as the destruction of all existing bombs. The Russian proposal was founded on the same perception of national self-interest as the American plan. The Russian army was still relatively strong, and the Soviet leaders wished to use its conventional strength to the utmost by outlawing the atomic bomb.

No agreement was possible. Neither the United States nor the Soviet Union could abandon its position without surrendering a vital national interest. America stressed the need for inspection and control; Russia advocated immediate disarmament. The two superpowers agreed to disagree. Trusting neither each other nor any form of international cooperation, each concentrated on taking maximum advantage of its wartime gains. Thus the Russians exploited the territory they had conquered in Europe while the United States retained its economic and strategic advantages over the Soviet Union. The result was the Cold War.

CONTAINMENT

A major departure in American foreign policy occurred in January 1947 when General George C. Marshall became secretary of state. He had the capacity to think in broad, strategic terms. An extraordinarily good judge of ability, he relied on gifted subordinates to handle the day-to-day implementation of his policies. In the months after taking office, he came to rely on two exceptionally gifted men in particular: Dean Acheson and George Kennan.

Acheson, an experienced Washington lawyer and bureaucrat, was appointed undersecretary of state and given free rein by Marshall to conduct American diplomacy. As an ardent Anglophile, he wanted to see the United States take over a faltering Britain's role as the supreme arbiter of world affairs. Recalling the lesson taught by the Munich Conference of 1938, he opposed appeasement and advocated a policy of negotiating only from strength.

Marshall's other mainstay was George Kennan, the Soviet expert who headed the newly created Policy Planning Staff. A career foreign-service officer, he had served in Moscow, where he developed a profound distrust for the Soviet regime. He believed that only a strong and sustained resistance could halt the outward flow of Russian power. In the spring of 1947, a sense of crisis impelled Marshall, Acheson, and Kennan to set out on a new course in American diplomacy: "A long-term, patient but firm containment of Russian expansionist tendencies." The new policy both consolidated the evolving postwar anticommunism and established guidelines that would shape America's role in the world for the next two decades.

THE TRUMAN DOCTRINE

The initial step came in response to an urgent British request. On February 21, 1947, the British informed the United States that they could no longer afford to aid the anti-Communist governments in Greece or Turkey. Believing that the Russians were responsible for the strife in Greece (in fact, they were not), Marshall, Acheson, and Kennan quickly decided that the United States would have to take over Britain's role in the eastern Mediterranean.

Attempting to secure congressional support for their policy, Acheson warned that if Greece went Communist, it would threaten Iran, all the Mideast, Africa, Italy, and France. The bipartisan group of congressional leaders was deeply impressed. Finally, Republican Senator Arthur M. Vandenberg spoke up, saying he would support the president, but adding that to ensure public backing, Truman would have to "scare hell" out of the American people.

The president followed Vandenberg's advice. On March 12, 1947, he asked Congress for $400 million for military and economic assistance to Greece and Turkey. He made clear that more was involved than just these two countries, that America must aid free peoples resisting subjugation. After a brief debate, both the House and the Senate approved the program.

The Truman Doctrine marked an informal declaration of cold war against the Soviet Union. Truman used the crisis in Greece to secure congressional approval and build a national consensus for the policy of containment. In less than two years, the civil war in Greece ended, but the American commitment to oppose Communist expansion, whether by internal subversion or external aggression, placed the United States on a collision course with the Soviet Union around the globe.

THE MARSHALL PLAN

By 1947 many Americans felt that Western Europe, far more vital to U.S. interests than the eastern Mediterranean, was open to Soviet penetration. The problem was economic in nature. World War II had taken a terrible toll on England, France, Italy, and other European countries. Food was scarce, industrial machinery was broken down and obsolete, and workers were demoralized by years of depression and war. Resentment and discontent led to growing Communist voting strength, especially in Italy and France. Unless the United States could do something to reverse the process, it seemed as though all Europe might drift into the Communist orbit.

Acheson believed that it was time to extend American "economic power" in Europe both "to call an effective halt to the Soviet Union's expansionism" and "to create a basis for political stability and economic well-being." The experts drew up a plan for the massive infusion of American capital to finance the economic recovery of Europe. In a speech at a Harvard commencement on June 5, 1947, Marshall presented the broad outline. He proposed American aid to foster the "political and social conditions in which free institutions can exist."

The fate of the Marshall Plan depended on the reaction of the Soviet Union and the U.S. Congress. Marshall had taken a gamble by including Russia in his offer of aid. At a meeting of the European nations in Paris in July 1947, the Soviet foreign minister ended the suspense by abruptly withdrawing. Neither Russia nor its satellites would take part, apparently because Moscow saw the Marshall Plan as an American attempt to weaken Soviet control over Eastern Europe. The other European countries then made a formal request for $17 billion in assistance over the next four years.

Congress responded cautiously to this proposal. The administration lobbied vigorously,

pointing out that the Marshall Plan would help the United States by stimulating trade with Europe as well as checking Soviet expansion. It was the latter argument, however, that proved decisive, especially after the Czech coup in March, 1948. Congress approved the Marshall Plan by heavy majorities. They quickly put forth loans, which generated a broad industrial revival in Western Europe that became self-sustaining by the 1950s. The threat of Communist domination faded, and a prosperous Europe proved to be a bonanza for American farmers, miners, and manufacturers.

THE WESTERN MILITARY ALLIANCE

The final phase of containment came in 1949 with the establishment of the North Atlantic Treaty Organization (NATO). NATO grew out of European fears of Russian military aggression. Recalling Hitler's tactics in the 1930s, the people of Western Europe wanted assurance that the United States would protect them from attack as they began to achieve economic recovery.

In January 1949, Truman called for a defense pact including the United States; ten European nations joined the United States and Canada in signing the North Atlantic Treaty. This historic departure from the traditional policy of isolation caused extensive debate, but the Senate ratified it in July 1949.

There were two main features of NATO. First, the United States committed itself to the defense of Europe in case of an attack. In effect, the United States was extending its atomic shield over Europe. The second feature was designed to reassure worried Europeans that the United States would honor this commitment. In late 1950, Truman appointed General Eisenhower to the post of NATO supreme commander and authorized the stationing of four American divisions in Europe to serve as the nucleus of the NATO army. Now any Russian assault would automatically involve American troops, a fact that would deter the Soviet Union.

The Western military alliance escalated the developing Cold War. It represented an overreaction to the Soviet danger. Americans and Europeans alike were attempting to apply the lesson of Munich to the Cold War. But there was no evidence of any Russian plan to invade Western Europe, and in the face of the American atomic bomb, none was likely. All NATO did was to intensify Russian fears of the West and thus increase the level of international tension. Russia and the Eastern bloc countries responded to NATO with the Warsaw Pact, a defense community of their own.

THE BERLIN BLOCKADE

The main Russian response to containment came in 1948 at the West's most vulnerable point. American, British, French, and Soviet troops each occupied a sector of Berlin, but the city was located more than one hundred miles within the Russian zone of Germany. Stalin decided to test his opponents' resolve by cutting off all rail and highway traffic to Berlin on June 20, 1948.

The timing was very awkward for Truman, who was locked in a tight presidential race. Immersed in election-year politics, he was caught unprepared by the Berlin blockade. The alternatives were not very appealing. The United States could withdraw its forces and lose not just the city, but the confidence of all Europe; it could try to send in reinforcements and fight for Berlin; or it could sit tight and attempt to find a diplomatic solution. Truman decided to fight to save Berlin.

The administration adopted a two-phase policy. The first part was a massive airlift of food, fuel, and supplies for both the troops and civilians in Berlin. Then, to guard against Soviet interruption of the airlift, Truman transferred sixty American B-29s, planes capable of delivering atomic bombs, to bases in England. The president was bluffing; the B-29s were not equipped with atomic bombs, but at the time the threat was effective.

For a few weeks, the world teetered on the edge of war. Stalin did not attempt to disrupt the flights to Berlin, but he rejected all American diplomatic initiatives. At any time the

The Berlin airlift of 1948–1949 broke the Soviet blockade. Called "Operation Vittles," it provided food and fuel for West Berliners. Children wait for candy dropped in handkerchief parachutes by American pilots.

Russians could have halted the airlift by jamming radar or shooting down the defenseless cargo planes. For Truman the tension was fierce. He feared America was dreadfully close to war.

Slowly the tension eased. The Russians did not shoot down any planes, and Truman was reelected, in part because the Berlin crisis had rallied the nation behind this leadership. In early 1949, the Soviets gave in, ending the blockade in return for another meeting of the Council of Foreign Ministers on Germany—a conclave that proved as unproductive as all the earlier ones.

The Berlin crisis marked the end of the initial phase of the Cold War. The airlift had given the United States a striking political victory, showing the world the triumph of American ingenuity over Russian stubbornness. Yet it could not disguise the fact that the Cold War had cut Europe in two. A divided Europe—politically, economically, and now militarily—was a far cry from the wartime hopes for a peaceful world. Such was the bitter legacy of World War II.

THE COLD WAR EXPANDS

The rivalry between the United States and the Soviet Union grew in the late 1940s and the early 1950s. Both sides ended the postwar demobilization and began to rebuild their military forces with new methods and advanced weapons. Equally significant, the diplomatic competition spread from Europe to Asia as each of the superpowers sought to enhance its influence in the Orient. By the time Truman left office in early 1953, the Cold War had taken on global proportions.

THE MILITARY DIMENSION

After World War II, American leaders were intent on reforming the nation's military system in light of the wartime experience. Two goals were uppermost. First, nearly everyone agreed in the aftermath of Pearl Harbor that the armed services should be unified into an integrated military system. The developing Cold War reinforced this decision. Equally important, planners realized the need for new institutions to coordinate military and diplomatic strategy so that the nation could cope effectively with threats to its security.

In 1947, Congress responded by passing the National Security Act, which established the Department of Defense. In addition, the act created the Central Intelligence Agency (CIA) to coordinate the intelligence-gathering activities of various government agencies. Finally, the act provided for a National Security Council (NSC) to advise the president on all matters regarding the nation's security.

Despite the appearance of equality among the services, the newly created air force quickly emerged as the dominant power in the atomic age. Both Truman and Congress allotted more money to the air force than to the other two branches of the military.

American military planners received a great boost in the fall of 1949 when the Soviet Union exploded its first atomic bomb. President Truman appointed a high-level committee to explore mounting an all-out effort to build a hydrogen bomb to maintain American nuclear supremacy.

Some scientists had technical objections to the H-bomb, while others opposed the new weapon on moral grounds, claiming its enormous destructive power (one thousand times greater than the atomic bomb) made it unthinkable. But Dean Acheson—who succeeded Marshall as secretary of state in early 1949—felt it was imperative that the United States develop the hydrogen bomb before the Soviet Union did. When Acheson presented the committee's favorable report to the president in January 1950, Truman took only seven minutes to decide to go ahead with the new bomb.

At the same time, Acheson ordered the Policy Planning Staff to draw up a new statement of national defense policy. NSC-68, as the document eventually became known, was based on the premise that the Soviet Union sought "to impose its absolute authority over the rest of the world" and thus "mortally challenged" the United States. Paul Nitze, who headed the Policy Planning Staff, advocated a massive expansion of American military power so that the United States could halt and overcome the Soviet threat. NSC-68 stood as a symbol of the Truman administration's determination to win the Cold War regardless of cost.

THE COLD WAR IN ASIA

The Soviet-American conflict developed more slowly in Asia. At Yalta, the two superpowers had agreed to a Far Eastern balance of power, with the Russians dominating Northeast Asia and the Americans in control of the Pacific, including Japan and its former island empire.

The United States moved quickly to consolidate its sphere of influence. General Douglas MacArthur, in charge of Japanese occupation, denied the Soviet Union any role in the reconstruction of Japan. Instead he supervised the transition of the Japanese government into a constitutional democracy in which Communists were barred from all government posts. The Japanese willingly renounced war in their new constitution, relying instead on American forces to protect their security. In addition, America held full control over the Marshall, Mariana, and Caroline Islands.

As defined at Yalta, China lay between the Soviet and American spheres. When World War II ended, the country was torn between Chiang Kai-shek's Nationalists in the South and Mao Tse-tung's Communists in the North. Although Chiang received American political and economic backing, his regime was corrupt, and a raging inflation rate devastated the Chinese middle classes and thus eroded his base of power. Mao used tight discipline and patriotic appeals to strengthen his hold on the peasantry and extend his influence. When the Soviets abruptly vacated Manchuria in 1946, Mao inherited control of this rich northern province. Ignoring American advice, Chiang rushed north to occupy Manchurian cities, overextending his supply lines and exposing his forces to Communist counterattack.

American policy aimed at averting a Chinese civil war by encouraging Chiang and Mao to form a coalition government. The policy failed. By 1947, as China plunged into full-scale civil war, the Truman administration had given up any meaningful effort to influence the outcome. Political mediation had failed, military intervention was out of the question, and a policy of continued American economic aid served only to appease domestic supporters of Chiang; 80 percent of the military supplies ended up in Communist hands.

The climax came at the end of the decade. Mao's forces drove the Nationalists out of Manchuria in late 1948 and advanced across the Yangtze River by mid-1949. Acheson released a lengthy White Paper justifying American policy in China on the grounds that the civil war there "was beyond the control of the government of the United States." Republican senators, however, disagreed, blaming American diplomats for sabotaging the Nationalists. While the domestic debate raged over responsibility for the loss of China, Chiang's forces fled the mainland for sanctuary on Formosa (Taiwan) in December 1949. Two months later, Mao and Stalin signed a Sino-Soviet treaty of mutual assistance that clearly placed China in the Russian orbit.

The American response to the Communist triumph in China was twofold. First, the State Department refused to recognize the legitimacy of the new regime in Peking, maintaining instead formal diplomatic relations with the Nationalists on Formosa. Then, to compensate for the loss of China, the United States focused on Japan as its main ally in Asia. The State Department encouraged the buildup of Japanese industry, and the Pentagon expanded American bases on the Japanese home islands and Okinawa. As it had done in Europe, the Cold War had now split Asia in two.

THE KOREAN WAR

The showdown between the United States and the Soviet Union in Asia came in Korea, which had been divided at the thirty-eighth parallel in 1945. The Russians occupied the industrial North, installing a Communist government under the leadership of Kim Il-Sung. In the

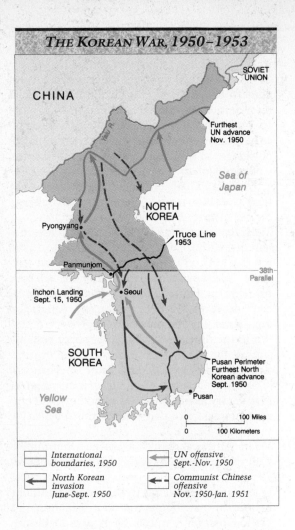

THE KOREAN WAR, 1950–1953

SOVIET UNION

CHINA

Furthest UN advance Nov. 1950

Sea of Japan

NORTH KOREA

Pyongyang

Truce Line 1953

Panmunjom

38th Parallel

Inchon Landing Sept. 15, 1950

Seoul

SOUTH KOREA

Yellow Sea

Pusan Perimeter Furthest North Korean advance Sept. 1950

Pusan

0   100 Miles
0   100 Kilometers

International boundaries, 1950

UN offensive Sept.-Nov. 1950

North Korean invasion June-Sept. 1950

Communist Chinese offensive Nov. 1950-Jan. 1951

eson, the president convened the UN Security Council and, taking advantage of a temporary Soviet boycott, secured a resolution condemning North Korea as an aggressor and calling on the member nations to engage in a collective-security action. Within a few days, American troops from Japan were in combat in South Korea. The conflict, which would last for more than three years, was technically a police action fought under UN auspices; in reality, the United States was at war with a Soviet satellite in Asia.

In the beginning, the fighting went badly as the North Koreans continued to drive down the peninsula. But by August, American forces had halted the Communist advance near Pusan. In September, General MacArthur changed the whole complexion of the war by carrying out a brilliant amphibious assault at Inchon, on the waist of Korea, cutting off and destroying most of the North Korean army in the South. Encouraged by this victory, Truman began to shift from his original goal of restoring the thirty-eighth parallel to a new one: the unification of Korea by military force.

The administration ignored warnings from Peking, sent by way of India, against an American invasion of North Korea. Both Acheson and MacArthur advised Truman that the Chinese would not enter the conflict. Rarely has an American president received worse advice. The UN forces crossed the thirty-eighth parallel in October, advanced confidently to the Yalu River in November, and then were completely routed by a massive Chinese counterattack that drove them out of all North Korea by December. MacArthur finally stabilized the fighting near the thirty-eighth parallel, but when Truman decided to give up his attempt to unify Korea, the general protested to Congress, calling for a renewed offensive and proclaiming, "There is no substitute for victory."

Truman courageously relieved the popular hero of the Pacific of his command on April 11, 1951. The Korean War then settled into a stalemate near the thirty-eighth parallel as truce talks with the Communists bogged down for the rest of Truman's term in office. The presi-

agrarian South, Syngman Rhee emerged as the American-sponsored ruler. The two superpowers pulled out most of their occupation forces by 1949. The Russians, however, helped train a well-equipped army in the North, while the United States gave much more limited military assistance to South Korea.

On June 25, 1950, the North Korean army suddenly crossed the thirty-eighth parallel in great strength. Whether Stalin ordered the invasion is unknown, but Truman saw the action as a clear-cut case of Soviet aggression reminiscent of the 1930s. Following the advice of Ach-

dent could take heart from the fact that he had achieved his primary goal, defense of South Korea and the principle of collective security. Yet by taking the gamble to unify Korea by force, he had confused the American people and humiliated the United States in the eyes of the world.

In the last analysis, the most significant result of the Korean conflict was massive American rearmament. The war led to the implementation of NSC-68—the army expanded to 3.5 million troops, the defense budget increased to $50 billion a year by 1952, and the United States acquired military bases in distant quarters of the world. America was now committed to waging a global contest against the Soviet Union with arms as well as words.

THE COLD WAR AT HOME

The Cold War cast a long shadow over American life in the late 1940s and early 1950s. Harry Truman tried to carry on the New Deal reform tradition he had inherited from FDR, but the American poeple were more concerned about events abroad. The Republican party used growing dissatisfaction with both postwar economic adjustment and fears of Communist penetration of the United States to revive its sagging fortunes and regain control of the White House in 1952 for the first time in twenty years.

TRUMAN'S TROUBLES AND VINDICATION

Matching his foreign policy successes with equal achievements at home was not easy for Harry S Truman. As a senator he had faithfully supported Roosevelt's policies, and he had earned a reputation as a hard-working, reliable legislator. But he was relatively unknown to the public, and his background as a Missouri county judge associated with Kansas City machine politics did not inspire confidence in his leadership abilities. Surprisingly well read, Tru-

man possessed sound judgment, the ability to reach decisions quickly, and a fierce and uncompromising sense of right and wrong.

Two weaknesses marred his performance in the White House. One was his fondness for old friends, which resulted in the appointment of many Missouri and Senate cronies to high office. These men brought little credit to his administration. Truman's other serious limitation was his lack of political vision. He tried to perpetuate FDR's New Deal, but he engaged in a running battle with Congress rather than pursuing a coherent legislative program.

The fact that the postwar mood was not conducive to a new outburst of reform, of course, handicapped Truman's performance. Not only were the American people enjoying material prosperity, but also the Cold War diverted attention from domestic problems. Congress did pass the Employment Act of 1946, which asserted the principle that the government was responsible for the state of the economy and created a Council of Economic Advisors to guide the president. But the original goal of mandatory federal planning to achieve full employment failed to survive the legislative process.

After the Republican victory in 1946, relations between the president and Congress became increasingly stormy. Truman successfully vetoed two GOP measures to give large tax cuts to the wealthy, but Congress overrode his veto of the Taft-Hartley Act in 1947. Designed to redress the imbalance in labor-management relations created by the Wagner Act, the Taft-Hartley Act outlawed specific unfair union practices, and it permitted the president to invoke an eighty-day cooling-off period to delay strikes that might endanger national health or safety.

Truman's political fortunes reached their lowest ebb in early 1948. Former Vice-President Henry A. Wallace announced his third-party (Progressive) candidacy in the presidential contest that year. Although Truman was renominated by the Democratic party, his prospects for victory looked very dim—especially after disgruntled Southerners, alarmed by Tru-

A jubilant Harry Truman, on the morning after his 1948 election win, displays the headline blazoned on the front page of the Chicago Tribune—a newspaper that believed the pollsters.

man's civil rights advocacy, bolted the Democratic party to nominate Strom Thurmond, the governor of South Carolina, on a States' Rights party ticket.

The defection of the Dixiecrats in the South and Wallace's liberal followers in the North led political experts to predict an almost certain victory for Republican candidate Governor Thomas E. Dewey of New York. While Dewey waged a cautious, uninspired campaign, Truman barnstormed around the country denouncing the "do-nothing" Republican Eightieth Congress. To the amazement of the pollsters, Truman won a narrow victory in November. The old Roosevelt coalition—farmers, organized labor, urban ethnic groups, and blacks—had held together, enabling Truman to remain in the White House and the Democrats to gain control of Congress.

There was one more reason for Truman's win in 1948. During the election, held at the height of the Berlin crisis, the GOP failed to challenge Truman's conduct of the Cold War. Locked in a tense rivalry with the Soviet Union, the American people saw no reason to reject a president who had countered aggression overseas with the Truman Doctrine and the Marshall Plan. Until the Republicans found a way to challenge Truman's Cold War policies, they had little chance to regain the White House.

THE LOYALTY ISSUE

Despite Truman's surprising victory in 1948, there was one area on which the Democrats were vulnerable. The fear of communism abroad that had led to the bipartisan containment policy could be used against them at home by politicians who were more willing to exploit the public's deep-seated anxiety.

Fear of radicalism has been a recurrent feature of American life since the early days of the Republic. The Cold War heightened the traditional belief that subversion from abroad endangered the Republic. Bold rhetoric from members of the Truman administration, portraying the men in the Kremlin as inspired revolutionaries bent on world conquest, frightened the American people. They viewed the Soviet Union as a successor of Nazi Germany—a totalitarian police state that threatened the basic liberties of a free people.

A series of revelations of Communist espionage activities reinforced these fears. A Soviet spy ring was uncovered in Canada in 1946, and the House Un-American Activities Committee held hearings that indicated Communist agents had flourished in government departments in the 1930s. Although Truman tried to dismiss the loyalty issue as a "red herring," he felt compelled to take protective measures, thus lending substance to the charges of subversion. In March 1947, he had initiated a loyalty program, ordering security checks on government employees in order to root out Communists. Originally intended to remove subversives for whom "reasonable grounds exist for belief that the person involved is disloyal," within four years the Loyalty Review Board was dismissing workers as security risks if there was "reasonable doubt" of their loyalty. Thousands of government workers lost their jobs, charged with guilt by association with radicals or with membership in left-wing organizations.

The most famous disclosure came in August 1948 when Whittaker Chambers, a repentant Communist, accused Alger Hiss of having been a Soviet spy in the 1930s. When Hiss, who had been a prominent State Department official, denied the charges, Chambers produced microfilms of confidential government documents that he claimed Hiss had given him in the late 1930s. Although the statute of limitations prevented a charge of treason against Hiss, he was convicted of perjury in January 1950 and sentenced to a five-year prison term.

Events abroad intensified the sense of danger. The Communist triumph in China in the fall of 1949 came as a shock; soon there were charges that "fellow travelers" in the State Department were responsible for "the loss of China." In September 1949, when the Truman administration announced that the Russians had detonated their first atomic bomb, the ending of America's nuclear monopoly was blamed on Soviet espionage. In early 1950, Klaus Fuchs—a British scientist who had worked on the wartime Manhattan Project—admitted giving the Russians vital information about the A-bomb.

A few months later, the government charged American Communists Ethel and Julius Rosenberg with conspiracy to transmit atomic secrets to the Soviet Union. They were found guilty of treason in 1951 and, despite their claims of innocence and worldwide appeals for clemency on their behalf, executed in 1953. Thus by the early 1950s, nearly all the ingredients were at hand for a new outburst of hysteria—fear of Russia, evidence of espionage, and a belief in a vast unseen conspiracy. The only element missing was a leader to release this new outburst of intolerance.

McCarthyism in Action

On February 12, 1950, Senator Joseph R. McCarthy of Wisconsin delivered a routine Lincoln's Birthday speech in Wheeling, West Virginia. This little known Republican suddenly attracted national attention when he declared, "I have here in my hand a list of 205—a list of names that were made known to the secretary of state as being members of the Communist party and who nevertheless are still working and shaping policy in the State Department." Although he never substantiated his charge, McCarthy's speech triggered a four-and-a-half-year crusade to hunt down alleged Communists in government. The stridency and sensationalism of the senator's accusations soon won the name "McCarthyism."

McCarthy's basic technique was the multiple untruth. He leveled a bevy of charges of

Three days before Julius and Ethel Rosenberg were executed for treason, their two young sons, ten and six years old, marched to the White House to plead for clemency for their parents.

treasonable activities in government. While officials were refuting his initial accusations, he brought forth a steady stream of new ones, so that the corrections never caught up with the latest blast. He failed to unearth a single confirmed Communist in government, but he kept the Truman administration in turmoil. He exploited the press with great skill, combining current accusations with promises of future disclosures to guarantee headlines.

The secret of McCarthy's power was the fear he engendered among his Senate colleagues. They believed McCarthy's opposition would doom their reelection bids. McCarthy delighted in making sweeping, startling charges of Communist sympathies against prominent public figures. A favorite target was aristocratic Secretary of State Dean Acheson, but General George Marshall and even fellow Republicans also were named in his charges.

These attacks on the wealthy, famous, and privileged won McCarthy a devoted national following, although the public opinion polls indicated his approval rating never rose above 50 percent. He drew a disproportionate backing from working-class Catholics and ethnic groups who normally voted Democratic. He offered a simple solution to the complicated Cold War: defeat the enemy at home rather than continue to engage in costly foreign-aid programs and entangling alliances abroad. Above all, McCarthy appealed to conservative Republicans in the Midwest who shared his right-wing views and felt cheated by Truman's upset victory in 1948. Even GOP leaders who viewed McCarthy's tactics with distaste quietly encouraged him to attack vulnerable Democrats.

THE REPUBLICANS
IN POWER

In 1952, the GOP capitalized on a growing sense of national frustration to capture the presidency. The stalemate in Korea and the second Red Scare created the desire for change; revelations of scandals by several individuals close to Truman intensified the feeling that someone needed to clean up "the mess in Washington." In Dwight D. Eisenhower, the

Senator Joseph McCarthy maintained a steady stream of unsubstantiated charges, always ready to make new accusations of Communist infiltration before the preceding ones could be proven untrue.

Republican party found the perfect candidate to explore what one senator called K C—Korea, communism, and corruption.

A war hero with amiable manner and a winning smile, Eisenhower seemed to have the gifts to unite a divided nation. While his vice-presidential running mate, Senator Richard M. Nixon of California, hammered away at the Democrats on communism and corruption, Ike promised that once elected he would go to Korea if necessary to bring "an early and honorable end" to the war. In the November election, Eisenhower handily defeated Adlai Stevenson.

Once elected, Eisenhower moved quickly to fulfill his campaign pledge. He went to Korea, assessed the battlefield options, ruled out a new offensive, and turned his attention to a diplomatic settlement, even hinting to China that he might use nuclear weapons to break the stalemate peace talks. That threat, together with the death of Joseph Stalin in early March, finally led to the signing of an armistice on July 27, 1953, which ended the fighting but left Korea divided—as it had been before the war—near the thirty-eighth parallel.

Eisenhower was less effective in dealing with the problem raised by Senator Joseph McCarthy. McCarthy did not end his crusade with the Republican victory in 1952. Instead, he used his new position as chairman of the Senate Committee on Government Operations as a base for ferreting out suspected Communists on the federal payroll. Eisenhower's advisors urged the president to use his own great prestige to stop McCarthy. But Ike refused such a confrontation, saying, "I will not get into a pissing contest with that skunk."

The Wisconsin senator finally overreached himself. In 1954, he uncovered an Army dentist suspected of disloyalty and proceeded to attack the upper echelons of the United States Army. The controversy culminated in the televised Army-McCarthy hearings. For six weeks, the senator revealed his crude, bullying behavior to the American people. Viewers were repelled by his frequent outbursts and by his attempt to slur the reputation of a young lawyer associated with the army counsel Joseph Welch. This last maneuver led Welch to condemn McCarthy for his "reckless cruelty" and ask rhetorically, as millions watched on television, "Have you no sense of decency, sir . . . ?"

Courageous Republicans, such as Margaret Chase Smith of Maine, joined with Democrats to bring about the Senate's censure of McCarthy in December 1954. The vote was 67 to 22. Once rebuked, McCarthy fell quickly from prominence. He died three years later virtually unnoticed and unmourned.

Yet his influence was profound. Not only did he paralyze national life with shameful activities, but he also helped impose a political and cultural conformity that froze dissent for the rest of the 1950s. Long after McCarthy's passing, the nation tolerated loyalty oaths for teachers, the banning of left-wing books in public libraries, and the blacklisting of entertainers in radio, television, and films. Freedom of expression was inhibited, and the opportunity to try out new ideas and approaches was lost as

CHRONOLOGY

1945	Truman meets Stalin at Potsdam Conference (July)
	World War II ends with Japanese surrender (August)
1946	Winston Churchill gives "Iron Curtain" speech
1947	Truman Doctrine announced to Congress (March)
	George Marshall outlines Marshall Plan (June)
	Truman orders loyalty program for government employees
1948	Soviets begin blockade of Berlin (June)
	Truman scores upset victory in presidential election
1949	North Atlantic Treaty signed in Washington
	Soviet Union tests its first atomic bomb (August)
1950	Truman authorizes building of hydrogen bomb (January)
	Senator Joseph McCarthy claims Communists in government (February)
	North Korea invades South Korea (June)
1951	Truman recalls MacArthur from Korea
1952	Dwight D. Eisenhower elected president
1953	Julius and Ethel Rosenberg executed for atomic-secrets spying
	Korean War truce signed at Panmunjom (July)

the United States settled into a sterile Cold War consensus.

While Dwight Eisenhower could claim that his policy of giving McCarthy enough rope to hang himself had worked, it is possible that a bolder and more forthright presidential attack on the senator might have spared the nation some of the excesses of the second Red Scare.

By the early 1950s, the Cold War had become an enduring reality of American life. The initial disagreements between the United States and the Soviet Union had settled down into a deadly rivalry with no end in sight. World War II had not led to an era of peace and tranquility and American world dominance. Although the United States emerged from the war more powerful than at any other time in the nation's history, it faced a seemingly endless struggle against a determined and dangerous foe. And as the second Red Scare had so vividly demonstrated, it was a contest that was bound to affect every aspect of American life in the postwar era.

❧ RECOMMENDED READING

The best general guide to American diplomacy since World War II is Walter LaFeber, *America, Russia and the Cold War, 1945–1950*, 5th ed. (1985). Other surveys of American foreign policy since 1945 include Stephen Ambrose, *Rise to Globalism*, 5th ed. (1988); Thomas G. Paterson, *Meeting the Communist Threat* (1988); and John Lewis Gaddis, *Strategies of Containment* (1982). Adam B. Ulam provides a perceptive summary of Soviet-American relations for this period in *The Rivals* (1971).

Gar Alperovitz began the revisionist controversy over the origins of the Cold War in *Atomic Diplomacy* (1965). Other revisionist accounts include Joyce Kolko and Gabriel Kolko, *The Limits of Power* (1972); Lawrence Wittner, *American Intervention in Greece, 1943–1949* (1982); and Thomas G. Paterson, *On Every Front* (1979). Post-revisionist studies include John L. Gaddis, *The United States and the Origins of the Cold War* (1972); and Daniel Yergin, *Shattered Peace* (1977).

The foreign policy of the Truman administration is covered in two works by Robert J. Donovan: *Conflict and Crisis* (1977) and *Tumultuous Years* (1982). See also Gaddis Smith, *Dean Acheson* (1972); Forrest Pogue, *George C. Marshall: Statesman, 1945–1959* (1987); Walter Isaacson and Evan Thomas, *The Wise Men* (1986); Michael Hogan, *The Marshall Plan* (1987); and Gregg Herken, *The Winning Weapon* (1980).

For the Cold War in the Far East, consult Akira Iriye, *The Cold War in Asia* (1974); and Russell D. Buhite, *Soviet-American Relations in Asia 1945–1954* (1982). Books on the Korean War include Bruce Cumings, *The Origins of the Korean War* (1981); Burton Kaufman, *The Korean War* (1986); and John W. Spanier, *The Truman-MacArthur Controversy and the Korean War* (1959). For the beginning of American involvement in Vietnam, consult Lloyd Gardner, *Approaching Vietnam* (1988).

Works on Eisenhower include Emmet J. Hughes, *The Ordeal of Power* (1962); Robert A. Divine, *Eisenhower and the Cold War* (1981); and Stephen Ambrose, *Eisenhower: The President* (1984). For information on specific topics, see Richard Immerman, *The CIA in Guatemala* (1982); Robert A. Divine, *Blowing on the Wind* (1978); Burton Kaufman, *Trade and Aid* (1982); Stephen G. Rabe, *Eisenhower and Latin America* (1988); Thomas Powers, *The Man Who Kept the Secrets* (1979), on the CIA; and Michael Beschloss, *May Day* (1986), on the U-2 incident.

29 AFFLUENCE AND ANXIETY: FROM THE FAIR DEAL TO THE GREAT SOCIETY

THE POSTWAR BOOM

THE GOOD LIFE?

FAREWELL TO REFORM

THE STRUGGLE OVER CIVIL RIGHTS

KENNEDY AND THE NEW FRONTIER

"LET US CONTINUE"

On May 7, 1947, William Levitt announced plans to build 2000 houses in a former potato field on Long Island, thirty miles from midtown Manhattan. Using mass-production techniques he had learned while erecting navy housing during the war, Levitt quickly built 4000 homes. In 1948, he began offering his houses for sale for a small amount down and a low monthly payment. Young couples, crowded in city apartments or still living with their parents, rushed out to buy Levitt's houses. By the time Levittown was completed in 1951, it contained more than 17,000 homes.

Levitt eventually built two more Levittowns, one in Pennsylvania and one in New Jersey. Each contained the same curving streets, neighborhood parks and playgrounds, and com-

munity swimming pools as did the first development. Some observers denounced Levittown, seeing it as the symbol of conformity and materialism, but William Levitt had tapped the postwar desire of young Americans to move to the suburbs and raise their children outside the central city.

Levitt's houses were ideal for young people just starting out in life. They were cheap, comfortable, and efficient, and each house came with a refrigerator, cooking range, and washing machine. Despite the conformity of the houses, the three Levittowns were surprisingly diverse communities; residents had a wide variety of religious, ethnic, and occupational backgrounds. Blacks, however, were rigidly excluded. In time, as the more successful families

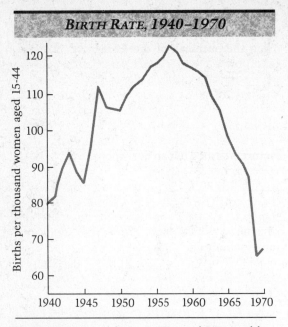

BIRTH RATE, 1940–1970

Births per thousand women aged 15–44

Source: U.S. Bureau of the Census, Historical Statistics of the United States, Colonial Times to 1970, Bicentennial Edition, Washington, D.C., 1975.

moved on to larger homes in more exclusive neighborhoods, the Levittowns became enclaves for lower-middle-class families.

Levittown symbolized the most significant social trend of the postwar era in the United States—the flight to the suburbs. While central cities remained relatively stagnant during the decade, suburbs grew by 46 percent; by 1960, one third of the nation lived in the suburbs. This massive shift in population from the central city was accompanied by a baby "boom" that started during World War II. Young married couples began to have three, four, even five children, and these larger families led to a 19 percent growth in the nation's population between 1950 and 1960, the greatest increase in growth rate since 1910.

The economy boomed as residential construction soared. A multitude of new consumer products—ranging from frozen foods to filter cigarettes, from high fidelity phonographs to cars equipped with automatic transmissions

and tubeless tires—appeared in stores and showrooms. And in the suburbs, the supermarket replaced the corner grocer.

Although a new affluence for most Americans replaced the poverty and hunger of the Great Depression, the haunting memories of the thirties remained vivid. The absorption of material goods took on an almost desperate quality, as if a profusion of houses, cars, and home appliances could guarantee that the nightmare of depression would never return. Critics were quick to condemn the conformity, charging the newly affluent with forsaking traditional American individualism to live in identical houses, drive look-alike cars, and accumulate the same material possessions.

Events abroad added to the feeling of anxiety in the postwar years. Nuclear war became a frighteningly real possibility. The rivalry with the Soviet Union led to a new red scare. Charges of treason and betrayal were leveled with great abandon; many loyal Americans were unjustly accused. Frustrated by the stalemate with Russia, many Americans cheered demagogues like Senator Joseph McCarthy, who looked for the Communist enemy at home rather than abroad. Thus beneath the bland surface of suburban affluence, a dark current of distrust and insecurity marred the picture of a nation fulfilling its economic destiny.

THE POSTWAR BOOM

For fifteen years following World War II, the nation witnessed a period of unparalleled economic growth. A pent-up demand for consumer goods fueled a steady industrial expansion, and heavy government spending during the Cold War added an extra stimulus to the economy, offsetting brief recessions in 1949 and 1953 and moderating a steeper one in 1957–1958. By the end of the fifties, the bulk of the population had achieved an affluence that finally dimmed the lingering memories of the Great Depression.

The task of reconverting American industry from its wartime production of tanks and bombers back to the creation of automobiles and household appliances led to considerable stress and tension. Prices and wages caused most of the concern. Congress voted in 1946 to weaken price controls. With returning servicemen and affluent civilians vying for scarce goods, prices rose 25 percent in less than two years. Workers, accustomed to wartime paychecks heavy with overtime, began to demand higher wages and shorter hours, and a wave of labor unrest swept over the country in the spring of 1946.

President Truman was caught in the middle. Sensitive to union demands, he permitted businessmen to negotiate large pay increases and then pass on the cost to consumers in the form of higher prices. He criticized Congress for weakening wartime price controls, but he offered nothing else to curb inflation. Housewives blamed him for the rising price of food, while labor condemned Truman as the Country's "No. 1 Strikebreaker" when he asked Congress for power to draft striking railway workers into the army.

The Republicans seized on the nation's economic woes to attack the Democrats. The American people, weary of inflation and labor unrest, responded in 1946 by electing a majority of Republicans to both the House and the Senate for the first time since 1930.

POSTWAR PROSPERITY

The economy began to move forward as the result of two long-term factors. First, American consumers—after being held in check by depression and then by wartime scarcities—finally had a chance to indulge their suppressed appetites for material goods. Initially, American factories could not turn out enough automobiles and appliances to satisfy the horde of buyers, whose personal savings at war's end stood at $37 billion. By 1950, however, production lines had finally caught up with the demand.

The Cold War provided the extra stimulus the economy needed when postwar expansion slowed. The Marshall Plan and other foreign-aid programs financed a heavy export trade. Then the outbreak of the Korean War helped overcome a brief recession and ensure continued prosperity as the government spent massive amounts on guns, planes, and munitions.

In the 1950s the baby boom and the spectacular growth of suburbia served as great stimulants to the consumer-goods industries. Manufacturers turned out an ever-increasing number of refrigerators, washing machines, and dishwashers to equip the kitchens in the houses that were being built across America. The automobile industry thrived with suburban expansion as two-car families became more and more common. The electronics industry boomed. Customers were eager to acquire the latest marvel of home entertainment—the television set.

Yet the economic abundance of the 1950s was not without its problems. While some sections of the nation (notably the emerging Sunbelt areas of the South and West) benefited enormously from the growth of the aircraft and electronics industries, older manufacturing regions did not fare as well. The steel industry fell behind the rate of national growth, agriculture did not share in the general affluence, and unemployment persisted despite the boom. Moreover, the rate of economic growth slowed in the second half of the decade, causing concern about the continuing vitality of the American economy.

None of these flaws, however, could disguise the fact that the nation was prospering to an extent no one dreamed possible in the 1930s. The GNP more than doubled its 1940 level. More important, workers now labored fewer than forty hours a week; they rarely worked on Saturdays, and nearly all enjoyed a two-week paid vacation each year. By the mid-1950s, the average American family had twice as much real income to spend as its counterpart had possessed in the boom years of the 1920s. The American people, in one generation, had moved from poverty and depression to the highest standard of living the world had ever known.

LIFE IN THE SUBURBS

Rather than forming a homogenous social group, the suburbs contained a surprising variety of people who ranged across the social classes. Doctors and lawyers, shoe salesmen and master plumbers, often lived in the same developments. The traditional distinctions of ancestry, education, and size of residence no longer differentiated people so easily.

Yet suburbs could vary widely, from working-class communities clustered near factories built in the countryside to old, elitist areas like Scarsdale, New York and Shaker Heights, Ohio. Most were almost exclusively white and Christian; a few enabled Jews and blacks to take part in the flight from the inner city.

Life in all these suburban communities depended on the automobile. Highways and expressways allowed husbands to commute to jobs in the cities. Wives drove to the shopping centers that began to dot the countryside by the mid-1950s. Children rode buses to school, then were driven to piano lessons and Little League ball games.

The home became the focus for activities and aspirations. Men and women who moved to the suburbs prized the new kitchens, extra bedrooms, large garages, and small, neat lawns. "Togetherness" became the code word of the fifties. Families did things together, whether gathering around the TV sets that dominated living rooms, attending community activities, or taking vacations in the huge station wagons of the era.

Emphasis on family life did not encourage the advancement of feminism. The end of the war saw many women who had entered the work force return to the home, where the role of wife and mother continued to be viewed as the ideal one for women in the 1950s. Trends toward getting married earlier and having larger families reinforced the tendency of women to devote all their efforts to housework and childraising rather than acquiring professional skills and pursuing careers outside the home. Dr. Benjamin Spock's 1946 best-seller, *Baby and Child Care*, became a fixture in millions of homes, while the traditional women's magazines like *McCall's* and *Good Housekeep-*

In the 1950s American consumers were able to acquire dream houses, home appliances, and tailfinned cars. The family car became an essential part of suburban life. It was used so much for shopping, commuting, and recreation that many families found it necessary to own a second vehicle.

ing thrived by featuring articles and inspirational pieces on such topics as "Homemaking Is My Vocation."

Nevertheless, the number of working wives doubled between 1940 and 1960. The heavy expenses involved in rearing and educating children led wives and mothers to seek ways to augment the family income, unintentionally preparing the way for a new demand for equality in the 1960s.

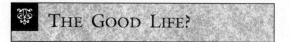

THE GOOD LIFE?

Consumerism was the dominant social theme of the 1950s. Yet even with an abundance of creature comforts and added hours of leisure time, the quality of life left many Americans anxious and dissatisfied.

AREAS OF GREATEST GROWTH

Organized religion flourished in the climate of the 1950s. Church and synagogue attendance rose, but some observers condemned the bland, secular nature of suburban churches, which seemed to be an integral part of the consumer society. Yet the emergence of neoorthodoxy in Protestant seminaries, and the rapid spread of radical forms of fundamentalism (such as the Assemblies of God), indicated that millions of Americans were searching for a deep inner faith.

Schools provided an immediate growth problem for the new suburban communities. The unprecedented increase in the number of school-age children overwhelmed the resources of many local districts, leading to demands for federal aid. Except for programs set up in reaction to Soviet scientific advances in space during the late 1950s, Congress and the Eisenhower administration provided only limited assistance to schools.

An important controversy arose over the nature of education in the 1950s. Critics of "progressive" education called for sweeping educational reforms and a new stress on traditional academic subjects. This issue often split suburban communities. The one thing all seemed to agree on was the desirability of a college education, and the number of young people attending college more than doubled between 1940 and 1960.

The largest growth area was the exciting new mass medium of television. From a shaky start just after the war, TV boomed in the fifties. By 1957, the three networks controlled the airways, reaching 40 million sets over nearly 500 stations. Advertisers soon took charge of the new medium, using many of the techniques first pioneered in radio—including pretaped commercials, quiz shows, and soap operas.

At first, the insatiable demand for programs encouraged a burst of creativity. Playwrights such as Reginald Rose, Rod Serling, and Paddy Chayefsky wrote a series of notable dramas for *Playhouse 90, Studio One,* and the *Goodyear Television Playhouse.* Broadcast live from cramped studios, these productions thrived on tight dramatic structures, movable scenery, and frequent close-ups of the actors.

Advertisers, however, quickly became disillusioned with the live anthology programs, which usually dealt with controversial subjects or focused on ordinary people and events. In contrast, sponsors wanted shows that stressed excitement, glamour, and instant success. Westerns and situation comedies soon prevailed after a fling with quiz shows ended in scandal. Despite its early promise of innovation, television soon became a technologically sophisticated but safe conveyor of the consumer culture.

CRITICS OF THE CONSUMER SOCIETY

One striking feature of the 1950s was the abundance of self-criticism. A number of widely read books explored the flaws in the new suburbia, criticizing the movement toward conformity and the obsession with material goods. The most sweeping indictment came in William H. Whyte's *The Organization Man* (1956), delineating the change from the old Protestant ethic, with its emphasis on hard work and personal responsibility, to a new social ethic, where everything centered on "the team" and the ultimate goal was "belongingness." The result was a stifling conformity and the loss of personal identity.

Harvard sociologist David Riesman was the most influential social critic of the fifties. His book, *The Lonely Crowd*, appeared in 1950 and set the tone for intellectual commentary about suburbia for the rest of the decade. Riesman described the shift from the "inner-directed" American of the past, who had relied on such traditional values as self-denial and frugality, to the "other directed" American of the consumer society, who constantly adapted his behavior to conform to social pressures. The consequence—a decline in individualism and a tendency for people to become acutely sensitive to the expectations of others—produced a bland and tolerant society of consumers short on creativity and adventuresomeness. More caustically, in *White Collar* (1951) and *The Power Elite* (1956), C. Wright Mills attacked the modern corporation for depriving workers of their own identities and imposing an impersonal discipline through manipulation and propaganda.

This disenchantment with the consumer culture reached its most eloquent expression with the "beats," a literary group that rebelled against the materialism of the 1950s. The name came from the quest for beatitude, a state of inner grace that is sought in Zen Buddhism. Jack Kerouac's novel, *On the Road* (1957) set the tone for the new movement. Flouting the respectability of suburbia, the "beatniks"—as middle-class America termed them—were easily identified by their long hair, bizarre clothing, and penchant for sexual promiscuity and drug experimentation. They were conspicuous dropouts from a society they found senseless. Yet as highly visible nonconformists in an era of stifling conformity, the beats demonstrated a style of social protest that would flower into the counterculture of the sixties.

THE REACTION TO *SPUTNIK*

The profound insecurity that underlay American life throughout the fifties surfaced in Oc-

tober 1957, when the Soviets sent the satellite *Sputnik* into orbit around the earth. The public's reaction to this impressive scientific feat was panic. The declining rate of economic growth; the recession of 1957–1958; the growing concern that American schools were lagging behind their Russian counterparts—all contributed to a conviction that the nation had somehow lost its previously unquestioned primacy in the eyes of the world.

In the late 1950s, the president and Congress moved to restore national confidence. In 1958 Congress created the National Aeronautics and Space Administration (NASA), appropriating vast sums to allow the agency to compete with the Russians in the space race. Soon a new group of heroes, the astronauts, began the training that led to suborbital flights and eventually to John Glenn's five-hour flight around the globe in 1962. Congress also sought to match the Soviet educational advances by passing the National Defense Education Act (NDEA). This legislation authorized federal financing of scientific and foreign-language programs in the nation's schools and colleges.

The belief persisted that in the midst of affluence and abundance Americans had lost their competitive edge. Disturbed by the charge that the nation had lost its sense of purpose, Eisenhower finally appointed a Commission on National Goals "to develop a broad outline of national objectives for the next decade and longer." The commission eventually issued a report that called for increased military spending abroad, greater economic growth at home, broader educational opportunities, and more government support for both scientific research and advancement of the arts. The consensus seemed to be that rather than a change of direction, all the United States needed was a renewed commitment to the pursuit of excellence.

FAREWELL TO REFORM

It is not surprising that the spirit of reform underlying the New Deal failed to flourish in the postwar years. Growing affluence took away the sense of grievance and the cry for change that was so strong in the thirties. Eager to enjoy the new prosperity after years of want and sacrifice, the American people lost their enthusiasm for federal regulation and welfare programs.

TRUMAN AND THE FAIR DEAL

After his 1948 victory, a triumphant Harry Truman announced his legislative program on January 5, 1949. He called for a "Fair Deal," a reform package that comprised a new program of national medical insurance, federal aid to education, enactment of a Fair Employment Practices Commission (FEPC) to prevent economic discrimination against blacks, and an overhaul of the farm subsidy program.

The Fair Deal was never enacted. Except for raising the minimum wage and broadening Social Security, Congress refused to pass any of Truman's health, education, or civil rights measures. In part, Truman was to blame for trying to secure too much too soon. More important, however, was the fact that Congress remained under the control of a bipartisan conservative coalition of northern Republicans and southern Democrats.

Although his legislative failure became certain in 1950 when war once again subordinated domestic issues to foreign policy, Truman deserves credit for maintaining and consolidating the New Deal. His spirited leadership prevented any Republican effort to repeal the gains of the 1930s. Moreover, even though he failed to get any new measures enacted, he broadened the reform agenda and laid the groundwork for future advances in health care, aid to education, and civil rights.

EISENHOWER'S MODERN REPUBLICANISM

Moderation was the keynote of the Eisenhower presidency. His major goal from the outset was to restore calm and tranquility to a badly divided nation. Unlike FDR and Truman, he had no commitment to social change or economic reform, yet he had no plans to dismantle the social programs of the New Deal. He sought instead to work toward balancing the budget, to keep military spending in check, to encourage as much private initiative as possible, and to reduce federal activities to the bare minimum. Defining his position as "Modern Republicanism," he claimed that he was "conservative when it comes to money and liberal when it comes to human beings."

On domestic issues, Eisenhower preferred to delegate authority and to play a passive role. He concentrated his own efforts on the Cold War abroad. The men he chose to run the nation reflected his preference for successful corporation executives. Eisenhower was equally reluctant to play an active role in dealing with Congress. A fervent believer in the separation of powers, Ike did not wish to engage in intensive lobbying. Such skillful aides as Sherman Adams, the White House chief of staff, insulated Eisenhower from many of the nation's pressing domestic problems.

Relations with Congress were weakened further by Republican losses in the midterm election of 1954. The Democrats regained control of both houses and kept it throughout the 1950s. The president had to rely on two Texas Democrats, Senate Majority Leader Lyndon B. Johnson and House Speaker Sam Rayburn, for legislative action; at best, it was an awkward and uneasy relationship.

The result was a very modest legislative record. Eisenhower extended Social Security benefits and raised the minimum wage. He consolidated the administration of welfare programs by creating the Department of Health, Education, and Welfare in 1953. But Ike steadfastly opposed Democratic plans for compulsory health insurance and comprehensive federal aid to education. The lack of presidential support and the continuing grip of the conservative coalition in Congress blocked any further reform in the 1950s.

The one significant legislative achievement of the Eisenhower years came with the passage of the Highway Act of 1956. After a twelve-year delay, Congress appropriated funds for a 41,000 mile interstate highway system consisting of multilane divided expressways that would connect all the nation's major cities. Although the act hurt railroad interests, it pleased a variety of highway users: the trucking industry, automobile clubs, organized labor (eager for construction jobs), farmers, and state highway officials. Built over the next twenty years, the interstate system had a profound influence on American life. It stimulated the economy and shortened travel time dramatically while intensifying the nation's dependence on the automobile and distorting metropolitan growth patterns into long strips paralleling the new expressways.

Overall, the Eisenhower years marked an era of political moderation. The American people, enjoying the abundance of the 1950s, seemed quite content with legislative inaction. He was sensitive to the nation's economic health; when recessions developed in 1953 and 1957, he quickly abandoned his goal of a balanced budget in favor of a policy advocating government spending to restore prosperity. Thus Eisenhower maintained the New Deal legacy of federal responsibility for social welfare and the state of the economy while successfully resisting demands for more extensive government involvement in American life.

THE STRUGGLE OVER CIVIL RIGHTS

Although the Cold War gave birth to the ugly loyalty issue, it had a more positive effect on another social problem—the denial of civil

Eisenhower neither enacted nor repealed any major reform legislation during his presidency. His landslide victories in 1952 and 1956 reflected the country's satisfaction with the status quo.

rights to African Americans. The contradiction between the denunciation of the Soviet Union for its human-rights violations and the second-class status of African Americans began to arouse the national conscience. Fighting for freedom against Communist tyranny abroad, Americans had to face the reality of the continued denial of freedom to a submerged minority at home.

Blacks had benefited economically from World War II, but they were still a seriously disadvantaged group. Those who moved for better opportunities to northern and western cities were concentrated in blighted and segregated neighborhoods, working at low-paying jobs, suffering economic and social discrimination, and failing to share fully in the postwar prosperity.

In the South, conditions were much worse. State laws forced blacks to live almost totally segregated from white society. Blacks attended separate schools and were rigidly excluded from all public facilities. They were forced to use separate waiting rooms in train stations, separate seats on all forms of transportation, and separate restrooms and drinking fountains. Segregation was enforced at all places of public entertainment and in hospitals, prisons, mental institutions, and nursing homes.

CIVIL RIGHTS AS A POLITICAL ISSUE

Truman was the first president to attempt to alter the historic pattern of racial discrimination in the United States. In his 1948 reform program, Truman included such measures as the establishment of a permanent Fair Employment Practices Commission (FEPC) and a civil rights commission. But southern resistance blocked any action by Congress, and the inclusion of a strong civil rights plank in the 1948 Democratic platform led to the walkout of some southern delegations and a separate States Rights (Dixiecrat) ticket in several states of the South that fall.

Black voters in the North responded by backing Truman overwhelmingly over Dewey in the 1948 election. In key states—California,

Ohio, and Illinois—it was the black voters in Los Angeles, Cleveland, and Chicago that ensured the Democratic victory. Truman responded by including civil rights legislation in his Fair Deal program in 1949. Once again, however, determined southern opposition blocked congressional action on a permanent FEPC and an antilynching measure.

Even though Truman had been unable to secure any significant legislation, he had succeeded in adding civil rights to the liberal, Democratic agenda, and was able to use his executive power to assist blacks seeking redress of grievances in school and housing issues. He strengthened the civil rights division of the Justice Department, which aided black groups in these issues. Most important, in 1948 Truman issued an order calling for the desegregation of the armed forces. By the end of the 1950s, the armed forces had become far more integrated than American society at large.

DESEGREGATING THE SCHOOLS

The nation's schools soon became the primary target of civil rights advocates. The NAACP concentrated first on the universities, successfully waging an intensive legal battle to win admission for qualified blacks to graduate and professional schools. Led by Thurgood Marshall, NAACP lawyers then took on the broader issue of segregation in the country's public schools. Challenging the 1896 Supreme Court decision (*Plessy* v. *Ferguson*) that upheld the constitutionality of separate but equal public facilities, Marshall argued that even substantially equal but separate schools did profound psychological damage to black children and thus violated the Fourteenth Amendment.

A unanimous Supreme Court agreed in its 1954 decision in the case of *Brown* v. *Board of Education of Topeka*. Chief Justice Earl Warren wrote the landmark opinion, which flatly declared that "separate educational facilities are inherently unequal." Recognizing that it would be difficult to change historic patterns of segregation quickly, in 1955 the Court ruled that implementation should proceed "with all deliberate speed" and left the details to the lower federal courts.

The process of desegregating the schools proved to be agonizingly slow. Southern states responded with a policy of massive resistance. Encouraged by a Southern Manifesto signed by 101 congressmen and senators, which denounced the Brown decision as "a clear abuse of judicial power," school boards found a variety of ways to evade the Court's ruling. By the end of the decade, less than 1 percent of the black children in the Deep South attended school with whites.

A conspicuous lack of presidential support further weakened the desegregation effort. Eisenhower was not a racist, but he believed that people's attitudes could not be changed by "cold lawmaking"—only "by appealing to reason, by prayer, and by constantly working at it through our own efforts." Quietly and unobtrusively, he worked to achieve desegregation in federal facilities. Yet he refrained from endorsing the *Brown* decision.

Southern leaders mistook Ike's silence for tacit support of segregation. In 1957, however, Eisenhower corrected this misunderstanding. Backing the federal courts, he used federal troops to ensure the integration of Little Rock's Central High School. The troops remained there for the rest of the school year. Then Little Rock authorities closed Central High School for the next two years; when it reopened, there were only three blacks in attendance.

Despite the snail's pace of school desegregation, the *Brown* decision led to other advances. In 1957, Eisenhower proposed and Congress passed a bill creating a permanent Commission for Civil Rights, one of Truman's original goals. It also provided for federal efforts aimed at "securing and protecting the right to vote." A second civil rights act in 1960 slightly strengthened the voting-rights section.

Like the desegregation effort, the attempt to ensure black voting rights in the South was still largely symbolic. Southern registrars used a variety of devices, ranging from intimidation to unfair tests, to deny blacks the suffrage. Yet the actions of Congress and the Supreme Court marked a vital turning point in national policy toward racial justice.

BEGINNINGS OF BLACK ACTIVISM

The most dynamic force for change came from blacks themselves. The shift from legal struggles in the courts to black protest in the streets began with an incident in Montgomery, Alabama. On December 1, 1955, Rosa Parks—a black seamstress who had been active in the local NAACP chapter—violated a city ordinance by refusing to give up her seat to a white person on a local bus. After her arrest, blacks gathered to protest and found a young, eloquent leader in Martin Luther King, Jr. He agreed to lead a massive boycott of the city's bus system, which depended heavily on black patronage.

The Montgomery bus boycott's goal was at first modest. King simply asked that seats be taken on a first-come, first-served basis, with blacks being seated from the back and whites from the front of each bus. The boycotters became more assertive as they endured both legal harassment and sporadic acts of violence. An

Rosa Parks' refusal to move to the back of the bus in Montgomery led to a citywide bus boycott in 1955 organized by Rev. Martin Luther King, Jr.

effective system of car pools enabled the protesters to avoid the city buses. Soon they were insisting on a total end to segregated seating.

The boycott ended in victory a year later when the Supreme Court ruled the Alabama segregated-seating law unconstitutional. King had won far more than this limited dent in the wall of segregation, however. He had provided blacks with a new weapon to fight racial oppression: a policy of passive resistance that stressed nonviolence and love.

A year after the successful bus boycott, King founded the Southern Christian Leadership Conference (SCLC) to direct the crusade against segregation. Then in February 1960 another spontaneous event sparked a further advance for passive resistance. Four black students from North Carolina Agricultural and Technical College sat down at a dime-store lunch counter in Greensboro, North Carolina, and refused to move after being denied service. Other students, both whites and blacks, joined in similar "sit-ins" across the South. By the end of the year, some 50,000 young people had succeeded in desegregating public facilities in over a hundred southern cities. Several thousand of the demonstrators were arrested and put in jail, but the movement gained strength, leading to

the formation of the Student Nonviolent Coordinating Committee (SNCC) in April 1960. From this time on, SCLC and SNCC, with their tactics of direct, though peaceful, confrontation would replace the NAACP, with its reliance on court action, in the forefront of the civil rights movement. The change would eventually lead to dramatic success, but it also ushered in a period of heightened tension and social turmoil in the 1960s.

KENNEDY AND THE NEW FRONTIER

On Monday evening, September 26, 1960, John F. Kennedy and Richard M. Nixon faced each other in the nation's first televised debate between two presidential candidates. Kennedy, as the relatively unknown Democratic challenger, had proposed the debates; Nixon, confident of his mastery of television, had accepted even though as Eisenhower's vice-president and the early front-runner in the election he had more to lose and less to gain.

Richard Nixon arrived an hour early, looking tired and ill at ease. He was still recuperating

An audience of 77 million viewers watched the four televised debates between presidential candidates John F. Kennedy and Richard Nixon. Kennedy's polished performance helped dispel fears that he was too young and inexperienced for the job.

from a knee injury that had slowed his campaign and left him pale and weak as he pursued a hectic catch-up schedule. Makeup experts offered to hide Nixon's heavy beard and soften his prominent jowls, but the GOP candidate declined. John Kennedy, tanned from open-air campaigning in California and rested by a day spent nearly free of distracting activity, wore no makeup but changed from a gray to a dark blue suit better adapted to the intense lighting on the set.

Before an audience estimated at 77 million, Kennedy led off, echoing Abraham Lincoln by saying that the nation faced the question of "whether the world will exist half-slave and half-free." Although the ground rules limited the first debate to domestic issues, Kennedy argued that foreign and domestic policy were inseparable. He accused the Republicans of letting the country drift at home and abroad. Nixon, caught off-guard, seemed to agree with Kennedy's assessment of the nation's problems, but he contended that he had better solutions.

For the rest of the hour, the two candidates answered questions from a panel of journalists. Radiating confidence and self-assurance, Kennedy used a flow of statistics and details to create the image of a man deeply knowledgeable about all aspects of government. Nixon seemed nervous and unsure of himself.

Polls taken over the next few weeks revealed a sharp swing to Kennedy. Nixon suffered more from his less attractive physical image than from what he said; those who heard the debate on radio thought that the Republican candidate more than held his own. Nixon improved his appearance and strategy in the three additional debates, but the damage had been done. A post-election poll revealed that of 4 million voters who were influenced by the debates, 3 million voted for Kennedy.

The television debates were only one of many factors influencing the outcome of the 1960 election. During the fall campaign, Kennedy exploited the national mood of frustration that had followed *Sputnik*. At home, he promised to stimulate the lagging economy and carry forward long-overdue reforms in education, health care, and civil rights under the ban-

ner of the "New Frontier." Abroad, he pledged a renewed commitment to the Cold War, vowing that he would lead the nation to victory over the Soviet Union.

The Democratic victory of 1960 was paper-thin. Kennedy's edge in the popular vote was only two tenths of 1 percent. Yet even though he had no mandate, Kennedy's triumph did mark a sharp political shift. In contrast to the aging Eisenhower, Kennedy symbolized youth, energy, and ambition. His mastery of the new medium of television reflected his sensitivity to the changes taking place in American life in the sixties. He came to office promising reform at home and advance abroad. Over the next five years, he and his vice-president, Lyndon Johnson, achieved many of their goals only to find the nation caught up in new and even greater dilemmas.

THE NEW FRONTIERSMEN

The election of John F. Kennedy marked the arrival of a new generation of leadership. For the first time, people born in the 20th century who had entered political life after World War II were in charge of national affairs. Kennedy himself had first been elected to Congress in 1946 at the age of 29 and then had won a Senate seat in 1952. Although he had not sponsored any significant legislation as a senator, he championed the traditional Democratic reforms during his presidential campaign, labeling them the New Frontier. Above all, he had criticized the Republicans for allowing sluggish economic growth and failing to deal with such pressing social problems as health care and education. His call to get the nation moving again was particularly attractive to young people, who had shunned political involvement during the Eisenhower years.

The new administration reflected Kennedy's aura of youth and energy. The most controversial cabinet choice was Robert F. Kennedy, the president's brother, as attorney general. Critics scoffed at his lack of legal experience, but the president prized his brother's loyalty and shrewd political advice. As important as his cabinet appointments were his White House staff appointments. Like their counterparts in foreign policy, these New Frontiersmen prided themselves on being tough-minded and pragmatic. In contrast to Eisenhower, Kennedy relied heavily on academics and intellectuals to help him infuse the nation with energy and a new sense of direction.

Kennedy's greatest asset was his personality. A cool, attractive, and intelligent man, he possessed a sense of style that endeared him to the American public. He seemed to be a new Lancelot, bent on calling forth the best in national life; admirers likened his inner circle to King Arthur's court at Camelot. Reporters loved him, both for his fact-filled and candid press conferences and for his witty comments.

THE CONGRESSIONAL OBSTACLE AND ECONOMIC ADVANCE

Neither Kennedy's wit nor charm proved strong enough to break the logjam in Congress. Since the late 1940s, a series of reform bills ranging from health care to federal aid to education had been stalled on Capitol Hill. Although Kennedy embraced these Democratic measures, labeling them the New Frontier, he was hurt by the loss of twenty seats in the House and two in the Senate. A conservative coalition of northern Republicans and southern Democrats opposed all efforts at reform.

The situation was especially critical in the House, where 101 southern representatives held the balance of power between 160 northern Democrats and 174 Republicans. Aided by Speaker Sam Rayburn, Kennedy was able to enlarge the Rules Committee and overcome a conservative roadblock, but the narrow vote, 217 to 212, revealed how difficult it would be to enact his education and health-care proposals. Thus the composition of Congress, coupled with Kennedy's distaste for legislative infighting, caused the New Frontier to languish.

Kennedy gave a higher priority to the sluggish American economy. JFK was determined to recover quickly from the recession he had in-

herited and to stimulate the economy to achieve a much higher rate of long-term growth. In part, he wanted to redeem his campaign pledge to get the nation moving again; he also felt that the United States had to surpass the Soviet Union in economic vitality.

Rejecting the idea of massive spending on public works, Kennedy sided with the experts who claimed the problem was essentially technological and urged manpower-training and area-redevelopment programs to modernize American industry. The actual stimulation of the economy, however, came not from such social programs but from greatly increased appropriations for defense and space. By 1962, over half the federal budget was devoted to space and defense; aircraft and computer companies in the South and West benefited, but unemployment remained uncomfortably high in the older industrial areas of the Northeast and Midwest.

The administration's desire to keep the inflation rate low led to a serious confrontation with the business community. Kennedy relied on informal wage and price guidelines to hold down the cost of living. But in April 1962, just after the president had persuaded the steelworkers' union to accept a new contract with no wage increases, U.S. Steel head Roger Blough informed Kennedy that his company was raising steel prices by $6 a ton. Outraged, Kennedy publicly criticized the action. Privately, he confided to aides, "My father always told me that all businessmen were sons-of-bitches, but I never believed it till now."

Faced with a cutoff in Pentagon steel orders, and the threat of an antitrust suit, Blough soon reconsidered. When several smaller steel companies refused to raise their prices in hopes of expanding their share of the market, U.S. Steel capitulated and rolled back its prices. But the business community deeply resented the president's action.

Troubled by his strained relations with business and by the continued lag in economic growth, Kennedy decided to adopt a more unorthodox approach in 1963. Walter Heller, chairman of the Council of Economic Advisors, had been arguing for a major cut in taxes since

1961 in the belief that it would stimulate consumer spending and give the economy the jolt it needed. The idea of a tax cut and resulting deficits during a period of prosperity went against economic orthodoxy, but Kennedy finally gave his approval. When enacted by Congress in 1964, the massive tax cut ($13.5 billion) led to the longest sustained economic advance in American history.

Kennedy's economic policy was far more successful than his legislative efforts. Although the rate of economic growth doubled to 4.5 percent by the end of 1963 and unemployment was reduced substantially, the cost of living rose only 1.3 percent a year. Personal income went up 13 percent in the early 1960s, but the greatest gains came in corporate profits—up 67 percent in this period. Critics pointed out that the Kennedy administration failed to close the glaring loopholes in the tax law that benefited the rich and that it made no effort to help those at the bottom by forcing a redistribution of national wealth. And in spite of the overall economic growth, the public sector remained neglected. Ecological and social problems continued to grow at an alarming rate.

MOVING SLOWLY ON CIVIL RIGHTS

Kennedy faced a genuine dilemma over the issue of civil rights. During the 1960 campaign, he had promised to launch an attack on segregation in the Deep South and had endeared himself to blacks across the nation when he helped win Martin Luther King's release from a Georgia jail. Fear of alienating the large bloc of southern Democrats, however, forced him to play down civil rights legislation.

The president's solution was to defer congressional action in favor of executive leadership in this area. He directed his brother, Attorney General Robert Kennedy, to continue and expand the Eisenhower administration's efforts to achieve voting rights for southern blacks. Working with the civil rights movement, the Justice Department labored to register previously disfranchised blacks. But the attorney general could not force the FBI to provide protection for the civil rights volunteers who risked their lives by encouraging blacks to register. Kennedy's other efforts to improve the conditions for blacks in America had limited results.

The civil rights movement refused to accept Kennedy's indirect approach. In May 1961, the Congress of Racial Equality (CORE) sponsored a "freedom ride" in which a biracial group attempted to test a 1960 Supreme Court decision outlawing segregation in all bus and train stations used in interstate commerce. When they arrived in Birmingham, Alabama, the freedom riders were attacked by a mob of angry whites. The attorney general quickly dispatched several hundred federal marshals to protect the freedom riders, but Kennedy was more upset at the distraction the protesters created. Deeply involved in the Berlin crisis, Kennedy directed an aide to get in touch with CORE leaders. "Tell them to call it off," he demanded. "Stop them."

In September, after the attorney general finally convinced the Interstate Commerce Commission to issue an order banning segregation in interstate terminals and buses, the freedom rides ended. The Kennedy administration then sought to prevent further confrontations by involving civil rights activists in its voting drive.

A pattern of belated reaction to southern racism marked the basic approach of the Kennedys. When James Meredith courageously sought admission to the all-white University of Mississippi in 1962, the president and the attorney general worked closely with Mississippi Governor Ross Barnett to avoid violence. But despite Barnett's later promise of cooperation, the night before Meredith enrolled at the University of Mississippi, a mob attacked the federal marshals and National Guard troops sent to protect him. The violence left two dead and 375 injured, but Meredith attended the university and eventually graduated.

"I HAVE A DREAM"

Martin Luther King, Jr., finally forced Kennedy to abandon his cautious tactics and come out

The attempts of African Americans to end discrimination and secure their civil rights met violent resistance in Birmingham, Alabama. Police used snarling dogs, fire hoses, clubs, and electric cattle prods to turn back unarmed demonstrators.

openly in behalf of racial justice. In the spring of 1963, King began a massive protest in Birmingham, one of the South's most segregated cities. Public marches and demonstrations aimed at integrating public facilities and opening up jobs for blacks quickly led to police harassment and many arrests, including that of King himself. Police Commissioner Eugene "Bull" Connor was determined to crush the civil rights movement; King was equally determined to prevail.

Bull Connor played directly into King's hands. On May 3, as 6000 children marched in place of the jailed protesters, authorities broke up a demonstration with clubs, snarling police dogs, and high-pressure water hoses. With a horrified nation watching scene after scene of this brutality on television, the Kennedy administration quickly intervened to arrange a settlement with the Birmingham civil leaders that ended the violence and granted the blacks most of their demands.

More important, Kennedy finally ended his long hesitation and sounded the call for action. Calling the problem a "moral issue," he sponsored civil rights legislation providing equal access to all public accommodations as well as an extension of voting rights for blacks.

Despite pleas from the government for an end to demonstrations and protests, the movement's leaders decided to keep pressure on the administration. On August 28, 1963, more than 200,000 marchers gathered in the nation's capital for a day-long rally in front of the Lincoln Memorial where they listened to hymns, speeches, and prayers for racial justice. The climax of the event was Martin Luther King's eloquent description of his dream for a united America.

By the time of Kennedy's death in November 1963, his civil rights legislation was well on its way to passage in Congress. Yet even this achievement did not fully satisfy his critics. They pointed to his failure to issue an executive order to end housing discrimination and to make good on his other campaign promises. For many, Kennedy had raised hopes for racial equality that he never fulfilled.

But unlike Eisenhower, he had provided presidential leadership for the civil rights movement. His emphasis on executive action gradually paid off, especially in extending voting rights. By early 1964, 40 percent of southern blacks had the franchise. Moreover, Kennedy's sense of caution and restraint, painful and frustrating as it was to black activists, had proved well founded. Avoiding an early, and possibly fatal, defeat in Congress, he had waited until a national consensus emerged and then had carefully channeled it behind effective legislation. Behaving very much the way Franklin Roosevelt did in guiding the nation into World War II, Kennedy chose to be a fox rather than a lion on civil rights.

THE SUPREME COURT AND REFORM

The most active impulse for social change in the early 1960s came from a surprising source; the usually staid and conservative Supreme Court. Under the leadership of Earl Warren, the Court ventured into new areas. A group of liberal judges—especially William O. Douglas, Hugo Black, and William J. Brennan, Jr.—argued for social reform, while advocates of judicial restraint (such as Felix Frankfurter) fought stubbornly against the new activism.

In addition to ruling against segregation, the Warren Court in the Eisenhower years had angered conservatives by protecting the constitutional rights of victims of McCarthyism. In *Yates* v. *U.S.* (1956), the judges reversed the conviction of fourteen Communist leaders, claiming that government prosecutors had failed to prove that the accused had actually organized a plot to overthrow the government. Mere advocacy of revolution, the Court said, did not justify conviction.

The resignation of Felix Frankfurter in 1962 enabled Kennedy to appoint Arthur Goldberg, a committed liberal, to the Supreme Court. With a clear majority now favoring judicial intervention, the Warren Court issued a series of landmark decisions designed to extend to state and local jurisdictions the traditional rights afforded the accused in federal courts. The Court in *Gideon* v. *Wainwright* (1963), *Escobedo* v. *Illinois* (1964), and *Miranda* v. *Arizona* (1966) decreed that defendants had to be provided lawyers, had to be informed of their constitutional rights, and could not be interrogated or induced to confess to a crime without defense counsel being present. In effect, the Court extended to the poor and the ignorant those constitutional guarantees that had always been available to the rich and to persons aware of their rights—notably hardened criminals.

The most far-reaching Warren Court decisions came in the area of legislative reapportionment. In *Baker* v. *Carr* (1962) the Court required Tennessee to redistrict its legislative seats to redress the rural overrepresentation in its state government. The Court proclaimed that places in all legislative bodies be allocated on the basis of "people, not land or trees or pastures." The principle of "one man, one vote" greatly increased the political power of cities at the expense of rural areas.

The activism of the Supreme Court stirred up a storm of criticism. The rulings that extended protection to criminals and those accused of subversive activity led some Americans to charge that the Court was encouraging crime and weakening national security. Decisions banning school prayers and permitting pornography incensed many conservative Americans who saw the Court as undermining moral values. Legal scholars worried more about the weakening of the Court's prestige as it became more directly involved in the political process. On balance, however, the Warren Court helped achieve greater social justice by protecting the rights of the underprivileged and by permitting dissent and free expression to flourish.

"LET US CONTINUE"

The New Frontier came to a sudden and violent end on November 22, 1963, when Lee Harvey Oswald assassinated John F. Kennedy as the president rode in a motorcade in downtown Dallas. The shock of losing the young leader, who had become a symbol of hope and promise for a whole generation, stunned the world. The American people were bewildered by the rapid sequence of events: the brutal killing of their beloved president; the televised slaying of Oswald by Jack Ruby; and the hurried Warren Commission report, which identified Oswald as the lone assassin.

Vice-President Lyndon B. Johnson moved quickly to fill the vacuum left by Kennedy's

Aboard Air Force One *on the return from Dallas to Washington, D.C., Judge Sarah Hughes administers the presidential oath of office to Lyndon Johnson.*

death. He soon met with a stream of world leaders to reassure them of American political stability. Five days after the tragedy in Dallas, Johnson spoke eloquently to a special joint session of Congress. Asking Congress to enact Kennedy's tax and civil rights bills as a tribute to the fallen leader, LBJ concluded, "Let us here highly resolve that John Fitzgerald Kennedy did not live or die in vain."

JOHNSON IN ACTION

Johnson suffered from the inevitable comparison with his young and stylish predecessor. LBJ was acutely aware of his own lack of polish, yet his assets were very real—an intimate knowledge of Congress, an incredible energy and determination to succeed, and a fierce ego. When a young marine officer tried to direct him to the proper helicopter, saying, "This one is yours," Johnson responded, "Son, they are all my helicopters."

LBJ's height and intensity gave him a powerful presence; he dominated any room he entered. Yet he found it impossible to project his intelligence and vitality to large audiences. Unlike Kennedy, he wilted before the camera, turning his televised speeches into stilted and awkward performances. Trying to belie his reputation as a riverboat gambler, he came across like a foxy grandpa, clever and calculating and not to be trusted.

Whatever his shortcomings in style, however, Johnson possessed far greater ability than Kennedy in dealing with Congress. He entered the White House with more than thirty years experience in Washington as a legislative aide, congressman, and senator. His encyclopedic knowledge of the legislative process and his shrewd manipulation of individual senators had enabled him to become the most influential Senate majority leader in history.

Above all, Johnson sought consensus. Indifferent to ideology, he had moved easily from New Deal liberalism to oil-and-gas conservatism as his career advanced. He could work easily with southern conservatives or liberals. Suddenly thrust into power, Johnson used his gifts wisely. Citing his favorite scriptural passage from Isaiah, "Come now, and let us reason together, saith the Lord," he concentrated on securing passage of Kennedy's tax and civil rights bills in 1964.

The tax cut came first. In February, after skillful maneuvering by Johnson, Congress reduced personal income taxes by more than $10 billion, touching off a sustained economic boom. Consumer spending increased by an impressive $43 billion in the next eighteen months, and new jobs opened up at the rate of one million a year.

Johnson was even more influential in passing the Kennedy civil-rights measure. Staying in the background, he encouraged liberal amendments that strengthened the bill in the House. With Hubert Humphrey leading the floor fight in the Senate, Johnson refused all efforts at compromise, counting on growing public pressure to force northern Republicans to abandon their traditional alliance with southern Democrats. After a fifty-five day filibuster failed, Johnson won the fight.

The 1964 Civil Rights Act, signed on June 2, made illegal the segregation of blacks in public facilities, established a Fair Employment Practices Committee to lessen racial discrimination in employment, and protected the voting rights of blacks. An amendment sponsored by segregationists in an effort to weaken the bill added sex to the prohibition of discrimination in Title VII of the act; in the future, women's groups would use this clause to secure government support for greater equality in employment and education.

THE ELECTION OF 1964

Passage of two key Kennedy measures within six months did not satisfy Johnson. Having established the theme of continuity, he now set out to win the presidency in his own right. Eager to surpass Kennedy's narrow victory in 1960, he hoped to win by a great landslide.

Searching for a cause of his own, LBJ found one in the issue of poverty. Beginning in the late 1950s, economists had warned that the prevailing affluence masked a persistent and deep-seated problem of poverty. In 1962 Michael Harrington's book, *The Other America*, attracted national attention. Writing with passion and eloquence, Harrington claimed that nearly one fifth of the nation lived in poverty.

Three groups predominated among the poor—blacks, the aged, and households headed by women. The problem, Harrington contended, was that the poor were invisible, living in slums or depressed areas like Appalachia and cut off from the educational facilities, medical care, and employment opportunities afforded more affluent Americans. Moreover, poverty was a vicious cycle. The children of the poor were trapped in the same culture of poverty as their parents.

Johnson quickly took over proposals that Kennedy had been developing and made them his own. In his State of the Union address in January 1964, LBJ announced, "This administration, today, here and now, declares unconditional war on poverty in America." Over the next eight months, Johnson fashioned a comprehensive poverty program.

The new Office of Economic Opportunity (OEO) set up a wide variety of programs, ranging from Head Start for preschoolers to the Job Corps for high school dropouts in need of vocational training. The emphasis was on self-help, with the government providing money and know-how, but the level of funding was never high enough to meet the OEO's ambitious goals. Nevertheless, the war on poverty, along with the economic growth provided by the tax cut, helped reduce the ranks of the poor by nearly 10 million between 1964 and 1967.

For Johnson, the new program established his reputation as a reformer in an election year. The man he faced in the election had a different sort of reputation. Senator Barry Goldwater, the Republican candidate, was an outspoken conservative from Arizona. An attractive and articulate man, Goldwater openly advocated a rejection of the welfare state and a return to unregulated free enterprise. He spoke out boldly against the Tennessee Valley Authority, denounced Social Security, and advocated a hawkish foreign policy.

Johnson stuck carefully to the middle of the road, embracing the liberal reform program—which he now called "The Great Society"—while stressing his concern for balanced budgets and fiscal orthodoxy. On election day, LBJ did even better than FDR had in 1936, receiving 61.1 percent of the popular vote and sweeping the electoral college 486 to 52. The Democrats also achieved huge gains in Congress. Kennedy's legacy and Goldwater's candor had enabled Johnson to break the conservative grip on Congress for the first time in a quarter of a century.

THE TRIUMPH OF REFORM

LBJ moved quickly to secure his legislative goals. He gave two traditional Democratic reforms—health care and education—top priority. Aware of strong opposition to a comprehensive medical program, LBJ settled for Medicare, which mandated health insurance under the Social Security program for Americans over age sixty-five, with a supplementary Medicaid program for the indigent.

On education, LBJ overcame the religious hurdle by supporting a child-benefit approach, allocating federal money to advance the education of students in parochial as well as public

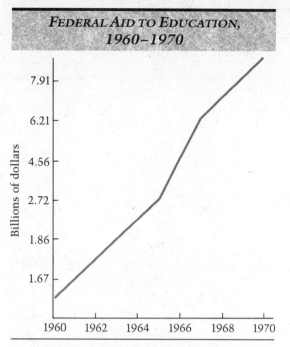

FEDERAL AID TO EDUCATION, 1960–1970

Billions of dollars

7.91
6.21
4.56
2.72
1.86
1.67

1960 1962 1964 1966 1968 1970

Source: Compiled from U.S. Bureau of the Census, Historical Statistics of the United States, Colonial Times to 1970, Bicentennial Edition, Washington, D.C. 1975.

schools. The Elementary and Secondary Education Act of 1965 provided over $1 billion in federal aid. During his administration, federal aid to education increased sharply.

Civil rights proved to be the most difficult test of Johnson's leadership. Martin Luther King, concerned that 3 million southern blacks were still denied the right to vote, in early 1965 chose Selma, Alabama, as a test case. The white authorities in Selma, led by Sheriff James Clark, used cattle prods and bullwhips to break up the demonstrations and jailed more than 2000 blacks. Johnson intervened in March, ordering the Alabama National Guard to federal duty to protect the demonstrators. He also had the Justice Department draw up a new voting-rights bill, and personally addressed the Congress on the need for civil rights.

Five months later, Congress passed the Voting Rights Act of 1965. The act banned literacy tests in states and counties in which less than

CHRONOLOGY

1946 Republicans win control of both houses of Congress in November elections

1947 William Levitt announces first Levittown

1954 Supreme Court orders schools desegregated in *Brown* v. *Board of Education of Topeka*

1955 African Americans begin boycott of Montgomery, Alabama, bus company (December)

1957 Soviets launch *Sputnik* (October)

1960 Kennedy elected president in narrow victory over Nixon

1962 James Meredith is first African American to enroll at University of Mississippi (September)

1963 Martin Luther King, Jr., tells crowd at rally in Washington, D.C., of his dream for a united America (August)
Kennedy assassinated, Lyndon B. Johnson sworn in as president (November)

1964 President Johnson declares war on poverty (January)
Johnson wins presidency in landslide victory

1965 Medicare legislation provides aged with medical care

African-American Voter Registration Before and After the Voting Rights Act of 1965

State	1960	1966	Increase	Percentage of Increase over 1960
Alabama	66,000	250,000	184,000	278.8
Arkansas	73,000	115,000	42,000	57.5
Florida	183,000	303,000	120,000	65.6
Georgia	180,000	300,000	120,000	66.7
Louisiana	159,000	243,000	84,000	52.8
Mississippi	22,000	175,000	153,000	695.4
North Carolina	210,000	282,000	72,000	34.3
South Carolina	58,000	191,000	133,000	229.3
Tennessee	185,000	225,000	40,000	21.6
Texas	227,000	400,000	173,000	76.2
Virginia	100,000	205,000	105,000	105.0

Source: Compiled from U.S. Bureau of the Census, Statistical Abstract of the United States: 1982–83 (103d edition) Washington, D.C., 1982.

half the population had voted in 1964 and provided for federal registrars in these areas to assure blacks the franchise. The results were dramatic. For the first time since Reconstruction, blacks were playing an active and effective role in southern politics.

Before the Eighty-ninth Congress ended its first session in the fall of 1965, it had passed eighty-nine bills. These measures ranged from ensuring clean air and water to improving education and housing. In nine months, Johnson had enacted the entire Democratic reform agenda, moving the nation beyond the New Deal by mandating federal concern for health, education, and the quality of life in both city and countryside.

The man responsible for this great leap forward, however, had failed to win the public adulation he so deeply desired. The people did not respond to Johnson's leadership with the warmth and praise they had showered on Kennedy, and reporters continued to portray him as a crude wheeler-dealer. No one was more aware of this lack of affection than LBJ himself. When foreign-policy problems soon eroded his popularity, few remembered his remarkable legislative achievement at home. Yet in one brief out-

burst of reform, he had accomplished more than any president since FDR.

Johnson's Great Society had a lasting impact on American life. Federal aid to education, the enactment of Medicare and Medicaid, and above all, the civil rights acts of 1964 and 1965, changed the nation irrevocably. The aged and the poor now were guaranteed access to medical care, communities saw an infusion of federal funds to improve local education, and African Americans could now begin to attend integrated schools, enjoy public facilities, and gain political power by exercising the right to vote. But even at this moment of triumph for liberal reform, new currents of dissent and rebellion were brewing.

RECOMMENDED READING

The two best general surveys of political trends in the 1960s are Jim F. Heath, *Decade of Disillusionment* (1975), a sympathetic view of the Kennedy and Johnson administrations, and Allen Matusow, *The Unraveling of America* (1984), a critical analysis of the failure of liberalism.

Laudatory views of the Kennedy presidency by JFK partisans include Arthur M. Schlesinger, Jr., *A Thou-*

sand Days (1965), and Theodore Sorensen, *Kennedy* (1965). For more critical evaluations, see Henry Fairlie, *The Kennedy Promise* (1973); Bruce Miroff, *Pragmatic Illusions* (1976); and Garry Wills, *The Kennedy Imprisonment* (1981). The best-balanced account is Herbert Parmet, *JFK: The Presidency of John F. Kennedy* (1983).

The most comprehensive account of the Johnson presidency is Eric Goldman's, *The Tragedy of Lyndon Johnson* (1969) by a historian who became a White House insider. Louis Heren, *No Hail, No Farewell* (1970) offers an objective and lucid survey of LBJ's presidential years, and Harry McPherson presents a candid portrait in *A Political Education* (1972). Other books on LBJ are the president's memoirs, *The Vantage Point* (1971); Doris Kearns, *Lyndon Johnson and the American Dream* (1976); George Reedy, *Lyndon Johnson: A Memoir* (1982); and Paul Conkin, *Big Daddy from the Pedernales* (1986). Two books edited by Robert Divine, *Exploring the Johnson Years* (1981), and *The Johnson Years: Vietnam, the Environment and Science* (1987), survey major themes of the Johnson administration.

Books on economic developments include Seymour Harris, *Economics of the Kennedy Years* (1964); Hobart Rowen, *The Free Enterprisers* (1964); and Jim F. Heath, *John F. Kennedy and the Business Community* (1969). Victor S. Navasky's account of Robert Kennedy as attorney general, *Kennedy Justice* (1971), is quite critical. More sympathetic on the same topic is Arthur Schlesinger, Jr., *Robert Kennedy and His Times* (1976). The Great Society, particularly in regard to welfare and the war on poverty, can be traced in John C. Donovan, *The Politics of Poverty* (1973); Sar Levitan, *The Great Society's Poor Law* (1969); James T. Patterson, *America's Struggle Against Poverty* (1982); and Julie Roy Jeffrey, *Education for the Children of the Poor* (1976). Robert H. Bremner, Gary Reichard, and Richard J. Hopkins, eds., *American Choices* (1986) contains informative essays on important domestic issues.

30 VIETNAM AND THE COLD WAR, 1953–1968

EISENHOWER WAGES THE COLD WAR

KENNEDY INTENSIFIES THE COLD WAR

JOHNSON ESCALATES THE VIETNAM WAR

On November 20, 1953, French planes dropped over 1800 elite paratroopers into Dien Bien Phu, a remote heart-shaped valley in North Vietnam. This move was the latest effort by the French to crush the rebellion of the Viet Minh, a Communist movement led by Ho Chi Minh, which had been fighting for the independence of Vietnam since 1946. The paratroopers quickly gained control of Dien Bien Phu, built airstrips to receive supplies and reinforcements, and then prepared for the expected onslaught from the Viet Minh. The French hoped to engage the elusive guerrilla forces in a pitched battle using the superior French firepower to gradually sap the strength of the Viet Minh insurgency.

By March 1954, the French garrison was in a desperate position. The Viet Minh had moved 50,000 troops into the hills surrounding Dien Bien Phu and had brought in heavy artillery pieces. Vietnamese soldiers had carried the disassembled cannons and mortars through the jungles to the hilltops overlooking the French positions in the valley below. From their commanding position, the Viet Minh attacked, overrunning three French outposts. Surprisingly accurate antiaircraft fire made it increasingly difficult for the French planes to bring in supplies and reinforcements. What had begun as an attempt to decimate the Viet Minh had turned into a showdown battle in which France's control of Indochina was thrown into jeopardy.

In desperation, the French turned to the United States. Although the United States had supported France since 1950 with military and financial assistance, President Dwight D. Eisenhower refused to commit American forces to save France's imperial dreams. The memory of the Korea War still loomed large in the minds of many American policy makers. When the French continued to press the United States for help, Eisenhower said that he would not act without the approval of Congress and America's European allies. Neither Congress nor Britain favored a more active role for the United States. Again Eisenhower turned down France's call for help. Years later, in 1960, Ike said that he had not wanted to sacrifice America's "tradition of anticolonialism" to bail out the French.

While Eisenhower and other political leaders searched for a negotiated settlement, the Viet Minh tightened the vice on Dien Bien Phu. The French were in a hopeless position. Their garrison was more than 200 miles behind the enemy's lines and was being pounded relentlessly by artillery shells. The trapped soldiers suffered from the lack of supplies and reinforcements. Finally on May 7, 1954, the Viet Minh attackers overcame the last stronghold at Dien Bien Phu. France's plan to regain control of Vietnam died in the mud of Dien Bien Phu.

At the international conference held in Geneva a few months later, Indochina was divided at the seventeenth parallel. Ho Chi Minh gained control of North Vietnam, while the French continued to rule in the South, with provision for a general election within two years to unify the country. The election was never held, largely because Eisenhower feared it would result in an overwhelming mandate for Ho. Instead the United States gradually took over from the French, sponsoring a new government in Saigon headed by Ngo Dinh Diem, a Vietnamese nationalist from a northern Catholic family. While Eisenhower can be given credit for refusing to engage American forces on behalf of French colonialism in Indochina, his determination to resist Communist expansion had committed the United States to a long and eventually futile struggle to prevent a unified Vietnam.

Ho Chi Minh and members of the Vietnam Workers' party discuss strategy during the Dien Bien Phu campaign.

EISENHOWER WAGES THE COLD WAR

Dwight D. Eisenhower came to the presidency in 1952 unusually well-prepared to lead the nation at the height of the Cold War. His long years of military service had exposed him to a wide variety of international issues and to an even broader array of world leaders. His gifts were political and diplomatic as well as military. He was blessed with a sharp, pragmatic mind and organizational genius that enabled him to plan and carry out large enterprises. Above all, he had a serene confidence in his own ability.

Eisenhower chose John Foster Dulles as his secretary of state. The myth soon developed that Ike gave Dulles free rein to conduct American diplomacy. Such was not the case. Eisenhower let Dulles make the public speeches and appearances before congressional committees, but Dulles carefully consulted with the president before every appearance. Ike respected Dulles' opinions, but he made all the major decisions himself.

From the outset, Eisenhower was determined to bring the Cold War under control. Ideally, he wanted to end it, but as a realist, he would settle for a relaxation of tensions with the Soviet Union. In part, he was motivated by a deeply held budgetary concern; Ike was convinced that the nation was in danger of going bankrupt unless military spending was reduced. As president, he inaugurated a "new look" for American defense, cutting back on the army and navy and relying even more heavily than Truman had on the air force and its nuclear striking power. As a result, the defense budget dropped from $50 billion to $40 billion annually. In 1954, Dulles announced reliance on massive retaliation—actually a continuation of Truman's policy of deterrence. Rather than becoming involved in limited wars such as Korea, the United States would consider the possibility of using nuclear weapons to halt any Communist aggression that threatened vital U.S. interests anywhere in the world.

While he permitted Dulles to make his veiled nuclear threats, Eisenhower's fondest dream was to end the arms race. Sobered by the development of the hydrogen bomb, the president began a new effort at disarmament with the Russians. Yet before this initiative could take effect, Ike had to weather a series of crises around the world that tested his skill and patience to the utmost.

CONTAINING CHINA

The Communist government in Peking posed a serious challenge to the Eisenhower administration. Senate Republicans blamed the Democrats for the "loss" of China. They viewed Mao as a puppet of the Soviet Union and insisted that the United States recognize the Nationalists on Formosa as the only legitimate government of China. While State Department experts realized that there were underlying tensions between China and the Soviet Union, Mao's intervention in the Korean War had con-

vinced most Americans that the Chinese Communists were an integral part of a larger Communist effort at world domination. Thus Truman and Acheson had abandoned any hope of trying to exploit differences between Mao and Stalin by wooing China away from the Soviet Union.

Eisenhower and Dulles chose to accentuate the potential conflict between China and the Soviet Union. They adopted a strong line, hoping to please congressional hawks and show China that the Soviet Union could not protect China's interests. Eisenhower and Dulles hoped that a policy of firmness would contain Communist Chinese expansion and drive a wedge between Moscow and Peking.

A crisis in the Formosa Straits provided the first test of the new policy.

In the fall of 1954, the mainland government threatened to seize islands off the coast of China occupied by the Nationalists. Fearful that this would be the first step toward an invasion of Formosa, Eisenhower committed the United States to defend Formosa. Once he received congressional support for his action, he and Dulles started to hint that they were prepared to use nuclear weapons to protect Formosa. The Chinese leaders, unsure whether Eisenhower was bluffing, decided not to test American resolve.

The apparent refusal of the Soviet Union to come to China's aid in the crisis contributed to the growing rift between the two Communist nations, but the Eisenhower administration failed to take full advantage of the opportunity that it had helped to create.

TURMOIL IN THE MIDDLE EAST

The gravest crisis came in the Middle East when Egyptian leader Gamal Nasser seized the Suez Canal in July 1956. England and France were ready to use force immediately; their citizens owned the canal company, and their economies were dependent on the canal for the flow of oil from the Persian Gulf. Eisenhower, however, was staunchly opposed to intervention, preferring to seek a diplomatic solution with

Nasser, who kept the canal running smoothly. The European allies, nevertheless, decided to take a desperate gamble—invade Egypt and seize the canal while relying on the United States to prevent any Russian interference.

Eisenhower was furious when England and France launched their attack in early November. Unhesitatingly, he instructed Dulles to sponsor a UN resolution calling for British and French withdrawal from Egypt. Yet when the Russians supported the proposal and went further, threatening rocket attacks on British and French cities and offering to send "volunteers" to fight in Egypt, Ike made it clear that he would not allow Soviet interference.

Just after noon on election day, November 6, 1956, British Prime Minister Anthony Eden called the president to inform him that England and France were ending their invasion. Eisenhower breathed a sigh of relief. American voters rallied behind Ike, electing him to a second term. As a result of the Suez crisis, the United States replaced England and France as the main Western influence in the Middle East. With Russia strongly backing Egypt and Syria, the Cold War had found yet another battleground.

Two years later, Eisenhower found it necessary to intervene in the strategic Middle Eastern country of Lebanon. Political power in this neutral nation was divided between Christian and Moslem elements. When the outgoing Christian president, Camille Chamoun, broke with tradition by seeking a second term, Moslem groups (aided by Egypt and Syria) threatened to launch a rebellion. After some hesitation, Ike decided to intervene in order to uphold the U.S. commitment to political stability in the Middle East.

American marines moved swiftly ashore on July 15, 1958, securing the Beirut airport and preparing the way for a force of some 14,000 troops. Lebanese political leaders quickly agreed on a successor to Chamoun, and American soldiers left the country before the end of October. This restrained use of force achieved Eisenhower's primary goal of quieting the explosive Middle East. It also served, as Dulles pointed out, "to reassure many small nations that they could call on us in a time of crisis."

COVERT ACTIONS

In addition to keeping the peace amid these dangerous crises, the Eisenhower administration worked behind the scenes in the 1950s to expand the nation's global influence. In 1953, the CIA was instrumental in overthrowing a popularly elected government in Iran and placing the Shah in full control of that country. American oil companies were rewarded with lucrative concessions, and Eisenhower felt that he had gained a valuable ally on the Russian border. But these short-run gains created a deep-seated animosity among Iranians that would haunt the United States in the years to come.

Closer to home in Latin America, Ike once again relied on covert action. In 1954, the CIA masterminded the overthrow of a leftist regime in Guatemala. The immediate advantage was in denying the Soviets a possible foothold in the Western Hemisphere, but Latin Americans resented the thinly disguised interference of the United States in their internal affairs. More important, when Fidel Castro came to power in Cuba in 1959, the Eisenhower administration adopted a hard line that helped drive Cuba into the Soviet orbit and led in turn to covert action against Castro.

Eisenhower's record as a Cold Warrior was thus mixed. His successful ending of the Korean War and his peacekeeping efforts in Indochina and Formosa and in the Suez crisis are all to his credit. Yet his reliance on coups and subversion directed by the CIA in Iran and Guatemala reveal Ike's corrupting belief that the ends justified the means. Nevertheless, because of his ability to stay calm, he could boast, as he did in 1962, of his ability to keep the peace.

WAGING PEACE

Eisenhower hoped to ease Cold War tensions by ending the nuclear arms race. The development of the hydrogen bomb and long-range ballistic missiles raised considerably the stakes in the arms race. By the mid-1950s, peace, as Winston Churchill noted, depended on a balance of terror.

Throughout the fifties, Eisenhower sought a way out of the nuclear dilemma. In April 1953, shortly after Stalin's death, he called on the Russians to join him in a new effort at disarmament. Even though the Soviets ignored this appeal, Eisenhower kept trying. He outlined an atoms-for-peace plan whereby both the U.S. and the Soviet Union would donate fissionable material to be used for peaceful purposes, and at the Geneva summit conference in 1955 he suggested an "open skies" mutual aerial surveillance program. Unfortunately, both times the Soviets rebuffed Eisenhower's overtures.

After his reelection in 1956, the president made a new effort to initiate nuclear-arms control. Concern over atmospheric fallout from nuclear testing led both Eisenhower and Khrushchev, who had emerged as Stalin's successor, to seek a ban on such experiments. In October 1958, Eisenhower and Khrushchev each voluntarily suspended further weapons tests pending the outcome of a conference held at Geneva to work out a test-ban treaty. Although the Geneva Conference failed to make progress, neither the United States nor the Soviet Union resumed testing for the remainder of Ike's term.

The suspension of testing halted the pollution of the world's atmosphere, but it did not lead to the improvement in Russian-American relations that Eisenhower sought. In the late 1950s, Khrushchev took advantage of the Soviet feat in launching *Sputnik*, the first artificial satellite to orbit the earth, to intensify the Cold War. Playing on Western fears that the Soviets had made a breakthrough in missile technology, the Russian leader began to issue threats, proclaiming, "We will bury capitalism." The most serious threat of all came in November 1958 when Khrushchev declared that within six months he would sign a separate peace treaty with East Germany, thereby ending American, British, and French occupation rights in Berlin. Eisenhower refused to abandon Berlin, however, and prudent diplomacy convinced Khrushchev not to go through with his threat.

In 1959 Khrushchev visited the United States and agreed to attend a summit conference in Paris in May 1960. This much-heralded meet-

The Soviets' successful launching of Sputnik *shook American confidence and triggered new interest and activity in the "space race." Both houses of Congress established Space Committees, and Eisenhower created the National Aeronautics and Space Administration (NASA).*

ing never took place. On May 1, the Soviets shot down an American U-2 plane piloted by Francis Gary Powers. The United States had been overflying Russia since 1956 in these high-altitude spy planes, gaining vital information about the Soviet missile program. When Eisenhower belatedly took full responsibility for the Powers' overflight, Khrushchev responded with a scathing personal denunciation and a refusal to meet with Eisenhower.

Ike deeply regretted the breakup of the Paris summit, telling an aide that "the stupid U-2 mess" had destroyed all his efforts for peace. Before he left office, however, Eisenhower made a final effort at peace. He delivered a farewell address in which he gave a somber warning about the danger of massive military spending. "In the councils of government, we must guard against the acquisition of unwarranted influence, whether sought or unsought, by the military-industrial complex," he declared. "The potential for the disastrous rise of misplaced power exists and will persist."

Rarely has an American president been more prophetic. In the years that followed, the level of defense spending skyrocketed as the Cold War escalated under his successors in the White House. The military-industrial complex reached its acme of power in the 1960s when the United States realized the full implications of Truman's doctrine of containment. Eisenhower had succeeded in keeping the peace for eight years, but he had failed to halt the momentum of the Cold War he had inherited from Truman. Ike's efforts to ease tension with the Soviet Union were dashed by his own distrust of communism and by Khrushchev's belligerent rhetoric and behavior. Still, he had begun the process of relaxing tensions that would survive the troubled sixties and, after a few false starts, would finally end the Cold War in the early nineties.

KENNEDY INTENSIFIES THE COLD WAR

John F. Kennedy was determined to succeed where he felt Eisenhower had failed. Critical of his predecessor for holding down defense spending and apparently allowing the Soviet Union to open up a dangerous lead in intercontinental ballistic missiles (ICBMs), Kennedy sought to warn the nation of its peril and lead it to victory in the Cold War. In his inaugural address, he ignored domestic issues and warned the world that "we shall pay any price, bear any burden, meet any hardship, support any friend, oppose any foe, to assure the survival and success of liberty."

From the day he took office, John F. Kennedy gave foreign policy top priority. In part, this decision reflected the perilous world situation, the immediate dangers ranging from a developing civil war in Vietnam to the emergence of Fidel Castro as a Soviet ally in Cuba. But it also corresponded to Kennedy's personal priorities. As a congressman and senator, he had been an intense Cold Warrior, supporting containment after World War II, lamenting the loss of China, and accusing the Eisenhower administration of allowing the Russians to open up a dangerous missile gap.

Kennedy's appointments reflected his determination to win the Cold War. His choice of Dean Rusk, an experienced but unassertive diplomat, to head the State Department indicated that Kennedy planned to be his own secretary of state. He surrounded himself with young, pragmatic advisors who prided themselves on toughness: McGeorge Bundy, dean of Harvard College, became national security advisor; Walt W. Rostow, an MIT economist, was Bundy's deputy; and Robert McNamara, the youthful president of the Ford Motor Company, took over as secretary of defense. These New Frontiersmen all shared a hard-line view of the Soviet Union and the belief that American security depended upon superior force and the willingness to use it.

FLEXIBLE RESPONSE

The first goal of the Kennedy administration was to build up the nation's armed forces. During the 1960 campaign, Kennedy had claimed that the Soviets were opening a missile gap. In fact, the United States had a significant lead in nuclear striking power by early 1961. Paying little heed to Eisenhower's somber farewell

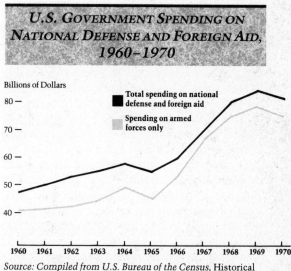

U.S. GOVERNMENT SPENDING ON NATIONAL DEFENSE AND FOREIGN AID, 1960–1970

Source: Compiled from U.S. Bureau of the Census, Historical Statistics of the United States, Colonial Times to 1970, Bicentennial Edition, Washington, D.C., 1975.

warning about the danger of massive military spending, the new administration, intent on putting the Soviets on the defensive, authorized the construction of an awesome nuclear arsenal that included 1000 Minuteman ICBMs. The United States thus opened a missile gap in reverse, creating the possibility of a successful American first strike.

At the same time, the Kennedy administration reinforced its conventional military strength. Secretary of Defense McNamara developed plans to add five combat-ready army divisions, three tactical air wings and a ten-division strategic reserve. The president took a personal interest in counterinsurgency. He expanded the Special Forces unit at Fort Bragg, North Carolina, and insisted, over army objections, that it adopt a distinctive green beret as a symbol of its elite status.

The purpose of this buildup was to create an alternative to Eisenhower's policy of massive retaliation. Instead of responding to Communist moves with nuclear threats, the United States could now call on a wide spectrum of force—ranging from ICBM missiles to Green Berets. The danger, however, of this new strategy of "flexible response" was that the existence of such a powerful arsenal would tempt the new administration to test its strength against the Soviet Union.

CRISIS OVER BERLIN

The first test came in Germany. Since 1958, Soviet Premier Khrushchev had been threatening to sign a peace treaty that would put access to the isolated western zones of Berlin under the control of East Germany. The steady flight of skilled workers to the West through the Berlin escape route weakened the East German regime dangerously, and the Soviets felt they had to resolve this issue quickly.

At a summit meeting in Vienna in June 1961, Kennedy and Khrushchev focused on Berlin as the key issue. In a series of meetings, the two leaders failed to find a solution. During their last session, the failure to reach agreement took on an ominous tone. "I want peace," Khrushchev declared, "but, if you want war,

that is your problem." "It is you, not I," the young president replied, "who wants to force a change." When the Soviet leader said he would sign a German peace treaty by December, Kennedy added, "It will be a cold winter."

The climax came sooner than either man expected. On July 25, Kennedy delivered an impassioned televised address to the American people in which he called the defense of Berlin "essential" to "the entire Free World." He took the unprecedented step of calling more than 150,000 reservists and National Guardsmen to active duty. Above all, he sought to convince Khrushchev of his determination and resolve.

Aware of superior American nuclear striking power, Khrushchev settled for a stalemate. On August 13, the Soviets sealed off their zone of the city. They began the construction of the Berlin Wall to stop the flow of brains and talent to the West. For a brief time, Russian and American tanks maneuvered within sight of each other at Checkpoint Charlie, but by fall the tension gradually eased. The Soviets signed the separate peace treaty; Berlin—like Germany and, indeed, all Europe—remained divided between the East and the West. Neither side could claim a victory, but Kennedy felt that at least he had proved America's willingness to honor its commitments.

CONTAINING FIDEL CASTRO

Two weeks before Kennedy's inaugural, Nikita Khrushchev gave a speech in Moscow in which he declared Soviet support for "wars of national liberation." The Russian leader's words were actually aimed more at China than the United States, but Kennedy concluded that the United States and Russia were now locked in a struggle for the hearts and minds of the uncommitted in Asia, Africa, and Latin America.

Calling for a new policy of nation building, Kennedy advocated financial and technical assistance designed to help Third World nations achieve economic modernization and stable, pro-Western governments. Measures ranging from the formation of the idealistic Peace Corps to the creation of the ambitious Alliance

To his great embarrassment, Kennedy's handling of the Bay of Pigs invasion backfired like the exploding Cuban cigar.

for Progress—a massive economic aid program for Latin America—were part of this effort. Unfortunately, Kennedy relied even more on counterinsurgency and the Green Berets to beat back the Communist challenge.

Kennedy's determination to check global Communist expansion reached a peak of intensity in Cuba. In the 1960 campaign, pointing to the growing ties between the Soviet Union and Fidel Castro's regime, he had accused the Republicans of permitting a "Communist satellite" to arise on "our very doorstep." Kennedy had even issued a statement backing "anti-Castro forces in exile."

In reality, the Eisenhower administration had been training a group of Cuban exiles in Guatemala since March 1960 as part of a CIA plan to topple the Castro regime. Many of Kennedy's advisors had tactical and moral doubts about the proposed invasion, but the president, committed by his own campaign rhetoric and

assured of success by the military, decided to go ahead.

On April 17, 1961, 1400 Cuban exiles moved ashore at the Bay of Pigs on the southern coast of Cuba. Even though the United States had masterminded the entire operation, Kennedy insisted on covert action, even canceling at the last minute a planned American air strike on the beachhead. With air superiority, Castro's well-trained forces had no difficulty in quashing the invasion.

Aghast at the swiftness of the defeat, Kennedy took personal responsibility for the failure. In his address to the American people, however, he showed no remorse for arranging the violation of a neighboring country's sovereignty, only regret at the outcome. Above all, he expressed renewed defiance, asserting that the United States would resist "Communist penetration" in the Western Hemisphere. For the remainder of his presidency, Kennedy continued to harass the Castro regime.

AT THE BRINK

The climax of Kennedy's crusade came in October 1962 with the Cuban missile crisis. Throughout the summer and early fall, the Soviets engaged in a massive arms buildup in Cuba, ostensibly to protect Castro from an American invasion. Although Kennedy had warned the Soviets against the introduction of any offensive weapons, Khrushchev secretly took a daring gamble and started to build missile sites in Cuba. Later he claimed his purpose was purely defensive, but most likely he was responding to the pressures from his own military to close the enormous strategic gap in nuclear striking power that Kennedy had opened.

On October 14, 1962, American U-2 planes finally discovered the missile sites that were nearing completion. As soon as he learned of the Russian action, Kennedy decided to seek a showdown with Khrushchev. Insisting on absolute secrecy, he convinced a special group of advisors to consider how to respond.

After weighing his alternatives, Kennedy finally decided on a two-step procedure. He would proclaim a quarantine of Cuba to prevent the arrival of new missiles and threaten a nuclear strike to force the removal of those already there. If the Russians did not cooperate, then the United States would invade Cuba and dismantle the missiles by force.

On the evening of October 22, Kennedy informed the nation of the existence of the Soviet missiles and his plans to remove them. He spared no words in blaming Khrushchev, and he made it clear that any missile attack from Cuba would lead to "a full retaliatory response upon the Soviet Union."

For the next six days, the world hovered on the brink of nuclear catastrophe. Khrushchev replied defiantly, and some sixteen Soviet ships continued on course toward Cuba. While the American navy deployed to intercept the Russian ships 500 miles from the island, American troops assembled in Florida in preparation for an invasion.

The first break came at midweek when the Soviet ships suddenly halted to avert a confrontation at sea. Kennedy felt better on Friday when Khrushchev sent him a long, rambling letter offering a face-saving way out—Russia would remove the missiles in return for an American promise never to invade Cuba. Kennedy was ready to accept when a second Russian message raised the stakes by insisting that American missiles be withdrawn from Turkey. Heeding his brother's advice, Kennedy decided to ignore the second Russian message and accept the original offer.

On Saturday night, October 27, Robert Kennedy—the president's brother and most trusted advisor—met with Soviet ambassador Anatoly Dobrynin to make it clear that this was the last chance to avert nuclear conflict. At nine the next morning, Khrushchev agreed to remove the missiles in return for Kennedy's promise not to invade Cuba. The crisis was over.

On the surface, Kennedy appeared to have won a striking personal and political victory. His party successfully overcame the Republican challenge in the November elections and his own popularity reached new heights in the Gallup poll. The American people, on the defensive since *Sputnik*, suddenly felt that they had proved their superiority over the Russians.

The Cuban missile crisis had more substantial results as well. Shaken by their close call, Kennedy and Khrushchev agreed to install a "hot line" to speed direct communication between Washington and Moscow in an emergency. Long-stalled negotiations over the reduction of nuclear testing suddenly resumed, leading to the limited test-ban treaty of 1963, which outlawed tests in the atmosphere while still permitting them underground. Above all, Kennedy displayed a new maturity as a result of the crisis. He shifted from the rhetoric of confrontation to that of conciliation.

Despite these hopeful signs, the missile crisis also had an unfortunate consequence. Those who believed that the Russians understood only the language of force were confirmed in their penchant for a hard line. Hawks who had backed Kennedy's military buildup felt that events had justified a policy of nuclear superiority. The Russian leaders drew similar conclusions. "Never will we be caught like this again," vowed one Russian official. After 1962, the Soviets embarked on a crash program to build up their navy and to overtake the American lead in nuclear missiles. Kennedy's moment of triumph thus ensured the escalation of the arms race. His legacy was one of short-term success and long-term anxiety.

JOHNSON ESCALATES THE VIETNAM WAR

Lyndon Johnson stressed continuity in foreign policy just as he had in enacting Kennedy's domestic reforms. He not only inherited the policy of containment from Kennedy, but he shared the same Cold War assumptions and convictions. And feeling less confident about dealing with international issues, he tended to rely heavily on Kennedy's advisors—notably Secretary of State Rusk, Secretary of Defense McNamara, and McGeorge Bundy (the national security advisor until he was replaced in 1966 by the even more hawkish Walt Rostow).

Although Johnson had had broad exposure to national security affairs, he fully accepted the common assumptions of Americans influenced by the "lessons" of World War II.

Like many people of his generation, he believed weakness, not strength, led to war. And he had also seen the devastating political impact of the Communist triumph in China on the Democratic party in the 1940s. "I am not going to lose Vietnam," he told the American ambassador to Saigon just after taking office in 1963. "I am not going to be the president who saw Southeast Asia go the way China went."

Aware of the problem Castro had caused John Kennedy, LBJ moved firmly to contain communism in the Western Hemisphere. When a military junta overthrew a leftist regime in Brazil, Johnson offered covert aid and open encouragement. In 1965, to block the possible emergence of a Castro-type government, LBJ sent 20,000 American troops to the Dominican Republic. His flimsy justification served only to alienate liberal critics in the United States. The intervention ended in 1966 with the election of a conservative government. But the cost of Johnson's victories was substantial. Such liberals as Senate Foreign Relations Committee Chairman William Fulbright deserted LBJ. The more Johnson struggled to uphold the traditional Cold War policies he had inherited from Kennedy, the more he found himself under attack from Congress, the media, and the universities.

CIVIL WAR IN VIETNAM

It was Vietnam rather than Latin America that became Lyndon Johnson's obsession and led ultimately to his political downfall. He inherited the Civil War in South Vietnam and the American commitment to Diem's regime in Saigon from Eisenhower and Kennedy.

The American decision to back Ngo Dinh Diem had prevented the holding of elections throughout Vietnam in 1956, as called for in the Geneva accords. Instead, Diem sought to establish a separate government in the South with large-scale American economic and military aid. By the time Kennedy entered the White House, however, the Communist government in North Vietnam, led by Ho Chi Minh, was directing the efforts of Viet Cong rebels in the South.

As the guerrilla war intensified in the fall of 1961, Kennedy sent two trusted advisors, Walt Rostow and General Maxwell Taylor, to South Vietnam. They returned favoring the dispatch of 8000 American combat troops. General Taylor described the risks of "backing" into a major Asian war by way of South Vietnam as "present but not impressive."

Kennedy decided against sending in combat troops in 1961, but he authorized substantial increases not only in economic aid to Diem but also in the size of the military mission in Saigon. The number of American advisors grew from fewer than a thousand in 1961 to more than 16,000 by late 1963. American aid slowed the Communist momentum, but by 1963 the situation had again become critical. Diem had failed to win the support of his own people; Buddhist monks set themselves aflame in public protests; and even Diem's own generals plotted his overthrow.

President Kennedy was in a quandary. He realized that the fate of South Vietnam would be determined not by Americans but by the Vietnamese. But at the same time, he was not prepared to accept the possible loss of all Southeast Asia. He did not want to "lose" South Vietnam. Although aides later claimed he planned to pull out after the 1964 election, Kennedy raised the stakes by tacitly approving a coup that led to Diem's overthrow and death on November 1, 1963. The resulting power vacuum in Saigon made further American involvement in Vietnam almost certain.

THE VIETNAM DILEMMA

The situation in Vietnam plagued Johnson from the outset. He took office only three weeks after the coup that had removed Diem and left a vacuum of power. In 1964, seven different governments ruled South Vietnam, and the mood in Saigon was tense and restless. Resisting pressure from the Joint Chiefs of Staff for direct American military involvement, LBJ simply continued Kennedy's policy of economic and technical assistance. He insisted it

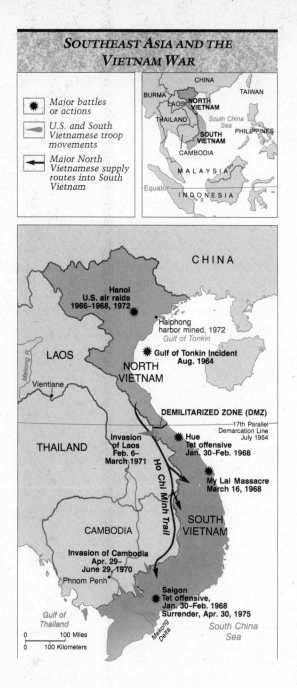

These undercover activities led directly to the Gulf of Tonkin affair. On August 2, 1964, North Vietnamese torpedo boats attacked the *Maddox*, an American destroyer engaged in electronic intelligence-gathering in the Gulf of Tonkin, in the belief that the American ship had been involved in a South Vietnamese raid nearby. The *Maddox* escaped unscathed, but to show American resolve, the navy sent in another destroyer, the *C. Turner Joy*. On the evening of August 4, the two destroyers, responding to sonar and radar contacts, opened fire on North Vietnamese gunboats in the area. Later investigation suggested that the North Vietnamese gunboats had not attacked the American ships, but Johnson ordered retaliatory air strikes on North Vietnamese naval bases.

The next day the president asked Congress to pass a resolution authorizing him to take "all necessary measures to repel any armed attack against the forces of the United States and to prevent further aggression." Later, critics charged that LBJ wanted a blank check from Congress to carry out the future escalation of the Vietnam War, but such a motive is unlikely. In part, he wanted the Gulf of Tonkin Resolution to demonstrate to North Vietnam the American determination to defend South Vietnam at any cost. He also wanted to preempt the Vietnam issue from his Republican opponent, Barry Goldwater, who had been advocating a tougher policy. By taking a firm stand on the Gulf of Tonkin incident, Johnson could both impress the North Vietnamese and outmaneuver a political rival at home. Later, after the incident had served its purpose, Johnson dismissed the attack with, "Hell, I think we may have fired at a whale."

Congress responded with alacrity. The House acted unanimously, while only two senators, both Democrats, voted against the Gulf of Tonkin Resolution. Johnson appeared to have won a spectacular victory, and his standing in the Gallup poll shot up from 42 to 72 percent.

In the long run, however, this easy victory proved very costly. Once having used force against North Vietnam, LBJ was more likely to

was still up to the Vietnamese themselves to win the war. At the same time, he expanded American support for covert operations, including amphibious raids on the North.

do so in the future, and the congressional resolution was phrased broadly enough to enable him to use whatever level of force he wished—including unlimited military intervention. Above all, when he did wage war in Vietnam, he left himself open to the charge of deliberately misleading Congress. Presidential credibility proved to be Johnson's ultimate Achilles heel; in that sense, his political downfall began with the Gulf of Tonkin Resolution.

ESCALATION

The full-scale American involvement in Vietnam began in 1965 in a series of steps designed primarily to prevent a North Vietnamese victory. With the political situation in Saigon growing more hopeless every day, the president's advisors urged the bombing of the North as the only conceivable solution. American air attacks would serve several purposes: They would block North Vietnamese infiltration routes, make Hanoi pay a heavy price for its role, and lift the sagging morale of the South Vietnamese. But most important, they would save South Vietnam from utter defeat. Johnson responded in February 1965 by ordering a long-planned aerial bombardment of selected North Vietnamese targets.

The air strikes proved ineffective. In April, Johnson authorized the use of American ground forces in South Vietnam, but he restricted them to defensive operations intended to protect American air bases. Rejecting the clear-cut alternatives of withdrawal or the massive use of force, LBJ settled for a steady military escalation designed to compel Hanoi to accept a diplomatic solution. In July, the president permitted a gradual increase in the bombing of North Vietnam and allowed American ground commanders to conduct combat operations in the South. Most ominously, he approved the immediate dispatch of 50,000 troops to Vietnam and the future commitment of 50,000 more.

These July decisions formed "an open-ended commitment to employ American military forces as the situation demanded," writes historian George Herring. Convinced that withdrawal would destroy American credibility before the world and that an invasion of the North would lead to World War III, Johnson opted for large-scale but limited military intervention. Moreover, LBJ feared the domestic consequences of either extreme. A pullout could cause a massive political backlash at home, as conservatives condemned him for betraying South Vietnam to communism. All-out war, however, would mean the end of his social programs. So he settled for a limited war, committing a half-million American troops to battle in Southeast Asia, all the while pretending it was a minor engagement and refusing to ask the American people for the support and sacrifice required for victory.

Johnson was not solely responsible for the Vietnam War. He inherited both a policy that assumed that Vietnam was a vital national interest and a deteriorating situation in Saigon that demanded a more active American role. Truman, Eisenhower, and Kennedy had taken the United States deep into the Vietnam maze; it was Johnson's fate to have to find a way out. But LBJ must bear full responsibility for the way he tried to resolve his dilemma. The failure to confront the people with the stark choices they faced, the insistence on secrecy and deceit, the refusal to acknowledge that he had committed the nation to a dangerous military involvement—these were Johnson's sins in Vietnam.

STALEMATE

For the next three years, Americans waged an intensive war in Vietnam and succeeded only in preventing a Communist victory. Bombing of North Vietnam proved ineffective, failing either to damage an essentially agrarian economy or to block the flow of supplies southward through Laos and Cambodia. In fact, the American air attacks, with their resultant civilian casualties, supplied North Vietnam with a powerful propaganda weapon, which it effectively used to sway world opinion against the United States.

Date	Event	Significance
May, 1950	Truman authorizes $10 million in aid to the French in Indochina fighting a war against guerrilla forces led by Ho Chi Minh.	Beginning of U.S. involvement in Vietnam.
May, 1954	Fall of Dien Bien Phu.	End of French dominance in Indochina.
July, 1954	Geneva Conference	Division of Vietnam at 17th parallel. Ho's forces gain control of North Vietnam.
Oct., 1954	Eisenhower backs Diem regime in Saigon, capital of South Vietnam.	U.S. replaces France as chief Western supporter of South Vietnam.
Nov., 1961	Kennedy sends thousands of military "advisors" to Vietnam.	The way is opened for an American combat role in Vietnam.
Nov., 1963	Overthrow and assassination of Ngo Dinh Diem after Kennedy gives tacit approval.	Political vacuum of power created in Saigon.
Aug., 1964	Congress passes Gulf of Tonkin Resolution.	President Johnson is given authority to use unlimited military force in Vietnam.
Feb., 1965	U.S. begins bombing of North Vietnam. It proves ineffective.	Johnson commits U.S. prestige to prevent defeat of South Vietnam.
July, 1965	Johnson announces decision to send 50,000 ground troops to Vietnam.	U.S. involvement escalates in an effort to compel a diplomatic settlement.
Jan., 1968	American ground troops reach the 500,000 mark. Viet Cong launch Tet offensive.	Public support for Vietnam War erodes in United States.
March, 1968	Johnson announces decision not to run for reelection.	End of American escalation in Vietnam.
May, 1968	Paris peace talks begin.	U.S. and North Vietnam quickly deadlock on peace terms.
June, 1969	Nixon announces withdrawal of 25,000 American troops from Vietnam.	Beginning of policy of Vietnamization.
April, 1970	Nixon orders invasion of Cambodia.	Widening of war to include all Indochina.
May, 1972	Nixon authorizes mining of Haiphong harbor and intensified bombing of North Vietnam.	U.S. attempts to pressure North Vietnam into agreeing to peace terms.
Jan., 1973	Cease-fire agreements signed in Paris. U.S. agrees to remove its troops within 60 days.	End of direct American military involvement in Vietnam.
Jan., 1975	North Vietnam invades South Vietnam.	U.S. unwilling to try again to rescue South Vietnam.
April, 1975	Fall of Saigon.	Abrupt U.S. withdrawal from South Vietnam.

The war in the South went no better. Despite the steady increase in American ground forces, from 184,000 in late 1965 to more than 500,000 in early 1968, the Viet Cong still controlled much of the countryside. The search-and-destroy tactics employed by the Americans proved ill-suited. The Viet Cong waged a war of insurgency, avoiding fixed positions and striking from ambush. In a vain effort to destroy the enemy, General William Westmoreland used superior American firepower wantonly, devastating the countryside, causing many civilian casualties, and driving the peasantry into the arms of the guerrillas.

The climax came in late January 1968 when the Viet Cong, aided by North Vietnamese regulars, launched the Tet offensive to mark the lunar New Year, recklessly attacking the South

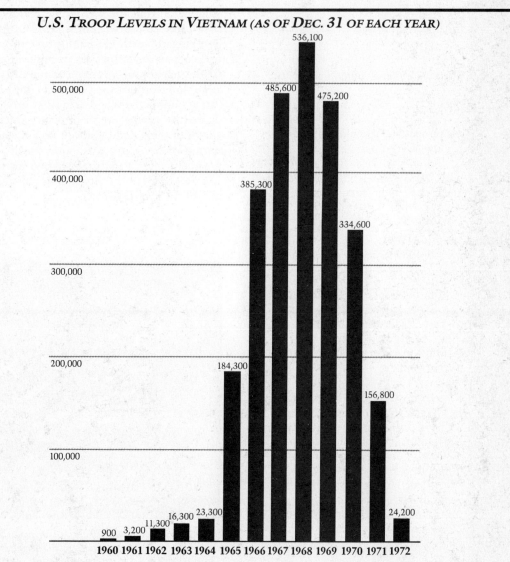

U.S. Troop Levels in Vietnam (as of Dec. 31 of each year)

Source: U.S. Department of Defense

CHRONOLOGY

Vietnamese cities and provincial capitals. American and government troops quickly beat back this bold assault, but at home, television viewers were shocked by scenes of VC fighting within the walls of the American embassy compound in Saigon. The outcome was a tactical defeat for the Communists but a decided political setback for the United States. President Johnson had been hammering away at the idea that the war was almost over; suddenly it appeared to be nearly lost.

President Johnson reluctantly came to the conclusion that the war would end in a stalemate. In mid-March, LBJ decided to limit the bombing of North Vietnam in an effort to open up peace negotiations with Hanoi. In a speech to the nation on Sunday evening, March 31, 1968, Johnson outlined his plans for a new effort at ending the war peacefully, and then concluded by saying, as proof of his sincerity, "I shall not seek, and I will not accept, the nomination of my party for another term as your president." Thus a stunned nation learned that LBJ had become the first major political casualty of the Vietnam War.

In 1967 British cartoonist Leslie Illingworth showed Lyndon Johnson caught in the gears of "The Time Machine," scrambling for escape.

In the twenty-four years since the siege of Dien Bien Phu, American policy had gone full cycle in Vietnam. Even though Eisenhower had decided against using force to rescue the French, his commitment to the Diem regime in Saigon had led eventually to American military involvement on a massive scale. Three years of inconclusive fighting and a steadily mounting loss of American lives had disillusioned the American people and finally cost Lyndon Johnson the presidency. And the full price the nation would have to pay for its folly in Southeast Asia was still unknown—the Vietnam experience would continue to cast a shadow over American life for years to come.

The failure in Vietnam reflected the difficulty the United States faced in pursuing containment on a global scale. The policies that had worked well in Europe in the 1940s had little relevance to a very different situation in Southeast Asia. Intent on halting the spread of communism, American leaders never grasped the political realities in Vietnam. The United States ended up backing a series of corrupt regimes in Saigon while the Viet Cong won the struggle for the hearts and minds of the Vietnamese people. More than anything else, the Vietnam War revealed the need for a thorough reexamination of the basic premises of American foreign policy in the Cold War.

❧ RECOMMENDED READING

The best introduction to the Vietnam War is the balanced survey by George Herring, *America's Longest War*, 2nd ed. (1985). Lloyd Gardner offers a persuasive analysis of the early American involvement through 1954 in *Approaching Vietnam* (1988), while George McT. Kahin, *Intervention* (1986) is excellent on what led to the escalation of the 1960s. Stephen E. Ambrose exemplifies the recent reevaluation of Dwight D. Eisenhower by historians in the second volume of his biography, *Eisenhower: The President* (1985). For an equally favorable analysis, see Robert A. Divine, *Eisenhower and the Cold War* (1981). Roger Hilsman, *To Move a Nation* (1967), is by far the most complete and analytical study of Kennedy's foreign policy.

H. W. Brands gives a good overview of Eisenhower's foreign policy team in *Cold Warriors* (1988).

Other books on Ike's foreign policy include Emmet J. Hughes, *The Ordeal of Power* (1962), a revealing memoir; Peter Lyon, *Eisenhower: Portrait of the Hero* (1974), a critical biography; William B. Ewald, *Eisenhower the President* (1981), a sympathetic account; and Blanche W. Cook, *The Declassified Eisenhower* (1981), a critique of his diplomacy. Eisenhower's two volumes of memoirs, *Mandate for Change* (1963) and *Waging Peace* (1966) are full and revealing accounts.

The best accounts of early American involvement in Vietnam are Andrew Rotter, *The Path to Vietnam* (1988), on events before 1954; Ellen J. Hammer, *The Struggle for Indochina, 1940–1955* (1966); Melvin Gurtov, *The First Vietnamese Crisis* (1967); Bernard B. Fall, *Hell in a Very Small Place* (1966), on the siege of Dien Bien Phu; and Melanie Billings-Yun, *Decision Against War* (1988) on Eisenhower and Dien Bien Phu. On Latin America, the best accounts are Richard Immerman, *The CIA in Guatemala* (1982) and Stephen Rabe, *Eisenhower and Latin America* (1988). For information on specific topics, see Chester Cooper, *The Lion's Last Roar* (1978) and Donald Neff, *Warriors at Suez* (1981) on the Suez crisis; David A. Mayers, *Cracking the Monolith* (1986) and Gordon Chang, *Friends and Enemies: The United States, China, and the Soviet Union, 1948–1972* (1990) on policy toward Communist China; Robert A. Divine, *Blowing on the Wind* (1978) and Richard Hewlett and Jack Holl, *Atoms for Peace and War, 1953–1961* (1989) on nuclear issues; Michael R. Beschloss, *May-Day* (1986) on the U-2 crisis; and Burton Kaufman, *Trade and Aid* (1982) on foreign economic policy.

Kennedy's foreign policy is subjected to critical scrutiny in Richard J. Walton, *Cold War and Counter-revolution* (1972) and Louise FitzSimmons, *The Kennedy Doctrine* (1972); the most recent scholarly reappraisal is Thomas Paterson, ed. *Kennedy's Quest for Victory* (1989). Philip Geyelin analyzes LBJ's foreign-policy weaknesses in *Lyndon B. Johnson and the World* (1966), while Walt W. Rostow defends both the Kennedy and Johnson records in *The Diffusion of Power* (1972). Desmond Ball, *Politics and Force Levels* (1981); Harland B. Moulton, *Nuclear Superiority and Parity* (1972); and two broader studies of the arms race since 1945, McGeorge Bundy, *Danger and Survival* (1989) and Ronald Powaski, *March to Armageddon* (1987).

On Latin America, Theodore Draper, *Castro's Revolution* (1962); Richard E. Welch, *Response to Revolution* (1985); Trumbull Higgins, *The Perfect Failure* (1987); Peter Wyden, *The Bay of Pigs* (1979); Elie Abel, *The Missile Crisis* (1966); Robert F. Kennedy, *Thirteen Days* (1968); Graham Allison, *The Essence of Decision* (1971); Raymond Garthoff, *Reflections* on the Cuban Missile Crisis (1987); James G. Blight and David A. Welch, *On the Brink* (1989); and Herbert Dinerstein, *The Making of the Missile Crisis* (1976) all deal with aspects of the Cuban problem. Books on Johnson's intervention in the Dominican Republic include John B. Martin, *Overtaken by Events* (1966); Jerome Slater, *Intervention and Negotiation* (1970); Abraham Lowenthal, *The Dominican Intervention* (1972); and Piero Gleijeses, *The Dominican Crisis* (1976).

Kennedy's handling of a key European problem is traced in Norman Gelb, *The Berlin Wall* (1986) and Honore Catudel, *Kennedy and the Berlin Wall Crisis* (1980). For African policy, see Richard D. Mahoney, *JFK: Ordeal in Africa* (1983) and Thomas J. Noer, *Cold War and Black Liberation* (1985).

Stanley Karnow offers a broad view of the Vietnam War in *Vietnam: A History* (1983). Other general accounts of the war in Vietnam include Guenther Lewy, *American in Vietnam* (1978); Gabriel Kolko, *Anatomy of a War* (1986); Chester Cooper, *The Lost Crusade* (1970); Leslie H. Gelb and Richard K. Betts, *The Irony of Vietnam* (1979); and David Halberstam, *The Best and the Brightest* (1972). For Kennedy's role, see William J. Rust, *Kennedy in Vietnam* (1985) and Ellen J. Hammer, *A Death in November* (1987). Neil Sheehan, ed., *The Pentagon Papers* (1971) contains important documents on the war.

Lyndon Johnson's Vietnam decisions and their consequences are traced in two books by Larry Berman, *Planning a Tragedy* (1982) and *Lyndon Johnson's War* (1989); two books on the Gulf of Tonkin incident, Joseph C. Goulden, *Truth is the First Casualty* (1969) and Anthony Austin, *The President's War* (1971); Kathleen Turner, *Lyndon Johnson's Dual War* (1985), on LBJ and the media; Townsend Hoopes, *The Limits of Intervention* (1969); Don Oberdorfer, *Tet!* (1971); and Herbert Y. Schandler, *The Unmaking of a President* (1977), on Johnson's change of heart in 1968.

31 PROTEST AND REACTION: FROM VIETNAM TO WATERGATE

YEARS OF TURMOIL

THE ELECTION OF 1968

NIXON IN POWER

THE CRISIS OF DEMOCRACY

"We are the people of this generation, bred in at least modest comfort, housed now in universities, looking uncomfortably to the world we inherit." So began the preamble to the Port Huron Statement, a manifesto of the newly reorganized Students for a Democratic Society (SDS) that became the call to arms for the vanguard of an entire generation. Like most revolutions, this one began small—fifty-nine delegates at a union summer camp in Michigan, in June 1962. The two main organizers, Al Haber and Tom Hayden, nevertheless hoped to transform their small student-protest group into the vehicle that would rid American society of poverty, racism, and violence.

Their timing was perfect. College enrollments were climbing rapidly as a result of the post-World War II baby boom and growing affluence. Before the end of the decade, more than half the American population would be under age thirty. And many, repelled by the crass materialism of American life, were ready to embrace a new life-style based on the belief that "man is sensitive, searching, poetic, and capable of love." They were ready to create a counterculture.

In some ways, the proposal adopted at Port Huron was prosaic, repeating many conventional liberal reforms. But it offered a startling new approach by advocating "participatory democracy" as its main tactic for social reform. In contrast to both traditional liberalism and old-fashioned socialism, the SDS sought salvation through the individual rather than the group.

Personal control of one's life and destiny, not simply the creation of new bureaucracies, became the hallmark of the New Left.

For the next few years, the SDS grew phenomenally. Spurred on by the Vietnam War and massive campus unrest, the SDS could count more than 100,000 followers and was responsible for disruptions at nearly 1000 colleges in 1968. Yet its very emphasis on the individual and its fear of entrenched cadres left it leaderless and subject to division and disunity. By 1970 a split between factions, based on their attitudes toward violence, led to its complete demise.

The meteoric career of the SDS symbolized the turbulence of the 1960s. For a brief time, it seemed as though the nation's youth had gone berserk, indulging in a wave of experimentation with drugs, sex, and rock music. Older Americans felt that all the nation's traditional values, from the Puritan work ethic to the family, were under attack.

Not all American youth joined in the cultural insurgency, however. In small towns and among blue-collar workers in the cities, young people went to Friday night high-school football games, cheered John Wayne as he wiped out the Viet Cong in the movie, *The Green Berets*, and attended church with their parents on Sunday. The rebellion was generally limited to children of the upper middle class. But like the flappers of the 1920s, they set the tone for an entire era and left a lasting impression on American society.

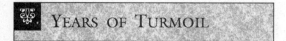

YEARS OF TURMOIL

The agitation of the 1960s was at its height from 1965 to 1968, the years that marked the escalation of the Vietnam War. Disturbances that began on college campuses quickly spread to infect the entire society, from the ghettos of the cities to the lettuce fields of the Southwest. All who felt disadvantaged—students, blacks, browns, women, hippies—took to the streets to give vent to their feelings.

THE STUDENT REVOLT

The first sign of student rebellion came in the fall of 1964 at the prestigious University of California at Berkeley. A small group of radical students resisted university efforts to deny them a place to solicit volunteers and funds for off-campus causes. Forming the Free Speech Movement (FSM), they struck back by occupying administration buildings and blocking the arrest of a nonstudent protester. For the next two months, the campus was in turmoil.

In the end, the protesters won the rights of free speech and association that they championed, and youth everywhere had a new model for effective direction. The hero was Mario Savio, a student who had eloquently summed up the cause by likening the university to a great machine and telling others "You've got to put your bodies upon the gears, and upon the wheels, upon the levers, upon all the apparatus, and you've got to make it stop."

The Free Speech Movement at Berkeley offered many insights into the causes of campus unrest. It was fueled in part by student suspicion of an older Depression-born generation that viewed affluence as the answer to all problems. The catchphrase of the movement was coined by activist Jack Weinberg: "Don't trust anyone over thirty." Unable to exert much influence on the power structure that directed the consumer society, the students turned on the university, which they viewed as the faithful servant of the corporate and political elite as it trained hordes of technicians to operate the new computers, harbored the research laboratories that perfected dreadful military weapons, and regimented its students with IBM punch cards.

War, racism, and poverty were the three great evils that student radicals addressed. Many were involved first in the civil rights cause, but after blacks began to take over the leadership in this area by 1965, white militants found a new issue—the Vietnam War. The first student teach-ins began at the University of Michigan in 1965, and they soon spread to campuses across the nation.

One of the great ironies of the Vietnam War was the system of student draft deferments, which enabled most of those enrolled in college to avoid military service. As a result, the children of the well-to-do, who were more likely to attend college, were able to escape the draft. Those too poor to attend college served in Vietnam in much larger numbers. One survey revealed that men from disadvantaged families, including a disproportionately large black and Hispanic representation, were twice as likely to be drafted and engage in combat in Vietnam as those from more privileged backgrounds. Consequently, a sense of guilt led many college activists, safe from Vietnam because of their student status, to take the lead in denouncing an unjust war.

As the fighting in Southeast Asia intensified in 1966 and 1967, the protests grew larger and the slogans more extreme. "Hey, Hey, LBJ, How Many Kids Have You Killed Today?" chanted students. At the Pentagon in October 1967, more than 100,000 demonstrators confronted a cordon of military policemen guarding the heart of the nation's war machine. From the windows above, Secretary of Defense McNamara and his generals looked down on the angry protesters.

The climax came in the spring of 1968. Driven both by opposition to the war and concern for social justice, the SDS and black radicals at Columbia University joined forces in April. They seized five buildings, effectively paralyzing one of the country's leading colleges. After eight days of tension, the New York City police regained control. In the melee more than 200 students were injured and 700 were arrested. The brutal repression quickened the pace of protest elsewhere. Sit-ins, violent marches, and arrests became common.

The students failed to stop the war, but they did succeed in gaining a voice in their education. University administrations allowed undergraduates to sit on faculty committees to plan the curriculum and gave up their once rigid control of dormitory and social life. But the students' greatest impact lay outside politics and the campus. They spawned a cultural uprising that transformed the manners and morals of America.

THE CULTURAL REVOLUTION

In contrast to the *political* revolt of the elitist SDS, the *cultural* rebellion by youth in the sixties was pervasive. Led by college students, young people challenged the prevailing adult values, in clothing, hairstyles, sexual conduct, work habits, and music. Blue jeans and love beads took the place of business suits and wristwatches, and family life gave way to communes for the "flower children" of the sixties.

Theorists quickly emerged to extol the new way of life. Theodore Roszak gloried in the rejection of modern science and technology in his influential book, *The Making of a Counter Culture* (1969). And Yale law school professor Charles Reich portrayed the emergence of a new world of love, beauty, and racial harmony in his rhapsodic work, *The Greening of America* (1970). He dubbed the new society "Consciousness III."

Music became the touchstone of the new departure. Folk singers like Joan Baez and Bob Dylan, popular for their songs of social protest in the mid-sixties, gave way to rock groups such as the Beatles, whose lyrics were often suggestive of drug use, and finally to "acid rock" as symbolized by the Grateful Dead. The climactic event of the decade came at the Woodstock concert when 400,000 young people indulged in a three-day orgy of rock music, drug experimentation, and public sexual activity.

The cultural revolution was heavily influenced by the drug scene. Former Harvard psychology professor Timothy Leary invited youth to "Tune in, turn on, drop out," literally, as they experimented with marijuana, LSD, and other drugs. Its ultimate expression of insurgency was the Yippie movement, led by such men as Jerry Rubin and Abbie Hoffman. The Yippies mocked the consumer culture and delighted in capitalizing on the mood of social protest to win attention. They succeeded in revealing the hypocrisy in American society, but in the process they fragmented the protest movement; serious radicals dismissed them as parasites.

"BLACK POWER"

The civil rights movement, which had conceived the mood of protest in the sixties, fell on hard times. The legislative triumphs of 1964 and 1965 were relatively easy victories over southern bigotry. Now the movement faced the far more complex problem of achieving economic equality in the cities of the North. Mired in poverty, crowded into ghettos, blacks had actually fallen further behind whites in disposable income since the beginning of the integration effort. The civil rights movement had the expectations of urban African Americans for improvement; frustration mounted as they failed to experience any significant economic gain.

The first sign of trouble came in the summer of 1964, when black teenagers in Harlem and Rochester, New York, rioted. The next summer, a massive outburst of rage and destruction swept over Watts in Los Angeles as the inhabitants burned buildings and looted stores. In 1967 the worst riots yet took place in Newark and Detroit, where forty-three were killed and hundreds injured. The mobs attacked the shops and stores, expressing a burning grievance against a consumer society from which they were excluded by their poverty.

The civil rights coalition fell apart, a victim of both its legislative success and economic failure. Black militants took over the leadership of the Student Nonviolent Coordinating Committee (SNCC); they disdained white help and even reversed Martin Luther King's insistence on nonviolence. SNCC's new leader, Stokely Carmichael, told blacks that they should seize power in those parts of the South where they outnumbered whites. "I am not going to beg the white man for anything I deserve," he said, "I'm going to take it." Soon his calls for "black power" became a rallying cry for more militant blacks who advocated the need for blacks to form their "own institutions,

The civil rights movement brought forth more than protest demonstrations. It raised the expectations of blacks and engendered a feeling of racial pride.

credit unions, co-ops, political parties" and even write their "own history."

Others went further than calls for ethnic separation. H. Rap Brown, who replaced Carmichael as the leader of SNCC in 1967, told a black crowd in Cambridge, Maryland, to "get your guns" and "burn this town down," while Huey Newton, one of the founders of the militant Black Panther party, proclaimed that "political power comes through the barrel of a gun."

King suffered most from this extremism. His denunciation of the Vietnam War cost him the support of the Johnson administration and the more conservative civil rights groups like the NAACP and the Urban League. Radical blacks rejected his nonviolent approach to change. King finally seized on poverty as the proper enemy for attack, but before he could lead his Poor People's March on Washington in 1968, he was assassinated in Memphis in early April.

Both blacks and whites realized that the nation had lost its most eloquent spokesman for racial harmony. His tragic death elevated King to the status of a martyr, but it also led to one last outbreak of widespread urban violence. Blacks exploded in angry riots in 125 cities across the nation; in Chicago and Baltimore, army units were needed to restore order in the ghettos. The worst rioting took place in Washington, D.C., where buildings were set on fire within a few blocks of the White House.

Yet there was a positive side to the emotions engendered by black nationalism. Spokespersons began to urge blacks to take pride in their ethnic heritage, to embrace their blackness as a positive value. Blacks began to wear Afro hairstyles and take interest in their African roots. The word "Negro"—identified with white supremacy of the past—virtually disappeared from usage overnight, replaced by "Afro-American" or "black." Singer James Brown best expressed the sense of racial identity: "Say It Loud—I'm Black and I'm Proud."

ETHNIC NATIONALISM

Other groups quickly emulated the black phenomenon. Native Americans decried the callous use of their identity as football mascots; Puerto Ricans demanded that their history be included in school and college texts; and Polish, Italian, and Czech groups insisted on respect for their nationalities. Congress acknowledged these demands with passage of the Ethnic Heritage Studies Act of 1972, which recognized ethnicity as a positive force in American society and appropriated money to subsidize ethnic studies courses.

Mexican Americans were in the forefront of the ethnic groups that became active in the 1970s. The primary impulse came from the efforts of César Chávez to organize the poorly paid grape pickers and lettuce workers in California into the National Farm Workers Association (NFWA). Chávez appealed to ethnic nationalism in mobilizing Mexican-American field hands to strike against grape growers in the San Joaquin Valley in 1965. Once Chávez had won the attention of the media, a national boycott of grapes by Mexican Americans and their sympathizers among the young people of the country led to a series of hard-fought victories over the growers. The five-year struggle brought union victory in 1970, but at an enormous cost—95 percent of the farm workers had lost their homes and their cars. Undaunted, Chávez turned next to the lettuce fields, and although he met with strong resistance, he succeeded in raising the hourly wage of farm workers in California to $3.53 by 1977 (it had been $1.20 in 1965).

Chávez's efforts helped spark an outburst of ethnic consciousness among Mexican Americans that swept through the urban barrios of the Southwest. Aware that a majority of their compatriots were functionally illiterate as a result of language difficulties and inferior schools, Mexican-American leaders campaigned for bilingual programs and improved educational opportunities. Young activists began to call themselves Chicanos, which had previously been a derogatory term, and to take pride in their cultural heritage; in 1968, they succeeded in establishing the first Mexican-American studies program at California State College at Los Angeles. In addition, student protests in several leading southwestern cities led to significant reforms, such as the introduction of bilingual programs in grade schools and the hiring of more Chicano teachers at all levels.

The Chicano movement had a broad cultural impact. In California and Texas, Mexican Americans began forming paramilitary organizations known as the Brown Berets. This militancy led inevitably to suspicion and hostility on the part of whites as well as to police harassment, which served only to intensify the Brown Berets' radical stance. A more significant cultural milestone came in 1967 with the founding of *El Grito: A Journal of Contemporary Mexican-American Thought*, which published scholarly articles on Chicano history and culture.

WOMEN'S LIBERATION

Active as they were in the civil rights and antiwar movements, women soon learned that the male leaders of protest causes were little different from corporate executives—they expected women to fix the food and type the communiqués while the men made the decisions. Understandably, women soon realized that they could only achieve respect and equality by mounting their own protest.

In some ways, the position of women in American society was worse in the 1960s than it had been in the 1920s. After forty years, there was a lower percentage of women enrolled in the nation's colleges and professional schools, and women with college degrees earned only half as much as similarly trained men. Women were still relegated to stereotyped occupations such as nursing and teaching. And sex roles, as portrayed on television commercials, continued to call for the husband to be the breadwinner and the wife to be the homemaker.

Betty Friedan was the first to seize upon the sense of grievance and discrimination that developed among women in the 1960s. The beginning of the effort to raise women's consciousness was her 1963 book, *The Feminine Mystique*. Calling the American home "a comfortable concentration camp," she attacked the prevailing view that women were completely contented with their housekeeping and child-rearing tasks, claiming that housewives had no self-esteem and no sense of identity.

The 1964 Civil Rights Act helped women attack economic inequality head-on by making it illegal to discriminate in employment on the basis of sex. Women filed suit for equal wages, demanded (with little success) that companies provide day care for their infants and preschool children, and entered politics to lobby against laws that were unfair to women. As the women's liberation movement grew, its advocates began to attack laws banning abortion and waged a campaign to toughen the enforcement of rape laws.

The women's movement met with many of the same obstacles as other protest groups in the 1960s. The moderate leadership of the National Organization for Women (NOW), founded by Betty Friedan in 1966, soon was challenged by those with more extreme views. The harsh rhetoric and militancy of the extremists repelled many women who expressed satisfaction with their lives. But despite these disagreements, most women supported the effort to achieve equal status with men, and in 1972 Congress responded by approving the Equal Rights Amendment to the Constitution.

In addition to concerns about unequal wages, many women felt stifled by their roles as wives and homemakers. Betty Friedan, a leader in the National Organization for Women (NOW), is shown here rallying support for the feminist cause.

This measure, first introduced in Congress in 1923, now faced a vote in the state legislatures, the final step toward ratification.

THE ELECTION OF 1968

The turmoil of the sixties reached a crescendo in 1968 as the American people responded to the two dominant events of the decade—the war in Vietnam and the cultural insurgency at home. To add to the chaos, this election year witnessed a series of bizarre events, including two assassinations, the withdrawal from the race of an incumbent president, and the emergence of the most effective third-party candidate in fifty years.

DEMOCRATS DIVIDE

Lyndon Johnson's withdrawal from the presidential race after the Tet offensive set the tone for the 1968 election. LBJ's decision had come in response to political as well as military realities. By 1966, the antiwar movement had spread from the college campuses to Capitol Hill. Former supporters such as Senator William Fulbright began to question the conflict. Housewives and middle-class professionals were attending the antiwar rallies. Johnson felt like a prisoner in the White House, since in his infrequent public appearances he was hounded by larger and larger gatherings of antiwar demonstrators.

The essentially leaderless protest against the war took on a new quality on January 3, 1968, when Senator Eugene McCarthy, a Democrat from Minnesota, announced that he was challenging LBJ for the party's presidential nomination. Cool, aloof, almost arrogant, McCarthy was an intellectual motivated primarily by a belief that Kennedy and Johnson had abused the power of the presidency. McCarthy's idealism proclaimed, "Whatever is morally necessary must be made politically possible." His stance against the war attracted the support of American youth. In the New Hampshire primary in early March, the nation's earliest polit-

ical test, McCarthy shocked the political experts by coming within a few thousand votes of defeating Johnson.

McCarthy's strong showing in New Hampshire led Robert Kennedy to enter the presidential race. Despite the obvious charge of opportunism he faced, Kennedy had a much better chance than did McCarthy to defeat LBJ and win in the fall. Unlike McCarthy, whose appeal was largely limited to upper-middle-class whites and college students, Kennedy attracted strong support among blue-collar workers, blacks, Chicanos, and other minorities who formed the nucleus of the continuing New Deal coalition.

LBJ's dramatic withdrawal caused an uproar in the Democratic party. With Johnson's tacit backing and strong support from party regulars and organized labor, Vice-President Hubert H. Humphrey, a classic Cold War liberal who had worked equally hard for social reform at home and American expansion abroad, declared his candidacy. The antiwar movement, however, considered him totally unacceptable. Accordingly, he decided to avoid the primaries and work for nomination within the framework of the party.

Kennedy and McCarthy, the two antiwar candidates, were thus left to contest the spring primaries, causing agonizing choices among those who stood for change. Kennedy won everywhere except in Oregon, but his narrow victory in California ended in tragedy when a Palestinian immigrant, Sirhan Sirhan, assassinated him in a Los Angeles hotel.

With his strongest opponent struck down, Humphrey had little difficulty turning back the challenges from McCarthy and George McGovern at the Chicago convention. Backed by party leaders, including Chicago's political boss, Mayor Richard Daley, Humphrey supporters defeated an antiwar resolution and won the nomination on the first ballot.

Humphrey's triumph was marred by violence outside the heavily guarded convention hall. Radical groups had urged their members to come to Chicago to agitate; the turnout was relatively small but included many who were ready to provoke the authorities in their despair

Alarmed by antiwar demonstrators drawn to the Democratic convention, Chicago Mayor Richard Daley erected barbed wire fences in an attempt to control access to the convention hall.

over the convention's outcome. Epithets and cries of "pigs" brought about a savage response from Daley's police, who shared their mayor's contempt for the protesters.

The bitter fumes of tear gas hung in the streets for days afterward; the battered heads and bodies of demonstrators and innocent bystanders alike flooded the city's hospital emergency rooms. What an official investigation later termed a "police riot" marred Humphrey's nomination and made a sad mockery out of his call for "the politics of joy." The Democratic party itself had become the next victim of the Vietnam War.

THE REPUBLICANS' RESURGENCE

The primary beneficiary of the Democratic debacle was Richard Nixon. Written off as politi-

cally dead after his unsuccessful race for governor of California in 1962, Nixon had slowly rebuilt his place within the party. Positioning himself squarely in the middle, with Governor Nelson Rockefeller of New York to his left and Governor Ronald Reagan of California, who had inherited Goldwater's following, on his right, he quickly became the front-runner for the Republican nomination. At the GOP convention in Miami Beach, Nixon won an easy first-ballot nomination and chose Maryland Governor Spiro Agnew as his running mate.

In the fall campaign, Nixon opened up a wide lead by avoiding controversy and reaping the benefit of discontent with the Vietnam War. He exploited television skillfully, appearing before carefully arranged panels to answer friendly questions. He played the peace issue shrewdly, appearing to advocate an end to the conflict without ever taking a definite stand. Above all, he chose the role of reconciler for a nation torn by emotion, a leader who promised to bring a divided country together again.

Humphrey, in contrast, found himself hounded by antiwar demonstrators who heckled him constantly. He walked a tightwire, desperate for the continued support of Johnson but handicapped by LBJ's stubborn refusal to speed up the diplomatic preliminaries in full-scale peace talks and to end all bombing of North Vietnam. His campaign gradually gained momentum, however, as he picked up support from union leaders and from blacks who remembered his strong stand on civil rights. When he broke with Johnson in late September by announcing that if elected he would "stop the bombing of North Vietnam as an acceptable risk for peace," he began to close in on Nixon.

Unfortunately for Humphrey, a third-party candidate cut deeply into the normal Democratic majority. George Wallace had first gained attention as the racist governor of Alabama whose motto was, "Segregation now . . . segregation tomorrow . . . segregation forever." His appeal was to blue-collar workers and white ethnics who believed that many of the gains made by blacks during the 1960s had come at their expense.

Running on the ticket of the American Independent Party, Wallace was a close third in the September polls, but as the election neared, his following declined. Humphrey continued to gain, especially after Johnson agreed in late October to end all bombing of North Vietnam. By the first week in November, the outcome was too close for the experts to call.

Nixon won the election by just 500,000 votes—the smallest share of the popular vote of any winning candidate since 1916, but scored a clear-cut victory in the electoral college, sweeping a broad band of states from Virginia and the Carolinas through the Midwest to the Pacific. As expected, Humphrey did well in the urban Northeast and Wallace made a strong showing in the Deep South.

The election marked a repudiation of the politics of protest and the cultural insurgency of the mid-sixties. The combined popular vote for Nixon and Wallace, 56.5 percent of the elector-ate, signified that there was a silent majority that was fed up with violence and confrontation. A growing concern over psychedelic drugs, rock music, lack of decorum in dress and behavior, and sexual permissiveness offset the usual Democratic advantage on economic issues and led to the election of a Republican president. By voting for Nixon and Wallace, the American people were sending out a message: They wanted a return to traditional values and an end to the war in Vietnam.

NIXON IN POWER

The man who took office as the thirty-sixth president of the United States on January 26, 1969, seemed to be a new Nixon. Gone was the fiery rhetoric and the penchant for making enemies. In their place, observers found an air of moderation and restraint. He appeared to have his emotions under firm control. But beneath the surface, he remained bitter, hurt, and sensitive to criticism.

An innately shy man, Nixon hoped to enjoy the power of the presidency in splendid solitude. He assembled a powerful White House staff whose main task was to isolate him from Congress, the press, and even his own cabinet. Loyal subordinates like H. R. Haldeman and John Ehrlichman took charge of domestic issues, often making decisions without even consulting Nixon. Foreign policy was Nixon's great passion, and here he relied heavily on Henry Kissinger, his national security adviser, to formulate policy, leaving Secretary of State William Rogers to keep the State Department bureaucrats busy with minor details.

The Nixon White House soon could be likened to a fortress under siege. Distrusting everyone, Nixon sought to preside without help from either Congress or his cabinet. An almost paranoid belief that he was surrounded by enemies led him to authorize wiretapping and covert surveillance to plug news leaks and to preserve secrecy. In his quest for privacy, Nixon cut himself off from the nation and thus sowed the seeds of his downfall.

RESHAPING THE GREAT SOCIETY

Beginning his first term on a hopeful note, Nixon promised the nation peace and respite from the chaos of the sixties. Rejecting the divisions that had split Americans apart, he pledged in his inaugural address to "bring us together."

Nixon's moderation indicated a return to the politics of accommodation that had characterized the Eisenhower era. Faced with a Democratic Congress, Nixon, like Ike, appeared ready to accept the main outlines of the welfare state. Instead of any massive overthrow of the Great Society, he focused on making the federal bureaucracy function more efficiently.

His advisers sought the passage of the Family Assistance Plan as a way to overhaul the clumsy welfare system. Instead of piecemeal handouts, each poor family would receive an annual payment of $1600, a variation of the guaranteed annual wage that had long been a goal of liberals. Democrats, however, quickly criticized the plan for the low level of payments. Despite its many attractive features, the Family Assistance Plan failed to win congressional appeal.

Nixon was more successful with his efforts to shift responsibility for social problems from Washington to state and local authorities. He developed the concept of revenue sharing, by which federal funds would be dispersed to state, county, and city agencies to meet local needs. In 1972 Congress approved a measure to share $30.1 billion with local governments over a five-year period. An accompanying ceiling of $2.5 billion a year on federal welfare payments, however, meant that much of the revenue-sharing payments had to be allocated by cities and states to programs previously paid for by the federal government.

In the area of civil rights Nixon made a shrewd political move. Action by Congress and the outgoing Johnson administration had ensured that massive desegregation of southern schools would finally begin just as Nixon took office. Nixon and his attorney general, John Mitchell, decided to shift the responsibility for the process to the courts. When the courts ordered action, the Nixon administration complied. But in the minds of southern white voters, it was the hated Supreme Court, not Richard Nixon, who had forced them to integrate their schools.

Nixon used similar tactics in his attempt to reshape the Supreme Court along more conservative lines. His appointment of Warren Burger, an experienced federal judge with moderate views to replace the retiring Earl Warren as Chief Justice, met with little objection. But when Nixon nominated Clement Haynesworth of South Carolina to fill another vacancy on the Court, liberal Democrats, troubled by conflict-of-interest charges against Haynesworth, led an all-out attack. The Senate rejected the appointment.

Nixon then responded by offering the name of G. Harrold Carswell, a Florida jurist with an undistinguished legal record. When the senators rejected Carswell by a narrow margin, Nixon denounced them for insulting "millions of Americans who live in the South." Once again, Nixon had used the Supreme Court to enhance his political appeal to Southerners.

Nixon finally filled the Court position with Harry Blackmun, a reputable conservative from Minnesota, who easily won confirmation. Subsequently, the president appointed Lewis Powell and William Rehnquist to the Supreme Court. Surprisingly, the Burger Court, despite its more conservative makeup, did not engage in any massive overturn of the Warren Court's decisions. It continued to uphold the legality of desegregation, restricted the government's right to wiretap suspected subversives, overturned state laws prohibiting abortion, and insisted that the death penalty only be invoked under very limited and precise circumstances.

The moderation of the Supreme Court and the legislative record of the Nixon administration demonstrated that the nation was not yet ready to abandon the reforms adopted in the 1960s. The pace of change slowed down in areas such as civil rights and welfare, but the commitment to social justice was still clear.

NIXONOMICS

The economy posed a more severe test for Richard Nixon. He inherited a rising inflationary rate, the product of LBJ's unsuccessful attempt to wage the Vietnam War without raising taxes. Strongly opposed to the idea of federal controls, Nixon rejected suggestions of national guideposts to hold down wages and prices. Instead, he opted for a reduction in government spending while encouraging the Federal Reserve Board to curtail the money supply, forcing up interest rates and slowing the rate of business expansion.

The result was disastrous. Inflation continued, reaching nearly 6 percent by the end of 1970, the highest rate since the Korean War. At the same time the economy underwent its first major recession since 1958. The stock market tumbled, the Dow-Jones average fell from over 900 to just above 600, the sharpest drop in thirty years, unemployment rose, and business failures jumped alarmingly. Democrats quickly coined a new word, "Nixonomics," to describe the disaster.

Conditions seemed to worsen in 1971. Inflation continued unabated, and the nation's balance of trade became negative as imports exceeded exports by a substantial margin. In mid-August, Nixon acted suddenly and boldly to halt the economic decline. Abandoning his earlier resistance to controls, he announced a ninety-day freeze on wages and prices to be followed by federally imposed guidelines in both areas. He also carried out a devaluation of the dollar which, along with a 10-percent surtax on all imports, led to a greatly improved balance of trade. The sudden Nixon economic reversal quickly ended the recession.

BUILDING A REPUBLICAN MAJORITY

"The Great Nixon Turnaround," as historian Lloyd Gardner termed it, came too late to help the Republicans in the 1970 congressional elections. From the time he took office in 1969, Nixon was obsessed with the fact that he had received only 43 percent of the popular vote. The Republicans were still a minority party, and to be reelected in 1972, Nixon would need to win over southern whites and blue-collar workers who had followed George Wallace out of the Democratic party.

Attorney General John Mitchell devised a southern strategy to help achieve a Republican majority by 1972. The administration's well-publicized objection to school desegregation in the South and the attempt to put Haynesworth and Carswell on the Court were part of this design. Advisers urged the Nixon administration to direct its appeal to "middle Americans"—southern whites, Catholic ethnic groups, blue-collar workers, and, above all, the new suburbanites of the South and West.

Nixon unleashed his vice-president, Spiro Agnew, in an attempt to exploit the social issue in the 1970 election. Blaming all social concerns—from sexual permissiveness to crime in the streets—on Democratic liberals and their allies in the media, Agnew delivered a series of scathing speeches. He denounced intellectuals as "an effete corps of impudent snobs" and damned the press as "nattering nabobs of negativism." Despite howls of protest, Agnew proved to be an effective political weapon.

The Democrats decided to change their tactics. Democratic candidates were careful to stress economic issues, blaming the Republicans for both inflation and recession. On the social issue, they joined the chorus against crime, pornography, and drugs.

The outcome was a standoff. Agnew's attacks helped the GOP to limit the usual off-year losses in the House to nine seats, while the Republicans actually gained two votes in the Senate. But the Democrats did well in state elections and proved once again that economic issues were crucial in American politics. Nixon and the Republicans still did not command a national majority.

IN SEARCH OF DÉTENTE

Nixon gave foreign policy top priority, and he proved surprisingly adept at it. In Kissinger, he had a White House specialist who had devoted his life to the study of diplomacy. Nixon and Kissinger approached foreign policy from a similar realistic perspective. "They recognized a cold and logical world without fated allies or enemies—only interested parties," commented one close observer. Instead of viewing the Cold War as an ideological struggle for survival with communism, they saw it as a traditional great-power rivalry, one to be managed and controlled rather than to be won.

Kissinger and Nixon had a grand design. Realizing that recent events, especially the Vietnam War and the rapid Soviet arms buildup of the 1960s, had eroded America's position of primacy in the world, they planned a strategic retreat. There were five major centers of power by the 1970s—the United States, Russia, China,

In a highly publicized visit, Nixon toured the Great Wall in China in 1972 and banqueted with heads of state. This was part of an intentional decision to improve relations with the USSR's next-door rival.

Japan, and the NATO countries of Western Europe. Russia had great military strength, but its economy was weak and it had a dangerous rival in China. Kissinger planned to use American trade—notably grain and high technology—to induce Soviet cooperation, while at the same time improving U.S. relations with China. With Russia neutralized, the United States would then focus on its economic rivalry with Japan and the countries of Western Europe.

Nixon and Kissinger shrewdly played the China card as their first step toward achieving *détente*—that is, a relaxation of tension—with the Soviet Union. After preliminary negotiations, Nixon traveled to China in February 1972. During his well-publicized tour he met with the Communist leaders and ended more than two decades of Sino-American hostility. The problem of Taiwan prevented full-scale diplomatic relations, but Nixon agreed to establish an American liaison mission in Peking as a first step toward ultimate recognition.

The Soviets, who viewed China as a dangerous adversary, responded by agreeing to reach an arms-control pact with the United States. The Strategic Arms Limitation Talks (SALT) had been underway since 1969. During a visit to Moscow in May 1972, Nixon signed two vital documents with Soviet leader Leonid Brezhnev. The first limited the two superpowers to 200 antiballistic missiles (ABMs) apiece; the second froze the number of offensive ballistic missiles for a five-year period.

The SALT I agreements were most important as a symbolic first step toward control of the nuclear-arms race. They signified that the United States and Russia were trying to achieve a settlement of their differences by peaceful means. The sale of American grain to the Soviets, along with proposed trade agreements to share more advanced American computer technology with them, seemed to promise a genuine relaxation of the dangerous tensions of the Cold War.

ENDING THE VIETNAM WAR

Vietnam remained the one foreign-policy challenge that Nixon could not overcome. He had a three-part plan to end the conflict: (1) renewed bombing, (2) a hard-line in negotiations with Hanoi, and (3) the gradual withdrawal of American troops. The last tactic, known as Vietnamization, proved the most successful. As South Vietnamese troops began to take over the major combat role, the number of American soldiers in Vietnam dropped from 543,000 in 1968 to 29,000 by 1972, and domestic opposition to the war declined.

The call for renewed bombing proved the most controversial part of the plan. As early as the spring of 1969, Nixon secretly ordered raids on Communist supply lines in neutral Cambodia. Then in April 1970, he ordered both air and ground strikes into Cambodia. These relieved pressure on hard-pressed South Vietnamese forces but caused a massive outburst of antiwar protests at home. Tragedy struck at Kent State University in Ohio in early May. After rioters had fire-bombed an ROTC building, the governor sent in national guard troops, who were taunted by irate students. The guardsmen then opened fire, killing four students and wounding eleven more. A week later two black students were killed at Jackson State College in Mississippi. Soon there were riots and protests on more than four hundred campuses across the country.

Nixon had little sympathy for the demonstrators, describing them as "bums," intent on "blowing up the campuses." The "silent majority" to whom he appealed seemed to agree. An "Honor America Day" program, held in Washington, D.C., on July 4 attracted 250,000 people who heard Billy Graham and Bob Hope endorse the president's policies. Nixon's Cambodian invasion did little to shorten the Vietnam War, but the public reaction reinforced his resolve not to surrender.

The second tactic, negotiation with Hanoi, finally proved successful. Beginning in the summer of 1969, Kissinger held a series of secret meetings with North Vietnam's foreign minister, Le Duc Tho. By the summer and fall of 1972, the two sides were near agreement, but South Vietnamese objections blocked a settlement before the 1972 elections. When the North Vietnamese tried to make last-minute

changes, Nixon ordered a series of savage B-52 raids on Hanoi that finally led to the signing of a truce on January 27, 1973. In return for the release of all American prisoners of war, the United States agreed to remove troops from South Vietnam in sixty days. The political clauses allowed the North Vietnamese to keep troops in the South, thus virtually guaranteeing future control over all of Vietnam by the Communists.

The agreement was, in fact, a disguised surrender, but finally the American combat role in Vietnam was over, after eight years of fighting, more than 57,000 Americans killed, more than $150 billion expended. The war ranks as America's second most expensive and fourth deadliest armed conflict. Yet even as the fighting wound down, the nation was already deeply enmeshed in another crisis—what Gerald R. Ford termed "the long national nightmare" of Watergate.

THE CRISIS OF DEMOCRACY

"The illegal we do immediately; the unconstitutional takes a little longer," Henry Kissinger once said jokingly of the Nixon administration. Unfortunately, he was far closer to the truth than anyone realized.

THE POLITICS OF DECEIT

Richard Nixon's consuming distrust of even his own associates quickly led to a series of underhanded and illegal activities. In the spring of 1969, when details of the secret bombing of Cambodia began to leak to the press, Nixon ordered wiretaps on the telephones of both reporters and members of Kissinger's National Security Council staff.

When the *New York Times* and the *Washington Post* began publishing the Pentagon Papers, a classified Defense Department study of the Vietnam War, Nixon decided to take drastic measures to plug any further leaks of secret documents. His aides created a self-styled "plumbers" unit within the White House directed by G. Gordon Liddy, a former FBI agent, and E. Howard Hunt, a veteran of the CIA. Charged with preserving secrecy and discrediting those who kept the press informed, Hunt and Liddy set out to embarrass Daniel Ellsberg, the Defense Department official who had leaked the Pentagon Papers. In a vain effort to find damaging information, they went so far as to break into the office of Ellsberg's psychiatrist in Los Angeles.

Operating under a siege mentality that justified any measure necessary to defeat its opponents, the White House went to extreme lengths to guarantee Nixon's reelection in 1972. A Committee to Reelect the President (CREEP) was formed, headed by Attorney General John Mitchell. Specialists in dirty tricks harassed Democratic contenders, while Liddy's "plumbers" developed an elaborate plan to spy on the opposition. Liddy's scheme included bugging the Democratic national headquarters in the Watergate complex in Washington. In the early morning hours of June 17, James McCord and four other men working under the direction of Hunt and Liddy were caught by police during a break-in at Watergate. The continuing abuse of power had finally culminated in an illegal act that soon threatened to bring down the entire Nixon administration.

THE ELECTION OF 1972

The irony of the Watergate break-in was that by the time it occurred Nixon's election was assured. Aided by Donald Segretti's dirty tricks, which included issuing phony press releases and campaign documents to embarrass such prominent contenders as Edmund Muskie and Hubert Humphrey, the Democrats destroyed themselves. First Muskie, the front-runner, replying in the New Hampshire primary to a Segretti-inspired letter accusing him of prejudice against New Englanders of French Canadian descent, lost his composure. Then an assassin shot and seriously wounded George Wallace. Paralyzed, Wallace was forced to drop out of the race, leaving Nixon with a complete monopoly over the political right.

Senator George McGovern of South Dakota emerged with the Democratic nomination. He ran on a platform that advocated a negotiated settlement in Vietnam, the right to abortion, and tolerance of diverse life-styles. The platform was perceived as "anti-establishment" by many middle-class Americans and greatly strengthened Nixon's appeal.

McGovern quickly lost what little strength he had by his inept handling of the vice-presidential nomination. Originally selecting Missouri Senator Thomas Eagleton, McGovern dumped him for R. Sargent Shriver of Maryland when it was disclosed that Eagleton had undergone psychiatric treatment for depression. Integrity had been McGovern's strongest point; when he dropped Eagleton from the ticket, that quality was called into question. His stiff speaking style and self-righteous manner only added to his problems.

Nixon shrewdly let McGovern's apparent extremism and New Left support become the main issue in the campaign, rather than the president's own record in office. Nixon's chances were further strengthened by the recent improvement in the economy and his foreign-policy triumphs with China and Russia.

The result was a stunning victory for Nixon. He won a popular landslide with 60.8 percent of the vote—second only to LBJ's record in 1964—and an even more decisive sweep of the electoral college. The voting patterns did suggest the beginning of a major political realignment, as only blacks, Jews, and low-income voters continued to vote overwhelmingly Democratic. The GOP made significant gains in the South and West and showed the emerging strength of the Sunbelt.

THE WATERGATE SCANDAL

Only Richard Nixon knew how fragile his victory was in 1972. The president apparently had no foreknowledge of the Watergate break-in, but he was deeply implicated in the attempt to cover up the involvement of White House aides in the original burglary. On June 23, only six days after the crime, he ordered the CIA to keep the FBI off the case, on the specious grounds that it involved national security. And he urged his aides to lie under oath, if necessary.

In the short run, the cover-up, directed by White House counsel John Dean, worked. Hunt and Liddy were convicted for their roles in the Watergate break-in, but they carefully avoided implicating either CREEP or Nixon's inner circle of advisers. Despite some very revealing stories by reporters Bob Woodward and Carl Bernstein in the *Washington Post*, the public was kept ignorant of the true dimensions of the Watergate affair.

The first thread unraveled when federal judge John Sirica sentenced the burglars to long jail terms. James McCord was the first to crack, informing Sirica that he had received money from the White House and had been promised a future pardon in return for his silence. By April 1973, Nixon was forced to fire John Dean, who refused to become the scapegoat for the cover-up, and to allow Haldeman and Ehrlichman, who were deeply implicated, to resign. The Senate then appointed a special committee to investigate the Watergate episode, with North Carolina Democrat Sam Ervin as chairman. In a week of dramatic testimony, Dean revealed Nixon's personal involvement in the cover-up. Still Nixon hoped to weather the storm, since it was basically the president of the United States' word against Dean's.

The existence of tapes of conversations in the Oval Office, recorded regularly since 1970, finally brought Nixon down. At first the president tried to invoke executive privilege to withhold the tapes. But his tactics merely delayed action; they did not end the matter. The Supreme Court ruled unanimously in June 1974 that the tapes had to be turned over to Judge Sirica.

By that time the House Judiciary Committee, acting on evidence uncovered by the Ervin committee, voted three articles of impeachment, charging Nixon with obstruction of justice, abuse of power, and contempt of Congress. Faced with the release of tapes that directly implicated him in the cover-up, Nixon finally chose to resign on August 9, 1974.

Nixon's resignation proved to be the culmination of the Watergate scandal. The entire episode revealed both the weaknesses and

Television viewers became acquainted with Senator Sam Ervin (seated), who with Senator Howard Baker (holding pencil) examines a message from the White House regarding the president's tapes during the Watergate scandal.

CHRONOLOGY

1963 Betty Friedan publishes *The Feminine Mystique*

1966 National Organization for Women (NOW) formed

1967 Riots in Detroit kill 43, injure 2000, leave 5000 homeless

1968 Viet Cong launch Tet offensive (January)
Johnson announces he will not seek reelection (March)
Martin Luther King, Jr., assassinated in Memphis, Tennessee (April)
Robert F. Kennedy assassinated in Los Angeles, California (June)
Nixon elected president

1970 U.S. forces invade Cambodia (April)
Ohio National Guardsmen kill four students at Kent State University (May)

1971 *New York Times* publishes the Pentagon Papers (June)
Nixon announces wage-and-price freeze (August)

1972 President Nixon visits China (February)
U.S. and USSR sign SALT 1 accords in Moscow (May)
White House "plumbers" unit breaks into Democratic headquarters in Watergate complex (June)
Richard Nixon wins reelection in landslide victory over McGovern

strengths of the American political system. Most regrettable was the abuse of presidential authority—a reflection both on the growing power of the modern presidency and the fatal flaws in Richard Nixon's character. Unlike such previous executive branch scandals as the Whisky Ring and Teapot Dome, Watergate involved a lust for power rather than for money.

But Watergate also demonstrated the vitality of a democratic society. The press showed how investigative reporting could unlock even the most closely guarded executive secrets. Judge Sirica proved that an independent judiciary was still the best bulwark for individual freedom. And Congress rose to the occasion, both by carrying out a successful investigation of executive misconduct and by following a scrupulous and nonpartisan impeachment process that left Nixon with no chance to escape his ultimate fate.

The nation survived the shock of Watergate with its institutions intact. Congress, in decline since Johnson's administration, was rejuvenated, with its members now intent on expanding congressional authority vis-à-vis the executive branch. There was, however, one lasting casualty. The people's faith in politicians was severely shaken. The events of the 1960s and the early 1970s had left the American people in a mood of cynicism and despair. After the Watergate experience, the ultimate challenge facing presidential aspirants was to offer the kind of inspired leadership that would rekindle the flagging democratic spirit.

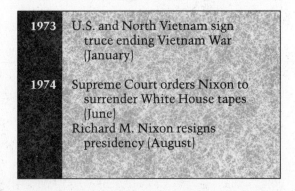

1973 U.S. and North Vietnam sign truce ending Vietnam War (January)

1974 Supreme Court orders Nixon to surrender White House tapes (June)
Richard M. Nixon resigns presidency (August)

✿ RECOMMENDED READING

The most penetrating analysis of the youthful protesters of the 1960s is Kenneth Keniston, *Young Radicals* (1968), a detailed assessment of the motives and aspirations of a group of antiwar activists. For a broader picture of the New Left see Irwin Unger, *The Movement* (1974).

The transition from the quest for integration to the assertion of black power is traced in James C. Harvey, *Black Civil Rights During the Johnson Administration* (1973); Clayborne Carson, *In Struggle* (1981); and Stokely Carmichael and C. V. Hamilton, *Black Power* (1967). Steven Lawson traces the growing importance of blacks in southern politics after 1965 in *In Pursuit of Power* (1985). For the urban riots of the sixties, see Robert Conot, *Rivers of Blood, Years of Darkness* (1967) on Watts; John Hersey, *The Algiers Hotel Incident* (1968) on Detroit; and James W. Button, *Black Violence* (1978). The growing self-consciousness of other minorities is described in Michael Novak, *The Rise of the Unmeltable Ethnics* (1973); Matt Meier and Feliciano Rivera, *The Chicanos* (1972); and Rodolfo Acuna, *Occupied America: A History of Chicanos*, 2d. ed. (1981). For the feminist movement, see two books by William Chafe, *The American Woman* (1972) and *Woman and Equality* (1977), and Sara Evans, *Personal Politics* (1979).

The tumultuous election of 1968 is described in Theodore White, *The Making of the President, 1968* (1969), and Lewis Chester, Godfrey Hodgson, and Bruce Page, *American Melodrama* (1969). Nixon's character and prepresidential career are traded in Garry Wills, *Nixon Agonistes* (1970), and Stephen E. Ambrose, *Nixon: The Education of a Politician, 1913–1962* (1987). Other important books on Nixon include William Safire, *Before the Fall* (1975); and the president's own memoir, *RN* (1978).

Henry Brandon, *The Retreat of American Power* (1973); Tad Szulc, *The Illusion of Peace* (1978); and Stanley Hoffman, *Primacy or World Order* (1978), all describe Nixon's foreign policy and the search for détente. Books that focus on Kissinger's role include his own memoir, *The White House Years* (1979); Seymour Hersh, *The Price of Power* (1983); Marvin Kalb and Bernard Kalb, *Kissinger* (1974); Roger Morris, *Uncertain Greatness* (1977); and Seyom Brown, *The Crisis of Power* (1979). For Soviet-American relations in the 1970s, see Adam Ulam, *Dangerous Relations* (1983); Raymond Garthoff, *Détente and Confrontation* (1985); and William G. Hyland, *Mortal Rivals* (1987).

Books on the antiwar movement include Alexander Kendrick, *The Wound Within* (1974); Lawrence M. Baskir and William A. Strauss, *Chance and Circumstance* (1978); and Melvin Small, *Nixon and the Doves* (1988). The different lessons drawn from the Vietnam experience are expounded in Early C. Ravenal, *Never Again* (1978), and Norman Podhoretz, *Why We Were in Vietnam* (1982).

General accounts of Watergate include two books by *Washington Post* reporters Bob Woodward and Carl Bernstein, *All the President's Men* (1974) and *The Final Days* (1976); Theodore White, *Breach of Faith* (1975); Jonathan Schell, *Time of Illusion* (1976); and J. Anthony Lukas, *Nightmare* (1976). Among the many memoirs by Watergate participants, the most revealing is John Dean, *Blind Ambition* (1976).

32 THE TROUBLED SEVENTIES

ENERGY AND THE ECONOMY

A TIME OF SOCIAL CHANGE

POLITICS AFTER WATERGATE

FROM DÉTENTE TO RENEWED COLD WAR

On October 6, 1973, Egypt and Syria launched a surprise attack on Israel. The invasion, which came while the Israelis were observing the Jewish holy day of atonement, Yom Kippur, caught American leaders completely offguard. After recovering from the initial shock, President Nixon and Henry Kissinger expected Israel to repel the Arab invaders and display the same military dominance it had used to win the Six Day War in 1967. In that conflict, Israel had devastated its Arab neighbors, taking possession of the Golan Heights from Syria, the Sinai peninsula from Egypt, and Jerusalem and the West Bank from Jordan. These conquests had added to Middle East tensions by unifying the Arab countries, which increasingly looked to the Soviet Union for arms and political support.

Henry Kissinger saw the outbreak of the Yom Kippur War as an opportunity to shift American policy from its traditional pro-Israeli position to a more neutral stance. If the war were to be brought to an end without a clear-cut victory for either side, the United States could play the role of honest broker between Israel and its Arab neighbors, step in, and arrange a diplomatic settlement. Events nearly betrayed Kissinger's strategy. Although the initial Egyptian and Syrian attack proved surprisingly successful, Israel soon drove the Syrians back toward Damascus and trapped the entire Egyptian army near the Suez Canal. At that point, Kissinger intervened forcefully, ordering a worldwide nuclear alert in response to the Soviet Union's warning to prevent a total victory for Israel. Kissinger's action quickly persuaded the

Israelis to halt their advance and led to a cease-fire in late October.

Kissinger's apparent diplomatic triumph, however, was offset by an unforeseen consequence of the Yom Kippur War. On October 17, the Arab members of the Organization of Petroleum Exporting Countries (OPEC) announced a 5-percent cut in oil production with additional cuts of 5 percent each month until Israel gave up the lands it had seized in 1967. President Nixon announced a $2.2-billion aid package for Israel on October 19, and the next day Saudi Arabia cut off oil shipments to the United States.

The Arab oil embargo had a disastrous impact on the American economy. First, it produced a worldwide shortage of oil. For the United States, which imported one third of its daily consumption, it meant a loss of nearly 2 million barrels a day. Increased imports from Iran, Libya, and Nigeria helped offset the Arab embargo, but American consumers began to panic.

A dramatic increase in oil prices proved to be a far more significant result of the embargo. In the United States, gasoline prices at the pumps nearly doubled in a few weeks time, while the cost of home heating fuel rose even more sharply. Nixon responded with a series of temporary measures, including pleas to turn down thermostats in homes and offices and reduce automobile speed limits to fifty-five miles per hour. He also outlined a plan for American energy independence, which encouraged conservation and the use of alternative sources of energy. When the Arab oil embargo ended in March, the American public relaxed. Gasoline once again became plentiful, thermostats were raised, and people rekindled their love affair with the automobile.

But the energy crisis did not end with the lifting of the embargo. The Arab action marked the beginning of a new era in American history. The United States, with only 6 percent of the world's population, had been using nearly 40 percent of the earth's energy supplies. Vast domestic reserves of petroleum and natural gas had fueled American economic expansion down through World War II, and then oil im-

ports had sustained postwar growth with artificially low energy costs. The embargo served only to highlight the fact that the nation was now dependent on other countries, notably those in the Persian Gulf, for its economic well-being.

The consequences soon became clear. The growing shortage of oil and natural gas led to a steady increase in energy costs, which contributed heavily to inflation. The price American consumers paid for oil went up sixfold during the 1970s. The revenues sent to OPEC members further weakened the American economy, leading to periodic recessions, higher interest rates, and the slowing of economic growth. A nation that based its way of life on abundance and expansion suddenly was faced with the reality of limited resources and economic stagnation. A land of plenty now had to face the challenge of scarcity.

ENERGY AND THE ECONOMY

The energy crisis that began with the Arab oil embargo in 1973 had a profound impact. The price American consumers paid for oil went up sixfold during the 1970s. The result was rampant inflation, rising unemployment, and the end to the postwar era of rapid economic growth.

THE OIL SHOCKS

Cheap energy had been the underlying force behind the amazing expansion of the American economy after World War II. The GNP had more than doubled between 1950 and 1973; the American people had come to base their way of life on gasoline prices that averaged about $.35 a gallon. The huge gas-guzzling cars, the flight to the suburbs, the long drive to work each day, the detached houses heated by fuel oil and natural gas and cooled by central air-conditioning represented a dependence on inexpensive energy that everyone took for granted.

The first great oil shock of the 1970s came with the Yom Kippur War and the resulting

Arab oil embargo. Global demand for oil, intensified by the explosive economic development of Western Europe and Japan as well as the United States, had caught up with oil production.

The effect on the American economy was devastating. In 1973 gasoline prices jumped from $.35 to $.65 a gallon; the cost of manufacturing went up proportionately, while utility rates rose sharply as a result of the higher cost of fuel oil and natural gas. Suddenly the American people faced drastic and unexpected increases in such everyday expenses as driving to work and heating their homes.

The result was a sharp decline in consumer spending and the worst recession since World War II. The GNP dropped by 6 percent in 1974 and unemployment rose to over 9 percent, the highest level since the Great Depression of the 1930s. Detroit was hit the hardest. Reacting to the high cost of gasoline, Americans turned away from big cars with low gas mileage.

President Gerald R. Ford, who followed Nixon into the White House, was concerned at first with inflation; he responded belatedly to the economic crisis by proposing a tax cut to stimulate consumer spending. Congress responded with a $22.8-billion reduction in taxes in 1975. With this stimulus, the economy gradually recovered by 1976, but the resulting budget deficits helped keep inflation above 5 percent and prevented a return to full economic health.

The next administration, headed by Jimmy Carter of Georgia, had little more success in achieving a rapid rate of economic growth. Continued federal deficits and relatively high interest rates kept the economy sluggish throughout 1977 and 1978. Then in 1979 the outbreak of the Iranian Revolution and the overthrow of the shah touched off another oil shock. The members of the OPEC cartel took advantage of the situation to raise prices to $30 a barrel—a staggering $21-a-barrel increase over the next eighteen months. Gasoline prices climbed to more than $1 a gallon at American service stations, and an even greater wave of inflation than the 1973 increase occurred.

The American people panicked. Gas lines formed as automobile drivers started filling

The age of cheap, abundant oil was ending. Prices climbed, supplies dwindled, and Americans waited in long lines for fuel or were faced with closed gas pumps.

their tanks every day or two. The long lines frustrated American drivers; incidents of violence began to mount, and the public took out its fury on the Carter administration.

By the fall of 1979, world supply had caught up with demand, and the oil scare ended. But the price of gasoline remained at over a dollar a gallon, and the inflation rate began to reach double-digit levels again. The twin oil shocks of the seventies had left the economy battered and had undermined the average American's faith in the future.

THE SEARCH FOR AN ENERGY POLICY

The oil shocks of 1973 and 1979 were but two symptoms of a much deeper energy crisis. Put simply, the United States was running out of the fossil fuels on which it had relied for its economic growth in the past. Domestic oil production peaked in 1970 and declined every year thereafter. Natural gas, another nonrenewable source, would also exhaust its supply eventually. American political leaders had to devise a national policy to meet the temporary shortfalls of the seventies and also the long-term energy problem inherent in past reliance on fossil fuels.

The success of the environmental movement in the late 1960s and early 1970s compounded the problem. Efforts to protect the environment and curtail pollution of the nation's air and water had led to significant legislative restrictions on American industry. Congress created the Environmental Protection Agency in 1970 to monitor industry and passed a Clean Air Act that encouraged public utilities to shift from using coal, which polluted the atmosphere, to clean-burning fuel oil and natural gas to generate electricity.

The energy crunch pitted the environmentalists and advocates of economic growth in direct confrontation. Those who put ecology first lost out. In the mid-1970s, Congress authorized construction of the Alaskan pipeline over environmentalists' objections and ordered public utilities to resume burning coal to produce electricity. During the rest of the decade, the government gradually relaxed environmental regulations to permit strip-mining of coal and offshore oil drilling.

The nation's leaders had an even more difficult time devising a coherent and workable long-term national energy policy. The Republicans advocated removing price controls on oil and natural gas to give wildcatters the incentive to bring in new supplies of these fuels. Greater production of coal, expanded nuclear power plants, and new technology to explore the possibilities of synthetic fuels and solar energy were all parts of the Republican approach to the energy problem.

The Democrats, in contrast, stressed price controls and conservation. They wanted to continue an elaborate system of price controls instituted by Nixon in 1973, and they favored standby plans for gas rationing as a better way to allocate scarce supplies than relying on the marketplace. Democrats' conservation measures included plans for tax breaks for those who insulated their homes, pressure on automakers to improve gas mileage for cars, and large appropriations for mass-transit systems for American cities.

The nation failed to adopt either the Republican or the Democratic energy plans; instead, Congress tried to muddle through with elements of both approaches. Thus Gerald Ford, who favored expanded production, was able to win approval for building the Alaskan pipeline. Carter placed a strong emphasis on reviving the lagging American coal industry. In late 1975, Congress extended the price controls on domestic oil for another forty months and in its most significant step toward conservation, mandated annual increases in gasoline mileage that forced Detroit to produce more fuel-efficient cars.

The overall outcome, however, was a patchwork that fell far short of a coherent national strategy for solving the energy problem. Neither Ford's appeal for decontrol nor Carter's call for a national conservation effort worked. Oil imports actually increased by 50 percent between 1973 and 1979. When the oil shock of 1979–1980 revealed how vulnerable the American economy was to OPEC, Carter reversed his policy and asked Congress to decontrol the price of domestic oil.

THE GREAT INFLATION

The gravest consequence of the oil shocks was inflation. The startling increase in price levels in the 1970s stemmed from many causes. The Vietnam War, particularly Johnson's early attempts to avoid a tax increase to pay for the fighting, created huge budget deficits. A worldwide shortage of food triggered a 20-percent rise in American food prices in 1973 alone. But above all else, it was the sixfold increase in petroleum prices, which raised the cost of every economic activity, that was the primary source of the great inflation of the 1970s.

The impact on the consumers was staggering. The price of an automobile jumped 72 percent between 1973 and 1978, and the prices of houses and food increased just as rapidly. Cor-

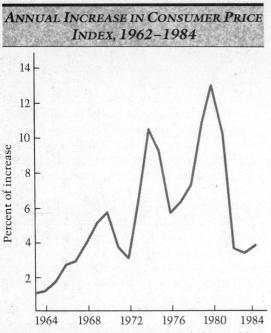

ANNUAL INCREASE IN CONSUMER PRICE INDEX, 1962–1984

Sources: U.S. Bureau of the Census, Statistical Abstract of the United States: 1982–83 (103rd edition) Washington, D.C., 1982; U.S. Department of Labor, Bureau of Labor Statistics.

responding wage increases merely kept most Americans even. For the first time since World War II, real wages did not increase in the 1970s, and in 1980 the real income of the average American family fell by 5.5 percent.

Curbing inflation proved to be beyond the power of the federal government. Neither Ford's nor Carter's efforts could abate the rise in inflation. Finally, in October 1979, the Federal Reserve Board began a sustained effort to halt inflation by mandating increased bank reserves to curtail the supply of money in circulation. But the new tight money policy served only to heighten inflation in the short run by driving interest rates up to record levels. By the spring of 1980, the prime interest rate reached 20 percent.

THE SHIFTING AMERICAN ECONOMY

Inflation and the oil shocks helped bring about significant changes in American business and industry in the 1970s. The most obvious result was the slowing of the rate of economic growth. More important, American industry began to lose its position of primacy in world markets. In all but one of the major industrial sectors—aerospace—U.S. corporations had declined between 1959 and 1976 in relation to Japanese and Western European competitors.

The most serious losses came in the heavy industries where the United States had once led the world. In 1946, American firms had produced 60 percent of the world's iron and steel; by 1978, they accounted for only 16 percent. As a result, by the end of the 1970s, fully 20 percent of all iron and steel used in the United States was imported, and American firms were closing down their obsolete mills in the East and Midwest, idling thousands of workers.

Foreign competition did even more damage in the automobile industry. The oil shocks led to a consumer demand for small, efficient cars. German and Japanese automakers seized the opportunity to expand their once small volume of sales in the United States. By 1977, imported cars had captured 18.3 percent of the American market. In response, Detroit spent $70 billion retooling to produce a new fleet of smaller, lighter, front-wheel-drive cars, but American manufacturers barely survived the foreign invasion.

In other areas, American corporations fared much better. Such multinationals as IBM and Pepsi-Cola continued to prosper all over the globe. The growth of high-technology industries proved to be the most profitable new trend of the 1970s. Computer companies and electronics firms grew at a rapid rate, especially after the development of the silicon chip—a small, wafer-thin microprocessor that can perform complex calculations almost instantly. The result was a geographic shift of American industry from the East and Midwest to the Sunbelt. At the same time, the decline of the steel and auto industries was leading to massive unemployment and economic stagnation in the northern industrial heartland.

The overall pattern was one of an economy in transition. The oil shocks had caused serious problems of inflation, slower economic growth, and rising unemployment rates. But American business still displayed the enterprise and the ability to develop new technologies that gave promise of continued economic vitality in the 1980s.

A TIME OF SOCIAL CHANGE

The 1970s and the 1980s witnessed a series of significant shifts in American society that paralleled the economic changes brought about by inflation and the oil shocks. According to the census at the end of the decade, the nation's population in 1980 stood at just over 226 million.

A PEOPLE ON THE MOVE

The most striking finding of the 1980 census was that for the first time in American history more than half of those 226 million people lived in the South and West. The states of the Northeast and Midwest had virtually stood still, while the Sunbelt, notably Florida, California, and Texas, had boomed. This population shift reflected the changing economic realities of the decade. College-educated people and blue-collar workers with skills in demand gravitated to the Sunbelt, where more and more American corporations were moving their offices and factories.

The cities of the North suffered the most from this mass exodus. New York City, which almost went bankrupt in mid-decade, lost nearly a million people between 1970 and 1980. The central cities of the North and West lost many of their best-educated and most affluent citizens, leaving them with large low-income populations—mainly minority groups—with very expensive social needs.

Another striking population trend was the nationwide rise in the number of the elderly. At the beginning of the century, only 4.1 percent of the population was age sixty-five or older; by

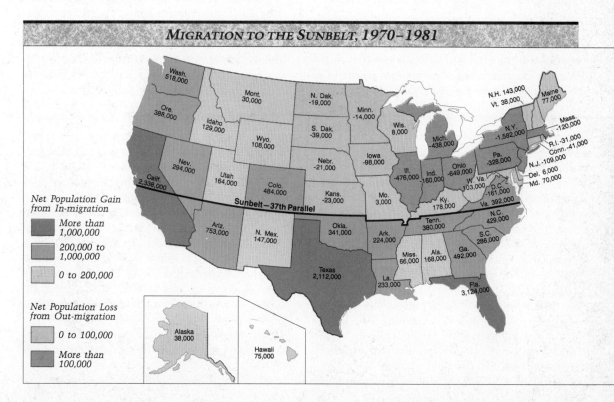

MIGRATION TO THE SUNBELT, 1970–1981

Wash. 518,000
Mont. 30,000
N. Dak. -19,000
Minn. -14,000
N.H. 143,000
Vt. 38,000
Maine 77,000
Ore. 388,000
Idaho 129,000
Wyo. 108,000
S. Dak. -39,000
Wis. 8,000
Mich. 438,000
N.Y. -1,582,000
Mass. -120,000
R.I. -31,000
Conn. -41,000
Nev. 294,000
Utah 164,000
Nebr. -21,000
Iowa -98,000
Ill. -476,000
Ind. -160,000
Ohio -649,000
Pa. -328,000
N.J. -109,000
Calif. 2,338,000
Colo. 484,000
Kans. -23,000
Mo. 3,000
W. Va. 103,000
Ky. 178,000
Del. 6,000
Md. 70,000
D.C. -161,000
Va. 392,000
Sunbelt—37th Parallel
Ariz. 753,000
N. Mex. 147,000
Okla. 341,000
Ark. 224,000
Tenn. 380,000
N.C. 429,000
S.C. 286,000
Miss. 66,000
Ala. 168,000
Ga. 492,000
Texas 2,112,000
La. 233,000
Fla. 3,124,000

Net Population Gain from In-migration
More than 1,000,000
200,000 to 1,000,000
0 to 200,000

Net Population Loss from Out-migration
0 to 100,000
More than 100,000

Alaska 38,000
Hawaii 75,000

1980, those over sixty-five made up 11.3 percent. Major advances in medicine had increased life expectancy from sixty-three years of age in the 1930s to seventy-two by the mid-1970s. Yet thanks to the indexing of Social Security payments to inflation, the elderly fared relatively well economically during the decade.

The postwar increase in the divorce rate continued unabated. Where marriages once outnumbered divorces by five to one in the 1950s, by 1980 the ratio was down to two to one. Marital breakup lost its stigma; for many, marriage ceased to be a sacred institution. The rise of the divorce rate resulted in a 79-percent increase in what the census dubbed "one-parent households," reflecting a sharp decline in traditional family units. By the end of the 1970s, 22 percent of all American children were reared in homes with only one parent.

A more traditional American process, that of immigration, underwent a surprising shift in the 1970s. A nation that had been built on a predominantly European influx suddenly found itself adding millions of Asians and Latin Americans to its population, with relatively fewer newcomers arriving from Europe. The newcomers from Asia and Latin America filled the traditional economic role of the immigrant, working at the dirty and difficult jobs that most Americans shunned, often for low wages and without receiving any government assistance. Their cultural, linguistic, and ethnic differences, however, created an assimilation problem at least as great as that of the "new" immigrants from southern and eastern Europe in the late nineteenth century.

Although the 1980 census revealed many departures from past experience, it also reaffirmed some traditional American patterns. In the face of inflation and unemployment, the majority of American people continued to be prosperous. Thanks to Medicare, Medicaid, and private health plans, Americans received better medical care than ever before. A declining birthrate lowered enrollments in elementary and secondary schools, leading to better teacher-student ratios, while college attendance continued to climb—nearly 12 million

by 1981, compared to 1.5 million forty years earlier.

The overall picture was of a society in transition. The rising figures of crime, teenage pregnancy, and drug use were balanced by better health and educational opportunities than any previous generation had enjoyed. Pockets of poverty were matched by boom areas. America was still the land of opportunity for immigrants, and despite the ravages of inflation and the shock of the energy crunch, people continued to look to the future, confident that they could still achieve the American dream.

THE CHANGING ROLE OF WOMEN

The entry of women into the work force accelerated in the 1970s. Some 10 million women took jobs in the period from 1965 to 1975, compared to 7 million men. By the end of the decade, 52 percent of all adult women were working, including 6 million more working wives than in 1970.

Women scored some impressive breakthroughs. They began to enter corporate boardrooms and were admitted to West Point and Annapolis. Equally important, they entered the blue-collar work force in factory and construction jobs that had traditionally been held by men. The appointment of Sandra Day O'Connor to the Supreme Court in 1981 marked a historic first. Yet despite the growing number of female elected officials, doctors, and lawyers, the vast majority of working women still suffered from economic discrimination. As late as 1980, the median pay for working women was only 60 percent of that for men.

Women had fewer children in the 1970s than in earlier decades. The birthrate, which had peaked at more than 3.5 births for every woman of childbearing age in the late 1950s, dropped to less than 2 by the mid-1970s. This trend toward smaller families was related to the great increase in working wives, which was itself intensified by the economic pressures of the 1970s. Many women put off childbearing until they had established themselves professionally; others decided to forego children entirely. The drop in the birthrate also reflected the later age of marriage in the 1970s, as well as the ever-larger number of single women.

The women's movement sought two different but related objectives in the 1970s. The first was ratification of the Equal Rights Amendment. Approved by Congress in 1972, the amendment simply stated "Equality of rights under law shall not be denied or abridged by the United States or any state on account of sex." The amendment fell three states short of ratification, opposed by right-wing activists such as Phyllis Schlafly and also in part by women workers who had fought for protective legislation regulating wages and hours of work for women. The National Organization for Women (NOW) persuaded Congress to extend the time for ratification by three years and waged intensive campaigns for approval in Florida and Illinois. But the deadline for ratification passed on June 30, 1982, with the ERA forces still three states short.

The women's movement was more successful in its fight for reproductive rights. Heartened by the 1973 Supreme Court decision, *Roe v. Wade*, which struck down state laws banning abortions, feminists worked hard to extend the right of women to choose whether to carry through a pregnancy. However, in 1981 the Supreme Court upheld a congressional act that forbade the use of federal money to pay for abortions. Despite this setback, pro-choice groups organized privately funded family-planning agencies and abortion clinics to give poor women the same opportunity to exercise choice as women who could afford to pay for these services. These efforts, however, continued to be attacked.

ADVANCE AND RETREAT FOR AFRICAN AMERICANS

For middle-class African Americans, the 1970s were a decade of progress; they began to reap the gains of the affirmative-action programs spawned by LBJ's Great Society. Education proved the key to black advances. With more than 1 million blacks enrolled in college by 1980, the opportunities for a middle-class style of life were greatly increased.

Many well-educated and affluent blacks tended to behave like whites in similar circumstances. Some joined the flight to the suburbs, while others flocked to the Sunbelt. In the 1970s, many young blacks, trained as doctors, lawyers, or business executives, returned to the cities of the South to pursue their careers.

Yet despite these gains, there were also setbacks for blacks in the 1970s. The whole affirmative-action process was brought into question by the case of Allen Bakke, a white applicant to the medical school of the University of California at Davis. When his application was rejected, even though his credentials were better than those of several minority applicants who were awarded some of the 16 places reserved for "disadvantaged students" in the class of 100, Bakke claimed that the use of explicit racial categories denied him equal protection under the Fourteenth Amendment. On June 28, 1978, the Supreme Court upheld a state court decision in Bakke's favor. Nevertheless, the Court also upheld the principle of affirmative action, claiming that universities could make race "simply one element" in their effort to select a diverse student body.

The plight of lower-class blacks, however, revealed that affirmative action had only a limited impact on their economic status. By the end of the seventies, fully one third of the nation's blacks lived below the poverty line, earning less than $8000 a year. Poor blacks, lacking education and job skills, could not join the migration to the Sunbelt cities and were stuck instead in the "rust belt," the decaying central cities of the East and Midwest. Unemployment rates for blacks ran about 14 percent, twice that for whites. As a result, most blacks did not share in the general affluence of the seventies.

THE EMERGING HISPANICS

People with Spanish surnames, labeled Hispanics in the census, were the fastest growing of all ethnic groups in the United States in the 1970s.

By 1989, there were more than 20 million Hispanics in the country, up from 14 million in 1980. The Hispanic groups were varied, with Mexican-Americans comprising the largest group, but they had several features in common. Most were relatively young and poor, and the great majority worked in either blue-collar or menial service jobs.

In the 1970s, Chicanos, as Mexican-American activists preferred to call themselves, became vocal in expressing their grievances. They succeeded in winning a federal mandate for bilingual education, compelling states like Texas and California to teach in Spanish and English. Mexican-American political leaders became active in local politics, leading the Democrats and Republicans to bid for their votes.

The entry of several million illegal immigrants from Mexico created a substantial social problem for the nation and especially for the Southwest. Critics charged that the flagrant violation of the nation's border with Mexico had led to an "invisible subculture outside the boundaries of law and legitimate institutions." They argued that these aliens took jobs away from American citizens, kept wages artificially low, and received extensive welfare benefits for which they were ineligible.

Defenders of the "illegals" contended that the nation gained from the abundant supply of workers who were willing to do the backbreaking jobs in fields and factories shunned by most Americans. Moreover, these illegal aliens usually paid sales and withholding taxes but rarely used government services for fear of being deported. In any case, by 1980 there was an exploited class of illegal aliens living on the edge of poverty.

Concern over economic competition from an estimated several million illegal aliens from Mexico led to legislative efforts to halt the flow across the border. In 1986 the Simpson-Mazzoli immigration bill was signed into law. It allowed illegal aliens who had resided in the United States since 1982 to stay and advance toward citizenship. (The amnesty for that group ended in May 1988.) At the same time, it

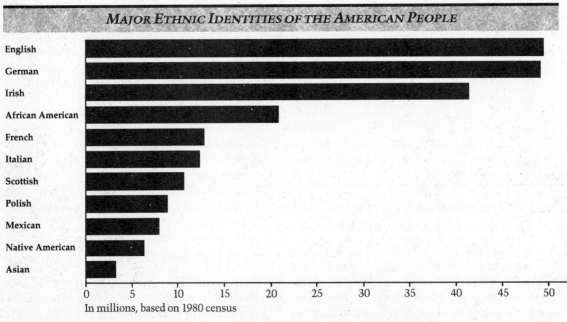

MAJOR ETHNIC IDENTITIES OF THE AMERICAN PEOPLE

In millions, based on 1980 census

Source: U.S. Bureau of the Census

stiffened penalties for employers who hired illegal aliens. The law, however, had little effect. Abject poverty drove many Mexicans over the border, and cutbacks in the Immigration and Naturalization Service (INS) reduced its ability to prevent the trek of "illegals."

Other substantial ethnic groups included Chinese, bolstered by a steady flow of immigrants from Taiwan, who achieved higher educational levels and greater affluence than other minorities, and South Vietnamese, mainly refugees who came to the United States after the North Vietnamese conquest in 1975. Like the blacks and Hispanics, the Asian immigrants—despite their educational advances and numerous individual success stories—tended to form an underclass that did not share fully in the benefits enjoyed by white America. In the late twentieth century, as in the nineteenth, the "melting pot" was inadequate as a description of the nation's ethnic mosaic.

POLITICS AFTER WATERGATE

The energy crisis and the economic dislocations of the mid-1970s could not have come at a worse time. Watergate had a paralyzing impact on the American political system. An awareness that the Cold War had led to an imperial presidency created a growing demand to weaken the power of the president and strengthen congressional authority. The result was an increasing tension between the White House and Capitol Hill, which prevented the kind of strong, effective leadership needed to meet the unprecedented problems of the 1970s.

THE FORD ADMINISTRATION AND THE 1976 CAMPAIGN

Gerald R. Ford of Michigan had the distinction of being the first president who had not been elected to national office. Richard Nixon had appointed him to the vice-presidency to succeed Spiro Agnew, who had been forced to resign in order to avoid prosecution for accepting bribes while he was governor of Maryland. The amiable Ford was a popular choice, and he seemed ready to restore public confidence in the presidency when he replaced Nixon in August 1974. Nelson Rockefeller, former governor of New York, was appointed vice-president.

Ford's honeymoon lasted only a month. On September 8, 1974, he shocked the nation by announcing that he had granted Nixon a full and unconditional pardon for all federal crimes he "committed or may have committed or taken part in" during his presidency. Ford apparently acted in an effort to end the bitterness over Watergate, but his attempt backfired, eroding public confidence in his leadership and linking him indelibly with the scandal.

Ford soon found himself fighting an equally difficult battle in behalf of the beleaguered CIA. The Watergate scandal and the Vietnam fiasco had eroded public confidence in the government and lent credibility to a startling series of disclosures about past covert actions. Americans were shocked to learn that the CIA had been involved in extensive domestic surveillance of antiwar protesters and attempts to assassinate such foreign leaders as Fidel Castro. In late 1975 Ford moved to limit the damage to the CIA. He appointed the respected, former congressman George Bush as the new CIA director and issued an executive order outlawing assassination as an instrument of American foreign policy. Congress also increased its own surveillance of the CIA.

Ford proved less successful in his dealings with Congress. As a congressman he had opposed virtually every Great Society measure, and he proved far more conservative than Nixon in the White House. In little more than a year, he vetoed thirty-nine separate bills, while he supported "maximum freedom for private enterprise."

Ford's weak record and the legacy of Watergate made the Democratic nomination a prize worth fighting for in 1976. A large field of candidates entered the contest, but a virtual unknown, the former Georgia Governor Jimmy Carter, quickly became the front-runner. Aware of the voters' disgust with politicians of both parties, Carter ran as an outsider who was untainted by Washington.

Appearing refreshingly candid and honest, Carter swept through the primaries and won the Democratic nomination easily. Victory in November seemed assured. The polls gave Carter a thirty-three-point lead over Ford when the campaign began, but he quickly lost ground as he began to hedge on the issues. Ford, however, also made costly mistakes, reinforcing his reputation as a bumbler. In a televised debate, responding to a question about Iron Curtain countries, he declared that "there is no Soviet domination of Eastern Europe."

Carter won an extremely narrow victory in 1976. Ford swept nearly the entire West, but Carter carried the South and key northern industrial states like New York and Ohio. Far more than most recent elections, the outcome turned on class and racial factors. The poor and especially the black vote clinched the victory for the Democrats.

DISENCHANTMENT WITH CARTER

The new president described by an associate as "superficially self-effacing but intensely shrewd," was an ambitious and intelligent politician. He was especially adept at utilizing symbols. He emerged from airplanes carrying his own garment bag and acted like an ordinary citizen who happened to be elected president. The substance, however, failed to match the style. He sought the White House convinced that he was brighter and better than his competitors, but once there he had no clear sense of direction, no discernible political philosophy.

The makeup of his administration reflected the conflicting tendencies that would eventually prove destructive. In the White House, he surrounded himself with close associates from Georgia. Yet he picked establishment Democrats such as Cyrus Vance and Joseph Califano for key cabinet positions. In the lower ranks, he selected followers of McGovern, Senator Edward Kennedy, and Ralph Nader, liberal activists who were intent on regulating business and preserving the environment. The result was

bound to be tension and conflict, as the White House staff and the federal bureaucracy worked at cross purposes.

President Carter strove hard for a balanced budget but was forced to accept mounting deficits. Federal agencies fought to save the environment and help consumers but served only to anger industry. Carter's unwillingness to take the political risks involved in revamping the overburdened Social Security system by reducing benefits and raising the retirement age blocked the efforts of Joseph Califano, head of the Department of Health, Education, and Welfare. And the HEW secretary finally gave up his attempt to draw up a workable National Health Insurance plan when he was caught in a cross-fire between President Carter and Senator Edward Kennedy.

Informed by his pollsters in 1979 that he was losing the nation's confidence, Carter sought desperately to redeem himself. He tried to pin responsibility for his failure on the American people's "crisis of confidence," and then on his advisers, but neither attempt could hide the fact that Carter, despite his good intentions and hard work, had failed to provide the bold leadership the nation needed.

FROM DÉTENTE TO RENEWED COLD WAR

America's position in the world declined sharply in the 1970s. In part, the fault was internal. The Vietnam War left the American people convinced that the nation should never again intervene abroad and the Watergate scandal discredited strong presidential leadership, shifting power over foreign policy to Congress. The new national consensus was symbolized by the War Powers Act (1973), which required the president to consult with Congress before sending American troops into action overseas. At the same time, external events and developments, notably the control over oil exercised by OPEC and the threats posed by revolutionary nationalism in the Middle East and Latin America, further weakened American foreign policy. No longer able to dominate the international scene, the United States began to play the role of spectator, and at times even of victim.

American diplomats tried three different strategies in the 1970s in an effort to adjust to the new realities of power. During the Ford presidency, Secretary of State Henry Kissinger continued the policy of détente. In the Carter administration, American foreign policy oscillated between two poles. While Secretary of State Cyrus Vance tried to maintain elements of détente, including a new strategic arms' limitation treaty (SALT II) and Carter called for an American crusade on behalf of human rights in the world, National Security Adviser Zbigniew Brzezinski was advocating more hawkish policies that stressed the Soviet arms buildup and the need for confrontation. By the late 1970s, Brzezinski's hard line had triumphed over both Vance's version of détente and Carter's concern for human rights.

RETREAT IN ASIA AND AFRICA

It was Gerald Ford's fate to reap where Nixon had sown. Once American aid stopped, South Vietnam was unable to halt the April 1975 North Vietnamese offensive. American forces concentrated on evacuating 150,000 loyal South Vietnamese, but many more were left behind when the last helicopter left the roof of the embassy in Saigon. Bitter and humiliated, the American people dejectedly watched the television scene as the North Vietnamese celebrated their conquest of the South. After a quarter century of futile effort, the United States finally had to admit defeat in the nation's longest and most humiliating foreign war.

Less than a month later, Ford had a chance to remind the world of American power. The Khmer Rouge government of Cambodia seized an American freighter, the *Mayaguez*, and imprisoned its crew. When the Communists ignored the initial American protest, Ford authorized an armed attack on Cambodia by 2000 marines from bases in Thailand. By the time the American forces landed on a small offshore island, Cambodia had freed the crewmen. The nation took pride in Ford's resort to force, but forty Americans paid for his decision with their lives.

Events in Africa, however, proved that caution and restraint were still the hallmarks of American foreign policy in the 1970s. The new nation of Angola had won its independence from Portugal in 1974, only to be caught up in a civil war between rival forces. The United States and China backed one group, but the Soviet Union, using several thousand Cuban troops, helped put a rival faction in power. Congress refused to sanction intervention, despite President Ford's pleas. Although Angola turned out to be surprisingly neutralist, Kissinger bemoaned the fact that the United States "was traumatized by Vietnam."

ACCOMMODATION IN LATIN AMERICA

President Carter was more successful than Ford in adjusting to the growing nationalism in the world, particularly in Central America, where the United States had imposed order for most of the twentieth century by backing reactionary regimes.

The first test came in Panama. Resentment over American ownership of the Panama Canal had led Lyndon Johnson to enter into negotiations aimed at the eventual return of the waterway to Panama. Carter completed the long diplomatic process in 1977 by signing two treaties. One restored sovereignty in the canal zone to Panama; the other provided for gradual Panamanian responsibility for operating the canal, with appropriate safeguards for its use and defense by the United States. In 1978, after a bitter struggle, the Senate ratified the treaties.

Carter was less successful, however, in dealing with a growing problem of left-wing uprisings in Central America. In mid-1979, dictator Anastasio Somoza fell before the Sandinista forces in Nicaragua. Despite American attempts to moderate the Sandinista revolution, the new regime moved steadily to the left, developing close ties with Castro's Cuba. In neighboring El Salvador, a growing leftist insurgency against a repressive regime put the United States in an awkward position. Unable to find a workable alternative between the extremes of reactionary dictatorship and radical revolution in Central America, Carter tried to use American economic aid to encourage the military junta in El Salvador to carry out democratic reforms. But after the guerrillas launched a major offensive in January 1981, he authorized large-scale military assistance to the government for its war against the insurgents, setting a precedent for the future.

THE QUEST FOR PEACE IN THE MIDDLE EAST

The inconclusive results of the Yom Kippur War gave Henry Kissinger the opportunity to play the role of peacemaker in the troubled Middle East. In arranging a pullback of Israeli forces in both the Sinai and the Golan Heights, he demonstrated that the United States could play the role of neutral mediator between Israelis and Arabs. And equally important, he detached Egypt from dependence on the Soviet Union, thereby weakening Russian influence in the Middle East.

A major change in Middle Eastern affairs occurred in November 1977 when Egyptian President Anwar Sadat stunned the world by traveling to Jerusalem in an effort to reach agreement directly with Israel. The next year, Carter invited both Sadat and Israeli Prime Minister Menachem Begin to negotiate under his guidance at Camp David. Eventually, the talks led to the ambiguous Camp David Accords—a framework for negotiations rather than a peace settlement. Then, in 1979, Israel and Egypt signed a peace treaty that provided for the gradual return of the entire Sinai to Egypt but left the fate of the Palestinian Arabs vague and unsettled. By excluding both the Palestine Liberation Organization (PLO) and the Soviet Union from the negotiations, however, the United States alienated Egypt from the other Arab nations and drove the more radical states closer to the Soviet Union.

Any sense of progress in the Middle East as a result of Camp David was quickly offset in

Signing of the Egypt-Israel peace treaty. President Anwar Sadat and Prime Minister Menachem Begin came together to negotiate with Jimmy Carter at Camp David.

1979 with the outbreak of the Iranian Revolution. Under Nixon and Kissinger, the United States had come to depend heavily on the shah and his powerful army for defense of the vital Persian Gulf. Carter continued the close relationship with the shah despite growing signs of domestic discontent with his leadership. When the exiled Ayatollah Khomeini led a fundamentalist Moslem revolt against the shah in 1978, the Carter administration misjudged the nature of the Iranian Revolution.

At first the United States encouraged the shah to remain in Iran, but when he decided to leave the country in January 1979, Carter tried to work with a moderate successor regime rather than encourage an army coup. With Khomeini's return from exile, Moslem militants quickly seized power in Teheran. In October 1979, Carter permitted the exiled shah to enter the United States for medical treatment. Incensed mobs in Iran railed against the United States and on November 4, militant students seized the U.S. embassy in Teheran and took fifty-eight Americans prisoner.

The prolonged hostage crisis revealed the extent to which American power had declined in the 1970s. Neither Carter's diplomatic efforts, economic sanctions, nor the concentration of U.S. naval forces in the Indian Ocean had any effect on the Iranian government. In his State of the Union message in January 1980, the president enunciated a new Carter Doctrine, telling the world that the United States would fight to protect the vital oil supplies of the Persian Gulf.

Carter was unable to back up these brave words with meaningful action. In April 1980, Carter authorized a desperate rescue mission that ended in failure when several helicopters broke down in the Iranian desert. The mission was aborted, an accident cost the lives of eight crewmen, and Secretary of State Cyrus Vance—who had opposed the rescue attempt—resigned in protest. The hostage crisis dragged on through the summer and fall of 1980, a symbol of American weakness that proved to be a powerful political handicap to Carter in the upcoming presidential election.

THE COLD WAR RESUMES

The policy of détente was already in trouble when Carter took office in 1977. Congressional refusal to relax trade restrictions on the Soviet Union had doomed Kissinger's attempts to win political concessions from the Soviets through economic incentives. The Kremlin's repression of the growing dissident movement and its harsh policy restricting the emigration of Soviet Jews had caused many Americans to doubt the wisdom of seeking accommodation with the Soviet Union.

Carter's emphasis on human rights appeared to the Russians to be a direct repudiation of détente. For Carter, his "absolute" commitment to human rights was easier said than done. He did withhold aid from authoritarian governments in Chile and Argentina, but equally repressive regimes such as South Korea and the Philippines continued to receive generous American support. Human rights proved, in the words of one presidential aide, "absolute in principle but flexible in application." The Soviets, however, were disturbed by the principle, particularly after Carter received Soviet exiles in the White House.

Secretary of State Vance concentrated on continuing the main pillar of détente, the SALT talks. In 1974, President Ford had met with Brezhnev and reached a tentative agreement on the outline of SALT II, which sought to limit each side to 2400 nuclear launchers. In March 1977, Vance went to Moscow to propose a drastic reduction in this level; the Soviets, already angry over human rights, rejected the American proposal. In 1980, however, Carter signed a SALT II agreement with Russia that did lower the ceiling on nuclear delivery systems to 2250 launchers.

Zbigniew Brzezinski, Carter's national security adviser, worked from the outset to reverse the policy of détente. He favored confrontation with the Kremlin. Toward this end, he prevailed on the president to advocate adoption of the new MX missile to replace the existing Minuteman ICBM's, which some experts thought were now vulnerable to a Soviet first strike. This new weapons system, together with the planned Trident submarine, ensured that regardless of SALT, the nuclear-arms race would be speeded up in the 1980s.

Brzezinski also was successful in persuading the president to use China to outmaneuver the Soviets. On January 1, 1979, the United States and China exchanged ambassadors, thereby completing the reconciliation that Nixon had begun in 1971. The new relationship between China and the United States presented the Soviet Union with the problem of defending itself against two distinct enemies.

The Cold War, in abeyance for nearly a decade, resumed with full fury in December 1979 when the Soviet Union invaded Afghanistan. Although this move was designed to ensure a regime friendly to the Soviet Union, it appeared to many as the beginning of a Soviet thrust toward the Indian Ocean and the Persian Gulf. Carter responded to this aggression with a series of stern measures. The United States banned the sale of high technology to Russia, embargoed the export of grain, resumed draft registration, and even boycotted the 1980 Moscow Olympics. These American moves did not halt the invasion of Afghanistan; instead, the results doomed détente. Right-wing groups in

CHRONOLOGY

1973	Arab oil embargo creates energy crisis in the United States
1974	Recession increases unemployment to over 9 percent
1975	Last evacuation helicopter leaves roof of U.S. embassy in Saigon, South Vietnam (April)
1976	Jimmy Carter elected president Imported cars account for 18.4 percent of total U.S. car sales
1977	President Carter signs Panama Canal treaties restoring sovereignty to Panama
1978	Supreme Court, in *Bakke* decision, reaffirms affirmative action if race not only factor (June) Jimmy Carter meets with Anwar Sadat of Egypt and Menachem Begin of Israel at Camp David to negotiate Middle East settlement (September)
1979	Iranian militants take fifty-eight Americans hostage in U.S. embassy in Teheran (November) Soviet invasion of Afghanistan provokes U.S. to ban grain sales to Russia and to withdraw from 1980 Moscow Olympics (December)
1980	One million black students enrolled in colleges and universities in U.S. U.S. attempt to rescue American hostages in Iran fails (April)

the United States began to warn of Soviet military superiority and call for a massive American arms build-up. Jimmy Carter, who had come into office hoping to advance human rights and control the nuclear-arms race, now found himself a victim of the renewed Cold War.

National frustration over the hostages in Iran and the Soviet invasion of Afghanistan, coupled with anxiety over the energy crunch and rampant inflation, eroded public confidence in the Carter administration. By mid-1980 the president's overall approval rating fell to 23 percent in the Gallup poll (and to 18 percent in foreign policy). The American people, disillusioned by the failures of Nixon, Ford, and Carter, yearned for new political leadership to meet the challenges facing the nation at home and abroad.

❦ RECOMMENDED READING

The most useful books on the Ford administration are Richard Reeves, *A Ford, Not a Lincoln* (1975); Robert Hartmann, *Palace Politics* (1980); and the president's own memoir, Gerald R. Ford, *A Time to Heal* (1979). On the election of 1976, see Jules Witcover, *Marathon* (1969). Books on the Carter administration include James Wooten, *Dasher* (1978), and Betty Glad, *Jimmy Carter* (1980), which deals with Carter's political career, and Charles O. Jones, *The Trustee Presidency* (1988), focusing on congressional relations. Memoirs that cover domestic issues include Joseph Califano, *On Governing America* (1981); Griffin Bell, *Taking Care of the Law* (1982); Jody Powell, *The Other Side of the Story* (1984); and Rosalynn Carter, *First Lady from Plains* (1985).

The best account of foreign policy during Nixon's abbreviated second term is the second volume of Henry Kissinger's memoirs, *Years of Upheaval* (1982). Developments in the Middle East are traced in Edward R. F. Sheehan, *The Arabs, Israelis and Kissinger* (1976), and William B. Quandt, *Decade of Decisions* (1977).

The best survey of Carter's foreign policy is Gaddis Smith, *Morality, Reason and Power* (1985). Jimmy Carter's memoir, *Keeping Faith* (1982), deals primarily with the Camp David agreement. For conflicting views of Carter's foreign policy by two key advisers, see Zbigniew Brzezinski, *Power and Principle* (1983), and Cyrus Vance, *Hard Choices* (1983). Other books on foreign policy issues of the 1970s are Strobe Talbott, *Endgame* (1979), on SALT II negotiations; John

Stockwell, *In Search of Enemies* (1976) on Angola; and two books by Walter LeFeber on Central America, *The Panama Canal* (1978) and *Inevitable Revolutions* (1983). On the Iranian hostage crisis, see Barry Rubin, *Paved with Good Intentions* (1980), and James Bill, *The Eagle and the Lion* (1988), which trace the course of post-World War II American relations with the shah, and Gary Sick, *All Fall Down* (1985), an insider's account of Carter's dilemma.

Richard Barnet, *The Lean Years* (1980) gives a thorough description of the impact of the energy crisis and foreign industrial competition on the American economy in the 1970s. Two superior collections of essays on the impact of the oil shocks are Robert Stobaugh and Daniel Yergin, eds., *Energy Future* (1980), and Daniel Yergin and Martin Hillenbrand, eds., *Global Insecurity* (1982). The fate of affirmative action in the 1970s is traced in Allan P. Sindler, *Bakke, DeFunis, and Minority Admissions* (1978), and J. Harvie Wilkinson, III, *From Brown to Bakke* (1979). For the changing nature of immigration patterns in the 1970s, see David Reimers, *Still the Golden Door: The Third World Comes to America* (1985).

33 THE REAGAN ERA AND BEYOND

THE CONSERVATIVE RESURGENCE: REPUBLICANS IN POWER

REAGAN AND THE WORLD

WHAT PRICE PROSPERITY?

SOCIAL DILEMMAS

THE REAGAN LEGACY

A WORLD IN FLUX

The Republican National Committee sponsored a televised address by Hollywood actor Ronald Reagan on behalf of Barry Goldwater's presidential candidacy in October 1964. In contrast to Goldwater's strident rhetoric, Reagan used relaxed, confident, and persuasive terms to put forth the case for a return to individual freedom. Instead of the usual choice between increased government activity and less governmental involvement, Reagan presented the options of either going up or down—"up to the maximum of human freedom consistent with law and order, or down to the ant heap of totalitarianism."

Although this speech did not rescue Goldwater's unpopular candidacy, it marked the beginning of Ronald Reagan's remarkable political career. A year later, a group of wealthy friends persuaded him, largely on the basis of the success of "the speech," to run for the California governorship. Reagan proved to be a masterful candidate. His friendly, relaxed manner and his mastery of television enabled him to present his strongly conservative message without appearing to be a rigid ideologue of the right. He won handily. Reagan's views addressed rising middle-class suburban resentment over high taxes, expanding welfare programs, and bureaucratic regulation. For a generation increasingly disenchanted with professionals in politics, he offered himself as a "civilian politician" who embodied the feelings and frustrations of most Americans in the modern consumer culture.

In two terms as governor, Reagan displayed natural ability as a political leader. Instead of insisting on implementing all of his conservative beliefs, he proved surprisingly flexible. Faced with a Democratic legislature, he yielded on raising taxes and increasing state spending while managing to trim the welfare rolls.

By the time Reagan left the governor's office in 1974, many signs pointed to a growing public frustration both with liberal reliance on government to solve most of the nation's problems and with increasing permissiveness in American society. In a popular rebellion against escalating property taxes in 1978, California's voters passed Proposition 13, which called for a 57 percent cut in taxes and resulted in a gradual reduction in social services. Concern over greater acceptance of homosexuality in society and rising abortion and divorce rates impelled religious groups to engage in political activity to defend traditional family values. Jerry Falwell, a successful Virginia radio and television evangelist, founded the Moral Majority, a fundamentalist group dedicated to preserving the "American way of life."

Conservatives proved far more skillful than liberals in mastering new political techniques. They developed direct-mail lists to elicit campaign contributions from millions of small givers; they used polls to single out the most effective issues to exploit; they perfected the system of telephone banks to get out the vote on behalf of conservative candidates on election day. Republicans especially benefited from a provision permitting PACs (political action committees) to raise and spend unlimited sums on behalf of favored candidates.

The population shift of the 1970s, especially the rapid growth of the Sunbelt region in the South and West (see Chapter 32), added momentum to the conservative upsurge. Those moving to the Sunbelt tended to be white, middle- and upper-class suburbanites—mainly skilled workers, young professionals, and business executives who were attracted both by economic opportunity and by a political climate stressing low taxes, less government regulation, and more reliance on the marketplace. In the West, the newcomers supported the dominant Republicans, while in the South, they could choose between a growing Republican party and conservative, "boll weevil" Democrats who advocated stronger national defense abroad and less government intrusion at home.

Conservatives also succeeded, for the first time since World War II, in making their cause intellectually respectable. Scholars and academics on the right flourished in new "think tanks." Writer William F. Buckley and economist Milton Friedman proved to be effective advocates of conservative causes in the print and television media. Neoconservative writers and spokespeople denounced liberals for being too soft on the Communist threat abroad and too willing to compromise high standards at home in the face of demands for equality from African Americans, women, and the disadvantaged. They called for a reaffirmation of capitalism and a new emphasis on what was right about America rather than an obsessive concern with social ills.

By the end of the 1970s, Ronald Reagan was recognized as the nation's most effective spokesman for the conservative resurgence. His personal charm softened the hard edges of his right-wing call to arms, and his conviction that America could regain its traditional self-confidence by reaffirming basic ideals had a broad appeal to a nation shaken by inflation at home and humiliation abroad. In 1980 he won the GOP presidential nomination handily.

In his acceptance speech at the Republican convention in Detroit, he set forth the themes that endeared him to conservatives—less government, balanced budget, family values, and peace through increased military spending. Reagan offered reassurance and hope for the future. He spoke of restoring to the federal government "the capacity to do the people's work without dominating their lives." As historian Robert Dallek has pointed out, Reagan "assured his listeners that he was no radical idealist courting defeat, but a sensible, thoroughly likable American with a surefire formula for success that would please everyone." In Ronald Reagan, the Republicans had found the perfect candidate to exploit both the American people's frustration with the domestic and foreign policy failures of the 1970s and the growing conservative mood of the nation.

THE CONSERVATIVE RESURGENCE: REPUBLICANS IN POWER

The liberal Democratic political coalition, originally created by Franklin D. Roosevelt in the Great Depression, finally split apart by the end of the 1970s. The Watergate scandal gave the Democrats a brief reprieve, but by the end of the decade, the Republicans were using the conservative upsurge to make inroads into such normally Democratic groups of voters as Jews, Southerners, and blue-collar workers. Yet the continuing appeal of the New Deal legacy prevented a total political realignment.

THE REAGAN VICTORY

In 1980, Jimmy Carter found himself in trouble. Inflation, touched off by the second oil shock of the 1970s, reached double-digit figures. The Federal Reserve Board's effort to shrink the money supply had led to a recession, with unemployment reaching 7.8 percent by July 1980. What Ronald Reagan dubbed the "misery index," the combined rate of inflation and unemployment, hit 28 percent early in 1980.

Foreign policy proved almost as damaging to Carter. The Soviet invasion of Afghanistan eroded hopes for continued détente; the hostage crisis in Iran highlighted the nation's sense of helplessness in the face of flagrant violations of its sovereignty. In the short run, Carter used that crisis to beat back the challenge to his renomination by fellow Democrat Edward Kennedy. The Democrats rallied behind Carter, although the delegates to the party's convention displayed a notable lack of enthusiasm in nominating him.

Ronald Reagan, in the meantime, chose George Bush as his running mate. In the fall campaign, the Republican candidates hammered away at the state of the economy and the world. Reagan scored heavily among traditionally Democratic blue-collar groups by blaming Carter for inflation, which robbed workers of any gain in real wages. Reagan also accused Carter of allowing the Soviets to outstrip the United States militarily and promised a massive buildup of American forces if he were elected. The Iranian situation helped Reagan by accentuating U.S. weakness in the world. Carter's position was further hurt by the independent candidacy of liberal Republican John Anderson of Illinois, who appealed to voters disenchanted with Carter but not yet ready to embrace Reagan.

The president struck back by claiming that Reagan was too reckless to conduct American foreign policy in the nuclear age. Carter tried to portray his Republican challenger as a warmonger. The attack backfired. In a televised debate Reagan assured the American people of his devotion to peace, leaving Carter with the onus of trying to land a low blow. At the end of the confrontation, Reagan scored impressively when he summed up the country's dire economic condition by suggesting voters ask themselves simply, "Are you better off now than you were four years ago?"

On election day, the American people answered with a resounding "no." Reagan carried forty-four states and gained 51 percent of the popular vote. Reagan clearly benefited from the growing political power of the Sunbelt. Even more impressive were his inroads into the old New Deal coalition. Reagan received 50.5 percent of the blue-collar vote and 46 percent of the Jewish vote, the best showing by a Republican since 1928. Only one group remained loyal to Carter; African-American voters gave him 85 percent of their ballots.

Even more surprising were the Republican gains in Congress. For the first time since 1954, the GOP gained control of the Senate, 53 to 46, and the party picked up 33 seats in the House to narrow the Democratic margin from 114 to 50. Liberals were the chief losers in the congressional swing to the right.

The meaning of the election was less clear than its outcome. Nearly all observers agreed that the voters had rendered an adverse judgment on the Carter administration. But most experts did not assess the outcome to be as major a realignment in American politics as the Democratic victory of FDR in 1932. Voters in 1980 expressed a distaste for current economic conditions, not a strongly held ideological preference. Political scientist Walter Dean Burnham termed the result "a conservative revitalization," but one that stopped short of making the GOP the dominant party.

Journalist Theodore White disagreed, viewing the outcome as a repudiation of the Democratic coalition that had dominated American politics since the days of Franklin D. Roosevelt and the New Deal. White may well have been right. The movement of the populations from the Northeast and Midwest to the South and West, along with the flight from the city, helped the Republicans far more than the Democrats. The Reagan victory in 1980 signaled a partial political realignment, ending a half-century of Democratic dominance.

CUTTING SPENDING AND TAXES

When Ronald Reagan took office in January, 1981, the ravages of inflation had cut $1400 in purchasing power from the median family income during the 1970s. High interest rates led to a decline in home building and auto sales. The government's share of the GNP had risen from 18.5 percent to over 23 percent since 1960, while the value of the dollar had dropped to just 36 cents over the same period. The new president blamed what he termed "the worst economic mess since the Great Depression" on high federal spending and excessive taxation. "Government is not the solution to our problems," Reagan announced in his inaugural address, "government is the problem."

The president embraced the concept of supply-side economics as the proper remedy for the nation's economic ills. In sharp contrast to the prevailing Keynesian theory, with its reliance on government spending to boost consumer demand, Reagan favored a reduction in both federal expenditures and revenues. Supply-side economists believed that the private sector, freed of the ever-increasing burden of government spending, would shift its resources from tax shelters to productive investment,

leading to an economic boom that would provide enough new income to offset the lost revenue. Although many other economists worried that the 30 percent cut in income taxes that Reagan favored would lead to staggering deficits, the president was confident that his program would both stimulate the economy and reduce the role of government. Reagan promised to increase national wealth, not just redistribute the existing wealth.

In pursuing his economic goals, Reagan relied on a mixed team of advisers. Neither his secretary of the treasury, Donald Regan, nor his chairman of the Council of Economic Advisers, Murray Weidenbaum, shared the president's faith in the supply-side theory. His new director of the Office of Management and Budget, David Stockman, was a former Michigan congressman who had become a convert to supply-side economics. Reagan entrusted Stockman with the primary responsibility for carrying out his policies of cutting government spending and sharply reducing taxes. At the same time, Reagan supported the efforts of Paul Volker, the banker Carter had appointed to head the Federal Reserve Board, to stem inflation by restricting the money supply, and even appointed him to a second four-year term in 1983.

The president and his budget director made spending the first target. Quickly deciding not to attack such popular middle-class entitlement programs as Social Security and Medicare, and sparing critical social services for the "truly deserving needy," the so-called "safety net," they concentrated on slashing $41.4 billion from the budget by cutting heavily into such other social services as food stamps, and by reducing public service jobs, student loans, and support for urban mass transit. Appearing before a joint session of Congress only weeks after an attempt on his life, Reagan won a commanding 253 to 176 margin of victory for his budget in the House, and an even more lopsided vote of 78 to 20 in the Senate in May. Reagan thus emerged from the budget struggle victorious.

The president proved equally successful in reducing taxes. He advocated a cut of 10 percent in personal income taxes for three consecutive years. When the Democrats countered with a two-year plan that would only reduce taxes 15 percent, Reagan compromised with 5 percent the first year, but insisted on the full 10 percent for the second and third years. Despite fears of the large deficit that would result from the loss of revenue, the president once again overcame Democratic resistance in Congress. Concessions to special interests offered by both sides, notably lower corporate rates and tax breaks for the oil industry and savings and loan associations, added to the loss of revenue. But regardless of the economic consequences, Reagan had demonstrated beyond any doubt his ability to wield presidential power effectively.

LIMITING THE ROLE OF GOVERNMENT

Reagan met with only mixed success in his other efforts to restrict governmental activity and reduce federal regulation of the economy. The concept of cutting back on the scope of federal agencies and limiting their impact on American business was a central tenet of the president's political philosophy. The goal of deregulation led to the appointment of men and women who shared his belief in relying on the marketplace rather than the bureaucracy to direct the nation's economy. Thus James Watt, the secretary of the interior, outraged environmentalists by opening up federal land to coal and timber production, halting the growth of national parkland, and making more than a billion acres available for offshore oil drilling. Though Watt was eventually forced to resign, the Reagan administration continued its policy of liberating business from governmental intervention.

Transportation Secretary Drew Lewis proved to be the most effective cabinet member in the administration's first two years. He helped relieve the troubled American automobile industry of many of the regulations adopted in the 1970s to reduce air pollution and increase passenger safety. At the same time, he played a key role in the behind-the-scenes negotiations that led Japan to agree in the spring of 1981 to restrict its automobile exports to the United States for the next three years. This unilateral Japanese action enabled the Reagan administration to help Detroit's carmakers without openly violating its free-market position by endorsing protectionist measures.

The Reagan administration was less successful in trying to cut back on the entitlement programs that it viewed as the primary cause of the

Vocal and determined opposition greeted the Reagan administration's proposal to reduce Social Security benefits.

growing budget deficits. Social Security was the greatest offender. The decision to index old-age pensions to the cost of living in the 1970s led to a 500 percent increase in benefits over the decade and threatened to bankrupt the system's trust fund by the end of the century. Buoyed by his May budget victory in Congress, Reagan permitted the Health and Human Services Department to propose a major reduction in future benefits. In late May, the Republican Senate rejected this proposal by a stinging 96 to 0 vote and the Democrats quickly charged that Reagan was trying to balance the budget on the backs of the elderly. In March 1983, Congress finally approved a series of changes that guaranteed the solvency of Social Security by gradually raising the retirement age, delaying cost-of-living increases for six months, and taxing pensions paid to the well-to-do elderly.

The administration's record in dealing with civil rights and women's concerns proved surprisingly clumsy and divisive. In regard to federal appointments, Reagan showed far less interest than Carter in advancing minority representation. In contrast to the 12 percent African-American representation in major government positions under the Democrats, the Republican figure totaled only 4.1 percent. Women were also slighted, falling from 12.1 percent under Carter to 8 percent under Reagan; the percentage of Hispanics dropped only slightly, from 4.1 percent to 3.8 percent.

Although feminist groups were disappointed by the administration's strong rhetorical attacks on legalized abortion and its lack of support for the Equal Rights Amendment, which ran out of time for consideration by the states in June 1982, the appointment of Sandra Day O'Connor to the Supreme Court pleased them. By this one shrewd move, Reagan was able both to fulfill a campaign pledge and make a symbolic gesture to women. At the same time, the president also buttressed the conservative tilt of the Court.

The administration's civil rights record proved especially revealing. Aware of how few African Americans had supported the GOP in 1980, Reagan made no effort to reward this group with government jobs or favors. Instead, the Justice Department actively opposed busing to achieve school integration and affirmative-action measures that resulted in minority hiring quotas.

Despite these lapses, in its first two years the Reagan administration had achieved most of its goals in the domestic area. The president had not only succeeded in cutting domestic spending and taxes, but he had reduced the degree of government involvement in everyday American life. The cuts in social programs helped achieve this goal, as did the efforts at deregulation by James Watt and Drew Lewis. For the first time since LBJ's Great Society, the rate of government growth had been slowed and more reliance placed on business to regulate itself.

REAGAN AND THE WORLD

Ronald Reagan was even more determined to reverse the course of American policy abroad than at home. He believed that under Carter, American prestige and standing in the world had dropped to an all-time low. Intent on restoring traditional American pride and self-respect, Reagan's mission was to strengthen America's defenses and recapture world supremacy from the Soviet Union.

In reality, the new president was simply continuing the hard line that Carter had begun to take after the invasion of Afghanistan. The Democrats had begun a massive military buildup in 1979 that included plans for cruise missiles in Europe, a rapid deployment force in the Middle East, and a 5-percent increase in the defense budget.

Under Reagan, the Pentagon flourished. Secretary of Defense Caspar Weinberger, once known as a budget cutter, presented a plan that would more than double defense spending. The emphasis was on new weapons, ranging from the B-1 bomber and the controversial MX nuclear missile to the expansion of the navy from 456 to 600 ships. Despite growing opposition in Congress, by 1985 the defense budget grew to over $300 billion at the very time the administration was cutting back on domestic spending.

Reagan was less than successful in resolving a recurring problem that had plagued the Carter administration—internal feuding between the secretary of state and the national security adviser in the White House. The appointment of Alexander Haig to head the State Department was a clear attempt to restore the dominant role of the secretary of state. Haig, a former general, NATO commander, Kissinger aide, and White House chief of staff under Nixon, was a well-known and forceful figure compared to Richard Allen, the conservative but relatively obscure national security adviser. Haig soon proved to be too outspoken and domineering for Reagan's White House staff, and after William Clark replaced Allen in the National Security Council post, the friction became intense. Finally, in mid-1982, Reagan replaced Haig as secretary of state with George Shultz, a professional economist with extensive government experience, whose low-key and relaxed style brought an air of calm reassurance to the conduct of American foreign policy.

Despite the steady increase in defense spending and the formation of a smoothly functioning foreign policy team, Reagan soon found that his diplomatic goals were more difficult to achieve than the budgetary and tax measures he had pushed through Congress so speedily.

CHALLENGING THE "EVIL EMPIRE"

The belief that the Soviet Union was a deadly enemy that threatened the well-being and security of the United States was the central tenet of Reagan's approach to foreign policy. He saw the Russians as bent on world revolution, ready "to commit any crime, to lie, to cheat" to advance their cause. Citing what he called a "record of tyranny," Reagan denounced the Russians before the UN in 1982, claiming that "Soviet-sponsored guerrillas and terrorists are at work in Central and South America, in Africa, the Middle East, in the Caribbean, and in Europe, violating human rights and unnerving the world with violence."

Given this view of Russia as "the focus of evil in the modern world," it is not surprising that the new president continued the hard line that Carter had adopted after the invasion of Afghanistan. Abandoning détente, Reagan proceeded to implement a 1979 decision to place 572 Pershing II and cruise missiles in Western Europe within range of Moscow and other Russian population centers to match Soviet deployment of medium range missiles aimed at NATO countries.

Strong protests from the Soviet Union, as well as growing uneasiness in Europe and an increasingly vocal nuclear freeze movement at home, led the Reagan administration to offer two new arms control initiatives by 1982. The first, called a "zero-option," proposed canceling the placement of all 572 American medium-range missiles in return for Russian removal of their missiles targeted on Western Europe. Secondly, in a new series of strategic arms talks, dubbed START, Reagan proposed that the two superpowers cut their nuclear warheads by one third, with no more than half of those remaining to be land-based. Since both proposals benefited the United States, the Soviets quickly turned down both proposals. Yet Reagan's proposals succeeded in blunting both the nuclear freeze movement at home and European doubts about Reagan's commitment to nuclear disarmament.

After Russian Foreign Minister Andrei Gromyko rejected an American offer to deploy only a portion of the 572 Pershing II and cruise missiles, the United States began putting these weapons in bases in Great Britain and Germany in November 1983. The Soviets, claiming that this move gave them only ten minutes warning time in case of an American attack, responded by breaking off the START negotiations in Geneva.

The nuclear arms race had now reached a more dangerous level than ever before. The United States stepped up research and development of the Strategic Defense Initiative (SDI), an antimissile system based on the use of lasers and particle beams to destroy incoming missiles in outer space. SDI was quickly dubbed

President Reagan steadfastly defended SDI ("Star Wars") against critics who questioned its huge, open-ended costs and scientists who doubted its feasibility.

"star wars" by the media. Although critics charged that SDI would increase the arms race, the Reagan administration defended "star wars" as a legitimate attempt to free the United States from the deadly trap of deterrence, with its reliance on the threat of nuclear retaliation to keep the peace. Meanwhile, the Soviet Union kept deploying larger and more accurate land-based ICBMs.

Reagan's reliance on harsh rhetoric and an arms buildup, reminiscent of Dean Acheson's policy of negotiating only from strength, had failed to force the Soviets to retreat. At the same time, the illness and death of Brezhnev in 1982, followed in rapid succession by the deaths of his aged successors, Yuri Andropov and Konstantin Chernenko, prevented any meaningful negotiations with the Soviet Union. The selection of Mikhail Gorbachev, a younger and more dynamic Soviet leader, led to a summit meeting in Geneva in November 1985. Reagan and Gorbachev failed to break the nuclear deadlock, but the two leaders did agree to begin a new effort at arms control, providing a glimmer of hope for future progress on the grimmest of all issues facing humanity.

FURTHER TURMOIL IN THE MIDDLE EAST

Reagan tried to continue Carter's basic policy in the turbulent Middle East. In April 1982, the Israelis honored a Camp David pledge by making their final withdrawal from the Sinai. Reagan hoped to complete the other Camp David objective of providing a homeland for the Palestinian Arabs on the West Bank, but Israel instead continued to extend Jewish settlements into this disputed area. The threat of the Palestine Liberation Organization (PLO), based in southern Lebanon and frequently raiding across the border into Israel, seemed to be the major obstacle to further progress.

On June 6, 1982, with tacit American encouragement, Israel's Prime Minister Menachem Begin began an invasion of southern Lebanon designed to secure Israel's northern border and destroy the PLO. The United States made no effort to halt this offensive, but did join with France and Italy in sending a multinational force to permit the PLO to evacuate to Tunisia. Reagan then tried to achieve an overall Arab-Israeli settlement by proposing the creation of a Palestinian homeland on the West Bank in close association with Jordan.

Unfortunately, Reagan's diplomacy soon became enmeshed in the Lebanese civil war, raging since 1975. Neither the PLO nor Syria, which occupied portions of Lebanon, would back his West Bank plan, and soon American marines, sent to Lebanon as part of the multinational force to restore order, were caught up in the renewed hostilities between Moslem and Christian militia. The Moslems perceived the marines as aiding the Christian-dominated government of Lebanon instead of acting as neutral peacekeepers, and began firing on the vulnerable American troops.

In the face of growing congressional demands for the withdrawal of the marines, Reagan declared that they were there to protect Lebanon from the designs of Soviet-backed Syria. But finally, after a Moslem terrorist drove a truck loaded with explosives into the American barracks, killing 239 marines, the president had no choice but to pull out. Despite his good intentions, Reagan had experienced a humiliation similar to Carter's in Iran—one that left Lebanon in shambles and the Arab-Israeli situation worse than ever.

CONFRONTATION IN CENTRAL AMERICA

Reagan faced a difficult situation in Central America (see Chapter 32). In an area marked by great extremes of wealth, the United States sought moderate, middle-class regimes to support. Washington usually ended up backing repressive, right-wing dictatorships rather than the more leftist groups who raised the radical issues of land reform and redistribution of wealth. Yet it was often oppression by U.S.-supported regimes that drove those seeking political change to embrace revolutionary tactics.

This is precisely what happened in Nicaragua, where the Sandinista coalition finally succeeded in overthrowing the repressive Somoza regime in 1979. In an effort to strengthen the many middle-class elements in the original Sandinista government and to avoid forcing

Nicaragua into the Cuban and Soviet orbit, Carter extended American economic aid.

The Reagan administration quickly reversed this policy. Alexander Haig cut off all aid to Nicaragua in the spring of 1981. The new policy became self-fulfilling, as Nicaragua became even more dependent on Cuba and the Soviet Union.

The United States and Nicaragua were soon on a collision course. In a speech to Congress in April 1983, the president declared that "the national security of all the Americas is at stake in Central America," but Congress, fearful of repeating the Vietnam fiasco, proved reluctant to seek a military solution. Reagan then opted for covert action. The CIA began supplying the Contras, exiles fighting against the Sandinistas from bases in Honduras and Costa Rica. Despite Democratic objections, the U.S.-backed rebels tried to disrupt the Nicaraguan economy, raiding villages, blowing up oil tanks and even mining harbors. The Contras succeeded only in turning Nicaragua into an armed camp, as the Sandinistas went on a war footing. Then, in 1984, Congress passed the Boland Amendment prohibiting any United States agency from spending money in Central America. The withdrawal of U.S. financial backing left the Contras stranded in a fight that might not have escalated without U.S. funding in the first place.

The situation in El Salvador proved little better. There a guerrilla war had broken out in the 1970s between left-wing groups and a reactionary regime dominated by wealthy landowners. Reagan stepped up support for a government headed by middle-of-the-roader José Napoleón Duarte. The Reagan administration, ignoring charges that right-wing death squads, which were not under Duarte's control, had killed 40,000 civilians, did all it could to help the Duarte government, which did succeed in winning a decisive election victory over the extreme right in 1984 and began modest reforms in an effort to undercut the appeal of the guerrillas.

The only clear-cut triumph that Reagan achieved in the hemisphere came in the Caribbean. In October 1983, a military coup led to the death of the prime minister of Grenada, a friend of Fidel Castro, who was subsequently replaced by an even more radical regime. The Reagan administration, already upset by Grenada's close ties to Cuba and the construction of a large airfield on this small Caribbean island, decided to intervene to prevent the Communists from acquiring a strategic military base.

Nearly 2000 American marines invaded Grenada on October 25, 1983. After brief but strong resistance from 800 Cuban workers and troops on the island, the American forces claimed a victory that cost eighteen lives. Reagan proudly pointed to the Grenada invasion as one of his successes in Latin America.

Aside from Grenada, however, the Reagan administration had little to show for its massive military buildup. In the Middle East, its well-intentioned use of marines had ended in disaster, while its determined opposition to left-wing groups in Central America had at best achieved a stalemate. Relations with the Soviet Union had fallen into one of the deepest chills of the entire Cold War with the nuclear arms race more intense than ever.

Yet Reagan appeared to succeed in his effort to restore American pride and self-confidence. Public opinion polls showed strong support for the president's hard line. And Russian behavior, notably the callous shooting down of a Korean civilian airliner in September 1983, underscored the administration's depiction of the Soviet Union as a dangerous and untrustworthy adversary.

What Price Prosperity?

The sweeping reductions in domestic spending and income taxes that Reagan achieved in 1981 gave rise to conflicting economic expectations. Supply-side economists believed that the tax relief granted to investors would lead to rapid business growth, which would raise more than enough new revenue to offset the lower rates. The administration's critics, on the other hand,

were sure that heavy defense spending coupled with tax reductions would create massive deficits and result in economic stagnation.

Both groups proved to be wrong. Over the next seven years, the nation experienced both recession and rapid growth, deficits as well as prosperity, and best of all, an unexpected easing of inflation. Even though Reagan was unable to reach all of his goals, the combination of lowered inflation and renewed economic growth gave him an enormous political advantage.

REAGANOMICS

The supply-side theory became the first economic casualty of the 1980s. The naive belief that a combination of cuts in social spending and sharply reduced taxes could unleash an economic boom that would avoid huge deficits was the victim of both Reagan's insistence on huge increases in defense spending and the Federal Reserve Board's tight money policy. It was the latter that touched off a recession that began in the fall of 1981 and steadily worsened throughout 1982, until factory utilization fell to less than 70 percent and unemployment reached a postwar high of 10.4 percent in October 1982.

Reagan responded by refusing to give up his income tax cuts. But he did prove flexible in other ways, slightly moderating the defense buildup, accepting fewer cuts in social programs than he proposed, and finally agreeing to a $98 billion increase in miscellaneous federal taxes under the guise of tax reform in order to hold the projected 1983 deficit under $100 billion. In addition, in early 1983 he accepted a Democratic proposal for spending $4.6 billion on an emergency jobs program to relieve unemployment. But at the same time he refused to cancel the final 10 percent cut in income taxes in mid-1983. Instead he declared that all signs pointed to "a strong recovery."

Whether by design or good luck, the president's optimism proved justified. In the second quarter of 1983, the economy came to life. The final 10 percent tax cut in July stimulated consumer spending, along with moderating inflation that kept prices from rising so quickly. The long-depressed automobile industry, helped by Japan's voluntary quotas on car exports, began to boom. The American people went on a great buying spree with consumer installment debt increasing as much in the first six months of 1983 as in all of 1982. Even the dormant stock market came to life; the Dow Jones industrial average set new record highs in 1983.

Best of all, inflation remained under control as the economy expanded. At the same time, interest rates, which had been hovering around 16.5 percent in 1982, fell to 10.5 percent and remained below 11 percent, enabling consumers to buy goods and corporations to expand their inventories much more easily. A combination of long-term Federal Reserve policy, the impact of the recession, and a worldwide decline in energy and food prices enabled the Reagan administration to take credit for solving the problem that had proved fatal for Carter and the Democrats.

THE TWIN DEFICITS

Two problems emerged in the mid-1980s to cloud Reagan's claims of economic recovery.

The first was the growing federal budget deficit. The 1982 recession undercut the rosy assumptions of the supply-siders. As the economy weakened and unemployment increased, tax revenues fell below projections while government spending on unemployment insurance and other social programs climbed. The deficit reached $207.8 billion in 1983, triple the pre-Reagan high of $66 billion in 1976.

Even more frightening, some economists were predicting that at current spending and tax rates, the deficit would rise to over $300 billion a year by the end of the decade. The result, many feared, would be soaring interest rates as the government competed with the private sector for the limited amount of investment capital in the nation. In fact, a slumping world economy led to a massive infusion of foreign investment, which kept the prime rate from rising above 11 percent.

When the deficit continued to climb during the economic recovery of the mid-1980s, Congress finally came forward with what appeared to be a drastic solution. Republican Senators Phil Gramm of Texas and Warren Rudman of New Hampshire joined with Democrat Ernest Hollings of South Carolina to set a series of

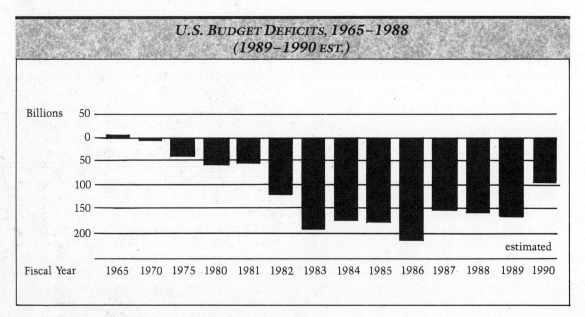

U.S. BUDGET DEFICITS, 1965–1988
(1989–1990 EST.)

Billions — 50, 0, 50, 100, 150, 200

Fiscal Year: 1965 1970 1975 1980 1981 1982 1983 1984 1985 1986 1987 1988 1989 1990

estimated

Source: Economic Report of the President, 1989. Washington, D.C., 1989

budgetary ceilings designed to eliminate the deficit entirely by 1991. If Congress and the administration exceeded these limits each year, then there would be automatic, across-the-board reductions in both defense and domestic spending. After the Supreme Court invalidated the compulsory feature, the revised Gramm-Rudman-Hollings Balanced Budget Act did succeed in halting the deficit spiral. As altered by Congress in 1986 and 1987, Gramm-Rudman, as it became known, stretched out the goal of ending the deficit until 1993. The president and Congress, thanks in part to temporary revenue gains from a 1986 tax reform bill, were able to lower the deficit from the all-time high of $221 billion in 1986 to a more manageable $155 billion by 1988. Even more important, the deficit as a percentage of the GNP fell from over 5 percent to close to 3 percent, a level common in many industrial nations.

In essence, Gramm-Rudman was a political compromise. The price Reagan had to pay for Democratic help in resolving his budgetary crisis was to stop the increase in defense spending. But at the same time, by agreeing to sizable budget deficits for the next few years, the Democrats, who controlled Congress, had to give up any hope of expanding existing social programs or enacting new ones, such as a comprehensive national health plan.

Concern over another alarming deficit—in the balance of overseas trade—became an equally important issue in the mid-1980s. American exports had been falling steadily since the 1970s as a result of the decline in traditional manufacturing industries—iron and steel, electronics, and automobiles. The Japanese had been the biggest gainers as they dominated the American market in consumer goods such as television sets and VCRs. Even the American advantage in high technology was threatened by the mid-1980s as Japan began to capture the lead in the manufacture of semiconductors, once an American monopoly.

A sharp rise in the value of the dollar, beginning in 1983, accentuated the problem by making American goods too expensive in foreign markets. The result was a trade deficit that grew from a modest $31 billion in 1981 to an alarming $171 billion by 1987. In late 1985, the

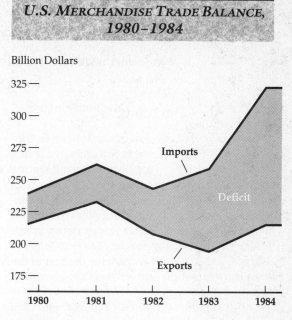

U.S. MERCHANDISE TRADE BALANCE, 1980–1984

Billion Dollars

Source: U.S. International Trade Commission of the U.S. Department of Commerce.

Reagan administration joined with the governments of Japan and Western Europe to devalue the dollar. The resulting decline in the dollar stimulated American exports and helped reduce the trade deficit to more manageable proportions by 1989.

The only way the United States could equalize the balance of international payments was to import even more capital from abroad. Led by the Japanese, foreign investors poured large sums into the United States, buying real estate, office buildings, and even banks. As a result, in 1985, the United States, a creditor nation since World War I, suddenly became the world's leading debtor.

The twin deficits had led to a dangerous financial dependence on other nations. In the 1980s, the American people had begun living beyond their means. Just as the government incurred large deficits rather than raising taxes to pay for the huge defense buildup, so consumers had cut back on personal saving in order to buy imported cars, television sets, and VCRs, encouraging further foreign investment. Reaganomics had succeeded in continuing America's traditional high standard of living, but with a very high price—massive borrowing that mortgaged the nation's future.

THE POLITICS OF PROSPERITY

"Are you better off now than you were four years ago?" Reagan had asked voters at the end of his 1980 debate with Jimmy Carter. By the mid-1980s, he appeared to have delivered on his implicit promise to stem inflation and revive the stagnant American economy. Yet not everyone benefited equally from Reaganomics.

The gains were impressive. Inflation dropped and remained below 4 percent for the rest of the decade. Meanwhile, the recovery that began in the final quarter of 1982 led to the creation of 16 million new jobs and a drop in the unemployment rate to just over 5 percent. The best measure of living standards, the median per capita family income, rose slowly but steadily.

Despite these gains, the average American family was no better off by the end of the Reagan years than it had been in 1973. Measured in 1987 dollars, family income, which had declined during the years of inflation, had just reached the level it enjoyed before the oil shocks hit so hard. Moreover, not everyone fared equally well. Those in the top 20 percent in terms of family income benefited the most from Reagan's economic policies and tax reforms. Those near the bottom were helped by the Reagan administration's willingness to preserve basic social programs, the so-called "safety net." But the lower middle class did not fare as well, gaining little from the income tax changes and seeing their weekly take-home pay drop as a result of rising Social Security taxes. The rich got richer, the poor stayed poor, while middle America struggled to make ends meet.

The most depressing development was the relatively bleak outlook for the next generation. Young people could no longer look forward to living better than their parents. Home ownership among those aged 25 to 35 declined because of the rise in interest rates and real estate. Being a home owner—the American Dream—was removed from the reach of many Americans.

Despite these mixed results, the Republicans were remarkably successful in persuading American voters that the Reagan administration had cured the nation's economic woes. The waning of inflation, which had been the most frightening development of the 1970s, along with the fact that wealthy Americans were far more likely to cast ballots than poorer ones, helps explain this seeming contradiction between public support of Reagan and the reality of Reaganomics. Even so, the GOP success was largely confined to the presidential level. The Democrats made solid gains in the 1982 elections.

The economic boom that began in 1983 came at just the right time for the Republican party. By early 1984, with personal income rising and unemployment shrinking rapidly, Democratic prospects dimmed for the 1984 election. After a long, bruising primary battle, Walter Mondale, former Minnesota senator and Carter's vice-president, won the Democratic nomination. In a bold break with tradition, he chose a woman as a running mate, Congresswoman Geraldine Ferraro of New York.

When the Republicans renominated Reagan and Bush, the campaign quickly came down to one issue—leadership. The GOP claimed that Reagan had overcome the problems that overwhelmed Carter, notably inflation at home and disrespect abroad. The president told voters if they reelected him, "You ain't seen nothin' yet."

Mondale and Ferraro, in contrast, accused Reagan of helping the rich at the expense of the poor, saddling future generations with huge deficits and risking war in the Middle East and Central America. In a surprise move, the Democratic candidate announced he intended to raise taxes to curb the deficit and then accused Reagan of harboring a "secret plan" to increase taxes himself.

The outcome was an even greater Reagan landslide than in 1980. With a solid base in the South and West, Reagan cut deeply into the normally Democratic states of the Northeast and the swing states of the Midwest to take the electoral votes of all but Minnesota and the District of Columbia. Exit surveys revealed that economic issues were uppermost in the minds of voters; in the midst of a strong economic recovery, Reagan won a majority among all voters earning more than $12,500 a year. More than two thirds of the white males in the nation voted for Reagan, who won even a majority of the blue-collar and women's vote. Of all the traditional Democratic groups, only African Americans proved loyal to the party.

The 1984 election was far more of a triumph for Reagan than for his party. The GOP made only small gains in the House and actually lost two seats in the Senate. Despite minor gains at the state level, the GOP failed to achieve the party realignment it hoped for. The nation seemed to be dividing politically along economic lines, with the wealthy and affluent who fared best from Reagan's economic policies supporting the president while a growing underclass of African Americans, Hispanics, and the working poor were voting solidly Democratic. Middle-class Americans who held the balance revealed their mixed feelings by backing a Republican for president and Democratic candidates for the House and Senate.

SOCIAL DILEMMAS

Two complex social issues arose in the 1980s that went against the grain of the general sense of well-being in the Reagan years. A massive viral epidemic and a new drug crisis threatened the social fabric of the United States, yet the administration failed to respond promptly or effectively to either one.

THE AIDS EPIDEMIC

The outbreak of AIDS (acquired immune deficiency syndrome) in the early 1980s took most Americans by surprise. Even health experts had difficulty grasping the nature and extent of the new public health threat. Doctors first noticed

a few cases of a rare form of pneumonia and an unusual type of skin cancer in male patients in New York and San Francisco in 1981, but it was several years before researchers finally identified it as a hitherto unknown virus that had spread from Central Africa by way of Haiti and had found its first American victims primarily among gay men.

Initially, AIDS was perceived as only a threat to gay men, a group that had fought hard in the 1970s to gain a larger degree of societal freedom and approval. With a growing sense of urgency as the death toll mounted, homosexual men began to confine their relationships to trusted partners.

It soon became apparent, however, that AIDS could not be so easily contained. It began to appear among intravenous drug users who shared the same needles and eventually among hemophiliacs and others receiving frequent blood transfusions. The possibility of a contaminated national blood supply terrified middle-class America, as did the possibility of the spread of AIDS to heterosexuals.

Scientists tried to reassure the public by explaining that the virus could be spread only by the exchange of bodily fluids, primarily blood and semen, and not by casual contact. The death of movie star Rock Hudson in the summer of 1985 intensified the sense of national panic. Controversy soon developed over proposals for mandatory blood tests for suspected carriers and the segregation of AIDS victims. The integrity of hospital blood supplies caused the most realistic concern; in 1985, a new test finally provided reassurance that transfusions could be performed safely.

The Reagan administration proved slow and halting in its approach to the AIDS epidemic. The lack of sympathy for gays and a need to reduce the deficit worked against any large increase in health spending; what little money was devoted to AIDS went almost entirely for research rather than for educational measures to slow its spread. The only real leadership came from Surgeon General C. Everett Koop who surprised his conservative backers in 1986 by coming out boldly with proposals for sex education, the use of condoms to ensure "safe sex," and confidential blood testing to help contain the disease.

While the administration dallied, the grim toll mounted. Since the average time between the initial infection and the first symptoms was five years and could be as long as fourteen years, efforts at prevention had little immediate impact. In November 1983, there were 2803 known cases and 1416 deaths; by the time Rock Hudson died in mid-1985, over 12,000 cases and more than 6000 deaths had been reported.

Growing public concern finally led to action. The president's own report criticized the administration's AIDS efforts as "inconsistent" and recommended a new effort that included antidiscrimination legislation and explicit prevention education. Koop responded by sending out a pamphlet entitled "Understanding AIDS" to 107 million households, while in the fall, Congress voted to spend $1.3 billion to fight AIDS.

Despite these new efforts, the epidemic continued to grow. In 1987, there were 50,000 cases; by mid-1989, the count had reached 100,000. The "gay" disease had spread far beyond that one group in society; by the end of the decade, most of the new victims were drug users among the urban poor, many of them racial minorities. Most frightening of all was the time bomb ticking away in those exposed to the virus in the 1980s, which made the experts' forecast of as many as 500,000 cases by the mid-1990s all too believable. With no cure in sight, AIDS promised to be the most deadly disease in American history.

THE WAR ON DRUGS

The 1980s witnessed the rapid spread of cocaine use in America, leading to a growing sense of social crisis by the end of the decade. Cocaine had long been viewed as a relatively harmless recreational drug used by only a few people—rock musicians, Hollywood producers, and the very wealthy. By the end of the 1970s, the snorting of cocaine had spread to the upper middle class. The "illusion of instant happiness" came at a high price—$100 for a few snorts and the danger of dying from an overdose or figuratively blowing one's mind. Nevertheless, the number of users reached over 4 million by 1982.

In the mid-1980s, cocaine suddenly was perceived as a danger to American society. The deaths of several celebrities from cocaine overdoses, notably movie star John Belushi and Maryland basketball player Len Bias, alarmed the public. More ominously, Jamaican drug gangs began to sell crack, a cheap cocaine derivative that could be smoked in a pipe to give a very intense high. Dealers sold this new form of cocaine for as little as $10 a dose, opening up a vast new market among the poor in the urban ghettos. By 1986, an estimated 5.8 million people were using cocaine at least once a month and over 600,000 were confirmed addicts.

Despite its relatively low cost, crack led to an explosion of urban crime. The brief, intense high lasted only a few minutes, leading users to keep smoking more, desensitizing their nervous systems and thus forcing them to use still larger amounts to achieve the by-now indispensable euphoria. Needing as much as $1000 of crack each day to sustain their habits, users began to go on literal crime sprees to gain the necessary funds. By 1987, over 70 percent of all those arrested for burglary in Manhattan tested positive for cocaine.

The Reagan administration tried several approaches to the problem posed by cocaine. In 1982, the First Lady, Nancy Reagan, chose drug education as her special project. Using the slogan "Just Say No," she urged schools, churches, and civic groups to inform young people about the dangers of cocaine. Her program helped educate the middle class but had little impact on the crack smokers in the ghetto.

In the mid-1980s, the administration began to place greater emphasis on interdiction, using agents of the Drug Enforcement Agency (DEA), the Customs Bureau, and the Coast Guard to try to seal off the nation's borders. An international cartel of drug dealers, led by a group of Colombians, overcame this effort by saturating the nation with cocaine. In reality, the Reagan administration was unwilling to devote the personnel and resources that truly effective interdiction required.

The very nature of the cocaine industry frustrated a third, and potentially most promising, countermeasure—wiping out the coca fields and processing plants in South America. The administration relied on diplomatic efforts in cooperation with the governments of Colombia, Bolivia, and Peru to curb the trade in cocaine, but with little success. For many South American farmers, coca was too valuable a crop to give up.

By the time Ronald Reagan left office, the problem remained as serious as ever, despite actions by Congress in 1986 and 1988 to allocate more funds for drug education and enforcement, to legalize the death sentence for some drug-related killings, and to create a new federal drug czar. More cocaine than ever was flooding the American market, and addiction continued its upswing.

Only one thing had changed dramatically— public awareness. A Gallup poll taken in the summer of 1989 showed that for the first time in recent history, the American people regarded illegal drugs as their greatest concern, a spot once reserved for economic and international concerns. Ronald Reagan thus bequeathed his successor a social problem that transcended even the Cold War and the state of the national economy in the minds of the American people.

THE REAGAN LEGACY

Ronald Reagan's second term in the White House proved much less successful than his first. Dubbed the "teflon president" for the way his charm and good luck enabled him to avoid being held responsible for administration failures, Reagan suddenly was forced to face intense criticism and growing public disenchantment. Yet in the end he was able to rescue his troubled presidency and maintain the Republican hold on the White House.

THE CHANGING PALACE GUARD

Ronald Reagan had always been unusually dependent on aides and assistants. He saw his own role as one above the heat of bureaucratic battle—providing the nation with a set of goals and a vision of the future. As the great communicator, he built the public consensus and let others manage the more mundane task of turning his dreams into reality.

His initial success depended heavily on the very effective White House team of James Baker, Edwin Meese, and Michael Deaver. Baker, a Texan with extensive Washington experience, became the chief of staff, managing the White House and directing legislative strategy. Meese accepted the role of counselor to the president, advising Reagan on policy but having little to do with its implementation. The final member of the trio, Mike Deaver, applied himself full time to the goal of enhancing Reagan's political image. Although Deaver and Meese were close to the president personally, it was Baker, the newcomer with keen political instincts and experience in dealing with Congress, who was mainly responsible for the Reagan administration's stunning early successes.

The president's laid-back style was misleading. Some thought he was little more than an actor playing the role of president, content to perform the ceremonial duties of a head of state while letting others run the country. Although it is true he preferred to be presented with solutions rather than problems, it was Reagan's determination to cut taxes, reduce domestic spending, and rebuild America's defenses that gave shape and coherence to his administration's policies. In the White House, he thrived on the interplay between Baker, Meese, and Deaver, letting them present various alternatives and then instinctively suggesting viable compromises. Neither brilliant nor well-read, Reagan had a quick mind and a remarkable feel for the public's emotions that enabled him to perform very effectively as a detached but charismatic chief executive.

An abrupt change in the White House staff in 1985 nearly proved disastrous for Reagan. Tired from the constant infighting, Baker agreed to Secretary of the Treasury Donald Regan's suggestion that the two men swap jobs. A self-made Wall Street operator, Regan possessed a confident, abrasive manner and a determination to assert his authority as White House chief of staff. When Meese became attorney general and Deaver left the government later in 1985, Regan took advantage of the president's passive nature, extending his own control and thus ending the give-and-take in the Oval Office that had allowed Reagan to shape the final policy choices during his first term. Lacking Baker's sensitivity to congressional concerns and Deaver's careful nurturing of Reagan's public image, Don Regan soon brought the administration into deep political trouble.

At first, Regan and Baker were able to score a major victory. Intent on lowering tax rates on the wealthy still more while capitalizing on growing congressional demands for a simpler and fairer revenue system, the two men pressed for a major overhaul of the income tax. Working with Congress, they shaped the 1986 Tax Reform Act. It cut the top rate from 50 to 28 percent while wiping out most shelters by severely restricting the tax breaks for losses in real estate ventures and many other speculative enterprises. An alternative minimum tax would end the injustice of many wealthy individuals paying no tax at all, while the new rates exempted 6 million people at the lower end from any tax liability at all. Although corporate rates were also cut, changes in depreciation and tax credits led to a short-term increase of $120 billion in business payments. This helped offset the loss from reductions in individual rates and thus did not add to the budget deficit.

The administration had only partial success in another area—altering the makeup of the federal judiciary. Long unhappy with judges who sought to carry out social change with their decisions, Reagan moved to fill the federal benches with conservative judges. The administration was able to fill the appeals courts with sympathetic judges, most of them wealthy, while males. And in 1986, Reagan succeeded in replacing outgoing Chief Justice Warren Burger with the court's strongest conservative, William Rehnquist. Equally conservative appeals court judge Antonin Scalia joined the Supreme Court at the same time. But in 1987, when the president nominated Robert Bork, an outspoken opponent of judicial activism, to fill the next vacancy, Democrats drew the line and rejected Bork's nomination. It was a bittersweet victory, however, as Reagan responded by appointing the moderately conservative, but far more diplomatic, Anthony Kennedy to the Court.

The Bork defeat was especially hard on Attorney General Ed Meese, who had been directing the administration's fight against judicial activism. But by then Meese himself had become an embarrassment to Reagan by symbolizing what came to be known as the "sleaze factor." During the hearing on his nomination to the post of Attorney General, charges of loose financial dealings and unethical conduct in office had raised doubts about his judgment. Although a special prosecutor found no evidence that the attorney general had broken the law, he admitted that some of Meese's dealings had the "appearance" of impropriety. The Meese affair was one of a number of episodes that stained the administration's reputation and left the Reagan administration with the appearance of tolerating corruption at the highest levels of government.

The "sleaze factor," however, was not the highest price that Reagan had to pay for his detached style of leadership. His inattention to detail nearly proved fatal to his presidency when he allowed trusted subordinates to subvert the will of Congress and flout the Constitution in a way the nation had not seen since the days of Watergate.

TRADING ARMS FOR HOSTAGES

The Iran-Contra affair began in mid-1985 when Robert McFarlane, Reagan's national security adviser, began a new initiative designed to restore American influence in the troubled Middle East. Concerned over the fate of six Americans held hostage in Lebanon by groups thought to be loyal to Ayatollah Khomeini, McFarlane proposed trading American anti-tank missiles to Iran in return for the hostages' release. Although he realized that the president was primarily concerned with the fate of the hostages, particularly CIA officer William Buckley, McFarlane's primary goal in proposing the exchange was to establish good relations with moderate elements in Iran, anticipating the aged Khomeini's death. The Iranians, desperate for weapons in the war they had been waging against Iraq since 1980, seemed willing to comply.

McFarlane soon found himself in over his head. He relied heavily on a young Marine lieutenant colonel assigned to the National Security Council, Oliver North, and North in turn sought the assistance of CIA Director William Casey. Casey soon took charge. By early 1986, when John Poindexter, a naval officer with little political experience, replaced a burned-out McFarlane as national security adviser, Casey was able to persuade the president to go ahead with shipments of both TOW antitank missiles and HAWK antiaircraft missiles to Iran.

The concept of trading arms for hostages was fatally flawed. The Reagan administration, in an effort to help end the war between Iran and Iraq, had imposed an arms embargo on Iran and had tried to prevent U.S. allies from sending weapons there. In addition, no sooner was one hostage released than several more Americans were taken hostage. As one observer commented, "As soon as Iran realized how highly we valued getting those hostages back, they apparently kept a good supply of hostages to ensure that we would do their bidding."

The arms deal with Iran was bad policy, but what came next was criminal. Ever since the Boland Amendment in late 1984 had cut off congressional funding, the Reagan administration had been searching for ways to supply the Contras. Reagan sought aid from friendly foreign governments, notably Saudi Arabia and Brunei, while Oliver North was put in charge of soliciting donations from wealthy, right-wing Americans. In early 1986, North had what he later described as a "neat idea" (apparently

shared by Casey as well)—he could use the enormous profits from the sale of weapons to Iran to finance the Contra campaign in Nicaragua. Despite the appeal of using Khomeini's money to pay the Contras and topple the Sandinistas, North's ploy was clearly not only illegal but also unconstitutional, since it meant usurping the congressional power of the purse.

Unlike the policy of trading arms for hostages, the diversion of the profits to the Contras was a closely held secret never debated among Reagan's advisers. Apparently, only North, Casey, and Poindexter were aware of this illegal activity until November 1986, when the press finally learned of the Iranian arms sales. While Attorney General Meese conducted an internal investigation, North hurriedly destroyed most of the incriminating documents, but overlooked one key memo that revealed the Contra diversion.

The political fallout was very heavy. The administration, having learned from the Watergate coverup, tried to control the damage by breaking the bad news itself. But the subsequent investigations led to the dismissal of Poindexter and North, and Donald Regan was

Despite Oliver North's questionable conduct, the public elevated him to near-heroic status during the televised Iran-Contra hearings. The bemedaled marine testified that he believed his deeds were justified as a defense of democracy.

forced to resign. Although every effort was made to protect Reagan himself, a poll taken in December 1986 revealed that his popularity had dropped from 67 percent to 46 percent in just a month, the steepest decline ever recorded.

The vital question of whether Ronald Reagan had approved of the Contra diversion was never answered satisfactorily. A special commission headed by John Tower to investigate the affair painted a very unflattering picture of a disengaged president, unaware of what his aides were doing, and concluded that he neither knew of nor consented to this illegal move. Public opinion polls indicated that most Americans suspected the president was at least aware of the Contra diversion. In the absence of firm evidence, however, they were willing to give Reagan the benefit of the doubt, and a protracted congressional hearing in the summer of 1987 did little to clear up the confusion.

While Reagan escaped from the Iran-Contra affair without being held fully responsible for it, his presidency was in serious trouble. In Congress, the Democrats, who gained control of the Senate as well as the House in the 1986 elections, began to override his vetoes, reject his nominees (notably Robert Bork), and bring a total halt to even humanitarian aid to the Contras. Ronald Reagan was still in the White House, but his reliance on others to conduct the affairs of state had robbed him of his power to lead the nation.

REAGAN THE PEACEMAKER

By the end of 1987, Ronald Reagan and his resourceful new chief of staff, former GOP Senate Majority Leader Howard Baker, made a remarkable recovery. Stepping into the foreign affairs arena, Reagan shed his image as a hawk and set out to reverse the course of Soviet-American relations.

The timing was fortunate. Mikhail Gorbachev was equally intent on improving relations as part of his new policy of *perestroika* (restructuring the Soviet economy) and *glasnost* (political openness). Soviet economic performance had been deteriorating steadily under Brezhnev and his successors, and the bloody war in Afghanistan had become a major liability. Gorbachev needed a breathing spell in the arms race and a reduction in Cold War tensions in order to carry out his sweeping changes at home.

The first meeting between the two leaders, at Geneva in 1985, had gone well, but had not led to any significant agreements. A hurried summit at Reykjavik, Iceland, in October 1986, just before the Iran-Contra affair had become public, nearly led to a historic breakthrough. The two men reached general agreement on the long disputed issue of Intermediate Nuclear Forces in Europe (INF), and then discussed the abolition of all nuclear weapons over the next decade. Although the two leaders could reach no agreement, it was clear that the Soviet Union was anxious to curtail the arms race.

The apparent failure at Reykjavik, however, did not halt the new momentum toward peace; both leaders needed a foreign policy triumph too much not to continue the dialogue. Throughout 1987, experts worked out the details of an INF agreement built on the original Reagan "zero option." What was once considered a propaganda ploy now became the basis for the most significant achievement in disarmament since SALT I in 1972. Meeting in Washington in December 1987, Reagan and Gorbachev agreed to remove and destroy all intermediate range missiles and to permit on-site inspection to verify this process. Thus, not only did Reagan succeed where Carter had failed in ending the Russian deployment of sophisticated SS-20 missiles targeted at Western Europe, but he also could claim that his policy of building up America's defenses and talking tough to the Russians had paid off handsomely.

Reagan's popularity soared to 70 percent, higher than it had been before the Iran-Contra affair. He had succeeded in making a major breakthrough in the nuclear arms race, and he could claim that his policies had led to a moderation in Soviet behavior. During the president's last year in office, the Soviets cooperated with the United States in pressuring Iran and Iraq to end their long war and opening negotiations to remove 50,000 Soviet-supplied Cuban troops from Angola. Most impressive of all, Gorbachev moved to end the invasion of Afghanistan that had renewed the Cold War in 1979. By the time Reagan left office in January 1989, he had scored a series of foreign policy triumphs that offset his dismal Iran-Contra fiasco and thus helped redeem his presidency.

THE ELECTION OF 1988

Despite the president's comeback, the outlook for the Democrats in 1988 was promising. Ronald Reagan would not be on the ballot. The Iran-Contra affair and the looming budget deficit undercut the Republican appeal to peace and prosperity, and most observers thought George Bush, the likely GOP nominee, would be a weak candidate. Michael Dukakis, the successful governor of Massachusetts, emerged from the grueling primary contests as the clearcut winner. With the selection of moderate Texas Senator Lloyd Bentsen as his vice-presidential running mate, Dukakis left the convention at Atlanta confident of victory, with polls showing him ahead by 17 points.

Bush quickly regained the lead, despite the controversial choice of Indiana Senator Dan Quayle as his running mate. The Republicans waged a ruthless attack on Dukakis, portraying him as soft on crime and defense, and turning the presidential contest away from potentially embarrassing issues such as the budget deficit and the Iran-Contra affair. Above all, the GOP candidate repeatedly promised not to raise taxes, reiterating his favorite line: "Read my lips—no new taxes."

The election's outcome confirmed the pollsters' projections. Bush won overwhelmingly in the South, carried most of the West, and defeated Dukakis in such key industrial states as Michigan and Pennsylvania. His victory reflected the continuing GOP dominance of the electoral college, as well as the natural advantage of an incumbent at a time when the economy was healthy and the world at relative peace. The Democrats, however, increased their margins in both the House and Senate.

The election of 1988 indicated that, at least on the presidential level, a significant change

had taken place in American politics in 1980. Bush consolidated the GOP's grip on the electoral college, winning in the Sunbelt states and cementing much of Reagan's inroads into the working-class vote. At the same time, racial polarization in politics continued, with Dukakis getting 88 percent of the African-American vote and 69 percent of the Hispanic ballots.

With Bush in office, major Reagan initiatives would continue, notably the shift away from the welfare state, a lower tax burden on the wealthy, more emphasis on the free market through deregulation, and a strong national defense. At the same time, Bush had to confront the consequences of Reagan's policies, particularly the large budget deficit, the trade imbalance, the growing opposition to heavy defense spending, and the failure of the Contras to overthrow the Sandinista regime. Above all, he had to face the challenge of meeting the high expectations that Reagan and Gorbachev had raised, not only in the United States but throughout the world, to end the Cold War and bring the frightening nuclear arms race under control. Winning the election had proved relatively easy; the real test of Bush's leadership still lay ahead.

A WORLD IN FLUX

Many people expected the Bush administration to reflect the reputation of the new president—bland and cautious, lacking in vision but safely predictable. A startling series of events abroad during his first year in office gave Bush the opportunity to preside over the end of the Cold War. At home, however, he was compelled to deal with issues he inherited from the Reagan years.

THE POLITICS OF POSTPONEMENT

Promised new initiatives in education, health care, and environmental protection were postponed as Bush faced three pressing domestic problems. First, the nation's savings and loan industry, based on U.S. government-insured deposits, was in grave trouble as a result of lax regulation and unwise, even possibly fraudulent, loan policies. Second, Congress began to probe into a scandal in the Department of Housing and Urban Development (HUD) in which former secretary Samuel Pierce and members of his staff had allowed favored operators to gain huge profits from urban renewal projects. Most serious of all was the continuing budget deficit. Despite Gramm-Rudman, the nation continued to spend beyond its means, with deficits still running about $150 billion a year.

The president and Congress finally did reach agreement on two outstanding issues. In August, Congress passed an administration bill to close or merge more than 700 ailing savings and loans at a cost of $157 billion over a ten-year period. At first hailed as a victory for Bush, the savings and loan bailout soon proved that critics were right in warning that the eventual cost would be far greater than the administration's original estimate.

Action on the budget proved more difficult. A conflict quickly developed between Bush and Congress. Bush held out against any tax increases; Congress insisted on keeping domestic programs intact. In November, the two sides finally compromised on a budget just under the Gramm-Rudman deficit limit of $110 billion for 1991. Both the administration and the Democratic-controlled Congress continued to engage in an elaborate charade, since actual spending was expected to raise the deficit far above the projected $105 billion level. Most important of all, Bush agreed to a tax increase of $134 billion that clearly violated his 1988 "read my lips" pledge.

THE END OF THE COLD WAR

Abroad, the Bush administration faced an unprecedented year of change that marked the end of the post-World War II era. In country after country, Communism gave way to freedom as the Cold War seemed to fade away more quickly than anyone had dared hope.

The first attempt at internal liberation proved tragically abortive. In May, students in China began a month-long demonstration for freedom in Beijing's Tiananmen Square that attracted worldwide attention. Watching American television coverage of Gorbachev's visit to China in mid-May, Americans were fascinated to see the Chinese students call for democracy with a hunger strike and a hand-crafted replica of the Statue of Liberty. But on the evening of June 4, the Chinese leaders sent tanks and troops to Tiananmen Square to crush the student demonstration. By the next day, full-scale repression swept over China. Chinese leaders imposed martial law to quell the dissent and shatter American hopes for a democratic China.

President Bush responded cautiously. While he did suspend sales of military equipment to China and stopped all government-to-government trade, he neither imposed stiffer sanctions nor engaged in harsh rhetoric. Bush wanted to preserve American influence with the Chinese government. Hence, despite official statements denouncing the crackdown, Bush permitted National Security Adviser Brent Scowcroft to undertake a secret mission to Beijing to maintain a working relationship with the Chinese leaders.

A far more promising trend toward freedom began in Europe in mid-1989. In June, Lech Walesa and his Solidarity movement came to power in free elections in Poland. Soon the winds of change were sweeping over the former Iron Curtain countries. A new regime in Hungary opened its borders to the West in September, allowing thousands of East German tourists in Hungary to flee to freedom. One by one, the repressive governments of East Germany, Czechoslovakia, Bulgaria, and Romania fell. The most heartening scene of all took place in East Germany in early November when the new Communist leaders suddenly announced the opening of the Berlin Wall. Workers quickly demolished a 12-foot high section of this despised physical symbol of the Cold War.

Most people realized it was Mikhail Gorbachev who was responsible for the liberation of Eastern Europe. In late 1988, he signaled the

Jubilant citizens from both East and West Germany joined to bring down the Berlin Wall in November 1989. Observers around the world cheered the triumph of freedom.

spread of his reforms to the Soviet satellites by announcing that the Brezhnev doctrine, which called for Soviet control of Eastern Europe, was now replaced with "the Sinatra doctrine," which meant the people of this region could now do things "their way." It was Gorbachev's refusal to use armed force to keep repressive regimes in power that permitted the long-delayed liberation of the captive peoples of Central and Eastern Europe.

Yet by the end of 1991, both Gorbachev and the Soviet Union had become victims of the demise of Communism. On August 19, 1991, eight right-wing plotters placed Gorbachev under arrest and attempted to seize control of the government in Moscow. Boris Yeltsin, the newly-elected president of the Russian Republic, however, broke up the coup by mounting a tank in Moscow and demanding Gorbachev's release. The Red Army rallied to Yeltsin's side. The coup failed and Gorbachev was released, only to resign in December, 1991 after the fifteen republics dissolved the Soviet Union. Russia, by far the largest and most powerful of the former Soviet republics, took the lead in joining with ten others to form a loose alignment called the Commonwealth of Independent States (CIS). Yeltsin then disbanded the Communist party and continued the reforms begun by Gorbachev to establish democracy and a free-market system in Russia.

The Bush administration, although criticized for its cautious approach, welcomed the demise of Communism and offered economic assistance to Russia and the other members of the new CIS. The most important steps came in the critical area of nuclear weapons. In 1991, Bush and Gorbachev signed START I, agreeing to reduce nuclear warheads to under 10,000 apiece; in late 1992, Bush and Yeltsin agreed on the terms for START II, which would eliminate land missiles with multiple warheads and reduce the number of nuclear weapons on each side to just over 3000, a level not seen since the mid-1960s. Although several of the republics had yet to agree even to START I, Bush could claim that by the time he left office in January 1993, the Cold War was over and the nuclear danger sharply curtailed.

The end of the Cold War, however, did not bring about a peaceful world. On August 2, 1990, Saddam Hussein, the leader of Iraq, stunned the world by conquering defenseless Kuwait and threatening Saudi Arabia and the

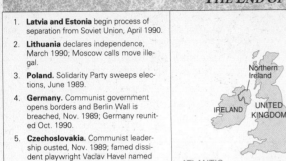

THE END OF THE COLD WAR

1. **Latvia and Estonia** begin process of separation from Soviet Union, April 1990.

2. **Lithuania** declares independence, March 1990; Moscow calls move illegal.

3. **Poland.** Solidarity Party sweeps elections, June 1989.

4. **Germany.** Communist government opens borders and Berlin Wall is breached, Nov. 1989; Germany reunited Oct. 1990.

5. **Czechoslovakia.** Communist leadership ousted, Nov. 1989; famed dissident playwright Vaclav Havel named president, Dec. 1989.

6. **Hungary.** Free election sweeps non-Communists into power, April 1990.

7. **Romania.** Communist dictator Ceausescu overthrown and executed, Dec. 1989; Salvation Front led by dissident former Communists wins elections, May 1990.

8. **Bulgaria.** Government disavows "dominant role" for Communist Party; pledges free elections and new constitution in 1990.

9. **Yugoslavia.** Government decides to hold free elections, Dec. 1989.

10. **Albania.** Communist Party still retains Leninist orientation.

11. **Russia.** Soviet Union dismantled, 1991; end of Cold War proclaimed, 1992.

oil-rich Persian Gulf. President Bush responded firmly, accusing Iraq of naked aggression and forming a United Nations coalition in behalf of what he termed "a new world order." Equally important, he quickly persuaded Saudi Arabia to accept a huge American troop buildup, dubbed Operation Desert Shield. Some critics questioned the meaning of the "new world order," but few could quarrel with the strategic need to prevent the bulk of the world's oil reserves from falling into the hands of Saddam Hussein. With the United States once again importing nearly half the oil the American people used, control of the Persian Gulf was clearly a vital national interest.

Debate raged, however, on the best way to meet the Iraqi threat. Many Democrats in Congress supported Bush's efforts to place international economic sanctions on Iraq, but opposed the use of force. Bush had clearly opted for a different solution by November, massing far more troops in the Persian Gulf area than were needed to defend Saudi Arabia—Desert Shield was giving way to Desert Storm. After securing UN support and winning a close vote in Congress, on January 17, 1991, Bush unleashed a devastating aerial assault on Iraq. The overwhelming American advantage in modern weaponry softened up Saddam Hussein's forces; when the ground offensive began on February 24, it took only 100 hours to bring about the collapse of Iraqi resistance.

Desert Storm brought mixed blessings. It was a great personal victory for George Bush, who saw his approval rating climb to nearly 90 percent in the Gallup poll. American military leaders felt that had finally atoned for Vietnam, a sentiment widely shared by a euphoric public. Best of all, the price of gasoline, which had climbed to a record $1.34 a gallon in October, fell back to just over $1 a gallon, enabling Americans to continue to enjoy a way of life based on the automobile. At the same time, however, Saddam Hussein continued to rule in Baghdad, persecuting Kurds in northern Iraq and Shiite Muslims in the south. Most alarming of all, the Persian Gulf War halted a slow recovery from a lingering recession and revived growing fears for America's economic health in the post-Cold War years.

DEMOCRATIC RESURGENCE

The persistence of the recession that had begun in mid-1990 became the dominant political reality of 1992. As unemployment rose from 5.2 percent in 1988 to over 7 percent in mid-1992, Bush's popularity plummeted. At the same time, a decline in tax revenues due to the sluggish economy, coupled with the continued high cost of the savings and loan bailout, added nearly $400 billion more to the deficit, which rose to over $3 trillion. Economists warned that the interest payments alone, already $300 billion a year, would become the largest single budget expenditure by the end of the 1990s, thereby threatening the nation's economic future.

Two men sought to capitalize on this bleak outlook. First, Arkansas Governor Bill Clinton defeated a field of five other challengers for the Democratic nomination by becoming the champion of economic renewal. Foregoing traditional liberal appeals to interest groups, Clinton emphasized the need for investment in the nation's future—rebuilding the infrastructure, training workers for high-tech jobs and solving

CHRONOLOGY

1980	Ronald Reagan wins presidency
1981	American hostages in Iran released after 444 days in captivity (January)
	Sandra Day O'Connor becomes first woman U.S. Supreme Court justice (September)
1982	Equal Rights Amendment fails state ratification (June) Unemployment reaches postwar record high of 10.4 percent (October)
1983	Soviets shoot down Korean airliner (September) Terrorist bomb kills 239 marines in Beirut barracks (October) U.S. invades Grenada (October)
1984	Ronald Reagan reelected president (November)
1985	Mikhail Gorbachev becomes leader of the Soviet Union (March) United States becomes debtor nation for first time since 1914
1986	Iran-Contra affair made public (November)
1987	Reagan and Gorbachev sign INF treaty at Washington summit
1988	George Bush defeats Michael Dukakis decisively in presidential election
1989	Communist governments in Eastern Europe fall Berlin Wall demolished (November)
1991	Attempted hardline coup in Russia fails (August) Soviet Union ends
1992	Bill Clinton elected president, defeating Republican George Bush and Independent H. Ross Perot

the growing national health crisis. One key statistic gave his message a vital appeal—in 1991, per capita income failed to keep pace with inflation. The average family income declined by 1.9 percent, the worst economic performance since 1970.

Despite his victories in the Democratic primaries, however, Clinton faced a sudden new rival in H. Ross Perot. An eccentric Texas billionaire, Perot singled out the deficit as the nation's greatest danger and agreed to run as an independent candidate in response to a grassroots movement to place his name on the fall ballot. As a businessman, Perot made sense to millions of Americans as he charged that during the Reagan-Bush era the Washington politicians had given the country $11.4 trillion worth of programs and services while raising only $9.3 trillion in taxes. Voters got 23 percent more government than they paid for, at a hidden cost to be paid for by future generations.

When Clinton succeeded in unifying the Democratic party and gaining agreement on a moderate platform that promised economic change, Perot stunned his supporters by suddenly dropping out of the race in July. Clinton immediately became the front-runner, rising from under 30 percent to over 50 percent in the polls, leaving Bush far behind. With unemployment continuing unabated and the economy failing to respond when the Federal Reserve Board dropped the interest rate to the lowest level since the 1960s, the American people turned their backs on George Bush and the Reagan revolution.

A relentless Democratic attack on the administration's lackluster economic performance overcame all of the president's efforts to remind the nation of Reagan prosperity and Bush triumphs abroad. The message that Clinton's political adviser tacked up at the Democratic candidate's headquarters, "THE ECONOMY, STUPID," provided the key to victory in November. Clinton wound up with 43 percent of the popular vote but with a commanding lead in the electoral college, 357 to 168 for Bush. Perot won 19 percent of the popular vote but failed to carry a single state.

For political scientists, 1992 was a clear case of a negative referendum. Voters had rejected the Reagan-Bush programs decisively. Troubled both by the frightening deficit and the sluggish

At the presidential debate held in October 1992 in Richmond, Virginia, ordinary citizens, rather than media representatives, had the opportunity to question the three candidates, Republican George Bush, Democrat Bill Clinton, and Independent H. Ross Perot.

economy, they had chosen Clinton's program of economic revitalization over Perot's call for short-term sacrifice to achieve long-term prosperity. In winning, Clinton had broken the GOP's grip on the South and West—only Texas and the interior western states had remained Republican strongholds. Clinton kept traditional Democratic voters, winning 83 percent support from African Americans and 62 percent from Hispanics, gained back the elderly by getting 50 percent of the votes of those over age sixty, and cut deeply into the crucial suburban vote by doing better than Bush among those earning between $30,000 and $75,000 a year.

As he took the oath of office on January 20, 1993, Bill Clinton seemed to have much in common with other Democratic presidents in the 20th century. Like Woodrow Wilson, Franklin D. Roosevelt, and Lyndon Johnson, he won election largely on domestic issues—his call for economic rebirth echoed the New Freedom, the New Deal, and the Great Society. Yet even before he entered the White House, it was becoming apparent that he would face severe challenges abroad as well as at home. Just as Wilson, Roosevelt, and Johnson soon became embroiled in conflicts in Europe and Asia, Clinton would have to deal with Bush's humanitarian intervention in Somalia, the threat of ethnic cleansing in what had been Yugoslavia, the continuing provocations of Saddam Hussein in Iraq, and the economic and political crisis in the former Soviet Union. Elected to revive the dormant American economy, his place in history could well depend on his ability to guide the United States through the perils of the post-Cold War world.

❧ RECOMMENDED READING

The best introduction to Ronald Reagan is Garry Wills, *Reagan's America* (1987), a provocative analysis of the various images of American life that the future president used as substitutes for reality. Robert Schieffer and Gary Paul Gates offer a critical overview of the Reagan administration in *The Acting President* (1989). Focusing on Reagan's detached style of leadership, they concentrate on the people to whom he delegated authority.

The best account by an insider, and the only one to give a positive view of the Reagan presidency, is Martin Anderson, *Revolution* (1988).

Theodore White offers a stimulating account of the political changes in the 1970s that led to Reagan's election to the presidency in *America in Search of Itself* (1982). Books on the 1980 election include Elizabeth Drew, *Portrait of an Election* (1981); Jack W. Germond and Jules Witcover, *Blue Smoke and Mirrors* (1981); and Thomas Ferguson and Joel Rogers, eds., *The Hidden Election of 1980* (1981). For the conservative resurgence see Peter Steinfels, *The Neo-Conservatives* (1979); Sidney Blumenthal, *The Rise of the Counter-Establishment* (1986), a critical account; and F. Clifton White and William Gil, *Why Reagan Won: The Conservative Movement, 1964–1981* (1982), a more sympathetic view.

Lou Cannon, *Reagan* (1982) offers the most thorough biography of the president. For more interpretive accounts, see Robert Dallek, *Ronald Reagan* (1984) and Michael Paul Rogin, *Ronald Reagan: The Movie* (1987). Reagan's early successes in cutting taxes and domestic spending can be traced in Rowland Evans and Robert Novak, *The Reagan Revolution* (1981); Lawrence Barrett, *Gambling with History* (1983); Fred Greenstein, ed., *The Reagan Presidency* (1983); and John L. Palmer and Isabel V. Sawhill, eds., *The Reagan Experiment* (1982). C. Brandt Short traces the conservation debate in *Ronald Reagan and the Public Lands* (1989).

The fullest account of the 1984 election is Peter Goldman and Tony Fuller, *The Quest for the Presidency 1984* (1985), but see also Elizabeth Drew, *Campaign Journal* (1985); Jack W. Germond and Jules Witcover, *Wake Us When It's Over* (1985); and Geraldine Ferraro, *My Story* (1985). Thomas Ferguson and Joel Rogers analyze the political realignment of the 1980s in *Right Turn* (1985).

Memoirs by White House staffers, many containing revelations embarrassing to the administration, include David Stockman, *The Triumph of Politics* (1986), critical of Reaganomics; Michael Deaver, *Behind the Scenes* (1987); Larry Speakes, *Speaking Out* (1988); and Donald Regan, *For the Record* (1988), a particularly vengeful account by the former White House chief of staff.

William G. Hyland provides an overview of American diplomacy in the 1980s in *The Reagan Foreign Policy* (1987) as does Coral Bell in *The Reagan Paradox* (1990). Reagan's first secretary of state, Alexander M. Haig, Jr., gives his views in *Caveat* (1984). On Central America, see the essays edited by Kenneth M. Coleman and George C. Herring, *The Central American Crisis* (1985) and two books on Nicaragua, Robert Pastor, *Condemned to Repetition* (1988) and Roy Gutman, *Banana Diplomacy* (1988). Paul B.

Stares traces the development of the Strategic Defense Initiative in *Space and National Security* (1987). The best studies of arms control in the 1980s are two books by Strobe Talbott, *Deadly Gambits* (1984), on the failure of Reagan's early efforts, and *The Master of the Game* (1988), on the role of Paul Nitze.

The Reagan administration's attempts to deal with the cocaine problem are traced in Elaine Shannon, *Desperados* (1988) and James A. Inciardi, *The War on Drugs* (1986). The best account of the impact of AIDS on American life in the 1980s is Randy Shilts, *And the Band Played On* (1987). For a spirited defense of Reaganomics, see Michael J. Boskin, *Reagan and the Economy* (1987), and Clyde V. Prestowitz, Jr., *Trading Places* (1988), critical of the administration's handling of the Japanese trade offensive.

The fullest account of the Iran-Contra affair is Jane Mayer and Doyle McManus, *Landslide* (1988). For views of insiders, see *Perilous Statecraft* (1988) by Michael A. Ledeen, one of the original conspirators, and *Men of Zeal* (1988) by William S. Cohen and George J. Mitchell, the two Maine senators who served on the congressional investigating committee. Bob Woodward traces CIA Director William Casey's role in the Iran-Contra affair, as well as other covert activities of the 1980s, in *Veil* (1987).

The best assessment of the overall impact of the Reagan presidency on American life can be found in the essays edited by Sidney Blumenthal and Thomas Byrne Edsall, *The Reagan Legacy* (1988). For information about the election of 1988, see Jack W. Germond and Jules Witcover, *Whose Broad Stripes and Bright Stars?* (1989).

APPENDIX

THE DECLARATION OF INDEPENDENCE

IN CONGRESS,
JULY 4, 1776

The Unanimous Declaration of the
thirteen United States of America,

When, in the course of human events, it becomes necessary for one people to dissolve the political bonds which have connected them with another, and to assume, among the powers of the earth, the separate and equal station to which the laws of nature and of nature's God entitle them, a decent respect to the opinions of mankind requires that they should declare the causes which impel them to the separation.

We hold these truths to be self-evident: That all men are created equal; that they are endowed by their Creator with certain unalienable rights; that among these are life, liberty, and the pursuit of happiness; that, to secure these rights, governments are instituted among men, deriving their just powers from the consent of the governed; that whenever any form of government becomes destructive of these ends, it is the right of the people to alter or to abolish it, and to institute new government, laying its foundation on such principles, and organizing its powers in such form, as to them shall seem most likely to effect their safety and happiness. Prudence, indeed, will dictate that governments long established should not be changed for light and transient causes; and accordingly all experience hath shown that mankind are more disposed to suffer, while evils are sufferable, than to right themselves by abolishing the forms to which they are accustomed. But when a long train of abuses and usurpations, pursuing invariably the same object, evinces a design to reduce them under absolute despotism, it is their right, it is their duty, to throw off such government, and to provide new guards for their future security. Such has been the patient sufferance of these colonies; and such is now the necessity which constrains them to alter their former systems of government. The history of the present King of Great Britain is a history of repeated injuries and usurpations, all having in direct object the establishment of an absolute tyranny over these states. To prove this, let facts be submitted to a candid world.

He has refused his assent to laws, the most wholesome and necessary for the public good.

He has forbidden his governors to pass laws of immediate and pressing importance, unless suspended in their operation till his assent should be obtained; and, when so suspended, he has utterly neglected to attend to them.

He has refused to pass other laws for the accommodation of large districts of people, unless those people would relinquish the right of representation in the legislature, a right inestimable to them, and formidable to tyrants only.

He has called together legislative bodies at places unusual, uncomfortable, and distant from the depository of their public records, for the sole purpose of fatiguing them into compliance with his measures.

He has dissolved representative houses repeatedly, for opposing, with manly firmness, his invasions on the rights of the people.

He has refused for a long time, after such dissolutions, to cause others to be elected; whereby the legislative powers, incapable of annihilation, have returned to the people at large for their exercise; the state remaining, in the mean time, exposed to all the dangers of invasions from without and convulsions within.

He has endeavored to prevent the population of these states; for that purpose obstructing the laws for naturalization of foreigners; refusing to pass others to encourage their migration hither, and raising the conditions of new appropriations of lands.

He has obstructed the administration of justice, by refusing his assent to laws for establishing judiciary powers.

He has made judges dependent on his will alone, for the tenure of their offices, and the amount and payment of their salaries.

He has erected a multitude of new offices, and sent hither swarms of officers to harass our people and eat out their substance.

He has kept among us, in times of peace, standing armies, without the consent of our legislatures.

He has affected to render the military independent of, and superior to, the civil power.

He has combined with others to subject us to a jurisdiction foreign to our constitution, and unacknowledged by our laws, giving his assent to their acts of pretended legislation:

For quartering large bodies of armed troops among us;

For protecting them, by a mock trial, from punishment for any murder which they should commit on the inhabitants of these states;

For cutting off our trade with all parts of the world;

For imposing taxes on us without our consent;

For depriving us, in many cases, of the benefits of trial by jury;

For transporting us beyond seas, to be tried for pretended offenses;

For abolishing the free system of English laws in a neighboring province, establishing therein an arbitrary government, and enlarging its boundaries, so as to render it at once an example and fit instrument for introducing the same absolute rule into these colonies;

For taking away our charters abolishing our most valuable laws, and altering fundamentally the forms of our governments;

For suspending our own legislatures, and declaring themselves invested with power to legislate for us in all cases whatsoever.

He has abdicated government here, by declaring us out of his protection and waging war against us.

He has plundered our seas, ravaged our coasts, burned our towns, and destroyed the lives of our people.

He is at this time transporting large armies of foreign mercenaries to complete the works of death, desolation, and tyranny already begun with circumstances of cruelty and perfidy scarcely paralleled in the most barbarous ages, and totally unworthy the head of a civilized nation.

He has constrained our fellow-citizens, taken captive on the high seas, to bear arms against their country, to become the executioners of their friends and brethren, or to fall themselves by their hands.

He has excited domestic insurrection among us, and has endeavored to bring on the inhabitants of our frontiers the merciless Indian savages, whose known rule of warfare is an undistinguished destruction of all ages, sexes, and conditions.

In every stage of these oppressions we have petitioned for redress in the most humble terms; our repeated petitions have been answered only by repeated injury. A prince, whose character is thus marked by every act which may define a tyrant, is unfit to be the ruler of a free people.

Nor have we been wanting in our attentions to our British brethren. We have warned them, from time to time, of attempts by their legislature to extend an unwarrantable jurisdiction over us. We have reminded them of the circumstances of our emigration and settlement here. We have appealed to their native justice and magnanimity; and we have conjured them, by the ties of our common kindred, to disavow these usurpations, which would inevitably interrupt our connections and correspondence. They, too, have been deaf to the voice of justice and of consanguinity. We must, therefore, acquiesce in the necessity which denounces our separation, and hold them, as we hold the rest of mankind, enemies in war, in peace friends.

We, therefore, the representatives of the United States of America, in General Congress assembled, appealing to the Supreme Judge of the world for the rectitude of our intentions, do, in the name and by the authority of the good people of these colonies, solemnly publish and declare, that these United Colonies are, and of right ought to be, FREE AND INDEPENDENT STATES; that they are absolved from all allegiance to the British crown, and that all political connection between them and the state of Great Britain is, and ought to be, totally dissolved; and that, as free and independent states, they have full power to levy war, conclude peace, contract alliances, establish commerce, and do all other acts and things which independent states may of right do. And for the support of this declaration, with a firm reliance on the protection of Divine Providence, we mutually pledge to each other our lives, our fortunes, and our sacred honor.

JOHN HANCOCK

BUTTON GWINNETT
LYMAN HALL
GEO. WALTON
WM. HOOPER
JOSEPH HEWES
JOHN PENN
EDWARD RUTLEDGE
THOS. HEYWARD, JUNR.
THOMAS LYNCH, JUNR.
ARTHUR MIDDLETON
SAMUEL CHASE
WM. PACA
THOS. STONE
CHARLES CARROLL OF CARROLLTON

GEORGE WYTHE
RICHARD HENRY LEE
TH. JEFFERSON
BENJ. HARRISON
THOS. NELSON, JR.
FRANCIS LIGHTFOOT LEE
CARTER BRAXTON
ROBT. MORRIS
BENJAMIN RUSH
BENJA. FRANKLIN
JOHN MORTON
GEO. CLYMER
JAS. SMITH
GEO. TAYLOR

JAMES WILSON
GEO. ROSS
CAESAR RODNEY
GEO. READ
THO. M'KEAN
WM. FLOYD
PHIL. LIVINGSTON
FRANS. LEWIS
LEWIS MORRIS
RICHD. STOCKTON
JNO. WITHERSPOON
FRAS. HOPKINSON
JOHN HART
ABRA. CLARK

JOSIAH BARTLETT
WM. WHIPPLE
SAML. ADAMS
JOHN ADAMS
ROBT. TREAT PAINE
ELBRIDGE GERRY
STEP. HOPKINS
WILLIAM ELLERY
ROGER SHERMAN
SAM'EL HUNTINGTON
WM. WILLIAMS
OLIVER WOLCOTT
MATTHEW THORNTON

THE CONSTITUTION OF THE UNITED STATES OF AMERICA

We the People of the United States, in Order to form a more perfect Union, establish Justice, insure domestic Tranquility, provide for the common defence, promote the general Welfare, and secure the Blessings of Liberty to ourselves and our Posterity, do ordain and establish this Constitution for the United States of America.

Article I.

Section 1

All legislative Powers herein granted shall be vested in a Congress of the United States, which shall consist of a Senate and House of Representatives.

Section 2

The House of Representatives shall be composed of Members chosen every second Year by the People of the several States, and the Electors in each State shall have the Qualifications requisite for Electors of the most numerous Branch of the State Legislature.

No Person shall be a Representative who shall not have attained to the Age of twenty five Years, and been seven Years a Citizen of the United States, and who shall not, when elected, be an inhabitant of that State in which he shall be chosen.

Representatives and direct Taxes shall be apportioned among the several States which may be included within this Union, according to their respective Numbers, *which shall be determined by adding to the whole Number of free Persons, including those bound to Service for a Term of Years, and excluding Indians not taxed, three fifths of all other Persons.* The actual Enumeration shall be made within three Years after the first Meeting of the Congress of the United States, and within every subsequent Term of ten Years, in such Manner as they shall by Law direct. The Number of Representatives shall not exceed one for every thirty Thousand, but each State shall have at Least one Representative; *and until such enumeration shall be made, the State of New Hampshire shall be entitled to chuse three, Massachusetts eight, Rhode-Island and Providence Plantations one, Connecticut five, New York six, New Jersey four, Pennsylvania eight, Delaware one,*

Passages no longer in effect are printed in italic type.

Maryland six, Virginia ten, North Carolina five, South Carolina five, and Georgia three.

When vacancies happen in the Representation from any State, the Executive Authority thereof shall issue Writs of Election to fill such Vacancies.

The House of Representatives shall chuse their Speaker and other Officers; and shall have the sole Power of Impeachment.

Section 3

The Senate of the United States shall be composed of two Senators from each State, *chosen by the Legislature thereof,* for six Years; and each Senator shall have one Vote.

Immediately after they shall be assembled in Consequence of the first Election, they shall be divided as equally as may be into three Classes. The Seats of the Senators of the first Class shall be vacated at the Expiration of the second Year, of the second Class at the Expiration of the fourth Year, and of the third Class at the Expiration of the sixth Year so that one third may be chosen every second Year; *and if Vacancies happen by Resignation, or otherwise, during the Recess of the Legislature of any state, the Executive thereof may make temporary Appointments until the next Meeting of the Legislature, which shall then fill such Vacancies.*

No Person shall be a Senator who shall not have attained to the Age of thirty Years, and been nine Years a Citizen of the United States, and who shall not, when elected, be an Inhabitant of that State for which he shall be chosen.

The Vice President of the United States shall be President of the Senate, but shall have no Vote, unless they be equally divided.

The Senate shall chuse their other Officers, and also a President *pro tempore,* in the Absence of the Vice President, or when he shall exercise the Office of President of the United States.

The Senate shall have the sole Power to try all Impeachments. When sitting for that Purpose, they shall be on Oath or Affirmation. When the President of the United States is tried the Chief Justice shall preside: And no Person shall be convicted without the Concurrence of two thirds of the Members present.

Judgment in Cases of Impeachment shall not extend further than to removal from Office, and disqualification to hold and enjoy any Office of honor, Trust or Profit under the United States: but the Party convicted shall nevertheless be liable and subject to Indictment, Trial, Judgment and Punishment, according to Law.

Section 4

The Times, Places and Manner of holding Elections for Senators and Representatives, shall be prescribed in each State by the Legislature thereof; but the Congress may at any time by Law make or alter such Regulations, except as to the Places of chusing Senators.

The Congress shall assemble at least once in every Year, and such Meeting *shall be on the first Monday in December, unless they shall by Law appoint a different Day.*

Section 5

Each House shall be the Judge of the Elections, Returns and Qualifications of its own Members, and a Majority of each shall constitute a Quorum to do Business; but a smaller Number may adjourn from day to day, and may be authorized to compel the Attendance of absent Members, in such Manner, and under such Penalties as each House may provide.

Each House may determine the Rules of its Proceedings, punish its Members for disorderly Behaviour, and, with the Concurrence of two thirds, expel a Member.

Each House shall keep a Journal of its Proceedings, and from time to time publish the same, excepting such Parts as may in their Judgment require Secrecy; and the Yeas and Nays of the Members of either House on any question shall, at the Desire of one fifth of those Present, be entered on the Journal.

Neither House, during the Session of Congress, shall, without the Consent of the other, adjourn for more than three days, nor to any other Place than that in which the two Houses shall be sitting.

Section 6

The Senators and Representatives shall receive a Compensation for their Services, to be ascertained by Law, and paid out of the Treasury of the United States. They shall in all Cases, except Treason, Felony and Breach of the Peace, be privileged from Arrest during their Attendance at the Session of their respective Houses, and in going to and returning from the same; and for any Speech or Debate in either House, they shall not be questioned in any other Place.

No Senator or Representative shall, during the Time for which he was elected, be appointed to any civil Office under the Authority of the United States, which shall have been created, or the Emoluments whereof shall have been encreased during such time, and no Person holding any Office under the United States, shall be a Member of either House during his Continuance in Office.

Section 7

All Bills for raising Revenue shall originate in the House of Representatives; but the Senate may propose or concur with Amendments as on other Bills.

Every Bill which shall have passed the House of Representatives and the Senate, shall, before it become a Law, be presented to the President of the United States; If he approve he shall sign it, but if not he shall return it, with his Objections to the House in which it shall have originated, who shall enter the Objections at large on their Journal, and proceed to reconsider it. If after such Reconsideration two thirds of that House shall agree to pass the Bill, it shall be sent, together with the Objections, to the other House, by which it shall likewise be reconsidered, and if approved by two thirds of that House, it shall become a Law. But in all such Cases the Votes of both Houses shall be determined by yeas and Nays, and the Names of the Persons voting for and against the Bill shall be entered on the Journal of each House respectively. If any Bill shall not be returned by the President within ten Days (Sundays excepted) after it shall have been presented to him, the Same shall be a Law, in like Manner as if he had signed it, unless the Congress by their Adjournment prevent its Return, in which Case it shall not be a Law.

Every Order, Resolution, or Vote to which the Concurrence of the Senate and House of Representatives may be necessary (except on a question of Adjournment) shall be presented to the President of the United States; and before the Same shall take Effect, shall be approved by him, or being disapproved by him, shall be repassed by two thirds of the Senate and House of Representatives, according to the Rules and Limitations prescribed in the Case of a Bill.

Section 8

The Congress shall have Power To lay and collect Taxes, Duties, Imposts and Excises, to pay the Debts and provide for the common Defence and general Welfare of the United States; but all Duties, Imposts and Excises shall be uniform throughout the United States;

To borrow Money on the credit of the United States;

To regulate Commerce with foreign Nations, and among the several States, and with the Indian Tribes;

To establish an uniform Rule of Naturalization, and uniform Laws on the subject of Bankruptcies throughout the United States;

To coin Money, regulate the Value thereof, and of foreign Coin, and fix the Standard of Weights and Measures;

To provide for the Punishment of counterfeiting the Securities and current Coin of the United States;

To establish Post Offices and post Roads;

To promote the Progress of Science and useful Arts, by securing for limited Times to Authors and Inventors the exclusive Right to their respective Writings and Discoveries;

To constitute Tribunals inferior to the supreme Court;

To define and punish Piracies and Felonies committed on the high Seas, and Offences against the Law of Nations;

To declare War, grant Letters of Marque and Reprisal, and make Rules concerning Captures on Land and Water;

To raise and support Armies, but no Appropriation of Money to that Use shall be for a longer Term than two Years;

To provide and maintain a Navy;

To make Rules for the Government and Regulation of the land and naval Forces;

To provide for calling forth the Militia to execute the Laws of the Union, suppress Insurrections and repel Invasions;

To provide for organizing, arming, and disciplining, the Militia, and for governing such Part of them as may be employed in the Service of the United States, reserving to the States respectively, the Appointment of the Officers, and the Authority of training the Militia according to the discipline prescribed by Congress;

To exercise exclusive Legislation in all Cases whatsoever, over such District (not exceeding ten Miles square) as may, by Cession of particular States, and the Acceptance of Congress, become the Seat of the Government of the United States, and to exercise like Authority over all Places purchased by the Consent of the Legislature of the State in which the Same shall be, for the Erection of Forts, Magazines, Arsenals, dock-Yards, and other needful Buildings;—And

To make all Laws which shall be necessary and proper for carrying into Execution the foregoing Powers, and all other Powers vested by this Constitution in the Government of the United States, or in any Department or Officer thereof.

Section 9

The Migration or Importation of such Persons as any of the States now existing shall think proper to admit, shall not be prohibited by the Congress prior to the Year one thousand eight hundred and eight, but a Tax or duty may be imposed on such Importation, not exceeding ten dollars for each Person.

The Privilege of the Writ of Habeas Corpus shall not be suspended, unless when in Cases of Rebellion or Invasion the public Safety may require it.

No Bill of Attainder or ex post facto Law shall be passed.

No Capitation, or other direct, Tax shall be laid, unless in Proportion to the Census or Enumeration herein before directed to be taken.

No Tax or Duty shall be laid on Articles exported from any State.

No Preference shall be given by any Regulation of Commerce or Revenue to the Ports of one State over those of another: nor shall Vessels bound to, or from, one State, be obliged to enter, clear, or pay Duties in another.

No Money shall be drawn from the Treasury, but in Consequence of Appropriations made by Law; and a regular Statement and Account of the Receipts and Expenditures of all public Money shall be published from time to time.

No Title of Nobility shall be granted by the United States: And no Person holding any Office of Profit or Trust under them, shall, without the Consent of the Congress, accept of any present, Emolument, Office, or Title, of any kind whatever, from any King, Prince, or foreign State.

Section 10

No State shall enter into any Treaty, Alliance, or Confederation; grant Letters of Marque and Reprisal; coin Money; emit Bills of Credit; make any Thing but gold and silver Coin a Tender in Payment of Debts; pass any Bill of Attainder, ex post facto Law, or Law impairing the obligation of Contracts, or grant any Title of Nobility.

No State shall, without the Consent of the Congress, lay any Imposts or Duties on Imports or Exports, except what may be absolutely necessary for executing its inspection Laws: and the net Produce of all Duties and Imposts, laid by any State on Imports or Exports, shall be for the Use of the Treasury of the United States; and all such Laws shall be subject to the Revision and Controul of the Congress.

No State shall, without the Consent of Congress, lay any Duty of Tonnage, keep Troops, or Ships of War in time of Peace, enter into any Agreement or Compact with another State, or with a foreign Power, or engage in War, unless actually invaded, or in such imminent Danger as will not admit of delay.

Article II.

Section 1

The executive Power shall be vested in a President of the United States of America. He shall hold his Office during the Term of four Years, and, together with the Vice President, chosen for the same Term, be elected, as follows:

Each State shall appoint, in such Manner as the Legislature thereof may direct, a Number of Electors, equal to the whole Number of Senators and Representatives to which the State may be entitled in the Congress: but no Senator or Representative, or Person holding an Office of Trust or Profit under the United States, shall be appointed an Elector.

The Electors shall meet in their respective States, and vote by Ballot for two Persons, of whom one at least

shall not be an Inhabitant of the same State with themselves. And they shall make a List of all the Persons voted for, and of the Number of Votes for each; which List they shall sign and certify, and transmit sealed to the Seat of the Government of the United States, directed to the President of the Senate. The President of the Senate shall, in the Presence of the Senate and House of Representatives, open all the Certificates, and the Votes shall then be counted. The Person having the greatest Number of Votes shall be the President, if such Number be a Majority of the whole number of Electors appointed; and if there be more than one who have such Majority, and have an equal Number of Votes, then the House of Representative shall immediately chuse by Ballot one of them for President; and if no Person have a Majority, then from the five highest on the List the said House shall in like Manner chuse the President. But in chusing the President, the Votes shall be taken by States, the Representation from each State having one Vote; A quorum for this Purpose shall consist of a Member or Members from two thirds of the States, and a Majority of all the States shall be necessary to a Choice. In every Case, after the Choice of the President, the Person having the greatest Number of Votes of the Electors shall be the Vice President. But if there should remain two or more who have equal Votes, the Senate shall chuse from them by Ballot the Vice President.

The Congress may determine the time of chusing the Electors, and the Day on which they shall give their Votes; which Day shall be the same throughout the United States.

No person except a natural born Citizen, or a Citizen of the United States, at the time of the Adoption of this Constitution, shall be eligible to the Office of President; neither shall any Person be eligible to that Office who shall not have attained to the Age of thirty five Years, and been fourteen Years a Resident within the United States.

In Case of the Removal of the President from Office, or of his Death, Resignation, or Inability to discharge the Powers and Duties of the said Office, the Same shall devolve on the Vice President, and the Congress may by Law provide for the Case of Removal, Death, Resignation or Inability, both of the President and Vice President, declaring what Officer shall then act as President, and such Officer shall act accordingly, until the Disability be removed, or a President shall be elected.

The President shall, at stated Times, receive for his Services, a Compensation, which shall neither be encreased nor diminished during the Period for which he shall have been elected, and he shall not receive within that period any other Emolument from the United States, or any of them.

Before he enter on the Execution of his Office, he shall take the following Oath or Affirmation:—"I do solemnly swear (or affirm) that I will faithfully execute the Office of President of the United States, and will to the best of my Ability, preserve, protect and defend the Constitution of the United States."

Section 2

The President shall be Commander in Chief of the Army and Navy of the United States, and of the Militia of the several States, when called into the actual Service of the United States; he may require the Opinion, in writing, of the principal Officer in each of the executive Departments, upon any Subject relating to the Duties of their respective Offices, and he shall have Power to grant Reprieves and Pardons for Offences against the United States, except in Cases of Impeachment.

He shall have Power, by and with the Advice and Consent of the Senate, to make Treaties, provided two thirds of the Senators present concur; and he shall nominate, and by and with the Advice and Consent of the Senate, shall appoint Ambassadors, other public Ministers and Consuls, Judges of the supreme Court, and all other Officers of the United States, whose Appointments are not herein otherwise provided for, and which shall be established by Law: but the Congress may by Law vest the Appointment of such inferior Officers, as they think proper in the President alone, in the Courts of Law, or in the Heads of Departments.

The President shall have Power to fill up all Vacancies that may happen during the Recess of the Senate, by granting Commissions which shall expire at the End of their next Session.

Section 3

He shall from time to time give to the Congress Information of the State of the Union, and recommend to their Consideration such Measures as he shall judge necessary and expedient; he may, on extraordinary Occasions, convene both Houses, or either of them, and in Case of disagreement between them, with Respect to the Time of Adjournment, he may adjourn them to such Time as he shall think proper; he shall receive Ambassadors and other public Ministers; he shall take Care that the Laws be faithfully executed, and shall Commission all the officers of the United States.

Section 4

The President, Vice President and all civil Officers of the United States, shall be removed from Office on Impeachment for, and Conviction of, Treason, Bribery or other high Crimes and Misdemeanors.

Article III.

Section 1

The judicial Power of the United States, shall be vested in one supreme Court, and in such inferior

Courts as the Congress may from time to time ordain and establish. The Judges, both of the supreme and inferior Courts, shall hold their offices during good Behaviour, and shall, at stated Times, receive for their Services, a Compensation, which shall not be diminished during their Continuance in Office.

Section 2

The judicial Power shall extend to all Cases, in Law and Equity, arising under this Constitution, the Laws of the United States, and Treaties made, or which shall be made, under their Authority;—to all Cases affecting Ambassadors, other public Ministers and Consuls;—to all Cases of admiralty and maritime Jurisdiction;—to Controversies to which the United States shall be a Party;—to Controversies between two or more States;—*between a State and Citizens of another State;*—between Citizens of different States,—between Citizens of the same State claiming Lands under Grants of different States, and between a State, or the Citizens thereof, and foreign States, Citizens or Subjects.

In all Cases affecting Ambassadors, other public Ministers and Consuls, and those in which a State shall be Party, the supreme Court shall have original Jurisdiction. In all the other Cases before mentioned, the supreme Court shall have appellate Jurisdiction, both as to Law and Fact, with such Exceptions, and under such Regulations as the Congress shall make.

The Trial of all Crimes, except in Cases of Impeachment, shall be by Jury; and such Trial shall be held in the State where the said Crimes shall have been committed, but when not committed within any State, the Trial shall be at such Place or Places as the Congress may by Law have directed.

Section 3

Treason against the United States, shall consist only in levying War against them, or in adhering to their Enemies, giving them Aid and Comfort. No person shall be convicted of Treason unless on the Testimony of two Witnesses to the same overt Act, or on Confession in open Court.

The Congress shall have Power to declare the Punishment of Treason, but no Attainder of Treason shall work Corruption of Blood, or Forfeiture except during the Life of the Person attainted.

Article IV.

Section 1

Full Faith and Credit shall be given in each State to the public Acts, Records, and judicial Proceedings of every other State. And the Congress may by general Laws prescribe the Manner in which such Acts, Records and Proceedings shall be proved, and the Effect thereof.

Section 2

The Citizens of each State shall be entitled to all Privileges and Immunities of Citizens in the several States.

A Person charged in any State with Treason, Felony, or other Crime, who shall flee from Justice, and be found in another State, shall on Demand of the executive Authority of the State from which he fled, be delivered up, to be removed to the State having Jurisdiction of the Crime.

No Person held to Service or Labour in one State, under the Laws thereof, escaping into another, shall, in Consequence of any Law or Regulation therein, be discharged from such Service or Labour, but shall be delivered up on Claim of the Party to whom such Service or Labour may be due.

Section 3

New States may be admitted by the Congress into this Union; but no new State shall be formed or erected within the Jurisdiction of any other State; nor any State be formed by the Junction of two or more States, or Parts of States, without the Consent of the Legislatures of the States concerned as well as of the Congress.

The Congress shall have Power to dispose of and make all needful Rules and Regulations respecting the Territory or other Property belonging to the United States; and nothing in this Constitution shall be so construed as to Prejudice any Claims of the United States, or of any particular States.

Section 4

The United States shall guarantee to every State in this Union a Republican Form of Government, and shall protect each of them against Invasion; and on Application of the Legislature, or of the Executive (when the Legislature cannot be convened) against domestic violence.

Article V.

The Congress, whenever two thirds of both Houses shall deem it necessary, shall propose Amendments to this Constitution, or, on the Application of the Legislatures of two thirds of the several States, shall call a Convention for proposing Amendments, which, in either Case, shall be valid to all Intents and Purposes, as Part of this Constitution, when ratified by the Legislatures of three fourths of the several States, or by Conventions in three fourths thereof, as the one or the other Mode of Ratification may be proposed by the Congress; Provided *that no Amendment which may be made prior to the Year One thousand eight hundred and eight shall in any Manner affect the first and fourth Clauses in the Ninth Section of the first Article;* and that no State without its Consent, shall be deprived of its equal Suffrage in the Senate.

Article VI.

All Debts contracted and Engagements entered into, before the Adoption of this Constitution, shall be as valid against the United States under this Constitution, as under the Confederation.

This Constitution, and Laws of the United States which shall be made in Pursuance thereof; and all Treaties made, or which shall be made, under the Authority of the United States, shall be the supreme Law of the Land; and the Judges in every State shall be bound thereby, any Thing in the Constitution or Laws of any State to the Contrary notwithstanding.

The Senators and Representatives before mentioned, and the Members of the several State Legislatures, and all executive and Judicial Officers, both of the United States and of the several States, shall be bound by Oath or Affirmation, to support this Constitution; but no religious Test shall ever be required as a Qualification to any Office of public Trust under the United States.

Article VII.

The Ratification of the Conventions of nine States, shall be sufficient for the Establishment of this Constitution between the States so ratifying the Same.

Done in Convention by the Unanimous Consent of the States present the Seventeenth Day of September in the Year of our Lord one thousand seven hundred and Eighty seven and of the Independence of the United States of America the Twelfth[1] IN WITNESS whereof We have hereunto subscribed our Names,

[1] The Constitution was submitted on September 17, 1787, by the Constitutional Convention, was ratified by the conventions of several states at various dates up to May 29, 1790, and became effective on March 4, 1789.

GEORGE WASHINGTON,
PRESIDENT AND DEPUTY FROM VIRGINIA

New Hampshire
JOHN LANGDON
NICHOLAS GILMAN

Massachusetts
NATHANIEL GORHAM
RUFUS KING

Connecticut
WILLIAM S. JOHNSON
ROGER SHERMAN

New York
ALEXANDER HAMILTON

New Jersey
WILLIAM LIVINGSTON
DAVID BREARLEY
WILLIAM PATERSON
JONATHAN DAYTON

Pennsylvania
BENJAMIN FRANKLIN
THOMAS MIFFLIN
ROBERT MORRIS
GEORGE CLYMER
THOMAS FITZSIMONS
JARED INGERSOLL
JAMES WILSON
GOUVERNEUR MORRIS

Delaware
GEORGE READ
GUNNING BEDFORD, JR.
JOHN DICKINSON
RICHARD BASSETT
JACOB BROOM

Maryland
JAMES MCHENRY
DANIEL OF ST. THOMAS JENIFER
DANIEL CARROLL

Virginia
JOHN BLAIR
JAMES MADISON, JR.

North Carolina
WILLIAM BLOUNT
RICHARD DOBBS SPRAIGHT
HU WILLIAMSON

South Carolina
J. RUTLEDGE
CHARLES G. PINCKNEY
PIERCE BUTLER

Georgia
WILLIAM FEW
ABRAHAM BALDWIN

AMENDMENTS TO THE CONSTITUTION

Amendment I

Congress shall make no law respecting an establishment of religion, or prohibiting the free exercise thereof; or abridging the freedom of speech, or of the press; or the right of the people peaceably to assemble, and to petition the Government for a redress of grievances.

Amendment II

A well regulated Militia being necessary to the security of a free State, the right of the people to keep and bear Arms, shall not be infringed.

Amendment III

No Soldier shall, in time of peace be quartered in any house, without the consent of the Owner, nor in time of war, but in a manner to be prescribed by law.

Amendment IV

The right of the people to be secure in their persons, houses, papers, and effects, against unreasonable searches and seizures, shall not be violated, and no Warrants shall issue, but upon probable cause, supported by Oath or affirmation, and particularly describing the place to be searched, and the persons or things to be seized.

Amendment V

No person shall be held to answer for a capital, or otherwise infamous crime, unless on a presentment or indictment of a Grand Jury, except in cases arising in the land or naval forces, or in the Militia, when in actual service in time of War or public danger; nor shall any person be subject for the same offense to be twice put in jeopardy of life or limb; nor shall be compelled in any criminal case to be a witness against himself, nor be deprived of life, liberty, or property, without due process of law; nor shall private property be taken for public use, without just compensation.

The first ten amendments (the Bill of Rights) were ratified and adoption certified on December 15, 1791.

Amendment VI

In all criminal prosecutions, the accused shall enjoy the right to a speedy and public trial, by an impartial jury of the State and district wherein the crime shall have been committed, which district shall have been previously ascertained by law, and to be informed of the nature and cause of the accusation; to be confronted with the witnesses against him; to have compulsory process for obtaining witnesses in his favor, and to have the Assistance of Counsel for his defence.

Amendment VII

In Suits at common law, where the value in controversy shall exceed twenty dollars, the right of trial by jury shall be preserved, and no fact trial by a jury, shall be otherwise re-examined in any Court of the United States, than according to the rules of the common law.

Amendment VIII

Excessive bail shall not be required, nor excessive fines imposed, nor cruel and unusual punishments inflicted.

Amendment IX

The enumeration in the Constitution, of certain rights, shall not be construed to deny or disparage others retained by the people.

Amendment X

The powers not delegated to the United States by the Constitution, nor prohibited by it to the States, are reserved to the States respectively, or to the people.

Amendment XI

[Adopted 1798]
The Judicial power of the United States shall not be construed to extend to any suit in law or equity, commenced or prosecuted against one of the United States by Citizens of another State, or by Citizens or Subjects of any Foreign State.

Amendment XII

[Adopted 1804]

The Electors shall meet in their respective states, and vote by ballot for President and Vice-President, one of whom, at least, shall not be an inhabitant of the same state with themselves; they shall name in their ballots the person voted for as President, and in distinct ballots the person voted for as Vice-President, and they shall make distinct lists of all persons voted for as President, and of all persons voted for as Vice-President, and of the number of votes for each, which lists they shall sign and certify, and transmit sealed to the seat of the government of the United States, directed to the President of the Senate;—The President of the Senate shall, in the presence of the Senate and House of Representatives, open all the certificates and the votes shall then be counted;—The person having the greatest number of votes for President, shall be the President, if such number be a majority of the whole number of Electors appointed; and if no person have such majority, then from the persons having the highest numbers not exceeding three on the list of those voted for as President, the House of Representatives shall choose immediately, by ballot, the President. But in choosing the President, the votes shall be taken by states, the representation from each state having one vote; a quorum for this purpose shall consist of a member or members from two-thirds of the states, and a majority of all the states shall be necessary to a choice. And if the House of Representatives shall not choose a President whenever the right of choice shall devolve upon them, before *the fourth day of March* next following, then the Vice-President shall act as President, as in the case of the death or other constitutional disability of the President.—The person having the greatest number of votes as Vice-President, shall be the Vice-President, if such number be a majority of the whole number of Electors appointed, and if no person have a majority, then from the two highest numbers on the list, the Senate shall choose the Vice-President; a quorum for the purpose shall consist of two-thirds of the whole number of Senators, and a majority of the whole number shall be necessary to a choice. But no person constitutionally ineligible to the office of President shall be eligible to that of Vice President of the United States.

Amendment XIII

[Adopted 1865]

Section 1

Neither slavery nor involuntary servitude, except as a punishment for crime whereof the party shall have been duly convicted, shall exist within the United States, or any place subject to their jurisdiction.

Section 2

Congress shall have power to enforce this article by appropriate legislation.

Amendment XIV

[Adopted 1868]

Section 1

All persons born or naturalized in the United States, and subject to the jurisdiction thereof, are citizens of the United States and of the State wherein they reside. No State shall make or enforce any law which shall abridge the privileges or immunities of citizens of the United States; nor shall any State deprive any person of life, liberty, or property, without due process of law; nor deny to any person within its jurisdiction the equal protection of the laws.

Section 2

Representatives shall be apportioned among the several States according to their respective numbers, counting the whole number of persons in each State, excluding Indians not taxed. But when the right to vote at any election for the choice of electors for President and Vice-President of the United States, Representatives in Congress, the Executive and Judicial officers of a State, or the members of the Legislature thereof, is denied to any of the male inhabitants of such State, being twenty-one years of age, and citizens of the United States, or in any way abridged, except for participation in rebellion, or other crime, the basis of representation therein shall be reduced in the proportion which the number of such male citizens shall bear to the whole number of male citizens twenty-one years of age in such State.

Section 3

No person shall be a Senator or Representative in Congress, or elector of President and Vice President, or hold any office, civil or military, under the United States, or under any State, who, having previously taken an oath, as a member of Congress, or as an officer of the United States, or as a member of any State legislature, or as an executive or judicial officer of any State, to support the Constitution of the United States, shall have engaged in insurrection or rebellion against the same, or given aid or comfort to the enemies thereof. But Congress may by a vote of two-thirds of each House, remove such disability.

Section 4

The validity of the public debt of the United States, authorized by law, including debts incurred for payment of pensions and bounties for services in suppressing insurrection or rebellion, shall not be questioned. But neither the United States nor any State shall assume or pay any debt or obligation incurred in aid of insurrection or rebellion against the United States, or any claim for the loss or emancipation of any slave; but all such debts, obligations and claims shall be held illegal and void.

Section 5

The Congress shall have power to enforce, by appropriate legislation, the provisions of this article.

Amendment XV

[Adopted 1870]

Section 1

The right of citizens of the United States to vote shall not be denied or abridged by the United States or by any State on account of race, color, or previous condition of servitude.

Section 2

The Congress shall have power to enforce this article by appropriate legislation.

Amendment XVI

[Adopted 1913]

The Congress shall have power to lay and collect taxes on incomes, from whatever source derived, without apportionment among the several States, and without regard to any census or enumeration.

Amendment XVII

[Adopted 1913]

The Senate of the United States shall be composed of two Senators from each State, elected by the people thereof, for six years; and each Senator shall have one vote. The electors in each State shall have the qualifications requisite for electors of the most numerous branch of the State legislatures.

When vacancies happen in the representation of any State in the Senate, the executive authority of such State shall issue writs of election to fill such vacancies: *Provided*, That the legislature of any State may empower the executive thereof to make temporary appointments until the people fill the vacancies by election as the legislature may direct.

This amendment shall not be so construed as to affect the election or term of any Senator chosen before it becomes valid as part of the Constitution.

Amendment XVIII

[Adopted 1919, repealed 1933]

Section 1

After one year from the ratification of this article the manufacture, sale, or transportation of intoxicating liquors within, the importation thereof into, or the exportation thereof from the United States and all territory subject to the jurisdiction thereof for beverage purposes is hereby prohibited.

Section 2

The Congress and the several States shall have concurrent power to enforce this article by appropriate legislation.

Section 3

This article shall be inoperative unless it shall have been ratified as an amendment to the Constitution by the legislatures of the several States, as provided in the Constitution, within seven years from the date of the submission hereof to the States by the Congress.

Amendment XIX

[Adopted 1920]

The right of citizens of the United States to vote shall not be denied or abridged by the United States or by any State on account of sex.

Congress shall have power to enforce this article by appropriate legislation.

Amendment XX

[Adopted 1933]

Section 1

The terms of the President and Vice President shall end at noon on the 20th day of January, and the terms of Senators and Representatives at noon on the 3d day of January, of the years in which such terms would have ended if this article had not been ratified; and the terms of their successors shall then begin.

Section 2

The Congress shall assemble at least once in every year, and such meeting shall begin at noon on the 3d day of January, unless they shall by law appoint a different day.

Section 3

If, at the time fixed for the beginning of the term of the President, the President elect shall have died, the Vice President elect shall become President. If a President shall not have been chosen before the time fixed for the beginning of his term, or if the President elect shall have failed to qualify, then the Vice President elect shall act as President until a President shall have qualified; and the Congress may by law provide for the case wherein neither a President elect nor a Vice President elect shall have qualified, declaring who shall then act as President, or the manner in which one who is to act shall be selected, and such person shall act accordingly until a President or Vice President shall have qualified.

Section 4

The Congress may by law provide for the case of the death of any of the persons from whom the House of Representatives may choose a President whenever the right of choice shall have devolved upon them, and for the case of the death of any of the persons from whom the Senate may choose a Vice President whenever the right of choice shall have devolved upon them.

Section 5

Sections 1 and 2 shall take effect on the 15th day of October following the ratification of this article.

Section 6

This article shall be inoperative unless it shall have been ratified as an amendment to the Constitution by the legislatures of three fourths of the several States within seven years from the date of its submission.

Amendment XXI

[Adopted 1933]

Section 1

The eighteenth article of amendment to the Constitution of the United States is hereby repealed.

Section 2

The transportation or importation into any State, Territory, or possession of the United States for delivery or use therein of intoxicating liquors in violation of the laws thereof, is hereby prohibited.

Section 3

This article shall be inoperative unless it shall have been ratified as an amendment to the Constitution by conventions in the several States, as provided in the Constitution, within seven years from the date of the submission hereof to the States by the Congress.

Amendment XXII

[Adopted 1951]

Section 1

No person shall be elected to the office of the President more than twice, and no person who has held the office of President, or acted as President, for more than two years of a term to which some other person was elected President shall be elected to the office of the President more than once. But this Article shall not apply to any person holding the office of President when this Article was proposed by the Congress, and shall not prevent any person who may be holding the office of President, or acting as President, during the term within which this Article becomes operative from holding the office of President or acting as President during the remainder of such term.

Section 2

This article shall be inoperative unless it shall have been ratified as an amendment to the Constitution by the legislatures of three-fourths of the several States within seven years from the date of its submission to the States by the Congress.

Amendment XXIII

[Adopted 1961]

Section 1

The District constituting the seat of Government of the United States shall appoint in such manner as the Congress shall direct:

A number of electors of President and Vice President equal to the whole number of Senators and Representatives in Congress to which the District would be entitled if it were a State, but in no event more than the least populous State; they shall be in addition to those appointed by the States, but they shall be considered, for the purposes of the election of President and Vice President, to be electors appointed by a State; and they shall meet in the District and perform such duties as provided by the twelfth article of amendment.

Section 2

The Congress shall have power to enforce this article by appropriate legislation.

Amendment XXIV

[Adopted 1964]

Section 1

The right of citizens of the United States to vote in any primary or other election for President or Vice President, for electors for President or Vice President, or for Senator or Representative in Congress, shall not be denied or abridged by the United States or any state by reason of failure to pay any poll tax or other tax.

Section 2

The Congress shall have the power to enforce this article by appropriate legislation.

Amendment XXV

[Adopted 1967]

Section 1

In case of the removal of the President from office or his death or resignation, the Vice President shall become President.

Section 2

Whenever there is a vacancy in the office of the Vice President, the President shall nominate a Vice President who shall take the office upon confirmation by a majority vote of both houses of Congress.

Section 3

Whenever the President transmits to the President pro tempore of the Senate and the Speaker of the House of Representatives his written declaration that he is unable to discharge the powers and duties of his office, and until he transmits to them a written declaration to the contrary, such powers and duties shall be discharged by the Vice President as Acting President.

Section 4

Whenever the Vice President and a majority of either the principal officers of the executive departments or of such other body as Congress may by law provide, transmit to the President pro tempore of the Senate and the Speaker of the House of Representatives their written declaration that the President is unable to discharge the powers and duties of his office, the Vice President shall immediately assume the powers and duties of the office as Acting President.

Thereafter, when the President transmits to the President pro tempore of the Senate and the Speaker of the House of Representatives his written declaration that no inability exists, he shall resume the powers and duties of his office unless the Vice President and a majority of either the principal officers of the executive department or of such other body as Congress may by law provide, transmit within four days to the President pro tempore of the Senate and the Speaker of the House of Representatives their written declaration that the President is unable to discharge the powers and duties of his office. Thereupon Congress shall decide the issue, assembling within 48 hours for that purpose if not in session. If the Congress, within 21 days after receipt of the latter written declaration, or, if Congress is not in session, within 21 days after Congress is required to assemble, determines by two-thirds vote of both houses that the President is unable to discharge the powers and duties of his office, the Vice President shall continue to discharge the same as Acting President; otherwise, the President shall resume the powers and duties of his office.

Amendment XXVI

[Adopted 1971]

Section 1

The right of citizens of the United States, who are 18 years of age or older, to vote shall not be denied or abridged by the United States or any state on account of age.

Section 2

The Congress shall have the power to enforce this article by appropriate legislation.

Choosing the President

	President	Party	Vice-President	Party
1789	George Washington		John Adams	Parties not yet established
1792	George Washington		John Adams	Federalist
1796	John Adams	Federalist	Thomas Jefferson	Democratic-Republican
1800	Thomas Jefferson	Democratic-Republican	Aaron Burr	Democratic-Republican
1804	Thomas Jefferson	Democratic-Republican	George Clinton	Democratic-Republican
1808	James Madison	Democratic-Republican	George Clinton	Democratic-Republican
1812	James Madison	Democratic-Republican	Elbridge Gerry	Democratic-Republican
1816	James Monroe	Democratic-Republican	Daniel D. Tompkins	Democratic-Republican
1820	James Monroe	Democratic-Republican	Daniel D. Tompkins	Democratic-Republican
1824	John Quincy Adams Elected by House of Representatives because no candidate received a majority of electoral votes.	National Republican	John C. Calhoun	Democratic
1828	Andrew Jackson	Democratic	John C. Calhoun	Democratic
1832	Andrew Jackson	Democratic	Martin Van Buren	Democratic

Major Opponents			Electoral Vote		Popular Vote
For President	*Party*				
			Washington	69	Electors selected by state legislatures
			J. Adams	34	
George Clinton	Democratic-Republican		Washington	132	Electors selected by state legislatures
			J. Adams	77	
			Clinton	50	
Thomas Pinckney	Federalist		J. Adams	71	Electors selected by state legislatures
Aaron Burr	Democratic-Republican		Jefferson	68	
			Pinckney	59	
John Adams	Federalist		Jefferson	73	Electors selected by state legislatures
Charles Cotesworth Pinckney	Federalist		J. Adams	65	
Charles Cotesworth Pinckney	Federalist		Jefferson	162	Electors selected by state legislatures
			Pinckney	14	
Charles Cotesworth Pinckney	Federalist		Madison	122	Electors selected by state legislatures
George Clinton	Eastern Republican		Pinckney	47	
De Witt Clinton	Democratic-Republican (antiwar faction) and Federalist		Madison	128	Electors selected by state legislatures
			Clinton	89	
Rufus King	Federalist		Monroe	183	Electors selected by state legislatures
			King	34	
			Monroe	231	Electors selected by state legislatures
			J. Q. Adams	1	
Andrew Jackson	Democratic		J. Q. Adams	84	113,122
Henry Clay	Democratic-Republican		Jackson	99	151,271
			Clay	37	47,531
William H. Crawford	Democratic-Republican		Crawford	41	40,856
John Quincy Adams	National Republican		Jackson	178	642,553
			J. Q. Adams	83	500,897
Henry Clay	National Republican		Jackson	219	701,780
			Clay	49	482,205
William Wirt	Anti-Masonic		Wirt	7	100,715
			*Floyd (Ind. Dem.)	11	*Delegates chosen by South Carolina legislature

	President	Party	Vice-President	Party
1836	Martin Van Buren	Democratic	Richard M. Johnson First and only Vice-President elected by the Senate (1837), having failed to receive a majority of electoral votes.	Democratic
1840	William Henry Harrison	Whig	John Tyler	Whig
1844	James K. Polk	Democratic	George M. Dallas	Democratic
1848	Zachary Taylor	Whig	Millard Fillmore	Whig
1852	Franklin Pierce	Democratic	William R. King	Democratic
1856	James Buchanan	Democratic	John C. Breckinridge	Democratic
1860	Abraham Lincoln	Republican	Hannibal Hamlin	Republican
1864	Abraham Lincoln	National Union Republican	Andrew Johnson	National Union Democratic
1868	Ulysses S. Grant	Republican	Schuyler Colfax	Republican
1872	Ulysses S. Grant	Republican	Henry Wilson	Republican
1876	Rutherford B. Hayes Contested result settled by special election commission in favor of Hayes	Republican	William A. Wheeler	Republican

Major Opponents		Electoral Vote		Popular Vote
For President	*Party*			
Daniel Webster	Whig	Van Buren	170	764,176
Hugh L. White	Whig	W. Harrison	73	550,816
William Henry Harrison	Anti-Masonic	White	26	146,107
		Webster	14	41,201
		* Mangum	11	
		(Ind. Dem.)		* Delegates chosen by South Carolina legislature
Martin Van Buren	Democratic	W. Harrison	234	1,274,624
James G. Birney	Liberty	Van Buren	60	1,127,781
Henry Clay	Whig	Polk	170	1,338,624
James G. Birney	Liberty	Clay	105	1,300,097
		Birney	—	62,300
Lewis Cass	Democratic	Taylor	163	1,360,967
Martin Van Buren	Free-Soil	Cass	127	1,222,342
		Van Buren	—	291,263
Winfield Scott	Whig	Pierce	254	1,601,117
John P. Hale	Free-Soil	Scott	42	1,385,453
		Hale	—	155,825
John C. Fremont	Republican	Buchanan	174	1,832,955
Millard Fillmore	American	Fremont	114	1,339,932
	(Know-Nothing)	Fillmore	8	871,731
John Bell	Constitutional Union	Lincoln	180	1,865,593
		Breckinridge	72	848,356
Stephen A. Douglas	Democratic	Douglas	12	1,382,713
John C. Breckinridge	Democratic	Bell	39	592,906
George B. McClellan	Democratic	Lincoln	212	2,218,388
		McClellan	21	1,812,807
		* Eleven secessionist states did not participate		
Horatio Seymour	Democratic	Grant	286	3,598,235
		Seymour	80	2,706,829
		* Texas, Mississippi, and Virginia did not participate		
Horace Greeley	Democratic and Liberal Republican	Grant	286	3,598,235
Charles O'Conor	Democratic	Greeley	80	* 2,834,761
James Black	Temperance	* Greeley died before the Electoral College met. His electoral votes were divided among the four minor candidates.		
Samuel J. Tilden	Democratic	Hayes	185	4,034,311
Peter Cooper	Greenback	Tilden	184	4,288,546
Green Clay Smith	Prohibition	Cooper	—	75,973

	President	Party	Vice-President	Party
1880	James A. Garfield	Republican	Chester A. Arthur	Republican
1884	Grover Cleveland	Democratic	Thomas A. Hendricks	Democratic
1888	Benjamin Harrison	Republican	Levi P. Morton	Republican
1892	Grover Cleveland	Democratic	Adlai E. Stevenson	Democratic
1896	William McKinley	Republican	Garret A. Hobart	Republican
1900	William McKinley	Republican	Theodore Roosevelt	Republican
1904	Theodore Roosevelt	Republican	Charles W. Fairbanks	Republican
1908	William Howard Taft	Republican	James S. Sherman	Republican
1912	Woodrow Wilson	Democratic	Thomas R. Marshall	Democratic
1916	Woodrow Wilson	Democratic	Thomas R. Marshall	Democratic

Major Opponents		Electoral Vote		Popular Vote
For President	*Party*			
Winfield S. Hancock	Democratic	Garfield	214	4,446,158
James B. Weaver	Greenback	Hancock	155	4,444,260
Neal Dow	Prohibition	Weaver	—	305,997
James G. Blaine	Republican	Cleveland	219	4,874,621
John P. St. John	Prohibition	Blaine	182	4,848,936
Benjamin F. Butler	Greenback	Butler	—	175,096
		St. John	—	147,482
Grover Cleveland	Democratic	B. Harrison	233	5,447,129
Clinton B. Fisk	Prohibition	Cleveland	168	5,537,857
Alson J. Streeter	Union Labor			
Benjamin Harrison	Republican	Cleveland	277	5,555,426
James B. Weaver	Populist	B. Harrison	145	5,182,600
John Bidwell	Prohibition	Weaver	22	1,029,846
William Jennings Bryan	Democratic, Populist, and National Silver Republican	McKinley	271	7,102,246
		Bryan	176	6,492,559
Joshua Levering	Prohibition			
John M. Palmer	National Democratic			
William Jennings Bryan	Democratic and Fusion Populist	McKinley	292	7,218,039
		Bryan	155	6,358,345
Wharton Barker	Anti-Fusion Populist	Woolley	—	209,004
Eugene V. Debs	Social Democratic	Debs	—	86,935
John G. Woolley	Prohibition			
Alton B. Parker	Democratic	T. Roosevelt	336	7,626,593
Eugene V. Debs	Socialist	Parker	140	5,082,898
Silas C. Swallow	Prohibition	Debs	—	402,489
		Swallow	—	258,596
William Jennings Bryan	Democratic	Taft	321	7,676,258
Eugene V. Debs	Socialist	Bryan	162	6,406,801
Eugene W. Chafin	Prohibition	Debs	—	420,380
		Chafin	—	252,821
William Howard Taft	Republican	Wilson	435	6,296,547
Theodore Roosevelt	Progressive (Bull Moose)	T. Roosevelt	88	4,118,571
		Taft	8	3,486,720
Eugene V. Debs	Socialist			
Eugene W. Chafin	Prohibition			
Charles E. Hughes	Republican	Wilson	277	9,127,695
Allen L. Benson	Socialist	Hughes	254	8,533,507
J. Frank Hanley	Prohibition			
Charles W. Fairbanks	Republican			

	President	Party	Vice-President	Party
1920	Warren G. Harding	Republican	Calvin Coolidge	Republican
1924	Calvin Coolidge	Republican	Charles G. Dawes	Republican
1928	Herbert C. Hoover	Republican	Charles Curtis	Republican
1932	Franklin D. Roosevelt	Democratic	John N. Garner	Democratic
1936	Franklin D. Roosevelt	Democratic	John N. Garner	Democratic
1940	Franklin D. Roosevelt	Democratic	Henry A. Wallace	Democratic
1944	Franklin D. Roosevelt	Democratic	Harry S Truman	Democratic
1948	Harry S Truman	Democratic	Alben W. Barkley	Democratic
1952	Dwight D. Eisenhower	Republican	Richard M. Nixon	Republican
1956	Dwight D. Eisenhower	Republican	Richard M. Nixon	Republican
1960	John F. Kennedy	Democratic	Lyndon B. Johnson	Democratic
1964	Lyndon B. Johnson	Democratic	Hubert H. Humphrey	Democratic
1968	Richard M. Nixon	Republican	Spiro T. Agnew	Republican
1972	Richard M. Nixon	Republican	Spiro T. Agnew	Republican
1976	Jimmy Carter	Democratic	Walter Mondale	Democratic

Major Opponents		Electoral Vote		Popular Vote
For President	Party			
James M. Cox	Democratic	Harding	404	16,133,314
Eugene V. Debs	Socialist	Cox	127	9,140,884
		Debs	—	913,664
John W. Davis	Democratic	Coolidge	382	15,717,553
Robert M. LaFollette	Progressive	Davis	136	8,386,169
		LaFollette	13	4,814,050
Alfred E. Smith	Democratic	Hoover	444	21,391,993
Norman Thomas	Socialist	Smith	87	15,016,169
Herbert C. Hoover	Republican	F. Roosevelt	472	22,809,638
Norman Thomas	Socialist	Hoover	59	15,758,901
Alfred M. Landon	Republican	F. Roosevelt	523	27,752,869
William Lemke	Union	Landon	8	16,674,665
Wendell L. Willkie	Republican	F. Roosevelt	449	27,263,448
		Willkie	82	22,336,260
Thomas E. Dewey	Republican	F. Roosevelt	432	25,611,936
		Dewey	99	22,013,372
Thomas E. Dewey	Republican	Truman	303	24,105,182
J. Strom Thurmond	States' Rights	Dewey	189	21,970,065
	Democratic	Thurmond	39	1,169,063
Henry A. Wallace	Progressive	H. Wallace	—	1,157,326
Adlai E. Stevenson	Democratic	Eisenhower	442	33,936,137
		Stevenson	89	27,314,649
Adlai E. Stevenson	Democratic	Eisenhower	457	35,585,245
		Stevenson	73	26,030,172
Richard M. Nixon	Republican	Kennedy	303	34,227,096
		Nixon	219	34,108,546
		H. Byrd	15	—
		(Ind. Dem.)		
Barry M. Goldwater	Republican	Johnson	486	43,126,584
		Goldwater	52	27,177,838
Hubert H. Humphrey	Democratic	Nixon	301	31,770,237
George C. Wallace	American	Humphrey	191	31,270,533
	Independent	G. Wallace	46	9,906,141
George S. McGovern	Democratic	Nixon	520	46,740,323
		McGovern	17	28,901,598
		Hospers (Va.)	1	—
Gerald R. Ford	Republican	Carter	297	40,830,763
Eugene McCarthy	Independent	Ford	240	39,147,793
		E. McCarthy	—	756,631

	President	Party	Vice-President	Party
1980	Ronald Reagan	Republican	George Bush	Republican
1984	Ronald Reagan	Republican	George Bush	Republican
1988	George Bush	Republican	J. Danforth Quayle	Republican
1992	William Clinton	Democratic	Albert Gore, Jr.	Democratic

Major Opponents			Electoral Vote		Popular Vote
For President	*Party*				
Jimmy Carter	Democratic		Reagan	489	43,899,248
John B. Anderson	Independent		Carter	49	35,481,435
Ed Clark	Libertarian		Anderson	—	5,719,437
Walter Mondale	Democratic		Reagan	525	54,451,521
David Bergland	Libertarian		Mondale	13	37,565,334
Michael Dukakis	Democratic		Bush	426	47,946,422
			Dukakis	111	41,016,429
			Bentsen	1	—
George Bush	Republican		Clinton	357	43,728,275
H. Ross Perot	Independent		Bush	168	38,167,416
			Perot	—	19,237,245

Cabinet Members for Each Administration

THE WASHINGTON ADMINISTRATION

Secretary of State	Thomas Jefferson	1789–1793
	Edmund Randolph	1794–1795
	Timothy Pickering	1795–1797
Secretary of Treasury	Alexander Hamilton	1789–1795
	Oliver Wolcott	1795–1797
Secretary of War	Henry Knox	1789–1794
	Timothy Pickering	1795–1796
	James McHenry	1796–1797
Attorney General	Edmund Randolph	1789–1793
	William Bradford	1794–1795
	Charles Lee	1795–1797
Postmaster General	Samuel Osgood	1789–1791
	Timothy Pickering	1791–1794
	Joseph Habersham	1795–1797

THE JOHN ADAMS ADMINISTRATION

Secretary of State	Timothy Pickering	1797–1800
	John Marshall	1800–1801
Secretary of Treasury	Oliver Wolcott	1797–1800
	Samuel Dexter	1800–1801
Secretary of War	James McHenry	1797–1800
	Samuel Dexter	1800–1801
Attorney General	Charles Lee	1797–1801
Postmaster General	Joseph Habersham	1797–1801
Secretary of Navy	Benjamin Stoddert	1798–1801

THE JEFFERSON ADMINISTRATION

Secretary of State	James Madison	1801–1809
Secretary of Treasury	Samuel Dexter	1801
	Albert Gallatin	1801–1809
Secretary of War	Henry Dearborn	1801–1809
Attorney General	Levi Lincoln	1801–1805
	Robert Smith	1805
	John Breckinridge	1805–1806
	Caesar Rodney	1807–1809
Postmaster General	Joseph Habersham	1801
	Gideon Granger	1801–1809
Secretary of Navy	Robert Smith	1801–1809

THE MADISON ADMINISTRATION

Secretary of State	Robert Smith	1809–1811
	James Monroe	1811–1817
Secretary of Treasury	Albert Gallatin	1809–1813
	George Campbell	1814
	Alexander Dallas	1814–1816
	William Crawford	1816–1817
Secretary of War	William Eustis	1809–1812
	John Armstrong	1813–1814
	James Monroe	1814–1815
	William Crawford	1815–1817
Attorney General	Caesar Rodney	1809–1811
	William Pinkney	1811–1814
	Richard Rush	1814–1817
Postmaster General	Gideon Granger	1809–1814
	Return Meigs	1814–1817
Secretary of Navy	Paul Hamilton	1809–1813
	William Jones	1813–1814
	Benjamin Crowninshield	1814–1817

THE MONROE ADMINISTRATION

Secretary of State	John Quincy Adams	1817–1825
Secretary of Treasury	William Crawford	1817–1825
Secretary of War	George Graham	1817
	John C. Calhoun	1817–1825
Attorney General	Richard Rush	1817
	William Wirt	1817–1825
Postmaster General	Return Meigs	1817–1823
	John McLean	1823–1825
Secretary of Navy	Benjamin Crowninshield	1817–1818
	Smith Thompson	1818–1823
	Samuel Southard	1823–1825

THE JOHN QUINCY ADAMS ADMINISTRATION

Secretary of State	Henry Clay	1825–1829
Secretary of Treasury	Richard Rush	1825–1829

Secretary of War	James Barbour	1825–1828
	Peter Porter	1828–1829
Attorney General	William Wirt	1825–1829
Postmaster General	John McLean	1825–1829
Secretary of Navy	Samuel Southard	1825–1829

THE JACKSON ADMINISTRATION

Secretary of State	Martin Van Buren	1829–1831
	Edward Livingston	1831–1833
	Louis McLane	1833–1834
	John Forsyth	1834–1837
Secretary of Treasury	Samuel Ingham	1829–1831
	Louis McLane	1831–1833
	William Duane	1833
	Roger B. Taney	1833–1834
	Levi Woodbury	1834–1837
Secretary of War	John H. Eaton	1829–1831
	Lewis Cass	1831–1837
	Benjamin Butler	1837
Attorney General	John M. Berrien	1829–1831
	Roger B. Taney	1831–1833
	Benjamin Butler	1833–1837
Postmaster General	William Barry	1829–1835
	Amos Kendall	1835–1837
Secretary of Navy	John Branch	1829–1831
	Levi Woodbury	1831–1834
	Mahlon Dickerson	1834–1837

THE VAN BUREN ADMINISTRATION

Secretary of State	John Forsyth	1837–1841
Secretary of Treasury	Levi Woodbury	1837–1841
Secretary of War	Joel Poinsett	1837–1841
Attorney General	Benjamin Butler	1837–1838
	Felix Grundy	1838–1840
	Henry D. Gilpin	1840–1841
Postmaster General	Amos Kendall	1837–1840
	John M. Niles	1840–1841
Secretary of Navy	Mahlon Dickerson	1837–1838
	James Paulding	1838–1841

THE WILLIAM HARRISON ADMINISTRATION

Secretary of State	Daniel Webster	1841
Secretary of Treasury	Thomas Ewing	1841
Secretary of War	John Bell	1841

Attorney General	John J. Crittenden	1841
Postmaster General	Francis Granger	1841
Secretary of Navy	George Badger	1841

THE TYLER ADMINISTRATION

Secretary of State	Daniel Webster	1841–1843
	Hugh S. Legaré	1843
	Abel P. Upshur	1843–1844
	John C. Calhoun	1844–1845
Secretary of Treasury	Thomas Ewing	1841
	Walter Forward	1841–1843
	John C. Spencer	1843–1844
	George Bibb	1844–1845
Secretary of War	John Bell	1841
	John C. Spencer	1841–1843
	James M. Porter	1843–1844
	William Wilkins	1844–1845
Attorney General	John J. Crittenden	1841
	Hugh S. Legaré	1841–1843
	John Nelson	1843–1845
Postmaster General	Francis Granger	1841
	Charles Wickliffe	1841
Secretary of Navy	George Badger	1841
	Abel P. Upshur	1841
	David Henshaw	1843–1844
	Thomas Gilmer	1844
	John Y. Mason	1844–1845

THE POLK ADMINISTRATION

Secretary of State	James Buchanan	1845–1849
Secretary of Treasury	Robert J. Walker	1845–1849
Secretary of War	William L. Marcy	1845–1849
Attorney General	John Y. Mason	1845–1846
	Nathan Clifford	1846–1848
	Isaac Toucey	1848–1849
Postmaster General	Cave Johnson	1845–1849
Secretary of Navy	George Bancroft	1845–1846
	John Y. Mason	1846–1849

THE TAYLOR ADMINISTRATION

Secretary of State	John M. Clayton	1849–1850
Secretary of Treasury	William Meredith	1849–1850
Secretary of War	George Crawford	1849–1850

Attorney General	Reverdy Johnson	1849–1850
Postmaster General	Jacob Collamer	1849–1850
Secretary of Navy	William Preston	1849–1850
Secretary of Interior	Thomas Ewing	1849–1850

THE FILLMORE ADMINISTRATION

Secretary of State	Daniel Webster	1850–1852
	Edward Everett	1852–1853
Secretary of Treasury	Thomas Corwin	1850–1853
Secretary of War	Charles Conrad	1850–1853
Attorney General	John J. Crittenden	1850–1853
Postmaster General	Nathan Hall	1850–1852
	Sam D. Hubbard	1852–1853
Secretary of Navy	William A. Graham	1850–1852
	John P. Kennedy	1852–1853
Secretary of Interior	Thomas McKennan	1850
	Alexander Stuart	1850–1853

THE PIERCE ADMINISTRATION

Secretary of State	William L. Marcy	1853–1857
Secretary of Treasury	James Guthrie	1853–1857
Secretary of War	Jefferson Davis	1853–1857
Attorney General	Caleb Cushing	1853–1857
Postmaster General	James Campbell	1853–1857
Secretary of Navy	James C. Dobbin	1853–1857
Secretary of Interior	Robert McClelland	1853–1857

THE BUCHANAN ADMINISTRATION

Secretary of State	Lewis Cass	1857–1860
	Jeremiah S. Black	1860–1861
Secretary of Treasury	Howell Cobb	1857–1860
	Philip Thomas	1860–1861
	John A. Dix	1861
Secretary of War	John B. Floyd	1857–1861
	Joseph Holt	1861
Attorney General	Jeremiah S. Black	1857–1860
	Edwin M. Stanton	1860–1861
Postmaster General	Aaron V. Brown	1857–1859
	Joseph Holt	1859–1861
	Horatio King	1861

Secretary of Navy	Isaac Toucey	1857–1861
Secretary of Interior	Jacob Thompson	1857–1861

THE LINCOLN ADMINISTRATION

Secretary of State	William H. Seward	1861–1865
Secretary of Treasury	Salmon P. Chase	1861–1864
	William P. Fessenden	1864–1865
	Hugh McCulloch	1865
Secretary of War	Simon Cameron	1861–1862
	Edwin M. Stanton	1862–1865
Attorney General	Edward Bates	1861–1864
	James Speed	1864–1865
Postmaster General	Horatio King	1861
	Montgomery Blair	1861–1864
	William Dennison	1864–1865
Secretary of Navy	Gideon Welles	1861–1865
Secretary of Interior	Caleb B. Smith	1861–1863
	John P. Usher	1863–1865

THE ANDREW JOHNSON ADMINISTRATION

Secretary of State	William H. Seward	1865–1869
Secretary of Treasury	Hugh McCulloch	1865–1869
Secretary of War	Edwin M. Stanton	1865–1867
	Ulysses S. Grant	1867–1868
	Lorenzo Thomas	1868
	John M. Schofield	1868–1869
Attorney General	James Speed	1865–1866
	Henry Stanbery	1866–1868
	William M. Evarts	1868–1869
Postmaster General	William Dennison	1865–1866
	Alexander Randall	1866–1869
Secretary of Navy	Gideon Welles	1865–1869
Secretary of Interior	John P. Usher	1865
	James Harlan	1865–1866
	Orville H. Browning	1866–1869

THE GRANT ADMINISTRATION

Secretary of State	Elihu B. Washburne	1869
	Hamilton Fish	1869–1877
Secretary of Treasury	George S. Boutwell	1869–1873
	William Richardson	1873–1874
	Benjamin Bristow	1874–1876
	Lot M. Morrill	1876–1877
Secretary of War	John A. Rawlins	1869
	William T. Sherman	1869
	William W. Belknap	1869–1876
	Alphonso Taft	1876

	James D. Cameron	1876–1877
Attorney General	Ebenezer Hoar	1869–1870
	Amos T. Ackerman	1870–1871
	G. H. Williams	1871–1875
	Edwards Pierrepont	1875–1876
	Alphonso Taft	1876–1877
Postmaster General	John A. Creswell	1869–1874
	James W. Marshall	1874
	Marshall Jewell	1874–1876
	James N. Tyner	1876–1877
Secretary of Navy	Adolph E. Borie	1869
	George M. Robeson	1869–1877
Secretary of Interior	Jacob D. Cox	1869–1870
	Columbus Delano	1870–1875
	Zachariah Chandler	1875–1877

THE HAYES ADMINISTRATION

Secretary of State	William B. Evarts	1877–1881
Secretary of Treasury	John Sherman	1877–1881
Secretary of War	George W. McCrary	1877–1879
	Alex Ramsey	1879–1881
Attorney General	Charles Devens	1877–1881
Postmaster General	David M. Key	1877–1880
	Horace Maynard	1880–1881
Secretary of Navy	Richard W. Thompson	1877–1880
	Nathan Goff, Jr.	1881
Secretary of Interior	Carl Schurz	1877–1881

THE GARFIELD ADMINISTRATION

Secretary of State	James G. Blaine	1881
Secretary of Treasury	William Windom	1881
Secretary of War	Robert T. Lincoln	1881
Attorney General	Wayne MacVeagh	1881
Postmaster General	Thomas L. James	1881
Secretary of Navy	William H. Hunt	1881
Secretary of Interior	Samuel J. Kirkwood	1881

THE ARTHUR ADMINISTRATION

Secretary of State	F. T. Frelinghuysen	1881–1885
Secretary of Treasury	Charles J. Folger	1881–1884
	Walter Q. Gresham	1884
	Hugh McCulloch	1884–1885

Secretary of War	Robert T. Lincoln	1881–1885
Attorney General	Benjamin H. Brewster	1881–1885
Postmaster General	Timothy O. Howe	1881–1883
	Walter Q. Gresham	1883–1884
	Frank Hatton	1884–1885
Secretary of Navy	William H. Hunt	1881–1882
	William E. Chandler	1882–1885
Secretary of Interior	Samuel J. Kirkwood	1881–1882
	Henry M. Teller	1882–1885

THE FIRST CLEVELAND ADMINISTRATION

Secretary of State	Thomas F. Bayard	1885–1889
Secretary of Treasury	Daniel Manning	1885–1887
	Charles S. Fairchild	1887–1889
Secretary of War	William C. Endicott	1885–1889
Attorney General	Augustus H. Garland	1885–1889
Postmaster General	William F. Vilas	1885–1888
	Don M. Dickinson	1888–1889
Secretary of Navy	William C. Whitney	1885–1889
Secretary of Interior	Lucius Q. C. Lamar	1885–1888
	William F. Vilas	1888–1889
Secretary of Agriculture	Norman J. Colman	1889

THE BENJAMIN HARRISON ADMINISTRATION

Secretary of State	James G. Blaine	1889–1892
	John W. Foster	1892–1893
Secretary of Treasury	William Windom	1889–1891
	Charles Foster	1891–1893
Secretary of War	Redfield Proctor	1889–1891
	Stephen B. Elkins	1891–1893
Attorney General	William H. H. Miller	1889–1891
Postmaster General	John Wanamaker	1889–1893
Secretary of Navy	Benjamin F. Tracy	1889–1893
Secretary of Interior	John W. Noble	1889–1893
Secretary of Agriculture	Jeremiah M. Rusk	1889–1893

THE SECOND CLEVELAND ADMINISTRATION

Secretary of State	Walter Q. Gresham	1893–1895
	Richard Olney	1895–1897
Secretary of Treasury	John G. Carlisle	1893–1897

Secretary of War	Daniel S. Lamont	1893–1897
Attorney General	Richard Olney	1893–1895
	James Harmon	1895–1897
Postmaster General	Wilson S. Bissell	1893–1895
	William L. Wilson	1895–1897
Secretary of Navy	Hilary A. Herbert	1893–1897
Secretary of Interior	Hoke Smith	1893–1896
	David R. Francis	1896–1897
Secretary of Agriculture	Julius S. Morton	1893–1897

THE MCKINLEY ADMINISTRATION

Secretary of State	John Sherman	1897–1898
	William R. Day	1898
	John Hay	1898–1901
Secretary of Treasury	Lyman J. Gage	1897–1901
Secretary of War	Russell A. Alger	1897–1899
	Elihu Root	1899–1901
Attorney General	Joseph McKenna	1897–1898
	John W. Griggs	1898–1901
	Philander C. Knox	1901
Postmaster General	James A. Gary	1897–1898
	Charles E. Smith	1898–1901
Secretary of Navy	John D. Long	1897–1901
Secretary of Interior	Cornelius N. Bliss	1897–1899
	Ethan A. Hitchcock	1899–1901
Secretary of Agriculture	James Wilson	1898–1901

THE THEODORE ROOSEVELT ADMINISTRATION

Secretary of State	John Hay	1901–1905
	Elihu Root	1905–1909
	Robert Bacon	1909
Secretary of Treasury	Lyman J. Gage	1901–1902
	Leslie M. Shaw	1902–1907
	George B. Cortelyou	1907–1909
Secretary of War	Elihu Root	1901–1904
	William H. Taft	1904–1908
	Luke E. Wright	1908–1909
Attorney General	Philander C. Knox	1901–1904
	William H. Moody	1904–1906
	Charles J. Bonaparte	1906–1909
Postmaster General	Charles E. Smith	1901–1902
	Henry C. Payne	1902–1904
	Robert J. Wynne	1904–1905
	George B. Cortelyou	1905–1907
	George von L. Meyer	1907–1909
Secretary of Navy	John D. Long	1901–1902
	William H. Moody	1902–1904
	Paul Morton	1904–1905
	Charles J. Bonaparte	1905–1906
	Victor H. Metcalf	1906–1908
	Truman H. Newberry	1908–1909
Secretary of Interior	Ethan A. Hitchcock	1901–1907
	James R. Garfield	1907–1909
Secretary of Agriculture	James Wilson	1901–1909
Secretary of Labor and Commerce	George B. Cortelyou	1903–1904
	Victor H. Metcalf	1904–1906
	Oscar S. Straus	1906–1909
	Charles Nagel	1909

THE TAFT ADMINISTRATION

Secretary of State	Philander C. Knox	1909–1913
Secretary of Treasury	Franklin MacVeagh	1909–1913
Secretary of War	Jacob M. Dickinson	1909–1911
	Henry L. Stimson	1911–1913
Attorney General	George W. Wickersham	1909–1913
Postmaster General	Frank H. Hitchcock	1909–1913
Secretary of Navy	George von L. Meyer	1909–1913
Secretary of Interior	Richard A. Ballinger	1909–1911
	Walter L. Fisher	1911–1913
Secretary of Agriculture	James Wilson	1909–1913
Secretary of Labor and Commerce	Charles Nagel	1909–1913

THE WILSON ADMINISTRATION

Secretary of State	William J. Bryan	1913–1915
	Robert Lansing	1915–1920
	Bainbridge Colby	1920–1921
Secretary of Treasury	William G. McAdoo	1913–1918
	Carter Glass	1918–1920
	David F. Houston	1920–1921
Secretary of War	Lindley M. Garrison	1913–1916
	Newton D. Baker	1916–1921
Attorney General	James C. McReynolds	1913–1914
	Thomas W. Gregory	1914–1919
	A. Mitchell Palmer	1919–1921
Postmaster General	Albert S. Burleson	1913–1921
Secretary of Navy	Josephus Daniels	1913–1921
Secretary of Interior	Franklin K. Lane	1913–1920
	John B. Payne	1920–1921

Secretary of Agriculture	David F. Houston	1913–1920
	Edwin T. Meredith	1920–1921
Secretary of Commerce	William C. Redfield	1913–1919
	Joshua W. Alexander	1919–1921
Secretary of Labor	William B. Wilson	1913–1921

THE HARDING ADMINISTRATION

Secretary of State	Charles E. Hughes	1921–1923
Secretary of Treasury	Andrew Mellon	1921–1923
Secretary of War	John W. Weeks	1921–1923
Attorney General	Harry M. Daugherty	1921–1923
Postmaster General	Will H. Hays	1921–1922
	Hubert Work	1922–1923
	Harry S. New	1923
Secretary of Navy	Edwin Denby	1921–1923
Secretary of Interior	Albert B. Fall	1921–1923
	Hubert Work	1923
Secretary of Agriculture	Henry C. Wallace	1921–1923
Secretary of Commerce	Herbert C. Hoover	1921–1923
Secretary of Labor	James J. Davis	1921–1923

THE COOLIDGE ADMINISTRATION

Secretary of State	Charles E. Hughes	1923–1925
	Frank B. Kellogg	1925–1929
Secretary of Treasury	Andrew Mellon	1923–1929
Secretary of War	John W. Weeks	1923–1925
	Dwight F. Davis	1925–1929
Attorney General	Henry M. Daugherty	1923–1924
	Harlan F. Stone	1924–1925
	John G. Sargent	1925–1929
Postmaster General	Harry S. New	1923–1929
Secretary of Navy	Edwin Denby	1923–1924
	Curtis D. Wilbur	1924–1929
Secretary of Interior	Hubert Work	1923–1928
	Roy O. West	1928–1929
Secretary of Agriculture	Henry C. Wallace	1923–1924
	Howard M. Gore	1924–1925
	William M. Jardine	1925–1929
Secretary of Commerce	Herbert C. Hoover	1923–1928
	William F. Whiting	1928–1929

Secretary of Labor	James J. Davis	1923–1929

THE HOOVER ADMINISTRATION

Secretary of State	Henry L. Stimson	1929–1933
Secretary of Treasury	Andrew Mellon	1929–1932
	Ogden L. Mills	1932–1933
Secretary of War	James W. Good	1929
	Patrick J. Hurley	1929–1933
Attorney General	William D. Mitchell	1929–1933
Postmaster General	Walter F. Brown	1929–1933
Secretary of Navy	Charles F. Adams	1929–1933
Secretary of Interior	Ray L. Wilbur	1929–1933
Secretary of Agriculture	Arthur M. Hyde	1929–1933
Secretary of Commerce	Robert P. Lamont	1929–1932
	Roy D. Chapin	1932–1933
Secretary of Labor	James J. Davis	1929–1930
	William N. Doak	1930–1933

THE FRANKLIN D. ROOSEVELT ADMINISTRATION

Secretary of State	Cordell Hull	1933–1944
	E. R. Stettinius, Jr.	1944–1945
Secretary of Treasury	William H. Woodin	1933–1934
	Henry Morgenthau, Jr.	1934–1945
Secretary of War	George H. Dern	1933–1936
	Henry A. Woodring	1936–1940
	Henry L. Stimson	1940–1945
Attorney General	Homer S. Cummings	1933–1939
	Frank Murphy	1939–1940
	Robert H. Jackson	1940–1941
	Francis Biddle	1941–1945
Postmaster General	James A. Farley	1933–1940
	Frank C. Walker	1940–1945
Secretary of Navy	Claude A. Swanson	1933–1940
	Charles Edison	1940
	Frank Knox	1940–1944
	James V. Forrestal	1944–1945
Secretary of Interior	Harold L. Ickes	1933–1945
Secretary of Agriculture	Henry A. Wallace	1933–1940
	Claude R. Wickard	1940–1945
Secretary of Commerce	Daniel C. Roper	1933–1939
	Harry L. Hopkins	1939–1940
	Jesse Jones	1940–1945
	Henry A. Wallace	1945
Secretary of Labor	Frances Perkins	1933–1945

THE TRUMAN ADMINISTRATION

Secretary of State	James F. Byrnes	1945–1947
	George C. Marshall	1947–1949
	Dean G. Acheson	1949–1953
Secretary of Treasury	Fred M. Vinson	1945–1946
	John W. Snyder	1946–1953
Secretary of War	Robert P. Patterson	1945–1947
	Kenneth C. Royall	1947
Attorney General	Tom C. Clark	1945–1949
	J. Howard McGrath	1949–1952
	James P. McGranery	1952–1953
Postmaster General	Frank C. Walker	1945
	Robert E. Hannegan	1945–1947
	Jessee M. Donaldson	1947–1953
Secretary of Navy	James V. Forrestal	1945–1947
Secretary of Interior	Harold L. Ickes	1945–1946
	Julius A. Krug	1946–1949
	Oscar L. Chapman	1949–1953
Secretary of Agriculture	Clinton P. Anderson	1945–1948
	Charles F. Brannan	1948–1953
Secretary of Commerce	Henry A. Wallace	1945–1946
	W. Averell Harriman	1946–1948
	Charles W. Sawyer	1948–1953
Secretary of Labor	Lewis B. Schwellenbach	1945–1948
	Maurice J. Tobin	1948–1953
Secretary of Defense	James V. Forrestal	1947–1949
	Louis A. Johnson	1949–1950
	George C. Marshall	1950–1951
	Robert A. Lovett	1951–1953

THE EISENHOWER ADMINISTRATION

Secretary of State	John Foster Dulles	1953–1959
	Christian A. Herter	1959–1961
Secretary of Treasury	George M. Humphrey	1953–1957
	Robert B. Anderson	1957–1961
Attorney General	Herbert Brownell, Jr.	1953–1958
	William P. Rogers	1958–1961
Postmaster General	Arthur E. Summerfield	1953–1961
Secretary of Interior	Douglas McKay	1953–1956
	Fred A. Seaton	1956–1961
Secretary of Agriculture	Ezra T. Benson	1953–1961
Secretary of Commerce	Sinclair Weeks	1953–1958
	Lewis L. Strauss	1958–1959
	Frederick H. Mueller	1959–1961
Secretary of Labor	Martin P. Durkin	1953
	James P. Mitchell	1953–1961
Secretary of Defense	Charles E. Wilson	1953–1957
	Neil H. McElroy	1957–1959
	Thomas S. Gates, Jr.	1959–1961

Secretary of Health, Education and Welfare	Oveta Culp Hobby	1953–1955
	Marion B. Folsom	1955–1958
	Arthur S. Flemming	1958–1961

THE KENNEDY ADMINISTRATION

Secretary of State	Dean Rusk	1961–1963
Secretary of Treasury	C. Douglas Dillon	1961–1963
Attorney General	Robert F. Kennedy	1961–1963
Postmaster General	J. Edward Day	1961–1963
	John A. Gronouski	1963
Secretary of Interior	Stewart I. Udall	1961–1963
Secretary of Agriculture	Orville L. Freeman	1961–1963
Secretary of Commerce	Luther H. Hodges	1961–1963
Secretary of Labor	Arthur J. Goldberg	1961–1962
	W. Willard Wirtz	1962–1963
Secretary of Defense	Robert S. McNamara	1961–1963
Secretary of Health, Education and Welfare	Abraham A. Ribicoff	1961–1962
	Anthony J. Celebrezze	1962–1963

THE LYNDON JOHNSON ADMINISTRATION

Secretary of State	Dean Rusk	1963–1969
Secretary of Treasury	C. Douglas Dillon	1963–1965
	Henry H. Fowler	1965–1969
Attorney General	Robert F. Kennedy	1963–1964
	Nicholas Katzenbach	1965–1966
	Ramsey Clark	1967–1969
Postmaster General	John A. Gronouski	1963–1965
	Lawrence F. O'Brien	1965–1968
	Marvin Watson	1968–1969
Secretary of Interior	Stewart L. Udall	1963–1969
Secretary of Agriculture	Orville L. Freeman	1963–1969
Secretary of Commerce	Luther H. Hodges	1963–1964
	John T. Connor	1964–1967
	Alexander B. Trowbridge	1967–1968
	Cyrus R. Smith	1968–1969
Secretary of Labor	W. Willard Wirtz	1963–1969
Secretary of Defense	Robert F. McNamara	1963–1968
	Clark Clifford	1968–1969

Secretary of Health, Education and Welfare	Anthony J. Celebrezze	1963–1965
	John W. Gardner	1965–1968
	Wilbur J. Cohen	1968–1969
Secretary of Housing and Urban Development	Robert C. Weaver	1966–1969
	Robert C. Wood	1969
Secretary of Transportation	Alan S. Boyd	1967–1969

THE NIXON ADMINISTRATION

Secretary of State	William P. Rogers	1969–1973
	Henry A. Kissinger	
Secretary of Treasury	David M. Kennedy	1969–1970
	John B. Connally	1971–1972
	George P. Shultz	1972–1974
	William E. Simon	1974
Attorney General	John N. Mitchell	1969–1972
	Richard G. Kleindienst	1972–1973
	Elliot L. Richardson	1973
	William B. Saxbe	1973–1974
Postmaster General	Winton M. Blount	1969–1971
Secretary of Interior	Walter J. Hickel	1969–1970
	Rogers Morton	1971–1974
Secretary of Agriculture	Clifford M. Hardin	1969–1971
	Earl L. Butz	1971–1974
Secretary of Commerce	Maurice H. Stans	1969–1972
	Peter G. Peterson	1972–1973
	Frederick B. Dent	1973–1974
Secretary of Labor	George P. Shultz	1969–1970
	James D. Hodgson	1970–1973
	Peter J. Brennan	1973–1974
Secretary of Defense	Melvin R. Laird	1969–1973
	Elliot L. Richardson	1973
	James R. Schlesinger	1973–1974
Secretary of Health, Education and Welfare	Robert H. Finch	1969–1970
	Elliot L. Richardson	1970–1973
	Casper W. Weinberger	1973–1974
Secretary of Housing and Urban Development	George Romney	1969–1973
	James T. Lynn	1973–1974
Secretary of Transportation	John A. Volpe	1969–1973
	Claude S. Brinegar	1973–1974

THE FORD ADMINISTRATION

Secretary of State	Henry A. Kissinger	1974–1977
Secretary of Treasury	William E. Simon	1974–1977
Attorney General	William Saxbe	1974–1975
	Edward Levi	1975–1977
Secretary of Interior	Rogers Morton	1974–1975
	Stanley K. Hathaway	1975
	Thomas Kleppe	1975–1977
Secretary of Agriculture	Earl L. Butz	1974–1976
	John A. Knebel	1976–1977
Secretary of Commerce	Frederick B. Dent	1974–1975
	Rogers Morton	1975–1976
	Elliot L. Richardson	1976–1977
Secretary of Labor	Peter J. Brennan	1974–1975
	John T. Dunlop	1975–1976
	W. J. Usery	1976–1977
Secretary of Defense	James R. Schlesinger	1974–1975
	Donald Rumsfeld	1975–1977
Secretary of Health, Education and Welfare	Casper Weinberger	1974–1975
	Forrest D. Mathews	1975–1977
Secretary of Housing and Urban Development	James T. Lynn	1974–1975
	Carla A. Hills	1975–1977
Secretary of Transportation	Claude Brinegar	1974–1975
	William T. Coleman	1975–1977

THE CARTER ADMINISTRATION

Secretary of State	Cyrus R. Vance	1977–1980
	Edmund Muskie	1980–1981
Secretary of Treasury	W. Michael Blumenthal	1977–1979
	G. William Miller	1979–1981
Attorney General	Griffin Bell	1977–1979
	Benjamin R. Civiletti	1979–1981
Secretary of Interior	Cecil D. Andrus	1977–1981
Secretary of Agriculture	Robert Bergland	1977–1981
Secretary of Commerce	Juanita M. Kreps	1977–1979
	Philip M. Klutznick	1979–1981
Secretary of Labor	F. Ray Marshall	1977–1981
Secretary of Defense	Harold Brown	1977–1981
Secretary of Health, Education and Welfare	Joseph A. Califano	1977–1979
	Patricia R. Harris	1979
Secretary of Health and Human Services	Patricia R. Harris	1979–1981

Secretary of Education	Shirley M. Hufstedler	1979–1981
Secretary of Housing and Urban Development	Patricia R. Harris Moon Landrieu	1977–1979 1979–1981
Secretary of Transportation	Brock Adams Neil E. Goldschmidt	1977–1979 1979–1981
Secretary of Energy	James R. Schlesinger Charles W. Duncan	1977–1979 1979–1981

THE REAGAN ADMINISTRATION

Secretary of State	Alexander M. Haig George P. Schultz	1981–1982 1982–1989
Secretary of Treasury	Donald T. Regan James A. Baker III Nicholas Brady	1981–1985 1985–1988 1988–1989
Attorney General	William French Smith Edwin Meese III Richard Thornburgh	1981–1985 1985–1988 1988–1989
Secretary of Interior	James Watt William P. Clark Donald P. Hodel	1981–1983 1983–1985 1985–1989
Secretary of Agriculture	John R. Block Richard E. Lyng	1981–1985 1985–1989
Secretary of Commerce	Malcolm Baldrige C. William Verity	1981–1987 1987–1989
Secretary of Labor	Raymond J. Donovan William E. Brock Ann Dore McLaughlin	1981–1985 1985–1988 1988–1989
Secretary of Defense	Caspar W. Weinberger Frank C. Carlucci	1981–1988 1988–1989
Secretary of Health and Human Services	Richard S. Schweiker Margaret M. Heckler Otis R. Bowen	1981–1983 1983–1985 1985–1989
Secretary of Education	Terrel H. Bell William J. Bennett Lauro F. Cavazos	1981–1985 1985–1988 1988–1989
Secretary of Housing and Urban Development	Samuel R. Pierce, Jr.	1981–1989
Secretary of Transportation	Drew Lewis Elizabeth H. Dole James L. Burnley IV	1981–1983 1983–1987 1987–1989
Secretary of Energy	James B. Edwards Donald P. Hodel John S. Herrington	1981–1982 1982–1985 1985–1989

THE BUSH ADMINISTRATION

Secretary of State	James A. Baker III Lawrence S. Eagleburger	1989–1992 1992–1993
Secretary of Treasury	Nicholas F. Brady	1989–1993
Attorney General	Richard Thornburgh William P. Barr	1989–1992 1992–1993
Secretary of Interior	Manuel Lujan, Jr.	1989–1993
Secretary of Agriculture	Clayton Yeutter Edward Madigan	1989–1991 1991–1993
Secretary of Commerce	Robert Mosbacher, Sr. Barbara H. Franklin	1989–1992 1992–1993
Secretary of Labor	Elizabeth H. Dole Lynn Martin	1989–1991 1991–1993
Secretary of Defense	Richard B. Cheney	1989–1993
Secretary of Health and Human Services	Louis W. Sullivan	1989–1993
Secretary of Education	Lauro F. Cavazos Lamar Alexander	1989–1991 1991–1993
Secretary of Housing and Urban Development	Jack F. Kemp	1989–1993
Secretary of Transportation	Samuel Skinner Andrew Card	1989–1992 1992–1993
Secretary of Energy	James D. Watkins	1989–1993
Secretary of Veterans Affairs	Edward J. Derwinski	1989–1993

THE CLINTON ADMINISTRATION

Secretary of State	Warren M. Christopher	1993–
Secretary of Treasury	Lloyd Bentsen	1993–
Attorney General	Janet Reno	1993–
Secretary of Interior	Bruce Babbitt	1993–
Secretary of Agriculture	Mike Espy	1993–
Secretary of Commerce	Ronald Brown	1993–

Secretary of Labor	Robert B. Reich	1993–	Secretary of Housing and Urban Development	Henry G. Cisneros	1993–
Secretary of Defense	Les Aspin	1993–			
Secretary of Health and Human Services	Donna Shalala	1993–	Secretary of Transportation	Federico F. Pena	1993–
			Secretary of Energy	Hazel R. O'Leary	1993–
Secretary of Education	Richard W. Riley	1993–	Secretary of Veterans Affairs	Jesse Brown	1993–

SUPREME COURT JUSTICES

Name	Terms of Service[1]	Appointed by	Name	Terms of Service[1]	Appointed by
John Jay	1789–1795	Washington	David J. Brewer	1890–1910	B. Harrison
James Wilson	1789–1798	Washington	Henry B. Brown	1891–1906	B. Harrison
John Rutledge	1790–1791	Washington	George Shiras, Jr.	1892–1903	B. Harrison
William Cushing	1790–1810	Washington	Howell E. Jackson	1893–1895	B. Harrison
John Blair	1790–1796	Washington	Edward D. White	1894–1910	Cleveland
James Iredell	1790–1799	Washington	Rufus W. Peckham	1896–1909	Cleveland
Thomas Johnson	1792–1793	Washington	Joseph McKenna	1898–1925	McKinley
William Paterson	1793–1806	Washington	Oliver W. Holmes	1902–1932	T. Roosevelt
John Rutledge[2]	1795	Washington	William R. Day	1903–1922	T. Roosevelt
Samuel Chase	1796–1811	Washington	William H. Moody	1906–1910	T. Roosevelt
Oliver Ellsworth	1796–1800	Washington	Horace H. Lurton	1910–1914	Taft
Bushrod Washington	1799–1829	J. Adams	Charles E. Hughes	1910–1916	Taft
Alfred Moore	1800–1804	J. Adams	Willis Van Devanter	1911–1937	Taft
John Marshall	1801–1835	J. Adams	Joseph R. Lamar	1911–1916	Taft
William Johnson	1804–1834	Jefferson	**Edward D. White**	1910–1921	Taft
William Johnson	1804–1834	Jefferson	Mahlon Pitney	1912–1922	Taft
Brockholst Livingston	1807–1823	Jefferson	James C. McReynolds	1914–1941	Wilson
Thomas Todd	1807–1826	Jefferson	Louis D. Brandeis	1916–1939	Wilson
Gabriel Duval	1811–1835	Madison	John H. Clarke	1916–1922	Wilson
Joseph Story	1812–1845	Madison	**William H. Taft**	1921–1930	Harding
Smith Thompson	1823–1843	Monroe	George Sutherland	1922–1938	Harding
Robert Trimble	1826–1828	J. Q. Adams	Pierce Butler	1923–1939	Harding
John McLean	1830–1861	Jackson	Edward T. Sanford	1923–1930	Harding
Henry Baldwin	1830–1844	Jackson	Harlan F. Stone	1925–1941	Coolidge
James M. Wayne	1835–1867	Jackson	**Charles E. Hughes**	1930–1941	Hoover
Roger B. Taney	1836–1864	Jackson	Owen J. Roberts	1930–1945	Hoover
Philip P. Barbour	1836–1841	Jackson	Benjamin N. Cardozo	1932–1938	Hoover
John Cartron	1837–1865	Van Buren	Hugo L. Black	1937–1971	F. Roosevelt
John McKinley	1838–1852	Van Buren	Stanley F. Reed	1938–1957	F. Roosevelt
Peter V. Daniel	1842–1860	Van Buren	Felix Frankfurter	1939–1962	F. Roosevelt
Samuel Nelson	1845–1872	Tyler	William O. Douglas	1939–1975	F. Roosevelt
Levi Woodbury	1845–1851	Polk	Frank Murphy	1940–1949	F. Roosevelt
Robert C. Grier	1846–1870	Polk	**Harlan F. Stone**	1941–1946	F. Roosevelt
Benjamin R. Curtis	1851–1857	Fillmore	James F. Byrnes	1941–1942	F. Roosevelt
John A. Campbell	1853–1861	Pierce	Robert H. Jackson	1941–1954	F. Roosevelt
Nathan Clifford	1858–1881	Buchanan	Wiley B. Rutledge	1943–1949	F. Roosevelt
Noah H. Swayne	1862–1881	Lincoln	Harold H. Burton	1945–1958	Truman
Samuel F. Miller	1862–1890	Lincoln	**Frederick M. Vinson**	1946–1953	Truman
David Davis	1862–1877	Lincoln	Tom C. Clark	1949–1967	Truman
Stephen J. Field	1863–1897	Lincoln	Sherman Minton	1949–1956	Truman
Salmon P. Chase	1864–1873	Lincoln	**Earl Warren**	1953–1969	Eisenhower
William Strong	1870–1880	Grant	John Marshall Harlan	1955–1971	Eisenhower
Joseph P. Bradley	1870–1892	Grant	William J. Brennan, Jr.	1956–1990	Eisenhower
Ward Hunt	1873–1882	Grant	Charles E. Whittaker	1957–1962	Eisenhower
Morrison R. Waite	1873–1888	Grant	Potter Stewart	1958–1981	Eisenhower
John M. Harlan	1877–1911	Hayes	Byron R. White	1962–	Kennedy
William B. Woods	1881–1887	Hayes	Arthur J. Goldberg	1962–1965	Kennedy
Stanley Matthews	1881–1889	Garfield	Abe Fortas	1965–1970	Johnson
Horace Gray	1882–1902	Arthur	Thurgood Marshall	1967–1991	Johnson
Samuel Blatchford	1882–1893	Arthur	**Warren E. Burger**	1969–1986	Nixon
Lucius Q. C. Lamar	1888–1893	Cleveland	Harry A. Blackmun	1970–	Nixon
Melville W. Fuller	1888–1910	Cleveland	Lewis F. Powell, Jr.	1971–1987	Nixon

Name	Terms of Service[1]	Appointed by	Name	Terms of Service[1]	Appointed by
William H. Rehnquist	1971–1986	Nixon	Antonin Scalia	1986–	Reagan
John Paul Stevens	1975–	Ford	Anthony M. Kennedy	1988–	Reagan
Sandra Day O'Connor	1981–	Reagan	David H. Souter	1990–	Bush
William H. Rehnquist	1986–	Reagan	Clarence Thomas	1991–	Bush

Chief Justices in bold type

1. The date on which the justice took his judicial oath is here used as the date of the beginning of his service, for until that oath is taken he is not vested with the prerogatives of his office. Justices, however, receive their commissions ("letters patent") before taking their oath—in some instances, in the preceding year.
2. Acting Chief Justice; Senate refused to confirm appointment.

POLITICAL AND PHYSICAL MAP OF THE UNITED STATES

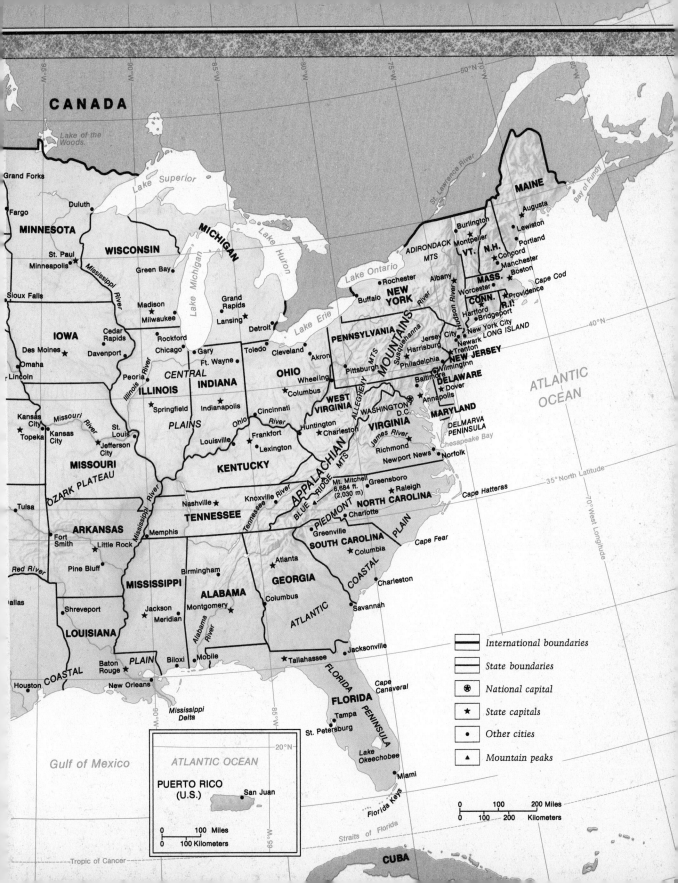

CANADA

Lake of the
Woods

Lake Superior

MINNESOTA
Grand Forks
Fargo
Duluth
St. Paul
Minneapolis
Sioux Falls

WISCONSIN
Green Bay
Madison
Milwaukee

MICHIGAN

Lake Michigan
Lake Huron

Grand
Rapids
Lansing

Lake Ontario
Rochester
Buffalo

ADIRONDACK
MTS
Albany
Burlington
Montpelier
VT. N.H.
Concord
Manchester

MAINE
Augusta
Lewiston
Portland

**NEW
YORK**

MASS.
Worcester
Boston
Providence
CONN.
R.I.
Hartford
Bridgeport
Cape Cod

IOWA
Cedar
Rapids
Des Moines
Davenport
Omaha
Lincoln

Rockford
Chicago
Gary
Ft. Wayne

Toledo
Cleveland
Akron

Detroit
Lake Erie

OHIO
Columbus
Wheeling

PENNSYLVANIA
Pittsburgh
Harrisburg
Susquehanna

Jersey City
Philadelphia
Newark
Trenton
New York City
LONG ISLAND

NEW JERSEY
Wilmington
Baltimore
DELAWARE
Dover
Annapolis

40°N

ATLANTIC
OCEAN

CENTRAL
Peoria
ILLINOIS
Springfield

INDIANA
Indianapolis

Cincinnati
Frankfort
Lexington
Louisville

Ohio River

**WEST
VIRGINIA**
Huntington
Charleston

WASHINGTON
D.C.

VIRGINIA
Richmond
Newport News
Norfolk

MARYLAND
DELMARVA
PENINSULA
Chesapeake Bay

Kansas
City
Topeka
Kansas
City
St.
Louis
Jefferson
City

Missouri River

MISSOURI
OZARK PLATEAU
Tulsa

PLAINS

Mississippi River

KENTUCKY

APPALACHIAN MTS
ALLEGHENY MTS
BLUE RIDGE MTS

Mt. Mitchell
6,684 ft.
(2,030 m)

Greensboro
Raleigh

NORTH CAROLINA
Charlotte

Cape Hatteras

35° North Latitude

Nashville
Knoxville

TENNESSEE
Memphis

Tennessee River

PIEDMONT
Greenville

SOUTH CAROLINA
Columbia

COASTAL
PLAIN
Cape Fear

ARKANSAS
Fort
Smith
Little Rock
Pine Bluff

Red River

MISSISSIPPI
Jackson
Meridian

Birmingham

ALABAMA
Montgomery

Alabama River

Atlanta

GEORGIA
Columbus

ATLANTIC

Charleston

Savannah

70° West Longitude

Dallas

LOUISIANA
Shreveport

Baton
Rouge
PLAIN
Biloxi
Mobile

COASTAL

Houston
New Orleans

Tallahassee
Jacksonville

FLORIDA

Cape
Canaveral

Mississippi
Delta

**FLORIDA
PENINSULA**
Tampa
St. Petersburg

Lake
Okeechobee

Miami

Gulf of Mexico

ATLANTIC OCEAN

**PUERTO RICO
(U.S.)**
San Juan

0   100 Miles
0 100 Kilometers

20°N

Florida Keys

Straits of Florida

CUBA

Tropic of Cancer

International boundaries

State boundaries

⊛ National capital

★ State capitals

• Other cities

▲ Mountain peaks

0   100   200 Miles
0 100   200 Kilometers

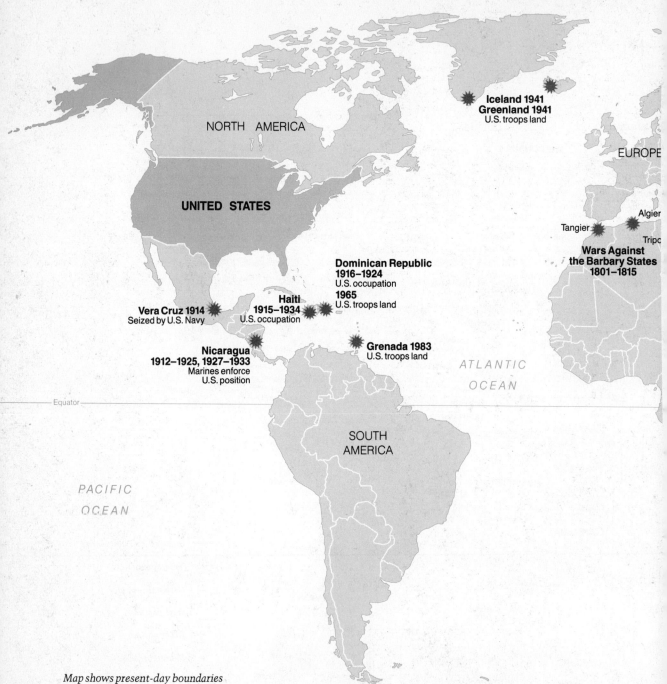

NORTH AMERICA

UNITED STATES

EUROPE

Iceland 1941
Greenland 1941
U.S. troops land

Tangier

Algier

Tripo

Wars Against
the Barbary States
1801–1815

Dominican Republic
1916–1924
U.S. occupation
1965
U.S. troops land

Vera Cruz 1914
Seized by U.S. Navy

Haiti
1915–1934
U.S. occupation

Grenada 1983
U.S. troops land

Nicaragua
1912–1925, 1927–1933
Marines enforce
U.S. position

ATLANTIC
OCEAN

Equator

SOUTH
AMERICA

PACIFIC

OCEAN

Map shows present-day boundaries

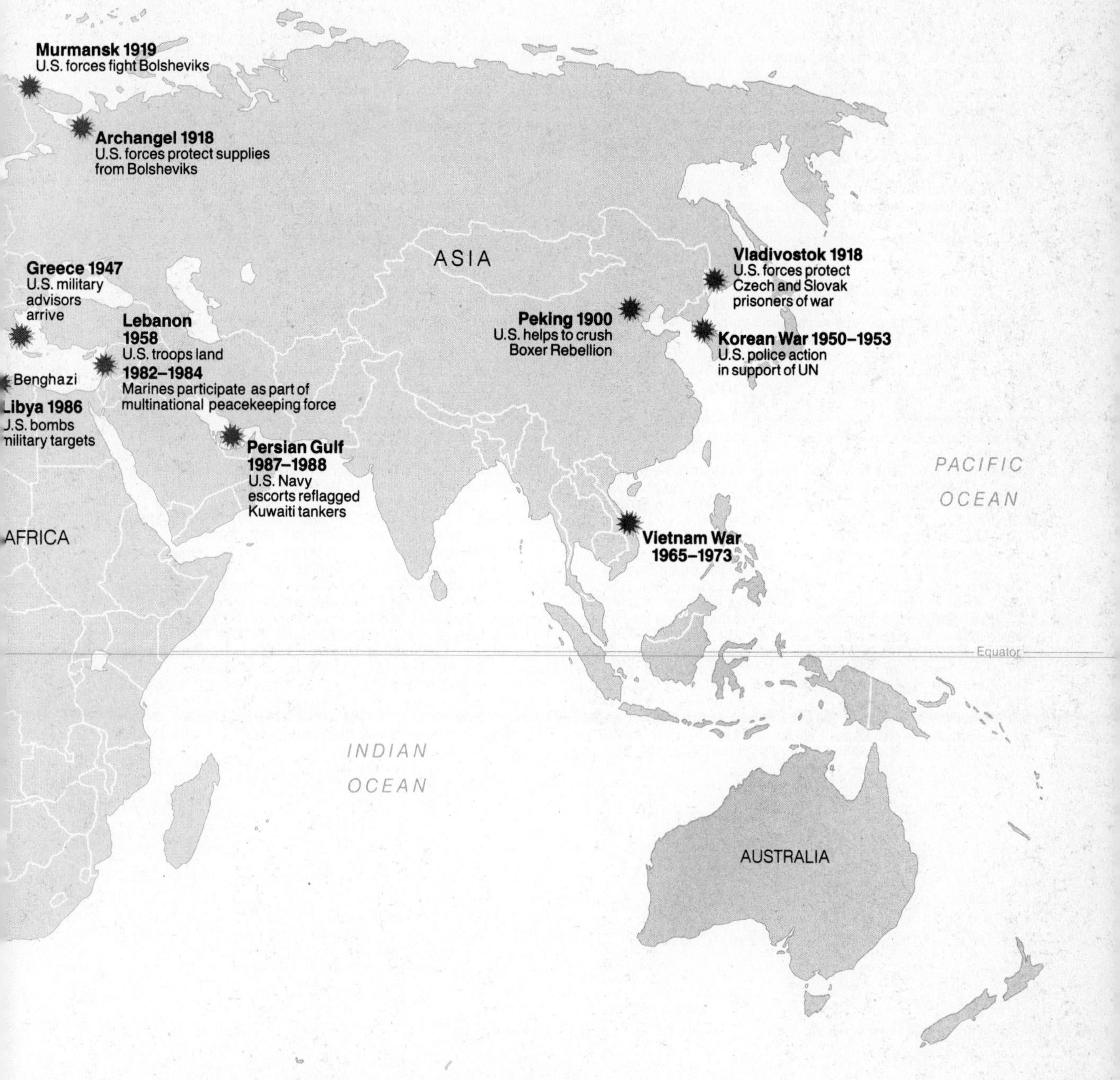

Murmansk 1919
U.S. forces fight Bolsheviks

Archangel 1918
U.S. forces protect supplies
from Bolsheviks

ASIA

Greece 1947
U.S. military
advisors
arrive

**Lebanon
1958**
U.S. troops land
1982–1984
Marines participate as part of
multinational peacekeeping force

Benghazi

Libya 1986
U.S. bombs
military targets

**Persian Gulf
1987–1988**
U.S. Navy
escorts reflagged
Kuwaiti tankers

Peking 1900
U.S. helps to crush
Boxer Rebellion

Vladivostok 1918
U.S. forces protect
Czech and Slovak
prisoners of war

Korean War 1950–1953
U.S. police action
in support of UN

**Vietnam War
1965–1973**

PACIFIC

OCEAN

AFRICA

Equator

INDIAN

OCEAN

AUSTRALIA

CREDITS

2 New York Public Library, Astor, Lenox and Tilden Foundations   **9** Museo de America, Madrid/foto MAS   **10** Courtesy of the Trustees of the British Museum   **12** George Catlina; *La Salle Crossing Lake Michigan on the Ice*, National Gallery of Art, Washington, DC   **21** Courtesy, A. H. Robins Company   **22** National Portrait Gallery, Smithson/Art Resource, NY   **23** Smithsonian Institution   **31** Courtesy, Museum of Fine Arts, Boston, Bequest of Maxim Karolik   **40** Massachusetts Historical Society   **46** Abby Aldrich Rockefeller Folk Art Center   **50** Shelburne Museum, Shelburne, Vermont   **57** Courtesy, Museum of Fine Arts, Boston   **60** Library Company of Philadelphia   **62** National Portrait Gallery, London   **69** Library of Congress   **73** The Colonial Williamsburg Foundation   **77** Library of Congress   **82** Chicago Historical Society   **83L** National Portrait Gallery, London   **83R** Library of Congress   **88** Library of Congress   **93** The Bettmann Archive   **100ALL** Smithsonian Institution   **102** Library of Congress   **113ALL** Independence Historical Park, Eastern National Parks and Monuments Association   **117** Bibliotheque Nationale   **120** From *Our First Century*   **123** Library of Congress   **130** Library of Congress   **131** Copyright Yale University Art Gallery   **133** Chicago Historical Society   **140** Pennsylvania Academy of the Fine Arts, Harrison Earl Fund Purchase   **148** Western History Collection, Denver Public Library   **151** The Hudson's Bay Company   **153** The New-York Historical Society, New York City   **168** Illustration from *Pathfinder*   **170** In the Collection of the Corcoran Gallery of Art, Gift of William Wilson Corcoran   **172** Woolaroc Museum, Bartlesville, Oklahoma   **177** The Mattatuck Museum, Waterbury, Connecticut   **182** Whaling Museum, New Bedford, MA   **187** Courtesy of The Newberry Library, Chicago   **188** The Bettmann Archive   **190** Library of Congress   **192** The Picture Collection, The New York Public Library   **200** Texas State Capitol   **223** From the Penn School Collection, Permission granted by Penn Center, St. Helena Island, SC   **224** Culver Pictures   **228** Sophia Smith Collection, Smith College, Northampton, MA   **237** The New-York Historical Society, New York City   **243** June 27, 1857/*Frank Leslie's Illustrated Newspaper*, **245** Library of Congress   **264** Library of Congress   **274** Library of Congress   **281ALL** Sophia Smith Collection, Smith College, Northampton, MA   **291** From *A Pictographic History of the Oglala Sioux* by Amos Bad Heart Bull,

University of Nebraska Press   **292** Amon Carter Museum of Western Art, Forth Worth, TX   **296** Dentzel Collection   **301** Nebraska State Historical Society   **312** March 6, 1901, *Puck*   **314** Brown Brothers   **316** Courtesy, Metropolitan Life Insurance Company   **319L** *Harper's Weekly*   **326** The Bryon Collection, The Museum of the City of New York   **332** Culver Pictures   **335L** Chicago Historical Society   **335R** Brown Brothers   **340** Culver Pictures   **345** The Kansas State Historical Society, Topeka   **346** Free Library of Philadelphia   **350** From *The Silent War*, Courtesy of The Newberry Library, Chicago   **351** From L. Frank Baum, *The Wizard of Oz*, Reilly & Lee Company, Chicago   **358** Library of Congress   **363** *New York Journal*, February 17, 1898   **365** Chicago Historical Society   **374** Courtesy, Ford Archives, From the Collections of Henry Ford Museum and Greenfield Villa   **376** Brown Brothers   **382** A. B. Walker in *LIFE*   **388** Chicago Historical Society   **393** Culver Pictures   **396** Brown Brothers   **402** The National Archives   **419** The National Archives   **427** Culver Pictures   **430** September 11, 1920, *Frank Leslie's Illustrated Newspaper*   **433** Chicago Historical Society   **436** *New York World*, May 19, 1925   **437** *LIFE*, 1922   **443** Chicago Historical Society   **446** Brown Brothers   **448** The National Archives   **451** Library of Congress   **453** AP/Wide World   **463** U. S. Army Photo   **467L** December 8, 1941, *San Francisco Chronicle*   **467R** AP/Wide World   **473** Margaret Bourke-White/*LIFE* Magazine, Time Warner Inc.   **477** AP/Wide World   **482** by Herblock in *The Washington Post*   **485** Consulate General of Germany   **490** UPI/Bettmann   **491** UPI/Bettmann   **492** UPI/Bettmann   **498** Bern Keating/Black Star   **502** AP/Wide World   **504** UPI/Bettmann   **505** AP/Wide World   **509** Charles Moore/Black Star   **511** UPI/Bettmann   **517** Black Star   **520** © 1957 by The New York Times Company, Reprinted by permission   **523** The Illingworth Collection, Courtesy The National Library of Wales   **530** by Leslie Illingworth, © Punch/Rothco   **536** Hal A. Franklin   **538** Werner Wolff/Black Star   **540** UPI/Bettmann   **544** Roger Pic/Gamma-Liaison   **547** J. P. Laffont/Sygma   **552** Alain DeJean/Sygma   **562** Bill Fitz-Patrick/The White House   **570** Bob North/Picture Group   **573** Jerry Robinson/© Cartoonists Writers Syndicate   **583** Brad Markel/Gamma-Liaison   **587** Juergen Mueller-Sceck Stern/Black Star   **590** Dennis Brack/Black Star

INDEX